Reviewers Praise *Real World XML*

The author's approach is definitely bottom up, written in a highly personable tone. He makes efficient use of example code, which sets this book apart from many I have read in the past. His examples bring to life the code without overwhelming the reader, and he does not present any examples for which the reader has not been prepared. In addition, no prior knowledge of XML is assumed. As such, this is an excellent book for both beginners and intermediate level web designers and programmers. Experts, too, will find this book of value, due to its emphasis on real world applicability. Overall, this book will benefit all web developers and programmers, with a special emphasis on beginner and intermediate developers.

~Donna A. Dulo, MS, MA, Senior Systems Engineer, U.S. Department of Defense

This book will provide a brilliant basis for anyone wishing to keep up to speed with the new XML developments.

~Mr. Andrew Madden, Department of Computer Science, University of Wales

I found this book's strengths to be: its exhaustive specification reference for the conscientious developer; access to the official specs, which is key; the wide variety of choices provided for all aspects of XML; several alternatives provided for each editor, browser, parser, stylesheet transform engine, and programming language; and working examples that show the power of the tools used.

~Jaime Ryan, Software Developer/Documentation Manager, Blue Titan Software

Comments from the Previous Edition

Steve Holzner has successfully given each topic good, detailed treatment—each chapter builds on the last providing the reader a solid understanding of XML, its related technologies, and how it fits into the current application development arena. This book will appeal to the novice and experienced XML programmers alike.

~Beth Breidenbach, Senior Software Engineer, MCSD Getronics

Inside XML's building block approach, clear explanations, and extensive examples are perfectly targeted for an introduction to XML.

~Tom Comerford, Director Supratext, LLC

Readers will find this book an excellent companion for XML development. Well-constructed examples are ample throughout, making this book not only a genuine learning tool, but a fine resource as well.

~Andrew J. Indovina, Software Engineer/e-Commerce Developer

Real World
XML

by

Steven Holzner

New Riders

Real World XML

By Steven Holzner
Copyright © 2003 by New Riders Publishing

New Riders Publishing is a division of Peachpit Publishing Group

210 W. 103rd St.
Indianapolis, IN 46290

Find us on the World Wide Web at: http://www.newriders.com

For resources mentioned in this book, see: http://www.newriders.com

Associate Publisher: Stephanie Wall
Production Manager: Gina Kanouse
Senior Product Marketing Manager: Tammy Detrich
Publicity Manager: Susan Nixon
Senior Project Editor: Lori Lyons
Copy Editor: Krista Hansing
Indexers: Chris Morris and Lisa Stumpf
Composition: Wil Cruz and Amy Parker
Interior Design: Jeff Carlson
Cover Illustration: Alan Clements

Colophon

This book was written and edited in Microsoft Word, and laid out in QuarkXPress. The fonts used for the body text are Minion and Mono. It was printed on 50# Husky Offset Smooth paper at Edwards Brothers, Inc. in Ann Arbor, Michigan. Prepress consisted of PostScript computer-to-plate technology (filmless process). The cover was printed at Moore Langen Printing in Terre Haute, Indiana, on 12 pt., coated on one side.

ISBN: 0-7357-1286-7

Library of Congress Catalog Card Number: 2002100320

06 05 04 03   7 6 5 4 3 2 1

Printed and bound in the United States of America

About the Author

Steven Holzner is an award-winning author who has been writing about XML for as long as it's been around. He's the author of 75 books on programming, and a former contributing editor to *PC Magazine*. A number of his books have been programming bestsellers, and he's had books translated into 16 languages around the world, selling more than 1.5 million copies. He received his Ph.D. at Cornell University, and has been on the faculty of both Cornell and MIT. His hobbies include travel, chess, classical music, and writing books on philosophy.

About the Technical Reviewers

These reviewers contributed their considerable hands-on expertise to the entire development process for *Real World XML*. As the book was being written, these dedicated professionals reviewed all the material for technical content, organization, and flow. Their feedback was critical to ensuring that *Real World XML* fits our reader's need for the highest-quality technical information.

Steve Heckler is President of Accelebrate, an IT training and technical writing firm in Atlanta. An avid ASP.NET, Java, and XML developer and trainer, Steve served more than six years as a senior manager and trainer at a leading east-coast IT training firm prior to founding Accelebrate. He holds a Bachelor and Masters degree from Stanford University.

Carl Burnham is a web developer, technology specialist, and author, with 17 years of experience supporting IT operations within the private/public sectors. He founded Southpoint.com, a popular travel destination guide, in 1996. Carl is author of the book, *Web Hosting, a Complete Strategy*, and has coauthored several technology books.

Dedication

To Nancy, of course!

Acknowledgments

A book like the one you're holding is the work of a great many people, not just the author. The people at New Riders have been great, and I'd like to thank Stephanie Wall, Associate Publisher extraordinaire; Lori Lyons and Krista Hansing, Project/Copy Editors, who kept things moving along; and finally, the Technical Reviewers, Steve Heckler and Carl Burnham, who did a great job of checking everything. Thanks, everyone, for all your much-appreciated hard work.

Preface

Welcome to *Real World XML*. This book is designed to be as comprehensive—and as accessible—as possible for a single book on XML. XML is a standard, not an implementation, and it's become an umbrella for a great number of topics. You'll find XML just about everywhere you look on the Internet today, and even in many places behind the scenes (such as internally in Netscape Navigator 6). I believe this book provides more complete coverage of what's going on in XML than any other XML book today.

You'll find coverage of all the official XML standards here. I'll also take a look at many of the most popular and important implementations of XML that are out there, and put them to work in this book.

That's just part of the story—we'll also put XML to work in depth, pushing the envelope as far as it can go. The best way to learn any topic like XML is by example, and this is an example-oriented book. You'll find hundreds of tested examples here, ready to be used.

Writing XML is not some ordinary and monotonous task: it inspires artistry, devotion, passion, exaltation, and eccentricity—not to mention exasperation and frustration. I'll try to be true to that spirit and capture as much of the excitement and power of XML in this book as I can.

What Is Inside This Book

This book is designed to give you as much of the whole XML story as one book can hold. We'll not only see the full XML syntax—from the most basic to the most advanced—but also dig into many of the ways in which XML is used.

There are hundreds of real-world topics covered in this book, like connecting XML to databases—both locally and on Web servers—styling XML for viewing in today's browsers, reading and using XML documents in browsers, creating our own graphically based browsers, and a great deal more.

Here's a sample of some of the topics in this book—note that each of these topics themselves have many subtopics (too many to list here):

- The complete XML syntax
- Well-formed XML documents
- Valid XML documents
- Document type definitions (DTDs)
- Namespaces
- The XML Document Object Model (DOM)
- Canonical XML
- XML schemas
- Parsing XML with JavaScript
- XML and data binding
- XML and Cascading Style Sheets (CSS)
- XML and Java
- XML and .NET
- DOM parsers
- SAX parsers
- Extensible Stylesheet Language (XSL) transformations
- XSL formatting objects
- XLinks
- XPointers
- XPath
- XBase
- XHTML 1.0 and 1.1
- Resource Description Framework (RDF)
- Simple Object Access Protocol (SOAP)
- Vector Markup Language (VML)
- Wireless Markup Language (WML)
- Server-side XML with JavaServer Pages (JSP), Active Server Pages (ASP), Java servlets, and Perl

This book starts with the basics. I do assume that you have some knowledge of HTML, but not necessarily much. We'll see how to create XML documents from scratch in this book, starting at the very beginning.

From there, we'll move up to see how to check the syntax of XML documents. The big attraction of XML is that you can define your own tags, like the <DOCUMENT> and <GREETING> tags in this document, which we'll see early in Chapter 1:

```
<?xml version="1.0" encoding="UTF-8"?>
<DOCUMENT>
    <GREETING>
        Hello From XML
    </GREETING>
    <MESSAGE>
        Welcome to the wild and woolly world of XML.
    </MESSAGE>
</DOCUMENT>
```

Because you can create your own tags in XML, it's also important to specify the syntax you want those tags to obey (for example, can a <MESSAGE> appear inside a <GREETING>?). XML puts a big emphasis on this, too, and there are two main ways to specify the syntax you want your XML to follow—with XML *document type definitions* (DTDs) and XML *schemas*. We'll see how to create both.

And because you can make up your own tags in XML, it's also up to you to specify how they should be used—Netscape Navigator won't know, for example, that a <KILLER> tag marks a favorite book in your collection. Because it's up to you to determine what a tag actually means, handling your XML documents in programming is an important part of learning XML, despite what some second-rate XML books try to claim. The two languages I'll use in this book are JavaScript and Java; before using them, I'll introduce them in special sections with plenty of examples, so even if you're not familiar with these languages, you won't have to go anywhere else to get the skills you need.

The major browsers today are becoming more and more XML-aware, and they use scripting languages to let you work with your XML documents. We'll be using the most popular and powerful of those scripting languages here, JavaScript. Using JavaScript, we'll be able to read XML documents directly in browsers like the Microsoft Internet Explorer.

It's also important to know how to handle XML outside browsers, because there are plenty of things that JavaScript can't handle. These days, most XML development is taking place in Java, and there is an endless arsenal of Java resources available for free on the Internet. In fact, the connection between Java and XML is a natural one, as we'll see. We'll use Java to read XML documents and interpret them, starting in Chapter 11. That doesn't mean you have to be a Java expert—far from it, in fact—because I'll introduce all the Java we'll need right here in this book. And because most XML development is done in Java today, we're going to find a wealth of tools here, ready for use.

You can also design your XML documents to be displayed directly in some modern browsers, and I'll take a look at doing that in two ways—with Cascading Style Sheets (CSS) and the Extensible Stylesheet Language (XSL). Using CSS and XSL, you can indicate exactly how a tag that you make up, like <PANIC> or <BIG_AND_BOLD> or <AZURE_UNDERLINED_TEXT>, should be displayed. I'll take a look at both parts of XSL—XSL transformations and formatting objects—in depth.

In addition, we'll see various other XML specifications in this book as well, such as XLinks, XBase, and XPointers, which let you point to particular items in XML documents in very specific ways. The XML specifications are made by a body called the World Wide Web Consortium, abbreviated W3C, and we'll become very familiar with those specifications here, seeing what they say—and seeing what they lack.

I'll wind up the book by taking a look at a number of the most popular uses of XML on the Internet in several chapters. XML is really a language for *defining* languages, and there are hundreds of such XML-based languages out there now. Some of them are gaining great popularity, and I'll cover them in some depth in this book.

There is an astonishing wealth of material on XML available on the Internet today, so I'm also going to fill this book with the URIs of dozens of those resources (in XML, you use *Uniform Resource Identifiers*, not URLs, although in practice they are the same thing for most purposes today). In nearly every chapter, you'll find lists of free online programs and other resources. (However, there's a hazard here that I should mention—URIs change frequently on the Internet, so don't be surprised if some of these URIs have changed by the time you look for them.)

Who Is This Book For?

This book is designed for just about anyone who wants to learn XML and how it's used today in the real world. The only assumption that I make is that you have some knowledge of how to create documents using Hypertext Markup Language (HTML). You don't have to be any great HTML expert, but a little knowledge of HTML will be helpful. That's really all you need.

However, it's a fact of life that most XML software these days is targeted at Windows. Among other things, this means you should have access to Windows for many of the topics covered in this book, and in Chapters 7 and 8, we'll be taking a look at the XML support in Microsoft Internet Explorer. I wish there was more support for the other operating systems I like, such as Unix, but right now a lot of it is Windows-only. I'll explore alternatives when I can. One hopeful note for the future is that there are more and more Java-based XML tools appearing daily, and those tools are platform-independent.

At What Level This Book Is Written

This book is written at several different levels—from basic to advanced—because the XML spectrum is so broad. The rule of thumb is that this book was written to follow HTML books in level. We start at the basic level and gradually get more advanced in a slow, steady way.

I'm not going to assume that you have any programming knowledge (at least until we get to the advanced topics in Chapter 20, such as JavaServer Pages and using Perl with XML) when you start this book. We'll be using both JavaScript and Java in this book, but all you need to know about those languages will be introduced before we use them, and it won't be hard to pick up.

Because there are so many uses of XML available today, this book involves many different software packages; all the ones I'll put to work in the text are free to download from the Internet; I'll tell you where to get them.

Conventions Used

There are several conventions that I use in this book that you should be aware of. The most important one is that when I add new sections of code, I'll mark them with gray highlighting to point out the actual lines I'm discussing so that they stand out. (This sample is written in one of the languages built on XML, the Wireless Markup Language (WML), which is targeted at "micro-browsers" in cellular phones and personal digital assistants, or PDAs.)

```
<?xml version="1.0"?>
<!DOCTYPE wml PUBLIC "-//WAPFORUM//DTD WML 1.1//EN"
"http://www.wapforum.org/DTD/wml_1.1.xml">
<wml>
    <card id="Card1" title="First WML Example">
        <!— This is a comment —>
        <p>
            Greetings from WML.
        </p>
    </card>
</wml>
```

Also, where there's something worth noting or some additional information that adds something to the discussion, I'll add a sidebar:

More on SOAP

With a common name like SOAP, it's hard to search the Internet for more information about the Simple Object Access Protocol unless you're really into pages on personal cleanliness and daytime television. For more information, you might check out this starter list: `http://msdn.microsoft.com/xml/general/soapspec.asp`, `www.oasis-open.org/cover/soap.html`, `www.develop.com/soap/`, and `www.develop.com/soap/soapfaq.xml`.

Well, we're ready to go. If you have comments, I encourage you to write to me, care of New Riders. This book is designed to be the new standard in XML coverage, truly more complete and more accessible than ever before. Please do keep in touch with me with ways to improve it and keep it on the forefront. If you think the book lacks anything, let me know—I'll add it, because I want to make sure this book stays on top.

Overview

Table of Contents

CHAPTER 2

Creating Well-Formed XML Documents 49

CHAPTER 3

Valid Documents: Creating Document Type Definitions 99

CHAPTER 6

Understanding JavaScript 239

CHAPTER 7

Handling XML Documents with JavaScript

CHAPTER 8

XML and Data Binding

CHAPTER 9

Cascading Style Sheets 401

CHAPTER 10

Understanding Java 461

CHAPTER 11

Java and the XML DOM 513

CHAPTER 12

Java and SAX 569

CHAPTER 13

XSL Transformations 623

CHAPTER 14

XSL Formatting Objects **687**

CHAPTER 15

XLinks and XPointers **739**

CHAPTER 18

SOAP and RDF 903

CHAPTER 19

Vector Markup Language 961

CHAPTER 20

WML, ASP, JSP, Servlets, and Perl 1019

APPENDIX A

The XML 1.0 Recommendation (Second Edition) 1069

CHAPTER 1
Essential XML

Welcome to the world of Extensible Markup Language, XML. This book is your guided tour to that world, so have no worries—you've come to the right place. That world is large and expanding in unpredictable ways every minute, but we're going to become familiar with the lay of the land in detail here. And there's a lot of territory to cover because XML is getting into the most amazing places, and in the most amazing ways, these days.

XML is a language defined by the World Wide Web Consortium (W3C, `www.w3c.org`), the body that sets the standards for the Web, and this first chapter is all about getting a solid overview of that language and how you can use it. For example, you probably already know that you can use XML to create your own elements, thus creating a customized markup language for your own use. In this way, XML supercedes other markup languages such as Hypertext Markup Language (HTML); in HTML, all the elements you use are predefined—and there are not enough of them. In fact, XML is a metamarkup language because it lets you create your own markup languages.

Markup Languages

Markup languages are all about describing the form of the document—that is, the way the content of the document should be interpreted. The markup language that most people are familiar with today is, of course, HTML, which you use to create standard Web pages. Here's an example HTML page:

Listing ch01_01.html

```
<HTML>
    <HEAD>
        <TITLE>Hello From HTML</TITLE>
    </HEAD>
    <BODY>
        <CENTER>
            <H1>
                Hello From HTML
            </H1>
        </CENTER>
        Welcome to the wild and woolly world of HTML.
    </BODY>
</HTML>
```

You can see the results of this HTML in Figure 1-1 in Netscape Navigator. Note that the HTML markup in this page—that is, *tags* such as <HEAD>, <CENTER>, <H1>, and so on—is there to give directions to the browser. That's what markup does; it specifies directions on the way the content is to be interpreted.

Figure 1-1
An HTML page in a browser.

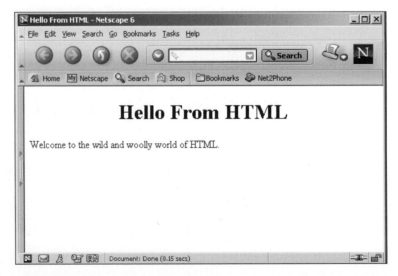

When you think of markup in terms of specifying how the content of a document is to be handled, it's easy to see that there are many kinds of markup languages all around already. For example, if you use a word processor to save a document in Rich Text Format (RTF), you'll find all kinds of markup codes embedded in the document. Here's an example; in this case, I've just created an RTF file with the letters abc underlined and in bold using Microsoft Word—try searching for the actual text (hint: it's near the very end):

```
{\rtf1\ansi\ansicpg1252\uc1 \deff0\deflang1033
\deflangfe1033{\fonttbl{\f0\froman\fcharset0\fprq2{\*\panose
02020603050405020304}Times New Roman;}}{\colortbl;\red0
\green0\blue0;\red0\green0\blue255;\red0\green255\blue255;
\red0\green255\blue0;\red255\green0\blue255;\red255\green0
\blue0;\red255\green255\blue0;\red255\green255\blue255;\red0
\green0\blue128;\red0\green128\blue128;\red0\green128\blue0;
\red128\green0\blue128;\red128\green0\blue0;\red128\green128
\blue0;\red128\green128\blue128;\red192\green192\blue192;}
{\stylesheet{\widctlpar\adjustright \fs20\cgrid \snext0 Normal;}
{\*\cs10 \additive Default Paragraph Font;}}{\info{\title  }
{\author Steven Holzner}{\operator Steven Holzner}{\creatim
\yr2000\mo\dy\hr\min}{\revtim\yr2000\mo4\dy17\hr13\min55}
{\version1}{\edmins1}{\nofpages1}{\nofwords0}{\nofchars1}
{\*\company SteveCo}{\nofcharsws1}{\vern89}}\widowctrl\ftnbj
\aenddoc\formshade\viewkind4\viewscale100\pgbrdrhead\pgbrdrfoot
\fet0\sectd \psz1\linex0\endnhere\sectdefaultcl {\*\pnseclvl1
\pnucrm\pnstart1\pnindent720\pnhang{\pntxta .}}{\*\pnseclvl2
\pnucltr\pnstart1\pnindent720\pnhang{\pntxta .}}{\*\pnseclvl3
\pndec\pnstart1\pnindent720\pnhang{\pntxta .}}{\*\pnseclvl4
\pnlcltr\pnstart1\pnindent720\pnhang{\pntxta )}}{\*\pnseclvl5
\pndec\pnstart1\pnindent720\pnhang{\pntxtb (}{\pntxta )}}
{\*\pnseclvl6\pnlcltr\pnstart1\pnindent720\pnhang{\pntxtb (}
{\pntxta )}}{\*\pnseclvl7\pnlcrm\pnstart1\pnindent720\pnhang
{\pntxtb (}{\pntxta )}}{\*\pnseclvl8\pnlcltr\pnstart1
\pnindent720\pnhang{\pntxtb (}{\pntxta )}}{\*\pnseclvl9\pnlcrm
\pnstart1\pnindent720\pnhang{\pntxtb (}{\pntxta )}}\pard\plain
\sl480\slmult1\widctlpar\adjustright \fs20\cgrid {\b\fs24\ul abc }{\b\ul \par }}
```

The markup language that most people are familiar with these days is HTML, but it's easy to see how that language doesn't provide enough power for anything beyond creating standard Web pages.

HTML 1.0 consisted of only a dozen or so tags, but the most recent version, HTML 4.01, consists of almost 100—and if you include the other tags added by the major browsers, that number is closer to 120. But as handling data on the Web and other nets intensifies, it's clear that 120 tags isn't enough—and, in fact, you can never have enough.

For example, what if your hobby was building model ships and you wanted to exchange specifications with others on the topic? HTML doesn't include tags such as <BEAMWIDTH>, <MIZZENHEIGHT>, <DRAFT>, <SHIPCLASS>, and the others you might want. What if you were a major bank that wanted to exchange financial data with other institutions—would you prefer tags such as <B>, <UL>, and <FONT>, or tags such as <FISCALYEAR>, <ACCOUNTNUMBER>, <TRANSFERACCOUNT>, and others? (In fact, such markup languages as Extensible Business Reporting Language exist now—and they're built on XML.)

What if you were a Web browser manufacturer and wanted to create your own markup language to let people configure your browser, adding scrollbars, toolbars, and other elements? You might create your own markup language to do that; in fact, Netscape has done just that with the XML-based User Interface Language, which we'll see in this chapter.

The upshot is that there are as many reasons to create markup languages as there are ways of handling data—and, of course, that's unlimited. That's where XML comes in: It's a metamarkup specification that lets you create your own markup languages.

What Does XML Look Like?

So what does XML look like and how does it work? Here's an example that mimics the HTML page just introduced:

Listing ch01_02.xml

```
<?xml version="1.0" encoding="UTF-8"?>
<DOCUMENT>
    <GREETING>
        Hello From XML
    </GREETING>
    <MESSAGE>
        Welcome to the wild and woolly world of XML.
    </MESSAGE>
</DOCUMENT>
```

We'll see the parts of an XML document in detail in the next chapter, but in overview, here's how this one works: I start with the XML *processing instruction* <?xml version="1.0" encoding="UTF-8"?> (all XML processing instructions start with <? and end with ?>), which indicates that I'm using XML version 1.0, the only version currently defined, and using the UTF-8 *character encoding*, which means that I'm using an 8-bit condensed version of Unicode (more on this later in the chapter):

```
<?xml version="1.0" encoding="UTF-8"?>
<DOCUMENT>
    <GREETING>
        Hello From XML
    </GREETING>
    <MESSAGE>
        Welcome to the wild and woolly world of XML.
    </MESSAGE>
</DOCUMENT>
```

Next, I create a new *tag* named <DOCUMENT>. As we'll see in the next chapter, you can use any name, not just DOCUMENT, for a tag, as long as the name starts with a letter or underscore (_) and the following characters consist of letters, digits, underscores, dots (.), or hyphens (-), but no spaces. In XML, tags always start with < and end with >.

XML documents are made up of XML *elements*, and (much like HTML) you create XML elements with an opening tag (such as <DOCUMENT>), followed by any element content (if any) (such as text or other elements) and ending with the matching closing tag that starts with </ (such as </DOCUMENT>). (There are additional rules we'll see in the next chapter if the element doesn't contain any content.) It's necessary to enclose the entire document, except for processing instructions, in one element, called the *root element*, and that's the <DOCUMENT> element here:

```
<?xml version="1.0" encoding="UTF-8"?>
<DOCUMENT>
    .
    .
    .
</DOCUMENT>
```

Now I'll add a new element that I made up, <GREETING>, which encloses text content (in this case, that's Hello From XML), to this XML document, like this:

```
<?xml version="1.0" encoding="UTF-8"?>
<DOCUMENT>
    <GREETING>
        Hello From XML
    </GREETING>
    .
    .
    .
</DOCUMENT>
```

Next, I can add a new element as well, `<MESSAGE>`, which also encloses text content:

```
<?xml version="1.0" encoding="UTF-8"?>
<DOCUMENT>
    <GREETING>
        Hello From XML
    </GREETING>
    <MESSAGE>
        Welcome to the wild and woolly world of XML.
    </MESSAGE>
</DOCUMENT>
```

Now the `<DOCUMENT>` root element contains two elements—`<GREETING>` and `<MESSAGE>`. And each of the `<GREETING>` and `<MESSAGE>` elements holds text. In this way, I've created a new XML document.

Note the similarity of this document to the HTML page we saw earlier. Note also, however, that in the HTML document, all the tags were predefined and a Web browser knows how to handle them. Here we've just created these tags, `<DOCUMENT>`, `<GREETING>`, and `<MESSAGE>`, from thin air—how can we use an XML document like this one? What would a browser make of these new tags?

What Does XML Look Like in a Browser?

It turns out that a browser such as Microsoft Internet Explorer version 5 or later lets you display raw XML documents directly. For example, if I saved the XML document just created in a document named ch01_02.xml and opened that document in Internet Explorer, I'd see something like Figure 1-2.

Figure 1-2
An XML document in Internet Explorer.

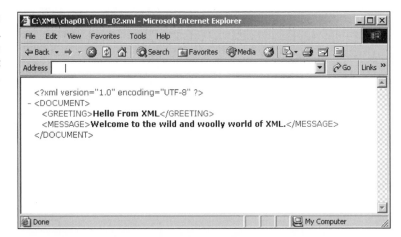

You can see the complete XML document in Figure 1-2, but it's nothing like the image you see in Figure 1-1; there's no particular formatting at all. So now that we've created our own markup elements, how do you tell a browser how to display them?

In fact, many people who are new to XML find the claim that you can use XML to create new markup languages very frustrating—after all, what then? It turns out that it's up to you to assign meaning to the new elements you create, and you can do that in two main ways. First, you can use a *stylesheet* to indicate to a browser how you want the content of the elements you've created formatted. The second way is to use a programming language, such as Java or JavaScript, to handle the XML document in programming code. We'll see both ways throughout this book, and I'll take a look at them in overview in this chapter as well. I'll start by adding a stylesheet to the XML document we've already created.

There are two main ways of specifying styles when you format XML documents: Cascading Style Sheets (CSS) and the Extensible Stylesheet Language (XSL). We'll see both in this book; here, I'll apply a CSS stylesheet using the XML processing instruction `<?xml-stylesheet type="text/css" href="ch01_04.css"?>`, which tells the browser that the type of the stylesheet I'll be using is CSS and that its name is ch01_04.css (and because I'm not giving any path to the stylesheet, the browser will assume that it's in the same directory as the XML document itself):

Listing ch01_03.xml

```
<?xml version="1.0" encoding="UTF-8"?>
<?xml-stylesheet type="text/css" href="ch01_04.css"?>
<DOCUMENT>
    <GREETING>
        Hello From XML
    </GREETING>
    <MESSAGE>
        Welcome to the wild and woolly world of XML.
    </MESSAGE>
</DOCUMENT>
```

Here's what ch01_04.css itself looks like. In this case, I'm customizing the <GREETING> element to display its content in red, centered in the browser and in 36-point font, and the <MESSAGE> element to display its text in black 18-point font. The display: block part indicates that I want the content of these elements to be displayed in a block, which translates here to being displayed on its own line:

Listing ch01_04.css

```
GREETING {display: block; font-size: 36pt; color: #FF0000; text-align:
➥center}
MESSAGE (display: block; font-size: 18pt; color: #000000}
```

You can see the results in two browsers that support XML in Figures 1-3 and 1-4. Figure 1-3 shows this XML document in Netscape 6, and Figure 1-4 shows the same document in Internet Explorer. As you can see, we've formatted the XML document as we like it using stylesheets—in fact, this result is already an advance over HTML because we've been able to format exactly how we want to display the text, not just rely on predefined elements such as <H1>.

Figure 1-3
An XML document in Netscape Navigator.

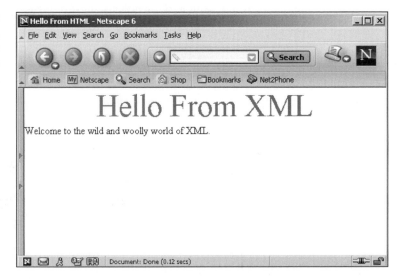

Figure 1-4
An XML
document in
Internet
Explorer.

That gives us a taste of XML. Now we've seen how to create a first XML document and how to use a stylesheet to display it in a browser. We've seen what it looks like—so what's so great about XML? Take a look at the overview, coming up next.

What's So Great About XML?

XML is so popular for many reasons. I'll examine some of them here as part of our overview of where XML is today. My own personal favorite is that XML allows easy data handling and exchange, and I'm going to start with that.

Easy Data Exchange

I've been involved with computing for a long time, and one of the things I've watched with misgiving is the growth of proprietary data formats. In earlier days, programs could exchange data easily because data was stored as text. Today, however, you need conversion programs or modules to let applications transfer data between themselves. In fact, proprietary data formats have become so complex that frequently one version of a complex application can't even read data from an earlier version of the same application.

In XML, data and markup is stored as text that you yourself can configure. If you like, you can use XML editors, as we'll see, to create XML documents. If something goes wrong, however, you can examine or modify the document directly because it's all just text. The data is also not encoded in some way that has been patented or copyrighted, which some formats are, so it's more accessible.

You might think that binary formats would be more efficient because they can store data more compactly, but that's not the way things have worked out. Microsoft Corporation, for example, is notorious for turning out huge applications that store even simple data in huge files (the not-so-affectionate name for this is "bloatware"). If you store only the letters abc in a Microsoft Word 2000 document, you might be surprised to find that the document is something like 20,000 bytes. A similar XML file might be 30 or 40 bytes. Even large amounts of data are not necessarily stored efficiently; Microsoft Excel, for example, routinely creates large files that are five times as long as the corresponding text, and Microsoft Access XP creates files that start at 96KB.

In addition, when you standardize markup languages, many different people can use them; I'll take a look at that next.

Customizing Markup Languages

As we've already seen, you can create customized markup languages using XML, and that represents its extraordinary power. When you and a number of other people agree on a markup language, you can create customized browsers or applications that handle that language. Hundreds of such languages are already being standardized now, including these:

- Banking Industry Technology Secretariat (BITS)
- Financial Exchange (IFX)
- Bank Internet Payment System (BIPS)
- Telecommunications Interchange Markup (TIM)
- Schools Interoperability Framework (SIF)
- Common Business Library (xCBL)
- Electronic Business XML Initiative (ebXML)
- Product Data Markup Language (PDML)
- Financial Information eXchange protocol (FIX)
- The Text Encoding Initiative (TEI)

Some customized markup languages, such as Chemical Markup Language (CML), let you represent complex molecules graphically, as we'll see later in this chapter. And you can imagine how useful a language would be that creates graphical building plans for architects when you open a document in a browser.

Not only can you create custom markup languages, but you can extend them using XML as well. So, if someone creates a markup language based on XML, you can add the extensions you want easily. In fact, that's what's happening now with Extensible Hypertext Markup Language (XHTML), which I'll take a look at briefly in this chapter and in detail later in the book. Using XHTML, you can add your own elements to what a browser displays as normal HTML.

Self-Describing Data

The data in XML documents is self-describing. Take a look at this document:

Listing ch01_05.xml

```
<?xml version="1.0" encoding="UTF-8"?>
<DOCUMENT>
    <GREETING>
        Hello From XML
    </GREETING>
    <MESSAGE>
        Welcome to the wild and woolly world of XML.
    </MESSAGE>
</DOCUMENT>
```

Based solely on the names we've given to each XML element here, you can figure out what's going on. This document has a greeting and a message to impart. Even if you came back to this document years later, you could figure out what's going on. This means that XML documents are, to a large extent, self-documenting. (We'll also see in the next chapter that you can add explicit comments to XML files.)

Structured and Integrated Data

Another powerful aspect of XML is that it lets you specify not only data, but also the structure of that data and how various elements are integrated into other elements. This is important when you're dealing with complex and important data. For example, you could represent a long bank statement in HTML, but in XML, you can actually build in the semantic rules that specify the structure of the document so that the document can be checked to make sure it's set up correctly.

Take a look at this XML document:

Listing ch01_06.xml

```xml
<?xml version="1.0"?>
<SCHOOL>
    <CLASS type="seminar">
        <CLASS_TITLE>XML In The Real World</CLASS_TITLE>
        <CLASS_NUMBER>6.031</CLASS_NUMBER>
        <SUBJECT>XML</SUBJECT>
        <START_DATE>6/1/2002</START_DATE>
        <STUDENTS>
            <STUDENT status="attending">
                <FIRST_NAME>Edward</FIRST_NAME>
                <LAST_NAME>Samson</LAST_NAME>
            </STUDENT>
            <STUDENT status="withdrawn">
                <FIRST_NAME>Ernestine</FIRST_NAME>
                <LAST_NAME>Johnson</LAST_NAME>
            </STUDENT>
        </STUDENTS>
    </CLASS>
</SCHOOL>
```

Here I've set up an XML seminar and added two students to it. As we'll see in Chapter 2, "Creating Well-Formed XML Documents" and Chapter 3, "Valid Documents: Creating Document Type Definitions," using XML, you can specify, for example, that each <STUDENT> element needs to enclose a <FIRST_NAME> and a <LAST_NAME> element, that the <START_DATE> element can't go in the <STUDENTS> element, and more.

In fact, this emphasis on the correctness of documents is strong in XML. In HTML, a Web author could (and frequently did) write sloppy HTML, knowing that the Web browser would take care of any syntax problems (some Web authors even exploited this intentionally to create special effects in some browsers). In fact, some people estimate that 50% or more of the code in modern browsers is there to take care of sloppy HTML in Web pages. For that kind of reason, the story is different in XML. In XML, browsers are supposed to check your document; if there's a problem, they are not supposed to proceed any further. They should let you know about the problem, but that's as far as they're supposed to go.

So how does an XML browser check your document? There are two main checks that XML browsers can make: checking that your document is *well-formed* and checking that it's *valid*. We'll see what these terms mean in more detail in the next chapter, and I'll look at them in overview here.

Well-Formed XML Documents

What does it mean for an XML document to be well formed? To be well formed, an XML document must follow the syntax rules set up for XML by the World Wide Web Consortium in the XML 1.0 specification (which you can find at `www.w3.org/TR/REC-xml`, and which we'll discuss in more detail in the next chapter). Informally, well-formedness often means that the document must contain one or more elements, and one element, the root element, must contain all the other elements. Also, each element must nest inside any enclosing elements properly. For example, this document is not well formed because the `</GREETING>` closing tag comes after the opening `<MESSAGE>` tag for the next element:

```
<?xml version="1.0" encoding="UTF-8"?>
<DOCUMENT>
    <GREETING>
        Hello From XML
    <MESSAGE>
    </GREETING>
        Welcome to the wild and woolly world of XML.
    </MESSAGE>
</DOCUMENT>
```

Valid XML Documents

Most XML browsers will check your document to see if it is well formed. Some of them can also check whether it's valid. An XML document is valid if there is a document type definition (DTD) or XML schema associated with it, and if the document complies with that DTD or schema.

A document's DTD or schema specifies the correct syntax of the document, as we'll see in Chapter 3, "Valid Documents: Creating Document Type Definitions," for DTDs and Chapter 5, "Creating XML Schemas," for schemas. For example, DTDs can be stored in a separate file, or they can be stored in the document itself using a `<!DOCTYPE>` element. Here's an example in which I add a `<!DOCTYPE>` element to the greeting XML document we developed earlier:

Listing ch01_07.xml

```
<?xml version="1.0" encoding="UTF-8"?>
<?xml-stylesheet type="text/css" href="first.css"?>
<!DOCTYPE DOCUMENT [
    <!ELEMENT DOCUMENT (GREETING, MESSAGE)>
```

continues

Listing ch01_07.xml Continued

```
    <!ELEMENT GREETING (#PCDATA)>
    <!ELEMENT MESSAGE (#PCDATA)>
]>
<DOCUMENT>
    <GREETING>
        Hello From XML
    </GREETING>
    <MESSAGE>
        Welcome to the wild and woolly world of XML.
    </MESSAGE>
</DOCUMENT>
```

We'll see more about DTDs in Chapter 3, but this DTD indicates that you can have <GREETING> and <MESSAGE> elements inside a <DOCUMENT> element, that the <DOCUMENT> element is the root element, and that the <GREETING> and <MESSAGE> elements can hold text.

Most XML browsers will check XML documents for well-formedness, but only a few will check for validity. I'll talk more about where to find XML validators later in this chapter.

We've gotten an overview of XML documents now, including how to display them using stylesheets and what a well-formed and valid document is. However, this is only part of the story: Many XML documents are not designed to be displayed in browsers at all—or, even if they are, they are not designed to be used with modern stylesheets (such as browsers that convert XML into industry-specific graphics such as molecular structure, physics equations, or even musical scales). The more powerful use of XML involves *parsing* an XML document to break it down into its component parts and then handling the resulting data yourself. I'll take a look at a few ways of parsing XML data that are available to us next.

Parsing XML Yourself

Say that you have this XML document, ch01_02.xml, which we developed earlier in this chapter:

```
<?xml version="1.0" encoding="UTF-8"?>
<DOCUMENT>
    <GREETING>
        Hello From XML
    </GREETING>
    <MESSAGE>
        Welcome to the wild and woolly world of XML.
    </MESSAGE>
</DOCUMENT>
```

Now say that you wanted to extract the greeting `Hello From XML` from this XML document. One way of doing that is by using XML data islands in Internet Explorer and then using a scripting language, such as JavaScript, to extract and display the text content of the `<GREETING>` element. Here's how that looks in a Web page:

Listing ch01_08.html

```
<HTML>
    <HEAD>
        <TITLE>
            Finding Element Values in an XML Document
        </TITLE>

        <XML ID="firstXML" SRC="ch01_02.xml"></XML>

        <SCRIPT LANGUAGE="JavaScript">
            function getData()
            {
                xmldoc= document.all("firstXML").XMLDocument;

                nodeDoc = xmldoc.documentElement;
                nodeGreeting = nodeDoc.firstChild;

                outputMessage = "Greeting: " +
                        nodeGreeting.firstChild.nodeValue;
                message.innerHTML=outputMessage;
            }
        </SCRIPT>
    </HEAD>

    <BODY>
        <CENTER>
            <H1>
                Finding Element Values in an XML Document
            </H1>

            <DIV ID="message"></DIV>
            <P>
            <INPUT TYPE="BUTTON" VALUE="Get The Greeting"
                ONCLICK="getData()">
        </CENTER>
    </BODY>
</HTML>
```

This Web page displays a button with the caption `Get The Greeting`, as you see in Figure 1-5. When you click the button, the JavaScript code in this page reads in ch01_02.xml, extracts the text from the `<GREETING>` element, and displays that text, as you can also see in Figure 1-5. In this way, you can see how you can create applications that handle XML documents in a customized way—even customized XML browsers.

Figure 1-5
Extracting data from an XML document in Internet Explorer.

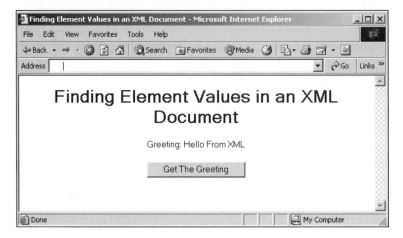

We'll see more about using JavaScript to work with XML later in this book. I'll also cover how JavaScript itself works first, so that if you haven't used it before, there won't be a problem.

Although JavaScript is useful for lightweight XML uses, most XML programming is done in Java today, and we'll take advantage of that in this book as well. Here's an example Java program, ch01_09.java. This program also reads ch01_02.xml and extracts the text content of the `<GREETING>` element (we'll see how to run this kind of program in Chapter 10, "Understanding Java"):

Listing ch01_09.java

```java
import javax.xml.parsers.*;
import org.w3c.dom.*;
import java.io.*;

public class ch01_09
{
    static public void main(String[] argv)
    {
```

```
try {

DocumentBuilderFactory dbf =
    DocumentBuilderFactory.newInstance();

DocumentBuilder db = null;
try {
    db = dbf.newDocumentBuilder();
}
catch (ParserConfigurationException pce) {}

Document doc = null;
    doc = db.parse("ch01_02.xml");

    for (Node node = doc.getDocumentElement().getFirstChild();
        node != null; node = node.getNextSibling()) {

        if (node instanceof Element) {
            if (node.getNodeName().equals("GREETING")) {

                StringBuffer buffer = new StringBuffer();

                for (Node subnode = node.getFirstChild();
                    subnode != null; subnode =
subnode.getNextSibling()){
                    if (subnode instanceof Text) {
                        buffer.append(subnode.getNodeValue());
                    }
                }
                System.out.println(buffer.toString());
            }
        }
    }
} catch (Exception e) {
    e.printStackTrace();
}
    }
}
```

When you run this program, the output looks like this (I'll use % to stand for the command-line prompt in this book. If you're using UNIX, this prompt might look familiar, or your prompt might look something like \home\steve:. If you're using Windows, you get a command-line prompt by opening an MS-DOS window, and your prompt might look something like C:\XML>):

```
%java ch01_09
        Hello From XML
```

(Note that this program returns all the text in the `<GREETING>` element, including the leading spaces.) We'll see how to use Java to parse XML documents later in this book, in Chapter 11, "Java and the XML DOM," and Chapter 12, "Java and SAX." I'll also cover the Java you need to know before getting into the programming; if you haven't programmed in Java before, that won't be a problem.

We've gotten a good overview of how XML works. Now it's time to take a look at how it's already working in the real world, starting with an overview of the XML resources available to you.

XML Resources

A great many XML resources are available to you online. Because it's very important to know about them to get a solid background in XML, I'm going to list them here.

The XML specification is defined by the World Wide Web Consortium (W3C), and that's where you should start looking for XML resources. Here's a good starter list (we'll see all these topics in this book):

- `www.w3c.org/xml`—The World Wide Web Consortium's main XML site, the starting point for all things XML.

- `www.w3.org/XML/1999/XML-in-10-points`—"XML in 10 Points" (actually only seven), an XML overview.

- `www.w3.org/TR/REC-xml`—The official W3C recommendation for XML 1.0, the current (and only) version. It won't be easy to read, however—that's what this book is all about, translating that kind of document to English.

- `www.w3.org/TR/xml-stylesheet/`—All about using stylesheets and XML.

- `www.w3.org/TR/REC-xml-names/`—All about XML namespaces.

- `www.w3.org/Style/XSL/`—All about Extensible Stylesheet Language, XSL.

- `www.w3.org/TR/xslt`—All about XSL transformations, XSLT.

- `www.w3.org/XML/Activity.html`—An overview of current XML activity at W3C.

- `www.w3.org/TR/xmlschema-0/`, `www.w3.org/TR/xmlschema-1/`, and `www.w3.org/TR/xmlschema-2/`—XML Schemas, the alternative to DTDs.

- `www.w3.org/TR/xlink/`—The XLinks specification.

- `www.w3.org/TR/xptr`—The XPointers specification.

- `www.w3.org/TR/xhtml1/`—The XHTML 1.0 specification.

- `www.w3.org/TR/xhtml11/`—The XHTML 1.1 specification.

- `www.w3.org/DOM/`—The W3C Document Object Model, DOM.

Many non-W3C XML resources are out there, too (a casual search for the word *XML* on the Web turns up more than 13 million matches). Here's a list to get started with:

- `www.xml.com` XML.com—This site is filled with XML resources, discussions, and notifications of public events.

- `www.oasis-open.org`—OASIS, the Organization for the Advancement of Structured Information Standards, is dedicated to the adoption of product-independent formats such as XML.

- `XML.org` `www.xml.org`—XML.ORG is designed to provide information about the use of XML in industrial and commercial settings. It's hosted by OASIS and is a reference for XML vocabularies, DTDs, schemas, and namespaces.

- `http://msdn.microsoft.com/xml/default.asp`—Microsoft's XML page.

There are also quite a few XML tutorials out there online (searching for "XML Tutorial" brings up more than 2,300 matches). Here are a few to start with:

- `www-105.ibm.com/developerworks/education.nsf/`
  `xml-onlinecourse-bytitle/`
  `8C8A8628B3DD7EDB852567BD000A8A64?OpenDocument`—
  IBM's free tutorials.

- `www.ucc.ie/xml/`—A comprehensive Frequently Asked Questions (FAQ) list about XML, kept up by some of the contributors to the W3C's XML Working Group. Considered by many the definitive FAQ on XML.

- `http://msdn.microsoft.com/xml/tutorial/default.asp`—Microsoft's XML tutorial.

- `www.xml.com/pub/98/10/guide0.html`—XML.com's XML overview.

In addition, you might find some newsgroups on Usenet useful (note that your news server might not carry all these groups):

- `comp.text.xml`—A good general-purpose, free-floating XML forum.

- `microsoft.public.dotnet.xml`—XML discussions and questions concerning using XML with Microsoft's .NET initiative.

- `microsoft.public.xml`—The general Microsoft XML forum.

That's a good start on XML resources available on the Internet (note that you can use a search engine such as `http://groups.google.com` to search these groups for XML material). What about XML software? I'll take a look at what's out there, starting with XML editors.

XML Editors

To create the XML documents we'll use in this book, all you need is a text editor of some kind, such as vi, emacs, pico, Macintosh's BBEdit or SimpleText, or Windows Notepad or Windows WordPad. By default, XML documents are supposed to be written in Unicode, although in practice you can write them in ASCII—and nearly all of them are written that way so far. Just make sure that when you write an XML document, you save it in your editor's plain text format.

Using Windows Text Editors

Windows text editors such as WordPad have an annoying habit of appending the extension .txt to a filename if they don't understand the extension you've given the file. That's not a problem with .xml files because WordPad understands the extension .xml. However, if you try to save, for example, an XML-based User Interface Language document with the correct extension, .xul, WordPad will give it the extension .xul.txt. To avoid that, place the name of the file in quotation marks when you save it, as in "scrollbars.xul".

However, it can be a lot easier to use an actual XML editor, which is designed explicitly for the job of handling XML. Here's a list of some programs that let you edit your XML:

- **Adobe FrameMaker,** `www.adobe.com`—Adobe includes great but expensive XML support in FrameMaker.

- **XML Pro,** `www.vervet.com/`—Costly but powerful XML editor.

- **XML Writer,** `http://xmlwriter.net/`—Color syntax highlighting, nice interface.

- **XML Notepad,** `msdn.microsoft.com/xml/notepad/intro.asp`—Microsoft's free XML editor, but a little obscure to use.

- **eNotepad,** `www.edisys.com/Products/eNotepad/enotepad.asp`—A WordPad replacement that does well with XML and has a good user interface.

- **XML Spy,** `www.xmlspy.com/`—A good user interface, and easy to use.

You can see XML Spy at work in Figure 1-6, XML Writer in Figure 1-7, XML Notepad in Figure 1-8, and eNotepad in Figure 1-9.

Figure 1-6
XML Spy
editing XML.

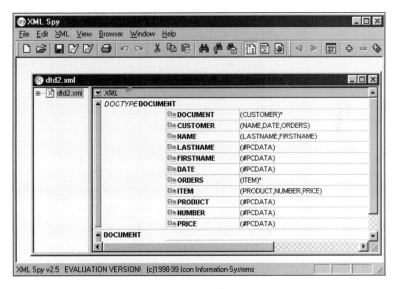

Figure 1-7
XML Writer
editing XML.

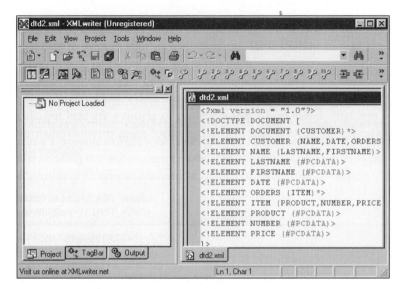

Figure 1-8
XML Notepad
editing XML.

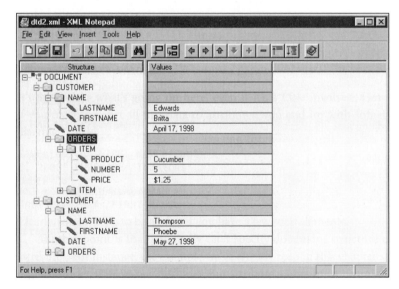

Figure 1-9
eNotepad
editing XML.

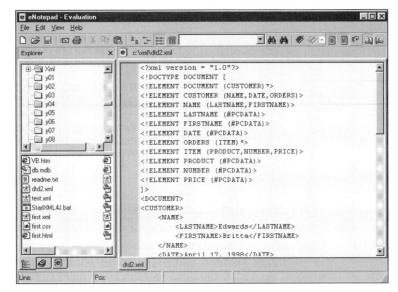

Now that we've gotten an overview of creating XML documents, what about XML browsers? The list is more limited, but there are a few out there. See the next topic.

XML Browsers

Creating a true XML browser is not easy because, besides XML, you have to support a style language such as CSS or XSL. You should also support a scripting language such as JavaScript. These are heavy requirements for most third-party vendors, so the true XML browsers out there are few. But there are a few.

Internet Explorer 6

Whether you love or hate Microsoft, the fact is that Internet Explorer is currently the most powerful XML browser available; you can get it at www.microsoft.com/windows/ie/downloads/ie6/default.asp (although, like many other URLs on the Microsoft site, that URL might change—if so, go to www.microsoft.com/windows/ie/).

Internet Explorer 6.0 can display XML documents directly, as you saw in Figure 1-2, and can also handle them in scripting languages (JScript, Microsoft's version of JavaScript, and Microsoft's VBScript are supported). There is good stylesheet support, and other useful features that we'll see in this book (including the <XML> element, which lets you create XML data islands that you can load XML documents into), and ways of binding XML to ActiveX Data Object (ADO) database recordsets. Internet Explorer 6 is the browser we use most in this book.

There's no question that Microsoft's XML commitment is strong—XML has been integrated even into the Office 2000 suite of applications—but Microsoft sometimes swerves significantly from the W3C standards (that is, when they're not the ones writing those standards themselves).

Netscape Navigator 6

You can get Netscape Navigator 6 or later at `http://wp.netscape.com/download`, which has some XML support. You can see Netscape Navigator 6 at work in Figure 1-3 shown earlier in this chapter.

As with Internet Explorer, support for stylesheets is good in Netscape Navigator. Netscape Navigator 6 also supports the XML-based User Interface Language (XUL), which lets you configure the browser. Netscape Navigator 7 is available in prerelease form as of this writing, but it's not yet stable enough for standard use.

Jumbo

There are relatively few other true XML browsers out there. One of the more famous ones is Jumbo, an XML browser designed to work with XML and the Chemical Markup Language (CML). You can pick up Jumbo for free at `www.xml-cml.org/`. This browser cannot only display XML (although not with stylesheets), but it also can use CML to draw molecules, as you see in Figure 1-10.

Although there are relatively few real XML browsers out there, there *are* a large number of XML *parsers*. You can use these parsers to read XML documents and break them up into their component parts.

Figure 1-10
Jumbo at
work.

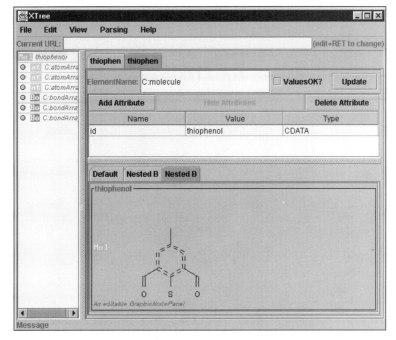

XML Parsers

XML parsers are software packages that you use as part of an application such as Oracle 8i, which includes good XML support, or as part of your own programs. You use an XML parser to dissect XML documents and gain access to the data in them. Starting in Chapter 10, you'll see how to put Sun Microsystems's Java language to work with XML. The current version of Java, version 1.4, contains a great deal of built-in support for working with XML. Here's a list of some of the other XML parsers out there:

- **SAX: The Simple API for XML**—SAX is a well-known parser written by David Megginson, et al. (`www.megginson.com/SAX/index.html`), that uses event-based parsing I'll use SAX in this book.

- **expat**—This is a famous XML parser written in the C programming language by James Clark (`www.jclark.com/xml/expat.html`). This is the parser that's used in Netscape Navigator 6 and in the Perl language's XML::Parser module.

- **expat as a Perl Module (XML::Parser)**—This parser is maintained by Clark Cooper (`ftp://ftp.perl.org/pub/CPAN/modules/by-module/XML/`).

- **TclExpat**—This is a parser written for use in the Tcl programming language (`http://tclxml.sourceforge.net/`)

- **LT XML**—This is an XML developers' toolkit from the Language Technology Group at the University of Edinburgh (`www.ltg.ed.ac.uk/software/xml/`).

- **XML for Java (XML4J)**—From IBM AlphaWorks (`www.alphaworks.ibm.com/tech/xml4j`), this is a famous and very widely used XML parser that adheres well to the W3C standards.

- **XML Microsoft's Validating XML Processor**—This parser and various tools, samples, tutorials, and online documentation can be found at `msdn.microsoft.com/xml/default.asp`.

- **XP**—This is a nonvalidating XML processor written in Java by James Clark (`www.jclark.com/xml/xp/index.html`).

- **Python and XML Processing Preliminary XML Parser**—This parser offers XML support to the Python programming language (`www.python.org/topics/xml/`).

- **XML Testbed**—This one was written by Steve Withall (`www.w3.org/XML/1998/08withall/`).

- **SXP Silfide XML Parser (SXP)**—This is another famous XML parser and, in fact, a complete XML application programming interface (API) for Java (`www.loria.fr/projets/XSilfide/EN/sxp/`).

Parsers will break up your document into its component pieces and make them accessible to other parts of a program, as we'll see later in this book; some parsers check for well-formedness, and fewer check for document validity. However, if you just want to check that your XML is both well formed and valid, all you need is an XML *validator*.

XML Validators

How do you know if your XML document is well formed and valid? One way is to check it with an XML validator, and there are plenty out there to choose from. Validators are packages that will check your XML and give you feedback. Here's a list of some of the XML validators on the Web:

- **W3C XML validator** (`http://validator.w3.org/`)—The official W3C HTML validator. Although it's officially for HTML, it also includes some XML support. Your XML document must be online to be checked with this validator.

- **Tidy** (`www.w3.org/People/Raggett/tidy/`)—Tidy is a beloved utility for cleaning up and repairing Web pages, and it includes limited support for XML. Your XML document must be online to be checked with this validator.

- `http://www.xml.com/pub/a/tools/ruwf/check.html`—This is XML.com's XML validator based on the Lark processor. Your XML document must be online to be checked with this validator.

- `www.ltg.ed.ac.uk/~richard/xml-check.html`—The Language Technology Group at the University of Edinburgh's validator, based on the RXP parser. Your XML document must be online to be checked with this validator.

- `http://www.stg.brown.edu/service/xmlvalid/`—The excellent XML validator from the Scholarly Technology Group at Brown University. This is the only online XML validator that I know of that allows you to check XML documents that are not online. You can use the Web page's file upload control to specify the name of the file on your hard disk that you want to have uploaded and checked.

To see a validator at work, take a look at Figure 1-11. There, I'm asking the XML validator from the Scholarly Technology Group to validate the XML document c:\xml\ch01_02.xml, where I've purposely exchanged the order of the `<MESSAGE>` and `</GREETING>` tags:

```
<?xml version="1.0" encoding="UTF-8"?>
<!DOCTYPE DOCUMENT [
    <!ELEMENT DOCUMENT (GREETING, MESSAGE)>
    <!ELEMENT GREETING (#PCDATA)>
    <!ELEMENT MESSAGE (#PCDATA)>
]>
<DOCUMENT>
    <GREETING>
        Hello From XML
```

continues

```
    <MESSAGE>
    </GREETING>
        Welcome to the wild and woolly world of XML.
    </MESSAGE>
</DOCUMENT>
```

You can see the results in Figure 1-12; the validator is indicating that there is a problem with these two tags.

XML validators give you a powerful way of checking your XML documents—and that's useful because XML is much stricter about making sure a document is correct than HTML browsers (recall that XML browsers are not supposed to make attempts to fix XML documents if they find a problem—they're just supposed to stop loading the document).

We've gotten a good overview of XML already in this chapter, and in a few pages I'll start taking a look at a number of XML languages that are already developed. However, there are a few more topics that are useful to cover first, especially if you have programmed in HTML and want to know the differences between XML and HTML.

Figure 1-11
Using an XML
validator.

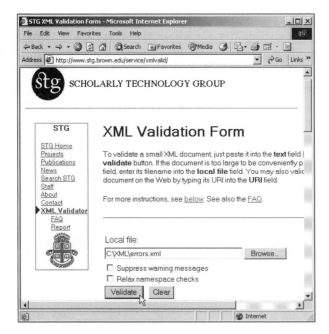

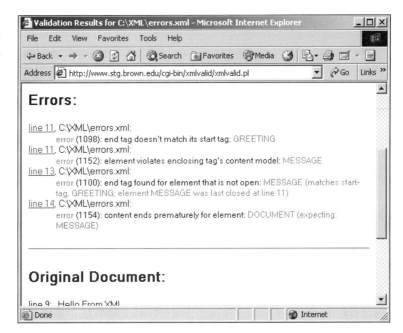

Figure 1-12
The results
from an XML
validator.

CSS and XSL

Stylesheets are becoming increasing important in HTML because, in HTML 4, many built-in style features such as the <CENTER> element have become deprecated (declared obsolete) in favor of stylesheets. However, most HTML programming ignores stylesheets entirely.

The story is different in XML, however. In XML, you create your own elements, which means that if you want a browser to display them, you have to tell it how. This is both good and bad: good because it allows you to use the powerful Cascading Style Sheet (CSS) and Extensible Stylesheet Language (XSL) specifications to customize the appearance of your XML elements far beyond what's possible with standard HTML, but bad because it can demand a lot of additional work. (One way of getting around the necessity of designing your own stylesheets is to use an established XML language that has its own stylesheets.)

All this is to say that XML defines the structure and semantics of the document, not its format; if you want to display XML directly, you can either use the default presentation in Internet Explorer or use a stylesheet to set up the presentation yourself.

Two main ways exist for specifying a stylesheet for an XML document: with CSS and with XSL, both of which I'll dig into in this book. CSS is popularly used with HTML documents and is widely supported. Using CSS, you can specify the formatting of individual elements, create style classes, and set up fonts, colors, and even placement of elements in the page.

XSL, on the other hand, is ultimately a better choice to work with XML documents because it's more powerful (in fact, XSL stylesheets are themselves well-formed XML documents). XSL documents are made up of rules that are applied to XML documents. When a pattern that you've specified in the XSL document is recognized in the XML document, the rules transform the matched XML into something entirely new. You can even transform XML into HTML this way.

Whereas CSS can only set the format and placement of elements, XSL can reorder elements in a document, change them entirely, display some but hide others, select styles based not just on elements but also on element attributes (XML elements can have attributes just as HTML elements can, and I'll introduce them in the next chapter), select styles based on element location, and much more. There are two ways to approach XSL: with XSL transformations and XSL formatting objects. We'll take a look at both in this book.

Here are some good online resources for stylesheets:

- `www.w3.org/Style/CSS/`—The W3C outline and overview of CSS programming
- `www.w3.org/TR/REC-CSS1/`—The W3C CSS1 specification
- `www.w3.org/TR/REC-CSS2/`—The W3C CSS2 specification
- `www.w3.org/Style/XSL/`—The W3C XSL page

XLinks and XPointers

It's hard to imagine the World Wide Web without hyperlinks, and, of course, HTML documents excel at letting you link from one to another. How about XML? In XML, it turns out, you use XLinks and XPointers.

XLinks let any element become a link, not just a single element as with the HTML <A> element. That's a good thing because XML doesn't have a built-in <A> element. In XML, you define your own elements, and it only makes sense that you can define which of those represent links to other documents.

In fact, XLinks are more powerful than simple hyperlinks. XLinks can be bidirectional, allowing the user to return after following a link. They can even be multidirectional—in fact, they can be sophisticated enough to point to the nearest mirror site from which a resource can be fetched.

XPointers, on the other hand, point not to a whole document, but to a part of a document. In fact, XPointers are smart enough to point to a specific element in a document, or the second instance of such an element, or the 11,904th instance. They can even point to the first child element of another element, and so on. The idea is that XPointers are powerful enough to locate specific parts of another document without forcing you to add more markup to the target document.

On the other hand, the whole idea of XLinks and XPointers is relatively new and not fully implemented in any browser. We will see what's possible today later in this book.

Here are some XLink and XPointer references online—take a look for more information on these topics:

- `www.w3.org/TR/xlink/`—The W3C XLink page
- `www.w3.org/TR/xptr`—The W3C XPointer page

URLs Versus URIs

Having discussed XLinks and XPointers, I should also mention that the XML specification expands the idea of standard URLs (uniform resource locators) into URIs (uniform resource identifiers).

URLs are well understood and well supported on the Internet today. On the other hand, as you'd expect given the addition of XLinks and XPointers to XML, the idea of URIs is more general than simple URLs.

URIs represent a way of finding resources on the Internet, and they center more on the resource than the actual location. The idea is that, at least in theory, URIs can locate the nearest mirror site for a resource or even track a document that has been moved from one location to another.

In practice, the concept of URIs is still being developed, and most software will still handle only URLs.

URI: Formal Definition

You might want to look up the formal definition of URIs, which you can find in its entirety at `www.ics.uci.edu/pub/ietf/uri/rfc2396.txt`.

ASCII, Unicode, and the Universal Character System

The actual characters in documents are stored as numeric codes, and today the most common code set is the American Standard Code for Information Interchange (ASCII). ASCII codes extend from 0 to 127; for example, the ASCII code for *A* is 65, the ASCII code for *B* is 66, and so on.

On the other hand, the World Wide Web is just that today—worldwide. And plenty of scripts are not handled by ASCII, including Bengali, Armenian, Hebrew, Thai, Tibetan, Japanese Katakana, Arabic, and Cyrillic.

For that reason, the default character set specified for XML by W3C is Unicode, not ASCII. Unicode codes are made up of 2 bytes, not 1, so they extend from 0 to 65,535 instead of just 0 to 255 (however, to make things easier, the Unicode codes 0 to 255 do indeed correspond to the ASCII 0 to 255 codes). Unicode can therefore include many of the symbols commonly used in worldwide character and ideograph sets today.

Only about 40,000 Unicode codes are reserved at this point (of which about 20,000 codes are used for Han ideographs, although there are more than 80,000 such ideographs defined and 11,000 for Korean Hangul syllables).

In practice, Unicode support, like many parts of the XML technology, is not fully supported on most platforms today. Windows 95/98 does not have full support for Unicode, although Windows NT and Windows 2000 come much closer (and XML Spy lets you use Unicode to write XML documents in Windows NT). What this means most often is that XML documents are written in simply ASCII or in UTF-8, which is a compressed version of Unicode that uses 8 bits to represent characters (in practice, this is well suited to ASCII documents because multiple bytes are needed for many non-ASCII symbols and because ASCII documents converted to Unicode are two times as long). Here's how to specify the UTF-8 character encoding in an XML document:

```
<?xml version="1.0" encoding="UTF-8"?>
<DOCUMENT>
    <GREETING>
        Hello From XML
    </GREETING>
    <MESSAGE>
        Welcome to the wild and woolly world of XML.
    </MESSAGE>
</DOCUMENT>
```

In fact, the default for XML processors today is to assume that your document is in UTF-8, so if you omit the encoding specification, UTF-8 is assumed. So if you're writing XML documents in ASCII, you'll have no trouble.

Actually, not even Unicode has enough space for all symbols in common use, so a new specification, the Universal Character System (UCS, also called ISO 10646) uses 4 bytes per symbol. This gives it a range of two billion symbols—far more than needed. You can specify that you want to use pure Unicode encoding in your XML documents by using the UCS-2 encoding (also called ISO-10646-UCS-2), which is compressed 2-byte UCS. You can also use UTF-16, which is a special encoding that represents UCS symbols using 2 bytes so that the result corresponds to UCS-2. Straight UCS encoding is referred to as UCS-4 (also called ISO-10646-UCS-4).

You can write documents in a local character set and use a translation utility to translate them to Unicode, or you can insert the actual Unicode codes directly into your documents. For example, the Unicode for π is 0x3C0 in hexadecimal, so you can insert π into your document with the character entity (more on entities in the next chapter) π.

More character sets are available than those mentioned here; for a longer list, take a look at the list posted by the Internet Assigned Numbers Authority (IANA), at www.iana.org/assignments/character-sets.

Converting ASCII to Unicode

If you want to convert ASCII files to straight Unicode, you can use the native2ascii program that comes with Sun Microsystems's Java Software Development Kit. Using this tool, you can convert to Unicode like this: `native2ascii file.txt file.uni`. You can also convert to a number of other encodings besides Unicode, such as compressed Unicode, UTF-8.

XML Applications

We've seen a lot of theory in this chapter, so I'm going to spend the rest of this chapter taking a look at how XML is used today in the real world. The world of XML is huge these days; in fact, XML is now used internally even in Netscape and Microsoft products, as well as installations of programming languages such as Perl. You can find a good list of organizations that produce their own XML-based languages at www.xml.org/xml/marketplace_company.jsp.

It's useful and encouraging to see how XML is being used today in these XML-based languages. Here's a new piece of terminology: As you know, XML is a metamarkup language, so it's actually used to create languages. The languages so created are applications of XML; as a result, they're called *XML applications.*

Note that the term *XML application* means an application of XML to a specific domain, such as MathML, the mathematics markup language; it does not refer to a program that uses XML (a fact that causes a lot of confusion among people who know nothing about XML).

Thousands of XML applications are around today, and we'll see some of them here. You can see the advantage to various groups when defining their own markup languages. For example, physicists or chemists can use the symbols and graphics of their discipline in customized browsers. In fact, I'll start with Chemical Markup Language (CML) now.

XML at Work: Chemical Markup Language

Peter Murray-Rust developed CML as a very early XML application, so it has been around quite a while. Many people think of CML as a sort of HTML+Molecules, and that's not a bad characterization. Using CML, you can display the structure of complex molecules.

With CML, chemists can create and publish molecule specifications for easy interchange. Note that the real value of this is not so much in looking at individual chemicals as it is in being able to search CML repositories for molecules matching specific characteristics.

I've already mentioned a famous CML browser available: Jumbo, which you can download for free from www.xml-cml.org/jumbo.html. Jumbo is not only for handling CML; you can also use it to display the structure of an XML document in general. However, there's no question that the novelty of Jumbo is that it can use CML to create graphical representations of molecules.

We've already seen an example in Jumbo in Figure 1-10, where Jumbo is displaying the molecule thiophenol. Here is the file thiophenol.xml that it's reading to display that molecule:

```
<?jumbo:namespace ns="http://www.xml-cml.org" prefix="C"
    java="jumbo.cmlxml.*Node" ?>
<C:molecule id="thiophenol">
    <C:atomArray builtin="elsym">
        C C C C C C S C C O O
```

```
    </C:atomArray>
    <C:atomArray builtin="x2" type="float">
        0 0.866 0.866 0 -0.866 -0.866
        0.0 0.0  1.732 -1.732 1.732 -1.732
    </C:atomArray>
    <C:atomArray builtin="y2" type="float">
        1 0.5   -0.5  -1.0 -0.5   0.5
        -2.0  2.0  1.0   1.0   2.0   2.0
    </C:atomArray>
    <C:bondArray builtin="atid1">
        1 2 3 4 5 6 1 4 2 9  6   10
    </C:bondArray>
    <C:bondArray builtin="atid2">
        2 3 4 5 6 1 8 7 9 11 10 12
    </C:bondArray>
    <C:bondArray builtin="order" type="integer">
        4 4 4 4 4 4 1 1 1 2  1   2
    </C:bondArray>
</C:molecule>
```

XML at Work:
Mathematical Markup Language

Mathematical Markup Language was designed to fill a significant gap in Web documents: equations. In fact, Tim Berners-Lee first developed the World Wide Web at CERN so that high-energy physicists could exchange papers and documents. However, there has been no way to display true equations in Web browsers for nearly a decade.

Mathematical Markup Language (MathML) fixes that. MathML is itself a W3C specification, and you can find it at www.w3.org/Math/. Using MathML, you can display equations and all kinds of mathematical terms. (It's not powerful enough for many specialized areas of the sciences or mathematics yet, but it's growing all the time.)

Because of the limited audience for this kind of presentation, no major browser yet supports MathML. However, the Amaya browser, which is W3C's own testbed browser for testing new HTML and XHTML elements (but it's not, unfortunately, an XML browser) has some limited support. You can download Amaya for free from www.w3.org/Amaya/.

Here's a MathML document that displays the equation $3Z^2 - 6Z + 12 = 0$ (this document uses an XML namespace, which we'll see more about in the next chapter):

```xml
<?xml version="1.0"?>
<html xmlns:m="http://www.w3.org/TR/REC-MathML/">
<math>
    <m:mrow>
        <m:mrow>
            <m:mn>3</m:mn>
            <m:mo>&InvisibleTimes;</m:mo>
            <m:msup>
                <m:mi>Z</m:mi>
                <m:mn>2</m:mn>
            </m:msup>
            <m:mo>-</m:mo>
            <m:mrow>
                <m:mn>6</m:mn>
                <m:mo>&InvisibleTimes;</m:mo>
                <m:mi>Z</m:mi>
            </m:mrow>
            <m:mo>+</m:mo>
            <m:mn>12</m:mn>
        </m:mrow>
        <m:mo>=</m:mo>
        <m:mn>0</m:mn>
    </m:mrow>
</math>
```

You can see the results of this document in the Amaya browser in Figure 1-13.

Figure 1-13
Displaying MathML in the Amaya browser.

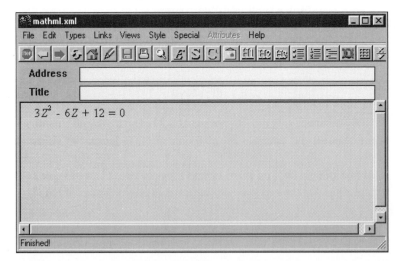

XML at Work: Synchronized Multimedia Integration Language

Synchronized Multimedia Integration Language (SMIL, pronounced "smile") has been around for quite some time. It's a W3C standard that you can find more about at www.w3.org/AudioVideo/#SMIL.

SMIL attempts to fix a problem with modern "multimedia" browsers. Usually, such browsers can handle only one aspect of multimedia at a time—video, audio, or images—and never more than that. SMIL lets you create television-like fast cuts and true multimedia presentations by letting you specify when various multimedia files are played.

The idea is that SMIL lets you specify what multimedia files are played when; SMIL itself does not describe or encapsulate any multimedia itself.

Microsoft, Macromedia, and Compaq have a semicompeting specification, HTML+TIME, which I'll take a look at next. Microsoft hasn't implemented much SMIL in Internet Explorer yet because of this reason. You can find a SMIL applet written in Java at www.empirenet.com/~joseram, as well as some stunning examples of symphonies coordinated with images.

Here's an example SMIL document that creates a multimedia sequence playing mozart1.wav and amadeus1.mov, displaying mozart1.htm, then playing mozart2.wav and amadeus2.mov, and displaying mozart2.htm:

```
<?xml version="1.0"?>
<!DOCTYPE smil PUBLIC "-//W3C//DTD SMIL 1.0//EN"
  "http://www.w3.org/TR/REC-smil/SMIL10.dtd">
<smil>
    <body>
        <seq id="mozart">
            <audio src="mozart1.wav"/>
            <video src="amadeus1.mov"/>
            <text src="mozart1.htm"/>
            <audio src="mozart2.wav"/>
            <video src="amadeus2.mov"/>
            <text src="mozart2.htm"/>
        </seq>
    </body>
</smil>
```

XML at Work: HTML+TIME

Microsoft, Macromedia, and Compaq have a multimedia alternative to SMIL called Timed Interactive Multimedia Extension (referred to as HTML+TIME), which is an XML application. Whereas SMIL documents let you manipulate other files, HTML+TIME lets you handle both HTML and multimedia presentations in the same page.

HTML+TIME is not nearly as powerful as SMIL, but Microsoft has shown relatively little interest in SMIL. You can find out about HTML+TIME at msdn.microsoft.com/workshop/Author/behaviors/time.asp. HTML+ TIME is implemented in the Internet Explorer as a *behavior*, which is a construct in Internet Explorer that lets you separate code from data. You can find more information about Internet Explorer behaviors at msdn.microsoft.com/workshop/c-frame.htm#/workshop/author/default.asp.

Here's an example HTML+TIME document that displays the words Hello, there, from, HTML+TIME, spacing the words' appearance apart by 2 seconds and then repeating:

Listing ch01_10.html

```
<HTML>
    <HEAD>
        <TITLE>
            Using HTML+TIME
        </TITLE>
        <STYLE>
            .time {behavior: url(#default#time);}
        </STYLE>
    </HEAD>

    <BODY>
        <DIV CLASS="time" t:REPEAT="5" t:DUR="10" t:TIMELINE="par">
            <DIV CLASS="time" t:BEGIN="0" t:DUR="10">Hello</DIV>
            <DIV CLASS="time" t:BEGIN="2" t:DUR="10">there</DIV>
            <DIV CLASS="time" t:BEGIN="4" t:DUR="10">from</DIV>
            <DIV CLASS="time" t:BEGIN="6" t:DUR="10">HTML+TIME.</DIV>
        </DIV>
    </BODY>
</HTML>
```

You can see the results of this HTML+TIME document in Figure 1-14.

Figure 1-14
An
HTML+TIME
document at
work.

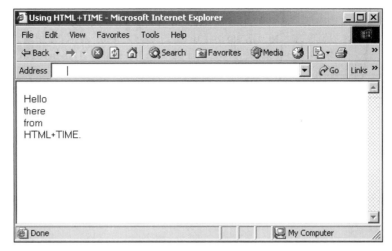

HTML+TIME actually builds on SMIL to a great extent. The example from the previous topic on SMIL would look this way in HTML+TIME:

```
<t:seq id="mozart">
    <t:audio src="mozart1.wav"/>
    <t:video src="amadeus1.mov"/>
    <t:textstream src="mozart1.htm"/>
    <t:audio src="mozart2.wav"/>
    <t:video src="amadeus2.mov"/>
    <t:textstream src="mozart2.htm"/>
</seq>
```

XML at Work: XHTML

One of the biggest XML applications around today is XHTML, the translation of HTML 4.0 into XML by W3C. It's attracting a lot of attention. I'll dig into XHTML in some depth in this book.

W3C introduced XHTML to bridge the gap between HTML and XML, and to introduce more people to XML. XHTML is simply an application that mimics HTML 4.0 in such a way that you can display the results—true XML documents—in current Web browsers. XHTML is an exciting development in the XML world, and we'll be spending some time with it later in this book.

Here are some XHTML resources online:

- www.w3.org/MarkUp/Activity.html—The W3C Hypertext Markup activity page, which has an overview of XHTML

- www.w3.org/TR/xhtml1/—The XHTML 1.0 specification (in more common use than XHTML 1.1 today)

- www.w3.org/TR/xhtml11/—The XHTML 1.1 working draft of the XHTML 1.1 module-based specification

XHTML 1.0 comes in three different versions: transitional, frameset, and strict. The transitional version is the most popular because it supports HTML more or less as it's used today. The frameset version supports XHTML documents that display frames (this version is different than the transitional version because documents in the transitional version are based on the <body> element, whereas documents that use frames are based on the <frameset> element). The strict version omits all the HTML elements deprecated in HTML 4.0 (of which there were quite a few).

XHTML 1.1 is a form of the XHTML 1.0 strict version made a little more strict by omitting support for some elements and adding support for a few more (such as <ruby> for annotated text). You can find a list of the differences between XHTML 1.0 and XHTML 1.1 at www.w3.org/TR/xhtml11/ changes.html#a_changes.

Here's an example XHTML document using the XHTML 1.0 transitional DTD. You can display this document in any standard HTML browser (note that tag names are all in lowercase in XHTML):

Listing ch01_11.html

```
<?xml version="1.0"?>
<!DOCTYPE html PUBLIC "-//W3C//DTD XHTML 1.0 Transitional//EN"
"http://www.w3.org/TR/xhtml1/DTD/xhtml1-transitional.dtd">
<html xmlns="http://www.w3.org/1999/xhtml" xml:lang="en" lang="en">
    <head>
        <title>
            Web page number one!
        </title>
    </head>

    <body>
        <h1>
            Welcome to XHTML!
        </h1>
        <center>
```

```
       This is simple text that appears in this page.
            <p>
                Here's a new paragraph!
            </p>
        </center>
    </body>
</html>
```

You can see the results of this XHTML in Figure 1-15. Writing XHTML is a lot like HTML, except that you have to adhere to XML syntax (such as making sure that every element has a closing tag).

Figure 1-15
Displaying
XHTML.

XML at Work: Microsoft's .NET

Microsoft's .NET initiative is based substantially on XML, which it uses to send data back and forth between .NET components. In .NET, you don't usually see the XML—it's handled behind the scenes automatically—but it's there.

Here's an example in VB .NET that will expose the behind-the-scenes XML: The data in .NET datasets is transported using XML, and this example explicitly writes the `authors` database table of the `pubs` example database to an XML file when the user clicks a button. When the user clicks another button, the code reads that file back into a second .NET dataset. You can see this example at work in Figure 1-16 (which also displays the data in the `authors` table).

Figure 1-16
Writing data
in XML in
VB .NET.

Here's the VB .NET code—when the user clicks the "Write existing dataset to XML file" button you see in Figure 1-16, the authors table in the dataset is written to the file dataset.xml; and when the user clicks the "Create new dataset from XML file" button, a new dataset is created and reads its data in from dataset.xml:

```
Private Sub Button1_Click(ByVal sender As System.Object, _
    ByVal e As System.EventArgs) Handles Button1.Click
    DataSet11.Clear()
    OleDbDataAdapter1.Fill(DataSet11)
    DataSet11.WriteXml("dataset.xml")
End Sub

Private Sub Button2_Click(ByVal sender As System.Object, _
    ByVal e As System.EventArgs) Handles Button2.Click
    Dim ds As New DataSet()
    ds.ReadXml("dataset.xml")
    DataGrid1.SetDataBinding(ds, "authors")
End Sub
```

You can see the dataset's data in the dataset.xml file, which looks like this—it's pure XML (and matches the data you see in Figure 1-16):

```
<?xml version="1.0" standalone="yes"?>
<DataSet1 xmlns="http://www.tempuri.org/DataSet1.xsd">
   <authors>
     <au_id>172-32-1176</au_id>
     <au_lname>White</au_lname>
     <au_fname>Johnson</au_fname>
     <phone>408 496-7223</phone>
     <address>10932 Bigge Rd.</address>
     <city>Menlo Park</city>
     <state>CA</state>
```

```
  <zip>94025</zip>
  <contract>true</contract>
</authors>
<authors>
  <au_id>213-46-8915</au_id>
  <au_lname>Green</au_lname>
  <au_fname>Marjorie</au_fname>
  <phone>415 986-7020</phone>
         .
         .
         .
```

And that provides us with a glimpse at the actual XML used behind the scenes to transport data in .NET—something that's usually handled automatically.

XML at Work: Open Software Description

Open Software Description (OSD) was developed by Marimba and Microsoft, and you can find more about this XML application at www.w3.org/TR/NOTE-OSD.html. OSD allows you to specify how and when software is updated via the Internet.

Not everyone thinks OSD is a great idea—after all, many users want control over when their software is updated. New versions might have incompatibilities with old versions, for example.

Here's an example .osd file that handles updates for a word processor named SuperDuperTextPro from SuperDuperSoft:

```
<?xml version="1.0"?>
<CHANNEL HREF="http://www.superdupersoft.com/updates.html">
    <TITLE>
        SuperDuperTextPro Updates
    </TITLE>
    <USAGE VALUE="SoftwareUpdate"/>
    <SOFTPKG
        HREF="http://updates.superdupersoft.com/updates.html"
        NAME="{34567A7E-8BE7-99C0-8746-0034829873A3}"
        VERSION="2,4,6">
        <TITLE>
            SuperDuperTextPro
        </TITLE>
        <ABSTRACT>
            SuperDuperTextPro version 206 with sideburns!!!
        </ABSTRACT>
        <IMPLEMENTATION>
            <CODEBASE HREF=
                "http://www.superdupersoft.com/new.exe"/>
        </IMPLEMENTATION>
    </SOFTPKG>
</CHANNEL>
```

XML at Work: Scalable Vector Graphics

Scalable Vector Graphics (SVG) is another W3C-based XML application that is a good idea but that has found only limited implementation so far (notably, in such programs as CorelDraw and various Adobe products such as Adobe Illustrator). Using SVG, you can draw two-dimensional graphics using markup. You can find the SVG specification at www.w3.org/TR/SVG/ and an overview at www.w3.org/Graphics/SVG/Overview.htm8.

Note that because SVG describes graphics, not text, it's harder for current browsers to implement, and are no browsers today have full SVG implementations. Other graphics standards have been proposed, such as the Precision Graphics Markup Language (PGML) proposed to the W3C (www.w3.org/TR/1998/NOTE-PGML) by IBM, Adobe, Netscape, and Sun.

Here's an example PGML document that draws a blue box:

```
<?xml version="1.0"?>
<!DOCTYPE pgml SYSTEM "/DTDs/pgml.dtd">
<pgml>
  <group fillcolor="blue">
    <path>
      <moveto x="0" y="0"/>
      <lineto x="0" y="1000"/>
      <lineto x="1000" y="1000"/>
      <lineto x="1000" y="0"/>
      <closepath/>
    </path>
  </group>
</pgml>
```

XML at Work: Vector Markup Language

Vector Markup Language (VML) is an alternative to SVG that is implemented in Microsoft Internet Explorer. You can find out more about VML at www.w3.org/TR/NOTE-VML. Using VML, you can draw many vector-based graphics figures; here's an example that draws a yellow oval, a blue box, and a red squiggle:

Listing ch01_12.html

```
<HTML xmlns:v="urn:schemas-microsoft-com:vml">

    <HEAD>
        <TITLE>
            Using Vector Markup Language
        </TITLE>
```

```
        <STYLE>
        v\:* {behavior: url(#default#VML);}
        </STYLE>
    </HEAD>

    <BODY>
        <CENTER>
            <H1>
                Using Vector Markup Language
            </H1>
        </CENTER>
        <P>
        <v:oval STYLE='width:100pt; height:75pt'
            fillcolor="yellow"> </v:oval>
        <P>
        <v:rect STYLE='width:100pt; height:75pt' fillcolor="blue"
            strokecolor="red" STROKEWEIGHT="2pt"/>
        <P>
        <v:polyline
            POINTS="20pt,55pt,100pt,-10pt,180pt,65pt,260pt,25pt"
            strokecolor="red" STROKEWEIGHT="2pt"/>
    </BODY>
</HTML>
```

You can see the results of this VML in Figure 1-17.

Figure 1-17
Vector Markup
Language
at work.

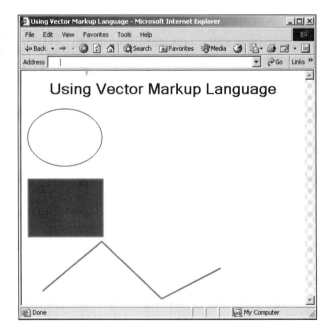

Extensible Business Reporting Language

Extensible Business Reporting Language (XBRL, formerly named XFRML) is an open specification that uses XML to describe financial statements. You can find more on XBRL at www.xbrl.org/. Using XBRL, you can codify business financial statements in a way that makes it easy to search them en masse and review them quickly, extracting the information you want.

Here's a sample XBRL document that gives you an idea of what this application looks like at work:

```xml
<?xml version="1.0" encoding="utf-8" ?>
    <group xmlns="http://www.xbrl.org/us/aicpa-us-gaap"
        xmlns:gpsi="http://www.xbrl.org/TaxonomyCustom.xsd"
        id="543-AB" entity="NASDAQ:GPSI" period="1999-05-31"
        schemaLocation="http://www.xbrl.org/TaxonomyCustom.xsd"
        scaleFactor="6" precision="9" type="USGAAP:Financial"
        unit="ISO4217:USD" decimalPattern="" formatName="">
        <item id="IS-025"
            type="operatingExpenses.researchExpense"
            period="P1Y/1999-05-31">20427</item>
        <item id="IS-026"
            type="operatingExpenses.researchExpense"
            period="P1Y/1998-05-31">12586</item>
    </group>
    <group type="gpsi:detail.quarterly" period="1998-05-31">
        <item period="1997-06-01/1998-07-31">0.12</item>
        <item period="1997-09-01/1997-11-30">0.16</item>
        <item period="1997-12-01/1998-02-28">0.17</item>
        <item period="1998-03-01/1998-05-31">-0.12</item>
        <item period="1998-06-01/1998-05-31">0.33</item>
    </group>
    <group type="gpsi:detail.quarterly" period="1999-05-31">
        <item period="1998-06-01/1998-08-31">0.15</item>
        <item period="1998-09-01/1998-11-30">0.20</item>
        <item period="1998-12-01/1999-02-28">0.23</item>
        <item period="1999-03-01/1999-05-31">0.28</item>
        <item period="1998-06-01/1999-05-31">0.86</item>
    </group>
    <group type="gpsi:detail.quarterly" period="1998-05-31">
        <item period="1997-06-01/1998-07-31">0.11</item>
        <item period="1997-09-01/1997-11-30">0.15</item>
        <item period="1997-12-01/1998-02-28">0.17</item>
        <item period="1998-03-01/1998-05-31">-0.12</item>
        <item period="1998-06-01/1998-05-31">0.32</item>
    </group>
```

Resource Description Framework

Resource Description Framework (RDF) is an XML application that specializes in metadata—that is, data about other data. You use RDF to specify information about other resources, such as Web pages, movies, automobiles, or practically anything. You can find more information about RDF at www.w3.org/RDF/; I'll be discussing it later in the book as well.

Using RDF, you create vocabularies that describe resources. For example, the Dublin Core is an RDF vocabulary that handles metadata for Web pages; you can find more information about it at http://dublincore.org/. Using the Dublin Core, you can specify a great deal of information about Web pages. The Dublin Core is designed ultimately to replace the unsystematic use of <META> tags in today's pages. When systemized, that information will be much more tractable to Web search engines.

Here's an example RDF page using the Dublin Core that gives information about a Web page:

```
<RDF:RDF xmlns:RDF="http://www.w3.org/1999/02/22-rdf-syntax-ns#"
    xmlns:DC="http://purl.org/DC/">
    <RDF:Description about="http://www.starpowder.com/xml">
        <DC:Format>HTML</DC:Format>
        <DC:Language>en</DC:Language>
        <DC:Date>2002-02-02</DC:date>
        <DC:Type>tutorial</DC:Type>
        <DC:Title>Welcome to XML!</DC:Title>
    </RDF:Description>
</RDF:RDF>
```

Note that many more XML applications exist than can be covered in one chapter—and plenty of them work behind the scenes. As mentioned earlier, Microsoft's .NET initiative uses XML extensively internally. Microsoft Office 2000 and Office XP can handle HTML as well as other types of documents, but HTML doesn't allow it to store everything it needs in a document; thus, it also includes some XML behind the scenes (in fact, Office 2000 and XP's vector graphics are done using VML). Even relatively early versions of Netscape Navigator allowed you to look for sites much like the current one you're viewing; to do that, it connected to a program that uses XML internally. As you can see, XML is everywhere you look on the Internet.

And that's it for our overview chapter. We've gotten a solid foundation in XML here, and it's a good place to begin. The next step is to get systematic and to start getting all the actual ground rules for creating XML documents under our belts. I'll turn to that in Chapter 2.

CHAPTER 2
Creating Well-Formed XML Documents

In the previous chapter, we got our start in XML and got an overview of how XML lets you structure your own documents, what XML is all about, and some of the uses you can make of it. It's time to take a look at XML in more depth and to sharpen our XML understanding until it's crystal clear.

In HTML, about 100 elements already are defined. Browsers can check the HTML in a Web page and display that page as they see fit. In XML, you have more freedom—and so more responsibility. In XML, you define your own elements, and it's up to you to decide how they should be used. Despite their apparently free-form nature, XML documents are subject to a number of rules that allow them to be handled in a useful and reproducible way.

In fact, the rules that XML documents are subject to are significantly more stringent than the rules that HTML documents are subject to. As mentioned in the previous chapter, if an XML document cannot be successfully understood by an XML processor, the processor is not supposed to make *any* guesses about the structure of the document at all—it's just supposed to quit, possibly returning an error.

As we also saw in the previous chapter, there are two specific constraints that XML documents are subject to: *well-formedness* and *validity*. As far as World Wide Web Consortium (W3C) is concerned, well-formedness is the more basic constraint. In the XML 1.0 specification itself, which represents the foundation of this and the next chapter, the W3C says that you can't even call a data object an XML document unless it's well formed:

> *A data object is an XML document if it is well-formed,*
> *as defined in this specification. A well-formed XML document may*
> *in addition be valid if it meets certain further constraints.*

Why is it so important that XML documents be well formed? Why does the W3C specify that XML processors should not attempt to fix documents that are not well formed?

The W3C makes this stipulation mainly to stop XML processors from doing the same thing that HTML browsers have done to HTML: By trying to fix things, the major browsers have introduced their own versions of HTML that authors now rely on. The result is that there are many "versions" of HTML current today, and the W3C wants to avoid this problem with XML.

In this chapter, we're going to see what makes an XML document well formed, which is the minimal requirement that a data object must satisfy to be an XML document. The second constraint that you can require of XML documents is that they be valid, which means that they must obey the document type definition (DTD) or schema that you use to specify the legal syntax of the document. This chapter is all about what makes XML documents well formed, and the next chapter is all about what makes them valid.

Now that we're taking a look at how to build XML documents in a formal way, I'm going to start from the beginning so the foundation we're building is complete and solid. And that means starting with the W3C itself.

The World Wide Web Consortium

We already know that the W3C is the body responsible for defining exactly what XML is, but what is the W3C? The W3C is not a government body. Instead, it's a group of member organizations (more than 400 at the moment) that have an interest in the World Wide Web. The W3C is hosted by the Massachusetts Institute of Technology, Laboratory for Computer Science (MIT/LCS) in the United States; the Institut National de Recherche en Informatique et en Automatique (INRIA) in Europe; and the Keio University Shonan Fujisawa Campus in Japan. Currently, it has about 50 full-time staff members.

How does the W3C set up specifications for the Web? It does so by publishing those standards in HTML (and recently, in XHTML) form at its Web site, www.w3c.org. These specifications are given three different levels:

- **Notes**—Specifications that were usually submitted to the W3C by a member organization and that the W3C is making public although not necessarily endorsing. For example, the note submitted by Microsoft to the W3C on the Vector Markup Language (VML) is www.w3.org/TR/NOTE-VML.

- **Working drafts**—A working draft is a specification that is under consideration and open to comment. It's inappropriate to refer to such works as standards or as anything other than working drafts. For example, the working draft for XHTML 1.1 is at www.w3.org/TR/xhtml11/.

- **Recommendations**—Working drafts that the W3C has accepted become recommendations, which is the term the W3C uses when it publishes its standards (because the W3C is not a government body, it does not use the term *standard*). For example, the XML 1.0 recommendation is at www.w3.org/TR/REC-xml.

Besides these official specification levels, the W3C has *candidate recommendations*, which are working drafts that have been proposed but not yet accepted as recommendations, and *companion recommendations*, which augment recommendations. In fact, there are plenty of companion recommendations for XML (such as schemas, XLinks, XPointers, and so on), and you'll find a good list of them at www.w3c.org/xml.

The recommendation for XML 1.0, which defines XML, is at www.w3.org/TR/REC-xml, and you'll also find it in Appendix A, "The XML Specification." That specification is the most important one as far as this book is concerned; together with the associated standards (Unicode and ISO/IEC 10646 for characters, Internet RFC 1766 for language identification tags, ISO 639 for language name codes, and ISO 3166 for country name codes), that recommendation gives you all you need to understand XML Version 1.0 and create XML documents. Now it's time to put that recommendation to work, creating well-formed XML documents.

What Is a Well-Formed XML Document?

The W3C, which is responsible for the term *well-formedness*, defines it this way in the XML 1.0 recommendation (I'll take a look at each of these stipulations later):

A textual object is a well-formed XML document if:

- *Taken as a whole, it matches the production labeled document.*

- *It meets all the well-formedness constraints given in this specification (that is,* www.w3.org/TR/REC-xml*).*

- *Each of the parsed entities that is referenced directly or indirectly within the document is well-formed.*

The W3C calls the individual specifications within a working draft or recommendation *productions*. In this case, to be well formed, a document must follow the "document" production, which means that the document itself must have three parts: a prolog (which can be empty), a root element, and an optional miscellaneous part.

The prolog, which I'll talk about in a few pages, can include an XML declaration (such as <?xml version = "1.0"?>) and an optional miscellaneous part that includes comments, processing instructions, and so on.

The root element of the document can itself hold other elements—in fact, it's hard to imagine useful XML documents in which the root element does not contain other elements. Note that each well-formed XML document must have exactly one root element and that all other elements in the document must be enclosed in the root element (this does not apply to the parts of the prolog, of course, because items such as processing instructions and comments are not considered elements).

The optional miscellaneous part can be made up of XML comments, processing instructions, and whitespace (including spaces, tabs, and so on). I'll take a look at each of these three parts in this chapter: the prolog, the root element, and the miscellaneous part.

The next stipulation in the list says that to be well formed, XML documents must also satisfy the well-formedness constraints listed in the XML 1.0 specification. This means that XML documents must adhere to the syntax rules specified in the XML 1.0 recommendation. I'll talk about those rules in this chapter, including the naming rules you should follow when naming tags, how to nest elements, and so on.

Well-Formedness Constraint

If you search the XML 1.0 specification, which also appears in Appendix A, you'll see that all constraints you need to satisfy to create a well-formed document are marked with the term "Well-Formedness Constraint."

Finally, the last stipulation in the W3C well-formed document list is that each *parsed entity* must itself be well formed. What does that mean?

The parts of an XML document are called *entities*. An entity is a part of a document that can hold text or binary data (but not both). An entity may refer to other entities and so cause them to be included in the document. You can have either parsed (character data) or unparsed (character data that can include non-XML text or binary data that the XML processor does not parse) entities. In other words, the term *entity* is just a generic way of referring to a data storage unit in XML—for example, a file with a few XML elements in it is an entity, but it's not a document unless it's also well formed.

The stipulation about parsed entities means that if you refer to an entity and so include that entity's data (which can include data from external sources) in your document, the included data must itself be well formed.

That's the W3C's definition of a well-formed document, but it's far from clear at this point. What are the well-formedness constraints we need to follow? What exactly can be in a prolog? To answer questions like that, the rest of this chapter is be devoted to examining what these constraints mean in detail.

I'm going to start by looking at an XML document that we can refer to throughout the chapter as we examine what it means for a document to be well formed. In this case, I'll store customer data for specific purchases in a document called ch02_01.xml. I start with the XML declaration itself:

```
<?xml version = "1.0"?>
```

Here, I'm using the `<?xml?>` declaration to indicate that this document is written in XML and is specifying the only version possible at this time, version 1.0. Because all the documents in this chapter are self-contained (they don't refer to or include any external entities), I can also use the `standalone` attribute, setting it to `"yes"` like this:

```
<?xml version = "1.0" standalone="yes"?>
```

This attribute, which may or may not be used by an XML parser, indicates that the document is completely self-contained. Technically, XML documents do not need to start with the XML declaration, but the W3C recommends it.

Next, I add the root element, which I'll call <DOCUMENT> in this case (although you can use any name):

```
<?xml version = "1.0" standalone="yes"?>
<DOCUMENT>
    .
    .
    .
</DOCUMENT>
```

The root element can contain other elements, of course, as here, where I add elements for three customers to the document:

```
<?xml version = "1.0" standalone="yes"?>
<DOCUMENT>
    <CUSTOMER>
    .
    .
    .
    </CUSTOMER>
    <CUSTOMER>
    .
    .
    .
    </CUSTOMER>
    <CUSTOMER>
    .
    .
    .
    </CUSTOMER>
</DOCUMENT>
```

For each customer, I will store a name in a <NAME> element, which itself encloses <LAST_NAME> and <FIRST_NAME> elements like this:

```
<?xml version = "1.0" standalone="yes"?>
<DOCUMENT>
    <CUSTOMER>
        <NAME>
            <LAST_NAME>Smith</LAST_NAME>
            <FIRST_NAME>Sam</FIRST_NAME>
        </NAME>
```

```
        .
        .
        .
    </CUSTOMER>
    <CUSTOMER>
        .
        .
        .
    </CUSTOMER>
    <CUSTOMER>
        .
        .
        .
    </CUSTOMER>
</DOCUMENT>
```

I can also store the details of customer orders with a new element, <DATE>, and an element named <ORDERS> like this:

```
<?xml version = "1.0" standalone="yes"?>
<DOCUMENT>
    <CUSTOMER>
        <NAME>
            <LAST_NAME>Smith</LAST_NAME>
            <FIRST_NAME>Sam</FIRST_NAME>
        </NAME>
        <DATE>October 15, 2003</DATE>
        <ORDERS>
        .
        .
        .
        </ORDERS>
        .
        .
        .
    </CUSTOMER>
    <CUSTOMER>
        .
        .
        .
    </CUSTOMER>
    <CUSTOMER>
        .
        .
        .
    </CUSTOMER>
</DOCUMENT>
```

I can also record each item a customer bought with an `<ITEM>` element, which itself is broken up into `<PRODUCT>`, `<NUMBER>`, and `<PRICE>` elements:

```
<?xml version = "1.0" standalone="yes"?>
<DOCUMENT>
    <CUSTOMER>
        <NAME>
            <LAST_NAME>Smith</LAST_NAME>
            <FIRST_NAME>Sam</FIRST_NAME>
        </NAME>
        <DATE>October 15, 2003</DATE>
        <ORDERS>
            <ITEM>
                <PRODUCT>Tomatoes</PRODUCT>
                <NUMBER>8</NUMBER>
                <PRICE>$1.25</PRICE>
            </ITEM>
            <ITEM>
                <PRODUCT>Oranges</PRODUCT>
                <NUMBER>24</NUMBER>
                <PRICE>$4.98</PRICE>
            </ITEM>
        </ORDERS>
        .
        .
        .
    </CUSTOMER>
    <CUSTOMER>
        .
        .
        .
    </CUSTOMER>
    <CUSTOMER>
        .
        .
        .
    </CUSTOMER>
</DOCUMENT>
```

That's what the data looks like for one customer; here's the full document, including data for all three customers:

Listing ch02_01.xml

```
<?xml version = "1.0" standalone="yes"?>
<DOCUMENT>
    <CUSTOMER>
        <NAME>
            <LAST_NAME>Smith</LAST_NAME>
            <FIRST_NAME>Sam</FIRST_NAME>
        </NAME>
```

```
            <DATE>October 15, 2003</DATE>
            <ORDERS>
                <ITEM>
                    <PRODUCT>Tomatoes</PRODUCT>
                    <NUMBER>8</NUMBER>
                    <PRICE>$1.25</PRICE>
                </ITEM>
                <ITEM>
                    <PRODUCT>Oranges</PRODUCT>
                    <NUMBER>24</NUMBER>
                    <PRICE>$4.98</PRICE>
                </ITEM>
            </ORDERS>
        </CUSTOMER>
        <CUSTOMER>
            <NAME>
                <LAST_NAME>Jones</LAST_NAME>
                <FIRST_NAME>Polly</FIRST_NAME>
            </NAME>
            <DATE>October 20, 2003</DATE>
            <ORDERS>
                <ITEM>
                    <PRODUCT>Bread</PRODUCT>
                    <NUMBER>12</NUMBER>
                    <PRICE>$14.95</PRICE>
                </ITEM>
                <ITEM>
                    <PRODUCT>Apples</PRODUCT>
                    <NUMBER>6</NUMBER>
                    <PRICE>$1.50</PRICE>
                </ITEM>
            </ORDERS>
        </CUSTOMER>
        <CUSTOMER>
            <NAME>
                <LAST_NAME>Weber</LAST_NAME>
                <FIRST_NAME>Bill</FIRST_NAME>
            </NAME>
            <DATE>October 25, 2003</DATE>
            <ORDERS>
                <ITEM>
                    <PRODUCT>Asparagus</PRODUCT>
                    <NUMBER>12</NUMBER>
                    <PRICE>$2.95</PRICE>
                </ITEM>
                <ITEM>
                    <PRODUCT>Lettuce</PRODUCT>
                    <NUMBER>6</NUMBER>
                    <PRICE>$11.50</PRICE>
                </ITEM>
            </ORDERS>
        </CUSTOMER>
</DOCUMENT>
```

Documents like these can grow very long and consist of markup that is many levels deep. Handling such documents is not a problem for XML parsers, however, as long as the document is well formed (and, if the parser is a validating parser, valid). In this chapter, I'll refer back to this document, modifying it and taking a look at its parts as we see what makes a document well formed.

We're ready now to take XML documents apart piece by piece. I'll start with the basics and work up through the prolog, root element, enclosed elements, and so on. We're going to see it all in this chapter.

At their most basic level, then, XML documents are combinations of *markup* and *character data*, and I'm going to start from that point.

Markup and Character Data

XML documents are made up of markup and character data (and possibly, one day, binary data, but there is no provision for enclosing binary data in a document made up of markup and character data yet—until there is, you refer to external binary data with entity references, as we'll see).

The markup in a document gives it its structure. Markup includes start tags, end tags, empty-element tags, entity references, character references, comments, CDATA section delimiters (we'll see more about CDATA sections in a few pages), DTDs, and processing instructions. So what's the character data in an XML document? All the text in a document that is not markup is character data.

Here's a quick example using markup and character data that we've already seen:

```
<?xml version="1.0" encoding="UTF-8"?>
<DOCUMENT>
    <GREETING>
        Hello From XML
    </GREETING>
    <MESSAGE>
        Welcome to the wild and woolly world of XML.
    </MESSAGE>
</DOCUMENT>
```

Tags begin with < and end with >, so it's easy to see that the markup here consists of tags such as <?xml version="1.0" encoding="UTF-8"?>, <DOCUMENT>, and so on. The text Hello From XML and Welcome to the wild and woolly world of XML. is the character data.

However, markup does not need to begin and end with < and >. Markup can also start with & and end with ; in the case of *general entity references* (an entity reference is replaced by the entity it refers to when it's parsed), or it can start with % and end with ; for *parameter entity references*, which are used in DTDs (as we'll see in the next chapter). Using entity references, some of the markup in a document can *become* character data when you process that document. For example, the markup > is a general entity reference that is turned into < when parsed. Likewise, the markup < is turned into > when parsed. Here's an example:

Listing ch02_02.xml

```
<?xml version="1.0" encoding="UTF-8"?>
<DOCUMENT>
    <GREETING>
        This text is inside the &lt;GREETING&gt; element.
    </GREETING>
</DOCUMENT>
```

You can see this XML document in Internet Explorer in Figure 2-1, where you see that the markup > was turned into <, and the markup < was turned into >.

Figure 2-1
Using markup
in Internet
Explorer.

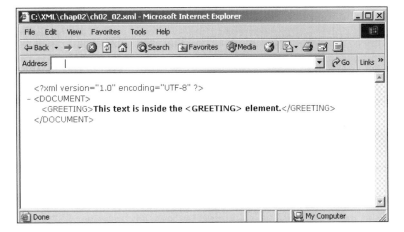

Because some markup can turn into character data when parsed, the character data that results after everything has been parsed—and markup that should be replaced by character data has been replaced—has a special name: *parsed character data*.

Whitespace

If you're ever been concerned about exactly what characters are legal in XML documents, you'll find them listed in the XML 1.0 specification, under the production named Char. It's worth noting that spaces, carriage returns, linefeeds, and tabs are all treated as whitespace in XML. So, practically speaking, this document:

```
<?xml version="1.0" encoding="UTF-8"?>
<DOCUMENT>
<GREETING>
Hello From XML
</GREETING>
<MESSAGE>
Welcome to the wild and woolly world of XML.
</MESSAGE>
</DOCUMENT>
```

is equivalent to this one:

```
<?xml version="1.0" encoding="UTF-8"?>
<DOCUMENT><GREETING>Hello From XML</GREETING>
<MESSAGE>Welcome to the wild and woolly world of XML.</MESSAGE></DOCUMENT>
```

It's also worth noting that the XML recommendation specifies that XML documents use the Unix convention for line endings, which means that lines are ended with a linefeed character only (ASCII code 10). In DOS files, lines are ended with carriage-return linefeed pairs (ASCII codes 13 and 10), but when parsed, that's treated simply as a single linefeed (ASCII code 10).

Handling of Whitespace

There is a special attribute named `xml:space` you can use in an element to indicate that whitespace should be preserved by applications (if you use `xml:space` in documents with a DTD, you must also declare it before using it). You can set this attribute to `default` to indicate that the default handling of whitespace is okay, or `preserve` to indicate that you want all applications to preserve whitespace as it is in the document.

That gets us started with what can go into XML documents: markup and character data. It's time to move to the next step up now and begin working on the actual structure of XML documents, starting with the prolog.

The Prolog

Prologs come at the very beginning of XML documents. In fact, XML documents do not need prologs to be considered well formed. However, the W3C recommends that you include at least the XML declaration, which indicates the version of XML, in the document's prolog. In general, prologs can contain XML declarations, comments, processing instructions, whitespace, and doctype declaration(s).

Here's an example. In this case, I've marked the document's prolog, which contains an XML declaration, a processing instruction, and a DTD (which we'll see more about in the next chapter):

```
<?xml version = "1.0" standalone="yes"?>
<?xml-stylesheet type="text/css" href="greeting.css"?>
<!DOCTYPE DOCUMENT [
<!ELEMENT DOCUMENT (CUSTOMER)*>
<!ELEMENT CUSTOMER (NAME,DATE,ORDERS)>
<!ELEMENT NAME (LAST_NAME,FIRST_NAME)>
<!ELEMENT LAST_NAME (#PCDATA)>
<!ELEMENT FIRST_NAME (#PCDATA)>
<!ELEMENT DATE (#PCDATA)>
<!ELEMENT ORDERS (ITEM)*>
<!ELEMENT ITEM (PRODUCT,NUMBER,PRICE)>
<!ELEMENT PRODUCT (#PCDATA)>
<!ELEMENT NUMBER (#PCDATA)>
<!ELEMENT PRICE (#PCDATA)>
]>
<DOCUMENT>
    <CUSTOMER>
        <NAME>
            <LAST_NAME>Smith</LAST_NAME>
            <FIRST_NAME>Sam</FIRST_NAME>
        </NAME>
        .
        .
        .
```

Each part of the prolog bears a closer look, and I'll examine them here (except for document type definitions, which we'll explore in the next chapter).

The XML Declaration

An XML document can (and should, according to the W3C) start with an XML declaration, which can indicate that the document is written in XML. If you use an XML declaration, it should be the first line in the document. Nothing should come before the XML declaration. Here's an example:

```
<?xml version = "1.0" standalone="yes" encoding="UTF-8"?>
```

The XML declaration uses the <?xml?> element; in earlier drafts of XML, that was <?XML?>, but it was made lowercase in the final recommendation, and it's an error to use upper case. (You'll still find applications out there that insist on the original uppercase version; browsers such as Internet Explorer accept either version.)

There are three possible attributes you can use in the XML declaration:

- version—The XML version. Currently, only 1.0 is possible here. This attribute is required if you use an XML declaration.

- encoding—The language encoding for the document. As discussed in the previous chapter, the default here is UTF-8. You can also use Unicode, UCS-2 or UCS-4, and many other character sets, such as ISO character sets. This attribute is optional.

- standalone—Set to yes if the document does not refer to any external entities; set to no otherwise. This attribute is optional; the default value is yes.

Comments

XML comments are very much like HTML comments. You can use comments to include explanatory notes in your document that are ignored by XML parsers; comments may appear anywhere in a document outside other markup. As in HTML, you start a comment with <!-- and end it with -->. Here's an example:

```
<?xml version="1.0" encoding="UTF-8"?>
<DOCUMENT>
    <!--Start the document off with a greeting.-->
    <GREETING>
    <!--Here's the greeting's text.-->
        Hello from XML!
    </GREETING>
</DOCUMENT>
```

You should follow a few rules when adding comments to an XML document: Comments must not come before an XML declaration. For example, this is incorrect:

```
<!--Here's my document.-->
<?xml version="1.0" encoding="UTF-8"?>
<DOCUMENT>
    <GREETING>
        Hello from XML!
    </GREETING>
</DOCUMENT>
```

You can't put a comment inside markup, like this:

```
<?xml version="1.0" encoding="UTF-8"?>
<DOCUMENT <!--Start the document-->>
    <GREETING>
        Hello from XML!
    </GREETING>
</DOCUMENT>
```

You cannot use -- inside a comment because XML parsers look for that string within a comment as indicating the end of the comment. For example, this is incorrect:

```
<?xml version="1.0" encoding="UTF-8"?>
<DOCUMENT>
    <!--Start the document off--politely--with a greeting.-->
    <GREETING>
        Hello from XML!
    </GREETING>
</DOCUMENT>
```

You can also use comments to remove parts of documents as far as a parser is concerned. For example, here I'm commenting out the <MESSAGE> element:

```
<?xml version="1.0" encoding="UTF-8"?>
<DOCUMENT>
    <GREETING>
        Hello From XML
    </GREETING>
<!--
    <MESSAGE>
        Welcome to the wild and woolly world of XML.
    </MESSAGE>
-->
</DOCUMENT>
```

Here's how a parser treats this document:

```
<?xml version="1.0" encoding="UTF-8"?>
<DOCUMENT>
    <GREETING>
        Hello From XML
    </GREETING>
</DOCUMENT>
```

Processing Instructions

As their name implies, processing instructions are instructions to the XML processor. These instructions start with <? and end with ?>. The only restriction here is that you can't use <?xml?> (or <?XML?>, which is also reserved). Processing instructions must be understood by the XML processor, so they're processor-dependant, not built into the XML recommendation.

A very common and well-understood processing instruction (although, like other processing instructions, not a part of the XML 1.0 recommendation) is <?xml-stylesheet?>, which connects a style sheet with the document. Here's an example:

```
<?xml version = "1.0" standalone="yes"?>
<?xml-stylesheet type="text/css" href="greeting.css"?>
<DOCUMENT>
    <GREETING>
        Hello From XML
    </GREETING>
    <MESSAGE>
        Welcome to the wild and woolly world of XML.
    </MESSAGE>
</DOCUMENT>
```

XML processors such as Internet Explorer 6 and Netscape Navigator 6 or later understand <?xml-stylesheet?> already.

I've taken a look at everything a prolog can contain (except DTDs): XML declarations, comments, processing instructions, and whitespace. It's time to take a look at the actual structure of an XML document, as created with tags and elements.

Tags and Elements

You give structure to an XML document by using markup, which consists of *elements*. An XML element, in turn, consists of a start tag and an end tag, except in the case of elements that are defined to be empty, which consist only of one tag.

A start tag (also called an opening tag) starts with < and ends with >. End tags (also called closing tags) begin with </ and end with >.

Tag Names

The XML specification is very specific about tag names; you can start a tag name with a letter, an underscore, or a colon. The next characters may be letters, digits, underscores, hyphens, periods, and colons (but no whitespace).

Avoid Colons in Tag Names

Although the XML 1.0 recommendation does not say so, you should definitely avoid using colons in tag names because you use a colon when specifying namespaces in XML. I'll discuss this later in the chapter.

Here are some allowed XML tags:

```
<DOCUMENT>
<document>
<_Record>
<customer>
<PRODUCT>
```

Note that because XML processors are case sensitive, the <DOCUMENT> tag is not the same as a <document> tag. (In fact, you can even have <DOCUMENT> and <document>—and even <DoCuMeNt>—tags as different tags in the same document, but I strongly recommend against it.)

Here are the corresponding closing tags:

```
</DOCUMENT>
</document>
</_Record>
</customer>
</PRODUCT>
```

Here are some tags that XML considers illegal:

```
<2003DOCUMENT>
<.document>
<Record Number>
<customer*name>
<PRODUCT(ID)>
```

Using start and end tags, you can create elements, as in this example, which has three elements, the `<DOCUMENT>`, `<GREETING>`, and `<MESSAGE>` elements. The `<DOCUMENT>` element contains the `<GREETING>` and `<MESSAGE>` elements:

```
<?xml version = "1.0" standalone="yes"?>
<DOCUMENT>
    <GREETING>
        Hello From XML
    </GREETING>
    <MESSAGE>
        Welcome to the wild and woolly world of XML.
    </MESSAGE>
</DOCUMENT>
```

You can also create elements without using end tags if the elements are explicitly declared to be *empty*.

Empty Elements

Empty elements have only one tag, not a start and end tag. You may be familiar with empty elements from HTML; for example, the HTML `<IMG>`, `<LI>`, `<HR>`, and `<BR>` elements are empty, which is to say that they do not enclose any content (either character data or markup).

Empty elements are represented with only one tag (in HTML, there are no closing `</IMG>`, `</LI>`, `</HR>`, and `</BR>` tags). In XML, you can declare elements to be empty in the document's DTD, as we'll see in the next chapter.

In XML, you close an empty element with `/>`. For example, if the `<GREETING>` element is empty, it might look like this in an XML document:

```
<?xml version = "1.0" standalone="yes"?>
<DOCUMENT>
    <GREETING TEXT = "Hello From XML" />
</DOCUMENT>
```

This usage might seem a little strange at first, but this is XML's way of making sure that an XML processor isn't left searching for a nonexistent closing tag. In fact, in XHTML, which is a derivation of HTML in XML, the `<IMG>`, `<LI>`, `<HR>`, and `<BR>` tags are actually used as `<IMG />`, `<LI />`, `<HR />`, and `<BR />` (except that XHTML tags actually use lower case). The additional / doesn't seem to give the major browsers any trouble. We'll see how to declare empty tags in the next chapter.

The Root Element

Each well-formed XML document must contain one element that contains all the other elements. The containing element is called the *root element*. The root element is a very important part of XML documents, especially when you look at them from a programming point of view, because you parse XML documents starting with the root element. In ch02_01.xml, developed at the start of this chapter, the root element is the `<DOCUMENT>` element (although you can give the root element any name):

```
<?xml version = "1.0" standalone="yes"?>
<DOCUMENT>
    <CUSTOMER>
        <NAME>
            <LAST_NAME>Smith</LAST_NAME>
            <FIRST_NAME>Sam</FIRST_NAME>
        </NAME>
        <DATE>October 15, 2003</DATE>
        <ORDERS>
            <ITEM>
                <PRODUCT>Tomatoes</PRODUCT>
                <NUMBER>8</NUMBER>
                <PRICE>$1.25</PRICE>
            </ITEM>
                .
                .
                .
            <ITEM>
                <PRODUCT>Lettuce</PRODUCT>
                <NUMBER>6</NUMBER>
                <PRICE>$11.50</PRICE>
            </ITEM>
        </ORDERS>
    </CUSTOMER>
</DOCUMENT>
```

Attributes

Attributes in XML are much like attributes in HTML: They're name-value pairs that let you specify additional data in start and empty tags. To assign a value to an attribute, you use an equals sign.

For example, I'm assigning values to the STATUS attribute of the <CUSTOMER> elements in the XML here to indicate the status of the customer's credit:

Listing ch02_03.xml

```xml
<?xml version = "1.0" standalone="yes"?>
<DOCUMENT>
    <CUSTOMER STATUS="Good credit">
        <NAME>
            <LAST_NAME>Smith</LAST_NAME>
            <FIRST_NAME>Sam</FIRST_NAME>
        </NAME>
        <DATE>October 15, 2003</DATE>
        <ORDERS>
            <ITEM>
                <PRODUCT>Tomatoes</PRODUCT>
                <NUMBER>8</NUMBER>
                <PRICE>$1.25</PRICE>
            </ITEM>
            <ITEM>
                <PRODUCT>Oranges</PRODUCT>
                <NUMBER>24</NUMBER>
                <PRICE>$4.98</PRICE>
            </ITEM>
        </ORDERS>
    </CUSTOMER>
    <CUSTOMER STATUS="Lousy credit">
        <NAME>
            <LAST_NAME>Jones</LAST_NAME>
            <FIRST_NAME>Polly</FIRST_NAME>
        </NAME>
        <DATE>October 20, 2003</DATE>
        <ORDERS>
            <ITEM>
                <PRODUCT>Bread</PRODUCT>
                <NUMBER>12</NUMBER>
                <PRICE>$14.95</PRICE>
            </ITEM>
            <ITEM>
                <PRODUCT>Apples</PRODUCT>
                <NUMBER>6</NUMBER>
                <PRICE>$1.50</PRICE>
```

```
            </ITEM>
        </ORDERS>
    </CUSTOMER>
    <CUSTOMER STATUS="Good credit">
        <NAME>
            <LAST_NAME>Weber</LAST_NAME>
            <FIRST_NAME>Bill</FIRST_NAME>
        </NAME>
        <DATE>October 25, 2003</DATE>
        <ORDERS>
            <ITEM>
                <PRODUCT>Asparagus</PRODUCT>
                <NUMBER>12</NUMBER>
                <PRICE>$2.95</PRICE>
            </ITEM>
            <ITEM>
                <PRODUCT>Lettuce</PRODUCT>
                <NUMBER>6</NUMBER>
                <PRICE>$11.50</PRICE>
            </ITEM>
        </ORDERS>
    </CUSTOMER>
</DOCUMENT>
```

You can see this XML document in Internet Explorer, including the attributes and their values, in Figure 2-2.

Figure 2-2
Using attributes in Internet Explorer.

An XML processor can read the attributes and their values, and you can put that data to work in your own applications. We'll see how to read attribute values in both JavaScript and Java in this book.

A lot of debate rages over when you should store data using attributes and when you should store data using elements. There simply is no hard and fast rule, but here are a couple of guidelines that I find useful. First, too many attributes definitely make documents hard to read. For example, take a look at this element:

```
<CUSTOMER>
    <NAME>
        <LAST_NAME>Smith</LAST_NAME>
        <FIRST_NAME>Sam</FIRST_NAME>
    </NAME>
    <DATE>October 15, 2003</DATE>
    <ORDERS>
        <ITEM>
            <PRODUCT>Tomatoes</PRODUCT>
            <NUMBER>8</NUMBER>
            <PRICE>$1.25</PRICE>
        </ITEM>
    </ORDERS>
</CUSTOMER>
```

It's fairly clear what's going on here, even if it's a little involved. However, if you try to convert all this data to attributes, you end up with something like this:

```
<CUSTOMER LAST_NAME="Smith" FIRST_NAME="Sam"
DATE="October 15, 2003" PURCHASE="Tomatoes"
PRICE="$1.25" NUMBER="8" />
```

Clearly, this is going to be a mess if you have a few such elements.

Another point is that you really can't specify document structure using attributes. For instance, the example we've already seen in this chapter stores multiple ordered items per customer. But attribute names must be unique, so it's much tougher to store data like this using attributes:

```
<CUSTOMER>
    <NAME>
        <LAST_NAME>Smith</LAST_NAME>
        <FIRST_NAME>Sam</FIRST_NAME>
    </NAME>
    <DATE>October 15, 2003</DATE>
    <ORDERS>
```

```
    <ITEM>
        <PRODUCT>Tomatoes</PRODUCT>
        <NUMBER>8</NUMBER>
        <PRICE>$1.25</PRICE>
    </ITEM>
    <ITEM>
        <PRODUCT>Oranges</PRODUCT>
        <NUMBER>24</NUMBER>
        <PRICE>$4.98</PRICE>
    </ITEM>
  </ORDERS>
</CUSTOMER>
```

The upshot is that deciding whether to store your data in attributes or create new elements is really a matter of taste—until you get beyond a few attributes per tag. If you find yourself using (not just defining, but using) more than four attributes in a tag, consider breaking up the tag into a number of enclosed tags. Doing so will make the document structure much easier to work with and edit later.

You should follow specific rules when creating attributes. Those include setting attribute names and specifying attribute values. I'll take a look at these rules now.

Attribute Names

According to the XML 1.0 specification, attribute names must follow the same rules as those for tag names, which means that you can start an attribute name with a letter, an underscore, or a colon. The next characters may be letters, digits, underscores, hyphens, periods, and colons (but no whitespace because you separate attribute name-value pairs with whitespace).

Here are some examples showing legal attribute names:

```
<circle origin_x="10.0" origin_y="20.0" radius="10.0" />

<image src="image1.jpg">

<pen color="red" width="5">

<book pages="1231" >
```

And here are some illegal attribute names:

```
<circle 2origin_x="10.0" 2origin_y="20.0" 2radius="10.0" />

<image src name="image1.jpg">

<pen color@="red" width@="5">

<book pages(excluding front matter)="1231" >
```

Attribute Values

Because markup is always text, attributes are also text. Even if you're assigning a number to an attribute, you treat that number as a text string and enclose it in quotation marks, like this:

```
<circle origin_x="10.0" origin_y="20.0" radius="10.0" />
```

Among other things, this means that XML processors will return attribute values as text strings. If you want to treat them as numbers, you'll have to make sure you translate them to numbers as the programming language you're using allows.

In XML, you must enclose attribute values in quotation marks. Usually you use double quotes, but consider the case in which the attribute value itself contains double quotes: You can't just surround such a value with double quotes because an XML processor will get confused as to where your text ends. In such a case, you can use single quotes to surround the text, like this:

```
<quotation text='He said, "Not that!"' />
```

What if the attribute value contains both single *and* double quotes? In that case, you can use the XML-defined entity references for a single quote, ', and for a double quote, ", like this (I'll discuss the five XML-defined entity references in a few pages):

```
<person height="5&apos;6&quot;" />
```

Assigning Values to Attributes

If you're going to use an attribute, you must assign it a value. Not doing so is a violation of well-formedness. That is, you cannot have "standalone" attributes in XML, such as the BORDER attribute in HTML tables, which need not be assigned a value.

A Useful Attribute: *xml:lang*

One general attribute bears mention: xml:lang. It's often convenient to specify the language of a document's content and attribute values, especially to help software such as Web search engines. You can specify the language in XML tags with the xml:lang attribute. (In valid documents, this attribute, like any other, must be declared if it is used.)

You can set the `xml:lang` attribute to these values:

- A two-letter language code as defined by [ISO 639].

- A language identifier registered with the Internet Assigned Numbers Authority (IANA). Such identifiers begin with the prefix "i-" (or "I-").

- A language identifier assigned by you or for private use. Such identifiers must begin with "x-" or "X-".

Here is an example. In this case, I'm using the `xml:lang` attribute to indicate that an element's language is English:

```
<p xml:lang="en">The color should be brown.</p>
```

You can also use language *subcodes* if you follow the language code with a hyphen and the subcode. A subcode indicates a dialect or regional variation. For example, here I'm indicating that one element holds British English content and one holds American English:

```
<p xml:lang="en-GB">The colour should be brown.</p>
<p xml:lang="en-US">The color should be brown.</p>
```

Here's an example where I'm using German:

```
<p farbe="braun" xml:lang="de">
```

Building Well-Formed Document Structure

We've learned a lot of the syntax and rules of creating XML documents at the element and character data levels. It's time to move on to the next level: actually giving your document structure.

The W3C has a lot of rules about how to structure your document in a way to make it well formed, and I'm going to take a look at those rules here. In this chapter, I'm going to talk about only standalone documents; in the next chapter, we'll see that we have to adjust these points somewhat for documents that have a DTD.

Checking Well-Formedness

If you have doubts about whether your XML document is well formed, use an online XML validator, such as the excellent one hosted by the Brown University Scholarly Technology Group at www.stg.brown.edu/service/xmlvalid/. You'll get a complete report on your document's well formedness and validity. To see all the well-formedness constraints as set up by the W3C, look at www.w3.org/TR/REC-xml (or Appendix A) and search for the text "Well-Formedness Constraint," which is how W3C names those constraints.

An XML Declaration Should Begin the Document

The first well-formedness structure constraint is that you should start the document with an XML declaration. Technically, you don't need to include an XML declaration in your document; if you do, to make the document well formed, the XML declaration must be absolutely the *first* thing in the document, like this (not even whitespace should come before the XML declaration):

```
<?xml version = "1.0" standalone="yes"?>
<DOCUMENT>
    <CUSTOMER STATUS="Good credit">
        <NAME>
            <LAST_NAME>Smith</LAST_NAME>
            <FIRST_NAME>Sam</FIRST_NAME>
        </NAME>
        <DATE>October 15, 2003</DATE>
        <ORDERS>
            <ITEM>
                <PRODUCT>Tomatoes</PRODUCT>
                <NUMBER>8</NUMBER>
                <PRICE>$1.25</PRICE>
            </ITEM>
            <ITEM>
                <PRODUCT>Oranges</PRODUCT>
                <NUMBER>24</NUMBER>
                <PRICE>$4.98</PRICE>
            </ITEM>
        </ORDERS>
    </CUSTOMER>
    .
    .
    .
```

Do You Need an XML Declaration?

The W3C says that XML documents should have an XML declaration, but documents really don't need to have one in all cases. For example, when you're combining XML documents into one large one, you don't want to include an XML declaration at the head of each section of the document.

Include One or More Elements

To be a well-formed document, a document must include one or more elements. The first element it includes, of course, is the root element; all other elements are enclosed by that element. The examples we've seen throughout this chapter show how this works, as here, where this XML document contains multiple elements within the root element:

```
<?xml version = "1.0" standalone="yes"?>
<DOCUMENT>
    <GREETING>
        Hello From XML
    </GREETING>
    <MESSAGE>
        Welcome to the wild and woolly world of XML.
    </MESSAGE>
</DOCUMENT>
```

Include Both Start and End Tags for Nonempty Elements

In HTML, Web browsers often handle the case in which you omit end tags for HTML elements, even if you shouldn't omit those end tags according to the HTML specification. For example, if you use the <p> tag and then follow it with another <p> tag—without using a </p> tag—the browser will have no problem.

In XML, the story is different. To make sure a document is well formed, every nonempty element must have both a start tag and an end tag, as in the example we just saw:

```
<?xml version = "1.0" standalone="yes"?>
<DOCUMENT>
    <GREETING>
        Hello From XML
    </GREETING>
```

continues

```
    <MESSAGE>
        Welcome to the wild and woolly world of XML.
    </MESSAGE>
</DOCUMENT>
```

In fact, there's another well-formedness constraint here: End tags must match start tags to complete an element.

Close Empty Tags with />

Some elements—empty elements—don't have closing tags (although they may have attributes). These tags have no content, which means that they do not enclose any character data or markup. Instead, these elements are made up entirely of one tag, like this:

```
<?xml version = "1.0" standalone="yes"?>
<DOCUMENT>
    <GREETING TEXT = "Hello From XML" />
</DOCUMENT>
```

In XML, you must always end empty elements with />, as shown here, if you want your document to be well formed. In general, the current crop of the major Web browsers deals well with elements such as <BR />. This is good because the alternative is to write such elements like
</BR>, and that can be confusing. In fact, some browsers, such as Netscape Navigator, interpret that markup as two <BR> elements.

The Root Element Must Contain All Other Elements

One element in well-formed documents contains all other elements. As we know, that element is called the root element. In this case, the root element is the <BOOKS> element:

```
<?xml version = "1.0" standalone="yes"?>
<BOOKS>
    <BOOK>
        <TITLE>
            Inside XML
        </TITLE>
        <REVIEW>
            Excellent
        </REVIEW>
    </BOOK>
```

```
    <BOOK>
        <TITLE>
            Other XML Book
        <TITLE>
        <REVIEW>
            OK
        </REVIEW>
    </BOOK>
</BOOKS>
```

In this case, the root element must contain all other elements (excluding the XML declaration, comments, and other nonelements). This makes it easy for XML processors to handle XML documents as *trees*, starting at the root element, as we'll see when we start parsing XML documents.

Nest Elements Correctly

A very big part of making sure documents are well formed is ensuring that elements nest correctly (in fact, that's one of the reasons for the term *well-formed*). The idea here is that if an element contains a start tag for a nonempty tag, it must also contain that element's end tag.

For example, this XML is fine:

```
<?xml version = "1.0" standalone="yes"?>
<DOCUMENT>
    <GREETING>
        Hello From XML
    </GREETING>
    <MESSAGE>
        Welcome to the wild and woolly world of XML.
    </MESSAGE>
</DOCUMENT>
```

However, there's a nesting problem in this next document because an XML processor will encounter the <MESSAGE> tag before finding the closing </GREETING> tag:

```
<?xml version = "1.0" standalone="yes"?>
<DOCUMENT>
    <GREETING>
        Hello From XML
    <MESSAGE>
    </GREETING>
        Welcome to the wild and woolly world of XML.
    </MESSAGE>
</DOCUMENT>
```

Because you should nest elements correctly to create a well-formed document, and because XML processors are supposed to refuse documents that are not well formed, you can always count on every nonroot element to have exactly one (and only one) *parent element* that encloses it. For example, in the example before the previous, non–well-formed, example, the `<GREETING>` and `<MESSAGE>` elements both have the same parent: the `<DOCUMENT>` element itself, which is also the root element. Note that a parent element can enclose an indefinite number of *child elements* (which can also mean zero child elements).

Use Unique Attribute Names

One of the well-formedness constraints that the XML 1.0 specification lists is that no attribute name may appear more than once in the same start tag or empty-element tag. It's hard to see how you would violate this one except by mistake, as in this case, where I give a person two last names:

```
<PERSON LAST_NAME="Wooster" LAST_NAME="Jeeves">
```

Note that because XML is case sensitive, attributes with different capitalization are different, as in this case (although it's still hard to see how you'd write this except by mistake):

```
<PERSON LAST_NAME="Wooster" last_name="Jeeves">
```

(In general, using attribute names that differ only in terms of capitalization is a really bad idea.)

Use Only the Five Pre-existing Entity References

XML has five predefined *entity references*. An entity reference is replaced by the corresponding entity when the XML document is processed. You may already know about entity references from HTML; for example, the HTML entity reference `&copy;` is replaced by the © symbol when it parses an HTML document.

As in HTML, general entity references in XML start with `&` and end with `;`. Parameter entity references, which we'll use in DTDs in the next chapter, start with `%` and end with `;`. Here are the five predefined entity references in XML and the characters they are replaced with when parsed:

- `&amp;`—The & character
- `&lt;`—The < character
- `&gt;`—The > character
- `&apos;`—The ' character
- `&quot;`—The " character

Normally, these characters are tricky to handle in XML documents because XML processors give them special importance. That is, < and > straddle markup tags, you use quotation marks to surround attribute values, and the & character starts entity references. Replacing them with the previous entity references makes them safe because the XML processor replaces them with the appropriate character when processing the document. Using an entity reference for a character is often called *escaping* that character (following the terminology of programming languages that use "escape sequences" to embed special characters in text).

For example, say that you wanted to use the term "The S&O Railway" in a document; you could use the `&amp;` entity reference for the ampersand this way:

```
<TOUR CAPTION="The S&amp;O Railway" />
```

Although there are only five predefined entity references in XML, you can define new entity references. I'll take a look at how to do that in the next chapter on DTDs.

The Final *;* in Entity References

HTML browsers often let you omit the final ; in entity references if the entity reference is followed by whitespace (if the entity reference is embedded in nonwhitespace text, you must include the final ;, even in HTML). However, you cannot omit the final ; in XML entity references.

Surround Attribute Values with Quotation Marks

In HTML, there's no problem if you omit the quotation marks around attribute values (as long as those values don't contain any whitespace). For example, this element presents no problem to HTML browsers:

```
<IMG SRC=image.jpg>
```

However, XML processors would refuse such an element because omitting the quotation marks around the attribute value `"image.jpg"` is a violation of well-formedness. Here's how this element would look when written properly:

```
<IMG SRC="image.jpg" />
```

You can also use single quotation marks, like this:

```
<IMG SRC='image.jpg' />
```

In fact, if the attribute value contains double quotes, you should surround it with single quotes, as we've seen:

```
<quotation text='He said, "Not that!"' />
```

XML makes provisions for handling single and double quotes inside attribute values—you can always replace single quotes with the entity reference for apostrophes, ', and double quotes with the entity reference ". For example, to assign the attribute `height` the value `5'6"`, you can do it this way:

```
<person height="5&apos;6&quot;" />
```

In XHTML, the XML-based version of HTML 4 in XML, you must surround attribute values in quotation marks, just as in any other XML document. I'm sure that requirement is going to be one of the most persistently troublesome for Web authors switching to XHTML, simply because it's so easy to forget.

A few more well-formedness constraints on attribute values bear mention. Attribute values cannot contain direct or indirect references to external entities (more on this in the next chapter), and you cannot use the < character in attribute values. If you must use <, use the entity reference < instead, like this, where I'm assigning the text < — to the TEXT attribute:

```
<ARROW TEXT="&lt;--" />
```

In fact, so strong is the prohibition against using < except to start markup that you shouldn't use it anywhere in the document except for that purpose (see the next topic).

Use < and & Only to Start Tags and Entities

XML processors assume that < always starts a tag and & always starts an entity reference, so you should avoid using those characters for anything else. We've already seen this example where the ampersand in `"The S&O Railway"` is replaced by &:

```
<TOUR CAPTION="The S&amp;O Railway" />
```

You should particularly avoid the < character in nonmarkup text. This can be difficult sometimes, as when the < character must be used as the less-than operator in JavaScript, as in this example in XHTML:

```
<?xml version="1.0"?>
<!DOCTYPE html PUBLIC "-//W3C//DTD XHTML 1.0 Transitional//EN"
"http://www.w3.org/tr/xhtml1/DTD/xhtml1-transitional.dtd">
<html xmlns="http://www.w3.org/1999/xhtml" xml:lang="en" lang="en">
    <head>

        <title>
            Using The if Statement In JavaScript
        </title>

    </head>

    <body>

        <script language="javascript">
            var budget
            budget = 234.77
            if (budget < 0) {
                document.writeln("Uh oh.")
            }
        </script>

        <center>
            <h1>
                Using The if Statement In JavaScript
            </h1>
        </center>
    </body>
</html>
```

W3C suggests that in cases like this, you should enclose the JavaScript code in a CDATA section (see the next topic in this chapter) so that the XML processor will ignore it. Unfortunately, no major browser today understands CDATA sections. Another possible solution is to enclose the JavaScript code in a comment, <!-- and -->. However, the W3C doesn't recommend this because XML processors are allowed to remove comments before passing the XML to the underlying application, and so they would remove the JavaScript code entirely from the document.

You can use < for the < operator—in fact, this is what you should do, like this:

```
<?xml version="1.0"?>
<!DOCTYPE html PUBLIC "-//W3C//DTD XHTML 1.0 Transitional//EN"
"http://www.w3.org/tr/xhtml1/DTD/xhtml1-transitional.dtd">
<html xmlns="http://www.w3.org/1999/xhtml" xml:lang="en" lang="en">
    <head>

        <title>
            Using The if Statement In JavaScript
        </title>

    </head>

    <body>

        <script language="javascript">
            var budget
            budget = 234.77
            if (budget &lt; 0) {
                document.writeln("Uh oh.")
            }
        </script>

        <center>
            <h1>
                Using The if Statement In JavaScript
            </h1>
        </center>
    </body>
</html>
```

Practically speaking, however, this still represents a problem for the major browsers, although it's the way you should go in the long run. In the short run, you should actually remove the whole problem from the scope of the browser by placing the script code in an external file, here named script.js:

```
<?xml version="1.0"?>
<!DOCTYPE html PUBLIC "-//W3C//DTD XHTML 1.0 Transitional//EN"
"http://www.w3.org/tr/xhtml1/DTD/xhtml1-transitional.dtd">
<html xmlns="http://www.w3.org/1999/xhtml" xml:lang="en" lang="en">
    <head>

        <title>
            Using The if Statement In JavaScript
        </title>

    </head>
```

```
    <body>

        <script language="javascript" src="script.js">
        </script>

        <center>
            <h1>
                Using The if Statement In JavaScript
            </h1>
        </center>
    </body>
</html>
```

CDATA Sections

As you know, XML processors are very sensitive to characters such as < and &. So what if you had a large section of text that contained a great many < and & characters that you didn't want to interpret as markup? You can escape those characters as < and &, of course—but with many such characters, that's awkward and hard to read. Instead, you can use a CDATA section.

CDATA sections hold character data that is supposed to remain unparsed by the XML processor. This is a useful asset to XML. Otherwise, all the text in an XML document is parsed and searched for characters such as < and &. You use CDATA sections simply to tell the XML processor to leave the enclosed text alone and pass it on unchanged to the underlying application.

You start a CDATA section with the markup <![CDATA[and end it with]]>. Note that this means that actually CDATA sections *are* searched, but only for the ending text]]>. Among other things, this means that you cannot include the text]]> inside a CDATA section—and it also means that you cannot nest CDATA sections.

Here's an example. In this case, I've added an element named <MARKUP> to a document, and this element itself contains markup that I want to preserve as character data (so that it can be printed out, for example). To make sure that the markup inside this element is preserved as text, I enclose it in a CDATA section like this:

```
<?xml version = "1.0" standalone="yes"?>
<DOCUMENT>
    <MARKUP>
    <![CDATA[
        <CUSTOMER>
            <NAME>
```

continues

```
                    <LAST_NAME>Smith</LAST_NAME>
                    <FIRST_NAME>Sam</FIRST_NAME>
             </NAME>
          <DATE>October 15, 2003</DATE>
          <ORDERS>
                 <ITEM>
                      <PRODUCT>Tomatoes</PRODUCT>
                      <NUMBER>8</NUMBER>
                      <PRICE>$1.25</PRICE>
                 </ITEM>
                 <ITEM>
                      <PRODUCT>Oranges</PRODUCT>
                      <NUMBER>24</NUMBER>
                      <PRICE>$4.98</PRICE>
                 </ITEM>
             </ORDERS>
       </CUSTOMER>
   ]]>
     </MARKUP>
</DOCUMENT>
```

As you can see, CDATA sections are powerful because they enable you to embed character data directly in XML documents without having it parsed (normally, character data in XML documents is parsed by the XML processor and becomes parsed character data).

Here's another example. In this case, I'm adapting the JavaScript example in the previous section to show how the W3C wants to handle script code in XHTML pages—by placing that code in a CDATA section:

```
<?xml version="1.0"?>
<!DOCTYPE html PUBLIC "-//W3C//DTD XHTML 1.0 Transitional//EN"
"http://www.w3.org/tr/xhtml1/DTD/xhtml1-transitional.dtd">
<html xmlns="http://www.w3.org/1999/xhtml" xml:lang="en" lang="en">
    <head>

        <title>
            Using The if Statement In JavaScript
        </title>

    </head>

    <body>

        <script language="javascript">
            <![CDATA[
                var budget
                budget = 234.77
```

```
                    if (budget < 0) {
                        document.writeln("Uh oh.")
                    }
                ]]>
        </script>

        <center>
            <h1>
                Using The if Statement In JavaScript
            </h1>
        </center>
    </body>
</html>
```

Unfortunately, as mentioned in the previous topic, the idea of a CDATA section, especially one that starts with the expression `<![CDATA[` and ends with the expression `]]>`, confuses the major browsers. When those browsers are configured to handle XHTML, the situation will improve.

XML Namespaces

There's considerable freedom in XML because you can define your own tags. However, as more XML applications came to be developed, a problem arose that was unforeseen by the creators of the original XML specification: tag name conflicts.

As we saw in the previous chapter, two popular XML applications are XHTML (that is, HTML 4 as written in XML) and MathML, which lets you display equations. XHTML is useful because it lets you handle all the standard HTML 4 tags. If you need to display equations, MathML can be essential. So what if you want to use MathML inside an XHTML Web page? That's a problem because the tags defined in XHTML and MathML overlap (specifically, both applications define `<var>` and `<select>` elements).

The solution is to use *namespaces*. Namespaces allow you to make sure that one set of tags cannot conflict with another. Namespaces work by letting you prepend a name followed by a colon to tag and attribute names, changing those names so they don't conflict.

XML namespaces are one of those XML companion recommendations that keep being added to the XML specification; you can find the specification for namespaces at `www.w3.org/TR/REC-xml-names/`. There's still a lot of debate about this one (largely because namespaces can make writing DTDs difficult), but it's now an official W3C recommendation.

Creating a Namespace

Here's an example. In this case, I'll use a fictitious XML application designed for cataloging books whose root element is <library>, and I'll add my own reviews to each book. I start off with a book as specified with the fictitious XML application:

```
<library>
    <book>
        <title>
            Earthquakes for Lunch.
        </title>
    </book>
</library>
```

Now I want to add my own comments to this <book> item. To do that, I will start by confining the book XML application to its own namespace, for which I'll use the prefix book:. To define a new namespace, you use the xmlns:*prefix* attribute, where *prefix* is the prefix you want to use for the namespace, like this:

```
<library
    xmlns:book="http://www.amazingterrificbooks.com/spec">
    <book>
        <title>
            Earthquakes for Lunch.
        </title>
    </book>
</library>
```

To define a namespace, you assign the xmlns:*prefix* attribute to a unique identifier, which in XML is usually a URI (read URL, in this case) that may direct the XML processor to a DTD for the namespace (but that doesn't have to). After defining the book namespace, you can preface every tag and attribute name in this namespace with book:, like this:

```
<book:library
    xmlns:book="http://www.amazingterrificbooks.com/spec">
    <book:book>
        <book:title>
            Earthquakes for Lunch.
        </book:title>
    </book:book>
</book:library>
```

Now the tag and attribute names have actually been changed; for example, <library> is now <book:library>, as far as the XML processor is concerned. (If you've defined tag and attribute names in a document's DTD, this means that you have to redefine the tags and attributes there as well to make the new names legal.)

Because all tag and attribute names from the book namespace are now in their own namespace, I'm free to add my own namespace to the document to allow me to add my own comments to each book entry. I start by defining a new namespace named steve:

```
<book:library
    xmlns:book="http://www.amazingterrificbooks.com/spec"
    xmlns:steve="http://www.starpowder.com/steve">
    <book:book>
        <book:title>
            Earthquakes for Lunch.
        </book:title>
    </book:book>
</book:library>
```

Now I can use the new steve namespace to add markup to the document like this, keeping it separate from the other markup:

```
<book:library
    xmlns:book="http://www.amazingterrificbooks.com/spec"
    xmlns:steve="http://www.starpowder.com/steve">
    <book:book>
        <book:title>
            Earthquakes for Lunch.
        </book:title>
        <steve:review>
            This book was OK, no great shakes.
        </steve:review>
    </book:book>
</book:library>
```

I can also use attributes in the steve namespace as long as I prefix them with steve:, like this:

```
<book:library
    xmlns:book="http://www.amazingterrificbooks.com/spec"
    xmlns:steve="http://www.starpowder.com/steve">
    <book:book>
        <book:title>
            Earthquakes for Lunch.
        </book:title>
```

continues

```
            <steve:review steve:ID="1000034">
                This book was OK, no great shakes.
            </steve:review>
        </book:book>
</book:library>
```

And that's how namespaces work—you can use them to separate tags, even tags with the same name, from each other. As you can see, using multiple namespaces in the same document is no problem at all. Just use the xmlns attribute in the enclosing element to define the appropriate namespaces.

xmlns in Child Elements

In fact, you can use the xmlns attribute in child elements to *redefine* an enclosing namespace if you want to.

Creating Local Namespaces

You don't need to use the xmlns attribute in the root element. You can use this attribute in any element as in this case, where I've moved the steve namespace definition to the element in which it's used:

```
<book:library
    xmlns:book="http://www.amazingterrificbooks.com/spec">
    <book:book>
        <book:title>
            Earthquakes for Lunch.
        </book:title>
        <steve:review
        xmlns:steve="http://www.starpowder.com/steve"
        steve:ID="1000034">
            This book was OK, no great shakes.
        </steve:review>
    </book:book>
</book:library>
```

Because namespace prefixes are really just text prepended to tag and attribute names, they follow the same rules for naming tags and attributes—that is, a namespace can start with a letter or an underscore. The following characters can include underscores, letters, digits, hyphens, and periods. Although colons are legal in tag names, you can't use a colon in a namespace name, for obvious reasons. In addition, two namespace names are reserved: xml and xmlns.

Note that because namespace prefixes are merely text prepended to tag and attribute names, followed by a colon (which is legal in names), XML processors that have never heard of namespaces can use them without problem.

Names of Attributes in Namespaces

You can use two names to refer to the same namespace. Note, however, that because you must use attributes with unique names, you cannot use attributes with two namespaces that share the same name in the same element.

Default Namespaces

Now I'll return to the example that introduced this topic: the idea of using MathML in an XHTML document. In this case, I'll assume that I want to display an equation in an XHTML document. I start off with an XHTML document that looks like this:

```
<?xml version="1.0"?>
<!DOCTYPE html PUBLIC "-//W3C//DTD XHTML 1.0 Transitional//EN"
"http://www.w3.org/tr/xhtml1/DTD/xhtml1-transitional.dtd">
<html xmlns="http://www.w3.org/1999/xhtml" xml:lang="en" lang="en">
    <head>
        <title>
            Embedding MathML In XHTML
        </title>
    </head>

    <body>
        <center>
            <h1>
                Embedding MathML In XHTML
            </h1>
        </center>
        Here's the MathML:
    </body>
</html>
```

This document has a `<!DOCTYPE>` element that you use to connect a DTD to a document, and the `<html>` element defines a namespace with the `xmlns` attribute. Note in particular that, this time, the `xmlns` attribute is used by itself, without defining any prefix to specify a namespace (`xmlns="http://www.w3.org/1999/xhtml"`). When you use the `xmlns` attribute alone without specifying any prefix, you are defining a *default* namespace. All the enclosed elements are assumed to belong to that namespace.

In XHTML documents, it's customary to make the W3C XHTML name-space, http://www.w3.org/1999/xhtml, into the default namespace for the document. When you do, you can then use the standard HTML tag names without any prefixes, as you see in this example.

However, I want to use MathML markup in this document. To do so, I add a new namespace, which I'll call m, to this document using the namespace that the W3C has specified for MathML, http://www.w3.org/1998/Math/MathML/:

```
<?xml version="1.0"?>
<!DOCTYPE html PUBLIC "-//W3C//DTD XHTML 1.0 Transitional//EN"
"http://www.w3.org/tr/xhtml1/DTD/xhtml1-transitional.dtd">
<html xmlns="http://www.w3.org/1999/xhtml" xml:lang="en" lang="en"
    xmlns:m="http://www.w3.org/1998/Math/MathML/">
    <head>
        <title>
            Embedding MathML In XHTML
        </title>
    </head>

    <body>
        <center>
            <h1>
                Embedding MathML In XHTML
            </h1>
        </center>
        Here's the MathML:
    </body>
</html>
```

Now I can add MathML as I like, as long as I restrict that markup to the m namespace like this:

```
<?xml version="1.0"?>
<!DOCTYPE html PUBLIC "-//W3C//DTD XHTML 1.0 Transitional//EN"
"http://www.w3.org/tr/xhtml1/DTD/xhtml1-transitional.dtd">
<html xmlns="http://www.w3.org/1999/xhtml" xml:lang="en" lang="en"
    xmlns:m="http://www.w3.org/1998/Math/MathML/">
    <head>
        <title>
            Embedding MathML In XHTML
        </title>
    </head>

    <body>
        <center>
            <h1>
                Embedding MathML In XHTML
            </h1>
```

```
          </center>
          Here's the MathML:
          <m:math>
              <m:mrow>
                  <m:mrow>
                  <m:mn>3</m:mn>
                      <m:mo>&InvisibleTimes;</m:mo>
                      <m:msup>
                          <m:mi>Z</m:mi>
                          <m:mn>2</m:mn>
                      </m:msup>
                      <m:mo>-</m:mo>
                      <m:mrow>
                          <m:mn>6</m:mn>
                          <m:mo>&InvisibleTimes;</m:mo>
                          <m:mi>Z</m:mi>
                      </m:mrow>
                      <m:mo>+</m:mo>
                      <m:mn>12</m:mn>
                  </m:mrow>
                  <m:mo>=</m:mo>
                  <m:mn>0</m:mn>
              </m:mrow>
          </m:math>
      </body>
</html>
```

This document works fine, and you can see the result in the W3C Amaya browser in Figure 2-3.

Figure 2-3
The MathML
markup in the
Amaya browser.

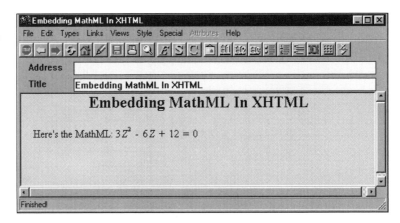

We'll have occasion to use namespaces throughout this book, as when we work with the XSL transformation language.

Infosets

While discussing creating XML documents, it's worth discussing another XML specification: the XML Information Set specification, which you'll find at www.w3.org/TR/xml-infoset.

XML documents excel at storing data, and this has led developers to wonder if XML will ultimately be able to solve an old problem: being able to directly compare and classify the data in multiple documents. For example, consider the World Wide Web as it stands today: There can be thousands of documents on a particular topic, but how can you possibly compare them? For example, a search for the term *XML* turns up millions of matches, but it would be extraordinarily difficult to write a program that would compare the data in those documents because all that data isn't stored in any remotely compatible format.

The idea behind XML information sets, also called *infosets*, is to set up an abstract way of looking at an XML document so that it can be compared to others. To have an infoset, XML documents may not use colons in tag and attribute names unless they are used to support namespaces. Documents do not need to be valid to have an infoset, but they need to be well formed.

An XML document's information set consists of two or more *information items* (the information set for any well-formed XML document contains at least the document information item and one element information item). An information item is an abstract representation of some part of an XML document, and each information item has a set of properties, some of which are considered *core* and some of which are considered *peripheral*.

An XML information set can contain 15 different types of information items:

- A document information item (core)
- Element information items (core)
- Attribute information items (core)
- Processing instruction information items (core)
- Reference to skipped entity information items (core)
- Character information items (core)
- Comment information items (peripheral)
- A document type definition information item (peripheral)
- Entity information items (core for unparsed entities, peripheral for others)
- Notation information items (core)

- Entity start marker information items (peripheral)
- Entity end marker information items (peripheral)
- CDATA start marker information items (peripheral)
- CDATA end marker information items (peripheral)
- Namespace declaration information items (core)

There is always one document information item in the information set. Here's a list of the core properties of the document information item:

- `[children]`—This property holds an ordered list of references to child information items, in the original document order.
- `[notations]`—This property holds an unordered set of references to notation information items (which we'll see more about in the next chapter).
- `[entities]`—This property holds an unordered set of references to entity information items, one for each unparsed entity declaration in the DTD.

The document information item can also have these properties:

- `[base URI]`—This property holds the absolute URI of the document entity.
- `[children - comments]`—This property holds a reference to a comment information item for each comment outside the document element.
- `[children - doctype]`—This property holds a reference to one document type definition information item.
- `[entities - other]`—This property holds a reference to an entity information item for each parsed general entity declaration in the DTD.

The other information items, such as element information items and processing instruction information items, have similar properties lists.

Currently, no applications create and work with infosets. However, W3C documentation often refers to the information stored in an XML document as its infoset, so it's an important term to know. The closest you come to working with infosets right now is working with *canonical* XML documents (see the next topic).

Canonical XML

Although infosets are a good idea, they are only abstract formulations of the information in an XML document. So without reducing an XML document to its infoset, how can you actually approach the goal of being able to actually compare XML documents byte by byte?

It turns out that there is a way: You can use canonical XML. Canonical XML is a companion standard to XML, and you can read all about it at www.w3.org/TR/xml-c14n. Essentially, canonical XML is a strict XML syntax; documents in canonical XML can be compared directly. The information included in the canonical XML version of a document is the same as would appear in its infoset.

As you can imagine, two XML documents that actually contain the same information can be arranged differently. They can differ in terms of their structure, attribute ordering, and even character encoding. That means that it's very hard to compare such documents. However, when you place these documents in canonical XML format, they can be compared on a byte-by-byte level. In the canonical XML syntax, logically equivalent documents are identical byte for byte.

The canonical XML syntax is very strict; for example, canonical XML uses UTF-8 character encoding only, carriage-return linefeed pairs are replaced with linefeeds, tabs in CDATA sections are replaced by spaces, all entity references must be expanded, and much more, as specified in www.w3.org/TR/xml-c14n. Because canonical XML is intended to be byte-by-byte correct, the upshot is that if you need a document in canonical form, you should use software to convert your XML documents to that form.

One such package that will convert valid XML documents to canonical form comes with the XML for Java software that you can get from IBM's AlphaWorks (the Web site is http://www.alphaworks.ibm.com/tech/xml4j). XML for Java comes with a Java program named DOMWriter that can convert documents to canonical XML form. To use this program, you need to make sure that your document is valid, which means giving it a DTD or schema to be checked against. I'll add a DTD to the example ch02_01.xml we've seen in this chapter (we'll see how to create DTDs in the next chapter):

Listing ch02_04.xml

```xml
<?xml version = "1.0" standalone="yes"?>
<!DOCTYPE DOCUMENT [
<!ELEMENT DOCUMENT (CUSTOMER)*>
<!ELEMENT CUSTOMER (NAME,DATE,ORDERS)>
<!ELEMENT NAME (LAST_NAME,FIRST_NAME)>
<!ELEMENT LAST_NAME (#PCDATA)>
<!ELEMENT FIRST_NAME (#PCDATA)>
<!ELEMENT DATE (#PCDATA)>
<!ELEMENT ORDERS (ITEM)*>
<!ELEMENT ITEM (PRODUCT,NUMBER,PRICE)>
<!ELEMENT PRODUCT (#PCDATA)>
<!ELEMENT NUMBER (#PCDATA)>
<!ELEMENT PRICE (#PCDATA)>
]>
<DOCUMENT>
    <CUSTOMER>
        <NAME>
            <LAST_NAME>Smith</LAST_NAME>
            <FIRST_NAME>Sam</FIRST_NAME>
        </NAME>
        <DATE>October 15, 2003</DATE>
        <ORDERS>
            <ITEM>
                <PRODUCT>Tomatoes</PRODUCT>
                <NUMBER>8</NUMBER>
                <PRICE>$1.25</PRICE>
            </ITEM>
            <ITEM>
                <PRODUCT>Oranges</PRODUCT>
                <NUMBER>24</NUMBER>
                <PRICE>$4.98</PRICE>
            </ITEM>
        </ORDERS>
    </CUSTOMER>
    <CUSTOMER>
        <NAME>
            <LAST_NAME>Jones</LAST_NAME>
            <FIRST_NAME>Polly</FIRST_NAME>
        </NAME>
        <DATE>October 20, 2003</DATE>
        <ORDERS>
            <ITEM>
                <PRODUCT>Bread</PRODUCT>
                <NUMBER>12</NUMBER>
                <PRICE>$14.95</PRICE>
```

continues

Listing ch02_04.xml Continued

```
                </ITEM>
                <ITEM>
                    <PRODUCT>Apples</PRODUCT>
                    <NUMBER>6</NUMBER>
                    <PRICE>$1.50</PRICE>
                </ITEM>
            </ORDERS>
        </CUSTOMER>
        <CUSTOMER>
            <NAME>
                <LAST_NAME>Weber</LAST_NAME>
                <FIRST_NAME>Bill</FIRST_NAME>
            </NAME>
            <DATE>October 25, 2003</DATE>
            <ORDERS>
                <ITEM>
                    <PRODUCT>Asparagus</PRODUCT>
                    <NUMBER>12</NUMBER>
                    <PRICE>$2.95</PRICE>
                </ITEM>
                <ITEM>
                    <PRODUCT>Lettuce</PRODUCT>
                    <NUMBER>6</NUMBER>
                    <PRICE>$11.50</PRICE>
                </ITEM>
            </ORDERS>
        </CUSTOMER>
</DOCUMENT>
```

Now you can use the DOMWriter program with the special `-c` switch to convert this document to canonical form (the `> canonical.xml` part at the end sends the output of the program to a file named canonical.xml):

```
%java dom.DOMWriter -c ch02_01.xml > canonical.xml
```

Here's the result (note that DOMWriter has preserved all the whitespace in the document, and the `&#10;` entity references stand for the UTF-8 code for a linefeed—you can also give codes in hexadecimal if you include an x before the number, like this, for a linefeed: `&#xA`):

```
<DOCUMENT>&#10;      <CUSTOMER>&#10;            <NAME>&#10;
<LAST_NAME>Smith</LAST_NAME>&#10;
<FIRST_NAME>Sam</FIRST_NAME>&#10;            </NAME>&#10;
<DATE>October 15, 2003</DATE>&#10;            <ORDERS>&#10;
<ITEM>&#10;                  <PRODUCT>Tomatoes</PRODUCT>&#10;
<NUMBER>8</NUMBER>&#10;
<PRICE>$1.25</PRICE>&#10;            </ITEM>&#10;
<ITEM>&#10;                  <PRODUCT>Oranges</PRODUCT>&#10;
<NUMBER>24</NUMBER>&#10;
<PRICE>$4.98</PRICE>&#10;            </ITEM>&#10;
</ORDERS>&#10;      </CUSTOMER>&#10;      <CUSTOMER>&#10;
<NAME>&#10;            <LAST_NAME>Jones</LAST_NAME>&#10;
<FIRST_NAME>Polly</FIRST_NAME>&#10;            </NAME>&#10;
<DATE>October 20, 2003</DATE>&#10;            <ORDERS>&#10;
<ITEM>&#10;                  <PRODUCT>Bread</PRODUCT>&#10;
<NUMBER>12</NUMBER>&#10;
<PRICE>$14.95</PRICE>&#10;            </ITEM>&#10;
<ITEM>&#10;                  <PRODUCT>Apples</PRODUCT>&#10;
<NUMBER>6</NUMBER>&#10;
<PRICE>$1.50</PRICE>&#10;            </ITEM>&#10;
</ORDERS>&#10;      </CUSTOMER>&#10;      <CUSTOMER>&#10;
<NAME>&#10;            <LAST_NAME>Weber</LAST_NAME>&#10;
<FIRST_NAME>Bill</FIRST_NAME>&#10;            </NAME>&#10;
<DATE>October 25, 2003</DATE>&#10;            <ORDERS>&#10;
<ITEM>&#10;                  <PRODUCT>Asparagus</PRODUCT>&#10;
<NUMBER>12</NUMBER>&#10;
<PRICE>$2.95</PRICE>&#10;            </ITEM>&#10;
<ITEM>&#10;                  <PRODUCT>Lettuce</PRODUCT>&#10;
<NUMBER>6</NUMBER>&#10;
<PRICE>$11.50</PRICE>&#10;            </ITEM>&#10;
</ORDERS>&#10;      </CUSTOMER>&#10;</DOCUMENT>
```

In their canonical form, documents can be compared directly, and any differences will be readily apparent.

This example is also useful because it shows exactly what a DTD looks like and provides us with the perfect starting point for the next chapter, which is where we're going to start writing DTDs ourselves and thus create valid XML documents.

CHAPTER 3

Valid Documents: Creating Document Type Definitions

In the previous chapter, we saw all about creating well-formed XML documents. However, there's more to creating good XML documents than the simple (although essential) requirement that they be well formed. Because you can create your own tags when you create an XML application, it's up to you to set their syntax. For example, can a `<HOUSE>` element contain plain text or only other elements such as `<TENANT>` or `<OWNER>`? Must a `<BOOK>` element contain a `<PAGE_COUNT>` element, or can it get by without one? It's up to you to decide. Making sure documents have been written using your XML syntax is not only good for making sure your documents are legible, it can also be essential for programs that deal with documents via code.

Valid XML Documents

XML documents whose syntax has been checked successfully are called *valid* documents; in particular, an XML document is considered valid if there is a *document type definition* (DTD) or XML schema associated with it and if the document complies with the DTD or schema. That's all there is to making a document valid. This chapter is all about creating basic DTDs. In the next chapter, I'll elaborate on the DTDs we create here and show how to declare entities, attributes, and notations.

You can find the formal rules for DTDs in the XML 1.0 recommendation, `www.w3.org/TR/REC-xml`, which also appears in Appendix A, "The XML Specification." The constraints that documents and DTDs must adhere to in order to create a valid document are marked with the text "Validity Constraint."

Note that DTDs are all about specifying the structure and syntax of XML documents (not their content). Various organizations can share a DTD to put an XML application into practice. We've seen quite a few examples of XML applications in Chapter 1, "Essential XML," and those applications can all be enforced with DTDs that the various organizations make public. We'll see how to create public DTDs in this chapter.

Most XML parsers, like the one in the Internet Explorer, require XML documents to be well formed but not necessarily valid (most XML parsers do not require a DTD, but if there is one, validating parsers will use it to check the XML document).

IE with DTDs

To see how to get Internet Explorer to work with DTDs, see the section "Validating XML Documents with DTDs in Internet Explorer" in Chapter 7, "Handling XML Documents with JavaScript."

In fact, we saw a DTD at the end of the previous chapter. In that chapter, I set up an example XML document named ch02_01.xml that stored customer orders. At the end of the chapter, I used the DOMWriter program that comes with IBM's XML for Java package to translate the document into canonical XML. To run it through that program, I needed to add a DTD to the document. Here's what it looked like:

Listing ch03_01.xml

```
<?xml version = "1.0" standalone="yes"?>
<!DOCTYPE DOCUMENT [
<!ELEMENT DOCUMENT (CUSTOMER)*>
<!ELEMENT CUSTOMER (NAME,DATE,ORDERS)>
<!ELEMENT NAME (LAST_NAME,FIRST_NAME)>
<!ELEMENT LAST_NAME (#PCDATA)>
<!ELEMENT FIRST_NAME (#PCDATA)>
<!ELEMENT DATE (#PCDATA)>
<!ELEMENT ORDERS (ITEM)*>
<!ELEMENT ITEM (PRODUCT,NUMBER,PRICE)>
<!ELEMENT PRODUCT (#PCDATA)>
<!ELEMENT NUMBER (#PCDATA)>
<!ELEMENT PRICE (#PCDATA)>
]>
```

```
<DOCUMENT>
    <CUSTOMER>
        <NAME>
            <LAST_NAME>Smith</LAST_NAME>
            <FIRST_NAME>Sam</FIRST_NAME>
        </NAME>
        <DATE>October 15, 2003</DATE>
        <ORDERS>
            <ITEM>
                <PRODUCT>Tomatoes</PRODUCT>
                <NUMBER>8</NUMBER>
                <PRICE>$1.25</PRICE>
            </ITEM>
            <ITEM>
                <PRODUCT>Oranges</PRODUCT>
                <NUMBER>24</NUMBER>
                <PRICE>$4.98</PRICE>
            </ITEM>
        </ORDERS>
    </CUSTOMER>
    <CUSTOMER>
        <NAME>
            <LAST_NAME>Jones</LAST_NAME>
            <FIRST_NAME>Polly</FIRST_NAME>
        </NAME>
        <DATE>October 20, 2003</DATE>
        <ORDERS>
            <ITEM>
                <PRODUCT>Bread</PRODUCT>
                <NUMBER>12</NUMBER>
                <PRICE>$14.95</PRICE>
            </ITEM>
            <ITEM>
                <PRODUCT>Apples</PRODUCT>
                <NUMBER>6</NUMBER>
                <PRICE>$1.50</PRICE>
            </ITEM>
        </ORDERS>
    </CUSTOMER>
    <CUSTOMER>
        <NAME>
            <LAST_NAME>Weber</LAST_NAME>
            <FIRST_NAME>Bill</FIRST_NAME>
        </NAME>
        <DATE>October 25, 2003</DATE>
        <ORDERS>
            <ITEM>
                <PRODUCT>Asparagus</PRODUCT>
                <NUMBER>12</NUMBER>
                <PRICE>$2.95</PRICE>
            </ITEM>
```

continues

Listing ch03_01.xml Continued

```
            <ITEM>
                <PRODUCT>Lettuce</PRODUCT>
                <NUMBER>6</NUMBER>
                <PRICE>$11.50</PRICE>
            </ITEM>
        </ORDERS>
    </CUSTOMER>
</DOCUMENT>
```

In this chapter, I'm going to take this DTD apart to see what makes it tick. Actually, this DTD is a pretty substantial one; to get us started and to show how DTDs work in overview, I'll start with a mini-example first. Here it is:

Listing ch03_02.xml

```
<?xml version="1.0"?>
<!DOCTYPE THESIS [
    <!ELEMENT THESIS (P*)>
    <!ELEMENT P (#PCDATA)>
]>
<THESIS>
    <P>
        This is my Ph.D. thesis.
    </P>
    <P>
        Pretty good, huh?
    </P>
    <P>
        So, give me a Ph.D. now!
    </P>
</THESIS>
```

Note the <!DOCTYPE> element here. This element is a document type *declaration* (DTDs are document type *definitions*). You use document type declarations to indicate the DTD used for the document. The basic syntax for the document type declaration is <!DOCTYPE *rootname* [*DTD*]> (there are other variations we'll see in this chapter), where *DTD* is the document type definition you want to use. DTDs can be internal or external, as we'll see in this chapter. In this case, the DTD is internal:

```
<?xml version="1.0"?>
<!DOCTYPE THESIS [
    <!ELEMENT THESIS (P*)>
    <!ELEMENT P (#PCDATA)>
]>
<THESIS>
    <P>
        This is my Ph.D. thesis.
    </P>
    <P>
        Pretty good, huh?
    </P>
    <P>
        So, give me a Ph.D. now!
    </P>
</THESIS>
```

This DTD follows the World Wide Web Consortium (W3C) syntax conventions, which means that I specify the syntax for each element with `<!ELEMENT>`. Using this element, you can specify that the contents of an element can be either parsed character data, #PCDATA or other elements that you've created, or both. In this example, I'm indicating that the `<THESIS>` element must contain only `<P>` elements, but that it can contain zero or more occurrences of the `<P>` element (which is what the * after P in `<!ELEMENT THESIS (P*)>` means).

In addition to defining the `<THESIS>` element, I define the `<P>` element so that it can hold only text—that is, parsed character data (which is pure text, without any markup)—with the term #PCDATA:

```
<?xml version="1.0"?>
<!DOCTYPE THESIS [
    <!ELEMENT THESIS (P*)>
    <!ELEMENT P (#PCDATA)>
]>
<THESIS>
    <P>
        This is my Ph.D. thesis.
    </P>
    <P>
        Pretty good, huh?
    </P>
    <P>
        So, give me a Ph.D. now!
    </P>
</THESIS>
```

In this way, I've specified the syntax of these two elements, <THESIS> and <P>. A validating XML processor can now validate this document using the DTD that it supplies.

And that's what a DTD looks like in overview; now it's time to dig into the full details. And we're going to take a look at all of them here and in the next chapter.

Creating Document Type Declarations

You define the syntax and structure of elements using a document type *definition* (DTD), and you declare that definition in a document using a document type *declaration*. We've seen that you use the <!DOCTYPE> element to create a document type declaration. This element can take many different forms, as you see here (here, *URL* is the URL of a DTD, and *rootname* is the name of the root element); we'll see all these forms in this chapter:

- <!DOCTYPE *rootname* [*DTD*]>
- <!DOCTYPE rootname SYSTEM URL>
- <!DOCTYPE rootname SYSTEM URL [DTD]>
- <!DOCTYPE rootname PUBLIC identifier URL>
- <!DOCTYPE rootname PUBLIC identifier URL [DTD]>

To use a DTD, you need a document type declaration, which means that you need a <!DOCTYPE> element. The <!DOCTYPE> element is part of a document's prolog. Here's how I add a document type declaration to the document ch02_01.xml that we developed in the previous chapter:

```
<?xml version = "1.0" standalone="yes"?>
<!DOCTYPE DOCUMENT [
    .
    .
    .
]>
<DOCUMENT>
    <CUSTOMER>
        <NAME>
            <LAST_NAME>Smith</LAST_NAME>
            <FIRST_NAME>Sam</FIRST_NAME>
        </NAME>
        <DATE>October 15, 2003</DATE>
        <ORDERS>
            <ITEM>
                <PRODUCT>Tomatoes</PRODUCT>
```

```
                   <NUMBER>8</NUMBER>
                   <PRICE>$1.25</PRICE>
              </ITEM>
                   .
                   .
                   .
              <ITEM>
                   <PRODUCT>Asparagus</PRODUCT>
                   <NUMBER>12</NUMBER>
                   <PRICE>$2.95</PRICE>
              </ITEM>
              <ITEM>
                   <PRODUCT>Lettuce</PRODUCT>
                   <NUMBER>6</NUMBER>
                   <PRICE>$11.50</PRICE>
              </ITEM>
         </ORDERS>
     </CUSTOMER>
</DOCUMENT>
```

Now it's up to us to supply the actual DTD that is part of this <!DOCTYPE> element.

Creating Document Type Definitions

To introduce DTDs, I'll start with a DTD that's internal to the document whose syntax it specifies (we'll see how to create external DTDs later in the chapter). In this case, the DTD itself goes inside the square brackets in the <!DOCTYPE> element (note that I've set the standalone attribute to yes here because this document does not rely on any external resources):

```
<?xml version = "1.0" standalone="yes"?>
<!DOCTYPE DOCUMENT [
<!ELEMENT DOCUMENT (CUSTOMER)*>
<!ELEMENT CUSTOMER (NAME,DATE,ORDERS)>
<!ELEMENT NAME (LAST_NAME,FIRST_NAME)>
<!ELEMENT LAST_NAME (#PCDATA)>
<!ELEMENT FIRST_NAME (#PCDATA)>
<!ELEMENT DATE (#PCDATA)>
<!ELEMENT ORDERS (ITEM)*>
<!ELEMENT ITEM (PRODUCT,NUMBER,PRICE)>
<!ELEMENT PRODUCT (#PCDATA)>
<!ELEMENT NUMBER (#PCDATA)>
<!ELEMENT PRICE (#PCDATA)>
]>
```

continues

```
<DOCUMENT>
    <CUSTOMER>
        <NAME>
            <LAST_NAME>Smith</LAST_NAME>
            <FIRST_NAME>Sam</FIRST_NAME>
        </NAME>
        <DATE>October 15, 2003</DATE>
        <ORDERS>
            <ITEM>
                <PRODUCT>Tomatoes</PRODUCT>
                <NUMBER>8</NUMBER>
                <PRICE>$1.25</PRICE>
            </ITEM>
                .
                .
                .
            <ITEM>
                <PRODUCT>Asparagus</PRODUCT>
                <NUMBER>12</NUMBER>
                <PRICE>$2.95</PRICE>
            </ITEM>
            <ITEM>
                <PRODUCT>Lettuce</PRODUCT>
                <NUMBER>6</NUMBER>
                <PRICE>$11.50</PRICE>
            </ITEM>
        </ORDERS>
    </CUSTOMER>
</DOCUMENT>
```

After a DTD is in place—and we'll see how to create this DTD in this chapter—you've got a valid document.

Validating Against a DTD

How do you really know if your XML document is valid? One way is to check it with an XML validator, and there are plenty out there to choose from. As we saw in Chapter 1, validators are packages that will check your XML and give you feedback. Here's a list of some of the XML validators on the Web:

- **W3C XML validator** (validator.w3.org/)—This is the official W3C HTML validator. Although it's officially for HTML, it also includes some XML support. Your XML document must be online to be checked with this validator.

- **Tidy** (www.w3.org/People/Raggett/tidy/)—Tidy is a beloved utility for cleaning up and repairing Web pages, and it includes limited support for XML. Your XML document must be online to be checked with this validator.

- **XML.com** (`www.xml.com/xml/pub/tools/ruwf/check.html`)—This is XML.com's XML validator based on the Lark processor. Your XML document must be online to be checked with this validator.

- **Language Technology Group** (`www.ltg.ed.ac.uk/~richard/xml-check.html`)—The Language Technology Group at the University of Edinburgh has this validator, based on the RXP parser. Your XML document must be online to be checked with this validator.

- **STG XML Validator** (`http://www.stg.brown.edu/service/xmlvalid/`)—This excellent XML validator is from the Scholarly Technology Group at Brown University. This is the only online XML validator that I know of that allows you to check XML documents that are not online; you can use the Web page's file upload control to specify the name of the file on your hard disk that you want to have uploaded and checked.

To see one of these online validators at work, take a look at Figure 1.11 back in Chapter 1. There, I'm asking the XML validator from the Scholarly Technology Group to validate greeting.xml after I've added a DTD and purposely exchanged the order of the `<MESSAGE>` and `</GREETING>` tags:

```
<?xml version="1.0" encoding="UTF-8"?>
<!DOCTYPE DOCUMENT [
    <!ELEMENT DOCUMENT (GREETING, MESSAGE)>
    <!ELEMENT GREETING (#PCDATA)>
    <!ELEMENT MESSAGE (#PCDATA)>
]>
<DOCUMENT>
    <GREETING>
        Hello From XML
    <MESSAGE>
    </GREETING>
        Welcome to the wild and woolly world of XML.
    </MESSAGE>
</DOCUMENT>
```

You can see the results in Figure 1.12 in Chapter 1; as you see there, the validator is indicating that there is a problem with these two tags. In general, then, you can use a validator to check your document. Validators can help a great deal, as you're writing long and difficult XML documents, because you can often check them at each development stage.

Having gotten the `<!DOCTYPE>` element in place, we're ready to start creating the DTD, starting with the `<!ELEMENT>` element.

Element Declarations

To declare the syntax of an element in a DTD, you use the `<!ELEMENT>` element like this: `<!ELEMENT NAME CONTENT_MODEL>`. Here, `NAME` is the name of the element you're declaring; `CONTENT_MODEL` can be set to `EMPTY` or `ANY`, or it can hold mixed content (other elements as well as parsed character data) or child elements.

Here are a few element examples—note the expressions starting with `%` and ending with `;`. Those expressions are parameter entity references, much like general entity references, except that you use them in DTDs, not the body of the document (we'll see parameter entities in the next chapter):

```
<!ELEMENT direction (left, right, top?)>
<!ELEMENT CHAPTER (INTRODUCTION, (P | QUOTE | NOTE)*, DIV*)>
<!ELEMENT HR EMPTY>
<!ELEMENT p (#PCDATA | I)* >
<!ELEMENT %title; %content; >
<!ELEMENT DOCUMENT ANY>
```

We're going to see how to create `<!ELEMENT>` elements like these in this chapter and the next one. I'll start by declaring the root element of the example document for this chapter, ch02_01.xml:

```
<?xml version = "1.0" standalone="yes"?>
<!DOCTYPE DOCUMENT [
<!ELEMENT DOCUMENT ANY>
]>
<DOCUMENT>
</DOCUMENT>
```

Note that I'm specifying a content model of `ANY` here; see the next topic for the details on this keyword.

ANY

When you declare an element with the content model of `ANY`, it means that the declared element can contain any type of content—any element in the document as well as parsed character data. (Effectively, this means that the contents of elements you declare with the `ANY` content model are not checked by XML validators.)

Here's how you specify a content model of `ANY`:

```
<?xml version = "1.0" standalone="yes"?>
<!DOCTYPE DOCUMENT [
<!ELEMENT DOCUMENT ANY>
```

```
]>
<DOCUMENT>
</DOCUMENT>
```

However, giving an element the content model ANY is often not a good idea because it removes syntax checking. It's usually far better to specify an actual content model, and I'll start doing that with a child list of elements.

Child Element Lists

Besides using the content model of ANY, you can specify that the element you're declaring contains another element by giving the name of that element in parentheses, like this:

```
<?xml version = "1.0" standalone="yes"?>
<!DOCTYPE DOCUMENT [
<!ELEMENT DOCUMENT (CUSTOMER)*>
]>
<DOCUMENT>
    .
    .
    .
</DOCUMENT>
```

In this case, I'm indicating that the root element, <DOCUMENT>, can contain any number (including zero) of <CUSTOMER> elements. (The way I specify that the <DOCUMENT> element can contain any number of <CUSTOMER> elements is with the asterisk after the parentheses, and we'll see how that works in a page or two.)

The <DOCUMENT> element can contain any number of <CUSTOMER> elements, so I can now add a <CUSTOMER> element to the document, like this:

```
<?xml version = "1.0" standalone="yes"?>
<!DOCTYPE DOCUMENT [
<!ELEMENT DOCUMENT (CUSTOMER)*>
]>
<DOCUMENT>
    <CUSTOMER>
    .
    .
    .
    </CUSTOMER>
</DOCUMENT>
```

However, this is not a valid document because I haven't declared the <CUSTOMER> element yet. I'll do that next.

#PCDATA

Say that we want to let the `<CUSTOMER>` element store some plain text—in particular, say that we want to store the name of a customer. All nonmarkup text is referred to as *parsed character data* in a DTD, and it's abbreviated as #PCDATA in element declarations. Parsed character data explicitly means text that does not contain markup; it's just simple character data.

The parsed character data is where you store the actual content of the document as plain text. Note, however, that this is the *only* way to specify the content of the document using DTDs. You can't say anything more about the actual *type* of content.

For example, even though you might be storing numbers, that data is only plain text as far as DTDs are concerned. This lack of precision is one of the reasons that XML schemas, the alternative to DTDs, were developed. With schemas, you can specify much more about the type of data you're storing, such as whether it's in an integer, a floating point, or even a date format, and XML processors can check to make sure that the data matches the format in which it's supposed to be expressed. I'll take a look at schemas in Chapter 5, "Creating XML Schemas."

Here's how I declare the `<CUSTOMER>` element so that it can contain PCDATA (and only PCDATA):

```
<?xml version = "1.0" standalone="yes"?>
<!DOCTYPE DOCUMENT [
<!ELEMENT DOCUMENT (CUSTOMER)*>
<!ELEMENT CUSTOMER (#PCDATA)>
]>
<DOCUMENT>
    <CUSTOMER>
    .
    .
    .
    </CUSTOMER>
</DOCUMENT>
```

Now I can add text to a `<CUSTOMER>` element in the document, like this:

```
<?xml version = "1.0" standalone="yes"?>
<!DOCTYPE DOCUMENT [
<!ELEMENT DOCUMENT (CUSTOMER)*>
<!ELEMENT CUSTOMER (#PCDATA)>
]>
<DOCUMENT>
    <CUSTOMER>
        Sam Smith
    </CUSTOMER>
</DOCUMENT>
```

Note that elements that have been declared to hold PCDATA can hold only PCDATA; you cannot, for example, place another element in the <CUSTOMER> element the way it has been declared now:

```
<?xml version = "1.0" standalone="yes"?>
<!DOCTYPE DOCUMENT [
<!ELEMENT DOCUMENT (CUSTOMER)*>
<!ELEMENT CUSTOMER (#PCDATA)>
]>
<DOCUMENT>
    <CUSTOMER>
        Sam Smith
        <CREDIT_RATING>
            Lousy
        </CREDIT_RATING>
    </CUSTOMER>
</DOCUMENT>
```

The content model that supports both PCDATA and other elements inside an element is called the *mixed-content model*, and I'll take a look at it in a few pages. (You can also support a mixed-content model using the ANY content model, of course.)

There's another thing to note here now that we're dealing with multiple declarations: The order in which you declare elements doesn't matter, so this DTD, in which I've declared the <DOCUMENT> element after the <CUSTOMER> element, works just as well:

```
<?xml version = "1.0" standalone="yes"?>
<!DOCTYPE DOCUMENT [
<!ELEMENT CUSTOMER (#PCDATA)>
<!ELEMENT DOCUMENT (CUSTOMER)*>
]>
<DOCUMENT>
    <CUSTOMER>
    .
    .
    .
    </CUSTOMER>
</DOCUMENT>
```

Order of Element Declarations

Although the order of element declarations is not supposed to matter (and, in practice, that's the way I've always seen it), it is possible that some XML processors will demand that you declare an element before using it in another declaration.

It's also possible to declare elements in such a way that they can contain multiple children. In fact, you can specify the exact types of child elements that an element can enclose, as well as in what order those child elements must appear. I'll take a look at that now.

Dealing with Multiple Children

When you want to declare an element that can contain multiple children, you have several options. DTDs use a syntax to deal with multiple children that is much like working with regular expressions in languages such as Perl, if you're familiar with that. Here's the syntax you can use (here, a and b are child elements of the element you're declaring):

- a+—One or more occurrences of a.
- a*—Zero or more occurrences of a.
- a?—a or nothing.
- a, b—a followed by b.
- a ¦ b—a or b, but not both.
- (*expression*)—Surrounding an expression with parentheses means that it is treated as a unit and may have the suffix operators ?, *, or +.

If you're not familiar with this kind of syntax, it's not much use asking why things are set up this way; this syntax has been around a long time, and the W3C adopted it for DTDs because many people were familiar with it. If this looks totally strange to you, it's just one of the skills you'll have to master when writing DTDs—but, fortunately, it soon becomes second nature. I'll take a look at each of these possibilities in detail now.

One or More Children

If you have to specify that the <DOCUMENT> element can contain only between 12 and 15 <CUSTOMER> elements, you'll have a problem when working with DTDs: the DTD syntax won't allow you to do that without getting very complex. You can, however, specify that the <DOCUMENT> element must contain one or more <CUSTOMER> elements like this, using the + operator:

```
<?xml version = "1.0" standalone="yes"?>
<!DOCTYPE DOCUMENT [
<!ELEMENT DOCUMENT (CUSTOMER)+>
<!ELEMENT CUSTOMER (#PCDATA)>
]>
```

```
<DOCUMENT>
    <CUSTOMER>
        Sam Smith
    </CUSTOMER>
    <CUSTOMER>
        Fred Smith
    </CUSTOMER>
</DOCUMENT>
```

In this case, the XML processor now knows that you want the <DOCUMENT> element to contain at least one or more <CUSTOMER> elements, which makes sense if you want a useful document that actually contains some data. In this way, we've been able to specify the syntax of the <DOCUMENT> element in some more detail.

Zero or More Children

Besides specifying one or more child elements, you can declare elements so that they can enclose zero or more of a particular child element. This is useful if you want to allow an element to have a particular child element, or any number of such elements, but you don't want to force it to have that particular child element.

For example, a <CHAPTER> element might be capable of containing an <FOOTNOTE> element, or even several <FOOTNOTE> elements, but you wouldn't necessarily want to force all <CHAPTER> elements to have <FOOTNOTE> elements. Using the * operator, you can do that.

The * operator means that the indicated child element can appear any number of times in the declared element (including zero times). Here's how I indicate that the <DOCUMENT> element can contain any number of <CUSTOMER> elements:

```
<?xml version = "1.0" standalone="yes"?>
<!DOCTYPE DOCUMENT [
<!ELEMENT DOCUMENT (CUSTOMER)*>
<!ELEMENT CUSTOMER (#PCDATA)>
]>
<DOCUMENT>
    <CUSTOMER>
        Sam Smith
    </CUSTOMER>
    <CUSTOMER>
        Fred Smith
    </CUSTOMER>
</DOCUMENT>
```

Zero or One Child

Besides using + to specify one or more occurrences of a particular child element and * to specify zero or more occurrences of a child element, you can use ? to specify zero or one occurrence of a child element. In other words, using ? indicates that a particular child element *may* be present in the element you're declaring, but it need not be.

For example, a <CHAPTER> element might be capable of containing one <OPENING_QUOTATION> element, but you wouldn't necessarily want to force all <CHAPTER> elements to have an <OPENING_QUOTATION> element. Using the ? operator, you can do that.

Here's an example. In this case, I'm allowing the <DOCUMENT> element to contain only zero or one <CUSTOMER> element (rather a limited clientele):

```
<?xml version = "1.0" standalone="yes"?>
<!DOCTYPE DOCUMENT [
<!ELEMENT DOCUMENT (CUSTOMER)?>
<!ELEMENT CUSTOMER (#PCDATA)>
]>
<DOCUMENT>
    <CUSTOMER>
        Sam Smith
    </CUSTOMER>
</DOCUMENT>
```

We've advanced a little in DTD power now by allowing multiple child elements, but so far, we've allowed only child elements of the same type in any one declared element. That's about to change.

DTD Sequences

You can specify exactly what child elements a particular element can contain, and in what order, by using a *sequence*. A sequence is a comma-separated list of element names that tells the XML processor what elements must appear and in what order.

For example, say that we wanted to change the <CUSTOMER> element so that instead of containing only PCDATA, it can contain other elements. Here, I'll let the <CUSTOMER> element contain one <NAME> element, one <DATE> element, and one <ORDERS> element, in exactly that order. The resulting declaration looks like this:

```
<!ELEMENT CUSTOMER (NAME,DATE,ORDERS)>
```

I can break this down further, of course. For example, I can specify that the <NAME> element must contain exactly one <LAST_NAME> element and one <FIRST_NAME> element, in that order, like this:

```
<!ELEMENT NAME (LAST_NAME,FIRST_NAME)>
```

Whitespace doesn't matter, of course, so the same declaration could look like this:

```
<!ELEMENT    NAME          (LAST_NAME,       FIRST_NAME)>
```

Being able to specify the exact order that the elements in your document must take can be great when you're working with software that relies on such an order.

Here's how I'll elaborate the ch02_01.xml document to include the previous two sequences as well as a third one that makes sure that the <ITEM> element contains exactly one <PRODUCT> element, one <NUMBER> element, and one <PRICE> element, in that order. The resulting DTD enforces the syntax of the ch02_01.xml document that we developed in the previous chapter; you can see the whole document, complete with working DTD, here:

```
<?xml version = "1.0" standalone="yes"?>
<!DOCTYPE DOCUMENT [
<!ELEMENT DOCUMENT (CUSTOMER)*>
<!ELEMENT CUSTOMER (NAME,DATE,ORDERS)>
<!ELEMENT NAME (LAST_NAME,FIRST_NAME)>
<!ELEMENT LAST_NAME (#PCDATA)>
<!ELEMENT FIRST_NAME (#PCDATA)>
<!ELEMENT DATE (#PCDATA)>
<!ELEMENT ORDERS (ITEM)*>
<!ELEMENT ITEM (PRODUCT,NUMBER,PRICE)>
<!ELEMENT PRODUCT (#PCDATA)>
<!ELEMENT NUMBER (#PCDATA)>
<!ELEMENT PRICE (#PCDATA)>
]>
<DOCUMENT>
    <CUSTOMER>
        <NAME>
            <LAST_NAME>Smith</LAST_NAME>
            <FIRST_NAME>Sam</FIRST_NAME>
        </NAME>
        <DATE>October 15, 2003</DATE>
        <ORDERS>
            <ITEM>
                <PRODUCT>Tomatoes</PRODUCT>
                <NUMBER>8</NUMBER>
                <PRICE>$1.25</PRICE>
            </ITEM>
```

continues

```
            <ITEM>
                  <PRODUCT>Oranges</PRODUCT>
                  <NUMBER>24</NUMBER>
                  <PRICE>$4.98</PRICE>
            </ITEM>
        </ORDERS>
    </CUSTOMER>
    <CUSTOMER>
        <NAME>
            <LAST_NAME>Jones</LAST_NAME>
            <FIRST_NAME>Polly</FIRST_NAME>
        </NAME>
        <DATE>October 20, 2003</DATE>
        <ORDERS>
            <ITEM>
                  <PRODUCT>Bread</PRODUCT>
                  <NUMBER>12</NUMBER>
                  <PRICE>$14.95</PRICE>
            </ITEM>
            <ITEM>
                  <PRODUCT>Apples</PRODUCT>
                  <NUMBER>6</NUMBER>
                  <PRICE>$1.50</PRICE>
            </ITEM>
        </ORDERS>
    </CUSTOMER>
    <CUSTOMER>
        <NAME>
            <LAST_NAME>Weber</LAST_NAME>
            <FIRST_NAME>Bill</FIRST_NAME>
        </NAME>
        <DATE>October 25, 2003</DATE>
        <ORDERS>
            <ITEM>
                  <PRODUCT>Asparagus</PRODUCT>
                  <NUMBER>12</NUMBER>
                  <PRICE>$2.95</PRICE>
            </ITEM>
            <ITEM>
                  <PRODUCT>Lettuce</PRODUCT>
                  <NUMBER>6</NUMBER>
                  <PRICE>$11.50</PRICE>
            </ITEM>
        </ORDERS>
    </CUSTOMER>
</DOCUMENT>
```

You can use the same element in a sequence a number of times, if you want. For example, here's how I make sure that the <CUSTOMER> element should hold exactly three <NAME> elements:

```
<!ELEMENT CUSTOMER (NAME,NAME,NAME)>
```

Here's another important note: You can use +, *, and ? operators that we've already seen inside sequences. For example, here's how I specify that there can be one or more <NAME> elements for an order, an optional <CREDIT_RATING> element, and any number of <DATE> elements:

```
<?xml version = "1.0" standalone="yes"?>
<!DOCTYPE DOCUMENT [
<!ELEMENT DOCUMENT (CUSTOMER)*>
<!ELEMENT CUSTOMER (NAME+,CREDIT_RATING?,DATE*,ORDERS)>
<!ELEMENT NAME (LAST_NAME,FIRST_NAME)>
<!ELEMENT LAST_NAME (#PCDATA)>
<!ELEMENT FIRST_NAME (#PCDATA)>
<!ELEMENT DATE (#PCDATA)>
<!ELEMENT ORDERS (ITEM)*>
<!ELEMENT ITEM (PRODUCT,NUMBER,PRICE)>
<!ELEMENT PRODUCT (#PCDATA)>
<!ELEMENT NUMBER (#PCDATA)>
<!ELEMENT PRICE (#PCDATA)>
<!ELEMENT CREDIT_RATING (#PCDATA)>
]>
<DOCUMENT>
    <CUSTOMER>
        <NAME>
            <LAST_NAME>Smith</LAST_NAME>
            <FIRST_NAME>Sam</FIRST_NAME>
            .
            .
            .
```

Using +, *, and ? inside sequences provides you with a lot of flexibility because now you can specify how many times an element can appear in a sequence— and even if it can be absent altogether.

Creating Subsequences with Parentheses

In fact, you can get even more powerful using the +, *, and ? operators inside sequences because, using parentheses, you can create *subsequences*—that is, sequences inside sequences.

For example, say that I wanted the <CUSTOMER> element to be capable of holding one or more <NAME> element. For each <NAME> element, I also want to allow a possible <CREDIT_RATING> element. I can do that like this, where I'm creating the subsequence (NAME,CREDIT_RATING?) and allowing that subsequence to appear one or more times in the <CUSTOMER> element:

Listing ch03_03.xml

```
<?xml version = "1.0" standalone="yes"?>
<!DOCTYPE DOCUMENT [
<!ELEMENT DOCUMENT (CUSTOMER)*>
<!ELEMENT CUSTOMER ((NAME,CREDIT_RATING?)+,DATE*,ORDERS)>
<!ELEMENT NAME (LAST_NAME,FIRST_NAME)>
<!ELEMENT LAST_NAME (#PCDATA)>
<!ELEMENT FIRST_NAME (#PCDATA)>
<!ELEMENT DATE (#PCDATA)>
<!ELEMENT ORDERS (ITEM)*>
<!ELEMENT ITEM (PRODUCT,NUMBER,PRICE)>
<!ELEMENT PRODUCT (#PCDATA)>
<!ELEMENT NUMBER (#PCDATA)>
<!ELEMENT PRICE (#PCDATA)>
<!ELEMENT CREDIT_RATING (#PCDATA)>
]>
<DOCUMENT>
    <CUSTOMER>
        <NAME>
            <LAST_NAME>Smith</LAST_NAME>
            <FIRST_NAME>Sam</FIRST_NAME>
        </NAME>
        <DATE>October 15, 2003</DATE>
        <ORDERS>
            <ITEM>
                <PRODUCT>Tomatoes</PRODUCT>
                <NUMBER>8</NUMBER>
                <PRICE>$1.25</PRICE>
            </ITEM>
            <ITEM>
                <PRODUCT>Oranges</PRODUCT>
                <NUMBER>24</NUMBER>
                <PRICE>$4.98</PRICE>
            </ITEM>
        </ORDERS>
    </CUSTOMER>
```

```
<CUSTOMER>
    <NAME>
        <LAST_NAME>Jones</LAST_NAME>
        <FIRST_NAME>Polly</FIRST_NAME>
    </NAME>
    <DATE>October 20, 2003</DATE>
    <ORDERS>
        <ITEM>
            <PRODUCT>Bread</PRODUCT>
            <NUMBER>12</NUMBER>
            <PRICE>$14.95</PRICE>
        </ITEM>
        <ITEM>
            <PRODUCT>Apples</PRODUCT>
            <NUMBER>6</NUMBER>
            <PRICE>$1.50</PRICE>
        </ITEM>
    </ORDERS>
</CUSTOMER>
<CUSTOMER>
    <NAME>
        <LAST_NAME>Weber</LAST_NAME>
        <FIRST_NAME>Bill</FIRST_NAME>
    </NAME>
    <DATE>October 25, 2003</DATE>
    <ORDERS>
        <ITEM>
            <PRODUCT>Asparagus</PRODUCT>
            <NUMBER>12</NUMBER>
            <PRICE>$2.95</PRICE>
        </ITEM>
        <ITEM>
            <PRODUCT>Lettuce</PRODUCT>
            <NUMBER>6</NUMBER>
            <PRICE>$11.50</PRICE>
        </ITEM>
    </ORDERS>
</CUSTOMER>
</DOCUMENT>
```

Defining subsequences like this, and using the +, *, and ? syntax, allows you to be very flexible when defining elements. Here's another example. In this case, I'm declaring an element named <COMMENTS> that must contain a <DATE> element and that then can contain one or more sequences of <TITLE>, <AUTHOR>, and <TEXT> elements:

```
<!ELEMENT COMMENTS (DATE,(TITLE,AUTHOR,TEXT)+)>
```

Choices

Besides using sequences, you can use *choices* in DTDs. A choice lets you specify that one of a number of elements will appear at that particular location. Here's how a choice specifying *one* of the elements <a> *or* <b> *or* <c> looks: (a | b | c). When you use this expression, the XML processor knows that exactly one of the <a> *or* <b> *or* <c> elements can appear.

I'll put choices to work in an example now. In this case, I'll specify that the <ITEM> element must enclose a <PRODUCT> element, a <NUMBER> element, and exactly one element from the list <PRICE>, <CHARGEACCT>, and <SAMPLE>:

Listing ch03_04.xml

```
<?xml version = "1.0" standalone="yes"?>
<!DOCTYPE DOCUMENT [
<!ELEMENT DOCUMENT (CUSTOMER)*>
<!ELEMENT CUSTOMER (NAME,DATE,ORDERS)>
<!ELEMENT NAME (LAST_NAME,FIRST_NAME)>
<!ELEMENT LAST_NAME (#PCDATA)>
<!ELEMENT FIRST_NAME (#PCDATA)>
<!ELEMENT DATE (#PCDATA)>
<!ELEMENT ORDERS (ITEM)*>
<!ELEMENT ITEM (PRODUCT, NUMBER, (PRICE | CHARGEACCT | SAMPLE))>
<!ELEMENT PRODUCT (#PCDATA)>
<!ELEMENT NUMBER (#PCDATA)>
<!ELEMENT PRICE (#PCDATA)>
<!ELEMENT CHARGEACCT (#PCDATA)>
<!ELEMENT SAMPLE (#PCDATA)>
]>
<DOCUMENT>
    <CUSTOMER>
        <NAME>
            <LAST_NAME>Smith</LAST_NAME>
            <FIRST_NAME>Sam</FIRST_NAME>
        </NAME>
        <DATE>October 15, 2003</DATE>
        <ORDERS>
            <ITEM>
                <PRODUCT>Tomatoes</PRODUCT>
                <NUMBER>8</NUMBER>
                <PRICE>$1.25</PRICE>
            </ITEM>
            <ITEM>
```

```
                    <PRODUCT>Oranges</PRODUCT>
                    <NUMBER>24</NUMBER>
                    <SAMPLE>$4.98</SAMPLE>
                </ITEM>
            </ORDERS>
        </CUSTOMER>
        <CUSTOMER>
            <NAME>
                <LAST_NAME>Jones</LAST_NAME>
                <FIRST_NAME>Polly</FIRST_NAME>
            </NAME>
            <DATE>October 20, 2003</DATE>
            <ORDERS>
                <ITEM>
                    <PRODUCT>Bread</PRODUCT>
                    <NUMBER>12</NUMBER>
                    <CHARGEACCT>$14.95</CHARGEACCT>
                </ITEM>
                <ITEM>
                    <PRODUCT>Apples</PRODUCT>
                    <NUMBER>6</NUMBER>
                    <CHARGEACCT>$1.50</CHARGEACCT>
                </ITEM>
            </ORDERS>
        </CUSTOMER>
        <CUSTOMER>
            <NAME>
                <LAST_NAME>Weber</LAST_NAME>
                <FIRST_NAME>Bill</FIRST_NAME>
            </NAME>
            <DATE>October 25, 2003</DATE>
            <ORDERS>
                <ITEM>
                    <PRODUCT>Asparagus</PRODUCT>
                    <NUMBER>12</NUMBER>
                    <PRICE>$2.95</PRICE>
                </ITEM>
                <ITEM>
                    <PRODUCT>Lettuce</PRODUCT>
                    <NUMBER>6</NUMBER>
                    <CHARGEACCT>$11.50</CHARGEACCT>
                </ITEM>
            </ORDERS>
        </CUSTOMER>
</DOCUMENT>
```

As you might expect, you can use the +, *, and ? with choices as well. Here, I'm allowing one or more elements selected from a choice to appear in the <ITEM> element—and allowing the choice to return any number of <CHARGEACCT> elements:

```
<?xml version = "1.0" standalone="yes"?>
<!DOCTYPE DOCUMENT [
<!ELEMENT DOCUMENT (CUSTOMER)*>
<!ELEMENT CUSTOMER (NAME,DATE,ORDERS)>
<!ELEMENT NAME (LAST_NAME,FIRST_NAME)>
<!ELEMENT LAST_NAME (#PCDATA)>
<!ELEMENT FIRST_NAME (#PCDATA)>
<!ELEMENT DATE (#PCDATA)>
<!ELEMENT ORDERS (ITEM)*>
<!ELEMENT ITEM (PRODUCT, NUMBER, (PRICE | CHARGEACCT* | SAMPLE)+)>
<!ELEMENT PRODUCT (#PCDATA)>
<!ELEMENT NUMBER (#PCDATA)>
<!ELEMENT PRICE (#PCDATA)>
<!ELEMENT CHARGEACCT (#PCDATA)>
<!ELEMENT SAMPLE (#PCDATA)>
]>
        .
        .
        .
```

As you can see, DTD syntax allows you to specify syntax fairly exactly (unless you want to specify a range on the number of times an element can appear or its exact data type, of course). In fact, there are two more content models that you can use as well: mixed-content models and empty-content models.

Mixed Content

It is actually possible to specify that an element can contain both PCDATA and other elements. Such a content model is called *mixed*. To specify a mixed-content model, just list #PCDATA along with the child elements you want to allow:

Listing ch03_05.xml

```
<?xml version = "1.0" standalone="yes"?>
<!DOCTYPE DOCUMENT [
<!ELEMENT DOCUMENT (CUSTOMER)*>
<!ELEMENT CUSTOMER (NAME,DATE,ORDERS)>
<!ELEMENT NAME (LAST_NAME,FIRST_NAME)>
<!ELEMENT LAST_NAME (#PCDATA)>
<!ELEMENT FIRST_NAME (#PCDATA)>
<!ELEMENT DATE (#PCDATA)>
<!ELEMENT ORDERS (ITEM)*>
```

```
<!ELEMENT ITEM (PRODUCT, NUMBER, PRICE)>
<!ELEMENT PRODUCT (#PCDATA | PRODUCT_ID)*>
<!ELEMENT NUMBER (#PCDATA)>
<!ELEMENT PRICE (#PCDATA)>
<!ELEMENT PRODUCT_ID (#PCDATA)>
]>
<DOCUMENT>
    <CUSTOMER>
        <NAME>
            <LAST_NAME>Smith</LAST_NAME>
            <FIRST_NAME>Sam</FIRST_NAME>
        </NAME>
        <DATE>October 15, 2003</DATE>
        <ORDERS>
            <ITEM>
                <PRODUCT>Tomatoes</PRODUCT>
                <NUMBER>8</NUMBER>
                <PRICE>$1.25</PRICE>
            </ITEM>
            <ITEM>
                <PRODUCT>
                    <PRODUCT_ID>
                        124829548702121
                    </PRODUCT_ID>
                </PRODUCT>
                <NUMBER>24</NUMBER>
                <PRICE>$4.98</PRICE>
            </ITEM>
        </ORDERS>
    </CUSTOMER>
    <CUSTOMER>
        <NAME>
            <LAST_NAME>Jones</LAST_NAME>
            <FIRST_NAME>Polly</FIRST_NAME>
        </NAME>
        <DATE>October 20, 2003</DATE>
        <ORDERS>
            <ITEM>
                <PRODUCT>Bread</PRODUCT>
                <NUMBER>12</NUMBER>
                <PRICE>$14.95</PRICE>
            </ITEM>
            <ITEM>
                <PRODUCT>Apples</PRODUCT>
                <NUMBER>6</NUMBER>
                <PRICE>$1.50</PRICE>
            </ITEM>
        </ORDERS>
    </CUSTOMER>
    <CUSTOMER>
        <NAME>
```

continues

Listing ch03_05.xml Continued

```
            <LAST_NAME>Weber</LAST_NAME>
            <FIRST_NAME>Bill</FIRST_NAME>
        </NAME>
        <DATE>October 25, 2003</DATE>
        <ORDERS>
            <ITEM>
                <PRODUCT>Asparagus</PRODUCT>
                <NUMBER>12</NUMBER>
                <PRICE>$2.95</PRICE>
            </ITEM>
            <ITEM>
                <PRODUCT>Lettuce</PRODUCT>
                <NUMBER>6</NUMBER>
                <PRICE>$11.50</PRICE>
            </ITEM>
        </ORDERS>
    </CUSTOMER>
</DOCUMENT>
```

However, there is a big drawback to using the mixed-content model: You can specify only the names of the child elements that can occur. You cannot set the child elements' order or number of occurrences. And inside the mixed-content model, you cannot use the +, *, or ? operators.

Because of these severe restrictions, I suggest avoiding the mixed-content model. You're almost always better off declaring a new element that can hold PCDATA and including that in a standard content model instead.

Why Use the Mixed Content Model?

One possible reason to use the mixed-content model is when you're translating simple text documents into XML. Using the mixed-content model can handle the case in which part of the document is in XML and part is in simple text.

Empty Elements

The last remaining DTD content model is the *empty-content model*. In this case, the elements you declare cannot hold any content (either PCDATA or other elements).

Declaring an element to be empty is easy; you just use the keyword EMPTY, like this:

```
<!ELEMENT CREDIT_WARNING EMPTY>
```

Now you can use this new element, `<CREDIT_WARNING>`, like this:

```
<CREDIT_WARNING />
```

Note that although empty elements cannot contain any content, they can have attributes (such as the XHTML `<img>` element). We'll see how to add attributes to element declarations in the next chapter. Here's how I declare and put the `<CREDIT_WARNING>` element to work:

Listing ch03_06.xml

```
<?xml version = "1.0" standalone="yes"?>
<!DOCTYPE DOCUMENT [
<!ELEMENT DOCUMENT (CUSTOMER)*>
<!ELEMENT CUSTOMER (CREDIT_WARNING?,NAME,DATE,ORDERS)>
<!ELEMENT NAME (LAST_NAME,FIRST_NAME)>
<!ELEMENT LAST_NAME (#PCDATA)>
<!ELEMENT FIRST_NAME (#PCDATA)>
<!ELEMENT DATE (#PCDATA)>
<!ELEMENT ORDERS (ITEM)*>
<!ELEMENT ITEM (PRODUCT, NUMBER, PRICE)>
<!ELEMENT PRODUCT (#PCDATA)>
<!ELEMENT NUMBER (#PCDATA)>
<!ELEMENT PRICE (#PCDATA)>
<!ELEMENT CREDIT_WARNING EMPTY>
]>
<DOCUMENT>
    <CUSTOMER>
        <NAME>
            <LAST_NAME>Smith</LAST_NAME>
            <FIRST_NAME>Sam</FIRST_NAME>
        </NAME>
        <DATE>October 15, 2003</DATE>
        <ORDERS>
            <ITEM>
                <PRODUCT>Tomatoes</PRODUCT>
                <NUMBER>8</NUMBER>
                <PRICE>$1.25</PRICE>
            </ITEM>
            <ITEM>
                <PRODUCT>Oranges</PRODUCT>
                <NUMBER>24</NUMBER>
                <PRICE>$4.98</PRICE>
            </ITEM>
        </ORDERS>
    </CUSTOMER>
    <CUSTOMER>
        <CREDIT_WARNING />
```

continues

Listing ch03_06.xml Continued

```
            <NAME>
                    <LAST_NAME>Jones</LAST_NAME>
                    <FIRST_NAME>Polly</FIRST_NAME>
            </NAME>
            <DATE>October 20, 2003</DATE>
            <ORDERS>
                    <ITEM>
                            <PRODUCT>Bread</PRODUCT>
                            <NUMBER>12</NUMBER>
                            <PRICE>$14.95</PRICE>
                    </ITEM>
                    <ITEM>
                            <PRODUCT>Apples</PRODUCT>
                            <NUMBER>6</NUMBER>
                            <PRICE>$1.50</PRICE>
                    </ITEM>
            </ORDERS>
        </CUSTOMER>
        <CUSTOMER>
            <NAME>
                    <LAST_NAME>Weber</LAST_NAME>
                    <FIRST_NAME>Bill</FIRST_NAME>
            </NAME>
            <DATE>October 25, 2003</DATE>
            <ORDERS>
                    <ITEM>
                            <PRODUCT>Asparagus</PRODUCT>
                            <NUMBER>12</NUMBER>
                            <PRICE>$2.95</PRICE>
                    </ITEM>
                    <ITEM>
                            <PRODUCT>Lettuce</PRODUCT>
                            <NUMBER>6</NUMBER>
                            <PRICE>$11.50</PRICE>
                    </ITEM>
            </ORDERS>
        </CUSTOMER>
</DOCUMENT>
```

DTD Comments

As you can see, DTDs can become fairly complex, especially in longer and more involved documents. To make things easier for the DTD author, the XML specification allows you to place comments inside DTDs.

DTD comments are just like normal XML comments—in fact, they *are* normal XML comments, and they're often stripped out by the XML processor. (The W3C allows XML processors to remove comments, but some processors pass comments on to the underlying application.) Here's an example in which I have added comments to ch02_01.xml:

Listing ch03_07.xml

```
<?xml version = "1.0" standalone="yes"?>
<!DOCTYPE DOCUMENT [
<!-- DOCUMENT is the root element -->
<!ELEMENT DOCUMENT (CUSTOMER)*>
<!-- CUSTOMER stores customer data -->
<!ELEMENT CUSTOMER (NAME,DATE,ORDERS)>
<!-- NAME stores the customer name-->
<!ELEMENT NAME (LAST_NAME,FIRST_NAME)>
<!-- LAST_NAME stores customer's last name -->
<!ELEMENT LAST_NAME (#PCDATA)>
<!-- FIRST_NAME stores customer's last name -->
<!ELEMENT FIRST_NAME (#PCDATA)>
<!-- DATE stores order data -->
<!ELEMENT DATE (#PCDATA)>
<!-- ORDERS stores customer orders -->
<!ELEMENT ORDERS (ITEM)*>
<!-- ITEM represents a customer purchase -->
<!ELEMENT ITEM (PRODUCT,NUMBER,PRICE)>
<!-- PRODUCT represents a purchased product -->
<!ELEMENT PRODUCT (#PCDATA)>
<!-- NUMBER indicates the number of item purchased -->
<!ELEMENT NUMBER (#PCDATA)>
<!-- PRICE is the item's price -->
<!ELEMENT PRICE (#PCDATA)>
]>
<DOCUMENT>
    <CUSTOMER>
        <NAME>
            <LAST_NAME>Smith</LAST_NAME>
            <FIRST_NAME>Sam</FIRST_NAME>
        </NAME>
        <DATE>October 15, 2003</DATE>
        <ORDERS>
            <ITEM>
                <PRODUCT>Tomatoes</PRODUCT>
```

continues

Listing ch03_07.xml Continued

```
                <NUMBER>8</NUMBER>
                <PRICE>$1.25</PRICE>
            </ITEM>
            <ITEM>
                <PRODUCT>Oranges</PRODUCT>
                <NUMBER>24</NUMBER>
                <PRICE>$4.98</PRICE>
            </ITEM>
        </ORDERS>
    </CUSTOMER>
    <CUSTOMER>
        <NAME>
            <LAST_NAME>Jones</LAST_NAME>
            <FIRST_NAME>Polly</FIRST_NAME>
        </NAME>
        <DATE>October 20, 2003</DATE>
        <ORDERS>
            <ITEM>
                <PRODUCT>Bread</PRODUCT>
                <NUMBER>12</NUMBER>
                <PRICE>$14.95</PRICE>
            </ITEM>
            <ITEM>
                <PRODUCT>Apples</PRODUCT>
                <NUMBER>6</NUMBER>
                <PRICE>$1.50</PRICE>
            </ITEM>
        </ORDERS>
    </CUSTOMER>
    <CUSTOMER>
        <NAME>
            <LAST_NAME>Weber</LAST_NAME>
            <FIRST_NAME>Bill</FIRST_NAME>
        </NAME>
        <DATE>October 25, 2003</DATE>
        <ORDERS>
            <ITEM>
                <PRODUCT>Asparagus</PRODUCT>
                <NUMBER>12</NUMBER>
                <PRICE>$2.95</PRICE>
            </ITEM>
            <ITEM>
                <PRODUCT>Lettuce</PRODUCT>
                <NUMBER>6</NUMBER>
                <PRICE>$11.50</PRICE>
            </ITEM>
        </ORDERS>
    </CUSTOMER>
</DOCUMENT>
```

A DTD Example

Because being able to create DTDs is an essential XML skill these days (at least until XML schemas are widely supported), I'll work through another example here.

This new example is a model for a book, complete with `<CHAPTER>`, `<SECTION>`, `<PART>`, and `<SUBTITLE>` elements. Here's what the document will look like:

Listing ch03_08.xml

```
<?xml version="1.0"?>
<!DOCTYPE BOOK [
    <!ELEMENT p (#PCDATA)>
    <!ELEMENT BOOK            (OPENER,SUBTITLE?,INTRODUCTION?,(SECTION |
➥PART)+)>
    <!ELEMENT OPENER         (TITLE_TEXT)*>
    <!ELEMENT TITLE_TEXT     (#PCDATA)>
    <!ELEMENT SUBTITLE       (#PCDATA)>
    <!ELEMENT INTRODUCTION (HEADER, p+)+>
    <!ELEMENT PART           (HEADER, CHAPTER+)>
    <!ELEMENT SECTION        (HEADER, p+)>
    <!ELEMENT HEADER         (#PCDATA)>
    <!ELEMENT CHAPTER        (CHAPTER_NUMBER, CHAPTER_TEXT)>
    <!ELEMENT CHAPTER_NUMBER (#PCDATA)>
    <!ELEMENT CHAPTER_TEXT (p)+>
]>
<BOOK>
    <OPENER>
        <TITLE_TEXT>
            All About Me
        </TITLE_TEXT>
    </OPENER>
    <PART>
        <HEADER>Welcome To My Book</HEADER>
        <CHAPTER>
            <CHAPTER_NUMBER>CHAPTER 1</CHAPTER_NUMBER>
            <CHAPTER_TEXT>
                <p>Glad you want to hear about me.</p>
                <p>There's so much to say!</p>
                <p>Where should we start?</p>
                <p>How about more about me?</p>
            </CHAPTER_TEXT>
        </CHAPTER>
    </PART>
</BOOK>
```

In this case, I'll start the DTD by declaring the <p> element, which I want to hold text only—that is, PCDATA, which you specify with #PCDATA:

```
<!ELEMENT p              (#PCDATA)>
            .
            .
            .
```

Next, I'll declare the <BOOK> element, which is the root element. In this case, the <BOOK> element can contain an <OPENER> element, possibly a <SUBTITLE> element, possibly an <INTRODUCTION> element, and one or more sections or parts declared with the <SECTION> and <PART> elements:

```
<!ELEMENT p              (#PCDATA)>
<!ELEMENT BOOK           (OPENER,SUBTITLE?,INTRODUCTION?,(SECTION | PART)+)>
            .
            .
            .
```

Now I will declare an <OPENER> element. This element will hold the title text for the chapter, which I'll store in <TITLE_TEXT> elements:

```
<!ELEMENT p              (#PCDATA)>
<!ELEMENT BOOK           (OPENER,SUBTITLE?,INTRODUCTION?,(SECTION | PART)+)>
<!ELEMENT OPENER         (TITLE_TEXT)*>
            .
            .
            .
```

I'll declare the <TITLE_TEXT> element so that it can contain plain text:

```
<!ELEMENT p              (#PCDATA)>
<!ELEMENT BOOK           (OPENER,SUBTITLE?,INTRODUCTION?,(SECTION | PART)+)>
<!ELEMENT OPENER         (TITLE_TEXT)*>
<!ELEMENT TITLE_TEXT     (#PCDATA)>
            .
            .
            .
```

And I'll declare the <SUBTITLE> element, which must also contain PCDATA:

```
<!ELEMENT p              (#PCDATA)>
<!ELEMENT BOOK           (OPENER,SUBTITLE?,INTRODUCTION?,(SECTION | PART)+)>
<!ELEMENT OPENER         (TITLE_TEXT)*>
<!ELEMENT TITLE_TEXT     (#PCDATA)>
<!ELEMENT SUBTITLE       (#PCDATA)>
            .
            .
            .
```

I'll set up the <INTRODUCTION> element up so that it can contain a <HEADER> element and must contain one or more <p> elements. I'll allow that sequence to repeat, like this:

```
<!ELEMENT p              (#PCDATA)>
<!ELEMENT BOOK           (OPENER,SUBTITLE?,INTRODUCTION?,(SECTION | PART)+)>
<!ELEMENT OPENER         (TITLE_TEXT)*>
<!ELEMENT TITLE_TEXT     (#PCDATA)>
<!ELEMENT SUBTITLE       (#PCDATA)>
<!ELEMENT INTRODUCTION (HEADER, p+)+>
      .
      .
      .
```

Next, the <PART> element can contain a <HEADER> and one or more <CHAPTER> elements:

```
<!ELEMENT p              (#PCDATA)>
<!ELEMENT BOOK           (OPENER,SUBTITLE?,INTRODUCTION?,(SECTION | PART)+)>
<!ELEMENT OPENER         (TITLE_TEXT)*>
<!ELEMENT TITLE_TEXT     (#PCDATA)>
<!ELEMENT SUBTITLE       (#PCDATA)>
<!ELEMENT INTRODUCTION (HEADER, p+)+>
<!ELEMENT PART           (HEADER, CHAPTER+)>
      .
      .
      .
```

In addition, I'll specify that the <CHAPTER> element must contain a <CHAPTER_NUMBER> and <CHAPTER_TEXT> element:

```
<!ELEMENT p              (#PCDATA)>
<!ELEMENT BOOK           (OPENER,SUBTITLE?,INTRODUCTION?,(SECTION | PART)+)>
<!ELEMENT OPENER         (TITLE_TEXT)*>
<!ELEMENT TITLE_TEXT     (#PCDATA)>
<!ELEMENT SUBTITLE       (#PCDATA)>
<!ELEMENT INTRODUCTION (HEADER, p+)+>
<!ELEMENT PART           (HEADER, CHAPTER+)>
<!ELEMENT SECTION        (HEADER, p+)>
<!ELEMENT HEADER         (#PCDATA)>
    <!ELEMENT CHAPTER    (CHAPTER_NUMBER, CHAPTER_TEXT)>
      .
      .
      .
```

The <CHAPTER_NUMBER> element contains parsed character data:

```
<!ELEMENT p                (#PCDATA)>
<!ELEMENT BOOK             (OPENER,SUBTITLE?,INTRODUCTION?,(SECTION | PART)+)>
<!ELEMENT OPENER           (TITLE_TEXT)*>
<!ELEMENT TITLE_TEXT       (#PCDATA)>
<!ELEMENT SUBTITLE         (#PCDATA)>
<!ELEMENT INTRODUCTION     (HEADER, p+)+>
<!ELEMENT PART             (HEADER, CHAPTER+)>
<!ELEMENT SECTION          (HEADER, p+)>
<!ELEMENT HEADER           (#PCDATA)>
<!ELEMENT CHAPTER          (CHAPTER_NUMBER, CHAPTER_TEXT)>
<!ELEMENT CHAPTER_NUMBER (#PCDATA)>
            .
            .
            .
```

Finally, the <CHAPTER_TEXT> element can contain <p> paragraph elements:

```
<!ELEMENT p (#PCDATA)>
<!ELEMENT BOOK                (OPENER,SUBTITLE?,INTRODUCTION?,(SECTION |
➥PART)+)>
<!ELEMENT OPENER           (TITLE_TEXT)*>
<!ELEMENT TITLE_TEXT       (#PCDATA)>
<!ELEMENT SUBTITLE         (#PCDATA)>
<!ELEMENT INTRODUCTION     (HEADER, p+)+>
<!ELEMENT PART             (HEADER, CHAPTER+)>
<!ELEMENT SECTION          (HEADER, p+)>
<!ELEMENT HEADER           (#PCDATA)>
<!ELEMENT CHAPTER          (CHAPTER_NUMBER, CHAPTER_TEXT)>
<!ELEMENT CHAPTER_NUMBER (#PCDATA)>
<!ELEMENT CHAPTER_TEXT (p)+>
```

And that's it; the DTD is finished.

External DTDs

The DTDs I've created in this chapter so far have all been built into the documents they are targeted for. However, you can also create *external* DTDs, in which the actual DTD is stored in an external file (usually with the extension .dtd).

Using external DTDs makes it easy to create an XML application that can be shared by many people. In fact, that's the way many XML applications are supported. There are two ways to specify external DTDs: as private DTDs or as public DTDs. I'll take a look at private DTDs first.

Private DTDs are intended for use by people or groups privately and are not intended for public distribution. You specify an external private DTD with the SYSTEM keyword in the <!DOCTYPE> element, like this (note also that because this document now depends on an external file, the DTD file ch03_10.dtd, I've changed the value of the standalone attribute from yes to no):

Listing ch03_09.xml

```
<?xml version = "1.0" standalone="no"?>
<!DOCTYPE DOCUMENT SYSTEM "ch03_10.dtd">
<DOCUMENT>
    <CUSTOMER>
        <NAME>
            <LAST_NAME>Smith</LAST_NAME>
            <FIRST_NAME>Sam</FIRST_NAME>
        </NAME>
        <DATE>October 15, 2003</DATE>
        <ORDERS>
            <ITEM>
                <PRODUCT>Tomatoes</PRODUCT>
                <NUMBER>8</NUMBER>
                <PRICE>$1.25</PRICE>
            </ITEM>
            <ITEM>
                <PRODUCT>Oranges</PRODUCT>
                <NUMBER>24</NUMBER>
                <PRICE>$4.98</PRICE>
            </ITEM>
        </ORDERS>
    </CUSTOMER>
    <CUSTOMER>
        <NAME>
            <LAST_NAME>Jones</LAST_NAME>
            <FIRST_NAME>Polly</FIRST_NAME>
        </NAME>
        <DATE>October 20, 2003</DATE>
        <ORDERS>
            <ITEM>
                <PRODUCT>Bread</PRODUCT>
                <NUMBER>12</NUMBER>
                <PRICE>$14.95</PRICE>
            </ITEM>
            <ITEM>
                <PRODUCT>Apples</PRODUCT>
                <NUMBER>6</NUMBER>
                <PRICE>$1.50</PRICE>
            </ITEM>
```

continues

Listing ch03_09.xml Continued

```
            </ORDERS>
        </CUSTOMER>
        <CUSTOMER>
            <NAME>
                <LAST_NAME>Weber</LAST_NAME>
                <FIRST_NAME>Bill</FIRST_NAME>
            </NAME>
            <DATE>October 25, 2003</DATE>
            <ORDERS>
                <ITEM>
                    <PRODUCT>Asparagus</PRODUCT>
                    <NUMBER>12</NUMBER>
                    <PRICE>$2.95</PRICE>
                </ITEM>
                <ITEM>
                    <PRODUCT>Lettuce</PRODUCT>
                    <NUMBER>6</NUMBER>
                    <PRICE>$11.50</PRICE>
                </ITEM>
            </ORDERS>
        </CUSTOMER>
</DOCUMENT>
```

Here's the file ch03_10.dtd that holds the external DTD. Note that it simply holds the part of the document that was originally between the [and] in the <!DOCTYPE> element:

Listing ch03_10.dtd

```
<!ELEMENT DOCUMENT (CUSTOMER)*>
<!ELEMENT CUSTOMER (NAME,DATE,ORDERS)>
<!ELEMENT NAME (LAST_NAME,FIRST_NAME)>
<!ELEMENT LAST_NAME (#PCDATA)>
<!ELEMENT FIRST_NAME (#PCDATA)>
<!ELEMENT DATE (#PCDATA)>
<!ELEMENT ORDERS (ITEM)*>
<!ELEMENT ITEM (PRODUCT,NUMBER,PRICE)>
<!ELEMENT PRODUCT (#PCDATA)>
<!ELEMENT NUMBER (#PCDATA)>
<!ELEMENT PRICE (#PCDATA)>
```

Using Document Type Definitions with URLs

The previous example just listed the name of an external DTD in the `<!DOCTYPE>` element. However, if the DTD is not in the same directory on the Web site as the document itself, you can specify a *Uniform Resource Indentifier* (URI) (which is currently implemented as URLs for today's XML processors) for the DTD, like this:

```
<?xml version = "1.0" standalone="no"?>
<!DOCTYPE DOCUMENT SYSTEM
    "http://www.starpowder.com/dtd/ch03_10.dtd">
<DOCUMENT>
    <CUSTOMER>
        <NAME>
            <LAST_NAME>Smith</LAST_NAME>
            <FIRST_NAME>Sam</FIRST_NAME>
        </NAME>
        <DATE>October 15, 2003</DATE>
        <ORDERS>
            <ITEM>
                <PRODUCT>Tomatoes</PRODUCT>
                <NUMBER>8</NUMBER>
                <PRICE>$1.25</PRICE>
            </ITEM>
            <ITEM>
                <PRODUCT>Oranges</PRODUCT>
                <NUMBER>24</NUMBER>
                <PRICE>$4.98</PRICE>
            </ITEM>
                .
                .
                .
            <ITEM>
                <PRODUCT>Asparagus</PRODUCT>
                <NUMBER>12</NUMBER>
                <PRICE>$2.95</PRICE>
            </ITEM>
            <ITEM>
                <PRODUCT>Lettuce</PRODUCT>
                <NUMBER>6</NUMBER>
                <PRICE>$11.50</PRICE>
            </ITEM>
        </ORDERS>
    </CUSTOMER>
</DOCUMENT>
```

This is also very useful, of course, if you're using someone else's DTD. In fact, there's a special way of using DTDs intended for public distribution.

Public Document Type Definitions

When you have a DTD that's intended for public use, you use the PUBLIC keyword instead of SYSTEM in the <!DOCTYPE> document type declaration. To use the PUBLIC keyword, you must also create a *formal public identifier* (FPI), and there are specific rules for FPIs:

- The first field in an FPI specifies the connection of the DTD to a formal standard. For DTDs that you're defining yourself, this field should be -. If a nonstandards body has approved the DTD, use +. For formal standards, this field is a reference to the standard itself (such as ISO/IEC 13449:2000).

- The second field must hold the name of the group or person that is going to maintain or be responsible for the DTD. In this case, you should use a name that is unique and identifies your group easily (for example, W3C simply uses W3C).

- The third field must indicate the type of document that is described, preferably followed by a unique identifier of some kind (such as Version 1.0). This part should include a version number that you'll update.

- The fourth field specifies the language your DTD uses. (For example, for English you use EN. Note that two-letter language specifiers allow only a maximum of $24 \times 24 = 576$ possible languages; expect to see three-letter language specifiers in the near future.)

- Fields in an FPI must be separated by a double slash (//).

Here's how I can modify the previous example to include a public DTD, complete with its own FPI:

```
<?xml version = "1.0" standalone="no"?>
<!DOCTYPE DOCUMENT PUBLIC "-//starpowder//Custom XML Version 1.0//EN"
"http://www.starpowder.com/steve/ch03_10.dtd">
<DOCUMENT>
    <CUSTOMER>
        <NAME>
            <LAST_NAME>Smith</LAST_NAME>
            <FIRST_NAME>Sam</FIRST_NAME>
        </NAME>
        <DATE>October 15, 2003</DATE>
        <ORDERS>
            <ITEM>
                <PRODUCT>Tomatoes</PRODUCT>
                <NUMBER>8</NUMBER>
                <PRICE>$1.25</PRICE>
            </ITEM>
```

```
            <ITEM>
                <PRODUCT>Oranges</PRODUCT>
                <NUMBER>24</NUMBER>
                <PRICE>$4.98</PRICE>
            </ITEM>
                .
                .
                .
            <ITEM>
                <PRODUCT>Asparagus</PRODUCT>
                <NUMBER>12</NUMBER>
                <PRICE>$2.95</PRICE>
            </ITEM>
            <ITEM>
                <PRODUCT>Lettuce</PRODUCT>
                <NUMBER>6</NUMBER>
                <PRICE>$11.50</PRICE>
            </ITEM>
        </ORDERS>
    </CUSTOMER>
</DOCUMENT>
```

Note the syntax of the <!DOCTYPE> element in this case: <!DOCTYPE *rootname* PUBLIC *FPI URL*>. Here's the external DTD, ch03_10.dtd, which is the same as in the previous example:

```
<!ELEMENT DOCUMENT (CUSTOMER)*>
<!ELEMENT CUSTOMER (NAME,DATE,ORDERS)>
<!ELEMENT NAME (LAST_NAME,FIRST_NAME)>
<!ELEMENT LAST_NAME (#PCDATA)>
<!ELEMENT FIRST_NAME (#PCDATA)>
<!ELEMENT DATE (#PCDATA)>
<!ELEMENT ORDERS (ITEM)*>
<!ELEMENT ITEM (PRODUCT,NUMBER,PRICE)>
<!ELEMENT PRODUCT (#PCDATA)>
<!ELEMENT NUMBER (#PCDATA)>
<!ELEMENT PRICE (#PCDATA)>
```

Using Both Internal and External DTDs

In fact, you can use *both* internal and external DTDs at the same time by using these forms of the <!DOCTYPE> element: <!DOCTYPE *rootname* SYSTEM *URL* [*DTD*]> for private external DTDs, and <!DOCTYPE *rootname* PUBLIC *FPI URL* [*DTD*]> for public external DTDs. In this case, the external DTD is specified by *URL* and the internal one by *DTD*.

Here's an example in which I've removed the `<PRODUCT>` element from the external DTD ch03_10.dtd:

```
<!ELEMENT DOCUMENT (CUSTOMER)*>
<!ELEMENT CUSTOMER (NAME,DATE,ORDERS)>
<!ELEMENT NAME (LAST_NAME,FIRST_NAME)>
<!ELEMENT LAST_NAME (#PCDATA)>
<!ELEMENT FIRST_NAME (#PCDATA)>
<!ELEMENT DATE (#PCDATA)>
<!ELEMENT ORDERS (ITEM)*>
<!ELEMENT ITEM (PRODUCT,NUMBER,PRICE)>
<!ELEMENT NUMBER (#PCDATA)>
<!ELEMENT PRICE (#PCDATA)>
```

Now I'll specify that I want to use this external DTD in the document's `<!DOCTYPE>` element and then also add square brackets, [and], to enclose an internal DTD:

```
<?xml version = "1.0" standalone="no"?>
<!DOCTYPE DOCUMENT SYSTEM "ch03_10.dtd" [
    .
    .
    .
]>
<DOCUMENT>
    <CUSTOMER>
        <NAME>
            <LAST_NAME>Smith</LAST_NAME>
            <FIRST_NAME>Sam</FIRST_NAME>
        </NAME>
        <DATE>October 15, 2003</DATE>
        <ORDERS>
            <ITEM>
                <PRODUCT>
                    <PRODUCT_ID>
                        198348209
                    </PRODUCT_ID>
                </PRODUCT>
                <NUMBER>8</NUMBER>
                <PRICE>$1.25</PRICE>
            </ITEM>
            .
            .
            .
            <ITEM>
                <PRODUCT>
                    <PRODUCT_ID>
                        198348206
                    </PRODUCT_ID>
                </PRODUCT>
                <NUMBER>6</NUMBER>
```

```
                    <PRICE>$11.50</PRICE>
                </ITEM>
            </ORDERS>
        </CUSTOMER>
</DOCUMENT>
```

Next, I add the declaration of the <PRODUCT> element to the internal part of the DTD, like this:

```
<?xml version = "1.0" standalone="no"?>
<!DOCTYPE DOCUMENT SYSTEM "ch03_10.dtd" [
<!ELEMENT PRODUCT (PRODUCT_ID)>
<!ELEMENT PRODUCT_ID (#PCDATA)>
]>
<DOCUMENT>
    <CUSTOMER>
        <NAME>
            <LAST_NAME>Smith</LAST_NAME>
            <FIRST_NAME>Sam</FIRST_NAME>
        </NAME>
        <DATE>October 15, 2003</DATE>
        <ORDERS>
            <ITEM>
                <PRODUCT>
                    <PRODUCT_ID>
                        198348209
                    </PRODUCT_ID>
                </PRODUCT>
                <NUMBER>8</NUMBER>
                <PRICE>$1.25</PRICE>
            </ITEM>
                .
                .
                .
            <ITEM>
                <PRODUCT>
                    <PRODUCT_ID>
                        198348206
                    </PRODUCT_ID>
                </PRODUCT>
                <NUMBER>6</NUMBER>
                <PRICE>$11.50</PRICE>
            </ITEM>
        </ORDERS>
    </CUSTOMER>
</DOCUMENT>
```

And that's all it takes; now this DTD uses both internal and external parts.

If It's Both Internal and External, Which Takes Precedence?

Theoretically, if an element or attribute is defined in both an internal and external DTD, the definition in the internal DTD is supposed to take precedence, overwriting the external definition. Things were arranged that way to let you customize external DTDs as you like. However, my experience is that most XML processors simply consider it an error if there is an element or attribute conflict between internal and external DTDs, and they usually just halt.

Namespaces and DTDs

There's one more topic that I want to cover now that we're discussing the basics of creating DTDs: how to use namespaces when you're using DTDs. In fact, this will give us an introduction to the next chapter, where we'll work with declaring attributes as well as elements.

The important thing to recall is that, as far as standard XML processors are concerned, namespace prefixes are just text prepended to tag and attribute names with a colon, so they change those tag and attribute names. That means those names have to be declared, with their prefixes, in the DTD.

Here's an example. I'll start with the easy case in which I'm using a default namespace, like this:

```
<?xml version = "1.0" standalone="yes"?>
<!DOCTYPE DOCUMENT [
<!ELEMENT DOCUMENT (CUSTOMER)*>
<!ELEMENT CUSTOMER (NAME,DATE,ORDERS)>
<!ELEMENT NAME (LAST_NAME,FIRST_NAME)>
<!ELEMENT LAST_NAME (#PCDATA)>
<!ELEMENT FIRST_NAME (#PCDATA)>
<!ELEMENT DATE (#PCDATA)>
<!ELEMENT ORDERS (ITEM)*>
<!ELEMENT ITEM (PRODUCT,NUMBER,PRICE)>
<!ELEMENT PRODUCT (#PCDATA)>
<!ELEMENT NUMBER (#PCDATA)>
<!ELEMENT PRICE (#PCDATA)>
]>
<DOCUMENT xmlns="http://www.starpowder.com/dtd/">
    <CUSTOMER>
        <NAME>
            <LAST_NAME>Smith</LAST_NAME>
            <FIRST_NAME>Sam</FIRST_NAME>
        </NAME>
        <DATE>October 15, 2003</DATE>
        <ORDERS>
            <ITEM>
                <PRODUCT>Tomatoes</PRODUCT>
                <NUMBER>8</NUMBER>
```

```
                        <PRICE>$1.25</PRICE>
                </ITEM>
        .
        .
        .

            </ORDERS>
        </CUSTOMER>
</DOCUMENT>
```

Some validating XML processors aren't going to understand the xmlns attribute that you use to declare a namespace. That means that you must declare the attribute as follows. Here, I'm using the <!ATTLIST> element (as we'll see how to do in the next chapter) to declare this attribute, indicating that the xmlns attribute has a fixed value, which I'm setting to the namespace identifier "http://www.starpowder.com/dtd/":

```
<?xml version = "1.0" standalone="yes"?>
<!DOCTYPE DOCUMENT [
<!ELEMENT DOCUMENT (CUSTOMER)*>
<!ATTLIST DOCUMENT
    xmlns CDATA #FIXED "http://www.starpowder.com/dtd/">
<!ELEMENT CUSTOMER (NAME,DATE,ORDERS)>
<!ELEMENT NAME (LAST_NAME,FIRST_NAME)>
<!ELEMENT LAST_NAME (#PCDATA)>
<!ELEMENT FIRST_NAME (#PCDATA)>
<!ELEMENT DATE (#PCDATA)>
<!ELEMENT ORDERS (ITEM)*>
<!ELEMENT ITEM (PRODUCT,NUMBER,PRICE)>
<!ELEMENT PRODUCT (#PCDATA)>
<!ELEMENT NUMBER (#PCDATA)>
<!ELEMENT PRICE (#PCDATA)>
]>
<DOCUMENT xmlns="http://www.starpowder.com/dtd/">
    <CUSTOMER>
        <NAME>
            <LAST_NAME>Smith</LAST_NAME>
            <FIRST_NAME>Sam</FIRST_NAME>
        </NAME>
        <DATE>October 15, 2003</DATE>
        <ORDERS>
            <ITEM>
                <PRODUCT>Tomatoes</PRODUCT>
                <NUMBER>8</NUMBER>
                <PRICE>$1.25</PRICE>
            </ITEM>
        .
        .
        .

            </ORDERS>
        </CUSTOMER>
</DOCUMENT>
```

Now I'm free to use the xmlns attribute in the root element, as I did earlier. That's all there is to setting up a default namespace when using DTDs.

However, if you want to use a namespace *prefix* throughout a document, the process is a little more involved. For instance, in this next example, use the namespace prefix doc: for the namespace "http://www.starpowder.com/dtd/". To do that, I declare a new attribute xmlns:doc and use that attribute in the root element like this to set up the namespace:

```
<?xml version = "1.0" standalone="yes"?>
<!DOCTYPE DOCUMENT [
<!ELEMENT DOCUMENT (CUSTOMER)*>
<!ATTLIST doc:DOCUMENT
    xmlns:doc CDATA #FIXED "http://www.starpowder.com/dtd/">
<!ELEMENT CUSTOMER (NAME,DATE,ORDERS)>
<!ELEMENT NAME (LAST_NAME;FIRST_NAME)>
<!ELEMENT LAST_NAME (#PCDATA)>
<!ELEMENT FIRST_NAME (#PCDATA)>
<!ELEMENT DATE (#PCDATA)>
<!ELEMENT ORDERS (ITEM)*>
<!ELEMENT ITEM (PRODUCT,NUMBER,PRICE)>
<!ELEMENT PRODUCT (#PCDATA)>
<!ELEMENT NUMBER (#PCDATA)>
<!ELEMENT PRICE (#PCDATA)>
]>
<DOCUMENT xmlns:doc="http://www.starpowder.com/dtd/">
    <CUSTOMER>
        <NAME>
            <LAST_NAME>Smith</LAST_NAME>
            <FIRST_NAME>Sam</FIRST_NAME>
        </NAME>
        <DATE>October 15, 2003</DATE>
        <ORDERS>
            <ITEM>
                <PRODUCT>Tomatoes</PRODUCT>
                <NUMBER>8</NUMBER>
                <PRICE>$1.25</PRICE>
            </ITEM>
    .
    .
    .
        </ORDERS>
    </CUSTOMER>
</DOCUMENT>
```

Now I can use the doc: prefix throughout the document, where necessary:

Listing ch03_11.xml

```xml
<?xml version = "1.0" standalone="yes"?>
<!DOCTYPE doc:DOCUMENT [
<!ELEMENT doc:DOCUMENT (doc:CUSTOMER)*>
<!ATTLIST doc:DOCUMENT
    xmlns:doc CDATA #FIXED "http://www.starpowder.com/dtd/">
<!ELEMENT doc:CUSTOMER (doc:NAME,doc:DATE,doc:ORDERS)>
<!ELEMENT doc:NAME (doc:LAST_NAME,doc:FIRST_NAME)>
<!ELEMENT doc:LAST_NAME (#PCDATA)>
<!ELEMENT doc:FIRST_NAME (#PCDATA)>
<!ELEMENT doc:DATE (#PCDATA)>
<!ELEMENT doc:ORDERS (doc:ITEM)*>
<!ELEMENT doc:ITEM (doc:PRODUCT,doc:NUMBER,doc:PRICE)>
<!ELEMENT doc:PRODUCT (#PCDATA)>
<!ELEMENT doc:NUMBER (#PCDATA)>
<!ELEMENT doc:PRICE (#PCDATA)>
]>
<doc:DOCUMENT xmlns:doc="http://www.starpowder.com/dtd/">
    <doc:CUSTOMER>
        <doc:NAME>
            <doc:LAST_NAME>Smith</doc:LAST_NAME>
            <doc:FIRST_NAME>Sam</doc:FIRST_NAME>
        </doc:NAME>
        <doc:DATE>October 15, 2003</doc:DATE>
        <doc:ORDERS>
            <doc:ITEM>
                <doc:PRODUCT>Tomatoes</doc:PRODUCT>
                <doc:NUMBER>8</doc:NUMBER>
                <doc:PRICE>$1.25</doc:PRICE>
            </doc:ITEM>
            <doc:ITEM>
                <doc:PRODUCT>Oranges</doc:PRODUCT>
                <doc:NUMBER>24</doc:NUMBER>
                <doc:PRICE>$4.98</doc:PRICE>
            </doc:ITEM>
        </doc:ORDERS>
    </doc:CUSTOMER>
    <doc:CUSTOMER>
        <doc:NAME>
            <doc:LAST_NAME>Jones</doc:LAST_NAME>
            <doc:FIRST_NAME>Polly</doc:FIRST_NAME>
        </doc:NAME>
        <doc:DATE>October 20, 2003</doc:DATE>
        <doc:ORDERS>
            <doc:ITEM>
                <doc:PRODUCT>Bread</doc:PRODUCT>
                <doc:NUMBER>12</doc:NUMBER>
                <doc:PRICE>$14.95</doc:PRICE>
            </doc:ITEM>
            <doc:ITEM>
```

continues

Listing ch03_11.xml Continued

```
                    <doc:PRODUCT>Apples</doc:PRODUCT>
                    <doc:NUMBER>6</doc:NUMBER>
                    <doc:PRICE>$1.50</doc:PRICE>
                </doc:ITEM>
            </doc:ORDERS>
        </doc:CUSTOMER>
        <doc:CUSTOMER>
            <doc:NAME>
                <doc:LAST_NAME>Weber</doc:LAST_NAME>
                <doc:FIRST_NAME>Bill</doc:FIRST_NAME>
            </doc:NAME>
            <doc:DATE>October 25, 2003</doc:DATE>
            <doc:ORDERS>
                <doc:ITEM>
                    <doc:PRODUCT>Asparagus</doc:PRODUCT>
                    <doc:NUMBER>12</doc:NUMBER>
                    <doc:PRICE>$2.95</doc:PRICE>
                </doc:ITEM>
                <doc:ITEM>
                    <doc:PRODUCT>Lettuce</doc:PRODUCT>
                    <doc:NUMBER>6</doc:NUMBER>
                    <doc:PRICE>$11.50</doc:PRICE>
                </doc:ITEM>
            </doc:ORDERS>
        </doc:CUSTOMER>
</doc:DOCUMENT>
```

And that's all it takes. Now this document, complete with namespace, is valid. This example has introduced us to a very important topic: declaring attributes in DTDs. I'll take a look at how that works in the next chapter.

CHAPTER 4
DTDs: Entities and Attributes

In the previous chapter, I discussed creating DTDs and declaring the elements you use in XML documents. But there's more to DTDs than that. You can also declare *attributes* and *entities* as well, and we're going to do that in this chapter. We'll also take a look at embedding non-XML data in XML documents.

Entities

In the previous chapter, we got an introduction to the idea of entities in XML documents. There are two kinds of entities: general entities and parameter entities. General entities are probably used by more XML authors because you use them in the content of your XML document. However, parameter entities, which you use in a document's DTD, are also available and very powerful.

So what exactly is an entity? An entity is simply XML's way of referring to a data item; entities are usually text, but they can also be binary data. You declare an entity in a DTD and then refer to it by *reference* in your document. General entity references start with & and end with ;. Parameter entity references start with % and end with ;. For text entities, the entity reference is replaced by the entity itself when parsed by an XML processor.

In other words, you declare an entity in the DTD and refer to it with an entity reference, either in the document's content for general entities or in the DTD for parameter entities.

Entities can be *internal* or *external*. An internal entity is defined completely inside the XML document that references it (and, in fact, the document itself is considered an entity in XML). External entities, on the other hand, derive their content from an external source, such as a file, and a reference to them usually includes a uniform resource identifer (URI) at which they can be found. Entities can also be *parsed* or *unparsed*. The content of parsed entities is well-formed XML text; unparsed entities hold data that you don't want parsed, such as simple text or binary data. We'll see how to deal with all kinds of entities here.

In fact, we've already seen the five predefined general entity references in XML: <, >, &, ", and '. They stand for the characters <, >, &, ", and ', respectively. Because these entities are predefined in XML, you don't need to define them in a DTD; for example, here's a document that uses all five predefined entity references:

Listing ch04_01.xml

```
<?xml version = "1.0" standalone="yes"?>
<TEXT>
    This text about the &quot;S&amp;O Railroad&quot;
    is the &lt;TEXT&gt; element&apos;s content.
</TEXT>
```

Each of these entity references is replaced by the appropriate character when parsed by an XML processor. For example, you can see this document open in Internet Explorer in Figure 4-1. As you see in that figure, every entity reference has indeed been replaced.

Figure 4-1 Using the predefined entities in Internet Explorer.

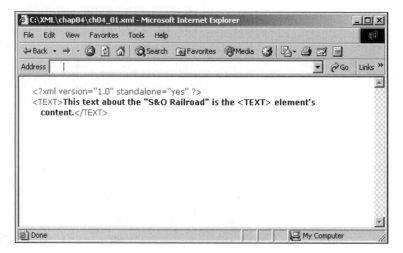

The five predefined entity references are very useful when you want to use as text the specific characters that are interpreted as markup.

You can also define your own entities by declaring them in a DTD. To declare an entity, you use the `<!ENTITY>` element (just as you use the `<!ELEMENT>` element to declare an element). Declaring a general entity looks like this:

```
<!ENTITY NAME DEFINITION>
```

Here, `NAME` is the entity's name and `DEFINITION` is its definition. The name of the entity is just the name you want to use to refer to the entity. The entity's definition can take several different forms, as we'll see in this chapter.

The simplest possible entity definition is just the text that you want a reference to that entity to be replaced with. Here's an example showing how that looks. In this case, I'm defining a general entity named TODAY to hold a date—October 15, 2003, in this DTD:

```
<?xml version = "1.0" standalone="yes"?>
<!DOCTYPE DOCUMENT [
<!ELEMENT DOCUMENT (CUSTOMER)*>
<!ELEMENT CUSTOMER (NAME,DATE,ORDERS)>
<!ELEMENT NAME (LAST_NAME,FIRST_NAME)>
<!ELEMENT LAST_NAME (#PCDATA)>
<!ELEMENT FIRST_NAME (#PCDATA)>
<!ELEMENT DATE (#PCDATA)>
<!ELEMENT ORDERS (ITEM)*>
<!ELEMENT ITEM (PRODUCT,NUMBER,PRICE)>
<!ELEMENT PRODUCT (#PCDATA)>
<!ELEMENT NUMBER (#PCDATA)>
<!ELEMENT PRICE (#PCDATA)>
<!ENTITY TODAY "October 15, 2003">
]>
       .
       .
       .
```

And that's all it takes. Now when I put a reference to this entity, `&TODAY;`, into the document, it'll be replaced with the text `October 15, 2003` by the XML processor:

Listing ch04_02.xml

```
<?xml version = "1.0" standalone="yes"?>
<!DOCTYPE DOCUMENT [
<!ELEMENT DOCUMENT (CUSTOMER)*>
<!ELEMENT CUSTOMER (NAME,DATE,ORDERS)>
<!ELEMENT NAME (LAST_NAME,FIRST_NAME)>
```

continues

Listing ch04_02.xml   Continued

```
<!ELEMENT LAST_NAME (#PCDATA)>
<!ELEMENT FIRST_NAME (#PCDATA)>
<!ELEMENT DATE (#PCDATA)>
<!ELEMENT ORDERS (ITEM)*>
<!ELEMENT ITEM (PRODUCT,NUMBER,PRICE)>
<!ELEMENT PRODUCT (#PCDATA)>
<!ELEMENT NUMBER (#PCDATA)>
<!ELEMENT PRICE (#PCDATA)>
<!ENTITY TODAY "October 15, 2003">
]>
<DOCUMENT>
<CUSTOMER>
        <NAME>
            <LAST_NAME>Smith</LAST_NAME>
            <FIRST_NAME>Sam</FIRST_NAME>
        </NAME>
        <DATE>&TODAY;</DATE>
        <ORDERS>
            <ITEM>
                <PRODUCT>Tomatoes</PRODUCT>
                <NUMBER>8</NUMBER>
                <PRICE>$1.25</PRICE>
            </ITEM>
            <ITEM>
                <PRODUCT>Oranges</PRODUCT>
                <NUMBER>24</NUMBER>
                <PRICE>$4.98</PRICE>
            </ITEM>
        </ORDERS>
    </CUSTOMER>
    <CUSTOMER>
        <NAME>
            <LAST_NAME>Jones</LAST_NAME>
            <FIRST_NAME>Polly</FIRST_NAME>
        </NAME>
        <DATE>&TODAY;</DATE>
        <ORDERS>
            <ITEM>
                <PRODUCT>Bread</PRODUCT>
                <NUMBER>12</NUMBER>
                <PRICE>$14.95</PRICE>
            </ITEM>
            <ITEM>
                <PRODUCT>Apples</PRODUCT>
                <NUMBER>6</NUMBER>
                <PRICE>$1.50</PRICE>
            </ITEM>
        </ORDERS>
    </CUSTOMER>
```

```
<CUSTOMER>
     <NAME>
          <LAST_NAME>Weber</LAST_NAME>
          <FIRST_NAME>Bill</FIRST_NAME>
     </NAME>
     <DATE>&TODAY;</DATE>
     <ORDERS>
          <ITEM>
               <PRODUCT>Asparagus</PRODUCT>
               <NUMBER>12</NUMBER>
               <PRICE>$2.95</PRICE>
          </ITEM>
          <ITEM>
               <PRODUCT>Lettuce</PRODUCT>
               <NUMBER>6</NUMBER>
               <PRICE>$11.50</PRICE>
          </ITEM>
     </ORDERS>
</CUSTOMER>
</DOCUMENT>
```

You can see the results of this document in Internet Explorer in Figure 4-2. As you see there, the &TODAY; entity references have been replaced with the full text we've specified.

Figure 4-2
Using user-defined entities in Internet Explorer.

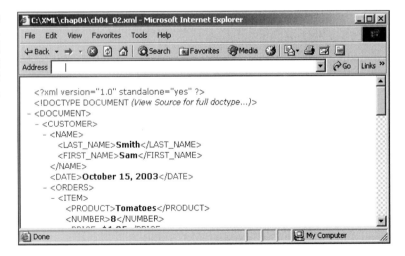

```
C:\XML\chap04\ch04_02.xml - Microsoft Internet Explorer

File   Edit   View   Favorites   Tools   Help

Back ▾  →  ▾  Search  Favorites  Media  

Address

<?xml version="1.0" standalone="yes" ?>
<!DOCTYPE DOCUMENT (View Source for full doctype...)>
- <DOCUMENT>
  - <CUSTOMER>
    - <NAME>
        <LAST_NAME>Smith</LAST_NAME>
        <FIRST_NAME>Sam</FIRST_NAME>
      </NAME>
        <DATE>October 15, 2003</DATE>
    - <ORDERS>
      - <ITEM>
          <PRODUCT>Tomatoes</PRODUCT>
          <NUMBER>8</NUMBER>

Done                                    My Computer
```

Besides general entities as in this example, we'll see parameter entities in this chapter, designed to be used in DTDs themselves. Declaring a parameter entity looks like this (note the %):

```
<!ENTITY % NAME DEFINITION>
```

Besides setting up your own entities in XML, you can customize your document's elements by declaring attributes for those elements.

Attributes

We've already discussed attributes in some detail; they're those name-value pairs that you can use in start tags and empty tags to provide additional information for an element. Here's an example. In this case, I'm adding an attribute named TYPE to the <CUSTOMER> tag to indicate what type of customer a person is:

```
<CUSTOMER TYPE = "excellent">
        <NAME>
            <LAST_NAME>Smith</LAST_NAME>
            <FIRST_NAME>Sam</FIRST_NAME>
        </NAME>
        <DATE>October 15, 2003</DATE>
    .
    .
    .
```

You can use attributes like this one and assign them values in XML documents, but unless you also declare them, your document won't be valid. You can declare a list of attributes for an element with the <!ATTLIST> element in the DTD. Here's the general form of an <!ATTLIST> element:

```
<!ATTLIST ELEMENT_NAME
    ATTRIBUTE_NAME TYPE DEFAULT_VALUE
    ATTRIBUTE_NAME TYPE DEFAULT_VALUE
    ATTRIBUTE_NAME TYPE DEFAULT_VALUE
    .
    .
    .
    ATTRIBUTE_NAME TYPE DEFAULT_VALUE>
```

In this case, ELEMENT_NAME is the name of the element that you're declaring attributes for, ATTRIBUTE_NAME is the name of an attribute you're declaring, TYPE is the attribute's type, and DEFAULT_VALUE specifies its default value. As we'll see in this chapter, DEFAULT_VALUE can take several forms.

Here's an example in which I'll declare the TYPE attribute we used previously. In this case, I'll use the simplest kind of declaration, making the attribute's type CDATA, which is simple character data, and using an #IMPLIED default value, which means that you can use this attribute in an element or skip it entirely. This is what the document, including the DTD, looks like:

```
<?xml version = "1.0" standalone="yes"?>
<!DOCTYPE DOCUMENT [
<!ELEMENT DOCUMENT (CUSTOMER)*>
<!ELEMENT CUSTOMER (NAME,DATE,ORDERS)>
<!ELEMENT NAME (LAST_NAME,FIRST_NAME)>
<!ELEMENT LAST_NAME (#PCDATA)>
<!ELEMENT FIRST_NAME (#PCDATA)>
<!ELEMENT DATE (#PCDATA)>
<!ELEMENT ORDERS (ITEM)*>
<!ELEMENT ITEM (PRODUCT,NUMBER,PRICE)>
<!ELEMENT PRODUCT (#PCDATA)>
<!ELEMENT NUMBER (#PCDATA)>
<!ELEMENT PRICE (#PCDATA)>
<!ATTLIST CUSTOMER
    TYPE CDATA #IMPLIED>
]>
<DOCUMENT>
<CUSTOMER TYPE = "excellent">
        <NAME>
            <LAST_NAME>Smith</LAST_NAME>
            <FIRST_NAME>Sam</FIRST_NAME>
        </NAME>
        <DATE>October 15, 2003</DATE>
        <ORDERS>
            <ITEM>
                <PRODUCT>Tomatoes</PRODUCT>
                <NUMBER>8</NUMBER>
                <PRICE>$1.25</PRICE>
            </ITEM>
            <ITEM>
                <PRODUCT>Oranges</PRODUCT>
                <NUMBER>24</NUMBER>
                <PRICE>$4.98</PRICE>
            </ITEM>
            .
            .
            .
            <ITEM>
                <PRODUCT>Asparagus</PRODUCT>
                <NUMBER>12</NUMBER>
                <PRICE>$2.95</PRICE>
            </ITEM>
            <ITEM>
                <PRODUCT>Lettuce</PRODUCT>
                <NUMBER>6</NUMBER>
```

continues

```
                <PRICE>$11.50</PRICE>
            </ITEM>
        </ORDERS>
    </CUSTOMER>
</DOCUMENT>
```

That introduces us to the idea of declaring attributes in DTDs. I'll get into the details on entities and attributes now, starting with entities—first general entities and then parameter entities.

Creating Internal General Entities

As discussed in the beginning of the chapter, entities can be either internal or external. We already saw how to create an internal general reference in the beginning of the chapter, when we created an internal general entity named TODAY and referenced it as &TODAY; in the document:

```
<?xml version = "1.0" standalone="yes"?>
<!DOCTYPE DOCUMENT [
<!ELEMENT DOCUMENT (CUSTOMER)*>
<!ELEMENT CUSTOMER (NAME,DATE,ORDERS)>
<!ELEMENT NAME (LAST_NAME,FIRST_NAME)>
<!ELEMENT LAST_NAME (#PCDATA)>
<!ELEMENT FIRST_NAME (#PCDATA)>
<!ELEMENT DATE (#PCDATA)>
<!ELEMENT ORDERS (ITEM)*>
<!ELEMENT ITEM (PRODUCT,NUMBER,PRICE)>
<!ELEMENT PRODUCT (#PCDATA)>
<!ELEMENT NUMBER (#PCDATA)>
<!ELEMENT PRICE (#PCDATA)>
<!ENTITY TODAY "October 15, 2003">
]>
<DOCUMENT>
<CUSTOMER>
        <NAME>
            <LAST_NAME>Smith</LAST_NAME>
            <FIRST_NAME>Sam</FIRST_NAME>
        </NAME>
        <DATE>&TODAY;</DATE>
        <ORDERS>
            <ITEM>
                <PRODUCT>Tomatoes</PRODUCT>
                <NUMBER>8</NUMBER>
                <PRICE>$1.25</PRICE>
            </ITEM>
            .
            .
            .
</DOCUMENT>
```

You can see the results in Figure 4-2. There are a few things to note here; one is that you can *nest* general references like this:

```
<!ENTITY NAME "Alfred Hitchcock">
<!ENTITY SIGNATURE "&NAME; 14 Mystery Drive">
```

Another point is that entity references can't be circular, or you'll drive the XML processor crazy. Here's an example:

```
<!ENTITY NAME "Alfred Hitchcock &SIGNATURE;">
<!ENTITY SIGNATURE "&NAME; 14 Mystery Drive">
```

In this case, when the XML processor tries to resolve the &NAME; reference, it finds that it needs to substitute the text for the SIGNATURE entity in the text for the NAME entity. However, the NAME entity needs the SIGNATURE entity's text, and so on, around in a circle that never ends. The result is that circular entity references have been made illegal in valid documents.

Also, it's worth noting that you can't use general entity references to insert text that is supposed to be used only in the DTD and not in the document content itself. Here's an example of something that's considered illegal:

```
<!ENTITY TAGS "(NAME,DATE,ORDERS)">
<!ELEMENT CUSTOMER &TAGS;>
```

The correct way to do this is with parameter entities, not general entities, and I'll cover them in a few pages. You can use general entities in the DTD to insert text that will become part of the document body, however.

Creating External General Entities

Entities can also be external, which means you should provide a URI directing the XML processor to the entity. You can use references to external entities to embed those entities in your document. As we'll see near the end of this chapter, you can also indicate that an external entity should not be parsed, which means that you can associate binary data with a document (much like associating images with an HTML document).

External entities can be simple strings of text, entire documents, or sections of documents. All that matters is that when they are inserted into the document's content, the XML processor is satisfied that the document is well formed and valid.

As with DTDs, you can declare external entities using the SYSTEM or PUB-LIC keywords. Entities declared with the SYSTEM keyword are for private use by an organization of individuals. Entities declared with PUBLIC are public, so they need a formal public identifier (FPI—see Chapter 3, "Valid Documents: Creating Document Type Definitions," for the rules on creating FPIs). Here's how you use the SYSTEM and PUBLIC keywords to declare an external entity:

```
<!ENTITY NAME SYSTEM URI>
<!ENTITY NAME PUBLIC FPI URI>
```

For example, say that you've stored a date as the text October 15, 2003 in a file named ch04_03.xml. Here's how you could set up an entity named TODAY connected to that file:

Listing ch04_03.xml

```
<!ENTITY TODAY SYSTEM "ch04_03.xml">
```

And here's how you could use a reference to that entity to insert the data into a document's content (note that I changed the value of the standalone attribute from "yes" to "no" here because we're working with an external entity):

Listing ch04_04.xml

```
<?xml version = "1.0" standalone="no"?>
<!DOCTYPE DOCUMENT [
<!ELEMENT DOCUMENT (CUSTOMER)*>
<!ELEMENT CUSTOMER (NAME,DATE,ORDERS)>
<!ELEMENT NAME (LAST_NAME,FIRST_NAME)>
<!ELEMENT LAST_NAME (#PCDATA)>
<!ELEMENT FIRST_NAME (#PCDATA)>
<!ELEMENT DATE (#PCDATA)>
<!ELEMENT ORDERS (ITEM)*>
<!ELEMENT ITEM (PRODUCT,NUMBER,PRICE)>
<!ELEMENT PRODUCT (#PCDATA)>
<!ELEMENT NUMBER (#PCDATA)>
<!ELEMENT PRICE (#PCDATA)>
<!ENTITY TODAY SYSTEM "ch04_03.xml">
]>
<DOCUMENT>
<CUSTOMER>
        <NAME>
             <LAST_NAME>Smith</LAST_NAME>
             <FIRST_NAME>Sam</FIRST_NAME>
        </NAME>
```

```
            <DATE>&TODAY;</DATE>
        <ORDERS>
            <ITEM>
                <PRODUCT>Tomatoes</PRODUCT>
                <NUMBER>8</NUMBER>
                <PRICE>$1.25</PRICE>
            </ITEM>
            <ITEM>
                <PRODUCT>Oranges</PRODUCT>
                <NUMBER>24</NUMBER>
                <PRICE>$4.98</PRICE>
            </ITEM>
        </ORDERS>
    </CUSTOMER>
    <CUSTOMER>
        <NAME>
            <LAST_NAME>Jones</LAST_NAME>
            <FIRST_NAME>Polly</FIRST_NAME>
        </NAME>
        <DATE>&TODAY;</DATE>
        <ORDERS>
            <ITEM>
                <PRODUCT>Bread</PRODUCT>
                <NUMBER>12</NUMBER>
                <PRICE>$14.95</PRICE>
            </ITEM>
            <ITEM>
                <PRODUCT>Apples</PRODUCT>
                <NUMBER>6</NUMBER>
                <PRICE>$1.50</PRICE>
            </ITEM>
        </ORDERS>
    </CUSTOMER>
    <CUSTOMER>
        <NAME>
            <LAST_NAME>Weber</LAST_NAME>
            <FIRST_NAME>Bill</FIRST_NAME>
        </NAME>
        <DATE>&TODAY;</DATE>
        <ORDERS>
            <ITEM>
                <PRODUCT>Asparagus</PRODUCT>
                <NUMBER>12</NUMBER>
                <PRICE>$2.95</PRICE>
            </ITEM>
            <ITEM>
                <PRODUCT>Lettuce</PRODUCT>
                <NUMBER>6</NUMBER>
                <PRICE>$11.50</PRICE>
            </ITEM>
        </ORDERS>
    </CUSTOMER>
</DOCUMENT>
```

Note how powerful this technique is: Now you can create documents that are themselves pieced together from other documents. If you wanted to use a public entity instead of a private one, you could use the SYSTEM keyword with a formal public identifier (FPI), like this:

```
<!ENTITY TODAY SYSTEM "-//starpowder//Custom Entity Version 1.0//EN"
"ch04_03.xml">
```

Defining external entities makes them available for multiple documents, which is useful in case you want to be able to have, say, the same text appear as a signature in all your documents, or work with text that will change frequently (such as a greeting for the day) that you want to edit in only one place.

Here's another note: Often nonvalidating XML processors will read a DTD to pick up any entity declarations you might have put there, even though they don't use the DTD to validate the document. That means that XML authors sometimes even add partial DTDs to documents that would not be considered valid so that they can use entity references. Here's an example (note that this DTD is not complete by any means, and that it carries only the declaration for the entity TODAY):

```
<?xml version = "1.0" standalone="no"?>
<!DOCTYPE DOCUMENT [
<!ENTITY TODAY SYSTEM "ch04_03.xml">
]>
<DOCUMENT>
<CUSTOMER>
        <NAME>
            <LAST_NAME>Smith</LAST_NAME>
            <FIRST_NAME>Sam</FIRST_NAME>
        </NAME>
        <DATE>&TODAY;</DATE>
        <ORDERS>
            <ITEM>
                <PRODUCT>Tomatoes</PRODUCT>
                <NUMBER>8</NUMBER>
                <PRICE>$1.25</PRICE>
            </ITEM>
            .
            .
            .
</DOCUMENT>
```

Building a Document from Pieces

One way to use external general entities is to build a document from pieces, treating each piece as a general entity. Here's an example. In this case, I'm including an entity that refers to the file ch04_06.xml in my document:

Listing ch04_05.xml

```
<?xml version = "1.0" standalone="no"?>
<!DOCTYPE DOCUMENT [
<!ELEMENT DOCUMENT (CUSTOMER)*>
<!ELEMENT CUSTOMER (NAME,DATE,ORDERS)>
<!ELEMENT NAME (LAST_NAME,FIRST_NAME)>
<!ELEMENT LAST_NAME (#PCDATA)>
<!ELEMENT FIRST_NAME (#PCDATA)>
<!ELEMENT DATE (#PCDATA)>
<!ELEMENT ORDERS (ITEM)*>
<!ELEMENT ITEM (PRODUCT,NUMBER,PRICE)>
<!ELEMENT PRODUCT (#PCDATA)>
<!ELEMENT NUMBER (#PCDATA)>
<!ELEMENT PRICE (#PCDATA)>
<!ENTITY data SYSTEM "ch04_06.xml">
]>
<DOCUMENT>
&data;
</DOCUMENT>
```

The file ch04_06.xml itself holds the actual data for the document:

Listing ch04_06.xml

```
<CUSTOMER>
    <NAME>
        <LAST_NAME>Smith</LAST_NAME>
        <FIRST_NAME>Sam</FIRST_NAME>
    </NAME>
    <DATE>October 15, 2003</DATE>
    <ORDERS>
        <ITEM>
            <PRODUCT>Tomatoes</PRODUCT>
            <NUMBER>8</NUMBER>
            <PRICE>$1.25</PRICE>
        </ITEM>
        <ITEM>
            <PRODUCT>Oranges</PRODUCT>
            <NUMBER>24</NUMBER>
            <PRICE>$4.98</PRICE>
```

continues

Listing ch04_06.xml   Continued

```
        </ITEM>
    </ORDERS>
</CUSTOMER>
<CUSTOMER>
    <NAME>
        <LAST_NAME>Jones</LAST_NAME>
        <FIRST_NAME>Polly</FIRST_NAME>
    </NAME>
    <DATE>October 20, 2003</DATE>
    <ORDERS>
        <ITEM>
            <PRODUCT>Bread</PRODUCT>
            <NUMBER>12</NUMBER>
            <PRICE>$14.95</PRICE>
        </ITEM>
        <ITEM>
            <PRODUCT>Apples</PRODUCT>
            <NUMBER>6</NUMBER>
            <PRICE>$1.50</PRICE>
        </ITEM>
    </ORDERS>
</CUSTOMER>
<CUSTOMER>
    <NAME>
        <LAST_NAME>Weber</LAST_NAME>
        <FIRST_NAME>Bill</FIRST_NAME>
    </NAME>
    <DATE>October 25, 2003</DATE>
    <ORDERS>
        <ITEM>
            <PRODUCT>Asparagus</PRODUCT>
            <NUMBER>12</NUMBER>
            <PRICE>$2.95</PRICE>
        </ITEM>
        <ITEM>
            <PRODUCT>Lettuce</PRODUCT>
            <NUMBER>6</NUMBER>
            <PRICE>$11.50</PRICE>
        </ITEM>
    </ORDERS>
</CUSTOMER>
```

In this way, you can put documents together from various pieces, choosing the pieces you want.

Predefined General Entity References

As we already know, there are five predefined entity references in XML, and they stand for characters that can be interpreted as markup or other control characters. Here they are:

- & becomes the & character.

- ' becomes the ' character.

- > becomes the > character.

- < becomes the < character.

- " becomes the " character.

It turns out that you can create entity references for individual characters yourself in XML. All you have to do is specify the correct character code in the encoding you're using. For example, in the UTF-8 encoding, the character code for @ is #64 (where the # indicates that this value is in hexadecimal), so you can define an entity named, say, at_new so that references to at_new will be replaced by @ when parsed. Here's how that entity would look:

```
<!ENTITY at_new "&#64;">
```

In fact, you can even define the predefined entity references yourself, in case you run across an XML processor that doesn't understand them. Here's how I modified the example document at the beginning of this chapter that uses those entity references—this time defining the entities myself:

```
<?xml version = "1.0" standalone="yes"?>
<!DOCTYPE TEXT [
<!ENTITY amp_new "&#38;#38;">
<!ENTITY apos_new "&#39;">
<!ENTITY gt_new "&#62;">
<!ENTITY lt_new "&#38;#60;">
<!ENTITY quot_new "&#34;">
]>
<TEXT>
    This text about the &quot_new;S&amp_new;O Railroad&quot_new;
    is the &lt_new;TEXT&gt_new; element&apos_new;s content.
</TEXT>
```

Creating Internal Parameter Entities

As we've seen, you use general entity references in documents so that the XML processor will replace them with the entity they refer to. However, you can use general entities in only a limited way in DTDs—that is, you can use them to insert text that will itself be inserted into the document content, but you can't use them to work with the declarations themselves in the DTD.

To actually work with element and attribute declarations, you use parameter entities. Parameter entity references can be used only in the DTD. In fact, there's an additional restriction: Any parameter entity references that you use in any DTD declaration must appear only in the DTD's *external subset* (the external subset is the part of the DTD that is external). You can use parameter entities in the internal subset, but only in a limited way, as we'll see.

Unlike general entity references, parameter entity references start with %, not &. Creating a parameter entity is just like creating a general entity, except that you include a % in the <!ENTITY> element, like this:

```
<!ENTITY % NAME DEFINITION>
```

You can also declare external parameter entities using the SYSTEM and PUBLIC keywords, like this (where FPI stands for a formal public identifier):

```
<!ENTITY % NAME SYSTEM URI>
<!ENTITY % NAME PUBLIC FPI URI>
```

Here's an example using an internal parameter entity. In this case, I'll declare a parameter entity named BR that stands for the text <!ELEMENT BR EMPTY> inside this DTD:

```
<?xml version = "1.0" standalone="yes"?>
<!DOCTYPE DOCUMENT [
<!ENTITY % BR "<!ELEMENT BR EMPTY>">
<!ELEMENT DOCUMENT (CUSTOMER)*>
<!ELEMENT CUSTOMER (NAME,DATE,ORDERS)>
<!ELEMENT NAME (LAST_NAME,FIRST_NAME)>
<!ELEMENT LAST_NAME (#PCDATA)>
<!ELEMENT FIRST_NAME (#PCDATA)>
<!ELEMENT DATE (#PCDATA)>
<!ELEMENT ORDERS (ITEM)*>
<!ELEMENT ITEM (PRODUCT,NUMBER,PRICE)>
<!ELEMENT PRODUCT (#PCDATA)>
<!ELEMENT NUMBER (#PCDATA)>
<!ELEMENT PRICE (#PCDATA)>
]>
    .
    .
    .
```

Now I can reference that parameter entity this way to include the element declaration `<!ELEMENT BR EMPTY>` in the DTD:

```
<?xml version = "1.0" standalone="yes"?>
<!DOCTYPE DOCUMENT [
<!ENTITY % BR "<!ELEMENT BR EMPTY>">
<!ELEMENT DOCUMENT (CUSTOMER)*>
<!ELEMENT CUSTOMER (NAME,DATE,ORDERS)>
<!ELEMENT NAME (LAST_NAME,FIRST_NAME)>
<!ELEMENT LAST_NAME (#PCDATA)>
<!ELEMENT FIRST_NAME (#PCDATA)>
<!ELEMENT DATE (#PCDATA)>
<!ELEMENT ORDERS (ITEM)*>
<!ELEMENT ITEM (PRODUCT,NUMBER,PRICE)>
<!ELEMENT PRODUCT (#PCDATA)>
<!ELEMENT NUMBER (#PCDATA)>
<!ELEMENT PRICE (#PCDATA)>
%BR;
]>
<DOCUMENT>
    <CUSTOMER>
        <NAME>
            <LAST_NAME>Smith</LAST_NAME>
            <FIRST_NAME>Sam</FIRST_NAME>
        </NAME>
        <DATE>October 15, 2003</DATE>
        <ORDERS>
            <ITEM>
                <PRODUCT>Tomatoes</PRODUCT>
                <NUMBER>8</NUMBER>
                <PRICE>$1.25</PRICE>
            </ITEM>
            <ITEM>
                <PRODUCT>Oranges</PRODUCT>
                <NUMBER>24</NUMBER>
                <PRICE>$4.98</PRICE>
            </ITEM>
            .
            .
            .
</DOCUMENT>
```

Note that I haven't really saved much time here; I might as well have just put the declaration `<!ELEMENT BR EMPTY>` directly into the DTD. On the other hand, you can't do much more with internal parameter entities (those that are defined in the DTD's internal subset) because you can't use them inside any other declarations. If you want to find out what people really use parameter entities for, we have to take a look at external parameter entities.

External Parameter Entities

When you use a parameter entity in the DTD's external subset, you can reference that entity anywhere in the DTD, including in element declarations.
Here's an example. In this case, I'm using an external DTD named
ch04_07.dtd for this document:

```
<?xml version = "1.0" standalone="no"?>
<!DOCTYPE DOCUMENT SYSTEM "ch04_07.dtd">
<DOCUMENT>
    <CUSTOMER>
        <NAME>
            <LAST_NAME>Smith</LAST_NAME>
            <FIRST_NAME>Sam</FIRST_NAME>
        </NAME>
        <DATE>October 15, 2003</DATE>
        <ORDERS>
            <ITEM>
                <PRODUCT>Tomatoes</PRODUCT>
                <NUMBER>8</NUMBER>
                <PRICE>$1.25</PRICE>
            </ITEM>
            <ITEM>
                <PRODUCT>Oranges</PRODUCT>
                <NUMBER>24</NUMBER>
                <PRICE>$4.98</PRICE>
            </ITEM>
                .
                .
                .
            <ITEM>
                <PRODUCT>Asparagus</PRODUCT>
                <NUMBER>12</NUMBER>
                <PRICE>$2.95</PRICE>
            </ITEM>
            <ITEM>
                <PRODUCT>Lettuce</PRODUCT>
                <NUMBER>6</NUMBER>
                <PRICE>$11.50</PRICE>
            </ITEM>
        </ORDERS>
    </CUSTOMER>
</DOCUMENT>
```

In the external DTD subset, ch04_07.dtd, I'm going to set things up so that
the <DOCUMENT> element can contain not only <CUSTOMER> elements, but also
<BUYER> and <DISCOUNTER> elements. Each of these two new elements,
<BUYER> and <DISCOUNTER>, has the same content model as the <CUSTOMER>

element (that is, these elements can contain <NAME>, <DATE>, and <ORDERS> elements); to save a little time, I'll assign that content model, (NAME,DATE,OR-DERS), to a parameter entity named record:

```
<!ENTITY % record "(NAME,DATE,ORDERS)">
<!ELEMENT DOCUMENT (CUSTOMER | BUYER | DISCOUNTER)*>
    .
    .
    .
```

Now I'm free to refer to the record parameter entity where I like. In this case, that means using it to declare the <CUSTOMER>, <BUYER>, and <DISCOUNTER> elements:

Listing ch04_07.xml

```
<!ENTITY % record "(NAME,DATE,ORDERS)">
<!ELEMENT DOCUMENT (CUSTOMER | BUYER | DISCOUNTER)*>
<!ELEMENT CUSTOMER %record;>
<!ELEMENT BUYER %record;>
<!ELEMENT DISCOUNTER %record;>
<!ELEMENT NAME (LAST_NAME,FIRST_NAME)>
<!ELEMENT LAST_NAME (#PCDATA)>
<!ELEMENT FIRST_NAME (#PCDATA)>
<!ELEMENT DATE (#PCDATA)>
<!ELEMENT ORDERS (ITEM)*>
<!ELEMENT ITEM (PRODUCT,NUMBER,PRICE)>
<!ELEMENT PRODUCT (#PCDATA)>
<!ELEMENT NUMBER (#PCDATA)>
<!ELEMENT PRICE (#PCDATA)>
```

Now the document works and parses as expected: I can use <CUSTOMER>, <BUYER>, and <DISCOUNTER> elements inside the <DOCUMENT> element, and all three of those elements have the same content model:

Listing ch04_08.xml

```
<?xml version = "1.0" standalone="no"?>
<!DOCTYPE DOCUMENT SYSTEM "ch04_07.dtd">
<DOCUMENT>
    <CUSTOMER>
        <NAME>
            <LAST_NAME>Smith</LAST_NAME>
            <FIRST_NAME>Sam</FIRST_NAME>
        </NAME>
```

continues

Listing ch04_08.xml   Continued

```
            <DATE>October 15, 2003</DATE>
            <ORDERS>
                <ITEM>
                    <PRODUCT>Tomatoes</PRODUCT>
                    <NUMBER>8</NUMBER>
                    <PRICE>$1.25</PRICE>
                </ITEM>
                <ITEM>
                    <PRODUCT>Oranges</PRODUCT>
                    <NUMBER>24</NUMBER>
                    <PRICE>$4.98</PRICE>
                </ITEM>
            </ORDERS>
        </CUSTOMER>
        <BUYER>
            <NAME>
                <LAST_NAME>Jones</LAST_NAME>
                <FIRST_NAME>Polly</FIRST_NAME>
            </NAME>
            <DATE>October 20, 2003</DATE>
            <ORDERS>
                <ITEM>
                    <PRODUCT>Bread</PRODUCT>
                    <NUMBER>12</NUMBER>
                    <PRICE>$14.95</PRICE>
                </ITEM>
                <ITEM>
                    <PRODUCT>Apples</PRODUCT>
                    <NUMBER>6</NUMBER>
                    <PRICE>$1.50</PRICE>
                </ITEM>
            </ORDERS>
        </BUYER>
        <DISCOUNTER>
            <NAME>
                <LAST_NAME>Weber</LAST_NAME>
                <FIRST_NAME>Bill</FIRST_NAME>
            </NAME>
            <DATE>October 25, 2003</DATE>
            <ORDERS>
                <ITEM>
                    <PRODUCT>Asparagus</PRODUCT>
                    <NUMBER>12</NUMBER>
                    <PRICE>$2.95</PRICE>
                </ITEM>
                <ITEM>
                    <PRODUCT>Lettuce</PRODUCT>
                    <NUMBER>6</NUMBER>
                    <PRICE>$11.50</PRICE>
```

```
        </ITEM>
      </ORDERS>
    </DISCOUNTER>
</DOCUMENT>
```

This example points out probably the biggest reason people use parameter entities: to handle text that's repeated often in element declarations in a DTD. In this case, I specified the content model of three elements using the same parameter entity, but I could just have easily set up a parameter entity to let me specify an attribute list that was the same for as many elements as I like. In this way, you can control the declarations of many elements and attributes, even in a huge DTD. And if you need to modify a declaration, you need to modify only the parameter entity, not each declaration in detail.

For example, you might divide your attributes in a big DTD into various types. When you declare some new element, you might want to give it only the image-handling and URI-handling attributes, which you could do like this (in fact, this is the way the XHTML DTDs are built):

```
<!ATTLIST NEW_ELEMENT %image_attributes; %URI_attributes;>
```

Here's another example showing how to use parameter entities; in this case, I'm going to base my document on the XHTML 1.0 transitional DTD, adding a few elements of my own to XHTML. To do that, I declare the elements I want to use and then simply include the entire XHTML 1.0 transitional DTD using a parameter reference like this:

```
<!ENTITY % record "(NAME,DATE,ORDERS)">
<!ELEMENT DOCUMENT (CUSTOMER | BUYER | DISCOUNTER)*>
<!ELEMENT CUSTOMER %record;>
<!ELEMENT BUYER %record;>
<!ELEMENT DISCOUNTER %record;>
<!ELEMENT NAME (LAST_NAME,FIRST_NAME)>
<!ELEMENT LAST_NAME (#PCDATA)>
<!ELEMENT FIRST_NAME (#PCDATA)>
<!ELEMENT DATE (#PCDATA)>
<!ELEMENT ORDERS (ITEM)*>
<!ELEMENT ITEM (PRODUCT,NUMBER,PRICE)>
<!ELEMENT PRODUCT (#PCDATA)>
<!ELEMENT NUMBER (#PCDATA)>
<!ELEMENT PRICE (#PCDATA)>
<!ENTITY % XHTML1-t.dtd PUBLIC "-//W3C//DTD XHTML 1.0 Transitional//EN"
➥"http://www.w3.org/TR/xhtml1/DTD/xhtml1-transitional.dtd">
%XHTML1-t.dtd;
```

Using *INCLUDE* and *IGNORE*

Two important DTD directives are often used with parameter entities: IN-CLUDE and IGNORE. You use these directives to include or remove sections of a DTD; here's how you use them: `<![ INCLUDE [DTD Section]]>` and `<![ IG-NORE [DTD Section]]>`. Using these directives, you can customize your DTD.

Here's an example showing what these two directives look like in practice:

```
<![ INCLUDE [
<!ELEMENT PRODUCT_ID (#PCDATA)>
<!ELEMENT SHIP_DATE (#PCDATA)>
<!ELEMENT SKU (#PCDATA)>
]]>
<![ IGNORE [
<!ELEMENT PRODUCT_ID (#PCDATA)>
<!ELEMENT SHIP_DATE (#PCDATA)>
<!ELEMENT SKU (#PCDATA)>
]]>
```

You might wonder what the big deal is here—after all, you can just use a comment to hide sections of a DTD. The usefulness of INCLUDE and IGNORE sections becomes more apparent when you use them together with parameter entities to *parameterize* DTDs. When you parameterize a DTD, you can include or ignore multiple sections of a DTD simply by changing the value of a parameter entity from IGNORE to INCLUDE or back again.

Here's an example. In this case, I'm going to let XML authors include or ignore sections of a DTD just by changing the value of a parameter entity named includer. To use a parameter entity in INCLUDE and IGNORE sections, you must work with the external DTD subset, so I'll set up an external DTD subset named ch04_09.dtd:

```
<?xml version = "1.0" standalone="no"?>
<!DOCTYPE DOCUMENT SYSTEM "ch04_09.dtd">
<DOCUMENT>
    <CUSTOMER>
        <NAME>
            <LAST_NAME>Smith</LAST_NAME>
            <FIRST_NAME>Sam</FIRST_NAME>
        </NAME>
        <DATE>October 15, 2003</DATE>
        <ORDERS>
            <ITEM>
                <PRODUCT>Tomatoes</PRODUCT>
                <NUMBER>8</NUMBER>
                <PRICE>$1.25</PRICE>
            </ITEM>
```

```
                      .
                      .
                      .
                   <ITEM>
                        <PRODUCT>Lettuce</PRODUCT>
                        <NUMBER>6</NUMBER>
                        <PRICE>$11.50</PRICE>
                   </ITEM>
              </ORDERS>
         </CUSTOMER>
</DOCUMENT>
```

Here's what ch04_09.dtd looks like. First I set up the includer parameter entity, setting it to the text "INCLUDE" by default:

```
<!ENTITY % includer "INCLUDE">
<!ELEMENT DOCUMENT (CUSTOMER)*>
<!ELEMENT CUSTOMER (NAME,DATE,ORDERS)>
<!ELEMENT NAME (LAST_NAME,FIRST_NAME)>
<!ELEMENT LAST_NAME (#PCDATA)>
<!ELEMENT FIRST_NAME (#PCDATA)>
<!ELEMENT DATE (#PCDATA)>
<!ELEMENT ORDERS (ITEM)*>
<!ELEMENT ITEM (PRODUCT,NUMBER,PRICE)>
<!ELEMENT PRODUCT (#PCDATA)>
<!ELEMENT NUMBER (#PCDATA)>
<!ELEMENT PRICE (#PCDATA)>
```

Now I can use the value of this entity to set up an INCLUDE (or IGNORE) section in the DTD, like this:

Listing ch04_09.dtd

```
<!ENTITY % includer "INCLUDE">
<!ELEMENT DOCUMENT (CUSTOMER)*>
<!ELEMENT CUSTOMER (NAME,DATE,ORDERS)>
<!ELEMENT NAME (LAST_NAME,FIRST_NAME)>
<!ELEMENT LAST_NAME (#PCDATA)>
<!ELEMENT FIRST_NAME (#PCDATA)>
<!ELEMENT DATE (#PCDATA)>
<!ELEMENT ORDERS (ITEM)*>
<!ELEMENT ITEM (PRODUCT,NUMBER,PRICE)>
<!ELEMENT PRODUCT (#PCDATA)>
<!ELEMENT NUMBER (#PCDATA)>
<!ELEMENT PRICE (#PCDATA)>
<![ %includer; [
<!ELEMENT PRODUCT_ID (#PCDATA)>
<!ELEMENT SHIP_DATE (#PCDATA)>
```

continues

Listing ch04_09.dtd   Continued

```
<!ELEMENT SKU (#PCDATA)>
]]>
```

At this point, you can include or ignore the indicated section of the DTD just by changing the value of the `includer` entity. Using a technique like this makes it easy to centralize the entities you need to use to customize a whole DTD at one time.

In fact, that's the way the XHTML 1.1 DTD works; XHTML is expressly built to be *modular* to allow devices that can't handle full XHTML to support partial implementations. The main XHTML 1.1 DTD is actually a DTD *driver*, which means that it includes the various XHTML 1.1 modules using parameter entities. For example, here's how the XHTML 1.1 DTD includes the DTD module (that is, a section of a DTD) that supports HTML tables, `xhtml11-table-1.mod`. Note that it declares a parameter entity corresponding to that module and then uses an entity reference to include the actual module:

```
<!-- Tables Module ............................................ -->
<!ENTITY % xhtml-table.mod
     PUBLIC "-//W3C//ELEMENTS XHTML 1.1 Tables 1.0//EN"
            "xhtml11-table-1.mod" >
%xhtml-table.mod;
```

However, not all devices that support XHTML are capable of supporting tables (for example, cell phones or PDAs). So, the XHTML 1.1 DTD also defines a parameter entity named `xhtml-table.module` that's set to `"INCLUDE"` by default, and includes the table module with an `INCLUDE` section, like this:

```
<!-- Tables Module ............................................ -->
<!ENTITY % xhtml-table.module "INCLUDE" >
<![%xhtml-table.module;[
<!ENTITY % xhtml-table.mod
     PUBLIC "-//W3C//ELEMENTS XHTML 1.1 Tables 1.0//EN"
            "xhtml11-table-1.mod" >
%xhtml-table.mod;]]>
```

Now you can customize the XHTML 1.1 DTD by changing the value of `xhtml-table.module` to `"IGNORE"` to exclude support for tables. Because all the various XHTML 1.1 DTD modules are part of `INCLUDE` sections based on parameter entities like this, that DTD is considered fully *parameterized*.

All About Attributes

Attributes are name/value pairs that you can use in start and empty tags to add additional information. We've already seen in Chapter 2, "Creating Well-Formed XML Documents," that you can set up attributes as easily in XML as in HTML. Here's an example showing several attributes:

```
<CUSTOMER LAST_NAME="Smith" FIRST_NAME="Sam"
    DATE="October 15, 2003" PURCHASE="Tomatoes"
    PRICE="$1.25" NUMBER="8" />
```

In this case, I'm indicating that the customer's last name is Smith and first name is Sam, that the date of the current purchase is October 15, 2003, and that Sam purchased eight tomatoes for a total cost of $1.25.

Because you can declare elements in DTDs, you might expect that you can declare attributes as well, and you'd be right. In fact, there's good support for attribute declarations in DTDs, and we'll take a look at how that works now.

Declaring Attributes in DTDs

Declaring attributes and their types is very useful in XML. If you want your document to be valid, you must declare any attributes that you use before using them. You can give attributes default values and even require XML authors who use your DTD to assign values to attributes.

As we saw at the beginning of this chapter, you declare a list of attributes for an element with the `<!ATTLIST>` element:

```
<!ATTLIST ELEMENT_NAME
    ATTRIBUTE_NAME TYPE DEFAULT_VALUE
    ATTRIBUTE_NAME TYPE DEFAULT_VALUE
    ATTRIBUTE_NAME TYPE DEFAULT_VALUE
    .
    .
    .
    ATTRIBUTE_NAME TYPE DEFAULT_VALUE>
```

In this case, *ELEMENT_NAME* is the name of the element that you're declaring attributes for, *ATTRIBUTE_NAME* is the name of an attribute you're declaring, *TYPE* is the attribute's type, and *DEFAULT_VALUE* represents its default value.

Here are the possible *TYPE* values you can use:

- CDATA—Simple character data (that is, text that does not include any markup).

- ENTITIES—Multiple entity names (which must be declared in the DTD), separated by whitespace.

- ENTITY—Names an entity (which must be declared in the DTD).

- *Enumerated*—Represents a list of values. Any one item from the list is an appropriate attribute value.

- ID—A proper XML name that must be unique (that is, not shared by any other attribute of the ID type).

- IDREF—Holds the value of an ID attribute of some element, usually another element that the current element is related to.

- IDREFS—Multiple IDs of elements separated by whitespace.

- NMTOKEN—A name token, made up of one or more letters, digits, hyphens, underscores, colons, and periods.

- NMTOKENS—Multiple NMTOKENs in a list, separated by whitespace.

- NOTATION—A notation name (which must be declared in the DTD).

I'll take a look at all these possibilities in this chapter.

Here are the possible *DEFAULT_VALUE* settings you can use:

- *VALUE*—A simple text value, enclosed in quotes.

- #IMPLIED—Indicates that there is no default value for this attribute and that this attribute need not be used.

- #REQUIRED—Indicates that there is no default value but that a value must be assigned to this attribute. If a required attribute is missing, the document is not valid.

- #FIXED *VALUE*—In this case, *VALUE* is the attribute's value, and the attribute must always have this value.

Here's a simple example in which I declare a TYPE attribute of the CDATA type for the <CUSTOMER> element and indicate that this attribute can be used or not, as the author prefers:

Listing ch04_10.xml

```
<?xml version = "1.0" standalone="yes"?>
<!DOCTYPE DOCUMENT [
<!ELEMENT DOCUMENT (CUSTOMER)*>
<!ELEMENT CUSTOMER (NAME,DATE,ORDERS)>
<!ELEMENT NAME (LAST_NAME,FIRST_NAME)>
<!ELEMENT LAST_NAME (#PCDATA)>
<!ELEMENT FIRST_NAME (#PCDATA)>
<!ELEMENT DATE (#PCDATA)>
```

```
<!ELEMENT ORDERS (ITEM)*>
<!ELEMENT ITEM (PRODUCT,NUMBER,PRICE)>
<!ELEMENT PRODUCT (#PCDATA)>
<!ELEMENT NUMBER (#PCDATA)>
<!ELEMENT PRICE (#PCDATA)>
<!ATTLIST CUSTOMER
    TYPE CDATA #IMPLIED>
]>
<DOCUMENT>
    <CUSTOMER TYPE = "excellent">
        <NAME>
            <LAST_NAME>Smith</LAST_NAME>
            <FIRST_NAME>Sam</FIRST_NAME>
        </NAME>
        <DATE>October 15, 2003</DATE>
        <ORDERS>
            <ITEM>
                <PRODUCT>Tomatoes</PRODUCT>
                <NUMBER>8</NUMBER>
                <PRICE>$1.25</PRICE>
            </ITEM>
            <ITEM>
                <PRODUCT>Oranges</PRODUCT>
                <NUMBER>24</NUMBER>
                <PRICE>$4.98</PRICE>
            </ITEM>
        </ORDERS>
    </CUSTOMER>
    <CUSTOMER TYPE = "lousy">
        .
        .
        .
    </CUSTOMER>
</DOCUMENT>
```

This example shows how to declare a single attribute. As its name implies, you can use <!ATTLIST> to declare an entire list of attributes for an element. Here's an example in which I declare the attributes OWES, LAYAWAY, and DEFAULTS for the <CUSTOMER> element all at once:

Listing ch04_11.xml

```
<?xml version = "1.0" standalone="yes"?>
<!DOCTYPE DOCUMENT [
<!ELEMENT DOCUMENT (CUSTOMER)*>
<!ELEMENT CUSTOMER (NAME,DATE,ORDERS)>
<!ELEMENT NAME (LAST_NAME,FIRST_NAME)>
<!ELEMENT LAST_NAME (#PCDATA)>
```

continues

Listing ch04_11.xml   Continued

```
<!ELEMENT FIRST_NAME (#PCDATA)>
<!ELEMENT DATE (#PCDATA)>
<!ELEMENT ORDERS (ITEM)*>
<!ELEMENT ITEM (PRODUCT,NUMBER,PRICE)>
<!ELEMENT PRODUCT (#PCDATA)>
<!ELEMENT NUMBER (#PCDATA)>
<!ELEMENT PRICE (#PCDATA)>
<!ATTLIST CUSTOMER
    OWES CDATA "0"
    LAYAWAY CDATA "0"
    DEFAULTS CDATA "0">
]>
<DOCUMENT>
    <CUSTOMER OWES="$12.13" LAYAWAY="$0" DEFAULTS="0">
        <NAME>
            <LAST_NAME>Smith</LAST_NAME>
            <FIRST_NAME>Sam</FIRST_NAME>
        </NAME>
        <DATE>October 15, 2003</DATE>
        <ORDERS>
            <ITEM>
                <PRODUCT>Tomatoes</PRODUCT>
                <NUMBER>8</NUMBER>
                <PRICE>$1.25</PRICE>
            </ITEM>
            <ITEM>
                <PRODUCT>Oranges</PRODUCT>
                <NUMBER>24</NUMBER>
                <PRICE>$4.98</PRICE>
            </ITEM>
        </ORDERS>
    </CUSTOMER>
    <CUSTOMER OWES="$132.69" LAYAWAY="$44.99" DEFAULTS="0">
        .
        .
        .
    </CUSTOMER>
</DOCUMENT>
```

Now that I've declared these attributes, the document is valid.

Setting Default Values for Attributes

I'm going to start the examination of declaring attributes in DTDs by seeing what kind of default values you can specify for attributes.

Immediate Values

You can supply a default value for an attribute simply by giving that value in quotes in the attribute's declaration in the `<!ATTLIST>` element, as we've seen:

```
<?xml version = "1.0" standalone="yes"?>
<!DOCTYPE DOCUMENT [
<!ELEMENT DOCUMENT (CUSTOMER)*>
<!ELEMENT CUSTOMER (NAME,DATE,ORDERS)>
<!ELEMENT NAME (LAST_NAME,FIRST_NAME)>
<!ELEMENT LAST_NAME (#PCDATA)>
<!ELEMENT FIRST_NAME (#PCDATA)>
<!ELEMENT DATE (#PCDATA)>
<!ELEMENT ORDERS (ITEM)*>
<!ELEMENT ITEM (PRODUCT,NUMBER,PRICE)>
<!ELEMENT PRODUCT (#PCDATA)>
<!ELEMENT NUMBER (#PCDATA)>
<!ELEMENT PRICE (#PCDATA)>
<!ATTLIST CUSTOMER
    OWES CDATA "0"
    LAYAWAY CDATA "0"
    DEFAULTS CDATA "0">
]>
    .
    .
    .
```

However, you can also use other keywords here, such as `#REQUIRED`.

#REQUIRED

When you use the `#REQUIRED` keyword as an attribute's default value, it means that you're actually not providing a default value, but you're requiring anyone using this DTD to do so. Here's an example in which I'm requiring anyone who uses this DTD to supply the `<CUSTOMER>` element with an `OWES` attribute:

Listing ch04_12.xml

```
<?xml version = "1.0" standalone="yes"?>
<!DOCTYPE DOCUMENT [
<!ELEMENT DOCUMENT (CUSTOMER)*>
<!ELEMENT CUSTOMER (NAME,DATE,ORDERS)>
<!ELEMENT NAME (LAST_NAME,FIRST_NAME)>
<!ELEMENT LAST_NAME (#PCDATA)>
<!ELEMENT FIRST_NAME (#PCDATA)>
<!ELEMENT DATE (#PCDATA)>
<!ELEMENT ORDERS (ITEM)*>
```

continues

Listing ch04_12.xml   Continued

```
<!ELEMENT ITEM (PRODUCT,NUMBER,PRICE)>
<!ELEMENT PRODUCT (#PCDATA)>
<!ELEMENT NUMBER (#PCDATA)>
<!ELEMENT PRICE (#PCDATA)>
<!ATTLIST CUSTOMER
    OWES CDATA #REQUIRED>
]>
<DOCUMENT>
    <CUSTOMER OWES="$0">
        <NAME>
            <LAST_NAME>Smith</LAST_NAME>
            <FIRST_NAME>Sam</FIRST_NAME>
        </NAME>
        <DATE>October 15, 2003</DATE>
        <ORDERS>
            <ITEM>
                <PRODUCT>Tomatoes</PRODUCT>
                <NUMBER>8</NUMBER>
                <PRICE>$1.25</PRICE>
            </ITEM>
            <ITEM>
                <PRODUCT>Oranges</PRODUCT>
                <NUMBER>24</NUMBER>
                <PRICE>$4.98</PRICE>
            </ITEM>
        </ORDERS>
    </CUSTOMER>
    <CUSTOMER OWES="$599.99">
        .
        .
        .
    </CUSTOMER>
</DOCUMENT>
```

Requiring a value for an attribute is useful for cases in which a document should be customized, as when you want to list the document author's name or email address. It's also useful, of course, when the element needs more information, as when you use a URI attribute for an element that displays an image or loads an applet.

#IMPLIED

You use the #IMPLIED keyword when you don't have a default value for an attribute in mind and you want to indicate that the document author doesn't even have to use this attribute at all. XML processors will know about this attribute and not be disturbed if the attribute is not used (note that some XML processors will explicitly inform the underlying software that no value is available for this attribute if no value is given). The #IMPLIED keyword is the one to use when you want to allow the document author to include this attribute but not require it.

Here's an example in which I'm making the OWES attribute of the <CUSTOMER> element implied, which means that not every element needs to use it:

Listing ch04_13.xml

```
<?xml version = "1.0" standalone="yes"?>
<!DOCTYPE DOCUMENT [
<!ELEMENT DOCUMENT (CUSTOMER)*>
<!ELEMENT CUSTOMER (NAME,DATE,ORDERS)>
<!ELEMENT NAME (LAST_NAME,FIRST_NAME)>
<!ELEMENT LAST_NAME (#PCDATA)>
<!ELEMENT FIRST_NAME (#PCDATA)>
<!ELEMENT DATE (#PCDATA)>
<!ELEMENT ORDERS (ITEM)*>
<!ELEMENT ITEM (PRODUCT,NUMBER,PRICE)>
<!ELEMENT PRODUCT (#PCDATA)>
<!ELEMENT NUMBER (#PCDATA)>
<!ELEMENT PRICE (#PCDATA)>
<!ATTLIST CUSTOMER
    OWES CDATA #IMPLIED>
]>
<DOCUMENT>
    <CUSTOMER OWES="$23.99">
        <NAME>
            <LAST_NAME>Smith</LAST_NAME>
            <FIRST_NAME>Sam</FIRST_NAME>
        </NAME>
        <DATE>October 15, 2003</DATE>
        <ORDERS>
            <ITEM>
                <PRODUCT>Tomatoes</PRODUCT>
                <NUMBER>8</NUMBER>
                <PRICE>$1.25</PRICE>
            </ITEM>
            <ITEM>
                <PRODUCT>Oranges</PRODUCT>
                <NUMBER>24</NUMBER>
                <PRICE>$4.98</PRICE>
            </ITEM>
        </ORDERS>
    </CUSTOMER>
    <CUSTOMER>
```

continues

Listing ch04_13.xml   Continued

```
            .
            .
            .
        </CUSTOMER>
</DOCUMENT>
```

It's very common to declare attributes as #IMPLIED because that means they can appear in elements or not, as the document author prefers.

#FIXED

You can even set the value of an attribute so that it must always have that value. To do that, you use the #FIXED keyword, which sets a fixed value for the attribute. Then you specify the value you want the attribute to have.

Here's an example in which I'm setting the LANGUAGE attribute of the <CUSTOMER> elements to English, EN, and specifying that that is the only valid value for the attribute. This makes the assumption that the underlying application can handle only English and so needs data provided in that language:

Listing ch04_14.xml

```
<?xml version = "1.0" standalone="yes"?>
<!DOCTYPE DOCUMENT [
<!ELEMENT DOCUMENT (CUSTOMER)*>
<!ELEMENT CUSTOMER (NAME,DATE,ORDERS)>
<!ELEMENT NAME (LAST_NAME,FIRST_NAME)>
<!ELEMENT LAST_NAME (#PCDATA)>
<!ELEMENT FIRST_NAME (#PCDATA)>
<!ELEMENT DATE (#PCDATA)>
<!ELEMENT ORDERS (ITEM)*>
<!ELEMENT ITEM (PRODUCT,NUMBER,PRICE)>
<!ELEMENT PRODUCT (#PCDATA)>
<!ELEMENT NUMBER (#PCDATA)>
<!ELEMENT PRICE (#PCDATA)>
<!ATTLIST CUSTOMER
    LANGUAGE CDATA #FIXED "EN">
]>
<DOCUMENT>
    <CUSTOMER>
        <NAME>
            <LAST_NAME>Smith</LAST_NAME>
            <FIRST_NAME>Sam</FIRST_NAME>
        </NAME>
        <DATE>October 15, 2003</DATE>
```

```
<ORDERS>
    <ITEM>
        <PRODUCT>Tomatoes</PRODUCT>
        <NUMBER>8</NUMBER>
        <PRICE>$1.25</PRICE>
    </ITEM>
    <ITEM>
        <PRODUCT>Oranges</PRODUCT>
        <NUMBER>24</NUMBER>
        <PRICE>$4.98</PRICE>
    </ITEM>
</ORDERS>
</CUSTOMER>
<CUSTOMER>
    .
    .
    .
</CUSTOMER>
</DOCUMENT>
```

Note that I didn't even use the LANGUAGE attribute in the <CUSTOMER> elements here. The XML processor passes that attribute and its value to the underlying application anyway because I've declared them #FIXED. If you do explicitly use this attribute, you must set its value to the value you've set as the default in the DTD, or the XML processor will generate an error.

That covers the possible default value types you can specify when declaring attributes; I'll take a look at the possible attribute *types* next.

Attribute Types

So far, I've used just the CDATA attribute type when declaring attributes—and, in fact, that's probably the most common declaration type for attributes because it allows you to use simple text for the attribute's value. However, you can specify a number of different attribute types, and I'll take a look at them here. These types are not (not yet, anyway) detailed enough to indicate specific data types such as float, int, or double, but they can provide you with some ability to check the syntax of a document.

CDATA

The most simple attribute type you can have is CDATA, which is simple character data. That means the attribute may be set to a value which is any string of text, as long as the string does not contain markup. The requirement that you can't use markup explicitly excludes any string that includes the characters <, ", or &. If you want to use those characters, use their predefined entity references (<, ", and &) instead: These entity references will be parsed and replaced with the corresponding characters. (Because these attribute values are parsed—which is why you have to be careful about including anything that looks like markup—you use the term CDATA for this type, not PCDATA, which is character data that has already been parsed.)

We've already seen a number of examples of attribute declared with the CDATA type, as here:

```
<?xml version = "1.0" standalone="yes"?>
<!DOCTYPE DOCUMENT [
<!ELEMENT DOCUMENT (CUSTOMER)*>
<!ELEMENT CUSTOMER (NAME,DATE,ORDERS)>
<!ELEMENT NAME (LAST_NAME,FIRST_NAME)>
<!ELEMENT LAST_NAME (#PCDATA)>
<!ELEMENT FIRST_NAME (#PCDATA)>
<!ELEMENT DATE (#PCDATA)>
<!ELEMENT ORDERS (ITEM)*>
<!ELEMENT ITEM (PRODUCT,NUMBER,PRICE)>
<!ELEMENT PRODUCT (#PCDATA)>
<!ELEMENT NUMBER (#PCDATA)>
<!ELEMENT PRICE (#PCDATA)>
<!ATTLIST CUSTOMER
    OWES CDATA "0"
    LAYAWAY CDATA "0"
    DEFAULTS CDATA "0">
]>
    .
    .
    .
```

The CDATA type is the most general type of attribute; from here, we get into more specific types, such as the enumerated type.

Enumerated

The enumerated type does not use a keyword like the other attribute types do. Instead, it provides a list (or *enumeration*) of possible values. Each possible value must be a valid XML name (following the usual rules that the first character must be a letter or underscore, and so on).

Here's an example; in this case, I'm declaring an attribute named CREDIT_OK that can have one of only two possible values—"TRUE" or "FALSE"—and which has the default value "TRUE":

Listing ch04_15.xml

```
<?xml version = "1.0" standalone="yes"?>
<!DOCTYPE DOCUMENT [
<!ELEMENT DOCUMENT (CUSTOMER)*>
<!ELEMENT CUSTOMER (NAME,DATE,ORDERS)>
<!ELEMENT NAME (LAST_NAME,FIRST_NAME)>
<!ELEMENT LAST_NAME (#PCDATA)>
<!ELEMENT FIRST_NAME (#PCDATA)>
<!ELEMENT DATE (#PCDATA)>
<!ELEMENT ORDERS (ITEM)*>
<!ELEMENT ITEM (PRODUCT,NUMBER,PRICE)>
<!ELEMENT PRODUCT (#PCDATA)>
<!ELEMENT NUMBER (#PCDATA)>
<!ELEMENT PRICE (#PCDATA)>
<!ATTLIST CUSTOMER
    CREDIT_OK (TRUE | FALSE) "TRUE">
]>
<DOCUMENT>
    <CUSTOMER CREDIT_OK = "FALSE">
        <NAME>
            <LAST_NAME>Smith</LAST_NAME>
            <FIRST_NAME>Sam</FIRST_NAME>
        </NAME>
        <DATE>October 15, 2003</DATE>
        <ORDERS>
            <ITEM>
                <PRODUCT>Tomatoes</PRODUCT>
                <NUMBER>8</NUMBER>
                <PRICE>$1.25</PRICE>
            </ITEM>
            <ITEM>
                <PRODUCT>Oranges</PRODUCT>
                <NUMBER>24</NUMBER>
                <PRICE>$4.98</PRICE>
            </ITEM>
        </ORDERS>
    </CUSTOMER>
    <CUSTOMER>
        .
        .
        .
    </CUSTOMER>
</DOCUMENT>
```

Using enumerations like this is great if you want to set the possible range of values that an attribute can take. For example, you might want to restrict an attribute named WEEKDAY to these possible values: "Sunday", "Monday", "Tuesday", "Wednesday", "Thursday", "Friday", or "Sunday".

NMTOKEN

Document authors commonly use another attribute type: NMTOKEN. An attribute of this type can take only values that are made up of proper XML name characters (that is, made up of one or more letters, digits, hyphens, underscores, colons, and periods). In particular, note that NMTOKEN values cannot include whitespace.

Using NMTOKEN attribute values can be useful in some applications. Note, for example, that XML names are very close to those that are legal for variables in C++, Java, and JavaScript, which means that you could even use those names in underlying applications in fancy ways. NMTOKEN values also mean that attribute values must consist of a single word because whitespace of any kind is not allowed; that can be a useful restriction.

Here's an example. In this case, I'm declaring an attribute named SHIP_STATE to hold the two-letter state code to which an order was shipped; I'm also declaring that the attribute with NMTOKEM rules out the possibility of values that are longer than a single term:

Listing ch04_16.xml

```
<?xml version = "1.0" standalone="yes"?>
<!DOCTYPE DOCUMENT [
<!ELEMENT DOCUMENT (CUSTOMER)*>
<!ELEMENT CUSTOMER (NAME,DATE,ORDERS)>
<!ELEMENT NAME (LAST_NAME,FIRST_NAME)>
<!ELEMENT LAST_NAME (#PCDATA)>
<!ELEMENT FIRST_NAME (#PCDATA)>
<!ELEMENT DATE (#PCDATA)>
<!ELEMENT ORDERS (ITEM)*>
<!ELEMENT ITEM (PRODUCT,NUMBER,PRICE)>
<!ELEMENT PRODUCT (#PCDATA)>
<!ELEMENT NUMBER (#PCDATA)>
<!ELEMENT PRICE (#PCDATA)>
<!ATTLIST CUSTOMER
    SHIP_STATE NMTOKEN #REQUIRED>
]>
<DOCUMENT>
    <CUSTOMER SHIP_STATE = "CA">
        <NAME>
            <LAST_NAME>Smith</LAST_NAME>
            <FIRST_NAME>Sam</FIRST_NAME>
        </NAME>
        <DATE>October 15, 2003</DATE>
        <ORDERS>
            <ITEM>
                <PRODUCT>Tomatoes</PRODUCT>
```

```
                <NUMBER>8</NUMBER>
                <PRICE>$1.25</PRICE>
            </ITEM>
            <ITEM>
                <PRODUCT>Oranges</PRODUCT>
                <NUMBER>24</NUMBER>
                <PRICE>$4.98</PRICE>
            </ITEM>
        </ORDERS>
    </CUSTOMER>
    <CUSTOMER SHIP_STATE = "LA">
        .
        .
        .
    </CUSTOMER>
</DOCUMENT>
```

NMTOKENS

You can even specify that an attribute value must be made up of NMTOKENs separated by whitespace if you use the NMTOKENS attribute type. For example, here I'm giving the attribute CONTACT_NAME the type NMTOKENS to allow attribute values to hold first and last names, separated by whitespace:

Listing ch04_17.xml

```
<?xml version = "1.0" standalone="yes"?>
<!DOCTYPE DOCUMENT [
<!ELEMENT DOCUMENT (CUSTOMER)*>
<!ELEMENT CUSTOMER (NAME,DATE,ORDERS)>
<!ELEMENT NAME (LAST_NAME,FIRST_NAME)>
<!ELEMENT LAST_NAME (#PCDATA)>
<!ELEMENT FIRST_NAME (#PCDATA)>
<!ELEMENT DATE (#PCDATA)>
<!ELEMENT ORDERS (ITEM)*>
<!ELEMENT ITEM (PRODUCT,NUMBER,PRICE)>
<!ELEMENT PRODUCT (#PCDATA)>
<!ELEMENT NUMBER (#PCDATA)>
<!ELEMENT PRICE (#PCDATA)>
<!ATTLIST CUSTOMER
    CONTACT_NAME NMTOKENS #IMPLIED>
]>
<DOCUMENT>
    <CUSTOMER CONTACT_NAME = "George Starr">
```

continues

Listing ch04_17.xml   Continued

```
        .
        .
        .
    </CUSTOMER>
    <CUSTOMER CONTACT_NAME = "Ringo Harrison">
        .
        .
        .
    </CUSTOMER>
    <CUSTOMER CONTACT_NAME = "Paul Lennon">
        .
        .
        .
    </CUSTOMER>
</DOCUMENT>
```

ID

There's another very important attribute type that you can declare: ID. XML gives special meaning to an element's ID value because that's the value that applications typically use to identify elements. For that reason, XML processors are supposed to make sure that no two elements have the same value for the attribute that is of the type ID in a document (and you can give elements only one attribute of this type). The actual value you assign to the attribute of this type must be a proper XML name.

Applications can use the ID value of elements to uniquely identify those elements—but note that you don't have to name the attribute ID, as you do in HTML, because simply specifying an attribute's type to be the ID type makes it into an ID attribute. Here's an example in which I add an ID attribute named CUSTOMER_ID to the <CUSTOMER> elements in this document:

Listing ch04_18.xml

```
<?xml version = "1.0" standalone="yes"?>
<!DOCTYPE DOCUMENT [
<!ELEMENT DOCUMENT (CUSTOMER)*>
<!ELEMENT CUSTOMER (NAME,DATE,ORDERS)>
<!ELEMENT NAME (LAST_NAME,FIRST_NAME)>
<!ELEMENT LAST_NAME (#PCDATA)>
<!ELEMENT FIRST_NAME (#PCDATA)>
<!ELEMENT DATE (#PCDATA)>
<!ELEMENT ORDERS (ITEM)*>
```

```
<!ELEMENT ITEM (PRODUCT,NUMBER,PRICE)>
<!ELEMENT PRODUCT (#PCDATA)>
<!ELEMENT NUMBER (#PCDATA)>
<!ELEMENT PRICE (#PCDATA)>
<!ATTLIST CUSTOMER
    CUSTOMER_ID ID #REQUIRED>
]>
<DOCUMENT>
    <CUSTOMER CUSTOMER_ID = "C1232231">
        .
        .
        .
    </CUSTOMER>
    <CUSTOMER CUSTOMER_ID = "C1232232">
        .
        .
        .
    </CUSTOMER>
    <CUSTOMER CUSTOMER_ID = "C1232233">
        .
        .
        .
    </CUSTOMER>
</DOCUMENT>
```

Note that you cannot use the ID type with #FIXED attributes (because all #FIXED attributes have same value). You usually use the #REQUIRED keyword instead.

ID Values Must Be Proper Names

One thing to realize is that because ID values must be proper XML names, they can't be simple numbers such as 12345; these values cannot start with a digit.

IDREF

The IDREF attribute type represents an attempt to let you use attributes to specify something about a document's structure—in particular, something about the relationship that exists between elements. IDREF attributes hold the ID value of another element in the document.

For example, say you wanted to set up a parent-child relationship between elements that was not reflected in the normal nesting structure of the document. In that case, you could set an IDREF attribute of an element to the ID of its parent. An application could then check the attribute with the IDREF type to determine the child's parent.

Here's an example. In this case, I'm declaring two attributes, a CUS-TOMER_ID attribute of type ID and an EMPLOYER_ID attribute of type IDREF that holds the ID value of the customer's employer:

Listing ch04_19.xml

```
<?xml version = "1.0" standalone="yes"?>
<!DOCTYPE DOCUMENT [
<!ELEMENT DOCUMENT (CUSTOMER)*>
<!ELEMENT CUSTOMER (NAME,DATE,ORDERS)>
<!ELEMENT NAME (LAST_NAME,FIRST_NAME)>
<!ELEMENT LAST_NAME (#PCDATA)>
<!ELEMENT FIRST_NAME (#PCDATA)>
<!ELEMENT DATE (#PCDATA)>
<!ELEMENT ORDERS (ITEM)*>
<!ELEMENT ITEM (PRODUCT,NUMBER,PRICE)>
<!ELEMENT PRODUCT (#PCDATA)>
<!ELEMENT NUMBER (#PCDATA)>
<!ELEMENT PRICE (#PCDATA)>
<!ATTLIST CUSTOMER
    CUSTOMER_ID ID #REQUIRED
    EMPLOYER_ID IDREF #IMPLIED>
]>
<DOCUMENT>
    <CUSTOMER CUSTOMER_ID = "C1232231">
        .
        .
        .
    </CUSTOMER>
    <CUSTOMER CUSTOMER_ID = "C1232232" EMPLOYER_ID="C1232231">
        .
        .
        .
    </CUSTOMER>
    <CUSTOMER CUSTOMER_ID = "C1232233">
        .
        .
        .
    </CUSTOMER>
</DOCUMENT>
```

An XML processor can pass on the ID and IDREF structure of a document to an underlying application, which can then use that information to reconstruct the relationships of the elements in the document.

ENTITY

You can also specify that an attribute be of type ENTITY, which means that the
attribute can be set to the name of an entity you've declared. For example, say
that I declared an entity named SNAPSHOT1 that referred to an external image
file. I could then create a new attribute named, say, IMAGE, that I could set to
the entity name SNAPSHOT1; here's how that looks:

```
<?xml version = "1.0" standalone="no"?>
<!DOCTYPE DOCUMENT [
<!ELEMENT DOCUMENT (CUSTOMER)*>
<!ELEMENT CUSTOMER (NAME,DATE,ORDERS)>
<!ELEMENT NAME (LAST_NAME,FIRST_NAME)>
<!ELEMENT LAST_NAME (#PCDATA)>
<!ELEMENT FIRST_NAME (#PCDATA)>
<!ELEMENT DATE (#PCDATA)>
<!ELEMENT ORDERS (ITEM)*>
<!ELEMENT ITEM (PRODUCT,NUMBER,PRICE)>
<!ELEMENT PRODUCT (#PCDATA)>
<!ELEMENT NUMBER (#PCDATA)>
<!ELEMENT PRICE (#PCDATA)>
<!ATTLIST CUSTOMER
    IMAGE ENTITY #IMPLIED>
<!ENTITY SNAPSHOT1 SYSTEM "image.gif">
]>
<DOCUMENT>
    <CUSTOMER IMAGE="SNAPSHOT1">
        <NAME>
            <LAST_NAME>Smith</LAST_NAME>
            <FIRST_NAME>Sam</FIRST_NAME>
        </NAME>
        <DATE>October 15, 2003</DATE>
        <ORDERS>
            <ITEM>
                <PRODUCT>Tomatoes</PRODUCT>
                <NUMBER>8</NUMBER>
                <PRICE>$1.25</PRICE>
            </ITEM>
            .
            .
            .
            <ITEM>
                <PRODUCT>Lettuce</PRODUCT>
                <NUMBER>6</NUMBER>
                <PRICE>$11.50</PRICE>
            </ITEM>
        </ORDERS>
    </CUSTOMER>
</DOCUMENT>
```

This points out how to use the ENTITY attribute type (but actually it's not a complete example because there are specific ways to set up entities to refer to external, non-XML data that we'll see at the end of this chapter). In general, the ENTITY attribute type is a useful one if you declare your own entities. For example, you might want to declare entities named SIGNATURE_HOME, SIGNA-TURE_WORK, and so on that hold your name and home address, work address, and so on. If you then declare an attribute named, say, SIGNATURE of the EN-TITY type, you can assign the SIGNATURE_HOME or SIGNATURE_WORK entities to the SIGNATURE attribute in the document.

ENTITIES

As with the NMTOKEN attribute type, which has a plural type, NMTOKENS, the EN-TITY attribute type has a plural type, ENTITIES. Attributes of this type can hold lists of entity names separated by whitespace.

Here's an example. In this case, I'm declaring two entities, SNAPSHOT1 and SNAPSHOT2, and an attribute named IMAGES that you can assign both SNAP-SHOT1 and SNAPSHOT2 to at the same time:

```
<?xml version = "1.0" standalone="no"?>
<!DOCTYPE DOCUMENT [
<!ELEMENT DOCUMENT (CUSTOMER)*>
<!ELEMENT CUSTOMER (NAME,DATE,ORDERS)>
<!ELEMENT NAME (LAST_NAME,FIRST_NAME)>
<!ELEMENT LAST_NAME (#PCDATA)>
<!ELEMENT FIRST_NAME (#PCDATA)>
<!ELEMENT DATE (#PCDATA)>
<!ELEMENT ORDERS (ITEM)*>
<!ELEMENT ITEM (PRODUCT,NUMBER,PRICE)>
<!ELEMENT PRODUCT (#PCDATA)>
<!ELEMENT NUMBER (#PCDATA)>
<!ELEMENT PRICE (#PCDATA)>
<!ATTLIST CUSTOMER
    IMAGES ENTITIES #IMPLIED>
<!ENTITY SNAPSHOT1 SYSTEM "image.gif">
<!ENTITY SNAPSHOT2 SYSTEM "image2.gif">
]>
<DOCUMENT>
    <CUSTOMER IMAGES="SNAPSHOT1 SNAPSHOT2">
        <NAME>
            <LAST_NAME>Smith</LAST_NAME>
            <FIRST_NAME>Sam</FIRST_NAME>
        </NAME>
        <DATE>October 15, 2003</DATE>
        <ORDERS>
            <ITEM>
```

```
            <PRODUCT>Tomatoes</PRODUCT>
            <NUMBER>8</NUMBER>
            <PRICE>$1.25</PRICE>
        </ITEM>
        .
        .
        .
        <ITEM>
            <PRODUCT>Lettuce</PRODUCT>
            <NUMBER>6</NUMBER>
            <PRICE>$11.50</PRICE>
        </ITEM>
      </ORDERS>
    </CUSTOMER>
</DOCUMENT>
```

As with the NMTOKENS attribute type, the reason for using the plural ENTITIES type is when you want to assign a number of entities to the same attributes. For example, you might have multiple entities defined that represent a customer's usernames, and you want to assign all of them to an attribute named USERNAMES. Because entities can be quite complex and even can include other entities, this is one way to store detailed data in a document simply using attributes.

NOTATION

The final attribute type is NOTATION. When you declare an attribute of this type, you can assign values to it that have been declared *notations*.

A notation specifies the format of non-XML data, and you use it to describe external entities. One popular type of notation is Multipurpose Internet Mail Extension (MIME) types such as image/gif, application/xml, text/html, and so on.

List of MIME Types

You can get a list of the registered MIME types at ftp://ftp.isi.edu/in-notes/iana/ assignments/media-types/media-types.

Here's an example. In this case, I'll declare two notations, GIF and JPG, that stand for the MIME types image/gif and image/jpeg. Then I'll set up an attribute that can be assigned either of these values.

To declare a notation, you use the `<!NOTATION>` element in a DTD, like this:

```
<!NOTATION NAME SYSTEM "EXTERNAL_ID">
```

Here, *NAME* is the name of the notation and *EXTERNAL_ID* is the external ID you want to use for the notation, often a MIME type.

You can also use the `PUBLIC` keyword for public notations if you supply an FPI (see the rules for constructing FPIs in the previous chapter), like this:

```
<!NOTATION NAME PUBLIC FPI "EXTERNAL_ID">
```

Here's how I create the `GIF` and `JPG` notations:

```
<?xml version = "1.0" standalone="no"?>
<!DOCTYPE DOCUMENT [
<!ELEMENT DOCUMENT (CUSTOMER)*>
<!ELEMENT CUSTOMER (NAME,DATE,ORDERS)>
<!ELEMENT NAME (LAST_NAME,FIRST_NAME)>
<!ELEMENT LAST_NAME (#PCDATA)>
<!ELEMENT FIRST_NAME (#PCDATA)>
<!ELEMENT DATE (#PCDATA)>
<!ELEMENT ORDERS (ITEM)*>
<!ELEMENT ITEM (PRODUCT,NUMBER,PRICE)>
<!ELEMENT PRODUCT (#PCDATA)>
<!ELEMENT NUMBER (#PCDATA)>
<!ELEMENT PRICE (#PCDATA)>
<!NOTATION GIF SYSTEM "image/gif">
<!NOTATION JPG SYSTEM "image/jpeg">
    .
    .
    .
```

Now I'm free to create an attribute named, say, `IMAGE_TYPE`, of type `NOTATION` that you can assign either the `GIF` or `JPG` notations to:

```
<?xml version = "1.0" standalone="no"?>
<!DOCTYPE DOCUMENT [
<!ELEMENT DOCUMENT (CUSTOMER)*>
<!ELEMENT CUSTOMER (NAME,DATE,ORDERS)>
<!ELEMENT NAME (LAST_NAME,FIRST_NAME)>
<!ELEMENT LAST_NAME (#PCDATA)>
<!ELEMENT FIRST_NAME (#PCDATA)>
<!ELEMENT DATE (#PCDATA)>
<!ELEMENT ORDERS (ITEM)*>
<!ELEMENT ITEM (PRODUCT,NUMBER,PRICE)>
<!ELEMENT PRODUCT (#PCDATA)>
<!ELEMENT NUMBER (#PCDATA)>
<!ELEMENT PRICE (#PCDATA)>
```

```
<!NOTATION GIF SYSTEM "image/gif">
<!NOTATION JPG SYSTEM "image/jpeg">
<!ATTLIST CUSTOMER
    IMAGE NMTOKEN #IMPLIED
    IMAGE_TYPE NOTATION (GIF | JPG) #IMPLIED>
]>
    .
    .
    .
```

At this point, I'm free to use the IMAGE_TYPE attribute:

```
<?xml version = "1.0" standalone="no"?>
<!DOCTYPE DOCUMENT [
<!ELEMENT DOCUMENT (CUSTOMER)*>
<!ELEMENT CUSTOMER (NAME,DATE,ORDERS)>
<!ELEMENT NAME (LAST_NAME,FIRST_NAME)>
<!ELEMENT LAST_NAME (#PCDATA)>
<!ELEMENT FIRST_NAME (#PCDATA)>
<!ELEMENT DATE (#PCDATA)>
<!ELEMENT ORDERS (ITEM)*>
<!ELEMENT ITEM (PRODUCT,NUMBER,PRICE)>
<!ELEMENT PRODUCT (#PCDATA)>
<!ELEMENT NUMBER (#PCDATA)>
<!ELEMENT PRICE (#PCDATA)>
<!NOTATION GIF SYSTEM "image/gif">
<!NOTATION JPG SYSTEM "image/jpeg">
<!ATTLIST CUSTOMER
    IMAGE NMTOKEN #IMPLIED
    IMAGE_TYPE NOTATION (GIF | JPG) #IMPLIED>
]>
<DOCUMENT>
    <CUSTOMER IMAGE="image.gif" IMAGE_TYPE="GIF">
        .
        .
        .
    </CUSTOMER>
</DOCUMENT>
```

Note that this example brings up an interesting point: Here, I've just set the value of an attribute, IMAGE, to the name of an image file, image.gif. But how do you actually make an unparsed entity like an image part of a document? There's a way of doing that explicitly; now that we know about notations, we're ready to do things that way.

xml:space and xml:lang

This completes our coverage of creating attributes. But don't forget that there are also two attributes that are in some sense predefined in XML (we've already covered those): xml:space, which you can use to preserve the whitespace in an element; and xml:lang, which you can use to specify the language used in an element and its attributes. They're not really predefined because you have to declare them if you want to use them, but you shouldn't use these attribute names for anything but their intended use.

Embedding Non-XML Data in a Document

In the previous example, I associated an image, image.gif, with a document, but only by setting an attribute to the text "image.gif". What if I wanted to make image.gif a real part of the document?

I can do that by treating image.gif as an external *unparsed entity*. The creators of XML realized that XML was not ideal for storing data that is not text. So, they added the idea of unparsed entities as a way of associating non-XML data, such as non-XML text, or binary data, with XML documents.

To declare an external unparsed entity, you use an <!ENTITY> element like this. Note the keyword NDATA, indicating that I'm referring to an unparsed entity:

```
<!ENTITY NAME SYSTEM VALUE NDATA TYPE>
```

Here, NAME is the name of the external unparsed entity, VALUE is the value of the entity (such as the name of an external file, as in image.gif), and TYPE is a declared notation.

You can also use public external unparsed entities if you use the PUBLIC keyword with an FPI:

```
<!ENTITY NAME PUBLIC FPI VALUE NDATA TYPE>
```

Here's an example. In this case, I start by declaring a notation named GIF that stands for the image/gif MIME type:

```
<?xml version = "1.0" standalone="no"?>
<!DOCTYPE DOCUMENT [
<!ELEMENT DOCUMENT (CUSTOMER)*>
<!ELEMENT CUSTOMER (NAME,DATE,ORDERS)>
<!ELEMENT NAME (LAST_NAME,FIRST_NAME)>
<!ELEMENT LAST_NAME (#PCDATA)>
<!ELEMENT FIRST_NAME (#PCDATA)>
<!ELEMENT DATE (#PCDATA)>
```

```
<!ELEMENT ORDERS (ITEM)*>
<!ELEMENT ITEM (PRODUCT,NUMBER,PRICE)>
<!ELEMENT PRODUCT (#PCDATA)>
<!ELEMENT NUMBER (#PCDATA)>
<!ELEMENT PRICE (#PCDATA)>
<!NOTATION GIF SYSTEM "image/gif">
       .
       .
       .
```

Now I create an external unparsed entity named SNAPSHOT1 to refer to the external image file, image.gif:

```
<?xml version = "1.0" standalone="no"?>
<!DOCTYPE DOCUMENT [
<!ELEMENT DOCUMENT (CUSTOMER)*>
<!ELEMENT CUSTOMER (NAME,DATE,ORDERS)>
<!ELEMENT NAME (LAST_NAME,FIRST_NAME)>
<!ELEMENT LAST_NAME (#PCDATA)>
<!ELEMENT FIRST_NAME (#PCDATA)>
<!ELEMENT DATE (#PCDATA)>
<!ELEMENT ORDERS (ITEM)*>
<!ELEMENT ITEM (PRODUCT,NUMBER,PRICE)>
<!ELEMENT PRODUCT (#PCDATA)>
<!ELEMENT NUMBER (#PCDATA)>
<!ELEMENT PRICE (#PCDATA)>
<!NOTATION GIF SYSTEM "image/gif">
<!ENTITY SNAPSHOT1 SYSTEM "image.gif" NDATA GIF>
       .
       .
       .
```

After you've declared an external unparsed entity such as SNAPSHOT1, you can't just embed it in an XML document directly. Instead, you create a new attribute of the ENTITY type that you can assign the entity to. I'll call this new attribute IMAGE:

```
<?xml version = "1.0" standalone="no"?>
<!DOCTYPE DOCUMENT [
<!ELEMENT DOCUMENT (CUSTOMER)*>
<!ELEMENT CUSTOMER (NAME,DATE,ORDERS)>
<!ELEMENT NAME (LAST_NAME,FIRST_NAME)>
<!ELEMENT LAST_NAME (#PCDATA)>
<!ELEMENT FIRST_NAME (#PCDATA)>
<!ELEMENT DATE (#PCDATA)>
<!ELEMENT ORDERS (ITEM)*>
<!ELEMENT ITEM (PRODUCT,NUMBER,PRICE)>
<!ELEMENT PRODUCT (#PCDATA)>
<!ELEMENT NUMBER (#PCDATA)>
```

continues

```
<!ELEMENT PRICE (#PCDATA)>
<!NOTATION GIF SYSTEM "image/gif">
<!ENTITY SNAPSHOT1 SYSTEM "image.gif" NDATA GIF>
<!ATTLIST CUSTOMER
    IMAGE ENTITY #IMPLIED>
]>
   .
   .
   .
```

Now, finally, I'm able to assign the IMAGE attribute the value SNAPSHOT1 like this, making image.gif an official part of the document:

```
<?xml version = "1.0" standalone="no"?>
<!DOCTYPE DOCUMENT [
<!ELEMENT DOCUMENT (CUSTOMER)*>
<!ELEMENT CUSTOMER (NAME,DATE,ORDERS)>
<!ELEMENT NAME (LAST_NAME,FIRST_NAME)>
<!ELEMENT LAST_NAME (#PCDATA)>
<!ELEMENT FIRST_NAME (#PCDATA)>
<!ELEMENT DATE (#PCDATA)>
<!ELEMENT ORDERS (ITEM)*>
<!ELEMENT ITEM (PRODUCT,NUMBER,PRICE)>
<!ELEMENT PRODUCT (#PCDATA)>
<!ELEMENT NUMBER (#PCDATA)>
<!ELEMENT PRICE (#PCDATA)>
<!NOTATION GIF SYSTEM "image/gif">
<!ENTITY SNAPSHOT1 SYSTEM "image.gif" NDATA GIF>
<!ATTLIST CUSTOMER
    IMAGE ENTITY #IMPLIED>
]>
<DOCUMENT>
    <CUSTOMER IMAGE="SNAPSHOT1">
        .
        .
        .
    </CUSTOMER>
</DOCUMENT>
```

If you use external unparsed entities like this, validating XML processors won't try to read and parse them, but they'll often check to make sure they're there. By doing so, they will confirm that the document is complete.

What if I wanted to embed multiple unparsed entities? Take a look at the next topic.

Embedding Multiple Unparsed Entities in a Document

Embedding multiple unparsed entities is no problem. Just create an attribute of the ENTITIES type and assign multiple entities to it, like this:

```
<?xml version = "1.0" standalone="no"?>
<!DOCTYPE DOCUMENT [
<!ELEMENT DOCUMENT (CUSTOMER)*>
<!ELEMENT CUSTOMER (NAME,DATE,ORDERS)>
<!ELEMENT NAME (LAST_NAME,FIRST_NAME)>
<!ELEMENT LAST_NAME (#PCDATA)>
<!ELEMENT FIRST_NAME (#PCDATA)>
<!ELEMENT DATE (#PCDATA)>
<!ELEMENT ORDERS (ITEM)*>
<!ELEMENT ITEM (PRODUCT,NUMBER,PRICE)>
<!ELEMENT PRODUCT (#PCDATA)>
<!ELEMENT NUMBER (#PCDATA)>
<!ELEMENT PRICE (#PCDATA)>
<!NOTATION GIF SYSTEM "image/gif">
<!ATTLIST CUSTOMER
    IMAGES ENTITIES #IMPLIED>
<!ENTITY SNAPSHOT1 SYSTEM "image.gif" NDATA GIF>
<!ENTITY SNAPSHOT2 SYSTEM "image2.gif" NDATA GIF>
<!ENTITY SNAPSHOT3 SYSTEM "image3.gif" NDATA GIF>
]>
<DOCUMENT>
    <CUSTOMER IMAGES="SNAPSHOT1 SNAPSHOT2 SNAPSHOT3">
        .
        .
        .
    </CUSTOMER>
</DOCUMENT>
```

That's it all it takes. And that's it for our coverage of constructing and using DTDs as well. In this chapter and the previous chapter, we've seen what goes into a DTD and how to handle elements, attributes, entities, and notations. In the next chapter, we'll take a look at the proposed alternate way of declaring those items in XML documents: XML schemas.

CHAPTER 5

Creating XML Schemas

For the past two chapters, we've been working with document type definitions (DTDs). Over time, many people have complained to the World Wide Web Consortium (W3C) about the complexity of DTDs and have asked for something simpler. The W3C listened, assigned a committee to work on the problem, and came up with a solution that is much more complex than DTDs ever were: XML schemas.

On the other hand, schemas are also far more powerful and precise than DTDs ever were. With schemas, you can specify not only the syntax of a document as you would with a DTD, but also the actual data types of each element's content, inherit syntax from other schemas, annotate schemas, use them with multiple namespaces, create simple and complex data types, specify the minimum and maximum number of times an element can occur, create list types, create attribute groups, restrict the ranges of values that elements can hold, restrict what other schemas can inherit from yours, merge fragments of multiple schemas, require that attribute or element values be unique, and much more.

Currently, the specification for XML schemas is in the working draft stage, which means it will probably change before becoming a recommendation. You can find the specification in these three documents:

- `http://www.w3.org/TR/xmlschema-0/`—XML schema primer, a tutorial introduction to schemas

- `http://www.w3.org/TR/xmlschema-1/`—XML schema structures, the formal details on creating schemas

- `http://www.w3.org/TR/xmlschema-2/`—XML schema data types, all about the data types you can use in schemas

There were a few issues that the schema working group expressly set out to tackle: using namespaces when validating documents, providing for data typing and restrictions, allowing and restricting inheritance between schemas, creating primitive data types, and other issues.

As with most issues in this book, this is all best seen with an example. One of the major applications that does support schemas is Internet Explorer, so let's take a look at that first.

Using XML Schemas in Internet Explorer

The XML support in Internet Explorer is built into the Microsoft XML (MSXML package). This package was called the Microsoft XML Parser until version 4.0, when it was named the Microsoft XML Core Services. Version 4.0 is the version that supports full schemas, also called XML Schema Definition Language (XSD) schemas. Before version 4.0, the MSXML package supported a smaller and different version of XML schemas, which Microsoft calls XML-Data Reduced (XDR) schemas. You can see the support for XML schemas by MSXML version in Table 5-1.

	Version	Support
Table 5-1 XML Schema Support by MSXML Version	MSXML	No support for schemas
	MSXML 2.0	Support for XDR schemas
	MSXML 2.6	Support for XDR schemas
	MSXML 3.0	Support for XDR schemas
	MSXML 4.0	Support for XSD and XDR schemas

If you're running Windows, how do you know what version of MSXML you have? Take a look in the directory where Windows stores your system dynamic link library (DLL) files—either system or system32 under the main Windows directory. If you see msxml3.dll and no later version, you have MSXML 3.0. If you see msxml4.dll and no later version, you have version 4.0.

To work with full schemas, you'll need MSXML version 4.0 or later. If you don't already have it installed, you can download it from Microsoft for free from the Microsoft XML site, currently at http://msdn.microsoft.com/library/default.asp?url=/nhp/Default.asp?contentid=28000438. The actual download site for MSXML 4.0 is http://msdn.microsoft.com/downloads/default.asp?url=/downloads/sample.asp?url=/msdnfiles/027/001/766/msdncompositedoc.xml currently (or if you don't feel like typing all that in, use the links from `http://msdn.microsoft.com/downloads/xml`).

Here's an example, ch05_01.html, that puts MSXML 4.0 to work. This example uses JavaScript, which you'll see in the next chapter, to load an XML schema in and use it to verify an XML document:

Listing ch05_01.html

```
<HTML>
    <HEAD>
        <TITLE>
            Using XML Schemas
        </TITLE>
    </HEAD>

    <BODY>
        <CENTER>
            <H1>Using XML Schemas</H1>
        </CENTER>

        <SCRIPT LANGUAGE="JavaScript">
            var schemaCache = new
            ➥ActiveXObject("MSXML2.XMLSchemaCache.4.0");
            schemaCache.add("http://starpowder", "ch05_02.xsd");

            var doc = new ActiveXObject("MSXML2.DOMDocument.4.0");
            doc.schemas = schemaCache;
            doc.validateOnParse = true;

            if (doc.load("ch05_03.xml")) {
                document.write("ch05_03.xml is valid.");
            } else {
                if (doc.parseError.errorCode != 0) {
                    document.write("Error: " + doc.parseError.reason);
                }
            }
        </SCRIPT>
    </BODY>
</HTML>
```

Here's the XML schema, ch05_02.xsd—note the namespace, `xs`, used by the schema elements, which corresponds to `"http://www.w3.org/2001/XMLSchema"`:

Listing ch05_02.xsd

```xml
<?xml version="1.0"?>
<xs:schema xmlns:xs="http://www.w3.org/2001/XMLSchema"
    targetNamespace = "http://starpowder"
    xmlns:ch05 = "http://starpowder"
    elementFormDefault = "qualified">
  <xs:element name="document"></xs:element>
</xs:schema>
```

And here's the XML document that we want to try to verify, ch05_03.xml:

Listing ch05_03.xml

```xml
<?xml version="1.0"?>
<ch05:document xmlns:ch05 = 'http://starpowder'>
    <ch05:data/>
</ch05:document>
```

If you take a close look at the XML schema here, you can probably figure out what's going on: It's declaring an element named document. If you look in the XML document, on the other hand, you can see that element in use, along with a namespace that corresponds to this chapter, `<ch05:document>`. Note, however, that the XML document also contains an element named `<ch05:data/>`, which is *not* in the schema. That's an error, and that's exactly what this example reports, as you see in Figure 5-1. (Note that to run this example, ch05_01.html, ch05_02.xsd, and ch05_03.xml should all be in the same directory.)

Figure 5-1
Using XML schemas in Internet Explorer.

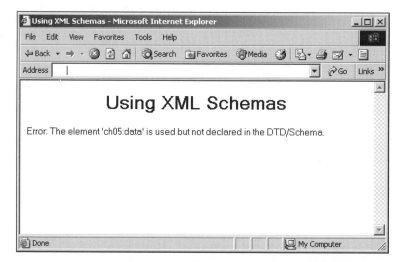

If you look closely at ch05_01.html, you'll see that the code in that example loads both the XML document and the XML schema. In fact, MSXML 4.0 lets you specify the location of the schema in the XML document, without having to specify it in your code. You can indicate where the schema is with the schemaLocation attribute in the XML document's root element; if you use that attribute, you don't have to load the schema separately, as you see in this new version of this example's HTML page (for details on how JavaScript works, see the next chapter):

Listing ch05_04.html

```
<HTML>
    <HEAD>
        <TITLE>
            Using XML Schemas
        </TITLE>
    </HEAD>

    <BODY>
        <CENTER>
            <H1>Using XML Schemas</H1>
        </CENTER>

        <SCRIPT LANGUAGE="JavaScript">

            var doc = new ActiveXObject("MSXML2.DOMDocument.4.0");
            doc.validateOnParse = true;

            if (doc.load("ch05_05.xml")) {
                document.write("ch05_05.xml is valid.");
            } else {
                if (doc.parseError.errorCode != 0) {
                    document.write("Error: " + doc.parseError.reason);
                }
            }
        </SCRIPT>
    </BODY>
</HTML>
```

Here's the new XML document that this HTML page uses. Note the use of the schemaLocation attribute to indicate both the namespace (ch05) and the location of the schema (ch05_02.xsd):

Listing ch05_05.xml

```xml
<?xml version="1.0"?>
<ch05:document xmlns:xsi='http://www.w3.org/2001/XMLSchema-instance'
    xmlns:ch05 = 'http://starpowder'
    xsi:schemaLocation='http://starpowder ch05_02.xsd'>
    <ch05:data/>
</ch05:document>
```

When you load this new HTML page, ch05_04.html, into Internet Explorer, you'll get the same results as you see in Figure 5-1 (to run this example, ch05_02.xsd, ch05_04.html, and ch05_05.xml should all be in the same directory). As you can see, Internet Explorer does indeed offer support for XML schemas.

Here's another example—as discussed in Chapter 1, "Essential XML," Visual Basic.NET uses XML to transfer data. And it uses XML schema to validate that data. In fact, you can take a look at such schema directly.

To do that, you need a data set from a database. To take a look at the XML schema Visual Basic .NET uses for a particular dataset, use the Data | View Dataset Schema menu item. This opens the data set's schema, in a Visual Basic designer window, as you see in Figure 5-2.

Figure 5-2
Using XML schemas in Visual Basic .NET.

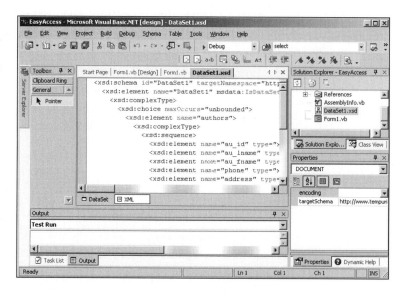

As you can see here and in many other applications, software support for XML schemas is now real. The next question is: Just how do you write a schema in the first place?

Writing XML Schemas

Most of this chapter centers on an example document, ch05_06.xml, and its accompanying schema, ch05_07.xsd. (You can use these examples with Internet Explorer's MSXML 4.0; it will validate ch05_06.xml using ch05_07.xsd.) This example is all about recording the books loaned by one person, Doug Glass, and borrowed by another, Britta Regensburg. I record the name and address of the borrower and lender, as well as data about the actual books borrowed, including their titles, publication date, replacement value, and the maximum number of days the book may be loaned for. Here's what ch05_06.xml looks like:

Listing ch05_06.xml

```
<?xml version="1.0"?>
<transaction borrowDate="2003-10-15">
    <Lender phone="607.555.2222">
        <name>Doug Glass</name>
        <street>416 Disk Drive</street>
        <city>Medfield</city>
        <state>MA</state>
    </Lender>
    <Borrower phone="310.555.1111">
        <name>Britta Regensburg</name>
        <street>219 Union Drive</street>
        <city>Medfield</city>
        <state>CA</state>
    </Borrower>
    <note>Lender wants these back in two weeks!</note>
    <books>
        <book bookID="123-4567-890">
            <bookTitle>Earthquakes for Breakfast</bookTitle>
            <pubDate>2003-10-20</pubDate>
            <replacementValue>15.95</replacementValue>
            <maxDaysOut>14</maxDaysOut>
        </book>
        <book bookID="123-4567-891">
            <bookTitle>Avalanches for Lunch</bookTitle>
            <pubDate>2003-10-21</pubDate>
            <replacementValue>19.99</replacementValue>
            <maxDaysOut>14</maxDaysOut>
        </book>
```

continues

Listing ch05_06.xml   Continued

```
        <book bookID="123-4567-892">
            <bookTitle>Meteor Showers for Dinner</bookTitle>
            <pubDate>2003-10-22</pubDate>
            <replacementValue>11.95</replacementValue>
            <maxDaysOut>14</maxDaysOut>
        </book>
        <book bookID="123-4567-893">
            <bookTitle>Snacking on Volcanoes</bookTitle>
            <pubDate>2003-10-23</pubDate>
            <replacementValue>17.99</replacementValue>
            <maxDaysOut>14</maxDaysOut>
        </book>
    </books>
</transaction>
```

Note in particular that this document has a root element named <transaction> and various subelements such as <Lender>, <Borrower>, and <books>. In fact, the subelements themselves have elements, such as the multiple <book> elements inside the <books> element.

In terms of XML schemas, elements that enclose subelements or that have attributes are *complex types*. Elements that enclose only simple data such as numbers, strings, or dates—but do not have any subelements—are *simple types*. In addition, attributes are always simple types because attribute values cannot contain any structure. If you look at a document as a tree, simple types have no subnodes, while complex types can have subnodes.

The distinction between simple and complex types is an important one because you declare these types differently. You declare complex types yourself; the XML schema specification comes with many simple types already declared, as we'll see. You can also declare your own simple types, and we'll how to do that as well.

Here's the schema for the document ch05_06.xml; this schema is named ch05_07.xsd, and the prefix xsd: is a prefix used by convention to indicate a W3C schema namespace. Besides xsd, you often find the prefix xs used for schema namespaces these days—which namespace you use is a matter of choice, or is up to the application you're working with. Note that like all schemas, ch05_07.xsd is a well-formed XML document:

Listing ch05_07.xsd

```
<xsd:schema xmlns:xsd="http://www.w3.org/2001/XMLSchema">

    <xsd:annotation>
        <xsd:documentation>
            Book borrowing transaction schema.
        </xsd:documentation>
    </xsd:annotation>

    <xsd:element name="transaction" type="transactionType"/>

    <xsd:complexType name="transactionType">
        <xsd:sequence>
            <xsd:element name="Lender" type="address"/>
            <xsd:element name="Borrower" type="address"/>
            <xsd:element ref="note" minOccurs="0"/>
            <xsd:element name="books" type="books"/>
        </xsd:sequence>
        <xsd:attribute name="borrowDate" type="xsd:date"/>
    </xsd:complexType>

    <xsd:element name="note" type="xsd:string"/>

    <xsd:complexType name="address">
        <xsd:sequence>
            <xsd:element name="name" type="xsd:string"/>
            <xsd:element name="street" type="xsd:string"/>
            <xsd:element name="city" type="xsd:string"/>
            <xsd:element name="state" type="xsd:NMTOKEN"/>
        </xsd:sequence>
        <xsd:attribute name="phone" type="xsd:string"
            use="optional"/>
    </xsd:complexType>

    <xsd:complexType name="books">
        <xsd:sequence>
            <xsd:element name="book" minOccurs="0" maxOccurs="10">
                <xsd:complexType>
                    <xsd:sequence>
                        <xsd:element name="bookTitle" type="xsd:string"/>
                        <xsd:element name="pubDate" type="xsd:date"
                        ➥minOccurs='0'/>
                        <xsd:element name="replacementValue"
                        ➥type="xsd:decimal"/>
                        <xsd:element name="maxDaysOut">
                            <xsd:simpleType>
                                <xsd:restriction base="xsd:integer">
                                    <xsd:maxExclusive value="14"/>
                                </xsd:restriction>
                            </xsd:simpleType>
```

continues

Listing ch05_07.xsd   Continued

```
                           </xsd:element>
                       </xsd:sequence>
                       <xsd:attribute name="bookID" type="catalogID"/>
                   </xsd:complexType>
               </xsd:element>
           </xsd:sequence>
       </xsd:complexType>

       <xsd:simpleType name="catalogID">
           <xsd:restriction base="xsd:string">
               <xsd:pattern value="\d{3}-\d{4}-\d{3}"/>
           </xsd:restriction>
       </xsd:simpleType>

</xsd:schema>
```

We'll go through the various parts of this schema in this chapter, but you can already see some of the structure here. Note, for example that you use a particular namespace in XML schemas (`"http://www.w3.org/2001/XMLSchema"`) and that the schema elements such as `<xsd:element>` are part of that namespace (you don't have to use the prefix `xsd:`, but it's conventional). As you can see, elements are declared with the `<xsd:element>` element, and attributes are declared with the `<xsd:attribute>` element. Furthermore, you specify the type of elements and attributes when you declare them. To create types, you can use the `<xsd:complexType>` and `<xsd:simpleType>` elements (you can then either create elements from the simple or complex types you've created or use the built-in simple types), schema annotations with the `<xsd:annotation>` element, and so on.

In this case, the root element of the document, `<transaction>`, is defined to be of the *type* `transactionType`. This element can contain several other elements, including those of the `address` and `books` types. The `address` type itself is defined to contain elements that hold a person's name and address. The `books` type holds elements named `<book>` that describe a book, including its title, publication date, and so on. Using this schema, you can describe the syntax of ch05_06.xml completely. I'll start taking this schema apart now as we explore it piece by piece.

What Elements Can You Use in Schemas?

So which elements do schemas support? You can see an overview in Table 5-2. You'll see many of these elements at work as you build schemas in this chapter.

Type	Description
all	Permits the elements in a group to appear in any order in the containing element.
annotation	Creates an annotation.
any	Permits any element from the given namespace(s) to appear in the containing sequence or choice element.
anyAttribute	Permits any attribute from the given namespace to appear in the containing complexType element or the containing attributeGroup element.
appinfo	Specifies information to be used by applications within an annotation element.
attribute	Creates an attribute.
attributeGroup	Groups attribute declarations so that they can be used as a group for complex type definitions.
choice	Permits one—and only one—of the elements contained in the group to appear in the containing element.
complexContent	Contains extensions or restrictions on a complex type that contains mixed content or elements only.
complexType	Defines a complex type, which supports attributes and element content.
documentation	Holds text to be read or used by users within an annotation element.
element	Creates an element.
extension	Extends a simple type or a complex type that has simple content.
field	Indicates an XML Path Language (XPath) expression that gives the value to define a constraint (unique, key, and keyref elements).
group	Groups a set of element declarations so that they can be incorporated as a group into complex type definitions.

Table 5-2
Schema Elements

continues

Type	Description
import	Imports a namespace whose schema components are referenced by the containing schema.
include	Includes the given schema document in the target namespace of the containing schema.
key key.	Indicates that an attribute or element value must be a
keyref	Indicates that an attribute or element value corresponds to the value of the given key or unique element.
list	Defines a simpleType element as a list of values of a given data type.
notation	Contains the definition of a notation to describe the format of non-XML data within an XML document.
redefine	Permits simple and complex types, as well as groups (and attribute groups from external schema files), to be redefined in the current schema.
restriction	Defines constraints, such as data types.
schema	Contains the definition of a schema.
selector	Indicates an XPath expression that selects a set of elements for an identity constraint for the unique, key, and keyref elements.
sequence	Requires the elements in the group to appear in the given sequence within the containing element.
simpleContent	Contains extensions or restrictions on a complexType element with character data or a simpleType element as content. Contains no elements.
simpleType	Defines a simple type.
union	Defines a simpleType element as a collection of values from given simple data types.
unique	Indicates that an attribute or element value must be unique.

Declaring Types and Elements

The most basic thing to understand about XML schemas is the concept of using simple and complex types, and how they relate to declaring elements. In schemas, unlike DTDs, you specify the type of the elements you declare.

That means that the first step in declaring elements is to make sure you have the types you want—and that often means defining new complex types. Complex types can enclose elements and have attributes, and simple types cannot do either. You can find the simple types built into XML schemas in Table 5-3. (When you specify these types in schemas, bear in mind that you'll preface them with the W3C schema prefix, usually `xsd:`.)

Type	Examples
anyURI	http://www.starpowder.com
base64Binary	GpM6
boolean	true, false, 1, 0
byte	-5, 116
date	2003-05-31
dateTime	2003-03-31T11:15:00.000-03:00
decimal	1.234, -1.234, 6000.00
double	12, 12.34E-5, 1.2222
duration	P1Y1M4DT10H50M11.7S
ENTITIES	(XML entities)
ENTITY	(XML entity)
float	12, 12.34E-5, 1.2222
gDay	---30
gMonth	--04--
gMonthDay	--03-30
gYear	2003
gYearMonth	2003-02
hexBinary	0BB6

Table 5-3
Simple Types
Built into XML
Schema

continues

Type	Examples
ID	(XML ID)
IDREF	(XML ID REF)
IDREFS	(XML ID REFS)
int	10, 12345678
integer	-123456, -1, 10
language	en-US, fr, de
long	-1234, 12345678901234
Name	George
NCName	USData
negativeInteger	-123, -1345
NMTOKEN	US
NMTOKENS	US UK, DE UK FR
nonNegativeInteger	0, 1, 12345
nonPositiveInteger	-1234, -1, 0
normalizedString	Here is some text
NOTATION	(XML NOTATION)
positiveInteger	1, 12345
QName	doc:Data
short	-12, 1234
string	Here is some text
time	11:15:00.000
token	Here is some text
unsignedByte	0, 127
unsignedInt	0, 12345678
unsignedLong	0, 12678967543233
unsignedShort	0, 12678

Compatibility Between XML Schema and DTDs

If you want to ensure compatibility between XML Schema and XML DTDs, you should use only the simple types ID, IDREF, IDREFS, ENTITY, ENTITIES, NOTATION, NMTOKEN, and NMTOKENS when declaring attributes.

You create new complex types using the <xsd:complexType> element in schemas. A complex type definition itself usually contains element declarations, references to other elements, and attribute declarations. You declare elements with the <xsd:element> element, and you declare attributes with the <xsd:attribute> element. As in DTDs, element declarations specify the syntax of an element. In schemas, though element declarations can specify the elements' type as well. You can specify the type of attributes as well.

Here's an example from ch05_07.xsd. In this case, I'm declaring a complex type named address, which holds the elements that make up a person's address, in this order. (The <xsd:sequence> element indicates that this is the order the contained elements should appear in. If you don't want to specify the order, use an element such as <xsd:all> instead—see "Creating all Groups," later in this chapter.)

```
<xsd:complexType name="address">
    <xsd:sequence>
        <xsd:element name="name" type="xsd:string"/>
        <xsd:element name="street" type="xsd:string"/>
        <xsd:element name="city" type="xsd:string"/>
        <xsd:element name="state" type="xsd:NMTOKEN"/>
    </xsd:sequence>
    <xsd:attribute name="phone" type="xsd:string"
        use="optional"/>
</xsd:complexType>
```

I'll use address as the type of the <Lender> and <Borrower> elements so that I can store the address of the books' lender and borrower. That declaration looks like this:

```
<xsd:complexType name="transactionType">
    <xsd:sequence>
        <xsd:element name="Lender" type="address"/>
        <xsd:element name="Borrower" type="address"/>
        <xsd:element ref="note" minOccurs="0"/>
        <xsd:element name="books" type="books"/>
    <xsd:sequence>
    <xsd:attribute name="borrowDate" type="xsd:date"/>
</xsd:complexType>
```

In the address type, I'm indicating that any element of this type must have four elements and one attribute. Those elements are <name>, <street>, <city>, and <state>; the attribute is phone. Note how the declarations for these elements set their data types as well: <name>, <street>, and <city> must all be of type xsd:string, and the <state> element must be of type NMTOKEN. The attribute phone must be of type xsd:string as well.

The definition of the address complex type contains only declarations based on the simple type xsd:string. On the other hand, complex types can themselves contain elements that are based on complex types. You can see how this works in the transactionType, which is the type of ch05_06.xml's root element, <transaction>. In this case, two of the elements, <Lender> and <Borrower>, are themselves of the address type.

Note that the transactionType type also includes an attribute, borrowDate, which is of the simple type xsd:date. Attributes are always of a simple type because attributes can't have internal content.

After you've defined a new type, you can declare new elements of that type. For example, after declaring the transactionType, you can declare the <transaction> element, which is the root element of the document, to be of that type, like this:

```
<xsd:element name="transaction" type="transactionType"/>

<xsd:complexType name="transactionType">
    <xsd:sequence>
        <xsd:element name="Lender" type="address"/>
        <xsd:element name="Borrower" type="address"/>
        <xsd:element ref="note" minOccurs="0"/>
        <xsd:element name="books" type="books"/>
    <xsd:sequence>
    <xsd:attribute name="borrowDate" type="xsd:date"/>
</xsd:complexType>
```

So far, then, we've gotten an overview of how to create new element and attribute declarations. You use <xsd:element> and <xsd:attribute> elements and set the type attribute of those elements to the type you want. If you want to use a complex type, you'll have to create it, and you do that with the <xsd:complexType> element (we'll see how to create simple types in a few pages).

Now take a look at the declaration for the `<note>` element in the transactionType type:

```xsd
<xsd:complexType name="transactionType">
    <xsd:sequence>
        <xsd:element name="Lender" type="address"/>
        <xsd:element name="Borrower" type="address"/>
        <xsd:element ref="note" minOccurs="0"/>
        <xsd:element name="books" type="books"/>
    </xsd:sequence>
    <xsd:attribute name="borrowDate" type="xsd:date"/>
</xsd:complexType>
```

Here, I'm not declaring a new element. Instead, I'm including an already existing element by *referring* to it. That is to say, the `<note>` element already exists because we've declared it separately like this:

```xsd
<xsd:complexType name="transactionType">
    <xsd:sequence>
        <xsd:element name="Lender" type="address"/>
        <xsd:element name="Borrower" type="address"/>
        <xsd:element ref="note" minOccurs="0"/>
        <xsd:element name="books" type="books"/>
    </xsd:sequence>
    <xsd:attribute name="borrowDate" type="xsd:date"/>
</xsd:complexType>
<xsd:element name="note" type="xsd:string"/>
```

Using the `ref` attribute lets you include an element that has already been defined in a complex type definition. However, you can't just include any element by reference—the element you refer to must have been declared *globally*, which means that it itself is not part of any other complex type. A global element or attribute declaration appears as an immediate child element of the `<xsd:schema>` element. When you declare an element or attribute globally, it can be used in any complex type. Using the `ref` attribute in this way is a powerful technique because it lets you avoid redefining elements that already exist globally.

Now I'll take a look at how to specify how many times elements can occur in a complex type.

Specifying How Often Elements Can Occur

I've indicated that the `<note>` element can either appear or not appear in elements of the `transactionType`. This is because I've set the `minOccurs` attribute like this, which indicates that the minimum number of times this element can occur is zero:

```
<xsd:complexType name="transactionType">
    <xsd:sequence>
        <xsd:element name="Lender" type="address"/>
        <xsd:element name="Borrower" type="address"/>
        <xsd:element ref="note" minOccurs="0"/>
        <xsd:element name="books" type="books"/>
    <xsd:sequence>
    <xsd:attribute name="borrowDate" type="xsd:date"/>
/xsd:complexType>
```

In general, you can specify the minimum number of times an element appears with the `minOccurs` attribute and the maximum number of times it can appear with the `maxOccurs` attribute. For example, here's how I would say that the `<note>` element can appear from zero to five times in the `transactionType` type:

```
<xsd:complexType name="transactionType">
    <xsd:sequence>
        <xsd:element name="Lender" type="address"/>
        <xsd:element name="Borrower" type="address"/>
    <xsd:element ref="note" minOccurs="0" maxOccurs="5"/>
        <xsd:element name="books" type="books"/>
    <xsd:sequence>
    <xsd:attribute name="borrowDate" type="xsd:date"/>
</xsd:complexType>
```

minOccurs and *maxOccurs*

The default value for `minOccurs` is 1. If you don't specify a value for `maxOccurs`, its default value is the value of `minOccurs`. To indicate that there is no upper bound to the `maxOccurs` attribute, set it to the value `unbounded`.

Specifying Default Values for Elements

In addition to the `minOccurs` and `maxOccurs` attributes, you can use the `<xsd:element>` element's `fixed` and `default` attributes to indicate values that an element must have (you use one of these attributes, not both together). For example, setting `fixed` to `400` means that the element's value must always be 400. Setting the default value to 400, on the other hand, means that the default value for the element is 400, but if the element appears in the document, its actual value is the value it encloses.

For example, here I'm setting the value of an element named <maxTrials> to 100 and specifying that it must always be 100, using the fixed attribute in the <xsd:element> element:

```
<xsd:element name="maxTrials" type="xsd:integer" fixed="100"/>
```

And here I'm giving this element the *default* value of 100 instead of fixing its value at 100:

```
<xsd:element name="maxTrials" type="xsd:integer" default="100"/>
```

Specifying Attribute Constraints and Defaults

As with elements, you can specify the type of attributes, but unlike elements, attributes must be of a simple type. And you don't use minOccurs and maxOccurs for attributes because attributes can appear only once, at most. Instead, you use a different syntax when constraining attributes.

You declare attributes with the <xsd:attribute> element, and the <xsd:attribute> element itself has a type attribute that gives the attribute's (simple) type. So how do you indicate whether an attribute is required or optional, or whether there's a default value, or even whether the value of the attribute is fixed at a certain value? You use the <xsd:attribute> element's use and value attributes.

The use attribute specifies whether the attribute is required or optional and, if optional, whether the attribute's value is fixed or whether there is a default. The second attribute, value, holds any value that is needed.

For example, I've added an attribute named phone to the Address type; this attribute is of type xsd:string, and its use is optional:

```
<xsd:complexType name="address">
    <xsd:sequence>
        <xsd:element name="name" type="xsd:string"/>
        <xsd:element name="street" type="xsd:string"/>
        <xsd:element name="city" type="xsd:string"/>
        <xsd:element name="state" type="xsd:NMTOKEN"/>
    </xsd:sequence>
```

```
    <xsd:attribute name="phone" type="xsd:string"
        use="optional"/>
</xsd:complexType>
```

Here are the possible values for the use attribute:

- required—The attribute is required and may have any value.

- optional—The attribute is optional and may have any value.

- fixed—The attribute value is fixed, and you set its value with the value attribute.

- default—If the attribute does not appear, its value is the default value set with the value attribute. If it does appear, its value is the value it is assigned in the document.

- prohibited—The attribute must not appear.

For example, this attribute declaration creates an integer attribute named counter whose value is always 400:

```
<xsd:attribute name="counter" type="xsd:int"
use="fixed" value="400">
```

And this attribute declaration means that the counter attribute has a default value of 400 if it is not used, and it has the value assigned to it if it is used:

```
<xsd:attribute name="counter" type="xsd:int"
use="default" value="400">
```

Creating Simple Types

Most of the types I've used in ch05_07.xsd are simple types that come built into the XML schema specification, such as xsd:string, xsd:integer, xsd:date, and so on. However, take a look at the attribute named bookID: this attribute is declared to be of the type catalogID:

```
<xsd:complexType name="books">
    <xsd:sequence>
        <xsd:element name="book" minOccurs="0" maxOccurs="10">
            <xsd:complexType>
                <xsd:sequence>
                    <xsd:element name="bookTitle" type="xsd:string"/>
                    <xsd:element name="pubDate" type="xsd:date"
                    ➥minOccurs='0'/>
```

```
              <xsd:element name="replacementValue" type="xsd:decimal"/>
                  <xsd:element name="maxDaysOut">
                      <xsd:simpleType>
                          <xsd:restriction base="xsd:integer">
                              <xsd:maxExclusive value="14"/>
                          </xsd:restriction>
                      </xsd:simpleType>
                  </xsd:element>
              </xsd:sequence>
                  <xsd:attribute name="bookID" type="catalogID"/>
          </xsd:complexType>
      </xsd:element>
  </xsd:sequence>
</xsd:complexType>
```

This type, `catalogID`, is itself a simple type that is not built into the XML schema specification; instead, I've defined it with the `<simpleType>` element like this:

```
<xsd:simpleType name="catalogID">
    <xsd:restriction base="xsd:string">
        <xsd:pattern value="\d{3}-\d{4}-\d{3}"/>
    </xsd:restriction>
</xsd:simpleType>
```

Note in particular that you must base new simple types such as `catalogID` on already existing simple type (either a built-in simple type or one you've created—here, I'm using the built-in `xsd:string` type). To do that, you use the base attribute in the `<xsd:restriction>` element. In the case of the `catalogID` type, I've based it on the `xsd:string` type with the attribute/value pair `base="xsd:string"`. To describe the properties of new simple types, XML schemas use *facets*.

Creating Simple Types Using Facets

Using facets lets you restrict the data a simple type can hold. For example, say that you want to create a simple type named `dayOfMonth` that can hold only values between 1 and 31, inclusive. In that case, you can define it this way, using the two facets `minInclusive` and `maxInclusive`:

```
<xsd:simpleType name="dayOfMonth">
    <xsd:restriction base="xsd:integer">
        <xsd:minInclusive value="1"/>
        <xsd:maxInclusive value="31"/>
    </xsd:restriction>
 </xsd:simpleType>
```

Now that you've created this new simple type, you can declare elements and attributes of this type.

In ch05_07.xsd, the catalogID simple type is even more powerful than this dayOfMonth simple type. The catalogID simple type uses the pattern *facet* to specify a *regular expression* (that is, a pattern set up to match text in the format you specify) that text strings values for this type must match:

```
<xsd:simpleType name="catalogID">
    <xsd:restriction base="xsd:string">
        <xsd:pattern value="\d{3}-\d{4}-\d{3}"/>
    </xsd:restriction>
</xsd:simpleType>
```

In this case, the text in the simpleType type must match the regular expression "\d{3}-\d{4}-\d{3}", which matches text strings made up of three digits, a hyphen, four digits, another hyphen, and three digits.

About Regular Expressions

The regular expressions used in XML schema facets are the same as those used in the Perl programming language. You can find the complete documentation for Perl regular expressions at the Comprehensive Perl Archive Network (CPAN) Web site: www.cpan.org/doc/manual/html/pod/perlre.html. (Regular expressions are not a skill you'll need in this book.)

The catalogID type is the type of the <book> element's bookID attribute, so I can specify book ID values like this in ch05_06.xml, matching the regular expression I've used for this attribute:

```
<book bookID="123-4567-890">
    <bookTitle>Earthquakes for Breakfast</bookTitle>
    <pubDate>2003-10-20</pubDate>
    <replacementValue>15.95</replacementValue>
    <maxDaysOut>14</maxDaysOut>
</book>
```

What facets are there, and what built-in simple types support them? You'll find the general facets, listed by the simple types that support them, in Table 5-4.

	Type	length	min Length	max Length	pattern	enumer- ation	White- space
Table 5-4 Simple Types and Applicable Facets	anyURI	X	X	X	X	X	X
	base64Binary	X	X	X	X	X	X
	boolean				X		X
	byte				X	X	X
	date				X	X	X
	dateTime				X	X	X
	decimal				X	X	X
	double				X	X	X
	duration				X	X	X
	ENTITIES	X	X	X		X	X
	ENTITY	X	X	X	X	X	X
	float				X	X	X
	gDay				X	X	X
	gMonth				X	X	X
	gMonthDay				X	X	X
	gYear				X	X	X
	gYearMonth				X	X	X
	hexBinary	X	X	X	X	X	X
	ID	X	X	X	X	X	X
	IDREF	X	X	X	X	X	X
	IDREFS	X	X	X		X	X
	int				X	X	X
	integer				X	X	X
	language	X	X	X	X	X	X
	long				X	X	X
	Name	X	X	X	X	X	X

continues

Type	length	min Length	max Length	pattern	enumeration	Whitespace
NCName	X	X	X	X	X	X
negativeInteger				X	X	X
NMTOKEN	X	X	X	X	X	X
NMTOKENS	X	X	X		X	X
nonNegativeInteger				X	X	X
nonPositiveInteger				X	X	X
normalizedString	X	X	X	X	X	X
NOTATION	X	X	X	X	X	X
positiveInteger				X	X	X
QName	X	X	X	X	X	X
short				X	X	X
string	X	X	X	X	X	X
time				X	X	X
token	X	X	X	X	X	X
unsignedBxte				X	X	X
unsignedInt				X	X	X
unsignedLong				X	X	X
unsignedShort				X	X	X

The numeric simple types and those simple types that can be ordered also have some additional facets, which you see in Table 5-5.

Table 5-5	Type	max Inclusive	max Exclusive	min Inclusive	min Exclusive	Total Digits	Fraction Digits
Ordered Simple Types and Applicable Facets	byte	X	X	X	X	X	X
	unsignedByte	X	X	X	X	X	X
	integer	X	X	X	X	X	X
	positiveInteger	X	X	X	X	X	X
	negativeInteger	X	X	X	X	X	X
	nonNegativeInteger	X	X	X	X	X	X
	nonPositiveInteger	X	X	X	X	X	X
	int	X	X	X	X	X	X
	unsignedInt	X	X	X	X	X	X
	long	X	X	X	X	X	X
	unsignedLong	X	X	X	X	X	X
	short	X	X	X	X	X	X
	unsignedShort	X	X	X	X	X	X
	decimal	X	X	X	X	X	X
	float	X	X	X	X		
	double	X	X	X	X		
	time	X	X	X	X		
	dateTime	X	X	X	X		
	duration	X	X	X	X		
	date	X	X	X	X		
	gMonth	X	X	X	X		
	gYear	X	X	X	X		
	gYearMonth	X	X	X	X		
	gDay	X	X	X	X		
	gMonthDay	X	X	X	X		

Of all the facets you see in Tables 5-4 and 5-5, my favorites are `minInclusive`, `maxInclusive`, `pattern`, and `enumeration`. We've seen the first three, but not the `enumeration` facet yet.

The `enumeration` facet lets you set up an enumeration of values, exactly as you can do in DTDs (as we saw in the previous chapter). Using an enumeration, you can restrict the possible values of a simple type to a list of values that you specify.

For example, to set up a simple type named `weekday` whose values can be `"Sunday"`, `"Monday"`, `"Tuesday"`, `"Wednesday"`, `"Thursday"`, `"Friday"`, and `"Saturday"`, you'd define that type like this:

```
<xsd:simpleType name="weekday">
    <xsd:restriction base="xsd:string">
        <xsd:enumeration value="Sunday"/>
        <xsd:enumeration value="Monday"/>
        <xsd:enumeration value="Tuesday"/>
        <xsd:enumeration value="Wednesday"/>
        <xsd:enumeration value="Thursday"/>
        <xsd:enumeration value="Friday"/>
        <xsd:enumeration value="Saturday"/>
    </xsd:restriction>
</xsd:simpleType>
```

Using Anonymous Type Definitions

So far, all the element declarations we've used in the ch05_07.xsd schema have used the `type` attribute to indicate the new element's type. But what if you want to use a type only once? Do you have to go to the trouble of declaring it and naming it, all to use it in only one element declaration?

It turns out that there is an easier way. You can use an *anonymous type definition* to avoid having to define a whole new type that you'll reference only once. Using an anonymous type definition simply means that you enclose a `<xsd:simpleType>` or `<xsd:complexType>` element inside an `<xsd:element>` element declaration. In this case, you don't assign an explicit value to the `type` attribute in the `<xsd:element>` element because the anonymous type you're using doesn't have a name. (In fact, you can tell that an anonymous type definition is being used if an `<xsd:complexType>` element does not include a `type` attribute.)

Here's an example from ch05_07.xsd. In this case, I'll use an anonymous type definition for the `<book>` element. This element holds `<bookTitle>`, `<pubDate>`, `<replacementValue>`, and `<maxDaysOut>` elements. It will also have an attribute named `bookID`, so it looks like a good one to create from a complex type. Instead of declaring a separate complex type, however, I'll just put a `<xsd:complexType>` element *inside* the `<xsd:element>` element that declares `<book>`:

```
<xsd:element name="book" minOccurs="0" maxOccurs="10">
    <xsd:complexType>
    .
    .
    .
    </xsd:complexType>
</xsd:element>
```

Now I'm free to add the elements I want inside the `<book>` element—without defining a named, separate complex type at all:

```
<xsd:element name="book" minOccurs="0" maxOccurs="10">
    <xsd:complexType>
        <xsd:sequence>
            <xsd:element name="bookTitle" type="xsd:string"/>
            <xsd:element name="pubDate" type="xsd:date" minOccurs='0'/>
            <xsd:element name="replacementValue" type="xsd:decimal"/>
            .
            .
            .
        </xsd:sequence>
    </xsd:complexType>
</xsd:element>
```

You can also use simple anonymous types. For example, the `<maxDaysOut>` element holds the maximum number of days that a book is supposed to be out. To set the maximum number of days that a book can be out to 14, I use a new simple anonymous type so that I can use the `maxExclusive` facet like this:

```
<xsd:element name="book" minOccurs="0" maxOccurs="10">
    <xsd:complexType>
        <xsd:sequence>
            <xsd:element name="bookTitle" type="xsd:string"/>
            <xsd:element name="pubDate" type="xsd:date" minOccurs='0'/>
        <xsd:element name="replacementValue" type="xsd:decimal"/>
            <xsd:element name="maxDaysOut">
                <xsd:simpleType>
                    <xsd:restriction base="xsd:integer">
                        <xsd:maxExclusive value="14"/>
                    </xsd:restriction>
                </xsd:simpleType>
            </xsd:element>
```

```
            .
            .
            .
        </xsd:sequence>
      </xsd:complexType>
</xsd:element>
```

You can also include attribute declarations in anonymous type definitions, like this:

```
xsd:element name="book" minOccurs="0" maxOccurs="10">
    <xsd:complexType>
        <xsd:sequence>
            <xsd:element name="bookTitle" type="xsd:string"/>
            <xsd:element name="pubDate" type="xsd:date" minOccurs='0'/>
             <xsd:element name="replacementValue" type="xsd:decimal"/>
            <xsd:element name="maxDaysOut">
                <xsd:simpleType>
                    <xsd:restriction base="xsd:integer">
                        <xsd:maxExclusive value="14"/>
                    </xsd:restriction>
                </xsd:simpleType>
            </xsd:element>
        </xsd:sequence>
        <xsd:attribute name="bookID" type="catalogID"/>
    </xsd:complexType>
</xsd:element>
```

Now I'll take a look at declaring empty elements.

Creating Empty Elements

Empty elements have no content, but they can have attributes. So how do you declare them in an XML schema? You do that by declaring a complex type and using the `<xsd:complexContent>` element. In effect, you are declaring an element that can contain only elements but that does not contain any elements, so it's an empty element.

Here's an example. In this case, I'm going to create a new empty element named `<image>` that can take three attributes—source, width, and height—like this: `<image source="/images/cover.gif" height="255" width=512 />`. I start by declaring this element:

```
<xsd:element name="image">
    .
    .
    .
</xsd:element>
```

I haven't used the type attribute in this element's declaration because I'll use an anonymous type definition to base this element on. To create the anonymous type, I use a `<complexType>` and a `<complexContent>` element:

```
<xsd:element name="image">
    <xsd:complexType>
        <xsd:complexContent>
            .
            .
            .
        </xsd:complexContent>
    </xsd:complexType>
</xsd:element>
```

Finally, I use a `<xsd:restriction>` element with the type attribute set to xsd:anyType, and add the attributes this element will use:

```
<xsd:element name="image">
    <xsd:complexType>
        <xsd:complexContent>
            <xsd:restriction base="xsd:anyType">
                <xsd:attribute name="source" type="xsd:string" />
                <xsd:attribute name="width" type="xsd:decimal" />
                <xsd:attribute name="height" type="xsd:decimal" />
            </xsd:restriction>
        </xsd:complexContent>
    </xsd:complexType>
</xsd:element>
```

And that's all it takes—now the empty element `<image>` is ready to be used.

Creating Mixed-Content Elements

So far, the plain text in the documents we've looked at in this chapter has been confined to the deepest elements in the document—that is, to elements that enclose no child elements, just text. However, as you know, you can also create elements that support *mixed content*—both text and other elements. You can create mixed-content elements with schemas as well as DTDs. In these elements, character data can appear at the same level as child elements.

Here's an example document that shows what mixed-content elements look like using the elements we've declared in ch05_07.xsd. In this case, I'm creating a new element named `<reminder>` that encloses a reminder letter to a book borrower reminding him to return a book:

```
<?xml version="1.0">
<reminder>
    Dear <name>Britta Regensburg</name>:
        The book <bookTitle>Snacking on Volcanoes</bookTitle>
```

```
was only supposed to be out for <maxDaysOut>14</maxDaysOut>
days. Please return it or pay
$<replacementValue>17.99</replacementValue>.
Thank you.
</reminder>
```

This document uses elements that we've defined before, character data, and the new `<reminder>` element. The `<reminder>` element is the one that has a mixed-content model; to declare it in a schema, I'll start by creating an anonymous new complex type like this inside the declaration for `<reminder>`. To indicate that this element can handle mixed content, you set the `<complexType>` element's mixed attribute to `true`:

```
<xsd:element name="reminder">
    <xsd:complexType mixed="true">
    .
    .
    .
    </xsd:complexType>
</xsd:element>
```

Now all I have to do is to add the declarations for the elements that you can use inside the `<reminder>` element, like this:

```
<xsd:element name="reminder">
    <xsd:complexType mixed="true">
        <xsd:sequence>
            <xsd:element name="name" type="xsd:string"/>
            <xsd:element name="bookTitle" type="xsd:string"/>
            <xsd:element name="maxDaysOut">
                <xsd:simpleType>
                    <xsd:restriction base="xsd:integer">
                        <xsd:maxExclusive value="14"/>
                    </xsd:restriction>
                </xsd:simpleType>
            </xsd:element>
            <xsd:element name="replacementValue" type="xsd:decimal"/>
        </xsd:sequence>
    </xsd:complexType>
</xsd:element>
```

As you might recall from our discussion of DTDs, you can't constrain the order or number of child elements appearing in a mixed-model element. There's more power available when it comes to schemas, however: Here, the order and number of child elements does have to correspond to the order and number of child elements that you specify in the schema. In other words, even though DTDs provide only partial syntax specifications for mixed-content models, schemas provide much more complete syntax specifications.

Annotating Schemas

In DTDs, you can use XML comments to add annotations and provide documentation. In schemas, you might expect that the situation would be a little more complex, and you'd be right. XML schemas define three additional elements that you use to add annotations to schemas: `<xsd:annotation>`, `<xsd:documentation>`, and `<xsd:appInfo>`.

Here's how things work: The `<xsd:annotation>` element is the container element for `<xsd:documentation>` and `<xsd:appInfo>` elements. The `<xsd:documentation>` element holds text of the kind you'd expect to see in a normal comment—that is, text designed for human readers. As its name implies, the `<xsd:appInfo>` element, on the other hand, holds annotations suitable for applications that read the document. Such applications can pick up information from `<xsd:appInfo>` elements if those elements are constructed in a way they recognize.

Here's an example using the `<xsd:annotation>` and `<xsd:documentation>` elements, adding an explanatory comment at the beginning of the ch05_07.xsd schema:

```
<xsd:schema xmlns:xsd="http://www.w3.org/2001/XMLSchema">

    <xsd:annotation>
        <xsd:documentation>
            Book borrowing transaction schema.
        </xsd:documentation>
    </xsd:annotation>
    .
    .
    .
```

In fact, you can use the `<xsd:annotation>` element at the beginning of most schema constructions, such as the `<xsd:schema>`, `<xsd:complexType>`, `<xsd:simpleType>`, `<xsd:element>`, and `<xsd:attribute>` elements, and so on. Here's an example in which I've added an annotation to a complex type in ch05_07.xsd:

```
<xsd:schema xmlns:xsd="http://www.w3.org/2001/XMLSchema">

    <xsd:annotation>
        <xsd:documentation>
            Book borrowing transaction schema.
        </xsd:documentation>
    </xsd:annotation>

    <xsd:element name="transaction" type="transactionType"/>
```

```
<xsd:complexType name="transactionType">
<xsd:annotation>
    <xsd:documentation>
        This type is used by the root element.
    </xsd:documentation>
</xsd:annotation>
    <xsd:sequence>
        <xsd:element name="Lender" type="address"/>
        <xsd:element name="Borrower" type="address"/>
        <xsd:element ref="note" minOccurs="0"/>
        <xsd:element name="books" type="books"/>
    <xsd:sequence>
    <xsd:attribute name="borrowDate" type="xsd:date"/>
</xsd:complexType>
.
.
.
```

As we've seen with DTDs, you can create choices and sequences of elements—and as you might expect, you can do the same with schemas.

Creating Choices

A choice lets you specify a number of elements, only one of which will be chosen. To create a choice in XML schemas, you use the <xsd:choice> element. The code that follows is an example. In this case, I'll change the transactionType type so that the borrower can borrow either several books or just one book. I do this by creating an <xsd:choice> element that holds both a <books> element and a <book> element. Note that, in this case, the <book> element needs to be made into a global element so I can refer to it in this choice. Thus, I remove it from the declaration of the <books> element, as you see here:

```
xsd:complexType name="transactionType">
    <xsd:sequence>
        <xsd:element name="Lender" type="address"/>
        <xsd:element name="Borrower" type="address"/>
        <xsd:element ref="note" minOccurs="0"/>
        <xsd:choice>
            <xsd:element name="books" type="books"/>
            <xsd:element ref="book"/>
        <xsd:choice>
    </xsd:sequence>
    <xsd:attribute name="borrowDate" type="xsd:date"/>
</xsd:complexType>
```

```
<xsd:complexType name="books">
    <xsd:sequence>
        <xsd:element ref="book" minOccurs="0" maxOccurs="10" />
    </xsd:sequence>
</xsd:complexType>

<xsd:element name="book">
    <xsd:complexType>
        <xsd:sequence>
            <xsd:element name="bookTitle" type="xsd:string"/>
            <xsd:element name="pubDate" type="xsd:date" minOccurs='0'/>
            <xsd:element name="replacementValue" type="xsd:decimal"/>
            <xsd:element name="maxDaysOut">
                <xsd:simpleType>
                    <xsd:restriction base="xsd:integer">
                        <xsd:maxExclusive value="14"/>
                    </xsd:restriction>
                </xsd:simpleType>
            </xsd:element>
        </xsd:sequence>
        <xsd:attribute name="bookID" type="catalogID"/>
    </xsd:complexType>
</xsd:element>
```

Next, I'll take a look at creating sequences.

Creating Element Groups

Say that I wanted to let the borrower borrow not just books, but also a magazine. To do that, I can create a new *group* named booksAndMagazine. A group collects elements together, and you can name groups. You can then include a group in other elements using the <xsd:group> element and referring to the group by name:

```
<xsd:complexType name="transactionType">
    <xsd:sequence>
        <xsd:element name="Lender" type="address"/>
        <xsd:element name="Borrower" type="address"/>
        <xsd:element ref="note" minOccurs="0"/>
        <xsd:choice>
            <xsd:element name="books" type="books"/>
            <xsd:element ref="book"/>
            <xsd:group ref="booksAndMagazine"/>
        </xsd:choice>
    </xsd:sequence>
    <xsd:attribute name="borrowDate" type="xsd:date"/>
</xsd:complexType>
```

To create the group named booksAndMagazine, I use the <xsd:group> element; to ensure that the elements inside that group appear in a specific sequence, I use the <xsd:sequence> element this way:

```
<xsd:complexType name="transactionType">
    <xsd:sequence>
        <xsd:element name="Lender" type="address"/>
        <xsd:element name="Borrower" type="address"/>
        <xsd:element ref="note" minOccurs="0"/>
        <xsd:choice>
            <xsd:element name="books" type="books"/>
            <xsd:element ref="book"/>
            <xsd:group ref="booksAndMagazine"/>
        </xsd:choice>
    </xsd:sequence>
    <xsd:attribute name="borrowDate" type="xsd:date"/>
</xsd:complexType>
```

```
<xsd:group name="booksAndMagazine">
    <xsd:sequence>
        <xsd:element ref="books"/>
        <xsd:element ref="magazine"/>
    </xsd:sequence>
</xsd:group>
```

Creating Attribute Groups

You can also create groups of attributes using the <xsd:attributeGroup> element. For example, say that I wanted to add a number of attributes to the <book> element that describe the book. To do that, I can create an attribute group named bookDescription and then reference that attribute group in the declaration for <book>:

```
<xsd:element name="book">
    <xsd:complexType>
        <xsd:sequence>
            <xsd:element name="bookTitle" type="xsd:string"/>
            <xsd:element name="pubDate" type="xsd:date" minOccurs='0'/>
            <xsd:element name="replacementValue" type="xsd:decimal"/>
            <xsd:element name="maxDaysOut">
                <xsd:simpleType>
                    <xsd:restriction base="xsd:integer">
                        <xsd:maxExclusive value="14"/>
                    </xsd:restriction>
                </xsd:simpleType>
            </xsd:element>
        </xsd:sequence>
```

```
            <xsd:attributeGroup ref="bookDescription"/>
        </xsd:complexType>
</xsd:element>
```

To create the attribute group bookDescription, I just use the <xsd:attributeGroup> element, enclosing the <xsd:attribute> elements that I use to declare the attributes in the <xsd:attributeGroup> element:

```
<xsd:element name="book">
    <xsd:complexType>
        <xsd:sequence>
            <xsd:element name="bookTitle" type="xsd:string"/>
            <xsd:element name="pubDate" type="xsd:date" minOccurs='0'/>
            <xsd:element name="replacementValue" type="xsd:decimal"/>
            <xsd:element name="maxDaysOut">
               <xsd:simpleType>
                   <xsd:restriction base="xsd:integer">
                       <xsd:maxExclusive value="14"/>
                   </xsd:restriction>
               </xsd:simpleType>
            </xsd:element>
        </xsd:sequence>
        <xsd:attributeGroup ref="bookDescription"/>
    </xsd:complexType>
</xsd:element>

<xsd:attributeGroup name="bookDescription">
    <xsd:attribute name="bookID" type="CatalogID"/>
    <xsd:attribute name="numberPages" type="xsd:decimal"/>
    <xsd:attribute name="coverType">
        <xsd:simpleType>
            <xsd:restriction base="xsd:string">
                <xsd:enumeration value="leather"/>
                <xsd:enumeration value="cloth"/>
                <xsd:enumeration value="vinyl"/>
            </xsd:restriction>
        </xsd:simpleType>
    </xsd:attribute>
</xsd:attributeGroup>
```

Using Groups

It's worth noticing that the process of creating a group of elements or attributes and then referencing that group in another element mimics the use of parameter entities in DTDs. You do the same thing in a fairly similar way: include a group or elements or attributes. There are no such things as parameter entities in schemas, but using groups, you can accomplish most of what parameter entities are used for in DTDs.

As you can see, schemas provide some sophisticated mechanisms for building documents from pieces.

Creating *all* Groups

Schemas support another type of group: the `all` group. All the elements in an `all` group may appear once or not at all, and they may appear in any order. This group must be used at the top level of the content model, and the group's children must be individual elements—that is, this group must itself contain no groups. In addition, any element in this content model can appear no more than once (which means that the allowed values of `minOccurs` and `maxOccurs` are `0` and `1` only).

Here's an example. In this case, I'm converting the `transactionType` type into an `all` group:

```
<xsd:complexType name="transactionType">
<xsd:all>
    <xsd:element name="Lender" type="address"/>
    <xsd:element name="Borrower" type="address"/>
    <xsd:element ref="note" minOccurs="0"/>
    <xsd:element name="books" type="books"/>
</xsd:all>
    <xsd:attribute name="borrowDate" type="xsd:date"/>
</xsd:complexType>
```

This means that the elements in this type may now appear in any order, but they can appear only once, at most. Another important point is that if you use it, an `<xsd:all>` group must contain all the element declarations in a content model (that is, you can't declare additional elements in the content model but outside the group).

Schemas and Namespaces

One of the big ideas behind schemas was to allow XML processors to validate documents that use namespaces (which DTDs have a problem with). Toward that end, the `<schema>` element has a new attribute: `targetNamespace`.

The `targetNamespace` attribute specifies the namespace the schema is *targeted* to (that is, intended for). This means that if an XML processor is validating a document and is checking elements in a particular namespace, it will know what schema to check based on the schema's target namespace. That's the idea behind target namespaces—you can indicate what namespace a schema is targeted to so that an XML processor can determine which schema(s) to use to validate a document. For an example using the `targetNamespace` attribute, see "Using XML Schemas in Internet Explorer," at the beginning of this chapter.

You can also specify whether the elements and attributes that were *locally* declared in a schema need to be qualified when used in a namespace. We've seen globally declared elements and attributes in schemas: They're declared at the top level in the schema, directly under the `<schema>` element. All the other elements and attributes declared in a schema—that is, those not declared as direct children of the `<schema>` element—are locally declared. Schemas allow you to indicate whether locals need to be qualified when used in a document.

Using Unqualified Locals

I'll start looking at how schemas work with target namespaces and locals by beginning with unqualified locals (which don't need to be qualified in a document). To indicate whether elements need to be qualified, you use the `elementFormDefault` attribute of the `<schema>` element; to indicate whether attributes need to be qualified, you use the `attributeFormDefault` attribute of the same element. You can set the `elementFormDefault` and `attributeFormDefault` attributes to either `"qualified"` or `"unqualified"`.

I'll take a look at an example to see how this works. Here, I'm indicating that the target namespace of a schema is `"http://www.starpowder.com/namespace"`. I'm also making the W3C XML schema namespace, `"http://www.w3.org/2001/XMLSchema"`, the default namespace for the document so that I don't have to qualify the XML schema elements such as `<annotation>` and `<complexType>` with a prefix such as `xsd`.

However, I have to be a little careful: When an XML processor dealing with this schema wants to check, say, the `transactionType` complex type, it will need to know what namespace to search—and it won't find the `transactionType` type in the default namespace, which is the W3C XML schema namespace. For that reason, I'll define a new namespace prefix, `t`, and associate that prefix with the same namespace as the target namespace. Now I can use `t:` to prefix types defined in this schema so that an XML processor will know what namespace to search for their definitions.

I'll also indicate that both elements and attributes should be unqualified in this case. Here's what this new schema looks like (note that I qualify types defined in this schema with the `t` prefix, but not types, such as `string`, that are defined in the default `"http://www.w3.org/2001/XMLSchema"` namespace):

```xml
<schema xmlns="http://www.w3.org/2001/XMLSchema"
    xmlns:t="http://www.starpowder.com/namespace"
    targetNamespace="http://www.starpowder.com/namespace"
    elementFormDefault="unqualified"
    attributeFormDefault="unqualified">

    <annotation>
        <documentation>
            Book borrowing transaction schema.
        </documentation>
    </annotation>

    <element name="transaction" type="t:transactionType"/>

    <complexType name="transactionType">
        <sequence>
            <element name="Lender" type="t:address"/>
            <element name="Borrower" type="t:address"/>
            <element ref="note" minOccurs="0"/>
            <element name="books" type="t:books"/>
        </sequence>
        <attribute name="borrowDate" type="date"/>
    </complexType>

    <element name="note" type="string"/>

    <complexType name="address">
        <sequence>
            <element name="name" type="string"/>
            <element name="street" type="string"/>
            <element name="city" type="string"/>
            <element name="state" type="NMTOKEN"/>
        </sequence>
        <attribute name="phone" type="string"
            use="optional"/>
    </complexType>

    <complexType name="books">
        <sequence>
            <element name="book" minOccurs="0" maxOccurs="10">
                <complexType>
                    <sequence>
                        <element name="bookTitle" type="string"/>
                        <element name="pubDate" type="date" minOccurs='0'/>
                        <element name="replacementValue" type="decimal"/>
                        <element name="maxDaysOut">
                            <simpleType>
                                <restriction base="integer">
                                    <maxExclusive value="14"/>
                                </restriction>
                            </simpleType>
```

```
                    </element>
                </sequence>
                <attribute name="bookID" type="t:catalogID"/>
            </complexType>
        </element>
    </sequence>
</complexType>

<simpleType name="catalogID" base="string">
    <restriction base="string">
        <pattern value="\d{3}-\d{4}-\d{3}"/>
    </restriction>
</simpleType>

</schema>
```

So how does a document that conforms to this schema look? The following code is an example. Note that locals are unqualified, but I do need to qualify globals such as <transaction>, <note>, and <books>. (Note also that the namespace of this document is the same as the target namespace of the schema that specifies its syntax, as it should be.)

```
<?xml version="1.0"?>
<at:transaction xmlns:at="http://www.starpowder.com/namespace"
    borrowDate="2003-10-15">
    <Lender phone="607.555.2222">
        <name>Doug Glass</name>
        <street>416 Disk Drive</street>
        <city>Medfield</city>
        <state>MA</state>
    </Lender>
    <Borrower phone="310.555.1111">
        <name>Britta Regensburg</name>
        <street>219 Union Drive</street>
        <city>Medfield</city>
        <state>CA</state>
    </Borrower>
    <at:note>Lender wants these back in two weeks!</at:note>
    <at:books>
        <book bookID="123-4567-890">
            <bookTitle>Earthquakes for Breakfast</bookTitle>
            <pubDate>2003-10-20</pubDate>
            <replacementValue>15.95</replacementValue>
            <maxDaysOut>14</maxDaysOut>
        </book>
        .
        .
        .
    </at:books>
</at:transaction>
```

Using Qualified Locals

You can also require that locals be qualified. Here's an example schema that requires that element names be qualified in conforming documents:

```
<schema xmlns="http://www.w3.org/2001/XMLSchema"
    xmlns:t="http://www.starpowder.com/namespace"
    targetNamespace="http://www.starpowder.com/namespace"
    elementFormDefault="qualified"
    attributeFormDefault="unqualified">

    <annotation>
        <documentation>
            Book borrowing transaction schema.
        </documentation>
    </annotation>
    .
    .
    .
```

What does a document that conforms to this schema look like? Here's an example. Note that I qualify all elements explicitly:

```
<?xml version="1.0"?>
<at:transaction xmlns:at="http://www.starpowder.com/namespace"
    borrowDate="2003-10-15">
    <at:Lender phone="607.555.2222">
        <at:name>Doug Glass</at:name>
        <at:street>416 Disk Drive</at:street>
        <at:city>Medfield</at:city>
        <at:state>MA</at:state>
    </at:Lender>
    <at:Borrower phone="310.555.1111">
        <at:name>Britta Regensburg</at:name>
        <at:street>219 Union Drive</at:street>
        <at:city>Medfield</at:city>
        <at:state>CA</at:state>
    </at:Borrower>
    <at:note>Lender wants these back in two weeks!</at:note>
    <at:books>
        <at:book bookID="123-4567-890">
            <at:bookTitle>Earthquakes for Breakfast</at:bookTitle>
            <at:pubDate>2003-10-20</at:pubDate>
            <at:replacementValue>15.95</at:replacementValue>
            <at:maxDaysOut>14</at:maxDaysOut>
        </at:book>
        .
        .
        .
    </at:books>
</at:transaction>
```

Another way of creating a document that conforms to this schema is to replace the explicit qualification of every element with an *implicit* qualification by using a default namespace. Here's what that looks like:

```
<?xml version="1.0"?>
<transaction xmlns="http://www.starpowder.com/namespace"
    borrowDate="2003-10-15">
    <Lender phone="607.555.2222">
        <name>Doug Glass</name>
        <street>416 Disk Drive</street>
        <city>Medfield</city>
        <state>MA</state>
    </Lender>
    <Borrower phone="310.555.1111">
        <name>Britta Regensburg</name>
        <street>219 Union Drive</street>
        <city>Medfield</city>
        <state>CA</state>
    </Borrower>
    <note>Lender wants these back in two weeks!</note>
    <books>
        <book bookID="123-4567-890">
            <bookTitle>Earthquakes for Breakfast</bookTitle>
            <pubDate>2003-10-20</pubDate>
            <replacementValue>15.95</replacementValue>
            <maxDaysOut>14</maxDaysOut>
        </book>
        .
        .
        .
    </books>
</transaction>
```

So far, we've indicated that *all* locals must be either qualified or unqualified. However, there is a way of specifying that individual locals can be either qualified or unqualified, and you do that with the form attribute.

Here's an example. In this case, I'll leave all locals unqualified except the bookID attribute, which I'll specify must be qualified:

```
<schema xmlns="http://www.w3.org/2001/XMLSchema"
    xmlns:t="http://www.starpowder.com/namespace"
    targetNamespace="http://www.starpowder.com/namespace"
    elementFormDefault="unqualified"
    attributeFormDefault="unqualified">

    <annotation>
        <documentation>
            Book borrowing transaction schema.
        </documentation>
```

```
    </annotation>

    <element name="transaction" type="t:transactionType"/>
        .
        .
        .
    <complexType name="books">
        <sequence>
            <element name="book" minOccurs="0" maxOccurs="10">
                <complexType>
                    <sequence>
                        <element name="bookTitle" type="string"/>
                        <element name="pubDate" type="date" minOccurs='0'/>
                        <element name="replacementValue" type="decimal"/>
                        <element name="maxDaysOut">
                            <simpleType base="integer">
                                <restriction base="integer">
                                    <maxExclusive value="14"/>
                                </restriction>
                            </simpleType>
                        </element>
                    </sequence>
                    <attribute name="bookID" type="t:catalogID"
                        form="qualified"/>
                </complexType>
            </element>
        </sequence>
    </complexType>

    <simpleType name="catalogID">
        <restriction base="string">
            <pattern value="\d{3}-\d{4}-\d{3}"/>
        </restriction>
    </simpleType>

</schema>
```

Here's a document that conforms to this schema. Note that all locals are un-qualified except the bookID attribute, which is qualified:

```
<?xml version="1.0"?>
<at:transaction xmlns:at="http://www.starpowder.com/namespace"
    borrowDate="2003-10-15">
    <Lender phone="607.555.2222">
        <name>Doug Glass</name>
        <street>416 Disk Drive</street>
        <city>Medfield</city>
        <state>MA</state>
    </Lender>
    <Borrower phone="310.555.1111">
```

```
        <name>Britta Regensburg</name>
        <street>219 Union Drive</street>
        <city>Medfield</city>
        <state>CA</state>
    </Borrower>
    <at:note>Lender wants these back in two weeks!</at:note>
    <at:books>
        <book at:bookID="123-4567-890">
            <bookTitle>Earthquakes for Breakfast</bookTitle>
            <pubDate>2003-10-20</pubDate>
            <replacementValue>15.95</replacementValue>
            <maxDaysOut>14</maxDaysOut>
        </book>
        .
        .
        .
    </at:books>
</at:transaction>
```

There's plenty more power wrapped up in schemas. For example, you can have one schema inherit functionality from another, and you can restrict the inheritance process, much as you would in an object-oriented programming language. This standard is one that's still evolving—and still expanding. Let's hope that it won't expand past the capabilities of XML processor authors and that we'll see more processors that support schemas—at least partially—in the future. You can find a good list of tools that handle schemas today at http://www.w3.org/XML/Schema.

CHAPTER 6

Understanding JavaScript

This book is written to require only knowledge of HTML before starting because we're covering XML from scratch—and that means many readers don't come to this book with a programming background. However, XML is a natural for programming because you can tell a browser how to handle your documents if you do use programming. Fortunately, we won't have to learn a lot about programming here; all we'll need to understand are the fundamentals of JavaScript to work with XML in a browser. If you already know JavaScript, feel free to skip this chapter; if not, this chapter is here so you don't have to run out and buy a book on JavaScript before proceeding with the work we'll be doing in the next few chapters.

JavaScript Coverage

If you already know JavaScript, you might want to go on to Chapter 7, "Handling XML Documents with JavaScript," now. We're now on the second edition of this book, and I've had so many emails from readers saying that the chapter on JavaScript and the upcoming chapter on Java were so useful to them that I'm leaving these chapters in the book.

These days, the browser that lets you interact with XML documents in the most powerful and general way is Microsoft Internet Explorer. Whatever you think of Microsoft, there's no denying that it's making a serious attempt at supporting XML. You can write code in Internet Explorer to work with XML documents in either VBScript (Microsoft's proprietary scripting language based on its Visual

Basic language) or JavaScript. Other browsers are going to follow suit. For example, Netscape Navigator 6 already offers some XML support, and although it will allow you to access XML documents from code in the future, Netscape hasn't said much publicly on the point yet. To support the largest number of browsers, I'll use JavaScript to access XML in browsers in this book (and we'll also use Java itself later in the book). This chapter will provide the foundation for that work.

What Is JavaScript?

JavaScript (which is *not* actually related to Java) is the most popular scripting language today. Using JavaScript, you can embed programs in Web pages and run those programs. In the next chapter, we'll see how to use those programs to retrieve the contents of XML elements and attributes, and we'll even see how to search XML documents for data.

Internet Explorer provides strong XML support with *XML islands*, which let you embed XML directly in HTML pages, and by letting you read XML documents directly. In this chapter, we'll learn how to use JavaScript. In Chapter 7, we'll use it to parse XML documents. In Chapter 8, "XML and Data Binding," we'll use JavaScript to load XML documents into database recordsets that have a great deal of support in Internet Explorer, letting you search, order, and display data in many ways.

The programs you write in JavaScript go in the <SCRIPT> HTML element, which itself usually goes into the <HEAD> section of a Web page (however, if you use the script to write text directly to the Web page itself, as we'll do often in this chapter, you should place the <SCRIPT> element in the page's <BODY> element because the <HEAD> section may be parsed before the document's body is available).

Here's an example to get us started. In this case, this JavaScript is writing the text Welcome to JavaScript! directly into a Web page when that Web page is first displayed by the browser:

Listing ch06_01.html

```
<HTML>
    <HEAD>
        <TITLE>
            Welcome To JavaScript
        </TITLE>
    </HEAD>
```

```
<BODY>
    <SCRIPT LANGUAGE="JavaScript">
    <!--
        document.writeln("Welcome to JavaScript!")
    //-->
    </SCRIPT>
    <CENTER>
        <H1>
            Welcome To JavaScript!
        </H1>
    </CENTER>
</BODY>
</HTML>
```

You can see the results of this HTML in Figure 6-1. The JavaScript code wrote the welcoming text you see in the upper-left corner of the page.

Figure 6-1
Using
JavaScript in
Internet
Explorer.

Let's take this example apart to get started. Note that I begin with the <SCRIPT> element and place the JavaScript code into that element. In the <SCRIPT> element, I set the LANGUAGE attribute to "JavaScript" to let the browser know what language the script is in:

```
<HTML>
    <HEAD>
        <TITLE>
            Welcome To JavaScript
        </TITLE>
    </HEAD>

    <BODY>
```

```
<SCRIPT LANGUAGE="JavaScript">
    .
    .
    .
</SCRIPT>

<CENTER>
    <H1>
        Welcome To JavaScript!
    </H1>
</CENTER>

</BODY>
</HTML>
```

I'll enclose the actual JavaScript code inside an HTML comment. What's the purpose of that? It's just general good practice in JavaScript. Unlike an XML browser, if an HTML browser can't understand the contents of an element, it ignores the markup and just displays the text directly. Because some browsers can't understand JavaScript and the <SCRIPT> tag, I place the code in an HTML comment so it won't be displayed in such browsers. JavaScript-enabled browsers ignore the comment markup. (Note that, by convention, you must end the HTML comment with //-->, not just -->, because // is the JavaScript way of creating a comment. I'll go into more depth about this in a few pages.) Otherwise, the browser might try to interpret the --> markup as JavaScript:

```
<HTML>
    <HEAD>
        <TITLE>
            Welcome To JavaScript
        </TITLE>
    </HEAD>

    <BODY>

        <SCRIPT LANGUAGE="JavaScript">
        <!--
            .
            .
            .
        //-->
        </SCRIPT>

        <CENTER>
            <H1>
                Welcome To JavaScript!
```

```
            </H1>
        </CENTER>

    </BODY>
</HTML>
```

Handling Browsers That Don't Support JavaScript

There's also a `<NOSCRIPT>` element that you can use to display messages in browsers that don't support JavaScript (such as `"You're missing some amazing JavaScript action!"`). Browsers that don't handle JavaScript won't understand either the `<SCRIPT>` or `<NOSCRIPT>` elements, but they will display the text in the `<NOSCRIPT>` element directly. (Remember, the JavaScript code in the `<SCRIPT>` element is usually in an HTML comment.) JavaScript-enabled browsers ignore the `<NOSCRIPT>` element.

At this point, we're ready for the JavaScript code. Here, that code is simply the JavaScript expression `document.writeln("Welcome to JavaScript!");` this expression just writes the text `Welcome to JavaScript!` to the Web page:

```
<HTML>
    <HEAD>
        <TITLE>
            Welcome To JavaScript
        </TITLE>
    </HEAD>

    <BODY>

        <SCRIPT LANGUAGE="JavaScript">
        <!--
            document.writeln("Welcome to JavaScript!")
        //-->
        </SCRIPT>

        <CENTER>
            <H1>
                Welcome To JavaScript!
            </H1>
        </CENTER>

    </BODY>
</HTML>
```

That's our first line of JavaScript: `document.writeln("Welcome to JavaScript!")`. When the Web page is loaded, this JavaScript is read and run by the browser.

Ending Semicolon in JavaScript Statements

The official standard for JavaScript says that each JavaScript statement should end with a semicolon (;). In other words, this first line of JavaScript should technically be `document.writeln("Welcome to JavaScript!");`. However, browsers no longer require the ending semicolon because it's so easy to forget it. It has become usual to omit the semicolon these days, so I have done the same here.

The big two implementations of JavaScript are Netscape's and Microsoft's. These two browser vendors are not exactly the best of friends; if you assumed that the two implementations of JavaScript have some differences, you'd be right.

Netscape's JavaScript

You can find documentation for Netscape Navigator's JavaScript at `http://developer.netscape.com/tech/javascript/index.html`. Netscape has also developed a version of JavaScript designed to be used on the server side, not in browsers at all; you can find Netscape's documentation for server-side JavaScript at `http://developer.netscape.com/docs/manuals/enterprise/wrijsap/index.htm`.

Microsoft's JScript

Microsoft's implementation of JavaScript is both different and more extensive than the Netscape standards. The implementation of JavaScript in Internet Explorer is actually called JScript, not JavaScript, although JScript is very close to JavaScript. You can find the official documentation for JScript at `http://msdn.microsoft.com/scripting/default.htm?/scripting/jscript/techinfo/jsdocs.htm`. (Note that Microsoft reorganizes its Web sites every 15 minutes or so; by the time you read this, this URL might have changed—if so, check `http://msdn.microsoft.com/scripting/`.)

ECMAScript

There's some animosity between the two main JavaScript implementers, so you might wonder if there isn't some third party that might be able to sort things out. In fact, there is: The European Computer Manufacturers Association (ECMA) in Geneva, Switzerland, has standardized JavaScript. You can find the current standard at www.ecma.ch/ecma1/stand/ecma-262.htm and www.ecma.ch/ecma1/stand/ecma-290.htm. Netscape Navigator's version of JavaScript is ECMA compliant.

You can find plenty of free JavaScript resources out there to learn from. To start, you can find the documentation for Netscape's JavaScript 1.5 online here:

- The JavaScript 1.5 user's guide is at http://developer.netscape.com/docs/manuals/js/core/jsguide15/contents.html.

- The JavaScript 1.5 reference manual is at http://developer.netscape.com/docs/manuals/js/core/jsref15/contents.html.

- You can download the JavaScript 1.5 user's guide and reference manual from http://developer.netscape.com/docs/manuals/index.html?content=javascript.html.

You can find the documentation for Microsoft's JScript 5.6 online as well:

- The JScript 5.6 user's guide and reference manual is available at http://msdn.microsoft.com/library/default.asp?url=/library/en-us/script56/html/js56jsconjscriptfundamentals.asp. Click the links in the navigation bar to find these items.

- You can also download the JScript 5.6 user's guide and reference manual. The URL for that currently is http://msdn.microsoft.com/downloads/default.asp?URL=/downloads/sample.asp?url=/msdn-files/027/001/733/msdncompositedoc.xml.

The ECMAScript specifications are also online:

- The ECMAScript Language Specification, 3rd edition, is at www.ecma.ch/ecma1/STAND/ECMA-262.HTM.

- The ECMAScript Components Specification is at www.ecma.ch/ecma1/STAND/ECMA-290.HTM.

- The ECMAScript 3rd Edition Compact Profile Specification is at www.ecma.ch/ecma1/STAND/ecma-327.htm.

Many general sites also have good JavaScript resources—here's a starter list:

- Netscape's JavaScript resources page is at `http://developer.netscape.com/docs/manuals/jsresource.html`.

- You can find some useful JavaScript resources at `http://javascript.com/`. This is a good JavaScript resource.

- A good source of JavaScript information is at `http://javascript.about.com/`.

- You can find additional JavaScript resources at `www.javascriptgate.com/`.

And here are a few free JavaScript tutorials on the Web:

- `www.scriptsearch.com/JavaScript/Tips_and_Tutorials/`

- `www.scriptsearch.com/JavaScript/Web_Sites/`

- `http://javascript.about.com/cs/beginner/index.htm`

- `www.w3schools.com/js/default.asp` (JavaScript school)

- `www.echoecho.com/javascript.htm`

- `www.iboost.com/build/programming/js/tutorial/876.htm`

- `www.bitafterbit.com/english/jscript/basic/index.html`

- `www.javascriptmall.com/learn/index.htm`

JavaScript Is Object-Based

JavaScript is an *object-based* language. The term *object-based* should not make you nervous: For us, object-based programming will be a lot easier. For our purposes, object-based programming just means that JavaScript makes available objects that give us access to some aspect of the browser or document.

For example, we already have used the `document` object, one of the most powerful JavaScript objects, in this chapter. That object refers to the body of the Web page in the browser. With this object, you have access to the HTML in the page. In the previous example, I used the `writeln` (which stands for "write line") *method* of the `document` object to write `"Welcome to JavaScript!"`, like this:

```
<SCRIPT LANGUAGE="JavaScript">
<!--
    document.writeln("Welcome to JavaScript!")
//-->
</SCRIPT>
```

You can use methods such as writeln to have an object perform some action, such as writing to the Web page. Other methods let you force the browser to navigate to a new page, send data back to scripts on the server, and so on.

The objects that you already have access to in JavaScript give you a great deal of power. For example, we'll use the document object to access XML documents in the next chapter. Here's an overview of some of the most popular JavaScript objects and what they're all about:

- document—Represents the current Web page's body. With this object, you can access all the elements in a Web page, such as links, images, anchors, and so on.

- history—Has a record of what sites the Web browser has been to before opening the current page. Using the methods of this object, you can move backward and forward though the *history list*.

- location—Holds information about the location of the current Web page, including its URL, domain name, path, server port, and so on.

- navigator—Actually refers to the Web browser itself. Using this object, you can determine the type of browser in use.

- window—Refers to the current browser window and provides many powerful methods. In Internet Explorer, you use the event subobject of this object to handle events, as we'll see at the end of the chapter.

Many more objects exist in JavaScript, and you can define your own objects—see the JavaScript documentation for the details. When you want to create your own objects, you first define a *class*, which you can consider the *type* of the object. Using the JavaScript new operator, you can create objects from classes; we won't create classes here, but we'll use the new operator later in this chapter to create objects in the next chapter.

You have to know about two aspects of objects to be able to get any-where—*methods*, which we've already seen, and *properties*.

Using Object Properties and Methods in JavaScript

JavaScript programming centers on objects, to a large extent. We've already seen the `document` object and seen that one way to use that object is to use methods such as `writeln` to indicate that you want to write to a Web page. To use a method, you use the object's name, followed by a dot (`.`) and then the method name, such as `document.writeln`. Here are a few examples of methods:

- `document.write`—Writes to the body of the current Web page

- `document.writeln`—Writes to the body of the current Web page and ends the text with a carriage return

- `history.go`—Makes the browser navigate to a particular location in the browser's history list

- `window.alert`—Makes the browser display an alert dialog box

- `window.open`—Makes the browser open a new browser window, possibly displaying a new document

There are hundreds of such methods available in JavaScript, and they let you work with a browser as it's running. In addition to using methods to cause the browser to perform some action, you can read and change the settings in the JavaScript objects using *properties*. For example, the `document.fgcolor` property holds the color of text in the current Web page. By changing the `document.fgcolor` property, you can change the color of that text.

Here are some examples of properties, including the objects they belong to:

- `document.bgcolor`—Holds the background color of the current page.

- `document.fgcolor`—Holds the foreground (that is, default text) color of the current page.

- `document.lastmodified`—Holds the date the page was last modified (although many documents do not provide this information).

- `document.title`—Holds the title of the current page (which appears in the browser's title bar).

- `navigator.appName`—Holds the actual name of the browser, which you can use to determine what browser the user is using. We'll use this property at the end of the chapter to distinguish between Internet Explorer and Netscape Navigator.

Using object methods and properties, you have access to what's going on in a Web page, and you have complete programmatic control over the browser in many areas. We'll be putting methods and properties to work in this chapter and the next two chapters.

We've taken a look at the idea of methods and properties, but there's one more concept to cover before getting the actual programming details: using *events* in JavaScript. That topic is coming up.

Using Events in JavaScript

When you load an XML document in a browser, the browser can keep track of the success or failure of the operation. When the user clicks a button in a Web page or uses the mouse, the browser keeps track of that, too. How does the browser inform your JavaScript code what's going on? It uses *events*.

For example, when the user clicks a Web page, a `mouseDown` event occurs. To handle that event in your code, you can connect code to that event. Most HTML tags now support events using attributes such as `onMouseDown` that you use to connect events to JavaScript code. Here's an example. In this case, when the user clicks the Web page, a `mouseDown` event occurs. Using the `onMouseDown` attribute, I can execute JavaScript code to perform some action, such as turning the background of the Web page green. (This example works only in Internet Explorer—you have to add a little additional code to make it work in the Netscape Navigator, as we'll see at the end of this chapter.)

Listing ch06_02.html

```
<HTML>
    <HEAD>
        <TITLE>
            Using JavaScript Events
        </TITLE>
    </HEAD>

    <BODY onMouseDown="document.bgColor='green'">

        <CENTER>
            <H1>
                Click anywhere to turn this page green!
            </H1>
        </CENTER>
    </BODY>
</HTML>
```

When the user clicks the Web page, the code `document.bgColor='green'` is executed, assigning a value of `"green"` to the `document.bgColor` property. You can see this page at work in Figure 6-2.

Figure 6-2
Using an event
in Internet
Explorer.

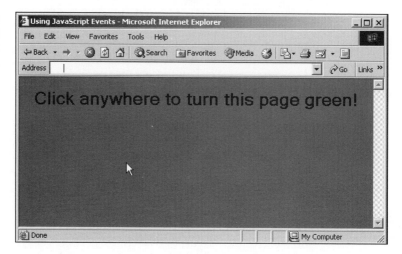

This example is a very simple one because the JavaScript code is in the `<BODY>` element itself. For longer code, you'll usually store the code in the `<SCRIPT>` element instead and *call* that code from elements such as `<BODY>`. We'll see how that works in the section "Creating Functions in JavaScript," later in this chapter.

A great number of events are available. Here's a starter list showing the commonly used ones (note that support for these attributes varies by browser and by HTML tag):

- `onBlur`—Happens when an element loses the input focus. (The element with the focus is the one keystrokes are sent to.)

- `onChange`—Happens when data in an HTML control changes. (HTML controls include text fields, buttons, lists, and so on.)

- `onClick`—Happens when an element is clicked.

- `onDblClick`—Happens when an element is double-clicked.

- `onError`—Happens when an error occurs while executing your code.

- `onFocus`—Happens when an element gets the focus. (The element with the focus is the one keystrokes are sent to.)

- `onKeyDown`—Happens when a key is pressed.

- `onKeyPress`—Happens when a key is pressed and the key code is available to be read in code.

- `onKeyUp`—Happens when a key is released.

- `onLoad`—Happens when the page first loads in the browser.

- `onMouseDown`—Happens when a mouse button is pressed.

- `onMouseMove`—Happens when the mouse moves.

- `onMouseOut`—Happens when the mouse leaves a visible HTML element.

- `onMouseOver`—Happens when the mouse cursor moves over an element.

- `onMouseUp`—Happens when a mouse button is released.

- `onMove`—Happens when an element is moved, either by code or by the user.

- `onReset`—Happens when the user clicks the Reset button in an HTML form.

- `onResize`—Happens when code or the user resizes an element or page.

- `onSelect`—Happens when the user makes a selection.

- `onSubmit`—Happens when the user clicks the Submit button in an HTML form.

- `onUnload`—Happens when the browser unloads a page.

You use events to handle user and browser actions in real time in your code, and dozens of events are available. These events are supported by the various HTML tags supported by the browser. You can see which HTML tags support what event attributes in Table 6-1 for Internet Explorer and Table 6-2 for the Netscape Navigator.

Table 6-1	Element	Event Attributes
Events Supported by Internet Explorer	A	onbeforecopy, onbeforecut, onbeforeeditfocus, onbeforefocusenter, onbeforefocusleave, onbeforepaste, onblur, onclick, oncontextmenu, oncontrolselect, oncopy, oncut, ondblclick, ondrag, ondragend, ondragenter, ondragleave, ondragover, ondragstart, ondrop, onfocus, onfocusenter, onfocusleave, onhelp, onkeydown, onkeypress, onkeyup, onlosecapture, onmousedown, onmouseenter, onmouseleave, onmousemove, onmouseout, onmouseover, onmouseup, onpaste, onpropertychange, onreadystatechange, onresize, onresizeend, onresizestart, onselectstart
	BODY	onafterprint, onbeforecut, onbeforefocusenter, onbeforefocusleave, onbeforepaste, onbeforeprint, onbeforeunload, onclick, oncontextmenu, oncontrolselect, oncut, ondblclick, ondrag, ondragend, ondragenter, ondragleave, ondragover, ondragstart, ondrop
	BUTTON	onbeforecut, onbeforeeditfocus, onbeforefocusenter, onbeforefocusleave, onbeforepaste, onblur, onclick, oncontextmenu, oncontrolselect, oncut, ondblclick, ondragenter, ondragleave, ondragover, ondrop, onfilterchange, onfocus, onfocusenter, onfocusleave, onhelp, onkeydown, onkeypress, onkeyup, onlosecapture, onmousedown, onmouseenter, onmouseleave, onmousemove, onmouseout, onmouseover, onmouseup, onpaste, onpropertychange, onreadystatechange, onresize, onresizeend, onresizestart, onselectstart
	DIV	onbeforecopy, onbeforecut, onbeforeeditfocus, onbeforefocusenter, onbeforefocusleave, onbeforepaste, onblur, onclick, oncontextmenu, oncontrolselect, oncopy, oncut, ondblclick, ondrag, ondragend, ondragenter, ondragleave, ondragover, ondragstart, ondrop, onfilterchange, onfocus, onfocusenter, onfocusleave, onhelp, onkeydown, onkeypress, onkeyup, onlayoutcomplete, onlosecapture, onmousedown, onmouseenter, onmouseleave, onmousemove, onmouseout, onmouseover, onmouseup, onpaste, onpropertychange, onreadystatechange, onresize, onresizeend, onresizestart, onscroll, onselectstart

Element	Event Attributes
FORM	onbeforecopy, onbeforecut, onbeforefocusenter, onbeforefocusleave, onbeforepaste, onblur, onclick, oncontextmenu, oncontrolselect, oncopy, oncut, ondblclick, ondrag, ondragend, ondragenter, ondragleave, ondragover, ondragstart, ondrop, onfocus, onfocusenter, onfocusleave, onhelp, onkeydown, onkeypress, onkeyup, onlosecapture, onmousedown, onmouseenter, onmouseleave, onmousemove, onmouseout, onmouseover, onmouseup, onpaste, onpropertychange, onreadystatechange, onreset, onresize, onresizeend, onresizestart, onselectstart, onsubmit
FRAME	onbeforefocusenter, onbeforefocusleave, onblur, oncontrolselect, onfocus, onfocusenter, onfocusleave, onresize, onresizeend, onresizestart
IFRAME	onbeforefocusenter, onbeforefocusleave, onblur, oncontrolselect, onfocus, onfocusenter, onfocusleave, onresizeend, onresizestart
IMG	onabort, onbeforecopy, onbeforecut, onbeforefocusenter, onbeforefocusleave, onbeforepaste, onblur, onclick, oncontextmenu, oncontrolselect, oncopy, oncut, ondblclick, ondrag, ondragend, ondragenter, ondragleave, ondragover, ondragstart, ondrop, onerror, onfilterchange, onfocus, onfocusenter, onfocusleave, onhelp, onload, onlosecapture, onmousedown, onmouseenter, onmouseleave, onmousemove, onmouseout, onmouseover, onmouseup, onpaste, onpropertychange, onreadystatechange, onresize, onresizeend, onresizestart, onselectstart
INPUT (button)	onbeforecut, onbeforeeditfocus, onbeforefocusenter, onbeforefocusleave, onbeforepaste, onblur, onclick, oncontextmenu, oncontrolselect, oncut, ondblclick, ondrag, ondragend, ondragenter, ondragleave, ondragover, ondragstart, ondrop, onfilterchange, onfocus, onfocusenter, onfocusleave, onhelp, onkeydown, onkeypress, onkeyup, onlosecapture, onmousedown, onmouseenter, onmouseleave, onmousemove, onmouseout, onmouseover, onmouseup, onpaste,

continues

Element	Event Attributes
	onpropertychange, onreadystatechange, onresize, onresizeend, onresizestart, onselectstart
INPUT (check box)	onbeforecut, onbeforeeditfocus, onbeforefocusenter onbeforefocusleave, onbeforepaste, onblur, onclick, oncontextmenu, oncontrolselect, oncut, ondblclick, ondrag, ondragend, ondragenter, ondragleave, ondragover, ondragstart, ondrop, onfilterchange, onfocus, onfocusenter, onfocusleave, onhelp, onkeydown, onkeypress, onkeyup, onlosecapture, onmousedown, onmouseenter, onmouseleave, onmousemove, onmouseout, onmouseover, onmouseup, onpaste, onpropertychange, onreadystatechange, onresizeend, onresizestart, onselectstart
INPUT (radio button)	onbeforecut, onbeforeeditfocus, onbeforefocusenter, onbeforefocusleave, onbeforepaste, onblur, onclick, oncontextmenu, oncontrolselect, oncut, ondblclick, ondrag, ondragend, ondragenter, ondragleave, ondragover, ondragstart, ondrop, onfilterchange, onfocus, onfocusenter, onfocusleave, onhelp, onkeydown, onkeypress, onkeyup, onlosecapture, onmousedown, onmouseenter, onmouseleave, onmousemove, onmouseout, onmouseover, onmouseup, onpaste, onpropertychange, onreadystatechange, onresizeend, onresizestart, onselectstart
INPUT (submit button)	onbeforecut, onbeforeeditfocus, onbeforefocusenter, onbeforefocusleave, onbeforepaste, onblur, onclick, oncontextmenu, oncontrolselect, oncut, ondblclick, ondrag, ondragend, ondragenter, ondragleave, ondragover, ondragstart, ondrop, onfilterchange, onfocus, onfocusenter, onfocusleave, onhelp, onkeydown, onkeypress, onkeyup, onlosecapture, onmousedown, onmouseenter, onmouseleave, onmousemove, onmouseout, onmouseover, onmouseup, onpaste, onpropertychange, onreadystatechange, onresize, onresizeend, onresizestart, onselectstart
INPUT (text field)	onafterupdate, onbeforecut, onbeforeeditfocus, onbeforefocusenter, onbeforefocusleave, onbeforepaste, onbeforeupdate, onblur, onchange, onclick, oncontextmenu, oncontrolselect, oncut,

Element	Event Attributes
	ondblclick, ondrag, ondragend, ondragenter, ondragleave, ondragover, ondragstart, ondrop, onerrorupdate, onfilterchange, onfocus, onfocusenter, onfocusleave, onhelp, onkeydown, onkeypress, onkeyup, onlosecapture, onmousedown, onmouseenter, onmouseleave, onmousemove, onmouseout, onmouseover, onmouseup, onpaste, onpropertychange, onreadystatechange, onresize, onresizeend, onresizestart, onselect, onselectstart
LI	onbeforecopy, onbeforecut, onbeforefocusenter, onbeforefocusleave, onbeforepaste, onblur, onclick, oncontextmenu, oncontrolselect, oncopy, oncut, ondblclick, ondrag, ondragend, ondragenter, ondragleave, ondragover, ondragstart, ondrop, onfocus, onfocusenter, onfocusleave, onhelp, onkeydown, onkeypress, onkeyup, onlayoutcomplete, onlosecapture, onmousedown, onmouseenter, object, onmouseleave, onmousemove, onmouseout, onmouseover, onmouseup, onpaste, onpropertychange, onreadystatechange, onresize, onresizeend, onresizestart, onselectstart
MARQUEE	onbeforecut, onbeforeeditfocus, onbeforefocusenter, onbeforefocusleave, onbeforepaste, onblur, onbounce, oncontextmenu, oncontrolselect, oncut, ondblclick, ondrag, ondragend, ondragenter, ondragleave, ondragover, ondragstart, ondrop, onfilterchange, onfinish, onfocus, onfocusenter, onfocusleave, onhelp, onkeydown, onkeypress, onkeyup, onlosecapture, onmousedown, onmouseenter, onmouseleave, onmousemove, onmouseout, onmouseover, onmouseup, onpaste, onpropertychange, onreadystatechange, onresize, onresizeend, onresizestart, onscroll, onselectstart, onstart
OBJECT	onbeforeeditfocus, onbeforefocusenter, onbeforefocusleave, onblur, oncellchange, onclick, oncontrolselect, ondataavailable, ondatasetchanged, ondatasetcomplete, ondblclick, ondrag, ondragend, ondragenter, ondragleave, ondragover, ondragstart, ondrop, onerror, onfocus, onfocusenter, onfocusleave,

contin

Element	Event Attributes
	onkeydown, onkeypress, onkeyup, onlosecapture, onpropertychange, onreadystatechange, onresize, onresizeend, onresizestart, onrowenter, onrowexit, onrowsdelete, onrowsinserted, onscroll, onselectstart
P	onbeforecopy, onbeforecut, onbeforefocusenter, onbeforefocusleave, onbeforepaste, onblur, onclick, oncontextmenu, oncontrolselect, oncopy, oncut, ondblclick, ondrag, ondragend, ondragenter, ondragleave, ondragover, ondragstart
PRE	onbeforecopy, onbeforecut, onbeforefocusenter, onbeforefocusleave, onbeforepaste, onblur, onclick, oncontextmenu, oncontrolselect, oncopy, oncut, ondblclick, ondrag, ondragend, ondragenter, ondragleave, ondragover, ondragstart, ondrop, onfocus, onfocusenter, onfocusleave, onhelp, onkeydown, onkeypress, onkeyup, onlosecapture, onmousedown, onmouseenter, onmouseleave, onmousemove, onmouseout, onmouseover, onmouseup, onpaste, onpropertychange, onreadystatechange, onresize, onresizeend, onresizestart, onselectstart
SELECT	onbeforecut, onbeforeeditfocus, onbeforefocusenter, onbeforefocusleave, onbeforepaste, onblur, onchange, onclick, oncontextmenu, oncontrolselect, oncut, ondblclick, ondragenter, ondragleave, ondragover, ondrop, onfocus, onfocusenter, onfocusleave, onhelp, onkeydown, onkeypress, onkeyup, onlosecapture, onmousedown, onmouseenter, onmouseleave, onmousemove, onmouseout, onmouseover, onmouseup, onpaste, onpropertychange, onreadystatechange, onresize, onresizeend, onresizestart, onscroll, onselectstart
SPAN	onbeforecopy, onbeforecut, onbeforeeditfocus, onbeforefocusenter, onbeforefocusleave, onbeforepaste, onblur, onclick, oncontextmenu, oncontrolselect, oncopy, oncut, ondblclick, ondrag, ondragend, ondragenter, ondragleave, ondragover, ondragstart, ondrop, onfilterchange,

Element	Event Attributes
	onfocus, onfocusenter, onfocusleave, onhelp, onkeydown, onkeypress, onkeyup, onlosecapture, onmousedown, onmouseenter, onmouseleave, onmousemove, onmouseout
TABLE	onbeforecut, onbeforeeditfocus, onbeforefocusenter, onbeforefocusleave, onbeforepaste, onblur, onclick, oncontextmenu, oncontrolselect, oncut, ondblclick, ondrag, ondragend, ondragenter, ondragleave, ondragover, ondragstart, ondrop, onfilterchange, onfocus, onfocusenter, onfocusleave, onhelp, onkeydown, onkeypress, onkeyup, onlosecapture, onmousedown, onmouseenter, onmouseleave, onmousemove, onmouseout, onmouseover, onmouseup, onpaste, onpropertychange, onreadystatechange, onresize, onresizeend, onresizestart, onscroll, onselectstart
TD	onbeforecopy, onbeforecut, onbeforeeditfocus, onbeforefocusenter, onbeforefocusleave, onbeforepaste, onblur, onclick, oncontextmenu, oncontrolselect, oncopy, oncut, ondblclick, ondrag, ondragend, ondragenter, ondragleave, ondragover, ondragstart, ondrop, onfilterchange, onfocus, onfocusenter, onfocusleave, onhelp, onkeydown, onkeypress, onkeyup, onlosecapture, onmousedown, onmouseenter, onmouseleave, onmousemove, onmouseout, onmouseover, onmouseup, onpaste, onpropertychange, onreadystatechange, onresizeend, onresizestart, onselectstart
TEXTAREA	onafterupdate, onbeforecopy, onbeforecut, onbeforeeditfocus, onbeforefocusenter, onbeforefocusleave, onbeforepaste, onbeforeupdate, onblur, onchange, onclick, oncontextmenu, oncontrolselect, oncut, ondblclick, ondrag, operation, ondragend, ondragenter, ondragleave, ondragover, ondragstart, ondrop, onerrorupdate, onfilterchange, onfocus, onfocusenter, onfocusleave, onhelp, onkeydown, onkeypress, onkeyup, onlosecapture, onmousedown, onmouseenter, onmouseleave, onmousemove, onmouseout, onmouseover, onmouseup, onpaste, onpropertychange, onreadystatechange, onresize, onresizeend, onresizestart, onscroll, onselect, onselectstart

Table 6-2	Element	Event Attributes
Events Supported by Netscape Navigator	A	onclick, onmouseout, onmouseover
	BODY	onload, onunload, onblur, onfocus
	DIV	None
	EMBED	None
	FORM	onreset, onsubmit
	FRAME	None
	ILAYER	None
	IMG	onabort, onerror, onload
	INPUT (button)	onclick
	INPUT (check box)	onclick
	INPUT (radio button)	onclick
	INPUT (submit button)	onclick
	INPUT (text field)	onblur, onchange, onfocus, onselect
	LAYER	onmouseover, onmouseout, onfocus, onblur, onload
	LI	None
	OBJECT	None
	P	None
	PRE	None
	SELECT	onblur, onchange, onclick, onfocus
	SPAN	None
	TABLE	None
	TD	None
	TEXTAREA	onblur, onchange, onfocus, onselect

This overview gives some indication of how powerful JavaScript is. It's time to turn to the details of writing code in JavaScript so we can put it to work in the next two chapters.

Programming in JavaScript

In this chapter, we'll build our JavaScript foundation by getting the syntax of the language down. For example, you can make decisions based on your data values with the JavaScript `if` statement. In this code, I'm comparing the value 143 to 719; and if 719 is greater than 143, displaying the message `The first value is greater than the second.`:

Listing ch06_03.html

```
<HTML>
    <HEAD>
        <TITLE>
            Using the JavaScript if Statement
        </TITLE>
    </HEAD>

    <BODY>
        <CENTER>
            <H1>
                Using the JavaScript if Statement
            </H1>
        </CENTER>
        <SCRIPT LANGUAGE="JavaScript">
            if(719 > 143){
                document.writeln(
                    "The first value is greater than the second."
                )
            }
        </SCRIPT>
    </BODY>
</HTML>
```

You can see this Web page at work in Figure 6-3. As indicated in that page, 719 is indeed greater than 143.

Testing for Errors in Your Code

While you are developing your JavaScript code, Internet Explorer displays an error icon at the lower left (in the status bar) that you can double-click to open a dialog box indicating what errors are in your code. However, Netscape Navigator simply refuses to run that code. To see what the trouble is, just type **"javascript:"** in the Location box and press Enter. Netscape Navigator opens a new window telling you what's wrong with the code. In Netscape Navigator 6, select the Tasks, Tools, JavaScript Console menu item.

Figure 6-3
Using the
JavaScript `if`
Statement in
Internet
Explorer.

We're going to see statements like the `if` statement in the remainder of this chapter—and we'll put them to work in the next two chapters.

Working with Data in JavaScript

Using data is basic to nearly any JavaScript program, and JavaScript supports quite a number of different data types: numbers, Boolean values, text strings, and so on. You store data values in *variables* in JavaScript.

As with other programming languages, variables are simply named locations in memory that you use to store data. You create variables in JavaScript with the `var` statement, and when a variable has been created, it's ready for you to store and retrieve data in.

Here's an example. In this case, I'm creating a new variable named `temperature` and storing a value of 72 in it using the = assignment operator. When I use this variable in code, JavaScript replaces it with the value 72, so I can display the temperature like this:

Listing ch06_04.html

```
<HTML>
    <HEAD>
        <TITLE>
            Using Variables in JavaScript
        </TITLE>
    </HEAD>
```

```
<BODY>
    <CENTER>
        <H1>
            Using Variables in JavaScript
        </H1>
    </CENTER>
    <SCRIPT LANGUAGE="JavaScript">
        var number
        temperature = 72
        document.writeln("The temperature is "
        +  temperature
        + " degrees.")
    </SCRIPT>
</BODY>
</HTML>
```

Note the text I'm passing to the document.writeln method this time: "The temperature is " + temperature + " degrees.". In this case, I'm using the JavaScript concatenation operator, + (which is also the addition operator for numbers), to join these three expressions into one string. The temperature variable is replaced with the value this variable contains, which is 72, as you see in Figure 6-4.

Figure 6-4
Using variables in JavaScript.

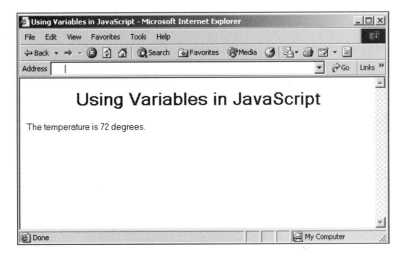

You can also create a variable *and* assign a value to it at the same time with the var statement. Here's what that looks like:

```
var temperature = 72
document.writeln("The temperature is "
+   temperature
+ " degrees.")
```

Besides storing numbers in JavaScript variables, you can store text strings. In this next example, I store the entire text The temperature is 72 degrees. in the variable named weatherReport, and I display the text like this:

```
<HTML>
    <HEAD>
        <TITLE>
            Using Variables in JavaScript
        </TITLE>
    </HEAD>

    <BODY>
        <CENTER>
            <H1>
                Using Variables in JavaScript
            </H1>
        </CENTER>
        <SCRIPT LANGUAGE="JavaScript">
        <!--
            var weatherReport
            weatherReport = "The temperature is 72 degrees."
            document.writeln(weatherReport)
        //-->
        </SCRIPT>
    </BODY>
</HTML>
```

This code produces the same display as you see in Figure 6-4.

Note the name weatherReport here. The convention in JavaScript is to use lowercase names for variables and, if you create a name by joining several words, to capitalize the first letter of the second word, the third word, and so on. Names for JavaScript variables obey the same rules as the names for XML elements. Here are a few examples:

- counter
- numberOfLinks
- countLeftUntilFinished
- oneOfThoseVeryVeryVeryLongVariableNames

Commenting Your JavaScript

As with HTML and XML, you can add comments to JavaScript code; in JavaScript, you use a double forward slash (//) to start a comment. The JavaScript interpreter in the browser stops reading anything on a line past //, so you can comment your code like this:

```
<HTML>
    <HEAD>
        <TITLE>
            Using Variables in JavaScript
        </TITLE>
    </HEAD>

    <BODY>
        <CENTER>
            <H1>
                Using Variables in JavaScript
            </H1>
        </CENTER>

        <SCRIPT LANGUAGE="JavaScript">
        <!--
            //Create the weatherReport variable
            var weatherReport
            //Assign a value to weatherReport
            weatherReport = "The temperature is 72 degrees."
            //Display the value in weatherReport
            document.writeln(weatherReport)
        //-->
        </SCRIPT>
    </BODY>
</HTML>
```

Working with JavaScript Operators

What if you wanted to manipulate your data in JavaScript code? Say, for example, that you needed to multiple 219 by 45—how would you do it? In JavaScript, you can use the multiplication *operator* (*). Here's an example showing how this works:

Listing ch06_05.html

```
<HTML>
    <HEAD>
        <TITLE>
            Using Operators In JavaScript
        </TITLE>
    </HEAD>

    <BODY>
        <CENTER>
            <H1>
                Using Operators In JavaScript
            </H1>
        </CENTER>

        <SCRIPT LANGUAGE="JavaScript">
            var result
            result = 219 * 45
            document.writeln("219 * 45 = " +  result)
        </SCRIPT>
    </BODY>
</HTML>
```

You can see the results of this code in Figure 6-5.

Figure 6-5
Using
JavaScript
operators in
Internet
Explorer.

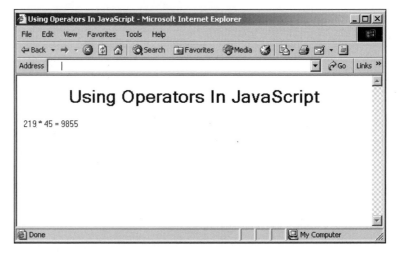

As you might expect, there are many operators available in JavaScript. For example, you can use the increment operator, ++, to add 1 to a numeric value. For example, if counter holds 400, then after you apply the ++ operator, as in ++counter, counter will hold 401.

Prefix Versus Postfix Operators

As C, C++, Perl, Java, and JavaScript programmers know, you can apply the increment (++) and decrement (--) operators as prefix or postfix operators: ++counter or counter++. Prefix operators are applied before the rest of the statement or expression is evaluated, and postfix operators are applied after the rest of the statement is evaluated.

These are the JavaScript operators (as with the rest of the material in this chapter, check the JavaScript documentation for more details):

- **Addition operator** (+)—Adds two numbers or concatenates two strings.

- **Assignment operator** (=)—Assigns a value or object to a variable.

- **Bitwise AND operator** (&)—Performs a bitwise AND on two values.

- **Bitwise left shift operator** (<<)—Shifts the bits of an expression to the left a specified number of times.

- **Bitwise NOT operator** (~)—Negation. Performs a bitwise NOT on a value.

- **Bitwise OR operator** (|)—Performs a bitwise OR operation on two values.

- **Bitwise right shift operator** (>>)—Shifts the bits of a value to the right (maintaining the sign of the value).

- **Bitwise XOR operator** (^)—Performs a bitwise exclusive OR on two values.

- **Comma operator** (,)—Causes two expressions to be evaluated sequentially.

- **Conditional (trinary) operator** (?:)—Executes one of two expressions, depending on whether a condition is true or false. For example, a > 5 ? exp1 : exp2 executes exp1 if the value in variable a is greater than 5, and exp2 otherwise.

- **Decrement operator** (--)—Decrements a value by 1.

- **Division operator** (/)—Divides two numbers and returns a numeric result.

- **Equality operator** (==)—Comparison operator. Compares two expressions to determine whether they are equal.

- **Greater than operator** (>)—Comparison operator. Compares two expressions to determine whether one is greater than the other.

- **Greater than or equal to operator** (>=)—Comparison operator. Compares two expressions to determine whether one is greater than or equal to the other.

- **Identity operator** (===)—Comparison operator. Compares two expressions to determine whether they are equal in value and of the same data type.

- **Increment operator** (++)—Increments a value by 1.

- **Inequality operator** (!=)—Comparison operator. Compares two expressions to determine whether they are unequal.

- **Less than operator** (<)—Comparison operator. Compares two values to determine whether one is less than the other.

- **Less than or equal to operator** (<=)—Comparison operator. Compares two expressions to determine whether one is less than or equal to the other.

- **Logical AND operator** (&&)—Performs a logical AND conjunction operation on two expressions.

- **Logical NOT operator** (!)—Performs logical negation on an expression.

- **Logical OR operator** (||)—Performs a logical OR disjunction operation on two expressions.

- **Modulus operator** (%)—Divides two numbers and returns the remainder.

- **Multiplication operator** (*)—Multiplies two numbers.

- **New operator** (new)—Creates a new object.

- **Nonidentity operator** (!==)—Comparison operator. Compares two expressions to determine whether they are equal in value or of the same data type.

- **Subtraction operator** (-)—Subtracts one value from another.

- **Typeof operator** (typeof)—Returns a string that identifies the data type of an expression.

- **Unary negation operator** (-)—Returns the negative value of a numeric expression.

- **Unsigned right shift operator** (>>>)—Performs an unsigned right shift of the bits in a value.

Besides the operators in this list, you can put together a number of combination operators from two operators. For example, `counterValue += 101` adds 101 to the value in `counterValue`. The combination operators in JavaScript are +=, -=, *=, /=, %=, &=, |=, ^=, <<=, >>=, and >>>=.

It's also worth noting that a number of these operators have to do with comparisons, and you use them to make decisions in code. We've already seen the greater than comparison operator (>), like this:

```
if(719 > 143){
    document.writeln(
        "The first value is greater than the second."
    )
}
```

What's really going on here? In this case, I'm using the `if` statement to compare two numbers. The `if` statement is fundamental to JavaScript, and it's the next step up from using simple operators.

Creating JavaScript *if* Statements

You use the `if` statement in JavaScript to test your data and to execute some code if the test is true. Here's the basic form of the `if` statement:

```
if (condition) {
    code
}
```

Here, `condition` is the test that you want to make, and `code` is the code you want to execute if the condition is true. One thing to note here is that you must enclose the code to execute in curly braces, { and }.

So what kind of conditions can you check, and how do you do so? To construct a condition to test, you use the comparison operators, such as < (less than), > (greater than), == (is equal to), <= (is less than or equal to), or >= (is greater than or equal to).

Here's an example. in this case, I'm making sure that the value in a variable named `temperature` is greater than 32:

Listing ch06_06.html

```
<HTML>
    <HEAD>
        <TITLE>
            Using the JavaScript if Statement
```

continues

Listing ch06_06.html   Continued

```
            </TITLE>
        </HEAD>

        <BODY>
            <CENTER>
                <H1>
                    Using the JavaScript if Statement
                </H1>
            </CENTER>

            <SCRIPT LANGUAGE="JavaScript">
                var temperature
                temperature = 45
                if (temperature > 32) {
                    document.writeln("We're above freezing.")
                }
            </SCRIPT>
        </BODY>
</HTML>
```

You can see the results of this code in Figure 6-6.

Figure 6-6
Using the `if` statement to check the temperature.

Here are some other `if` statement examples:

```
if (year == 2001) {
    document.writeln("The year is 2001.")
}

if (color == "red") {
```

```
        document.writeln("Stop the car.")
}

if (price < 2000.00) {
    document.writeln("Be careful, the price has fallen too low!")
}
```

Besides using the comparison operators, you can use the *and* operator, &&, and the *or* operator, ||, to combine conditions. Here's how you can use the && operator:

```
if (temperature < 75 && temperature > 65) {
    document.writeln("We're in the comfort zone.")
}
```

Here, the value in the variable named temperature must be less than 75 *and* greater than 65 for the code to be executed. If the temperature is indeed in that range, the message We're in the comfort zone. is displayed.

In this example, both conditions must be true for the overal condition to be considered true. However, you can use the || operator as well to connect conditions. Here's an example:

```
if (temperature < 65 || temperature > 75) {
    document.writeln("Outside the comfort zone!")
}
```

In this case, if the value in temperature is less than 65 *or* greater than 75, the overall condition is considered true and the code is executed, which means that the message Outside the comfort zone! is displayed in the Web page.

Creating JavaScript *if...else* Statements

In fact, the more general form of the if statement has an else clause, which can also hold code. The else clause is optional, but if you include it, the code in that clause is executed if the condition in the associated if statement is false. Here's how the if...else statement looks in general:

```
if (condition) {
    code executed if condition is true
}
else {
    code executed if condition is false
}
```

Here's an example showing how this works. In this case, I'm elaborating our previous example that made sure that the temperature is above freezing. I've added an else clause that is executed if the temperature is less than 32°, and the code in that clause displays the message Time to drain the pool.:

Listing ch06_07.html

```
<HTML>
    <HEAD>
        <TITLE>
            Using the JavaScript else Clause
        </TITLE>
    </HEAD>

    <BODY>
        <CENTER>
            <H1>
                Using the JavaScript else Clause
            </H1>
        </CENTER>

        <SCRIPT LANGUAGE="JavaScript">
            var temperature
            temperature = 5
            if (temperature > 32) {
                document.writeln("We're above freezing.")
            }
            else {
                document.writeln("Time to drain the pool.")
            }
        </SCRIPT>
    </BODY>
</HTML>
```

You can see the results of this code in Figure 6-7.

Figure 6-7
Using the
else clause.

Figure 6-7
Using the
else clause.

Creating *switch* Statements

The JavaScript switch statement is the next step up in decision making after the if statement. You use the switch statement if you want to test a large number of cases and don't want to construct a long ladder of if...else statements.

Here's how it works: You compare a test expression against a number of values. If one of those values matches, the code associated with the value is executed until the JavaScript interpreter finds a break statement. Here's what the switch statement looks like in outline:

```
switch(test){
    case value1:
        .
        .
        .
        code executed if test matches value1
        .
        .
        .
        break;
    case value2:
        .
        .
        .
        code executed if test matches value2
        .
        .
        .
```

```
        break;
    case value3:
           .

           .

           .
        code executed if test matches value3
           .

           .

           .
        break;
    default:
           .

           .

           .
        code executed if test doesn't matches any case
           .

           .

           .
        break;
}
```

Here, you list the possible values to match against with the case statement. When a value given in a case statement matches, the corresponding code (that is, the code that follows the case statement up to a break statement) is executed.

You might also note that I've added a default statement to the end of the list of case statements. If no case statement's values have matched the text expression, the code in the default statement is executed, in case you want to make sure *some* code is executed. The default statement is optional.

Here's an example putting the switch statement to work. In this case, I'm checking user input, which I've stored in a variable named userInput, against various test strings, and displaying messages to match the various possibilities:

```
switch(userInput){
    case "EDIT":
        document.writeln("Now entering EDIT mode.")
        break;
    case "HELP":
        //This response should look familiar to users...
        document.writeln("Sorry, no help is available.")
        break;
    case "QUIT":
        document.writeln("Are you sure you want to quit?")
        break;
    default:
        document.writeln("I do not understand that response.")
        break;
}
```

Creating JavaScript *for* Loop Statements

Using loops, you can execute code as many times as you want—which is one of the things computers excel at. The most basic loop is the `for` loop statement, and here's what this statement looks like in general:

```
for (initialization; test; increment) {
    code
}
```

Here's what's happening: You place an expression in the *initialization* part of the `for` loop (which often initializes a variable, called a loop index, to 0), Then you insert a test condition in the *test* part of the loop to be tested each time the code in the loop has been executed. If the test is false, the loop ends (often the test condition checks whether the value in the loop index exceeds a specified maximum value). On the other hand, if the test condition is true, the body of the loop is executed and the code in the *increment* part of the loop is executed to get the loop ready for the next iteration (often by incrementing the loop index).

Here's an example to make this clear. In this case, I'll set up a loop to execute 10 times; each time, it will print out the value in a loop index. This example works by setting a loop index variable named `loopIndex` to `0` to start; then it increments it each time when the loop code has executed (using the increment operator, `++`) and checks to make sure the loop index does not exceed `10`. When the loop index does exceed `10`, the loop terminates. Here's the code (the HTML `<BR>` element makes the Web browser skip to the next line):

Listing ch06_08.html

```
<HTML>
    <HEAD>
        <TITLE>
            Using the for Statement
        </TITLE>
    </HEAD>

    <BODY>
        <CENTER>
            <H1>
                Using the for Statement
            </H1>
        </CENTER>

        <SCRIPT LANGUAGE = "JavaScript">
```

continues

Listing ch06_08.html   Continued

```
            for(var loopIndex = 1; loopIndex <= 10; loopIndex++){
                document.writeln("The loop index value is " +
                loopIndex + "<BR>")
            }
        </SCRIPT>
    </BODY>
</HTML>
```

Here's another thing to note in this example: Because loopIndex is a variable that we're using in our code, we must declare it. JavaScript allows you the shortcut of declaring a variable like this right in the for loop itself, and you can see the var statement inside the initialization part of the for loop. This is a common practice, and I'm including it here because you'll see it often.

When you open this page in a browser, you'll see a message displaying the value of the loop index from 1 to 10, as you see in Figure 6-8.

Figure 6-8
Using a JavaScript for loop in Internet Explorer.

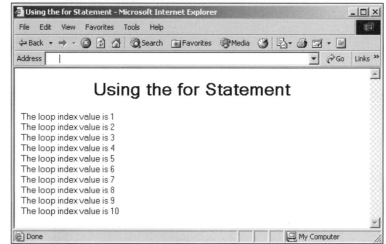

Creating *while* Loop Statements

There are other loops besides the for loop in JavaScript, such as the while loop. The while loop tests a condition each time the loop is executed. If the condition is true, it executes the code in the loop. Here's what this loop looks like in outline:

```
while (condition){
    code
}
```

For example, here's how you write the example we used in the discussion of for loops as a while loop:

Listing ch06_09.html

```
<HTML>
    <HEAD>
        <TITLE>
            Using the while Statement
        </TITLE>
    </HEAD>

    <BODY>
        <CENTER>
            <H1>
                Using the while Statement
            </H1>
        </CENTER>

        <SCRIPT LANGUAGE = "JavaScript">
            var loopIndex = 0

            while(loopIndex < 10){
                loopIndex++
                document.writeln("The loop index value is " +
                loopIndex + "<BR>")
            }
        </SCRIPT>
    </BODY>
</HTML>
```

You can see the results of this code in Figure 6-9.

Figure 6-9
Using a JavaScript while loop in Internet Explorer.

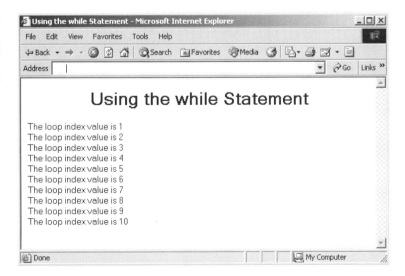

Creating *do...while* Loops

There's another form of the while loop available: the do...while loop. This loop is much like the while loop, except that it checks the loop condition at the end, after the code in the loop has been executed, not at the beginning. Here's what this loop looks like in outline:

```
do {
    code
} while (condition)
```

Actually, there's a big difference between the while and do...while loops in programmatic terms: The code in a do...while loop is always executed at least once, although that's not true of a while loop. Take a look at this example:

```
var number = 25
do {
    document.writeln("The reciprocal of "
    + number + " is "
    + 1/number + "<BR>")
    --number
} while (number > 0)
```

Here I'm displaying a sequence of reciprocal values, from 1/25 up to 1/1, using a do...while loop. However, this would be a problem if number were initialized to 0 because the first reciprocal that the code would attempt to calculate is 1/0:

```
var number = 0
do {
    document.writeln("The reciprocal of "
    + number + " is "
    + 1/number + "<BR>")
    --number
} while (number > 0)
```

A better choice is to use the while loop here: It checks the value in number first and won't attempt to calculate a reciprocal if that value equals 0:

```
var number = 25
while (number > 0) {
    document.writeln("The reciprocal of "
    + number + " is "
    + 1/number + "<BR>")
    --number
}
```

Both forms of the `while` loop have their places, however. For example, if you need to execute the body of the loop before testing to see if the loop should continue, use the `do...while` loop.

Creating Functions in JavaScript

Functions are a crucial part of JavaScript programming. With a function, you can wrap some code into a programming construct, a function, and you then call that function to execute that code.

You create functions with the `function` statement. Here's how that statement looks in outline:

```
function functionname([argument1 [, argument2 [, ...argumentn]]])
{
    code
}
```

In this case, I'm *passing* the values `argument1`, `argument2`, and so on to this function. The code in the function has access to these values. A function can also *return* a value; to do that, you use the `return` statement.

Here's an example. In this case, I'm creating a function named `getTime`, which will return the current time. Notice the syntax of the `function` statement here—I'm adding an empty set of parentheses after the name of the function. Those parentheses are always necessary; when we pass values to a function, they'll be listed in the parentheses. The `getTime` function doesn't accept any passed values, so the parentheses are empty:

```
function getTime()
{
    var now = new Date
    var returnValue = now.getHours() + ":"
    + now.getMinutes()
    return(returnValue)
}
```

In this case, we're using the JavaScript `Date` class and creating a new object of that class named `now` using the `new` operator. I can use the `getHours` and `getMinutes` methods of this new object (these methods are built into the `Date` class) to get the current time.

In fact, methods are just functions built into objects. If you continue on in JavaScript to creating your own classes and objects, the functions you add to a class will be called methods.

In this example, I place the current time into a string named returnValue. That string is what I return from the function, using the return statement. After creating this function, you're free to use it in your code. Here's how I place that function in a <SCRIPT> element. Note that the code in functions is not run automatically when the page loads; it's run only when the function is actually called:

Listing ch06_10.html

```
<HTML>
    <HEAD>
        <TITLE>
            Using JavaScript Functions
        </TITLE>
    </HEAD>

    <BODY>
        <CENTER>
            <H1>
                Using JavaScript Functions
            </H1>
        </CENTER>

        <SCRIPT LANGUAGE = "JavaScript">
            document.writeln("The time is " + getTime()
            + " right now.")

            function getTime()
            {
                var now = new Date
                var returnValue = now.getHours() + ":"
                + now.getMinutes()
                return(returnValue)
            }
        </SCRIPT>
    </BODY>
</HTML>
```

You can see this page in Internet Explorer in Figure 6-10. As you can see there, things have worked out as we expected. When the page is loaded, the docu-ment.writeln statement is executed, which means that the call to the getTime function is also executed. The getTime function returns the current time as a string, which is incorporated into the text that's displayed in the page.

Figure 6-10
Using a
JavaScript
function in
Internet
Explorer.

We've seen how to write a function that returns a value now, but what about passing values to functions so they can work on them? I'll take a look at how that works next.

Passing Values to Functions

The values you pass to functions are called *arguments*. When you pass data in arguments to a function, the code in the function has access to those values. When you create a function, you specify which arguments are to be passed to the function in an *argument list*.

Here's an example. In this case, I'll create a function named adder that will add two values and return their sum. Here's how I start creating adder:

```
function adder()
{
    .
    .
    .
}
```

This time, we're going to pass arguments to the function. So, we list the arguments that we'll pass by giving them names in the argument list, which is enclosed in the parentheses following the function name. Here, I'll call the two arguments passed to adder value1 and value2:

```
function adder(value1, value2)
{
    .
    .
    .
}
```

Calling by Value

By default in JavaScript, what's really passed to functions are not the actual arguments themselves, but *copies* of those arguments, provided that those arguments evaluate to primitive (nonobject) values. This process is named *calling by value*. On the other hand, in JavaScript, objects are passed by *reference*, which means that what's actually passed is not the object itself, or even a copy of the object, but the location of the object in memory.

Now you're free to refer to the passed values by the names you've given them in the argument list. To return the sum of value1 and value2, all I have to do is to add those values and use the return statement, like this:

```
function adder(value1, value2)
{
    return(value1 + value2)
}
```

To make use of this function, you pass values to it in parentheses like this, where I'm finding the sum of the values 47 and 99:

Listing ch06_11.html

```
<HTML>
    <HEAD>
        <TITLE>
            Passing Arguments to Functions in JavaScript
        </TITLE>
    </HEAD>

    <BODY>
        <CENTER>
            <H1>
                Passing Arguments to Functions in JavaScript
            </H1>
        </CENTER>

        <SCRIPT LANGUAGE = "JavaScript">
```

```
        document.writeln("47 + 99 = " +  adder(47, 99))

        function adder(value1, value2)
        {
            return(value1 + value2)
        }
    </SCRIPT>
  </BODY>
</HTML>
```

That's all it takes; now we're passing arguments to the adder function. You can see the results in Figure 6-11. As you see there, everything is working perfectly: The sum of 47 and 99 is displayed as it should be. (You might also note that even though the value returned from the adder function is a number, JavaScript is smart enough to treat that number as a text string when it's time to print it with document.writeln.)

Figure 6-11
Passing
arguments to
functions in
JavaScript.

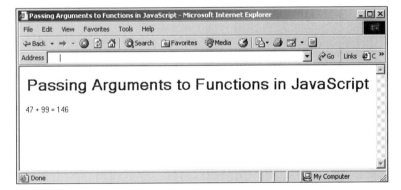

Using a Variable Number of Arguments

In case you're interested, you can actually call a function with fewer arguments than those that appear in its formal argument list (that is, the number of arguments that you've defined it with). There's no problem unless you try to access arguments by name that had no value passed to them. In addition, you can pass *more* arguments than a function's formal argument list specifies. If you do that, you can access the additional arguments from the arguments *array* (and we'll see more about arrays in a few pages). For example, the first argument passed to adder can also be referenced inside the adder function as adder.arguments[0], the next as adder.arguments[1], and so on.

Creating Objects in JavaScript

As we already know, JavaScript comes with a number of built-in objects ready for you to use, such as the `document`, `location`, `navigator`, and `history` objects. JavaScript also comes with many classes built in, including classes such as the `Date` class, which handles dates and times, and the `Math` class, which has many built-in methods such as `min` and `max` to compare numbers. You can use built-in classes (and those you create yourself, although we're not going to do that here) to create objects using the `new` operator.

You can think of a class as an object's *type* because, using the new operator, you create objects from classes. Objects can have methods and properties built into them—in fact, most do. We'll be using the new operator in the next chapter to create objects that will let us handle XML documents. We've already seen new at work in this chapter in this example:

```
<HTML>
    <HEAD>
        <TITLE>
            Using JavaScript Functions
        </TITLE>

    </HEAD>

    <BODY>
        <CENTER>
            <H1>
                Using JavaScript Functions
            </H1>
        </CENTER>

        <SCRIPT LANGUAGE = "JavaScript">
            document.writeln("The time is " + getTime()
            + " right now.")

            function getTime()
            {
                var now = new Date
                var returnValue = now.getHours() + ":"
                + now.getMinutes()
                return(returnValue)
            }
        </SCRIPT>
    </BODY>
</HTML>
```

The new operator uses the Date class's *constructor*, which is a special method that classes use to create and return objects. In this case, we didn't pass any arguments to the Date class's constructor, so the object that it returns and that we call now here will reflect the current date. On the other hand, you could pass a date to the Date class's constructor when you use the new operator, and the Date object returned will reflect that date instead. Here's what that might look like:

```
var then = new Date("10/15/2001")
```

Class Affects Value Types

How do you know what kind of values you can pass to a JavaScript class's constructor? Take a look at the JavaScript documentation; what arguments, and what order you pass them in, varies by class.

One important class that's built into JavaScript is the String class, which you use to handle text strings. To get a better idea of how classes, objects, and constructors work, I'll take a look at that class next.

Using *String* Objects in JavaScript

You handle text strings in JavaScript using the String class. This class lets you create objects that can hold text strings, and it provides you with plenty of methods to let you work on those strings. You'll find the JavaScript methods of this class in Table 6-3 and the JScript methods of this class in Table 6-4.

Table 6-3	Methods			
Methods of the JavaScript *String* Class	anchor	big	blink	bold
	charAt	charCodeAt	concat	fixed
	fontcolor	fontsize	indexOf	italics
	lastIndexOf	link	match	replace
	search	slice	small	split
	strike	sub	substr	substring
	sup	toLowerCase	toSource	toString
	toUpperCase	valueOf		

Table 6-4	**Methods**			
Methods of the JScript *String* Class	anchor	big	blink	bold
	charAt	charCodeAt	concat	fixed
	fontcolor	fontsize	fromCharCode	indexOf
	italics	lastIndexOf	link	match
	replace	search	slice	small
	split	strike	sub	substr
	substring	sup	toLowerCase	toString
	toUpperCase	valueOf		

Here's an example. In this case, I'll create an object of the String class. Then I'll use the object's italics method to display it in italics, and its length property to find its length:

Listing ch06_12.html

```
<HTML>
    <HEAD>
        <TITLE>
            Using the String Class
        </TITLE>
    </HEAD>

    <BODY>
        <CENTER>
            <H1>
                Using the String Class
            </H1>
        </CENTER>

        <SCRIPT LANGUAGE = "JavaScript">
            var string1 = new String("JavaScript and XML are a good mix")

            document.writeln("The text string, " + string1.italics() +
            ", is " + string1.length + " characters long.")
        </SCRIPT>
    </BODY>
</HTML>
```

In this case, I'm passing the text I want in the string "JavaScript and XML are a good mix" to the String class's constructor. That constructor creates a new String object with that text in it and returns it. Now I'm able to use the new object's italics method to display the string in italics, and I can use the length property to determine the string's length. You can see the results in Figure 6-12.

Figure 6-12
Using the
String class
in Internet
Explorer.

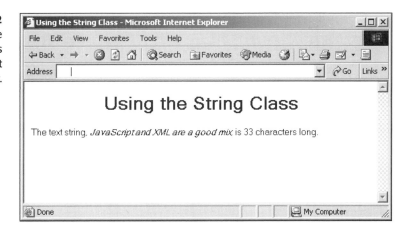

Here's another important aspect of the String class: JavaScript treats this class in a special way, which means that you can actually use it without the new operator. You can declare an object of the String class as a normal variable (without using the new operator or even mentioning the String class), and JavaScript will know just what you mean. Behind the scenes, it uses the String class, but you never need to know it, as in this code:

```
<HTML>
    <HEAD>
        <TITLE>
            Using the String Class
        </TITLE>
    </HEAD>

    <BODY>
        <CENTER>
            <H1>
                Using the String Class
            </H1>
        </CENTER>

        <SCRIPT LANGUAGE = "JavaScript">
```

```
var string1 = "JavaScript and XML are a good mix"
```

```
        document.writeln("The text string, " + string1.italics() +
        ", is " + string1.length + " characters long.")
    </SCRIPT>
  </BODY>
</HTML>
```

Using the *Array* Class to Create Arrays

Arrays are programming constructs that can hold a set of data items that you access item by item with a numeric index. Arrays are perfect for programming because, using the array index, you can reach each item in the array. So, you can easily iterate over every item in the array using a loop.

To create arrays, you use the JavaScript Array class. You can find the methods of this class in Table 6-5 and the methods of the JScript Array class in Table 6-6.

Table 6-5
Methods of the JavaScript Array Class

concat	join	pop	push
reverse	shift	slice	splice
sort	toSource	toString	unshift
valueOf			

Table 6-6
Methods of the JScript Array Class

concat	join	reverse	slice
sort	toString	valueOf	

Let's see an example to make this concrete. In this case, I'll create an array that will hold the student scores from an exam. I'll use a for loop to add them all, finding the average score by dividing the total sum by the number of elements in the array.

I start by creating a new array named scores to hold the student scores, and a variable named runningSum to hold the sum of all the scores:

```
var scores = new Array()
var runningSum = 0
    .
    .
    .
```

You can refer to the first item in the `scores` array as `scores[0]`, the next as `scores[1]`, and so on. So, I can store the students' scores in the `scores` array like this (you can also pass those values to the `Array` class's constructor):

```
var scores = new Array()
var runningSum = 0

scores[0] = 43
scores[1] = 87
scores[2] = 92
scores[3] = 70
scores[4] = 55
scores[5] = 61
    .
    .
    .
```

Now I can add the scores in a `for` loop this way:

```
var scores = new Array()
var runningSum = 0

scores[0] = 43
scores[1] = 87
scores[2] = 92
scores[3] = 70
scores[4] = 55
scores[5] = 61

for(var loopIndex = 0; loopIndex < scores.length; loopIndex++){
    runningSum += scores[loopIndex]
}
    .
    .
    .
```

All that's left is to divide the total of all the scores by the number of elements in the array; you can find the length of an array with its `length` property, this way:

```
var scores = new Array()
var runningSum = 0

cores[0] = 43
cores[1] = 87
cores[2] = 92
cores[3] = 70
cores[4] = 55
cores[5] = 61
```

```
for(var loopIndex = 0; loopIndex < scores.length; loopIndex++){
    runningSum += scores[loopIndex]
}

document.write("The average student score is " +
    runningSum / scores.length)
```

Here's the final code in a Web page:

Listing ch06_13.html

```
<HTML>
    <HEAD>
        <TITLE>
            Using Arrays in JavaScript
        </TITLE>
    </HEAD>

    <BODY>
        <CENTER>
            <H1>
                Using Arrays in JavaScript
            </H1>
        </CENTER>

        <SCRIPT LANGUAGE = "JavaScript">
            var scores = new Array()
            var runningSum = 0

            scores[0] = 43
            scores[1] = 87
            scores[2] = 92
            scores[3] = 70
            scores[4] = 55
            scores[5] = 61

            for(var loopIndex = 0; loopIndex < scores.length; loopIndex++){
                runningSum += scores[loopIndex]
            }

            document.write("The average student score is " +
                runningSum / scores.length)
        </SCRIPT>
    </BODY>
</HTML>
```

You can see the results of this JavaScript in Figure 6-13, where you see that the average score is 68.

Figure 6-13
Using arrays in
JavaScript.

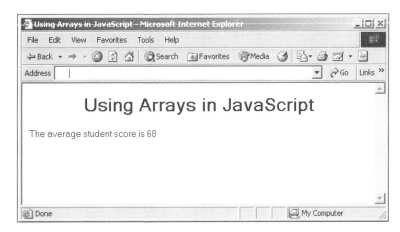

Working with Events

One important aspect of JavaScript is interacting with the user, and you do that through *events*. As discussed earlier, when the user takes some action, such as clicking a button, dragging the mouse, or typing keys, an event happens. In the next chapter, we'll handle not only ordinary events such as button clicks, but also the events that occur as an XML document is loaded into the browser and parsed.

Events are handled tag by tag in browsers, and you use special event attributes to connect code, such as JavaScript code, to an event. For example, when the user presses the mouse button in a Web page, the code connected to the <BODY> element with that element's onMouseDown attribute is executed. You can see the complete list of events for various HTML tags in Table 6-1 for Internet Explorer and Table 6-2 for the Netscape Navigator.

Let's put this technology to work. In this case, I'll use events with two HTML controls (which are what you call the buttons, text fields, lists, and so on in HTML pages): buttons and text fields. When the user clicks the button, the JavaScript code in the page will display the message Welcome to event handling. in the text field.

You create both button and text field controls with the HTML <INPUT> element, setting this element's TYPE attribute to "text" to create a text field and to "button" to create a button. You can also give the button a caption with this element's VALUE attribute, give the text field a length (in characters) with the LENGTH attribute, and supply a name with the NAME attribute. When you give a control a name, you can refer to it in code.

You must create controls inside an HTML form to use them, and you create an HTML form with the `<FORM>` element. (A form is just a programming construct. It does not appear in the Web page. When you click a Submit button, if there is one, all the data from the controls in a form is sent back to the Web server.) Here's how I add a button and a text field to an HTML page:

```
<HTML>
    <HEAD>
        <TITLE>
            Working With Events in JavaScript
        </TITLE>
    </HEAD>

    <BODY>

        <CENTER>
            <FORM name = "form1">
                <H1>
                    Working With Events in JavaScript
                </H1>
                <BR>
                <H2>
                    Click the button!
                </H2>
                <BR>
                <INPUT TYPE = "text" NAME = "Text" SIZE = "60">
                <BR>
                <BR>
                <INPUT TYPE="button" VALUE="Click Here">
            </FORM>
        </CENTER>

    </BODY>

</HTML>
```

The next step is to connect the button to some JavaScript code so that when the button is clicked, a JavaScript function named `displayMessage` is called. In that function, I'll add the code we need to display the message `Welcome to event handling.` in the text field. To connect the `displayMessage` function to the button, I set the button's `onClick` event attribute to the JavaScript I want executed when the button is clicked—`"displayMessage()"`, which will call the `displayMessage` function:

```
<HTML>
    <HEAD>
        <TITLE>
```

```
            Working With Events in JavaScript
        </TITLE>
    </HEAD>

    <BODY>

        <CENTER>
            <FORM name = "form1">
                <H1>
                    Working With Events in JavaScript
                </H1>
                <BR>
                <H2>
                    Click the button!
                </H2>
                <BR>
                <INPUT TYPE = "text" NAME = "Text" SIZE = "60">
                <BR>
                <BR>
                <INPUT TYPE="button" VALUE="Click Here"
                    onClick="displayMessage()">
            </FORM>
        </CENTER>
    </BODY>
</HTML>
```

All that we need to do now is create the JavaScript function named displayMessage that places the message Welcome to event handling. in the text field. So how do you actually access the text in a text field? All the items in a Web page can be accessed as subobjects of the document object. In particular, I've given the text field the name Text by setting the <INPUT> element's NAME attribute to "Text". It's in the <FORM> element, which I've given the name form1. This means that you can refer to the text field object as document.form1.Text. The actual text in the text field object appears in its value property, so you can refer to that text as document.form1.Text.value, like this:

Listing ch06_14.html

```
<HTML>
    <HEAD>
        <TITLE>
            Working With Events in JavaScript
        </TITLE>

        <SCRIPT LANGUAGE= "JavaScript">
```

continues

Listing ch06_14.html   Continued

```
            function displayMessage(e)
            {
                document.form1.Text.value = "Welcome to event handling."
            }
        </SCRIPT>
    </HEAD>

    <BODY>

        <CENTER>
            <FORM name = "form1">
                <H1>
                    Working With Events in JavaScript
                </H1>
                <BR>
                <H2>
                    Click the button!
                </H2>
                <BR>
                <INPUT TYPE = "text" NAME = "Text" SIZE = "60">
                <BR>
                <BR>
                <INPUT TYPE="button" VALUE="Click Here"
                    onClick="displayMessage()">
            </FORM>
        </CENTER>
    </BODY>
</HTML>
```

That's all it takes. Now when the user clicks the button, the message is displayed in the text field, as you can see in Figure 6-14.

Figure 6-14
Using a button
and a text field
in Internet
Explorer.

Getting Event Information

You might have noticed that I declared the function `displayMessage` as `displayMessage(e)` in the previous example. Why did I indicate that this function would be passed an argument? The answer is that it *is* passed an argument in the Netscape Navigator. This argument is an object of the `event` class, and you can get information about the event (such as where a mouse click occurred) using this object, which I've named e. You'll find the properties of the `event` class in Netscape Navigator in Table 6-7.

However, Internet Explorer handles things differently, of course. In Internet Explorer, event-handling functions are not passed an `event` object. (JavaScript is flexible enough that even if you declare a function as we have here to handle both browsers, as though it does receive an argument—although it really doesn't—there's no problem.) Instead of passing an `event` object to event-handling functions, you use the `window.event` object (that is, the `event` subobject of the `window` object), which is available globally in code and doesn't have to be passed to a function. You'll find the properties of the `window.event` property in Internet Explorer in Table 6-8.

	Property	Means
Table 6-7 Netscape Navigator's Event Object Properties	`data`	Holds an array of strings containing the URLs of the dropped objects. It is used with the `dragdrop` event.
	`height`	Holds a height associated with the event.
	`layerX`	Holds the cursor's horizontal position in pixels, relative to the layer in which the event occurred.
	`layerY`	Holds the cursor's vertical position in pixels, relative to the layer in which the event occurred.
	`modifiers`	Holds modifier keys associated with a mouse or key event. Possible values are ALT_MASK, CONTROL_MASK, SHIFT_MASK, and META_MASK.
	`pageX`	Holds the cursor's horizontal position in pixels, relative to the page.
	`pageY`	Holds the cursor's vertical position in pixels, relative to the page.
	`screenX`	Holds the cursor's horizontal position in pixels, relative to the screen.
	`screenY`	Holds a vertical position in pixels, relative to the screen.

continues

Property	Means
type	Holds the type of event.
which	Indicates the mouse button that was pressed or the ASCII value of a pressed key.
width	Holds a width associated with the event.

Table 6-8	Property	Means
Internet Explorer's *window.* *event* Object Properties	altKey	Is true if the Alt key was down
	altLeft	Is true if the left Alt key was down
	button	Specifies which mouse button, if any, was pressed
	cancelBubble	Indicates whether this event should move up the event hierarchy
	clientX	Holds an x coordinate with respect to the client area
	clientY	Holds a y coordinate with respect to the client area
	ctrlKey	Is true if the Ctrl key was down
	ctrlLeft	Is true if the left Ctrl key was down
	fromElement	Specifies an element being moved
	keyCode	Holds the code of the struck key
	offsetX	Holds a container-relative x position
	offsetY	Holds a container-relative y position
	reason	Holds information about a data transfer
	returnValue	Specifies the return value of the event
	screenX	Holds an x coordinate relative to physical screen size
	screenY	Holds a y coordinate relative to physical screen size
	shiftKey	Is true if the Shift key was down
	shiftLeft	Is true if the left Shift key was down
	srcElement	Holds the element that caused the event
	srcFilter	Holds a filter event if this is a filterChange event
	toElement	Specifies the element being moved to

Property	Means
`type`	Property event type as a string
`x`	Holds an x position of the event in context
`y`	Holds a y position of the event in context

For an example that uses the event objects in Tables 6-7 and 6-8, see the next section.

Handling Mouse Events

I'll close this chapter with a reasonably full-scale example that uses the mouse. You can use it in either the Netscape Navigator or Internet Explorer (even though event handling works differently in those two browsers). I determine what browser the user has by checking the appName property of the navigator object; the two possible values of navigator.appName are "Microsoft Internet Explorer" or "Netscape" in these two browsers.

Here are the JavaScript events that this program will use:

- onMouseDown—Happens when a mouse button goes down in the page
- onMouseUp—Happens when a mouse button goes up in the page

When you press or release the mouse button in this page, the code reports the location of the mouse. To find the (x, y) location of the mouse, you use the window.event.x and window.event.y properties in Internet Explorer; you use the e.pageX and e.pageY properties, in which e is the name I've given the event object passed to the mouse event-handler function in the Netscape Navigator.

There's one more point I should mention. In Internet Explorer, you connect the mouseDown and mouseUp events to the <BODY> element this way:

```
<BODY onMouseDown = "mouseDownHandler()" onMouseUp = "mouseUpHandler()">
```

But in Netscape Navigator, the <BODY> element does *not* support the onMouseDown and onMouseUp event attributes. In Netscape Navigator, you connect mouse event handlers using the document.onMouseDown and document.onMouseUp properties in the <SCRIPT> element, like this:

```
<SCRIPT LANGUAGE= "JavaScript">
```

```
document.onMouseDown = mouseDownHandler
document.onMouseUp = mouseUpHandler
      .
      .
      .
```

Here's what the full code looks like for this example:

Listing ch06_15.html

```
<HTML>
    <HEAD>
        <TITLE>
            Using JavaScript and the Mouse
        </TITLE>

        <SCRIPT LANGUAGE= "JavaScript">
            document.onMouseDown = mouseDownHandler
            document.onMouseUp = mouseUpHandler

            function mouseDownHandler(e)
            {
                if (navigator.appName == "Microsoft Internet Explorer") {
                    document.form1.Text.value = "Mouse button down at: " +
                    window.event.x + ", " + window.event.y
                }

                if(navigator.appName == "Netscape" &&
                    parseInt(navigator.appVersion) == 4) {
                    document.form1.Text.value = "Mouse button down at: "
                    + e.pageX + ", " + e.pageY
                }

                if(navigator.appName == "Netscape" &&
                    parseInt(navigator.appVersion) > 4) {
                    document.form1.Text.value = "Mouse button down at: "
                    + e.clientX + ", " + e.clientY
                }
            }

            function mouseUpHandler(e)
            {
                if (navigator.appName == "Microsoft Internet Explorer") {
                    document.form1.Text.value = "Mouse button up at: " +
                    window.event.x + ", " + window.event.y
                }

                if(navigator.appName == "Netscape" &&
                    parseInt(navigator.appVersion) == 4) {
                    document.form1.Text.value = "Mouse button up at: "
                    + e.pageX + ", " + e.pageY
                }
```

```
                    if(navigator.appName == "Netscape" &&
                        parseInt(navigator.appVersion) > 4) {
                        document.form1.Text.value = "Mouse button up at: "
                        + e.clientX + ", " + e.clientY
                    }
                }
        </SCRIPT>
    </HEAD>

    <BODY onMouseDown = "mouseDownHandler(event)" onMouseUp =
        "mouseUpHandler(event)">
        <CENTER>
            <FORM name = "form1">
            <H1>
                Using JavaScript and the Mouse
            </H1>
            <BR>
            Click the mouse.
            <BR>
            <BR>
            <BR>
            <INPUT TYPE = "text" name = "Text" SIZE = 60>
            </FORM>
        </CENTER>
    </BODY>
</HTML>
```

You can see this example at work in Figure 6-15. If you press or release the mouse button in the page, the JavaScript code lets you know what's going on—and *where* it's going on, as you see in the figure.

Figure 6-15
Using the mouse in JavaScript.

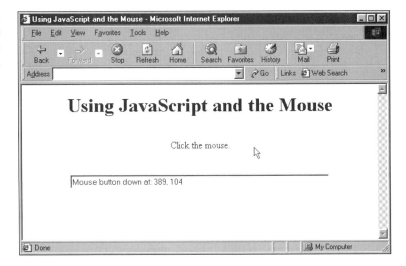

That brings us up to speed in JavaScript. We're ready to put it to work in the next chapter—using a scripting language such as JavaScript is how you gain access to XML in a document in the browser. I'll turn to that now.

CHAPTER 7

Handling XML Documents with JavaScript

Having successfully mastered JavaScript in the previous chapter (for our purposes, anyway), we're going to use it in this chapter to work with the World Wide Web Consortium (W3C) Document Object Model (DOM), the W3C-standardized programming interface for handling XML documents. Before the introduction of the DOM, all XML parsers and processors had different ways of interacting with XML documents—and, worse, they kept changing all the time. With the introduction of the XML DOM, things have settled down (to some extent).

The W3C DOM

The W3C DOM specifies a way of treating a document as a *tree of nodes*. In this model, every discrete data item is a *node*, and child elements or enclosed text become subnodes. Treating a document as a tree of nodes is one good way of handling XML documents (although there are others, as we'll see when we start working with Java): It makes it explicit which elements contain which other elements because the contained elements become subnodes (called child nodes) of the container nodes. Everything in a document becomes a node in this model—elements, element attributes, text, and so on. Here are the possible node types in the W3C DOM:

- Element
- Attribute

- Text
- CDATA section
- Entity reference
- Entity
- Processing instruction
- Comment
- Document
- Document type
- Document fragment
- Notation

For example, take a look at this document:

```
<?xml version="1.0" encoding="UTF-8"?>
<DOCUMENT>
    <GREETING>
        Hello From XML
    </GREETING>
    <MESSAGE>
        Welcome to the wild and woolly world of XML.
    </MESSAGE>
</DOCUMENT>
```

This document has a processing instruction node and a root element node corresponding to the <DOCUMENT> element. The <DOCUMENT> node has two subnodes, the <GREETING> and <MESSAGE> nodes. These nodes are *child* nodes of the <DOCUMENT> node and are *sibling* nodes of each other. Both the <GREETING> and <MESSAGE> elements themselves have one subnode: a text node that holds character data. We'll get used to handling documents like this one as a tree of nodes in this chapter. Looked at as a tree, this is what this document looks like:

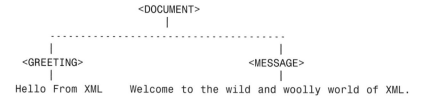

Every discrete data item is itself treated as a node. Using the methods defined in the W3C DOM, you can navigate along the various branches of a document's tree using methods such as `nextChild` to move to the `nextChild` node, or `lastSibling` to move to the last sibling node of the current node. Working with a document this way takes a little practice, and that's what this chapter is all about.

There are a number of different levels of DOM:

- **Level 0**—There is no official DOM "Level 0," but that's the way the W3C refers to the DOM, as implemented in relatively early versions of the popular browsers—in particular, Netscape Navigator 3.0 and Microsoft Internet Explorer 3.0.

- **Level 1**—This level of the DOM is the current W3C recommendation, and it concentrates on the HTML and XML document models. You can find the documentation for this level at `www.w3.org/TR/REC-DOM-Level-1/`.

- **Level 2**—Currently at the Candidate Recommendation stage, this level of the DOM is more advanced and includes a stylesheet object model. It also adds functionality for manipulating the style information attached to a document. In addition, it lets you traverse a document, has a built-in event model, and supports XML namespaces. You can find the documentation for this level at `www.w3.org/TR/DOM-Level-2/`.

- **Level 3**—This level is still in the planning stage and will address document loading and saving, and content models (such as DTDs and schemas) with document validation support. In addition, it will address document views and formatting, key events, and event groups. There is no documentation on this level yet.

Practically speaking, the only nearly complete implementation of the XML DOM today is that in Internet Explorer version 5 or later; you can find the documentation for the Microsoft DOM at `http://msdn.microsoft.com/library/psdk/xmlsdk/xmld20ab.htm` as of this writing. However, the Microsoft sites are continually (and annoyingly) being reorganized, so it's quite possible that by the time you read this, that page will be long gone. In that case, your best bet is to go to `http://msdn.microsoft.com` and search for "xml dom." (The general rule is not to trust a URL at a Microsoft site for more than about two months.)

Because Internet Explorer provides substantial support for the W3C DOM Level 1, I'm going to use it in this chapter. Let us hope that translation to other W3C-compliant browsers as those browsers begin to support the W3C DOM won't be terribly difficult.

The XML DOM Objects

Here are the official W3C DOM Level 1 objects:

- Document—The document object.
- DocumentFragment—A fragment of a document.
- DocumentType—Reference to the <!DOCTYPE> element.
- EntityReference—Reference to an entity.
- Element—An element.
- Attr—An attribute.
- ProcessingInstruction—A processing instruction.
- Comment—The content of an XML comment.
- Text—Text content of an element or attribute.
- CDATASection—Refers to CDATA section
- Entity—Stands for a parsed or unparsed entity in the XML document.
- Notation—Holds a notation.
- Node—A single node in the document tree.
- NodeList—A list of node objects. Allows iteration and indexed access operations.
- NamedNodeMap—Allows iteration and access by name to the collection of attributes.

Microsoft uses different names for these objects and adds its own. In particular, Microsoft defines a set of "base objects" that form the foundation of its XML DOM. The top-level object is the DOMDocument object, and it's the only one you create directly—you reach the other objects through that object. Here's the list of base objects in Internet Explorer. Note the objects designed to treat a document as a tree of nodes—XMLDOMNode, XMLDOMNodeList, and so on:

- DOMDocument—The top node of the XML DOM tree.
- XMLDOMNode—A single node in the document tree. Includes support for data types, namespaces, DTDs, and XML schemas.

- `XMLDOMNodeList`—A list of node objects. Allows iteration and indexed access operations.

- `XMLDOMNamedNodeMap`—Object that allows iteration and access by name to the collection of attributes.

- `XMLDOMParseError`—Information about the most recent error. Includes error number, line number, character position, and a text description.

- `XMLHttpRequest`—Object that allows communication with HTTP servers.

- `XSLRuntime`—Object that supports methods that you can call from XSL stylesheets.

Besides these base objects, the Microsoft XML DOM provides these XML DOM objects that you use when working with documents in code. This includes the various types of nodes, which you see supported with objects of types such as `XMLDOMAttribute`, `XMLDOMCharacterData`, and `XMLDOMElement`:

- `XMLDOMAttribute`—Stands for an attribute object

- `XMLDOMCDATASection`—Handles `CDATA` sections so that text is not interpreted as markup language

- `XMLDOMCharacterData`—Provides methods used for text manipulation

- `XMLDOMComment`—Provides the content of an XML comment

- `XMLDOMDocumentFragment`—Is a lightweight object useful for tree insert operations

- `XMLDOMDocumentType`—Holds information connected to the document type declaration

- `XMLDOMElement`—Stands for the element object

- `XMLDOMEntity`—Stands for a parsed or unparsed entity in the XML document

- `XMLDOMEntityReference`—Stands for an entity reference node

- `XMLDOMImplementation`—Supports general DOM methods

- `XMLDOMNotation`—Holds a notation (as declared in the DTD or schema)

- `XMLDOMProcessingInstruction`—Is a processing instruction

- `XMLDOMText`—Provides text content of an element or attribute

We'll put many of these objects to work in this chapter, seeing how to parse and access XML documents using the Microsoft XML DOM and handling events as documents are loaded. We'll also see how to alter an XML document at run time.

The previous list of objects is pretty substantial, and each object can contain its own properties, methods, and events. Although most of these properties, methods, and events are specified in the W3C XML DOM, many are added by Microsoft as well. If we're going to work with the XML DOM in practice, it's essential to have a good understanding of these objects, both practically for the purposes of this chapter and for reference. I'll go through the major objects in some detail to make handling the XML DOM clear, starting with the main object, the DOMDocument object.

The *DOMDocument* Object

The DOMDocument object is the main object you work with, and it represents the top node in every document tree. When working with the DOM, this is the only object you create directly.

As we'll see in this chapter, there are two ways to create document objects in Internet Explorer: using the Microsoft.XMLDOM class and using XML *data islands*. Creating a document object with the Microsoft.XMLDOM class looks like this—you explicitly load a document into the object with the load method:

```
function readXMLDocument()
{
    var xmldoc
    xmldoc = new ActiveXObject("Microsoft.XMLDOM")
    xmldoc.load("ch07_01.xml")
    .
    .
    .
```

Microsoft.XMLDOM represents a fairly early version of Microsoft's XML (MSXML) support, but it also represents a common denominator for that support. You can specify that you want to use a later version of the MSXML package like this, which explicitly uses version 4.0 (you can also use "MSXML2.DOMDocument.2.0" or "MSXML2.DOMDocument.3.0"):

```
function readXMLDocument()

    var xmldoc
    xmldoc = new ActiveXObject("MSXML2.DOMDocument.4.0")
```

```
xmldoc.load("ch07_01.xml")
    .
    .
    .
```

The problem with this is that not all users will have MSXML 4.0 installed. Of course, if you need the advanced functionality of a recent version of MSXML (such as the capability to work with full XML schemas with MSXML 4.0, as we saw in Chapter 5, "Creating XML Schemas"), you don't have any other options.

We'll also see that you can use the <XML> HTML element to create a data island in Internet Explorer and then use the XMLDocument property of that element to gain access to the corresponding document object:

```
<XML ID="meetingsXML" SRC="ch07_01.xml"></XML>

<SCRIPT LANGUAGE="JavaScript">
    function readXMLDocument()
    {
        xmldoc = document.all("meetingsXML").XMLDocument
        .
        .
        .
```

Here is the base set of properties for this object. (MSXML version 4.0 will have more properties, for example, as you can see in the documentation that comes with version 4.0.) Throughout this chapter, those items marked with an asterisk (*) represent a Microsoft extension to the W3C DOM:

- async*—Indicates whether asynchronous download is allowed. Read/write.

- attributes—Holds the list of attributes for this node. Read-only.

- baseName*—Is the base name qualified with the namespace. Read-only.

- childNodes—Holds a node list containing child nodes for nodes that may have children. Read-only.

- dataType*—Gives the data type for this node. Read/write.

- definition*—Gives the definition of the node in the DTD or schema. Read-only.

- doctype—Is the document type node, which is what specifies the DTD for this document. Read-only.

- documentElement—Specifies the root element of the document. Read/write.

- firstChild—Is the first child of the current node. Read-only.

- implementation—Is the XMLDOMImplementation object for this document. Read-only.

- lastChild—Is the last child node of the current node. Read-only.

- namespaceURI*—Gives the uniform resource identifier (URI) for the namespace. Read-only.

- nextSibling—Is the next sibling of the current node. Read-only.

- nodeName—Is the qualified name of the element, attribute, or entity reference. Holds a fixed string for other node types. Read-only.

- nodeType—Specifies the XML DOM node type. Read-only.

- nodeTypedValue*—Holds this node's value. Read/write.

- nodeTypeString*—Gives the node type expressed as a string. Read-only.

- nodeValue—Gives the text associated with the node. Read/write.

- ondataavailable*—Is the event handler for the ondataavailable event. Read/write.

- onreadystatechange*—Is the event handler that handles readyState property changes. Read/write.

- ontransformnode*—Is the event handler for the ontransformnode event. Read/write.

- ownerDocument—Specifies the root of the document that contains this node. Read-only.

- parentNode—Is the parent node (for nodes that can have parents). Read-only.

- parsed*—Is true if this node and all descendants have been parsed; is false otherwise. Read-only.

- parseError*—Is an XMLDOMParseError object with information about the most recent parsing error. Read-only.

- prefix*—Is the namespace prefix. Read-only.

- preserveWhiteSpace*—Is true if processing should preserve whitespace; is false otherwise. Read/write.

- previousSibling—Is the previous sibling of this node. Read-only.

- readyState*—Specifies the current state of the XML document. Read-only.

- `resolveExternals*`—Indicates whether external definitions are to be resolved at parse time. Read/write.

- `given*`—Indicates whether the node is explicitly given or derived from a default value. Read-only.

- `text*`—Holds the text content of the node and its subtrees. Read/write.

- `url*`—Gives the canonicalized uniform resource locator (URL) for the most recently loaded XML document. Read-only.

- `validateOnParse*`—Indicates whether the parser should validate this document. Read/write.

- `xml*`—Gives the XML representation of the node and all its descendants. Read-only.

Here is the base set of methods of the `document` object (as before, this is the base set; MSXML versions such as 4.0 will have more methods). Again, those items marked with an asterisk (*) represent a Microsoft extension to the W3C DOM:

- `abort*`—Aborts an asynchronous download

- `appendChild`—Appends a new child as the last child of the current node

- `cloneNode`—Returns a new node that is a copy of this node

- `createAttribute`—Returns a new attribute with the given name

- `createCDATASection`—Returns a `CDATA` section node that contains the given data

- `createComment`—Returns a comment node

- `createDocumentFragment`—Returns an empty `DocumentFragment` object

- `createElement`—Returns an element node using the given name

- `createEntityReference`—Returns a new `EntityReference` object

- `createNode*`—Returns a node using the given type, name, and namespace

- `createProcessingInstruction`—Returns a processing instruction node

- `createTextNode`—Returns a text node that contains the given data

- `getElementsByTagName`—Yields a collection of elements that have the given name
- `hasChildNodes`—Is true if this node has children
- `insertBefore`—Inserts a child node to the before the given node
- `load*`—Loads an XML document from the given location
- `loadXML*`—Loads an XML document using the given string
- `nodeFromID*`—Yields the node whose ID attribute matches the given value
- `removeChild`—Removes the given child node from the list of children
- `replaceChild`—Replaces the given child node with the given new child node
- `save*`—Saves an XML document to the given location
- `selectNodes*`—Applies the given pattern-matching operation to this node's context, returning a list of matching nodes
- `selectSingleNode*`—Applies the given pattern-matching operation to this node's context, returning the first matching node
- `transformNode*`—Transforms this node and its children using the given XSL stylesheet
- `transformNodeToObject*`—Transforms this node and its children using the given XSL stylesheet and returns the an object

Here is the base set of the events of the `document` object:

- `ondataavailable*`—Indicates that XML document data is available
- `onreadystatechange*`—Indicates when the `readyState` property changes
- `ontransformnode*`—Happens before each node in the stylesheet is applied in the XML source

The *XMLDOMNode* Object

The Microsoft `XMLDOMNode` object extends the core XML DOM node interface by adding support for data types, namespaces, DTDs, and schemas as implemented in Internet Explorer. We'll use this object a good deal as we traverse document trees. Here is the base set of properties for this object. As before, those items marked with an asterisk (*) represent a Microsoft extension to the W3C DOM:

- `attributes`—The list of attributes for this node. Read-only.
- `baseName`*—The base name for the name qualified with the namespace. Read-only.
- `childNodes`—A node list containing the child nodes of the current node. Read-only.
- `dataType`*—The data type for this node. Read/write.
- `definition`*—The definition of the node in the DTD or schema. Read-only.
- `firstChild`—The first child of the current node. Read-only.
- `given`*—Indication of whether a node is explicitly given or derived from a default value. Read-only.
- `lastChild`—The last child of the current node. Read-only.
- `namespaceURI`*—The URI for the namespace. Read-only.
- `nextSibling`—The next sibling of this node. Read-only.
- `nodeName`—Property that holds a qualified name for an element, attribute, or entity reference, or a string for other node types. Read-only.
- `nodeType`—The XML DOM node type. Read-only.
- `nodeTypedValue`*—The node's value. Read/write.
- `nodeTypeString`*—The node type in string form. Read-only.
- `nodeValue`—The text associated with the node. Read/write.
- `ownerDocument`—The root of the document. Read-only.
- `parentNode`—The parent node. Read-only.
- `parsed`*—True if this node and all descendants have been parsed; false otherwise. Read-only.
- `prefix`*—The namespace prefix. Read-only.
- `previousSibling`—The previous sibling of this node. Read-only.

- text*—The text content of the node and its subtrees. Read/write.
- xml*—The XML representation of the node and all its descendants. Read-only.

Here is the base set of methods for this object:

- appendChild—Appends a new child as the last child of this node
- cloneNode—Creates a new node that is a copy of this node
- hasChildNodes—Is true if this node has children
- insertBefore—Inserts a child node before the given node
- removeChild—Removes the given child node
- replaceChild—Replaces the given child node with the given new child node
- selectNodes*—Applies the given pattern-matching operation to this node's context, returning a list of matching nodes
- selectSingleNode*—Applies the given pattern-matching operation to this node's context, returning the first matching node
- transformNode*—Transforms this node and its children using the given XSL stylesheet
- transformNodeToObject*—Transforms this node and its children using the given XSL stylesheet, returning the result as an object

This object has no events.

The *XMLDOMNodeList* Object

You use the XMLDOMNodeList to handle lists of nodes, and node lists are useful because a node can itself have many child nodes. Using a node list, you can handle all the children of a node at once.

For example, here I'm loading a document and getting a list of all <PERSON> elements as a node list, using the document object's getElementsByTagName method:

```
function readXMLDocument()
{
    var xmldoc, nodeList
    xmldoc = new ActiveXObject("Microsoft.XMLDOM")
    xmldoc.load("ch07_01.xml")
    nodeList = xmlDoc.getElementsByTagName("PERSON")
    .
    .
    .
```

Here is the base set of properties for the XMLDOMNodeList object:

- length—Number of items in the collection. Read-only.

Here is the base set of methods for the XMLDOMNodeList object:

- item—Allows random access to nodes in the collection
- nextNode*—Shows the next node in the collection
- reset*—Resets the list iterator

This object has no events.

The *XMLDOMNamedNodeMap* Object

The Microsoft XML DOM also supports an XMLDOMNamedNodeMap object, which provides support for namespaces. Here is the base set of properties for this object:

- item—Allows random access to nodes in the collection. Read-only.
- length—Specifies the number of items in the collection. Read-only.

Here is the base set of methods for this object:

- getNamedItem—Gets the attribute with the given name
- getQualifiedItem*—Gets the attribute with the given namespace and attribute name
- nextNode—Gets the next node
- removeNamedItem—Removes an attribute
- removeQualifiedItem—Removes the attribute with the given namespace and attribute name
- reset—Resets the list iterator
- setNamedItem—Adds the given node

This object has no events.

The *XMLDOMParseError* Object

The Microsoft XMLDOMParseError object holds information about the most recent parse error, including the error number, line number, character position, and a text description. Although it's not obvious to anyone who loads an

XML document into Internet Explorer, the browser does validate the document using either a DTD or a schema, if one is supplied. It's not obvious that this happens because, by default, Internet Explorer does not display any validation error messages. However, if you use the XMLDOMParseError object, you can get a full validation report, and I'll do so in this chapter.

Here are the base properties of this object:

- errorCode—The error code of the most recent parse error. Read-only.

- filepos—The file position where the error occurred. Read-only.

- line—The line number that contains the error. Read-only.

- linepos—The character position in the line where the error happened. Read-only.

- reason—The reason for the error. Read-only.

- srcText—The full text of the line containing the error. Read-only.

- url—The URL of the XML document containing the last error. Read-only.

Note that this object does not have any methods or events, and it does not correspond to any official W3C object in the W3C DOM.

The *XMLDOMAttribute* Object

In both the W3C DOM and the Microsoft DOM, attribute objects are node objects (that is, they are based on the node object), but they are not actually child nodes of an element and are *not* considered part of the document tree. Instead, attributes are considered *properties* of their associated elements (this means that properties such as parentNode, previousSibling, and nextSibling are meaningless for attributes). We'll see how to work with attributes in this chapter.

Here are the base properties of the XMLDOMAttribute object:

- attributes—The list of attributes for this node. Read-only.

- baseName*—The base name for the name qualified with the namespace. Read-only.

- childNodes—A node list containing child nodes. Read-only.

- dataType*—The data type of this node. Read/write.

- `definition*`—The definition of the node in the DTD or schema. Read-only.

- `firstChild`—The first child of the current node. Read-only.

- `lastChild`—The last child of the current node. Read-only.

- `name`—The attribute name. Read-only.

- `namespaceURI*`—The URI for the namespace. Read-only.

- `nextSibling`—The next sibling of this node. Read-only.

- `nodeName`—The qualified name for an element, attribute, or entity reference, or a string for other node types. Read-only.

- `nodeType`—The XML DOM node type. Read-only.

- `nodeTypedValue*`—The node's value. Read/write.

- `nodeTypeString*`—The node type in string form. Read-only.

- `nodeValue`—The text associated with the node. Read/write.

- `ownerDocument`—The root of the document. Read-only.

- `parentNode`—The parent node (for nodes that can have parents). Read-only.

- `parsed*`—True if this node and all descendants have been parsed; false otherwise. Read-only.

- `prefix*`—The namespace prefix. Read-only.

- `previousSibling`—The previous sibling of this node. Read-only.

- `specified`—Indication of whether the node (usually an attribute) is explicitly specified or derived from a default value. Read-only.

- `text`—The text content of the node and its subtrees. Read/write.

- `value`—The attribute's value. Read/write.

- `xml`—The XML representation of the node and all its descendants. Read-only.

Here are the base methods of the `XMLDOMAttribute` object:

- `appendChild`—Appends a new child as the last child of this node

- `cloneNode`—Returns a new node that is a copy of this node

- `hasChildNodes`—True if this node has children

- `insertBefore`—Inserts a child node before the given node

- `removeChild`—Removes the given child node from the list

- `replaceChild`—Replaces the given child node with the given new child node
- `selectNodes`—Applies the given pattern-matching operation to this node's context, returning a list of matching nodes
- `selectSingleNode`—Applies the given pattern-matching operation to this node's context, returning the first matching node
- `transformNode`—Transforms this node and its children using the given XSL stylesheet
- `transformNodeToObject`—Transforms this node and its children using the given XSL stylesheet, and returns the result in an object

This object does not support any events.

The *XMLDOMElement* Object

The XMLDOMElement object represents elements and is probably the most common node object you'll deal with. Because attributes are not considered child nodes of an element object, you use special methods to get the attributes of an element. For example, you can use the getAttribute method, which returns an XMLDOMNamedNodeMap object that contains all the element's attributes.

Here are the base properties of the XMLDOMElement object:

- `attributes`—The list of attributes for this node. Read-only.
- `baseName`*—The base name for the name qualified with the namespace. Read-only.
- `childNodes`—A node list containing the children. Read-only.
- `dataType`*—The data type for this node. Read/write.
- `definition`*—The definition of the node in the DTD or schema.
- `firstChild`—The first child of this node. Read-only.
- `lastChild`—The last child node of this node. Read-only.
- `namespaceURI`*—The URI for the namespace. Read-only.
- `nextSibling`—The next sibling of this node. Read-only.
- `nodeName`—The qualified name of an element, attribute, or entity reference, or a string for other node types. Read-only.
- `nodeType`—The XML DOM node type. Read-only.
- `nodeTypeString`*—The node type in string form. Read-only.
- `nodeValue`—The text associated with the node. Read/write.

- `ownerDocument`—The root of the document. Read-only.

- `parentNode`—The parent node of the current node. Read-only.

- `parsed`*—True if this node and all descendants have been parsed; false otherwise. Read-only.

- `prefix`*—The namespace prefix. Read-only.

- `previousSibling`—The previous sibling of this node. Read-only.

- `specified`*—Indication of whether the node is explicitly specified or derived from a default value in the DTD or schema. Read-only.

- `tagName`—The element name. Read-only.

- `text`*—The text content of the node and its subtrees. Read/write.

- `xml`*—The XML representation of the node and all its descendants. Read-only.

Here are the base methods of the `XMLDOMElement` object:

- `appendChild`—Appends a new child as the last child of the current node

- `cloneNode`—Returns a new node that is a copy of this node

- `getAttribute`—Gets the value of the named attribute

- `getAttributeNode`—Gets the named attribute node

- `getElementsByTagName`—Returns a list of all descendant elements that match the given name

- `hasChildNodes`—Is true if this node has children

- `insertBefore`—Inserts a child node before the given node

- `normalize`—Normalizes all descendent elements, combining two or more text nodes next to each other into one text node

- `removeAttribute`—Removes or replaces the named attribute

- `removeAttributeNode`—Removes the given attribute from this element

- `removeChild`—Removes the given child node

- `replaceChild`—Replaces the given child node with the given new child node

- `selectNodes`*—Applies the given pattern-matching operation to this node's context, returning the list of matching nodes

- `selectSingleNode*`—Applies the given pattern-matching operation to this node's context, returning the first matching node

- `setAttribute`—Sets the value of a named attribute

- `setAttributeNode`—Adds or changes the given attribute node on this element

- `transformNode*`—Transforms this node and its children using the given XSL stylesheet

- `transformNodeToObject*`—Transforms this node and its children using the given XSL stylesheet, and returns the resulting transformation as an object

This object has no events.

The *XMLDOMText* Object

The `XMLDOMText` object holds the text content of an element or attribute. If there is no markup inside an element but there is text, that element will contain only one node: a text node that holds the text. (In mixed-content models, text nodes can have sibling element nodes.)

When a document is first made available to the XML DOM, all text is *normalized*, which means that there is only one text node for each block of text. You can actually create text nodes that are adjacent to each other, although they will not be saved as distinct the next time the document is opened. (It's worth noting that the `normalize` method on the `XMLDOMElement` object merges adjacent text nodes into single nodes.)

Here are the base properties of the `XMLDOMText` object:

- `attributes`—The list of attributes for this node. Read-only.

- `baseName*`—The base name for the name qualified with the namespace. Read-only.

- `childNodes`—A node list containing the child nodes. Read-only.

- `data`—This node's data (what's actually stored depends on the node type). Read/write.

- `dataType*`—The data type for this node. Read/write.

- `definition*`—The definition of the node in the DTD or schema. Read-only.

- `firstChild`—The first child of the current node. Read-only.

- `lastChild`—The last child of the current node. Read-only.

- `length`—The length, in characters, of the data. Read-only.

- `namespaceURI*`—The URI for the namespace. Read-only.

- `nextSibling`—The next sibling of this node. Read-only.

- `nodeName`—The qualified name of an element, attribute, or entity reference, or a string for other node types. Read-only.

- `nodeType`—The XML DOM node type. Read-only.

- `nodeTypedValue*`—This node's value. Read/write.

- `nodeTypeString*`—The node type in string form. Read-only.

- `nodeValue`—The text associated with the node. Read/write.

- `ownerDocument`—The root of the document. Read-only.

- `parentNode`—The parent node. Read-only.

- `parsed*`—True if this node and all descendants have been parsed; false otherwise. Read-only.

- `prefix*`—The namespace prefix. Read-only.

- `previousSibling`—The previous sibling of this node. Read-only.

- `specified`—Indication of whether the node is explicitly specified or derived from a default value. Read-only.

- `text*`—The text content of the node and its subtrees. Read/write.

- `xml*`—The XML representation of the node and all its descendants. Read-only.

Here are the methods of the `XMLDOMText` object:

- `appendChild`—Appends a new child as the last child of this node

- `appendData`—Appends the given string to the existing string data

- `cloneNode`—Returns a new node that is a copy of this node

- `deleteData`—Removes the given substring within the string data

- `hasChildNodes`—Is true if this node has children

- `insertBefore`—Inserts a child node before the specified node

- `insertData`—Inserts the supplied string at the specified offset

- `removeChild`—Removes the specified child node from the list of children

- `replaceChild`—Replaces the specified child node with the given new child node

- `selectNodes`*—Replaces the given number of characters with the given string

- `selectSingleNode`*—Applies the given pattern-matching operation to this node's context, returning a list of matching nodes

- `specified`*—Applies the specified pattern-matching operation to this node's context, returning an object

- `splitText`—Breaks this text node into two text nodes

- `substringData`—Returns a substring of the full string

- `transformNode`*—Transforms this node and its children using the given XSL stylesheet

- `transformNodeToObject`*—Transforms this node and its children using the given XSL stylesheet, and returns the resulting transformation as an object

This object does not support any events.

That gives us an overview of the most commonly used objects in the Microsoft XML DOM, and I'm going to put them to work in the rest of the chapter. I'll start at the beginning: loading an XML document.

Loading XML Documents

Our first step will be to load an XML document into Internet Explorer using code, and to create a document object. Using this object, we'll be able to access all aspects of the document itself.

As mentioned earlier in this chapter, there are two ways to load an XML document into Internet Explorer so that you have access to it using JavaScript. To see how this works, I'll use this XML document, ch07_01.xml, throughout this chapter. This document records business meetings, including who was present and when the meeting occurred:

Listing ch07_01.xml

```
<?xml version="1.0"?>
<MEETINGS>
    <MEETING TYPE="informal">
        <MEETING_TITLE>XML In The Real World</MEETING_TITLE>
```

```
<MEETING_NUMBER>2079</MEETING_NUMBER>
<SUBJECT>XML</SUBJECT>
<DATE>6/1/2003</DATE>
<PEOPLE>
    <PERSON ATTENDANCE="present">
        <FIRST_NAME>Edward</FIRST_NAME>
        <LAST_NAME>Samson</LAST_NAME>
    </PERSON>
    <PERSON ATTENDANCE="absent">
        <FIRST_NAME>Ernestine</FIRST_NAME>
        <LAST_NAME>Johnson</LAST_NAME>
    </PERSON>
    <PERSON ATTENDANCE="present">
        <FIRST_NAME>Betty</FIRST_NAME>
        <LAST_NAME>Richardson</LAST_NAME>
    </PERSON>
</PEOPLE>
    </MEETING>
</MEETINGS>
```

The first way of loading an XML document into Internet Explorer is to create a document object using the `Microsoft.XMLDOM` class. (Bear in mind that you can also specify the version of MSXML you want, for example, as `MSXML2.DOMDocument.4.0`.)

To see this in action, I'm going to create an example that reads in ch07_01.xml and retrieves the name of the third person in that document (Betty Richardson). I start by creating a new document object like this (recall that you use the `new` operator to create a new object): `xmldoc = new ActiveXObject("Microsoft.XMLDOM")`. Here's how it looks in code, in which I'm loading in the XML document ch07_01.xml:

```
<HTML>
    <HEAD>
        <TITLE>
            Reading XML element values
        </TITLE>

        <SCRIPT LANGUAGE="JavaScript">
            function readXMLDocument()
            {
                var xmldoc
                xmldoc = new ActiveXObject("Microsoft.XMLDOM")
                xmldoc.load("ch07_01.xml")
                .
                .
                .
    </HEAD>
</HTML>
```

The next step is to get a node object corresponding to the document's root element, <MEETINGS>, and you do that with the documentElement method:

```
var xmldoc, meetingsNode
xmldoc = new ActiveXObject("Microsoft.XMLDOM")
xmldoc.load("ch07_01.xml")

meetingsNode = xmldoc.documentElement
    .
    .
    .
```

At this point, I'm free to move around the document as I like, using methods such as firstChild, nextChild, previousChild, and lastChild, which let you access the child elements of an element, and the firstSibling, nextSibling, previousSibling, and lastSibling methods, which let you access elements on the same nesting level. For example, the <MEETING> element is the first child of the document root element, <MEETINGS>, so I can get a node corresponding to the <MEETING> element using the firstChild method:

```
var xmldoc, meetingsNode, meetingNode,
xmldoc = new ActiveXObject("Microsoft.XMLDOM")
xmldoc.load("ch07_01.xml")

meetingsNode = xmldoc.documentElement
meetingNode = meetingsNode.firstChild
    .
    .
    .
```

I want to track down the third <PERSON> element inside the <PEOPLE> element. The <PEOPLE> element is the last child of the <MEETING> element, so I can get a node corresponding to the <PEOPLE> element this way:

```
var xmldoc, meetingsNode, meetingNode, peopleNode
var first_nameNode, last_nameNode
xmldoc = new ActiveXObject("Microsoft.XMLDOM")
xmldoc.load("ch07_01.xml")

meetingsNode = xmldoc.documentElement
meetingNode = meetingsNode.firstChild
peopleNode = meetingNode.lastChild
    .
    .
    .
```

I want the third person in the <PEOPLE> element, which is the last child of this element, so I get access to that person with the lastChild method:

```
var xmldoc, meetingsNode, meetingNode, peopleNode
xmldoc = new ActiveXObject("Microsoft.XMLDOM")
xmldoc.load("ch07_01.xml")

meetingsNode = xmldoc.documentElement
meetingNode = meetingsNode.firstChild
peopleNode = meetingNode.lastChild
personNode = peopleNode.lastChild
    .
    .
    .
```

Finally, I can get a node corresponding to the <FIRST_NAME> and <LAST_NAME> elements that hold the person's name using the firstChild and nextSibling (which gets the current node's next sibling node) methods:

```
var xmldoc, meetingsNode, meetingNode, peopleNode
var first_nameNode, last_nameNode
xmldoc = new ActiveXObject("Microsoft.XMLDOM")
xmldoc.load("ch07_01.xml")

meetingsNode = xmldoc.documentElement
meetingNode = meetingsNode.firstChild
peopleNode = meetingNode.lastChild
personNode = peopleNode.lastChild
first_nameNode = personNode.firstChild
last_nameNode = first_nameNode.nextSibling
    .
    .
    .
```

Now I've walked the tree to get nodes corresponding to the actual elements I want. Note, however, that the node I want is actually the text node *inside* the <FIRST_NAME> and <LAST_NAME> elements, which holds the person's name. That means that I have to get the first child of those elements (that is, the text node) and then use the nodeValue property of that text node to read the person's name.

To actually display the person's first and last names, I'll use a little dynamic HTML. Here, I'm going to use an HTML <DIV> element and the innerHTML property of that element (which holds the text content of the <DIV> element) to display the person's name like this:

Listing ch07_02.html

```
<HTML>
    <HEAD>
        <TITLE>
            Reading XML element values
        </TITLE>

        <SCRIPT LANGUAGE="JavaScript">
            function readXMLDocument()
            {
                var xmldoc, meetingsNode, meetingNode, peopleNode
                var first_nameNode, last_nameNode, outputText
                xmldoc = new ActiveXObject("Microsoft.XMLDOM")
                xmldoc.load("ch07_01.xml")

                meetingsNode = xmldoc.documentElement
                meetingNode = meetingsNode.firstChild
                peopleNode = meetingNode.lastChild
                personNode = peopleNode.lastChild
                first_nameNode = personNode.firstChild
                last_nameNode = first_nameNode.nextSibling

                outputText = "Third name: " +
                        first_nameNode.firstChild.nodeValue + ' '
                    + last_nameNode.firstChild.nodeValue
                messageDIV.innerHTML=outputText
            }
        </SCRIPT>
    </HEAD>

    <BODY>
        <CENTER>
            <H1>
                Reading XML element values
            </H1>

            <INPUT TYPE="BUTTON" VALUE="Get the name of the third person"
                ONCLICK="readXMLDocument()">
            <P>
            <DIV ID="messageDIV"></DIV>
        </CENTER>
    </BODY>
</HTML>
```

I've also added a button with the caption Get the name of the third person that will call the JavaScript function we've defined, readXMLDocument; that function reads and displays the document.

You can see this page at work in Internet Explorer in Figure 7-1. When the user clicks the button, the XML document ch07_01.xml is read and parsed, and we retrieve and display the third person's name. We've made substantial progress.

Figure 7-1
Reading an XML element in Internet Explorer.

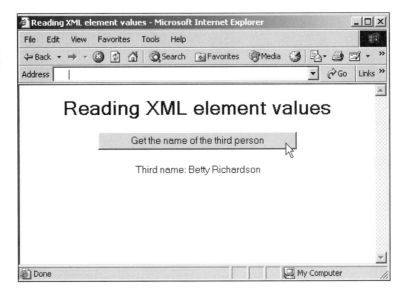

Using XML Data Islands

As of version 5 in Internet Explorer, you can also use *XML data islands* to actually embed XML inside HTML pages. Internet Explorer supports an HTML <XML> element (which is not part of the HTML standard) that you can simply enclose an XML document inside, like this:

```
<XML ID="greeting">
    <DOCUMENT>
        <GREETING>Hi there XML!</GREETING>
    </DOCUMENT>
</XML>
```

The Internet Explorer <XML> element has some attributes worth noting:

- ID—The ID with which you can refer to the <XML> element in code. Set to an alphanumeric string.

- NS—The URI of the XML namespace used by the XML content. Set to a URI.

- PREFIX—Namespace prefix of the XML contents. Set to an alphanumeric string.

- SRC—Source for the XML document, if the document is external. Set to an URI.

When you use this element, you access it using its ID value in code. To reach the element, you can use the all collection, passing it the ID you gave the element like this for the previous example: document.all("greeting"). To get the document object corresponding to the XML document, you can then use the XMLDocument property. Here's how I convert the previous example to use a data island instead of the Microsoft.XMLDOM object:

Listing ch07_03.html

```
<HTML>
    <HEAD>
        <TITLE>
            Reading element values with XML data islands
        </TITLE>

        <XML ID="meetingsXML" SRC="ch07_01.xml"></XML>

        <SCRIPT LANGUAGE="JavaScript">
            function readXMLDocument()
            {
                var xmldoc, meetingsNode, meetingNode, peopleNode
                var first_nameNode, last_nameNode, outputText

                xmldoc= document.all("meetingsXML").XMLDocument

                meetingsNode = xmldoc.documentElement
                meetingNode = meetingsNode.firstChild
                peopleNode = meetingNode.lastChild
                personNode = peopleNode.lastChild
                first_nameNode = personNode.firstChild
                last_nameNode = first_nameNode.nextSibling

                outputText = "Third name: " +
                        first_nameNode.firstChild.nodeValue + ' '
                    + last_nameNode.firstChild.nodeValue
                messageDIV.innerHTML=outputText
            }
        </SCRIPT>
    </HEAD>

    <BODY>
```

```
      <CENTER>
          <H1>
              Reading element values with XML data islands
          </H1>

          <INPUT TYPE="BUTTON" VALUE="Get the name of the third person"
              ONCLICK="readXMLDocument()">
          <P>
          <DIV ID="messageDIV"></DIV>
      </CENTER>
  </BODY>
</HTML>
```

This example works as the previous example did, as you see in Figure 7-2.

Figure 7-2
Using XML
data islands in
Internet
Explorer.

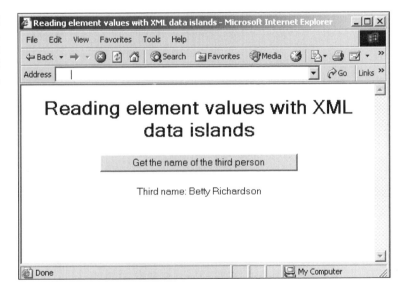

In the previous example, I used an external XML document, ch07_01.xml, which I referenced with the <XML> element's SRC attribute. However, you can also enclose the entire XML document in the <XML> element, like this:

```
<HTML>
    <HEAD>
        <TITLE>
            Creating An XML Data Island
        </TITLE>
```

```
<XML ID="meetingsXML">
    <?xml version="1.0"?>
    <MEETINGS>
        <MEETING TYPE="informal">
            <MEETING_TITLE>XML In The Real World</MEETING_TITLE>
            <MEETING_NUMBER>2079</MEETING_NUMBER>
            <SUBJECT>XML</SUBJECT>
            <DATE>6/1/2003</DATE>
            <PEOPLE>
                <PERSON ATTENDANCE="present">
                    <FIRST_NAME>Edward</FIRST_NAME>
                    <LAST_NAME>Samson</LAST_NAME>
                </PERSON>
                <PERSON ATTENDANCE="absent">
                    <FIRST_NAME>Ernestine</FIRST_NAME>
                    <LAST_NAME>Johnson</LAST_NAME>
                </PERSON>
                <PERSON ATTENDANCE="present">
                    <FIRST_NAME>Betty</FIRST_NAME>
                    <LAST_NAME>Richardson</LAST_NAME>
                </PERSON>
            </PEOPLE>
        </MEETING>
    </MEETINGS>
</XML>

<SCRIPT LANGUAGE="JavaScript">
    function readXMLDocument()
    {
        var xmldoc, meetingsNode, meetingNode, peopleNode
        var first_nameNode, last_nameNode, outputText

        xmldoc = document.all("meetingsXML").XMLDocument

        meetingsNode = xmldoc.documentElement
        meetingNode = meetingsNode.firstChild
        peopleNode = meetingNode.lastChild
        personNode = peopleNode.lastChild
        first_nameNode = personNode.firstChild
        last_nameNode = first_nameNode.nextSibling

        outputText = "Third name: " +
            first_nameNode.firstChild.nodeValue + ' '
            + last_nameNode.firstChild.nodeValue
        messageDIV.innerHTML=outputText
    }
</SCRIPT>
</HEAD>

<BODY>
    <CENTER>
        <H1>
            Reading element values with XML data islands
        </H1>
```

```
            <INPUT TYPE="BUTTON" VALUE="Get the name of the third person"
                ONCLICK="readXMLDocument()">
            <P>
            <DIV ID="messageDIV"></DIV>
        </CENTER>
    </BODY>
</HTML>
```

So far, I've used the XMLDocument property of the object corresponding to the XML data island to get the document object. However, you can also use the documentElement property of the data island directly to get the root element of the XML document, like this:

```
<HTML>
    <HEAD>
        <TITLE>
            Reading XML element values
        </TITLE>

        <XML ID="meetingsXML" SRC="ch07_01.xml"></XML>

        <SCRIPT LANGUAGE="JavaScript">
            function readXMLDocument()
            {
                var xmldoc, meetingsNode, meetingNode, peopleNode
                var first_nameNode, last_nameNode, outputText

                meetingsNode = meetingsXML.documentElement
                meetingNode = meetingsNode.firstChild
                peopleNode = meetingNode.lastChild
                personNode = peopleNode.lastChild
                first_nameNode = personNode.firstChild
                last_nameNode = first_nameNode.nextSibling
                .
                .
                .
</HTML>
```

Getting Elements by Name

So far in this chapter, I've used navigation methods such as nextSibling and nextChild to move through XML documents. However, you can also get individual elements by searching for them by name. Here's an example. In this case, I'll use the document object's getElementsByTagName method to return a node list object holding all elements of a given name. In particular, I'm searching for <FIRST_NAME> and <LAST_NAME> elements, so I get lists of those elements like this:

```
<HTML>
    <HEAD>
        <TITLE>
            Reading XML element values
        </TITLE>

        <SCRIPT LANGUAGE="JavaScript">
            function loadDocument()
            {
                var xmldoc, listNodesFirstName, listNodesLastName

                xmldoc = new ActiveXObject("Microsoft.XMLDOM")
                xmldoc.load("ch07_01.xml")

                listNodesFirstName =
                ➥xmldoc.getElementsByTagName("FIRST_NAME")
                listNodesLastName =
                ➥xmldoc.getElementsByTagName("LAST_NAME")<HTML>
                        .
                        .
                        .
```

Like all node lists, the listNodesFirstName and listNodesLastName node lists are indexed by number starting at 0, so the third element in these lists is element number 2, which you refer to as listNodesLastName.item(2). That means I can find the first and last name of the third person like this in the whole listing (recall that I actually need the first child of the <FIRST_NAME> and <LAST_NAME> nodes, which is the text node inside those elements that holds the person's name, so I use the firstChild method here):

Listing ch07_04.html

```
<HTML>
    <HEAD>
        <TITLE>
            Reading XML element values
        </TITLE>

        <SCRIPT LANGUAGE="JavaScript">
            function loadDocument()
            {
                var xmldoc, listNodesFirstName, listNodesLastName

                xmldoc = new ActiveXObject("Microsoft.XMLDOM")
```

```
            xmldoc.load("ch07_01.xml")

            listNodesFirstName =
xmldoc.getElementsByTagName("FIRST_NAME")
            listNodesLastName =
xmldoc.getElementsByTagName("LAST_NAME")

            outputText = "Third name: " +
                listNodesFirstName.item(2).firstChild.nodeValue + ' '
                + listNodesLastName.item(2).firstChild.nodeValue
            messageDIV.innerHTML=outputText
        }
    </SCRIPT>
</HEAD>

<BODY>
    <CENTER>
        <H1>
            Reading XML element values
        </H1>

        <INPUT TYPE="BUTTON" VALUE="Get the name of the third person"
            ONCLICK="loadDocument()">
        <P>
        <DIV ID="messageDIV"></DIV>
    </CENTER>
</BODY>
</HTML>
```

We've made some progress here. We've been able to read in an XML document in various ways, and we've been able to access specific elements in the document. I'll move on to the next step now: accessing not just an element's text content, but also the element's *attributes*.

Getting Attribute Values from XML Elements

To show you how to read attribute values from an XML document, I'll read the value of the ATTENDANCE attribute of the third person in the XML document ch07_01.xml:

```
<?xml version="1.0"?>
<MEETINGS>
    <MEETING TYPE="informal">
        <MEETING_TITLE>XML In The Real World</MEETING_TITLE>
        <MEETING_NUMBER>2079</MEETING_NUMBER>
```

```
<SUBJECT>XML</SUBJECT>
<DATE>6/1/2003</DATE>
<PEOPLE>
    <PERSON ATTENDANCE="present">
        <FIRST_NAME>Edward</FIRST_NAME>
        <LAST_NAME>Samson</LAST_NAME>
    </PERSON>
    <PERSON ATTENDANCE="absent">
        <FIRST_NAME>Ernestine</FIRST_NAME>
        <LAST_NAME>Johnson</LAST_NAME>
    </PERSON>
    <PERSON ATTENDANCE="present">
        <FIRST_NAME>Betty</FIRST_NAME>
        <LAST_NAME>Richardson</LAST_NAME>
    </PERSON>
</PEOPLE>
</MEETING>
</MEETINGS>
```

How do you read attribute values? You start by getting a named node map object of the attributes of the current element using that element's `attributes` property. In this case, we want the attributes of the third `<PERSON>` element, and we get a named node map of those attributes like this:

```
<HTML>
    <HEAD>
        <TITLE>
            Reading attribute values from XML documents
        </TITLE>

        <XML ID="meetingsXML" SRC="ch07_01.xml"></XML>

        <SCRIPT LANGUAGE="JavaScript">
            function readXMLDocument()
            {
                var xmldoc, meetingsNode, meetingNode, peopleNode
                var first_nameNode, last_nameNode, outputText
                var attributes

                xmldoc= document.all("meetingsXML").XMLDocument

                meetingsNode = xmldoc.documentElement
                meetingNode = meetingsNode.firstChild
                peopleNode = meetingNode.lastChild
                personNode = peopleNode.lastChild
                first_nameNode = personNode.firstChild
                last_nameNode = first_nameNode.nextSibling
                attributes = personNode.attributes
                    .
                    .
                    .

</HTML>
```

Now I can recover the actual node for the ATTENDANCE node with the named node map object's getNamedItem method:

```
attributes = personNode.attributes
attendancePerson = attributes.getNamedItem("ATTENDANCE")
   .
   .
   .
```

Now I have a node corresponding to the ATTENDANCE attribute, and I can get the value of that attribute using the value property (attribute nodes don't have internal text nodes):

```
attributes = personNode.attributes
attendancePerson = attributes.getNamedItem("ATTENDANCE")
outputText = first_nameNode.firstChild.nodeValue
       + ' ' + last_nameNode.firstChild.nodeValue
       + " is " + attendancePerson.value
messageDIV.innerHTML=outputText
   .
   .
   .
```

And that's all it takes. Here's what the whole listing looks like:

Listing ch07_05.html

```
<HTML>
    <HEAD>
        <TITLE>
            Reading attribute values from XML documents
        </TITLE>

        <XML ID="meetingsXML" SRC="ch07_01.xml"></XML>

        <SCRIPT LANGUAGE="JavaScript">
            function readXMLDocument()
            {
                var xmldoc, meetingsNode, meetingNode, peopleNode
                var first_nameNode, last_nameNode, outputText
                var attributes, attendancePerson

                xmldoc = document.all("meetingsXML").XMLDocument

                meetingsNode = xmldoc.documentElement
                meetingNode = meetingsNode.firstChild
                peopleNode = meetingNode.lastChild
                personNode = peopleNode.lastChild
                first_nameNode = personNode.firstChild
```

continues

Listing ch07_05.html   Continued

```
                      last_nameNode = first_nameNode.nextSibling
                      attributes = personNode.attributes
                      attendancePerson = attributes.getNamedItem("ATTENDANCE")
                      outputText = first_nameNode.firstChild.nodeValue
                          + ' ' + last_nameNode.firstChild.nodeValue
                          + " is " + attendancePerson.value
                      messageDIV.innerHTML=outputText
                  }
            </SCRIPT>
      </HEAD>

      <BODY>
          <CENTER>
              <H1>
                  Reading attribute values from XML documents
              </H1>

              <INPUT TYPE="BUTTON" VALUE="Get attendance of the third person"
                  ONCLICK="readXMLDocument()">
              <P>
              <DIV ID="messageDIV"></DIV>
          </CENTER>
      </BODY>
</HTML>
```

You can see the results in Figure 7-3, where you see that the attendance of the third person is "present."

Figure 7-3
Reading
attributes in
Internet
Explorer.

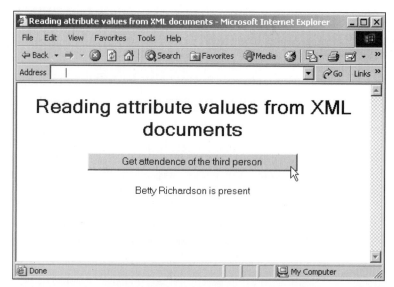

Parsing XML Documents in Code

Up to this point, I've gone after a specific element in a Web page, but there are other ways of handling documents, too. For example, you can parse—that is, read and interpret—the entire document at once. Here's an example. In this case, I'll work through this entire XML document, ch07_01.xml, displaying all its nodes in an HTML Web page.

To handle this document, I'll create a function, `iterateChildren`, that will read and display all the children of a node. As with most parsers, this function is a recursive function, which means that it can call itself to get the children of the current node. To get the name of a node, I will use the `nodeName` property. To parse an entire document, then, you just have to pass the root node of the entire document to the `iterateChildren` function, and it'll work through the entire document, displaying all the nodes in that document:

```
function parseDocument()
{
    documentXML = document.all("meetingsXML").XMLDocument
    resultsDIV.innerHTML = iterateChildren(documentXML, "")
}
    .
    .
    .
```

Note that I've also passed an empty string, `""`, to the `iterateChildren` function. I'll use this string to indent the various levels of the display, to indicate what nodes are nested inside what other nodes. In the `iterateChildren` function, I start by creating a new text string with the current indentation string (which is either an empty string or a string of spaces), as well as the name of the current node and a `<BR>` element that so the browser will skip to the next line:

```
function parseDocument()
{
    documentXML = document.all("meetingsXML").XMLDocument
    resultsDIV.innerHTML = iterateChildren(documentXML, "")
}

function iterateChildren(theNode, indentSpacing)
{
    var text = indentSpacing + theNode.nodeName + "<BR>"
        .
        .
        .
```

```
        return text
    }
```

.
.
.

I can determine whether the current node has children by checking the `childNodes` property, which holds a node list of the children of the current node. I can determine whether the current node has any children by checking the length of this list with its `length` property, and if so, I call `iterateChildren` on all child nodes (note also that I indent this next level of the display by adding four non-breaking spaces—which you specify with the ` ` entity reference in HTML—to the current indentation string):

```
function iterateChildren(theNode, indentSpacing)
{
    var text = indentSpacing + theNode.nodeName + "<BR>"

    if (theNode.childNodes.length > 0) {
        for (var loopIndex = 0; loopIndex <
            theNode.childNodes.length; loopIndex++) {
            text +=
            iterateChildren(theNode.childNodes(loopIndex),
            indentSpacing + "    ")
        }
    }
    return text
}
```

.
.
.

And that's all it takes. Here's the whole Web page:

Listing ch07_06.html

```
<HTML>
    <HEAD>
        <TITLE>
            Parsing an XML Document
        </TITLE>

        <XML ID="meetingsXML" SRC="ch07_01.xml"></XML>

        <SCRIPT LANGUAGE="JavaScript">
            function parseDocument()
```

```
        {
            documentXML = document.all("meetingsXML").XMLDocument
            resultsDIV.innerHTML = iterateChildren(documentXML, "")
        }

        function iterateChildren(theNode, indentSpacing)
        {
            var text = indentSpacing + theNode.nodeName + "<BR>"

            if (theNode.childNodes.length > 0) {
                for (var loopIndex = 0; loopIndex <
                    theNode.childNodes.length; loopIndex++) {
                    text +=
                    ➥iterateChildren(theNode.childNodes(loopIndex),
                    indentSpacing + "    ")
                }
            }
            return text
        }
    </SCRIPT>
</HEAD>

<BODY>
    <CENTER>
        <H1>
            Parsing an XML Document
        </H1>
    </CENTER>

    <CENTER>
        <INPUT TYPE="BUTTON" VALUE="Parse and display the document"
            ONCLICK="parseDocument()">
    </CENTER>
    <DIV ID="resultsDIV"></DIV>
</BODY>
</HTML>
```

When you click the button in this page, it will read ch07_01.xml and display its structure as you see in Figure 7-4. You can see all the nodes listed there, indented as they should be. Note also the "metanames" that Internet Explorer gives to document and text nodes: #document and #text.

Figure 7-4
Parsing a
document in
Internet
Explorer.

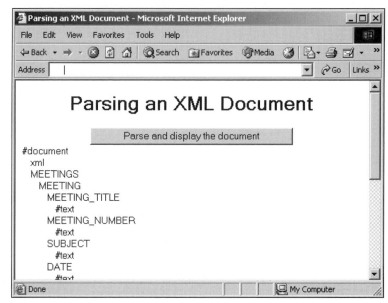

Parsing an XML Document to Display Node Type and Content

In the previous example, the code listed the names of each node in the ch07_01.xml document. However, you can do more than that: You can also use the `nodeValue` property to list the value of each node, and I'll do that in this section. In addition, you can indicate the type of each node you come across by checking the `nodeType` property. Here are the possible values for this property:

- 1: Element
- 2: Attribute
- 3: Text
- 4: CDATA section
- 5: Entity reference
- 6: Entity
- 7: Processing instruction
- 8: Comment
- 9: Document
- 10: Document type

- 11: Document fragment

- 12: Notation

Here's how I determine the type of a particular node, using a JavaScript `switch` statement of the kind we saw in the previous chapter:

```
function parseDocument()
{
    documentXML = document.all("meetingsXML").XMLDocument
    resultsDIV.innerHTML = iterateChildren(documentXML, "")
}

function iterateChildren(theNode, indentSpacing)
{
    var typeData
    switch (theNode.nodeType) {
        case 1:
            typeData = "element"
            break
        case 2:
            typeData = "attribute"
            break
        case 3:
            typeData = "text"
            break
        case 4:
            typeData = "CDATA section"
            break
        case 5:
            typeData = "entity reference"
            break
        case 6:
            typeData = "entity"
            break
        case 7:
            typeData = "processing instruction"
            break
        case 8:
            typeData = "comment"
            break
        case 9:
            typeData = "document"
            break
        case 10:
            typeData = "document type"
            break
        case 11:
            typeData = "document fragment"
            break
```

```
            case 12:
                typeData = "notation"
        }
            .
            .
            .
```

If the node has a value (which I check by comparing `nodeValue` to `null`, which is the value it will have if there is no actual node value), I can display that value like this, as you see in the whole listing:

Listing ch07_07.html

```html
<HTML>
    <HEAD>
        <TITLE>
            Parsing an XML document and displaying node type and content
        </TITLE>

        <XML ID="meetingsXML" SRC="ch07_01.xml"></XML>

        <SCRIPT LANGUAGE="JavaScript">
            function parseDocument()
            {
                documentXML = document.all("meetingsXML").XMLDocument
                resultsDIV.innerHTML = iterateChildren(documentXML, "")
            }

            function iterateChildren(theNode, indentSpacing)
            {
                var typeData

                switch (theNode.nodeType) {
                    case 1:
                        typeData = "element"
                        break
                    case 2:
                        typeData = "attribute"
                        break
                    case 3:
                        typeData = "text"
                        break
                    case 4:
                        typeData = "CDATA section"
                        break
                    case 5:
                        typeData = "entity reference"
                        break
```

```
                    case 6:
                        typeData = "entity"
                        break
                    case 7:
                        typeData = "processing instruction"
                        break
                    case 8:
                        typeData = "comment"
                        break
                    case 9:
                        typeData = "document"
                        break
                    case 10:
                        typeData = "document type"
                        break
                    case 11:
                        typeData = "document fragment"
                        break
                    case 12:
                        typeData = "notation"
                }
                var text

                if (theNode.nodeValue != null) {
                    text = indentSpacing + theNode.nodeName
                    + "  = " + theNode.nodeValue
                    + "  (Node type: " + typeData
                    + ")<BR>"
                } else {
                    text = indentSpacing + theNode.nodeName
                    + "  (Node type: " + typeData
                    + ")<BR>"
                }

                if (theNode.childNodes.length > 0) {
                    for (var loopIndex = 0; loopIndex <
                        theNode.childNodes.length; loopIndex++) {
                        text +=
                        ➥iterateChildren(theNode.childNodes(loopIndex),
                        indentSpacing + "    ")
                    }
                }
                return text
            }
        </SCRIPT>
</HEAD>

<BODY>
    <CENTER>
        <H1>
```

continues

Listing ch07_07.html   Continued

```
               Parsing an XML document and displaying node type and content
          </H1>
      </CENTER>

      <CENTER>
          <INPUT TYPE="BUTTON" VALUE="Parse and display the document"
              ONCLICK="parseDocument()">
      </CENTER>

      <DIV ID="resultsDIV"></DIV>
   </BODY>
</HTML>
```

And that's all it takes. Now you can see the results in Figure 7-5. As you see there, the entire document is listed, as is the type of each node. In addition, if the node has a value, that value is displayed.

Figure 7-5
Using
JavaScript to
display
element
content and
type.

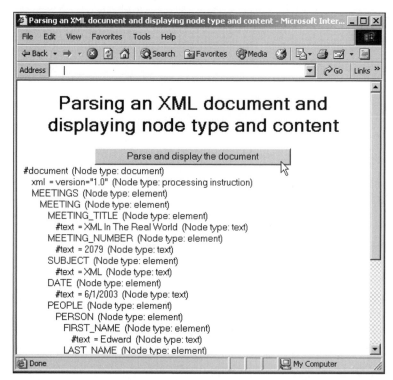

This example listed the nodes of a document. On the other hand, some of the elements in ch07_01.xml have attributes as well. So how do you handle attributes?

Parsing an XML Document to Display Attribute Values

You can get access to an element's attributes with the element's `attributes` property. You can get attribute names and values with the `name` and `value` properties of attribute objects, and I used the `value` property earlier in this chapter. It's also worth noting that because attributes are themselves nodes, you can use the `nodeName` and `nodeValue` properties to do the same thing; I'll do that in this example to show how it works.

Here's how I augment the previous example in our final parsing example in this chapter, looping over all the attributes an element has and listing them (note that you could use the `name` and `value` properties here instead of `nodeName` and `nodeValue`):

Listing ch07_08.html

```
<HTML>
    <HEAD>
        <TITLE>
            Parsing XML to read attributes
        </TITLE>

        <XML ID="meetingsXML" SRC="ch07_01.xml"></XML>

        <SCRIPT LANGUAGE="JavaScript">

            function parseDocument()
            {
                documentXML = document.all("meetingsXML").XMLDocument
                resultsDIV.innerHTML = iterateChildren(documentXML, "")
            }

            function iterateChildren(theNode, indentSpacing)
            {
                var typeData

                switch (theNode.nodeType) {
                    case 1:
                        typeData = "element"
                        break
```

continues

Listing ch07_08.html   Continued

```
            case 2:
                typeData = "attribute"
                break
            case 3:
                typeData = "text"
                break
            case 4:
                typeData = "CDATA section"
                break
            case 5:
                typeData = "entity reference"
                break
            case 6:
                typeData = "entity"
                break
            case 7:
                typeData = "processing instruction"
                break
            case 8:
                typeData = "comment"
                break
            case 9:
                typeData = "document"
                break
            case 10:
                typeData = "document type"
                break
            case 11:
                typeData = "document fragment"
                break
            case 12:
                typeData = "notation"
        }
        var text

        if (theNode.nodeValue != null) {
            text = indentSpacing + theNode.nodeName
            + "  = " + theNode.nodeValue
            + "  (Node type: " + typeData
            + ")"
        } else {
            text = indentSpacing + theNode.nodeName
            + "  (Node type: " + typeData
            + ")"
        }

        if (theNode.attributes != null) {
            if (theNode.attributes.length > 0) {
                for (var loopIndex = 0; loopIndex <
```

```
                                theNode.attributes.length; loopIndex++) {
                                text += " (Attribute: " +
                                        theNode.attributes(loopIndex).nodeName +
                                        " = \"" +
                                        theNode.attributes(loopIndex).nodeValue
                                        + "\")"
                            }
                        }
                    }

                    text += "<BR>"

                    if (theNode.childNodes.length > 0) {
                        for (var loopIndex = 0; loopIndex <
                            theNode.childNodes.length; loopIndex++) {
                            text += iterateChildren(theNode.childNodes
                            ➥(loopIndex),
                            indentSpacing + "    ")
                        }
                    }
                    return text
                }

            </SCRIPT>
    </HEAD>

    <BODY>
        <CENTER>
            <H1>
                Parsing XML to read attributes
            </H1>
        </CENTER>

        <CENTER>
            <INPUT TYPE="BUTTON" VALUE="Parse and display the document"
                ONCLICK="parseDocument()">
        </CENTER>
        <DIV ID="resultsDIV"></DIV>
    </BODY>
</HTML>
```

You can see the results of this page in Figure 7-6. As you can see, both elements and attributes are listed in that figure.

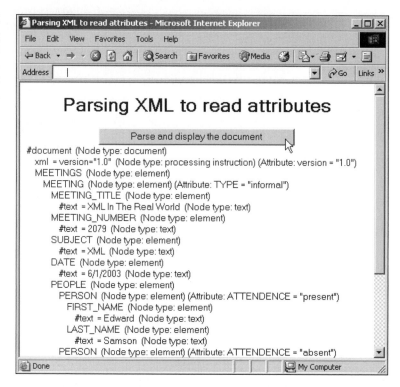

Figure 7-6
Listing
elements and
attributes in
Internet
Explorer.

Handling Events While Loading XML Documents

Internet Explorer also lets you track the progress of an XML document as it's being loaded. In particular, you can use the onreadystatechange and ondataavailable events to watch what's happening. The readyState property in the onreadystatechange event informs you about the current status of a document. Here's an example showing how this works:

Listing ch07_09.html

```
<HTML>
    <HEAD>
        <TITLE>
            Handling document loading events
        </TITLE>

        <SCRIPT LANGUAGE="JavaScript">
            var xmldoc
```

```
function loadDocument()
{
    xmldoc = new ActiveXObject("microsoft.XMLDOM")

    xmldoc.ondataavailable = dataAvailableHandler
    xmldoc.onreadystatechange = stateChangeHandler

    xmldoc.load('ch07_01.xml')
}

function dataAvailableHandler()
{
    messageDIV.innerHTML += "Status: data available.<BR>"
}

function stateChangeHandler()
{
    switch (xmldoc.readyState)
    {
        case 1:
            messageDIV.innerHTML += "Status: data
            ➥uninitialized.<BR>"
            break
        case 2:
            messageDIV.innerHTML += "Status: data loading.<BR>"
            break
        case 3:
            messageDIV.innerHTML += "Status: data loaded.<BR>"
            break
        case 4:
            messageDIV.innerHTML += "Status: data loading
            ➥complete.<BR>"
            if (xmldoc.parseError.errorCode != 0) {
                messageDIV.innerHTML += "Status: error.<BR>"
            }
            else {
                messageDIV.innerHTML += "Status: data loaded
                ➥alright.<BR>"
            }
            break
    }
}
</SCRIPT>
</HEAD>

<BODY>
    <CENTER>
        <H1>
            Handling document loading events
        </H1>
    </CENTER>
```

continues

Listing ch07_09.html   Continued

```
        <CENTER>
            <INPUT TYPE="BUTTON" VALUE="Load the document"
                ONCLICK="loadDocument()">
        </CENTER>
        <DIV ID="messageDIV"></DIV>
    </BODY>
</HTML>
```

The results of this Web page appears in Figure 7-7, and you can see the progress that Internet Explorer made in loading a document in that page.

Figure 7-7
Monitoring XML loading events in Internet Explorer.

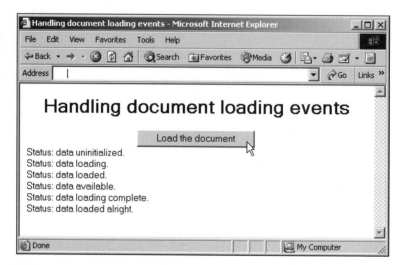

Validating XML Documents with DTDs in Internet Explorer

By default, Internet Explorer actually does validate XML documents with DTDs as it loads them, but you won't see any validation errors unless you check the parseError object.

Turning Validation On and Off

You can turn document validation on or off with the document object's validateOnParse property, which is set to true by default.

Here's an example. In this case, I'll load this XML document, ch07_10.xml. This document has a validation problem because the <NAME> element is declared to contain only a <FIRST_NAME> element, not a <LAST_NAME> element:

Listing ch07_10.xml

```
<?xml version = "1.0" standalone="yes"?>
<!DOCTYPE DOCUMENT [
<!ELEMENT DOCUMENT (CUSTOMER)*>
<!ELEMENT CUSTOMER (NAME,DATE,ORDERS)>
<!ELEMENT NAME (FIRST_NAME)>
<!ELEMENT LAST_NAME (#PCDATA)>
<!ELEMENT FIRST_NAME (#PCDATA)>
<!ELEMENT DATE (#PCDATA)>
<!ELEMENT ORDERS (ITEM)*>
<!ELEMENT ITEM (PRODUCT,NUMBER,PRICE)>
<!ELEMENT PRODUCT (#PCDATA)>
<!ELEMENT NUMBER (#PCDATA)>
<!ELEMENT PRICE (#PCDATA)>
]>
<DOCUMENT>
    <CUSTOMER>
        <NAME>
            <LAST_NAME>Smith</LAST_NAME>
            <FIRST_NAME>Sam</FIRST_NAME>
        </NAME>
        <DATE>October 15, 2003</DATE>
        <ORDERS>
            <ITEM>
                <PRODUCT>Tomatoes</PRODUCT>
                <NUMBER>8</NUMBER>
                <PRICE>$1.25</PRICE>
            </ITEM>
            <ITEM>
                <PRODUCT>Asparagus</PRODUCT>
                <NUMBER>12</NUMBER>
                <PRICE>$2.95</PRICE>
            </ITEM>
            <ITEM>
                <PRODUCT>Lettuce</PRODUCT>
                <NUMBER>6</NUMBER>
                <PRICE>$11.50</PRICE>
            </ITEM>
        </ORDERS>
    </CUSTOMER>
</DOCUMENT>
```

Here's what the Web page that reads in and checks this document looks like. Here I'm using the `parseError` object's errorCode, url, line, linepos, errorString, and reason properties to track down the error:

Listing ch07_11.html

```
<HTML>
    <HEAD>
        <TITLE>
            Validating documents
        </TITLE>

        <SCRIPT LANGUAGE="JavaScript">
            var xmldoc

            function loadDocument()
            {
                xmldoc = new ActiveXObject("microsoft.XMLDOM")

                xmldoc.onreadystatechange = stateChangeHandler
                xmldoc.ondataavailable = dataAvailableHandler

                xmldoc.load('ch07_10.xml')
            }

            function dataAvailableHandler()
            {
                messageDIV.innerHTML += "Status: data available.<BR>"
            }

            function stateChangeHandler()
            {
                if(xmldoc.readyState == 4){
                    var errorString = xmldoc.parseError.srcText
                    errorString = xmldoc.parseError.srcText.replace
                    ➥(/\</g, "&lt;")
                    errorString = errorString.replace(/\>/g, "&gt;")
                    if (xmldoc.parseError.errorCode != 0) {
                        messageDIV.innerHTML = "Problem in " +
                        xmldoc.parseError.url +
                        " line " + xmldoc.parseError.line +
                        " position " + xmldoc.parseError.linepos +
                        ":<BR>Error source: " + errorString +
                        "<BR>" + xmldoc.parseError.reason +
                        "<BR>" +   "Error: " +
                        xmldoc.parseError.errorCode
                    }
                    else {
                        messageDIV.innerHTML = "Status: document loaded
                        ➥alright.<BR>"
```

```
                        }
                    }
                }
        </SCRIPT>
    </HEAD>

    <BODY>
        <CENTER>
            <H1>
                Validating documents
            </H1>
        </CENTER>

        <DIV ID="messageDIV"></DIV>

        <CENTER>
            <INPUT TYPE="BUTTON" VALUE="Load the document"
                ONCLICK="loadDocument()">
        </CENTER>
    </BODY>
</HTML>
```

You can see the results of this Web page in Figure 7-8, where the validation error is reported.

Figure 7-8
Validating XML documents in Internet Explorer.

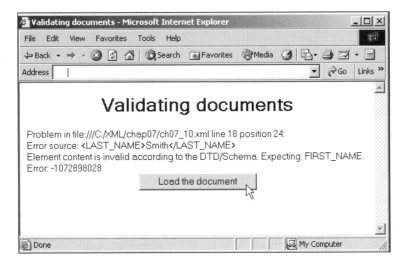

Replace < with *<* and > with *>*

You might note that the `errorString` property holds the error-causing text from the XML document. Because that text is `<LAST_NAME>Smith</LAST_NAME>`, there's a problem. The browser will try to interpret this as markup. To avoid that, I use the JavaScript `String` object's `replace` method to replace < with < and > with >. (You pass a regular expression to the `replace` method.) To change all < characters to <, you use the regular expression /\</g;. To change all > characters to >, you match to the regular expression /\>/g.

Scripting XML Elements

Internet Explorer provides limited support for scripting XML elements. For example, I can add an `onclick` event attribute to an XML element named `<xlink>` (we'll take a look at XLinks later in this book) in an XHTML document (we'll also take a look at XHTML later in this book):

Listing ch07_12.html

```
<?xml version="1.0" encoding="UTF-8"?>
<?xml-stylesheet TYPE="text/css" href="ch07_13.css"?>

<html>
    <head>
    </head>

    <body>
    Want to check out <xlink xml:link = "simple" inline="false"
    href = "http://www.w3c.org"
    onclick="location.href='http://www.w3c.org'">W3C</xlink>?
    </body>
</html>
```

I can specify in a stylesheet, ch07_13.css, that `<xlink>` elements should be displayed in blue and underlined as a hyperlink might appear. I can also specify that the mouse cursor should change to a hand when over this element, just as it would for an HTML hyperlink:

Listing ch07_13.css

```
xlink {color: #0000FF; text-decoration: underline; cursor: hand}
```

The results appear in Figure 7-9. When the user clicks the `<xlink>` element, Internet Explorer executes the code in the `onClick` event attribute. In this case, that navigates the browser to `www.w3c.org`. As you can see, you can script XML elements in Internet Explorer, adding event attributes such as `onclick`.

Figure 7-9
Creating a "hyperlink" in an XML document in Internet Explorer.

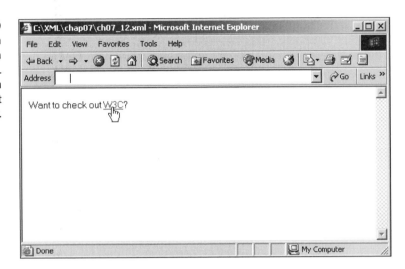

Editing XML Documents with Internet Explorer

You can alter the contents of an XML document in Internet Explorer. To do this, you use methods such as `createElement`, `insertBefore`, `createTextNode`, and `appendChild`.

As an example, I'll alter the document ch07_01.xml by inserting a new element, `<MEETING_CHAIR>`, like this:

```
<?xml version="1.0"?>
<MEETINGS>
    <MEETING TYPE="informal">
        <MEETING_CHAIR>Ted Bond</MEETING_CHAIR>
        <MEETING_TITLE>XML In The Real World</MEETING_TITLE>
        <MEETING_NUMBER>2079</MEETING_NUMBER>
        <SUBJECT>XML</SUBJECT>
        <DATE>6/1/2003</DATE>
        <PEOPLE>
            <PERSON ATTENDANCE="present">
                <FIRST_NAME>Edward</FIRST_NAME>
                <LAST_NAME>Samson</LAST_NAME>
            </PERSON>
            .
            .
            .
```

I begin by creating the new node, corresponding to the <MEETING_CHAIR> element, and inserting it into the document with the insertBefore method:

```
<HTML>
    <HEAD>
        <XML ID="meetingsXML" SRC="ch07_01.xml"></XML>

        <SCRIPT LANGUAGE="JavaScript">
        <!--
            function alterDocument()
            {
                var xmldoc, rootNode, meetingsNode, meetingNode,
                ➥createdNode, createdTextNode

                xmldoc = document.all.meetingsXML
                rootNode = xmldoc.documentElement
                meetingsNode = rootNode.firstChild
                meetingNode = meetingsNode.firstChild

                createdNode = xmldoc.createElement("MEETING_CHAIR")
                createdNode = meetingsNode.insertBefore(createdNode,
                ➥meetingNode)
                    .
                    .
                    .
```

Now I will create the text node inside this new element. The text node will hold the text "Ted Bond". I'll create it with the createTextNode method and append it to the <MEETING_CHAIR> element with the appendChild method:

```
<HTML>
    <HEAD>
        <XML ID="meetingsXML" SRC="ch07_01.xml"></XML>

        <SCRIPT LANGUAGE="JavaScript">
        <!--
            function alterDocument()
            {
                var xmldoc, rootNode, meetingsNode, meetingNode,
                ➥createdNode, createdTextNode

                xmldoc = document.all.meetingsXML
                rootNode = xmldoc.documentElement
                meetingsNode = rootNode.firstChild
                meetingNode = meetingsNode.firstChild

                createdNode = xmldoc.createElement("MEETING_CHAIR")
                createdNode = meetingsNode.insertBefore(createdNode,
                ➥meetingNode)
                createdTextNode = xmldoc.createTextNode("Ted Bond")
                createdNode.appendChild(createdTextNode)
                    .
                    .
                    .
```

Now I've altered the document—but at this point, it exists only inside the xmldoc object. How do I display it in the browser? The DOMDocument object actually has a save method that allows you to save the document to a new file like this: xmldoc.save("new.xml"). However, you can't use that method without changing the security settings in Internet Explorer because, by default, browsers aren't supposed to be capable of writing files on the host machine.

I'll take a different approach. In this case, I'll store the XML document's text in a hidden control in an HTML form (a hidden control simply holds text invisible to the user), and I'll send the data in that form to a server-side Active Server Pages (ASP) script. That script will just echo the document back to the browser, which, in turn, will display it. Here's the ASP script, ch07_14.asp, where I set the MIME type of this document to "text/xml", add an <?xml?> processing instruction, and echo the XML data back to Internet Explorer (ASP scripts like this one are beyond the scope of this book, but we'll take a look at them in brief in Chapter 20, "WML, ASP, JSP, Servlets, and Perl"):

Listing ch07_14.asp

```
<%@ LANGUAGE="VBSCRIPT" %>
<%
Response.ContentType = "text/xml"
Response.Write "<?xml version=" & Chr(34) & "1.0" & Chr(34) & "?>" & Chr(13)
& Chr(10)
Response.Write Request("data")
%>
```

I have an ASP server on my host machine (Microsoft Internet Information Server, IIS), so the URI I'll send the XML document to is http://steve/ch07_14.asp. I do that by using the HTML form's submit method (which works exactly as if the user had clicked a Submit button in the form) after loading the XML document into the page's hidden control:

Listing ch07_15.html

```
<HTML>
    <HEAD>
        <XML ID="meetingsXML" SRC="ch07_01.xml"></XML>

        <SCRIPT LANGUAGE="JavaScript">
        <!--
            function alterDocument()
            {
```

continues

Listing ch07_15.html   Continued

```
            var xmldoc, rootNode, meetingsNode, meetingNode,
            ➡createdNode, createdTextNode

            xmldoc = document.all.meetingsXML
            rootNode = xmldoc.documentElement
            meetingsNode = rootNode.firstChild
            meetingNode = meetingsNode.firstChild

            createdNode = xmldoc.createElement("MEETING_CHAIR")
            createdNode = meetingsNode.insertBefore(createdNode,
            ➡meetingNode)

            createdTextNode = xmldoc.createTextNode("Ted Bond")
            createdNode.appendChild(createdTextNode)

            document.all.data.value = meetingsXML.documentElement.xml
            document.form1.submit()
        }
    //-->
    </SCRIPT>
</HEAD>

<BODY>
    <CENTER>
        <FORM NAME="form1" ACTION="http://steve/ch07_14.asp"
        ➡METHOD="POST">
        <INPUT TYPE="HIDDEN" NAME="data">
        <INPUT TYPE="BUTTON" VALUE="Alter the document"
        ➡onclick="alterDocument()">
        </FORM>
    </CENTER>
</BODY>
</HTML>
```

And that's it. Now when the user clicks the button with the caption Alter the Document, the code in this page alters the XML document and sends it to the server. The ASP script on the server echoes the XML document back to the browser, which displays it, as you see in Figure 7-10. You can see the new <MEETING_CHAIR> element in that figure.

Figure 7-10
Altering an
XML
document in
Internet
Explorer.

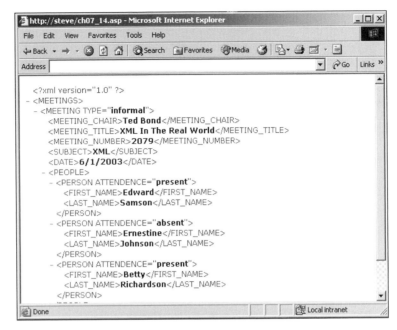

We've put JavaScript to work in this chapter, parsing and accessing XML documents. In the next chapter, I'm going to put JavaScript to work treating XML data as database objects, and I'll turn to that now.

CHAPTER 8

XML and Data Binding

XML is all about storing data. It turns out that Internet Explorer supports a number of techniques to let you extract that data without needing any programming at all: You can use *data binding*. We'll see how that works in this chapter.

In the previous chapter, we took a look at working with XML documents in Internet Explorer using the DOM. In that chapter, we used methods such as `firstChild`, `lastChild`, `lastSibling`, and so on to work through a document. Using methods such as those give you complete access to the data in an XML document. Regarding an XML document as a node tree can be confusing, however, especially if you forget that the character data in an element is stored in its own node.

There's another way of handling XML documents in Internet Explorer, and it also bears exploration. Internet Explorer lets you read both HTML and XML documents and store them in a database. Using the database methods that we'll see in this chapter, you can move from record to record through your data in a way that many programmers find easier to use than the DOM methods.

Data Binding in Internet Explorer

Internet Explorer specializes in data binding. With data binding, you can connect the data in documents to an ActiveX Data Object (ADO) database and work with that data in an easy way. This technique is useful because data from a database can be sent as an XML document over the Internet and immediately converted back to a database in the browser. This means that programmers familiar with database programming can concentrate on using database methods, not DOM methods.

I'll take a look at data binding in Internet Explorer in general first. Then I'll work specifically with XML documents in this chapter. There are two parts to working with bound data in Internet Explorer: using Data Source Objects (DSOs) and binding data to the HTML elements in a Web page.

For More on Data Binding

You can find information about data binding in Internet Explorer at `http://msdn.microsoft.com/workshop/c-frame.htm#/workshop/author/default.asp`.

Using Data Source Objects

There are four DSOs in Internet Explorer—the Microsoft HTML (MSHTML) control, the tabular data control (TDC), the XML DSO, and XML data islands. (In fact, Internet Explorer also supports the relatively sophisticated Remote Data Service (RDS) DSO, which you use to connect to database applications, such as those that run in SQL-enabled applications on a Web server.) Two of these DSOs, the XML DSO and XML data islands, support XML documents.

A DSO doesn't appear in a Web page (although, as we'll see at the end of the chapter, the XML DSO can display status messages in a page). You use a DSO to read a document and make its data available to the rest of the page. For a DSO to read data from a document, that data must be formatted correctly.

Here's an example HTML document, ch08_01.html, that holds data on sales made to customers. Here, I'm recording the customers' names, their IDs, the date of the purchase, the department of the item purchased, and the name of the item. Note how I'm structuring an HTML page to hold data for Internet Explorer—by using the <SPAN> element (you can also use other elements such as <DIV>) and assigning a type to each data item with the enclosing element's ID tag (as you can see, this technique cries out for XML formatting):

Listing ch08_01.html

```
<HTML>
    <HEAD>
        <TITLE>
            Customer Data
        </TITLE>
    </HEAD>
```

```
<BODY>
    Name: <SPAN ID="NAME">Charles</SPAN><BR>
    ID: <SPAN ID="CUSTOMER_ID">58704</SPAN><BR>
    Purchase date: Date: <SPAN ID="PURCHASE_DATE">
        10/15/2003</SPAN><BR>
    Department: <SPAN ID="DEPARTMENT">
        Meat</SPAN><BR>
    Product: <SPAN ID="PRODUCT_NAME">Ham</SPAN><BR>

    Name: <SPAN ID="NAME">Franklin</SPAN><BR>
    ID: <SPAN ID="CUSTOMER_ID">58705</SPAN><BR>
    Purchase date: <SPAN ID="PURCHASE_DATE">
        10/15/2003</SPAN><BR>
    Department: <SPAN ID="DEPARTMENT">
        Produce</SPAN><BR>
    Product: <SPAN ID="PRODUCT_NAME">Tomatoes</SPAN><BR>

    Name: <SPAN ID="NAME">Phoebe</SPAN><BR>
    ID: <SPAN ID="CUSTOMER_ID">58706</SPAN><BR>
    Purchase date: <SPAN ID="PURCHASE_DATE">
        10/15/2003</SPAN><BR>
    Department: <SPAN ID="DEPARTMENT">
        Meat</SPAN><BR>
    Product: <SPAN ID="PRODUCT_NAME">Turkey</SPAN><BR>

    Name: <SPAN ID="NAME">Mark</SPAN><BR>
    ID: <SPAN ID="CUSTOMER_ID">58707</SPAN><BR>
    Purchase date: <SPAN ID="PURCHASE_DATE">
        10/15/2003</SPAN><BR>
    Department: <SPAN ID="DEPARTMENT">
        Meat</SPAN><BR>
    Product: <SPAN ID="PRODUCT_NAME">Beef</SPAN><BR>

    Name: <SPAN ID="NAME">Nancy</SPAN><BR>
    ID: <SPAN ID="CUSTOMER_ID">58708</SPAN><BR>
    Purchase date: <SPAN ID="PURCHASE_DATE">
        10/15/2003</SPAN><BR>
    Department: <SPAN ID="DEPARTMENT">
        Frozen</SPAN><BR>
    Product: <SPAN ID="PRODUCT_NAME">Broccoli</SPAN><BR>

    </BODY>
</HTML>
```

The most common way of handling data formatted as HTML documents is with the MSHTML DSO, and I'm going to use it here. A DSO reads a document like this one and converts it into a *recordset*. Each record in the recordset comes from the HTML or XML elements you've used to store the data. For example, here's what the HTML for one record looks like:

```
Name: <SPAN ID="NAME">Charles</SPAN><BR>
ID: <SPAN ID="CUSTOMER_ID">58704</SPAN><BR>
Purchase date: Date: <SPAN ID="PURCHASE_DATE">
     10/15/2003</SPAN><BR>
Department: <SPAN ID="DEPARTMENT">
     Meat</SPAN><BR>
Product: <SPAN ID="PRODUCT_NAME">Ham</SPAN><BR>
```

This record has five *fields*: NAME, CUSTOMER_ID, PURCHASE_DATE, DEPARTMENT, and PRODUCT_NAME. A recordset is much like an array holding records; when you work with a particular record, you can access the data in the fields in each record individually. For example, to determine what item Charles has purchased, you only need to find his record and then check the PRODUCT_NAME field in that record.

Using the Internet Explorer <OBJECT> element, you can create an MSHTML DSO and bind it to employee.htm. Here, I'm naming this DSO dsoCustomer:

```
<OBJECT ID="dsoCustomer" DATA="ch08_01.html" HEIGHT="0" WIDTH="0">
</OBJECT>
```

The DSO will read and interpret ch08_01.html and convert that document into an ADO recordset (the type of recordset actually used in Internet Explorer is read-only, called an ADOR recordset). The DSO holds data from only one record at a time, and that record is called the *current record*. You can use the built-in methods of a recordset to navigate through your data by making other records the current record. Some common methods are moveFirst, moveLast, moveNext, and movePrevious, which let you navigate from record to record, and we'll see these methods here. To actually display the data from this DSO, you can bind it to HTML elements.

Binding Data to HTML Elements

Quite a few elements in Internet Explorer support data properties that you can use to bind them to DSO. To connect to those properties, you use the DATASRC and DATAFLD attributes in those elements. You set the DATASRC attribute to the name of a DSO, and you set the DATAFLD attribute to the name of the data field that you want to bind the element to. The element then displays the data in the current record in the DSO. You can use the moveFirst, moveLast, moveNext, and movePrevious methods to make other records the current record, and the data in the bound elements is updated automatically.

For example, if you've bound a text field control to the dsoCustomer DSO and to the NAME field in the DSO's records, that control will display the name Charles when the page first loads. Executing the moveNext method will make the next record in the record set the current record, and the text field will display the name Franklin.

Here's a list of HTML elements in Internet Explorer detailing what property is actually bound when you use the DATASRC and DATAFLD attributes:

- A—Binds to the href property. Does not update data.

- APPLET—Binds to the param property. Updates data.

- BUTTON—Binds to the value property. Does not update data.

- DIV—Binds to the innerText and innerHTML properties. Does not update data.

- FRAME—Binds to the src property. Does not update data.

- IFRAME—Binds to the src property. Does not update data.

- IMG—Binds to the src property. Does not update data.

- INPUT TYPE=BUTTON—Binds to the value property. Does not update data.

- INPUT TYPE=CHECKBOX—Binds to the checked property. Updates data.

- INPUT TYPE=HIDDEN—Binds to the value property. Updates data.

- INPUT TYPE=PASSWORD—Binds to the value property. Updates data.

- INPUT TYPE=RADIO—Binds to the checked property. Updates data.

- INPUT TYPE=TEXT—Binds to the value property. Updates data.

- LABEL—Binds to the value property. Does not update data.

- MARQUEE—Binds to the innerText and innerHTML properties. Does not update data.

- OBJECT—Binds to the objects property. Updates data.

- PARAM—Binds to the param property. Updates data.

- SELECT—Binds to the text property of an option. Updates data.

- SPAN—Bind to the innerText and innerHTML properties. Does not update data.

- TABLE—Constructs an entire table. Does not update data.

- TEXTAREA—Binds to the value property. Updates data.

In addition, HTML tags have certain events that you use with data bindings:

- `onafterupdate`—Happens after the data in the element is updated to the DSO
- `onbeforeunload`—Happens before the page is unloaded
- `onbeforeupdate`—Happens when the data in the element is updated in the DSO
- `onerrorupdate`—Happens if an error stops data being updated in the DSO

It's time to put this to work. I'll start by adding an MSHTML control named `dsoCustomer` to a Web page and connecting that DSO to ch08_01.html:

```
<HTML>
    <HEAD>
        <TITLE>
            Data Binding With the MSHTML DSO
        </TITLE>
    </HEAD>

    <BODY>
        <CENTER>
            <H1>
                Data Binding With the MSHTML DSO
            </H1>

            <OBJECT ID="dsoCustomer" DATA="ch08_01.html" HEIGHT="0"
            ➥WIDTH="0">
            </OBJECT>
            .
            .
            .
```

Now I'll bind this DSO to a text field by setting that text field's `DATASRC` attribute to `#dsoCustomer` (Internet Explorer requires the # symbol before a DSO's name). Because a text field can display only one field of data at a time, I'll bind the `NAME` field to this control by setting its `DATAFLD` attribute to `"NAME"`:

```
<OBJECT ID="dsoCustomer" DATA="ch08_01.html" HEIGHT="0" WIDTH="0">
</OBJECT>

Name: <INPUT TYPE="TEXT" DATASRC="#dsoCustomer"
    DATAFLD="NAME" SIZE="10">
    .
    .
    .
```

I'll bind the CUSTOMER_ID field to another text field as well. I can also display text data from the DSO directly in a Web page—without using a text field control—by binding that DSO to a <SPAN> element this way:

```
<OBJECT ID="dsoCustomer" DATA="ch08_01.html" HEIGHT="0" WIDTH="0">
</OBJECT>

Name: <INPUT TYPE="TEXT" DATASRC="#dsoCustomer"
    DATAFLD="NAME" SIZE="10">

<P>
ID: <INPUT TYPE="TEXT" DATASRC="#dsoCustomer"
    DATAFLD="CUSTOMER_ID" SIZE="5">

<P>
Purchase date: <SPAN DATASRC="#dsoCustomer"
    DATAFLD="PURCHASE_DATE"></SPAN>
    .
    .
    .
```

To show how to bind to other controls, I'll bind the DEPARTMENT field, which can take the values Produce, Meat, or Frozen, to a <SELECT> control, which displays a drop-down list. You bind this control to the dsoCustomer DSO as you do other controls; however, you must also specify all possible values that the field you're binding, DEPARTMENT, can take as <OPTION> elements in the <SELECT> control, like this:

```
<OBJECT ID="dsoCustomer" DATA="ch08_01.html" HEIGHT="0" WIDTH="0">
</OBJECT>

Name: <INPUT TYPE="TEXT" DATASRC="#dsoCustomer"
    DATAFLD="NAME" SIZE="10">

P>
D: <INPUT TYPE="TEXT" DATASRC="#dsoCustomer"
    DATAFLD="CUSTOMER_ID" SIZE="5">

<P>
Purchase date: <SPAN DATASRC="#dsoCustomer"
    DATAFLD="PURCHASE_DATE"></SPAN>

    <P>
Department: <SELECT DATASRC="#dsoCustomer"
    DATAFLD="DEPARTMENT" SIZE="1">
    <OPTION VALUE="Produce">Produce
    <OPTION VALUE="Meat">Meat
    <OPTION VALUE="Frozen">Frozen
```

continues

```
</SELECT>

<P>
Product: <SPAN DATASRC="#dsoCustomer" DATAFLD="PRODUCT_NAME">
</SPAN>
```

.
.
.

Note that I'm binding the PRODUCT_NAME field to another <SPAN> element as well. When the page first loads, you'll see the customer name, customer ID, purchase date, department, and product ID of the first record displayed in the elements we've put in the page. But there's a problem: As you recall, DSOs don't appear in the page, so how can the user move from record to record?

To let the user navigate through the recordset, you use the recordset's moveFirst, moveLast, moveNext, and movePrevious methods, and I'll connect those methods to buttons. You can reach the recordset object inside the DSO as dsoCustomer.recordset, so using the moveFirst method to move to the first record in the recordset looks like this: dsoCustomer.recordset.moveFirst(). Following common usage, I'll give the buttons the captions << (move to the first record), < (move to the previous record), > (move to the next record), and >> (move to the last record). Here's what the HTML for these buttons looks like:

```
<BUTTON ONCLICK=
    "dsoCustomer.recordset.moveFirst()" >&lt;&lt;
</BUTTON>
<BUTTON ONCLICK
    "dsoCustomer.recordset.movePrevious()" >&lt;
</BUTTON>
<BUTTON ONCLICK
    "dsoCustomer.recordset.moveNext()" >&gt;
</BUTTON>
<BUTTON ONCLICK=
    "dsoCustomer.recordset.moveLast()">&gt;&gt;
</BUTTON>
```

Before using the moveNext and movePrevious methods, however, it's worth checking to make sure that there actually is a next or previous record to move to—if you move past the end of the recordset, the bound elements in your page will appear blank. You can use the recordset object's BOF (beginning of file) property to see if you're at the beginning of the record set, and you can use the EOF (end of file) property to see if you're at the end of the recordset. To make sure we're not trying to move outside the recordset, I'll use this code:

Listing ch08_02.html

```
<HTML>
    <HEAD>
        <TITLE>
            Data Binding With the MSHTML DSO
        </TITLE>
    </HEAD>

    <BODY>

        <CENTER>
            <H1>
                Data Binding With the MSHTML DSO
            </H1>

            <OBJECT ID="dsoCustomer" DATA="ch08_01.html" HEIGHT="0"
            ➥WIDTH="0">
            </OBJECT>

            Name: <INPUT TYPE="TEXT" DATASRC="#dsoCustomer"
                DATAFLD="NAME" SIZE="10">

            <P>
            ID: <INPUT TYPE="TEXT" DATASRC="#dsoCustomer"
                DATAFLD="CUSTOMER_ID" SIZE="5">

            <P>
            Purchase date: <SPAN DATASRC="#dsoCustomer"
                DATAFLD="PURCHASE_DATE"></SPAN>

            <P>
            Department: <SELECT DATASRC="#dsoCustomer"
                DATAFLD="DEPARTMENT" SIZE="1">
                <OPTION VALUE="Produce">Produce
                <OPTION VALUE="Meat">Meat
                <OPTION VALUE="Frozen">Frozen
            </SELECT>

            <P>
            Product: <SPAN DATASRC="#dsoCustomer" DATAFLD="PRODUCT_NAME">
            </SPAN>

            <P>
            <BUTTON ONCLICK=
                "dsoCustomer.recordset.moveFirst()" >&lt;&lt;
            </BUTTON>
            <BUTTON ONCLICK="if (!dsoCustomer.recordset.BOF)
                dsoCustomer.recordset.movePrevious()" >&lt;
            </BUTTON>
            <BUTTON ONCLICK="if (!dsoCustomer.recordset.EOF)
```

continues

Listing ch08_02.html   Continued

```
                dsoCustomer.recordset.moveNext()" >&gt;
            </BUTTON>
            <BUTTON ONCLICK=
                "dsoCustomer.recordset.moveLast()">&gt;&gt;
            </BUTTON>
        </CENTER>
    </BODY>
</HTML>
```

You can see this page in operation in Figure 8-1. As you see in that page, the data from ch08_01.html is displayed. The user can move from record to record using the buttons at the bottom of the page.

Figure 8-1
Using data binding in Internet Explorer.

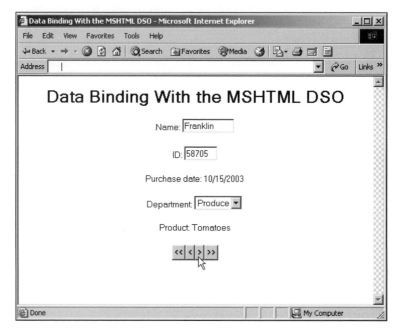

So much for data binding and HTML; it's time to start working with XML.

Using Data Binding with XML

I'll start by converting ch08_01.html to XML. In ch08_01.html, I had to use the ID attribute of <SPAN> elements to name the fields in a record; in XML, I can simply create a new element. Here's what ch08_01.html looks like in XML format, ch08_03.xml:

Listing ch08_03.xml

```
<?xml version="1.0"?>
<CUSTOMERS>

    <CUSTOMER>
        <NAME>Charles</NAME>
        <CUSTOMER_ID>58704</CUSTOMER_ID>
        <PURCHASE_DATE>10/15/2003</PURCHASE_DATE>
        <DEPARTMENT>Meat</DEPARTMENT>
        <PRODUCT_NAME>Ham</PRODUCT_NAME>
    </CUSTOMER>

    <CUSTOMER>
        <NAME>Franklin</NAME>
        <CUSTOMER_ID>58705</CUSTOMER_ID>
        <PURCHASE_DATE>10/15/2003</PURCHASE_DATE>
        <DEPARTMENT>Produce</DEPARTMENT>
        <PRODUCT_NAME>Tomatoes</PRODUCT_NAME>
    </CUSTOMER>

    <CUSTOMER>
        <NAME>Phoebe</NAME>
        <CUSTOMER_ID>58706</CUSTOMER_ID>
        <PURCHASE_DATE>10/15/2003</PURCHASE_DATE>
        <DEPARTMENT>Meat</DEPARTMENT>
        <PRODUCT_NAME>Turkey</PRODUCT_NAME>
    </CUSTOMER>

    <CUSTOMER>
        <NAME>Mark</NAME>
        <CUSTOMER_ID>58707</CUSTOMER_ID>
        <PURCHASE_DATE>10/15/2003</PURCHASE_DATE>
        <DEPARTMENT>Meat</DEPARTMENT>
<PRODUCT_NAME>Beef</PRODUCT_NAME>
    </CUSTOMER>

    <CUSTOMER>
        <NAME>Nancy</NAME>
        <CUSTOMER_ID>58708</CUSTOMER_ID>
        <PURCHASE_DATE>10/15/2003</PURCHASE_DATE>
        <DEPARTMENT>Frozen</DEPARTMENT>
        <PRODUCT_NAME>Broccoli</PRODUCT_NAME>
    </CUSTOMER>

</CUSTOMERS>
```

As you can see, each record has become a `<CUSTOMER>` element. You can use whatever name you want for elements, and Internet Explorer will understand what you mean. In the previous HTML example, I used the MSHTML control as a DSO, but that's not going to work here. Instead, you can use either an

XML data island or a special applet-based XML DSO that comes with
Internet Explorer. I'm going to start with XML data islands.

XML Single-Record Binding Using XML Data Islands

To see how to bind HTML elements to an XML data island, I'll write an example. In this case, I'll add a data island for ch08_03.xml with the ID of customers to a new Web page, like this:

```
<HTML>
    <HEAD>
        <TITLE>
            Single Record Binding Using XML Data Islands
        </TITLE>
    </HEAD>

    <XML SRC="ch08_03.xml" ID="customers"></XML>
    .
    .
    .
```

Now customers can act like a DSO, just like any other DSO (which is why
data islands are called data islands). I can bind this DSO to assorted HTML
elements, as we've already seen in this chapter:

```
<XML SRC="ch08_03.xml" ID="customers"></XML>

BODY>
    <CENTER>
        <H1>
            Single Record Binding Using XML Data Islands
        </H1>

        Name: <INPUT TYPE="TEXT" DATASRC="#customers"
            DATAFLD="NAME" SIZE=10>

        <P>
        CUSTOMER_ID: <INPUT TYPE="TEXT" DATASRC="#customers"
            DATAFLD="CUSTOMER_ID" SIZE=5>

        <P>
        Department: <SELECT DATASRC="#customers"
            DATAFLD="DEPARTMENT" SIZE=1>

            <OPTION VALUE="Meat">Meat
            <OPTION VALUE="Produce">Produce
```

```
                <OPTION VALUE="Frozen">Frozen
          </SELECT>

          <P>
          Purchase date: <SPAN DATASRC="#customers"
                DATAFLD="PURCHASE_DATE"></SPAN>

          <P>
          Product: <SPAN DATASRC="#customers"
          ➥DATAFLD="PRODUCT_NAME"></SPAN><P>
            .
            .
            .
        </CENTER>
    </BODY>
</HTML>
```

The Properties, Methods, and Events of XML DSOs

In the example at the beginning of this chapter, we saw that you can use recordset methods such as moveFirst, moveLast, moveNext, and movePrevious to move around in a recordset. I'll make that more systematic now. In particular, the recordset object in an XML DSO has these properties:

- absolutePage—The page where the current record is

- absolutePosition—The position in a recordset of the current record

- BOF—True if the current record position is before the first record

- cacheSize—The number of records from a recordset object that are cached locally

- cursorLocation—The location of the cursor for the recordset

- cursorType—The type of database cursor used

- editMode—Specification of whether editing is in progress

- EOF—True if the current position is after the last record

- lockType—The type of database locking in force

- maxRecords—The maximum number of records to return to a recordset from a query

- pageCount—The number of pages of data the recordset contains

- `pageSize`—The number of records that make up one page
- `recordCount`—The number of records in the recordset
- `state`—The state of the recordset (open or closed)
- `status`—The status of the current record
- `stayInSync`—Specification of whether a hierarchical recordset should remain in contact with the data source

Here are the methods of the recordset objects inside XML DSOs:

- `addNew`—Adds a new record to the recordset.
- `cancel`—Cancels execution of a pending Execute or Open request.
- `cancelUpdate`—Cancels a pending update operation.
- `clone`—Creates a copy of the recordset.
- `close`—Closes a recordset.
- `delete`—Deletes the current record (or group of records).
- `find`—Searches the recordset (although the Structured Query Language syntax required here is not supported by Internet Explorer yet).
- `getRows`—Reads records and stores them in an array.
- `getString`—Gets the recordset as a string.
- `move`—Moves the position of the current record.
- `moveFirst, moveLast, moveNext, movePrevious`—Let you navigate to various positions in the recordset.
- `nextRecordSet`—Clears the current recordset object and returns the next recordset. Used with hierarchical recordsets.
- `open`—Opens a database.
- `requery`—Re-executes the query that created the recordset.
- `save`—Saves the recordset in a file.
- `supports`—Indicates the features supported by the recordset. You must pass long integer values that correspond to the various ADO methods, as defined in the Microsoft ADO documentation. For example passing this method a value of `0x1000400` (`0x` specifies a hexadecimal value) returns a value of `true`, indicating that the record set supports the `addNew` method; passing a value of `0x10000` returns a value of `false`, indicating that the record set does not support the `updateBatch` method.

XML DSOs also have a number of events that you can handle. (Recall that we saw how to handle XML document events in Internet Explorer at the end of the previous chapter.) Here they are:

- onCellChange—Happens when the data in a bound control changes and the focus leaves that cell

- onDataAvailable—Happens each time a batch of data is downloaded

- onDatasetChanged—Happens when the data set was changed

- onDatasetComplete—Happens when the data is downloaded and ready for use

- onReadyStateChange—Happens when the ReadyState property changes

- onRowEnter—Happens when the a new record becomes the current one

- onRowExit—Happens just before exiting the current record

- onRowsDelete—Happens when a row is deleted

- onRowsInserted—Happens when a row is inserted

To let the user navigate around in the recordset created from ch08_03.xml, I'll add the same buttons we saw in the earlier HTML example, using methods such as customers.recordset.moveNext() to navigate, like this:

Listing ch08_04.html

```
<HTML>
    <HEAD>
        <TITLE>Single Record Binding Using XML Data Islands</TITLE>
    </HEAD>

    <XML SRC="ch08_03.xml" ID="customers"></XML>

    <BODY>
        <CENTER>
            <H1>
                Single Record Binding Using XML Data Islands
            </H1>

            Name: <INPUT TYPE="TEXT" DATASRC="#customers"
                DATAFLD="NAME" SIZE=10>
            <P>
```

continues

Listing ch08_04.html   Continued

```
            Customer ID: <INPUT TYPE="TEXT" DATASRC="#customers"
                DATAFLD="CUSTOMER_ID" SIZE=5>

            <P>
            Purchase date: <SPAN DATASRC="#customers"
                DATAFLD="PURCHASE_DATE"></SPAN><P>
            Product: <SPAN DATASRC="#customers"
            ➥DATAFLD="PRODUCT_NAME"></SPAN>

            <P>
            Department: <SELECT DATASRC="#customers"
                DATAFLD="DEPARTMENT" SIZE=1>

            <OPTION VALUE="Meat">Meat
            <OPTION VALUE="Produce">Produce
            <OPTION VALUE="Frozen">Frozen
            </SELECT>

            <P>
            <BUTTON ONCLICK="customers.recordset.moveFirst()" >
                &lt;&lt;
            </BUTTON>
            <BUTTON ONCLICK="if (!customers.recordset.BOF)
                customers.recordset.movePrevious()" >
                &lt;
            </BUTTON>
            <BUTTON ONCLICK="if (!customers.recordset.EOF)
                customers.recordset.moveNext()" >
                &gt;
            </BUTTON>
            <BUTTON ONCLICK="customers.recordset.moveLast()">
                &gt;&gt;
            </BUTTON>
        </CENTER>
    </BODY>
</HTML>
```

You can see this page in Figure 8-2, where you see the fields of the current record displayed in bound HTML elements. The user can click the buttons in the page to navigate through the recordset.

As you can see in the previous list, there's a lot more you can do with a recordset than just navigate through the recordset. For example, it's often useful to access the individual fields in a record. Say that you wanted to get the value in the CUSTOMER_ID field of the current record in the DSO; you can use the expression customers.recordset("CUSTOMER_ID") to do that.

Figure 8-2
Using data binding to display an XML document in Internet Explorer.

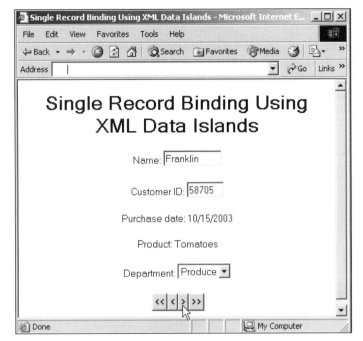

Accessing Data

You might note how much easier accessing data in recordset fields is than using DOM methods, such as `nextChild` and `lastSibling`, to navigate a node tree. If you can treat an XML document as a database, it can make life a good deal easier for you.

I'll access individual fields in records now in an example to make this concrete. In this case, I'll loop over all the records in the database (which I can do with a `while` loop, looping until the recordset's `EOF` property is `true`) and display the customer name, the item purchased, and what department the purchase was made in. Here's what the code looks like:

Listing ch08_05.html

```
<HTML>
    <HEAD>
        <TITLE>
            Accessing individual data fields
        </TITLE>
```

continues

Listing ch08_05.html   Continued

```
<XML ID="customer" SRC="ch08_03.xml"></XML>

<SCRIPT LANGUAGE="JavaScript">
    function viewData()
    {
        while (!customer.recordset.EOF) {
            div1.innerHTML +=
            customer.recordset("NAME") +
            " bought " +
            customer.recordset("PRODUCT_NAME") +
            " from the " +
            customer.recordset("DEPARTMENT") +
            " department.<BR>"
            customer.recordset.moveNext()
        }
    }
</SCRIPT>
</HEAD>

<BODY>
    <CENTER>
        <H1>
            Accessing individual data fields
        </H1>
    </CENTER>

    <FORM>
        <CENTER>
            <INPUT TYPE="BUTTON" VALUE="View data"
                ONCLICK="viewData()">
        </CENTER>
    </FORM>
    <DIV ID="div1">
    </DIV>
</BODY>
</HTML>
```

You can see this page in operation in Figure 8-3. As you can see there, the data from the individual fields in the various records has been assembled and displayed.

Besides working with single records as we have up to this point, you can work with all the data in an XML document at once when you bind it to a table.

Figure 8-3
Accessing
individual data
fields.

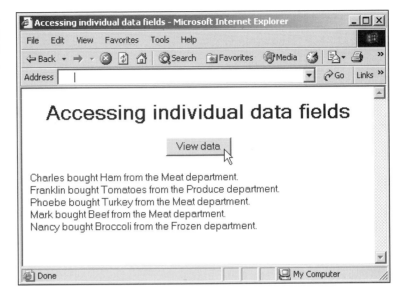

Tabular Data Binding and XML

When you bind a recordset to an HTML table, the table can display the entire recordset. Here's an example. In this case, I'll bind the data in ch08_03.xml to a table. I start by creating an XML data island, giving the data island the ID of customers:

```
<HTML>
    <HEAD>
        <TITLE>
            Tabular Binding with XML Data Islands
        </TITLE>
    </HEAD>

    <BODY>
        <CENTER>
            <H1>
                Tabular Binding with XML Data Islands
            </H1>

            <XML SRC="ch08_03.xml" ID="customers"></XML>
            .
            .
            .
```

To bind the data in ch08_03.xml to a table, all I have to do is set a table's DATASRC attribute to customers:

```
<XML SRC="ch08_03.xml" ID="customers"></XML>
```

```
<TABLE DATASRC="#customers" CELLSPACING="10">
    .
    .
    .
```

The fields in the records of ch08_03.xml are NAME, CUSTOMER_ID, PURCHASE_DATE, DEPARTMENT, and PRODUCT. I will bind those fields to the individual cells in a table like this using the DATAFLD attribute:

Listing ch08_06.html

```
<HTML>
    <HEAD>
        <TITLE>
            Tabular Binding with XML Data Islands
        </TITLE>
    </HEAD>

    <BODY>
        <CENTER>
            <H1>
                Tabular Binding with XML Data Islands
            </H1>

            <XML SRC="ch08_03.xml" ID="customers"></XML>

            <TABLE DATASRC="#customers" CELLSPACING="10">
                <THEAD>
                    <TR>
                        <TH>Name</TH>
                        <TH>Customer ID</TH>
                        <TH>Purchase Date</TH>
                        <TH>Department</TH>
                        <TH>Product</TH>
                    </TR>
                </THEAD>

                <TBODY>
                    <TR>
                        <TD>
                            <SPAN DATAFLD="NAME">
                            </SPAN>
                        </TD>
```

```
                    <TD>
                         <SPAN DATAFLD="CUSTOMER_ID">
                         </SPAN>
                    </TD>
                    <TD>
                         <SPAN DATAFLD="PURCHASE_DATE">
                         </SPAN>
                    </TD>
                    <TD>
                         <SPAN DATAFLD="DEPARTMENT">
                         </SPAN>
                    </TD>
                    <TD>
                         <SPAN DATAFLD="PRODUCT_NAME">
                         </SPAN>
                    </TD>
               </TR>
          </TBODY>
     </TABLE>
   </CENTER>
 </BODY>
</HTML>
```

You can see the results in Figure 8-4, where the data from ch08_03.xml is displayed in a table.

Figure 8-4
Binding data
to a table in
Internet
Explorer.

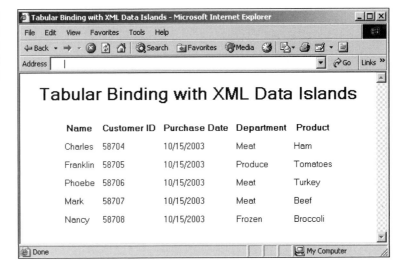

There's another DSO you can use with XML documents in Internet Explorer: the XML DSO.

Single-Record Data Binding with the XML DSO

Starting in Internet Explorer 4, Microsoft has included an XML DSO expressly designed to be used with XML. This DSO is a little odd because it's not internal to Internet Explorer; instead, it's implemented as a Java applet. You can
embed this applet in a page and create an XML DSO like this with the HTML
<APPLET> element:

```
<APPLET
    CODE="com.ms.xml.dso.XMLDSO.class"
    ID="IDNAME"
    WIDTH="0"
    HEIGHT="0"
    MAYSCRIPT="true">
    <PARAM NAME="URL" VALUE="XMLPageURL">
</APPLET>
```

Here, you pass the URL of the XML document as a parameter to the XML
DSO applet, using the <PARAM> element; you give this DSO a name with the
<APPLET> ID attribute.

In the next example, I'll put the XML DSO to work, connecting it to
ch08_03.xml. To bind ch08_03.xml to HTML elements, I start by adding the
XML applet to a Web page, calling this DSO dsoCustomer. Then I pass it the
URL of the document to read as a parameter:

```
<HTML>
    <HEAD>
        <TITLE>
            Single Record Binding Using the XML DSO
        </TITLE>
    </HEAD>

    <BODY>
        <CENTER>
            <H1>
                Single Record Binding Using the XML DSO
            </H1>

            <APPLET CODE="com.ms.xml.dso.XMLDSO.class"
                ID="dsoCustomer"
                WIDTH="0" HEIGHT="0"
                MAYSCRIPT="true">
                <PARAM NAME="URL" VALUE="ch08_03.xml">
            </APPLET>
            .
            .
            .
```

That's all it takes. This DSO exposes a recordset object as XML data islands do, so I can bind HTML elements to it as we've done before:

```
<APPLET CODE="com.ms.xml.dso.XMLDSO.class"
    ID="dsoCustomer"
    WIDTH="0" HEIGHT="0"
    MAYSCRIPT="true">
    <PARAM NAME="URL" VALUE="ch08_03.xml">
</APPLET>
```

```
Name:
<INPUT TYPE="TEXT" DATASRC="#dsoCustomer"
    DATAFLD="NAME" SIZE=10>

<P>
Customer ID:
<INPUT TYPE="TEXT" DATASRC="#dsoCustomer"
    DATAFLD="CUSTOMER_ID" SIZE=5>

<P>
Purchase date:
<SPAN DATASRC="#dsoCustomer"
    DATAFLD="PURCHASE_DATE"></SPAN>

<P>
Department:
<SELECT DATASRC="#dsoCustomer"
    DATAFLD="DEPARTMENT" SIZE=1>

    <OPTION VALUE="Meat">Meat
    <OPTION VALUE="Produce">Produce
    <OPTION VALUE="Frozen">Frozen
</SELECT>

<P>
Product:
<SPAN DATASRC="#dsoCustomer" DATAFLD="PRODUCT_NAME">
</SPAN>
```

.
.
.

I can use the recordset object's methods, such as moveNext to move to the next record and movePrevious to move to the previous one, with buttons like this. Here's the whole code:

Listing ch08_07.html

```
<HTML>
    <HEAD>
        <TITLE>
            Single Record Binding Using the XML DSO
        </TITLE>
    </HEAD>

    <BODY>
        <CENTER>
            <H1>
                Single Record Binding Using the XML DSO
            </H1>

            <APPLET CODE="com.ms.xml.dso.XMLDSO.class"
                ID="dsoCustomer"
                WIDTH="0" HEIGHT="0"
                MAYSCRIPT="true">
                <PARAM NAME="URL" VALUE="ch08_03.xml">
            </APPLET>

            Name:
            <INPUT TYPE="TEXT" DATASRC="#dsoCustomer"
                DATAFLD="NAME" SIZE=10>

            <P>
            Customer ID:
            <INPUT TYPE="TEXT" DATASRC="#dsoCustomer"
                DATAFLD="CUSTOMER_ID" SIZE=5>

            <P>
            Purchase date:
            <SPAN DATASRC="#dsoCustomer"
                DATAFLD="PURCHASE_DATE"></SPAN>

            <P>
            Department:
            <SELECT DATASRC="#dsoCustomer"
                DATAFLD="DEPARTMENT" SIZE=1>

                <OPTION VALUE="Meat">Meat
                <OPTION VALUE="Produce">Produce
                <OPTION VALUE="Frozen">Frozen
            </SELECT>

            <P>
            Product:
            <SPAN DATASRC="#dsoCustomer" DATAFLD="PRODUCT_NAME">
            </SPAN>

            <P>
```

```
<BUTTON ONCLICK="dsoCustomer.recordset.moveFirst()" >
    &lt;&lt;
</BUTTON>
<BUTTON ONCLICK="if (!dsoCustomer.recordset.BOF)
    dsoCustomer.recordset.movePrevious()" >
    &lt;
</BUTTON>
<BUTTON ONCLICK="if (!dsoCustomer.recordset.EOF)
    dsoCustomer.recordset.moveNext()" >
    &gt;
</BUTTON>
<BUTTON ONCLICK="dsoCustomer.recordset.moveLast()">
    &gt;&gt;
</BUTTON>
```

```
        </CENTER>

    </BODY>
</HTML>
```

You can see this page at work in Figure 8-5. The XML DOS applet works as expected, but the fact that it has remained an applet external to Internet Explorer suggests that Microsoft might discard it sooner or later in favor of XML islands.

Figure 8-5
Single-record binding using the XML DSO in Internet Explorer.

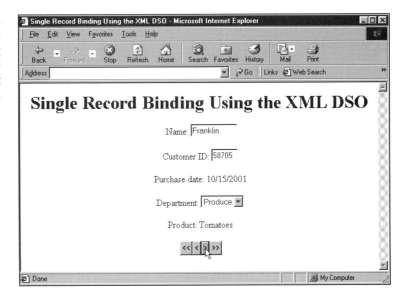

As with XML data islands, you can also bind the XML DSO to tables.

Tabular Data Binding with the XML DSO

It's as easy to bind the XML DSO to tables as it was to bind XML data islands to tables. Here's an example showing how this works. In this case, I'm just binding ch08_03.xml to a table using the XML DSO, and I'm displaying all the fields in the various records of ch08_03.xml at once:

Listing ch08_08.html

```
<HTML>
    <HEAD>
        <TITLE>
            Binding the XML DSO to Tables
        </TITLE>
    </HEAD>

    <BODY>
        <CENTER>
            <H1>
                Binding the XML DSO to Tables
            </H1>

            <APPLET CODE="com.ms.xml.dso.XMLDSO.class"
                ID="customers"
                WIDTH="0" HEIGHT="0"
                MAYSCRIPT="true">
                <PARAM NAME="URL" VALUE="ch08_03.xml">
            </APPLET>

            <TABLE DATASRC="#customers" CELLSPACING="10">
                <THEAD>
                    <TR>
                        <TH>Name</TH>
                        <TH>Customer ID</TH>
                        <TH>Purchase Date</TH>
                        <TH>Department</TH>
                        <TH>Product</TH>
                    </TR>
                </THEAD>

                <TBODY>
                    <TR>
                        <TD>
                            <SPAN DATAFLD="NAME">
                            </SPAN>
                        </TD>
                        <TD>
                            <SPAN DATAFLD="CUSTOMER_ID">
                            </SPAN>
```

```
                    </TD>
                    <TD>
                        <SPAN DATAFLD="PURCHASE_DATE">
                        </SPAN>
                    </TD>
                    <TD>
                        <SPAN DATAFLD="DEPARTMENT">
                        </SPAN>
                    </TD>
                    <TD>
                        <SPAN DATAFLD="PRODUCT_NAME">
                        </SPAN>
                    </TD>
                </TR>
            </TBODY>
        </TABLE>
    </CENTER>
  </BODY>
</HTML>
```

That's all it takes. You can see this page in action in Figure 8-6.

Figure 8-6
Tabular data
binding with
the XML DSO
in Internet
Explorer.

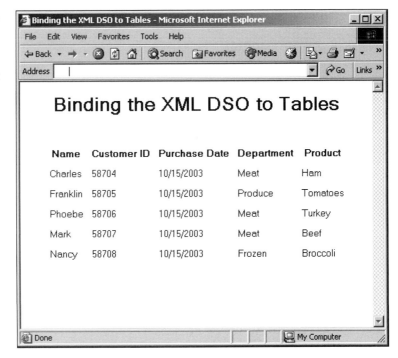

XML and Hierarchical Data

One of the most interesting developments in database handling is the capability to create hierarchical recordsets, in which a record can actually contain an entire new recordset. XML documents represent a perfect way of storing hierarchical recordsets because you can enclose one set of elements inside another easily.

Here's an example. In this case, I'm adding records about deliveries made to the customers in ch08_03.xml in a new XML document, ch08_09.xml:

Listing ch08_09.xml

```xml
<?xml version="1.0"?>
<CUSTOMERS>
    <CUSTOMER>
        <NAME>Charles</NAME>
        <RECORD>
            <CUSTOMER_ID>58704</CUSTOMER_ID>
            <PURCHASE_DATE>10/15/2003</PURCHASE_DATE>
            <DEPARTMENT>Meat</DEPARTMENT>
            <PRODUCT_NAME>Ham</PRODUCT_NAME>
            <DELIVERY>
                <DATE>10/20/2003</DATE>
                <TOTAL_COST>$1.99</TOTAL_COST>
            </DELIVERY>
            <DELIVERY>
                <DATE>10/25/2003</DATE>
                <TOTAL_COST>$1.49</TOTAL_COST>
            </DELIVERY>
        </RECORD>
    </CUSTOMER>
    <CUSTOMER>
        <NAME>Franklin</NAME>
        <RECORD>
            <CUSTOMER_ID>58705</CUSTOMER_ID>
            <PURCHASE_DATE>10/15/2003</PURCHASE_DATE>
            <DEPARTMENT>Produce</DEPARTMENT>
            <PRODUCT_NAME>Tomatoes</PRODUCT_NAME>
            <DELIVERY>
                <DATE>10/20/2003</DATE>
                <TOTAL_COST>$3.00</TOTAL_COST>
            </DELIVERY>
            <DELIVERY>
                <DATE>10/25/2003</DATE>
                <TOTAL_COST>$2.95</TOTAL_COST>
            </DELIVERY>
        </RECORD>
    </CUSTOMER>
```

```
    <CUSTOMER>
        <NAME>Phoebe</NAME>
        <RECORD>
            <CUSTOMER_ID>58706</CUSTOMER_ID>
            <PURCHASE_DATE>10/15/2003</PURCHASE_DATE>
            <DEPARTMENT>Meat</DEPARTMENT>
            <PRODUCT_NAME>Turkey</PRODUCT_NAME>
            <DELIVERY>
                <DATE>10/20/2003</DATE>
                <TOTAL_COST>$4.99</TOTAL_COST>
            </DELIVERY>
            <DELIVERY>
                <DATE>10/25/2003</DATE>
                <TOTAL_COST>$8.99</TOTAL_COST>
            </DELIVERY>
        </RECORD>
    </CUSTOMER>
    <CUSTOMER>
        <NAME>Mark</NAME>
        <RECORD>
            <CUSTOMER_ID>58707</CUSTOMER_ID>
            <PURCHASE_DATE>10/15/2003</PURCHASE_DATE>
            <DEPARTMENT>Meat</DEPARTMENT>
            <PRODUCT_NAME>Beef</PRODUCT_NAME>
            <DELIVERY>
                <DATE>10/20/2003</DATE>
                <TOTAL_COST>$3.95</TOTAL_COST>
            </DELIVERY>
            <DELIVERY>
                <DATE>10/25/2003</DATE>
                <TOTAL_COST>$6.95</TOTAL_COST>
            </DELIVERY>
        </RECORD>
    </CUSTOMER>
    <CUSTOMER>
        <NAME>Nancy</NAME>
        <RECORD>
            <CUSTOMER_ID>58708</CUSTOMER_ID>
            <PURCHASE_DATE>10/15/2003</PURCHASE_DATE>
            <DEPARTMENT>Frozen</DEPARTMENT>
            <PRODUCT_NAME>Broccoli</PRODUCT_NAME>
            <DELIVERY>
                <DATE>10/20/2003</DATE>
                <TOTAL_COST>$1.99</TOTAL_COST>
            </DELIVERY>
            <DELIVERY>
                <DATE>10/25/2003</DATE>
                <TOTAL_COST>$2.99</TOTAL_COST>
            </DELIVERY>
        </RECORD>
    </CUSTOMER>
</CUSTOMERS>
```

In this case, each <RECORD> element itself contains two <DELIVERY> elements (which contain <DATE> and <TOTAL_COST> elements). A DSO can't simply treat multiple enclosed records like this as a single record because that would give two or more fields in the record the same name. Instead, Internet Explorer makes the recordset into a hierarchical recordset and gives each <DE-LIVERY> element its own subrecordset.

How do you refer to a subrecordset in a hierarchical database? For example, how can you refer to the <DELIVERY> elements in each <RECORD> element? You do that by referring to a new recordset, RECORD.DELIVERY. This expression refers to the child recordset made up of the <DELIVERY> elements in the current record.

As usual, this is made easier to understand with an example, so take a look at this code, where I'm binding ch08_09.xml to a table and displaying the <DELIVERY> records for each customer using tables. I start by binding a table to an XML data island and displaying the name of each customer, like this:

```
<HTML>
    <HEAD>
        <TITLE>
            Using XML With Hierarchical Records
        </TITLE>
    </HEAD>

    <BODY>

        <CENTER>
            <H1>
                Using XML With Hierarchical Records
            </H1>

            <XML SRC="ch08_09.xml" ID=dsoCustomer></XML>

            <TABLE DATASRC="#dsoCustomer" BORDER="1">
                <TR>
                    <TH><DIV DATAFLD="NAME"></DIV></TH>
                    <TD>
            .
            .
            .
```

Next, I bind a table to the RECORD field in the current record:

```
<XML SRC="ch08_09.xml" ID=dsoCustomer></XML>

<TABLE DATASRC="#dsoCustomer" BORDER="1">
    <TR>
```

```
    <TH><DIV DATAFLD="NAME"></DIV></TH>
    <TD>
        <TABLE DATASRC="#dsoCustomer"
        DATAFLD="RECORD">
```

   .
   .
   .

To display the data from the <DATE> and <TOTAL_COST> elements in each <DE-LIVERY> record, I bind one final internal table to the RECORD.DELIVERY recordset. Here's the whole code:

Listing ch08_10.html

```
<HTML>
    <HEAD>
        <TITLE>
            Using XML With Hierarchical Records
        </TITLE>
    </HEAD>

    <BODY>

        <CENTER>
            <H1>
                Using XML With Hierarchical Records
            </H1>

            <XML SRC="ch08_09.xml" ID=dsoCustomer></XML>

            <TABLE DATASRC="#dsoCustomer" BORDER="1">
                <TR>
                    <TH><DIV DATAFLD="NAME"></DIV></TH>
                    <TD>
                        <TABLE DATASRC="#dsoCustomer"
                        DATAFLD="RECORD">
                            <TR>
                                <TD>
                                    <TABLE DATASRC="#dsoCustomer"
                                        CELLPADDING = "5"
                                        DATAFLD="RECORD.DELIVERY">
                                        <TR ALIGN = "LEFT">
                                            <TH>Date</TH>
                                            <TH>Total Cost</TH>
                                        </TR>
                                        <TR ALIGN = "LEFT">
                                            <TD><DIV DATAFLD="DATE">
                                            </DIV></TD>
                                            <TD><DIV
```

continues

Listing ch08_10.html   Continued

```
                                          DATAFLD="TOTAL_COST">
                                        </DIV></TD>
                                    </TR>
                                </TABLE>
                            </TD>
                        </TR>
                    </TABLE>
                </TD>
            </TR>
        </TABLE>
    </CENTER>
</BODY>
</HTML>
```

This page appears in Internet Explorer in Figure 8-7. As you can see there, each customer's name is displayed next to the dates and costs of the deliveries. Now you're handling hierarchical recordsets and XML.

Figure 8-7
Displaying hierarchical recordsets in Internet Explorer.

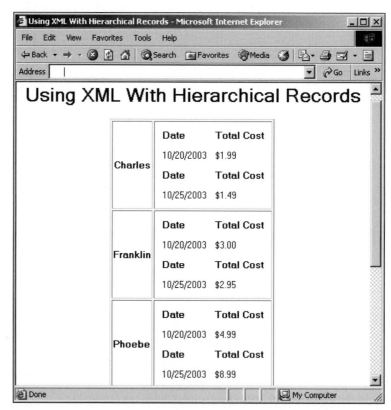

Handling Variable-Size Hierarchical Data in XML Documents

We've seen that Internet Explorer DSOs can handle hierarchical recordsets in which each record itself has an internal recordset. The internal recordsets I used each contained two records, but that's hardly a realistic example; in real-world documents, recordsets can be of any length. How do the DSOs in Internet Explorer stack up here? Take a look at this new document, ch08_11.xml, in which each internal recordset has between one and three `<DELIVERY>` records:

Listing ch08_11.xml

```
<?xml version="1.0"?>
<CUSTOMERS>

    <CUSTOMER>
        <NAME>Charles</NAME>
        <RECORD>
            <CUSTOMER_ID>58704</CUSTOMER_ID>
            <PURCHASE_DATE>10/15/2003</PURCHASE_DATE>
            <DEPARTMENT>Meat</DEPARTMENT>
            <PRODUCT_NAME>Ham</PRODUCT_NAME>
            <DELIVERY>
                <DATE>10/20/2003</DATE>
                <TOTAL_COST>$1.99</TOTAL_COST>
            </DELIVERY>
            <DELIVERY>
                <DATE>10/25/2003</DATE>
                <TOTAL_COST>$1.49</TOTAL_COST>
            </DELIVERY>
            <DELIVERY>
                <DATE>10/25/2003</DATE>
                <TOTAL_COST>$1.49</TOTAL_COST>
            </DELIVERY>
        </RECORD>
    </CUSTOMER>

    <CUSTOMER>
        <NAME>Franklin</NAME>
        <RECORD>
            <CUSTOMER_ID>58705</CUSTOMER_ID>
            <PURCHASE_DATE>10/15/2003</PURCHASE_DATE>
            <DEPARTMENT>Produce</DEPARTMENT>
            <PRODUCT_NAME>Tomatoes</PRODUCT_NAME>
            <DELIVERY>
                <DATE>10/20/2003</DATE>
```

continues

Listing ch08_11.xml   Continued

```xml
                <TOTAL_COST>$3.00</TOTAL_COST>
            </DELIVERY>
        </RECORD>
    </CUSTOMER>

    <CUSTOMER>
        <NAME>Phoebe</NAME>
        <RECORD>
            <CUSTOMER_ID>58706</CUSTOMER_ID>
            <PURCHASE_DATE>10/15/2003</PURCHASE_DATE>
            <DEPARTMENT>Meat</DEPARTMENT>
            <PRODUCT_NAME>Turkey</PRODUCT_NAME>
            <DELIVERY>
                <DATE>10/20/2003</DATE>
                <TOTAL_COST>$4.99</TOTAL_COST>
            </DELIVERY>
            <DELIVERY>
                <DATE>10/25/2003</DATE>
                <TOTAL_COST>$8.99</TOTAL_COST>
            </DELIVERY>
        </RECORD>
    </CUSTOMER>

    <CUSTOMER>
        <NAME>Mark</NAME>
        <RECORD>
            <CUSTOMER_ID>58707</CUSTOMER_ID>
            <PURCHASE_DATE>10/15/2003</PURCHASE_DATE>
            <DEPARTMENT>Meat</DEPARTMENT>
            <PRODUCT_NAME>Beef</PRODUCT_NAME>
            <DELIVERY>
                <DATE>10/20/2003</DATE>
                <TOTAL_COST>$3.95</TOTAL_COST>
            </DELIVERY>
            <DELIVERY>
                <DATE>10/25/2003</DATE>
                <TOTAL_COST>$6.95</TOTAL_COST>
            </DELIVERY>
        </RECORD>
    </CUSTOMER>

    <CUSTOMER>
        <NAME>Nancy</NAME>
        <RECORD>
            <CUSTOMER_ID>58708</CUSTOMER_ID>
            <PURCHASE_DATE>10/15/2003</PURCHASE_DATE>
            <DEPARTMENT>Frozen</DEPARTMENT>
            <PRODUCT_NAME>Broccoli</PRODUCT_NAME>
            <DELIVERY>
```

```
            <DATE>10/20/2003</DATE>
            <TOTAL_COST>$1.99</TOTAL_COST>
        </DELIVERY>
        <DELIVERY>
            <DATE>10/25/2003</DATE>
            <TOTAL_COST>$2.99</TOTAL_COST>
        </DELIVERY>
        <DELIVERY>
            <DATE>5-3-2002</DATE>
            <TOTAL_COST>$7200.00</TOTAL_COST>
        </DELIVERY>
    </RECORD>
    </CUSTOMER>
</CUSTOMERS>
```

In fact, this is not a problem; here's the page I'll use to display this data:

Listing ch08_12.html

```
<HTML>
    <HEAD>
        <TITLE>
            Variable Size Hierarchical Records
        </TITLE>
    </HEAD>

    <BODY>

        <CENTER>
            <H1>
                Variable Size Hierarchical Records
            </H1>

            <XML SRC="ch08_11.xml" ID="customers"></XML>

            <TABLE DATASRC="#customers" BORDER="1">
                <TR>
                    <TH><DIV DATAFLD="NAME"></DIV></TH>
                    <TD>
                        <TABLE DATASRC="#customers"
                        DATAFLD="RECORD">
                            <TR>
                                <TD>
                                <TABLE DATASRC="#customers"
                                    CELLPADDING = "3"
                                    DATAFLD="RECORD.DELIVERY">
                                    <TR ALIGN = "LEFT">
                                        <TH>Date</TH>
                                        <TH>Amount</TH>
```

continues

Listing ch08_12.html   Continued

```
                                    </TR>
                                    <TR ALIGN = "LEFT">
                                        <TD><DIV DATAFLD="DATE">
                                        </DIV></TD>
                                        <TD><DIV
                                        DATAFLD="TOTAL_COST">
                                        </DIV></TD>
                                    </TR>
                                </TABLE>
                            </TD>
                        </TR>
                    </TABLE>
                </TD>
            </TR>
        </TABLE>
    </CENTER>
    </BODY>
</HTML>
```

You can see the results in Figure 8-8, in which each <DELIVERY> recordset is correctly displayed, even though they all have different numbers of records.

Figure 8-8
Variable-size
hierarchical
records in
Internet
Explorer.

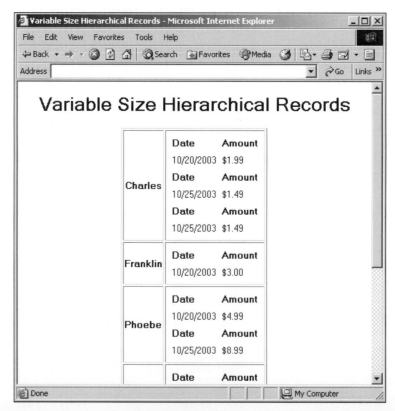

You can also create the same page using the XML DSO applet instead of data islands:

```
<HTML>
    <HEAD>
        <TITLE>
            Variable Size Hierarchical Records
        </TITLE>
    </HEAD>

    <BODY>
        <CENTER>
            <H1>
                Variable Size Hierarchical Records
            </H1>

            <APPLET CODE="com.ms.xml.dso.XMLDSO.class"
                ID="customers"
                WIDTH="0" HEIGHT="0"
                MAYSCRIPT="true">
                <PARAM NAME="URL" VALUE="ch08_11.xml">
            </APPLET>

            <TABLE DATASRC="#customers" BORDER="1">
                <TR>
                    <TH><DIV DATAFLD="NAME"></DIV></TH>
                    <TD>
                        <TABLE DATASRC="#customers"
                        DATAFLD="RECORD">
                            <TR ALIGN = CENTER>
                                <TD>Sales</TD>
                            </TR>
                            <TR>
                                .
                                .
                                .
                            </TR>
                        </TABLE>
                    </TD>
                </TR>
            </TABLE>
        </CENTER>
    </BODY>
</HTML>
```

Searching XML Data

You can do a great many things with recordsets, as we've seen in this chapter. In this chapter's final example, I'll take a look at how to search a database for a specific item. In particular, I'll let the user search for a match to a customer's name that the user specifies.

For this example, I'll modify ch08_03.xml by adding a second customer with the name Nancy to make sure we catch all instances of a match, and I'll name this new document ch08_13.xml:

Listing ch08_13.xml

```
<?xml version="1.0"?>
<CUSTOMER>

    <CUSTOMER>
        <NAME>Charles</NAME>
        <CUSTOMER_ID>58704</CUSTOMER_ID>
        <PURCHASE_DATE>10/15/2003</PURCHASE_DATE>
        <DEPARTMENT>Meat</DEPARTMENT>
        <PRODUCT_NAME>Ham</PRODUCT_NAME>
    </CUSTOMER>

    <CUSTOMER>
        <NAME>Franklin</NAME>
        <CUSTOMER_ID>58705</CUSTOMER_ID>
        <PURCHASE_DATE>10/15/2003</PURCHASE_DATE>
        <DEPARTMENT>Produce</DEPARTMENT>
        <PRODUCT_NAME>Tomatoes</PRODUCT_NAME>
    </CUSTOMER>

    <CUSTOMER>
        <NAME>Phoebe</NAME>
        <CUSTOMER_ID>58706</CUSTOMER_ID>
        <PURCHASE_DATE>10/15/2003</PURCHASE_DATE>
        <DEPARTMENT>Meat</DEPARTMENT>
        <PRODUCT_NAME>Turkey</PRODUCT_NAME>
    </CUSTOMER>

    <CUSTOMER>
        <NAME>Mark</NAME>
        <CUSTOMER_ID>58707</CUSTOMER_ID>
        <PURCHASE_DATE>10/15/2003</PURCHASE_DATE>
        <DEPARTMENT>Meat</DEPARTMENT>
<PRODUCT_NAME>Beef</PRODUCT_NAME>
    </CUSTOMER>

    <CUSTOMER>
        <NAME>Nancy</NAME>
        <CUSTOMER_ID>58708</CUSTOMER_ID>
        <PURCHASE_DATE>10/15/2003</PURCHASE_DATE>
        <DEPARTMENT>Frozen</DEPARTMENT>
        <PRODUCT_NAME>Broccoli</PRODUCT_NAME>
    </CUSTOMER>

    <CUSTOMER>
        <NAME>Nancy</NAME>
        <CUSTOMER_ID>58709</CUSTOMER_ID>
```

```
        <PURCHASE_DATE>10/15/2003</PURCHASE_DATE>
        <DEPARTMENT>Produce</DEPARTMENT>
        <PRODUCT_NAME>Tomatoes</PRODUCT_NAME>
    </CUSTOMER>
```

```
</CUSTOMER>
```

After setting up an XML data island and connecting it to ch08_13.xml, I'll define a new function named findMatches that will search for matches to the customer name that the user wants to search for. Although ADOR recordset objects do have a method called find to search databases with, you set the search criterion in that method using a Structured Query Language (SQL, the language many database applications use) expression, and Internet Explorer doesn't appear to support such expressions. Instead, I'll set up a JavaScript loop that will find matches to the name that the user is searching for.

The user can enter the name to search for in a text field I'll call text1. When the user clicks a button, the findMatches function is called. I'll convert the name to search for into lower case (using the JavaScript String object's toLowerCase method), to make the search non–case sensitive, and I'll store it in a variable named searchFor:

```
<HTML>
    <HEAD>
        <TITLE>
            Searching XML-Based Databases
        </TITLE>

        <XML ID="customers" SRC="ch08_13.xml"></XML>

        <SCRIPT LANGUAGE="JavaScript">
            function findMatches()
            {
                var searchFor = form1.text1.value.toLowerCase()
```

.
.
.

Now I'll loop over all the records in the recordset, storing the name in the current record in a variable named currentName, which I also convert to lower case:

```
function findMatches()
{
    var searchFor = form1.text1.value.toLowerCase()
```

```
            while (!customers.recordset.EOF) {
                var currentName = new
                ➥String(customers.recordset("NAME"))
                currentName = currentName.toLowerCase()
                    .
                    .
                    .
                customers.recordset.moveNext()
            }
        }
```

I'll use the JavaScript String object's indexOf method to see if the current name matches the name that the user is searching for. The indexOf method returns a value of 0 or greater if a match was found, so I use that method like this:

```
function findMatches()
{
    var searchFor = form1.text1.value.toLowerCase()

    while (!customers.recordset.EOF) {
        var currentName = new
String(customers.recordset("NAME"))
        currentName = currentName.toLowerCase()
        if (currentName.indexOf(searchFor) >= 0) {
            .
            .
            .
        }
        customers.recordset.moveNext()
    }
    .
    .
    .
```

All that remains is to display the matching records in a <DIV> element, as we have before in this chapter, and add the button and text field that we'll use to let the user interact with our code:

Listing ch08_14.html

```
<HTML>
    <HEAD>
        <TITLE>
            Searching XML-Based Databases
        </TITLE>
```

```
<XML ID="customers" SRC="ch08_13.xml"></XML>

<SCRIPT LANGUAGE="JavaScript">
    function findMatches()
    {
        var searchFor = form1.text1.value.toLowerCase()

        while (!customers.recordset.EOF) {
            var currentName = new
            ➥String(customers.recordset("NAME"))
            currentName = currentName.toLowerCase()
            if (currentName.indexOf(searchFor) >= 0) {
                divMessage.innerHTML +=
                customers.recordset("NAME") +
                " (ID " +
                customers.recordset("CUSTOMER_ID") +
                ") bought " +
                customers.recordset("PRODUCT_NAME") +
                " from the " +
                customers.recordset("DEPARTMENT") +
                " department on " +
                customers.recordset("PURCHASE_DATE") +
                ".<BR>"
            }
            customers.recordset.moveNext()
        }
    }
</SCRIPT>
</HEAD>

<BODY>
    <CENTER>
        <H1>
            Searching XML-Based Databases
        </H1>

        <FORM ID="form1">
            Search for this name: <INPUT TYPE="TEXT" NAME="text1">
            <BR>
            <BR>
            <INPUT TYPE="BUTTON" VALUE="Search for matches"
                ONCLICK="findMatches()">
        </FORM>
    </CENTER>
    <DIV ID="divMessage">
    </DIV>
</BODY>
</HTML>
```

You can see the results in Figure 8-9, where we've matched both customers named Nancy.

Figure 8-9
Searching for
matches in
XML-based
databases.

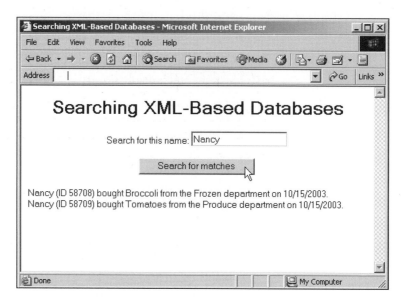

In this example, I've used XML data islands, but of course you can also use the XML DSO applet to load the file ch08_13.xml. I'll do that here to demonstrate another aspect of the XML DSO applet—up until now, I've given the applet a zero width and height, but in fact, this applet does display the status of its operations if you give it some space in the Web page. I'll do that like this:

Listing ch08_15.html

```
<HTML>
    <HEAD>
        <TITLE>
            Searching XML-Based Databases
        </TITLE>

        <SCRIPT LANGUAGE="JavaScript">
            function findMatches()
            {
                var searchFor = form1.text1.value.toLowerCase()

                while (!customers.recordset.EOF) {
                    var currentName = new
                    ➥String(customers.recordset("NAME"))
```

```
                        currentName = currentName.toLowerCase()
                        if (currentName.indexOf(searchFor) >= 0) {
                            divMessage.innerHTML +=
                            customers.recordset("NAME") +
                            " (ID " +
                            customers.recordset("CUSTOMER_ID") +
                            ") bought " +
                            customers.recordset("PRODUCT_NAME") +
                            " from the " +
                            customers.recordset("DEPARTMENT") +
                            " department on " +
                            customers.recordset("PURCHASE_DATE") +
                            ".<BR>"
                        }
                        customers.recordset.moveNext()
                    }
                }
        </SCRIPT>
    </HEAD>

    <BODY>
        <CENTER>
            <H1>
                Searching XML-Based Databases
            </H1>
            <APPLET CODE="com.ms.xml.dso.XMLDSO.class"
                ID="customers"
                WIDTH="400" HEIGHT="50"
                MAYSCRIPT="true">
                <PARAM NAME="URL" VALUE="ch08_13.xml">
            </APPLET>

            <FORM ID="form1">
                Search for this name: <INPUT TYPE="TEXT" NAME="text1">
                <BR>
                <BR>
                <INPUT TYPE="BUTTON" VALUE="Search for matches"
                    ONCLICK="findMatches()">
            </FORM>
        </CENTER>
        <DIV ID="divMessage">
        </DIV>
    </BODY>
</HTML>
```

You can see the results in Figure 8-10, where the XML DSO is displaying the message `Successfully loaded XML from "file:/C:/xml/chap08/ch08_13.xml"`. The background of this applet is green because there was no error. If there was an error, however, the background would be red and the applet would display error messages.

Figure 8-10
Searching for matches in XML-based databases using the XML DSO.

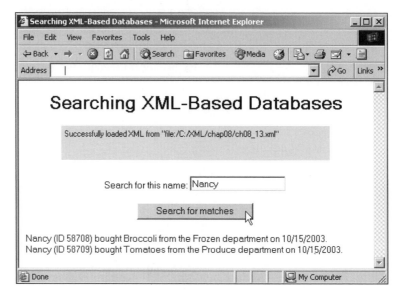

CHAPTER 9

Cascading Style Sheets

If you want to display XML pages in a browser, you've got a problem: Unless the browser you're using can handle your XML markup (such as the Jumbo browser, which handles Chemical Markup Language), the best it can do is to display your document in some default way. For example, take a look at this document, which holds the beginning text of the stoic philosopher (and Roman emperor) Marcus Aurelius's *The Meditations*:

Listing ch09_01.xml

```
<?xml version="1.0" standalone="yes"?>
<DOCUMENT>
    <TITLE>The Meditations</TITLE>
    <AUTHOR>By Marcus Aurelius</AUTHOR>
    <SECTION>Book One</SECTION>
    <P>
        From my grandfather, Verus, I learned good morals
        and the government of my temper.
    </P>
    <P>
        From the reputation and remembrance of my father,
        modesty and a manly character.
    </P>
    <P>
        From my mother, piety and beneficence, and abstinence,
        not only from evil deeds, but even from evil
        thoughts; and further, simplicity in my way of living,
        far removed from the habits of the rich.
    </P>
    <P>
        From my great-grandfather, not to have frequented
        public schools, and to have had good teachers at home,
        and to know that on such things a man should spend
        freely.
    </P>
</DOCUMENT>
```

Internet Explorer can display this document, but because it has no idea what you want to do with the various tags as far as presentation goes, it leaves them in, as you see in Figure 9-1.

Figure 9-1
Displaying an
XML
document in
Internet
Explorer.

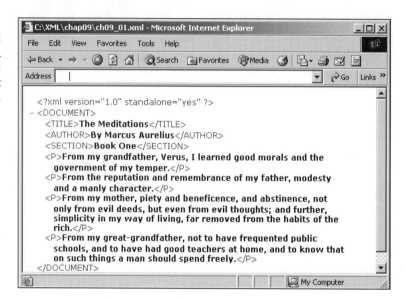

This chapter is all about fixing this situation by telling browsers exactly how to display the elements you've created in a document. To do this, I'll use Cascading Style Sheets (CSS), which were first introduced in December 1996. CSS is now widely supported in the major browsers. Using CSS, you can specify exactly how you want your documents to appear in browsers. Although CSS was developed for use with HTML, it works with XML—in fact, it works even better with XML because there are some conflicts between CSS and HTML (such as the CSS nowrap specification and the HTML NOWRAP attribute) that XML doesn't have. Furthermore, in HTML, you're restricted to working with the predefined HTML elements, while in XML, you can style sophisticated nestings of elements and more.

There are two levels of CSS today, and they're both W3C specifications—CSS1 and CSS2. You'll find these specifications at www.w3.org/TR/REC-CSS1 and www.w3.org/TR/REC-CSS2. CSS2 includes all of CSS1 and adds some additional features, such as aural stylesheets, support for various media types, and other advanced features. In fact, CSS3 is under development, and you can read all about it at www.w3.org/Style/CSS/current-work.

The actual support you'll find in browsers for CSS varies widely, as you might expect. The support in both Netscape Navigator and Internet Explorer is good, although somewhat different, so some experimentation in both browsers is usually a good idea. In fact, until fairly recently, no browser even supported CSS1 completely (Internet Explorer 5.0 for the Macintosh shipped March 27, 2000, and is apparently the first complete CSS1 browser). I can't stress this enough: Test your stylesheets in as many browsers as you can because stylesheet implementation varies a great deal from browser to browser.

More on Stylesheets

Many more styles are found in CSS2—such as aural stylesheets—than I can include in this chapter. See `www.w3.org/TR/REC-CSS2/` for the details.

Here are a few online CSS resources:

- The W3C CSS validator is at `http://jigsaw.w3.org/css-validator/`. It checks the CSS in your pages for you.

- The W3C TIDY program can convert styles in HTML document to CSS for you. You can find TIDY at `www.w3.org/People/Raggett/tidy`.

- Many CSS resources are available at the W3C CSS page, `www.w3.org/Style/CSS/`, including CSS tutorials and links to free tools. If you will be using a lot of CSS, take a look at this page first.

So what are stylesheets? A stylesheet is a list of style *rules*, and it's attached to a document to indicate how you want the elements in the document displayed. For example, the document we've just seen uses `<TITLE>`, `<AUTHOR>`, `<SECTION>`, and `<P>` elements. In a stylesheet, I can supply a rule for all of these elements. A rule consists of a *selector*, which specifies what element or elements you want the rule to apply to, and the rule specification itself, which is enclosed in curly braces, { and }. Here's a sample stylesheet, ch09_02.css, for the XML document we've already seen:

Listing ch09_02.css

```
TITLE {display: block; font-size: 24pt; font-weight: bold;
    text-align: center; text-decoration: underline}
AUTHOR {display: block; font-size: 18pt; font-weight: bold;
    text-align: center}
SECTION {display: block; font-size: 16pt; font-weight: bold;
    text-align: center; font-style: italic}
P {display: block; margin-top: 10}
```

How do you attach this stylesheet to the XML document we saw at the beginning of this chapter? Take a look at the next section.

Attaching Stylesheets to XML Documents

In HTML, there are three ways of connecting stylesheets to documents: You can use the <STYLE> HTML element to attach an internal or external stylesheet, or you can use the STYLE attribute in HTML elements to style an individual element. In XML, there's really only one way of connecting a stylesheet to an XML document, and that's by using the <?xml-stylesheet?> processing instruction (in fact, <?xml-stylesheet?> is only an agreed-upon convention and does *not* appear in the XML 1.0 W3C recommendation). To use <?xml-stylesheet?> with CSS stylesheets, you set the type attribute to "text/css" and set the href attribute to the URI of the stylesheet. For example, to attach ch09_02.css to the XML document, I can use a <?xml-stylesheet?> processing instruction like this:

Listing ch09_03.xml

```
<?xml version="1.0" standalone="yes"?>
<?xml-stylesheet type="text/css" href="ch09_02.css"?>
<DOCUMENT>
    <TITLE>The Meditations</TITLE>
    <AUTHOR>By Marcus Aurelius</AUTHOR>
    <SECTION>Book One</SECTION>
    <P>
        From my grandfather, Verus, I learned good morals
        and the government of my temper.
    </P>
    <P>
        From the reputation and remembrance of my father,
        modesty and a manly character.
    </P>
    <P>
        From my mother, piety and beneficence, and abstinence,
        not only from evil deeds, but even from evil
        thoughts; and further, simplicity in my way of living,
        far removed from the habits of the rich.
    </P>
    <P>
        From my great-grandfather, not to have frequented
        public schools, and to have had good teachers at home,
        and to know that on such things a man should spend
        freely.
    </P>
</DOCUMENT>
```

That's all it takes. Now you can open this document in a browser, as you see in Figure 9-2, and the browser will know how to handle the document.

Figure 9-2
A style XML document.

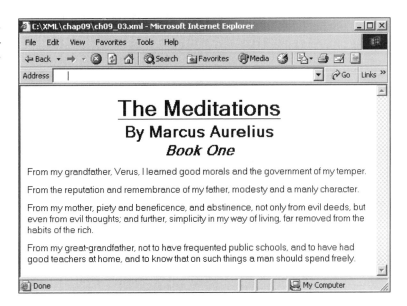

Although I've said that using the `<?xml-stylesheet?>` processing instruction is the only way to attach a stylesheet to an XML document, some browsers, such as Internet Explorer, also support a `STYLE` attribute in XML elements. You can specify styles using this attribute, like this:

```
From my grandfather, <UL STYLE="text-decoration: underline">Verus</UL>,
➥I learned good morals
and the government of my temper.
```

I'll take a look at this way of styling individual elements, called *inline styling*, as well. However, it's worth noting that it's even less standard than the `<?xml-stylesheet?>` processing instruction, and its use is discouraged by style purists (mainly because it decentralizes your style specification for a document).

Selecting Elements in Stylesheet Rules

This chapter is dedicated to understanding how to create stylesheets. After going through the mechanics, we'll first see a lot of examples at work; then we'll spend some time with the actual CSS specification.

I'll start by taking a look at how to create *selectors*, which indicate what element or elements you want to attach a style rule to. In the stylesheet we've already seen, ch09_02.css, the selectors are of the simplest kind and select just one element by giving the name of that element:

```
TITLE {display: block; font-size: 24pt; font-weight: bold;
text-align: center; text-decoration: underline}
AUTHOR {display: block; font-size: 18pt; font-weight: bold;
text-align: center}
SECTION {display: block; font-size: 16pt; font-weight: bold;
text-align: center; font-style: italic}
P {display: block; margin-top: 10}
```

For example, here I'm applying the style specification {display: block; font-size: 24pt; font-weight: bold; text-align: center; text-decoration: underline} to the <TITLE> element, {display: block; font-size: 18pt; font-weight: bold; text-align: center} to the <AUTHOR> element, and so on. As you can see, one type of selector just lists the element you want to style. However, you can create many other types of selectors, such as *grouping* elements.

Grouping Elements in Selectors

Another way of creating an element selector in a style rule is to list a number of elements, separated by commas. The same rule will apply to the whole group of elements, as in this case, where I'm styling the <TITLE> and <AUTHOR> elements the same way:

Listing ch09_04.css

```
TITLE, AUTHOR {display: block; font-size: 24pt; font-weight: bold;
text-align: center; text-decoration: underline}
SECTION {display: block; font-size: 16pt; font-weight: bold;
text-align: center; font-style: italic}
P {display: block; margin-top: 10}
```

You can see this stylesheet applied to the XML document we've been using in Figure 9-3. As you see in that figure, the <TITLE> and <AUTHOR> elements are indeed styled the same way.

Figure 9-3
Using a group
selector in a
stylesheet.

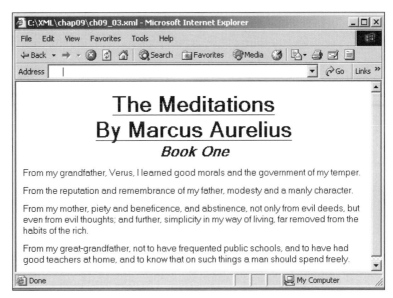

Creating Pseudo-Elements

Besides using elements as selectors for rules, you can use *pseudo-elements*. Two pseudo-elements exist in CSS1: `first-letter`, which refers to the first letter of a block of text, and `first-line`, which refers to the block's first line. Two more pseudo-elements were introduced in CSS2—`before` and `after`, which let you specify what should go immediately before and after elements. You use these pseudo-elements like this: `P:first-letter` to refer to the first letter of a `<P>` element.

Here's an example. In this case, I'm styling the first letter of `<P>` elements to be larger than the rest of the text and to be a "drop cap," which means that it'll appear lower than the rest of the text on the first line (I'll specify that the top of the first letter should align with the top of the rest of the text on the first line with `vertical-align: text-top`, and we'll see how this works later in the chapter):

Listing ch09_05.css

```
TITLE {display: block; font-size: 24pt; font-weight: bold;
text-align: center; text-decoration: underline}
AUTHOR {display: block; font-size: 18pt; font-weight: bold;
text-align: center}
SECTION {display: block; font-size: 16pt; font-weight: bold;
text-align: center; font-style: italic}
P {display: block; margin-top: 10}
P:first-letter {font-size: 18pt; float: left; vertical-align: text-top}
```

These pseudo-elements are not implemented in Internet Explorer, but they are implemented in Netscape Navigator 6. You can see this stylesheet applied to the XML document in Figure 9-4.

Figure 9-4
Using pseudo-
elements in
Netscape
Navigator 6.

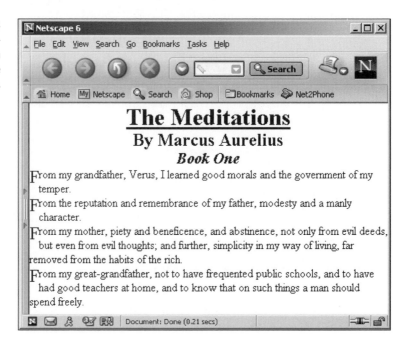

You can also use the `before` and `after` pseudo-elements to specify what comes before or after another element. In this case, I'm adding a line of hyphens and asterisks after the `<P>` element (the `\A` characters refer to line breaks—A is the hexadecimal digit for 10 decimal, and that's the UTF-8 code for a line-feed character.)

```
P:after {content: "\A-*-*-*-*-*-*-*-*-*-*-*-*-*-*-*-*-*-*-*-*-*\A"}
```

Classes

Besides elements, you can create selectors using *classes*. Here's an example. In this case, I'll create a class named RED that specifies that elements it's applied to must use a foreground (text) color of red and a background color of pink; to define a general class such as RED, you must preface it with a dot (.), as in .RED:

Listing ch09_06.css

```
TITLE {display: block; font-size: 24pt; font-weight: bold;
text-align: center; text-decoration: underline}
AUTHOR {display: block; font-size: 18pt; font-weight: bold;
text-align: center}
SECTION {display: block; font-size: 16pt; font-weight: bold;
text-align: center; font-style: italic}
P {display: block; margin-top: 10}
.RED {color:red; background-color: pink}
```

To apply this class to an individual element, such as the <TITLE> element in our XML document, I can add a CLASS attribute to that element, assuming that the browser I'm using can understand that attribute:

Listing ch09_07.xml

```
<?xml version="1.0" standalone="yes"?>
<?xml-stylesheet type="text/css" href="ch09_06.css"?>
<DOCUMENT>
    <TITLE CLASS="RED">The Meditations</TITLE>
    <AUTHOR>By Marcus Aurelius</AUTHOR>
    <SECTION>Book One</SECTION>
    <P>
        From my grandfather, Verus, I learned good morals
        and the government of my temper.
    </P>
    <P>
        From the reputation and remembrance of my father,
        modesty and a manly character.
    </P>
    <P>
        From my mother, piety and beneficence, and abstinence,
        not only from evil deeds, but even from evil
        thoughts; and further, simplicity in my way of living,
        far removed from the habits of the rich.
    </P>
    <P>
        From my great-grandfather, not to have frequented
        public schools, and to have had good teachers at home,
        and to know that on such things a man should spend
        freely.
    </P>
</DOCUMENT>
```

Browsers such as Internet Explorer understand the CLASS attribute, so you can see what this document looks like in Figure 9-5.

Figure 9-5
Using style
classes.

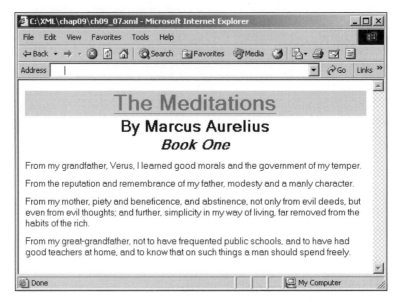

Note that if you want to make this a valid document, you must declare the
CLASS attribute. That might look like this in a DTD:

```
<!ELEMENT TITLE (CDATA)*>
<!ATTLIST TITLE CLASS CDATA #IMPLIED>
```

You can also create classes that apply only to specific elements. For example,
here's how I style the first paragraph in a document to add some space before
that paragraph, creating a class named TOP that applies only to <P> elements.
I specify this by calling this class P.TOP (note that general classes such as RED
apply to all elements, which is why you declare them as .RED):

Listing ch09_08.css

```
TITLE {display: block; font-size: 24pt; font-weight: bold;
text-align: center; text-decoration: underline}
AUTHOR {display: block; font-size: 18pt; font-weight: bold;
text-align: center}
SECTION {display: block; font-size: 16pt; font-weight: bold;
text-align: center; font-style: italic}
P {display: block; margin-top: 10}
P.TOP {display: block; margin-top: 30}
```

Now I can use this new class with the first paragraph in the document:

Listing ch09_09.xml

```
<?xml version="1.0" standalone="yes"?>
<?xml-stylesheet type="text/css" href="ch09_08.css"?>
<DOCUMENT>
    <TITLE>The Meditations</TITLE>
    <AUTHOR>By Marcus Aurelius</AUTHOR>
    <SECTION>Book One</SECTION>
    <P CLASS="TOP">
        From my grandfather, Verus, I learned good morals
        and the government of my temper.
    </P>
    <P>
        From the reputation and remembrance of my father,
        modesty and a manly character.
    </P>
    <P>
        From my mother, piety and beneficence, and abstinence,
        not only from evil deeds, but even from evil
        thoughts; and further, simplicity in my way of living,
        far removed from the habits of the rich.
    </P>
    <P>
        From my great-grandfather, not to have frequented
        public schools, and to have had good teachers at home,
        and to know that on such things a man should spend
        freely.
    </P>
</DOCUMENT>
```

You can see the results in Figure 9-6.

Figure 9-6
Styling
just one
paragraph.

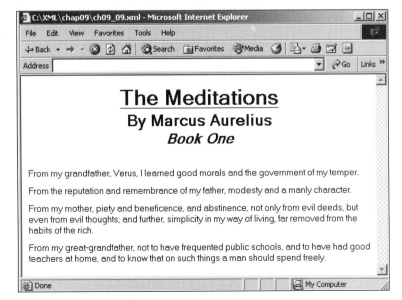

Creating Pseudo-Classes

CSS also defines a number of *pseudo-classes*. Here's a sampling of pseudo-classes that can act as selectors:

- :focus—Refers to the element with the focus (the item that is the target of keystrokes). For example, P:focus selects the <P> element with the focus.

- :first-child—Refers to the first child of the indicated element. For example, P:first-child selects the first child of the <P> element.

- :link, :visited, :active, :hover—Refer to hyperlink-like elements. The :link pseudo-class refers to elements that have been designated as links, :visited specifies the style of visited links, :active specifies the style of links as they're being activated, and :hover specifies the style as the mouse hovers over them.

- :lang()—Refers to elements that use a specified language. The language is usually set in elements with the xml:lang attribute.

Selecting by ID

Another way of selecting elements is by their ID values, which you set with an ID attribute. To create a selector that targets elements with a certain ID, you use the syntax *ELEMENT_NAME#ID_VALUE*. For example, here's how I create a rule for <P> elements with the ID value of "TOP":

Listing ch09_10.css

```
TITLE {display: block; font-size: 24pt; font-weight: bold;
text-align: center; text-decoration: underline}
AUTHOR {display: block; font-size: 18pt; font-weight: bold;
text-align: center}
SECTION {display: block; font-size: 16pt; font-weight: bold;
text-align: center; font-style: italic}
P {display: block; margin-top: 10}
P#TOP {display: block; margin-top: 30}
```

To give an element the ID "TOP", I can add an ID attribute like this, assuming that the browser can understand this attribute:

Listing ch09_11.xml

```
<?xml version="1.0" standalone="yes"?>
<?xml-stylesheet type="text/css" href="ch09_10.css"?>
<DOCUMENT>
    <TITLE>The Meditations</TITLE>
    <AUTHOR>By Marcus Aurelius</AUTHOR>
    <SECTION>Book One</SECTION>
    <P ID="TOP">
        From my grandfather, Verus, I learned good morals
        and the government of my temper.
    </P>
    <P>
        From the reputation and remembrance of my father,
        modesty and a manly character.
    </P>
    <P>
        From my mother, piety and beneficence, and abstinence,
        not only from evil deeds, but even from evil
        thoughts; and further, simplicity in my way of living,
        far removed from the habits of the rich.
    </P>
    <P>
        From my great-grandfather, not to have frequented
        public schools, and to have had good teachers at home,
        and to know that on such things a man should spend
        freely.
    </P>
</DOCUMENT>
```

Internet Explorer lets you use ID attributes to XML elements, so selecting by ID like this gives you the same results that you see in Figure 9-6. Note that, as with the CLASS attribute, you must declare the ID attribute if you want to use it. Such a declaration might look like this in a document type definition (DTD)—note that I'm declaring this attribute of type ID:

```
<!ELEMENT P (#PCDATA)>
<!ATTLIST P ID ID #REQUIRED>
```

Using Contextual Selectors

You can use *contextual* selectors to specify the style of elements that appear within other elements. For example, you might want an element to appear one way when it's by itself, but another way when enclosed in another element. Here's how that might look. In this case, I'm specifying that when used inside <P> elements, the <U> element must underline its enclosed text:

Listing ch09_12.css

```
TITLE {display: block; font-size: 24pt; font-weight: bold;
text-align: center; text-decoration: underline}
AUTHOR {display: block; font-size: 18pt; font-weight: bold;
text-align: center}
SECTION {display: block; font-size: 16pt; font-weight: bold;
text-align: center; font-style: italic}
P {display: block; margin-top: 10}
P U {text-decoration: underline}
```

Now I can use the `<U>` element inside a `<P>` element:

Listing ch09_13.xml

```
<?xml version="1.0" standalone="yes"?>
<?xml-stylesheet type="text/css" href="ch09_12.css"?>
<DOCUMENT>
    <TITLE>The Meditations</TITLE>
    <AUTHOR>By Marcus Aurelius</AUTHOR>
    <SECTION>Book One</SECTION>
    <P>
        From my grandfather, <U>Verus</U>, I learned good morals
        and the government of my temper.
    </P>
    <P>
        From the reputation and remembrance of my father,
        modesty and a manly character.
    </P>
    <P>
        From my mother, piety and beneficence, and abstinence,
        not only from evil deeds, but even from evil
        thoughts; and further, simplicity in my way of living,
        far removed from the habits of the rich.
    </P>
    <P>
        From my great-grandfather, not to have frequented
        public schools, and to have had good teachers at home,
        and to know that on such things a man should spend
        freely.
    </P>
</DOCUMENT>
```

You can see the results in Figure 9-7, where you can see the `<U>` tag doing its job.

Figure 9-7
Using
contextual
selectors.

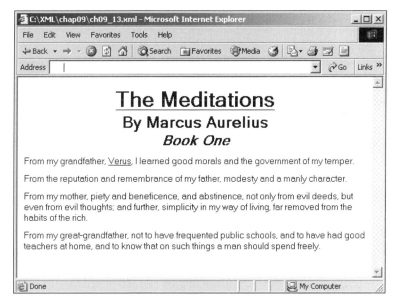

Using Inline Styles

As mentioned earlier, you can also create inline styles using the STYLE attribute, if the browser you're using understands that attribute in XML documents. Using the STYLE attribute, you can specify a rule directly. For example, here's how I style the `<U>` element used in the previous example using the STYLE attribute:

```
<?xml version="1.0" standalone="yes"?>
<?xml-stylesheet type="text/css" href="ch09_02.css"?>
<DOCUMENT>
    <TITLE>The Meditations</TITLE>
    <AUTHOR>By Marcus Aurelius</AUTHOR>
    <SECTION>Book One</SECTION>
    <P>
        From my grandfather,
        <U STYLE="text-decoration: underline">Verus</U>,
        I learned good morals and the government of my temper.
    </P>
    <P>
        From the reputation and remembrance of my father,
        modesty and a manly character.
    </P>
    <P>
        From my mother, piety and beneficence, and abstinence,
        not only from evil deeds, but even from evil
        thoughts; and further, simplicity in my way of living,
```

```
        far removed from the habits of the rich.
    </P>
    <P>
        From my great-grandfather, not to have frequented
        public schools, and to have had good teachers at home,
        and to know that on such things a man should spend
        freely.
    </P>
</DOCUMENT>
```

This document gives the same results you see in Figure 9-7. Note that if you want to make this document valid, you'll have to declare the STYLE attribute, which might look like this in a DTD:

```
<!ELEMENT U (CDATA)*>
<!ATTLIST U STYLE CDATA #IMPLIED>
```

Style purists recommend that you stay away from the STYLE attribute because using this attribute means that your style declarations will be all over the document, not just in a centralized stylesheet. However, this attribute is certainly recognized by browsers, so the choice is up to you.

Using Inheritance

You might have noticed that although the <U> element in the previous examples specified only one aspect of the element's style—that is, that text should be underlined (by using this rule: U {text-decoration: underline})—the underlined text appeared in the same font as the surrounding text, as you see in Figure 9-7. The reason is that styled elements *inherit* the styles of their parent elements. In this case, the <U> element's parent element is <P>:

```
<?xml-stylesheet type="text/css" href="ch09_02.css"?>
<DOCUMENT>
    <TITLE>The Meditations</TITLE>
    <AUTHOR>By Marcus Aurelius</AUTHOR>
    <SECTION>Book One</SECTION>
    <P>
        From my grandfather, <U>Verus</U>, I learned good morals
        and the government of my temper.
    </P>
    <P>
        From the reputation and remembrance of my father,
        modesty and a manly character.
    </P>
    <P>
```

```
        From my mother, piety and beneficence, and abstinence,
        not only from evil deeds, but even from evil
        thoughts; and further, simplicity in my way of living,
        far removed from the habits of the rich.
    </P>
    <P>
        From my great-grandfather, not to have frequented
        public schools, and to have had good teachers at home,
        and to know that on such things a man should spend
        freely.
    </P>
</DOCUMENT>
```

Inheritance is very useful because, as you see, you don't have to specify all aspects of a child element's style if you want it to retain those aspects from the parent element. When you want to override some aspects of a style from the parent's style, you just need to define them in a rule for the child element.

Because style rules can inherit other rules, the order in which rules are applied becomes important. This ordering process is called a style *cascade*, which is where Cascading Style Sheets take their name.

Understanding Cascades

You can use multiple stylesheets for one XML document in several ways because there are multiple ways of attaching stylesheets. For example, you can use the `<?xml-stylesheet?>` processing instruction, and you can use the `@import` directive (for example, this directive will import a stylesheet: `@import url(http://www.starpowder.com/ch09_02.css);`) in a stylesheet to *import* another stylesheet. The reader of a document may use browser-specific techniques to use stylesheets, and the reader's software can even supply default stylesheets.

In addition, the author or reader of a document can use another declaration, the `!important` declaration, to specify that some aspect of a style should not be overridden by inheritance. (For example, this declaration specifies that it's important for `<U>` elements to color their text red: `U {color: red !important text-decoration: underline}`.)

So when multiple style rules are involved, what order are they applied in? Generally, the most *specific* rules are the ones that are applied if there is a conflict. For example, rules that you apply by ID are preferred to those applied by class. However, rules applied by class are preferred to those applied to all elements of the same type. If no selector fits the situation, the element will inherit styles from its parent; if there is no parent, a default style is used.

If there's a conflict, rules that the document author specified as important are preferred, followed by rules that the reader specified as important, followed by general author rules (that is, those not marked as important), followed by general reader rules, and finally followed by the most recent rule in the applicable stylesheet(s).

Creating Style Rules

We've seen how to create selectors in rules; it's time to take a look at creating rules themselves. A rule is composed of a selector followed by a semicolon-separated list of *property-value* pairs enclosed in curly braces, like this:

```
TITLE {display: block; font-size: 24pt; font-weight: bold;
text-align: center; text-decoration: underline}
```

In this case, I'm setting values for the `display`, `font-size`, `font-weight`, `text-align`, and `text-decoration` properties. You assign a value to a property by following the name of the property with a colon, whitespace, and the value you want to assign.

Quite a number of properties are defined in CSS. The best way to get a grip on what's going on is to actually *use* them, so we're about to see a lot of examples.

Creating Block Elements

You might have noticed the property-value pair `display: block` in the rules in ch09_02.css:

```
TITLE {display: block; font-size: 24pt; font-weight: bold;
text-align: center; text-decoration: underline}
AUTHOR {display: block; font-size: 18pt; font-weight: bold;
text-align: center}
SECTION {display: block; font-size: 16pt; font-weight: bold;
text-align: center; font-style: italic}
P {display: block; margin-top: 10}
```

In particular, `display: block` specifies that the element in question get its own *block*, which means that these elements start on a new line and that the element following them starts on a new line as well. That is, you use `display: block` to create *block-level* elements.

The `display` property is more important in XML stylesheets than it is in HTML stylesheets because HTML styles such as `<H1>` already inherit the `display: block` style. To create elements that you want set off from other elements, such as paragraphs and headers, use `display: block`. (For example, using this style specification is the reason the `<TITLE>`, `<AUTHOR>`, and `<SECTION>` elements appear on their own lines in Figure 9-2.)

Specifying Width and Height

You can specify the width and height of a block using the `width` and `height` properties; see the topic "Displaying Images," later in this chapter, for more details.

Styling Text

Setting text styles is one of the most important aspects of cascading style sheets, but the process is not straightforward. Here are some properties that you can use with text:

- `float`—Indicates how text should flow around this element. Set this to `left` to move the element to the left of the display area and have text flow around it to the right, set it to `right` to move the element to the right and have text flow around the element to the left, or set it to `none`.

- `font-family`—Sets the font face. (Note that you can specify a number of options here, separated by commas; the first face available on the user's system is used.)

- `font-size`——Sets the size of the text's font.

- `font-stretch`—Indicates the desired amount of condensing or expanding in the letters used to draw the text.

- `font-style`—Specifies whether the text is to be rendered using a normal, italic, or oblique face.

- `font-variant`—Indicates whether the text is to be rendered using the normal letters for lowercase characters or rendered using small-cap letters for lowercase characters.

- `font-weight`—Refers to the boldness or lightness used to render the text, relative to other fonts in the same font family.

- `font-weight`—Makes text bold.

- `line-height`—Indicates the height given to each line. Set this to an absolute measurement or a percentage value such as 200% to create double spacing.

- `text-align`—Sets the alignment of text. You can set this to `left`, `right`, `center`, or `justify`.

- `text-decoration`—Underlines the text. You can set this to `underline`, `overline`, `line-through`, or `blink`; to remove inherited decorations, set this to `none`.

- `text-indent`—Sets the indentation of the first line of block-level elements. Set this to an absolute value, such as 10 pixels, `10px`, or 4 points, `4pt`.

- `text-transform`—Indicates whether you want to display text in all upper case, all lower case, or with initial letters capitalized. You can set this to `capitalize`, `uppercase`, `lowercase`, or `none`.

- `vertical-align`—Sets the vertical alignment of text. You can set this to `baseline`, `sub`, `super`, `top`, `text-top`, `middle`, `bottom`, or `text-bottom`.

Here's an example that puts some of these properties to use. In this case, I'll specify 18-point (a point is 1/72 of an inch) centered text in italic Arial (or Helvetica, if the browser can't find the Arial font face):

Listing ch09_14.css

```
TITLE {display: block; font-size: 24pt; font-weight: bold;
text-align: center; text-decoration: underline}
AUTHOR {display: block; font-size: 18pt; font-weight: bold;
text-align: center}
SECTION {display: block; font-size: 16pt; font-weight: bold;
text-align: center; font-style: italic}
P {display: block; font-size: 18pt; font-style: italic; font-family:
Arial, Helvetica; text-align: center; margin-top: 10}
```

You can see the results in Figure 9-8.

Figure 9-8
Using font
properties.

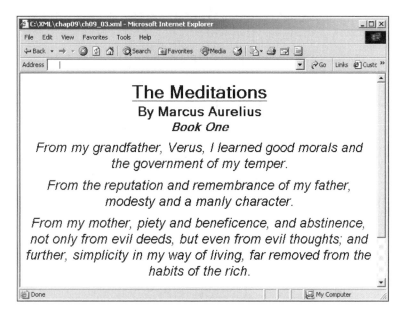

As with many groups of properties, there's a *shortcut* property that you can use to set the font-style, font-variant, font-weight, font-size, line-height, and font-family properties all at once: the font property. To use this shortcut property, you just specify values for all of these properties (in the order I've given here), separating the font-size and line-height values with a forward slash (/) and listing all values without commas (except between font family names, if you list more than one). Here's an example using the font shorthand property:

```
TITLE {display: block; font-size: 24pt; font-weight: bold;
text-align: center; text-decoration: underline}
AUTHOR {display: block; font-size: 18pt; font-weight: bold;
text-align: center}
SECTION {display: block; font-size: 16pt; font-weight: bold;
text-align: center; font-style: italic}
P {display: block; font: italic normal bold 12pt/10pt arial,
        helvetica; text-align: center}
```

Most groups of properties—such as the font properties, or those you use to set borders—have a shortcut property that lets you set multiple property values at once. I'll list some of these shortcut properties and show you how to use them at the end of this chapter.

Generic Font Selections

As a last resort, you can assign a generic font family to `font-family` to use in case the user's computer doesn't have the one you specified. The browser will select a font family that's similar. Generic font families include serif, sans serif, cursive, fantasy, and monospace.

Setting Colors and Backgrounds

These are the properties you use to set color and backgrounds:

- `color`—Sets the foreground (text) color.
- `background-color`—Sets the background color.
- `background-image`—Sets the background image.
- `background-repeat`—Specifies whether the background image should be tiled. You can set this to `repeat`, `repeat-x`, `repeat-y`, or `no-repeat`.
- `background-attachment`—Specifies whether the background scrolls with the rest of the document.
- `background-position`—Sets the initial position of the background.

You also can use a `background` shorthand property to set the background `color`, `image`, `repeat`, `attachment`, and `position` all at once (list those values in order). I'll cover how to use this shorthand property at the end of the chapter.

In this next example, I'm styling both the background and the foreground (that is, the text color) of a document. In this case, I'm setting the background color of the `<DOCUMENT>` element to coral. Note that because all the other elements in the document are children of this element, they'll all inherit this background color—except for the `<P>` element, in which I'm specifically setting the background to white and coloring the text blue:

Listing ch09_15.css

```
DOCUMENT {background-color: coral}
TITLE {display: block; font-size: 24pt; font-weight: bold;
text-align: center; text-decoration: underline}
AUTHOR {display: block; font-size: 18pt; font-weight: bold;
text-align: center}
SECTION {display: block; font-size: 16pt; font-weight: bold;
text-align: center; font-style: italic}
P {display: block; background-color: white; color: blue}
```

You can see the results in Figure 9-9.

Although dozens of colors are predefined in most browsers, the CSS standards define only 16 colors:

- Aqua
- Black
- Blue
- Fuchsia
- Gray
- Green
- Lime
- Maroon
- Navy
- Olive
- Purple
- Red
- Silver
- Teal
- White
- Yellow

Figure 9-9
Using font
properties.

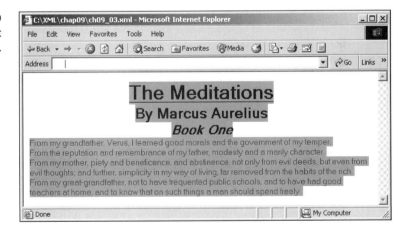

In this example, I used the predefined colors coral, blue, and white, but you can also define your own colors as color triplets: *#rrggbb*. Here, *rr*, *gg*, and *bb* are two-digit hexadecimal values that you use to specify the red, green, and blue components of a color, just as you do in HTML. For example, white is #ffffff, black is #000000, pure blue is #0000ff, pure red is #ff0000, pink is #ffcccc, orange is #ffcc00, and coral is #ff7f50. (You can find good selections of color values online, along with the corresponding colors; see http://www.ecn.bgu.edu/users/gallery/webwork/11_hexcolors.html for an example.) Using color triplets, here's what the previous stylesheet looks like:

```
DOCUMENT {background-color: #ff7f50}
TITLE {display: block; font-size: 24pt; font-weight: bold;
text-align: center; text-decoration: underline}
AUTHOR {display: block; font-size: 18pt; font-weight: bold;
text-align: center}
SECTION {display: block; font-size: 16pt; font-weight: bold;
text-align: center; font-style: italic}
P {display: block; background-color: #ffffff; color: #0000ff}
```

Here's another example that we saw in the beginning of this chapter, in which I gave the <TITLE> element a pink background and red foreground:

```
<?xml version="1.0" standalone="yes"?>
<?xml-stylesheet type="text/css" href="ch09_02.css"?>
<DOCUMENT>
    <TITLE CLASS="RED">The Meditations</TITLE>
    <AUTHOR>By Marcus Aurelius</AUTHOR>
    <SECTION>Book One</SECTION>
    <P>
        From my grandfather, Verus, I learned good morals
        and the government of my temper.
    </P>
    <P>
        From the reputation and remembrance of my father,
        modesty and a manly character.
    </P>
    <P>
        From my mother, piety and beneficence, and abstinence,
        not only from evil deeds, but even from evil
        thoughts; and further, simplicity in my way of living,
        far removed from the habits of the rich.
    </P>
    <P>
        From my great-grandfather, not to have frequented
        public schools, and to have had good teachers at home,
        and to know that on such things a man should spend
        freely.
    </P>
</DOCUMENT>
```

The RED class was defined this way:

```
TITLE {display: block; font-size: 24pt; font-weight: bold;
text-align: center; text-decoration: underline}
AUTHOR {display: block; font-size: 18pt; font-weight: bold;
text-align: center}
SECTION {display: block; font-size: 16pt; font-weight: bold;
text-align: center; font-style: italic}
P {display: block; margin-top: 10}
.RED {color:red; background-color: pink}
```

Margins, Indentations, and Alignments

These are the properties you use to work with margins, indentations, and alignments:

- line-height—Indicates the height given to each line. Set this to an absolute measurement or a percentage value, such as 200% to create double spacing.

- margin-left—Sets the left margin of a block element.

- margin-right—Sets the right margin of a block element.

- margin-top—Sets the top margin of a block element.

- text-align—Sets the alignment of text. You can set this to left, right, center, or justify.

- text-indent—Sets the indentation of the first line of block-level elements. Set this to an absolute value such as 10 pixels, 10px, or 4 points, 4pt.

- vertical-align—Sets the vertical alignment of text. You can set this to baseline, sub, super, top, text-top, middle, bottom, or text-bottom.

Here's an example showing how to put some of these properties to work. In this stylesheet, I'm indenting the first line of each paragraph by 40 pixels (for more on the kinds of units you use to specify lengths, see Table 9-1 later in this chapter) and indenting all the text in paragraphs by 20 pixels:

Listing ch09_16.css

```
TITLE {display: block; font-size: 24pt; font-weight: bold;
text-align: center; text-decoration: underline}
AUTHOR {display: block; font-size: 18pt; font-weight: bold;
text-align: center}
SECTION {display: block; font-size: 16pt; font-weight: bold;
text-align: center; font-style: italic}
P {display: block; text-indent: 40px; margin-left: 20px}
```

You can see the results in Figure 9-10. As you see there, the first line of each paragraph is indeed indented, and the paragraph text is also moved to the left.

Figure 9-10
Indenting text
using a
stylesheet.

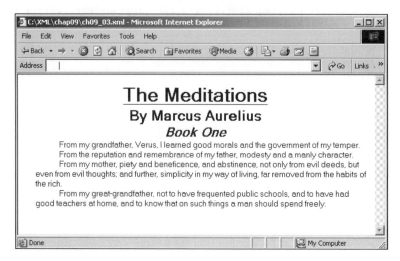

Applying Styles to Lists

These are the properties you typically use with lists:

- `list-item`—Sets the `display` property to this value to create a list.

- `list-style-image`—Sets the image that will be used as the list item marker. Internet Explorer only.

- `list-style-type`—Sets the appearance of the list item marker, such as disc, circle, square, decimal, lowercase Roman, uppercase Roman, and others.

Here's an example. In this case, I'm setting the marker in front of each list item in an unordered list to a square using `list-style-type`. Note that you have to set the `display` property to `list-item`:

```
TITLE {display: block; font-size: 24pt; font-weight: bold;
text-align: center; text-decoration: underline}
AUTHOR {display: block; font-size: 18pt; font-weight: bold;
text-align: center}
SECTION {display: block; font-size: 16pt; font-weight: bold;
text-align: center; font-style: italic}
P {display:list-item; list-style-type: square}
```

Creating Borders

You can also create borders for elements using CSS, setting the border style, border width, border color, and so on. Here are the border properties that are available:

- `border-bottom-width`—Sets the width of the bottom of the border. Set this to an absolute measurement, such as `10px` for 10 pixels, or `4pt` for 4 points; or use a keyword, as in `thin`, `medium`, or `thick`.

- `border-color`—Specifies the color you want the border to be displayed in (use a predefined color or a color triplet). Setting this property to one value sets the color of the whole border; two values set the top and bottom borders to the first value and the right and left borders to the second; four values set the color of all border parts in order: top, right, bottom, and left.

- `border-left-width`—Sets the width of the left edge of the border; set to an absolute measurement like 10px for 10 pixels, or 4pt for four points, or a keyword: `thin`, `medium`, or `thick`.

- `border-right-width`—Sets the width of the right edge of the border. Set this to an absolute measurement, such as `10px` for 10 pixels, or `4pt` for 4 points; or use a keyword, as in `thin`, `medium`, or `thick`.

- `border-style`—Sets the border style. Possible values include `dotted`, `dashed`, `solid`, `double`, `groove`, `ridge`, `inset`, and `outset`.

- `border-top-width`—Sets the width of the top of the border. Set this to an absolute measurement, such as `10px` for 10 pixels, or `4pt` for 4 points; or use a keyword, as in `thin`, `medium`, or `thick`.

You also can use five shorthand border properties:

- `border-top`—Sets the style of the top border
- `border-right`—Sets the style of the right border
- `border-bottom`—Sets the style of the bottom border
- `border-left`—Sets the style of the left border
- `border`—Sets the border style all at once

You set the shorthand properties to a width, style, and color all at once like this:

```
P {border 10pt solid cyan}
```

Here's an example. In this case, I'm adding a border to the <SECTION> element in our XML document:

Listing ch09_17.css

```
TITLE {display: block; font-size: 24pt; font-weight: bold;
text-align: center; text-decoration: underline}
AUTHOR {display: block; font-size: 18pt; font-weight: bold;
text-align: center}
SECTION {display: block; font-size: 16pt; font-weight: bold;
text-align: center; font-style: italic; border-style: solid}
P {display:block}
```

You can view the results in Figure 9-11, where you can see the solid border around the <SECTION> element. (I might note in passing that it's a good thing we selected a solid border for this element because Internet Explorer cannot draw anything but solid borders around elements presently.)

Figure 9-11
Enclosing an element in a border.

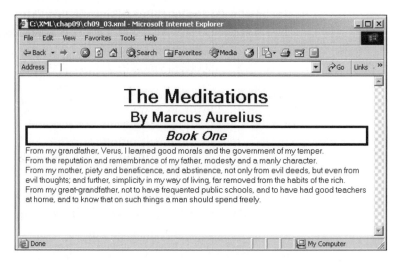

Displaying Images

You can use several properties with images:

- `background-image`—Sets a background image. Set this to a URL.

- `background-repeat`—Specifies whether the background image should be tiled. You can set this to `repeat`, `repeat-x`, `repeat-y`, or `no-repeat`.

- `background-attachment`—Specifies whether the background scrolls with the rest of the document.

- `background-position`—Sets the initial position of the background. Specify an x and y coordinate here (where the origin is at the upper left), such as `background-position: 0% 100%` to add a background image to the lower left.

There's also a `background` shorthand property that you can set to the background `color`, `image`, `repeat`, `attachment`, and `position` all at once (list those values in order).

Here's an example showing how to use a background image. In this case, I'll add a background image to appear behind text in <P> elements, making that image repeat until it fills all the space behind the <P> element. Note that you specify an URL with the `url` keyword:

Listing ch09_18.css

```
TITLE {display: block; font-size: 24pt; font-weight: bold;
text-align: center; text-decoration: underline}
AUTHOR {display: block; font-size: 18pt; font-weight: bold;
text-align: center}
SECTION {display: block; font-size: 16pt; font-weight: bold;
text-align: center; font-style: italic}
P {background-image: url(image.jpg);
    background-repeat: repeat}
```

For this example, I'll condense all the <P> elements in our XML document into one <P> element so that the result, showing the background image, will be clearer:

Listing ch09_19.xml

```xml
<?xml version="1.0" standalone="yes"?>
<?xml-stylesheet type="text/css" href="ch09_02.css"?>
<DOCUMENT>
    <TITLE CLASS="RED">The Meditations</TITLE>
    <AUTHOR>By Marcus Aurelius</AUTHOR>
    <SECTION>Book One</SECTION>
    <P>
        From my grandfather, Verus, I learned good morals
        and the government of my temper.
        From the reputation and remembrance of my father,
        modesty and a manly character.
        From my mother, piety and beneficence, and abstinence,
        not only from evil deeds, but even from evil
        thoughts; and further, simplicity in my way of living,
        far removed from the habits of the rich.
        From my great-grandfather, not to have frequented
        public schools, and to have had good teachers at home,
        and to know that on such things a man should spend
        freely.
    </P>
</DOCUMENT>
```

You can see the results in Figure 9-12, where the background image does indeed appear behind the text.

Figure 9-12
Displaying a background image.

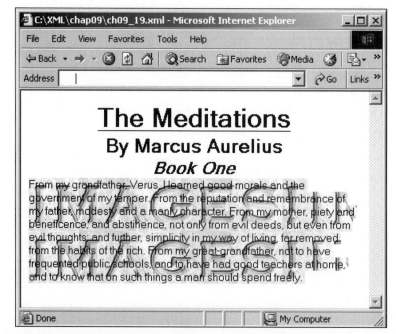

What if you want to display an image by itself? In that case, you can create a dedicated element that uses the image as its background image. Here's an example. Note that I'm setting the `height` and `width` properties to the size of the image; I'm also using the `float` property to indicate that text should flow around the left of this element:

Listing ch09_20.css

```
TITLE {display: block; font-size: 24pt; font-weight: bold;
text-align: center; text-decoration: underline}
AUTHOR {display: block; font-size: 18pt; font-weight: bold;
text-align: center}
SECTION {display: block; font-size: 16pt; font-weight: bold;
text-align: center; font-style: italic}
P {display:block}
IMG {background: url(image.jpg) no-repeat center center;
    height: 66px;
    width: 349px;
    float: right}
```

Here's how I add the `<IMG>` element to the document:

Listing ch09_21.xml

```
<?xml version="1.0" standalone="yes"?>
<?xml-stylesheet type="text/css" href="ch09_20.css"?>
<DOCUMENT>
    <TITLE CLASS="RED">The Meditations</TITLE>
    <AUTHOR>By Marcus Aurelius</AUTHOR>
    <SECTION>Book One</SECTION>
    <IMG></IMG>
    <P>
        From my grandfather, Verus, I learned good morals
        and the government of my temper.
        From the reputation and remembrance of my father,
        modesty and a manly character.
        From my mother, piety and beneficence, and abstinence,
        not only from evil deeds, but even from evil
        thoughts; and further, simplicity in my way of living,
        far removed from the habits of the rich.
        From my great-grandfather, not to have frequented
        public schools, and to have had good teachers at home,
        and to know that on such things a man should spend
        freely.
    </P>
</DOCUMENT>
```

You can see the results in Figure 9-13.

Figure 9-13
Displaying an
image.

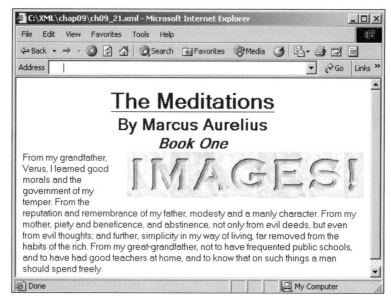

Absolute Positioning

You can use the `position` property to set the position of elements in a Web page. I'll take a look at positioning items in absolute terms in this section and in relative terms in the next section. Here are the properties you commonly use when working with positioning:

- `position`—Can hold values such as `absolute` and `relative`
- `top`—Specifies the offset of the top of the element
- `bottom`—Specifies the offset of the bottom of the element
- `left`—Specifies the offset of the left edge of the element
- `right`—Specifies the offset of the right edge of the element

In this example, I'll set the absolute position of the image we used in the previous example so that it's directly on top of the text:

Listing ch09_22.css

```
TITLE {display: block; font-size: 24pt; font-weight: bold;
text-align: center; text-decoration: underline}
AUTHOR {display: block; font-size: 18pt; font-weight: bold;
text-align: center}
SECTION {display: block; font-size: 16pt; font-weight: bold;
text-align: center; font-style: italic}
P {display: block; }
IMG {background: url(image.jpg) no-repeat center center;
    height: 66px;
    width: 349px;
    position:absolute; left:50; top:160;
    border-width: thick}
```

You can see the results in Figure 9-14. As you see there, the image has indeed moved so that it's now on top of the text. Using this technique, you can place elements as you like.

Figure 9-14
Using absolute
positioning.

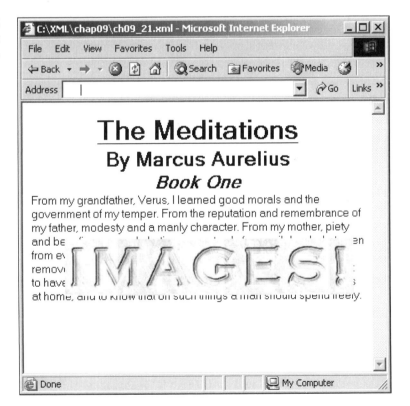

Relative Positioning

In addition to absolute positioning, you can use *relative* positioning. When you use relative positioning, elements are positioned relative to the location they would have had in the normal flow of elements in the Web browser.

To position items in a relative way, you set the `position` property to `relative`. You can also set the other properties to indicate the new relative position. In this example, I'm moving some text—the word *Verus*—up 5 pixels from the normal position at which the browser would place this text with a new element, `<SUP>`. I'm using a `STYLE` attribute to set the relative position:

Listing ch09_23.xml

```
<?xml version="1.0" standalone="yes"?>
<?xml-stylesheet type="text/css" href="ch09_02.css"?>
<DOCUMENT>
    <TITLE>The Meditations</TITLE>
    <AUTHOR>By Marcus Aurelius</AUTHOR>
    <SECTION>Book One</SECTION>
    <P>
        From my grandfather,
        <SUP STYLE="position: relative; top: -5">Verus</SUP>,
        I learned good morals and the government of my temper.
    </P>
    <P>
        From the reputation and remembrance of my father,
        modesty and a manly character.
    </P>
    <P>
        From my mother, piety and beneficence, and abstinence,
        not only from evil deeds, but even from evil
        thoughts; and further, simplicity in my way of living,
        far removed from the habits of the rich.
    </P>
    <P>
        From my great-grandfather, not to have frequented
        public schools, and to have had good teachers at home,
        and to know that on such things a man should spend
        freely.
    </P>
</DOCUMENT>
```

You can see the results in Figure 9-15, where the text inside the `<SUP>` element is positioned higher than the rest.

Figure 9-15
Using relative
positioning.

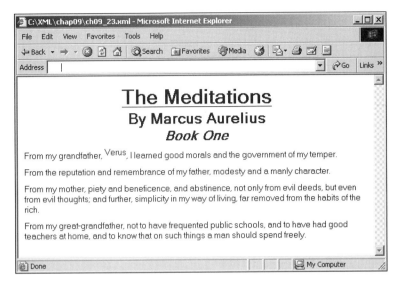

The Formal Style Property Specifications

We've seen quite a few CSS examples in this chapter. When you get more serious about CSS, you're going to need very in-depth information. For that reason, the rest of this chapter covers the most commonly used CSS styles and their formal specifications.

The World Wide Web Consortium (W3C) CSS style specifications give the possible values that CSS properties can take, the default value of those properties, and so on. The syntax that the W3C specifications use is a little complex. Here's an example: the style specification for the background-color property:

background-color

- CSS1 values: <color>|transparent

- CSS2 values: inherit

- Default value: transparent

- Element support: All elements

- Browser support: [IE4, IE5, IE6, NS4, NS6]

- Style inherited: No

Here you can see the way a style is specified, listing the possible values that the property can take for the CSS1 level specification, as well as the possible values that CSS2 adds, the property's default value, which types of elements are supported (such as block-level elements), and whether the style is inherited by child elements. I'm also adding which of the two major browsers support the property and what versions of those browsers do.

Note the expression <color>|transparent, which indicates the possible values you can assign this property. This expression means that you can set the background-color property to *either* a valid color value *or* the word transparent. The W3C syntax for style properties like this is worth getting to know so that you can refer to the W3C documentation when you need it. Here's the syntax the W3C uses:

- Terms in angle brackets (< and >) specify valid units for values. See Table 9-1 for the details.

- Values separated with | specify alternatives. Only one alternative may be used.

- Values separated with || specify options. You can use one or more of them in any order.

- Brackets ([and]) group statements. These are evaluated like mathematical statements.

- A * means that the preceding term can occur zero or more times (as in DTD syntax).

- A + means that the preceding term occurs one or more times (as in DTD syntax).

- A ? means that the preceding term is optional (as in DTD syntax).

- Curly braces ({ and }) enclose a comma-separated pair of numbers giving the minimum and maximum number of times a term may occur, such as {0, 10}.

The expressions you see in angle brackets, such as <color>, use a specific format, and I list those formats in Table 9-1. For example, there you'll see that <color> can be set to a red, green, blue triplet color value or a predefined color. That means you could assign a color value to the background-color property like this in a style rule: {background-color: #0000ff} or {background-color: azure}.

Table 9-1	Unit Measurement	Means
Units in the W3C Property Style Specifications	`<absolute-size>`	Absolute font sizes. May be `xx-small`, `x-small`, `small`, `medium`, `large`, `x-large`, or `xx-large`.
	`<angle>`	Angle. May be deg, grad, or rad.
	`<border-style>`	Border style. May be `none`, `dotted`, `dashed`, `solid`, `double`, `groove`, `ridge`, `inset`, or `outset`.
	`<border-width>`	Width of a border. May be `thin`, `medium`, `thick`, or an explicit length.
	`<color>`	Color. May be specified with a predefined color value (theoretically one of the 16 predefined CSS colors but, in practice, any color name that the browser recognizes) or RGB triplet color value.
	`<family-name>`	Name of a font family, such as Times New Roman, Courier New, or Arial.
	`<frequency>`	Frequency values. Units may be Hz or kHz.
	`<generic-family>`	Generic names for fonts specified as a last resort if the browser can't find a specific font face. For example, you can set this type to `serif` (for a serif font), `sans-serif` (for a sans-serif font), or `monospace` (for a monospace font).
	`<generic-voice>`	Aural voices. May be set to `male`, `female`, or `child`.
	`<integer>`	Standard integer values.
	`<length>`	Length. Can start with + or - followed by a number. The number can include a decimal point and can be followed by a unit identifier, which may be em (font size of the relevant font), ex (the x height of the font), px (pixels), pt (points, 1/72 of an inch), in (inches), cm (centimeters), mm (millimeters), or pc (picas, 1/6 of an inch).
	`<number>`	Number. Can include a sign and a decimal point.
	`<percentage>`	Percentage. Can include a sign followed by a percent sign (%).
	`<relative-size>`	Font size relative to the parent element. Can be either larger or smaller.
	`<shape>`	Shape. Can be only a rectangle currently, like this: rect (`<top>` `<right>` `<bottom>` `<left>`).
	`<time>`	Time units. Given as a number followed by ms (milliseconds) or s (seconds).
	`<uri>`	Uniform resource identifier.

You also should know about two special property values: `auto` and a new CSS2 value, `inherit`. You set a property to `auto` when you want the browser to assign an automatic value to the property. Usually, the value set depends on the context, such as the style or color of surrounding text. The `inherit` value is new in CSS2 and means that the value of this property should be *inherited* from its parent (instead of using the default initial value), if the element has a parent.

There's one more term to understand as well: *box.* A box is the area in which an element is drawn in the browser. That is, the box is the invisible rectangle surrounding the display area of the element. Because boxes are constructed with borders, padding, and margins, many style properties refer to them.

That's all the introduction we need to the actual style property specifications. I'll look at the most common style properties now, as well as the values they can take and what kind of elements you can use them with. Bear in mind that you can find the complete CSS property specifications at `www.w3.org/TR/REC-CSS1` and `www.w3.org/TR/REC-CSS2`.

Style Properties

Another thing to keep in mind is that I'm listing the style properties as the W3C defines them here. The way your browser uses these style properties might differ.

Text Properties

Probably the most common reason people think of stylesheets is to format text, so I'll start with the CSS text properties.

letter-spacing

- CSS1 values: normal|<length>
- CSS2 values: inherit
- Default value: normal
- Element support: All elements
- Browser support: [IE4, IE5, IE6]
- Style inherited: Yes

This property sets the spacing between text characters. It is implemented in Internet Explorer, but the implementation appears to be a little spotty.

line-height

- CSS1 values: normal|<number>|<length>|<percentage>
- CSS2 values: inherit
- Default value: normal
- Element support: All elements
- Browser support: [IE3, IE4, IE5, IE6, NS4, NS6]
- Style inherited: Yes

This property gives the minimum height of the element's box. Usually it is used to specify single or double spacing.

text-align

- CSS1 values: left|right|center|justify
- CSS2 values: <string>|inherit
- Default value: Varies
- Element support: Block-level elements
- Browser support: [IE3, IE4, IE5, IE6, NS4, NS6]
- Style inherited: Yes

This property indicates the alignment of the content of a block: `left`, `right`, `center`, or `justify`. Note that in CSS2, you can specify a string to align with respect to.

text-decoration

- CSS1 values: None|[underline||overline||line-through||blink]
- CSS2 values: inherit
- Default value: None
- Element support: All elements
- Browser support: [IE3, IE4, IE5, IE6, NS4, NS6]
- Style inherited: No

This property indicates the "decorations" for text display, including underlining, overlining, and line-through (strike-through). The `blink` value is not implemented anywhere yet, as far as I know.

text-indent

- CSS1 values: <length>I<percentage>
- CSS2 values: inherit
- Default value: 0
- Element support: Block-level elements
- Browser support: [IE3, IE4, IE5, IE6, NS4, NS6]
- Style inherited: Yes

This property indicates the indentation of the first line of text. Note that this property applies only to block-level elements (which you set with `display: block`).

text-shadow

- CSS2 values:
  NoneI[<color>II<length><length><length>?,]*[<color>II
  <length><length><length>?]Iinherit
- Default value: None
- Element support: All elements
- Browser support: [IE5, IE6]
- Style inherited: No

This property gives a comma-separated list of shadow effects that should be used for text.

vertical-align

- CSS1 values: baselineIsubIsuperItopItext-topImiddleIbottomItext-bottomI<percentage>I<length>
- CSS2 values: inherit
- Default value: baseline
- Element support: Inline-level and table cell elements
- Browser support: [IE4, IE5, IE6]
- Style inherited: No

This property indicates the vertical alignment of text in the element. For example, setting this value to `text-top` and using a larger initial character in a block of text is how you create drop caps.

white-space

- CSS1 values: normal|pre|nowrap
- CSS2 values: inherit
- Default value: normal
- Element support: Block-level elements
- Browser support: [NS4, NS6]
- Style inherited: Yes

This property indicates how whitespace should be handled. Theoretically, setting this property to pre should be like setting xml:space to preserve.

word-spacing

- CSS1 values: normal|<length>
- CSS2 values: inherit
- Default value: normal
- Element support: All elements
- Browser support: [None]
- Style inherited: Yes

This property sets the spacing between words. So far, however, it's not implemented anywhere, as far as I know.

Font Properties

Besides the text properties, probably the next most common set of style properties used is the font properties. I'll take a look at them here, starting with the font shorthand property.

font

- CSS1 values: [[<font-style>||<font-variant>||<font-weight>]?<font-size>[/<line-height>]?<font-family>
- CSS2 values: caption|icon|menu|message-box|small-caption|status-bar|inherit
- Default value: Varies
- Element support: All elements

- Browser support: [IE3, IE4, IE5, IE6]
- Style inherited: Yes

This shorthand property indicates `font-style`, `font-variant`, `font-weight`, `font-size`, `line-height`, and `font-family` properties. You list those properties in that order—and without commas between them, except between items in a list of alternate font families. You can also set all these properties individually.

font-family

- CSS1 values: [[<family-name>|<generic-family>],]*[<family-name>|<generic-family>]
- CSS2 values: inherit
- Default value: Depends on the browser
- Element support: All elements
- Browser support: [IE3, IE4, IE5, IE6, NS4, NS6]
- Style inherited: Yes

You set this property to a list of font family names or generic family names. Your document can be viewed in a browser that doesn't support the font face you want, so you can list alternates, as we have in this chapter. You can also list generic font families, such as `serif` or `sans-serif`.

font-size

- CSS1 values: |<relative-size>|<length>|<percentage>
- CSS2 values: inherit
- Default value: medium
- Element support: All elements
- Browser support: [IE3, IE4, IE5, IE6, NS4, NS6]
- Style inherited: Yes

This property sets the size of a font face. It is usually set in terms of points, but, of course, you can use any valid measurement.

font-stretch

- CSS2 values: normal|wider|narrower|ultra-condensed|extra-condensed|condensed|semi-condensed|semi-expanded|expanded|extra-expanded|ultra-expanded|inherit
- Default value: normal
- Element support: All elements
- Browser support: [None]
- Style inherited: Yes

You use this property to set a normal, condensed, or extended font face. It's not supported anywhere yet, as far as I know.

font-style

- CSS1 values: normal|italic|oblique
- CSS2 values: inherit
- Default value: normal
- Element support: All elements
- Browser support: [IE3, IE4, IE5, IE6, NS4, NS6]
- Style inherited: Yes

This property specifies font styles, such as `normal` (also called upright or standard), `italic`, and `oblique` fonts.

font-variant

- CSS1 values: normal|small-caps
- CSS2 values: inherit
- Default value: normal
- Element support: All elements
- Browser support: [IE4, IE5, IE6]
- Style inherited: Yes

This property indicates whether a font is a normal or special "small-caps" font.

font-weight

- CSS1 values:
  normal|bold|bolder|lighter|100|200|300|400|500|600|700|800|900

- CSS2 values: inherit

- Default value: normal

- Element support: All elements

- Browser support: [IE3, IE4, IE5, IE6, NS4, NS6]

- Style inherited: Yes

This property gives the *weight* of a font, such as normal, bold, or a numeric value.

Background and Color Properties

You can also use CSS to specify backgrounds, images, and colors. What follows is a synopsis of these properties.

background

- CSS1 values: [<background-color>||<background-image>||<background-repeat>||<background-attachment>||<background-position>]

- CSS2 values: inherit

- Default value: Not defined

- Element support: All elements

- Browser support: [IE3, IE4, IE5, IE6, NS4, NS6]

- Style inherited: No

This shorthand property lets you list the background properties (such as background-color, background-image, background-repeat, background-attachment, and background-position) all at the same time. Of course, you can set these properties individually as well.

background-attachment

- CSS1 values: scroll|fixed
- CSS2 values: inherit
- Default value: scroll
- Element support: All elements
- Browser support: [IE4, IE5, IE6]
- Style inherited: No

This property indicates whether a background image is fixed or moves when as user scrolls the rest of the document. You can create some interesting effects by letting text "float" over a background this way.

background-color

- CSS1 values: <color>|transparent
- CSS2 values: inherit
- Default value: transparent
- Element support: All elements
- Browser support: [IE4, IE5, IE6, NS4, NS6]
- Style inherited: No

This property indicates the background color of an element. You set it to either a <color> value or the keyword `transparent`. The `transparent` setting makes the underlying color visible.

background-image

- CSS1 values: <uri>|none
- CSS2 values: inherit
- Default value: None
- Element support: All elements
- Browser support: [IE4, IE5, IE6, NS4, NS6]
- Style inherited: No

This property sets an element's background image. One thing to keep in mind is that, when setting a background image, you might also want to set a background color in case the image is unavailable.

background-position

- CSS1 values: [[<percentage>|<length>]{1,2}|[[top|center|bottom]
  ||[left|center|right]]]
- CSS2 values: inherit
- Default value: 0% 0%
- Element support: Block-level and replaced elements
- Browser support: [IE4, IE5, IE6]
- Style inherited: No

You set this property to indicate a background image's starting position. For example, setting this property to 50% 50% starts it at the middle of the page.

background-repeat

- CSS1 values: repeat|repeat-x|repeat-y|no-repeat
- CSS2 values: inherit
- Default value: repeat
- Element support: All elements
- Browser support: [IE4, IE5, IE6]
- Style inherited: No

You use this property to specify whether a background image is repeated—called "tiling" the background—and, if so, how it is to be repeated.

color

- CSS1 values: <color>
- CSS2 values: inherit
- Default value: Browser dependent
- Element support: All elements
- Browser support: [IE3, IE4, IE5, IE6, NS4, NS6]
- Style inherited: Yes

This property sets a foreground (text) color. You set it to a color value.

Table Properties

CSS also supports a number of properties targeted especially at tables. There are quite a few table properties, but as yet the support for them is slight.

border-collapse

- CSS2 values: collapse|separate|inherit
- Default value: collapse
- Element support: Table and inline table elements
- Browser support: [IE5, IE6]
- Style inherited: Yes

This property gives a table's border model. For more information on table models, see the W3C CSS documentation.

border-spacing

- CSS2 values: <length><length>?|inherit
- Default value: 0
- Element support: Table and inline table elements
- Browser support: [None]
- Style inherited: Yes

Although it's not supported anywhere yet, this property is supposed to give the distance between cell borders.

column-span, row-span

- CSS2 values: <integer>|inherit
- Default value: 1
- Element support: Table cells, table columns, and table-column-group elements
- Browser support: [None]
- Style inherited: No

This property indicates how many columns or rows are spanned by a cell.

empty-cells

- CSS2 values: show|hide|inherit
- Default value: show
- Element support: Table cell elements
- Browser support: [None]
- Style inherited: Yes

You use this property to control how borders are drawn around cells that are empty.

table-layout

- CSS2 values: auto|fixed|inherit
- Default value: auto
- Element support: Table and inline table elements
- Browser support: [IE5, IE6]
- Style inherited: No

This property specifies how to lay out table cells, rows, and columns. For more information on table layouts, see the W3C CSS documentation.

Positioning and Block Properties

As you might recall, we took a look at absolute and relative positioning in this chapter, moving text and images around. Because the positioning style properties refer to position, they also refer to an element's box quite a bit. As mentioned earlier, an element's box is just the invisible rectangle it's drawn in.

bottom, top, left, right

- CSS2 values: <length>|<percentage>|auto|inherit
- Default value: auto
- Element support: All elements
- Browser support: [IE3, IE4, IE5, IE6, NS4, NS6]
- Style inherited: No

This property specifies how far a box's bottom, top, left, or right content edges should be from the box's containing area. You use these properties to position the box.

direction

- CSS1 values: ltr|rtl
- CSS2 values: inherit
- Default value: ltr
- Element support: All elements
- Browser support: [IE5, IE6]
- Style inherited: Yes

This property gives the base writing direction of text (left to right or right to left).

display

- CSS1 values: inline|block|list-item
- CSS2 values: run-in|compact|marker|table|inline-table|table-row-group|table-header-group|table-footer-group|table-row|table-col-umn-group|table-column|table-cell|table-caption|none|inherit
- Default value: inline
- Element support: All elements
- Browser support: [IE4, IE5, IE6]
- Style inherited: No

This property indicates how an element should be displayed. If you set this property to `block`, creating a block-level element, the element is displayed starting on a new line, and the following element also starts on a new line. The `inline` value, which is the default, specifies that elements should be displayed in the normal flow of elements.

float

- CSS1 values: left|right|none
- CSS2 values: inherit
- Default value: None
- Element support: All but positioned elements
- Browser support: [IE4, IE5, IE6, NS4, NS6]
- Style inherited: No

You use this property to indicate whether a box should be positioned to the left, right, or not at all. Text will flow around the element.

position

- CSS2 values: static|relative|absolute|fixed|inherit
- Default value: static
- Element support: All elements, but not generated content
- Browser support: [IE4, IE5, IE6, NS4, NS6]
- Style inherited: No

This property indicates which positioning algorithm to use. This setting is important when you set properties such as `left` or `right`.

unicode-bidi

- CSS2 values: normal|embed|bidi-override|inherit
- Default value: normal
- Element support: All elements
- Browser support: [IE5, IE6]
- Style inherited: No

You use this property to work with elements with reversed Unicode order.

z-index

- CSS2 values: auto|<integer>|inherit
- Default value: auto
- Element support: Positioned elements
- Browser support: [IE4, IE5, IE6, NS4, NS6]
- Style inherited: No

This property indicates the *stacking* level of a box. You use it when you position elements to indicate which element goes on top of which other element.

Box Properties

An element's box is an important part of its display, and quite a few style properties work with the box.

border

- CSS1 values: [<border-width>||<border-style>||<color>]
- CSS2 values: inherit
- Default value: Varies
- Element support: All elements
- Browser support: [IE4, IE5, IE6, NS4, NS6]
- Style inherited: No

This shorthand property lets you set the `border-width`, `border-style`, and `color` for all four borders of a box at once. List values for those properties in that order. Of course, you can also set these properties individually.

border-top, border-right, border-bottom, border-left

- CSS1 values: [<border-top/right/bottom/left-width>||<border-style>||<color>]
- CSS2 values: inherit
- Default value: Varies

- ▪ Element support: All elements
- ▪ Browser support: [IE4, IE5, IE6]
- ▪ Style inherited: No

These properties give the width, style, and color of the top, right, bottom, and left borders of a box. See Table 9-1 for possible settings.

border-color

- ▪ CSS1 values: <color>{1,4}|transparent
- ▪ CSS2 values: inherit
- ▪ Default value: Varies
- ▪ Element support: All elements
- ▪ Browser support: [IE4, IE5, IE6, NS4, NS6]
- ▪ Style inherited: No

This property gives the color of all four borders of a box.

border-top-color, border-right-color, border-bottom-color, border-left-color

- ▪ CSS1 values: <color>
- ▪ CSS2 values: inherit
- ▪ Default value: Varies
- ▪ Element support: All elements
- ▪ Browser support: [IE4, IE5, IE6]
- ▪ Style inherited: No

These properties give the color of one border of a box, such as the border's top.

border-style

- CSS1 values: <border-style>{1,4}
- CSS2 values: inherit
- Default value: varies
- Element support: All elements
- Browser support: [IE4, IE5, IE6, NS4, NS6]
- Style inherited: No

This property indicates the style of the four borders of a box. It can have from one to four values (the values are set on the different sides of the box).

border-top-style, border-right-style, border-bottom-style, border-left-style

- CSS1 values: <border-style>
- CSS2 values: inherit
- Default value: None
- Element support: All elements
- Browser support: [IE4, IE5, IE6]
- Style inherited: No

This property lets you specify the style of a one border edge of a box. See Table 9-1 for possible values.

border-width

- CSS1 values: <border-width>{1,4}
- CSS2 values: inherit
- Default value: Not defined
- Element support: All elements
- Browser support: [IE4, IE5, IE6, NS4, NS6]
- Style inherited: No

This property lets you set specify the border width, setting the `border-top-width`, `border-right-width`, `border-bottom-width`, and `border-left-width` properties all at the same time.

border-top-width, border-right-width, border-bottom-width, border-left-width

- CSS1 values: <border-width>
- CSS2 values: inherit
- Default value: medium
- Element support: All elements
- Browser support: [IE4, IE5, IE6, NS4, NS6]
- Style inherited: No

These properties let you set the border widths of a box's sides, one by one.

clear

- CSS1 values: none|left|right|both
- CSS2 values: inherit
- Default value: None
- Element support: Block-level elements
- Browser support: [IE4, IE5, IE6, NS4, NS6]
- Style inherited: No

This property lets you specify how another box should "clear" the current one, much like the CLEAR attribute in HTML. In particular, it specifies which borders of an element's boxes may not be next to an earlier floating element.

height, width

- CSS1 values: <length>|<percentage>|auto
- CSS2 values: inherit
- Default value: auto
- Element support: All elements except inline elements, table columns, and column groups
- Browser support: [IE4, IE5, IE6, NS4, NS6]
- Style inherited: No

These properties set the height or width of boxes.

margin

- CSS1 values: <margin-width>{1,4}
- CSS2 values: inherit
- Default value: Not defined
- Element support: All elements
- Browser support: [IE3, IE4, IE5, IE6, NS4, NS6]
- Style inherited: No

This shorthand property sets the `margin-top`, `margin-right`, `margin-bottom`, and `margin-left` properties all at the same time.

margin-top, margin-right, margin-bottom, margin-left

- CSS1 values: <margin-width>
- CSS2 values: inherit
- Default value: 0
- Element support: All elements
- Browser support: [IE3, IE4, IE5, IE6, NS4, NS6]
- Style inherited: No

These properties let you set the width of the top, right, bottom, or left margins of a box.

max-height, max-width

- CSS2 values: <length>|<percentage>|none|inherit
- Default value: None
- Element support: All elements except non-replaced inline elements and table elements
- Browser support: [IE4, IE5, IE6]
- Style inherited: No

These properties let you restrict box heights and widths to a range that you specify.

min-height

- CSS2 values: <length>|<percentage>inherit
- Default value: 0
- Element support: All elements except non-replaced inline elements and table elements
- Browser support: [None]
- Style inherited: No

This property lets you set the minimum height of a box.

min-width

- CSS2 values: <length>|<percentage>inherit
- Default value: 0
- Element support: All elements except non-replaced inline elements and table elements
- Browser support: [None]
- Style inherited: No

This property lets you set the minimum width of a box.

padding

- CSS1 values: <length>|<percentage>
- CSS2 values: inherit
- Default value: Not defined
- Element support: All elements
- Browser support: [IE4, IE5, IE6, NS4, NS6]
- Style inherited: No

This property lets you set the `padding-top`, `padding-right`, `padding-bottom`, and `padding-left` properties all at the same time and to the same value.

padding-top, padding-right, padding-bottom, padding-left

- CSS1 values: <length>|<percentage>
- CSS2 values: inherit
- Default value: 0
- Element support: All elements
- Browser support: [IE4, IE5, IE6, NS4, NS6]
- Style inherited: No

These properties let you set the top, right, bottom, and left padding of a box, which surrounds the content of the box.

Visual Effects Properties

New in CSS2, visual effect properties let you describe how elements are drawn. I'm including a sampling of these properties here.

clip

- CSS2 values: <shape>|auto|inherit
- Default value: auto
- Element support: Block-level and replaced elements
- Browser support: [IE5, IE6]
- Style inherited: No

The clipping region of an element indicates what part of the element is drawn and, therefore, what part is visible. This property lets you set an element's clipping region.

overflow

- CSS2 values: visible|hidden|scroll|auto|inherit
- Default value: visible
- Element support: Block-level and replaced elements
- Browser support: [IE5, IE6]
- Style inherited: No

This property specifies whether the content of a block-level element should be clipped if it extends past the edges of the element's box.

visibility

- CSS2 values: visible|hidden|collapse|inherit
- Default value: inherit
- Element support: All elements
- Browser support: [IE5, IE6]
- Style inherited: No

This property indicates whether the element should displayed.

List Properties

CSS also includes a number of styles that you use with lists. Although Internet Explorer indicates that it supports many of them, I've found the support to be spotty. To use these styles, you should set the display property to `list-item`.

list-style

- CSS1 values: [<list-style-type>||<list-style-position>||<list-style-image>]
- CSS2 values: inherit
- Default value: Not defined
- Element support: List items
- Browser support: [IE4, IE5, IE6]
- Style inherited: Yes

This shorthand property sets the values of the `list-style-type`, `list-style-position`, and `list-style-image` properties all at the same time and in the specified order.

list-style-image

- CSS1 values: <uri>| none
- CSS2 values: inherit
- Default value: None
- Element support: List items
- Browser support: [IE4, IE5, IE6]
- Style inherited: Yes

You can use this property to indicate an image that should be used next to every list item.

list-style-position

- CSS1 values: inside|outside
- CSS2 values: inherit
- Default value: outside
- Element support: List items
- Browser support: [IE4, IE5, IE6]
- Style inherited: Yes

This property sets the position of the list item marker; outside means that the marker should appear to the left of the text, and inside indicates that the marker should appear where the text's first character would normally appear.

list-style-type

- CSS1 values: disc|circle|square|decimal|decimal-leading-zero|lower-roman|upper-roman|lower-alpha|upper-alpha|none
- CSS2 values: lower-greek|lower-latin|upper-latin|hebrew|armenian|georgian|cjk-ideographic|hiragana|katakana|hiragana-iroha|katakana-iroha|inherit
- Default value: Disc
- Element support: List items
- Browser support: [IE4, IE5, IE6, NS4, NS6]
- Style inherited: Yes

This property lets you set the type of list item marker if you don't use the `list-style-image` property, or it has the value none (which is the default)—or if the image specified by that property cannot be displayed.

As you can see, there is a great deal to CSS, and it gives you a great deal of power formatting XML. In the next chapter, we'll start taking a look at the Java language to give us even more XML power.

CHAPTER 10

Understanding Java

In Chapter 7, "Handling XML Documents with JavaScript," and Chapter 8, "XML and Data Binding," we saw how to work with XML and JavaScript in Internet Explorer. However, JavaScript is a relatively lightweight language, and most serious XML programming does not take place in browsers such as Internet Explorer. Today, the most common way of handling XML in code is to use Java. Working with XML by using Java has become a central XML topic, and no XML book can ignore this connection. This book is designed to assume no more knowledge than HTML, so this chapter provides a painless introduction to Java. Java itself is a huge topic, but the Java we'll use in the coming chapters is limited; it turns out that we can get all the Java knowledge we need in this chapter. If you already know Java, feel free to skip this chapter.

Java should not be confused with JavaScript; despite their names and similar syntax, the two are not truly related. Java is a creation of Sun Microsystems, and JavaScript is a Netscape creation. Java is far deeper and far more extensive than JavaScript.

On the other hand, now that we've used JavaScript, we've got a good leg up on Java because much of their basic syntax is similar (because both are based on the C++ model, not because JavaScript and Java are directly related). In the next two chapters, we'll see how to work with XML package using Java.

In this chapter, we'll come up to speed with Java, building on what we already know of JavaScript. We'll get the skills we need for the next two chapters in this chapter, including creating Java classes and windowed applications.

In general, creating serious applications with Java is more involved than working with JavaScript because Java is so much more extensive. As you can imagine, there's way more Java than we can cover in one chapter—if you want to learn more, pick up a good book on the subject. On the other hand, this chapter introduces all the Java coding skills we'll use in the next two chapters. If you're already comfortable with Java, feel free to skip on to the next chapter, where I work with the XML DOM in Java, not JavaScript, as we did in Chapter 7.

Java Resources

Java is a product of Sun Microsystems. Here are some Web sites that contain Java resources online, most of them at Sun:

- `http://developer.netscape.com/tech/java/`—Netscape's "Java Developer Central" contains a good amount of useful information.

- http://java.sun.com—This is the main Java site, and it's filled with information.

- `http://java.sun.com/docs/`—The Java documentation is available online here. It's a good place to refer to.

- `http://java.sun.com/j2se/`—You can find Java 2 Standard Edition 1.4, which is the current version of the Java software development kit, at this site.

- `http://java.sun.com/j2se/1.4/docs/index.html`—This is the Java documentation for version 1.4.

- `www.javaworld.com`—This site carries a great number of Java resources and discussions.

Here's another list you might want to look into; these are free online tutorials that you can use to develop your Java skills:

- `http://java.sun.com/docs/books/tutorial/`
  `index.html`—Sun's own Java tutorial, which is very extensive

- `www.thejavatutorial.com/`—A useful Java tutorial

- `www.javacoffeebreak.com`—A good online Java tutorial

- `www-105.ibm.com/developerworks/education.nsf/`
  `java-onlinecourse-bytitle/FCCCC34D4124A8C086256997006B7146?`
  `OpenDocument`—IBM's Java tutorial with some outstanding features

Here's an important note: Java programming is not for everyone. Java is a complex language, and to cover it fully would take thousands of pages. We can't ignore it because it has come to play such a big part in the XML world. If you're not into programming, though, you can skip the Java chapters (this and the next two chapters) and continue on with the rest of the book. Many people prefer to get their Java XML applications written by someone else, and that's fine. However, these days, to really work with XML, it often comes down to working with Java sooner or later.

Writing Java Programs

You're probably already familiar with Java, if only because of Java *applets*. Applets, windowed Java applications designed to work in browsers, took the world by storm when first introduced, and all major browsers support Java these days. You can find millions of applets on the Internet, and whole banks of them you can pick up for free. There are even applets out there that work with XML.

A Java applet takes up a predefined area in a browser and can display graphics, controls such as buttons and text fields, text, and more. It's interactive because it runs in your browser. As mentioned, applets took the Internet by storm when they were first introduced. However, they're on the wane now, largely because of other solutions that are easier to program, such as Dynamic HTML, or more powerful, such as Macromedia Flash.

Don't worry about Java, though; as applets have become less popular (although they're still very popular), Java *applications* have gathered strength. The main reason that Java applications have become so powerful is that they're nearly as powerful as C++, but they're also cross-platform: You can use the same application in Windows or UNIX, for example. Many large corporations have switched from using C++ internally to using Java for most programming. (Another option is to use Java Servlets or JavaServer Pages, JSP, on the server to handle XML—I'll take a look at these options in Chapter 20, "WML, ASP, JSP, Servlets, and Perl.")

A Java application does not run in a browser like an applet—it's a freestanding program. Java applications can themselves create windows, like applets can, and we'll see how to do that here. In fact, Java applications can act as browsers, and we'll see an example of that in the next chapter with a Java application that reads an XML document from the Internet and uses it to display graphics. In that case, the XML document specifies circles to draw, and we'll be creating a graphical, not text-based, browser that is typical of the kinds of things you can do when you create your own XML applications.

Our XML Java work will center on writing Java applications, not applets. (For security reasons, applets are very restricted in terms of what they can do—they can't handle most types of file access, and we don't want to restrict our XML programs to work only in browsers.) So how do you create a Java application? You write applications as Java code and then *compile* them with the Java Software Development Kit (the Java SDK—before Java 2, the SDK was called the Java Development Kit [JDK], and some people and some Web pages at Sun still call it that). The compiled application is ready to run, and we'll see how to do that here.

I'll make this more concrete with an example. Here's how to create an application named ch10_01, which I'll store in a file named ch10_01.java (I'll go through the details of this application in this chapter):

Listing ch10_01.java

```
public class ch10_01
{
    public static void main(String[] args)
    {
        System.out.println("Welcome to Java");
    }
}
```

I can use the Java compiler, which is named javac, to compile this file into a bytecode file named ch10_01.class, and ch10_01.class is what you actually run. The bytecodes in the ch10_01.class are what Java reads and executes. (Java bytecodes are very compact compared to text, which makes applets fast to download. You can run the same bytecode file on many different operating systems, which makes it cross-platform.) Here's how you use javac to compile ch10_01.java (I'm using % as a generic command-line prompt, following the UNIX usage, where the prompt often is %; on an operating platform like Windows, this prompt will be something like C:\XML>):

```
%javac ch10_01.java
```

This creates ch10_01.class, and you use that file when running that application. To run the application, you use the tool named java (which comes with the Java SDK) like this:

```
%javac ch10_01.java
%java ch10_01
Welcome to Java
```

As you can see, the java tool executes the bytecode file ch10_01.class, and the result—the text `Welcome to Java`—appears. As mentioned, I'm using `%` as a generic command-line prompt because Java is available on many platforms. In Windows, you use these tools in an MS DOS window like this:

```
C:\>java ch10_01
Welcome to Java
```

That's what running a Java application looks like. As we'll see, there are many similarities between Java and JavaScript—but there are also significant differences. For example, we'll need to indicate the *type* of variables in Java, which you don't have to do in JavaScript. Java is also a lot more object-oriented than JavaScript.

Java Is Object-Oriented from the Ground Up

We first got a look at object-oriented programming when working with JavaScript, but that was only a quick glance. Object-oriented programming is integral to every aspect of Java. For example, take a look at the application we just saw:

```
public class ch10_01
{
    public static void main(String[] args)
    {
        System.out.println("Welcome to Java");
    }
}
```

Note the very first line, `public class ch10_01`, which defines a class named `ch10_01`. Our whole program is based on that class because, unlike in JavaScript, every line of code you write in Java has to be contained in a class (or an *interface*, which is a more generalized form of classes that we'll see in the next chapter). When Java runs this application, it creates an object of this class and gives that object control. So while you can optionally use objects in JavaScript, there's no avoiding them in Java.

I'll take a closer look at the idea behind classes now because we'll have to understand more about them than we did when discussing JavaScript. Object-oriented programming is really just another technique to let you implement that famous programming dictum: "Divide and conquer."

Here's the idea: You *encapsulate* data and functions into objects, which makes objects into self-contained units. The data inside an object can be purely internal to the object, in which case it's called private data, or it can be accessible externally, in which case it's called public data.

The functions built into an object can also be either purely private or public. In fact, ideally, the object should interact with the rest of the program only through a well-defined interface, as created by its public functions. As we saw in Chapter 6, "Understanding JavaScript," functions that are part of classes or objects are called methods.

Object-oriented programming was first developed to let programmers handle larger programs by breaking them into functional units that can be easily conceptualized. As you know, you can already break your code into functions. Object-oriented programming goes a step farther than that, letting you create objects that can contain not just one function, but many, as well as internal data items. When you encapsulate part of your code into an object, it lets you think of that part of the program in an easily conceptualized way, and that's the motivation behind object-oriented programming.

For example, consider a car—but consider it not as a sleek new automobile, but as an assemblage of pipes, wires, valves, switches, gasoline, and all the various parts that make it work. Now imagine that you are responsible for handling everything that the car usually does itself, such as pumping the fuel, igniting the fuel, transmitting power to the wheels, regulating electrical power, and more. A device requiring such attention would be impossible to drive. Now imagine all those functions back where they should be, internal to the car and interacting with each other automatically as needed when you step on the gas. You think of the result simply as a car—an easily imagined (and used) single concept. All you have to do is turn it on and step on the gas.

That's the idea behind encapsulation: You can turn a complex system that requires a lot of attention into an object that handles the details internally when you pass control to it. If the first dictum of object-oriented programming is "Divide and conquer," the second is surely "Out of sight, out of mind."

In Java, object-oriented programming revolves around a few key concepts: classes, data members, inheritance, methods, and objects. This list summarizes these terms:

- **Class**—A class can be thought of as a template from which you create objects. The definition of the class includes the formal specifications for the class and any data and methods in it.

- **Data members**—The data members of a class are the variables that are part of an object. You store the data that the object uses in its data members.

- **Inheritance**—This is the process of deriving one class, called the *derived* class, from another, the *base* class, and being able to make use of the base class's methods in the derived class.

- **Method**—A method is a function built into an object. Methods can be part of classes (*class methods*) or objects (*object methods*), as we'll see in this chapter.

- **Object**—An object is an *instance* of a class—what you create with classes. You can think of a class as the *type* of an object. When you've created an object, you can customize it by storing data in it (which you can't do with a class).

All these constructs are important to object-oriented programming, and we'll get more details on each of them in this chapter as we see how to create our own classes.

Getting the Java SDK

To create your own Java applications, you'll need to get and install the Java SDK; you can find it at `http://java.sun.com/j2se/` (download the Software Development Kit, SDK, not the Java Runtime Environment, JRE). The current version of Java as of this writing is 1.4. After downloading the Java SDK, usually as one executable package that installs itself, follow the installation instructions on the `http://java.sun.com` site.

The Java SDK

At this point, I'd love to be able to give detailed instructions on how to install the Java SDK, but that's a trap too many books have fallen into. The actual installation procedure has changed so often and so many times that any book that covers Java (and I've written many on Java) and tries to give those instructions is sure to make itself obsolete immediately. On the other hand, in recent versions, all you have to do is run an executable program that you download, and it'll do all the work for you.

As indicated in the Sun installation instructions, you have to make sure your machine can find the Java tools, including the Java compiler, javac. To do this, make sure that the Java bin subdirectory is in your computer's *path*. For example, in Windows, the bin subdirectory might be c:\jdk1.4\bin for the Java 2 SDK, version 1.4. You can use a line like this at the command prompt to put that directory into your path:

```
C:\>SET PATH=%PATH%;C:\JDK1.4\BIN
```

You can also set the computer's PATH environment variable permanently so that the path is set up correctly each time you reboot. How you do that varies by operating system. Take a look at the installation instructions for Java to see how to do this; you'll find them at http://java.sun.com/j2se/1.4/install.html for Java 1.4, http://java.sun.com/j2se/1.4.1/install.html for Java 1.4.1, and so on.

Now that the bin directory is in the path, you'll be able to use the Java tools from the command line without specifying their full path; otherwise, you'll have to preface them with a pathname each time you want to use them, like this in Windows:

```
C:\>C:\jdk1.4\bin\javac ch10_01.java
```

Creating Java Files

The actual Java code we'll write is stored in plain-text files holding Java statements and declarations. To store Java code in a file, you can use a simple text editor or as fancy a word processor as you like, as long as the result is a plain-text file without any fancy formatting that the Java compiler can't handle. You can use whatever text editor you prefer, such as vi in UNIX or WordPad in Windows.

You must give such files the extension .java because the Java compiler expects that extension. As you saw, I saved the application named ch10_01 in a file named ch10_01.java. This Java file is the one you'll pass to the Java compiler to create a bytecode file.

The tools we'll use are ready; it's time to start writing code.

Writing Code: Creating an Application

Here's the sample Java application that I'll develop through to the compiling and running stages over the next few sections. Place this code in a file named ch10_01.java:

```
public class ch10_01
{
    public static void main(String[] args)
    {
        System.out.println("Welcome to Java");
    }
}
```

As we've seen, this application will print out the text Welcome to Java when you run it. For example, here's how things would look in a DOS window under Windows:

```
C:\>java ch10_01
Welcome to Java
```

As you can see, this is not the most powerful of programs, but it's simple enough to get us started. We'll work up from this point to windowed Java applications at the end of the chapter. To see what's going on in ch10_01.java, I'm going to take it apart line by line now.

public class ch10_01

Note the first line in ch10_01.java:

```
public class ch10_01
{
    .
    .
    .
}
```

This line of code says that we're creating a new Java class named ch10_01. When we translate this file into a bytecode file, Java itself will create an object of this class and give it control.

Note also the keyword public in this line of code. This keyword is an *access specifier*. When you use the public access specifier for a class, that class is accessible anywhere in your program. The main class for a Java application must always be public. In fact, Java insists that you name the file after the public class in it, which is why this file is named ch10_01.java (note that capitalization counts—ch10_01.java must hold a public class named ch10_01, not Ch10_01 or cH10_01). Because the name of a public class sets the name of the file where that class is defined, you can have only one public class in a file.

Following the public class ch10_01 line is the actual implementation of the class, which goes in curly braces:

```
public class ch10_01
{
    .
    .
    .
}
```

As with the code you write for methods, the code you write for objects must go inside curly braces. The first line of code in the curly braces is coming up next.

public static void main(String[ ] args)

The next line of code in the application is as follows:

```
public class ch10_01
{
    public static void main(String[] args)
    {
         .
         .
         .
    }
}
```

What's going on here? In this case, I'm defining a function that's part of an object (because it's defined inside the object's definition), which makes it a *method*. I'm also declaring this method public, which means that it's accessible (may be called) outside the object. Methods that I declare private cannot be called from outside the object (and are usually utility methods that other methods inside the object call). As with functions in JavaScript, you can pass arguments to Java methods, and you can have methods return values. I'll go into more detail on this process later in the chapter, but here I'm indicating that this method is named main and does not return any value, which I specify with the void keyword. The main method is a special one in Java because it is called automatically when Java starts this application. When Java finds the main method, it passes control to it (applets don't need a main method—in fact, that's a major programming difference between programming applets and applications). You place the code that you want run as soon as the application starts in the main method.

In addition, I'm indicating that this method is passed an array of Java String objects by enclosing the code String[] args in parentheses after the method name. You must declare the type of every argument you pass to a method. I'm listing that type as String[] here, which is an array of strings. I'm also naming that array args, which is how I can refer to it in the method's code. This array is passed to every application's main method. As we'll see later in this chapter, you can use it to read the command-line arguments passed to the application. (For example, if you were to start the application like this %java ch10_01 Welcome to Java, the command-line arguments are Welcome, to, and Java.)

There's one more point here: Note the `static` keyword. Technically, the `main` method is a method of the application's main class, `ch10_01`. You don't create an object of the `ch10_01` class yourself in code; it remains as a class. For that reason, the methods and data items in the `ch10_01` class are class methods and data items (as opposed to object methods and data items). There is a rule for class methods and data items: They must be declared `static`, which gives Java a special way of storing them. When you've declared them `static`, you have access to the methods and data items in a class without having to create an object of that class.

This line of code starts the `main` method; the rest of this method's code is inside curly braces, as usual:

```
public class ch10_01
{
    public static void main(String[] args)
    {
        .
        .
        .
    }
}
```

The purpose of this method is to print the text `Welcome to Java`, and I'll do that in the next line of code.

System.out.println("Welcome to Java");

The `main` method has just one line of code in it, and here it is:

```
public class ch10_01
{
    public static void main(String[] args)
    {
        System.out.println("Welcome to Java");
    }
}
```

This line of code is the only one that actually produces anything as far as the user sees; it prints `Welcome to Java`. So what's going on here?

In this case, I'm using some of the built-in functionality that comes with Java. Like JavaScript, Java has plenty of classes and objects ready for you to use. In Java, that functionality is available in Java *packages* (which are class libraries). One of the Java packages that is available in any Java program is java.lang, the Java language package itself. This package makes an object named System available to us, which itself contains an object named out that lets you communicate with the user. In particular, I'm using the out object's println method here to display text on the user's console.

Here's another thing to notice: This line of code ends with a semicolon (;). Ending each simple statement with a semicolon has become standard in languages such as C, C++, Java, and even JavaScript. In JavaScript, we were able to omit the semicolon because browsers don't require it, and most people do. In Java, it's another story: The semicolons are required. In fact, if you're coming to Java from JavaScript, you might get the feeling that Java is a very prickly language by comparison to JavaScript. Not only do you have to put in the semicolons, but you also have to specify a data type for each data item. When you try to assign a value of one type to a variable of another (which might be legal in JavaScript), Java will give you warning and error reports.

At this point, you've created your new application and stored it in a file named ch10_01.java. What's the next step? How do you get it to actually *run*? Take a look at the next section.

Compiling Code

We have the complete file, ch10_01.java, and we're ready to run it. The first step is compiling it into a bytecode file, ch10_01.class. To compile ch10_01.java, you use the Java tool javac, the Java compiler (on Windows machines, this program is called javac.exe and is located in the bin subdirectory). Here's how you use javac in general (all the arguments here are optional, and I'll place them in square brackets to indicate that, which is the convention Sun itself uses in the java documentation):

```
javac [options] [sourcefiles] [files]
```

Here are the arguments to javac:

- options—Command-line options. See the Java documentation for the details; we won't need any command-line options here.
- sourcefiles—One or more code files to be compiled. (Here, that'll be just ch10_01.java.)
- files—One or more files that list command-line options code files to compile.

In this case, I'll compile ch10_01.java with this command:

```
%javac ch10_01.java
```

The Java compiler, javac, compiles the file ch10_01.java (assuming that there are no errors), translating it and creating a new file named ch10_01.class. If there are errors, the Java compiler will tell you what they are, including what line of code is wrong, as in this case, in which I've forgotten the name of the `println` method and tried to use one called `printText`:

```
%javac ch10_01.java
ch10_01.java:5: Method printText(java.lang.String) not found in class
java.io.Print
Stream.
        System.out.printText("Welcome to Java");
                           ^
1 error
```

At this point, we've created the file ch10_01.class, the bytecode file that Java will need to run the application. This bytecode file will run unchanged on any system that supports Java.

So how do you actually run ch10_01.class? I'll take a look at that in the next section.

Running Java Applications

You actually run Java applications with the Java tool named, appropriately enough, java. This tool is a program that comes with the Java SDK (java.exe in Windows, in the Java bin directory).

Running Java Apps Without the SDK

You don't need the full Java SDK to simply run Java applications. You can get the java tool in the Java Runtime Environment (JRE), which you can get from the Sun Java site at `http://java.sun.com/jdk`.

To run the ch10_01 application, I use the java tool like this on the command line:

```
%java ch10_01
```

The result appears at once:

```
%java ch10_01
Welcome to Java
```

You can see what this looks like in Figure 10-1, where I'm running this application in a DOS window in Windows.

Figure 10-1
Running a Java
application.

That's all it takes. You've created, compiled, and run your first Java application. (Note that if your application isn't responding or you want to stop it for some reason, you can type Ctrl+C in Windows. If that doesn't work, try the Escape key.)

While we're on the topic of compiling and running code, there is another detail that we should cover: commenting your Java code.

Commenting Your Code

As with JavaScript, you can comment your Java code. Comments serve the same purpose here as they do in XML and JavaScript: They hold descriptive code that explains what's going on in your code. There are two ways to insert comments in a Java program. The first way is to surround comments, especially multiline comments, with the characters /* and */, like this:

```
/* This application is designed to display
   the message "Welcome to Java" on the console
*/

public class ch10_01
{
    public static void main(String[] args)
    {
        System.out.println("Welcome to Java");
    }
}
```

As with any type of comment, the Java compiler ignores the text in the comment—that is, any text between the /* and */ markers.

As with JavaScript, Java supports a one-line comment using a double slash (//). The Java compiler ignores everything on a line after the // marker, so you can create whole lines that are comments or just add a comment to an individual line, like this:

```
/* This application is designed to display
   the message "Welcome to Java" on the console
*/

public class ch10_01   //Define the class ch10_01
{
    //Define main(), the first method to be called.
    public static void main(String[] args)
    {
        //Display the message "Welcome to Java"
        System.out.println("Welcome to Java");
    }
}
```

Importing Java Packages and Classes

As mentioned, the classes that Sun has put together for you to use are stored in class libraries called packages. The classes we'll use to interact with XML documents in the next two chapters are also stored in packages. Although the java.lang package is already available to your code by default, the classes in other packages are not, and you must *import* those packages to use them. You can also import individual classes as well as whole packages. Knowing how to do this is very important in Java programming because a great deal of the resources that most programs use are in packages that you have to import.

To import a package, you use the Java import statement, which looks like this (following the Sun conventions, items in square brackets are optional, and the upright bar, |, means "or", much as it does when you write DTDs):

```
import [package1[.package2...].](classname|*);
```

Note that you put a dot (.) between package and class names to keep them separate. The standard java packages themselves are stored in a large package called java, so the util package is really called the java.util package. (There are other large packages, including the java package, available. For example, the extensive Swing package is stored in the javax package.)

Here's an example. In this case, I want to use the `Date` class in the java.util package. To do that, I can import that class this way in code:

```
import java.util.Date;

public class ch10_02
{
    public static void main(String[] args)
    {
    .
    .
    .
    }
}
```

Now I'm able to use the `Date` class in code. To do that, I create a new `Date` object with the new operator—which is how you create objects from classes in JavaScript as well. (In fact, we used the JavaScript `Date` class and created a new object of that class in Chapter 6.) The new `Date` object represents today's date, which I can display like this. Note that I'm also adding a pair of empty parentheses after the `Date` class to indicate that I'm not passing any value to that class's constructor (as we saw in Chapter 6, a class's constructor is a method that runs when an object is created from the class, allowing you to initialize the object):

Listing ch10_02.java

```
import java.util.Date;

public class ch10_02
{
    public static void main(String[] args)
    {
        System.out.println("Today's date is " + new Date());
    }
}
```

When you compile and run this application, this is the kind of result you'll see:

```
%java ch10_02
Today's date is Mon May 22 16:28:53 EDT 2003
```

In this case, I imported a specific class, the Date class, from the java.util package. However, you can import all classes from a package at once with the * wildcard like this, where I'm importing all java.util classes (note that this does not make the ch10_02.class file any larger—only those classes that are actually referenced in the code are used when building the final bytecode file—the bytecode file ch10_02.class will be the same size if you use either the statement import java.util.Date; or import java.util.*;.):

```java
import java.util.*;

public class ch10_02
{
    public static void main(String[] args)
    {
        System.out.println("Today's date is " + new Date());
    }
}
```

You can also import classes that you've created. For example, say that you've created a class named Display that uses a method named showImage to display an image on the user's screen. You might create a new object of the Display class and use the showImage method something like this:

```java
public class ch10_02
{
    public static void main(String[] args)
    {
        (new Display()).showImage("flowers.gif");
    }
}
```

When you've created the file Display.class, you can import the Display class into your program like this:

```java
import Display;

public class ch10_02
{
    public static void main(String[] args)
    {
        (new Display()).showImage("flowers.gif");
    }
}
```

Storing *Display.class*

This technique relies on having `Display.class` in the same directory as the application you're compiling so that the `import` statement can find it. On the other hand, you might want to store `Display.class` in another directory, such as c:\display. In that case, you have to add `c:\display` to the Java environment variable `CLASSPATH`. We'll see more about this in the next chapter, or you can see the Java documentation for all the details.

Creating Variables in Java

We've seen that Java applications are class based, and we've gotten enough Java down now to create basic programs. The next step in Java programming is to start storing your data so that you can work on that data. As with JavaScript, variables serve as locations in memory in which you can store your data. However, unlike JavaScript, Java variables are strongly *typed*, which means that you have to declare a type for each variable and be careful about mixing those types.

For example, one of the most common variable types is int, which stands for "integer." This type sets aside 4 bytes of memory, which means that you can store values between -2,147,483,648 and 2,147,483,647 in int variables. Quite a few different variable types are built into Java, such as integers, floating-point numbers, and individual characters.

When you want to use a variable in Java, you must declare it, specifying the variable's type:

```
type name [= value][, name [= value]...];
```

Here's an example showing how to declare a variable of the int type. This variable is named counter:

```
public class ch10_03
{
    public static void main(String[] args)
    {
        int counter;
        .
        .
        .
    }
}
```

I've set aside 4 bytes of memory for the variable named counter. I can store a value of 2003 in that counter like this, using the Java assignment operator:

```java
public class ch10_03
{
    public static void main(String[] args)
    {
        int counter;

        counter = 2003;

        .
        .
        .
    }
}
```

And I can display the value in the counter variable with a println statement, like this:

Listing ch10_03.java

```java
public class ch10_03
{
    public static void main(String[] args)
    {
        int counter;

        counter = 2003;

        System.out.println("The current counter value is " + counter);
    }
}
```

Here's the result of this code:

```
%java ch10_03
The current counter value is 2003
```

As in JavaScript, there's a shortcut you can use to both declare a variable and assign a value to it at the same time like this:

```java
public class ch10_03
{
    public static void main(String[] args)
    {
        int counter = 2003;
```

```
        System.out.println("The current counter value is " + counter);
    }
}
```

Plenty of variable types are built into Java besides int:

- **Boolean**—The boolean type holds only two types of values: true and false.

- **Characters**—The char type holds representations of characters, such as letters and numbers.

- **Floating-point numbers**—There are two types here: float and double (for double precision), which hold signed floating-point numbers.

- **Integers**—There are a number of integer types, such as byte (1 byte of storage), short (usually 2 bytes), int (usually 4 bytes), and long (usually 8 bytes), which hold signed, whole-value numbers.

Java is a very strongly typed language, which means that it's very particular about mixing data types. For example, look at this code, in which I'm declaring a floating-point number and an integer, and then assigning the floating-point number to the integer:

```
public class ch10_03
{
    public static void main(String[] args)
    {
        float counter = 2003;
        int counter2;

        counter2 = counter;

        System.out.println("The current counter2 value is " + counter2);
    }
}
```

Java regards this as a problem because the floating-point type can hold numbers with greater precision than the int type. So, it returns an error when you try to compile this code, saying that an "explicit cast" is required to convert a floating-point number to an integer:

```
%javac ch10_03.java
ch10_03.java:8: Incompatible type for =. Explicit cast
needed to convert float to int.
```

```
    counter2 = counter;
                ^
1 error
```

To solve a problem like this, you can explicitly request that Java convert the floating-point number to an integer with the *cast* (int):

```
public class ch10_03
{
    public static void main(String[] args)
    {
        float counter = 2003;
        int counter2;

        counter2 = (int) counter;

        System.out.println("The current counter2 value is " + counter2);
    }
}
```

You can convert between types like this if required, but bear in mind that you could lose some numerical precision this way.

Creating Arrays in Java

Simple data types of the kind we saw in the previous section are fine for storing single data items, but data is often more complex. Like JavaScript, Java supports arrays as well. Here's an example. In this case, I'll store the balances in customers' charge accounts in an array named chargesDue. I start by declaring that array, making it of type double:

```
public class ch10_04
{
    public static void main(String[] args)
    {
        double chargesDue[];
        .
        .
        .
```

Besides declaring the array, you have to allocate the number of elements you want the array to hold. You do that using the new operator:

```
public class ch10_04
{
    public static void main(String[] args)
    {
        double chargesDue[];
```

```
        chargesDue = new double[100];
    .
    .
    .
```

You can combine the array declaration and definition into one statement like this:

```
public class ch10_04
{
    public static void main(String[] args)
    {
        double chargesDue[] = new double[100];
    .
    .
    .
```

After the array has been created, you can address individual elements using square brackets and an array index, like this:

Listing ch10_04.java

```
public class ch10_04
{
    public static void main(String[] args)
    {
        double chargesDue[] = new double[100];

        chargesDue[4] = 99.06;

        System.out.println("Customer 4 owes $" + chargesDue[4]);
    }
}
```

Here's the results of this code:

```
%java ch10_04
Customer 4 owes $99.06
```

Java Arrays

In Java, the lower bound of an array that you declare this way is 0, so the statement `chargesDue = new double[100]` creates an array with a first item of `chargesDue[0]` and a last item of `chargesDue[99]`.

You can also initialize arrays with values at the same time you create them. You do that by specifying a comma-separated list of values in curly braces like this (note that the number of elements in the created array will be the number of elements in the list):

```java
public class ch10_04
{
    public static void main(String[] args)
    {
        double chargesDue[] = {1093.66, 667.19, 45.99, 890.30, 99.06};

        System.out.println("Customer 4 owes $" + chargesDue[4]);
    }
}
```

I'll elaborate this example now. Say that the store we're handling customer balances for opens a new branch, so now there are both eastern and western branches. If customers can open accounts in both branches, we'll need to keep track of two balances for each customer. You can do that by using a two-dimensional array like this:

```java
public class ch10_05
{
    public static void main(String[] args)
    {
        double chargesDue[][] = new double[2][100];
        .
        .
        .
```

Now you refer to every element in the array with two array indices, not just one, as in the previous one-dimensional version of this array:

```java
public class ch10_05
{
    public static void main(String[] args)
    {
        double chargesDue[][] = new double[2][100];

        chargesDue[0][4] = 99.06;
        chargesDue[1][4] = 23.17;
        .
        .
        .
```

I can display the balance in both a customer's eastern and western branch accounts like this:

Listing ch10_05.java

```
public class ch10_05
{
    public static void main(String[] args)
    {
        double chargesDue[][] = new double[2][100];

        chargesDue[0][4] = 99.06;
        chargesDue[1][4] = 23.17;

        System.out.println("Customer 4 owes $" + chargesDue[0][4] + " in the
        ➥eastern branch.");
        System.out.println("Customer 4 owes $" + chargesDue[1][4] + " in the
        ➥Western branch.");
    }
}
```

Here's the result:

```
%java ch10_05
Customer 4 owes $99.06 in the eastern branch.
Customer 4 owes $23.17 in the western branch.
```

You can also initialize a two-dimensional array by assigning values when declaring such an array:

```
public class ch10_05
{
    public static void main(String[] args)
    {
        double chargesDue[][] = {{1093.66, 667.19, 45.99, 890.30, 99.06},
                                 {2019.00, 129.99, 19.01, 630.90, 23.17}};

        System.out.println("Customer 4 owes $" + chargesDue[0][4] + " in the
        ➥Eastern branch.");
        System.out.println("Customer 4 owes $" + chargesDue[1][4] + " in the
        ➥Western branch.");
    }
}
```

Find the Length of an Array

Need to find the length of an array? Just use the array's `length` property, like this: `scores.length`.

Creating Strings in Java

You might have noticed that you can add strings together with the + operator in Java, just as you can in JavaScript:

```
public class ch10_05
{
    public static void main(String[] args)
    {
        double chargesDue[][] = {{1093.66, 667.19, 45.99, 890.30, 99.06},
                                 {2019.00, 129.99, 19.01, 630.90, 23.17}};

        System.out.println("Customer 4 owes $" + chargesDue[0][4] + " in the
        ➥Eastern branch.");
        System.out.println("Customer 4 owes $" + chargesDue[1][4] + " in the
        ➥Western branch.");
    }
}
```

This works because strings are supported by the built-in class `String` in Java. In fact, the `String` class is treated in a special way in Java; you can use it just as you would any built-in data type, as in this case (note that I don't have to use the new operator or call the `String` class's constructor here):

```
public class ch10_05
{
    public static void main(String[] args)
    {
        String welcome = "Welcome to Java";
            .
            .
            .
```

You can treat this new `String` variable as you would other simple variables, including printing it like this:

```
public class ch10_05
{
    public static void main(String[] args)
    {
        String welcome = "Welcome to Java";

        System.out.println(welcome);
    }
}
```

Java String Classes

In fact, really two string classes are available in Java: the String and StringBuffer classes. For most purposes, String objects are read-only because they don't allow you to change their internal data. However, you can change the internal text in the StringBuffer class. Both these classes have a great many methods built into them, which you can find in the Java documentation.

Java Operators

As in JavaScript, operators are an important part of programming in Java. Here's an example of adding two values using the Java + operator:

Listing ch10_06.java

```
public class ch10_06
{
    public static void main(String[] args)
    {
        int int1 = 130, int2 = 250, sum;

        sum = int1 + int2;

        System.out.println(int1 + " + " + int2 +
            " = " + sum);
    }
}
```

Here are the results of this code:

```
%java ch10_06
130 + 250 = 380
```

So what operators are available in Java? Table 10-1 contains all of them. Note that nearly all of them are shared by JavaScript as well.

Table 10-1	**Operator**	**Operation Performed**
Java Operators	++	Increment
	- -	Decrement
	=	Assignment
	==	Equal to
	+	Addition
	+=	Addition assignment
	-	Subtraction
	-=	Subtraction assignment
	*	Multiplication
	*=	Multiplication assignment
	/	Division
	/=	Division assignment
	<	Less than
	<=	Less than or equal to
	<<	Shift left
	<<=	Shift left assignment
	>	Greater than
	>=	Greater than or equal to
	>>	Shift right
	>>=	Shift right assignment
	>>>	Shift right with zero fill
	>>>=	Shift right zero fill assignment
	^	Logical Xor
	^=	Bitwise Xor assignment
	|	Logical Or
	||	Short-circuit Or

continues

Operator	Operation Performed
|=	Bitwise Or assignment
~	Bitwise unary Not
!	Logical unary Not
!=	Not equal to
&	Logical And
&&	Short-circuit And
&=	Bitwise And assignment
?:	Ternary `if...else`
%	Modulus
%=	Modulus assignment

Java Conditional Statements: *if, if...else, switch*

After operators, the next level up is to use conditional statements. Java supports the same conditional statements as JavaScript: `if`, `if...else`, and `switch`.

The `if` statement allows you to check a condition, which you create using the Java conditional operators, such as <, >, and ==:

```
if (condition) {
    code executed if condition is true
}
else {
    code executed if condition is false
}
```

For example, say you had two `double` variables, `assets` and `debts`, and you wanted to compare the two to make sure you're solvent. You might want the code to display a message, such as `"You're solvent."`. You can do that like this:

Listing ch10_07.java

```
public class ch10_07
{
    public static void main(String[] args)
    {
        double assets = 175.99;
        double debts = 115.99;

        if (assets > debts) {
            System.out.println("You're solvent.");
        }
    }
}
```

As we've seen when discussing JavaScript, the `if` statement checks its condition and, if that condition evaluates to `true`, executes the code in the `if` statement's body. In this case, the code displays the message; here are the results:

```
%java ch10_07
You're solvent.
```

You can also explicitly handle the case in which the condition in an `if` statement turns out to be `false` by including an `else` clause. If the condition in the `if` statement evaluates to `false`, the code in the `else` clause is executed if the `if` statement has such a clause. Here's an example. In this case, the second message is displayed if the amount in `assets` is less than or equal to the amount in `debts`:

```
public class ch10_07
{
    public static void main(String[] args)
    {
        double assets = 175.99;
        double debts = 115.99;

        if (assets > debts) {
            System.out.println("You're solvent.");
        }
        else {
            System.out.println("Uh oh.");
        }
    }
}
```

You can also create "ladders" of if..else statements like this; I'm handling the cases in which the amount in assets is either the same or greater than that in debts:

```java
public class ch10_07
{
    public static void main(String[] args)
    {
        double assets = 175.99;
        double debts = 115.99;

        if (assets > debts) {
            System.out.println("You're solvent.");
        }
        else {
            if(assets == debts) {
                System.out.println("You're broke.");
            }
            else {
                System.out.println("Uh oh.");
            }
        }
    }
}
```

As with JavaScript, Java supports a switch statement:

```java
switch(test){
    case value1:
        .
        .
        .
        code executed if test matches value1
        .
        .
        .
        break;
    case value2:
        .
        .
        .
        code executed if test matches value2
        .
        .
        .
        break;
    default:
        .
        .
        .
```

```
                    code executed if test doesn't matches any case
                        .
                        .
                        .
                    break;
                }
```

But there's a catch—you can't use it with most of the many variable types that Java defines. The only values you can check in switch statements are `byte`, `char`, `short`, and `int` values. Here's an example in which I'm working with integers:

Listing ch10_08.java

```java
public class ch10_08
{
    public static void main(String[] args)
    {
        int day = 5;

        switch(day) {
            case 0:
                System.out.println("Today is Monday.");
                break;
            case 1:
                System.out.println("Today is Monday.");
                break;
            case 2:
                System.out.println("Today is Tuesday.");
                break;
            case 3:
                System.out.println("Today is Wednesday.");
                break;
            case 4:
                System.out.println("Today is Thursday.");
                break;
            case 5:
                System.out.println("Today is Friday.");
                break;
            default:
                System.out.println("It must be Saturday.");
        }
    }
}
```

There's another useful way of handling if...else situations: You can use the Java ?: operator. This operator returns one of two values depending on whether an expression evaluates to true or false. You put the condition in front of the ?, the value that this operator should return if the condition is true immediately after the ?, and the value that the operator should return if the condition is false after the colon. Here's an example in which I've converted the earlier if...else example to use the ?: operator:

Listing ch10_09.java

```java
public class ch10_09
{
    public static void main(String[] args)
    {
        double assets = 175.99;
        double debts = 115.99;
        String output;

        output = assets > debts ? "You're solvent." : "Uh oh.";

        System.out.println(output);
    }
}
```

Java Loops: *for, while, do...while*

The next step after working with conditional statements is to handle loops. Like JavaScript, Java supports a for loop, a while loop, and a do...while loop.

Here's how you use a Java for loop in general, Note that the statement that makes up the body of the for loop can be a compound statement; it can be made up of several single statements enclosed in curly braces:

```java
for (initialization_expression; end_conditon; iteration_expression) {
    statement
}
```

You place an expression in the *initialization* part of the for loop (which often initializes a variable—that is, a loop index—to 0), and then you place a test condition in the *test* part of the loop that is tested each time the code in the loop executes. If the test is false, the loop ends (often the test condition checks whether the value in the loop index exceeds a specified maximum value). On the other hand, if the test condition is `true`, the body of the loop is executed and the code in the *increment* part of the loop is executed to get the loop ready for the next iteration (often by incrementing the loop index).

Here's an example. In this case, I'm summing the values in five bank accounts, as stored in an array named `accounts`, using a `for` loop:

Listing ch10_10.java

```java
public class ch10_10
{
    public static void main(String[] args)
    {
        double accounts[] =
            {365.55, 789.19, 532.11, 1079.96, 185.19};
        double sum = 0;

        for (int loopIndex = 0; loopIndex < accounts.length;
            loopIndex++) {
            sum += accounts[loopIndex];
        }

        System.out.println("The total in all accounts is $" + sum);
    }
}
```

Here are the results of this code:

```
%java ch10_10
The total in all accounts is $2952
```

Java also supports a `while` loop. I'll create an example showing how to use this loop and how you can read input from the keyboard. In this case, I'll keep reading from the keyboard until the user types the word `quit`.

You can use the `System.in.read` method to read character by character from the keyboard. This method waits until the user presses Enter at the end of the line, at which point Java stores all those typed characters. When you call this method, it reads the next character from those that were typed and returns it.

To read what the user has typed using this method, I'll start by creating a string named `input`. I'll add all the waiting characters to this string in succession by repeatedly calling the `System.in.read` method and then searching the string for the word `quit`. I can use the `String` class's `indexOf` method to search this string for that word and keep looping until that word is found. The indexOf method returns either the starting location of the string you're searching for or -1 if that string is not found. Here's how I can keep waiting for quit until it's found:

```
public class ch10_11
{
    public static void main(String[] args)
    {
        String input = "";

        while (input.indexOf("quit") < 0){
            .
            .
            .
        }
    }
}
```

Each time the user enters a new line, I can use System.in.read to read the characters the user has typed and add them one by one to the input string. The System.in.read method actually returns ASCII codes as integers, so we'll need an explicit cast, (char), to convert those values to characters that we can add to the input string.

The creators of Java knew that I/O operations are prone to errors, so they allowed the System.in.read to generate errors that your program can handle, called *trappable* errors or *exceptions* in Java. Generating such an error is called *throwing an exception*. You must enclose the code that can cause errors in a special construct called a try block:

```
public class ch10_11
{
    public static void main(String[] args)
    {
        String input = "";

        while (input.indexOf("quit") < 0){
            try {
                input += (char) System.in.read();
            }
            .
            .
            .
        }
    }
}
```

You follow the try block with a catch block to catch any errors that occurred. The catch block is passed an object of class Exception, and I'll name that object e here. I can use that object's printStackTrace method to display the error that occurred, sending the text from that method to the System.err output channel (which corresponds to the console by default) like this:

Listing ch10_11.java

```java
public class ch10_11
{
    public static void main(String[] args)
    {
        String input = "";

        while (input.indexOf("quit") < 0){
            try {
                input += (char) System.in.read();
            } catch (Exception e) {
                e.printStackTrace(System.err);
            }
        }
    }
}
```

That's all we need, Now the user can enter text, which the application will read. When the user types the word quit anywhere in that text, the application will terminate:

```
%java ch10_11
Hi there!
This is great.
Anything happening?
Well, looks like it's time to quit.
```

Not bad—now we've seen one way to read from the keyboard as well as use the while loop.

Declaring and Creating Objects

In Java, you have to declare new objects and then create them with the new operator. For example, here's how I create an object of the Java String class, passing the text "Welcome to Java" to that class's constructor:

```java
public class ch10_12
{
    public static void main(String[] args)
    {
```

```
        String greeting1;

        greeting1 = new String("Welcome to Java");
    .
    .
    .
```

Note that I first declared the `greeting1` object, giving the object's class, `String`, as its type. Then I create the object with the `new` operator.

Overloaded Constructors

Classes can have different constructors that handle different types of data. For example, I passed a string to the `String` class's constructor in the previous example, but I can also pass an array of characters this way:

```
public class ch10_12
{
    public static void main(String[] args)
    {
        String greeting1, greeting2, greeting3;

        greeting1 = new String("Welcome to Java");

        char characters[] = {'W', 'e', 'l', 'c', 'o', 'm', 'e',
                    ' ', 't', 'o', ' ', 'J', 'a', 'v', 'a'};

        greeting2 = new String(characters);
        .
        .
        .
    }
}
```

Constructors and methods that can take different argument lists are said to be *overloaded*.

Overloading

To overload a constructor or method, you just define it a number of times, each with a different argument list. You can also overload operators. For example, the + operator is overridden for the `String` class, which means that you can add strings with the + operator.

Assigning Objects

You can also assign one object to another using the = assignment operator:

```
public class ch10_12
{
    public static void main(String[] args)
    {
        String greeting1, greeting2, greeting3;

        greeting1 = new String("Welcome to Java");

        char characters[] = {'W', 'e', 'l', 'c', 'o', 'm', 'e',
                    ' ', 't', 'o', ' ', 'J', 'a', 'v', 'a'};

        greeting2 = new String(characters);

        greeting3 = greeting2;
        .
        .
        .
    }
}
```

To end this example, I'll print all the strings we've created:

Listing ch10_12.java

```
public class ch10_12
{
    public static void main(String[] args)
    {
        String greeting1, greeting2, greeting3;

        greeting1 = new String("Welcome to Java");

        char characters[] = {'W', 'e', 'l', 'c', 'o', 'm', 'e',
                    ' ', 't', 'o', ' ', 'J', 'a', 'v', 'a'};

        greeting2 = new String(characters);

        greeting3 = greeting2;

        System.out.println(greeting1);
        System.out.println(greeting2);
        System.out.println(greeting3);
    }
}
```

Here's what this application looks like when run:

```
%java ch10_12
Welcome to Java
Welcome to Java
Welcome to Java
```

That's how to declare and create objects in Java. It's similar to the way you declare and create simple variables, with the added power of configuring objects by passing data to a class's constructor.

Creating Methods in Java

In JavaScript, we created functions; in Java, everything is object-oriented, so we'll be creating methods. A method is just a function that's part of a class or object. As an example, I'll create a method now named `adder` that will add two integers and return their sum.

To start, I'll need two numbers to add, and I'll let the user enter them as command-line arguments. I can read those arguments from the array passed to the `main` method, which I name `args`, and store them in integers `value1` and `value2`, like this:

```
public class ch10_13
{
    public static void main(String[] args)
    {
        int value1 = Integer.parseInt(args[0]);
        int value2 = Integer.parseInt(args[1]);
        .
        .
        .
}
```

Now I display those values, pass them to the `adder` method, and display the value that `adder` returned, like this:

```
public class ch10_13
{
    public static void main(String[] args)
    {
        int value1 = Integer.parseInt(args[0]);
        int value2 = Integer.parseInt(args[1]);

        System.out.println(value1 + " + " + value1 +
            " = " + adder(value1, value2));
```

```
        }
        .
        .
        .

}
```

All that remains is to create the `adder` method. You can give methods access specifiers such as `public` or `private`. If you give it the access specifier `public`, the method is accessible outside the object or class. If you give it the access specifier `private` (which is the default if you don't use an access specifier), it's accessible only inside the object or class. If you use the `protected` keyword, the method is accessible in objects of the current class or in classes based on the current class. I'll use `public` here (we won't use the `protected` or `private` keywords in this book).

In addition, you must specify the return type of the value the method returns (you can use the keyword `void` if the method does not return a value). And you must give a comma-separated argument list for the method, giving the type of each argument in parentheses following the method's name (if the method takes no arguments, leave the parentheses empty). All of this gives us the following skeleton for the definition of `adder`:

```
public class ch10_13
{
    public static void main(String[] args)
    {
        int value1 = Integer.parseInt(args[0]);
        int value2 = Integer.parseInt(args[1]);

        System.out.println(value1 + " + " + value1 +
        " = " + adder(value1, value2));
    }

    public static int adder(int int1, int int2)
    {
        .
        .
        .
    }
}
```

In the body of the method, I can refer to the two values passed using the names I've given them in the argument list, `int1` and `int2`. I add those values and return the result using the `return` statement:

Listing ch10_13.java

```java
public class ch10_13
{
    public static void main(String[] args)
    {
        int value1 = Integer.parseInt(args[0]);
        int value2 = Integer.parseInt(args[1]);

        System.out.println(value1 + " + " + value1 +
        " = " + adder(value1, value2));
    }

    public static int adder(int int1, int int2)
    {
        return int1 + int2;
    }
}
```

Now the user can enter values to add on the command line, and the application will handle them without a problem:

```
%java ch10_13 180 120
180 + 180 = 300
```

Using the *return* Statement

You can use the `return` statement even in methods from which you don't return any value if you want to terminate execution and return from the method. Just use the `return` statement alone, without specifying any values to return.

Creating Java Classes

We've already seen how to create classes in a rudimentary way: You need to create a class to do anything at all, as when we created the main class for the applications we've built:

```java
public class ch10_01
{
    public static void main(String[] args)
    {
        System.out.println("Welcome to Java");
    }
}
```

In preparation for the next chapter, let's take a look at a more advanced example. In this case, I'll create a new class named `AppFrame` based on the Java `Frame` class. This class is what you use to create frame windows (a frame window has a frame including a border and title bar) in Java.

Here's what it will look like in the `main` method. I'll create a new object named `f` of the `AppFrame` class, passing the text we want to appear in that window to that class's constructor:

```
public class ch10_14
{
    public static void main(String argv[]) {

        AppFrame f = new AppFrame("Creating windowed Java applications...");
            .
            .
            .
    }
}
```

Because the `AppFrame` class is built on the Java `Frame` class, I can use the `Frame` class's `setSize` method to give this new window a size of 400×200 pixels. I can use the `show` method to display it onscreen:

```
public class ch10_14
{
    public static void main(String argv[]) {

        AppFrame f = new AppFrame("Creating windowed Java applications...");

        f.setSize(400, 200);

        f.show();
    }
}
```

Creating New Classes

The `AppFrame` class is based on the Java `Frame` class, which means that `AppFrame` has all the built-in `Frame` class's methods. You can find those methods in Table 10-2.

Table 10-2	**Methods**	**Does This**
Methods of the *Frame* Class	`void addNotify()`	Allows this frame to be displayed by connecting it to a native screen resource
	`protected void finalize()`	Called when the frame is about to be disposed of
	`int getCursorType()`	Replaced by `Component.getCursor()`
	`int getExtendedState()`	Gets the state of this frame
	`static Frame[] getFrames()`	Returns an array containing all frames created by the application
	`Image getIconImage()`	Returns the image to be displayed in the minimized icon
	`Rectangle getMaximizedBounds()`	Gets maximized bounds for this frame
	`MenuBar getMenuBar()`	Returns the menu bar
	`int getState()`	Returns the current state of the frame
	`String getTitle()`	Returns the frame's title
	`boolean isResizable()`	Sets whether this frame is resizable by the user
	`boolean isUndecorated()`	Indicates whether this frame is undecorated
	`protected String paramString()`	Returns the parameter string of this frame
	`void remove(MenuComponent m)`	Removes the given menu bar from this frame
	`void removeNotify()`	Makes this frame undisplayable
	`void setCursor(int cursorType)`	Replaced by `Component.setCursor(Cursor)`
	`void setExtendedState(int state)`	Sets the state of this frame

Methods	Does This
void setIconImage(Image image)	Sets the image to display in the minimized icon for this frame
void setMaximizedBounds (Rectangle bounds)	Sets maximized bounds for this frame
void setMenuBar(MenuBar mb)	Sets the menu bar for this frame to the specified menu bar
void setResizable (boolean resizable)	Sets whether this frame is resizable by the user
void setState(int state)	Sets the state of this frame
void setTitle(String title)	Sets the title for this frame to the given string
void setUndecorated (boolean undecorated)	Disables or enables decorations for this frame

You can create your own classes with the class statement in Java, as we've seen. The AppFrame class is built on the Frame class, which in object-oriented terms means that AppFrame *inherits* the Frame class. To indicate that you want one class to be based on another, you use the extends keyword like this (note that I'm not using an access specifier when defining AppFrame, which means this class will use the default access specifier, which is private):

```
import java.awt.*;

public class ch10_14
{
    public static void main(String argv[]) {

        AppFrame f = new AppFrame("Creating windowed Java applications...");

        f.setSize(400, 200);

        f.addWindowListener(new WindowAdapter() {public void
            windowClosing(WindowEvent e) {System.exit(0);}});

        f.show();
    }
}

class AppFrame extends Frame
{
    .
    .
    .
}
```

Note also that the Java `Frame` class is part of the Java Abstract Windowing Toolkit (AWT) package. That means that I must import this package with the statement `import java.awt.*;`.

Creating a Constructor

This new class needs a constructor because I want to pass the text that the window should display to that constructor. You create a constructor simply by creating a method in a class that has the same name as the class. In this case, that's `AppFrame` (constructors do not specify any return value):

```
import java.awt.*;
import java.awt.event.*;

public class ch10_14
{
    public static void main(String argv[]) {

        AppFrame f = new AppFrame("Creating windowed Java applications...");

        f.setSize(400, 200);

        f.addWindowListener(new WindowAdapter() {public void
            windowClosing(WindowEvent e) {System.exit(0);}});

        f.show();
    }
}

class AppFrame extends Frame
{
    String displayText;

    public AppFrame(String text)
    {
        .
        .
        .
    }
}
```

AppFrame

You might note that the methods I'm adding to the `AppFrame` class are not declared `static`. That's because these methods will be used only as part of an object, not as class methods. In particular, I create an object of the `AppFrame` class named `f` in the `main` method and then use the methods of that object.

I'll store the text passed to the constructor in a string named `displayText`, this way:

```
import java.awt.*;
import java.awt.event.*;

public class ch10_14
{
    public static void main(String argv[]) {

        AppFrame f = new AppFrame("Creating windowed Java applications...");

        f.setSize(400, 200);

        f.addWindowListener(new WindowAdapter() {public void
            windowClosing(WindowEvent e) {System.exit(0);}});

        f.show();
    }
}

class AppFrame extends Frame
{
    String displayText;

    public AppFrame(String text)
    {
        displayText = text;
    }
}
```

Using Graphics Objects

The next step is to display the text in the window itself. The `Frame` class has a method named `paint` that is automatically called whenever the window needs to be drawn on the screen. This method is passed an object of the Java `Graphics` class, which I will call g:

```
import java.awt.*;
import java.awt.event.*;

public class ch10_14
{
    public static void main(String argv[]) {

        AppFrame f = new AppFrame("Creating windowed Java applications...");
```

```
        f.setSize(400, 200);

        f.addWindowListener(new WindowAdapter() {public void
            windowClosing(WindowEvent e) {System.exit(0);}});

        f.show();
    }
}

class AppFrame extends Frame
{
    String displayText;

    public AppFrame(String text)
    {
        displayText = text;
    }

    public void paint(Graphics g)
    {
        .
        .
        .
    }
}
```

You can use the `Graphics` object's methods to draw in a window, and you'll find a selection of those methods in Table 10-3. With the methods declared with the `abstract` keyword, you must base your own class on the `Graphics` class before using those methods (we won't use abstract methods in this book).

Table 10-3	Method	Does This
Methods of the *Graphics* Class	abstract void clearRect (int x, int y, int width, int height)	Clears a rectangle (fills it with the background color)
	abstract void clipRect (int x, int y, int width, int height)	Clips a rectangle
	abstract void copyArea (int x, int y, int width, int height, int dx, int dy)	Copies an area of size dx and dy
	abstract Graphics create()	Creates a new Graphics object and makes it a copy of the current one

Method	Does This

`Graphics create`
`(int x, int y, int width,`
`int height)`
	Creates a new `Graphics` object, with a new translation and clip area

`abstract void dispose()`	Disposes of a graphics context

`void draw3DRect`
`(int x, int y, int width,`
`int height, boolean raised)`
	Displays a 3D rectangle

`abstract void drawArc`
`(int x, int y, int width,`
`int height, int startAngle,`
`int arcAngle)`
	Draws a circular or elliptical arc

`void drawBytes`
`(byte[] data, int offset,`
`int length, int x, int y)`
	Draws the text stored in the byte array

`void drawChars`
`(char[] data, int offset,`
`int length, int x, int y)`
	Draws the text stored in the character array

`abstract boolean drawImage`
`(Image img, int x, int y,`
`Color bgcolor, ImageObserver`
`observer)`
	Draws as much of the specified image as possible

`abstract boolean drawImage`
`(Image img, int x, int y,`
`ImageObserver observer)`
	Draws as much of the given image as possible

`abstract boolean drawImage`
`(Image img, int x, int y,`
`int width, int height,`
`Color bgcolor, ImageObserver`
`observer)`
	Draws as much of the image as can fit inside the rectangle

`abstract boolean drawImage`
`(Image img, int x, int y,`
`int width, int height,`
`ImageObserver observer)`
	Draws as much of the given image as has been scaled to fit inside the rectangle

`abstract boolean drawImage`
`(Image img, int dx1, int`
`dy1,int dx2, int dy2, int`
`sx1,int sy1, int sx2, int`
`sy2, Color bgcolor,`
`ImageObserver observer)`
	Draws as much of the image as possible, scaling it to fit inside the given area

continues

Method	Does This
`abstract boolean drawImage` `(Image img, int dx1,` `int dy1, int dx2, int dy2,` `int sx1, int sy1, int sx2,` `int sy2, ImageObserver` `observer)`	Draws as much of the area of the image as possible, scaling it to fit inside the given area of the destination surface
`abstract void drawLine` `(int x1, int y1, int x2,` `int y2)`	Draws a line, in the current default color between the points (x1, y1) and (x2, y2)
`abstract void drawOval` `(int x, int y, int width,` `int height)`	Draws the outline of an oval
`abstract void drawPolygon` `(int[] xPoints, int[] yPoints,` `int nPoints)`	Draws a closed polygon with vertices defined by the x and y coordinate arrays
`void drawPolygon(Polygon p)`	Draws a polygon defined by the given `Polygon` object
`abstract void drawPolyline` `(int[] xPoints, int[] yPoints,` `int nPoints)`	Draws a sequence of connected lines
`void drawRect` `(int x, int y, int width,` `int height)`	Draws the specified rectangle
`abstract void drawRoundRect` `(int x, int y, int width,` `int height, int arcWidth,` `int arcHeight)`	Draws a round-cornered rectangle
`abstract void drawString` `(AttributedCharacterIterator` `iterator, int x, int y)`	Draws the text given by the iterator
`abstract void drawString` `(String str, int x, int y)`	Draws the text given by the string
`void fill3DRect` `(int x, int y, int width,` `int height, boolean raised)`	Paints a filled 3D rectangle
`abstract void fillArc` `(int x, int y, int width,` `int height, int startAngle,` `int arcAngle)`	Fills a circular or elliptical arc

Method	Does This

`abstract void fillOval`
`(int x, int y, int width,`
`int height)`
	Fills an oval bounded by the given rectangle

`abstract void fillPolygon`
`(int[] xPoints, int[] yPoints,`
`int nPoints)`
	Fills a closed polygon defined by arrays of x and y coordinates

`void fillPolygon(Polygon p)`	Fills the polygon defined by the `Polygon` object with the current color

`abstract void fillRect`
`(int x, int y, int width,`
`int height)`
	Fills the specified rectangle

`abstract void fillRoundRect`
`(int x, int y, int width,`
`int height, int arcWidth,`
`int arcHeight)`
	Fills a rounded corner rectangle

`void finalize()`	Called when the object is about to be disposed of
`abstract Shape getClip()`	Returns the clipping area
`abstract Rectangle` `getClipBounds()`	Returns the bounding rectangle of the clipping area
`Rectangle getClipBounds` `(Rectangle r)`	Returns the bounding rectangle of the clipping area
`Rectangle getClipRect()`	Replaced by `getClipBounds()`
`abstract Color getColor()`	Returns this graphics context's current foreground color
`abstract Font getFont()`	Returns the current font
`FontMetrics getFontMetrics()`	Returns the font metrics of the font
`abstract FontMetrics` `getFontMetrics(Font f)`	Returns the font metrics for the given font

`boolean hitClip`
`(int x, int y, int width,`
`int height)`
	True if the given area intersects the rectangle of the clipping area

continues

Method	Does This
`abstract void setClip` `(int x, int y, int width,` `int height)`	Sets the current clip to the given rectangle
`abstract void setClip` `(Shape clip)`	Sets the clipping area to a shape
`abstract void setColor(Color c)`	Sets the graphics context's foreground color
`abstract void setFont` `(Font font)`	Sets the graphics context's font.
`abstract void setPaintMode()`	Sets the paint mode
`abstract void setXORMode` `(Color c1)`	Sets the paint mode to use XOR painting
`String toString()`	Returns a `String` object that represents the `Graphics` object
`abstract void translate` `(int x, int y)`	Translates the origin of the graphics context to a new origin

In this case, I'll use the `drawString` method to display the text in the window, like this:

```java
import java.awt.*;
import java.awt.event.*;

public class ch10_14
{
    public static void main(String argv[]) {

        AppFrame f = new AppFrame("Creating windowed Java
applications...");

        f.setSize(400, 200);

        f.addWindowListener(new WindowAdapter() {public void
            windowClosing(WindowEvent e) {System.exit(0);}});

        f.show();
    }
}

class AppFrame extends Frame
{
```

```
    String displayText;

    public AppFrame(String text)
    {
        displayText = text;
    }

    public void paint(Graphics g)
    {
        g.drawString(displayText, 60, 100);
    }
}
```

Closing Application Windows

There's one more refinement to make. When the user clicks the Close button at the upper right in the window we're creating, we'll need to handle the window-closing event that occurs. To handle events in Java, you use an *event listener*. In this case, I'll use an event listener to catch the window-closing event and, when that event occurs, end the program using the call System.exit(0);. This call ends the program and passes a value of 0 (which indicates normal termination) as an exit code to the operating system.

Handling Java events in detail is beyond the scope of this book, but here's how it works here. In this case, I'll add a window listener to the AppFrame object that will "listen" for window-closing events and, when one occurs, end the program. Note that to handle events with AWT objects, you must import the classes in the java.awt.event package:

Listing ch10_14.java

```
import java.awt.*;
import java.awt.event.*;

public class ch10_14
{
    public static void main(String argv[]) {

        AppFrame f = new AppFrame("Creating windowed Java applications...");

        f.setSize(400, 200);

        f.addWindowListener(new WindowAdapter() {public void
            windowClosing(WindowEvent e) {System.exit(0);}});
```

continues

Listing ch10_14.java   Continued

```java
        f.show();
    }
}

class AppFrame extends Frame
{
    String displayText;

    public AppFrame(String text)
    {
        displayText = text;
    }

    public void paint(Graphics g)
    {
        g.drawString(displayText, 60, 100);
    }
}
```

You can see the results of this code in Figure 10-2. When you start this application, the window appears, displaying the text as shown.

Figure 10-2
Running a
windowed
Java
application.

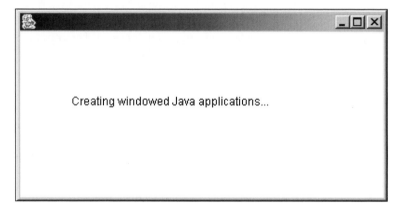

Now that we're in the Java business, it's time to put all this technology to work with XML. I'll do that in the next chapter.

CHAPTER 11

Java and the XML DOM

This chapter is all about using XML with Java to create standalone programs. I'll even create a few browsers in this chapter. As of Java 1.4, the current version at this time, Java includes a great deal of support for working with XML; I'll use Java 1.4 in this and the next chapter.

If you're using a version of Java before 1.4, you should install Java 1.4 to run the examples in this chapter and the next one. Alternatively, you can download and install the Java XML pack; currently, the download page is `http://java.sun.com/xml/downloads/javaxmlpack.html` (if that page doesn't exist when you read this, go to `http://java.sun.com/xml`). After downloading and unzipping, you must include the files jaxp-api.jar and xalan.jar in the CLASSPATH environment variable to run the Java XML examples coming up in this book (a JAR file holds a Java Archive, full of compressed .class files). The CLASSPATH variable tells Java where to search for .class files; when it is set it to the names of these JAR files, Java can find the .class files it needs.

Setting the CLASSPATH variable is just like setting the PATH environment variable you saw in the previous chapter. For example, if jaxp-api.jar and xalan.jar are in the current directory, you can set the CLASSPATH variable this way in Windows:

```
C:\>SET CLASSPATH=jaxp-api.jar;xalan.jar
```

If jaxp-api.jar and xalan.jar are in another directory, such as c:\javaxmlpack, you must include that path when setting the CLASSPATH variable:

```
C:\>SET CLASSPATH=c:\javaxmlpack\jaxp-api.jar;c:\javaxmlpack\xalan.jar
```

You can also set the CLASSPATH variable permanently, just as you could with the PATH variable in the previous chapter—see http://java.sun.com/j2se/ 1.4.1/install.html for instructions on how to set environment variables such as CLASSPATH permanently.

There's a shortcut if you can't get the CLASSPATH variable working: You can use the -classpath "switch" when working with the javac and java tools. For example, here's how I compile and run a program named browser.java using that switch to specify the classpath I want to use:

```
%javac -classpath c:\javaxmlpack\jaxp-api.jar;c:\javaxmlpack\
xalan.jar browser.java
```

You don't need to do any of this if you have Java 1.4 installed—you won't need the Java XML Pack until Chapter 18, "SOAP and RDF," where we discuss the XML SOAP. We're ready to start working with code now. I'll start by writing an example that parses an XML document.

Creating a Parser

This first Java example will get us started by parsing an XML document and displaying the number of a certain element in it. In this chapter, I'm taking a look at using the XML DOM with Java, and I'll use the Java DocumentBuilder class, which creates a W3C DOM tree as its output. Here's the document we'll parse:

Listing ch11_01.xml

```
<?xml version = "1.0" standalone="yes"?>
<DOCUMENT>
    <CUSTOMER>
        <NAME>
            <LAST_NAME>Smith</LAST_NAME>
            <FIRST_NAME>Sam</FIRST_NAME>
        </NAME>
        <DATE>October 15, 2003</DATE>
        <ORDERS>
            <ITEM>
                <PRODUCT>Tomatoes</PRODUCT>
                <NUMBER>8</NUMBER>
                <PRICE>$1.25</PRICE>
```

```
            </ITEM>
            <ITEM>
                <PRODUCT>Oranges</PRODUCT>
                <NUMBER>24</NUMBER>
                <PRICE>$4.98</PRICE>
            </ITEM>
        </ORDERS>
    </CUSTOMER>
    <CUSTOMER>
        <NAME>
            <LAST_NAME>Jones</LAST_NAME>
            <FIRST_NAME>Polly</FIRST_NAME>
        </NAME>
        <DATE>October 20, 2003</DATE>
        <ORDERS>
            <ITEM>
                <PRODUCT>Bread</PRODUCT>
                <NUMBER>12</NUMBER>
                <PRICE>$14.95</PRICE>
            </ITEM>
            <ITEM>
                <PRODUCT>Apples</PRODUCT>
                <NUMBER>6</NUMBER>
                <PRICE>$1.50</PRICE>
            </ITEM>
        </ORDERS>
    </CUSTOMER>
    <CUSTOMER>
        <NAME>
            <LAST_NAME>Weber</LAST_NAME>
            <FIRST_NAME>Bill</FIRST_NAME>
        </NAME>
        <DATE>October 25, 2003</DATE>
        <ORDERS>
            <ITEM>
                <PRODUCT>Asparagus</PRODUCT>
                <NUMBER>12</NUMBER>
                <PRICE>$2.95</PRICE>
            </ITEM>
            <ITEM>
                <PRODUCT>Lettuce</PRODUCT>
                <NUMBER>6</NUMBER>
                <PRICE>$11.50</PRICE>
            </ITEM>
        </ORDERS>
    </CUSTOMER>
</DOCUMENT>
```

In this first example, the code will scan ch11_01.xml and report how many
<CUSTOMER> elements the document has.

To start this program, I'll import the Java classes we'll need (which support the W3C DOM interfaces, such as Node and Element) and the XML parser classes we'll use:

```
import javax.xml.parsers.*;
import org.w3c.dom.*;
   .
   .
   .
```

I'll call this first program ch11_02.java, so the public class in that file is ch11_02:

```
import javax.xml.parsers.*;
import org.w3c.dom.*;

public class ch11_02
{
    public static void main(String[] args)
    {
       .
       .
       .
}
```

To parse the XML document, you need a DocumentBuilderFactory object, which you use to create an object of the DocumentBuilder class (it's called a document builder *factory* because you can use it to create parsers using Java classes from different parser vendors, not just the default Java XML parser that we'll use here):

```
import javax.xml.parsers.*;
import org.w3c.dom.*;

public class ch11_02
{
    public static void main(String[] args)
    {
        try {

            DocumentBuilderFactory dbf =
                DocumentBuilderFactory.newInstance();

            DocumentBuilder db = null;
            try {
                db = dbf.newDocumentBuilder();
            }
```

```
catch (ParserConfigurationException pce) {}
        .
        .
        .
    }
}
```

You can find the constructors for the DocumentBuilderFactory class in Table 11-1 and the methods of the DocumentBuilder class in Table 11-2.

	Method	Does This
Table 11-1 Methods of the *javax.xml.parsers.* *DocumentBuilder* *Factory* Class	`protected` `DocumentBuilderFactory()`	The default constructor

	`abstract`
	`Object getAttribute`
	`(String name)`
		Returns specific attribute values

	`boolean isCoalescing()`	Is true if the factory is configured to produce parsers that convert CDATA nodes to text nodes
	`boolean` `isExpandEntityReferences()`	Is true if the factory is configured to produce parsers that expand XML entity reference nodes
	`boolean isIgnoringComments()`	Is true if the factory will produce parsers that ignore comments
	`boolean isIgnoring` `ElementContentWhitespace()`	Is true if the factory will produce parsers that ignore ignorable whitespace (such as that used to indent elements) in element content
	`boolean isNamespaceAware()`	Is true if the factory will produce parsers that can use XML namespaces
	`boolean isValidating()`	Is true if the factory will produce parsers that validate the XML content during parsing operations
	`abstract   DocumentBuilder` `newDocumentBuilder()`	Creates a new DocumentBuilder object
	`static DocumentBuilder` `FactorynewInstance()`	Returns a new DocumentBuilderFactory object

continues

Method	Does This
abstract void setAttribute (String name, Object value)	Sets specific attributes
void setCoalescing (boolean coalescing)	Requires the parser produced to convert CDATA nodes to text nodes
void setExpandEntityReferences (boolean expandEntityRef)	Requires the parser produced to expand XML entity reference nodes
void setIgnoringComments (boolean ignoreComments)	Requires the parser produced to ignore comments
void setIgnoringElementContent Whitespace(boolean whitespace)	Requires the parsers created to eliminate ignorable whitespace
void setNamespaceAware (boolean awareness)	Requires the parser produced to provide support for XML namespaces
void setValidating (boolean validating)	Requires the parser produced to validate documents as they are parsed

Table 11-2
Methods
of the
javax.xml.parsers.
DocumentBuilder
Class

Method	Does This
protected DocumentBuilder()	The default constructor
abstract DOMImplementation getDOMImplementation()	Returns a DOMImplementation object
abstract boolean isNamespaceAware()	Is true if this parser is configured to understand namespaces
abstract boolean isValidating()	Is true if this parser is configured to validate XML documents
abstract Document newDocument() tree	Returns a new instance of a DOM Document object to build a DOM
Document parse(File f)	Parses the content of the file as an XML document and returns a new DOM Document object
abstract Document parse (InputSource is)	Parses the content of the specified source as an XML document and returns a new DOM Document object

Method	Does This
`Document parse(InputStream is)`	Parses the content of the specified `InputStream` as an XML document and returns a new DOM `Document` object
`Document parse(InputStream is, String systemId)`	Parses the content of the specified `InputStream` as an XML document and returns a new DOM `Document` object
`Document parse(String uri)`	Parses the content of the specified URI as an XML document and returns a new DOM `Document` object
`abstract void setEntityResolver (EntityResolver er)`	Specifies the `EntityResolver` object to be used to resolve entities
`abstract  void setErrorHandler (ErrorHandler eh)`	Specifies the ErrorHandler to be used to report errors

To actually parse the XML document, you use the parse method of the DocumentBuilder object. I'll let the user specify the name of the document to parse on the command line by parsing args[0]. Note that you don't need to pass the name of a local file to the parse method—you can pass the URL of a document on the Internet, and the parse method will retrieve that document.

Here's how you can use the parse method:

```
import javax.xml.parsers.*;
import org.w3c.dom.*;

public class ch11_02
{
    public static void main(String[] args)
    {

        try {

            DocumentBuilderFactory dbf =
                DocumentBuilderFactory.newInstance();

            DocumentBuilder db = null;
            try {
                db = dbf.newDocumentBuilder();
            }
            catch (ParserConfigurationException pce) {}
```

```
            Document doc = null;
            doc = db.parse(args[0]);
    .
    .
    .
    } catch (Exception e) {
        e.printStackTrace(System.err);
    }
  }
}
```

If the document is successfully parsed, this code creates a Document object based on the W3C DOM. The Document interface is part of the W3C DOM, and you can find the methods of this interface in Table 11-3.

	Method	Does This
Table 11-3 Methods of the *org.w3c.dom. Document* Interface	Attr createAttribute(String name)	Creates an Attr object of the specified name
	Attr createAttributeNS (String namespaceURI, String qualifiedName)	Creates an attribute of the specified name and name space
	CDATASection createCDATASection (String data)	Creates a CDATASection node whose value is the specified string
	Comment createComment(String data)	Creates a Comment node using the specified string
	DocumentFragment createDocumentFragment()	Creates an empty DocumentFragment object
	Element createElement (String tagName)	Creates an element of the type specified
	Element createElementNS (String namespaceURI, String qualifiedName)	Creates an element of the specified qualified name and namespace uniform resource identifier (URI)
	EntityReference createEntityReference(String name)	Creates an EntityReference object
	ProcessingInstruction createProcessingInstruction (String target, String data)	Creates a ProcessingInstruction node

Method	Does This
`Text createTextNode(String data)`	Creates a text node using the specified string
`DocumentType getDoctype()`	Returns the document type definition (DTD) for this document
`Element getDocumentElement()`	Provides direct access to the `Document` element
`Element getElementById (String elementId)`	Returns the element whose ID is specified
`NodeList getElementsByTagName (String tagname)`	Returns all the elements with a specified tag name
`NodeList getElementsByTagNameNS (String namespaceURI, String localName)`	Returns all the elements with a specified name and name space
`DOMImplementation getImplementation()`	Gets the `DOMImplementation` object that handles this document
`Node importNode(Node importedNode, boolean deep)`	Imports a node from another document to this document

The `Document` interface is based on the `Node` interface, which supports the W3C `Node` object. Nodes represent a single node in the document tree (as you recall, everything in the document tree, including text and comments, is treated as nodes). The `Node` interface has many methods that you can use to work with nodes. For example, you can use methods such as `getNodeName` and `getNodeValue` to get information about the node, and we'll use this kind of information a great deal in this chapter. This interface also has data members, called *fields*, which hold constant values corresponding to various node types; we'll see them in this chapter as well. You'll find the `Node` interface fields in Table 11-4 and the methods of this interface in Table 11-5. As you see in Table 11-4, the `Node` interface contains all the standard W3C DOM methods for navigating in a document that we've already used with JavaScript in Chapter 7, "Handling XML Documents with JavaScript." These include `getNextSibling`, `getPreviousSibling`, `getFirstChild`, `getLastChild`, and `getParent`. We'll put those methods to work here as well.

Table 11-4	Field Summary
Node Interface Fields	static short ATTRIBUTE_NODE
	static short CDATA_SECTION_NODE
	static short COMMENT_NODE
	static short DOCUMENT_FRAGMENT_NODE
	static short DOCUMENT_NODE
	static short DOCUMENT_TYPE_NODE
	static short ELEMENT_NODE
	static short ENTITY_NODE
	static short ENTITY_REFERENCE_NODE
	static short NOTATION_NODE
	static short PROCESSING_INSTRUCTION_NODE
	static short TEXT_NODE

Table 11-5	Method	Does This
Methods of the *org.w3c.dom.Node* Interface	Node appendChild(Node newChild)	Adds the specified node to the end of the list of children of the current node
	Node cloneNode(boolean deep)	Returns a duplicate of this node
	NamedNodeMap getAttributes()	Returns the attributes of this node if it is an element
	NodeList getChildNodes()	Returns all the children of this node
	Node getFirstChild()	Returns the first child of this node
	Node getLastChild()	Returns the last child of this node
	String getLocalName()	Returns the local part of the full name of this node

Method	Does This
`String getNamespaceURI()`	Returns the namespace URI of this node
`Node getNextSibling()`	Returns the node following this node
`String getNodeName()`	Returns the name of this node
`short getNodeType()`	Returns the type of the node's object
`String getNodeValue()`	Returns the value of this node
`Document getOwnerDocument()`	Returns the `Document` object for this node
`Node getParentNode()`	Returns the parent of this node
`String getPrefix()`	Returns the namespace prefix of this node
`Node getPreviousSibling()`	Returns the node preceding this node
`boolean hasAttributes()`	Is true if this node has any attributes
`boolean hasChildNodes()`	Is true if this node has any children
`Node insertBefore` `(Node newChild, Node refChild)`	Inserts the new node before the existing reference child node
`boolean isSupported` `(String feature, String version)`	Is true if the specific feature is implemented
`void normalize()`	Puts all text nodes into XML "normal" form
`Node removeChild(Node oldChild)`	Removes the child node and returns it
`Node replaceChild` `(Node newChild, Node oldChild)`	Replaces the child node in the list of children and returns the old child node
`void setNodeValue(String nodeValue)`	Sets the value of a node
`void setPrefix(String prefix)`	Sets the namespace prefix of this node

At this point, we've gotten access to the root node of the document in Java. Our goal here is to check how many <CUSTOMER> elements the document has. I'll use the getElementsByTagName method to get a Java NodeList object containing a list of all <CUSTOMER> elements:

```java
import javax.xml.parsers.*;
import org.w3c.dom.*;

public class ch11_02
{
    public static void main(String[] args)
    {

        try {

            DocumentBuilderFactory dbf =
                DocumentBuilderFactory.newInstance();

            DocumentBuilder db = null;
            try {
                db = dbf.newDocumentBuilder();
            }
            catch (ParserConfigurationException pce) {}

            Document doc = null;
            doc = db.parse(args[0]);

            NodeList nodelist = doc.getElementsByTagName("CUSTOMER");
                .
                .
                .
        } catch (Exception e) {
            e.printStackTrace(System.err);
        }
    }
}
```

The NodeList interface supports an ordered collection of nodes. You can access nodes in such a collection by index, and we'll do that in this chapter. You can find the methods of the NodeList interface in Table 11-6.

Table 11-6	Method	Summary
NodeList Interface Methods	int getLength()	Gets the number of nodes in this list
	Node item(int index)	Gets the item at index in the collection

If you take a look at Table 11-6, you'll see that the NodeList interface supports a getLength method that returns the number of nodes in the list. This means that we can find how many <CUSTOMER> elements there are in the document like this:

Listing ch11_02.java

```java
import javax.xml.parsers.*;
import org.w3c.dom.*;

public class ch11_02
{
    public static void main(String[] args)
    {

        try {

            DocumentBuilderFactory dbf =
                DocumentBuilderFactory.newInstance();

            DocumentBuilder db = null;
            try {
                db = dbf.newDocumentBuilder();
            }
            catch (ParserConfigurationException pce) {}

            Document doc = null;
            doc = db.parse(args[0]);

            NodeList nodelist = doc.getElementsByTagName("CUSTOMER");
            System.out.println(args[0] + " has " + nodelist.getLength() + "
            <CUSTOMER> elements.");

        } catch (Exception e) {
            e.printStackTrace(System.err);
        }
    }
}
```

And that's it. You can see the results of this code here, indicating that ch11_01.xml has three <CUSTOMER> elements, which is correct:

```
%java ch11_02 ch11_01.xml
ch11_01.xml has 3 <CUSTOMER> elements.
```

That's all it takes to get started with the Java XML parsers.

Displaying an Entire Document

In this next example, I'm going to write a program that will parse and display an entire document, indenting each element, processing instruction, and so on, as well as displaying attributes and their values. For example, if you pass ch11_01.xml to this program, which I'll call ch11_03.java, that program will display the whole document properly indented.

I start by letting the user specify what document to parse and parsing that document as before. To actually parse the document, I'll call a new method, displayDocument, from the main method:

```
public static void main(String args[])
{
    displayDocument(args[0]);
    .
    .
    .
}
```

In the displayDocument method, I'll parse the document and get an object corresponding to that document:

```
import javax.xml.parsers.*;
import org.w3c.dom.*;

public class ch11_03
{
    static String displayStrings[] = new String[1000];
    static int numberDisplayLines = 0;

    public static void displayDocument(String uri)
    {
        try {

            DocumentBuilderFactory dbf =
                DocumentBuilderFactory.newInstance();

            DocumentBuilder db = null;
            try {
                db = dbf.newDocumentBuilder();
            }
            catch (ParserConfigurationException pce) {}

            Document document = null;
            document = db.parse(uri);
            .
            .
            .
```

```
        } catch (Exception e) {
            e.printStackTrace(System.err);
        }
```

.
.
.

The actual method that will parse the document, display, will be recursive (we saw recursion when working with JavaScript). I'll pass the document to parse to that method, as well as the current indentation string (which will grow by four spaces for every successive level of recursion):

```
import javax.xml.parsers.*;
import org.w3c.dom.*;

public class ch11_03
{
    static String displayStrings[] = new String[1000];
    static int numberDisplayLines = 0;

    public static void displayDocument(String uri)
    {
        try {

            DocumentBuilderFactory dbf =
                DocumentBuilderFactory.newInstance();

            DocumentBuilder db = null;
            try {
                db = dbf.newDocumentBuilder();
            }
            catch (ParserConfigurationException pce) {}

            Document document = null;
            document = db.parse(uri);

            display(document, "");

        } catch (Exception e) {
            e.printStackTrace(System.err);
        }
```

.
.
.

In the `display` method, I'll check to see whether the node passed to us is really a node and, if not, return. The next job is to display the node. How we do that depends on the type of node we're working with. To get the type of node, you can use the node's `getNodeType` method. I'll set up a long `switch` statement to handle the different types:

```
public static void display(Node node, String indent)
{
    if (node == null) {
        return;
    }

    int type = node.getNodeType();

    switch (type) {
    .
    .
    .
```

To handle output from this program, I'll create an array of strings, `displayStrings`, placing each line of the output into one of those strings. I'll also store our current location in that array in an integer named `numberDisplayLines`:

```
public class ch11_03
{
    static String displayStrings[] = new String[1000];
    static int numberDisplayLines = 0;
    .
    .
    .
```

I'll start handling various types of nodes in this switch statement now.

Handling Document Nodes

At the beginning of the document is the XML declaration; the type of this node matches the constant `Node.DOCUMENT_NODE` defined in the `Node` interface (see Table 11-6). This declaration takes up one line of output, so I'll start the first line of output with the current indent string, followed by a default XML declaration.

The next step is to get the document element of the document we're pars-ing (the root element), and you do that with the `getDocumentElement` method. The root element contains all other elements, so I pass that element to the `display` method, which will display all those elements:

```java
public static void display(Node node, String indent)
{
    if (node == null) {
        return;
    }

    int type = node.getNodeType();

    switch (type) {
        case Node.DOCUMENT_NODE: {
            displayStrings[numberDisplayLines] = indent;
            displayStrings[numberDisplayLines] += "<?xml version=\"1.0\"
            ➥encoding=\""+
                "UTF-8" + "\"?>";
            numberDisplayLines++;
            display(((Document)node).getDocumentElement(), "");
            break;
        }
        .
        .
        .
```

Handling Element Nodes

To handle an element node, we should display the name of the element as well as any attributes the element has. I start by checking whether the current node type is `Node.ELEMENT_NODE`; if so, I place the current indent string into a dis-play string, followed by a < and the element's name, which I can get with the `getNodeName` method:

```java
switch (type) {
    .
    .
    .

    case Node.ELEMENT_NODE: {
        displayStrings[numberDisplayLines] = indent;
        displayStrings[numberDisplayLines] += "<";
        displayStrings[numberDisplayLines] += node.getNodeName();
        .
        .
        .
```

Handling Attributes

Now we've got to handle the attributes of this element, if it has any. Because the current node is an element node, you can use the method `getAttributes` to get a `NodeList` object that holds all its attributes, which are stored as `Attr` objects. I'll convert the node list to an array of `Attr` objects, `attributes`, like this. Note that I first create the `attributes` array after finding the number of items in the `NodeList` object with the `getLength` method:

```
switch (type) {
    .
    .
    .
    case Node.ELEMENT_NODE: {
        displayStrings[numberDisplayLines] = indent;
        displayStrings[numberDisplayLines] += "<";
        displayStrings[numberDisplayLines] += node.getNodeName();

        int length = (node.getAttributes() != null) ?
        ➥node.getAttributes().getLength() : 0;
        Attr attributes[] = new Attr[length];
        for (int loopIndex = 0; loopIndex < length; loopIndex++) {
            attributes[loopIndex] = (Attr)node.getAttributes().item
            ➥(loopIndex);
        }
        .
        .
        .
```

You can find the methods of the `Attr` interface in Table 11-7.

Table 11-7	Method	Summary
Attr Interface Methods	`java.lang.String getName()`	Gets the name of this attribute
	`Element getOwnerElement()`	Gets the `Element` node this attribute is attached to
	`boolean getSpecified()`	Is `true` if this attribute was explicitly given a value in the original document
	`java.lang.String getValue()`	Gets the value of the attribute as a string
	`void setValue(String value)`	Sets the value of the attribute as a string

Because the `Attr` interface is built on the `Node` interface, you can use either the `getNodeName` and `getNodeValue` methods to get the attribute's name and value, or the `Attr` `getName` and `getValue` methods. I'll use `getNodeName` and `getNodeValue` here. In this case, I'm going to loop over all the attributes in the `attributes` array, adding them to the current display like this: *`AttrName`* = "*`AttrValue`*" (note that I escape the quotation marks around the attribute values as `\"` so that Java doesn't interpret them as the end of the string):

```
switch (type) {
    .
    .
    .
    case Node.ELEMENT_NODE: {
        displayStrings[numberDisplayLines] = indent;
        displayStrings[numberDisplayLines] += "<";
        displayStrings[numberDisplayLines] += node.getNodeName();

       int length = (node.getAttributes() != null) ? node.getAttributes()
       ➥.getLength() : 0;
        Attr attributes[] = new Attr[length];
        for (int loopIndex = 0; loopIndex < length; loopIndex++) {
            attributes[loopIndex] = (Attr)node.getAttributes().item
            ➥(loopIndex);
        }

       for (int loopIndex = 0; loopIndex < attributes.length; loopIndex++){
           Attr attribute = attributes[loopIndex];
           displayStrings[numberDisplayLines] += " ";
           displayStrings[numberDisplayLines] += attribute.getNodeName();
                     displayStrings[numberDisplayLines] += "=\"";
                     displayStrings[numberDisplayLines] +=
                     attribute.getNodeValue();
           displayStrings[numberDisplayLines] += "\"";
       }
       displayStrings[numberDisplayLines] += ">";

       numberDisplayLines++;
       .
       .
       .
```

This element might have child elements, of course, and we've got to handle them as well. I do that by storing all the child nodes in a `NodeList` object with the `getChildNodes` method. If there are any child nodes, I add four spaces to the indent string and loop over those child nodes, calling `display` to display each of them:

```
switch (type) {
    .
    .
    .
    case Node.ELEMENT_NODE: {
        displayStrings[numberDisplayLines] = indent;
        displayStrings[numberDisplayLines] += "<";
        displayStrings[numberDisplayLines] += node.getNodeName();

        int length = (node.getAttributes() != null) ? node.getAttributes().
        ➥getLength() : 0;
        Attr attributes[] = new Attr[length];
        for (int loopIndex = 0; loopIndex < length; loopIndex++) {
            attributes[loopIndex] = (Attr)node.getAttributes().item
            ➥(loopIndex);
        }

        for (int loopIndex = 0; loopIndex < attributes.length; loopIndex++){
            Attr attribute = attributes[loopIndex];
            displayStrings[numberDisplayLines] += " ";
            displayStrings[numberDisplayLines] += attribute.getNodeName();
            displayStrings[numberDisplayLines] += "=\"";
            displayStrings[numberDisplayLines] += attribute.getNodeValue();
            displayStrings[numberDisplayLines] += "\"";
        }
        displayStrings[numberDisplayLines] += ">";

        numberDisplayLines++;

        NodeList childNodes = node.getChildNodes();
        if (childNodes != null) {
            length = childNodes.getLength();
            indent += "    ";
            for (int loopIndex = 0; loopIndex < length; loopIndex++ ) {
                display(childNodes.item(loopIndex), indent);
            }
        }
        break;
    }
    .
    .
    .
```

That's it for handling elements. I'll handle CDATA sections next.

Handling *CDATA* Section Nodes

Handling CDATA sections is particularly easy. All I have to do here is enclose the value of the CDATA section's node inside "<![CDATA[" and "[[>", and that looks like this:

```
case Node.CDATA_SECTION_NODE: {
    displayStrings[numberDisplayLines] = indent;
    displayStrings[numberDisplayLines] += "<![CDATA[";
    displayStrings[numberDisplayLines] += node.getNodeValue();
    displayStrings[numberDisplayLines] += "]]>";
    numberDisplayLines++;
    break;
}
.
.
.
```

Handling Text Nodes

The W3C DOM specifies that the text in elements must be stored in text nodes, and those nodes have the type Node.TEXT_NODE. For these nodes, I'll add the current indent string to the display string and then trim off leading and trailing whitespace from the node's value with the Java String object's trim method:

```
case Node.TEXT_NODE: {
    displayStrings[numberDisplayLines] = indent;
    String newText = node.getNodeValue().trim();
    .
    .
    .
```

XML parsers treat all text as text nodes, including the spaces used for indenting elements in ch11_01.xml. I'll filter out the text nodes corresponding to indentation spacing. If a text node contains only displayable text, on the other hand, I'll add that text to the strings in the displayStrings array:

```
case Node.TEXT_NODE: {
    displayStrings[numberDisplayLines] = indent;
    String newText = node.getNodeValue().trim();
    if(newText.indexOf("\n") < 0 && newText.length() > 0) {
        displayStrings[numberDisplayLines] += newText;
        numberDisplayLines++;
    }
```

```
    break;
}
.
.
.
```

Handling Processing Instruction Nodes

The W3C DOM also lets you handle processing instructions. Here, the node type is `Node.PROCESSING_INSTRUCTION_NODE` and the node value is simply the processing instruction itself. For example, if the processing instruction is `<?xml-stylesheet type="text/css" href="style.css"?>`, the value of the associated processing instruction node is `xml-stylesheet type="text/css" href="style.css"`. That means all we have to do is straddle the value of a processing instruction node with <? and ?>. Here's what the code looks like:

```
case Node.PROCESSING_INSTRUCTION_NODE: {
    displayStrings[numberDisplayLines] = indent;
    displayStrings[numberDisplayLines] += "<?";
    String text = node.getNodeValue();
    if (text != null && text.length() > 0) {
        displayStrings[numberDisplayLines] += text;
    }
    displayStrings[numberDisplayLines] += "?>";
    numberDisplayLines++;
    break;
}
}
.
.
.
```

And that finishes the `switch` statement that handles the various types of nodes. There's only one more point to cover.

Closing Element Tags

Displaying element nodes takes a little more thought than displaying other types of nodes because, in addition to displaying <, the name of the element, and >, you also have to display a closing tag, </, the name of the element, and > at the end of the element.

For that reason, I'll place some code after the `switch` statement to add closing tags to elements after all their children have been displayed (note that I'm also subtracting four spaces from the indent string, using the Java String `substr` method so that the closing tag lines up vertically with the opening tag):

```
    if (type == Node.ELEMENT_NODE) {
        displayStrings[numberDisplayLines] = indent.substring(0, indent
        ➥.length() - 4);
        displayStrings[numberDisplayLines] += "</";
        displayStrings[numberDisplayLines] += node.getNodeName();
        displayStrings[numberDisplayLines] += ">";
        numberDisplayLines++;
        indent += "    ";
    }
}
```

And that's it. Here's the entire code, ch11_03.java:

Listing ch11_03.java

```java
import javax.xml.parsers.*;
import org.w3c.dom.*;

public class ch11_03
{
    static String displayStrings[] = new String[1000];
    static int numberDisplayLines = 0;

    public static void displayDocument(String uri)
    {
        try {

            DocumentBuilderFactory dbf =
                DocumentBuilderFactory.newInstance();

            DocumentBuilder db = null;
            try {
                db = dbf.newDocumentBuilder();
            }
            catch (ParserConfigurationException pce) {}

            Document document = null;
            document = db.parse(uri);

            display(document, "");

        } catch (Exception e) {
```

continues

Listing ch11_03.java   Continued

```java
            e.printStackTrace(System.err);
        }

    }

    public static void display(Node node, String indent)
    {
        if (node == null) {
            return;
        }

        int type = node.getNodeType();

        switch (type) {
            case Node.DOCUMENT_NODE: {
                displayStrings[numberDisplayLines] = indent;
                displayStrings[numberDisplayLines] += "<?xml version=
                ➥\"1.0\" encoding=\""+
                  "UTF-8" + "\"?>";
                numberDisplayLines++;
                display(((Document)node).getDocumentElement(), "");
                break;
            }

            case Node.ELEMENT_NODE: {
                displayStrings[numberDisplayLines] = indent;
                displayStrings[numberDisplayLines] += "<";
                displayStrings[numberDisplayLines] += node.getNodeName();

                int length = (node.getAttributes() != null) ?
                node.getAttributes().getLength() : 0;
                Attr attributes[] = new Attr[length];
                for (int loopIndex = 0; loopIndex < length; loopIndex++) {
                    attributes[loopIndex] =
                    ➥(Attr)node.getAttributes().item(loopIndex);
                }

                for (int loopIndex = 0; loopIndex < attributes.length;
                ➥loopIndex++) {
                    Attr attribute = attributes[loopIndex];
                    displayStrings[numberDisplayLines] += " ";
                    displayStrings[numberDisplayLines] +=
                    ➥attribute.getNodeName();
                    displayStrings[numberDisplayLines] += "=\"";
                    displayStrings[numberDisplayLines] +=
                    ➥attribute.getNodeValue();
                    displayStrings[numberDisplayLines] += "\"";
                }
                displayStrings[numberDisplayLines] += ">";
```

```java
                numberDisplayLines++;

                NodeList childNodes = node.getChildNodes();
                if (childNodes != null) {
                    length = childNodes.getLength();
                    indent += "    ";
                    for (int loopIndex = 0; loopIndex < length;
                    ➥loopIndex++ ) {
                        display(childNodes.item(loopIndex), indent);
                    }
                }
                break;
            }

        case Node.CDATA_SECTION_NODE: {
            displayStrings[numberDisplayLines] = indent;
            displayStrings[numberDisplayLines] += "<![CDATA[";
            displayStrings[numberDisplayLines] += node.getNodeValue();
            displayStrings[numberDisplayLines] += "]]>";
            numberDisplayLines++;
            break;
        }

        case Node.TEXT_NODE: {
            displayStrings[numberDisplayLines] = indent;
            String newText = node.getNodeValue().trim();
            if(newText.indexOf("\n") < 0 && newText.length() > 0) {
                displayStrings[numberDisplayLines] += newText;
                numberDisplayLines++;
            }
            break;
        }

        case Node.PROCESSING_INSTRUCTION_NODE: {
            displayStrings[numberDisplayLines] = indent;
            displayStrings[numberDisplayLines] += "<?";
            displayStrings[numberDisplayLines] += node.getNodeName();
            String text = node.getNodeValue();
            if (text != null && text.length() > 0) {
                displayStrings[numberDisplayLines] += text;
            }
            displayStrings[numberDisplayLines] += "?>";
            numberDisplayLines++;
            break;
        }
    }
}

if (type == Node.ELEMENT_NODE) {
    displayStrings[numberDisplayLines] = indent.substring(0,
    ➥indent.length() - 4);
    displayStrings[numberDisplayLines] += "</";
```

continues

Listing ch11_03.java   Continued

```
            displayStrings[numberDisplayLines] += node.getNodeName();
            displayStrings[numberDisplayLines] += ">";
            numberDisplayLines++;
            indent += "      ";
        }
    }

    public static void main(String args[])
    {
        displayDocument(args[0]);

        for(int loopIndex = 0; loopIndex < numberDisplayLines; loopIndex++){
            System.out.println(displayStrings[loopIndex]);
        }
    }
}
```

I'll parse and display ch11_01.xml like this after compiling ch11_03.java. In this case, I'll pipe the output through the more filter to stop it from scrolling off the screen (the more filter is available in MS DOS and certain UNIX ports):

```
%java ch11_03 ch11_01.xml | more
```

You can see the results in Figure 11-1. As you see in this figure, the program works as it should: The document appears with all elements and text intact, indented properly. Congratulations, now you're able to handle most of what you'll find in XML documents using Java! Note that you can use this program as a text-based browser: You can give it the name of any XML document on the Internet—not just local documents—to parse, and it'll fetch that document and parse it.

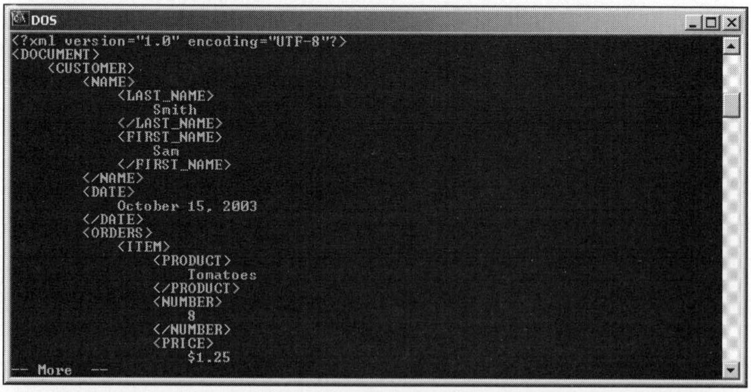

Figure 11-1
Parsing an
XML
document.

Filtering XML Documents

The previous example displayed the entire document, but you can be more selective than that through a process called *filtering*. When you filter a document, you extract only those elements you're interested in.

Here's an example named ch11_04.java. In this case, I'll let the user specify what document to search and what element name to search for like this, which will display all <ITEM> elements in ch11_01.xml:

```
%java ch11_04 ch11_01.xml ITEM
```

I'll start this program by creating a new class, FindElements, to make the programming a little easier. All I have to do is pass the document to search and the element name to search for to the contructor of this new class:

```
import javax.xml.parsers.*;
import org.w3c.dom.*;

public class ch11_04
{
    public static void main(String args[])
    {
        FindElements findElements = new FindElements(args[0], args[1]);
    }
}
```

In the FindElements class constructor, I'll save the name of the element to search for in a string named searchFor and call the displayDocument method as we did in the previous example to display the document. That method will fill the displayStrings array with the output strings, which we print:

```
class FindElements
{
    static String displayStrings[] = new String[1000];
    static int numberDisplayLines = 0;
    static String searchFor;

    public FindElements (String uri, String searchString)
    {
        searchFor = searchString;
        displayDocument(uri);

        for(int loopIndex = 0; loopIndex < numberDisplayLines; loopIndex++){
            System.out.println(displayStrings[loopIndex]);
        }
    }
```

In the `displayDocument` method, we want to display only the elements with the name in the `searchFor` string. To find those elements, I use the `getElementsByTagName` method, which returns a node list of matching elements. I loop over all elements in that list, calling the `display` method to display each element and its children:

```
public static void displayDocument(String uri)
{
    try {

        DocumentBuilderFactory dbf =
        DocumentBuilderFactory.newInstance();

        DocumentBuilder db = null;
        try {
            db = dbf.newDocumentBuilder();
        }
        catch (ParserConfigurationException pce) {}

        Document document = null;
            document = db.parse(uri);

        NodeList nodeList = document.getElementsByTagName(searchFor);

        if (nodeList != null) {
            for (int loopIndex = 0; loopIndex < nodeList.getLength();
            ➥loopIndex++ ) {
                display(nodeList.item(loopIndex), "");
            }
        }

    } catch (Exception e) {
        e.printStackTrace(System.err);
    }
}
```

The `display` method is the same as in the previous example.

That's all it takes. Here I search ch11_01.xml for all `<ITEM>` elements:

```
%java ch11_04 ch11_01.xml ITEM | more
```

You can see the results in Figure 11-2.

Figure 11-2
Filtering an
XML
document.

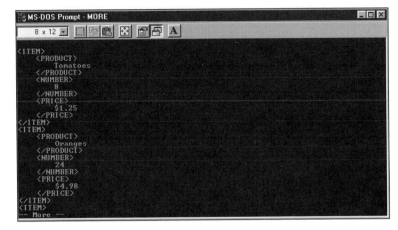

Here's the complete code for ch11_04.java:

Listing ch11_04.java

```java
import javax.xml.parsers.*;
import org.w3c.dom.*;

public class ch11_04
{
    public static void main(String args[])
    {
        FindElements findElements = new FindElements(args[0], args[1]);
    }
}

class FindElements
{
    static String displayStrings[] = new String[1000];
    static int numberDisplayLines = 0;
    static String searchFor;

    public FindElements (String uri, String searchString)
    {

        searchFor = searchString;
        displayDocument(uri);

        for(int loopIndex = 0; loopIndex < numberDisplayLines; loopIndex++){
            System.out.println(displayStrings[loopIndex]);
        }
```

continues

```java
    }

    public static void displayDocument(String uri)
    {
        try {

            DocumentBuilderFactory dbf =
            DocumentBuilderFactory.newInstance();

            DocumentBuilder db = null;
            try {
                db = dbf.newDocumentBuilder();
            }
            catch (ParserConfigurationException pce) {}

            Document document = null;
                document = db.parse(uri);

            NodeList nodeList = document.getElementsByTagName(searchFor);

            if (nodeList != null) {
                for (int loopIndex = 0; loopIndex < nodeList.getLength();
                ➥loopIndex++ ) {
                    display(nodeList.item(loopIndex), "");
                }
            }

        } catch (Exception e) {
            e.printStackTrace(System.err);
        }
    }

    public static void display(Node node, String indent)
    {
        if (node == null) {
            return;
        }

        int type = node.getNodeType();

        switch (type) {
            case Node.DOCUMENT_NODE: {
                displayStrings[numberDisplayLines] = indent;
                displayStrings[numberDisplayLines] += "<?xml
                ➥version=\"1.0\" encoding=\""+
                    "UTF-8" + "\"?>";
                numberDisplayLines++;
                display(((Document)node).getDocumentElement(), "");
                break;
```

```
        }

        case Node.ELEMENT_NODE: {
            displayStrings[numberDisplayLines] = indent;
            displayStrings[numberDisplayLines] += "<";
            displayStrings[numberDisplayLines] += node.getNodeName();

            int length = (node.getAttributes() != null) ?
            ➥node.getAttributes().getLength() : 0;
            Attr attrs[] = new Attr[length];
            for (int loopIndex = 0; loopIndex < length; loopIndex++) {
                attrs[loopIndex] =
                ➥(Attr)node.getAttributes().item(loopIndex);
            }

            for (int loopIndex = 0; loopIndex < attrs.length;
            ➥loopIndex++) {
                Attr attr = attrs[loopIndex];
                displayStrings[numberDisplayLines] += " ";
                displayStrings[numberDisplayLines] +=
                ➥attr.getNodeName();
                displayStrings[numberDisplayLines] += "=\"";
                displayStrings[numberDisplayLines] +=
                ➥attr.getNodeValue();
                displayStrings[numberDisplayLines] += "\"";
            }
            displayStrings[numberDisplayLines] += ">";

            numberDisplayLines++;

            NodeList childNodes = node.getChildNodes();
            if (childNodes != null) {
                length = childNodes.getLength();
                indent += "    ";
                for (int loopIndex = 0; loopIndex < length;
                ➥loopIndex++ ) {
                    display(childNodes.item(loopIndex), indent);
                }
            }
            break;
        }

        case Node.CDATA_SECTION_NODE: {
            displayStrings[numberDisplayLines] = indent;
            displayStrings[numberDisplayLines] += "<![CDATA[";
            displayStrings[numberDisplayLines] += node.getNodeValue();
            displayStrings[numberDisplayLines] += "]]>";
            numberDisplayLines++;
            break;
        }
```

continues

```
            case Node.TEXT_NODE: {
                displayStrings[numberDisplayLines] = indent;
                String newText = node.getNodeValue().trim();
                if(newText.indexOf("\n") < 0 && newText.length() > 0) {
                    displayStrings[numberDisplayLines] += newText;
                    numberDisplayLines++;
                }
                break;
            }

            case Node.PROCESSING_INSTRUCTION_NODE: {
                displayStrings[numberDisplayLines] = indent;
                displayStrings[numberDisplayLines] += "<?";
                displayStrings[numberDisplayLines] += node.getNodeName();
                String text = node.getNodeValue();
                if (text != null && text.length() > 0) {
                    displayStrings[numberDisplayLines] += text;
                }
                displayStrings[numberDisplayLines] += "?>";
                numberDisplayLines++;
                break;
            }
        }
    }

    if (type == Node.ELEMENT_NODE) {
        displayStrings[numberDisplayLines] = indent.substring(0,
        ➥indent.length() - 4);
        displayStrings[numberDisplayLines] += "</";
        displayStrings[numberDisplayLines] += node.getNodeName();
        displayStrings[numberDisplayLines] += ">";
        numberDisplayLines++;
        indent+= "    ";
    }
    }
}
}
```

The examples we've created so far have all created text-based output using the System.out.println method. However, few browsers these days work that way. In the next topic, I'll take a look at creating a windowed browser.

Creating a Windowed Browser

Converting the code we've written to display a document in a window isn't difficult because that code was purposely written to store the output in an array of strings and because I can display those strings in a Java window. In this example, I'll upgrade that code to a new program, browser.java, that will use Java to display XML documents in a window.

Here's how it works. I start by parsing the document the user wants to parse in the `main` method:

```
public static void main(String args[]) {

    displayDocument(args[0]);
    .
    .
    .
```

Then I'll create a new window using the techniques we saw in the previous chapter. Specifically, I'll create a new class named `AppFrame`, create an object of that class, and display it:

```
public static void main(String args[]) {

    displayDocument(args[0]);

    AppFrame f = new AppFrame(displayStrings, numberDisplayLines);

    f.setSize(300, 500);

    f.addWindowListener(new WindowAdapter() {public void
        windowClosing(WindowEvent e) {System.exit(0);}});

    f.show();
}
```

The `AppFrame` class is specially designed to display the output strings in the `displayStrings` array in a Java window. To do that, I pass that array and the number of lines to display to the `AppFrame` constructor, and I store them in this new class:

```
class AppFrame extends Frame
{
    String displayStrings[];
    int numberDisplayLines;

    public AppFrame(String[] strings, int number)
    {
        displayStrings = strings;
        numberDisplayLines = number;
    }
        .
        .
        .
```

All that's left is to display the strings in the displayStrings array. When you display text in a Java window, you're responsible for positioning that text as you want it. To display multiline text, we'll need to know the height of a line of text in the window, and you can find that with the Java FontMetrics class's getHeight method.

Here's how I display the output text in the AppFrame window. I create a new Java Font object using Courier font, and I install it in the Graphics object passed to the paint method. Then I find the height of each line of text:

```
public void paint(Graphics g)
{
    Font font = new Font("Courier", Font.PLAIN, 12);
    g.setFont(font);

    FontMetrics fontmetrics = getFontMetrics(getFont());
    int y = fontmetrics.getHeight();
        .
        .
        .
```

Finally, I loop over all lines of text using the Java Graphics object's drawString method:

```
public void paint(Graphics g)
{
    Font font = new Font("Courier", Font.PLAIN, 12);
    g.setFont(font);

    FontMetrics fontmetrics = getFontMetrics(getFont());
    int y = fontmetrics.getHeight();

    for(int index = 0; index < numberDisplayLines; index++){
        y += fontmetrics.getHeight();
        g.drawString(displayStrings[index], 5, y);
    }
}
```

You can see the result in Figure 11-3. As you see in this figure, ch11_01.xml is displayed in our windowed browser.

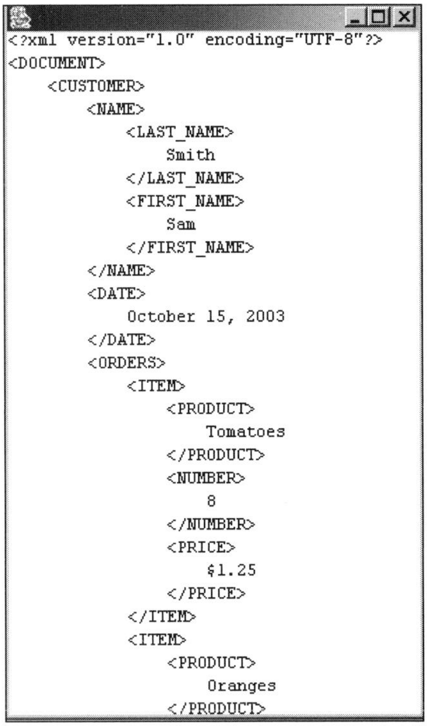

Figure 11-3
A graphical
browser.

```
<?xml version="1.0" encoding="UTF-8"?>
<DOCUMENT>
    <CUSTOMER>
        <NAME>
            <LAST_NAME>
                Smith
            </LAST_NAME>
            <FIRST_NAME>
                Sam
            </FIRST_NAME>
        </NAME>
        <DATE>
            October 15, 2003
        </DATE>
        <ORDERS>
            <ITEM>
                <PRODUCT>
                    Tomatoes
                </PRODUCT>
                <NUMBER>
                    8
                </NUMBER>
                <PRICE>
                    $1.25
                </PRICE>
            </ITEM>
            <ITEM>
                <PRODUCT>
                    Oranges
                </PRODUCT>
```

Here's the code for this example, ch11_05.java:

Listing ch11_05.java

```java
import javax.xml.parsers.*;
import org.w3c.dom.*;

import java.awt.*;
import java.awt.event.*;

public class ch11_05
{
```

continues

```java
static String displayStrings[] = new String[1000];
static int numberDisplayLines = 0;

public static void displayDocument(String uri)
{
    try {

    DocumentBuilderFactory dbf =
        DocumentBuilderFactory.newInstance();

    DocumentBuilder db = null;
    try {
        db = dbf.newDocumentBuilder();
    }
    catch (ParserConfigurationException pce) {}

    Document document = null;
        document = db.parse(uri);

        display(document, "");

    } catch (Exception e) {
        e.printStackTrace(System.err);
    }

}

public static void display(Node node, String indent)
{
    if (node == null) {
        return;
    }

    int type = node.getNodeType();

    switch (type) {
        case Node.DOCUMENT_NODE: {
            displayStrings[numberDisplayLines] = indent;
            displayStrings[numberDisplayLines] += "<?xml
        ➥version=\"1.0\" encoding=\""+
            "UTF-8" + "\"?>";
            numberDisplayLines++;
            display(((Document)node).getDocumentElement(), "");
            break;
        }

        case Node.ELEMENT_NODE: {
            displayStrings[numberDisplayLines] = indent;
            displayStrings[numberDisplayLines] += "<";
```

```
        displayStrings[numberDisplayLines] += node.getNodeName();

        int length = (node.getAttributes() != null) ?
        ➥node.getAttributes().getLength() : 0;
        Attr attrs[] = new Attr[length];
        for (int loopIndex = 0; loopIndex < length; loopIndex++) {
            attrs[loopIndex] =
            ➥(Attr)node.getAttributes().item(loopIndex);
        }

        for (int loopIndex = 0; loopIndex < attrs.length;
        ➥loopIndex++) {
            Attr attr = attrs[loopIndex];
            displayStrings[numberDisplayLines] += " ";
            displayStrings[numberDisplayLines] +=
            ➥attr.getNodeName();
            displayStrings[numberDisplayLines] += "=\"";
            displayStrings[numberDisplayLines] +=
            ➥attr.getNodeValue();
            displayStrings[numberDisplayLines] += "\"";
        }
        displayStrings[numberDisplayLines] += ">";

        numberDisplayLines++;

        NodeList childNodes = node.getChildNodes();
        if (childNodes != null) {
            length = childNodes.getLength();
            indent += "    ";
            for (int loopIndex = 0; loopIndex < length;
            ➥loopIndex++ ) {
                display(childNodes.item(loopIndex), indent);
            }
        }
        break;
}

case Node.CDATA_SECTION_NODE: {
    displayStrings[numberDisplayLines] = indent;
    displayStrings[numberDisplayLines] += "<![CDATA[";
    displayStrings[numberDisplayLines] += node.getNodeValue();
    displayStrings[numberDisplayLines] += "]]>";
    numberDisplayLines++;
    break;
}

case Node.TEXT_NODE: {
    displayStrings[numberDisplayLines] = indent;
    String newText = node.getNodeValue().trim();
    if(newText.indexOf("\n") < 0 && newText.length() > 0) {
        displayStrings[numberDisplayLines] += newText;
```

continues

Listing ch11_05.java   Continued

```java
                    numberDisplayLines++;
                }
                break;
        }

        case Node.PROCESSING_INSTRUCTION_NODE: {
            displayStrings[numberDisplayLines] = indent;

            displayStrings[numberDisplayLines] += "<?";
            displayStrings[numberDisplayLines] += node.getNodeName();
            String text = node.getNodeValue();
            if (text != null && text.length() > 0) {
                displayStrings[numberDisplayLines] += text;
            }
            displayStrings[numberDisplayLines] += "?>";
            numberDisplayLines++;
            break;
        }
    }

    if (type == Node.ELEMENT_NODE) {
        displayStrings[numberDisplayLines] = indent.substring(0,
        ➥indent.length() - 4);
        displayStrings[numberDisplayLines] += "</";
        displayStrings[numberDisplayLines] += node.getNodeName();
        displayStrings[numberDisplayLines] += ">";
        numberDisplayLines++;
        indent+= "    ";
    }
}

public static void main(String args[]) {

    displayDocument(args[0]);

    AppFrame f = new AppFrame(displayStrings, numberDisplayLines);

    f.setSize(300, 500);

    f.addWindowListener(new WindowAdapter() {public void
        windowClosing(WindowEvent e) {System.exit(0);}});

    f.show();
    }
}

class AppFrame extends Frame
{
    String displayStrings[];
```

```
    int numberDisplayLines;

    public AppFrame(String[] strings, int number)
    {
        displayStrings = strings;
        numberDisplayLines = number;
    }

    public void paint(Graphics g)
    {
        Font font = new Font("Courier", Font.PLAIN, 12);
        g.setFont(font);

        FontMetrics fontmetrics = getFontMetrics(getFont());
        int y = fontmetrics.getHeight();

        for(int index = 0; index < numberDisplayLines; index++){
            y += fontmetrics.getHeight();
            g.drawString(displayStrings[index], 5, y);
        }
    }
}
```

Now that we're parsing and displaying XML documents in windows, there's no reason to restrict ourselves to displaying the text form of an XML document. Take a look at the next topic.

Creating a Graphical Browser

In Java, text is just a form of graphics, so we've already been working with graphics. In this next example, I'll create a nontext browser that reads an XML document and uses it to draw graphics figures—circles. Here's what a document that this browser might read, ch11_06.xml, looks like. I'm specifying the (x, y) origin of the circle and the radius of the circle as attributes of the <CIRCLE> element:

Listing ch11_06.xml

```
<?xml version = "1.0" ?>
<!DOCTYPE DOCUMENT [
<!ELEMENT DOCUMENT (CIRCLE|ELLIPSE)*>
<!ELEMENT CIRCLE EMPTY>
<!ELEMENT ELLIPSE EMPTY>
<!ATTLIST CIRCLE
    X CDATA #IMPLIED
    Y CDATA #IMPLIED
```

continues

Listing ch11_06.xml   Continued

```
    RADIUS CDATA #IMPLIED>
<!ATTLIST ELLIPSE
    X CDATA #IMPLIED
    Y CDATA #IMPLIED
    WIDTH CDATA #IMPLIED
    HEIGHT CDATA #IMPLIED>
]>
<DOCUMENT>
    <CIRCLE X='200' Y='160' RADIUS='50' />
    <CIRCLE X='170' Y='100' RADIUS='15' />
    <CIRCLE X='80' Y='200' RADIUS='45' />
    <CIRCLE X='200' Y='140' RADIUS='35' />
    <CIRCLE X='130' Y='240' RADIUS='25' />
    <CIRCLE X='270' Y='300' RADIUS='45' />
    <CIRCLE X='210' Y='240' RADIUS='25' />
    <CIRCLE X='60' Y='160' RADIUS='35' />
    <CIRCLE X='160' Y='260' RADIUS='55' />
</DOCUMENT>
```

I'll call this example circles.java. We'll need to decode the XML document and store the specification of each circle. To store that data, I'll create an array named x to hold the x coordinates of the circles, y to hold the y coordinates, and radius to hold the radii of the circles. I'll also store our current location in these arrays in an integer named numberFigures:

```
public class circles
{
    static int numberFigures = 0;
    static  int x[] = new int[100];
    static int y[] = new int[100];
    static int radius[] = new int[100];
    .
    .
    .
```

As we parse the document, I'll filter out elements and search for <CIRCLE> elements. When I find a <CIRCLE> element, I'll store its x, y, and radius values in the appropriate array. To check whether the current node is a <CIRCLE> element, I'll compare the node's name, which I get with the getNodeName method, to "CIRCLE" using the Java String method equals, which you must use with String objects instead of the == operator:

```
if (node.getNodeType() == Node.ELEMENT_NODE) {

    if (node.getNodeName().equals("CIRCLE")) {
        .
        .
        .
    }
    .
    .
    .
```

To find the value of the X, Y, and RADIUS attributes, I'll use the getAttributes method to get a NamedNodeMap object representing all the attributes of this element. To get the value of specific attributes, I get the node corresponding to that attribute with the getNamedItem method. I get the attribute's actual value with getNodeValue like this, where I'm converting the attribute data from strings to integers using the Java Integer class's parseInt method:

```
if (node.getNodeType() == Node.ELEMENT_NODE) {

    if (node.getNodeName().equals("CIRCLE")) {

        NamedNodeMap attrs = node.getAttributes();

        x[numberFigures] =
        ➥Integer.parseInt((String)attrs.getNamedItem("X").getNodeValue());

        y[numberFigures] =
        ➥Integer.parseInt((String)attrs.getNamedItem("Y").getNodeValue());

        radius[numberFigures] = Integer.parseInt
        ➥((String)attrs.getNamedItem("RADIUS").getNodeValue());

        numberFigures++;
    }
    .
    .
    .
```

You can find the methods of the NamedNodeMap interface in Table 11-8.

	Method	**Summary**
Table 11-8 *NamedNodeMap* Interface Methods	`int getLength()`	Returns the number of nodes in this map
	`Node getNamedItem (java.lang.String name)`	Gets a node indicated by name
	`Node getNamedItemNS(java.lang. String namespaceURI, java.lang. String localName)`	Gets a node indicated by local name and namespace URI
	`Node item(int index)`	Gets an item in the map by index
	`Node removeNamedItem (java.lang.String name)`	Removes a node given by name
	`Node removeNamedItemNS (java.lang.String namespaceURI, java.lang.String localName)`	Removes a node given by local name and namespace URI
	`Node setNamedItem(Node arg)`	Adds a node specified by its `nodeName` attribute
	`Node setNamedItemNS(Node arg)`	Adds a node specified by its `namespaceURI` and `localName` attribute

After parsing the document, the required data is in the x, y, and radius arrays. All that's left is to display the corresponding circles, and I'll use the Java Graphics object's drawOval method to do that. This method draws ellipses and takes the (x, y) location of the figure's upper-left corner, as well as the minor and major axes lengths. To draw circles, I'll set both those lengths to the radius value for the circle. It all looks like this in the AppFrame class, which is where we draw the browser's window:

```
class AppFrame extends Frame
{
    int numberFigures;
    int[] xValues;
    int[] yValues;
    int[] radiusValues;

    public AppFrame(int number, int[] x, int[] y, int[] radius)
    {
```

```
        numberFigures = number;
        xValues = x;
        yValues = y;
        radiusValues = radius;
    }

    public void paint(Graphics g)
    {
        for(int loopIndex = 0; loopIndex < numberFigures; loopIndex++){
            g.drawOval(xValues[loopIndex], yValues[loopIndex],
            ➥radiusValues[loopIndex], radiusValues[loopIndex]);
        }
    }
}
```

And that's all it takes. You can see the results in Figure 11-4, where the browser is displaying ch11_06.xml. The complete listing appears in Listing ch11_04.java.

Figure 11-4
Creating a
graphical XML
browser.

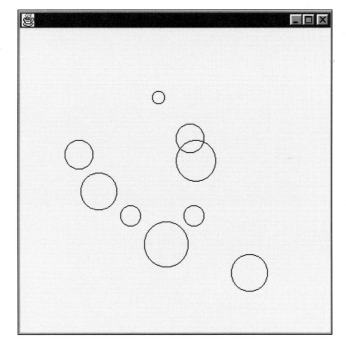

Listing ch11_07.java

```java
import java.awt.*;
import java.awt.event.*;

import javax.xml.parsers.*;
import org.w3c.dom.*;

public class ch11_07
{
    static int numberFigures = 0;
    static  int x[] = new int[100];
    static int y[] = new int[100];
    static int radius[] = new int[100];

    public static void displayDocument(String uri)
    {
        try {

        DocumentBuilderFactory dbf =
            DocumentBuilderFactory.newInstance();

        DocumentBuilder db = null;
        try {
            db = dbf.newDocumentBuilder();
        }
        catch (ParserConfigurationException pce) {}

        Document document = null;
            document = db.parse(uri);

            display(document);

        } catch (Exception e) {
            e.printStackTrace(System.err);
        }

    }

    public static void display(Node node)
    {
        if (node == null) {
            return;
        }

        int type = node.getNodeType();

        if (node.getNodeType() == Node.DOCUMENT_NODE) {
            display(((Document)node).getDocumentElement());
        }
```

```
        if (node.getNodeType() == Node.ELEMENT_NODE) {

            if (node.getNodeName().equals("CIRCLE")) {

                NamedNodeMap attrs = node.getAttributes();

                x[numberFigures] = Integer.parseInt((String)
                ↪attrs.getNamedItem("X").getNodeValue());

                y[numberFigures] = Integer.parseInt((String)
                ↪attrs.getNamedItem("Y").getNodeValue());

                radius[numberFigures] = Integer.parseInt((String)
                ↪attrs.getNamedItem("RADIUS").getNodeValue());

                numberFigures++;
            }

            NodeList childNodes = node.getChildNodes();

            if (childNodes != null) {
                int length = childNodes.getLength();
                for (int loopIndex = 0; loopIndex < length; loopIndex++) {
                    display(childNodes.item(loopIndex));
                }
            }
        }
    }
}

public static void main(String args[])
{
    displayDocument(args[0]);

    AppFrame f = new AppFrame(numberFigures, x, y, radius);

    f.setSize(400, 400);

    f.addWindowListener(new WindowAdapter() {public void
        windowClosing(WindowEvent e) {System.exit(0);}});

    f.show();
    }
}

class AppFrame extends Frame
{
    int numberFigures;
    int[] xValues;
    int[] yValues;
    int[] radiusValues;
```

continues

Listing ch11_07.java   Continued

```java
    public AppFrame(int number, int[] x, int[] y, int[] radius)
    {
        numberFigures = number;
        xValues = x;
        yValues = y;
        radiusValues = radius;
    }

    public void paint(Graphics g)
    {
        for(int loopIndex = 0; loopIndex < numberFigures; loopIndex++){
            ➥g.drawOval(xValues[loopIndex], yValues[loopIndex],
            radiusValues[loopIndex], radiusValues[loopIndex]);
        }
    }
}
```

Navigating in XML Documents

As you see in Table 11-5, the `Node` interface contains all the standard W3C DOM methods for navigating in a document that we've already used with JavaScript in Chapter 7. This includes `getNextSibling`, `getPreviousSibling`, `getFirstChild`, `getLastChild`, and `getParent`. You can put those methods to work here as easily as in Chapter 7. For example, here's the XML document that we navigated through in Chapter 7, which I'll call ch11_08.xml here:

Listing ch11_08.xml

```xml
<?xml version="1.0"?>
<MEETINGS>
    <MEETING TYPE="informal">
        <MEETING_TITLE>XML In The Real World</MEETING_TITLE>
        <MEETING_NUMBER>2079</MEETING_NUMBER>
        <SUBJECT>XML</SUBJECT>
        <DATE>6/1/2002</DATE>
        <PEOPLE>
            <PERSON ATTENDANCE="present">
                <FIRST_NAME>Edward</FIRST_NAME>
                <LAST_NAME>Samson</LAST_NAME>
            </PERSON>
            <PERSON ATTENDANCE="absent">
                <FIRST_NAME>Ernestine</FIRST_NAME>
                <LAST_NAME>Johnson</LAST_NAME>
```

```
        </PERSON>
        <PERSON ATTENDANCE="present">
            <FIRST_NAME>Betty</FIRST_NAME>
            <LAST_NAME>Richardson</LAST_NAME>
        </PERSON>
      </PEOPLE>
    </MEETING>
</MEETINGS>
```

In Chapter 7, we navigated through this document to display the third person's name, and I'll do the same here. The main difference between the Java and the JavaScript implementations in this case is that the Java implementation treats all text as text nodes—including the spacing used to indent meetings.xml. That means I can use essentially the same code to navigate through the document here that we used in Chapter 7, bearing in mind that we must step over the text nodes that contain only indentation text. Here's what that looks like in a program named ch11_09.java:

Listing ch11_09.java

```java
import javax.xml.parsers.*;
import org.w3c.dom.*;

public class ch11_09
{
    public static void displayDocument(String uri)
    {
        try {

        DocumentBuilderFactory dbf =
            DocumentBuilderFactory.newInstance();

        DocumentBuilder db = null;
        try {
            db = dbf.newDocumentBuilder();
        }
        catch (ParserConfigurationException pce) {}

        Document document = null;
            document = db.parse(uri);

            display(document);

        } catch (Exception e) {
            e.printStackTrace(System.err);
        }
```

continues

```
    }

    public static void display(Node node)
    {
        Node textNode;
        Node meetingsNode = ((Document)node).getDocumentElement();
        textNode = meetingsNode.getFirstChild();
        Node meetingNode = textNode.getNextSibling();
        textNode = meetingNode.getLastChild();
        Node peopleNode = textNode.getPreviousSibling();
        textNode = peopleNode.getLastChild();
        Node personNode = textNode.getPreviousSibling();
        textNode = personNode.getFirstChild();
        Node first_nameNode = textNode.getNextSibling();
        textNode = first_nameNode.getNextSibling();
        Node last_nameNode = textNode.getNextSibling();

        System.out.println("Third name: " +
            first_nameNode.getFirstChild().getNodeValue() + ' '
            + last_nameNode.getFirstChild().getNodeValue());
    }

    public static void main(String args[])
    {
        displayDocument("ch11_08.xml");
    }
}
```

And here are the results of this program:

```
%java ch11_09
Third name: Betty Richardson
```

Modifying XML Documents

As you can see in Table 11-5, the Node interface contains a number of methods for modifying documents by adding or removing nodes. These methods include appendChild, insertBefore, removeChild, replaceChild, and so on. You can use these methods to modify XML documents on the fly.

If you do modify a document, however, you still have to write it out (in Chapter 7, we couldn't do that using JavaScript in a browser, so I sent the whole document to an ASP script that echoed it back to be displayed in the browser). The Java packages do support an interface named Serializer that you can use to serialize (store) documents. However, that interface is not included in the standard JAR files that we've already downloaded; in fact, it's easy enough to simply store the modified XML document ourselves because we print that document anyway. Instead of using `System.out.println` to display the modified document on the console, I'll use a Java `FileWriter` object to write that document to disk.

In this example, I'll assume that all the people listed in ch11_01.xml (you can see this document at the beginning of this chapter) are experienced XML programmers. In addition to the `<FIRST_NAME>` and `<LAST_NAME>` elements, I'll give each of them "XML" as a middle name by adding a `<MIDDLE_NAME>` element. Like `<FIRST_NAME>` and `<LAST_NAME>`, `<MIDDLE_NAME>` will be a child element of the `<NAME>` element:

```
<NAME>
    <LAST_NAME>
        Jones
    </LAST_NAME>
    <FIRST_NAME>
        Polly
    </FIRST_NAME>
    <MIDDLE_NAME>
        XML
    </MIDDLE_NAME>
</NAME>
```

Adding a `<MIDDLE_NAME>` element to every `<NAME>` element is easy enough to do—all I have to do is make sure we're parsing the `<NAME>` element and then use the `createElement` method to create a new element named `<MIDDLE_NAME>`:

```
case Node.ELEMENT_NODE: {

    if(node.getNodeName().equals("NAME")) {
        Element middleNameElement = document.createElement("MIDDLE_NAME");
    .
    .
    .
```

Because all text is stored in text nodes, I also create a new text node with the `createTextNode` method to hold the text "XML":

```
case Node.ELEMENT_NODE: {

    if(node.getNodeName().equals("NAME")) {
        Element middleNameElement = document.createElement("MIDDLE_NAME");
        Text textNode = document.createTextNode("XML");
    .
    .
    .
```

Now I can append the text node to the new element with `appendChild`:

```
case Node.ELEMENT_NODE: {

    if(node.getNodeName().equals("NAME")) {
        Element middleNameElement = document.createElement("MIDDLE_NAME");
        Text textNode = document.createTextNode("XML");
        middleNameElement.appendChild(textNode);
    .
    .
    .
```

Finally, I append the new element to the <NAME> node like this:

```
case Node.ELEMENT_NODE: {

    if(node.getNodeName().equals("NAME")) {
        Element middleNameElement = document.createElement("MIDDLE_NAME");
        Text textNode = document.createTextNode("XML");
        middleNameElement.appendChild(textNode);
        node.appendChild(middleNameElement);
    }
    .
    .
    .
```

Using this code, I'm able to modify the document in memory. As before, the lines of this document are stored in the array `displayStrings`, and I can write that array to a file called ch11_11.xml. To do that, I use the Java `FileWriter` class, which writes text stored as character arrays in files. To create those character arrays, I can use the Java `String` object's handy `toCharArray` method, like this:

```
public static void main(String args[])
{
    displayDocument(args[0]);

    try {
        FileWriter filewriter = new FileWriter("ch11_11.xml");

        for(int loopIndex = 0; loopIndex < numberDisplayLines; loopIndex++){
            filewriter.write(displayStrings[loopIndex].toCharArray());
            filewriter.write('\n');
        }

        filewriter.close();
    }
    catch (Exception e) {
        e.printStackTrace(System.err);
    }
}
```

That's all there is to it. After running this code, this is the result complete with the new <MIDDLE_NAME> elements:

```xml
<?xml version="1.0" encoding="UTF-8"?>
<DOCUMENT>
    <CUSTOMER>
        <NAME>
            <LAST_NAME>
                Smith
            </LAST_NAME>
            <FIRST_NAME>
                Sam
            </FIRST_NAME>
            <MIDDLE_NAME>
                XML
            </MIDDLE_NAME>
        </NAME>
        <DATE>
            October 15, 2003
        </DATE>
        <ORDERS>
            <ITEM>
                <PRODUCT>
                    Tomatoes
                </PRODUCT>
                <NUMBER>
                    8
                </NUMBER>
                <PRICE>
                    $1.25
                </PRICE>
            </ITEM>
            <ITEM>
                <PRODUCT>
                    Oranges
                </PRODUCT>
                <NUMBER>
                    24
                </NUMBER>
                <PRICE>
                    $4.98
                </PRICE>
            </ITEM>
        </ORDERS>
    </CUSTOMER>
    <CUSTOMER>
        <NAME>
            <LAST_NAME>
                Jones
            </LAST_NAME>
            <FIRST_NAME>
```

```
                Polly
            </FIRST_NAME>
            <MIDDLE_NAME>
                XML
            </MIDDLE_NAME>
        </NAME>
        <DATE>
            October 20, 2003
        </DATE>
        <ORDERS>
            <ITEM>
                <PRODUCT>
                    Bread
                </PRODUCT>
                <NUMBER>
                    12
                </NUMBER>
                <PRICE>
                    $14.95
                </PRICE>
            </ITEM>
            <ITEM>
                <PRODUCT>
                    Apples
                </PRODUCT>
                <NUMBER>
                    6
                </NUMBER>
                <PRICE>
                    $1.50
                </PRICE>
            </ITEM>
        </ORDERS>
    </CUSTOMER>
    <CUSTOMER>
        <NAME>
            <LAST_NAME>
                Weber
            </LAST_NAME>
            <FIRST_NAME>
                Bill
            </FIRST_NAME>
            <MIDDLE_NAME>
                XML
            </MIDDLE_NAME>
        </NAME>
        <DATE>
            October 25, 2003
        </DATE>
        <ORDERS>
            <ITEM>
```

```
                <PRODUCT>
                    Asparagus
                </PRODUCT>
                <NUMBER>
                    12
                </NUMBER>
                <PRICE>
                    $2.95
                </PRICE>
            </ITEM>
            <ITEM>
                <PRODUCT ID="5231" TYPE="3133">
                    Lettuce
                </PRODUCT>
                <NUMBER>
                    6
                </NUMBER>
                <PRICE>
                    $11.50
                </PRICE>
            </ITEM>
        </ORDERS>
    </CUSTOMER>
</DOCUMENT>
```

Here's the code for this example, ch11_10.java:

Listing ch11_10.java

```
import java.awt.*;
import java.io.*;
import java.awt.event.*;

import org.w3c.dom.*;
import javax.xml.parsers.*;
import org.w3c.dom.*;

public class ch11_10
{
    static String displayStrings[] = new String[1000];
    static int numberDisplayLines = 0;
    static Document document;
    static Node c;

    public static void displayDocument(String uri)
    {
        try {

            DocumentBuilderFactory dbf =
```

continues

```
                    DocumentBuilderFactory.newInstance();

            DocumentBuilder db = null;
            try {
                db = dbf.newDocumentBuilder();
            }
            catch (ParserConfigurationException pce) {}

            document = db.parse(uri);

            display(document, "");

        } catch (Exception e) {
            e.printStackTrace(System.err);
        }

    }

    public static void display(Node node, String indent)
    {
        if (node == null) {
            return;
        }

        int type = node.getNodeType();

        switch (type) {
            case Node.DOCUMENT_NODE: {
                displayStrings[numberDisplayLines] = indent;
                displayStrings[numberDisplayLines] += "<?xml
                ➥version=\"1.0\" encoding=\""+
                   "UTF-8" + "\"?>";
                numberDisplayLines++;
                display(((Document)node).getDocumentElement(), "");
                break;
            }

            case Node.ELEMENT_NODE: {

                if(node.getNodeName().equals("NAME")) {
                    Element middleNameElement =
                    document.createElement("MIDDLE_NAME");
                    ➥Text textNode = document.createTextNode("XML");
                    middleNameElement.appendChild(textNode);
                    node.appendChild(middleNameElement);
                }

                displayStrings[numberDisplayLines] = indent;
                displayStrings[numberDisplayLines] += "<";
                displayStrings[numberDisplayLines] += node.getNodeName();
```

```java
        int length = (node.getAttributes() != null) ?
        ➥node.getAttributes().getLength() : 0;
        Attr attributes[] = new Attr[length];
        for (int loopIndex = 0; loopIndex < length; loopIndex++) {
            attributes[loopIndex] =
            ➥(Attr)node.getAttributes().item(loopIndex);
        }

        for (int loopIndex = 0; loopIndex < attributes.length;
        ➥loopIndex++) {
            Attr attribute = attributes[loopIndex];
            displayStrings[numberDisplayLines] += " ";
            displayStrings[numberDisplayLines] +=
            ➥attribute.getNodeName();
            displayStrings[numberDisplayLines] += "=\"";
            displayStrings[numberDisplayLines] +=
            ➥attribute.getNodeValue();
            displayStrings[numberDisplayLines] += "\"";
        }
        displayStrings[numberDisplayLines]+=">";

        numberDisplayLines++;

        NodeList childNodes = node.getChildNodes();
        if (childNodes != null) {
            length = childNodes.getLength();
            indent += "     ";
            for (int loopIndex = 0; loopIndex < length;
            ➥loopIndex++ ) {
                display(childNodes.item(loopIndex), indent);
            }
        }
        break;
}

case Node.CDATA_SECTION_NODE: {
    displayStrings[numberDisplayLines] = indent;
    displayStrings[numberDisplayLines] += "<![CDATA[";
    displayStrings[numberDisplayLines] += node.getNodeValue();
    displayStrings[numberDisplayLines] += "]]>";
    numberDisplayLines++;
    break;
}

case Node.TEXT_NODE: {
    displayStrings[numberDisplayLines] = indent;
    String newText = node.getNodeValue().trim();
    if(newText.indexOf("\n") < 0 && newText.length() > 0) {
        displayStrings[numberDisplayLines] += newText;
        numberDisplayLines++;
    }
    break;
}
```

continues

Listing ch11_10.java   Continued

```
            case Node.PROCESSING_INSTRUCTION_NODE: {
                displayStrings[numberDisplayLines] = indent;
                displayStrings[numberDisplayLines] += "<?";
                displayStrings[numberDisplayLines] += node.getNodeName();
                String text = node.getNodeValue();
                if (text != null && text.length() > 0) {
                    displayStrings[numberDisplayLines] += text;
                }
                displayStrings[numberDisplayLines] += "?>";
                numberDisplayLines++;
                break;
            }
        }

        if (type == Node.ELEMENT_NODE) {
            displayStrings[numberDisplayLines] = indent.substring(0,
            ➥indent.length() - 4);
            displayStrings[numberDisplayLines] += "</";
            displayStrings[numberDisplayLines] += node.getNodeName();
            displayStrings[numberDisplayLines] += ">";
            numberDisplayLines++;
            indent += "    ";
        }
    }

    public static void main(String args[])
    {
        displayDocument(args[0]);

        try {
            FileWriter filewriter = new FileWriter("ch11_11.xml");

            for(int loopIndex = 0; loopIndex < numberDisplayLines;
            ➥loopIndex++){
                filewriter.write(displayStrings[loopIndex].toCharArray());
                filewriter.write('\n');
            }

            filewriter.close();
        }
        catch (Exception e) {
            e.printStackTrace(System.err);
        }
    }
}
```

As you see, there's a lot of power in Java when it comes to XML. In fact, there's another way to do all this besides using the DOM. It's called Simple API for XML (SAX), and I'll take a look at it in the next chapter.

CHAPTER 12
Java and SAX

The previous chapter was all about using Java and the XML DOM. However, some people find using the DOM difficult and think that the whole concept of treating an XML document as a tree is unnecessarily complex. Rather than having to navigate through the whole document, they say, wouldn't it be great if the whole document came to you? That's the idea behind the Simple API for XML (SAX), and this chapter is dedicated to it. SAX really is a lot easier to use for many—possibly even most—XML parsing that you have to do. If you need to know the hierarchy of a document, use DOM methods; if you don't, you might try SAX.

You may be surprised to learn that we've already been putting the ideas behind SAX to work throughout the entire previous chapter. You may recall that in that chapter, I set up a recursive method named `display` that was called for every node in the DOM tree. In `display`, I used a `switch` statement to make things easier. That `switch` statement had `case` statements to handle different types of nodes:

```
public static void display(Node node, String indent)
{
    if (node == null) {
        return;
    }

    int type = node.getNodeType();

    switch (type) {
        case Node.DOCUMENT_NODE: {
            displayStrings[numberDisplayLines] = indent;
            displayStrings[numberDisplayLines] += "<?xml version=\"1.0\"
            ➥encoding=\""+
              "UTF-8" + "\"?>";
            numberDisplayLines++;
            display(((Document)node).getDocumentElement(), "");
```

```
        break;
    }

    case Node.ELEMENT_NODE: {
        displayStrings[numberDisplayLines] = indent;
        displayStrings[numberDisplayLines] += "<";
        displayStrings[numberDisplayLines] += node.getNodeName();

        int length = (node.getAttributes() != null) ?
        ➥node.getAttributes().getLength() : 0;
        Attr attributes[] = new Attr[length];
        for (int loopIndex = 0; loopIndex < length; loopIndex++) {
            attributes[loopIndex] = (Attr)node.getAttributes()
            ➥.item(loopIndex);
        }
        .
        .
        .
```

I was able to add the code that handled elements to one case statement, add the code to handle processing instructions to another case statement, and so on.

In essence, we were handling XML documents the same way that SAX does. Instead of navigating through the document ourselves, we let the document come to us, having the code call various case statements for the various nodes in the document. That's what SAX does. It's *event-based*, which means that when the SAX parser encounters an element, it treats that as an event and calls the code you specify for handling elements; when it encounters a processing instruction, it treats that as an event and calls the code you specify for handling processing instructions, and so on. In this way, you don't have to navigate through the document yourself—it comes to you. (SAX is simpler and usually faster than DOM techniques, partially because SAX is read-only and DOM techniques are read/write.) The fact that we've already done a significant amount of programming with this technique indicates how useful it is.

Working with SAX

This first example shows how to work with SAX. In this case, I'll use SAX to count the number of <CUSTOMER> elements in the same example we saw in the previous chapter. Here's that file, renamed ch12_01.xml for this chapter:

Listing ch12_01.xml

```xml
<?xml version = "1.0" standalone="yes"?>
<DOCUMENT>
    <CUSTOMER>
        <NAME>
            <LAST_NAME>Smith</LAST_NAME>
            <FIRST_NAME>Sam</FIRST_NAME>
        </NAME>
        <DATE>October 15, 2003</DATE>
        <ORDERS>
            <ITEM>
                <PRODUCT>Tomatoes</PRODUCT>
                <NUMBER>8</NUMBER>
                <PRICE>$1.25</PRICE>
            </ITEM>
            <ITEM>
                <PRODUCT>Oranges</PRODUCT>
                <NUMBER>24</NUMBER>
                <PRICE>$4.98</PRICE>
            </ITEM>
        </ORDERS>
    </CUSTOMER>
    <CUSTOMER>
        <NAME>
            <LAST_NAME>Jones</LAST_NAME>
            <FIRST_NAME>Polly</FIRST_NAME>
        </NAME>
        <DATE>October 20, 2003</DATE>
        <ORDERS>
            <ITEM>
                <PRODUCT>Bread</PRODUCT>
                <NUMBER>12</NUMBER>
                <PRICE>$14.95</PRICE>
            </ITEM>
            <ITEM>
                <PRODUCT>Apples</PRODUCT>
                <NUMBER>6</NUMBER>
                <PRICE>$1.50</PRICE>
            </ITEM>
        </ORDERS>
    </CUSTOMER>
    <CUSTOMER>
        <NAME>
            <LAST_NAME>Weber</LAST_NAME>
            <FIRST_NAME>Bill</FIRST_NAME>
        </NAME>
        <DATE>October 25, 2003</DATE>
        <ORDERS>
            <ITEM>
                <PRODUCT>Asparagus</PRODUCT>
```

continues

Listing ch12_01.xml   Continued

```
                <NUMBER>12</NUMBER>
                <PRICE>$2.95</PRICE>
            </ITEM>
            <ITEM>
                <PRODUCT>Lettuce</PRODUCT>
                <NUMBER>6</NUMBER>
                <PRICE>$11.50</PRICE>
            </ITEM>
        </ORDERS>
    </CUSTOMER>
</DOCUMENT>
```

Here, I'll base the new program on a new class named ch12_02:

```
public class ch12_02 extends DefaultHandler
{
        .
        .
        .
}
```

Note the keywords extends DefaultHandler here. This means that our class, ch12_02, is based on the Java DefaultHandler class. The DefaultHandler class already has a number of methods predefined for you that the SAX parser will call, including these *callback* methods:

- startDocument—Called when the start of the document is encountered

- endDocument—Called when the end of the document is encountered

- startElement—Called when the opening tag of an element is encountered

- endElement—Called when the closing tag of an element is encountered

- characters—Called when the XML parser sees text characters

All the required callback methods are already implemented in the DefaultHandler class, but they don't do anything. That means you have to implement only the methods you want to use, such as startDocument to catch the beginning of the document, or endDocument to catch the end of the document, as we'll see. You can see all the methods of the DefaultHandler class in Table 12-1.

Table 12-1 Methods of the *DefaultHandler* Class	Method	Does This
	`DefaultHandler()`	The class constructor
	`void characters(char[] ch, int start, int length)`	Handles character data inside an element
	`void endDocument()`	Handles the end of the document
	`void endElement(String uri, String localName, String qName)`	Handles the end of an element
	`void endPrefixMapping (String prefix)`	Handles the end of a namespace mapping
	`void error(SAXParseException e)`	Handles a recoverable parser error
	`void fatalError (SAXParseException e)`	Reports a fatal parsing error
	`void ignorableWhitespace(char[] ch, int start, int length)`	Handles ignorable whitespace (such as that used to indent a document) in element content
	`void notationDecl(String name, String publicId, String systemId)`	Handles a notation declaration
	`void processingInstruction (String target, String data)`	Handles an XML processing instruction (such as a JSP directive)
	`InputSource resolveEntity (String publicId, String systemId)`	Resolves an external entity
	`void setDocumentLocator (Locator locator)`	Sets a `Locator` object for document events
	`void skippedEntity(String name)`	Handles a skipped XML entity
	`void startDocument()`	Handles the beginning of the document
	`void startElement(String uri, String localName, String qName, Attributes attributes)`	Handles the start of an element
	`void startPrefixMapping (String prefix, String uri)`	Handles the start of a namespace mapping
	`void unparsedEntityDecl (String name, String publicId, String systemId, String notationName)`	Handles an unparsed entity declaration
	`void warning(SAXParseException e)`	Handles a parser warning

You have to pass the SAX handler an object based on a handler class such as DefaultHandler so that it can call the methods you see in Table 12-1. Our main class, ch12_02, is based on the DefaultHandler class, so we can pass an object of the ch12_02 class to the SAX parser. I begin by creating an object of the ch12_02 class named obj and then calling that object's displayDocument method, which creates the SAX parser. (The reason I create a new object from the current class instead of just calling displayDocument directly is that we have to pass an object to the SAX parser so that the parser can call that object's callback methods; we'll use obj itself for that purpose.)

```
public static void main(String args[])
{
    ch12_02 obj = new ch12_02();
    obj.displayDocument(args[0]);
}
```

In the displayDocument method, I'll create the SAX parser. To do that, you can use the Java SAXParserFactory class to create an object of the SAXParser class. (As with the DocumentBuilderFactory class in Chapter 11, "Java and the XML DOM," the Java SAXParserFactory class is called a factory because you can use it to create parsers using Java classes from different parser vendors, not just the default Java XML SAX parser that we'll use here.)

The actual parsing is done by the SAXParser object's parse method. You pass it the object whose methods it is supposed to call when the parser sees the beginning of an XML element, the end of an element, and so on. In this case, that's the current object (that is, obj, whose displayDocument method we're inside right now). In Java, you can refer to the present object with the this keyword. That means we can parse the file the user is asking us to parse like this:

```
public static void main(String args[])
{
    ch12_02 obj = new ch12_02();
    obj.displayDocument(args[0]);
}

public void displayDocument(String uri)
{
    DefaultHandler handler = this;
    SAXParserFactory factory = SAXParserFactory.newInstance();
    try {
        SAXParser saxParser = factory.newSAXParser();
        saxParser.parse(new File(uri), handler);
    } catch (Throwable t) {}
}
}
```

You'll find the methods of the `SAXParserFactory` class in Table 12-2 and the methods of the `SAXParser` class in Table 12-3.

Table 12-2
Methods
of the
*javax.xml.parsers.SAX
ParserFactory*
Interface

Method	Does This
protected SAXParserFactory()	The default constructor
abstract boolean getFeature (String name)	Returns the particular property requested
boolean isNamespaceAware()	True if the factory will produce parsers that use XML namespaces
boolean isValidating()	True if the factory will produce parsers that validate the XML content
static SAXParserFactory newInstance()	Gets a new SAXParserFactory object
abstract SAXParser newSAXParser()	Creates a new SAXParser object
abstract void setFeature (String name, boolean value)	Sets the particular feature requested
void setNamespaceAware (boolean awareness)	Requires the parser produced to support XML namespaces
void setValidating (boolean validating)	Requires the parser produced to validate XML documents

Table 12-3
Methods of
the *SAXParser*
Class

Method	Does This
protected SAXParser()	The default constructor
abstract Parser getParser()	Returns the SAX parser
abstract Object getProperty (String name)	Returns the particular property requested
abstract XMLReader getXMLReader()	Returns the XMLReader object used
abstract boolean isNamespaceAware()	True if this parser is configured to understand namespaces
abstract boolean isValidating()	True if this parser is configured to validate XML documents

continues

Method	Does This
`void parse` `(File f, DefaultHandler dh)`	Parses the content of the file specified using the specified `DefaultHandler` object
`void parse(File f,` `HandlerBase hb)`	Parses the content of the file specified using the specified `HandlerBase` object
`void parse(InputSource is,` `DefaultHandler dh)`	Parses the content specified by `InputSource` using the specified `DefaultHandler` object
`void parse(InputSource is,` `HandlerBase hb)`	Parses the content specified by `InputSource` using the specified `HandlerBase` object
`void parse(InputStream is,` `DefaultHandler dh)`	Parses the content of the specified `InputStream` instance using the specified `DefaultHandler` object

`void parse(InputStream is,`
`DefaultHandler dh, String`
`systemId)`
	Parses the content of the specified `InputStream` instance using the specified `DefaultHandler` object

`void parse(InputStream is,` `HandlerBase hb)`	Parses the content of the specified `InputStream` instance using the specified `HandlerBase` object
`void parse(InputStream is,` `HandlerBase hb, String systemId)`	Parses the content of the specified `InputStream` instance using the specified `HandlerBase` object and system ID
`void parse(String uri,` `DefaultHandler dh)`	Parses the content described by the giving uniform resource identifier (URI) using the specified `DefaultHandler` object
`void parse(String uri,` `HandlerBase hb)`	Parses the content described by the specified URI using the specified `HandlerBase` object
`abstract  void setProperty` `(String name, Object value)`	Sets a particular property in the `XMLReader` object

Now the SAX parser calls the various methods in the ch12_02 class when it encounters elements in the document we're parsing. In this case, the goal is to determine how many <CUSTOMER> elements the document has, so I implement the startElement method like this:

```
import org.xml.sax.*;
import org.xml.sax.helpers.DefaultHandler;
import javax.xml.parsers.*;
import java.io.*;

public class ch12_02 extends DefaultHandler
{
    public void startElement(String uri, String localName, String
    ➥qualifiedName,
        Attributes attributes)
    {
        .
        .
        .
    }
}
```

The startElement method is called each time the SAX parser sees the start of an element, and the endElement method is called when the SAX parser sees the end of an element.

Note that two element names are passed to the startElement method: localName and qualifiedName. You use the localName argument with namespace processing; this argument holds the name of the element without any namespace prefix. The qualifiedName argument holds the full, qualified name of the element, including any namespace prefix.

We're just going to count the number of <CUSTOMER> elements, so I'll take a look at the element's qualifiedName argument. If that argument equals "CUSTOMER", I'll increment a variable named customerCount:

```
import org.xml.sax.*;
import org.xml.sax.helpers.DefaultHandler;
import javax.xml.parsers.*;
import java.io.*;

public class ch12_02 extends DefaultHandler
{
    int customerCount = 0;

    public void startElement(String uri, String localName, String
    ➥qualifiedName,
        Attributes attributes)
    {
```

```
        if (qualifiedName.equals("CUSTOMER")) {
            customerCount++;
        }
    }
```

How do you know when you've reached the end of the document and there are no more <CUSTOMER> elements to count? You use the endDocument method, which is called when the end of the document is reached. I'll display the number of tallied <CUSTOMER> elements in that method:

Listing ch12_02.java

```java
import org.xml.sax.*;
import org.xml.sax.helpers.DefaultHandler;
import javax.xml.parsers.*;
import java.io.*;

public class ch12_02 extends DefaultHandler
{
    int customerCount = 0;

    public void startElement(String uri, String localName, String
    ↪qualifiedName,
        Attributes attributes)
    {
        if (qualifiedName.equals("CUSTOMER")) {
            customerCount++;
        }
    }

    public void endDocument()
    {
        System.out.println("The document has " + customerCount + "
        ↪<CUSTOMER> elements.");
    }

    public static void main(String args[])
    {
        ch12_02 obj = new ch12_02();
        obj.displayDocument(args[0]);
    }

    public void displayDocument(String uri)
    {
        DefaultHandler handler = this;
        SAXParserFactory factory = SAXParserFactory.newInstance();
        try {
            SAXParser saxParser = factory.newSAXParser();
```

```
        saxParser.parse(new File(uri), handler);
    } catch (Throwable t) {}
    }
}
```

You can compile and then run this program like this:

```
%java ch12_02 ch12_01.xml
The document has 3 <CUSTOMER> elements.
```

And that's all it takes to get started with SAX.

Displaying an Entire Document

In this next example, as in the previous chapter, I'm going to write a program that parses and displays an entire document, indenting each element, processing instruction, and so on, as well as displaying attributes and their values. Here, however, I'll use SAX methods, not DOM methods. If you pass ch12_01.xml to this program, which I'll call ch12_03.java, that program will display the whole document properly indented.

I start by letting the user specify what document to parse and parsing that document. To actually parse the document, I'll create an object of the current class and call that object's displayDocument method from the main method, as before. The displayDocument method will fill the array displayStrings with the formatted document, and the main method will print it:

```
import org.xml.sax.*;
import org.xml.sax.helpers.DefaultHandler;
import javax.xml.parsers.*;
import java.io.*;

public class ch12_03 extends DefaultHandler
{
    public static void displayDocument(String uri)
    {
        .
        .
        .
    }

    public static void main(String args[])
    {
        ch12_03 obj = new ch12_03();
        obj.displayDocument(args[0]);
```

```
        for(int index = 0; index < numberDisplayLines; index++){
            System.out.println(displayStrings[index]);
        }
    }
}
```

In the `displayDocument` method, I'll create a SAX parser. You need to register an object with the SAX parser whose callback methods the parser will call. We can use the current object for that, as in the previous example in this chapter:

```java
import org.xml.sax.*;
import org.xml.sax.helpers.DefaultHandler;
import javax.xml.parsers.*;
import java.io.*;

public class ch12_03 extends DefaultHandler
{
    public void displayDocument(String uri)
    {
        DefaultHandler handler = this;
        SAXParserFactory factory = SAXParserFactory.newInstance();
        try {
            SAXParser saxParser = factory.newSAXParser();
            saxParser.parse(new File(uri), handler);
        } catch (Throwable t) {}
    }

    public static void main(String args[])
    {
        ch12_03 obj = new ch12_03();
        obj.displayDocument(args[0]);

        for(int index = 0; index < numberDisplayLines; index++){
            System.out.println(displayStrings[index]);
        }
    }
}
```

All that's left is to create the various methods that will be called for SAX events, and I'll start with the beginning of the document.

Handling the Beginning of Documents

When the SAX parser encounters the beginning of the document to parse, it calls the startDocument method. This method is not passed any arguments, so I'll just have the program display the XML declaration. As in the previous chapter, I'll store the text to display in the array of String objects named displayStrings, our location in that array in the integer variable numberDisplayLines, and the current indentation level in a String object named indent. Using an array of strings like this facilitates the conversion process when we adapt this program to display in a Java window.

Here's how I add the XML declaration to the display strings in startDocument:

```java
import org.xml.sax.*;
import org.xml.sax.helpers.DefaultHandler;
import javax.xml.parsers.*;
import java.io.*;

public class ch12_03 extends DefaultHandler
{
    static String displayStrings[] = new String[1000];
    static int numberDisplayLines = 0;
    static String indent = "";

    public void displayDocument(String uri)
    {
        DefaultHandler handler = this;
        SAXParserFactory factory = SAXParserFactory.newInstance();
        try {
            SAXParser saxParser = factory.newSAXParser();
            saxParser.parse(new File(uri), handler);
        } catch (Throwable t) {}
    }

    public void startDocument()
    {
        displayStrings[numberDisplayLines] = indent;
        displayStrings[numberDisplayLines] += "<?xml version=\"1.0\"
    ➥encoding=\""+
            "UTF-8" + "\"?>";
        numberDisplayLines++;
    }
        .
        .
        .
    public static void main(String args[])
    {
        ch12_03 obj = new ch12_03();
```

```
            obj.displayDocument(args[0]);

            for(int index = 0; index < numberDisplayLines; index++){
                System.out.println(displayStrings[index]);
            }
        }
    }
```

I'll take a look at handling processing instructions next.

Handling Processing Instructions

You can handle processing instructions with the `processingInstruction` callback. This method is called with two arguments, the processing instruction's target and its data. For example, in the `<?xml-stylesheet type="text/css" href="style.css"?>`, its target is `xml-stylesheet` and its data is `type="text/css" href="style.css"`.

Here's how I handle processing instructions, adding them to the display strings. Note that I check first to make sure there is some data before adding it to the processing instruction's display:

```
import org.xml.sax.*;
import org.xml.sax.helpers.DefaultHandler;
import javax.xml.parsers.*;
import java.io.*;

public class ch12_03 extends DefaultHandler
{
    static String displayStrings[] = new String[1000];
    static int numberDisplayLines = 0;
    static String indent = "";

    public void processingInstruction(String target, String data)
    {
        displayStrings[numberDisplayLines] = indent;
        displayStrings[numberDisplayLines] += "<?";
        displayStrings[numberDisplayLines] += target;
        if (data != null && data.length() > 0) {
            displayStrings[numberDisplayLines] += ' ';
            displayStrings[numberDisplayLines] += data;
        }
        displayStrings[numberDisplayLines] += "?>";
        numberDisplayLines++;
    }

    public static void main(String args[])
    {
```

```
        .
        .
        .
    }
}
```

Handling the Beginning of Elements

You can handle the start of elements with the startElement method. Because we've found a new element, I'll add four spaces to the current indentation to handle any children the element has, and I'll display its name using the qualifiedName argument:

```
import org.xml.sax.*;
import org.xml.sax.helpers.DefaultHandler;
import javax.xml.parsers.*;
import java.io.*;

public class ch12_03 extends DefaultHandler
{
    static String displayStrings[] = new String[1000];
    static int numberDisplayLines = 0;
    static String indent = "";

    public void startElement(String uri, String localName, String
    ➥qualifiedName,
        Attributes attributes)
    {
        displayStrings[numberDisplayLines] = indent;

        indent += "    ";

        displayStrings[numberDisplayLines] += '<';
        displayStrings[numberDisplayLines] += qualifiedName;
        displayStrings[numberDisplayLines] += '>';
        numberDisplayLines++;
    }

    public static void main(String args[])
    {
        .
        .
        .
    }
}
```

That's enough to display the opening tag of an element, but what if the element has attributes?

Handling Attributes

One of the arguments passed to the startElement method is an object that implements the Attributes interface:

```
public void startElement(String uri, String localName, String qualifiedName,
    Attributes attributes)
{
.
.
.
}
```

This object gives you access to the attributes of the element, and you can find the methods of the Attributes interface in Table 12-4. You can reach the attributes in an object that implements this interface based on index, name, or namespace-qualified name.

Table 12-4 Attributes Interface Methods	Method	Summary
	int getIndex (java.lang.String qualifiedName)	Gets the index of an attribute, given its qualified name
	int getIndex(java.lang. String uri, java.lang.String localPart)	Gets the index of an attribute by namespace and local name
	int getLength()	Gets the number of attributes in the list
	java.lang.String getLocalName (int index)	Gets an attribute's local name by index
	java.lang.String getQName (int index)	Gets an attribute's qualified name by index
	java.lang.String getType (int index)	Gets an attribute's type by index
	java.lang.String getType (java.lang.String qualifiedName)	Gets an attribute's type by qualified name
	java.lang.String getType (java.lang.String uri, java.lang.String localName)	Gets an attribute's type by namespace and local name

Method	Summary
`java.lang.String getURI (int index)`	Gets an attribute's namespace URI by index
`java.lang.String getValue (int index)`	Gets an attribute's value by index
`java.lang.String getValue (java.lang.String qualifiedName)`	Gets an attribute's value by qualified name
`java.lang.String getValue (java.lang.String uri, java.lang. String localName)`	Gets an attribute's value by namespace name and local name

How do we find and display all the attributes an element has? I'll find the number of attributes using the `Attributes` interface's `getLength` method. Then I'll get the names and values of the attributes with the `getLocalName` and `getValue` methods, referring to attributes by index. Note that I first ensure that this element actually has attributes by checking to make sure that the `attributes` argument is not null:

```java
import org.xml.sax.*;
import org.xml.sax.helpers.DefaultHandler;
import javax.xml.parsers.*;
import java.io.*;

public class ch12_03 extends DefaultHandler
{
    static String displayStrings[] = new String[1000];
    static int numberDisplayLines = 0;
    static String indent = "";

    public void startElement(String uri, String localName, String
    ➥qualifiedName,
        Attributes attributes)
    {
        displayStrings[numberDisplayLines] = indent;

        indent += "    ";

        displayStrings[numberDisplayLines] += '<';
        displayStrings[numberDisplayLines] += qualifiedName;

        if (attributes != null) {
            int numberAttributes = attributes.getLength();
            for (int loopIndex = 0; loopIndex < numberAttributes;
            ➥loopIndex++) {
                displayStrings[numberDisplayLines] += ' ';
```

```
                        displayStrings[numberDisplayLines] +=
                        ➥attributes.getLocalName(loopIndex);
                        displayStrings[numberDisplayLines] += "=\"";
                        displayStrings[numberDisplayLines] +=
                        ➥attributes.getValue(loopIndex);
                        displayStrings[numberDisplayLines] += '"';
                }
        }

        displayStrings[numberDisplayLines] += '>';
        numberDisplayLines++;
    }

    public static void main(String args[])
    {
        .
        .
        .
    }
}
```

That's all it takes; now we're handling the element's attributes as well.

Handling Text

Many of the elements in ch12_01.xml, such as the <FIRST_NAME> and
<LAST_NAME> elements, contain text; we want to display that text. To handle
element text, you use the `characters` callback.

This method is called with three arguments: an array of type char that
holds the actual character text, the starting location in the array, and the
length of the text. For elements that contain only one text node, the starting
location is always 0 in the character array.

To add the text inside an element to the display strings, I implement the
`characters` method, converting the character array to a Java `String` object
named `characterData` like this. Note that I use the `String` class's `trim`
method to trim the text of leading and trailing spaces:

```
import org.xml.sax.*;
import org.xml.sax.helpers.DefaultHandler;
import javax.xml.parsers.*;
import java.io.*;

public class ch12_03 extends DefaultHandler
{
    static String displayStrings[] = new String[1000];
    static int numberDisplayLines = 0;
```

```
    static String indent = "";

    public void characters(char characters[], int start, int length)
    {
        String characterData = (new String(characters, start,
        ➥length)).trim();
            .
            .
            .

    }

    public static void main(String args[])
    {
        .
        .
        .
    }
}
```

To eliminate indentation text—the spaces used to indent the elements in the file ch12_01.xml—I add an `if` statement and then add the text itself to the display strings, this way:

```
import org.xml.sax.*;
import org.xml.sax.helpers.DefaultHandler;
import javax.xml.parsers.*;
import java.io.*;

public class ch12_03 extends DefaultHandler
{
    static String displayStrings[] = new String[1000];
    static int numberDisplayLines = 0;
    static String indent = "";

    public void characters(char characters[], int start, int length)
    {
        String characterData = (new String(characters, start,
        ➥length)).trim();
        if(characterData.indexOf("\n") < 0 && characterData.length() > 0) {
            displayStrings[numberDisplayLines] = indent;
            displayStrings[numberDisplayLines] += characterData;
            numberDisplayLines++;
        }
    }

    public static void main(String args[])
    {
        .
        .
        .
    }
}
```

That's all there is to it. By default, the Java SAX parser reports the whitespace that a document uses for indentation, which is called "ignorable" whitespace.

Handling Ignorable Whitespace

So how do you actually ignore "ignorable" whitespace? The SAX parser needs to know only what text it can ignore, so you must indicate what the proper grammar of the document is. You could do this with a DTD in ch12_01.xml:

```
<?xml version = "1.0" standalone="yes"?>
<!DOCTYPE DOCUMENT [
<!ELEMENT DOCUMENT (CUSTOMER)*>
<!ELEMENT CUSTOMER (NAME,DATE,ORDERS)>
<!ELEMENT NAME (LAST_NAME,FIRST_NAME)>
<!ELEMENT LAST_NAME (#PCDATA)>
<!ELEMENT FIRST_NAME (#PCDATA)>
<!ELEMENT DATE (#PCDATA)>
<!ELEMENT ORDERS (ITEM)*>
<!ELEMENT ITEM (PRODUCT,NUMBER,PRICE)>
<!ELEMENT PRODUCT (#PCDATA)>
<!ELEMENT NUMBER (#PCDATA)>
<!ELEMENT PRICE (#PCDATA)>
]>
<DOCUMENT>
    <CUSTOMER>
        <NAME>
            <LAST_NAME>Smith</LAST_NAME>
            <FIRST_NAME>Sam</FIRST_NAME>
        </NAME>
        <DATE>October 15, 2003</DATE>
        <ORDERS>
            .
            .
            .
        <ORDERS>
            <ITEM>
                <PRODUCT>Asparagus</PRODUCT>
                <NUMBER>12</NUMBER>
                <PRICE>$2.95</PRICE>
            </ITEM>
            <ITEM>
                <PRODUCT ID = "5231" TYPE = "3133">Lettuce</PRODUCT>
                <NUMBER>6</NUMBER>
                <PRICE>$11.50</PRICE>
            </ITEM>
        </ORDERS>
    </CUSTOMER>
</DOCUMENT>
```

Now, the SAX parser will not call the `characters` callback when it sees ignorable whitespace (such as indentation spaces); it will call a method named `ignorableWhitespace`. That means you can comment out the `if` statement I used to filter out ignorable whitespace before:

```
public void characters(char characters[], int start, int length)
{
    String characterData = (new String(characters, start, length)).trim();
    //if(characterData.indexOf("\n") < 0 && characterData.length() > 0) {
        displayStrings[numberDisplayLines] = indent;
        displayStrings[numberDisplayLines] += characterData;
        numberDisplayLines++;
    //}
}
```

That's all it takes. To filter out ignorable whitespace, just give the SAX parser some way of figuring out what is ignorable, such as adding a DTD to your document.

Note that you can add code to the `ignorableWhitespace` to handle that whitespace, if you like. In fact, you can even pass it on to the `characters` callback, as I'm doing here:

```
public void ignorableWhitespace(char characters[], int start, int length)
{
    characters(characters, start, length);
}
```

Handling the End of Elements

So far, we've handled the start of each element and incremented the indentation level each time to handle any possible children. We also have to display the end tag for each element and decrement the indentation level. I'll do that in the `endElement` callback, which is called each time the SAX parser reaches the end of an element. Here's what that looks like in code:

```
import org.xml.sax.*;
import org.xml.sax.helpers.DefaultHandler;
import javax.xml.parsers.*;
import java.io.*;

public class ch12_03 extends DefaultHandler
{
    static String displayStrings[] = new String[1000];
    static int numberDisplayLines = 0;
    static String indent = "";
```

```
    public void endElement(String uri, String localName, String
➥qualifiedName)
    {
        indent = indent.substring(0, indent.length() - 4);
        displayStrings[numberDisplayLines] = indent;
        displayStrings[numberDisplayLines] += "</";
        displayStrings[numberDisplayLines] += qualifiedName;
        displayStrings[numberDisplayLines] += '>';
        numberDisplayLines++;
    }

    public static void main(String args[])
    {
        .
        .
        .
    }
}
```

There's one last topic to cover: handling errors and warnings.

Handling Errors and Warnings

The DefaultHandler interface defines several callbacks to handle warnings and errors from the parser. These methods are warning, which handles parser warnings; error, which handles parser errors; and fatalError, which handles errors so severe that the parser can't continue.

Each of these methods is passed an object of the class SAXParseException. That object supports a method, getMessage, that will return the warning or error message. I display those messages using System.err.println message, which prints to the Java err output channel, which corresponds to the console by default:

```
import org.xml.sax.*;
import org.xml.sax.helpers.DefaultHandler;
import javax.xml.parsers.*;
import java.io.*;

public class ch12_03 extends DefaultHandler
{
    static String displayStrings[] = new String[1000];
    static int numberDisplayLines = 0;
    static String indent = "";
        .
        .
        .
```

```
public void warning(SAXParseException exception)
{
    System.err.println("WARNING! " +
        exception.getMessage());
}

public void error(SAXParseException exception)
{
    System.err.println("ERROR! " +
        exception.getMessage());
}

public void fatalError(SAXParseException exception)
{
    System.err.println("FATAL ERROR! " +
        exception.getMessage());
}

public static void main(String args[])
{
    .
    .
    .
    }
}
```

That's all we need. You can see the results of parsing ch12_01.xml in Figure 12-1, where I'm using the MS DOS more filter to stop the display from scrolling off the top of the window.

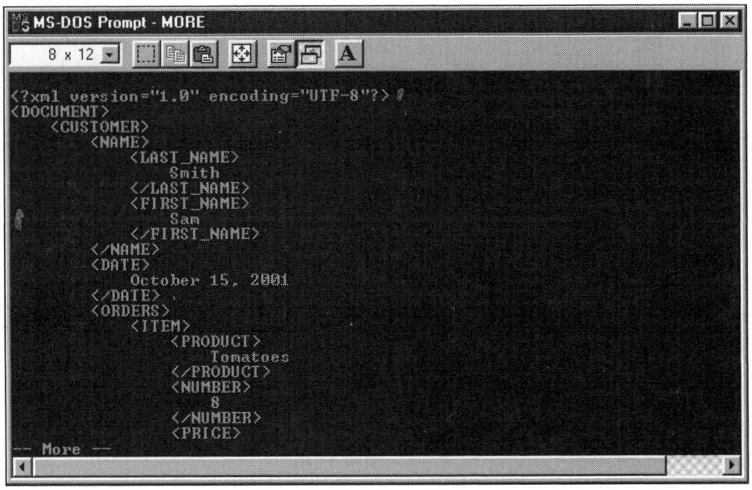

Figure 12-1
Parsing an XML document with a SAX parser.

This program is a success, and here's the complete code:

Listing ch12_03.java

```java
import org.xml.sax.*;
import org.xml.sax.helpers.DefaultHandler;
import javax.xml.parsers.*;
import java.io.*;

public class ch12_03 extends DefaultHandler
{
    static String displayStrings[] = new String[1000];
    static int numberDisplayLines = 0;
    static String indent = "";

    public void displayDocument(String uri)
    {
        DefaultHandler handler = this;
        SAXParserFactory factory = SAXParserFactory.newInstance();
        try {
            SAXParser saxParser = factory.newSAXParser();
            saxParser.parse(new File(uri), handler);
        } catch (Throwable t) {}
    }

    public void startDocument()
    {
        displayStrings[numberDisplayLines] = indent;
        displayStrings[numberDisplayLines] += "<?xml version=\"1.0\"
    ➥encoding=\""+
            "UTF-8" + "\"?>";
        numberDisplayLines++;
    }

    public void processingInstruction(String target, String data)
    {
        displayStrings[numberDisplayLines] = indent;
        displayStrings[numberDisplayLines] += "<?";
        displayStrings[numberDisplayLines] += target;
        if (data != null && data.length() > 0) {
            displayStrings[numberDisplayLines] += ' ';
            displayStrings[numberDisplayLines] += data;
        }
        displayStrings[numberDisplayLines] += "?>";
        numberDisplayLines++;
    }

    public void startElement(String uri, String localName, String
    ➥qualifiedName,
        Attributes attributes)
```

```
{
    displayStrings[numberDisplayLines] = indent;

    indent += "    ";

    displayStrings[numberDisplayLines] += '<';
    displayStrings[numberDisplayLines] += qualifiedName;
    if (attributes != null) {
        int numberAttributes = attributes.getLength();
        for (int loopIndex = 0; loopIndex < numberAttributes;
        ➥loopIndex++) {
            displayStrings[numberDisplayLines] += ' ';
            displayStrings[numberDisplayLines] +=
            ➥attributes.getLocalName(loopIndex);
            displayStrings[numberDisplayLines] += "=\"";
            displayStrings[numberDisplayLines] +=
            ➥attributes.getValue(loopIndex);
            displayStrings[numberDisplayLines] += '"';
        }
    }
    displayStrings[numberDisplayLines] += '>';
    numberDisplayLines++;
}

public void characters(char characters[], int start, int length)
{
    String characterData = (new String(characters, start,
    ➥length)).trim();
    if(characterData.indexOf("\n") < 0 && characterData.length() > 0) {
        displayStrings[numberDisplayLines] = indent;
        displayStrings[numberDisplayLines] += characterData;
        numberDisplayLines++;
    }
}

public void ignorableWhitespace(char characters[], int start, int
➥length)
{
    //characters(characters, start, length);
}

public void endElement(String uri, String localName, String
➥qualifiedName)
{
    indent = indent.substring(0, indent.length() - 4);
    displayStrings[numberDisplayLines] = indent;
    displayStrings[numberDisplayLines] += "</";
    displayStrings[numberDisplayLines] += qualifiedName;
    displayStrings[numberDisplayLines] += '>';
    numberDisplayLines++;
}
```

continues

Listing ch12_03.java   Continued

```java
    public void warning(SAXParseException exception)
    {
        System.err.println("WARNING! " +
            exception.getMessage());
    }

    public void error(SAXParseException exception)
    {
        System.err.println("ERROR! " +
            exception.getMessage());
    }

    public void fatalError(SAXParseException exception)
    {
        System.err.println("FATAL ERROR! " +
            exception.getMessage());
    }

    public static void main(String args[])
    {
        ch12_03 obj = new ch12_03();
        obj.displayDocument(args[0]);

        for(int index = 0; index < numberDisplayLines; index++){
            System.out.println(displayStrings[index]);
        }
    }
}
```

Filtering XML Documents

The previous example displayed the entire document, but as we saw in the previous chapter, you can be more selective than that through a process called filtering. When you filter a document, you extract only those elements you're interested in.

Here's a new example named ch12_04.java. In this case, I'll let the user specify what document to search and what element name to search for. This will display all <ITEM> elements in ch12_01.xml:

```
%java ch12_04 ch12_01.xml ITEM
```

This program is not difficult to write, now that we've written the indenting parser example. Note, however, that we have to handle not just the specific element that the user is searching for, but also the element's children that are contained inside the element. I'll adapt the ch12_03.java application to create ch12_04.java; all we'll have to control is when we display elements and when we do not. If the current element matches the element the user is searching for, I'll set a Boolean variable named printFlag to true:

```
public void startElement(String uri, String localName, String
➥qualifiedName, Attributes attributes)
{
    if(qualifiedName.equals(searchFor)){
        printFlag=true;
    }
      .
      .
      .
}
```

Now I can check whether printFlag is true and, if so, add the current element and its attributes to the display strings:

```
public void startElement(String uri, String localName, String
➥qualifiedName, Attributes attributes)
{
    if(qualifiedName.equals(searchFor)){
        printFlag=true;
    }

    if (printFlag){
        displayStrings[numberDisplayLines] = indent;

        indent += "    ";

        displayStrings[numberDisplayLines] += '<';
        displayStrings[numberDisplayLines] += qualifiedName;
        if (attributes != null) {
            int numberAttributes = attributes.getLength();
            for (int loopIndex = 0; loopIndex < numberAttributes;
            ➥loopIndex++) {
                displayStrings[numberDisplayLines] += ' ';
                displayStrings[numberDisplayLines] +=
                ➥attributes.getLocalName(loopIndex);
                displayStrings[numberDisplayLines] += "=\"";
                displayStrings[numberDisplayLines] +=
                ➥attributes.getValue(loopIndex);
                displayStrings[numberDisplayLines] += '"';
            }
```

```
        }
        displayStrings[numberDisplayLines] += '>';
        numberDisplayLines++;
    }
}
```

And I can do the same in other callback methods that add text to the displayStrings array, such as the character callback:

```
public void characters(char characters[], int start, int length) {
    if(printFlag){
        String characterData = (new String(characters, start,
        ➥length)).trim();
        if(characterData.indexOf("\n") < 0 && characterData.length() > 0) {
            displayStrings[numberDisplayLines] = indent;
            displayStrings[numberDisplayLines] += characterData;
            numberDisplayLines++;
        }
    }
}
```

Note that we don't want to set printFlag to false until after the element that the user is searching for ends, at which point we've displayed the whole element and all its children. When the element ends, I set printFlag to false this way:

```
public void endElement(String uri, String localName, String qualifiedName)
{
    if(printFlag){
        indent = indent.substring(0, indent.length() - 4);
        displayStrings[numberDisplayLines] = indent;
        displayStrings[numberDisplayLines] += "</";
        displayStrings[numberDisplayLines] += qualifiedName;
        displayStrings[numberDisplayLines] += '>';
        numberDisplayLines++;
    }
    if(qualifiedName.equals(searchFor)){
        printFlag=false;
    }
}
```

That's all it takes. I'll filter ch12_01.xml for <ITEM> elements like this:

```
%java ch12_04 ch12_01.xml ITEM | MORE
```

You can see the results in Figure 12-2, where I'm filtering ch12_01.xml to find all <ITEM> elements.

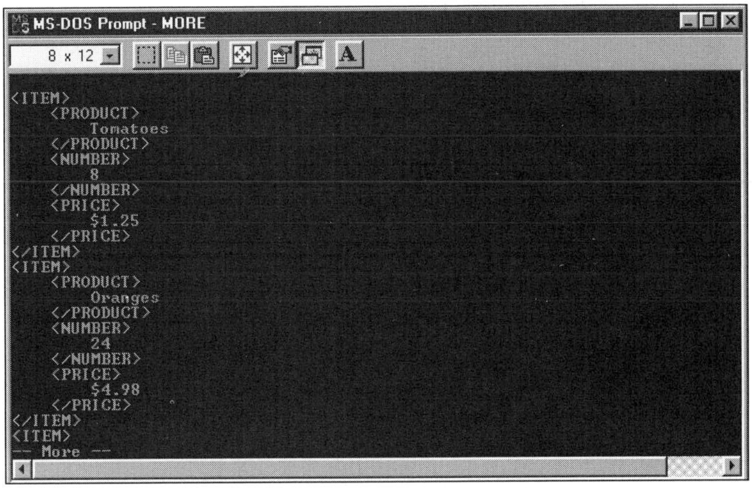

Figure 12-2
Filtering an
XML
document
using a SAX
parser.

Here's the complete code:

Listing ch12_04.java

```java
import org.xml.sax.*;
import org.xml.sax.helpers.DefaultHandler;
import javax.xml.parsers.*;
import java.io.*;

public class ch12_04 extends DefaultHandler
{
    static String displayStrings[] = new String[1000];
    static int numberDisplayLines = 0;
    static String indent = "";
    static boolean printFlag;
    static String searchFor;

    public void displayDocument(String uri)
    {
        DefaultHandler handler = this;
        SAXParserFactory factory = SAXParserFactory.newInstance();
        try {
            SAXParser saxParser = factory.newSAXParser();
            saxParser.parse(new File(uri), handler);
        } catch (Throwable t) {}
    }

    public void processingInstruction(String target, String data)
    {
        if(printFlag){
```

continues

Listing ch12_04.java   Continued

```java
            displayStrings[numberDisplayLines] = indent;
            displayStrings[numberDisplayLines] += "<?";
            displayStrings[numberDisplayLines] += target;
            if (data != null && data.length() > 0) {
                displayStrings[numberDisplayLines] += ' ';
                displayStrings[numberDisplayLines] += data;
            }
            displayStrings[numberDisplayLines] += "?>";
            numberDisplayLines++;
        }
    }

    public void startDocument()
    {
        if(printFlag){
            displayStrings[numberDisplayLines] = indent;
            displayStrings[numberDisplayLines] += "<?xml version=\"1.0\""
    ➥encoding=\""+
                "UTF-8" + "\"?>";
            numberDisplayLines++;
        }
    }

    public void startElement(String uri, String localName, String
    ➥qualifiedName, Attributes attributes)
    {
        if(qualifiedName.equals(searchFor)){
            printFlag=true;
        }

        if (printFlag){
            displayStrings[numberDisplayLines] = indent;

            indent += "    ";

            displayStrings[numberDisplayLines] += '<';
            displayStrings[numberDisplayLines] += qualifiedName;
            if (attributes != null) {
                int numberAttributes = attributes.getLength();
                for (int loopIndex = 0; loopIndex < numberAttributes;
                ➥loopIndex++) {
                    displayStrings[numberDisplayLines] += ' ';
                    displayStrings[numberDisplayLines] +=
                    ➥attributes.getLocalName(loopIndex);
                    displayStrings[numberDisplayLines] += "=\"";
                    displayStrings[numberDisplayLines] +=
                    ➥attributes.getValue(loopIndex);
                    displayStrings[numberDisplayLines] += '"';
                }
```

```
        }
        displayStrings[numberDisplayLines] += '>';
        numberDisplayLines++;
    }
}

public void characters(char characters[], int start, int length) {
    if(printFlag){
        String characterData = (new String(characters, start,
        ➥length)).trim();
        if(characterData.indexOf("\n") < 0 && characterData.length() >
        ➥0) {
            displayStrings[numberDisplayLines] = indent;
            displayStrings[numberDisplayLines] += characterData;
            numberDisplayLines++;
        }
    }
}

public void ignorableWhitespace(char characters[], int start, int
➥length)
{
    if(printFlag){
        //characters(ch, start, length);
    }
}

public void endElement(String uri, String localName, String
➥qualifiedName)
{
    if(printFlag){
        indent = indent.substring(0, indent.length() - 4);
        displayStrings[numberDisplayLines] = indent;
        displayStrings[numberDisplayLines] += "</";
        displayStrings[numberDisplayLines] += qualifiedName;
        displayStrings[numberDisplayLines] += '>';
        numberDisplayLines++;
    }
    if(qualifiedName.equals(searchFor)){
        printFlag=false;
    }
}

public void warning(SAXParseException exception)
{
    System.err.println("WARNING! " +
        exception.getMessage());
}

public void error(SAXParseException exception)
{
```

continues

Listing ch12_04.java   Continued

```java
        System.err.println("ERROR! " +
            exception.getMessage());
    }

    public void fatalError(SAXParseException exception)
    {
        System.err.println("FATAL ERROR! " +
            exception.getMessage());
    }

    public static void main(String args[])
    {
        ch12_04 obj = new ch12_04();
        searchFor = args[1];
        obj.displayDocument(args[0]);

        for(int index = 0; index < numberDisplayLines; index++){
            System.out.println(displayStrings[index]);
        }
    }
}
```

The examples we've created so far have all created text-based output using the `System.out.println` method. As noted in the previous chapter, however, few browsers these days work that way. In the next section, I'll take a look at creating a windowed browser.

Creating a Windowed Browser

We wrote the indenting parser example to store the display text in an array named `displayStrings`, so it's easy to display that text in a Java window as we did in the previous chapter. To do that, I'll create a new example named ch12_05.java. In this program, I'll create a new object of a class that I'll call `AppFrame`, and I'll pass `displayStrings` and the number of lines to display to the `AppFrame` class's constructor. Then I'll call the `AppFrame` object's show method to show the window:

```java
import java.awt.*;
import java.awt.event.*;

import org.xml.sax.*;
import org.xml.sax.helpers.DefaultHandler;
import javax.xml.parsers.*;
import java.io.*;

public class ch12_05 extends DefaultHandler
{
```

```
     .
     .
     .
    public static void main(String args[])
    {
        ch12_05 obj = new ch12_05();
        obj.displayDocument(args[0]);

        AppFrame f = new AppFrame(displayStrings, numberDisplayLines);

        f.setSize(300, 500);

        f.addWindowListener(new WindowAdapter() {public void
            windowClosing(WindowEvent e) {System.exit(0);}});

        f.show();
    }
}
```

The AppFrame class is based on the Java Frame class, and it displays the text we've passed to it:

```
class AppFrame extends Frame
{
    String displayStrings[];
    int numberDisplayLines;

    public AppFrame(String[] d, int n)
    {
        displayStrings = d;
        numberDisplayLines = n;
    }

    public void paint(Graphics g)
    {
        Font font;

        font = new Font("Courier", Font.PLAIN, 12);
        g.setFont(font);

        FontMetrics fontmetrics = g.getFontMetrics(getFont());
        int y = fontmetrics.getHeight();

        for(int index = 0; index < numberDisplayLines; index++){
            y += fontmetrics.getHeight();
            g.drawString(displayStrings[index], 5, y);
        }
    }
}
```

You can see this new application at work in Figure 12-3, where ch12_01.xml is displayed in a Java window.

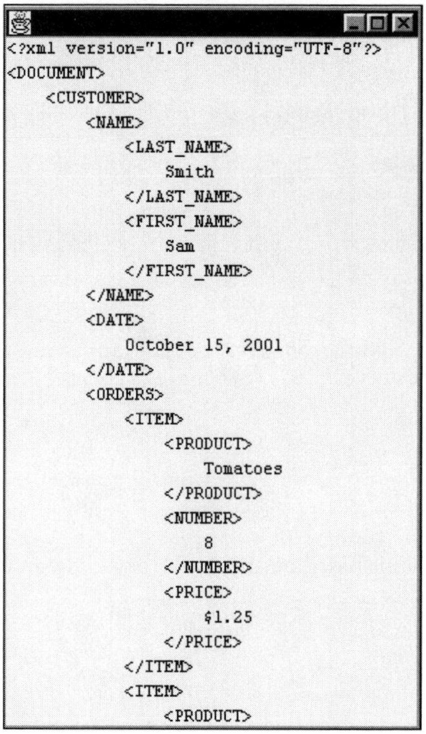

Figure 12-3
A window-based browser using a SAX parser.

```
<?xml version="1.0" encoding="UTF-8"?>
<DOCUMENT>
    <CUSTOMER>
        <NAME>
            <LAST_NAME>
                Smith
            </LAST_NAME>
            <FIRST_NAME>
                Sam
            </FIRST_NAME>
        </NAME>
        <DATE>
            October 15, 2001
        </DATE>
        <ORDERS>
            <ITEM>
                <PRODUCT>
                    Tomatoes
                </PRODUCT>
                <NUMBER>
                    8
                </NUMBER>
                <PRICE>
                    $1.25
                </PRICE>
            </ITEM>
            <ITEM>
                <PRODUCT>
```

Here's the code for this example:

Listing ch12_05.java

```java
import java.awt.*;
import java.awt.event.*;

import org.xml.sax.*;
import org.xml.sax.helpers.DefaultHandler;
import javax.xml.parsers.*;
import java.io.*;

public class ch12_05 extends DefaultHandler
{
    static String displayStrings[] = new String[1000];
    static int numberDisplayLines = 0;
    static String indent = "";
```

```java
public void displayDocument(String uri)
{
    DefaultHandler handler = this;
    SAXParserFactory factory = SAXParserFactory.newInstance();
    try {
        SAXParser saxParser = factory.newSAXParser();
        saxParser.parse(new File(uri), handler);
    } catch (Throwable t) {}
}

public void processingInstruction(String target, String data)
{
    displayStrings[numberDisplayLines] = indent;
    displayStrings[numberDisplayLines] += "<?";
    displayStrings[numberDisplayLines] += target;
    if (data != null && data.length() > 0) {
        displayStrings[numberDisplayLines] += ' ';
        displayStrings[numberDisplayLines] += data;
    }
    displayStrings[numberDisplayLines] += "?>";
    numberDisplayLines++;
}

public void startDocument()
{
    displayStrings[numberDisplayLines] = indent;
    displayStrings[numberDisplayLines] += "<?xml version=\"1.0\"
    ➥encoding=\""+
        "UTF-8" + "\"?>";
    numberDisplayLines++;
}

public void startElement(String uri, String localName, String
➥qualifiedName,
    Attributes attributes)
{
    displayStrings[numberDisplayLines] = indent;

    indent += "    ";

    displayStrings[numberDisplayLines] += '<';
    displayStrings[numberDisplayLines] += qualifiedName;
    if (attributes != null) {
        int numberAttributes = attributes.getLength();
        for (int loopIndex = 0; loopIndex < numberAttributes;
        ➥loopIndex++) {
```

continues

Listing ch12_05.java   Continued

```java
                displayStrings[numberDisplayLines] += ' ';
                displayStrings[numberDisplayLines] +=
                ➥attributes.getLocalName(loopIndex);
                displayStrings[numberDisplayLines] += "=\"";
                displayStrings[numberDisplayLines] +=
                ➥attributes.getValue(loopIndex);
                displayStrings[numberDisplayLines] += '"';
            }
        }
        displayStrings[numberDisplayLines] += '>';
        numberDisplayLines++;
    }

    public void characters(char characters[], int start, int length)
    {
        String characterData = (new String(characters, start,
        ➥length)).trim();
        if(characterData.indexOf("\n") < 0 && characterData.length() > 0) {
            displayStrings[numberDisplayLines] = indent;
            displayStrings[numberDisplayLines] += characterData;
            numberDisplayLines++;
        }
    }

    public void ignorableWhitespace(char characters[], int start, int
    ➥length)
    {
        //characters(characters, start, length);
    }

    public void endElement(String uri, String localName, String
    ➥qualifiedName)
    {
        indent = indent.substring(0, indent.length() - 4);
        displayStrings[numberDisplayLines] = indent;
        displayStrings[numberDisplayLines] += "</";
        displayStrings[numberDisplayLines] += qualifiedName;
        displayStrings[numberDisplayLines] += '>';
        numberDisplayLines++;
    }

    public void warning(SAXParseException exception)
    {
        System.err.println("WARNING! " +
            exception.getMessage());
    }

    public void error(SAXParseException exception)
    {
        System.err.println("ERROR! " +
            exception.getMessage());
```

```java
    }

    public void fatalError(SAXParseException exception)
    {
        System.err.println("FATAL ERROR! " +
            exception.getMessage());
    }

    public static void main(String args[])
    {
        ch12_05 obj = new ch12_05();
        obj.displayDocument(args[0]);

        AppFrame f = new AppFrame(displayStrings, numberDisplayLines);

        f.setSize(300, 500);

        f.addWindowListener(new WindowAdapter() {public void
            windowClosing(WindowEvent e) {System.exit(0);}});

        f.show();
    }
}

class AppFrame extends Frame
{
    String displayStrings[];
    int numberDisplayLines;

    public AppFrame(String[] d, int n)
    {
        displayStrings = d;
        numberDisplayLines = n;
    }

    public void paint(Graphics g)
    {
        Font font;

        font = new Font("Courier", Font.PLAIN, 12);
        g.setFont(font);

        FontMetrics fontmetrics = g.getFontMetrics(getFont());
        int y = fontmetrics.getHeight();

        for(int index = 0; index < numberDisplayLines; index++){
            y += fontmetrics.getHeight();
            g.drawString(displayStrings[index], 5, y);
        }
    }
}
```

Now that we're parsing and displaying XML documents in windows, there's no reason to restrict ourselves to displaying the text form of an XML document, just as we did in the previous chapter. But this time, we'll use the SAX parser. Take a look at the next section.

Creating a Graphical Browser

In the previous chapter, I adapted the DOM parser browser that we wrote to display circles. It will be instructive to do the same here for the SAX parser browser because it will show how to retrieve specific attribute values. Here's the document that this browser might read—in this chapter, I'll call this document ch12_06.xml. As in the previous chapter, I'm specifying the (x, y) origin of each circle and the radius of the circle as attributes of the <CIRCLE> element:

Listing ch12_06.xml

```
<?xml version = "1.0" ?>
<!DOCTYPE DOCUMENT [
<!ELEMENT DOCUMENT (CIRCLE|ELLIPSE)*>
<!ELEMENT CIRCLE EMPTY>
<!ELEMENT ELLIPSE EMPTY>
<!ATTLIST CIRCLE
    X CDATA #IMPLIED
    Y CDATA #IMPLIED
    RADIUS CDATA #IMPLIED>
<!ATTLIST ELLIPSE
    X CDATA #IMPLIED
    Y CDATA #IMPLIED
    WIDTH CDATA #IMPLIED
    HEIGHT CDATA #IMPLIED>
]>
<DOCUMENT>
    <CIRCLE X='200' Y='160' RADIUS='50' />
    <CIRCLE X='170' Y='100' RADIUS='15' />
    <CIRCLE X='80' Y='200' RADIUS='45' />
    <CIRCLE X='200' Y='140' RADIUS='35' />
    <CIRCLE X='130' Y='240' RADIUS='25' />
    <CIRCLE X='270' Y='300' RADIUS='45' />
    <CIRCLE X='210' Y='240' RADIUS='25' />
    <CIRCLE X='60' Y='160' RADIUS='35' />
    <CIRCLE X='160' Y='260' RADIUS='55' />
</DOCUMENT>
```

Here the trick will be to recover the values of the attributes X, Y, and RADIUS. I'll store those values in arrays named x, y, and radius. It turns out that getting an element's attribute values is easier using Java's SAX parser than it is with the DOM parser. The startElement method is passed an object of Attributes interface; all you have to do is to use that object's getValue method, passing it the name of the attribute you're interested in:

```java
import java.awt.*;
import java.awt.event.*;

import org.xml.sax.*;
import org.xml.sax.helpers.DefaultHandler;
import javax.xml.parsers.*;
import java.io.*;

public class ch12_07 extends DefaultHandler
{
    static int numberFigures = 0;
    static int x[] = new int[100];
    static int y[] = new int[100];
    static int radius[] = new int[100];
    .
    .
    .
    public void startElement(String uri, String localName, String
    ➥qualifiedName, Attributes attrs)
    {
        if (qualifiedName.equals("CIRCLE")) {
            x[numberFigures] = Integer.parseInt(attrs.getValue("X"));
            y[numberFigures] = Integer.parseInt(attrs.getValue("Y"));
            radius[numberFigures] = Integer.parseInt
            ➥(attrs.getValue("RADIUS"));
            numberFigures++;
        }
    }
    .
    .
    .
    public static void main(String args[])
    {
        .
        .
        .
    }
}
```

Having stored all the circles' data, I display them in the AppFrame class as we did in the previous chapter:

```
class AppFrame extends Frame
{
    int numberFigures;
    int[] xValues;
    int[] yValues;
    int[] radiusValues;

    public AppFrame(int number, int[] x, int[] y, int[] radius)
    {
        numberFigures = number;
        xValues = x;
        yValues = y;
        radiusValues = radius;
    }

    public void paint(Graphics g)
    {
        for(int loopIndex = 0; loopIndex < numberFigures; loopIndex++){
            g.drawOval(xValues[loopIndex], yValues[loopIndex],
            ➥radiusValues[loopIndex], radiusValues[loopIndex]);
        }
    }
}
```

And that's all it takes. You can see the results in Figure 12-4, where the browser is displaying circles.xml.

Figure 12-4
Creating a graphical XML browser using a SAX parser.

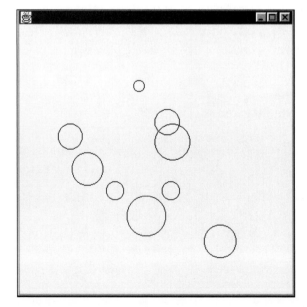

Here's the code for this example:

Listing ch12_07.java

```java
import java.awt.*;
import java.awt.event.*;

import org.xml.sax.*;
import org.xml.sax.helpers.DefaultHandler;
import javax.xml.parsers.*;
import java.io.*;

public class ch12_07 extends DefaultHandler
{
    static int numberFigures = 0;
    static int x[] = new int[100];
    static int y[] = new int[100];
    static int radius[] = new int[100];

    public void displayDocument(String uri)
    {
        DefaultHandler handler = this;
        SAXParserFactory factory = SAXParserFactory.newInstance();
        try {
            SAXParser saxParser = factory.newSAXParser();
            saxParser.parse(new File(uri), handler);
        } catch (Throwable t) {}
    }

    public void startElement(String uri, String localName, String
    ➥qualifiedName, Attributes attrs)
    {
        if (qualifiedName.equals("CIRCLE")) {
            x[numberFigures] = Integer.parseInt(attrs.getValue("X"));
            y[numberFigures] = Integer.parseInt(attrs.getValue("Y"));
            radius[numberFigures] = Integer.parseInt
            ➥(attrs.getValue("RADIUS"));
            numberFigures++;
        }
    }

    public void warning(SAXParseException exception)
    {
        System.err.println("WARNING! " +
            exception.getMessage());
    }

    public void error(SAXParseException exception)
    {
```

continues

Listing ch12_07.java   Continued

```java
        System.err.println("ERROR! " +
            exception.getMessage());
    }

    public void fatalError(SAXParseException exception)
    {
        System.err.println("FATAL ERROR! " +
            exception.getMessage());
    }

    public static void main(String args[])
    {
        ch12_07 obj = new ch12_07();
        obj.displayDocument(args[0]);

        AppFrame f = new AppFrame(numberFigures, x, y, radius);

        f.setSize(400, 400);

        f.addWindowListener(new WindowAdapter() {public void
            windowClosing(WindowEvent e) {System.exit(0);}});

        f.show();
    }
}

class AppFrame extends Frame
{
    int numberFigures;
    int[] xValues;
    int[] yValues;
    int[] radiusValues;

    public AppFrame(int number, int[] x, int[] y, int[] radius)
    {
        numberFigures = number;
        xValues = x;
        yValues = y;
        radiusValues = radius;
    }

    public void paint(Graphics g)
    {
        for(int loopIndex = 0; loopIndex < numberFigures; loopIndex++){
            g.drawOval(xValues[loopIndex], yValues[loopIndex],
            ➥radiusValues[loopIndex], radiusValues[loopIndex]);
        }
    }
}
```

Navigating in XML Documents

The Node interface available when you use the DOM parser contains all the standard W3C DOM methods for navigating in a document, such as getNextSibling, getPreviousSibling, getFirstChild, getLastChild, and getParent. It's different when you use a SAX parser: This parser does not create a tree of nodes, so those methods don't apply.

Instead, if you want to find a particular element, you have to find it yourself. In the previous chapter, I found the third person's name in this document, which we'll call ch12_08.xml here:

Listing ch12_08.xml

```
<?xml version="1.0"?>
<MEETINGS>
    <MEETING TYPE="informal">
        <MEETING_TITLE>XML In The Real World</MEETING_TITLE>
        <MEETING_NUMBER>2079</MEETING_NUMBER>
        <SUBJECT>XML</SUBJECT>
        <DATE>6/1/2002</DATE>
        <PEOPLE>
            <PERSON ATTENDANCE="present">
                <FIRST_NAME>Edward</FIRST_NAME>
                <LAST_NAME>Samson</LAST_NAME>
            </PERSON>
            <PERSON ATTENDANCE="absent">
                <FIRST_NAME>Ernestine</FIRST_NAME>
                <LAST_NAME>Johnson</LAST_NAME>
            </PERSON>
            <PERSON ATTENDANCE="present">
                <FIRST_NAME>Betty</FIRST_NAME>
                <LAST_NAME>Richardson</LAST_NAME>
            </PERSON>
        </PEOPLE>
    </MEETING>
</MEETINGS>
```

It's not difficult to do the same thing here, but in SAX programming, finding a specific element takes a little code. I start by finding the third <PERSON> element and setting a variable named thirdPersonFlag to true when I find it:

```
public void startElement(String uri, String localName, String qualifiedName,
➥Attributes attributes)
{
    if(qualifiedName.equals("PERSON")) {
        personCount++;
```

```
        }

        if(personCount == 3) {
            thirdPersonFlag = true;
        }
        .
        .
        .
}
```

When the SAX parser is parsing the third person's <FIRST_NAME> element, I'll set a variable named firstNameFlag to true. When it's parsing the third person's <LAST_NAME> element, I'll set a variable named lastNameFlag to true:

```
public void startElement(String uri, String localName, String qualifiedName,
➥Attributes attributes)
{
    if(qualifiedName.equals("PERSON")) {
        personCount++;
    }

    if(personCount == 3) {
        thirdPersonFlag = true;
    }

    if(qualifiedName.equals("FIRST_NAME") && thirdPersonFlag) {
        firstNameFlag = true;
    }

    if(qualifiedName.equals("LAST_NAME")  && thirdPersonFlag) {
        firstNameFlag = false;
        lastNameFlag = true;
    }
}
```

Watching the variables firstNameFlag and lastNameFlag, I can store the person's first and last names in the character callback:

```
public void characters(char characters[], int start, int length)
{
    String characterData = (new String(characters, start, length)).trim();
    if(characterData.indexOf("\n") < 0 && characterData.length() > 0) {
        if(firstNameFlag) {
            firstName = characterData;
        }
        if(lastNameFlag) {
            lastName = characterData;
        }
    }
}
```

When the SAX parser is done parsing the third `<PERSON>` element, I'll display that person's name:

```java
public void endElement(String uri, String localName, String qualifiedName)
{
    if(thirdPersonFlag && lastNameFlag){
        System.out.println("Third name: " + firstName + " " + lastName);
        thirdPersonFlag = false;
        firstNameFlag = false;
        lastNameFlag = false;
    }
}
```

And that's the technique you use when you're hunting a specific element using a SAX parser. You just wait until the parser hands it to you. Here are the results:

```
%java ch12_09 ch12_08.xml
Third name: Betty Richardson
```

Here's the full code for this program, ch12_09.java:

Listing ch12_09.java

```java
import org.xml.sax.*;
import org.xml.sax.helpers.DefaultHandler;
import javax.xml.parsers.*;
import java.io.*;

public class ch12_09 extends DefaultHandler
{
    int personCount;
    boolean thirdPersonFlag = false, firstNameFlag = false, lastNameFlag =
    ➥false;
    String firstName, lastName;

    public void displayDocument(String uri)
    {
        DefaultHandler handler = this;
        SAXParserFactory factory = SAXParserFactory.newInstance();
        try {
            SAXParser saxParser = factory.newSAXParser();
            saxParser.parse(new File(uri), handler);
        } catch (Throwable t) {}
    }

    public void startElement(String uri, String localName, String
    ➥qualifiedName, Attributes attributes)
```

continues

Listing ch12_09.java   Continued

```java
{
    if(qualifiedName.equals("PERSON")) {
        personCount++;
    }

    if(personCount == 3) {
        thirdPersonFlag = true;
    }

    if(qualifiedName.equals("FIRST_NAME") && thirdPersonFlag) {
        firstNameFlag = true;
    }

    if(qualifiedName.equals("LAST_NAME")  && thirdPersonFlag) {
        firstNameFlag = false;
        lastNameFlag = true;
    }

}

public void characters(char characters[], int start, int length)
{
    String characterData = (new String(characters, start,
    ➥length)).trim();
    if(characterData.indexOf("\n") < 0 && characterData.length() > 0) {
        if(firstNameFlag) {
            firstName = characterData;
        }
        if(lastNameFlag) {
            lastName = characterData;
        }
    }
}

public void endElement(String uri, String localName, String
➥qualifiedName)
{
    if(thirdPersonFlag && lastNameFlag){
        System.out.println("Third name: " + firstName + " " +
        ➥lastName);
        thirdPersonFlag = false;
        firstNameFlag = false;
        lastNameFlag = false;
    }
}

public void warning(SAXParseException exception)
{
    System.err.println("WARNING! " +
```

```
            exception.getMessage());
    }

    public void error(SAXParseException exception)
    {
        System.err.println("ERROR! " +
            exception.getMessage());
    }

    public void fatalError(SAXParseException exception)
    {
        System.err.println("FATAL ERROR! " +
            exception.getMessage());
    }

    public static void main(String args[])
    {
        ch12_09 obj = new ch12_09();
        obj.displayDocument(args[0]);
    }
}
```

Modifying XML Documents

In the previous chapter, we saw that the Java DOM parser has several methods, such as insertBefore and addChild, that let you modify a document in memory. SAX parsers don't give you access to the whole document tree at once, so no similar methods exist here.

However, you can "modify" the structure of a document when using a SAX parser simply by calling various callback methods yourself. For example, you can modify ch12_01.xml to create ch12_11.xml, adding a <MIDDLE_NAME> element with the text "XML" to each <PERSON> element in addition to the <FIRST_NAME> and <LAST_NAME> elements. It's easy enough to do the same here using SAX methods. All I have to do is to wait for a <FIST_NAME> element and then "create" a new element by calling the startElement, characters, and endElement callbacks myself:

```
public void endElement(String uri, String localName, String qualifiedName)
{
    indent = indent.substring(0, indent.length() - 4);
    displayStrings[numberDisplayLines] = indent;
    displayStrings[numberDisplayLines] += "</";
    displayStrings[numberDisplayLines] += qualifiedName;
    displayStrings[numberDisplayLines] += '>';
    numberDisplayLines++;
```

```
    if (qualifiedName.equals("FIRST_NAME")) {
        startElement("", "MIDDLE_NAME", "MIDDLE_NAME", null);
        characters("XML".toCharArray(), 0, "XML".length());
        endElement("", "MIDDLE_NAME", "MIDDLE_NAME");
    }
}
```

In the main method, I'll write this new document out to ch12_11.xml:

```
public static void main(String args[])
{
    displayDocument(args[0]);

    try {
        FileWriter filewriter = new FileWriter("ch12_11.xml");

        for(int loopIndex = 0; loopIndex < numberDisplayLines;
        ➥loopIndex++){
            filewriter.write(displayStrings[loopIndex].toCharArray());
            filewriter.write('\n');
        }

        filewriter.close();
    }
    catch (Exception e) {
        e.printStackTrace(System.err);
    }
}
}
```

And that's it—here's the whole code:

Listing ch12_10.java

```
import org.xml.sax.*;
import org.xml.sax.helpers.DefaultHandler;
import javax.xml.parsers.*;
import java.io.*;

public class ch12_10 extends DefaultHandler
{
    static String displayStrings[] = new String[1000];
    static int numberDisplayLines = 0;
    static String indent = "";

    public void displayDocument(String uri)
    {
        DefaultHandler handler = this;
```

```
    SAXParserFactory factory = SAXParserFactory.newInstance();
    try {
        SAXParser saxParser = factory.newSAXParser();
        saxParser.parse(new File(uri), handler);
    } catch (Throwable t) {}
}

public void startDocument()
{
    displayStrings[numberDisplayLines] = indent;
    displayStrings[numberDisplayLines] += "<?xml version=\"1.0\"
    ➥encoding=\""+
        "UTF-8" + "\"?>";
    numberDisplayLines++;
}

public void processingInstruction(String target, String data)
{
    displayStrings[numberDisplayLines] = indent;
    displayStrings[numberDisplayLines] += "<?";
    displayStrings[numberDisplayLines] += target;
    if (data != null && data.length() > 0) {
        displayStrings[numberDisplayLines] += ' ';
        displayStrings[numberDisplayLines] += data;
    }
    displayStrings[numberDisplayLines] += "?>";
    numberDisplayLines++;
}

public void startElement(String uri, String localName, String
➥qualifiedName,
    Attributes attributes)
{
    displayStrings[numberDisplayLines] = indent;

    indent += "     ";

    displayStrings[numberDisplayLines] += '<';
    displayStrings[numberDisplayLines] += qualifiedName;
    if (attributes != null) {
        int numberAttributes = attributes.getLength();
        for (int loopIndex = 0; loopIndex < numberAttributes;
        ➥loopIndex++) {
            displayStrings[numberDisplayLines] += ' ';
            displayStrings[numberDisplayLines] +=
            ➥attributes.getLocalName(loopIndex);
            displayStrings[numberDisplayLines] += "=\"";
            displayStrings[numberDisplayLines] +=
            ➥attributes.getValue(loopIndex);
            displayStrings[numberDisplayLines] += '"';
        }
```

continues

Listing ch12_10.java   Continued

```java
        }
        displayStrings[numberDisplayLines] += '>';
        numberDisplayLines++;
    }

    public void characters(char characters[], int start, int length)
    {
        String characterData = (new String(characters, start,
        ➥length)).trim();
        if(characterData.indexOf("\n") < 0 && characterData.length() > 0) {
            displayStrings[numberDisplayLines] = indent;
            displayStrings[numberDisplayLines] += characterData;
            numberDisplayLines++;
        }
    }

    public void ignorableWhitespace(char characters[], int start, int
    ➥length)
    {
        //characters(characters, start, length);
    }

    public void endElement(String uri, String localName, String
    ➥qualifiedName)
    {
        indent = indent.substring(0, indent.length() - 4);
        displayStrings[numberDisplayLines] = indent;
        displayStrings[numberDisplayLines] += "</";
        displayStrings[numberDisplayLines] += qualifiedName;
        displayStrings[numberDisplayLines] += '>';
        numberDisplayLines++;

        if (qualifiedName.equals("FIRST_NAME")) {
            startElement("", "MIDDLE_NAME", "MIDDLE_NAME", null);
            characters("XML".toCharArray(), 0, "XML".length());
            endElement("", "MIDDLE_NAME", "MIDDLE_NAME");
        }
    }

    public void warning(SAXParseException exception)
    {
        System.err.println("WARNING! " +
            exception.getMessage());
    }

    public void error(SAXParseException exception)
    {
        System.err.println("ERROR! " +
            exception.getMessage());
    }
```

```
public void fatalError(SAXParseException exception)
{
    System.err.println("FATAL ERROR! " +
        exception.getMessage());
}

public static void main(String args[])
{
    ch12_10 obj = new ch12_10();
    obj.displayDocument(args[0]);

    try {
        FileWriter filewriter = new FileWriter("ch12_11.xml");

        for(int loopIndex = 0; loopIndex < numberDisplayLines;
        ➥loopIndex++){
            filewriter.write(displayStrings[loopIndex].toCharArray());
            filewriter.write('\n');
        }

        filewriter.close();
    }
    catch (Exception e) {
        e.printStackTrace(System.err);
    }
}
}
```

And here's what the resulting document, ch12_11.xml, looks like, with the new <MIDDLE_NAME> elements:

Listing ch12_11.xml

```xml
<?xml version="1.0" encoding="UTF-8"?>
<DOCUMENT>
    <CUSTOMER>
        <NAME>
            <LAST_NAME>
                Smith
            </LAST_NAME>
            <FIRST_NAME>
                Sam
            </FIRST_NAME>
            <MIDDLE_NAME>
                XML
            </MIDDLE_NAME>
        </NAME>
        <DATE>
            October 15, 2003
```

continues

Listing ch12_11.xml   Continued

```
            </DATE>
            <ORDERS>
                <ITEM>
                    <PRODUCT>
                        Tomatoes
                    </PRODUCT>
                    <NUMBER>
                        8
                    </NUMBER>
                    <PRICE>
                        $1.25
                    </PRICE>
                </ITEM>
                <ITEM>
                    <PRODUCT>
                        Oranges
                    </PRODUCT>
                    <NUMBER>
                        24
                    </NUMBER>
                    <PRICE>
                        $4.98
                    </PRICE>
                </ITEM>
            </ORDERS>
        </CUSTOMER>
        <CUSTOMER>
            <NAME>
                <LAST_NAME>
                    Jones
                </LAST_NAME>
                <FIRST_NAME>
                    Polly
                </FIRST_NAME>
                <MIDDLE_NAME>
                    XML
                </MIDDLE_NAME>
            </NAME>
            <DATE>
                October 20, 2003
            </DATE>
            <ORDERS>
                <ITEM>
                    <PRODUCT>
                        Bread
                    </PRODUCT>
                    <NUMBER>
                        12
                    </NUMBER>
```

```
            <PRICE>
                $14.95
            </PRICE>
        </ITEM>
        <ITEM>
            <PRODUCT>
                Apples
            </PRODUCT>
            <NUMBER>
                6
            </NUMBER>
            <PRICE>
                $1.50
            </PRICE>
        </ITEM>
    </ORDERS>
</CUSTOMER>
<CUSTOMER>
    <NAME>
        <LAST_NAME>
            Weber
        </LAST_NAME>
        <FIRST_NAME>
            Bill
        </FIRST_NAME>
        <MIDDLE_NAME>
            XML
        </MIDDLE_NAME>
    </NAME>
    <DATE>
        October 25, 2003
    </DATE>
    <ORDERS>
        <ITEM>
            <PRODUCT>
                Asparagus
            </PRODUCT>
            <NUMBER>
                12
            </NUMBER>
            <PRICE>
                $2.95
            </PRICE>
        </ITEM>
        <ITEM>
            <PRODUCT>
                Lettuce
            </PRODUCT>
            <NUMBER>
                6
            </NUMBER>
```

continues

Listing ch12_11.xml   Continued

```
                <PRICE>
                    $11.50
                </PRICE>
            </ITEM>
        </ORDERS>
    </CUSTOMER>
</DOCUMENT>
```

That finishes our work with the Java XML parsers for the moment. In the next chapter, I'm going to start working with XSL transformations.

CHAPTER 13
XSL Transformations

In this chapter, I'm going to start working with Extensible Stylesheet Language, (XSL). XSL has two parts, a transformation language and a formatting language.

The transformation language lets you transform the structure of documents into different forms (such as PDF, WML, HTML, or another schema type), while the formatting language actually formats and styles documents in various ways. These two parts of XSL can function quite independently, and you can think of XSL as two languages, not one. In practice, you often transform a document before formatting it because the transformation process lets you add the tags that the formatting process requires. In fact, this is one of the main reasons the World Wide Web Consortium (W3C) supports XSLT—it's the first stage in the formatting process, as we'll see in the next chapter.

This chapter is about the transformation language, and the next is about the formatting language. The XSL transformation language is often called XSLT, and it has been a W3C recommendation since November 16, 1999. You can find the W3C recommendation for XSLT (the current version is XSLT 1.0) at www.w3.org/TR/xslt.

XSLT 2.0 Working Draft

XSLT 2.0 is in the works, but it's only a working draft with frequent changes at this point. You can see the current version of the XSLT 2.0 Working Draft at www.w3.org/TR/xslt20/. There is some support for XSLT 2.0 in the Saxon XSLT processor, which you can download for free from http://saxon.sourceforge.net/. (There also was an XSLT version 1.1, but it never got past the working draft stage.)

I'll start this chapter with an example to show how XSLT works.

Using XSLT Stylesheets in XML Documents

You use XSLT to manipulate documents, changing and working with their markup as you want. You can use XSLT to translate XML into formatted HTML that is readily viewed, for example. Or, you can change XML into plain text, or another restructured XML document, or even a JavaScript document. XSLT provides a way of gaining access to the content of XML documents and building new documents that use and manipulate that content. For that reason, it's worthy of our study.

One of the most common transformations is from XML documents to HTML documents, and that's the kind of transformation we'll see in the examples in this chapter.

To create an XSLT transformation, you need two documents: the document to transform and the stylesheet that specifies the transformation. Both documents are XML documents.

Here's an example: This document, ch13_01.xml, is a well-formed XML document that holds data about three planets, Mercury, Venus, and Earth. Throughout this chapter, I'll transform this document to HTML in various ways. For programs that can understand it, you can use the `<?xml-stylesheet?>` processing instruction to indicate what XSLT stylesheet to use; you set the `type` attribute to `"text/xml"` and the `href` attribute to the uniform resource identifier (URI) of the XSLT stylesheet, such as ch13_02.xsl in this example (XSLT stylesheets usually have to extension .xsl):

Listing ch13_01.xml

```
<?xml version="1.0"?>
<?xml-stylesheet type="text/xml" href="ch13_02.xsl"?>
<PLANETS>

    <PLANET>
        <NAME>Mercury</NAME>
        <MASS UNITS="(Earth = 1)">.0553</MASS>
        <DAY UNITS="days">58.65</DAY>
        <RADIUS UNITS="miles">1516</RADIUS>
        <DENSITY UNITS="(Earth = 1)">.983</DENSITY>
        <DISTANCE UNITS="million miles">43.4</DISTANCE><!--At perihelion-->
    </PLANET>

    <PLANET>
        <NAME>Venus</NAME>
```

```
        <MASS UNITS="(Earth = 1)">.815</MASS>
        <DAY UNITS="days">116.75</DAY>
        <RADIUS UNITS="miles">3716</RADIUS>
        <DENSITY UNITS="(Earth = 1)">.943</DENSITY>
        <DISTANCE UNITS="million miles">66.8</DISTANCE><!--At perihelion-->
    </PLANET>

    <PLANET>
        <NAME>Earth</NAME>
        <MASS UNITS="(Earth = 1)">1</MASS>
        <DAY UNITS="days">1</DAY>
        <RADIUS UNITS="miles">2107</RADIUS>
        <DENSITY UNITS="(Earth = 1)">1</DENSITY>
        <DISTANCE UNITS="million miles">128.4</DISTANCE><!--At perihelion-->
    </PLANET>

</PLANETS>
```

XSL Stylesheets

Here's what the stylesheet ch13_02.xsl might look like. In this case, I'm converting ch13_01.xml into HTML, stripping out the names of the planets, and surrounding those names with HTML <P> elements:

Listing ch13_02.xsl

```
<?xml version="1.0"?>
<xsl:stylesheet version="1.0"
xmlns:xsl="http://www.w3.org/1999/XSL/Transform">

    <xsl:template match="PLANETS">
        <HTML>
            <xsl:apply-templates/>
        </HTML>
    </xsl:template>

    <xsl:template match="PLANET">
        <P>
            <xsl:value-of select="NAME"/>
        </P>
    </xsl:template>

</xsl:stylesheet>
```

Alright, we've got an XML document and the stylesheet we'll use to transform it. So how exactly do you transform the document?

Making a Transformation Happen

You can transform documents in three ways:

- **On the server**—A server program, such as a Java servlet or a JavaServer Page (JSP), can use a stylesheet to transform a document automatically and serve it to the client. One such example is the XML Enabler, which is a servlet you'll find at the XML For Java Web site, www.alphaworks.ibm.com/tech/xml4j.

- **On the client**—A client program, such as a browser, can perform the transformation, reading in the stylesheet that you specify with the `<?xml-stylesheet?>` processing instruction. Internet Explorer can handle transformations this way, to some extent.

- **With a separate program**—Several standalone programs, usually based on Java, will perform XSLT transformations. I'll take a look at these programs in this chapter.

In this chapter, I'm going to use standalone programs to perform transformations because those programs offer by far the most complete implementations of XSLT. I'll also take a look at using XSLT in Internet Explorer and on the server.

On the Server

Here's an example showing how to use JavaServer Pages (JSP) to transform ch13_01.xml using ch13_02.xsl. JSP is not a skill you have to know in this book, but it provides some interesting examples of using Java, which we're already familiar with, and using XML on a Web server. Here's a JSP page that will perform the XSLT operation we want:

Listing ch13_03.jsp

```
<%@ page import="javax.xml.transform.*, javax.xml.transform.stream.*,
➥java.io.*" %>

<%
    try
    {
        TransformerFactory transformerfactory =
        ➥TransformerFactory.newInstance();
        Transformer transformer = transformerfactory.newTransformer(new
        ➥StreamSource(new File
            (application.getRealPath("/") + "ch13_02.xsl")));
```

```
        transformer.transform(new StreamSource(new
    ➥File(application.getRealPath("/") +
            "ch13_01.xml")),
        new StreamResult(new File(application.getRealPath("/") +
    ➥"temp.html")));

    }
    catch(Exception e) {}

    FileReader filereader = new FileReader(application.getRealPath("/") +
    ➥"temp.html");
    BufferedReader bufferedreader = new BufferedReader(filereader);
    String instring;

    while((instring = bufferedreader.readLine()) != null) {
%>
        <%= instring %>
<%
        }
        filereader.close();
%>
```

As we'll see in Chapter 18, "SOAP and RDF," the Tomcat server is the most popular one for use with JSP. You can see the results of this transformation using that server in Figure 13-1.

Figure 13-1
Performing
an XSL
transformation
on the server.

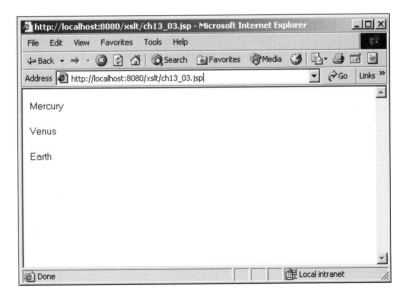

You can see what has happened here: The names of the planets were stripped out of ch13_01.xml and displayed. That provides us with a starting point, and we'll take apart the XSL stylesheet used here in a few pages. We'll also see how to perform all kinds of fancy formatting operations on the data we extract from XML documents in this chapter.

There's another way to transform XML documents without a standalone program: You can use a client program such as a browser to transform documents.

Using Browsers to Transform XML Documents

To use ch13_01.xml with Internet Explorer, I have to make a few modifications. For example, I have to convert the `type` attribute in the `<?xml-stylesheet?>` processing instruction from `"text/xml"` to `"text/xsl"` in a new version of this document, ch13_04.xml:

Listing ch13_04.xml

```
<?xml version="1.0"?>
<?xml-stylesheet type="text/xsl" href="ch13_02.xsl"?>
<PLANETS>

    <PLANET>
        <NAME>Mercury</NAME>
        <MASS UNITS="(Earth = 1)">.0553</MASS>
        <DAY UNITS="days">58.65</DAY>
        <RADIUS UNITS="miles">1516</RADIUS>
        <DENSITY UNITS="(Earth = 1)">.983</DENSITY>
        <DISTANCE UNITS="million miles">43.4</DISTANCE><!--At perihelion-->
    </PLANET>

    <PLANET>
        <NAME>Venus</NAME>
        <MASS UNITS="(Earth = 1)">.815</MASS>
        <DAY UNITS="days">116.75</DAY>
        <RADIUS UNITS="miles">3716</RADIUS>
        <DENSITY UNITS="(Earth = 1)">.943</DENSITY>
        <DISTANCE UNITS="million miles">66.8</DISTANCE><!--At perihelion-->
    </PLANET>

    <PLANET>
        <NAME>Earth</NAME>
        <MASS UNITS="(Earth = 1)">1</MASS>
        <DAY UNITS="days">1</DAY>
        <RADIUS UNITS="miles">2107</RADIUS>
        <DENSITY UNITS="(Earth = 1)">1</DENSITY>
        <DISTANCE UNITS="million miles">128.4</DISTANCE><!--At perihelion-->
    </PLANET>

</PLANETS>
```

Now you can navigate Internet Explorer to ch13_04.xml. You can see the results of this transformation in Figure 13-2.

Figure 13-2
Performing an XSL transformation in Internet Explorer.

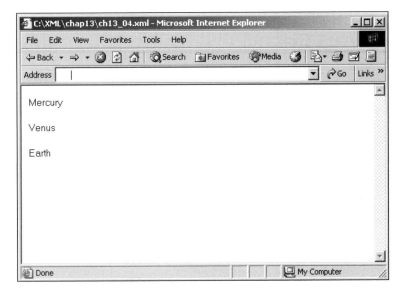

Using Standalone Programs to Transform XML Documents

In earlier days, you had to download separate Java JAR files from various sources to perform XSLT transformations, but as of Java 1.4, Java includes everything you need. Here's an example showing how it works, ch13_05.java. You can use this Java application to transform ch13_01.xml, using ch13_02.xsl, into a new document called result.html:

```
%java ch13_05 ch13_01.xml ch13_02.xsl result.html
```

To write ch13_05.java, you start by using the TransformerFactory class to create a new object of the Transformer class, passing it the XSL stylesheet:

```
import javax.xml.transform.*;
import javax.xml.transform.stream.*;
import java.io.*;

public class ch13_05
{
    public static void main(String args[])
    {
        try
        {
```

```
        TransformerFactory transformerfactory =
        ➥TransformerFactory.newInstance();
        Transformer transformer = transformerfactory.newTransformer
        ➥(new StreamSource(new File(args[1])));
          .
          .
          .
        }
          .
          .
          .
      }
    }
```

You can see the methods of the TransformerFactory class in Table 13-1, and the methods of the Transformer class in Table 13-2.

Table 13-1	Method	Does This
Methods of the *TransformerFactory* class	protected TransformerFactory()	The default constructor
	abstract Source getAssociatedStylesheet (Source source, String media, String title, String charset)	Gets the stylesheet specification(s)
	abstract Object getAttribute (String name)	Returns specific attributes
	abstract ErrorListener getErrorListener()	Returns the error event handler for the TransformerFactory
	abstract boolean getFeature (String name)	Returns the value of a feature
	abstract URIResolver getURIResolver()	Gets the object that is used by default during the transformation to resolve URIs
	static TransformerFactory newInstance()	Obtains a new TransformerFactory object
	abstract Templates newTemplates (Source source)	Processes the Source into a Templates object (a compiled representation of the source)
	abstract Transformer newTransformer()	Creates a new Transformer object that copies of the source to the result

Method	Does This
abstract Transformer) newTransformer(Source source	Creates a new Transformer object that uses the Source for transformations
abstract void setAttribute (String name, Object value)	Sets specific attributes
abstract void setErrorListener (ErrorListener listener)	Sets the Java error event listener
abstract void setURIResolver (URIResolver resolver)	Sets an object that is used by default during the transformation to resolve URIs

	Method	Does This
Table 13-2	protected Transformer()	The default constructor
Methods of the *javax.xml. transform. Transformer* Class	abstract void clearParameters()	Clears all the parameters that were set with setParameter
	abstract ErrorListener getErrorListener()	Returns the error event handler
	abstract Properties getOutputProperties()	Returns a copy of the output properties
	abstract String getOutputProperty(String name)	Returns the value of an output property
	abstract Object getParameter (String name)	Returns a parameter that was set with setParameter or setParameters
	abstract URIResolver getURIResolver()	Returns an object that will be used to resolve URIs
	abstract void setErrorListener (ErrorListener listener)	Sets the Java error event listener
	abstract void setOutputProperties (Properties oformat)	Sets the output properties
	abstract void setOutputProperty (String name, String value)	Sets an output property
	abstract void setParameter (String name, Object value)	Sets a parameter

continues

Method	Does This
abstract void setURIResolver (URIResolver resolver)	Sets an object that will be used to resolve URIs
abstract void transform (Source xmlSource, Result outputTarget)	Performs the transformation

To actually perform the transformation, you use the `Transformer` object's transform method, passing it the XML document to transform:

```
import javax.xml.transform.*;
import javax.xml.transform.stream.*;
import java.io.*;

public class ch13_05
{
    public static void main(String args[])
    {
        try
        {
            TransformerFactory transformerfactory =
            ➥TransformerFactory.newInstance();
            Transformer transformer = transformerfactory.newTransformer
            ➥(new StreamSource(new File(args[1])));

            transformer.transform(new StreamSource(new File(args[0])),
            new StreamResult(new File(args[2])));
        }
        .
        .
        .
    }
}
```

Note that files are handled with the `StreamSource` and `StreamResult` classes here, to fit the requirements of the `Transformer` class. You can see the methods of the `StreamSource` class in Table 13-3, and the methods of the `StreamResult` class in Table 13-4.

Table 13-3	Method	Does This
Methods of the *javax.xml. transform. stream. Stream Source* Class	`StreamSource()`	The default constructor
	`StreamSource(File f)`	Constructs a `StreamSource` from a `File` object
	`StreamSource(InputStream inputStream)`	Constructs a `StreamSource` from a byte stream
	`StreamSource(InputStream inputStream, String systemId)`	Constructs a `StreamSource` from a byte stream
	`StreamSource(Reader reader)`	Constructs a `StreamSource` from a character reader object
	`StreamSource(String systemId)`	Constructs a `StreamSource` from a URL
	`InputStream getInputStream()`	Gets the byte stream that was set with `setByteStream`
	`String getPublicId()`	Gets the public identifier that was set with `setPublicId`
	`Reader getReader()`	Gets the character stream that was set with `setReader`
	`String getSystemId()`	Gets the system identifier that was set with `setSystemId`
	`void setInputStream (InputStream inputStream)`	Sets the byte stream to be used as input
	`void setPublicId(String publicId)`	Sets the public identifier for this Source
	`void setReader(Reader reader)`	Sets the input to be a character reader
	`void setSystemId(File f)`	Sets the system ID from a File reference
	`void setSystemId(String systemId)`	Sets the system identifier for this Source

Table 13-4	Method	Does This
Methods of the *javax.xml. transform. stream. Stream Result* Class	`StreamResult()`	The default constructor
	`StreamResult(File f)`	Constructs a `StreamResult` from a `File` object
	`StreamResult(OutputStream outputStream)`	Constructs a `StreamResult` from a byte stream
	`StreamResult(String systemId)`	Constructs a `StreamResult` from a URL
	`StreamResult(Writer writer)`	Constructs a `StreamResult` from a character stream
	`OutputStream getOutputStream()`	Gets the byte stream that was set with `setOutputStream`
	`String getSystemId()`	Gets the system identifier that was set with `setSystemId`
	`Writer getWriter()`	Gets the character stream that was set with `setWriter`
	`void setOutputStream (OutputStream outputStream)`	Sets the `ByteStream` that is to be written to
	`void setSystemId(File f)`	Sets the system ID from a File reference
	`void setSystemId(String systemId)`	Sets the `systemID` that may be used in association with the byte or character stream
	`void setWriter(Writer writer)`	Sets the writer object that is used to get the result.

And that's all you need; here's the whole code:

Listing ch13_05.java

```java
import javax.xml.transform.*;
import javax.xml.transform.stream.*;
import java.io.*;

public class ch13_05
{
```

```
public static void main(String args[])
{
    try
    {
        TransformerFactory transformerfactory =
        ➥TransformerFactory.newInstance();
        Transformer transformer = transformerfactory.newTransformer
        ➥(new StreamSource(new File(args[1])));

        transformer.transform(new StreamSource(new File(args[0])),
        new StreamResult(new File(args[2])));
    }
    catch(Exception e) {}
}
}
```

After compiling ch13_05.java into ch13_05.class, you can execute this command at the command prompt. This command assumes that all needed files are in the current directory, `java  ch13_05  ch13_01.xml  ch13_02.xsl  result.html`. This produces result.html, which looks like this:

```
<HTML>

<P>Mercury</P>

<P>Venus</P>

<P>Earth</P>

</HTML>
```

We've gotten an overview of XSL transformations now and seen them at work. It's time to see how to create XSLT stylesheets in detail.

Creating XSLT Stylesheets

XSLT transformations accept a document tree as input and produce a tree as output. From the XSLT point of view, documents are trees built of nodes. XSLT recognizes seven types of nodes XSLT; here are those nodes, along with how XSLT processors treat them:

- **The document root**—This is the very start of the document.
- **Attribute**—This node holds the value of an attribute after entity references have been expanded and surrounding whitespace has been trimmed.

- **Comment**—This node holds the text of a comment, not including `<!--` and `-->`.
- **Element**—This node consists of all character data in the element, including character data in any of the children of the element.
- **Namespace**—This node holds the namespace's URI.
- **Processing instruction**—This node holds the text of the processing instruction, which does not include `<?` and `?>`.
- **Text**—This node holds the text of the node.

To indicate what node or nodes you want to work on, XSLT supports various ways of matching or selecting nodes. For example, the character / stands for the root node. To get us started, I'll create a short example here that will replace the root node—and, therefore, the whole document—with an HTML page.

As you might expect, XSLT stylesheets must be well-formed XML documents, so you start a stylesheet with the XML declaration. Next, you use a `<stylesheet>` element; XSLT stylesheets use the namespace xsl, which, now that XSLT has been standardized, corresponds to `www.w3.org/1999/XSL/Transform`. You must also include the `version` attribute in the `<stylesheet>` element, setting that attribute to the only current version, 1.0:

```
<?xml version="1.0"?>
<xsl:stylesheet version="1.0"
xmlns:xsl="http://www.w3.org/1999/XSL/Transform">
    .
    .
    .
```

That's how you start an XSLT stylesheet (in fact, if you're using a standalone program that requires you to give the name of the stylesheet you're using, you can usually omit the `<xsl:stylesheet>` element). To work with specific nodes in an XML document, XSLT uses *templates*. When you match or select nodes, a template tells the XSLT processor how to transform the node for output. In this example, I want to replace the root node with a whole new HTML document. I start by creating a template with the `<xsl:template>` element, setting the match attribute to the node to match, "/":

```
<?xml version="1.0"?>
<xsl:stylesheet version="1.0"
xmlns:xsl="http://www.w3.org/1999/XSL/Transform">
```

```
<xsl:template match="/">
    .
    .
    .
</xsl:template>
```

```
</xsl:stylesheet>
```

When the root node is matched, the template is applied to that node. In this case, I want to replace the root node with an HTML document, so I just include that HTML document directly as the content of the `<xsl:template>` element:

```
<?xml version="1.0"?>
<xsl:stylesheet version="1.0"
xmlns:xsl="http://www.w3.org/1999/XSL/Transform">

    <xsl:template match="/">
        <HTML>
            <HEAD>
                <TITLE>
                    A trivial transformation
                </TITLE>
            </HEAD>
            <BODY>
                This transformation has replaced
                the entire document.
            </BODY>
        </HTML>
    </xsl:template>

</xsl:stylesheet>
```

And that's all it takes. By using the `<xsl:template>` element, I've set up a *rule* in the stylesheet. When the XSL processor reads the document, the first node it sees is the root node. This rule matches that root node, so the XSL processor replaces it with the HTML document, producing this result:

```
<HTML>
    <HEAD>
        <TITLE>
            A trivial transformation
        </TITLE>
    </HEAD>
    <BODY>
        This transformation has replaced
        the entire document.
    </BODY>
</HTML>
```

That's our first rudimentary transformation. All we've done is replace the entire document with another one. But, of course, that's just the beginning.

The *xsl:apply-templates* Element

The template I used in the previous section applied only to one node, the root node, and it performed a trivial action, replacing the entire XML document with an HTML document. However, you can also apply templates to the *children* of a node that you've matched, and you do that with the <xsl:apply-templates> element.

For example, say that I want to convert ch13_01.xml to HTML. The document node in that document is <PLANETS>, so I can match that element with a template, setting the match attribute to the name of the element I want to match. Then I can replace the <PLANETS> element with an <HTML> element, like this:

```
<?xml version="1.0"?>
<xsl:stylesheet version="1.0"
xmlns:xsl="http://www.w3.org/1999/XSL/Transform">

    <xsl:template match="PLANETS">
        <HTML>

          .
          .
          .

        </HTML>
    </xsl:template>

  .
  .
  .

</xsl:stylesheet>
```

But what about the children of the <PLANETS> element? To make sure they are transformed correctly, you use the <xsl:apply-templates> element this way:

```
<?xml version="1.0"?>
<xsl:stylesheet version="1.0"
xmlns:xsl="http://www.w3.org/1999/XSL/Transform">

    <xsl:template match="PLANETS">
        <HTML>
            <xsl:apply-templates/>
        </HTML>
    </xsl:template>

  .
  .
  .

</xsl:stylesheet>
```

Now you can provide templates for the child nodes. In this case, I'll just replace each of the three <PLANET> elements with some text that I place directly into the template for the <PLANET> element:

Listing ch13_06.xsl

```
<?xml version="1.0"?>
<xsl:stylesheet version="1.0"
xmlns:xsl="http://www.w3.org/1999/XSL/Transform">

    <xsl:template match="PLANETS">
        <HTML>
            <xsl:apply-templates/>
        </HTML>
    </xsl:template>

    <xsl:template match="PLANET">
        <P>
            Planet data will go here....
        </P>
    </xsl:template>

</xsl:stylesheet>
```

And that's it. Now the <PLANETS> element is replaced by an <HTML> element, and the <PLANET> elements are also replaced:

```
<HTML>

    <P>
        Planet data will go here....
    </P>

    <P>
        Planet data will go here....
    </P>

    <P>
        Planet data will go here....
    </P>

</HTML>
```

You can see that this transformation works, but it's still less than useful; all we've done is replace the <PLANET> elements with some text. What if we want to access some of the data in the <PLANET> element? For example, say that we want to place the text from the <NAME> element in each <PLANET> element in the output document:

```
<PLANET>
    <NAME>Mercury</NAME>
    <MASS UNITS="(Earth = 1)">.0553</MASS>
    <DAY UNITS="days">58.65</DAY>
    <RADIUS UNITS="miles">1516</RADIUS>
    <DENSITY UNITS="(Earth = 1)">.983</DENSITY>
    <DISTANCE UNITS="million miles">43.4</DISTANCE><!--At perihelion-->
</PLANET>
```

To gain access to this kind of data, you can use the select attribute of the <xsl:value-of> element.

Getting the Value of Nodes with *xsl:value-of*

In this example, I'll extract the name of each planet and insert that name into the output document. To get the name of each planet, I'll use the <xsl:value-of> element in a template targeted at the <PLANET> element. I'll select the <NAME> element with the select attribute, like this:

Listing ch13_07.xsl

```
<?xml version="1.0"?>
<xsl:stylesheet version="1.0"
xmlns:xsl="http://www.w3.org/1999/XSL/Transform">

    <xsl:template match="PLANETS">
        <HTML>
            <xsl:apply-templates/>
        </HTML>
    </xsl:template>

    <xsl:template match="PLANET">
        <xsl:value-of select="NAME"/>
    </xsl:template>

</xsl:stylesheet>
```

Using `select` like this, you can select nodes. The `select` attribute is much like the `match` attribute of the `<xsl:template>` element, except that the `select` attribute is more powerful: You can specify the node or nodes to select using the full XPath specification, as we'll see in this chapter. XPath lets you select a node or a set of nodes in an XML document. The `select` attribute is an attribute of the `<xsl:apply-templates>`, `<xsl:value-of>`, `<xsl:for-each>`, and `<xsl:sort>` elements, all of which we'll also see in this chapter.

Applying the previous stylesheet, the `<xsl:value-of select="NAME"/>` element directs the XSLT processor to insert the name of each planet into the output document. That document looks like this:

```
<HTML>

  Mercury

  Venus

  Earth

</HTML>
```

Handling Multiple Selections with *xsl:for-each*

The `select` attribute selects only the first node that matches its selection criterion. However, what if you have multiple nodes that could match? For example, say you can have multiple `<NAME>` elements for each planet:

```
<PLANET>
    <NAME>Mercury</NAME>
    <NAME>Closest planet to the sun</NAME>
    <MASS UNITS="(Earth = 1)">.0553</MASS>
    <DAY UNITS="days">58.65</DAY>
    <RADIUS UNITS="miles">1516</RADIUS>
    <DENSITY UNITS="(Earth = 1)">.983</DENSITY>
    <DISTANCE UNITS="million miles">43.4</DISTANCE><!--At perihelion-->
</PLANET>
```

The `<xsl:value-of>` element's `select` attribute by itself selects only the first `<NAME>` element. To loop over all possible matches, you can use the `<xsl:for-each>` element, like this:

Listing ch13_08.xsl

```
<?xml version="1.0"?>
<xsl:stylesheet version="1.0"
xmlns:xsl="http://www.w3.org/1999/XSL/Transform">

    <xsl:template match="PLANETS">
        <HTML>
            <xsl:apply-templates/>
        </HTML>
    </xsl:template>

<xsl:template match="PLANET">
    <xsl:for-each select="NAME">
        <P>
            <xsl:value-of select="."/>
        </P>
    </xsl:for-each>
</xsl:template>

</xsl:stylesheet>
```

This stylesheet catches all <NAME> elements, places their values in a <P> element, and adds them to the output document, like this:

```
<HTML>

    <P>Mercury</P>
<P>Closest planet to the sun</P>

    <P>Venus</P>

    <P>Earth</P>

</HTML>
```

We've seen now that you can use the match and select attributes to indicate what nodes you want to work with. The actual syntax that you can use with these attributes is fairly complex but worth knowing. I'll take a look at the match attribute in more detail first, and I'll examine the select attribute later in this chapter.

Specifying Patterns for the *match* Attribute

You can use an involved syntax with the `<xsl:template>` element's `match` attribute, and you can use an even more involved syntax with the `select` attribute of the `<xsl:apply-templates>`, `<xsl:value-of>`, `<xsl:for-each>`, `<xsl:copy-of>`, and `<xsl:sort>` elements. We'll see them both in this chapter, starting with the syntax you can use with the `match` attribute.

Matching the Root Node

As we've already seen, you can match the root node with `/`, like this:

```
<xsl:template match="/">
    <HTML>
        <xsl:apply-templates/>
    </HTML>
</xsl:template>
```

Matching Elements

You can match elements simply by giving their name, as we've also seen:

```
<xsl:template match="PLANETS">
   <HTML>
     <xsl:apply-templates/>
   </HTML>
</xsl:template>
```

Matching Children

You can use the `/` operator to separate element names when you want to refer to a child of a particular node. For example, say that you want to create a rule that applies only to `<NAME>` elements that are children of `<PLANET>` elements. In that case, you can match to the expression `"PLANET/NAME"`. Here's a rule that will surround the text of such elements in an `<H3>` element:

```
<xsl:template match="PLANET/NAME">
  <H3><xsl:value-of select="."/></H3>
</xsl:template>
```

Note the expression "`.`" here. You use "`.`" with the `select` attribute to specify the current node, as we'll see when discussing the `select` attribute.

You can also use the `*` character as a wildcard, standing for any element (`*` can match only elements). For example, this rule applies to all `<NAME>` elements that are *grandchildren* of `<PLANET>` elements:

```
<xsl:template match="PLANET/*/NAME">
  <H3><xsl:value-of select="."/></H3>
</xsl:template>
```

Matching Element Descendants

In the previous section, I used the expression "`PLANET/NAME`" to match all `<NAME>` elements that are direct children of `<PLANET>` elements, and I used the expression "`PLANET/*/NAME`" to match all `<NAME>` elements that are grandchildren of `<PLANET>` elements. However, there's an easier way to perform both matches: Just use the expression "`PLANET//NAME`", which matches all `<NAME>` elements that are inside `<PLANET>` elements, no matter how many levels deep (the matched elements are called *descendants* of the `<PLANET>` element). In other words, "`PLANET//NAME`" matches "`PLANET/NAME`", "`PLANET/*/NAME`", "`PLANET/*/*/NAME`", and so on:

```
<xsl:template match="PLANETS//NAME">
  <H3><xsl:value-of select="."/></H3>
</xsl:template>
```

Matching Attributes

You can match an attribute if you preface its name with `@`. Here's an example; in this case, I'll display the data in ch13_01.xml in an HTML table. You might note, however, that the units for the various measurements are stored in attributes, like this:

```
<PLANET>
    <NAME>Earth</NAME>
    <MASS UNITS="(Earth = 1)">1</MASS>
    <DAY UNITS="days">1</DAY>
    <RADIUS UNITS="miles">2107</RADIUS>
    <DENSITY UNITS="(Earth = 1)">1</DENSITY>
    <DISTANCE UNITS="million miles">128.4</DISTANCE><!--At perihelion-->
</PLANET>
```

To recover the units and display them as well as the values for the mass and so on, I'll match the UNITS attribute with @UNITS. Here's how that looks. Note that I'm using the element <xsl:text> to insert a space into the output document (more on <xsl:text> later):

Listing ch13_09.xsl

```xml
<?xml version="1.0"?>
<xsl:stylesheet version="1.0"
xmlns:xsl="http://www.w3.org/1999/XSL/Transform">

    <xsl:template match="/PLANETS">
        <HTML>
            <HEAD>
                <TITLE>
                    The Planets Table
                </TITLE>
            </HEAD>
            <BODY>
                <H1>
                    The Planets Table
                </H1>
                <TABLE BORDER="1">
                    <TD>Name</TD>
                    <TD>Mass</TD>
                    <TD>Radius</TD>
                    <TD>Day</TD>
                    <xsl:apply-templates/>
                </TABLE>
            </BODY>
        </HTML>
    </xsl:template>

    <xsl:template match="PLANET">
        <TR>
            <TD><xsl:value-of select="NAME"/></TD>
            <TD><xsl:apply-templates select="MASS"/></TD>
            <TD><xsl:apply-templates select="RADIUS"/></TD>
            <TD><xsl:apply-templates select="DAY"/></TD>
        </TR>
    </xsl:template>

    <xsl:template match="MASS">
        <xsl:value-of select="."/>
        <xsl:text> </xsl:text>
        <xsl:value-of select="@UNITS"/>
    </xsl:template>

    <xsl:template match="RADIUS">
        <xsl:value-of select="."/>
        <xsl:text> </xsl:text>
```

continues

Listing ch13_09.xsl   Continued

```
        <xsl:value-of select="@UNITS"/>
    </xsl:template>

    <xsl:template match="DAY">
        <xsl:value-of select="."/>
        <xsl:text> </xsl:text>
        <xsl:value-of select="@UNITS"/>
    </xsl:template>

</xsl:stylesheet>
```

Now the resulting HTML table includes not only values, but also their units of measurement. (The spacing leaves a little to be desired, but HTML browsers will have no problem with it; we'll take a look at ways of handling whitespace later in this chapter.)

```
<HTML>
<HEAD>
<TITLE>
                    The Planets Table
        </TITLE>
</HEAD>
<BODY>
<H1>
                    The Planets Table
        </H1>
<TABLE BORDER="1">
<TD>Name</TD><TD>Mass</TD><TD>Radius</TD><TD>Day</TD>


<TR>
<TD>Mercury</TD><TD>.0553 (Earth = 1)</TD><TD>1516 miles</TD><TD>58.65
➥days</TD>
</TR>


<TR>
<TD>Venus</TD><TD>.815 (Earth = 1)</TD><TD>3716 miles</TD><TD>116.75
➥days</TD>
</TR>


<TR>
<TD>Earth</TD><TD>1 (Earth = 1)</TD><TD>2107 miles</TD><TD>1 days</TD>
</TR>


</TABLE>
</BODY>
</HTML>
```

You can see this result in Figure 13-3 in Internet Explorer.

Figure 13-3
An XSL
transformation
that creates an
HTML table.

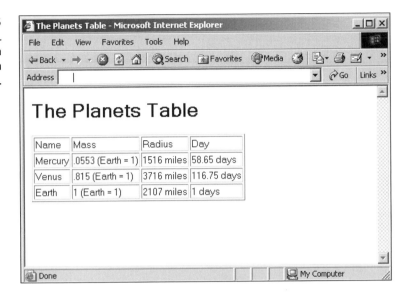

You can also use the @* wildcard to select all attributes of an element. For example, "PLANET/@*" selects all attributes of <PLANET> elements.

Matching by ID

You can also match elements that have a specific ID value using the pattern id(). To use this selector, you must give elements an ID attribute, and you must declare that attribute of type ID, as you can do in a DTD. Here's an example rule that adds the text of all elements that have the ID Christine:

```
<xsl:template match = "id('Christine')">
    <H3><xsl:value-of select="."/></H3>
</xsl:template>
```

Matching Comments

You can match the text of comments with the pattern comment(). You shouldn't store data that should go into the output document in comments in the input document, of course. However, you might want to convert comments from the <!--*comment*--> form into something that another markup language might use, such as a <COMMENT> element.

Here's an example; ch13_01.xml was designed to include comments so that we could see how to extract them:

```
<PLANET>
    <NAME>Venus</NAME>
    <MASS UNITS="(Earth = 1)">.815</MASS>
    <DAY UNITS="days">116.75</DAY>
    <RADIUS UNITS="miles">3716</RADIUS>
    <DENSITY UNITS="(Earth = 1)">.943</DENSITY>
    <DISTANCE UNITS="million miles">66.8</DISTANCE><!--At perihelion-->
</PLANET>
```

To extract comments and put them into <COMMENT> elements, I'll include a rule just for comments:

Listing ch13_10.xsl

```
<?xml version="1.0"?>
<xsl:stylesheet version="1.0"
xmlns:xsl="http://www.w3.org/1999/XSL/Transform">

    <xsl:template match="PLANETS">
        <HTML>
            <xsl:apply-templates/>
        </HTML>
    </xsl:template>

<xsl:template match="comment()">
    <COMMENT>
        <xsl:value-of select="."/>
    </COMMENT>
</xsl:template>

</xsl:stylesheet>
```

Here's what the result is for Venus; I've transformed the comment into a <COMMENT> element:

```
Venus
.815
116.75
3716
.943
66.8<COMMENT>At perihelion</COMMENT>
```

Note that the text for the other elements in the *<PLANET>* element is also inserted into the output document. This is because the *default rule* for each element is to include its text in the output document. Because I haven't provided a rule for elements, their text is simply included in the output document. I'll take a closer look at default rules later in the chapter.

Matching Text Nodes with *text( )*

You can match the text in a node with the pattern text(). There's really not much reason to ever use text() because XSLT includes a default rule: If there are no other rules for a text node, the text in that node is inserted into the output document. If you were to make that default rule explicit, it might look like this:

```
<xsl:template match="text()">
    <xsl:value-of select="."/>
</xsl:template>
```

You can override this rule by not sending the text in text nodes to the output document, like this:

```
<xsl:template match="text()">
</xsl:template>
```

In the previous example, you can see that a great deal of text made it from the input document to the output document because there was no explicit rule besides the default one for text nodes: The only output rule I used was for comments. If you turn off the default rule for text nodes by adding the previous two lines to ch13_10.xsl, the text of those text nodes does not go into the output document, and this is the result:

```
<HTML>
<COMMENT>At perihelion</COMMENT>
<COMMENT>At perihelion</COMMENT>
<COMMENT>At perihelion</COMMENT>
</HTML>
```

Matching Processing Instructions

You can use the pattern processing-instruction() to match processing instructions.

```
<xsl:template match="/processing-instruction()">
    <I>
        Found a processing instruction.
    </I>
</xsl:template>
```

You can also specify what processing instruction you want to match by giving the name of the processing instruction (excluding the <? and ?>), as in this case, where I'm matching the processing instruction <?xml-include?>:

```
<xsl:template match="/processing-instruction(xml-include)">
    <I>
        Found an xml-include processing instruction.
    </I>
</xsl:template>
```

Distinction Between Root Node and Document Node

One of the major reasons why XML makes a distinction between the root node at the very beginning of the document and the document node is so that you have access to the processing instructions and other nodes in the document's prolog.

Using the *Or* Operator

You can match to a number of possible patterns, which is very useful when your documents get a little more involved than the ones we've been using so far in this chapter. Here's an example. In this case, I want to display <NAME> and <MASS> elements in bold, which I'll do with the HTML <B> tag. To match either <NAME> or <MASS> elements, I'll use the Or operator, which is a vertical bar (|) in a new rule, like this:

Listing ch13_11.xsl

```
<?xml version="1.0"?>
<xsl:stylesheet version="1.0"
xmlns:xsl="http://www.w3.org/1999/XSL/Transform">

    <xsl:template match="PLANETS">
        <HTML>
            <xsl:apply-templates/>
        </HTML>
    </xsl:template>

    <xsl:template match="PLANET">
        <P>
            <xsl:apply-templates/>
        </P>
    </xsl:template>
```

```
    <xsl:template match="NAME | MASS">
        <B>
            <xsl:apply-templates/>
        </B>
    </xsl:template>
```

```
</xsl:stylesheet>
```

Here are the results. Note that the name and mass values are both enclosed in <B> elements. (Also note that, because of the XSL default rules, the text from the other child elements of the <PLANET> element is also displayed.)

```
<HTML>

  <P>
    <B>Mercury</B>
    <B>.0553</B>
    58.65
    1516
    .983
    43.4
  </P>

  <P>
    <B>Venus</B>
    <B>.815</B>
    116.75
    3716
    .943
    66.8
  </P>

  <P>
    <B>Earth</B>
    <B>1</B>
    1
    2107
    1
    128.4
  </P>

</HTML>
```

You can use any valid pattern with the | operator, such as the expressions PLANET | PLANET//NAME. You also can use multiple | operators, as in NAME | MASS | DAY, and so on.

Testing with *[ ]*

You can use the [ ] operator to test whether a certain condition is true. For example, you can test the following:

- Whether the value of an attribute is a given string
- The value of an element
- Whether an element encloses a particular child, attribute, or other element
- The position of a node in the node tree

Here are some examples. This expression matches <PLANET> elements that have child <NAME> elements:

```
<xsl:template match = "PLANET[NAME]">
```

This expression matches any element that has a <NAME> child element:

```
<xsl:template match = "*[NAME]">
```

This expression matches any <PLANET> element that has either a <NAME> or a <MASS> child element:

```
<xsl:template match="PLANET[NAME | MASS]">
```

Say that we gave the <PLANET> elements a new attribute—COLOR, which holds the planet's color:

Listing ch13_12.xml

```
<?xml version="1.0"?>
<?xml-stylesheet type="text/xml" href="ch13_02.xsl"?>
<PLANETS>

  <PLANET COLOR="RED">
    <NAME>Mercury</NAME>
    <MASS UNITS="(Earth = 1)">.0553</MASS>
    <DAY UNITS="days">58.65</DAY>
    <RADIUS UNITS="miles">1516</RADIUS>
    <DENSITY UNITS="(Earth = 1)">.983</DENSITY>
    <DISTANCE UNITS="million miles">43.4</DISTANCE><!--At perihelion-->
  </PLANET>

  <PLANET COLOR="WHITE">
    <NAME>Venus</NAME>
    <MASS UNITS="(Earth = 1)">.815</MASS>
    <DAY UNITS="days">116.75</DAY>
```

```
      <RADIUS UNITS="miles">3716</RADIUS>
      <DENSITY UNITS="(Earth = 1)">.943</DENSITY>
      <DISTANCE UNITS="million miles">66.8</DISTANCE><!--At perihelion-->
  </PLANET>

  <PLANET COLOR="BLUE">
      <NAME>Earth</NAME>
      <MASS UNITS="(Earth = 1)">1</MASS>
      <DAY UNITS="days">1</DAY>
      <RADIUS UNITS="miles">2107</RADIUS>
      <DENSITY UNITS="(Earth = 1)">1</DENSITY>
      <DISTANCE UNITS="million miles">128.4</DISTANCE><!--At perihelion-->
  </PLANET>

</PLANETS>
```

This expression matches `<PLANET>` elements that have `COLOR` attributes:

```
<xsl:template match="PLANET[@COLOR]">
```

What if you wanted to match planets whose `COLOR` attribute was `"BLUE"`? You can do that with the = operator, like this:

Listing ch13_13.xsl

```
<?xml version="1.0"?>
<xsl:stylesheet version="1.0"
xmlns:xsl="http://www.w3.org/1999/XSL/Transform">

    <xsl:template match="PLANETS">
        <HTML>
            <xsl:apply-templates/>
        </HTML>
    </xsl:template>

    <xsl:template match="PLANET[@COLOR = 'BLUE']">
            The <xsl:value-of select="NAME"/> is blue.
    </xsl:template>

    <xsl:template match="text()">
    </xsl:template>

</xsl:stylesheet>
```

This style sheet filters out all planets whose color is blue and omits the others by turning off the default rule for text nodes. Here's the result:

```
<HTML>
        The Earth is blue.
    </HTML>
```

In fact, the expressions you can use in the [] operators are W3C XPath expressions. XPath expressions give you ways of specifying nodes in an XML document using a fairly involved syntax. And because the select attribute, which we're about to cover, uses XPath, I'll take a look at XPath as well.

Specifying Patterns for the *select* Attribute

I've taken a look at the kinds of expressions you can use with the <xsl:template> element's match attribute. You can use an even more involved syntax with the select attribute of the <xsl:apply-templates>, <xsl:value-of>, <xsl:for-each>, <xsl:copy-of>, and <xsl:sort> elements.

The select attribute uses XPath expressions, and XPath is a W3C recommendation as of November 16, 1999. You can find the XPath recommendation (the current version is 1.0) at www.w3.org/TR/xpath.

XPath 2.0 Working Draft

As with XSLT, version 2.0 of XPath is in the works, but it's only a working draft at this point, with frequent changes. No software supports it yet, except for some support in the Saxon XSLT processor (http://saxon.sourceforge.net/). You can see the current version of the XPath 2.0 Working Draft at www.w3.org/TR/xpath20/.

We've seen that you can use the match attribute to find nodes by name, child element(s), attributes, or even descendants. And we've seen that you can make some tests to see if elements or attributes have certain values. You can do all that and more with the XPath specification supported by the select attribute, including finding nodes by parent or sibling elements and performing much more involved tests. XPath is much more of a true language than the expressions you can use with the match attribute; for example, XPath expressions can return not only lists of nodes, but also Boolean, string, and numeric values.

XPath expressions are more powerful than the `match` expressions we've seen; for one thing, they're not restricted to working with the current node or child nodes because you can work with parent nodes, ancestor nodes, and more. Specifying the node in relation to which you want to work is called specifying an *axis* in XPath. I'll take a look at XPath syntax in detail next.

Understanding XPath

To specify a node or set of nodes in XPath, you use a *location path*. A location path, in turn, consists of one or more *location steps*, separated by / or //. If you start the location path with /, the location path is called an *absolute location path* because you're specifying the path from the root node; otherwise, the location path is *relative*, starting with the current node, which is called the *context node*. Got all that? Good, because there's more.

A location step is made up of an *axis*, a *node test*, and zero or more *predicates*. For example, in the expression `child::PLANET[position() = 5]`, `child` is the name of the axis, `PLANET` is the node test, and `[position() = 5]` is a predicate. You can create location paths with one or more location steps, as in `/descendant::PLANET/child::NAME`, which selects all the <NAME> elements that have an <PLANET> parent. The best way to understand all this is by example, and we'll see plenty of them in a few pages. In the meantime, I'll take a look at what kind of axes, node tests, and predicates XPath supports.

XPath Axes

In the location path `child::NAME`, which refers to a <NAME> element that is a child of the current node, `child` is called the axis. XPath supports many different axes, and it's important to know what they are. Here's the list:

- The `ancestor` axis holds the ancestors of the context node; the ancestors of the context node are the parent of context node and the parent's parent and so forth, back to and including the root node.

- The `ancestor-or-self` axis holds the context node and the ancestors of the context node.

- The `attribute` axis holds the attributes of the context node.

- The `child` axis holds the children of the context node.

- The `descendant` axis holds the descendants of the context node. A descendant is a child or a child of a child, and so on.

- The `descendant-or-self` axis contains the context node and the descendants of the context node.

- The `following` axis holds all nodes in the same document as the context node that come after the context node.

- The `following-sibling` axis holds all the following siblings of the context node. A sibling is a node on the same level as the context node.

- The `namespace` axis holds the namespace nodes of the context node.

- The `parent` axis holds the parent of the context node.

- The `preceding` axis contains all nodes that come before the context node.

- The `preceding-sibling` axis contains all the preceding siblings of the context node. A sibling is a node on the same level as the context node.

- The `self` axis contains the context node.

You can use axes to specify a location step or path, as in this example. I'm using the `child` axis to indicate that I want to match to child nodes of the context node, which is a `<PLANET>` element (we'll see later that there's an abbreviated version that lets you omit the `child::` part):

```
<xsl:template match="PLANET">
    <HTML>
        <CENTER>
            <xsl:value-of select="child::NAME"/>
        </CENTER>
        <CENTER>
            <xsl:value-of select="child::MASS"/>
        </CENTER>
        <CENTER>
            <xsl:value-of select="child::DAY"/>
        </CENTER>
    </HTML>
</xsl:template>
```

In these expressions, `child` is the axis, and the element names `NAME`, `MASS`, and `DAY` are *node tests*.

XPath Node Tests

You can use names of nodes as node tests, or you can use the wildcard `*` to select element nodes. For example, the expression `child::*/child::NAME` selects all `<NAME>` elements that are grandchildren of the context node. Besides nodes and the wildcard character, you can use these node tests:

- The `comment()` node test selects comment nodes.
- The `node()` node test selects any type of node.
- The `processing-instruction()` node test selects a processing instruction node. You can specify the name of the processing instruction to select in the parentheses.
- The `text()` node test selects a text node.

XPath Predicates

The predicate part of an XPath step is perhaps its most intriguing part because it gives you the most power. You can work with all kinds of expressions in predicates; here are the possible types:

- Node sets
- Booleans
- Numbers
- Strings
- Result tree fragments

I'll take a look at these various types in turn.

XPath Node Sets

As its name implies, a node set is simply a set of nodes. An expression such as `child::PLANET` returns a node set of all `<PLANET>` elements. The expression `child::PLANET/child::NAME` returns a node list of all `<NAME>` elements that are children of `<PLANET>` elements. To select a node or nodes from a node set, you can use various functions that work on node sets in predicates. Here are those functions:

- `last()`—Returns the number of nodes in a node set.
- `position()`—Returns the position of the context node in the context node set (starting with 1).

- count(*node-set*)—Returns the number of nodes in the node set. Omitting *node-set* makes this function use the context node.

- id(string *ID*)—Returns a node set containing the element whose ID matches the string passed to the function, or an empty node set if no element has the specified ID. You can list multiple IDs separated by whitespace, and this function will return a node set of the elements with those IDs.

- local-name(*node-set*)—Returns the local name of the first node in the node set. Omitting *node-set* makes this function use the context node.

- namespace-uri(*node-set*)—Returns the URI of the namespace of the first node in the node set. Omitting *node-set* makes this function use the context node.

- name(*node-set*)—Returns the full, qualified name of the first node in the node set. Omitting *node-set* makes this function use the context node.

Here's an example. In this case, I'll number the elements in the output document using the position() function:

Listing ch13_14.xsl

```
<?xml version="1.0"?>
<xsl:stylesheet version="1.0"
xmlns:xsl="http://www.w3.org/1999/XSL/Transform">

    <xsl:template match="PLANETS">
        <HTML>
            <HEAD>
                <TITLE>
                    The Planets
                </TITLE>
            </HEAD>
            <BODY>
                <xsl:apply-templates select="PLANET"/>
            </BODY>
        </HTML>
    </xsl:template>

    <xsl:template match="PLANET">
        <P>
            <xsl:value-of select="position()"/>.
            <xsl:value-of select="NAME"/>
```

```
        </P>
    </xsl:template>

</xsl:stylesheet>
```

Here's the result, where you can see that the planets are numbered:

```
<HTML>
<HEAD>
<TITLE>
                The Planets
        </TITLE>
</HEAD>
<BODY>
<P>1.
        Mercury</P>
<P>2.
        Venus</P>
<P>3.
        Earth</P>
</BODY>
</HTML>
```

You can use functions that operate on node sets in predicates, as in `child::PLANET[position() = last()]`, which selects the last `<PLANET>` child of the context node.

XPath Booleans

You can also use Boolean values in XPath expressions. Numbers are considered false if they're zero; otherwise, they're considered true. An empty string, `""`, is also considered false; all other strings are considered true.

You can use XPath logical operators to produce Boolean `true`/`false` results; here are the logical operators:

- `!=` means "is not equal to."
- `<` means "is less than." (Use `&lt;` in XML documents.)
- `<=` means "is less than or equal to." (Use `&lt;=` in XML documents.)
- `=` means "is equal to." (C, C++, Java, and JavaScript programmers take note: This operator is one = sign, not two.)
- `>` means "is greater than."
- `>=` means "is greater than or equal to."

Use < and >

Note in particular that you shouldn't use < directly in XML documents; you should use the entity reference < instead. Some processors require you to use > for > as well.

You can also use the keywords and or or to connect Boolean clauses with a logical And or Or operation, as we've seen when working with JavaScript and Java.

Here's an example using the logical operator >. This rule applies to all <PLANET> elements after position 5:

```
<xsl:template match="PLANET[position() > 5]">
    <xsl:value-of select="."/>
</xsl:template>
```

There is also a true() functions that always returns a value of true, and a false() function that always returns a value of false.

You can also use the not() function to reverse the logical sense of an expression, as in this case, where I'm selecting all but the last <PLANET> element:

```
<xsl:template match="PLANET[not(position() = last())]">
    <xsl:value-of select="."/>
</xsl:template>
```

Finally, the lang() function returns true or false depending on whether the language of the context node (which is given by xml:lang attributes) is the same as the language you pass to this function.

XPath Numbers

In XPath, numbers are actually stored in double floating-point format (see Chapter 10, "Understanding Java," for more details on doubles—technically, all XPath numbers are stored in 64-bit IEEE 754 floating-point double format). All numbers are stored as doubles, even integers such as 5, as in the example we just saw:

```
<xsl:template match="PLANET[position() > 5]">
    <xsl:value-of select="."/>
</xsl:template>
```

You can use several operators on numbers:

Operator	Function
+	Addition.
-	Subtraction.
*	Multiplication.
div	Division. (The / character that stands for division in other languages is already used heavily in XML and Xpath.)
mod	Returns the modulus of two numbers (the remainder after dividing the first by the second).

For example, the element `<xsl:value-of select="180 + 420"/>` inserts the string `"600"` into the output document. This example selects all planets whose day (measured in Earth days) divided by its mass (where the mass of the Earth equals 1) is greater than 100:

```
<xsl:template match="PLANETS">
    <HTML>
        <BODY>
            <xsl:apply-templates select="PLANET[DAY div MASS > 100]"/>
        </BODY>
    </HTML>
</xsl:template>
```

XPath also supports these functions that operate on numbers:

- `ceiling()`—Returns the smallest integer larger than the number you pass it
- `floor()`—Returns the largest integer smaller than the number you pass it
- `round()`—Rounds the number you pass it to the nearest integer
- `sum()`—Returns the sum of the numbers you pass it

For example, here's how you can find the average mass of the planets in ch13_01.xml:

```
<xsl:template match="PLANETS">
    <HTML>
        <BODY>
```

```
            The average planetary mass is:
            <xsl:value-of select="sum(child::MASS) div count(child::MASS)"/>
        </BODY>
      </HTML>
</xsl:template>
```

XPath Strings

In XPath, strings are made up of Unicode characters. A number of functions are specially designed to work on strings:

- starts-with(string *string1*, string *string2*)—Returns true if the first string starts with the second string

- contains(string *string1*, string *string2*)—Returns true if the first string contains the second string

- substring(string *string1*, number *offset*, number *length*)—Returns *length* characters from the string, starting at *offset*

- substring-before(string *string1*, string *string2*)—Returns the part of *string1* up to the first occurrence of *string2*

- substring-after(string *string1*, string *string2*)—Returns the part of *string1* after the first occurrence of *string2*

- string-length(string *string1*)—Returns the number of characters in *string1*

- normalize-space(string *string1*)—Returns *string1* after leading and trailing whitespace is stripped and multiple consecutive whitespace characters are replaced with a single space

- translate(string *string1*, string *string2*, string *string3*)—Returns *string1* with all occurrences of the characters in *string2* replaced by the matching characters in *string3*

- concat(string *string1*, string *string2*, ...)—Returns all strings concatenated (that is, joined) together

- format-number(number *number1*, string *string2*, string *string3*)—Returns a string holding the formatted string version of *number1*, using *string2* as a formatting string (create formatting strings as you would for java's java.text.DecimalFormat method) and *string3* as the optional locale string

XPath Result Tree Fragments

A result tree fragment is a part of an XML document that is not a complete node or complete set of nodes. You can create result tree fragments in various ways, such as with the `document()` function when you point to somewhere inside another document.

You really can't do much with result tree fragments in XPath. Actually, you can do only two things: use the `string()` or `boolean()` functions to turn them into strings or Booleans.

XPath Examples

We've seen a lot of XPath in theory, how about some examples? Here's a number of location path examples—note that XPath allows you to use and or or in predicates to apply logical tests using multiple patterns:

- `child::PLANET`—Returns the `<PLANET>` element children of the context node.

- `child::*`—Returns all element children (`*`matches only elements) of the context node.

- `child::text()`—Returns all text node children of the context node.

- `child::node()`—Returns all the children of the context node, no matter what their node type is.

- `attribute::UNIT`—Returns the UNITS attribute of the context node.

- `descendant::PLANET`—Returns the `<PLANET>` element descendants of the context node.

- `ancestor::PLANET`—Returns all `<PLANET>` ancestors of the context node.

- `ancestor-or-self::PLANET`—Returns the `<PLANET>` ancestors of the context node. If the context node is a `<PLANET>` as well, also returns the context node.

- `descendant-or-self::PLANET`—Returns the `<PLANET>` element descendants of the context node. If the context node is a `<PLANET>` as well, also returns the context node.

- `self::PLANET`—Returns the context node if it is a `<PLANET>` element.

- `child::NAME/descendant::PLANET`—Returns the `<PLANET>` element descendants of the child `<NAME>` elements of the context node.

- `child::*/child::PLANET`—Returns all `<PLANET>` grandchildren of the context node.

- `/`—Returns the document root (that is, the parent of the document element).

- `/descendant::PLANET`—Returns all the `<PLANET>` elements in the document.

- `/descendant::PLANET/child::NAME`—Returns all the `<NAME>` elements that have a `<PLANET>` parent.

- `child::PLANET[position() = 3]`—Returns the third `<PLANET>` child of the context node.

- `child::PLANET[position() = last()]`—Returns the last `<PLANET>` child of the context node.

- `/descendant::PLANET[position() = 3]`—Returns the third `<PLANET>` element in the document.

- `child::PLANETS/child::PLANET[position() = 4]/child::NAME[position() = 3]`—Returns the third `<NAME>` element of the fourth `<PLANET>` element of the `<PLANETS>` element.

- `child::PLANET[position() > 3]`—Returns all the `<PLANET>` children of the context node after the first three.

- `preceding-sibling::NAME[position() = 2]`—Returns the second previous `<NAME>` sibling element of the context node.

- `child::PLANET[attribute::COLOR = "RED"]`—Returns all `<PLANET>` children of the context node that have a `COLOR` attribute with value of `"RED"`.

- `child::PLANET[attribute::COLOR = "RED"][position() = 3]`—Returns the third `<PLANET>` child of the context node that has a `COLOR` attribute with value of `"RED"`.

- `child::PLANET[position() = 3][attribute::COLOR="RED"]`—Returns the third `<PLANET>` child of the context node only if that child has a `COLOR` attribute with value of `"RED"`.

- `child::MASS[child::NAME = "VENUS"]`—Returns the `<MASS>` children of the context node that have `<NAME>` children whose text is `"VENUS"`.

- `child::PLANET[child::NAME]`—Returns the `<PLANET>` children of the context node that have `<NAME>` children.

- `child::*[self::NAME or self::MASS]`—Returns both the `<NAME>` and `<MASS>` children of the context node.

- `child::*[self::NAME or self::MASS][position() = first()]`—Returns the first `<NAME>` or `<MASS>` child of the context node.

As you can see, some of this syntax is pretty involved and a little lengthy to type. However, there is an abbreviated form of XPath syntax.

XPath Abbreviated Syntax

You can take advantage of a number of abbreviations in XPath syntax. Here are the rules:

- `self::node()` can be abbreviated as .

- `parent::node()` can be abbreviated as ..

- `child::childname` can be abbreviated as *childname*

- `attribute::childname` can be abbreviated as *@childname*

- `/descendant-or-self::node()/` can be abbreviated as //

You can also abbreviate predicate expressions, as in `[position() = 3]` as `[3]`, `[position() = last()]` as `[last()]`, and so on. Using the abbreviated syntax makes XPath expressions a lot easier to use. Here are some examples of location paths using abbreviated syntax—note how well these fit the syntax we saw with the `match` attribute earlier in the chapter:

Abbreviated Syntax	Description
`PLANET`	Returns the `<PLANET>` element children of the context node.
`*`	Returns all element children of the context node.
`text()`	Returns all text node children of the context node.
`@UNITS`	Returns the `UNITS` attribute of the context node.
`@*`	Returns all the attributes of the context node.
`PLANET[3]`	Returns the third `<PLANET>` child of the context node.

continues

Abbreviated Syntax	Description
PLANET[first()]	Returns the first <PLANET> child of the context node.
*/PLANET	Returns all <PLANET> grandchildren of the context node.
/PLANETS/PLANET[3]/NAME[2]	Returns the second <NAME> element of the third <PLANET> element of the <PLANETS> element.
//PLANET	Returns all the <PLANET> descendants of the document root.
PLANETS//PLANET	Returns the <PLANET> element descendants of the <PLANETS> element children of the context node.
//PLANET/NAME	Returns all the <NAME> elements that have an <PLANET> parent.
.	Returns the context node itself.
.//PLANET	Returns the <PLANET> element descendants of the context node.
..	Returns the parent of the context node.
../@UNITS	Returns the UNITS attribute of the parent of the context node.
PLANET[NAME]	Returns the <PLANET> children of the context node that have <NAME> children.
PLANET[NAME="Venus"]	Returns the <PLANET> children of the context node that have <NAME> children with text equal to "Venus".
PLANET[@UNITS = "days"]	Returns all <PLANET> children of the context node that have a UNITS attribute with the value "days".
PLANET[6][@UNITS = "days"]	Returns the sixth <PLANET> child of the context node, only if that child has a UNITS attribute with the value "days". Can also be written as PLANET[@UNITS = "days"][6].
PLANET[@COLOR and @UNITS]	Returns all the <PLANET> children of the context node that have both a COLOR attribute and an UNITS attribute.

Here's an example in which I put the abbreviated syntax to work, moving up and down inside a <PLANET> element:

Listing ch13_15.xsl

```
<?xml version="1.0"?>
<xsl:stylesheet version="1.0"
xmlns:xsl="http://www.w3.org/1999/XSL/Transform">

    <xsl:template match="PLANETS">
        <HTML>
            <xsl:apply-templates select="PLANET"/>
        </HTML>
    </xsl:template>

    <xsl:template match="PLANET">
        <xsl:apply-templates select="MASS"/>
    </xsl:template>

    <xsl:template match="MASS">
        <xsl:value-of select="../NAME"/>
        <xsl:value-of select="../DAY"/>
        <xsl:value-of select="."/>
    </xsl:template>

</xsl:stylesheet>
```

The Default XSLT Rules

XSLT has some built-in, default rules that we've already seen in action. For example, the default rule for text nodes is to add the text in that node to the output document.

The most important default rule applies to elements and can be expressed like this:

```
<xsl:template match="/ | *">
    <xsl:apply-templates/>
</xsl:template>
```

This rule is simply there to make sure that every element, from the root on down, is processed with `<xsl:apply-templates/>` if you don't supply some other rule. If you do supply another rule, it overrides the corresponding default rule.

The default rule for text can be expressed like this, where by default, the text of a text node is added to the output document:

```
<xsl:template match="text()">
    <xsl:value-of select="."/>
</xsl:template>
```

The same kind of default rule applies to attributes, which are added to the output document with a default rule like this:

```
<xsl:template match="@*">
    <xsl:value-of select="."/>
</xsl:template>
```

By default, processing instructions are not inserted in the output document, so their default rule can be expressed simply like this:

```
<xsl:template match="processing-instruction()"/>
```

And the same goes for comments, whose default rule can be expressed this way:

```
<xsl:template match="comment()"/>
```

The upshot of the default rules is that if you don't supply any rules, all the parsed character data in the input document is inserted in the output document. Here's what an XSLT stylesheet with no explicit rules looks like:

```
<?xml version="1.0"?>
<xsl:stylesheet version="1.0"
xmlns:xsl="http://www.w3.org/1999/XSL/Transform">
</xsl:stylesheet>
```

Here's the result of applying this stylesheet to ch13_01.xml:

```
<?xml version="1.0" encoding="UTF-8"?>



    Mercury
    .0553
    58.65
    1516
    .983
    43.4
```

```
Venus
.815
116.75
3716
.943
66.8


Earth
1
1
2107
1
128.4
```

Altering Document Structure Based on Input

So far, the templates in this chapter have been fairly rigid skeletons, specifying exactly what should go into the output document, in what order. But you can use XSLT elements such as `<xsl:element>`, `<xsl:attribute>`, `<xsl:text>`, and so on to create new nodes on the fly, based on what you find in the input document. I'll take a look at how this works now.

Creating Attribute Templates

Say that you wanted to convert the text in some elements to attributes in other elements; how could you do it? Attribute values must be quoted in XML, but you can't just use expressions like these, where I'm taking the values of `<NAME>`, `<MASS>`, and `<DAY>` elements and trying to make them into attribute values:

```
<xsl:template match="PLANET">
    <PLANET NAME="<xsl:value-of select="NAME"/>"
        MASS="<xsl:value-of select="MASS"/>"
        DAY="<xsl:value-of select="DAY"/>"
    />
```

This won't work because you can't use < inside attribute values as I have here. Instead, you must use an expression such as {NAME}. Here's the proper XSLT:

Listing ch13_16.xsl

```
<?xml version="1.0"?>
<xsl:stylesheet version="1.0"
xmlns:xsl="http://www.w3.org/1999/XSL/Transform">

<xsl:template match="PLANETS">
    <HTML>
        <HEAD>
            <TITLE>
                    Planets
            </TITLE>
        </HEAD>
        <BODY>
            <xsl:apply-templates select="PLANET"/>
        </BODY>
    </HTML>
</xsl:template>

<xsl:template match="PLANET">
    <PLANET NAME="{NAME}"
        MASS="{MASS}"
        DAY="{DAY}"
    />
</xsl:template>

</xsl:stylesheet>
```

Here's the resulting document. Note that I've been able to convert the values in various elements to attributes:

```
<HTML>
<HEAD>
<TITLE>
                Planets
            </TITLE>
</HEAD>
<BODY>
<PLANET DAY="58.65" MASS=".0553" NAME="Mercury">
</PLANET>
<PLANET DAY="116.75" MASS=".815" NAME="Venus">
</PLANET>
<PLANET DAY="1" MASS="1" NAME="Earth">
</PLANET>
</BODY>
</HTML>
```

You can even include multiple expressions in curly braces, like this, where I'm adding the units for mass and day measurements from the UNITS attribute in the original elements:

Listing ch13_17.xsl

```
<?xml version="1.0"?>
<xsl:stylesheet version="1.0"
xmlns:xsl="http://www.w3.org/1999/XSL/Transform">

<xsl:template match="PLANETS">
    <HTML>
        <HEAD>
            <TITLE>
                Planets
            </TITLE>
        </HEAD>
        <BODY>
            <xsl:apply-templates select="PLANET"/>
        </BODY>
    </HTML>
</xsl:template>

<xsl:template match="PLANET">
    <PLANET NAME="{NAME}"
        MASS="{MASS} {@UNITS}"
        DAY="{DAY} {@UNITS}"
    />
</xsl:template>

</xsl:stylesheet>
```

Creating New Elements

You can create new elements with the `<xsl:element>` element. For example, say that I store the name of planets in a NAME attribute instead of a `<NAME>` element in ch13_01.xml, like this:

```
<?xml version="1.0"?>
<?xml-stylesheet type="text/xml" href="ch13_02.xsl"?>
<PLANETS>

    <PLANET NAME="Mercury">
        <MASS UNITS="(Earth = 1)">.0553</MASS>
        <DAY UNITS="days">58.65</DAY>
        <RADIUS UNITS="miles">1516</RADIUS>
```

```
      <DENSITY UNITS="(Earth = 1)">.983</DENSITY>
      <DISTANCE UNITS="million miles">43.4</DISTANCE><!--At perihelion-->
   </PLANET>
      .
      .
      .
```

I could create a new element using the name of the planet with <xsl:element>, supplying the name of the new planet with the name attribute and enclosing a <MASS> element this way:

Listing ch13_18.xsl

```
<?xml version="1.0"?>
<xsl:stylesheet version="1.0"
xmlns:xsl="http://www.w3.org/1999/XSL/Transform">

<xsl:template match="PLANETS">
    <HTML>
        <HEAD>
            <TITLE>
                Planets
            </TITLE>
        </HEAD>
        <BODY>
            <xsl:apply-templates select="PLANET"/>
        </BODY>
    </HTML>
</xsl:template>

<xsl:template match="PLANET">
    <xsl:element name="{@NAME}">
        <MASS><xsl:value-of select="MASS"/></MASS>
    </xsl:element>
</xsl:template>

</xsl:stylesheet>
```

Here is the result, where I've created a new <mercury> element:

```
<HTML>
<HEAD>
<TITLE>
                Planets
            </TITLE>
</HEAD>
<BODY>
```

```
<Mercury>
<MASS>.0553</MASS>
</Mercury>
     .
     .
     .
```

In this way, you can create new elements and name them when the XSLT transformation takes place.

Creating New Attributes

Just as you can create new elements with `<xsl:element>` and set the element name and content under programmatic control, you can do the same for attributes using the `<xsl:attribute>` element.

Here's an example. In this case, I'm creating new `<PLANET>` elements with attributes corresponding to the various planet names and values taken from the `COLOR` attribute in the original `<PLANET>` elements:

Listing ch13_19.xsl

```
<?xml version="1.0"?>
<xsl:stylesheet version="1.0"
xmlns:xsl="http://www.w3.org/1999/XSL/Transform">

<xsl:template match="PLANETS">
    <HTML>
        <HEAD>
            <TITLE>
                Planets
            </TITLE>
        </HEAD>
        <BODY>
            <xsl:apply-templates select="PLANET"/>
        </BODY>
    </HTML>
</xsl:template>

<xsl:template match="PLANET">
    <PLANET>
        <xsl:attribute name="{NAME}">
            <xsl:value-of select="@COLOR"/>
        </xsl:attribute>
    </PLANET>
</xsl:template>

</xsl:stylesheet>
```

Here are the results; as you can see, I've created new attributes on the fly, using the names of the planets:

```
<HTML>
<HEAD>
<TITLE>
                Planets
        </TITLE>
</HEAD>
<BODY>
<PLANET Mercury="RED">
</PLANET>
<PLANET Venus="WHITE">
</PLANET>
<PLANET Earth="BLUE">
</PLANET>
</BODY>
</HTML>
```

Generating Comments with *xsl:comment*

You can also create comments on the fly with the `<xsl:comment>` element. Here's an example. In this case, I'm creating comments that will replace `<PLANET>` elements. I'll include the name of the planet in the text of the comment:

Listing ch13_20.xsl

```
<?xml version="1.0"?>
<xsl:stylesheet version="1.0"
xmlns:xsl="http://www.w3.org/1999/XSL/Transform">

<xsl:template match="PLANETS">
    <HTML>
        <HEAD>
            <TITLE>
                Planets
            </TITLE>
        </HEAD>
        <BODY>
            <xsl:apply-templates select="PLANET"/>
        </BODY>
    </HTML>
</xsl:template>

<xsl:template match="PLANET">
```

```
    <xsl:comment>This was the <xsl:value-of select="NAME"/>
    ➥element</xsl:comment>
</xsl:template>

</xsl:stylesheet>
```

Here's the result:

```
<HTML>
<HEAD>
<TITLE>
                Planets
        </TITLE>
</HEAD>
<BODY>
<!--This was the Mercury element-->
<!--This was the Venus element-->
<!--This was the Earth element-->
</BODY>
</HTML>
```

Generating Text with *xsl:text*

You can create text nodes with the <xsl:text> element, allowing you to do
things such as replace whole elements with text on the fly. One reason you can
use <xsl:text> is to preserve whitespace, as in this example from earlier in
the chapter, where I used <xsl:text> to insert spaces:

Listing ch13_21.xsl

```
<?xml version="1.0"?>
<xsl:stylesheet version="1.0"
xmlns:xsl="http://www.w3.org/1999/XSL/Transform">

    <xsl:template match="/PLANETS">
        <HTML>
            <HEAD>
                <TITLE>
                    The Planets Table
                </TITLE>
            </HEAD>
            <BODY>
                <H1>
                    The Planets Table
                </H1>
```

continues

Listing ch13_21.xsl   Continued

```
                <TABLE BORDER="1">
                    <TD>Name</TD>
                    <TD>Mass</TD>
                    <TD>Radius</TD>
                    <TD>Day</TD>
                    <xsl:apply-templates/>
                </TABLE>
            </BODY>
        </HTML>
    </xsl:template>

    <xsl:template match="PLANET">
      <TR>
        <TD><xsl:value-of select="NAME"/></TD>
        <TD><xsl:apply-templates select="MASS"/></TD>
        <TD><xsl:apply-templates select="RADIUS"/></TD>
      </TR>
    </xsl:template>

    <xsl:template match="MASS">
      <xsl:value-of select="."/>
      <xsl:text> </xsl:text>
      <xsl:value-of select="@UNITS"/>
    </xsl:template>

    <xsl:template match="RADIUS">
      <xsl:value-of select="."/>
      <xsl:text> </xsl:text>
      <xsl:value-of select="@UNITS"/>
    </xsl:template>

    <xsl:template match="DAY">
      <xsl:value-of select="."/>
      <xsl:text> </xsl:text>
      <xsl:value-of select="@UNITS"/>
    </xsl:template>

</xsl:stylesheet>
```

Another situation to use <xsl:text> is when you want characters such as < and &, not < and &, to appear in your output document. To do that, you set the <xsl:text> element's disable-output-escaping attribute to "yes":

Listing ch13_22.xsl

```
<?xml version="1.0"?>
<xsl:stylesheet version="1.0"
xmlns:xsl="http://www.w3.org/1999/XSL/Transform">

<xsl:template match="PLANETS">
    <HTML>
        <HEAD>
            <TITLE>
                    Planets
            </TITLE>
        </HEAD>
        <BODY>
                <xsl:apply-templates select="PLANET"/>
        </BODY>
    </HTML>
</xsl:template>

<xsl:template match="PLANET">
    <xsl:text disable-output-escaping = "yes">
        &lt;PLANET&gt;
    </xsl:text>
</xsl:template>

</xsl:stylesheet>
```

Here is the result:

```
<HTML>
<HEAD>
<TITLE>
                    Planets
                </TITLE>
</HEAD>
<BODY>
        <PLANET>

        <PLANET>

        <PLANET>
    </BODY>
</HTML>
```

Copying Nodes

You can use the `<xsl:copy>` element to copy nodes, specifying just what parts you want to copy. The default rule for elements is that only the text in the element is copied. However, you can change that with `<xsl:copy>`, which can copy whole elements, text nodes, attributes, processing instructions, and more, as you direct.

Here's an example. In this case, I'll strip all comments, processing instructions, and attributes out of ch13_01.xml, simply by copying only text and elements:

Listing ch13_23.xsl

```
<?xml version="1.0"?>
<xsl:stylesheet version="1.0"
➥xmlns:xsl="http://www.w3.org/1999/XSL/Transform">

<xsl:template match="* | text()">
    <xsl:copy>
        <xsl:apply-templates select="* | text()"/>
    </xsl:copy>
</xsl:template>

</xsl:stylesheet>
```

Here's the output of this transformation:

```
<?xml version="1.0" encoding="UTF-8"?>
<PLANETS>

  <PLANET>
    <NAME>Mercury</NAME>
    <MASS>.0553</MASS>
    <DAY>58.65</DAY>
    <RADIUS>1516</RADIUS>
    <DENSITY>.983</DENSITY>
    <DISTANCE>43.4</DISTANCE>
  </PLANET>
    .
    .
    .
```

Sorting Elements

You can use the `<xsl:sort>` element to sort node sets. You use this element inside `<xsl:apply-templates>` and then use its `select` attribute to specify what to sort on. For example, here's how I sort the planets based on density:

Listing ch13_24.xsl

```
<?xml version="1.0"?>
<xsl:stylesheet version="1.0"
➥xmlns:xsl="http://www.w3.org/1999/XSL/Transform">

    <xsl:template match="PLANETS">
        <HTML>
            <HEAD>
                <TITLE>
                    Planets
                </TITLE>
            </HEAD>
            <BODY>
                <H1>Planets sorted by density</H1>
                <TABLE BORDER="1">
                    <TD>Planet</TD>
                    <TD>Mass</TD>
                    <TD>Day</TD>
                    <TD>Density</TD>
                    <xsl:apply-templates>
                        <xsl:sort select="DENSITY"/>
                    </xsl:apply-templates>
                </TABLE>
            </BODY>
        </HTML>
    </xsl:template>

    <xsl:template match="PLANET">
        <TR>
            <TD><xsl:apply-templates select="NAME"/></TD>
            <TD><xsl:apply-templates select="MASS"/></TD>
            <TD><xsl:apply-templates select="DAY"/></TD>
            <TD><xsl:apply-templates select="DENSITY"/></TD>
        </TR>
    </xsl:template>

</xsl:stylesheet>
```

Here are the results of this transformation:

```
<HTML>
<HEAD>
<TITLE>

                    Planets
            </TITLE>
</HEAD>
<BODY>
<H1>Planets sorted by density</H1>
<TABLE BORDER="1">
<TD>Planet</TD><TD>Mass</TD><TD>Day</TD><TD>Density</TD>

<TR>
<TD>Venus</TD><TD>.815</TD><TD>116.75</TD><TD>.943</TD>
</TR>
<TR>
<TD>Mercury</TD><TD>.0553</TD><TD>58.65</TD><TD>.983</TD>
</TR>
<TR>
<TD>Earth</TD><TD>1</TD><TD>1</TD><TD>1</TD>
</TR>
</TABLE>
</BODY>
</HTML>
```

You can see this HTML page in Figure 13-4.

Figure 13-4
Sorting planets
by density.

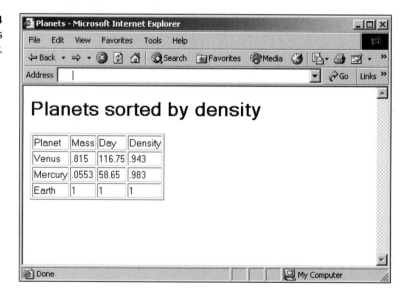

Note that, by default, `<xsl:sort>` performs a an alphabetic sort, which means that 10 will come before 2. You can perform a true numeric sort by setting the `data-type` attribute to `"number"`, like this:

```
<xsl:sort data-type="number" select="DENSITY"/>
```

Descending Sorts

You can also create descending sorts by setting the `<xsl:sort>` element's order attribute to `"descending"`.

Using *xsl:if*

You can make choices based on the input document using the `<xsl:if>` element. To use this element, you simply set its `test` attribute to an expression that evaluates to a Boolean value.

Here's an example. In this case, I'll list the planets one after the other and add a HTML horizontal rule, `<HR>`, element after the last element—but only after the last element. I can do that with `<xsl:if>` like this:

Listing ch13_25.xsl

```
<?xml version="1.0"?>
<xsl:stylesheet version="1.0"
➥xmlns:xsl="http://www.w3.org/1999/XSL/Transform">

<xsl:template match="PLANETS">
    <HTML>
        <HEAD>
            <TITLE>
                Planets
            </TITLE>
        </HEAD>
        <BODY>
            <xsl:apply-templates select="PLANET"/>
        </BODY>
    </HTML>
</xsl:template>

<xsl:template match="PLANET">
    <P>
    <xsl:value-of select="NAME"/>
    is planet number <xsl:value-of select="position()"/> from the sun.
    </P>
    <xsl:if test="position() = last()"><xsl:element name="HR"/></xsl:if>
</xsl:template>

</xsl:stylesheet>
```

Here is the result; as you can see, the `<HR>` element appears after only the last planet has been listed:

```
<HTML>
<HEAD>
<TITLE>
                Planets
        </TITLE>
</HEAD>
<BODY>
<P>Mercury
    is planet number 1 from the sun.
    </P>
<P>Venus
    is planet number 2 from the sun.
    </P>
<P>Earth
    is planet number 3 from the sun.
    </P>
<HR>
</BODY>
</HTML>
```

You can see this result in Figure 13-5.

Figure 13-5
Using *xsl:if*.

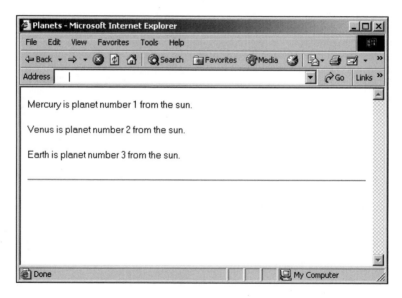

Using *xsl:choose*

The `<xsl:choose>` element is much like the Java `switch` statement, which lets you compare a test value against several possible matches. Suppose, for example, that we add COLOR attributes to each `<PLANET>` element in ch13_26.xml:

Listing ch13_26.xml

```
<?xml version="1.0"?>
<?xml-stylesheet type="text/xml" href="ch13_02.xsl"?>
<PLANETS>

  <PLANET COLOR="RED">
    <NAME>Mercury</NAME>
    <MASS UNITS="(Earth = 1)">.0553</MASS>
    <DAY UNITS="days">58.65</DAY>
    <RADIUS UNITS="miles">1516</RADIUS>
    <DENSITY UNITS="(Earth = 1)">.983</DENSITY>
    <DISTANCE UNITS="million miles">43.4</DISTANCE><!--At perihelion-->
  </PLANET>

  <PLANET COLOR="WHITE">
    <NAME>Venus</NAME>
    <MASS UNITS="(Earth = 1)">.815</MASS>
    <DAY UNITS="days">116.75</DAY>
    <RADIUS UNITS="miles">3716</RADIUS>
    <DENSITY UNITS="(Earth = 1)">.943</DENSITY>
    <DISTANCE UNITS="million miles">66.8</DISTANCE><!--At perihelion-->
  </PLANET>

  <PLANET COLOR="BLUE">
    <NAME>Earth</NAME>
    <MASS UNITS="(Earth = 1)">1</MASS>
    <DAY UNITS="days">1</DAY>
    <RADIUS UNITS="miles">2107</RADIUS>
    <DENSITY UNITS="(Earth = 1)">1</DENSITY>
    <DISTANCE UNITS="million miles">128.4</DISTANCE><!--At perihelion-->
  </PLANET>

</PLANETS>
```

Now say that we want to display the names of the various planets, formatted in different ways using HTML `<B>`, `<I>`, and `<U>` tags, depending on the value of the COLOR attribute. I can do this with an `<xsl:choose>` element. Each case in the `<xsl:choose>` element is specified with an `<xsl:when>` element, and you specify the actual test for the case with the `test` attribute. Here's what it looks like:

Listing ch13_27.xsl

```xml
<?xml version="1.0"?>
<xsl:stylesheet version="1.0"
➥xmlns:xsl="http://www.w3.org/1999/XSL/Transform">

<xsl:template match="PLANETS">
    <HTML>
        <HEAD>
            <TITLE>
                Planets
            </TITLE>
        </HEAD>
        <BODY>
            <xsl:apply-templates select="PLANET"/>
        </BODY>
    </HTML>
</xsl:template>

<xsl:template match="PLANET">
    <xsl:choose>
        <xsl:when test="@COLOR = 'RED'">
            <B>
                <xsl:value-of select="NAME"/>
            </B>
        </xsl:when>
        <xsl:when test="@COLOR = 'WHITE'">
            <I>
                <xsl:value-of select="NAME"/>
            </I>
        </xsl:when>
        <xsl:when test="@COLOR = 'BLUE'">
            <U>
                <xsl:value-of select="NAME"/>
            </U>
        </xsl:when>
        <xsl:otherwise>
            <PRE>
                <xsl:value-of select="."/>
            </PRE>
        </xsl:otherwise>
    </xsl:choose>
</xsl:template>

</xsl:stylesheet>
```

Note also the `<xsl:otherwise>` element in this example, which acts the same way as the `default:` case in a `switch` statement. That is, if no other case matches, the `<xsl:otherwise>` element is applied. Here is the result of this XSLT:

```
<HTML>
<HEAD>
<TITLE>
                Planets
        </TITLE>
</HEAD>
<BODY>
<B>Mercury</B>
<I>Venus</I>
<U>Earth</U>
</BODY>
</HTML>
```

Controlling Output Type

A lot of the examples in this chapter have converted XML into HTML, and you might have wondered how an XSLT processor knows to omit the `<?xml?>` declaration from the beginning of such output documents. It turns out that there's a special rule here: If the document node of the output document is `<HTML>`, the XSLT processor knows that the output document type is HTML and writes the document accordingly.

In fact, you can specify three types of output documents:

- **XML**—This is the default, and such documents start with an `<?xml?>` declaration. In addition, entity references are not replaced with characters such as < or & in the output document; the actual entity reference appears in the output.

- **HTML**—This is standard HTML 4.0, without an XML declaration or any need to close elements that don't normally have a closing tag in HTML 4.0. Empty elements can end with >, not `/>`. In addition, < and & characters in text are not escaped with the corresponding character entity references.

- **Text**—This type of output represents pure text. In this case, the output document is simply the plain text of the document tree.

You can set the output method by setting the `<xsl:output>` element's `method` attribute to `"xml"`, `"html"`, or `"text"`. For example, if you want to create an

HTML document, even though the root element is not <HTML>, you can use this <xsl:output> element:

```
<xsl:output method = "html"/>
```

Another useful attribute of <xsl:output> is the indent attribute, which allows the XSLT processor (but does not force it) to insert whitespace to indent the output. Here's how you can use this attribute:

```
<xsl:output indent = "yes"/>
```

Here are some <xsl:output> attributes you can use to create or modify XML declarations:

- encoding—Specifies the value for the XML declaration's encoding attribute.

- omit-xml-declaration—Specifies whether the processor should omit the XML declaration. Set to "yes" or "no".

- standalone—Specifies the value for the XML declaration's standalone attribute. Set to "yes" or "no".

- version—Specifies the value for the XML declaration's version attribute.

Another useful attribute of <xsl:output> is media-type, which lets you specify the MIME type of the output document. Here's an example:

```
<xsl:output media-type="text/xml"/>
```

You can also use the <xsl:output> doctype-system and doctype-public attributes to specify an external DTD. For example, this <xsl:output> element

```
<xsl:output doctype-system = "planets.dtd"/>
```

produces a <!DOCTYPE> element in the output document like this:

```
<!DOCTYPE PLANETS SYSTEM "planets.dtd">
```

As you can see, there's a tremendous amount going on in XSL transformations. In fact, there's more that we can cover here. For plenty of additional details, take a look at New Riders' *Inside XSLT* (it's a great book—well, that's what I think, anyway, because I wrote it), the W3C XSLT specification at www.w3.org/TR/xslt, and the XPath specification at www.w3.org/TR/xpath.

There's more to XSL. Besides XSL transformations, XSL includes a whole formatting language. I'm going to take a look at that next.

CHAPTER 14
XSL Formatting Objects

In the previous chapter, we took a look at the XSL transformation language. In this chapter, we'll take a look at the second half of XSL: formatting objects.

The World Wide Web Consortium (W3C) has defined formatting objects as `root`, `block`, and `character` that support different properties such as `font-weight`, `line-height`, and `border`. Using these predefined objects, you can specify the exact formatting for a document. At the time of this writing, there are 56 formatting objects and 177 properties that apply to these objects. Each of these objects has its own XML tag, and the properties it supports are attributes of that tag (many of these properties come from CSS2).

Like other XML applications, XSL formatting objects have their own namespace, `http://www.w3.org/1999/XSL/Format`, and the namespace prefix people use for that namespace is almost invariably `fo` for formatting objects. For example, here's how I can create a block (recall from CSS that blocks are rectangular areas in the output document) that displays the text `Welcome to XSL formatting.` in 36-point sans-serif font using the `<fo:block>` formatting object:

```
<fo:block font-family="sans-serif" line-height="48pt" font-size="36pt">
    Welcome to XSL formatting.
</fo:block>
```

The formatting object I'm using here is `fo:block`, and the properties I'm assigning values to are `font-family`, `line-height`, and `font-size`. After you've created a document using the XSL formatting objects, you can let an XSL processor format that document. We'll see one such program in this chapter that creates PDF (Portable Document Format, the common format you see on the Web for document exchange) files from documents written with the XSL formatting objects.

That's the idea: If you write your documents using the formatting objects, you can actually specify how that document will be displayed, down to the last comma and figure. Unfortunately, very little software actually interprets and uses the XSL formatting objects yet. In this chapter, we'll use the only such package I know of: the Apache XML project's fop processor.

The `<fo:block>` formatting object and all the others are defined by the W3C; you can find the W3C recommendation for the XSL formatting objects at `www.w3.org/TR/xsl`. The specification for all the formatting objects is at `www.w3.org/TR/xsl/slice6.html`, and the specification of the properties you can use with these objects is at `www.w3.org/TR/xsl/slice7.html`.

For More Info on Formatting Objects

We can't cover the entire field of formatting objects here because that would take a book by itself. For all the details, make sure you refer to `www.w3.org/TR/xsl`.

Formatting an XML Document

Writing an entire document using the XSL formatting objects is not an easy task for anything but short documents. I have a hard time imagining anyone using the formatting objects to write a book, for example. The W3C foresaw that difficulty, and that's one of the main reasons it also introduced the transformation language we took a look at in the previous chapter. You can write a document using your own tags, and you can use XSLT to transform the document so that it uses the XSL formatting objects. In practice, that's almost invariably the way it's done, which means all you have to supply is an XSLT stylesheet that can be used to convert your document to use formatting objects. In this way, an XSLT processor can do all the work for you, transforming a document from a form you're comfortable working with to a formatting object form, which you can then feed to a program that can handle formatting objects and display the formatted result.

To make all this self-evident, I'll write an example here using the XML document we saw in the previous chapter; I'll call this ch14_01.xml here:

Listing ch14_01.xml

```xml
<?xml version="1.0"?>
<?xml-stylesheet type="text/xml" href="ch14_02.xsl"?>
<PLANETS>

  <PLANET COLOR="RED">
    <NAME>Mercury</NAME>
    <MASS UNITS="(Earth = 1)">.0553</MASS>
    <DAY UNITS="days">58.65</DAY>
    <RADIUS UNITS="miles">1516</RADIUS>
    <DENSITY UNITS="(Earth = 1)">.983</DENSITY>
    <DISTANCE UNITS="million miles">43.4</DISTANCE><!--At perihelion-->
  </PLANET>

  <PLANET COLOR="WHITE">
    <NAME>Venus</NAME>
    <MASS UNITS="(Earth = 1)">.815</MASS>
    <DAY UNITS="days">116.75</DAY>
    <RADIUS UNITS="miles">3716</RADIUS>
    <DENSITY UNITS="(Earth = 1)">.943</DENSITY>
    <DISTANCE UNITS="million miles">66.8</DISTANCE><!--At perihelion-->
  </PLANET>

  <PLANET COLOR="BLUE">
    <NAME>Earth</NAME>
    <MASS UNITS="(Earth = 1)">1</MASS>
    <DAY UNITS="days">1</DAY>
    <RADIUS UNITS="miles">2107</RADIUS>
    <DENSITY UNITS="(Earth = 1)">1</DENSITY>
    <DISTANCE UNITS="million miles">128.4</DISTANCE><!--At perihelion-->
  </PLANET>

</PLANETS>
```

In this chapter, I'll write an XSLT stylesheet for this document, transforming it so that it uses formatting objects. Then I'll use the fop processor to turn the new document into a PDF file. And I'll take a look at the formatted document with Adobe Acrobat.

Creating the XSLT Stylesheet

I could translate ch14_01.xml into a document using the formatting objects by hand. As mentioned, however, that doesn't really work for anything but short documents in general. The usual technique is to create an XSLT stylesheet that you can use to transform a document so that it uses the XSL formatting objects, and I'll do that in this chapter. Here's what that stylesheet, ch14_02.xsl, is going to look like; in this case, I'm using a large font for text, 36 point:

Listing ch14_02.xsl

```
<?xml version='1.0'?>
<xsl:stylesheet xmlns:xsl="http://www.w3.org/1999/XSL/Transform"
    xmlns:fo="http://www.w3.org/1999/XSL/Format"
    version='1.0'>

    <xsl:template match="PLANETS">
        <fo:root>

            <fo:layout-master-set>
                <fo:simple-page-master master-name="page"
                    page-height="400mm" page-width="300mm"
                    margin-top="10mm" margin-bottom="10mm"
                    margin-left="20mm" margin-right="20mm">

                    <fo:region-body
                      margin-top="0mm" margin-bottom="10mm"
                      margin-left="0mm" margin-right="0mm"/>

                    <fo:region-after extent="10mm"/>
                </fo:simple-page-master>
            </fo:layout-master-set>

            <fo:page-sequence master-reference="page">
                <fo:flow flow-name="xsl-region-body">
                    <xsl:apply-templates/>
                </fo:flow>
            </fo:page-sequence>

        </fo:root>
    </xsl:template>

    <xsl:template match="PLANET/NAME">
        <fo:block font-weight="bold" font-size="36pt"
```

```
                line-height="48pt" font-family="sans-serif">
                Name:
                <xsl:apply-templates/>
        </fo:block>
    </xsl:template>

    <xsl:template match="PLANET/MASS">
        <fo:block font-size="36pt" line-height="48pt"
            font-family="sans-serif">
            Mass (Earth = 1):
            <xsl:apply-templates/>
        </fo:block>
    </xsl:template>

    <xsl:template match="PLANET/DAY">
        <fo:block font-size="36pt" line-height="48pt" font-family=
        ➥"sans-serif">
            Day (Earth = 1):
            <xsl:apply-templates/>
        </fo:block>
    </xsl:template>

    <xsl:template match="PLANET/RADIUS">
        <fo:block font-size="36pt" line-height="48pt" font-family=
        "sans-serif">
            Radius (in miles):
            <xsl:apply-templates/>
        </fo:block>
    </xsl:template>

    <xsl:template match="PLANET/DENSITY">
        <fo:block font-size="36pt" line-height="48pt" font-family=
        ➥"sans-serif">
            Density (Earth = 1):
            <xsl:apply-templates/>
        </fo:block>
    </xsl:template>

    <xsl:template match="PLANET/DISTANCE">
        <fo:block font-size="36pt" line-height="48pt" font-family=
        ➥"sans-serif">
            Distance (million miles):
            <xsl:apply-templates/>
        </fo:block>
    </xsl:template>

</xsl:stylesheet>
```

Transforming a Document into Formatting Object Form

To transform ch14_01.xml into a document that uses formatting objects, which I'll call ch14_03.fo, all I have to do is apply the stylesheet ch14_02.xsl to ch14_01.xml. You can do that using the XSLT techniques we saw in the previous chapter. For example, you can use the ch13_05.class application like this (this assumes that ch13_05.class, ch14_01.xml, and ch14_02.xsl are all in the current directory):

```
%java ch13_05 ch14_01.xml ch14_02.xsl ch14_03.fo
```

The document ch14_03.fo uses the XSL formatting objects to specify how the document should be formatted. Here's what ch14_03.po looks like:

Listing ch14_03.po

```xml
<?xml version="1.0" encoding="UTF-8"?>

<fo:root xmlns:fo="http://www.w3.org/1999/XSL/Format">
    <fo:layout-master-set>
        <fo:simple-page-master margin-right="20mm"
            margin-left="20mm" margin-bottom="10mm"
            margin-top="10mm" page-width="300mm"
            page-height="400mm" master-name="page">
            <fo:region-body margin-right="0mm"
                margin-left="0mm" margin-bottom="10mm"
                margin-top="0mm"/>
            <fo:region-after extent="10mm"/>
        </fo:simple-page-master>
    </fo:layout-master-set>

    <fo:page-sequence master-reference="page">
        <fo:flow flow-name="xsl-region-body">

            <fo:block font-family="sans-serif" line-height="48pt"
                font-size="36pt"
                font-weight="bold">
                    Name:
                    Mercury</fo:block>
            <fo:block font-family="sans-serif" line-height="48pt"
                font-size="36pt">
                    Mass (Earth = 1):
                    .0553</fo:block>
            <fo:block font-family="sans-serif" line-height="48pt"
                font-size="36pt">
                    Day (Earth = 1):
                    58.65</fo:block>
```

```
<fo:block font-family="sans-serif" line-height="48pt"
    font-size="36pt">
        Radius (in miles):
        1516</fo:block>
<fo:block font-family="sans-serif" line-height="48pt"
    font-size="36pt">
        Density (Earth = 1):
        .983</fo:block>
<fo:block font-family="sans-serif" line-height="48pt"
    font-size="36pt">
        Distance (million miles):
        43.4</fo:block>

<fo:block font-family="sans-serif" line-height="48pt"
    font-size="36pt" font-weight="bold">
        Name:
        Venus</fo:block>
<fo:block font-family="sans-serif" line-height="48pt"
    font-size="36pt">
        Mass (Earth = 1):
        .815</fo:block>
<fo:block font-family="sans-serif" line-height="48pt"
    font-size="36pt">
        Day (Earth = 1):
        116.75</fo:block>
<fo:block font-family="sans-serif" line-height="48pt"
    font-size="36pt">
        Radius (in miles):
        3716</fo:block>
<fo:block font-family="sans-serif" line-height="48pt"
    font-size="36pt">
        Density (Earth = 1):
        .943</fo:block>
<fo:block font-family="sans-serif" line-height="48pt"
    font-size="36pt">
        Distance (million miles):
        66.8</fo:block>

<fo:block font-family="sans-serif" line-height="48pt"
    font-size="36pt" font-weight="bold">
        Name:
        Earth</fo:block>
<fo:block font-family="sans-serif" line-height="48pt"
    font-size="36pt">
        Mass (Earth = 1):
        1</fo:block>
<fo:block font-family="sans-serif" line-height="48pt"
    font-size="36pt">
        Day (Earth = 1):
        1</fo:block>
```

continues

Listing ch14_03.po   Continued

```
        <fo:block font-family="sans-serif" line-height="48pt"
            font-size="36pt">
                Radius (in miles):
                2107</fo:block>
        <fo:block font-family="sans-serif" line-height="48pt"
            font-size="36pt">
                Density (Earth = 1):
                1</fo:block>
        <fo:block font-family="sans-serif" line-height="48pt"
            font-size="36pt">
                Distance (million miles):
                128.4</fo:block>

            </fo:flow>
    </fo:page-sequence>
</fo:root>
```

Okay, now we have ch14_03.po. How can we use it to create a formatted PDF file?

Creating a Formatted Document

To process ch14_03.po and create a formatted document, I'll use James Tauber's FOP (Formatting Objects Processor), which has now been donated to the Apache XML Project. (The alphaWorks XML for Java parsers that I've been using for several chapters are based on the Apache XML project's Xerces XML parser.)

Here's how the Apache XML Project describes FOP:

FOP (Formatting Objects Processor) is the world's first print formatter driven by XSL formatting objects and the world's first output independent formatter. It is a Java application that reads a formatting object tree and then renders the resulting pages to a specified output. Output formats currently supported are PDF, PCL, PS, SVG, XML (area tree representation), Print, AWT, MIF, and TXT. The primary output target is PDF.

Here's how the objectives of FOP are described:

The goals of the Apache XML FOP Project are to deliver an XSL FO–PDF formatter that is compliant to at least the Basic conformance level described in the 27 March 2000 XSL WD (W3C Working Draft) and that complies with the 11 March 1999 Portable Document Format Specification (Version 1.3) from Adobe Systems.

You can get FOP at `http://xml.apache.org/fop`; just click the Download button to download it. The FOP package, including documentation, comes zipped, so you have to unzip it. The current version as of this writing is 0.20.4 and it's written in Java; the compressed file that you download is fop-0.20.4-bin.tar.gz (even though it's a .tar.gz file, even Windows unzip utilities, such as WinZip, can unzip it). To convert ch14_03.fo into a PDF file, ch14_04.pdf, you can navigate to the fop-0.20.4 directory created when you unzip fop-0.20.4-bin.tar.gz and enter this command (this assumes that ch14_03.fo is in the fop-0.20.4 directory also):

```
%java -cp build\fop.jar;lib\batik.jar;lib\xalan-2.3.1.jar;lib\xercesImpl-
➥2.0.1.jar;lib\xml-apis.jar;lib\avalon-framework-cvs-20020315.jar;lib\logkit-
➥1.0.jar;lib\jimi-1.0.jar org.apache.fop.apps.Fop ch14_03.fo ch14_04.pdf
```

That's quite a mouthful, so FOP comes with a script for most shells, including a .bat file for Windows. This means that you only have to enter this command in the fop-0.20.4 directory to do the same thing:

```
%fop ch14_03.fo ch14_04.pdf
```

And that's it. You can see the final results, ch14_04.pdf, in the Adobe Acrobat PDF reader (which you can get for free at `www.adobe.com/products/acrobat/readermain.html`—currently, the download process starts at `www.adobe.com/products/acrobat/readstep.html`) in Figure 14-1. The ch14_01.xml document appears in that figure formatted exactly as it should be. The PDF format is a good one for formatting object output, although it has some limitations. For example, it can't handle dynamic tables that can expand or collapse at the click of a mouse, or interactive multiple-target links, both of which are part of the formatting objects specification.

Figure 14-1
A PDF document created with formatting objects.

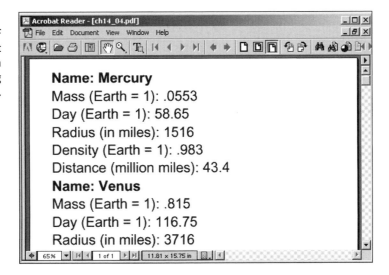

Now you've seen how the process works; it's time to get to the details, starting with an overview.

The XSL Formatting Objects

Here's an overview of the 56 formatting objects that exist as of this writing. We'll see a good number of them in action in this chapter:

- `bidi-override`—Overrides the default Unicode bidirectionality algorithm direction in mixed-language documents.

- `block`—Creates a display block. Often used for formatting paragraphs, titles, headlines, figure and table captions, and so on.

- `block-container`—Generates a block-level reference area.

- `character`—Represents a character that is associated with a glyph for display.

- `color-profile`—Declares a color profile for a stylesheet.

- `conditional-page-master-reference`—Specifies a page master to be used when the given conditions are met.

- `declarations`—Groups global declarations for a stylesheet.

- `external-graphic`—Adds an inline graphic to the document, where the graphics data is outside the xml result document.

- `float`—Can specify that some content is formatted in a separate area at the beginning of the page or is placed to one side.

- `flow`—Supports the flowing text content that is displayed in pages.

- `footnote`—Creates a footnote citation and the associated footnote.

- `footnote-body`—Creates the content of the footnote.

- `initial-property-set`—Sets the formatting properties for the first line of a block.

- `inline`—Usually used to format part of the text with a background or give it a border.

- `inline-container`—Creates an inline reference area.

- `instream-foreign-object`—Used to insert an inline graphic or other object, where the object data is a descendant of `fo:instream-foreign-object`.

- `layout-master-set`—Wrapper for all the masters used in the document.

- `leader`—Creates a rule or row of a repeating characters or repeating pattern of characters that is used between two text-formatting objects.

- `list-block`—Used to format a list.

- `list-item`—Holds the label and the body of an item in a list.

- `list-item-body`—Holds the content of the body of a `list-item`.

- `list-item-label`—Holds the content of the label of a `list-item`.

- `marker`—Used with `fo:retrieve-marker` to create on-the-fly headers or footers.

- `multi-case`—Adds flow objects that the parent object, which is `fo:multi-switch`, can show or hide.

- `multi-properties`—Switches between two or more property sets that are connected to a given part of the content.

- `multi-property-set`—Indicates an alternative set of formatting properties that can be applied to the content.

- `multi-switch`—Switches between two or more subtrees of formatting objects.

- `multi-toggle`—Used inside a `fo:multi-case` object to switch to another `fo:multi-case`.

- `page-number`—Holds the current page number.

- `page-number-citation`—References the page number for the page containing the cited formatting object.

- `page-sequence`—Specifies how to create a sequence of pages within a document.

- `page-sequence-master`—Contains sequences of page masters that are used to generate sequences of pages.

- `region-after`—Refers to the region located after a `fo:region-body` region.

- `region-before`—Refers to the region before a `fo:region-body` region.

- `region-body`—Refers to the region in the center of `fo:simple-page-master`.

- `region-end`—Refers to the region at the end of a `fo:region-body` region.

- `region-start`—Refers to the region starting a `fo:region-body` region.
- `repeatable-page-master-alternatives`—Indicates a subsequence made up of repeated instances of a set of alternative page masters.
- `repeatable-page-master-reference`—Indicates a subsequence of repeated instances of a single page master.
- `retrieve-marker`—Used with `fo:marker` to create on-the-fly headers or footers.
- `root`—The top node of an XSL-formatted document.
- `simple-link`—Represents the start location in a simple link.
- `simple-page-master`—Gives the geometry of a page, which may be divided into up to five regions.
- `single-page-master-reference`—Indicates a subsequence made up of a single instance of a single page master.
- `static-content`—Contains a sequence of formatting objects that should be presented in a single region or repeated in like-named regions on one or more pages in the page sequence. Most often used for repeating headers and footers.
- `table`—Formats the data in a table.
- `table-and-caption`—Formats the data and caption of a table.
- `table-body`—Holds the content of the table body.
- `table-caption`—Holds block-level formatting objects, which, in turn, hold the caption for a table.
- `table-cell`—Groups content to be placed in a table cell.
- `table-column`—Sets characteristics for table cells that have the same column.
- `table-footer`—Holds the content of the table footer.
- `table-header`—Holds the content of the table header.
- `table-row`—Groups table cells into rows.
- `title`—Gives a document a title. The content of the `fo:title` object can be formatted and displayed in the document.
- `wrapper`—Indicates inherited properties for a group of formatting objects.

The XSL Formatting Properties

The formatting objects in the previous section have properties that you can use to customize what they do. As we'll see in this chapter, a typical formatting object can support quite a few properties. Here are the current formatting properties that the W3C formatting objects specification supports. Many of these properties are taken from CSS and behave the same there. You set lengths and other units exactly as you do in CSS (using units such as px for pixels, pt for points, mm for millimeters, % for percentages, and so on):

- `absolute-position`
- `active-state`
- `alignment-adjust`
- `auto-restore`
- `azimuth`
- `background`
- `background-attachment`
- `background-color`
- `background-image`
- `background-position`
- `background-position-horizontal`
- `background-position-vertical`
- `background-repeat`
- `baseline-identifier`
- `baseline-shift`
- `blank-or-not-blank`
- `block-progression-dimension`
- `border`
- `border-after-color`
- `border-after-style`
- `border-after-width`
- `border-before-color`
- `border-before-style`
- `border-before-width`
- `border-bottom`
- `border-bottom-color`
- `border-bottom-style`
- `border-bottom-width`
- `border-collapse`
- `border-color`
- `border-end-color`
- `border-end-style`
- `border-end-width`
- `border-left`
- `border-left-color`
- `border-left-style`
- `border-left-width`
- `border-right`
- `border-right-color`
- `border-right-style`
- `border-right-width`
- `border-separation`
- `border-spacing`
- `border-start-color`
- `border-start-style`
- `border-start-width`

- border-style
- border-top
- border-top-color
- border-top-style
- border-top-width
- border-width
- bottom
- break-after
- break-before
- caption-side
- case-name
- case-title
- character
- clear
- clip
- color
- color-profile-name
- column-count
- column-gap
- column-number
- column-width
- content-height
- content-type
- content-width
- country
- cue
- cue-after
- cue-before
- destination-placement-offset
- direction
- display-align

- dominant-baseline
- elevation
- empty-cells
- end-indent
- ends-row
- extent
- external-destination
- float
- flow-name
- font
- font-family
- font-height-override-after
- font-height-override-before
- font-size
- font-size-adjust
- font-stretch
- font-style
- font-variant
- font-weight
- force-page-count
- format
- glyph-orientation-horizontal
- glyph-orientation-vertical
- grouping-separator
- grouping-size
- height
- hyphenate
- hyphenation-character
- hyphenation-keep
- hyphenation-ladder-count

- hyphenation-push-character-count
- hyphenation-remain-character-count
- id
- indicate-destination
- initial-page-number
- inline-progression-dimension
- internal-destination
- keep-together
- keep-with-next
- keep-with-previous
- language
- last-line-end-indent
- leader-alignment
- leader-length
- leader-pattern
- leader-pattern-width
- left
- letter-spacing
- letter-value
- linefeed-treatment
- line-height
- line-height-shift-adjustment
- line-stacking-strategy
- margin
- margin-bottom
- margin-left
- margin-right
- margin-top
- marker-class-name
- master-name
- max-height
- maximum-repeats
- max-width
- min-height
- min-width
- number-columns-repeated
- number-columns-spanned
- number-rows-spanned
- odd-or-even
- orphans
- overflow
- padding
- padding-after
- padding-before
- padding-bottom
- padding-end
- padding-left
- padding-right
- padding-start
- padding-top
- page-break-after
- page-break-before
- page-break-inside
- page-height
- page-position
- page-width
- pause
- pause-after
- pause-before
- pitch
- pitch-range

- play-during
- position
- precedence
- provisional-distance-between-starts
- provisional-label-separation
- ref-id
- reference-orientation
- region-name
- relative-align
- relative-position
- rendering-intent
- retrieve-boundary
- retrieve-class-name
- retrieve-position
- richness
- right
- role
- rule-style
- rule-thickness
- scaling
- scaling-method
- score-spaces
- script
- show-destination
- size
- source-document
- space-after
- space-before
- space-end
- space-start

- space-treatment
- span
- speak
- speak-header
- speak-numeral
- speak-punctuation
- speech-rate
- src
- start-indent
- starting-state
- starts-row
- stress
- suppress-at-line-break
- switch-to
- table-layout
- table-omit-footer-at-break
- table-omit-header-at-break
- text-align
- text-align-last
- text-decoration
- text-indent
- text-shadow
- text-transform
- top
- treat-as-word-space
- unicode-bidi
- vertical-align
- visibility
- voice-family
- volume
- white-space

- `white-space-collapse`

- `widows`

- `width`

- `word-spacing`

- `wrap-option`

- `writing-mode`

- `xml:lang`

- `z-index`

Working with Formatting Objects

This chapter is all about working with the XSL formatting objects, and I'm going to cover those objects in depth. Knowing how to use these objects is crucial to the whole formatting process. Even if you use a transformation stylesheet to transform XML documents to formatting-object form, you still have to know how to create the stylesheet to do so. By the end of this chapter, you'll have a solid idea of exactly how that works.

The first formatting object I'll cover is `fo:root`, the root object of any formatting object document.

The Document Root: *fo:root*

The `fo:root` object is the top node of the formatting object tree that makes up a formatting object document. That is, document node of the formatting object document *must* be `fo:root`.

The children of the `fo:root` formatting object are a single `fo:layout-master-set` and a sequence of one or more `fo:page-sequences`. The `fo:layout-master-set` formatting object holds all "masters" used in the document, which you use to specify how each page will actually be built. Each `fo:page-sequence` represents a sequence of pages formatted the way you want them. For example, each chapter of a book could be made up of its own page sequence, and you can give each sequence the same header and footer such as `Chapter 2: The Plot Thickens`.

In ch14_01.xml, the document node is `<PLANETS>`; however, the document node of a formatting object document is `<fo:root>`, which means we have to replace `<PLANETS>` with `<fo:root>`. That looks like this in ch14_02.xsl, the transformation stylesheet:

```
<?xml version='1.0'?>
<xsl:stylesheet xmlns:xsl="http://www.w3.org/1999/XSL/Transform"
    xmlns:fo="http://www.w3.org/1999/XSL/Format"
    version='1.0'>

    <xsl:template match="PLANETS">
        <fo:root>
        .
        .
        .
```

The `fo:root` object can contain both master set layouts and page sequences. I'll take a look at the `fo:layout-master-set` object first.

The Master Set Layout:
fo:layout-master-set

The `fo:layout-master-set` object contains all the masters used in the document, including page sequence master objects, page master objects, and region master objects, which you apply to create page sequences, pages, and regions. You use *masters* to create templates for pages, page sequences, and regions.

The name of each master ends in `-master` in XSL. For example, the page master we'll use is the `simple-page-master` object. Page masters specify the subdivisions of a page and the geometry of these subdivisions. Page sequence masters specify the sequence of page masters that will be used to generate pages during the formatting.

You list the masters you want to use in the document in the `<fo:layout-master-set>` element, so I'll add that element to ch14_02.xsl now:

```
<?xml version='1.0'?>
<xsl:stylesheet xmlns:xsl="http://www.w3.org/1999/XSL/Transform"
    xmlns:fo="http://www.w3.org/1999/XSL/Format"
    version='1.0'>

    <xsl:template match="PLANETS">
        <fo:root>

            <fo:layout-master-set>
        .
        .
        .
```

To configure each page, you use a page master; the one I'll use here is the `fo:simple-page-master` object.

Using a Page Master:
fo:simple-page-master

A page master is a master template that is used to generate a page, and it specifies the actual layout of the page. You can use a page master whenever you want to in a document. Each page master has a unique name.

In the current XSL specification, there is only one kind of page master, the `fo:simple-page-master` object; in the future, the XSL specification may support additional page masters. You use the `fo:simple-page-master` object to generate pages and define the geometry of the page.

To set the overall geometry of the page, you can use these properties of the `fo:simple-page-master` object:

- Common margin properties for blocks: `margin-top`, `margin-bottom`, `margin-left`, `margin-right`, `space-before`, `space-after`, `start-indent`, `end-indent`
- `master-name`
- `page-height`
- `page-width`
- `reference-orientation`
- `writing-mode`

In ch14_02.xsl, I'll name the simple page master page using the `master-name` property. When I want to create pages using this master, I'll be able to refer to it by name. I'll also specify the page dimensions and margins like this:

```
<?xml version='1.0'?>
<xsl:stylesheet xmlns:xsl="http://www.w3.org/1999/XSL/Transform"
    xmlns:fo="http://www.w3.org/1999/XSL/Format"
    version='1.0'>

    <xsl:template match="PLANETS">
        <fo:root>

            <fo:layout-master-set>
                <fo:simple-page-master master-name="page"
                    page-height="400mm" page-width="300mm"
                    margin-top="10mm" margin-bottom="10mm"
                    margin-left="20mm" margin-right="20mm">
            .
            .
            .
```

Besides laying out the margins of a page, a `fo:simple-page-master` has children that specify one or more *regions* in the page, letting you customize the layout in detail.

Creating Regions

In version 1.0 of the XSL recommendation, page masters have up to five regions. The central region, which corresponds to the body of the page, is called the *body region*. The top part of the page, the header, is called the *before region*; the bottom part of the page, the footer, is called the *after region*. In languages that read left to right, such as English, the left side of the page is called the *start region* and the right side is called the *end region*. In languages that read right to left, the start and end regions are reversed. You can think of start and end regions as sidebars that flank the body region.

XSL formatting objects correspond to these regions:

- `fo:region-before`
- `fo:region-after`
- `fo:region-body`
- `fo:region-start`
- `fo:region-end`

You can use these properties with these formatting objects:

- Common border, padding, and background properties: `background-attachment, background-color, background-image, background-repeat, background-position-horizontal, background-position-vertical, border-before-color, border-before-style, border-before-width, border-after-color, border-after-style, border-after-width, border-start-color, border-start-style, border-start-width, border-end-color, border-end-style, border-end-width, border-top-color, border-top-style, border-top-width, border-bottom-color, border-bottom-style, border-bottom-width, border-left-color, border-left-style, border-left-width, border-right-color, border-right-style, border-right-width, padding-before, padding-after, padding-start, padding-end, padding-top, padding-bottom, padding-left, padding-right`

- Common margin properties for blocks: `margin-top`, `margin-bottom`, `margin-left`, `margin-right`, `space-before`, `space-after`, `start-indent`, `end-indent`

- `clip`

- `column-count`

- `column-gap`

- `display-align`

- `extent`

- `overflow`

- `region-name`

- `reference-orientation`

- `writing-mode`

You can customize the regions of a page as you like, as in ch14_02.xsl, where I'm setting margins for the body region. The four outer regions (but not the body region) have an `extent` property that sets their size, and I'll use that here:

```
<?xml version='1.0'?>
<xsl:stylesheet xmlns:xsl="http://www.w3.org/1999/XSL/Transform"
    xmlns:fo="http://www.w3.org/1999/XSL/Format"
    version='1.0'>

    <xsl:template match="PLANETS">
        <fo:root>

            <fo:layout-master-set>
                <fo:simple-page-master master-name="page"
                    page-height="400mm" page-width="300mm"
                    margin-top="10mm" margin-bottom="10mm"
                    margin-left="20mm" margin-right="20mm">

                    <fo:region-body
                       margin-top="0mm" margin-bottom="10mm"
                       margin-left="0mm" margin-right="0mm"/>

                    <fo:region-after extent="10mm"/>
                </fo:simple-page-master>
            </fo:layout-master-set>
            .
            .
            .
```

That ends the only master I'll have in this document: the simple page master named page. That completes the `fo:layout-master-set` object.

As mentioned, besides the `fo:layout-master-set`, a formatting object document usually also contains one or more `fo:page-sequence` objects that define page sequences using the masters you define in the `fo:layout-master-set`.

Creating Page Sequences: *fo:page-sequence*

The pages in the output document are actually created when the XSL processor processes `fo:page-sequence` objects. A page sequence consists of a run of pages that share the same characteristics, such as a chapter in a book.

Each `fo:page-sequence` object references either a `fo:page-sequence-master` or a page master, and the actual layout of the pages is specified by those masters. You can get fairly involved here, creating sequences in which the page numbering alternates from side to side on the page as when you're creating pages for a book. Here are the properties that apply to the `fo:page-sequence` object:

- country
- format
- language
- letter-value
- grouping-separator
- grouping-size
- id
- initial-page-number
- force-page-count
- master-name

In the current W3C XSL recommendation, you specify what page master you want to use for a page sequence with the `<fo:page-sequence>` element's `master-reference` attribute. I named the simple page master we created page, so I'll set that attribute to that name here:

```
<?xml version='1.0'?>
<xsl:stylesheet xmlns:xsl="http://www.w3.org/1999/XSL/Transform"
```

```
xmlns:fo="http://www.w3.org/1999/XSL/Format"
version='1.0'>

<xsl:template match="PLANETS">
    <fo:root>

        <fo:layout-master-set>
            <fo:simple-page-master master-name="page"
                page-height="400mm" page-width="300mm"
                margin-top="10mm" margin-bottom="10mm"
                margin-left="20mm" margin-right="20mm">

                <fo:region-body
                   margin-top="0mm" margin-bottom="10mm"
                   margin-left="0mm" margin-right="0mm"/>

                <fo:region-after extent="10mm"/>
            </fo:simple-page-master>
        </fo:layout-master-set>

        <fo:page-sequence master-reference="page">
             .
             .
             .
```

That specifies what page master we want to use for a page sequence. Next, you have to specify the *content* of the page sequence. And the content of these pages comes from *flow* children of the fo:page-sequence.

Creating Flows: *fo:flow*

Flow objects are called that because the text in them "flows" and is arranged to fit the page by the displaying software. The content of a page is handled with flow objects.

There are two kinds of flow objects: fo:static-content and fo:flow. A fo:static-content flow object holds content, such as the text that goes into headers and footers that are repeated on the pages of the page sequence. The fo:flow flow object, on the other hand, holds the text itself that makes up the content of the document. The following fo:flow object has a single property: flow-name.

I'll add a fo:flow object to ch14_02.xsl to handle the text content of ch14_01.xml. To make sure that the text content of ch14_01.xml is transformed into that flow, I'll use an <xsl:apply-templates> element, which we first saw in the previous chapter. The <xsl:apply-templates> element will make the XSL processor process the various elements in ch14_01.xml (note that I also add the declaration of the xsl namespace) and insert them into the flow:

```
<?xml version='1.0'?>
<xsl:stylesheet xmlns:xsl="http://www.w3.org/1999/XSL/Transform"
    xmlns:fo="http://www.w3.org/1999/XSL/Format"
    version='1.0'>

    <xsl:template match="PLANETS">
        <fo:root>

            <fo:layout-master-set>
                <fo:simple-page-master master-name="page"
                    page-height="400mm" page-width="300mm"
                    margin-top="10mm" margin-bottom="10mm"
                    margin-left="20mm" margin-right="20mm">

                    <fo:region-body
                        margin-top="0mm" margin-bottom="10mm"
                        margin-left="0mm" margin-right="0mm" />

                    <fo:region-after extent="10mm" />
                </fo:simple-page-master>
            </fo:layout-master-set>

            <fo:page-sequence master-reference="page">
                <fo:flow flow-name="xsl-region-body">
                    <xsl:apply-templates/>
                </fo:flow>
            </fo:page-sequence>

        </fo:root>
    </xsl:template>
        .
        .
        .
```

That completes the fo:page-sequence object; we've specified a master to use for this sequence and provided the XSL processor a way to get the content that will go into the pages in the formatted document. Besides fo:flow, there's another flow object: fo:static-content.

Creating Static Content: *fo:static-content*

The `fo:static-content` formatting object holds formatting objects that are to be presented in a single region or repeated in regions on one or more pages in the page sequence. It is most often used to create repeating headers and footers, because its content is repeated on every page to which it is assigned.

You can use the property `flow-name` with the `fo:static-content` formatting object.

Creating Block-level Content: *fo:block*

You use blocks in XSL just as we did in CSS—to create a rectangular display area set off from other display areas in a document. You use the `fo:block` formatting object for formatting such items as paragraphs, titles, headlines, figure and table captions, and so on. Here's an example from the beginning of the chapter:

```
<fo:block font-family="sans-serif" line-height="48pt" font-size="36pt">
    Welcome to XSL formatting.
</fo:block>
```

You can use these properties with `fo:block`:

- Common accessibility properties: `source-document`, `role`
- Common aural properties: `azimuth`, `cue-after`, `cue-before`, `elevation`, `pause-after`, `pause-before`, `pitch`, `pitch-range`, `play-during`, `richness`, `speak`, `speak-header`, `speak-numeral`, `speak-punctuation`, `speech-rate`, `stress`, `voice-family`, `volume`
- Common border, padding, and background properties: `background-attachment`, `background-color`, `background-image`, `background-repeat`, `background-position-horizontal`, `background-position-vertical`, `border-before-color`, `border-before-style`, `border-before-width`, `border-after-color`, `border-after-style`, `border-after-width`, `border-start-color`, `border-start-style`, `border-start-width`, `border-end-color`, `border-end-style`, `border-end-width`, `border-top-color`, `border-top-style`, `border-top-width`, `border-bottom-color`, `border-bottom-style`, `border-bottom-width`, `border-left-color`, `border-left-style`, `border-left-width`, `border-right-color`, `border-right-style`, `border-right-width`, `padding-before`, `padding-after`, `padding-start`, `padding-end`, `padding-top`, `padding-bottom`, `padding-left`, `padding-right`

- Common font properties: `font-family`, `font-size`, `font-stretch`, `font-size-adjust`, `font-style`, `font-variant`, `font-weight`

- Common hyphenation properties: `country`, `language`, `script`, `hyphenate`, `hyphenation-character`, `hyphenation-push-character-count`, `hyphenation-remain-character-count`

- Common margin properties for blocks: `margin-top`, `margin-bottom`, `margin-left`, `margin-right`, `space-before`, `space-after`, `start-indent`, `end-indent`

- `break-after`

- `break-before`

- `color`

- `font-height-override-after`

- `font-height-override-before`

- `hyphenation-keep`

- `hyphenation-ladder-count`

- `id`

- `keep-together`

- `keep-with-next`

- `keep-with-previous`

- `last-line-end-indent`

- `linefeed-treatment`

- `line-height`

- `line-height-shift-adjustment`

- `line-stacking-strategy`

- `orphans`

- `relative-position`

- `space-treatment`

- `span`

- `text-align`

- `text-align-last`

- `text-indent`

- `visibility`

- white-space-collapse

- widows

- wrap-option

- z-index

Note that the data in ch14_01.xml is broken up into various child elements of a <PLANET> element, such as <NAME>, <MASS>, and so on, like this:

```
<PLANET COLOR="RED">
  <NAME>Mercury</NAME>
  <MASS UNITS="(Earth = 1)">.0553</MASS>
  <DAY UNITS="days">58.65</DAY>
  <RADIUS UNITS="miles">1516</RADIUS>
  <DENSITY UNITS="(Earth = 1)">.983</DENSITY>
  <DISTANCE UNITS="million miles">43.4</DISTANCE><!--At perihelion-->
</PLANET>
```

In this example, I'll give the data in each of the children of a <PLANET> element its own block in the formatted document. To do that, I add a rule to ch14_02.xsl for each of those children, specifying the font to use for each block:

```
<?xml version='1.0'?>
<xsl:stylesheet xmlns:xsl="http://www.w3.org/1999/XSL/Transform"
    xmlns:fo="http://www.w3.org/1999/XSL/Format"
    version='1.0'>

    <xsl:template match="PLANETS">
        <fo:root>

            <fo:layout-master-set>
                <fo:simple-page-master master-name="page"
                    page-height="400mm" page-width="300mm"
                    margin-top="10mm" margin-bottom="10mm"
                    margin-left="20mm" margin-right="20mm">

                    <fo:region-body
                        margin-top="0mm" margin-bottom="10mm"
                        margin-left="0mm" margin-right="0mm"/>

                    <fo:region-after extent="10mm"/>
                </fo:simple-page-master>
            </fo:layout-master-set>

            <fo:page-sequence master-reference="page">
                <fo:flow flow-name="xsl-region-body">
```

```
                    <xsl:apply-templates/>
                </fo:flow>
            </fo:page-sequence>

        </fo:root>
    </xsl:template>
```

```
<xsl:template match="PLANET/NAME">
    <fo:block font-weight="bold" font-size="36pt"
        line-height="48pt" font-family="sans-serif">
        Name:
        <xsl:apply-templates/>
    </fo:block>
</xsl:template>

<xsl:template match="PLANET/MASS">
    <fo:block font-size="36pt" line-height="48pt"
        font-family="sans-serif">
        Mass (Earth = 1):
        <xsl:apply-templates/>
    </fo:block>
</xsl:template>

<xsl:template match="PLANET/DAY">
    <fo:block font-size="36pt" line-height="48pt" font-family="sans-serif">
        Day (Earth = 1):
        <xsl:apply-templates/>
    </fo:block>
</xsl:template>

<xsl:template match="PLANET/RADIUS">
    <fo:block font-size="36pt" line-height="48pt" font-family="sans-serif">
        Radius (in miles):
        <xsl:apply-templates/>
    </fo:block>
</xsl:template>

<xsl:template match="PLANET/DENSITY">
    <fo:block font-size="36pt" line-height="48pt" font-family="sans-serif">
        Density (Earth = 1):
        <xsl:apply-templates/>
    </fo:block>
</xsl:template>

<xsl:template match="PLANET/DISTANCE">
    <fo:block font-size="36pt" line-height="48pt" font-family="sans-serif">
        Distance (million miles):
        <xsl:apply-templates/>
    </fo:block>
</xsl:template>
```

```
</xsl:stylesheet>
```

Now we've handled all the elements in ch14_01.xml, so that completes ch14_02.xsl. You can see the results in Figure 14-1. Congratulations, you've completed your first transformation to XSL formatting objects!

Inline-Level Formatting Objects

Besides block objects, you can also create *inline* objects. Inline objects are usually used to format part of text as that text follows the normal flow in the page. For example, you can make the first character in a paragraph larger, make the whole first line smaller, insert page numbers into text, and so on.

Here are the inline formatting objects:

- fo:bidi-override
- fo:character
- fo:initial-property-set
- fo:external-graphic
- fo:instream-foreign-object
- fo:inline
- fo:inline-container
- fo:leader
- fo:page-number
- fo:page-number-citation

I'll take a look at a few of the most common of these next.

Using *fo:character*

The fo:character object lets you handle the characters in a document individually, which is very useful if you want to write an XSL processor, but not necessarily that useful otherwise. You can use fo:character to replace characters with other characters. Here's an example; in this case, I'm matching an element named <MASKED> and replacing the characters in it with the character -:

```
<xsl:template match="MASKED">
    <fo:character character="-">
        <xsl:value-of select="."/>
    </fo:character>
</xsl:template>
```

You can use these properties with `fo:character`:

- Common aural properties: `azimuth`, `cue-after`, `cue-before`, `elevation`, `pause-after`, `pause-before`, `pitch`, `pitch-range`, `play-during`, `richness`, `speak`, `speak-header`, `speak-numeral`, `speak-punctuation`, `speech-rate`, `stress`, `voice-family`, `volume`

- Common border, padding, and background properties: `background-attachment`, `background-color`, `background-image`, `background-repeat`, `background-position-horizontal`, `background-position-vertical`, `border-before-color`, `border-before-style`, `border-before-width`, `border-after-color`, `border-after-style`, `border-after-width`, `border-start-color`, `border-start-style`, `border-start-width`, `border-end-color`, `border-end-style`, `border-end-width`, `border-top-color`, `border-top-style`, `border-top-width`, `border-bottom-color`, `border-bottom-style`, `border-bottom-width`, `border-left-color`, `border-left-style`, `border-left-width`, `border-right-color`, `border-right-style`, `border-right-width`, `padding-before`, `padding-after`, `padding-start`, `padding-end`, `padding-top`, `padding-bottom`, `padding-left`, `padding-right`

- Common font properties: `font-family`, `font-size`, `font-stretch`, `font-size-adjust`, `font-style`, `font-variant`, `font-weight`

- Common hyphenation properties: `country`, `language`, `script`, `hyphenate`, `hyphenation-character`, `hyphenation-push-character-count`, `hyphenation-remain-character-count`

- Common margin properties, inline: `space-end`, `space-start`

- `alignment-adjust`

- `baseline-identifier`

- `baseline-shift`

- `character`

- `color`

- `dominant-baseline`

- `font-height-override-after`

- `font-height-override-before`
- `glyph-orientation-horizontal`
- `glyph-orientation-vertical`
- `id`
- `keep-with-next`
- `keep-with-previous`
- `letter-spacing`
- `line-height`
- `line-height-shift-adjustment`
- `relative-position`
- `score-spaces`
- `suppress-at-line-break`
- `text-decoration`
- `text-shadow`
- `text-transform`
- `treat-as-word-space`
- `word-spacing`

fo:initial-property-set

You can format the first line of a `fo:block` object with `fo:initial-property-set` (it's much like the CSS `first-line` pseudo-element). Here's an example in which I'm setting the first line of a block in small caps:

```
<fo:block>
    <fo:initial-property-set font-variant="small-caps" />
    Here is the actual text of the paragraph; the first line,
    and only the first line, will be displayed in small caps.
</fo:block>
```

You can use these properties with `fo:initial-property-set`:

- Common accessibility properties: `source-document`, `role`
- Common aural properties: `azimuth`, `cue-after`, `cue-before`, `elevation`, `pause-after`, `pause-before`, `pitch`, `pitch-range`, `play-during`, `richness`, `speak`, `speak-header`, `speak-numeral`, `speak-punctuation`, `speech-rate`, `stress`, `voice-family`, `volume`

- Common border, padding, and background properties: `background-attachment`, `background-color`, `background-image`, `background-repeat`, `background-position-horizontal`, `background-position-vertical`, `border-before-color`, `border-before-style`, `border-before-width`, `border-after-color`, `border-after-style`, `border-after-width`, `border-start-color`, `border-start-style`, `border-start-width`, `border-end-color`, `border-end-style`, `border-end-width`, `border-top-color`, `border-top-style`, `border-top-width`, `border-bottom-color`, `border-bottom-style`, `border-bottom-width`, `border-left-color`, `border-left-style`, `border-left-width`, `border-right-color`, `border-right-style`, `border-right-width`, `padding-before`, `padding-after`, `padding-start`, `padding-end`, `padding-top`, `padding-bottom`, `padding-left`, `padding-right`

- Common font properties: `font-family`, `font-size`, `font-stretch`, `font-size-adjust`, `font-style`, `font-variant`, `font-weight`

- `color`

- `id`

- `letter-spacing`

- `line-height`

- `line-height-shift-adjustment`

- `relative-position`

- `score-spaces`

- `text-decoration`

- `text-shadow`

- `text-transform`

- `word-spacing`

Adding Graphics: *fo:external-graphic*

Another inline formatting object that is available is `fo:external-graphic`. You use this object to embed an image in a document (unfortunately, `fo:external-graphic` is not supported by fop yet).

You can set the size of the image in the document with the `content-height`, `content-width`, and `scaling` properties; if you don't set these properties, the image is displayed in its original size. Here's an example, ch14_05.fo, displaying an image, ch14_06.jpg, and a caption:

Listing ch14_05.fo

```
<?xml version="1.0" encoding="UTF-8"?>
<fo:root xmlns:fo="http://www.w3.org/1999/XSL/Format">

    <fo:layout-master-set>
        <fo:simple-page-master margin-right="20mm"
            margin-left="20mm" margin-bottom="10mm"
            margin-top="10mm" page-width="300mm"
            page-height="400mm" master-name="page">

            <fo:region-body margin-right="0mm"
                margin-left="0mm" margin-bottom="10mm"
                margin-top="0mm"/>

          <fo:region-after extent="10mm"/>

        </fo:simple-page-master>
    </fo:layout-master-set>

    <fo:page-sequence master-reference="page">
        <fo:flow flow-name="xsl-region-body">
            <fo:block>
                <fo:external-graphic src="file:ch14_06.jpg"/>
            </fo:block>

            <fo:block space-before="10pt" start-indent="10mm"
                end-indent="0mm" font-size="24pt">
                Embedding images!
            </fo:block>
        </fo:flow>
    </fo:page-sequence>
</fo:root>
```

You can create the PDF file ch14_07.pdf from ch14_05.po like this:

```
%fop ch14_05.fo ch14_07.pdf
```

You can see the results in Figure 14-2.

Figure 14-2
Embedding
images in a
PDF
document.

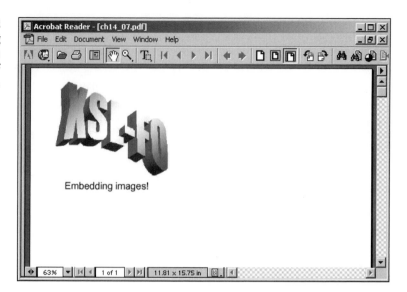

You can use these properties with fo:external-graphic:

- Common accessibility properties: source-document, role

- Common aural properties: azimuth, cue-after, cue-before, elevation, pause-after, pause-before, pitch, pitch-range, play-during, richness, speak, speak-header, speak-numeral, speak-punctuation, speech-rate, stress, voice-family, volume

- Common border, padding, and background properties: background-attachment, background-color, background-image, background-repeat, background-position-horizontal, background-position-vertical, border-before-color, border-before-style, border-before-width, border-after-color, border-after-style, border-after-width, border-start-color, border-start-style, border-start-width, border-end-color, border-end-style, border-end-width, border-top-color, border-top-style, border-top-width, border-bottom-color, border-bottom-style, border-bottom-width, border-left-color, border-left-style, border-left-width, border-right-color, border-right-style, border-right-width, padding-before, padding-after, padding-start, padding-end, padding-top, padding-bottom, padding-left, padding-right

- Common margin properties, inline: `space-end`, `space-start`
- `alignment-adjust`
- `baseline-identifier`
- `baseline-shift`
- `block-progression-dimension`
- `content-height`
- `content-type`
- `content-width`
- `dominant-baseline`
- `height`
- `id`
- `inline-progression-dimension`
- `keep-with-next`
- `keep-with-previous`
- `line-height`
- `line-height-shift-adjustment`
- `relative-position`
- `overflow`
- `scaling`
- `scaling-method`
- `src`
- `width`

The Inline Formatting Object: *fo:inline*

You can use the `fo:inline` formatting object to format a part of your text with a background or surround it with a border. This object is fairly general, and it lets you format an inline area almost as though it were a block.

You can use these properties with `fo:inline`:

- Common accessibility properties: `source-document`, `role`
- Common aural properties: `azimuth`, `cue-after`, `cue-before`, `elevation`, `pause-after`, `pause-before`, `pitch`, `pitch-range`, `play-during`, `richness`, `speak`, `speak-header`, `speak-numeral`, `speak-punctuation`, `speech-rate`, `stress`, `voice-family`, `volume`

- Common border, padding, and background properties: `background-attachment, background-color, background-image, background-repeat, background-position-horizontal, background-position-vertical, border-before-color, border-before-style, border-before-width, border-after-color, border-after-style, border-after-width, border-start-color, border-start-style, border-start-width, border-end-color, border-end-style, border-end-width, border-top-color, border-top-style, border-top-width, border-bottom-color, border-bottom-style, border-bottom-width, border-left-color, border-left-style, border-left-width, border-right-color, border-right-style, border-right-width, padding-before, padding-after, padding-start, padding-end, padding-top, padding-bottom, padding-left, padding-right`

- Common font properties: `font-family, font-size, font-stretch, font-size-adjust, font-style, font-variant, font-weight`

- Common margin properties, inline: `space-end, space-start`

- `alignment-adjust`

- `baseline-identifier`

- `baseline-shift`

- `color`

- `dominant-baseline`

- `id`

- `keep-together`

- `keep-with-next`

- `keep-with-previous`

- `line-height`

- `line-height-shift-adjustment`

- `relative-position`

- `text-decoration`

- `visibility`

- `z-index`

Creating Page Numbers: *fo:page-number*

Another useful inline formatting object is fo:page-number, which creates an inline area displaying the current page number. Here's an example:

```
<fo:block>
    <xsl:text>This is page </xsl:text><fo:page-number/>.
</fo:block>
```

You can use these properties with fo:page-number:

- Common accessibility properties: source-document, role
- Common aural properties: azimuth, cue-after, cue-before, elevation, pause-after, pause-before, pitch, pitch-range, play-during, richness, speak, speak-header, speak-numeral, speak-punctuation, speech-rate, stress, voice-family, volume
- Common border, padding, and background properties: background-attachment, background-color, background-image, background-repeat, background-position-horizontal, background-position-vertical, border-before-color, border-before-style, border-before-width, border-after-color, border-after-style, border-after-width, border-start-color, border-start-style, border-start-width, border-end-color, border-end-style, border-end-width, border-top-color, border-top-style, border-top-width, border-bottom-color, border-bottom-style, border-bottom-width, border-left-color, border-left-style, border-left-width, border-right-color, border-right-style, border-right-width, padding-before, padding-after, padding-start, padding-end, padding-top, padding-bottom, padding-left, padding-right
- Common font properties: font-family, font-size, font-stretch, font-size-adjust, font-style, font-variant, font-weight
- Common margin properties, inline: space-end, space-start
- alignment-adjust
- baseline-identifier
- baseline-shift
- dominant-baseline

- `id`
- `keep-with-next`
- `keep-with-previous`
- `letter-spacing`
- `line-height`
- `line-height-shift-adjustment`
- `relative-position`
- `score-spaces`
- `text-decoration`
- `text-shadow`
- `text-transform`
- `word-spacing`

Creating Tables

Some of the most useful constructs that you can format with XSL are tables. A table in XSL is much like one in HTML—a rectangular grid of rows and columns of cells. You can use nine formatting objects to create tables:

- `fo:table-and-caption`
- `fo:table`
- `fo:table-column`
- `fo:table-caption`
- `fo:table-header`
- `fo:table-footer`
- `fo:table-body`
- `fo:table-row`
- `fo:table-cell`

Creating tables is a little involved in XSL. You create a `fo:table object` and then format each column with a `fo:table-column` object. Then you create a `table-body object`, as well as `table-row` objects for each row and `table-cell` objects for each cell in each row. Here's an example creating a 3×3 table with the words `Tic`, `Tac`, and `Toe` repeated on each line:

Listing ch14_08.fo

```
<?xml version="1.0" encoding="UTF-8"?>
<fo:root xmlns:fo="http://www.w3.org/1999/XSL/Format">
    <fo:layout-master-set>
        <fo:simple-page-master margin-right="20mm"
            margin-left="20mm" margin-bottom="20mm"
            margin-top="20mm" page-width="300mm"
            page-height="400mm" master-name="page">

            <fo:region-body margin-right="0mm" margin-left="0mm"
                margin-bottom="20mm" margin-top="0mm"/>

            <fo:region-after extent="20mm"/>

        </fo:simple-page-master>
    </fo:layout-master-set>

    <fo:page-sequence master-reference="page">
        <fo:flow flow-name="xsl-region-body">
            <fo:table width="12cm" table-layout="fixed">
                <fo:table-column column-number="1" column-width="25mm">
                </fo:table-column>
                <fo:table-column column-number="2" column-width="25mm">
                </fo:table-column>
                <fo:table-column column-number="3" column-width="25mm">
                </fo:table-column>
                <fo:table-body>
                    <fo:table-row line-height="20mm">
                        <fo:table-cell column-number="1">
                            <fo:block font-family="sans-serif"
                                font-size="36pt">
                                Tic
                            </fo:block>
                        </fo:table-cell>
                        <fo:table-cell column-number="2">
                            <fo:block font-family="sans-serif"
                                font-size="36pt">
                                Tac
                            </fo:block>
                        </fo:table-cell>
                        <fo:table-cell column-number="3">
                            <fo:block font-family="sans-serif"
                                font-size="36pt">
                                Toe
                            </fo:block>
                        </fo:table-cell>
                    </fo:table-row>
                    <fo:table-row line-height="20mm">
                        <fo:table-cell column-number="1">
                            <fo:block font-family="sans-serif"
```

continues

```
                                        font-size="36pt">
                                        Tic
                                </fo:block>
                        </fo:table-cell>
                        <fo:table-cell column-number="2">
                                <fo:block font-family="sans-serif"
                                        font-size="36pt">
                                        Tac
                                </fo:block>
                        </fo:table-cell>
                        <fo:table-cell column-number="3">
                                <fo:block font-family="sans-serif"
                                        font-size="36pt">
                                        Toe
                                </fo:block>
                        </fo:table-cell>
                </fo:table-row>
                <fo:table-row line-height="20mm">
                        <fo:table-cell column-number="1">
                                <fo:block font-family="sans-serif"
                                        font-size="36pt">
                                        Tic
                                </fo:block>
                        </fo:table-cell>
                        <fo:table-cell column-number="2">
                                <fo:block font-family="sans-serif"
                                        font-size="36pt">
                                        Tac
                                </fo:block>
                        </fo:table-cell>
                        <fo:table-cell column-number="3">
                                <fo:block font-family="sans-serif"
                                        font-size="36pt">
                                        Toe
                                </fo:block>
                        </fo:table-cell>
                </fo:table-row>
            </fo:table-body>
        </fo:table>
    </fo:flow>
  </fo:page-sequence>
</fo:root>
```

Running this file, ch14_08.fo, through fop creates ch14_09.pdf, which you can see in Figure 14-3.

Figure 14-3
An XSL-
formatted
table in Adobe
Acrobat.

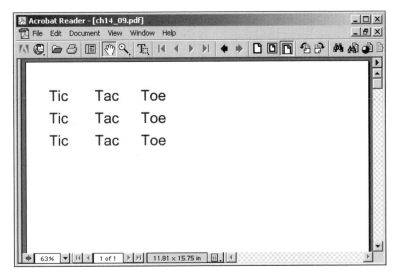

I'll take a look at the various objects you use to create tables now.

fo:table

You use the fo:table object to create a new table. The table itself consists of an optional header, an optional footer, and one or more table bodies. The actual grid of cells, arranged into rows and columns, appears in a table body.

You can use these properties with the fo:table object:

- Common accessibility properties: source-document, role

- Common aural properties: azimuth, cue-after, cue-before, elevation, pause-after, pause-before, pitch, pitch-range, play-during, richness, speak, speak-header, speak-numeral, speak-punctuation, speech-rate, stress, voice-family, volume

- Common border, padding, and background properties: background-attachment, background-color, background-image, background-repeat, background-position-horizontal, background-position-vertical, border-before-color, border-before-style, border-before-width, border-after-color, border-after-style, border-after-width, border-start-color, border-start-style, border-start-width, border-end-color, border-end-style, border-end-width, border-top-color, border-top-style, border-top-width, border-bottom-color, border-bottom-style, border-bottom-width, border-left-color, border-left-style, border-left-width, border-right-color, border-right-style, border-right-width, padding-before, padding-after, padding-start, padding-end, padding-top, padding-bottom, padding-left, padding-right

- Common margin properties, block: margin-top, margin-bottom, margin-left, margin-right, space-before, space-after, start-indent, end-indent
- block-progression-dimension
- border-collapse
- border-separation
- break-after
- break-before
- id
- inline-progression-dimension
- height
- keep-together
- keep-with-next
- keep-with-previous
- relative-position
- table-layout
- table-omit-footer-at-break
- table-omit-header-at-break
- width
- writing-mode

fo:table-column

You can use the fo:table-column formatting object to indicate characteristics that apply to table cells that have the same column. Probably the most important property here is the column-width property, which you use to set the width of each column.

You can use these properties with the `fo:table-column` object:

- Common border, padding, and background properties:
  `background-attachment, background-color, background-image, background-repeat, background-position-horizontal, background-position-vertical, border-before-color, border-before-style, border-before-width, border-after-color, border-after-style, border-after-width, border-start-color, border-start-style, border-start-width, border-end-color, border-end-style, border-end-width, border-top-color, border-top-style, border-top-width, border-bottom-color, border-bottom-style, border-bottom-width, border-left-color, border-left-style, border-left-width, border-right-color, border-right-style, border-right-width, padding-before, padding-after, padding-start, padding-end, padding-top, padding-bottom, padding-left, padding-right`

- `column-number`

- `column-width`

- `number-columns-repeated`

- `number-columns-spanned`

- `visibility`

fo:table-body

The actual content of tables appears in `fo:table-body` objects. The object is the one that contains the actual `fo:table-row` objects, which, in turn, contain the `fo:table-cell` objects that hold the data for the table.

You can use these properties with the `fo:table-body` object:

- Common border, padding, and background properties:
  `background-attachment, background-color, background-image, background-repeat, background-position-horizontal, background-position-vertical, border-before-color, border-before-style, border-before-width, border-after-color, border-after-style, border-after-width, border-start-color, border-start-style, border-start-width, border-end-color, border-end-style, border-end-width, border-top-color, border-top-style, border-top-width, border-bottom-color, border-bottom-style, border-bottom-width, border-left-color, border-left-style, border-left-width, border-right-color, border-right-style, border-right-width, padding-before, padding-after, padding-start, padding-end, padding-top, padding-bottom, padding-left, padding-right`

- id
- relative-position

fo:table-row

You use the fo:table-row object to group table cells into rows. The XSL processor determines the dimensions of the table by how many rows you've added to the table.

You can use these properties with the fo:table-row object:

- Common accessibility properties: source-document, role
- Common aural properties: azimuth, cue-after, cue-before, elevation, pause-after, pause-before, pitch, pitch-range, play-during, richness, speak, speak-header, speak-numeral, speak-punctuation, speech-rate, stress, voice-family, volume
- Common border, padding, and background properties: background-attachment, background-color, background-image, background-repeat, background-position-horizontal, background-position-vertical, border-before-color, border-before-style, border-before-width, border-after-color, border-after-style, border-after-width, border-start-color, border-start-style, border-start-width, border-end-color, border-end-style, border-end-width, border-top-color, border-top-style, border-top-width, border-bottom-color, border-bottom-style, border-bottom-width, border-left-color, border-left-style, border-left-width, border-right-color, border-right-style, border-right-width, padding-before, padding-after, padding-start, padding-end, padding-top, padding-bottom, padding-left, padding-right
- block-progression-dimension
- break-after
- break-before
- id
- height
- keep-together

- keep-with-next
- keep-with-previous
- relative-position

fo:table-cell

You place the content for each cell in a fo:table-cell object. To specify the font and other characteristics of that content, you can enclose a fo:block object inside each fo:table-cell object. You can connect a table cell with a table column using the column-number property.

You can use these properties with the fo:table-cell object:

- Common accessibility properties: source-document, role

- Common aural properties: azimuth, cue-after, cue-before, elevation, pause-after, pause-before, pitch, pitch-range, play-during, richness, speak, speak-header, speak-numeral, speak-punctuation, speech-rate, stress, voice-family, volume

- Common border, padding, and background properties: background-attachment, background-color, background-image, background-repeat, background-position-horizontal, background-position-vertical, border-before-color, border-before-style, border-before-width, border-after-color, border-after-style, border-after-width, border-start-color, border-start-style, border-start-width, border-end-color, border-end-style, border-end-width, border-top-color, border-top-style, border-top-width, border-bottom-color, border-bottom-style, border-bottom-width, border-left-color, border-left-style, border-left-width, border-right-color, border-right-style, border-right-width, padding-before, padding-after, padding-start, padding-end, padding-top, padding-bottom, padding-left, padding-right

- block-progression-dimension

- column-number

- display-align

- relative-align

- empty-cells

- ends-row

- height

- id

- number-columns-spanned

- number-rows-spanned

- relative-position

- starts-row

- width

Creating Lists

Besides tables, an XSL construct that is very close to the corresponding construct in HTML are lists. An XSL list presents a vertical arrangement of items, just as in HTML. You use four formatting objects to construct lists:

- fo:list-block

- fo:list-item

- fo:list-item-label

- fo:list-item-body

You enclose the whole list in a fo:list-block object and enclose each item in the list in a fo:list-item object. To create a label for the list item, you use a fo:list-item-label object; to insert the actual data for each list item, you use a fo:list-item-body object.

Here's an example creating a numbered list with three list items: Tic, Tac, and Toe:

Listing ch14_10.fo

```
<?xml version="1.0" encoding="UTF-8"?>
<fo:root xmlns:fo="http://www.w3.org/1999/XSL/Format">
    <fo:layout-master-set>
        <fo:simple-page-master margin-right="20mm" margin-left="20mm"
            margin-bottom="10mm" margin-top="10mm" page-width="300mm"
            page-height="400mm" master-name="page">

            <fo:region-body margin-right="0mm" margin-left="0mm"
            margin-bottom="10mm" margin-top="0mm"/>

            <fo:region-after extent="10mm"/>
        </fo:simple-page-master>
    </fo:layout-master-set>
```

```
    <fo:page-sequence master-reference="page">
        <fo:flow flow-name="xsl-region-body">
            <fo:list-block
                provisional-distance-between-starts="15mm"
                provisional-label-separation="5mm">

                <fo:list-item line-height="20mm">
                    <fo:list-item-label>
                        <fo:block font-family="sans-serif"
                            font-size="36pt">
                            1.
                        </fo:block>
                    </fo:list-item-label>
                    <fo:list-item-body start-indent="body-start()">
                        <fo:block font-family="sans-serif"
                            font-size="36pt">
                            Tic.
                        </fo:block>
                    </fo:list-item-body>
                </fo:list-item>
                <fo:list-item line-height="20mm">
                    <fo:list-item-label>
                        <fo:block font-family="sans-serif"
                            font-size="36pt">
                            2.
                        </fo:block>
                    </fo:list-item-label>
                    <fo:list-item-body start-indent="body-start()">
                        <fo:block font-family="sans-serif"
                            font-size="36pt">
                            Tac.
                        </fo:block>
                    </fo:list-item-body>
                </fo:list-item>
                <fo:list-item line-height="20mm">
                    <fo:list-item-label>
                        <fo:block font-family="sans-serif"
                            font-size="36pt">
                            3.
                        </fo:block>
                    </fo:list-item-label>
                    <fo:list-item-body start-indent="body-start()">
                        <fo:block font-family="sans-serif"
                            font-size="36pt">
                            Toe.
                        </fo:block>
                    </fo:list-item-body>
                </fo:list-item>
            </fo:list-block>
        </fo:flow>
    </fo:page-sequence>
</fo:root>
```

You can see the resulting PDF file displayed in the Adobe Acrobat in Figure 14-4, showing the list.

Figure 14-4
An XSL-
formatted list
in Adobe
Acrobat.

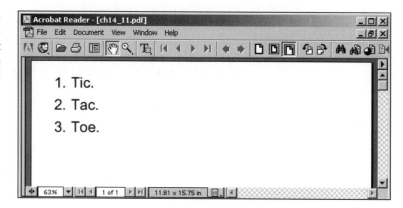

I'll take a look at the list-formatting objects in more detail now.

fo:list-block

You use `fo:list-block` to format create a list; this object encloses `fo:list-item` objects.

You can use these properties with the `fo:list-block` object:

- Common accessibility properties: `source-document`, `role`

- Common aural properties: `azimuth`, `cue-after`, `cue-before`, `elevation`, `pause-after`, `pause-before`, `pitch`, `pitch-range`, `play-during`, `richness`, `speak`, `speak-header`, `speak-numeral`, `speak-punctuation`, `speech-rate`, `stress`, `voice-family`, `volume`

- Common border, padding, and background properties: `background-attachment`, `background-color`, `background-image`, `background-repeat`, `background-position-horizontal`, `background-position-vertical`, `border-before-color`, `border-before-style`, `border-before-width`, `border-after-color`, `border-after-style`, `border-after-width`, `border-start-color`, `border-start-style`, `border-start-width`, `border-end-color`, `border-end-style`, `border-end-width`, `border-top-color`, `border-top-style`, `border-top-width`, `border-bottom-color`, `border-bottom-style`, `border-bottom-width`, `border-left-color`, `border-left-style`, `border-left-width`, `border-right-color`, `border-right-style`, border-right-width, padding-before, padding-after, padding-start, padding-end, padding-top, padding-bottom, padding-left, padding-right

- Common margin properties: margin-top, margin-bottom, margin-left, margin-right, space-before, space-after, start-indent, end-indent

- break-after

- break-before

- id

- keep-together

- keep-with-next

- keep-with-previous

- provisional-distance-between-starts

- provisional-label-separation

- relative-position

fo:list-item

You use a fo:list-item object to contain the label and the body of an item in a list.

You can use these properties with the fo:list-item object:

- Common accessibility properties: source-document, role

- Common aural properties: azimuth, cue-after, cue-before, elevation, pause-after, pause-before, pitch, pitch-range, play-during, richness, speak, speak-header, speak-numeral, speak-punctuation, speech-rate, stress, voice-family, volume

- Common border, padding, and background properties: background-attachment, background-color, background-image, background-repeat, background-position-horizontal, background-position-vertical, border-before-color, border-before-style, border-before-width, border-after-color, border-after-style, border-after-width, border-start-color, border-start-style, border-start-width, border-end-color, border-end-style, border-end-width, border-top-color, border-top-style, border-top-width, border-bottom-color, border-bottom-style, border-bottom-width, border-left-color, border-left-style, border-left-width, border-right-color, border-right-style, border-right-width, padding-before, padding-after, padding-start, padding-end, padding-top, padding-bottom, padding-left, padding-right

- Common margin properties, block: margin-top, margin-bottom, margin-left, margin-right, space-before, space-after, start-indent, end-indent
- break-after
- break-before
- id
- keep-together
- keep-with-next
- keep-with-previous
- relative-align
- relative-position

fo:list-item-label

You use the fo:list-item-label object to hold the label of a list item, usually to enumerate or decorate (as with a bullet) the body of the list item.

You can use these properties with the fo:list-item-label object:

- Common accessibility properties: source-document, role
- id
- keep-together

fo:list-item-body

You use the fo:list-item-body object to hold the actual body of a list item. To format the item's body the way you want it, you can enclose a fo:block object in a fo:list-item-body object.

You can use these properties with the `fo:list-item-body` object:

- Common accessibility properties: `source-document, role`
- `id`
- `keep-together`

As you can see, there's a lot to XSL formatting objects. In fact, there's a lot more that we don't have the space to cover here. For more details, take a look at the W3C site. Not a lot of software packages can put formatting objects to work yet, however, although that should change in the future.

In the next chapter, I'm going to start taking an in-depth look at another important part of the XML specification: XLinks and XPointers.

CHAPTER 15
XLinks and XPointers

This chapter is all about creating connections between documents and part of documents—the XLink and XPointer specifications. In HTML, you have hyperlinks, but XML has gone far beyond that and uses the XLink, XPointer, XPath, and XBase specifications.

Unfortunately, this is an area of XML where the World Wide Web Consortium (W3C) is far ahead of the rest of the world. No concrete implementations of any of these specifications exist yet. We'll see all these specifications implemented in future software, but for now, most of the material in this chapter is waiting for actual software implementation.

XLinks specify how one document links to another document, and XPointers specify locations inside a document, building on the XPath recommendation that we covered in Chapter 13, "XSL Transformations." I'll take a look at an overview now.

XLinks

As of this writing, the XLink specification is a W3C recommendation, released on June 27, 2001. You can find the most current version of this recommendation at `www.w3.org/TR/xlink`. You use XLinks to link one document to another. Here's what the W3C says in the W3C working draft:

> This specification defines the XML Linking Language (XLink), which allows elements to be inserted into XML documents in order to create and describe links between resources. It uses XML syntax to create structures that can describe links similar to the simple unidirectional hyperlinks of today's HTML, as well as more sophisticated links.

Here's an example to give you an idea of what an XLink looks like. Unlike HTML hyperlinks, any element can be a link in XML. You specify that an element is a link with the attribute `xlink:type` like this, where I'm creating a simple XLink:

```
<MOVIE_REVIEW xmlns:xlink = "http://www.w3.org/1999/xlink"
    xlink:type = "simple"
    xlink:show = "new"
    xlink:href = "http://www.starpowdermovies.com/reviews.xml">
    Mr. Blandings Builds His Dream House
</MOVIE_REVIEW>
```

In this case, I'm creating a simple XLink, which is much like an HTML hyperlink, by setting the `xlink:type` attribute to `"simple"`. I'm also setting the `xlink:show` attribute to `"new"`, which means that XLink-aware software should open the linked-to document in a new window or other display context. In addition, I'm setting the `xlink:href` attribute to the unifrom resource identifier (URI) of the new document (which can be quite general and need not be in the uniform resource locator [URL] form I've used here).

For the sake of familiarity, I'm starting with a simple XLink because it's much like an HTML link. However, XLinks can become quite involved, as we'll see in this chapter. Besides basic unidirectional links such as the simple link I've created here, you can also create bidirectional links, links between many documents and even document sets, and much more—you can even store your links in link databases called *linkbases*.

Some tools that are designed to help in working with XLink are starting to appear. These include the open source XTooX available at `www.xlinkit.com:8080/xtoox/index.html`.

XPointers

XLinks let you link to a particular document, but you often need to be more precise than that. XPointers let you point to specific locations inside a document—without having to modify that document by embedding special tags or markers.

To point to a specific location in a document, the XPointer specification builds on the XPath specification. As you recall, we covered the XPath specification in Chapter 13; it let you identify specific nodes in a document with expressions such as `/child::*[position()=126]/child::*[position()=first()]`.

XPointers are in the W3C candidate recommendation stage. As of this writing, the version is September 11, 2001. You can find the most current version of this specification at `www.w3.org/TR/xptr`. Here's what W3C says about XPointers:

> *This specification defines the XML Pointer Language (XPointer), the language to be used as the basis for a fragment identifier for any URI reference that locates a resource whose Internet media type is one of text/xml, application/xml, text/xml-external-parsed-entity, or application/xml-external-parsed-entity.*
>
> *XPointer, which is based on the XML Path Language (XPath), supports addressing into the internal structures of XML documents and external parsed entities. It allows for examination of a hierarchical document structure and choice of its internal parts based on various properties, such as element types, attribute values, character content, and relative position.*

Although XPointer is built on the XPath specification (which is covered in Chapter 13 and is at `www.w3.org/TR/xpath`), the XPointer specification extends XPath in ways we'll see in this chapter.

How do you add an XPointer to a document's URI to specify a specific location in a document? You can append # (following the HTML usage for URLs that specify link targets) and then `xpointer()`, placing the XPath expression you want to use in the parentheses. Here's an example:

```
<MOVIE_REVIEW xmlns:xlink = "http://www.w3.org/1999/xlink"
     xlink:type = "simple"
     xlink:show = "new"
     xlink:href = "http://www.starpowdermovies.com/
     ➥reviews.xml#xpointer(/child::*[position()=126]/child::*
     ➥[position()=first()])">
     Mr. Blandings Builds His Dream House
</MOVIE_REVIEW>
```

That gives us an overview of XLinks and XPointers. I'm going to cover both of these specifications, as well as the XBase specification, starting now with XLinks.

All About XLinks

Hyperlinks have long been an important part of HTML. You create them with the HTML <A> element, like this:

```
<A HREF = "http://www.starpowdermovies.com/reviews.html#blandings">
    Mr. Blandings Builds His Dream House
<A>
```

The hyperlink appears in an HTML document either as text, typically underlined and colored, or as a clickable image. When clicked, the hyperlink can perform a variety of actions: navigate to a new document or a specific location in that document, open the new document in an existing frame, even open a new window if you use the TARGET attribute, or execute JavaScript if you use the javascript: URL. Here are the official HTML attributes for the <A> element:

- ACCESSKEY—Assigns a keyboard shortcut to the hyperlink.
- CHARSET—Specifies the character encoding of the target of the hyperlink. You set this to an RFC 2045 language character set string (the default value is ISO-8859-1).
- CLASS—Gives the style class of the element.
- COORDS—Sets the coordinate values (in pixels) appropriate to the accompanying SHAPE attribute to define a region of an image for image maps.
- DIR—Gives the direction of directionally neutral text. You set it to LTR for left-to-right text or RTL for right-to-left text.
- HREF—Holds the target URL of the hyperlink. Either this attribute or the NAME attribute must be used.
- HREFLANG—Specifies the base language of the target indicated in the HREF attribute. Set this to RFC 1766 values.
- ID—A unique identifier for the tag.
- LANG—Base language used for the tag.
- METHODS—Can specify methods to be used in accessing the target.
- NAME—Set to an anchor name, the name you want to use to refer to the enclosed items (such as text, images, and so on). Either this attribute or the HREF attribute must be used.
- REL—Specifies the relationship described by the hyperlink.
- REV—Essentially is the same as the REL attribute, but the syntax works in the reverse direction.
- SHAPE—Defines the type of region to be defined for mapping in the HTML AREA tag.
- STYLE—Inline style indicating how to render the element.
- TABINDEX—Sets the tab sequence of hyperlinks in the page.

- TARGET—Indicates the named frame for the HREF hyperlink to jump to. Set this to the name of a frame.

- TITLE—Holds title information for the element.

- TYPE—Specifies the MIME type of the target given in the HREF attribute.

There's a lot of functionality here, but it all relies on the <A> element and the simplest type of hyperlink—one that waits to be clicked and then navigates to a new document or document location.

Relationships between documents can be far more complex than that. For example, you might want a link to point to 10 mirror sites of a main site and let the browser select the one that's closest. Or, you might want to link to an entire set of documents, complete with subsets, that the browser should search for the resource you want. Or, you might want to set up a series of paths that lets the user navigate through a set of documents in various directions but not in others, and so on. XLinks let you perform all these kinds of linking.

XLinks are not restricted to any one element such as the <A> element, which is to say that XLinks may not always appear in your documents in the traditional blue, underlined text (although, of course, they could if you wanted them that way). Being able to make any element into an XLink is great because you can create elements that are always links to other resources. Users might even come to expect that if they come across anything formatted with, say, the <CITATION> element, that element will be linked to the cited material.

You create an XLink with attributes, not with specific elements. Specifically, you use the xlink:type attribute to describe the kind of link and to create an XLink, setting it to one of the allowable types of XLinks: simple, extended, locator, arc, resource, title, or none.

Here are current XLink attributes:

- xlink:arcrole—This attribute holds the link's role in an arc (which can support multiple resources and various traversal paths), which may be different for different arcs. More on arcs and traversal paths comes later in this chapter.

- xlink:actuate—This attribute determines when linking operations occur. You can set this attribute to the official values of onLoad, onRequest, other, or none, or other values required by the software you're using.

- xlink:from—This attribute defines starting resources.

- xlink:href—This is the *locator* attribute. It supplies the data that allows an XLink application to find a remote resource.

- xlink:label—This attribute holds a human-readable label for the link.

- xlink:role—You use the role attribute to describe the function of a link's remote resource in a machine-readable fashion and, in the case of extended-type elements, to serve as a resource category label for traversal rules in arc-type elements. For example, search engines can read this attribute.

- xlink:show—You use this attribute to indicate how you want to display the linked-to resource. XLink applications must recognize the following values: new (opens a new display space), replace (replaces the currently displayed data), embed (embeds the new re-source in the current one), other (leaves the show function up to the displaying software), or none (doesn't show the resource).

- xlink:title—You use the title attribute to describe the function of a link's remote resource, for people to understand.

- xlink:to—This attribute defines target or ending resources.

- xlink:type—This attribute sets the type of the Xlink. This can be simple, extended, locator, arc, resource, title, or none. We'll see what these types mean in this chapter.

Using the XLink attributes, you can make an XLink mockup in browsers such as Internet Explorer. As an example, I'll create a mockup of a simple XLink here. Internet Explorer supports the onClick attribute if you use it with an XML element, and I'll add some JavaScript to that attribute that will make the browser navigate to a new URI, using Internet Explorer's location object:

Listing ch15_01.xml

```
<?xml version="1.0" encoding="UTF-8"?>
<?xml-stylesheet type="text/css" href="ch15_02.css"?>

<DOCUMENT>
    <P>
        Want to check out
        <LINK xml:type = "simple" href = "http://www.w3c.org"
        onClick="location.href='http://www.w3c.org'">W3C</LINK>?
    </P>
</DOCUMENT>
```

I'm even supplying a stylesheet, xlink_example.css, to make this XLink appear in the standard blue, underlined font. In fact, you can even make Internet Explorer's cursor change to a hand, as it does for HTML hyperlinks, with the cursor CSS property:

Listing ch15_02.css

```
LINK {color: #0000FF; text-decoration: underline; cursor: hand}
```

The result appears in Figure 15-1, where the simple XLink functions much like an HTML hyperlink (which, of course, limits the whole concept of XLinks badly). You can click this link to make Internet Explorer navigate to a new document.

So when do you use which XLink attributes? It all depends on the type of link you're creating, as given by the xlink:type attribute. Depending on the link type, some of these attributes are required and some are optional. You can find the complete rules in Table 15-1, where the rows correspond to the various XLink attributes and the columns correspond to the various XLink types.

Figure 15-1
A mockup of a simple XLink in Internet Explorer.

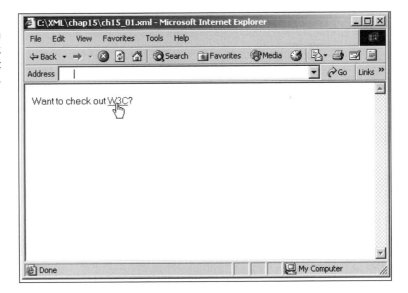

Table 15-1	simple	extended	locator	arc	resource	title
actuate	Optional	Omitted	Omitted	Optional	Omitted	Omitted
arcrole	Optional	Omitted	Omitted	Optional	Omitted	Omitted
from	Omitted	Omitted	Omitted	Optional	Omitted	Omitted
href	Optional	Omitted	Required	Omitted	Omitted	Omitted
label	Omitted	Omitted	Optional	Omitted	optional	Omitted
role	Optional	Optional	Optional	Optional	Optional	Omitted
show	Optional	Omitted	Omitted	Optional	Omitted	Omitted
title	Optional	Optional	Optional	Optional	Optional	Omitted
to	Omitted	Omitted	Omitted	Optional	Omitted	Omitted
type	Required	Required	Required	Required	Required	Required

Required and Optional Attributes by *xlink:type*

Note that each of these attributes uses the `xlink` namespace; this namespace always has the value `"http://www.w3.org/1999/xlink"`, as we saw in the earlier simple link example:

```
<MOVIE_REVIEW xmlns:xlink = "http://www.w3.org/1999/xlink"
    xlink:type = "simple"
    xlink:show = "new"
    xlink:href =
"http://www.starpowdermovies.com/reviews.xml#xpointer(/child::*[position()=
➥126]/child::*[position()=first()])">
    Mr. Blandings Builds His Dream House
</MOVIE_REVIEW>
```

XML Base (XBase)

Another W3C specification bears discussion while talking about linking and the relationship between documents: the XBase specification.

As of this writing, the XBase specification is in recommendation form, released on June 27, 2001. You can find the current version of this document at `www.w3.org/TR/xmlbase`. This specification lets you provide a base URI for XML documents, just like the HTML `<BASE>` element. In fact, the HTML `<BASE>` element is exactly the reason XBase exists: The W3C is committed to giving XLink all the power that HTML 4.0 linking has and then building on that. One of the aspects of linking in HTML 4.0 is the `<BASE>` element.

Here's how it works. You can use the `xml:base` element in an XML document to set the document's base URI. The other URIs in the document are then resolved using that value as a base. Note that `xml:base` uses the `xml` namespace, not the `xlink` namespace; the `xml` namespace is predefined in XML (that is, you don't have to define it to be able to use it in most XML parsers—in other words, almost any element can be linked) as `"http://www.w3.org/XML/1998/namespace"`. Here's an example:

```
<MOVIE_REVIEW xmlns:xlink = "http://www.w3.org/1999/xlink"
    xml:base="http://www.starpowder.com"
    xlink:type = "simple"
    xlink:show = "new"
    xlink:href = "reviews.xml">
    Mr. Blandings Builds His Dream House
</MOVIE_REVIEW>
```

Using the value assigned to the `xml:base` attribute, the URI in this example's `xlink:href` attribute, `"reviews.xml"`, is resolved to the full URI `http://www.starpowder.com/reviews.xml`. In this way, you can use `xml:base` to provide a base URI for a document (or even a specific element).

Declaring the XLink Attributes

Note that if you're creating valid XML documents, you must declare XLink attributes just like any other attributes. For example, you might use a declaration in a DTD like this for the previous example:

Listing ch15_03.xml

```
<?xml version = "1.0" standalone="yes"?>
<!DOCTYPE MOVIE_REVIEW [
<!ELEMENT MOVIE_REVIEW (#PCDATA)>
<!ATTLIST MOVIE_REVIEW
    xmlns:xlink CDATA #IMPLIED
    xml:base CDATA #IMPLIED
    xlink:type CDATA #REQUIRED
    xlink:href CDATA #IMPLIED
    xlink:show CDATA #IMPLIED
    xlink:actuate CDATA #IMPLIED
    xlink:title CDATA #IMPLIED>
]>
<MOVIE_REVIEW xmlns:xlink = "http://www.w3.org/1999/xlink"
    xml:base="http://www.starpowder.com"
    xlink:type = "simple"
    xlink:show = "new"
    xlink:href = "reviews.xml">
    Mr. Blandings Builds His Dream House
</MOVIE_REVIEW>
```

You can also hard-code the values for most of the values in the XLink attributes if you prefer, in which case you have to supply a value for only the `xlink:href` attribute:

Listing ch15_04.xml

```
<?xml version = "1.0" standalone="yes"?>
<!DOCTYPE MOVIE_REVIEW [
<!ELEMENT MOVIE_REVIEW (#PCDATA)>
<!ATTLIST MOVIE_REVIEW
    xmlns:xlink CDATA #FIXED "http://www.w3.org/1999/xlink"
    xml:base CDATA #FIXED "http://www.starpowder.com"
    xlink:type CDATA #FIXED "simple"
    xlink:href CDATA #REQUIRED
    xlink:show CDATA #FIXED "new"
    xlink:actuate CDATA #FIXED "onRequest"
    xlink:title CDATA #IMPLIED>
]>
<MOVIE_REVIEW xlink:href = "reviews.xml">
    Mr. Blandings Builds His Dream House
</MOVIE_REVIEW>
```

Because XLink is so general, declaring your XLink elements can get fairly involved. XLink elements may even have child XLink elements, which have their own XLink children, and so on. But keep in mind that if you want to create a valid document, you have to declare them all in a DTD or schema.

We've seen the attributes you can use with XLinks in overview now. Because these attributes define XLinks, I'll take a look at each of them in more detail now, starting with the most important one of all, the `xlink:type` attribute.

The *xlink:type* Attribute

The `xlink:type` attribute defines the type of XLink you're creating. You can set this attribute to these values:

- `simple`—Creates a simple link.
- `extended`—Creates an extended link.
- `locator`—Creates a locator link that points to a resource.
- `arc`—Creates an arc with multiple resources and various traversal paths. This attribute sets restrictions on paths where a link goes.

- `resource`—Creates a resource link, which indicates a specific resource.

- `title`—Creates a title link. Such elements are useful, for example, when human-readable label information needs further element markup or when multiple titles are necessary for internationalization purposes.

We've already seen how to create simple links:

```
<MOVIE_REVIEW xmlns:xlink = "http://www.w3.org/1999/xlink"
    xlink:type = "simple"
    xlink:show = "new"
    xlink:href =
"http://www.starpowdermovies.com/reviews.xml#xpointer(/child::*
➥[position()=126]/child::*[position()=first()])">
    Mr. Blandings Builds His Dream House
</MOVIE_REVIEW>
```

I'll take a look at the various other kinds of links in this chapter.

Locating Resources with *xlink:href*

The `xlink:href` attribute is also called the *locator* attribute. This is the attribute that supplies the data that allows an XLink application to find a remote resource.

URI Definition

Although XLinks can be quite general, they commonly use URIs to locate resources. You usually use a URI in `xlink:href`. Now that we're examining the way linking works in XML, you might want to look up the formal definition of URIs, which you can find in its entirety at `www.ics.uci.edu/pub/ietf/uri/rfc2396.txt`.

We've seen that you can set the `xlink:href` attribute to specify a document and an XPointer:

```
<MOVIE_REVIEW xmlns:xlink = "http://www.w3.org/1999/xlink"
    xlink:type = "simple"
    xlink:show = "new"
    xlink:href = "http://www.starpowdermovies.com/reviews.xml#xpointer
    ➥(/child::*[position()=126]/child::*[position()=first()])">
    Mr. Blandings Builds His Dream House
</MOVIE_REVIEW>
```

We'll see how the values you assign to this attribute can become fairly involved when we work with XPointers.

Describing Resources: *xlink:role* and *xlink:title*

Two important XLink attributes are `xlink:role` and `xlink:title`, which let you describe a remote resource. Both of these attributes are optional. Here's an example that puts both of these attributes to work:

Listing ch15_05.xml

```
<MOVIE_REVIEW xmlns:xlink = "http://www.w3.org/1999/xlink"
    xlink:type = "simple"
    xlink:show = "new"
    xlink:role = "MOVIE_REVIEW[EN]"
    xlink:title = "Review of 'Mr. Blandings Builds His Dream House'"
    xlink:href = "http://www.starpowdermovies.com/reviews.xml#xpointer
    ➥(/child::*[position()=126]/child::*[position()=first()])">
    Mr. Blandings Builds His Dream House
</MOVIE_REVIEW>
```

The `xlink:title` attribute here has the value `"Review of 'Mr. Blandings Builds His Dream House'"`. This is a human-readable description of the resource that the link links to; the idea here is that a person can read this text to get more information about the remote resource that the link points to. An application might display this text on demand.

The text of the `xlink:role` attribute, on the other hand, is designed to be read by software. A link's role indicates the category of a link. In this case, the text of the link's role is `"MOVIE_REVIEW[EN]"`.

No attempt has been made to standardize roles as there has been in the Remote Description Framework language we first saw in Chapter 1, "Essential XML"; there are simply too many possibilities. Although search engines can use the link's role to classify the link, you usually use roles to define directional links when creating extended links, and I'll take a look at that soon.

If you want to create valid documents, you have to declare the `xlink:role` and `xlink:title` attributes, as in this case where I'm using a DTD and giving `xlink:role` the fixed value `"MOVIE_REVIEW[EN]"` in `<MOVIE_REVIEW>` elements:

```
<!ELEMENT MOVIE_REVIEW (#PCDATA)>
```

```
<!ATTLIST MOVIE_REVIEW
    xmlns:xlink CDATA  #FIXED "http://www.w3.org/1999/xlink"
    xlink:type  CDATA  #FIXED "simple"
    xlink:href  CDATA  #REQUIRED
    xlink:title CDATA  #IMPLIED
    xlink:role  CDATA  #FIXED "MOVIE_REVIEW[EN]"
>
```

The *xlink:show* Attribute

You use the XLink `xlink:show` attribute to indicate how you want the linked-to resource displayed when the link is activated. The `xlink:show` attribute has five values that are predefined:

- `embed`—Embeds the linked-to resource in the current resource.

- `new`—Opens a new display area, such as a new window, to display the new resource.

- `none`—Does not show the resource. (It can also mean that the application's behavior is not constrained by this markup.)

- `other`—Indicates some setting other than those that are predefined (and usually means that the application should refer to other markup for more information).

- `replace`—Replaces the current resource, in the same window, if there is one.

Even though `xlink:show` has these predefined values, you can set your own values.

The default behavior of HTML links is to navigate to a linked-to document, replacing the current document with the new one. You can mimic that operation by assigning `xlink:show` a value of `"replace"`:

```
<MOVIE_REVIEW xmlns:xlink = "http://www.w3.org/1999/xlink"
    xlink:type = "simple"
    xlink:show = "replace"
    xlink:href = "http://www.starpowdermovies.com/reviews.xml">
    Mr. Blandings Builds His Dream House
</MOVIE_REVIEW>
```

In practice, this is application-specific. Although you'd expect the current document to be replaced with a new one, there are plenty of other possibilities. For example, a spreadsheet application may replace the displayed data, but not the overall display, with data from the linked-to resource. Or, the xlink:show attribute can make the application use a different stylesheet when the link is activated. Once again, the actual implementation is up to the software designer.

If the value of xlink:show is "new", activating the link typically opens a new window that displays the linked-to resource:

```
<MOVIE_REVIEW xmlns:xlink = "http://www.w3.org/1999/xlink"
    xlink:type = "simple"
    xlink:show = "new"
    xlink:href = "http://www.starpowdermovies.com/reviews.xml">
    Mr. Blandings Builds His Dream House
</MOVIE_REVIEW>
```

However, as before, there are plenty of possibilities. A value of "new" might simply mean that a new column is added to a table or that a new line displayed in a graph. It's a good idea to be considerate here. Bear in mind that users coming from HTML will not be used to having links that automatically open new windows, if that's what your link is going to do—you might make sure that you add some explanatory text because otherwise such behavior might be annoying.

Similarly, the attribute value "embed" is subject to interpretation. The idea here is that when a link is activated, the linked-to resource is embedded in the current display or document, although what is actually embedded and how this is done is up to the application. For example, say that we linked to our planetary example, which I'll call ch15_06.xml here for the sake of reference:

Listing ch15_06.xml

```
<?xml version="1.0"?>
<PLANETS>

    <PLANET>
        <NAME>Mercury</NAME>
        <MASS UNITS="(Earth = 1)">.0553</MASS>
        <DAY UNITS="days">58.65</DAY>
        <RADIUS UNITS="miles">1516</RADIUS>
        <DENSITY UNITS="(Earth = 1)">.983</DENSITY>
        <DISTANCE UNITS="million miles">43.4</DISTANCE><!--At perihelion-->
    </PLANET>
```

```
<PLANET>
    <NAME>Venus</NAME>
    <MASS UNITS="(Earth = 1)">.815</MASS>
    <DAY UNITS="days">116.75</DAY>
    <RADIUS UNITS="miles">3716</RADIUS>
    <DENSITY UNITS="(Earth = 1)">.943</DENSITY>
    <DISTANCE UNITS="million miles">66.8</DISTANCE><!--At perihelion-->
</PLANET>

<PLANET>
    <NAME>Earth</NAME>
    <MASS UNITS="(Earth = 1)">1</MASS>
    <DAY UNITS="days">1</DAY>
    <RADIUS UNITS="miles">2107</RADIUS>
    <DENSITY UNITS="(Earth = 1)">1</DENSITY>
    <DISTANCE UNITS="million miles">128.4</DISTANCE><!--At perihelion-->
</PLANET>

</PLANETS>
```

Here's how the links to the various planets might look. I'm anticipating the use of XPointers here to pick out the specific planets in ch15_06.xml. Note that the xlink:show values are all "embed" here:

Listing ch15_07.xml

```
<?xml version = "1.0">
<ASTRO_NEWS>
    <PLANET_DATA xmlns:xlink = "http://www.w3.org/1999/xlink"
        xlink:type = "simple"
        xlink:show = "embed"
        xlink:href = "http://www.starpowdermovies.com/
        ➥ch15_06.xml#xpointer(/descendant::PLANET[position() = 1]">
        Mercury
    </PLANET_DATA>
    <PLANET_DATA xmlns:xlink = "http://www.w3.org/1999/xlink"
        xlink:type = "simple"
        xlink:show = "embed"
        xlink:href = "http://www.starpowdermovies.com/
        ➥ch15_06.xml#xpointer(/descendant::PLANET[position() = 2]">
        Venus
    </PLANET_DATA>
    <PLANET_DATA xmlns:xlink = "http://www.w3.org/1999/xlink"
        xlink:type = "simple"
        xlink:show = "embed"
        xlink:href = "http://www.starpowdermovies.com/
        ➥ch15_06.xml#xpointer(/descendant::PLANET[position() = 3]">
        Earth
    </PLANET_DATA>
<ASTRO_NEWS>
```

After all these links are activated, the data from the various <PLANET> elements might be inserted into the current display, something like this (again, the details are up to the host application):

```
<?xml version = "1.0">
<ASTRO_NEWS>
    <PLANET_DATA xmlns:xlink = "http://www.w3.org/1999/xlink"
        <NAME>Mercury</NAME>
        <MASS UNITS="(Earth = 1)">.0553</MASS>
        <DAY UNITS="days">58.65</DAY>
        <RADIUS UNITS="miles">1516</RADIUS>
        <DENSITY UNITS="(Earth = 1)">.983</DENSITY>
        <DISTANCE UNITS="million miles">43.4</DISTANCE><!--At perihelion-->
    </PLANET_DATA>
    <PLANET_DATA xmlns:xlink = "http://www.w3.org/1999/xlink"
        <NAME>Venus</NAME>
        <MASS UNITS="(Earth = 1)">.815</MASS>
        <DAY UNITS="days">116.75</DAY>
        <RADIUS UNITS="miles">3716</RADIUS>
        <DENSITY UNITS="(Earth = 1)">.943</DENSITY>
        <DISTANCE UNITS="million miles">66.8</DISTANCE><!--At perihelion-->
    </PLANET_DATA>
    <PLANET_DATA xmlns:xlink = "http://www.w3.org/1999/xlink"
        <NAME>Earth</NAME>
        <MASS UNITS="(Earth = 1)">1</MASS>
        <DAY UNITS="days">1</DAY>
        <RADIUS UNITS="miles">2107</RADIUS>
        <DENSITY UNITS="(Earth = 1)">1</DENSITY>
        <DISTANCE UNITS="million miles">128.4</DISTANCE><!--At perihelion-->
    </PLANET_DATA>
<ASTRO_NEWS>
```

You can also set xlink:show to a value of "other", in which case you're indicating to the application that your markup is not constraining this attribute (which usually means that the application should refer to other markup). In fact, it's up to the application to decide what happens because it may ignore any of the values that you carefully assign to xlink:show, especially if it's not capable of handling what you want (as when you set xlink:show to "new" in a browser that can't handle multiple windows). The xlink:show value of "none" usually is an instruction not to show the associated resource (although it can also mean that the application's behavior is not constrained by this markup).

You're also free to set xlink:show to your own values. For example, setting it to "new_row" might add a new row to a table to display data in. You might also use this attribute to indicate something about the format in which documents are displayed rather than how they are displayed, as when you set `xlink:show` to the name of a stylesheet. Or, you might set JavaScript code to execute in this attribute's value when the link is activated.

Don't forget that you need to declare `xlink:show` if you want to create valid documents. That might look something like this in a DTD:

```
<!ELEMENT ASTRO_NEWS>
<!ATTLIST ASTRO_NEWS
    xmlns:xlink CDATA #FIXED "http://www.w3.org/1999/xlink"
    xlink:type CDATA #FIXED "simple"
    xlink:href CDATA #REQUIRED
    xlink:show (new | replace | embed | none | other) #IMPLIED "replace">
```

The *xlink:actuate* Attribute

You can use the `xlink:actuate` attribute to indicate when a link should be traversed. The `xlink:actuate` attribute has these predefined values:

- `onRequest`—The link should be traversed only at the user's request.

- `onLoad`—The link should be traversed when the document or resource is loaded.

- `other`—This is a custom preference, as defined by the application.

- `none`—This indicates no actuation (or indicates that the behavior of the application is not constrained by the markup).

You can also set your own values for `xlink:actuate`.

The first of the predefined values, `"onRequest"`, indicates that the user should request the link to be traversed before any action takes place. Typically, the user request takes the form of a mouse click, as in our earlier mockup of a simple link in Internet Explorer, where we can use the `"onRequest"` value:

```
<?xml version="1.0" encoding="UTF-8"?>
<?xml-stylesheet type="text/css" href="xlink_example.css"?>

<!DOCTYPE html SYSTEM "xlink_example.dtd">

<DOCUMENT>
    <P>
        Want to check out
        <LINK xml:type = "simple" href = "http://www.w3c.org"
        xlink:actuate = "onRequest" onClick=
        "location.href='http://www.w3c.org'">W3C</LINK>?
    </P>
</DOCUMENT>
```

If you set the value of xlink:actuate to "onLoad", the link is traversed when the resource containing it is loaded. For example, you might have a link to an image map's image and want to load it as soon as the containing document is loaded. That might look something like this:

```
<IMAGE_MAP xmlns:xlink="http://www.w3.org/1999/xlink"
    xlink:type="simple"
    xlink:href="http://www.starpowder.com/gifs/image_map.gif"
    xlink:actuate="onLoad">
</IMAGE_MAP>
```

You can also set xlink:actuate to other, which means that when the link is actually actuated is up to the application. (Of course, it's up to the application in any case, even when you specify another value for xlink:actuate.) The last choice, none, means no actuation or indicates that the markup does not constrain the application as far as the xlink:actuate attribute is concerned.

You can also set you own values for xlink:actuate. For example, you might define your own application-specific values, such as onLoadData, onShowImage, or onUnload.

If you want to create valid XML documents, of course, you'll have to declare xlink:actuate, and that might look something like this in a DTD:

```
<!ELEMENT ASTRO_NEWS>
<!ATTLIST ASTRO_NEWS
    xmlns:xlink CDATA #FIXED "http://www.w3.org/1999/xlink"
    xlink:type CDATA #FIXED "simple"
    xlink:href CDATA #REQUIRED
    xlink:show (new | replace | embed | other | none) #IMPLIED "replace"
    xlink:actuate (onRequest | onLoad | other | none) #IMPLIED "onRequest">
```

The *xlink:arcrole* and *xlink:label* Attributes

The xlink:arcrole attribute is set to a URI and holds the "role" of the link in an arc. (Arcs can support multiple resources and various traversal paths—see the section "Creating Arcs with the xlink:from and xlink:to Attributes," later in this chapter, for more on arcs.) Such links can be in multiple arcs and can have a different meaning in each. For example, a link may represent a person who is a son in one arc and a father in another. The xlink:label attribute holds, as you might guess, a human-readable label for the link.

Don't forget that you need to declare `xlink:arcrole` and `xlink:label` if you want to create valid documents. That might look something like this in a DTD:

```
<!ELEMENT ASTRO_NEWS>
<!ATTLIST ASTRO_NEWS
    xmlns:xlink CDATA #FIXED "http://www.w3.org/1999/xlink"
    xlink:type CDATA #FIXED "simple"
    xlink:arcrole CDATA #REQUIRED
    xlink:label CDATA #REQUIRED
    xlink:show (new | replace | embed | other | none) #IMPLIED "replace">
```

Extended Links

You may be used to the idea of simple links much as they work in HTML and as I've discussed them here, but here's where we broaden things by getting into extended links. Extended links are very general and really indicate relationships between resources. An extended link can involve multiple resources, multiple paths between those resources, bidirectional paths, and "out-of-line" links. It helps to think very generally here, in terms of all the possible relationships you might have between data resources.

The upcoming concepts may seem very vague when compared to the concrete functionality of simple links. Keep in mind that the W3C is trying to let you describe, in XML terms, all the possible relationships that might exist among multiple resources, as well as how those relationships work. It's a big job. In technical terms, an extended link is called a directed labeled graph. The resources it connects are called the vertices, and the actual links between resources are the edges of the graph.

In general terms, then, an extended link is made up of the connections between a set of resources. Such resources may be *local*, which means they're actually part of the extended link element, or *remote*, which means they're not part of the extended link element (but does not mean that they have to be in another document). If a link does not contain any local resources at all, it's called an *out-of-line* link.

So how does an application use an extended link? That's completely up to the application. I'll provide some ideas here, but so far, things are really up in the air. No generally available software packages that I know of implement true extended links.

A hypothetical example might be a so-called expert system, in which the links among multiple resources are traversed depending on "yes" or "no" answers to questions. The idea here is that by answering a series of questions, an expert system can progressively narrow a search and direct you to a resource that will provide the answer to quite complex queries.

As mentioned, resources that participate in an extended link can be either local or remote. A local resource is part of the extended link itself and is contained in an element that has its xlink:type attribute set to "resource".

On the other hand, remote resources are outside the extended link element, but not necessarily in another document. You use *locator elements* to point to remote resources, and those elements have their xlink:type attributes set to "locator". When you create a locator element, you must also give its xlink:href attribute a value that points to the remote resource.

Here's an example of an extended link. This link contains four resources: two inline links and two out-of-line links:

```
<ASTRO_DATA xmlns:xlink="http://www.w3.org/1999/xlink"
        xlink:type="extended" xlink:title="Planetary Data">
    <NAME xlink:type="resource" xlink:role="NAME">
        Planetary Data
    </NAME>
    <DATE xlink:type="resource" xlink:role="LAST_UPDATED">
        September 1, 2003
    </DATE>
    <PLANET_DATA xmlns:xlink = "http://www.w3.org/1999/xlink"
        xlink:type = "locator"
        xlink:show = "embed"
        xlink:href = "http://www.starpowdermovies.com/
        ➥ch15_06.xml#xpointer(/descendant::PLANET[position() = 1]">
        xlink:title="Mercury"
        xlink:role="PLANETARY_DATA"
    </PLANET_DATA>
    <PLANET_DATA xmlns:xlink = "http://www.w3.org/1999/xlink"
        xlink:type = "locator"
        xlink:show = "embed"
        xlink:href = "http://www.starpowdermovies.com/
        ➥ch15_06.xml#xpointer(/descendant::PLANET[position() = 2]">
        xlink:title="Venus"
        xlink:role="PLANETARY_DATA"
    </PLANET_DATA>
    <PLANET_DATA xmlns:xlink = "http://www.w3.org/1999/xlink"
        xlink:type = "locator"
        xlink:show = "embed"
        xlink:href = "http://www.starpowdermovies.com/
        ➥ch15_06.xml#xpointer(/descendant::PLANET[position() = 3]">
        xlink:title="Earth"
        xlink:role="PLANETARY_DATA"
    </PLANET_DATA>
</ASTRO_DATA>
```

The inline links here are those links that have the `xlink:type` value "resource" and whose resources are actually contained in the linking element. In this case, that's the <NAME> and <DATE> links. Both of these contain a local resource, which is simply text here, although it could consist of multiply-nested XML elements, if you prefer.

The out-of-link links here have the `xlink:type` attribute value "locator". These links serve to locate remote resources, which may be in the same document or in another document. In this example, the remote resources are all in another document, ch15_06.xml.

As before, if you want to create valid documents, you must declare the attributes and elements you're using. That might look like this, where I'm adding a DTD:

Listing ch15_08.xml

```
<?xml version = "1.0"?>
<!DOCTYPE ASTRO_DATA  [
<!ELEMENT ASTRO_DATA (NAME, DATE, PLANET_DATA*) >
<!ATTLIST ASTRO_DATA
    xmlns:xlink CDATA #FIXED "http://www.w3.org/1999/xlink"
    xlink:type (extended) #FIXED "extended"
    xlink:title CDATA #IMPLIED
    xlink:role CDATA #IMPLIED>

<!ELEMENT NAME (#PCDATA)>
<!ATTLIST NAME
    xmlns:xlink CDATA #FIXED "http://www.w3.org/1999/xlink"
    xlink:type CDATA #FIXED "resource"
    xlink:role CDATA #IMPLIED
    xlink:title CDATA #IMPLIED
>

<!ELEMENT DATE (#PCDATA)>
<!ATTLIST DATE
    xmlns:xlink CDATA #FIXED "http://www.w3.org/1999/xlink"
    xlink:type CDATA #FIXED "resource"
    xlink:role CDATA #IMPLIED
    xlink:title CDATA #IMPLIED
>

<!ELEMENT PLANET_DATA (#PCDATA)>
<!ATTLIST PLANET_DATA
    xmlns:xlink CDATA #FIXED "http://www.w3.org/1999/xlink"
    xlink:type CDATA #FIXED "locator"
    xlink:href CDATA #REQUIRED
    xlink:role CDATA #IMPLIED
    xlink:title CDATA #IMPLIED
```

continues

Listing ch15_08.xml   Continued

```
      xlink:show CDATA #IMPLIED
>
]>

<ASTRO_DATA xmlns:xlink="http://www.w3.org/1999/xlink"
          xlink:type="extended" xlink:title="Planetary Data">
     <NAME xlink:type="resource" xlink:role="NAME">
         Planetary Data
     </NAME>
     <DATE xlink:type="resource" xlink:role="LAST_UPDATED">
         September 1, 2003
     </DATE>
     <PLANET_DATA xmlns:xlink = "http://www.w3.org/1999/xlink"
         xlink:type = "locator"
         xlink:show = "embed"
         xlink:href = "http://www.starpowdermovies.com/
         ➥ch15_06.xml#xpointer(/descendant::PLANET[position() = 1]">
         xlink:title="Mercury"
         xlink:role="PLANETARY_DATA">
     </PLANET_DATA>
     <PLANET_DATA xmlns:xlink = "http://www.w3.org/1999/xlink"
         xlink:type = "locator"
         xlink:show = "embed"
         xlink:href = "http://www.starpowdermovies.com/
         ➥ch15_06.xml#xpointer(/descendant::PLANET[position() = 2]">
         xlink:title="Venus"
         xlink:role="PLANETARY_DATA">
     </PLANET_DATA>
     <PLANET_DATA xmlns:xlink = "http://www.w3.org/1999/xlink"
         xlink:type = "locator"
         xlink:show = "embed"
         xlink:href = "http://www.starpowdermovies.com/
         ➥ch15_06.xml#xpointer(/descendant::PLANET[position() = 3]">
         xlink:title="Earth"
         xlink:role="PLANETARY_DATA">
     </PLANET_DATA>
</ASTRO_DATA>
```

So far, all we've done is indicate whether elements that participate in an extended link represent local or remote resources. You can do more if you use the xlink:from and xlink:to attributes—they allow you to create directed links, or *arcs*.

Creating Arcs with the *xlink:from* and *xlink:to* Attributes

In simple links, there's little question where to go when the link is activated: The xlink:href attribute tells you all you need to know. However, extended links are more complex. When you want to traverse the link we've created in the last section, what should happen? There are all kinds of paths among the various resources.

Each of the possible paths between resources is called an arc. You represent an arc in XML elements by setting the xlink:type attribute to "arc".

To specify how an arc works, you can use attributes such as xlink:show and xlink:actuate. Here's the important part: Arc elements also have xlink:from and xlink:to elements to specify traversal paths. The xlink:from attribute indicates what resource an arc comes from, and the xlink:to attribute indicates what resource it goes to. You set the values of xlink:from and xlink:to to match the xlink:role attribute of the source and target resources.

Here's an example. In this case, I'll modify the previous example by renaming the <NAME> element as <START> and including three arcs, one from the <START> element to each of the three <PLANET_DATA> elements (individual arcs always go from one source resource to one target resource). I'll support the arcs with elements named <LOOKUP>. Here's what it looks like:

```
<?xml version = "1.0"?>
<ASTRO_DATA xmlns:xlink="http://www.w3.org/1999/xlink"
        xlink:type="extended" xlink:title="Planetary Data">

    <START xlink:type="resource" xlink:role="START">
        Planetary Data
    </START>

    <DATE xlink:type="resource" xlink:role="LAST_UPDATED">
        September 1, 2003
    </DATE>

    <PLANET_DATA xmlns:xlink = "http://www.w3.org/1999/xlink"
        xlink:type = "locator"
        xlink:show = "embed"
        xlink:href = "http://www.starpowdermovies.com/
        ➥ch15_06.xml#xpointer(/descendant::PLANET[position() = 1]">
        xlink:title="Mercury"
        xlink:role="Mercury">
    </PLANET_DATA>
```

```
<PLANET_DATA xmlns:xlink = "http://www.w3.org/1999/xlink"
    xlink:type = "locator"
    xlink:show = "embed"
    xlink:href = "http://www.starpowdermovies.com/
    ➥ch15_06.xml#xpointer(/descendant::PLANET[position() = 2]">
    xlink:title="Venus"
    xlink:role="Venus">
</PLANET_DATA>

<PLANET_DATA xmlns:xlink = "http://www.w3.org/1999/xlink"
    xlink:type = "locator"
    xlink:show = "embed"
    xlink:href = "http://www.starpowdermovies.com/
    ➥ch15_06.xml#xpointer(/descendant::PLANET[position() = 3]">
    xlink:title="Earth"
    xlink:role="Earth">
</PLANET_DATA>

<LOOKUP xlink:type = "arc" xlink:from = "START"
    xlink:to = "Mercury" xlink:show="new"
    xlink:actuate="onRequest">
</LOOKUP>

<LOOKUP xlink:type = "arc" xlink:from = "START"
    xlink:to = "Venus" xlink:show="new"
    xlink:actuate="onRequest">
</LOOKUP>

<LOOKUP xlink:type = "arc" xlink:from = "START"
    xlink:to = "Earth" xlink:show="new"
    xlink:actuate="onRequest">
</LOOKUP>
</ASTRO_DATA>
```

As usual, you need to declare the elements and attributes you're using if you want a valid document. That might look something like this with a DTD:

Listing ch15_09.xml

```
<?xml version = "1.0"?>
<!DOCTYPE ASTRO_DATA  [
<!ELEMENT ASTRO_DATA (START, DATE, PLANET_DATA*, LOOKUP*) >
<!ATTLIST ASTRO_DATA
    xmlns:xlink CDATA #FIXED "http://www.w3.org/1999/xlink"
    xlink:type (extended) #FIXED "extended"
    xlink:title CDATA #IMPLIED
    xlink:role CDATA #IMPLIED>
```

```
<!ELEMENT START (#PCDATA)>
<!ATTLIST START
    xmlns:xlink CDATA #FIXED "http://www.w3.org/1999/xlink"
    xlink:type CDATA #FIXED "resource"
    xlink:role CDATA #IMPLIED
    xlink:title CDATA #IMPLIED>

<!ELEMENT DATE (#PCDATA)>
<!ATTLIST DATE
    xmlns:xlink CDATA #FIXED "http://www.w3.org/1999/xlink"
    xlink:type CDATA #FIXED "resource"
    xlink:role CDATA #IMPLIED
    xlink:title CDATA #IMPLIED>

<!ELEMENT PLANET_DATA (#PCDATA)>
<!ATTLIST PLANET_DATA
    xmlns:xlink CDATA #FIXED "http://www.w3.org/1999/xlink"
    xlink:type CDATA #FIXED "locator"
    xlink:href CDATA #REQUIRED
    xlink:role CDATA #IMPLIED
    xlink:title CDATA #IMPLIED
    xlink:show CDATA #IMPLIED>

<!ELEMENT LOOKUP (#PCDATA)>
<!ATTLIST LOOKUP
    xlink:type CDATA #FIXED "arc"
    xlink:from CDATA #IMPLIED
    xlink:to CDATA #IMPLIED
    xlink:show CDATA #IMPLIED
    xlink:actuate (onRequest | onLoad | other | none) #IMPLIED>
]>

<ASTRO_DATA xmlns:xlink="http://www.w3.org/1999/xlink"
        xlink:type="extended" xlink:title="Planetary Data">

    <START xlink:type="resource" xlink:role="START">
        Planetary Data
    </START>

    <DATE xlink:type="resource" xlink:role="LAST_UPDATED">
        September 1, 2003
    </DATE>

    <PLANET_DATA xmlns:xlink = "http://www.w3.org/1999/xlink"
        xlink:type = "locator"
        xlink:show = "embed"
        xlink:href = "http://www.starpowdermovies.com/
        ➥ch15_06.xml#xpointer(/descendant::PLANET[position() = 1]">
        xlink:title="Mercury"
        xlink:role="Mercury">
    </PLANET_DATA>
```

continues

Listing ch15_09.xml   Continued

```
    <PLANET_DATA xmlns:xlink = "http://www.w3.org/1999/xlink"
        xlink:type = "locator"
        xlink:show = "embed"
        xlink:href = "http://www.starpowdermovies.com/
        ➥ch15_06.xml#xpointer(/descendant::PLANET[position() = 2]">
        xlink:title="Venus"
        xlink:role="Venus">
    </PLANET_DATA>

    <PLANET_DATA xmlns:xlink = "http://www.w3.org/1999/xlink"
        xlink:type = "locator"
        xlink:show = "embed"
        xlink:href = "http://www.starpowdermovies.com/
        ➥ch15_06.xml#xpointer(/descendant::PLANET[position() = 3]">
        xlink:title="Earth"
        xlink:role="Earth">
    </PLANET_DATA>

    <LOOKUP xlink:type = "arc" xlink:from = "START"
        xlink:to = "Mercury" xlink:show="new"
        xlink:actuate="onRequest">
    </LOOKUP>

    <LOOKUP xlink:type = "arc" xlink:from = "START"
        xlink:to = "Venus" xlink:show="new"
        xlink:actuate="onRequest">
    </LOOKUP>

    <LOOKUP xlink:type = "arc" xlink:from = "START"
        xlink:to = "Earth" xlink:show="new"
        xlink:actuate="onRequest">
    </LOOKUP>
</ASTRO_DATA>
```

You don't need to have an arc refer to one specific resource as I've done here. For example, here all three <PLANET_DATA> elements have the same role, PLANETARY_DATA. So, this single <LOOKUP> element defines three arcs, one to each <PLANET_DATA> resource:

Listing ch15_10.xml

```
<?xml version = "1.0"?>
<ASTRO_DATA xmlns:xlink="http://www.w3.org/1999/xlink"
        xlink:type="extended" xlink:title="Planetary Data">

    <START xlink:type="resource" xlink:role="START">
        Planetary Data
```

```
</START>

<DATE xlink:type="resource" xlink:role="LAST_UPDATED">
    September 1, 2003
</DATE>

<PLANET_DATA xmlns:xlink = "http://www.w3.org/1999/xlink"
    xlink:type = "locator"
    xlink:show = "embed"
    xlink:href = "http://www.starpowdermovies.com/
    ➥ch15_06.xml#xpointer(/descendant::PLANET[position() = 1]">
    xlink:title="Mercury"
    xlink:role="PLANETARY_DATA">
</PLANET_DATA>

<PLANET_DATA xmlns:xlink = "http://www.w3.org/1999/xlink"
    xlink:type = "locator"
    xlink:show = "embed"
    xlink:href = "http://www.starpowdermovies.com/
    ➥ch15_06.xml#xpointer(/descendant::PLANET[position() = 2]">
    xlink:title="Venus"
    xlink:role="PLANETARY_DATA">
</PLANET_DATA>

<PLANET_DATA xmlns:xlink = "http://www.w3.org/1999/xlink"
    xlink:type = "locator"
    xlink:show = "embed"
    xlink:href = "http://www.starpowdermovies.com/
    ➥ch15_06.xml#xpointer(/descendant::PLANET[position() = 3]">
    xlink:title="Earth"
    xlink:role="PLANETARY_DATA">
</PLANET_DATA>

<LOOKUP xlink:type = "arc" xlink:from = "START"
    xlink:to = "PLANETARY_DATA" xlink:show="new"
    xlink:actuate="onRequest">
</LOOKUP>
</ASTRO_DATA>
```

In fact, you can omit an `xlink:from` or `xlink:to` attribute altogether. In that case, arcs are created between the particular element and all the locator elements in the extended link (which can include the element that omits the `xlink:from` or `xlink:to` attribute itself).

The way the `xlink:from` and `xlink:to` attributes are actually used is up to the application that's reading the containing document.

Inline Versus Out-of-Line Links

When a link does not contain any of the resources it's linking to, it's called an out-of-line link. Inline links are part of the resources they provide links for, but out-of-link links are not part of the same resource. There's a big movement to try to separate markup from content as much as possible (this is the motivation behind the big switch in HTML 4.0 to working with stylesheets instead of dedicated elements, such as <CENTER>, and the external code modules called *behaviors* in Internet Explorer). Using out-of-links is very attractive if that's the way you want to go.

You can place out-of-link links in their own documents, called *linkbases*. The actual set of out-of-line links in a linkbase is called a *linkset*.

Here's an example. In this case, all the links in this document are to resources that are not part of the document, so this is a linkbase:

```
<?xml version = "1.0"?>
<ASTRO_DATA xmlns:xlink="http://www.w3.org/1999/xlink"
        xlink:type="extended" xlink:title="Planetary Data">

    <PLANET_DATA xmlns:xlink = "http://www.w3.org/1999/xlink"
        xlink:type = "locator"
        xlink:show = "embed"
        xlink:href = "http://www.starpowdermovies.com/ch15_06.xml">
        xlink:title="START"
        xlink:role="START">
    </PLANET_DATA>

    <PLANET_DATA xmlns:xlink = "http://www.w3.org/1999/xlink"
        xlink:type = "locator"
        xlink:show = "embed"
        xlink:href = "http://www.starpowdermovies.com/
        ➥ch15_06.xml#xpointer(/descendant::PLANET[position() = 1]">
        xlink:title="Mercury"
        xlink:role="Mercury">
    </PLANET_DATA>

    <PLANET_DATA xmlns:xlink = "http://www.w3.org/1999/xlink"
        xlink:type = "locator"
        xlink:show = "embed"
        xlink:href = "http://www.starpowdermovies.com/
        ➥ch15_06.xml#xpointer(/descendant::PLANET[position() = 2]">
        xlink:title="Venus"
        xlink:role="Venus">
    </PLANET_DATA>

    <PLANET_DATA xmlns:xlink = "http://www.w3.org/1999/xlink"
        xlink:type = "locator"
        xlink:show = "embed"
```

```
        xlink:href = "http://www.starpowdermovies.com/
        ➥ch15_06.xml#xpointer(/descendant::PLANET[position() = 3]">
        xlink:title="Earth"
        xlink:role="Earth">
    </PLANET_DATA>

    <LOOKUP xlink:type = "arc" xlink:from = "START"
        xlink:to = "Mercury" xlink:show="new"
        xlink:actuate="onRequest">
    </LOOKUP>

    <LOOKUP xlink:type = "arc" xlink:from = "START"
        xlink:to = "Venus" xlink:show="new"
        xlink:actuate="onRequest">
    </LOOKUP>

    <LOOKUP xlink:type = "arc" xlink:from = "START"
        xlink:to = "Earth" xlink:show="new"
        xlink:actuate="onRequest">
    </LOOKUP>
</ASTRO_DATA>
```

In this case, all the resources linked to are outside the document. I've added locator links to all the planets in ch15_06.xml, and I've added arcs from the starting position in that document to the planets as well. You typically have three types of links in a linkbase: extended links, locator links, and arcs. You cannot have any links that are of type resource.

Linkbases are subject to the same rules as other XML documents. You can provide them with DTDs if you want to validate them, like I've done here:

Listing ch15_11.xml

```
<?xml version = "1.0"?>
<!DOCTYPE ASTRO_DATA  [
<!ELEMENT ASTRO_DATA (PLANET_DATA*, LOOKUP*) >
<!ATTLIST ASTRO_DATA
    xmlns:xlink CDATA #FIXED "http://www.w3.org/1999/xlink"
    xlink:type (extended) #FIXED "extended"
    xlink:title CDATA #IMPLIED
    xlink:role CDATA #IMPLIED>

<!ELEMENT PLANET_DATA (#PCDATA)>
<!ATTLIST PLANET_DATA
    xmlns:xlink CDATA #FIXED "http://www.w3.org/1999/xlink"
    xlink:type CDATA #FIXED "locator"
    xlink:href CDATA #REQUIRED
    xlink:role CDATA #IMPLIED
```

Listing ch15_11.xml   Continued

```
      xlink:title CDATA #IMPLIED
      xlink:show CDATA #IMPLIED>

<!ELEMENT LOOKUP (#PCDATA)>
<!ATTLIST LOOKUP
      xlink:type CDATA #FIXED "arc"
      xlink:from CDATA #IMPLIED
      xlink:to CDATA #IMPLIED
      xlink:show CDATA #IMPLIED
      xlink:actuate (onRequest | onLoad | other | none) #IMPLIED>
]>
```

```
<ASTRO_DATA xmlns:xlink="http://www.w3.org/1999/xlink"
            xlink:type="extended" xlink:title="Planetary Data">

    <PLANET_DATA xmlns:xlink = "http://www.w3.org/1999/xlink"
        xlink:type = "locator"
        xlink:show = "embed"
        xlink:href = "http://www.starpowdermovies.com/ch15_06.xml">
        xlink:title="START"
        xlink:role="START">
    </PLANET_DATA>

    <PLANET_DATA xmlns:xlink = "http://www.w3.org/1999/xlink"
        xlink:type = "locator"
        xlink:show = "embed"
        xlink:href = "http://www.starpowdermovies.com/
        ➥ch15_06.xml#xpointer(/descendant::PLANET[position() = 1]">
        xlink:title="Mercury"
        xlink:role="Mercury">
    </PLANET_DATA>

    <PLANET_DATA xmlns:xlink = "http://www.w3.org/1999/xlink"
        xlink:type = "locator"
        xlink:show = "embed"
        xlink:href = "http://www.starpowdermovies.com/
        ➥ch15_06.xml#xpointer(/descendant::PLANET[position() = 2]">
        xlink:title="Venus"
        xlink:role="Venus">
    </PLANET_DATA>

    <PLANET_DATA xmlns:xlink = "http://www.w3.org/1999/xlink"
        xlink:type = "locator"
        xlink:show = "embed"
        xlink:href = "http://www.starpowdermovies.com/
        ➥ch15_06.xml#xpointer(/descendant::PLANET[position() = 3]">
        xlink:title="Earth"
        xlink:role="Earth">
    </PLANET_DATA>
```

```
    <LOOKUP xlink:type = "arc" xlink:from = "START"
        xlink:to = "Mercury" xlink:show="new"
        xlink:actuate="onRequest">
    </LOOKUP>

    <LOOKUP xlink:type = "arc" xlink:from = "START"
        xlink:to = "Venus" xlink:show="new"
        xlink:actuate="onRequest">
    </LOOKUP>

    <LOOKUP xlink:type = "arc" xlink:from = "START"
        xlink:to = "Earth" xlink:show="new"
        xlink:actuate="onRequest">
    </LOOKUP>
</ASTRO_DATA>
```

You can elaborate out-of-line linksets as much as you like. Here, I'm adding arcs that will add a "next" and "previous" link to each planet:

Listing ch15_12.xml

```
<?xml version = "1.0"?>
<ASTRO_DATA xmlns:xlink="http://www.w3.org/1999/xlink"
        xlink:type="extended" xlink:title="Planetary Data">

    <PLANET_DATA xmlns:xlink = "http://www.w3.org/1999/xlink"
        xlink:type = "locator"
        xlink:show = "embed"
        xlink:href = "http://www.starpowdermovies.com/ch15_06.xml">
        xlink:title="START"
        xlink:role="START">
    </PLANET_DATA>

    <PLANET_DATA xmlns:xlink = "http://www.w3.org/1999/xlink"
        xlink:type = "locator"
        xlink:show = "embed"
        xlink:href = "http://www.starpowdermovies.com/
        ➥ch15_06.xml#xpointer(/descendant::PLANET[position() = 1]">
        xlink:title="Mercury"
        xlink:role="Mercury">
    </PLANET_DATA>

    <PLANET_DATA xmlns:xlink = "http://www.w3.org/1999/xlink"
        xlink:type = "locator"
        xlink:show = "embed"
        xlink:href = "http://www.starpowdermovies.com/
        ➥ch15_06.xml#xpointer(/descendant::PLANET[position() = 2]">
        xlink:title="Venus"
```

continues

Listing ch15_12.xml   Continued

```
            xlink:role="Venus">
    </PLANET_DATA>

    <PLANET_DATA xmlns:xlink = "http://www.w3.org/1999/xlink"
        xlink:type = "locator"
        xlink:show = "embed"
        xlink:href = "http://www.starpowdermovies.com/ch15_06.xml#xpointer
(/descendant::PLANET[position() = 3]">
        xlink:title="Earth"
        xlink:role="Earth">
    </PLANET_DATA>

    <LOOKUP xlink:type = "arc" xlink:from = "START"
        xlink:to = "Mercury" xlink:show="new"
        xlink:actuate="onRequest">
    </LOOKUP>

    <LOOKUP xlink:type = "arc" xlink:from = "START"
        xlink:to = "Venus" xlink:show="new"
        xlink:actuate="onRequest">
    </LOOKUP>

    <LOOKUP xlink:type = "arc" xlink:from = "START"
        xlink:to = "Earth" xlink:show="new"
        xlink:actuate="onRequest">
    </LOOKUP>

    <NEXT xlink:type = "arc" xlink:from = "Mercury"
        xlink:to = "Venus" xlink:show="new"
        xlink:actuate="onRequest">
    </NEXT>

    <NEXT xlink:type = "arc" xlink:from = "Venus"
        xlink:to = "Earth" xlink:show="new"
        xlink:actuate="onRequest">
    </NEXT>

    <NEXT xlink:type = "arc" xlink:from = "Earth"
        xlink:to = "Mercury" xlink:show="new"
        xlink:actuate="onRequest">
    </NEXT>

    <PREVIOUS xlink:type = "arc" xlink:from = "Earth"
        xlink:to = "Venus" xlink:show="new"
        xlink:actuate="onRequest">
    </PREVIOUS>

    <PREVIOUS xlink:type = "arc" xlink:from = "Venus"
        xlink:to = "Mercury" xlink:show="new"
```

```
            xlink:actuate="onRequest">
      </PREVIOUS>

      <PREVIOUS xlink:type = "arc" xlink:from = "Mercury"
            xlink:to = "Earth" xlink:show="new"
            xlink:actuate="onRequest">
      </PREVIOUS>
</ASTRO_DATA>
```

The next question is: Because out-of-link links are outside all resources that they reference, how does application software that deals with those resources know how to find those links? According to the W3C, you can do that with a special arc whose arc role is www.w3.org/1999/xlink/properties/ linkbase. Here's what that looks like:

```
<load xlink:type="arc" xlink:from="start.xml"
    xlink:to="linkbase.xml" actuate="onLoad"
    xlink:arcrole=
    "http://www.w3.org/1999/xlink/properties/linkbase"/>
```

So far in this chapter, I've said that you use the xlink:href attribute to locate resources, and I've left it at that. However, there is more to it than that: You can do more than just place a URI in this attribute; you can also use XPointers to locate specific locations or sections of a document.

All About XPointers

At the beginning of this chapter, I took a look at a link that used an XPointer to locate a specific element in a document. That example looked like this:

```
<MOVIE_REVIEW xmlns:xlink = "http://www.w3.org/1999/xlink"
    xlink:type = "simple"
    xlink:show = "new"
    xlink:href = "http://www.starpowdermovies.com/reviews.xml#xpointer
    ➥(/child::*[position()=126]/child::*[position()=first()])">
    Mr. Blandings Builds His Dream House
</MOVIE_REVIEW>
```

You can see the XPointer part here: xpointer(/child::* [position()=126]/child::*[position()=first()]). This XPointer is appended to the URI I'm using here, following a # character.

You might notice that this XPointer expression looks a lot like the XPath expressions we used in Chapter 13, and with good reason: XPointers are built on XPaths, with certain additions that I'll note here.

Because XPointers are built on XPaths, they have all the power of XPaths. Among other things, that means that you can use an XPointer made up of location steps that target an individual location in a document, without having to add any markup to that document. You can also use the id() function to target specific elements if you do want to add ID attributes to those elements.

However, because XPointers extend XPaths, there are some differences. The biggest difference is that because users can select parts of documents using the mouse, if they prefer, XPointers allow you to select *points* and *ranges* in addition to the normal XPath nodes. A point is just what it sounds like: a specific location in a document. A range is made up of all the XML between two points, which can include part of elements and text strings.

To support points and ranges, XPointer extends the idea of nodes into *locations*. Every location is an XPath node, a point, or a range. Node sets therefore become *location sets* in the XPointer specification. XPointer specifically extends the defined node types to include points and ranges so that node tests can return any of those types.

How do you create an XPointer? Like XPaths, XPointers are made up of location paths that are divided into location steps, separated by the / character. A location step is made up of an axis, a node test, and zero or more predicates, like this: `axis::node_test[predicate]`. For example, in the expression `child::PLANET[position() = 5]`, `child` is the name of the axis, `PLANET` is the node test, and `[position() = 5]` is a predicate.

You can create location paths with one or more location steps, as in `/descendant::PLANET/child::NAME`, which selects all the <NAME> elements that have an <PLANET> parent.

XPointers augment what's available with XPaths, so I'm going to take a look these three parts— axes, node tests, and predicates—for XPointers now.

XPointer Axes

The XPointer axes are the same as the XPath axes, and we're already familiar with them. Axes tell you which direction you should search and give you a starting position to search from. Here's the list of possible axes:

- The `ancestor` axis holds the ancestors of the context node. The ancestors of the context node are the parent of context node and the parent's parent, and so forth, back to and including the root node.

- The `ancestor-or-self` axis holds the context node and the ancestors of the context node.

- The `attribute` axis holds the attributes of the context node.

- The `child` axis holds the children of the context node.

- The `descendant` axis holds the descendants of the context node. A descendant is a child or a child of a child, and so on.

- The `descendant-or-self` axis contains the context node and the descendants of the context node.

- The `following` axis holds all nodes in the same document as the context node that come after the context node.

- The `following-sibling` axis holds all the following siblings of the context node. A sibling is a node on the same level as the context node.

- The `namespace` axis holds the namespace nodes of the context node.

- The `parent` axis holds the parent of the context node.

- The `preceding` axis contains all nodes that come before the context node.

- The `preceding-sibling` axis contains all the preceding siblings of the context node. A sibling is a node on the same level as the context node.

- The `self` axis contains the context node.

Although XPointers use the same axes as XPaths, there are some new node tests.

XPointer Node Tests

These are the node tests you can use with XPointers, along with what they match:

`*`	Any element
`node()`	Any node
`text()`	A text node
`comment()`	A comment node
`processing-instruction()`	A processing instruction node
`point()`	A point in a resource
`range()`	A range in a resource

Note in particular the last two: `point()` and `range()`. These correspond to the two new constructs added in XPointers, points and ranges. I'll talk more about them at the end of this chapter. As you can see here, in XPointer, XPath node tests are extended to be able to include points and ranges as well.

XPointer Predicates

XPointers support the same types of expressions as XPaths. As in Chapter 13, these are the possible types of expressions you can use in predicates (refer to Chapter 13 for more information):

- Node sets (although they're called location sets in XPointer)
- Booleans
- Numbers
- Strings
- Result tree fragments

XPointer also makes some additions to the functions that return location sets, and I'll take a look at those functions now.

XPointer Location Set Functions

Two XPointer functions return location sets:

- `here()`—Returns a location set with one location, the current location
- `origin()`—The same as here(), except that this function is used with out-of-link links

The `here()` function refers to the current element. This is useful because XPointers are usually stored in text nodes or attribute values, and you might want to refer to the current element (not just the current node). For example, you might want to refer to the second previous <NAME> sibling element of the element that contains an Xpointer; you can use an expression like this to do so: `here()/preceding-sibling::NAME[position() = 2]`.

The `origin()` function is much like the `here()` function, but you use it with out-of-line links. It refers to the original element, which may be in another document, from which the current link was activated. This can be very helpful if the link itself is in a linkbase and needs to refer not to the element the link is in, but to the original element from which the link is activated.

You can use the abbreviated XPath syntax in XPointers as well. I'll take a look at a few examples using our planetary XML document, ch15_06.xml, as the document we'll be navigating. Note that, as with XPath, you can use the [ ] operator; here, it extracts a particular location from a location set:

- `PLANET`—Returns the `<PLANET>` element children of the context node.
- `*`—Returns all element children of the context node.
- `text()`—Returns all text node children of the context node.
- `@UNITS`—Returns the `UNITS` attribute of the context node.
- `@*`—Returns all the attributes of the context node.
- `PLANET[3]`—Returns the third `<PLANET>` child of the context node.
- `PLANET[first()]`—Returns the first `<PLANET>` child of the context node.
- `*/PLANET`—Returns all `<PLANET>` grandchildren of the context node.
- `/PLANETS/PLANET[3]/NAME[2]`—Returns the second `<NAME>` element of the third `<PLANET>` element of the `<PLANETS>` element.
- `//PLANET`—Returns all the `<PLANET>` descendants of the document root.
- `PLANETS//PLANET`—Returns the `<PLANET>` element descendants of the `<PLANETS>` element children of the context node.
- `//PLANET/NAME`—Returns all the `<NAME>` elements that have a `<PLANET>` parent.
- `.`—Returns the context node itself.
- `.//PLANET`—Returns the `<PLANET>` element descendants of the context node.
- `..`—Returns the parent of the context node.
- `../@UNITS`—Returns the `UNITS` attribute of the parent of the context node.
- `PLANET[NAME]`—Returns the `<PLANET>` children of the context node that have `<NAME>` children.
- `PLANET[NAME="Venus"]`—Returns the `<PLANET>` children of the context node that have `<NAME>` children with text equal to `"Venus"`.
- `PLANET[@UNITS = "days"]`—Returns all `<PLANET>` children of the context node that have a `UNITS` attribute with the value `"days"`.

- PLANET[6][@UNITS = "days"]—Returns the sixth <PLANET> child of the context node, only if that child has a UNITS attribute with the value "days". Can also be written as PLANET[@UNITS = "days"][6].
- PLANET[@COLOR and @UNITS]—Returns all the <PLANET> children of the context node that have both a COLOR attribute and a UNITS attribute.

In XPath, you can locate data only at the node level. That's fine when you're working with software that handles XML data in terms of nodes, such as XSL transformations, but it's not good enough for all purposes. For example, a user working with a displayed XML document might be able to click the mouse at a particular point or even select a range of XML content. (Note that such ranges might not start and end on node boundaries at all—they might contain parts of various trees and subtrees.) To give you finer control over XML data, you can work with *points* and *ranges* in XPointer.

Using XPointer Points

How do you define a point in the XPointer specification? To do so, you must use two items: a node and an index that can hold a positive integer or zero. The node specifies an origin for the point, and the index indicates how far the point you want is from that origin.

But what should the index be measured in terms of—characters in the document or number of nodes? In fact, there are two different types of points, and the index value that you use is measured differently for those types.

Node-Points

When the origin node, also called the *container* node, of a point can have child nodes (which means it's an element node or the root node), the point is called a *node-point*.

The index of a node-point is measured in child nodes. Here, the index of a node-point must be equal to or less than the number of child nodes in the origin node. If you use an index of 0, the point is immediately before any child nodes. An index of 5 locates a point immediately after the fifth child node.

You can use axes with node-points: A node-point's siblings are the children of the container node before or after the node-point. Points don't have any children, however.

Character-Points

If the origin node can't contain any child nodes, only text, the index is measured in characters. Points like these are called *character-points*.

The index of a character-point must be a positive integer or 0, and must be less than or equal to the length of the text string in the node. If the index is 0, the point is immediately before the first character; an index of 5 locates the point immediately after the fifth character. Character-points do not have preceding or following siblings or children.

For example, you can treat <DOCUMENT> as a container node in this document:

```
<DOCUMENT>
Hi there!
</DOCUMENT>
```

In this case, there are nine character-points, one before every character. The character-point at index 0 is right before the first character, H; the character-point at index 1 is right before the i; and so on.

In addition, you should note that the XPointer specification collapses all consecutive whitespace into a single space, so four spaces is the same as one when calculating an index for a character-point. Also, you cannot place points inside a start tag, end tag, processing instruction, comment, or any markup.

Point Functions

To create a point, you can use the point() function with a predicate like this: point()[position()=10]. Here's an example; say that I wanted to position a point just before the e in the text in Mercury's <NAME> element:

```
<?xml version="1.0"?>
<?xml-stylesheet type="text/xml" href="planets.xsl"?>
<PLANETS>

    <PLANET>
        <NAME>Mercury</NAME>
        <MASS UNITS="(Earth = 1)">.0553</MASS>
        <DAY UNITS="days">58.65</DAY>
        <RADIUS UNITS="miles">1516</RADIUS>
        <DENSITY UNITS="(Earth = 1)">.983</DENSITY>
        <DISTANCE UNITS="million miles">43.4</DISTANCE><!--At perihelion-->
    </PLANET>
    .
    .
    .
```

In this case, I could use an expression like this to refer to the point right before the character e:

```
xpointer(/PLANETS/PLANET[1]/NAME/text()/point()[position() = 1])
```

Similarly, I can access the point right before the 6 in the text in Mercury's <DAY> element, 58.65 (which, of course is text, not a number), this way:

```
xpointer(/PLANETS/PLANET[1]/DAY/text()/point()[position() = 3])
```

XPointer also supports these point-related functions:

- start-point(*location-set*)—Returns a location set with start points in it. Those points are the start points of ranges that would cover the passed locations. For example, start-point(//PLANET[2]) would return the point immediately before the second <PLANET> element in the document, and start-point(//PLANET) would return a location set of the points just before each <PLANET> element.

- end-point(*location-set*)—Is the same as start-point, except that it returns the corresponding end points of the ranges that cover the locations passed to it.

Using XPointer Ranges

You can create ranges with two points, a start point and an end point, as long as they are in the same document and the start point is not after the end point. (If the start point and the end point are the same, the range is said to be *collapsed*.) A range is all of the XML structure between those two points.

A range doesn't have to be a neat subsection of a document; it can extend from one subtree to another in the document, for example. All you need are a valid start point and a valid end point in the same document.

Range Functions

The XPointer specification adds a number of functions to those available in XPath to handle ranges:

- range(*location-set*)—This function takes the locations you pass to it and returns a range that completely covers the location. For example, an element location is converted to a range by returning the element's parent as the origin node, the start point as the number of previous siblings the element has, and the end point as one greater than the start point. In other words, this function is intended to cover locations with ranges.

- `range-inside(location-set)`—This function returns a range or ranges covering each location in the argument location set. For example, if you pass an element location, the result is a range that encloses all that is inside the element.

- `range-to(location-set)`—This function returns a range for each location in the location set. The start point of the range is the start point of the context location (as determined by the `start-point` function). The end point of the range is the end point (as determined by the `end-point` function) of the location found by evaluating the expression argument.

String Ranges

The XPointer specification also includes a function for basic string matching, `string-range()`. This function returns a location set with one range for every nonoverlapping match to the search string. The match operation is case sensitive.

You can also specify optional index and length arguments to specify how many characters after the match the range should start and how many characters should be in the range. Here's how you use `string-range()` in general:

```
string-range(location_set, string, [index, [length]])
```

Matching an Empty String

An empty string, `""`, matches the location immediately before any character, so you can use an empty string to match to the very beginning of any string.

For example, this expression returns a location set containing ranges covering all matches to the word Saturn:

```
string-range(/, "Saturn")
```

To extract a specific match from the location set returned, you use the `[]` operator. For example, this expression returns a range covering the second occurrence of Saturn in the document:

```
string-range(/, "Saturn")[2]
```

This expression returns a range covering the third occurrence of the word Jupiter in the `<NAME>` element of the sixth `<PLANET>` element in a document:

```
string-range(//PLANET[6]/NAME, "Jupiter")[3]
```

You can also specify the range you want to return using the `index` (which starts with a value of 1) and `length` arguments. For example, this expression returns a range covering the letters er in the third occurrence of the word Jupiter in the `<NAME>` element of the sixth `<PLANET>` element:

```
string-range(//PLANET[6]/NAME, "Jupiter", 6, 2)[3]
```

If you want to locate a specific point, you can create a collapsed (zero-length) range like this:

```
string-range(//PLANET[6]/NAME, "Jupiter", 6, 0)[3]
```

Another way to get a specific point is to use the `start-point()` function, which returns the start point of a range:

```
start-point(string-range(//PLANET[6]/NAME, "Jupiter", 6, 2)[3])
```

Here's an expression that locates the second @ character in any text node in the document and the five characters following it:

```
string-range(/, "@", 1, 6)[2]
```

XPointer Abbreviations

Because it's so common to refer to elements by location or ID, XPointer adds a few abbreviated forms of reference. Here's an example; suppose that you wanted to locate Venus's `<DAY>` element:

```
<?xml version="1.0"?>
<?xml-stylesheet type="text/xml" href="planets.xsl"?>
<PLANETS>

    <PLANET>
        <NAME>Mercury</NAME>
        <MASS UNITS="(Earth = 1)">.0553</MASS>
        <DAY UNITS="days">58.65</DAY>
        <RADIUS UNITS="miles">1516</RADIUS>
        <DENSITY UNITS="(Earth = 1)">.983</DENSITY>
        <DISTANCE UNITS="million miles">43.4</DISTANCE><!--At perihelion-->
    </PLANET>

    <PLANET>
        <NAME>Venus</NAME>
        <MASS UNITS="(Earth = 1)">.815</MASS>
```

```
      <DAY UNITS="days">116.75</DAY>
      <RADIUS UNITS="miles">3716</RADIUS>
      <DENSITY UNITS="(Earth = 1)">.943</DENSITY>
      <DISTANCE UNITS="million miles">66.8</DISTANCE><!--At perihelion-->
  </PLANET>
     .
     .
     .
```

You could do so with this rather formidable expression:

```
http://www.starpowdermovies.com/ch15_06.xml#xpointer(/child::*
➡[position()=1]/child::*[position()=2]/child::*[position()=3])
```

As you know from Chapter 13, the `child::` part is optional in XPath expressions, and the predicate [position() = *x*] can be abbreviated as [*x*]. In XPointer, you can abbreviate this still more, omitting the [and]. Here's the result, which, as you can see, is fairly compact:

```
http://www.starpowdermovies.com/ch15_06.xml#1/2/3
```

When you see location steps made up of single numbers in this way, those locations steps correspond to the location of elements.

In a similar way, you can use words as location steps, not just numbers, if those words correspond to ID values of elements in the document. For example, say I give Venus's `<PLANET>` element the ID "Planet_Of_Love" (here I'm assuming that this element's ID attribute is declared with the type ID in a DTD):

```
<?xml version="1.0"?>
<?xml-stylesheet type="text/xml" href="planets.xsl"?>
<PLANETS>

    <PLANET>
        <NAME>Mercury</NAME>
        <MASS UNITS="(Earth = 1)">.0553</MASS>
        <DAY UNITS="days">58.65</DAY>
        <RADIUS UNITS="miles">1516</RADIUS>
        <DENSITY UNITS="(Earth = 1)">.983</DENSITY>
        <DISTANCE UNITS="million miles">43.4</DISTANCE><!--At perihelion-->
    </PLANET>

    <PLANET ID = "Planet_Of_Love">
        <NAME>Venus</NAME>
        <MASS UNITS="(Earth = 1)">.815</MASS>
        <DAY UNITS="days">116.75</DAY>
        <RADIUS UNITS="miles">3716</RADIUS>
        <DENSITY UNITS="(Earth = 1)">.943</DENSITY>
```

```
    <DISTANCE UNITS="million miles">66.8</DISTANCE><!--At perihelion-->
</PLANET>
```

.
.
.

Now you could reach the `<DAY>` element in Venus's `<PLANET>` element like this:

```
http://www.starpowdermovies.com/ch15_06.xml#xpointer(//child::*[id("Planet_Of
➥_Love")]/child::*[position()=3]
```

However, there's also an abbreviated version that's much shorter. In this case, I take advantage of the fact that you can use an element's ID value as a location step, and the result looks like this:

```
http://www.starpowdermovies.com/ch15_06.xml#Planet_Of_Love/3
```

As you can see, this form is considerably shorter.

In this example, I used the `id()` function; to use that function, you should declare ID attributes to have the type ID. However, not all documents have a DTD or schema, so XPointer allows you to specify *alternative* patterns using multiple XPointers. Here's how that might look in this case, where I specify two XPointers in one location step:

```
http://www.starpowdermovies.com/ch15_06.xml#xpointer(id("Planet_Of_Love"))xpo
➥inter(//*[@id="Planet_Of_Love"])/3
```

If the first XPointer, which relies on the `id()` function, fails, the second XPointer is supposed to be used instead; that one locates any element that has an attribute named ID with the required value. It remains to be seen how much of this syntax applications will actually implement.

That's it for XLinks and XPointers. As you can see, there's a lot of power here—far more than with simple HTML hyperlinks. However, the XLink and XPointer standards have been proposed for quite a few years now, and there have been practically no implementations of them. Hopefully the future will bring more concrete results.

In the next chapter, I'm going to take a look at some popular XML applications in depth, starting with the most popular one of all: XHTML.

CHAPTER 16
Essential XHTML

Probably the biggest XML application today is XHTML, which is the World Wide Web Consortium (W3C's)implementation of HTML 4.0 in XML. XHTML is a true XML application, which means that XHTML documents are XML documents that can be checked for well-formedness and validity.

There are two big advantages to using XHTML. HTML predefines all its elements and attributes, and that's not something you can change—unless you use XHTML. Because XHTML is really XML, you can extend it with your own elements, and we'll see how to do that in the next chapter. Need `<INVOICE>`, `<DELIVERY_DATE>`, and `<PRODUCT_ID>` elements in your Web page? Now you can add them. (This aspect of XHTML isn't supported by the major browsers yet, but it's coming.) The other big advantage, as far as HTML authors are concerned, is that you can display XHTML documents in today's browsers without modification. That's the whole idea behind XHTML—it's supposed to provide a bridge between XML and HTML. XHTML is true XML, but you can use it today in browsers. And that has made it very popular.

Here's an example; this page is written in standard HTML:

Listing ch16_01.html

```
<HTML>
    <HEAD>
        <TITLE>
            Welcome to my page
        </TITLE>
    </HEAD>

    <BODY>
        <H1>
            Welcome to HTML!
        </H1>
    </BODY>
</HTML>
```

Here's the same page written in XHTML, with the message changed from `Welcome to HTML!` to `Welcome to XHTML!`:

Listing ch16_02.html

```
<?xml version="1.0"?>
<!DOCTYPE html PUBLIC "-//W3C//DTD XHTML 1.0 Transitional//EN"
"http://www.w3.org/TR/xhtml1/DTD/xhtml1-transitional.dtd">
<html xmlns="http://www.w3.org/1999/xhtml" xml:lang="en" lang="en">
    <head>
        <title>
            Welcome to my page
        </title>
    </head>

    <body>
        <h1>
            Welcome to XHTML!
        </h1>
    </body>
</html>
```

I'll go through exactly what's happening here in this chapter.

You save XHTML documents with the extension .html to make sure browsers treat those documents as HTML. This document produces the same result as the previous HTML document, except that this document says `Welcome to XHTML!` instead, as you can see in Figure 16-1.

Figure 16-1
An XHTML document in Netscape Navigator.

Take a look at this XHTML document. As you can see, it's true XML, starting with the XML declaration:

```
<?xml version="1.0"?>
    .
    .
    .
```

Next comes a `<!DOCTYPE>` element:

```
<?xml version="1.0"?>
<!DOCTYPE html PUBLIC "-//W3C//DTD XHTML 1.0 Transitional//EN"
"http://www.w3.org/TR/xhtml1/DTD/xhtml1-transitional.dtd">
    .
    .
    .
```

This is just a standard `<!DOCTYPE>` element; in this case, it indicates that the document element is `<html>`. Note the lowercase here: `<html>`, not `<HTML>`. All elements in XHTML (except the `<!DOCTYPE>` element) are in lowercase. That's the XHTML standard; if you're accustomed to using uppercase tag names, it'll take a little getting used to.

The document type definitions (DTDs) that XHTML uses are public DTDs, created by the W3C. Here, the formal public identifier (FPI) for the DTD I'm using is `-//W3C//DTD XHTML 1.0 Transitional//EN`, which is one of several DTDs available, as we'll see. I'm also giving the uniform resource locator (URL) for the DTD, which for this DTD is `http://www.w3.org/TR/xhtml1/DTD/xhtml1-transitional.dtd`.

Using an XHTML DTD, browsers can validate XHTML documents—at least theoretically. (In fact, browsers such as Internet Explorer will read in the DTD and check the document against it. However, as we've seen, you have to explicitly check whether there were errors because the browser won't announce them.)

Note also that the URI for the DTD is at the W3C itself: `http://www.w3.org/TR/xhtml1/DTD/xhtml1-transitional.dtd`. Now imagine 40 million browsers trying to validate XHTML documents all at the same time by downloading XHTML DTDs such as this one from the W3C site—quite a problem. To avoid bottlenecks like this, you can copy the XHTML DTDs and store them locally (I'll give their URIs and discuss this in a few pages), or you can do without a DTD in your documents. However, my guess is that when we get fully enabled validating XHTML browsers, they'll have the various XHTML DTDs stored internally for immediate access, without having to download the XHTML DTDs from the Internet. (As it stands now, it takes Internet Explorer 10–20 seconds to download a typical XHTML DTD at 56K speeds.)

After the `<!DOCTYPE>` element comes the `<html>` element, which is the document element and starts the actual document content:

```
<?xml version="1.0"?>
<!DOCTYPE html PUBLIC "-//W3C//DTD XHTML 1.0 Transitional//EN"
"http://www.w3.org/TR/xhtml1/DTD/xhtml1-transitional.dtd">
<html xmlns="http://www.w3.org/1999/xhtml" xml:lang="en" lang="en">
    .
    .
    .
```

I'm using three attributes of this XHTML element here, as is usual: `xmlns` to define an XML namespace for the document, `xml:lang` to set the language for the document when it's interpreted as XML, and the standard HTML attribute `lang` to set the language when the document is treated as HTML. Note in particular the namespace used for XHTML: "`http://www.w3.org/1999/xhtml`", which is the official XHTML namespace. All the XHTML elements must be in this namespace.

The remainder of the page is very like the HTML document we saw earlier—the only real difference is that the tag names are now in lowercase:

```
<?xml version="1.0"?>
<!DOCTYPE html PUBLIC "-//W3C//DTD XHTML 1.0 Transitional//EN"
"http://www.w3.org/TR/xhtml1/DTD/xhtml1-transitional.dtd">
<html xmlns="http://www.w3.org/1999/xhtml" xml:lang="en" lang="en">
    <head>
        <title>
            Welcome to my page
        </title>
    </head>

    <body>
        <h1>
            Welcome to XHTML!
        </h1>
    </body>
</html>
```

As you see in the `<!DOCTYPE>` element, I'm using the XHTML DTD that's called XHTML 1.0 Transitional. That's only one of the XHTML DTDs available, although it's currently the most popular one. So what XHTML DTDs are available, and what do they mean? That all depends on what version of XHTML you are using.

XHTML Version 1.0

The standard version of XHTML, version 1.0, is just a rewrite of HTML 4.0 in XML. You can find the W3C recommendation for XHTML 1.0 at `www.w3.org/TR/xhtml1`. Essentially, it's just a set of DTDs that provide validity checks for documents that are supposed to mimic HTML 4.0 (actually HTML 4.01). The W3C has created several DTDs for HTML 4.0, and the XHTML DTDs are based on those, translated into straight XML. As with HTML 4.0, XHTML 1.0 has three versions, which correspond to three DTDs here:

- **The strict XHTML 1.0 DTD**—The strict DTD is based on straight HTML 4.0 and does not include support for elements and attributes that the W3C considers deprecated. This is the version of XHTML 1.0 that the W3C hopes people will migrate to in time.

- **The transitional XHTML 1.0 DTD**—The transitional DTD is based on the *transitional* HTML 4 DTD. This DTD has support for the many elements and attributes that were deprecated in HTML 4.0 but are still popular, such as the <CENTER> and <FONT> elements. This DTD is also named the "loose" DTD. It is the most popular version of XHTML at the moment.

- **The frameset XHTML 1.0 DTD**—The frameset DTD is based on the frameset HTML 4.0 DTD. This is the DTD you should work with when you're creating pages based on frames. In that case, you replace the <BODY> element with a <FRAMESET> element. The DTD has to reflect that, so you use the frameset DTD when working with frames. That's the difference between the XHTML 1.0 transitional and frameset DTDs: The frameset DTD replaces the <BODY> element with the <FRAMESET> element.

XFrames

Speaking of frames, the W3C has recently come out with a working draft for a new specification, XFrames (see `www.w3.org/TR/xframes/`), which are designed to replace HTML frames.

Here are the actual `<!DOCTYPE>` elements you should use in XHTML for these various DTDs—strict, transitional, and frameset—including the URIs for these DTDs:

```
<!DOCTYPE html
     PUBLIC "-//W3C//DTD XHTML 1.0 Strict//EN"
     "http://www.w3.org/TR/xhtml1/DTD/xhtml1-strict.dtd">

<!DOCTYPE html
     PUBLIC "-//W3C//DTD XHTML 1.0 Transitional//EN"
     "http://www.w3.org/TR/xhtml1/DTD/xhtml1-transitional.dtd">

<!DOCTYPE html
     PUBLIC "-//W3C//DTD XHTML 1.0 Frameset//EN"
     "http://www.w3.org/TR/xhtml1/DTD/xhtml1-frameset.dtd">
```

I'm giving the DTDs' uniform resource indicators (URIs) here, so you can copy them and cache a local copy if you want for faster access. For example, if you place the DTD files in a directory named DTD in your Web site, your `<!DOCTYPE>` elements might look more like this:

```
<!DOCTYPE html
     PUBLIC "-//W3C//DTD XHTML 1.0 Strict//EN"
     "DTD/xhtml1-strict.dtd">

<!DOCTYPE html
     PUBLIC "-//W3C//DTD XHTML 1.0 Transitional//EN"
     "DTD/xhtml1-transitional.dtd">

<!DOCTYPE html
     PUBLIC "-//W3C//DTD XHTML 1.0 Frameset//EN"
     "DTD/xhtml1-frameset.dtd">
```

If you cache these DTDs locally, there should be less of a bottleneck when XHTML becomes very popular and users try to download your documents.

XHTML Version 1.1

There's also another version of XHTML available, version 1.1. This version is in W3C recommendation form. You can find the current version of XHTML 1.1 at `www.w3.org/TR/xhtml11`.

XHTML 1.1 is a strict version of XHTML, and it's clear that the W3C wants to wean HTML authors from their loose ways into writing very tight XML. How far those HTML authors will follow is yet to be determined.

XHTML 1.1 removes all the elements and attributes deprecated in HTML 4.0, and a few more as well.

<APPLET> Versus *<OBJECT>*

There's another interesting thing going on in XHTML 1.1: The W3C has long said that it wants to replace <APPLET> and other elements with the Microsoft-supported <OBJECT> element. However, and surprisingly, <OBJECT> is missing from XHTML 1.1. And, surprise, the <APPLET> element is back.

XHTML 1.1 is so far ahead of the pack that many features that today's HTML authors and browsers use aren't supported there at all. So, I'm going to stick to XHTML 1.0 transitional in the examples in this chapter and the next one. However, I'll also indicate which elements and attributes are supported by what versions of XHTML, including XHTML 1.1, throughout these chapters.

The Differences Between XHTML 1.0 and XHTML 1.1

You can find the differences between XHTML 1.0 and XHTML 1.1 at www.w3.org/TR/xhtml11/changes.html#a_changes.

When you want to use XHTML 1.1, here's the <!DOCTYPE> element you should use (there's only in XHTML 1.1 DTD, not three as in XHTML 1.0):

```
<!DOCTYPE html PUBLIC "-//W3C//DTD XHTML 1.1//EN"
    "http://www.w3.org/TR/xhtml11/DTD/xhtml11.dtd">
```

Another big difference between XHTML 1.1 and XHTML 1.0 goes beyond the support offered for various elements and attributes. XHTML is designed to be *modular*. In practice, that means that the XHTML 1.1 DTD is actually relatively short. It's a *driver* DTD, which inserts various other DTDs as modules. The benefit of modular DTDs is that you can omit the modules that your application doesn't support.

For example, if you're supporting XHTML 1.1 on a nonstandard device such as a PDA or even a cell phone or pager (the W3C has all kinds of big ideas for the future), you might not be able to support everything, such as tables or hyperlinks. With XHTML 1.1, all you need to do is omit the DTD modules corresponding to tables and hyperlinks (several modules are marked as required in the XHTML 1.1 DTD, and those cannot be omitted).

XHTML Version 2.0

There's growth coming up in the future, too: The W3C has just released a working draft for XHTML 2.0, and you can find it at www.w3.org/TR/xhtml2/. Here's what the W3C says about this new version:

> XHTML 2.0 is a next generation markup language, intended for rich, portable web-based applications. Note that while the ancestry of XHTML 2 comes from HTML 4, XHTML 1.0, and XHTML 1.1, it is not intended to be backward compatible with its earlier versions. Also, this first draft does not include the implementations of XHTML 2.0 in either DTD or XML Schema form yet.

XHTML 2.0 is module-based, and although the W3C indicates that there will be changes from earlier versions of XHTML, the XHTL 2.0 working draft is very sketchy on what these changes will be. A number of elements, such as <br> and <img>, will be deprecated. Other elements will get new attributes— the href attribute will be added to most visible elements to let them act as hyperlinks. And there will be some new elements, such as the <nl> element, which is used to define collections of selectable items.

The working draft is studded with "To Do" notes on items to be added and filled out in the future—this specification is still in rough outline form. Obviously, there's more to come here. We'll see more on XHTML 2.0 in the next chapter.

XHTML Basic

There's another version of XHTML, which is also in recommendation status: XHTML Basic. XHTML Basic is a very small subset of XHTML, reduced to the bare minimum so that it can be supported by devices considerably simpler than standard PCs. You can find the XHTML Basic recommendation at www.w3.org/TR/xhtml-basic.

If you want to use XML Basic, here's the <!DOCTYPE> element you should use:

```
<!DOCTYPE html PUBLIC "-//W3C//DTD XHTML Basic 1.0//EN"
    "http://www.w3.org/TR/xhtml-basic/xhtml-basic10.dtd">
```

XHTML Checklist

The W3C has a number of requirements for documents before they can be called true XHTML documents. Here's the list of requirements that documents must meet:

- The document must successfully validate against one of the W3C XHTML DTDs.

- The document element must be `<html>`.

- The document element, `<html>`, must set an XML namespace for the document, using the `xmlns` attribute. This namespace must be `"http://www.w3.org/1999/xhtml"`.

- There must be a `<!DOCTYPE>` element, and it must appear before the document element.

XHTML is designed to be displayed in today's browsers, and it works well (largely because those browsers ignore elements that they don't understand, such as `<?xml?>` and `<!DOCTYPE>`). However, because XHTML is also XML, there are a number of differences between legal HTML and legal XHTML.

Differences Between XHTML and HTML

As you know, XML is more particular about many aspects of writing documents than HTML is. For example, you need to place all attribute values in quotation marks in XML, although HTML documents can use unquoted values because HTML browsers will accept that. One of the problems the W3C is trying to solve with XHTML, in fact, is the thicket of nonstandard HTML that's out there on the Web, mostly because browsers support it. Some observers estimate that half of the code in browsers is there to handle nonstandard use of HTML, and that discourages any but the largest companies from creating HTML browsers. XHTML is supposed to be different: If a document isn't in perfect XHTML, the browser is supposed to quit loading it and display an error, *not* guess what the document author was trying to do. Hopefully, that'll make it easier to write XHTML browsers.

Here are some of the major differences between HTML and XHTML:

- XHTML documents must be well-formed XML documents.

- Element and attribute names must be in lowercase.

- Non-empty elements need end tags; end tags can't be omitted as they can sometimes in HTML.

- Attribute values must always be quoted.

- You cannot use "standalone" attributes that are not assigned values. If need be, assign a dummy value to an attribute, as in `action = "action"`.

- Empty elements must end with the `/>` characters. In practice, this does not seem to be a problem for the major browsers, which is a lucky thing for XHTML because it's definitely not standard HTML.

- The `<a>` element cannot contain other `<a>` elements.

- The `<pre>` element cannot contain the `<img>`, `<object>`, `<big>`, `<small>`, `<sub>`, or `<sup>` elements.

- The `<button>` element cannot contain the `<input>`, `<select>`, `<textarea>`, `<label>`, `<button>`, `<form>`, `<fieldset>`, `<iframe>`, or `<isindex>` elements.

- The `<label>` element cannot contain other `<label>` elements.

- The `<form>` element cannot contain other `<form>` elements.

- You must use the `id` attribute and not the `name` attribute, even for elements that have also had a `name` attribute. In XHTML 1.0, the name attribute of the `<a>`, `<applet>`, `<form>`, `<frame>`, `<iframe>`, `<img>`, and `<map>` elements is formally deprecated. In practice, this is a little difficult in browsers such as Netscape Navigator, which support `name` and not `id`; in that case, you should both attributes in the same element (even though it's not legal XHTML).

- You must escape sensitive characters. For example, when an attribute value contains an ampersand (`&`), the ampersand must be expressed as a character entity reference, as `&amp;`.

As we'll see in the next chapter, there are some additional requirements. For example, if you use the `<` character in your scripts, you should either escape it as `&lt;` or, if the browser can't handle that, place the script in an external file (the W3C's suggestion of placing scripts in CDATA sections is definitely not understood by any major browser today).

Automatic Conversion from HTML to XHTML

You may already have a huge Web site full of HTML pages, and you might be reading all this with some trepidation. How are you going to convert all those pages to the far more strict XHTML? In fact, there's a utility out there that can do it for you: the Tidy utility, created by Dave Raggett. This utility is available for a wide variety of platforms, and you can download it for free from `http://tidy.sourceforge.net/`. There's also a complete set of instructions on that page. (Other options include the HTML Kit at `http://www.chami.com/html-kit/.`)

Here's an example: I'll use Tidy in Windows to convert a file from HTML to XHTML. In this case, I'll use the example HTML file we developed earlier, as saved in a file named ch16_01.html:

```
<HTML>
    <HEAD>
        <TITLE>
            Welcome to my page
        </TITLE>
    </HEAD>

    <BODY>
        <H1>
            Welcome to XHTML!
        </H1>
    </BODY>
</HTML>
```

After downloading Tidy, you run it at the command prompt. Here are the command-line switches, or options, you can use with Tidy:

- `-config` *file*—Uses the configuration file named *file*
- `-indent` *or* `-i`—Indents element content
- `-omit` *or* `-o`—Omits optional end tags
- `-wrap 72`—Wraps text at column 72 (default is 68)
- `-upper` *or* `-u`—Forces tags to upper case (default is lowercase)
- `-clean` *or* `-c`—Replaces `font`, `nobr`, `&amp;`, and `center` tags, by Cascading Style Sheets (CSS)
- `-raw`—Doesn't substitute entities for characters 128 to 255
- `-ascii`—Uses ASCII for output, Latin-1 for input

- -latin1—Uses Latin-1 for both input and output
- -utf8—Uses UTF-8 for both input and output
- -iso2022—Uses ISO2022 for both input and output
- -numeric *or* -n—Outputs numeric rather than named entities
- -modify *or* -m—Modifies original files
- -errors *or* -e—Shows only error messages
- -quiet *or* -q—Suppresses nonessential output
- -f file—Writes errors to file
- -xml—Use this when input is in XML
- -asxml—Converts HTML to XML
- -slides—Bursts into slides on h2 elements
- -help—Lists command-line options
- -version—Shows release date

In this example, I'll use three switches: -m to indicate that I want Tidy to modify the file I pass to it, which will be index.html; -i to indicate that I want it to indent the resulting XHTML elements; and -config to indicate that I want to use a configuration file named config.txt. Here's how I use Tidy from the command line:

```
%tidy -m -i -config ch16_02.txt ch16_01.html
```

Tidy is actually a utility that cleans up HTML, as you might gather from its name. To make it create XHTML, you have to use a configuration file, which I've named ch16_02.txt here. You can see all the configuration file options on the Tidy Web site. Here are the contents of ch16_02.txt, which I'll use to convert ch16_01.html to XHTML:

Listing ch16_03.txt

```
output-xhtml: yes
add-xml-pi: yes
doctype: loose
```

Here, output-xhtml indicates that I want Tidy to create XHTML output. Using add-xml-pi indicates that the output should also include an XML declaration, and doctype: loose means that I want to use the transitional

XHTML DTD. If you don't specify what DTD to use, Tidy will guess, based on your HTML.

Here's the resulting XHTML document:

```
<?xml version="1.0"?>
<!DOCTYPE html PUBLIC "-//W3C//DTD XHTML 1.0 Transitional//EN"
    "http://www.w3.org/TR/xhtml1/DTD/xhtml1-transitional.dtd">

<html xmlns="http://www.w3.org/1999/xhtml">
  <head>
    <meta name="generator" content="HTML Tidy, see www.w3.org" />

    <title>Welcome to my page</title>
  </head>

  <body>
    <h1> Welcome to XHTML!</h1>
  </body>
</html>
```

You can even teach Tidy about new XHTML tags that you've added. If you're ever stuck and want a quick way of translating HTML into XHTML, check out Tidy; it's fast, it's effective, and it's free.

Validating Your XHTML Document

The W3C has a validator that you can use to check the validity of your XHTML document, and you can find this validator at http://validator.w3.org. To use the XHTML validator, you just enter the URI of your document and click the Validate This Page button. The W3C validator will check the document and give you a full report. Here's an example response:

```
Congratulations, this document validates as XHTML1.0 Transitional!
To show your readers that you have taken the care to create an
interoperable Web page, you may display this icon on any page that
validates. Here is the HTML you could use to add this icon to your
Web page:
  <p>
    <a href="http://validator.w3.org/check/referer"><img
        src="http://validator.w3.org/images/vxhtml10"
        alt="Valid XHTML 1.0!" height="31" width="88" /></a>
  </p>
```

In this case, the document I tested validated properly, and the W3C validator says I can add the official W3C XHTML 1.0 Transitional logo to the document. That logo appears in Figure 16-2.

Figure 16-2
The W3C
transitional
XHTML logo.

Actually, the W3C XHTML validator does not do a complete job: It doesn't check to see whether values are supplied for required attributes, for example, or make sure that child elements are allowed to be nested inside the particular type of their parents. However, it does a reasonably good job.

In the remainder of this chapter, I'm going to get to the actual XHTML programming, starting with the document element, `<html>`.

< html >—The Document Element

This element is supported in XHTML 1.0 Strict, XHTML 1.0 Transitional, XHTML 1.0 Frameset, and XHTML 1.1. Here are its attributes:

- `dir`—Sets the direction of text that doesn't have an inherent direction in which you should read it, called directionally neutral text. You can set this attribute to `LTR`, for left-to-right text, or `RTL`, for right-to-left text. (XHTML 1.0 Strict, XHTML 1.0 Transitional, XHTML 1.0 Frameset, XHTML 1.1.)

- `lang`—Specifies the base language used in the element. This applies only when the document is interpreted as HTML. (XHTML 1.0 Strict, XHTML 1.0 Transitional, XHTML 1.0 Frameset, XHTML 1.1.)

- `xml:lang`—Specifies the base language for the element when the document is interpreted as XML. (XHTML 1.0 Strict, XHTML 1.0 Transitional, XHTML 1.0 Frameset, XHTML 1.1.)

- `xmlns`—Required. Set this attribute to `http://www.w3.org/1999/ xhtml`. (XHTML 1.0 Strict, XHTML 1.0 Transitional, XHTML 1.0 Frameset, XHTML 1.1.)

The document element for all XHTML elements is `<html>`, which is how XHTML matched the `<HTML>` element in HTML documents. This element must contain all the content of the document, as in this example:

```
<?xml version="1.0"?>
<!DOCTYPE html PUBLIC "-//W3C//DTD XHTML 1.0 Transitional//EN"
"http://www.w3.org/TR/xhtml1/DTD/xhtml1-transitional.dtd">
<html xmlns="http://www.w3.org/1999/xhtml" xml:lang="en" lang="en">
    <head>
        <title>
```

```
            Welcome to my page
        </title>
    </head>

    <body>
        <h1>
            Welcome to XHTML!
        </h1>
    </body>
</html>
```

The document element is very important in XML documents, of course. Note that this is one of the big differences between XHTML and HTML: In HTML, the <HTML> tag is optional because it's the default. To be valid XHTML, a document must have a <html> element.

Of all the attributes of this element, only one is required: xmlns, which sets the XML namespace. Most XML applications set up their own namespace to avoid overlap, and XHTML is no exception; you must set the xmlns attribute to "http://www.w3.org/1999/xhtml" in XHTML documents.

This tag also supports the lang and xml:lang attributes to let you specify the language of the document. If you specify values for both these attributes, the xml:lang attribute takes precedence in XHTML.

In XHTML, the <html> element can contain a <head> and a <body> element (or a <head> and <frameset> element in the XHTML 1.0 Frameset document).

< head >—Creating a Web Page's Head

The <head> element contains the head of an XHTML document, which should contain at least a <title> element. The <head> element is supported in XHTML 1.0 Strict, XHTML 1.0 Transitional, XHTML 1.0 Frameset, and XHTML 1.1. Here are the attributes of this element:

- dir—Sets the direction of text that doesn't have an inherent direction in which you should read it, called directionally neutral text. You can set this attribute to LTR, for left-to-right text, or RTL, for right-to-left text. (XHTML 1.0 Strict, XHTML 1.0 Transitional, XHTML 1.0 Frameset, XHTML 1.1.)

- lang—Specifies the base language used in the element. This applies only when the document is interpreted as HTML. (XHTML 1.0 Strict, XHTML 1.0 Transitional, XHTML 1.0 Frameset, XHTML 1.1.)

- profile—Specifies the location of one or more whitespace-separated metadata profile URIs. (XHTML 1.0 Strict, XHTML 1.0 Transitional, XHTML 1.0 Frameset, XHTML 1.1.)

- xml:lang—Specifies the base language for the element when the document is interpreted as an XML document. (XHTML 1.0 Strict, XHTML 1.0 Transitional, XHTML 1.0 Frameset, XHTML 1.1.)

Each XHTML document should have a <head> element, like the one in this example:

```
<?xml version="1.0"?>
<!DOCTYPE html PUBLIC "-//W3C//DTD XHTML 1.0 Transitional//EN"
"http://www.w3.org/TR/xhtml1/DTD/xhtml1-transitional.dtd">
<html xmlns="http://www.w3.org/1999/xhtml" xml:lang="en" lang="en">
    <head>
        <title>
            Welcome to my page
        </title>
    </head>

    <body>
        <h1>
            Welcome to XHTML!
        </h1>
    </body>
</html>
```

The head of an XHTML document holds information that isn't directly displayed in the document itself, such as a title for the document (which usually appears in the browser's title bar), keywords that search engines can pick up, the base address for URIs, and so on. The head of every XHTML document is supposed to contain a <title> element, which holds the title of the document.

This element also supports the usual attributes, such as lang and xml:lang, as well as one attribute that is specific to <head> elements: profile. The profile attribute can hold a whitespace-separated list of URIs that hold information about the document, such as a description of the document, the author's name, copyright information, and so forth. (None of the major browsers implements this attribute yet.)

Here are the elements that can appear in the head:

- <base>—Specifies the base URI for the document

- <isindex>—Supports rudimentary input control

- `<link>`—Specifies the relationship between the document and an external object
- `<meta>`—Contains information about the document
- `<noscript>`—Contains text that appears only if the browser does not support the `<script>` tag
- `<object>`—Embeds an object
- `<script>`—Contains programming scripts, such as JavaScript code
- `<style>`—Contains style information used for rendering elements
- `<title>`—Contains the document's title, which appears in the browser

As mentioned, each `<head>` element should contain exactly one `<title>` element.

< title >–The Document's Title

As in HTML, the `<title>` element contains a title for the document, stored as simple text. Most browsers will read the document's title and display it in the title bar. The title of a document is also used by search engines. This element is supported in XHTML 1.0 Strict, XHTML 1.0 Transitional, XHTML 1.0 Frameset, and XHTML 1.1. Here are the attributes for this element:

- `dir`—Sets the direction of text that doesn't have an inherent direction in which you should read it, called directionally neutral text. You can set this attribute to `LTR`, for left-to-right text, or `RTL`, for right-to-left text. (XHTML 1.0 Strict, XHTML 1.0 Transitional, XHTML 1.0 Frameset, XHTML 1.1.)
- `lang`—Specifies the base language used in the element. This applies only when the document is interpreted as HTML. (XHTML 1.0 Strict, XHTML 1.0 Transitional, XHTML 1.0 Frameset, XHTML 1.1.)
- `xml:lang`—Specifies the base language for the element when the document is interpreted as an XML document. (XHTML 1.0 Strict, XHTML 1.0 Transitional, XHTML 1.0 Frameset, XHTML 1.1.)

You use the `<title>` element to specify the document's title to browsers and search engines; browsers usually display the title in the title bar. The W3C XHTML DTDs say, "Exactly one title is required per document." However, the W3C XHTML validator doesn't complain if you omit a title. Nonetheless, you should put a `<title>` element in every document.

We saw an example `<title>` element at the beginning of this chapter:

```
<?xml version="1.0"?>
<!DOCTYPE html PUBLIC "-//W3C//DTD XHTML 1.0 Transitional//EN"
"http://www.w3.org/TR/xhtml1/DTD/xhtml1-transitional.dtd">
<html xmlns="http://www.w3.org/1999/xhtml" xml:lang="en" lang="en">
    <head>
        <title>
            Welcome to my page
        </title>
    </head>

    <body>
        <h1>
            Welcome to XHTML!
        </h1>
    </body>
</html>
```

No major browser will react badly if you don't give a document a title. However, XHTML documents should have one, according to the W3C.

We've completed the head section of XHTML documents; next comes the body.

< body >—The Document's Body

The document's body is where the action is—the content that the document is designed to contain, that is. The `<body>` element is supported in XHTML 1.0 Strict, XHTML 1.0 Transitional, and XHTML 1.1. Here are this element's attributes:

- `alink`—Deprecated in HTML 4.0 (you use styles instead now). Sets the color of hyperlinks when they're being activated. (XHTML 1.0 Transitional, XHTML 1.0 Frameset.)

- `background`—Deprecated in HTML 4.0. Holds the URI of an image to be used in tiling the browser's background. (XHTML 1.0 Transitional, XHTML 1.0 Frameset.)

- `bgcolor`—Deprecated in HTML 4.0 (you use styles instead now). Sets the color of the browser's background. (XHTML 1.0 Transitional, XHTML 1.0 Frameset.)

- `class`—Gives the style class of the element. (XHTML 1.0 Strict, XHTML 1.0 Transitional, XHTML 1.0 Frameset, XHTML 1.1.)

- `dir`—Sets the direction of text that doesn't have an inherent direction in which you should read it, called directionally neutral text. You can set this attribute to `LTR`, for left-to-right text, or `RTL`, for right-to-left text. (XHTML 1.0 Strict, XHTML 1.0 Transitional, XHTML 1.0 Frameset, XHTML 1.1.)

- `id`—Refers to the element; set this attribute to a unique identifier. (XHTML 1.0 Strict, XHTML 1.0 Transitional, XHTML 1.0 Frameset, XHTML 1.1.)

- `lang`—Specifies the base language used in the element. Applies only when the document is interpreted as HTML. (XHTML 1.0 Strict, XHTML 1.0 Transitional, XHTML 1.0 Frameset, XHTML 1.1.)

- `link`—Deprecated in HTML 4.0 (you use styles now). Sets the color of hyperlinks that have not yet been visited. (XHTML 1.0 Transitional, XHTML 1.0 Frameset.)

- `style`—Set to an inline style to specify how the browser should display the element. (XHTML 1.0 Strict, XHTML 1.0 Transitional, XHTML 1.0 Frameset, XHTML 1.1.)

- `text`—Deprecated in HTML 4.0. Sets the color of the text in the document. (XHTML 1.0 Transitional, XHTML 1.0 Frameset.)

- `title`—Contains the title of the body (which might be displayed in ToolTips). (XHTML 1.0 Strict, XHTML 1.0 Transitional, XHTML 1.0 Frameset, XHTML 1.1.)

- `vlink`—Deprecated in HTML 4.0 (you use styles instead now). Sets the color of hyperlinks that have been visited already. (XHTML 1.0 Transitional, XHTML 1.0 Frameset.)

- `xml:lang`—Specifies the base language for the element when the document is interpreted as an XML document. (XHTML 1.0 Strict, XHTML 1.0 Transitional, XHTML 1.0 Frameset, XHTML 1.1.)

This element also supports these events in XHTML: `onclick`, `ondblclick`, `onload`, `onmousedown`, `onmouseup`, `onmouseover`, `onmousemove`, `onmouseout`, `onkeypress`, `onkeydown`, `onkeyup`, and `onunload`. You can use scripts such as JavaScript with events like these; I'll take a look at how in the next chapter.

If you place descriptions of your document in the `<head>` element, you place the actual content of the document in the `<body>` element—unless you're sectioning your page into frames, in which case you should use the `<frameset>` element instead of the `<body>` element.

We've already seen a simple example in which the content of a page is just an <h1> heading, like this:

```
<?xml version="1.0"?>
<!DOCTYPE html PUBLIC "-//W3C//DTD XHTML 1.0 Transitional//EN"
"http://www.w3.org/TR/xhtml1/DTD/xhtml1-transitional.dtd">
<html xmlns="http://www.w3.org/1999/xhtml" xml:lang="en" lang="en">
    <head>
        <title>
            Welcome to my page
        </title>
    </head>

    <body>
        <h1>
            Welcome to XHTML!
        </h1>
    </body>
</html>
```

If you've written HTML, you may be startled to discover that many cherished attributes are now considered deprecated in XHTML, which means they're omitted from XHTML 1.0 Strict and XHTML 1.1. Deprecated attributes of the <body> element include these:

- alink
- background
- bgcolor
- link
- text
- vlink

Instead of using these attributes, you're now supposed to use stylesheets. Here's an example showing how to replace deprecated attributes. In this case, I'll set the browser's background to white, the color of displayed text to black, the color of hyperlinks (created with the <a> element, which I'll take a look at in the next chapter) to red, the color of activated links to blue, and the color of visited links to green, all using deprecated attributes of the <body> element:

Listing ch16_04.html

```
<?xml version="1.0"?>
<!DOCTYPE html PUBLIC "-//W3C//DTD XHTML 1.0 Transitional//EN"
"http://www.w3.org/TR/xhtml1/DTD/xhtml1-transitional.dtd">
<html xmlns="http://www.w3.org/1999/xhtml" xml:lang="en" lang="en">
    <head>
        <title>
            Welcome to my page
        </title>
    </head>
    <body bgcolor="white" text="black" link="red" alink="blue"
        vlink="green">
        Welcome to my XHTML document.
        Want to check out more about XHTML?
        Go to
        <a href="http://www.w3c.org">W3C</a>.
    </body>
</html>
```

You can see this document displayed in Netscape Navigator in Figure 16-3. It works as it should, but it's not strict XHTML.

Figure 16-3
Displaying a hyperlink in Netscape Navigator.

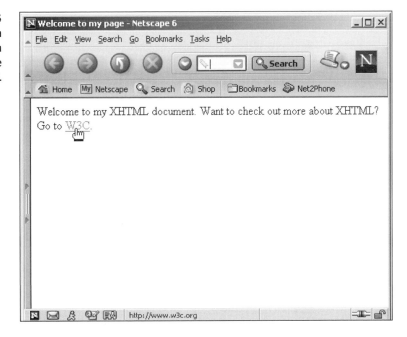

To make the same page adhere to the XHTML strict standard, you use stylesheets. Here's how this page looks using a `<style>` element to set up the same colors (I'll take a look at the `<style>` element more closely in the next chapter):

Listing ch16_05.html

```
<?xml version="1.0"?>
<!DOCTYPE html PUBLIC "-//W3C//DTD XHTML 1.0 Transitional//EN"
"http://www.w3.org/TR/xhtml1/DTD/xhtml1-transitional.dtd">
<html xmlns="http://www.w3.org/1999/xhtml" xml:lang="en" lang="en">
    <head>
        <title>
            Welcome to my page
        </title>
        <style type="text/css">
            body {background: white; color: black}
            a:link {color: red}
            a:visited {color: green}
            a:active {color: blue}
        </style>
    </head>

    <body>
        Welcome to my XHTML document.
        Want to check out more about XHTML?
        Go to
        <a href="http://www.w3c.org">W3C</a>.
    </body>
</html>
```

In this case, I'm using CSS to style this document. To separate content from markup, W3C is relying on stylesheets a great deal these days. However, note that the contents of a `<style>` element are still part of the XHTML document, which means that if you use sensitive characters such as & or < in it, you should either escape those characters or use an external stylesheet. I'll take a look at external stylesheets in the next chapter.

`<!- ->` Comments

Because XHTML documents are actually XML, they support XML comments, which you can use to annotate your document. These annotations will not be displayed by the browser. XHTML comments are supported in XHTML 1.0 Strict, XHTML 1.0 Transitional, XHTML 1.0 Frameset, and XHTML 1.1. Comments have no attributes.

We're familiar with comments from XML; you enclose the text in a comment like this: `<!--This page was last updated July 3.-->`. Using comments, you can describe to readers what's going on in your document.

Here's how I might add comments to an XHTML document:

```
<?xml version="1.0"?>
<!DOCTYPE html PUBLIC "-//W3C//DTD XHTML 1.0 Transitional//EN"
"http://www.w3.org/TR/xhtml1/DTD/xhtml1-transitional.dtd">
<html xmlns="http://www.w3.org/1999/xhtml" xml:lang="en" lang="en">
    <!-- This is the document head -->
    <head>
        <!-- This is the document title -->
        <title>
            Welcome to my page
        </title>
    </head>

    <!-- This is the document body element -->
    <body>
        <h1>
            <!-- This is an h1 heading element -->
            Welcome to XHTML!
        </h1>
    </body>
</html>
```

As with any XML documents, the comments are supposed to be stripped out by the XML processor that reads the document. On the other hand, keep in mind that comments are text; if you have a lot of them in a lengthy document, you can increase the download time of your document significantly.

Headings: *<h1>* Through *<h6>*

You use the <h1> through <h6> elements to create headings in your documents. These are the familiar headings from HTML: <h1> creates the largest text and <h6> produces the smallest. These elements are supported in 1.0 Strict, 1.0 Transitional, 1.0 Frameset, and XHTML 1.1. Here are the possible attributes of these elements and which versions of XHTML support them:

- align—Gives the alignment of text in the heading. The possible values are left (the default), center, right, and justify. (XHTML 1.0 Transitional, XHTML 1.0 Frameset.)

- class—Gives the style class of the element. (XHTML 1.0 Strict, XHTML 1.0 Transitional, XHTML 1.0 Frameset, XHTML 1.1.)

- `dir`—Sets the direction of text that doesn't have an inherent direction in which you should read it, called directionally neutral text. You can set this attribute to `LTR`, for left-to-right text, or `RTL`, for right-to-left text. (XHTML 1.0 Strict, XHTML 1.0 Transitional, XHTML 1.0 Frameset, XHTML 1.1.)

- `id`—Refers to the element; set this attribute to a unique identifier. (XHTML 1.0 Strict, XHTML 1.0 Transitional, XHTML 1.0 Frameset, XHTML 1.1.)

- `lang`—Specifies the base language used in the element. Applies only when the document is interpreted as HTML. (XHTML 1.0 Strict, XHTML 1.0 Transitional, XHTML 1.0 Frameset, XHTML 1.1.)

- `style`—Set to an inline style to specify how the browser should display the element. (XHTML 1.0 Strict, XHTML 1.0 Transitional, XHTML 1.0 Frameset, XHTML 1.1.)

- `title`—Contains the title of the element (which might be displayed in ToolTips). (XHTML 1.0 Strict, XHTML 1.0 Transitional, XHTML 1.0 Frameset, XHTML 1.1.)

- `xml:lang`—Specifies the base language for the element when the document is interpreted as an XML document. (XHTML 1.0 Strict, XHTML 1.0 Transitional, XHTML 1.0 Frameset, XHTML 1.1.)

These elements also support these events in XHTML: `onclick`, `ondblclick`, `onmousedown`, `onmouseup`, `onmouseover`, `onmousemove`, `onmouseout`, `onkeypress`, `onkeydown`, and `onkeyup`.

Headings act much like headlines in newspapers. They are block elements that present text in bold and often are larger than other text. There are six heading tags: `<h1>`, `<h2>`, `<h3>`, `<h4>`, `<h5>`, and `<h6>`. `<h1>` creates the largest text, and `<h6>` creates the smallest. Because headings are block elements, they get their own line in a displayed XHTML document.

Here's an example that shows these headings in action:

Listing ch16_06.html

```
<?xml version="1.0"?>
<!DOCTYPE html PUBLIC "-//W3C//DTD XHTML 1.0 Transitional//EN"
"http://www.w3.org/TR/xhtml1/DTD/xhtml1-transitional.dtd">
<html xmlns="http://www.w3.org/1999/xhtml" xml:lang="en" lang="en">
    <head>
        <title>
```

```
        The &lt;h1&gt; - &lt;h6&gt; Elements
    </title>
</head>

<body>
    <center>
        <h1>This is an &lt;h1&gt; heading</h1>
        <h2>This is an &lt;h2&gt; heading</h2>
        <h3>This is an &lt;h3&gt; heading</h3>
        <h4>This is an &lt;h4&gt; heading</h4>
        <h5>This is an &lt;h5&gt; heading</h5>
        <h6>This is an &lt;h6&gt; heading</h6>
    </center>
</body>
</html>
```

You can see this XHTML displayed in Netscape Navigator in Figure 16-4. Headings such as these help break up the text in a page, just as they do in newspapers, and they make the structure of your document stand out.

Figure 16-4
Displaying the six levels of headings in Netscape Navigator.

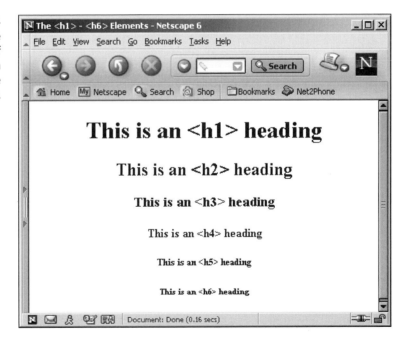

Text Handling

Displaying simple text works the same way in XHTML as it does in HTML: You just place the text directly in a document. XHTML elements that display text have mixed-content models, so they can contain both text and other elements, as in this example we saw earlier:

```
<?xml version="1.0"?>
<!DOCTYPE html PUBLIC "-//W3C//DTD XHTML 1.0 Transitional//EN"
"http://www.w3.org/TR/xhtml1/DTD/xhtml1-transitional.dtd">
<html xmlns="http://www.w3.org/1999/xhtml" xml:lang="en" lang="en">
    <head>
        <title>
            Welcome to my page
        </title>
    </head>
    <body bgcolor="white" text="black" link="red" alink="blue"
        vlink="green">
        Welcome to my XHTML document.
        Want to check out more about XHTML?
        Go to
        <a href="http://www.w3c.org">W3C</a>.
    </body>
</html>
```

The text in this document is displayed directly in the browser, as you see in Figure 16-3. It's up to you to format the text the way you want it. In early versions of HTML, you used elements such as <b> (bold), <i> (italics), and <u> (underline) to format text; as formatting has become more sophisticated, though, the emphasis has switched to using stylesheets.

As you know, XML has five predefined entity references, and they stand for characters that can be interpreted as markup or other control characters:

- & becomes the & character.
- ' becomes the ' character.
- > becomes the > character.
- < becomes the < character.
- " becomes the " character.

A great many more character entities exist in HTML 4.0, and they're supported in XHTML as well. You can find them in Table 16-1.

Table 16-1	Entity	Numerical	Does This
Character Entities in XHTML (Support Varies by Browser)	Aacute	&#193;	Latin capital letter *A* with acute accent
	aacute	&#225;	Latin small letter *a* with acute accent
	Acirc	&#194;	Latin capital letter *A* with circumflex
	acirc	&#226;	Latin small letter *a* with circumflex
	acute	&#180;	Acute accent
	AElig	&#198;	Latin capital letter *AE*
	aelig	&#230;	Latin small letter *ae*
	Agrave	&#192;	Latin capital letter *A* with grave accent
	agrave	&#224;	Latin small letter *a* with grave accent
	alefsym	&#8501;	Alef symbol; first transfinite cardinal
	Alpha	&#913;	Greek capital letter alpha
	alpha	&#945;	Greek small letter alpha
	amp	&#38;	Ampersand
	and	&#8743;	Logical and
	ang	&#8736;	Angle
	Aring	&#197;	Latin capital letter *A* with ring above
	aring	&#229;	Latin small letter *a* with ring above
	asymp	&#8776;	Almost equal to; asymptotic to
	Atilde	&#195;	Latin capital letter *A* with tilde
	atilde	&#227;	Latin small letter *a* with tilde
	Auml	&#196;	Latin capital letter *A* with dieresis (umlaut)
	auml	&#228;	Latin small letter *a* with dieresis (umlaut)
	bdquo	&#8222;	Double low-9 quotation mark
	Beta	&#914;	Greek capital letter beta

continues

Entity	Numerical	Does This
beta	β	Greek small letter beta
brvbar	¦	Broken bar; broken vertical bar
bull	•	Bullet; black small circle
cap	∩	Intersection; cap
Ccedil	Ç	Latin capital letter *C* with cedilla
ccedil	ç	Latin small letter *c* with cedilla
cedil	¸	Cedilla
cent	¢	Cent sign
Chi	Χ	Greek capital letter chi
chi	χ	Greek small letter chi
circ	ˆ	Modifier letter circumflex accent
clubs	♣	Black club suit; shamrock
cong	≅	Approximately equal to
copy	©	Copyright sign
crarr	↵	Downward arrow with corner leftward
cup	∪	Union; cup
curren	¤	Currency sign
Dagger	‡	Double dagger
dagger	†	Dagger
darr	↓	Downward arrow
dArr	⇓	Downward double arrow
deg	°	Degree sign
Delta	Δ	Greek capital letter delta
delta	δ	Greek small letter delta
diams	♦	Black diamond suit

Entity	Numerical	Does This
divide	÷	Division sign
Eacute	É	Latin capital letter *E* with acute accent
eacute	é	Latin small letter *e* with acute accent
Ecirc	Ê	Latin capital letter *E* with circumflex
ecirc	ê	Latin small letter *e* with circumflex
Egrave	È	Latin capital letter *E* with grave accent
egrave	è	Latin small letter *e* with grave accent
empty	∅	Empty set; null set; diameter
emsp		Em space
ensp		En space
Epsilon	Ε	Greek capital letter epsilon
epsilon	ε	Greek small letter epsilon
equiv	≡	Identical to
Eta	Η	Greek capital letter eta
eta	η	Greek small letter eta
ETH	Ð	Latin capital letter ETH
eth	ð	Latin small letter eth
Euml	Ë	Latin capital letter *E* with dieresis (umlaut)
euml	ë	Latin small letter *e* with dieresis (umlaut)
euro	€	Euro sign
exist	∃	There exists
fnof	ƒ	Latin small *f* with hook; function
forall	∀	For all
frac12	½	Vulgar fraction one half

continues

Entity	Numerical	Does This
frac14	¼	Vulgar fraction one quarter
frac34	¾	Vulgar fraction three quarters
frasl	⁄	Fraction slash
Gamma	Γ	Greek capital letter gamma
gamma	γ	Greek small letter gamma
ge	≥	Greater than or equal to
gt	>	Greater-than sign
hArr	⇔	Left/right double arrow
harr	↔	Left/right arrow
hearts	♥	Black heart suit; valentine
hellip	…	Horizontal ellipsis; three-dot leader
Iacute	Í	Latin capital letter *I* with acute accent
iacute	í	Latin small letter *i* with acute accent
Icirc	Î	Latin capital letter *I* with circumflex
icirc	î	Latin small letter *i* with circumflex
iexcl	¡	Inverted exclamation mark
Igrave	Ì	Latin capital letter *I* with grave accent
igrave	ì	Latin small letter *i* with grave accent
image	ℑ	Blackletter capital *I*; imaginary part
infin	∞	Infinity
int	∫	Integral
Iota	Ι	Greek capital letter iota
iota	ι	Greek small letter iota
iquest	¿	Inverted question mark

Entity	Numerical	Does This
isin	&#8712;	Element of
Iuml	&#207;	Latin capital letter *I* with dieresis (umlaut)
iuml	&#239;	Latin small letter *i* with dieresis (umlaut)
Kappa	&#922;	Greek capital letter kappa
kappa	&#954;	Greek small letter kappa
Lambda	&#923;	Greek capital letter lambda
lambda	&#955;	Greek small letter lambda
lang	&#9001;	Left-pointing angle bracket; bra
laquo	&#171;	Left-pointing double-angle quotation mark
lArr	&#8656;	Leftward double arrow
larr	&#8592;	Leftward arrow
lceil	&#8968;	Left ceiling; apl upstile
ldquo	&#8220;	Left double quotation mark
le	&#8804;	Less than or equal to
lfloor	&#8970;	Left floor; apl downstile
lowast	&#8727;	Asterisk operator
loz	&#9674;	Lozenge
lrm	&#8206;	Left-to-right mark
lsaquo	&#8249;	Single left-pointing angle quotation mark
lsquo	&#8216;	Left single quotation mark
lt	&#60;	Less-than sign
macr	&#175;	Macron; spacing macron
mdash	&#8212;	Em dash

continues

Entity	Numerical Does This	
micro	`&#181;`	Micro sign
middot	`&#183;`	Middle dot
minus	`&#8722;`	Minus sign
Mu	`&#924;`	Greek capital letter mu
mu	`&#956;`	Greek small letter mu
nabla	`&#8711;`	Nabla; backward difference
nbsp	` `	No-break space; nonbreaking space
ndash	`&#8211;`	En dash
ne	`&#8800;`	Not equal to
ni	`&#8715;`	Contains as member
not	`&#172;`	Not sign
notin	`&#8713;`	Not an element of
nsub	`&#8836;`	Not a subset of
Ntilde	`&#209;`	Latin capital letter *N* with tilde
ntilde	`&#241;`	Latin small letter *n* with tilde
Nu	`&#925;`	Greek capital letter nu
nu	`&#957;`	Greek small letter nu
Oacute	`&#211;`	Latin capital letter *O* with acute accent
oacute	`&#243;`	Latin small letter *o* with acute accent
Ocirc	`&#212;`	Latin capital letter *O* with circumflex
ocirc	`&#244;`	Latin small letter *o* with circumflex
OElig	`&#338;`	Latin capital ligature *OE*
oelig	`&#339;`	Latin small ligature *oe*
Ograve	`&#210;`	Latin capital letter *O* with grave accent

Entity	Numerical Does This	
ograve	&#242;	Latin small letter *o* with grave accent
oline	&#8254;	Overline; spacing overscore
Omega	&#937;	Greek capital letter omega
omega	&#969;	Greek small letter omega
Omicron	&#927;	Greek capital letter omicron
omicron	&#959;	Greek small letter omicron
oplus	&#8853;	Circled plus; direct sum
or	&#8744;	Logical or; vee
ordf	&#170;	Feminine ordinal indicator
ordm	&#186;	Masculine ordinal indicator
Oslash	&#216;	Latin capital letter *O* with stroke
oslash	&#248;	Latin small letter *o* with stroke
Otilde	&#213;	Latin capital letter *O* with tilde
otilde	&#245;	Latin small letter *o* with tilde
otimes	&#8855;	Circled times; vector product
Ouml	&#214;	Latin capital letter *O* with dieresis (umlaut)
ouml	&#246;	Latin small letter *o* with dieresis (umlaut)
para	&#182;	Pilcrow sign
part	&#8706;	Partial differential
permil	&#8240;	Per mille sign
perp	&#8869;	Up tack; orthogonal to; perpendicular
Phi	&#934;	Greek capital letter phi
phi	&#966;	Greek small letter phi
Pi	&#928;	Greek capital letter pi

continues

Entity	Numerical	Does This
pi	π	Greek small letter pi
piv	ϖ	Greek pi symbol
plusmn	±	Plus or minus sign
pound	£	Pound sign
Prime	″	Double prime; seconds; inches
prime	′	Prime; minutes; feet
prod	∏	N-ary product; product sign
prop	∝	Proportional to
Psi	Ψ	Greek capital letter psi
psi	ψ	Greek small letter psi
quot	"	Quotation mark; APL quote
radic	√	Square root; radical sign
rang	〉	Right-pointing angle bracket; ket
raquo	»	Right-pointing double-angle quotation mark
rArr	⇒	Rightward double arrow
rarr	→	Rightward arrow
rceil	⌉	Right ceiling
rdquo	”	Right double quotation mark
real	ℜ	Blackletter capital R; real part symbol
reg	®	Registered sign
rfloor	⌋	Right floor
Rho	Ρ	Greek capital letter rho
rho	ρ	Greek small letter rho
rlm	‏	Right-to-left mark
rsaquo	›	Single right-pointing angle quotation mark

Entity	Numerical Does This	
rsquo	&#8217;	Right single quotation mark
sbquo	&#8218;	Single low-9 quotation mark
Scaron	&#352;	Latin capital letter *S* with caron
scaron	&#353;	Latin small letter *s* with caron
sdot	&#8901;	Dot operator
sect	&#167;	Section sign
shy	&#173;	Soft hyphen
Sigma	&#931;	Greek capital letter sigma
sigma	&#963;	Greek small letter sigma
sigmaf	&#962;	Greek small letter final sigma
sim	&#8764;	Tilde operator
spades	&#9824;	Black spade suit
sub	&#8834;	Subset of
sube	&#8838;	Subset of or equal to
sum	&#8721;	N-ary summation
sup	&#8835;	Superset of
sup1	&#185;	Superscript 1
sup2	&#178;	Superscript 2
sup3	&#179;	Superscript 3
supe	&#8839;	Superset of or equal to
szlig	&#223;	Latin small letter sharp *s*
Tau	&#932;	Greek capital letter tau
tau	&#964;	Greek small letter tau
there4	&#8756;	Therefore
Theta	&#920;	Greek capital letter theta
theta	&#952;	Greek small letter theta

continues

Entity	Numerical Does This	
thetasym	&#977;	Greek small letter theta symbol
thinsp		Thin space
THORN	&#222;	Latin capital letter THORN
thorn	&#254;	Latin small letter thorn
tilde	&#732;	Small tilde
times	&#215;	Multiplication sign
trade	&#8482;	Trademark sign
Uacute	&#218;	Latin capital letter U with acute accent
uacute	&#250;	Latin small letter u with acute accent
uArr	&#8657;	Upward double arrow
uarr	&#8593;	Upward arrow
Ucirc	&#219;	Latin capital letter U with circumflex
ucirc	&#251;	Latin small letter u with circumflex
Ugrave	&#217;	Latin capital letter U with grave accent
ugrave	&#249;	Latin small letter u with grave accent
uml	&#168;	Dieresis (umlaut)
upsih	&#978;	Greek upsilon with hook symbol
Upsilon	&#933;	Greek capital letter upsilon
upsilon	&#965;	Greek small letter upsilon
Uuml	&#220;	Latin capital letter U with dieresis (umlaut)
uuml	&#252;	Latin small letter u with dieresis
weierp	&#8472;	Script capital P; power set
Xi	&#926;	Greek capital letter xi
xi	&#958;	Greek small letter xi

Entity	Numerical	Does This
Yacute	Ý	Latin capital letter *Y* with acute accent
yacute	ý	Latin small letter *y* with acute accent
yen	¥	Yen sign; Yuan sign
Yuml	Ÿ	Latin capital letter *Y* with dieresis
yuml	ÿ	Latin small letter *y* with dieresis
Zeta	Ζ	Greek capital letter zeta
zeta	ζ	Greek small letter zeta
zwj	‍	Zero width joiner
zwnj	‌	Zero width nonjoiner

As I mentioned, as in HTML, XHTML supports various text-formatting tags, such as <b> for bold text, <i> for italic text, and <u> for underlined text. I'll take a look at them briefly because they're still very popular.

<b>–Making Text Bold

The <b> element makes its enclosed text appear in boldface. This element is supported in XHTML 1.0 Strict, XHTML 1.0 Transitional, XHTML 1.0 Frameset, and XHTML 1.1. Here are its attributes:

- class—Gives the style class of the element. (XHTML 1.0 Strict, XHTML 1.0 Transitional, XHTML 1.0 Frameset, XHTML 1.1.)

- dir—Sets the direction of text that doesn't have an inherent direction in which you should read it, called directionally neutral text. You can set this attribute to LTR, for left-to-right text, or RTL, for right-to-left text. (XHTML 1.0 Strict, XHTML 1.0 Transitional, XHTML 1.0 Frameset, XHTML 1.1.)

- id—Refers to the element; set this attribute to a unique identifier. (XHTML 1.0 Strict, XHTML 1.0 Transitional, XHTML 1.0 Frameset, XHTML 1.1.)

- lang—Specifies the base language used in the element. Applies only when the document is interpreted as HTML. (XHTML 1.0 Strict, XHTML 1.0 Transitional, XHTML 1.0 Frameset, XHTML 1.1.)

- style—Set to an inline style to specify how the browser should display the element. (XHTML 1.0 Strict, XHTML 1.0 Transitional, XHTML 1.0 Frameset, XHTML 1.1.)

- title—Contains the title of the element (which might be displayed in ToolTips). (XHTML 1.0 Strict, XHTML 1.0 Transitional, XHTML 1.0 Frameset, XHTML 1.1.)

- xml:lang—Specifies the base language for the element when the document is interpreted as an XML document. (XHTML 1.0 Strict, XHTML 1.0 Transitional, XHTML 1.0 Frameset, XHTML 1.1.)

Here are the official XHTML events this element supports: onclick, ondblclick, onmousedown, onmouseup, onmouseover, onmousemove, onmouseout, onkeypress, onkeydown, and onkeyup.

The <b> element gives you a simple inline way of bolding text. Although plenty of experts would prefer that you use stylesheets to display text in bold, you can still use the <b> element. The following listing displays text in both italics and bold. (I'm using the line break element, <br>, which we'll see later, to separate the lines of text.)

Listing ch16_07.html

```
<?xml version="1.0"?>
<!DOCTYPE html PUBLIC "-//W3C//DTD XHTML 1.0 Transitional//EN"
"http://www.w3.org/TR/xhtml1/DTD/xhtml1-transitional.dtd">
<html xmlns="http://www.w3.org/1999/xhtml" xml:lang="en" lang="en">
    <head>
        <title>
            Bold and Italic Text
        </title>
    </head>

    <body>
        <i>This text is italic.</i>
        <br />
        <b>This text is bold.</b>
        <br />
        <b><i>This text is both.</i></b>
    </body>
</html>
```

The results of this XHTML appear in Figure 16-5; you can see text that's bold, italic, and both bold and italic. The <b> tag is a favorite one among Web page authors because it's so easy to use.

Figure 16-5
Displaying
bold and italic
text in
Netscape
Navigator.

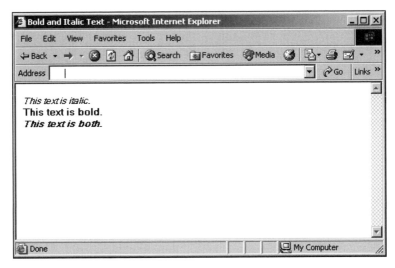

<*i*>–Making Text Italic

Like the <b> element, the <i> element offers some rudimentary text formatting—in this case, creating italic text. The <i> element is supported in XHTML 1.0 Strict, XHTML 1.0 Transitional, XHTML 1.0 Frameset, and XHTML 1.1. Here are its attributes:

- class—Gives the style class of the element. (XHTML 1.0 Strict, XHTML 1.0 Transitional, XHTML 1.0 Frameset, XHTML 1.1.)

- dir—Sets the direction of text that doesn't have an inherent direction in which you should read it, called directionally neutral text. You can set this attribute to LTR, for left-to-right text, or RTL, for right-to-left text. (XHTML 1.0 Strict, XHTML 1.0 Transitional, XHTML 1.0 Frameset, XHTML 1.1.)

- id—Refers to the element; set this attribute to a unique identifier. (XHTML 1.0 Strict, XHTML 1.0 Transitional, XHTML 1.0 Frameset, XHTML 1.1.)

- lang—Specifies the base language used in the element. Applies only when the document is interpreted as HTML. (XHTML 1.0 Strict, XHTML 1.0 Transitional, XHTML 1.0 Frameset, XHTML 1.1.)

- style—Set to an inline style to specify how the browser should display the element. (XHTML 1.0 Strict, XHTML 1.0 Transitional, XHTML 1.0 Frameset, XHTML 1.1.)

- title—Contains the title of the element (which might be displayed in ToolTips). (XHTML 1.0 Strict, XHTML 1.0 Transitional, XHTML 1.0 Frameset, XHTML 1.1.)

- xml:lang—Specifies the base language for the element when the document is interpreted as an XML document. (XHTML 1.0 Strict, XHTML 1.0 Transitional, XHTML 1.0 Frameset, XHTML 1.1.)

Here are the events this element supports in XHTML: onclick, ondblclick, onmousedown, onmouseup, onmouseover, onmousemove, onmouseout, onkeypress, onkeydown, and onkeyup.

You use the <i> element to display italicized text, as in this example we saw in the previous topic:

```
<?xml version="1.0"?>
<!DOCTYPE html PUBLIC "-//W3C//DTD XHTML 1.0 Transitional//EN"
"http://www.w3.org/TR/xhtml1/DTD/xhtml1-transitional.dtd">
<html xmlns="http://www.w3.org/1999/xhtml" xml:lang="en" lang="en">
    <head>
        <title>
            Bold and Italic Text
        </title>
    </head>

    <body>
        <i>This text is italic.</i>
        <br />
        <b>This text is bold.</b>
        <br />
        <b><i>This text is both.</i></b>
    </body>
</html>
```

You can see the results of this XHTML in Figure 16-5.

<u>–Underlining Text

The <u> element displays underlined text. This element was deprecated in HTML 4.0 (you're supposed to use styles instead now), so it is not supported in XHTML 1.0 Strict or XHTML 1.1. It is supported in XHTML 1.0 Transitional and XHTML 1.0 Frameset, however. Here are the attributes of this element:

- class—Gives the style class of the element. (XHTML 1.0 Transitional, XHTML 1.0 Frameset.)

- **dir**—Sets the direction of text that doesn't have an inherent direction in which you should read it, called directionally neutral text. You can set this attribute to **LTR**, for left-to-right text, or **RTL**, for right-to-left text. (XHTML 1.0 Transitional, XHTML 1.0 Frameset.)

- **id**—Refers to the element; set this attribute to a unique identifier. (XHTML 1.0 Transitional, XHTML 1.0 Frameset.)

- **lang**—Specifies the base language used in the element. Applies only when the document is interpreted as HTML. (XHTML 1.0 Transitional, XHTML 1.0 Frameset.)

- **style**—Set to an inline style to specify how the browser should display the element. (XHTML 1.0 Transitional, XHTML 1.0 Frameset.)

- **title**—Contains the title of the element (which might be displayed in ToolTips). (XHTML 1.0 Transitional, XHTML 1.0 Frameset.)

- **xml:lang**—Specifies the base language for the element when the document is interpreted as an XML document. (XHTML 1.0 Transitional, XHTML 1.0 Frameset.)

Here are the official XHTML events this element supports: `onclick`, `ondblclick`, `onmousedown`, `onmouseup`, `onmouseover`, `onmousemove`, `onmouseout`, `onkeypress`, `onkeydown`, and `onkeyup`.

The <u> element offers another easy formatting option, underlining its enclosed text. This element is deprecated in HTML 4.0, so you can't use it in strict XHTML 1.0 or XHTML 1.1. Here's an example putting <u> to work:

Listing ch16_08.html

```
<?xml version="1.0"?>
<!DOCTYPE html PUBLIC "-//W3C//DTD XHTML 1.0 Transitional//EN"
"http://www.w3.org/TR/xhtml1/DTD/xhtml1-transitional.dtd">
<html xmlns="http://www.w3.org/1999/xhtml" xml:lang="en" lang="en">
    <head>
        <title>
            Using the &lt;u&gt; Element
        </title>
    </head>

    <body>
        You can <u>underline</u> text for a little more emphasis.
    </body>
</html>
```

The results of this XHTML appear in Figure 16-6.

Figure 16-6
Displaying
underlined
text in
Netscape
Navigator.

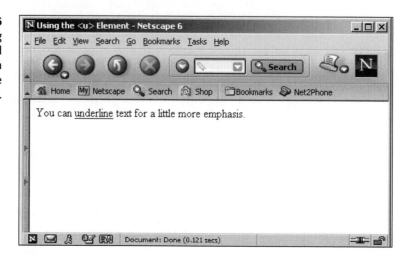

‹font›–Specifying a Text Font

Using the `<font>` element, you can you select text size, color, and face. However, this element was deprecated in HTML 4.0, so it's not available in XHTML 1.1 or XHTML 1.0 Strict. It's supported in XHTML 1.0 Transitional and XHTML 1.0 Frameset. Here are this element's attributes:

- `class`—Gives the style class of the element. (XHTML 1.0 Transitional, XHTML 1.0 Frameset.)

- `color`—Deprecated. Sets the color of the text. (XHTML 1.0 Transitional, XHTML 1.0 Frameset.)

- `dir`—Sets the direction of text that doesn't have an inherent direction in which you should read it, called directionally neutral text. You can set this attribute to `LTR`, for left-to-right text, or `RTL`, for right-to-left text. (XHTML 1.0 Transitional, XHTML 1.0 Frameset.)

- `face`—Deprecated (you're supposed to use styles instead now). You can set this attribute to a single font name or a list of names separated by commas. The browser will select the first font face from the list that it can find. (XHTML 1.0 Transitional, XHTML 1.0 Frameset.)

- `id`—Refers to the element; set this attribute to a unique identifier. (XHTML 1.0 Transitional, XHTML 1.0 Frameset.)

- `lang`—Specifies the base language used in the element. Applies only when the document is interpreted as HTML. (XHTML 1.0 Transitional, XHTML 1.0 Frameset.)

- `size`—Deprecated (you're supposed to use styles instead now). Sets the size of the text. Possible values range from 1 through 7. (XHTML 1.0 Transitional, XHTML 1.0 Frameset.)

- `style`—Set to an inline style to specify how the browser should display the element. (XHTML 1.0 Transitional, XHTML 1.0 Frameset.)

- `title`—Contains the title of the element (which might be displayed in ToolTips). (XHTML 1.0 Transitional, XHTML 1.0 Frameset.)

- `xml:lang`—Specifies the base language for the element when the document is interpreted as an XML document. (XHTML 1.0 Transitional, XHTML 1.0 Frameset.)

This element does not support any XHTML events.

The `<font>` element has always been very popular among HTML authors, but with the new emphasis on handling styles in stylesheets, you can imagine that it was headed for extinction. And it has indeed been deprecated in HTML 4.0, which means you'll find it only in the XHTML 1.0 Transitional and Frameset DTDs. Because it's so popular still, I'll cover it here briefly.

You can use the `<font>` element to set a font face, size, and color for text. Here's an example; in this case, I'm displaying text in a large red Arial font:

Listing ch16_09.html

```
<?xml version="1.0"?>
<!DOCTYPE html PUBLIC "-//W3C//DTD XHTML 1.0 Transitional//EN"
"http://www.w3.org/TR/xhtml1/DTD/xhtml1-transitional.dtd">
<html xmlns="http://www.w3.org/1999/xhtml" xml:lang="en" lang="en">
    <head>
        <title>
            Using the &lt;font&gt; Element
        </title>
    </head>

    <body>
        <font size="6" color="#ff0000" face="Arial">
        Putting the &lt;font&gt; element to work.
        </font>
    </body>
</html>
```

The results of this XHTML appear in Figure 16-7.

Figure 16-7
Using the
<*font*>
element in
Netscape
Navigator.

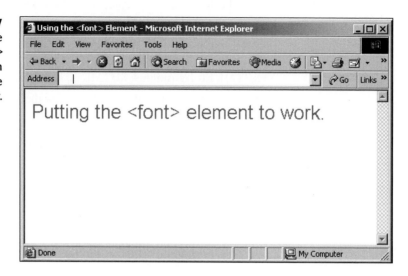

You specify font sizes by using the values 1 through 7. In practice, font size 1 is about 6 points, font size 2 is about 12 points, and so on, but actual sizes vary by system. Here's an example showing the range of possible sizes:

Listing ch16_10.html

```
<?xml version="1.0"?>
<!DOCTYPE html PUBLIC "-//W3C//DTD XHTML 1.0 Transitional//EN"
"http://www.w3.org/TR/xhtml1/DTD/xhtml1-transitional.dtd">
<html xmlns="http://www.w3.org/1999/xhtml" xml:lang="en" lang="en">
    <head>
        <title>
            Using the &lt;font&gt; Element
        </title>
    </head>

    <body>
        <center>
            <h1>
                Using the &lt;font&gt; Element
            </h1>
            <font size="1">This is font size 1.</font>
            <br />
            <font size="2">This is font size 2.</font>
            <br />
```

```
            <font size="3">This is font size 3.</font>
            <br />
            <font size="4">This is font size 4.</font>
            <br />
            <font size="5">This is font size 5.</font>
            <br />
            <font size="6">This is font size 6.</font>
            <br />
            <font size="7">This is font size 7.</font>
        </center>
    </body>
</html>
```

The results of this XHTML appear in Figure 16-8. Note that <font> has been deprecated in HTML 4.0 in favor of stylesheets. So how should you replace the <font> element? See the topic "<span>—Formatting Text Inline" at the end of this chapter for a good substitute.

Besides the simple text-formatting elements, HTML contains elements to arrange text in the display; XHTML supports those elements as well.

Figure 16-8
Displaying various fonts sizes in Netscape Navigator.

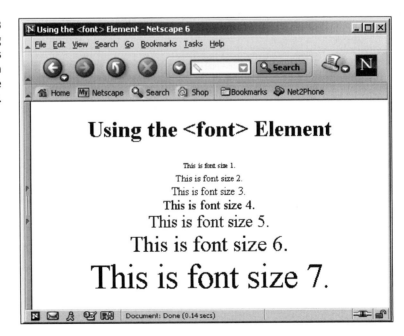

< br >–Creating Line Breaks

The <br> element is an empty element that inserts a line break into text. Because this element is empty, you use it like this in XHTML: <br />. This element is supported in XHTML 1.0 Strict, XHTML 1.0 Transitional, XHTML 1.0 Frameset, and XHTML 1.1. Here are the attributes of this element:

- class—Gives the style class of the element. (XHTML 1.0 Strict, XHTML 1.0 Transitional, XHTML 1.0 Frameset, XHTML 1.1.)

- clear—Used to move images or other elements that were aligned in the past. Set to none (the default—just a normal break), left (breaks line and moves down until there is a clear left margin past the aligned element), right (breaks line and moves down until there is a clear right margin past the aligned element), or all (breaks line and moves down until both margins are clear of the aligned element). (XHTML 1.0 Transitional, XHTML 1.0 Frameset.)

- id—Refers to the element; set this attribute to a unique identifier. (XHTML 1.0 Strict, XHTML 1.0 Transitional, XHTML 1.0 Frameset, XHTML 1.1.)

- style—Set to an inline style to specify how the browser should display the element. (XHTML 1.0 Strict, XHTML 1.0 Transitional, XHTML 1.0 Frameset, XHTML 1.1.)

- title—Contains the title of the element (which might be displayed in ToolTips). (XHTML 1.0 Strict, XHTML 1.0 Transitional, XHTML 1.0 Frameset, XHTML 1.1.)

This element does not support any XHTML events.

You use the <br> element to arrange the text in a document by adding a line break, making the browser skip to the next text line.

This element is an empty element, so you use it like this: <br />. This usage actually does not cause any problems in the major browsers, and the fact that those browsers are able to handle empty elements with the usual XML /> closing characters is one of the reasons that XHTML actually works as it should in HTML browsers. In fact, you can also insert line breaks as
</br>, but that usage is confusing to some browsers and XML validators.

Here's an example; in this case, I'm using <br> elements to introduce line breaks and a <p> element to create a new paragraph:

Listing ch16_11.html

```
<?xml version="1.0"?>
<!DOCTYPE html PUBLIC "-//W3C//DTD XHTML 1.0 Transitional//EN"
"http://www.w3.org/TR/xhtml1/DTD/xhtml1-transitional.dtd">
<html xmlns="http://www.w3.org/1999/xhtml" xml:lang="en" lang="en">
    <head>
        <title>
            Using the &lt;br&gt; and &lt;p&gt; Elements
        </title>
    </head>

    <body>
        <center>
            <h1>
                Using the &lt;br&gt; and &lt;p&gt; Elements
            </h1>
        </center>
        This is a line of text.
        <br />
        Using a line break skips to the next line.
        <p style="font-weight: bold">
            This is a line of bold text in a paragraph.
            <br />
            Here's a new line of text in the same paragraph.
        </p>
    </body>
</html>
```

The results of this code appear in Figure 16-9. As you can see, inserting a <br> element makes the browser move to the next line of text.

Figure 16-9
Using line breaks and paragraphs in Netscape Navigator.

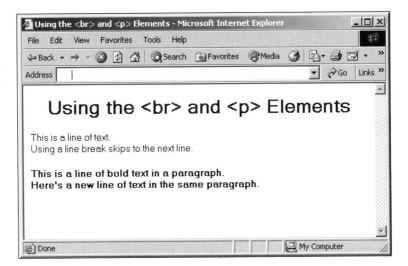

Let the Browser Handle the Formatting

Ideally, you should let the browser handle text formatting as much as possible. The text flow is supposed to be handled by the browser to display that text as best as possible to fit the display area. If you add a lot of line breaks, you may interfere with the best possible display (unless you're adding line breaks to specifically separate discrete elements, such as images). It's usually best to format your text into paragraphs that the browser can handle appropriately rather than expressly adding line breaks to text yourself.

<p>–Organizing Text into Paragraphs

The <p> element is a very popular one when dealing with text in Web pages; it allows you to break text up into paragraphs. Paragraphs are block elements that you can format as you like in stylesheets or with style attributes, including indenting the first line and so forth. If you're coming to XHTML from HTML, one issue to flag is that every <p> tag needs a corresponding </p> tag, which is easy to forget because HTML doesn't require that. In addition, note that paragraphs are block elements, which in XHTML means that you cannot display other block elements, such as headings, in them. The <p> element is supported in XHTML 1.0 Strict, XHTML 1.0 Transitional, XHTML 1.0 Frameset, and XHTML 1.1. Here are this element's attributes:

- align—Deprecated in HTML 4 (you're supposed to use styles now instead). Sets the alignment of the text. Possible values include left (the default), right, center, and justify. (XHTML 1.0 Transitional, XHTML 1.0 Frameset.)

- class—Gives the style class of the element. (XHTML 1.0 Strict, XHTML 1.0 Transitional, XHTML 1.0 Frameset, XHTML 1.1.)

- dir—Sets the direction of text that doesn't have an inherent direction in which you should read it, called directionally neutral text. You can set this attribute to LTR, for left-to-right text, or RTL, for right-to-left text. (XHTML 1.0 Strict, XHTML 1.0 Transitional, XHTML 1.0 Frameset, XHTML 1.1.)

- id—Refers to the element; set this attribute to a unique identifier. (XHTML 1.0 Strict, XHTML 1.0 Transitional, XHTML 1.0 Frameset, XHTML 1.1.)

- lang—Specifies the base language used in the element. Applies only when the document is interpreted as HTML. (XHTML 1.0 Strict, XHTML 1.0 Transitional, XHTML 1.0 Frameset, XHTML 1.1.)

- style—Set to an inline style to specify how the browser should display the element. (XHTML 1.0 Strict, XHTML 1.0 Transitional, XHTML 1.0 Frameset, XHTML 1.1.)

- title—Contains the title of the element (which might be displayed in ToolTips). (XHTML 1.0 Strict, XHTML 1.0 Transitional, XHTML 1.0 Frameset, XHTML 1.1.)

- xml:lang—Specifies the base language for the element when the document is interpreted as an XML document. (XHTML 1.0 Strict, XHTML 1.0 Transitional, XHTML 1.0 Frameset, XHTML 1.1.)

This element supports these XHTML events: onclick, ondblclick, onmousedown, onmouseup, onmouseover, onmousemove, onmouseout, onkeypress, onkeydown, and onkeyup.

You use the <p> element to organize your text into paragraphs. Paragraphs are rudimentary formatting structures that separate text into easily handled block elements. The browser adds a little vertical space on top to separate them from other elements. The browser formats the text in a paragraph to fit the current page width.

Here's the XHTML example using the <p> tag we saw in the previous topic:

```
<?xml version="1.0"?>
<!DOCTYPE html PUBLIC "-//W3C//DTD XHTML 1.0 Transitional//EN"
"http://www.w3.org/TR/xhtml1/DTD/xhtml1-transitional.dtd">
<html xmlns="http://www.w3.org/1999/xhtml" xml:lang="en" lang="en">
    <head>
        <title>
            Using the &lt;br&gt; and &lt;p&gt; Elements
        </title>
    </head>

    <body>
        <center>
            <h1>
                Using the &lt;br&gt; and &lt;p&gt; Elements
            </h1>
        </center>
        This is a line of text.
        <br />
        Using a line break skips to the next line.
```

```
        <p style="font-weight: bold">
            This is a line of bold text in a paragraph.
            <br />
            Here's a new line of text in the same paragraph.
        </p>
    </body>
</html>
```

This example points out the difference between <br> and <p>. The <br> element is empty and just makes the flow of text skip to the next line. The <p> element, on the other hand, is a block element that encloses content. You can apply styles to the content in a <p> element, and those styles are applied to all text in the paragraph, even if broken up with line breaks. You can see this in Figure 16-9, where the bold style of text applies to both lines in the paragraph.

< hr >–Creating Horizontal Rules

Another handy element to arrange text is the <hr> horizontal rule element. This element just causes the browser to draw a horizontal line to separate or group elements vertically. It's supported in XHTML 1.0 Strict, XHTML 1.0 Transitional, XHTML 1.0 Frameset, and XHTML 1.1. Here are the attributes of this element—note that it includes a few attributes that have been deprecated:

- align—Deprecated (you're supposed to use styles now instead). Sets the alignment of the rule to left, center (the default), or right. To set this attribute, you must also set the width attribute. (XHTML 1.0 Transitional, XHTML 1.0 Frameset.)

- class—Gives the style class of the element. (XHTML 1.0 Strict, XHTML 1.0 Transitional, XHTML 1.0 Frameset, XHTML 1.1.)

- id—Refers to the element; set this attribute to a unique identifier. (XHTML 1.0 Strict, XHTML 1.0 Transitional, XHTML 1.0 Frameset, XHTML 1.1.)

- noshade—Deprecated. Displays the rule with a two-dimensional, not three-dimensional (the default), appearance. (XHTML 1.0 Transitional, XHTML 1.0 Frameset.)

- size—Deprecated. Sets the vertical size of the horizontal rule in pixels. (XHTML 1.0 Transitional, XHTML 1.0 Frameset.)

- style—Set to an inline style to specify how the browser should display the element. (XHTML 1.0 Strict, XHTML 1.0 Transitional, XHTML 1.0 Frameset, XHTML 1.1.)

- title—Contains the title of the element (which might be displayed in ToolTips). (XHTML 1.0 Strict, XHTML 1.0 Transitional, XHTML 1.0 Frameset, XHTML 1.1.)

- width—Deprecated. Sets the horizontal width of the rule. You can set this attribute to a pixel measurement or a percentage of the display area. (XHTML 1.0 Transitional, XHTML 1.0 Frameset.)

- xml:lang—Specifies the base language for the element when the document is interpreted as an XML document. (XHTML 1.0 Strict, XHTML 1.0 Transitional, XHTML 1.0 Frameset, XHTML 1.1.)

Here are the XHTML events supported by this element: onclick, ondblclick, onmousedown, onmouseup, onmouseover, onmousemove, onmouseout, onkeypress, onkeydown, and onkeyup.

It's easy to break up your text with horizontal rules using the <hr> element. This can be very useful in longer documents, and it organizes your document visually into sections. This element is empty and just instructs the browser to insert a horizontal rule.

As with many style attributes in HTML 4.0, the <hr> element's align, width, noshade, and size attributes are all deprecated. However, they're still in the XHTML 1.0 Transitional or Frameset DTDs. Here's an example that displays a few horizontal rules of varying width and alignment:

Listing ch16_12.html

```
<?xml version="1.0"?>
<!DOCTYPE html PUBLIC "-//W3C//DTD XHTML 1.0 Transitional//EN"
"http://www.w3.org/TR/xhtml1/DTD/xhtml1-transitional.dtd">
<html xmlns="http://www.w3.org/1999/xhtml" xml:lang="en" lang="en">
    <head>
        <title>
            Using the &lt;hr&gt; Element
        </title>
    </head>

    <body>
        <center>
            <h1>
                Using the &lt;hr&gt; Element
            </h1>
        </center>
        This is &lt;hr /&gt;:
        <hr />
        <br />
```

continues

Listing ch16_12.html   Continued

```
        This is &lt;hr align="left" width="60%" /&gt;:
        <hr align="left" width="60%" />
        <br />
        This is &lt;hr align="center" width="60%" /&gt;:
        <hr align="center" width="60%" />
        <br />
        This is &lt;hr align="right" width="60%" /&gt;:
        <hr align="right" width="60%" />
        <br />
    </body>
</html>
```

You can see the results of this XHTML in Figure 16-10, which shows a number of ways to configure horizontal rules. Here's another note: When you set the align attribute, you must also set the width attribute.

Figure 16-10
Displaying horizontal rules in Netscape Navigator.

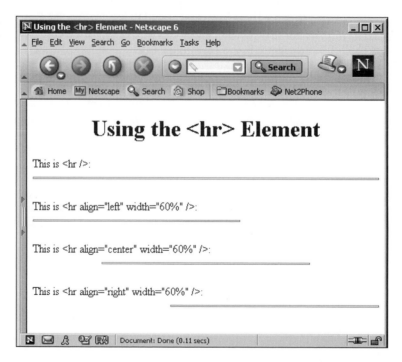

< center >–Centering Displayed Text

The `<center>` element is a very popular one that centers its enclosed text in the display area of the Web browser. Like many other styling elements and attributes in HTML 4.0, it was deprecated in favor of stylesheets, so it's supported only in XHTML 1.0 Transitional and XHTML 1.0 Frameset. Here are the attributes of this element:

- `class`—Gives the style class of the element. (XHTML 1.0 Transitional, XHTML 1.0 Frameset.)

- `dir`—Sets the direction of text that doesn't have an inherent direction in which you should read it, called directionally neutral text. You can set this attribute to `LTR`, for left-to-right text, or `RTL`, for right-to-left text. (XHTML 1.0 Transitional, XHTML 1.0 Frameset.)

- `id`—Refers to the element; set this attribute to a unique identifier. (XHTML 1.0 Transitional, XHTML 1.0 Frameset.)

- `lang`—Specifies the base language used in the element. Applies only when the document is interpreted as HTML. (XHTML 1.0 Transitional, XHTML 1.0 Frameset.)

- `style`—Set to an inline style to specify how the browser should display the element. (XHTML 1.0 Transitional, XHTML 1.0 Frameset.)

- `title`—Contains the title of the element (which might be displayed in ToolTips). (XHTML 1.0 Transitional, XHTML 1.0 Frameset.)

- `xml:lang`—Specifies the base language for the element when the document is interpreted as an XML document. (XHTML 1.0 Transitional, XHTML 1.0 Frameset.)

This element supports the following XHTML events: `onclick`, `ondblclick`, `onmousedown`, `onmouseup`, `onmouseover`, `onmousemove`, `onmouseout`, `onkeypress`, `onkeydown`, and `onkeyup`.

The `<center>` element does just what its name implies: centers text and elements in the browser's display area. The W3C deprecated `<center>` in HTML 4, so you won't find it in the XHTML 1.0 Strict or XHTML 1.1 DTDs. Nonetheless, `<center>` remains a favorite element and will be in use for a long time to come.

Here's an example of <center> at work centering multiline text:

Listing ch16_13.html

```
<?xml version="1.0"?>
<!DOCTYPE html PUBLIC "-//W3C//DTD XHTML 1.0 Transitional//EN"
"http://www.w3.org/TR/xhtml1/DTD/xhtml1-transitional.dtd">
<html xmlns="http://www.w3.org/1999/xhtml" xml:lang="en" lang="en">
    <head>
        <title>
            Using the &lt;center&gt; Element
        </title>
    </head>

    <body>
        <center>
            <h1>
                Using the &lt;center&gt; Element
            </h1>
        </center>
        <center>
            The &lt;center&gt; element is a
            <br />
            useful one for centering
            <br />
            text made up of
            <br />
            multiple lines.
        </center>
    </body>
</html>
```

You can see the results of this XHTML in Figure 16-11.

Figure 16-11
Using the
<center>
element.

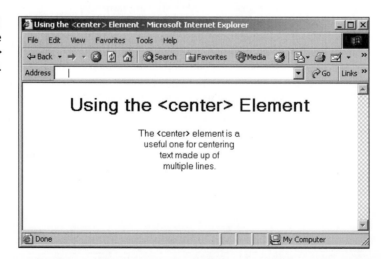

The <center> element is still in widespread use, which is why I'm taking a look at it here. However, it has been deprecated, which means that it will disappear from XHTML one day. So what are you supposed to use instead? Take a look at the next topic, the <div> element.

< *div* >—Formatting Text Blocks

You can use the <div> element to select or enclose a block of text, usually so that you can apply styles to it. This element is supported in XHTML 1.0 Strict, XHTML 1.0 Transitional, XHTML 1.0 Frameset, and XHTML 1.1. Here are its attributes:

- align—Deprecated. Sets the horizontal alignment of the element. Set to left (the default), right, center, or justify. (XHTML 1.0 Transitional, XHTML 1.0 Frameset.)

- class—Gives the style class of the element. (XHTML 1.0 Strict, XHTML 1.0 Transitional, XHTML 1.0 Frameset, XHTML 1.1.)

- dir—Sets the direction of text that doesn't have an inherent direction in which you should read it, called directionally neutral text. You can set this attribute to LTR, for left-to-right text, or RTL, for right-to-left text. (XHTML 1.0 Strict, XHTML 1.0 Transitional, XHTML 1.0 Frameset, XHTML 1.1.)

- id—Refers to the element; set this attribute to a unique identifier. (XHTML 1.0 Strict, XHTML 1.0 Transitional, XHTML 1.0 Frameset, XHTML 1.1.)

- lang—Specifies the base language used in the element. Applies only when the document is interpreted as HTML. (XHTML 1.0 Strict, XHTML 1.0 Transitional, XHTML 1.0 Frameset, XHTML 1.1.)

- style—Set to an inline style to specify how the browser should display the element. (XHTML 1.0 Strict, XHTML 1.0 Transitional, XHTML 1.0 Frameset, XHTML 1.1.)

- title—Contains the title of the element (which might be displayed in ToolTips). (XHTML 1.0 Strict, XHTML 1.0 Transitional, XHTML 1.0 Frameset, XHTML 1.1.)

- xml:lang—Specifies the base language for the element when the document is interpreted as an XML document. (XHTML 1.0 Strict, XHTML 1.0 Transitional, XHTML 1.0 Frameset, XHTML 1.1.)

This element supports these XHTML events: onclick, ondblclick, onmousedown, onmouseup, onmouseover, onmousemove, onmouseout, onkeypress, onkeydown, and onkeyup.

The <div> element allows you to refer to an entire section of your document by name. You can replace the text in it from JavaScript code, as we did in Chapter 7, "Handling XML Documents with JavaScript." There we read in XML documents and worked with them, displaying results using the <div> element's innerHTML property in Internet Explorer, as in this HTML document, ch07_02.html:

```
<HTML>
    <HEAD>
        <TITLE>
            Reading XML element values
        </TITLE>

        <SCRIPT LANGUAGE="JavaScript">
            function readXMLDocument()
            {
                var xmldoc, meetingsNode, meetingNode, peopleNode
                var first_nameNode, last_nameNode, outputText
                xmldoc = new ActiveXObject("Microsoft.XMLDOM")
                xmldoc.load("ch07_01.xml")

                meetingsNode = xmldoc.documentElement
                meetingNode = meetingsNode.firstChild
                peopleNode = meetingNode.lastChild
                personNode = peopleNode.lastChild
                first_nameNode = personNode.firstChild
                last_nameNode = first_nameNode.nextSibling

                outputText = "Third name: " +
                    first_nameNode.firstChild.nodeValue + ' '
                    + last_nameNode.firstChild.nodeValue
                messageDIV.innerHTML=outputText
            }
        </SCRIPT>
    </HEAD>

    <BODY>
        <CENTER>
            <H1>
                Reading XML element values
            </H1>

            <INPUT TYPE="BUTTON" VALUE="Get the name of the third person"
                ONCLICK="readXMLDocument()">
            <P>
            <DIV ID="messageDIV"></DIV>
        </CENTER>
    </BODY>
</HTML>
```

Here's an XHTML example. In this case, I'm enclosing some text in a `<div>` element and styling the text in bold red italics with an XHTML `<style>` element (more on the `<style>` element in the next chapter):

Listing ch16_14.html

```
<?xml version="1.0"?>
<!DOCTYPE html PUBLIC "-//W3C//DTD XHTML 1.0 Transitional//EN"
"http://www.w3.org/TR/xhtml1/DTD/xhtml1-transitional.dtd">
<html xmlns="http://www.w3.org/1999/xhtml" xml:lang="en" lang="en">
    <head>
        <title>
            Using the &lt;div&gt; tag
        </title>
        <style>
            div {color: red; font-weight: bold; font-style: italic}
        </style>
    </head>

    <body>
        <center>
            <h1>
                Using the &lt;div&gt; Element
            </h1>
        </center>

        <p>
            <div>
                This text, which
                <br />
                takes up multiple lines,
                <br />
                was formatted all at once
                <br />
                in a single &lt;div&gt; element.
            </div>
        </p>
    </body>
</html>
```

You can see the results of this XHTML in Figure 16-12, where, as you see, all the lines in the `<div>` element were styled in the same way.

Figure 16-12
Styling text
with the *<div>*
element.

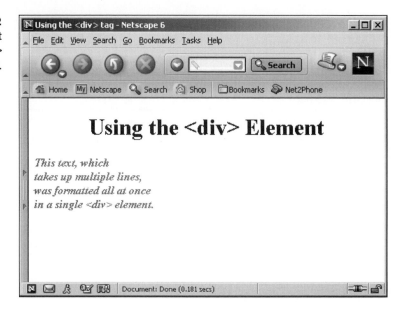

Figure 16-12
Styling text
with the *<div>*
element.

The W3C suggests that you use the `<div>` element's `align` attribute to replace the now deprecated `<center>` element, by setting `align` to "center". That would look like this, where I'm modifying the example from the previous section:

Listing ch16_15.html

```
<?xml version="1.0"?>
<!DOCTYPE html PUBLIC "-//W3C//DTD XHTML 1.0 Transitional//EN"
"http://www.w3.org/TR/xhtml1/DTD/xhtml1-transitional.dtd">
<html xmlns="http://www.w3.org/1999/xhtml" xml:lang="en" lang="en">
    <head>
        <title>
            Using the &lt;div&gt; Element
        </title>
    </head>

    <body>
        <div align="center">
            <h1>
                Using the &lt;div&gt; Element
            </h1>
        </div>
        <div align="center">
            The &lt;div&gt; element is a
            <br />
            useful one for centering
```

```
            <br />
            text made up of
            <br />
            multiple lines.
        </div>
    </body>
</html>
```

In fact, although W3C documentation suggests that you use the `align` attribute, the W3C seems to have forgotten that it deprecated that attribute in HTML 4.0. The way to center text now is to set a `<div>` element's `text-align` style property to `"center"`. That might look like this:

Listing ch16_16.html

```
<?xml version="1.0"?>
<!DOCTYPE html PUBLIC "-//W3C//DTD XHTML 1.0 Transitional//EN"
"http://www.w3.org/TR/xhtml1/DTD/xhtml1-transitional.dtd">
<html xmlns="http://www.w3.org/1999/xhtml" xml:lang="en" lang="en">
    <head>
        <title>
            Using the &lt;div&gt; Element
        </title>
        <style>
            div {text-align: center}
        </style>
    </head>

    <body>
        <div>
            <h1>
                Using the &lt;div&gt; Element
            </h1>
        </div>
        <div>
            The &lt;div&gt; element is a
            <br />
            useful one for centering
            <br />
            text made up of
            <br />
            multiple lines.
        </div>
    </body>
</html>
```

This works as planned—the text is indeed centered in the browser.

Using the positioning style properties, you can also position text with the <div> tag, even overlapping displayed text blocks. There's another handy element that you can use to select text and apply styles: <span>.

<*span*>–Formatting Text Inline

The <span> element lets you select inline text to apply styles. It's supported in XHTML 1.0 Strict, XHTML 1.0 Transitional, XHTML 1.0 Frameset, and XHTML 1.1. Here are the attributes of this element:

- class—Gives the style class of the element. (XHTML 1.0 Strict, XHTML 1.0 Transitional, XHTML 1.0 Frameset, XHTML 1.1.)

- dir—Sets the direction of text that doesn't have an inherent direction in which you should read it, called directionally neutral text. You can set this attribute to LTR, for left-to-right text, or RTL, for right-to-left text. (XHTML 1.0 Strict, XHTML 1.0 Transitional, XHTML 1.0 Frameset, XHTML 1.1.)

- id—Refers to the element; set this attribute to a unique identifier. (XHTML 1.0 Strict, XHTML 1.0 Transitional, XHTML 1.0 Frameset, XHTML 1.1.)

- lang—Specifies the base language used in the element. Applies only when the document is interpreted as HTML. (XHTML 1.0 Strict, XHTML 1.0 Transitional, XHTML 1.0 Frameset, XHTML 1.1.)

- style—Set to an inline style to specify how the browser should display the element. (XHTML 1.0 Strict, XHTML 1.0 Transitional, XHTML 1.0 Frameset, XHTML 1.1.)

- title—Contains the title of the element (which might be displayed in ToolTips). (XHTML 1.0 Strict, XHTML 1.0 Transitional, XHTML 1.0 Frameset, XHTML 1.1.)

- xml:lang—Specifies the base language for the element when the document is interpreted as an XML document. (XHTML 1.0 Strict, XHTML 1.0 Transitional, XHTML 1.0 Frameset, XHTML 1.1.)

This element supports these XHTML events: onclick, ondblclick, onmousedown, onmouseup, onmouseover, onmousemove, onmouseout, onkeypress, onkeydown, and onkeyup.

You usually use `<span>` to apply styles inline, such as in the middle of a sentence, to a few words or even characters. When styling blocks of text, you can use `<div>`; for individual characters, words, or sentences, use `<span>`.

As we saw, you can use `<div>` to replace the deprecated `<center>` element; there's also a deprecated element that you can replace with `<span>`: the `<font>` element. Using `<span>`, you can apply styles inline to a few characters or words, which is what Web authors previously used `<font>` for. For example, here I'm applying a style to a section of text using `<span>`, displaying that text in bold red italics:

Listing ch16_17.html

```
<?xml version="1.0"?>
<!DOCTYPE html PUBLIC "-//W3C//DTD XHTML 1.0 Transitional//EN"
"http://www.w3.org/TR/xhtml1/DTD/xhtml1-transitional.dtd">
<html xmlns="http://www.w3.org/1999/xhtml" xml:lang="en" lang="en">
    <head>
        <title>
            Using the &lt;span&gt; Element
        </title>
        <style>
            span {color: red; font-weight: bold; font-style: italic}
        </style>
    </head>

    <body>
        <center>
            <h1>
                Using the &lt;span&gt; Element
            </h1>
        </center>
        <h2>
            Sometimes, for <span>emphasis</span>, you might want to
            target <span>specific words</span> in your text.
        </h2>
    </body>
</html>
```

You can see the results of this XHTML in Figure 16-13, where the words we want styled in a specific way are styled correctly.

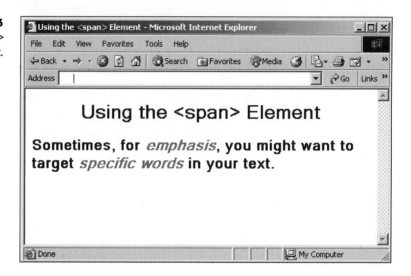

There's more XHTML to come—take a look at the next chapter.

CHAPTER 17
XHTML at Work

We got started with XHTML in the previous chapter, and I'll continue exploring it here. In this chapter, I'll take a look at how XHTML implements images, hyperlinks, stylesheets, tables, and forms. I'll also look at how to extend XHTML by creating custom tags. I'll start with handling images.

< img >–Displaying an Image

As in HTML, the `<img>` element is an empty element that you use to insert images into Web pages. This element is supported in XHTML 1.0 Strict, XHTML 1.0 Transitional, XHTML 1.0 Frameset, and XHTML 1.1. Here are its attributes:

- `align`—Sets the alignment of text relative to the image on the screen. Possible settings are `left`, `right`, `top`, `texttop`, `middle`, `absmiddle`, `baseline`, `bottom`, and `absbottom`. (XHTML 1.0 Transitional, XHTML 1.0 Frameset.)

- `alt`—Required. This attribute holds the text that should be displayed instead of an image for browsers that cannot handle graphics or have graphics disabled. (XHTML 1.0 Strict, XHTML 1.0 Transitional, XHTML 1.0 Frameset, XHTML 1.1.)

- `border`—Specifies whether the image has a border and, if so, how thick the border is. Set this to `0` for no border or to a positive integer pixel value. (XHTML 1.0 Transitional, XHTML 1.0 Frameset.)

- `class`—Gives the style class of the element. (XHTML 1.0 Strict, XHTML 1.0 Transitional, XHTML 1.0 Frameset, XHTML 1.1.)

- `height`—Specifies the height of the image, in pixels. (XHTML 1.0 Strict, XHTML 1.0 Transitional, XHTML 1.0 Frameset, XHTML 1.1.)

- `hspace`—Sets the horizontal spacing (both left and right sides) around the image. Set this to pixel measurements. (XHTML 1.0 Transitional, XHTML 1.0 Frameset.)

- id—Refers to the element; set this attribute to a unique identifier. (XHTML 1.0 Strict, XHTML 1.0 Transitional, XHTML 1.0 Frameset, XHTML 1.1.)

- ismap—Specifies that this image is to be used as an image map along with a map file. (XHTML 1.0 Strict, XHTML 1.0 Transitional, XHTML 1.0 Frameset, XHTML 1.1.)

- lang—Specifies the base language used in the element. Applies only when the document is interpreted as HTML. (XHTML 1.0 Strict, XHTML 1.0 Transitional, XHTML 1.0 Frameset, XHTML 1.1.)

- longdesc—Contains a longer description of the image. Allows descriptions that can contain markup. Set this to a URI. (XHTML 1.0 Strict, XHTML 1.0 Transitional, XHTML 1.0 Frameset, XHTML 1.1.)

- src—Required. Specifies the URI of the image to display. (XHTML 1.0 Strict, XHTML 1.0 Transitional, XHTML 1.0 Frameset, XHTML 1.1.)

- style—Inline style indicating how to render the element. (XHTML 1.0 Strict, XHTML 1.0 Transitional, XHTML 1.0 Frameset, XHTML 1.1.)

- title—Contains the title of the body (which might be displayed in ToolTips). (XHTML 1.0 Strict, XHTML 1.0 Transitional, XHTML 1.0 Frameset, XHTML 1.1.)

- usemap—Specifies the URI—usually inside the current document—of a client-side image map. (XHTML 1.0 Strict, XHTML 1.0 Transitional, XHTML 1.0 Frameset, XHTML 1.1.)

- vspace—Sets the vertical spacing around the image. Set this to pixel measurements. (XHTML 1.0 Transitional, XHTML 1.0 Frameset.)

- width—Indicates the width of the image. Set this to pixel measurements. (XHTML 1.0 Strict, XHTML 1.0 Transitional, XHTML 1.0 Frameset, XHTML 1.1.)

- xml:lang—Specifies the base language for the element when the document is interpreted as an XML document. (XHTML 1.0 Strict, XHTML 1.0 Transitional, XHTML 1.0 Frameset, XHTML 1.1.)

This element supports these XHTML events: onclick, ondblclick, onmousedown, onmouseup, onmouseover, onmousemove, onmouseout, onkeypress, onkeydown, and onkeyup.

Deprecated Attribute

In XHTML 2.0, the `<img>` element is deprecated in favor of the `<object>` element.

You use the XHTML `<img>` element to insert images into a Web page and image maps. When you use this element, you supply the URI of the image in the `src` attribute. Besides `src`, the `alt` attribute, which specifies alternate text to display in case the image can't be displayed, is required. Interestingly, the `align` attribute is not deprecated in the `<img>` element as it is for virtually every other XHTML element that supports it.

Here's a simple example using the `<img>` element to display an image, ch17_02.jpg:

Listing ch17_01.html

```
<?xml version="1.0"?>
<!DOCTYPE html PUBLIC "-//W3C//DTD XHTML 1.0 Transitional//EN"
"http://www.w3.org/TR/xhtml1/DTD/xhtml1-transitional.dtd">
<html xmlns="http://www.w3.org/1999/xhtml" xml:lang="en" lang="en">
    <head>
        <title>
            Using the &lt;img&gt; Element
        </title>
    </head>

    <body>
        <center>
            <h1>
                Using the &lt;img&gt; Element
            </h1>
            <img src="ch17_02.jpg"
                width="428" height="86" alt="An image" />
        </center>
    </body>
</html>
```

You can see the result in Figure 17-1.

Figure 17-1
Displaying an
image in
XHTML.

Figure 17-1
Displaying an
image in
XHTML.

<a>–Creating a Hyperlink or Anchor

The <a> element creates a hyperlink (use the href attribute) or anchor (use the id and/or the deprecated name attribute for browsers that need to use name, such as Netscape Navigator). This element is supported in XHTML 1.0 Strict, XHTML 1.0 Transitional, XHTML 1.0 Frameset, and XHTML 1.1. Here are this element's attributes:

- accesskey—Assigns a keyboard access key to the hyperlink. (XHTML 1.0 Strict, XHTML 1.0 Transitional.)

- charset—Indicates the character encoding of the hyperlink's target. Set this to Request for Comments (RFC) 2045 language character set string. The default value is ISO-8859-1. (XHTML 1.0 Strict, XHTML 1.0 Transitional, XHTML 1.0 Frameset, XHTML 1.1.)

- class—Gives the style class of the element. (XHTML 1.0 Strict, XHTML 1.0 Transitional, XHTML 1.0 Frameset, XHTML 1.1.)

- coords—Sets the coordinate values (in pixels) appropriate to the corresponding shape attribute to define a region of an image for image maps. (XHTML 1.0 Strict, XHTML 1.0 Transitional, XHTML 1.0 Frameset, XHTML 1.1.)

- `dir`—Sets the direction of text that doesn't have an inherent direction in which you should read it, called directionally neutral text. You can set this attribute to `ltr`, for left-to-right text, or `rtl`, for right-to-left text. (XHTML 1.0 Strict, XHTML 1.0 Transitional, XHTML 1.0 Frameset, XHTML 1.1.)

- `href`—Holds the target URI of the hyperlink. You must assign a value to either this attribute or the `id` attribute. (XHTML 1.0 Strict, XHTML 1.0 Transitional, XHTML 1.0 Frameset, XHTML 1.1.)

- `hreflang`—Gives the base language of the target indicated in the `href` attribute. Set this to RFC 1766 values. (XHTML 1.0 Strict, XHTML 1.0 Transitional, XHTML 1.0 Frameset, XHTML 1.1.)

- `id`—Refer to the element; set this attribute to a unique identifier. (XHTML 1.0 Strict, XHTML 1.0 Transitional, XHTML 1.0 Frameset, XHTML 1.1.)

- `lang`—Specifies the base language used in the element. Only applies when the document is interpreted as HTML. (XHTML 1.0 Strict, XHTML 1.0 Transitional, XHTML 1.0 Frameset, XHTML 1.1.)

- `name`—Available in the three XHTML 1.0 DTDs, but deprecated; not available in the XHTML 1.1 DTD (use `id` instead). Gives the anchor a name, which may be used as the target of a hyperlink. (XHTML 1.0 Strict, XHTML 1.0 Transitional, XHTML 1.0 Frameset.)

- `rel`—Specifies the relationship described by the hyperlink. (XHTML 1.0 Strict, XHTML 1.0 Transitional, XHTML 1.0 Frameset, XHTML 1.1.)

- `rev`—Same as the `rel` attribute, but the syntax works in the reverse direction. For example, a link from A to B with `rel="X"` signifies the same relationship as a link from B to A with `rev="X"`. (XHTML 1.0 Strict, XHTML 1.0 Transitional, XHTML 1.0 Frameset, XHTML 1.1.)

- `shape`—Specifies the type of region for mapping in an `<area>` element. This is used with the `coords` attribute. Possible values include `rect` (the default), `circ`, `circle`, `POLY`, and `polygon`. (XHTML 1.0 Strict, XHTML 1.0 Transitional, XHTML 1.0 Frameset, XHTML 1.1.)

- `style`—Inline style indicating how to render the element. (XHTML 1.0 Strict, XHTML 1.0 Transitional, XHTML 1.0 Frameset, XHTML 1.1.)

- `tabindex`—Specifies the tab sequence of hyperlinks in the page for keyboard navigation. (XHTML 1.0 Strict, XHTML 1.0 Transitional, XHTML 1.0 Frameset.)

- `target`—Indicates the named frame that serves as the target of the hyperlink. (XHTML 1.0 Transitional, XHTML 1.0 Frameset.)

- `title`—Contains the title of the element (which might be displayed in ToolTips). (XHTML 1.0 Strict, XHTML 1.0 Transitional, XHTML 1.0 Frameset, XHTML 1.1.)

- `type`—Specifies the Multipurpose Internet Mail Extensions (MIME) type of the target given in the `href` attribute. (XHTML 1.0 Strict, XHTML 1.0 Transitional, XHTML 1.0 Frameset, XHTML 1.1.)

- `xml:lang`—Specifies the base language for the element when the document is interpreted as an XML document. (XHTML 1.0 Strict, XHTML 1.0 Transitional, XHTML 1.0 Frameset, XHTML 1.1.)

This element supports these XHTML events: `onclick`, `ondblclick`, `onfocus`, `onblur`, `onmousedown`, `onmouseup`, `onmouseover`, `onmousemove`, `onmouseout`, `onkeypress`, `onkeydown`, and `onkeyup`.

New *href* Attribute

In XHTML 2.0, any element can be a hyperlink with the new `href` attribute, which is a part of the new XHTML 2.0 Common Attribute Collection.

The `<a>` element is a big part of what makes the Web work. You use this element to create hyperlinks and anchors (an anchor can serve as the target of a hyperlink). In this element, you must set either the `href` attribute to set the target URI of a hyperlink, or the `id` attribute to create an anchor. Here's an example using `href`, specifying the W3C site as the target of a hyperlink:

Listing ch17_03.html

```
<?xml version="1.0"?>
<!DOCTYPE html PUBLIC "-//W3C//DTD XHTML 1.0 Transitional//EN"
"http://www.w3.org/TR/xhtml1/DTD/xhtml1-transitional.dtd">
<html xmlns="http://www.w3.org/1999/xhtml" xml:lang="en" lang="en">
    <head>
        <title>
            Using the &lt;a&gt; Element
        </title>
```

```
    </head>

    <body>
        <center>
            <h1>
              Using the &lt;a&gt; Element
            </h1>

            Want to learn more about XHTML? Go to:
            <a href="http://w3c.org">W3C</a>.
        </center>
    </body>
</html>
```

You can see the results of this XHTML in Figure 17-2. As is standard in HTML browsers, the hyperlink appears as underlined text (largely because the browser thinks this *is* standard HTML). You can also use graphical hyperlinks if you enclose an <img> element in the <a> element.

Figure 17-2
Displaying a
hyperlink.

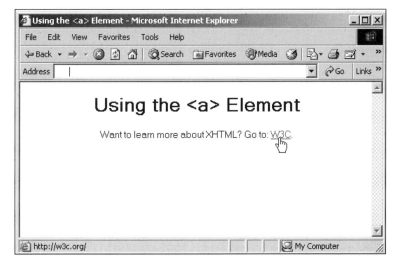

<link>–Setting Link Information

You use the XHTML <link> element to indicate the relationship of other documents to the current one, such as specifying an external stylesheet. This element is empty and goes in the <head> section of a document. This element is supported in XHTML 1.0 Strict, XHTML 1.0 Transitional, XHTML 1.0 Frameset, and XHTML 1.1. Here are the attributes of <link>:

- charset—Specifies the character encoding of the linked document. Set this to an RFC 2045 language character set string; the default value is ISO-8859-1. (XHTML 1.0 Strict, XHTML 1.0 Transitional, XHTML 1.0 Frameset, XHTML 1.1.)

- class—Gives the style class of the element. (XHTML 1.0 Strict, XHTML 1.0 Transitional, XHTML 1.0 Frameset, XHTML 1.1.)

- dir—Sets the direction of text that doesn't have an inherent direction in which you should read it, called directionally neutral text. You can set this attribute to ltr, for left-to-right text, or rtl, for right-to-left text. (XHTML 1.0 Strict, XHTML 1.0 Transitional, XHTML 1.0 Frameset, XHTML 1.1.)

- href—Contains the target URI of the resource. You must assign a value to either this attribute or the id attribute. (XHTML 1.0 Strict, XHTML 1.0 Transitional, XHTML 1.0 Frameset, XHTML 1.1.)

- hreflang—Indicates the base language of the target indicated in the href attribute. Set this to RFC 1766 values. (XHTML 1.0 Strict, XHTML 1.0 Transitional, XHTML 1.0 Frameset, XHTML 1.1.)

- id—Refers to the element; set this attribute to a unique identifier. (XHTML 1.0 Strict, XHTML 1.0 Transitional, XHTML 1.0 Frameset, XHTML 1.1.)

- lang—Specifies the base language used in the element. Applies only when the document is interpreted as HTML. (XHTML 1.0 Strict, XHTML 1.0 Transitional, XHTML 1.0 Frameset, XHTML 1.1.)

- media—Specifies the device that the document will be displayed on. Possible values are screen (the default), print, projection, braille, speech, or all (style information should be used for all devices). (XHTML 1.0 Strict, XHTML 1.0 Transitional, XHTML 1.0 Frameset, XHTML 1.1.)

- rel—Gives the relationship described by the hyperlink. (XHTML 1.0 Strict, XHTML 1.0 Transitional, XHTML 1.0 Frameset, XHTML 1.1.)

- rev—Same as the `rel` attribute, but the syntax works in the reverse direction. For example, a link from A to B with `rel="X"` signifies the same relationship as a link from B to A with `rev="X"`. (XHTML 1.0 Strict, XHTML 1.0 Transitional, XHTML 1.0 Frameset, XHTML 1.1.)

- `style`—Inline style indicating how to render the element. (XHTML 1.0 Strict, XHTML 1.0 Transitional, XHTML 1.0 Frameset, XHTML 1.1.)

- `target`—Indicates the named frame that serves as the target of the link. (XHTML 1.0 Transitional, XHTML 1.0 Frameset.)

- `title`—Contains the title of the element. (XHTML 1.0 Strict, XHTML 1.0 Transitional, XHTML 1.0 Frameset, XHTML 1.1.)

- `type`—Indicates the MIME type of the target given in the `href` attribute. (XHTML 1.0 Strict, XHTML 1.0 Transitional, XHTML 1.0 Frameset, XHTML 1.1.)

- `xml:lang`—Specifies the base language for the element when the document is interpreted as an XML document. (XHTML 1.0 Strict, XHTML 1.0 Transitional, XHTML 1.0 Frameset, XHTML 1.1.)

This element supports these event attributes: `onclick`, `ondblclick`, `onmousedown`, `onmouseup`, `onmouseover`, `onmousemove`, `onmouseout`, `onkeypress`, `onkeydown`, and `onkeyup`.

The `<link>` element specifies the relationship of the current document to other documents. I'll use this element to handle external stylesheets. You indicate the relationship with the `rel` attribute, which can take these values:

- `rel=alternate`—Links to an alternate resource

- `rel=appendix`—Links to an appendix

- `rel=bookmark`—Links to bookmarks, which provide links to entry points into a document

- `rel=chapter`—Links to a chapter

- `rel=contents`—Links to the contents section

- `rel=copyright`—Links to a copyright document for the current document

- `rel=glossary`—Links to a document providing a glossary of terms

- `rel=help`—Links to a document providing help

- `rel=home`—Links to a home page

- `rel=index`—Links to a document providing an index

- `rel=next`—Links to the next document

- `rel=previous`—Links to the previous document

- rel=section—Links to a section
- rel=start—Links to the start of a resource
- rel=stylesheet—Links to an external stylesheet
- rel=subsection—Links to a subsection
- rel=toc—Links to a document that holds a table of contents
- rel=up—Links to the parent of the current document.

Here's an example showing how to use an external stylesheet. I'm setting rel to stylesheet to indicate that the linked-to item is a stylesheet and href to the URI of the stylesheet:

Listing ch17_04.html

```
<!DOCTYPE html PUBLIC "-//W3C//DTD XHTML 1.0 Transitional//EN"
"http://www.w3.org/tr/xhtml1/DTD/xhtml1-transitional.dtd">
<html xmlns="http://www.w3.org/1999/xhtml" xml:lang="en" lang="en">
    <head>
        <title>
            Working With External Style Sheets
        </title>
        <link rel="stylesheet" href="ch17_05.css">
    </head>

    <body>
        <center>
            <h1>
                Working With External Style Sheets
            </h1>
            <p>
            This document is displayed using an external style sheet.
            </p>
        </center>
    </body>
</html>
```

Here's the stylesheet I'm using, ch17_05.css:

Listing ch17_05.css

```
body {background-color: #FFFFCC; font-family: Arial}
a:link {color: #0000FF}
a:visited {color: #FFFF00}
a:hover {color: #00FF00}
a:active {color: #FF0000}
p {font-style: italic}
```

That's all it takes. You can see the results in Figure 17-3. I'll take a closer look at working with stylesheets later in this chapter.

Figure 17-3
Using an external stylesheet in Netscape Navigator.

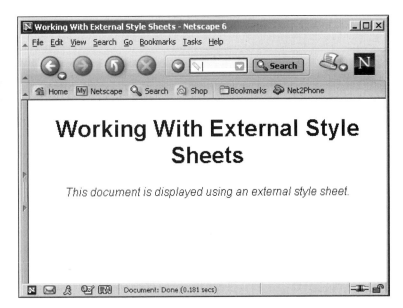

< table >—Creating Tables

The <table> element is always a popular one, and you use it to create tables. To build a table, you enclose other elements in <table>, such as <caption>, <tr>, <th>, <td>, <colspan>, <col>, <thead>, <tbody>, and <tfoot>. This element is supported in XHTML 1.0 Strict, XHTML 1.0 Transitional, XHTML 1.0 Frameset, and XHTML 1.1. Here are its attributes:

- align—Deprecated in HTML 4.0. Sets the horizontal alignment of the table in the browser window. You can set this to left, center, or right. (XHTML 1.0 Transitional, XHTML 1.0 Frameset.)

- bgcolor—Deprecated in HTML 4.0. Sets the background color of table cells. Even though this attribute is deprecated, stylesheet support for tables is still limited and inconsistent across browsers. (XHTML 1.0 Transitional, XHTML 1.0 Frameset.)

- border—Sets the border width, as measured in pixels. If you set this attribute to 0, the border is invisible. (XHTML 1.0 Transitional, XHTML 1.0 Frameset.)

- `cellpadding`—Specifies the spacing between cell walls and cell contents in pixels. (XHTML 1.0 Strict, XHTML 1.0 Transitional, XHTML 1.0 Frameset, XHTML 1.1.)

- `cellspacing`—Specifies the distance between cells. Set this to a value in pixels. (XHTML 1.0 Strict, XHTML 1.0 Transitional, XHTML 1.0 Frameset, XHTML 1.1.)

- `class`—Gives the style class of the element. (XHTML 1.0 Strict, XHTML 1.0 Transitional, XHTML 1.0 Frameset, XHTML 1.1.)

- `dir`—Sets the direction of text that doesn't have an inherent direction in which you should read it, called directionally neutral text. You can set this attribute to `ltr`, for left-to-right text, or `rtl`, for right-to-left text. (XHTML 1.0 Strict, XHTML 1.0 Transitional, XHTML 1.0 Frameset, XHTML 1.1.)

- `frame`—Determines the outer border display of the table using the Complex Table Model. You use this attribute with the `rules` attribute. Possible values are `void` (no borders), `above` (border on top side only), `below` (border on bottom side only), `hsides` (horizontal borders only), `vsides` (vertical borders only), `lhs` (border on left side only), `rhs` (border on right side only), `box` (border on all four sides), and `border` (the default, the same as `box`). (XHTML 1.0 Strict, XHTML 1.0 Transitional, XHTML 1.0 Frameset, XHTML 1.1.)

- `id`—Refers to the element; set this attribute to a unique identifier. (XHTML 1.0 Strict, XHTML 1.0 Transitional, XHTML 1.0 Frameset, XHTML 1.1.)

- `lang`—Specifies the base language used in the element. Applies only when the document is interpreted as HTML. (XHTML 1.0 Strict, XHTML 1.0 Transitional, XHTML 1.0 Frameset, XHTML 1.1.)

- `rules`—Specifies the interior struts in a table using the Complex Table Model. You can set this to `none` (no interior struts), `groups` (horizontal struts displayed between table groups created with the `thead`, `tbody`, `tfoot` and `colgroup` tags), `rows` (horizontal struts displayed between all table rows), `cols` (vertical struts displayed between all table columns), and `all` (struts displayed between all table cells). (XHTML 1.0 Strict, XHTML 1.0 Transitional, XHTML 1.0 Frameset, XHTML 1.1.)

- `style`—Inline style indicating how to render the element. (XHTML 1.0 Strict, XHTML 1.0 Transitional, XHTML 1.0 Frameset, XHTML 1.1.)

- `summary`—Gives summary information for nonvisual browsers. (XHTML 1.0 Strict, XHTML 1.0 Transitional, XHTML 1.0 Frameset, XHTML 1.1.)

- `title`—Contains the title of the element. (XHTML 1.0 Strict, XHTML 1.0 Transitional, XHTML 1.0 Frameset, XHTML 1.1.)

- `width`—Sets the width of the table. Set this to a pixel value or a percentage of the display area (add a percent sign [%] to such values). (XHTML 1.0 Strict, XHTML 1.0 Transitional, XHTML 1.0 Frameset, XHTML 1.1.)

- `xml:lang`—Specifies the base language for the element when the document is interpreted as an XML document. (XHTML 1.0 Strict, XHTML 1.0 Transitional, XHTML 1.0 Frameset, XHTML 1.1.)

Here are the XHTML events that this element supports: `onclick`, `ondblclick`, `onfocus`, `onblur`, `onmousedown`, `onmouseup`, `onmouseover`, `onmousemove`, `onmouseout`, `onkeypress`, `onkeydown`, and `onkeyup`.

The `<table>` element is what you use to create tables in XHTML. To create a table, you enclose everything in a `<table>` element:

```
<table>
    .
    .
    .
</table>
```

That creates a table, but nothing happens on the screen with this markup—you need to give the table some rows. See the next section to start fleshing things out.

\<tr\>–Creating Table Rows

You use `<tr>` to create rows in a table. This element can contain `<th>` (table header) and `<td>` (table data) elements. It is supported in XHTML 1.0 Strict, XHTML 1.0 Transitional, XHTML 1.0 Frameset, and XHTML 1.1. Here are this element's attributes:

- `align`—Specifies the horizontal alignment of the text in this table row. You can set this to `left`, `center`, `right`, `justify`, or `char`. Unlike other `align` attributes, this one is not deprecated. (XHTML 1.0 Strict, XHTML 1.0 Transitional, XHTML 1.0 Frameset, XHTML 1.1.)

- `bgcolor`—Deprecated in HTML 4.0. Specifies the background color of the table cells. (XHTML 1.0 Transitional, XHTML 1.0 Frameset.)

- `char`—Specifies a character to align text on. (XHTML 1.0 Strict, XHTML 1.0 Transitional, XHTML 1.0 Frameset, XHTML 1.1.)

- `charoff`—Sets the alignment offset to the first character to align on (which you set with `char`). (XHTML 1.0 Strict, XHTML 1.0 Transitional, XHTML 1.0 Frameset, XHTML 1.1.)

- `class`—Gives the style class of the element. (XHTML 1.0 Strict, XHTML 1.0 Transitional, XHTML 1.0 Frameset, XHTML 1.1.)

- `dir`—Sets the direction of text that doesn't have an inherent direction in which you should read it, called directionally neutral text. You can set this attribute to `ltr`, for left-to-right text, or `rtl`, for right-to-left text. (XHTML 1.0 Strict, XHTML 1.0 Transitional, XHTML 1.0 Frameset, XHTML 1.1.)

- `id`—Refers to the element; set this attribute to a unique identifier. (XHTML 1.0 Strict, XHTML 1.0 Transitional, XHTML 1.0 Frameset, XHTML 1.1.)

- `lang`—Specifies the base language used in the element. Applies only when the document is interpreted as HTML. (XHTML 1.0 Strict, XHTML 1.0 Transitional, XHTML 1.0 Frameset, XHTML 1.1.)

- `style`—Inline style indicating how to render the element. (XHTML 1.0 Strict, XHTML 1.0 Transitional, XHTML 1.0 Frameset, XHTML 1.1.)

- `title`—Contains the title of the element. (XHTML 1.0 Strict, XHTML 1.0 Transitional, XHTML 1.0 Frameset, XHTML 1.1.)

- `valign`—Sets the vertical alignment of the data in this row. Possible values are `top`, `middle`, `bottom`, and `baseline`. (XHTML 1.0 Strict, XHTML 1.0 Transitional, XHTML 1.0 Frameset, XHTML 1.1.)

- `xml:lang`—Specifies the base language for the element when the document is interpreted as an XML document. (XHTML 1.0 Strict, XHTML 1.0 Transitional, XHTML 1.0 Frameset, XHTML 1.1.)

Here are the events supported by this element: `onclick`, `ondblclick`, `onfocus`, `onblur`, `onmousedown`, `onmouseup`, `onmouseover`, `onmousemove`, `onmouseout`, `onkeypress`, `onkeydown`, and `onkeyup`.

You use <tr> inside <table> to create a row in a table. Here's how that looks:

```
<table>
    <tr>
        <td>
            Table Data
        </td>
        .
        .
        .
    </tr>
    .
    .
    .
</table>
```

There's a <tr> element for every row in an XHTML table, and the browser knows how many rows there will be in the table by counting the number of <tr> elements. This element contains <tr> elements, which you use to create table headers, and <td> elements, which hold the actual data in the cells in a table.

<*th*>–Creating Table Headings

You use the <th> element to create table headings, which are usually displayed in bold text, and label the columns in a table. This element is supported in XHTML 1.0 Strict, XHTML 1.0 Transitional, XHTML 1.0 Frameset, and XHTML 1.1. Here are its attributes:

- abbr—Holds an abbreviated name for a header. (XHTML 1.0 Strict, XHTML 1.0 Transitional, XHTML 1.0 Frameset, XHTML 1.1.)

- align—Sets the horizontal alignment of content in table cells. Possible values are left, center, right, justify, and char. (XHTML 1.0 Strict, XHTML 1.0 Transitional, XHTML 1.0 Frameset, XHTML 1.1.)

- axis—Contains a name for a cell (usually used only with table heading cells). Allows the table to be mapped to a tree hierarchy. (XHTML 1.0 Strict, XHTML 1.0 Transitional, XHTML 1.0 Frameset, XHTML 1.1.)

- bgcolor—Deprecated in HTML 4.0. Sets the background color of table cells. (XHTML 1.0 Transitional, XHTML 1.0 Frameset.)

- `char`—Specifies a character to align text on. (XHTML 1.0 Strict, XHTML 1.0 Transitional, XHTML 1.0 Frameset, XHTML 1.1.)

- `charoff`—Sets the alignment offset to the first character to align on (which you set with `char`). (XHTML 1.0 Strict, XHTML 1.0 Transitional, XHTML 1.0 Frameset, XHTML 1.1.)

- `class`—Gives the style class of the element. (XHTML 1.0 Strict, XHTML 1.0 Transitional, XHTML 1.0 Frameset, XHTML 1.1.)

- `colspan`—Specifies how many columns of the table this header should span (the default is 1). (XHTML 1.0 Strict, XHTML 1.0 Transitional, XHTML 1.0 Frameset, XHTML 1.1.)

- `dir`—Sets the direction of text that doesn't have an inherent direction in which you should read it, called directionally neutral text. You can set this attribute to `ltr`, for left-to-right text, or `rtl`, for right-to-left text. (XHTML 1.0 Strict, XHTML 1.0 Transitional, XHTML 1.0 Frameset, XHTML 1.1.)

- `headers`—Specifies a list of header cells that supply header information. (XHTML 1.0 Strict, XHTML 1.0 Transitional, XHTML 1.0 Frameset, XHTML 1.1.)

- `height`—Deprecated in HTML 4.0. Sets the height of the header in pixels. (XHTML 1.0 Transitional, XHTML 1.0 Frameset.)

- `id`—Refers to the element; set this attribute to a unique identifier. (XHTML 1.0 Strict, XHTML 1.0 Transitional, XHTML 1.0 Frameset, XHTML 1.1.)

- `lang`—Specifies the base language used in the element. Applies only when the document is interpreted as HTML. (XHTML 1.0 Strict, XHTML 1.0 Transitional, XHTML 1.0 Frameset, XHTML 1.1.)

- `nowrap`—Deprecated in HTML 4.0. Indicates that content should not be wrapped by the browser by adding line breaks. (XHTML 1.0 Transitional, XHTML 1.0 Frameset.)

- `rowspan`—Specifies how many rows of the table this header should span. (XHTML 1.0 Strict, XHTML 1.0 Transitional, XHTML 1.0 Frameset, XHTML 1.1.)

- `scope`—Specifies a set of data cells for which the header cell provides header information. You can set this to `row`, `col`, `rowgroup`, or `colgroup`. (XHTML 1.0 Strict, XHTML 1.0 Transitional, XHTML 1.0 Frameset, XHTML 1.1.)

- `style`—Inline style indicating how to render the element. (XHTML 1.0 Strict, XHTML 1.0 Transitional, XHTML 1.0 Frameset, XHTML 1.1.)

- `title`—Contains the title of the element. (XHTML 1.0 Strict, XHTML 1.0 Transitional, XHTML 1.0 Frameset, XHTML 1.1.)

- `valign`—Sets the vertical alignment of the data in this cell. You can set this to `top`, `middle`, `bottom`, or `baseline`. (XHTML 1.0 Strict, XHTML 1.0 Transitional, XHTML 1.0 Frameset, XHTML 1.1.)

- `width`—Deprecated in HTML 4.0. Gives the width of the header. (XHTML 1.0 Transitional, XHTML 1.0 Frameset.)

- `xml:lang`—Specifies the base language for the element when the document is interpreted as an XML document. (XHTML 1.0 Strict, XHTML 1.0 Transitional, XHTML 1.0 Frameset, XHTML 1.1.)

Here are the XHTML events supported by this element: `onclick`, `ondblclick`, `onfocus`, `onblur`, `onmousedown`, `onmouseup`, `onmouseover`, `onmousemove`, `onmouseout`, `onkeypress`, `onkeydown`, and `onkeyup`.

You use the `<th>` element to put a header on top of columns in a table. Headers like these can span several columns if you use the `colspan` attribute. Here's an example:

```
<table>
    <tr>
        <th>TIC</th>
        <th>TAC</th>
        <th>TOE</th>
    </tr>
    .
    .
    .
</table>
```

This adds three table headers on top of three columns: `TIC`, `TAC`, and `TOE`. The next step is adding cells to the table that can contain some data, and you do that with the `<td>` element.

<td>—Creating Table Data

The `<td>` element is where you place the data that you want in a cell in a table. You use this element inside the `<tr>` element. It's supported in XHTML 1.0 Strict, XHTML 1.0 Transitional, XHTML 1.0 Frameset, and XHTML 1.1. Here are this element's attributes:

- `abbr`—Gives an abbreviated name for a cell. (XHTML 1.0 Strict, XHTML 1.0 Transitional, XHTML 1.0 Frameset, XHTML 1.1, 4.)

- `align`—Sets the horizontal alignment of content in the table cell. You can set this to `left`, `center`, `right`, `justify`, or `char`. (XHTML 1.0 Strict, XHTML 1.0 Transitional, XHTML 1.0 Frameset, XHTML 1.1.)

- `axis`—Contains a name for a cell (usually used only with table heading cells). Allows the table to be mapped to a tree hierarchy. (XHTML 1.0 Strict, XHTML 1.0 Transitional, XHTML 1.0 Frameset, XHTML 1.1.)

- `bgcolor`—Deprecated in HTML 4.0. Sets the background color of table cells. (XHTML 1.0 Transitional, XHTML 1.0 Frameset.)

- `char`—Specifies a character to align text on. (XHTML 1.0 Strict, XHTML 1.0 Transitional, XHTML 1.0 Frameset, XHTML 1.1.)

- `charoff`—Sets the alignment offset to the first character to align on (which you set with `char`). (XHTML 1.0 Strict, XHTML 1.0 Transitional, XHTML 1.0 Frameset, XHTML 1.1.)

- `class`—Gives the style class of the element. (XHTML 1.0 Strict, XHTML 1.0 Transitional, XHTML 1.0 Frameset, XHTML 1.1.)

- `colspan`—Specifies how many columns this cell should span. (XHTML 1.0 Strict, XHTML 1.0 Transitional, XHTML 1.0 Frameset, XHTML 1.1.)

- `dir`—Sets the direction of text that doesn't have an inherent direction in which you should read it, called directionally neutral text. You can set this attribute to `ltr`, for left-to-right text, or `rtl`, for right-to-left text. (XHTML 1.0 Strict, XHTML 1.0 Transitional, XHTML 1.0 Frameset, XHTML 1.1.)

- `headers`—Specifies a list of header cells that supply header information. (XHTML 1.0 Strict, XHTML 1.0 Transitional, XHTML 1.0 Frameset, XHTML 1.1.)

- `height`—Deprecated in HTML 4.0. Sets the height of the cell in pixels. (XHTML 1.0 Transitional, XHTML 1.0 Frameset.)

- `id`—Refers to the element; set this attribute to a unique identifier. (XHTML 1.0 Strict, XHTML 1.0 Transitional, XHTML 1.0 Frameset, XHTML 1.1.)

- `lang`—Specifies the base language used in the element. Applies only when the document is interpreted as HTML. (XHTML 1.0 Strict, XHTML 1.0 Transitional, XHTML 1.0 Frameset, XHTML 1.1.)

- `nowrap`—Deprecated in HTML 4.0. Indicates that content should not be wrapped by the browser by adding line breaks. (XHTML 1.0 Transitional, XHTML 1.0 Frameset.)

- `rowspan`—Specifies how many rows of the table this cell should span. (XHTML 1.0 Strict, XHTML 1.0 Transitional, XHTML 1.0 Frameset, XHTML 1.1.)

- `scope`—Specifies a set of data cells for which the header cell provides header information. You can set this to `row`, `col`, `rowgroup`, or `colgroup`. (XHTML 1.0 Strict, XHTML 1.0 Transitional, XHTML 1.0 Frameset, XHTML 1.1.)

- `style`—Inline style indicating how to render the element. (XHTML 1.0 Strict, XHTML 1.0 Transitional, XHTML 1.0 Frameset, XHTML 1.1.)

- `title`—Contains the title of the element. (XHTML 1.0 Strict, XHTML 1.0 Transitional, XHTML 1.0 Frameset, XHTML 1.1.)

- `valign`—Sets the vertical alignment of the data in this cell. You can set this to `top`, `middle`, `bottom`, or `baseline`. (XHTML 1.0 Strict, XHTML 1.0 Transitional, XHTML 1.0 Frameset, XHTML 1.1.)

- `width`—Deprecated in HTML 4.0. Gives the width of the header. (XHTML 1.0 Transitional, XHTML 1.0 Frameset.)

- `xml:lang`—Specifies the base language for the element when the document is interpreted as an XML document. (XHTML 1.0 Strict, XHTML 1.0 Transitional, XHTML 1.0 Frameset, XHTML 1.1.)

Here are the events this element supports: `onclick`, `ondblclick`, `onfocus`, `onblur`, `onmousedown`, `onmouseup`, `onmouseover`, `onmousemove`, `onmouseout`, `onkeypress`, `onkeydown`, and `onkeyup`.

You use `<td>` elements to hold the data in a table's cells. The browser knows how many columns to create in the table depending on how many `<td>` or `<th>` elements you put into a row. For example, here's how I add data to the rows of a table using `<td>` elements:

Listing ch17_06.html

```
<!DOCTYPE html PUBLIC "-//W3C//DTD XHTML 1.0 Transitional//EN"
"http://www.w3.org/tr/xhtml1/DTD/xhtml1-transitional.dtd">
<html xmlns="http://www.w3.org/1999/xhtml" xml:lang="en" lang="en">
    <head>
        <title>
            Working With XHTML Tables
        </title>
    </head>

    <body>
        <center>
            <h1>
                Working With XHTML Tables
            </h1>
            <table>
                <tr>
                    <th>TIC</th>
                    <th>TAC</th>
                    <th>TOE</th>
                </tr>
                <tr>
                    <td>O</td>
                    <td>X</td>
                    <td>O</td>
                </tr>
                <tr>
                    <td>X</td>
                    <td>O</td>
                    <td>X</td>
                </tr>
                <tr>
                    <td>O</td>
                    <td>X</td>
                    <td>O</td>
                </tr>
            </table>
        </center>
    </body>
</html>
```

You can see the results in Figure 17-4. That's all it takes to create simple tables in XHTML. The process is just like HTML—you enclose everything in a `<table>` element, use `<tr>` to create the rows of a table, and enter the data in each cell using `<td>` (or `<th>` for header text).

Figure 17-4
A table written
in XHTML.

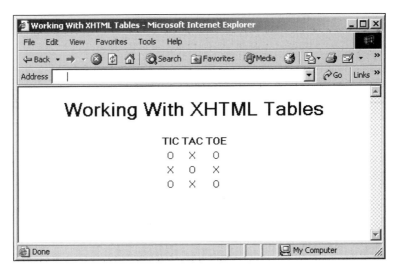

<*frameset*>—Creating Documents with Frames

You use the `<frameset>` element when you want to display frames in a document. The `<frameset>` element replaces the `<body>` element in such documents; in XHTML 1.0, that means you use the XHTML 1.0 Frameset DTD. This element is supported in XHTML 1.0 Frameset only. The `<frame>` and `<frameset>` elements are *not* supported in XHTML 1.1; the XHTML 1.1 DTD does not makes any mention of these elements or of frames at all, and these elements are specifically listed as unsupported in XHTML 1.1. Why aren't frames supported in XHTML 1.1? They're not supported because W3C expects stylesheets to handle the presentation techniques that you use frames for today. Whether the Web community will ultimately accept that is anyone's guess.

Here are the attributes of this element:

- `class`—Gives the style class of the element. (XHTML 1.0 Frameset.)

- `cols`—Sets the number of columns (vertical framed bands) in the frameset. (XHTML 1.0 Frameset.)

- `dir`—Sets the direction of text that doesn't have an inherent direction in which you should read it, called directionally neutral text. You can set this attribute to `ltr`, for left-to-right text, or `rtl`, for right-to-left text. (XHTML 1.0 Frameset.)

- `id`—Refers to the element; set this attribute to a unique identifier. (XHTML 1.0 Frameset.)

- `lang`—Specifies the base language used in the element. Applies only when the document is interpreted as HTML. (XHTML 1.0 Frameset.)

- `rows`—Sets the number of rows (horizontal framed bands) in the frameset. (XHTML 1.0 Frameset.)

- `style`—Inline style indicating how to render the element. (XHTML 1.0 Frameset.)

- `title`—Contains the title of the element. (XHTML 1.0 Frameset.)

- `xml:lang`—Specifies the base language for the element when the document is interpreted as an XML document. (XHTML 1.0 Frameset.)

This element supports no XHTML events.

You use the `<frameset>` element and the XHTML frameset DTD to format a page into frames. This element takes the place of the `<body>` element in documents that display frames. To create the frames themselves, you use the `<frame>` element.

To format the display into frames, you use the `rows` or `cols` attributes of the `<frameset>` element. You indicate the number of rows or columns you want to use by giving their heights or widths in a comma-separated list. To specify those heights or widths, you can give pixel measurements or a percentage measurement (such as `"40%"`) to request a percentage of the available display area. If you use an asterisk, the browser will try to give you the remaining display area; for example, `cols="200, *"` creates one vertical frame of 200 pixels and a second vertical frame filling the remainder of the display area. I recommend using percentage measurements rather than pixel measurements because the user may resize the browser window, unless you're using wide graphics or table with set widths.

For example, here's how I creates two columns—that is, two vertical frames—each of which take up half the available width (note that I'm using the XHTML 1.0 Frameset DTD):

```
<?xml version="1.0"?>
<!DOCTYPE html PUBLIC "-//W3C//DTD XHTML 1.0 Frameset//EN"
"http://www.w3.org/TR/xhtml1/DTD/xhtml1-frameset.dtd">
<html xmlns="http://www.w3.org/1999/xhtml" xml:lang="en" lang="en">
    <head>
```

```
    <title>
        Using XHTML Frames
    </title>
</head>

<frameset cols = "50%, 50%">
    .
    .
    .
</frameset>
</html>
```

So how do you actually create the frames that should be displayed? Take a look at the next section.

<frame>—Creating Individual Frames

You use the `<frame>` element to create an individual frame. This element is an empty element, and you use it inside the `<frameset>` element. It's supported in XHTML 1.0 Frameset only. Here are its attributes:

- `class`—Gives the style class of the element. (XHTML 1.0 Frameset.)

- `dir`—Sets the direction of text that doesn't have an inherent direction in which you should read it, called directionally neutral text. You can set this attribute to `ltr`, for left-to-right text, or `rtl`, for right-to-left text. (XHTML 1.0 Frameset.)

- `frameborder`—Sets whether borders enclose the frame. In Netscape Navigator, you set this attribute to `yes` (the default) or `no`; in the Internet Explorer you set it to `1` (the default) or `0` (no border). (XHTML 1.0 Frameset.)

- `id`—Refer to the element; set this attribute to a unique identifier. (XHTML 1.0 Frameset.)

- `lang`—Specifies the base language used in the element. Applies only when the document is interpreted as HTML. (XHTML 1.0 Frameset.)

- `longdesc`—Specifies the URI for a long description of the frame contents, which may include markup. (XHTML 1.0 Frameset.)

- `marginheight`—Sets the height of the top and bottom margins used in the frame. (XHTML 1.0 Frameset.)

- marginwidth—Sets the width of the right and left margins used in the frame. (XHTML 1.0 Frameset.)

- name—Sets the name of the frame, which you can use as a target destination for <a>, <area>, <base>, and <form> elements. (XHTML 1.0 Frameset.)

- noresize—Indicates that the frame may not be resized. The default is that frames may be resized by dragging the border. (XHTML 1.0 Frameset.)

- scrolling—Sets scrollbar action. Possible values are auto, yes, and no. (XHTML 1.0 Frameset.)

- src—Required. Holds the URI of the frame document. (XHTML 1.0 Frameset.)

- style—Inline style indicating how to display the element. (XHTML 1.0 Frameset.)

- title—Contains the title of the element. (XHTML 1.0 Frameset.)

- xml:lang—Specifies the base language for the element when the document is interpreted as an XML document. (XHTML 1.0 Frameset.)

This element does not support any XHTML events.

You can use the <frame> element inside a <frameset> element to create a frame. This element exists so that you can specify the document that is displayed in a URI. That's the one required attribute in this element: src, which holds the URI of the document the frame is to display.

For example, here's how I might display two frames, placing the contents of the document ch17_08.html in one and ch17_09.html in the other:

Listing ch17_07.html

```
<?xml version="1.0"?>
<!DOCTYPE html PUBLIC "-//W3C//DTD XHTML 1.0 Frameset//EN"
"http://www.w3.org/TR/xhtml1/DTD/xhtml1-frameset.dtd">
<html xmlns="http://www.w3.org/1999/xhtml" xml:lang="en" lang="en">
    <head>
        <title>
            Using XHTML Frames
        </title>
    </head>

    <frameset cols = "50%, 50%">
```

```
            <frame src="ch17_08.html" />
            <frame src="ch17_09.html" />
    </frameset>
</html>
```

Here's ch17_08.html:

Listing ch17_08.html

```
<?xml version="1.0"?>
<!DOCTYPE html PUBLIC "-//W3C//DTD XHTML 1.0 Frameset//EN"
"http://www.w3.org/TR/xhtml1/DTD/xhtml1-frameset.dtd">
<html xmlns="http://www.w3.org/1999/xhtml" xml:lang="en" lang="en">
    <head>
        <title>
            Using XHTML Frames
        </title>
    </head>

    <body bgcolor=red>
    <h1>
        <center>
        This is frame 1.
        </center>
    </h1>
    </body>
</html>
```

And here's ch17_09.html:

Listing ch17_09.html

```
<?xml version="1.0"?>
<!DOCTYPE html PUBLIC "-//W3C//DTD XHTML 1.0 Frameset//EN"
"http://www.w3.org/TR/xhtml1/DTD/xhtml1-frameset.dtd">
<html xmlns="http://www.w3.org/1999/xhtml" xml:lang="en" lang="en">
    <head>
        <title>
            Using XHTML Frames
        </title>
    </head>

    <body bgcolor=cyan>
    <h1>
        <center>
        This is frame 2.
        </center>
    </h1>
    </body>
</html>
```

The result of this XHTML appears in Figure 17-5.

Figure 17-5
Displaying
XHTML frames.

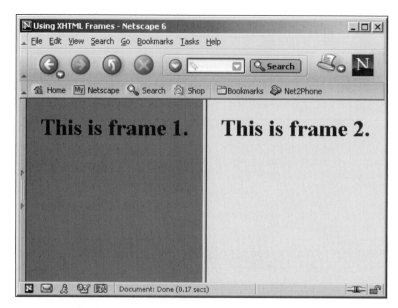

That's all it takes to create and display frames in XHTML, but bear in mind that the W3C has apparently targeted frames for extinction. Will stylesheets be able to take over what frames do today? What about XFrames? That remains to be seen. I'll take a look at handling stylesheets now.

Using Stylesheets in XHTML

You can use stylesheets in several ways in XHTML. As we already saw in this chapter, you can use the `<link>` element to connect an external stylesheet to a document, like this:

```
<!DOCTYPE html PUBLIC "-//W3C//DTD XHTML 1.0 Transitional//EN"
"http://www.w3.org/tr/xhtml1/DTD/xhtml1-transitional.dtd">
<html xmlns="http://www.w3.org/1999/xhtml" xml:lang="en" lang="en">
    <head>
        <title>
            Working With External Style Sheets
        </title>
        <link rel="stylesheet" href="style.css">
    </head>

    <body>
        <center>
            <h1>
                Working With External Style Sheets
```

```
            </h1>
            <p>
            This document is displayed using an external style sheet.
            </p>
        </center>
    </body>
</html>
```

This XHTML links the Web page to an external stylesheet named style.css, written in CSS (refer to Chapter 9, "Cascading Style Sheets," for more on CSS). Here's how that stylesheet looks:

```
body {background-color: #FFFFCC; font-family: Arial}
a:link {color: #0000FF}
a:visited {color: #FFFF00}
a:hover {color: #00FF00}
a:active {color: #FF0000}
p {font-style: italic}
```

XHTML documents can be interpreted in two ways by browsers today: as HTML or as XML (and, in the future, presumably as XHTML). If you treat an XHTML document as XML (that is, by giving it the extension .xml), you use an XML processing instruction, `<?xml-stylesheet?>`, to indicate what stylesheet you want to use, as we did in Chapter 9:

```
<?xml version="1.0"?>
<!DOCTYPE html PUBLIC "-//W3C//DTD XHTML 1.0 Transitional//EN"
"http://www.w3.org/tr/xhtml1/DTD/xhtml1-transitional.dtd">
<?xml-stylesheet type="text/css" href="style.css"?>
<html xmlns="http://www.w3.org/1999/xhtml" xml:lang="en" lang="en">
    <head>
        <title>
            Working With External Style Sheets
        </title>
        <link rel="stylesheet" href="style.css">
    </head>

    <body>
        <center>
            <h1>
                Working With External Style Sheets
            </h1>

            <p>
            This document is displayed using an external style sheet.
            </p>
        </center>
    </body>
</html>
```

Besides linking to external stylesheets, XHTML documents that are interpreted as HTML can use *embedded* stylesheets if you use the `<style>` element.

<style>—Creating Embedded Stylesheets in XHTML

The `<style>` element lets you embed full stylesheets in XHTML documents. It is supported in XHTML 1.0 Strict, XHTML 1.0 Transitional, XHTML 1.0 Frameset, and XHTML 1.1. Here are the attributes of this element:

- `dir`—Sets the direction of text that doesn't have an inherent direction in which you should read it, called directionally neutral text. You can set this attribute to `ltr`, for left-to-right text, or `rtl`, for right-to-left text. (XHTML 1.0 Strict, XHTML 1.0 Transitional, XHTML 1.0 Frameset, XHTML 1.1.)

- `lang`—Specifies the base language used in the element. Applies only when the document is interpreted as HTML. (XHTML 1.0 Strict, XHTML 1.0 Transitional, XHTML 1.0 Frameset, XHTML 1.1.)

- `media`—Specifies the target media for stylesheet. Possible values are `screen` (the default), `print`, `projection`, `braille`, `speech`, and `all`. (XHTML 1.0 Strict, XHTML 1.0 Transitional, XHTML 1.0 Frameset, XHTML 1.1.)

- `title`—Names the stylesheet so the browser can build a menu of alternative stylesheets. (XHTML 1.0 Strict, XHTML 1.0 Transitional, XHTML 1.0 Frameset, XHTML 1.1.)

- `type`—Required. Indicates the MIME type of the `<style>` element content. (XHTML 1.0 Strict, XHTML 1.0 Transitional, XHTML 1.0 Frameset, XHTML 1.1.)

- `xml:lang`—Specifies the base language for the element when the document is interpreted as an XML document. (XHTML 1.0 Strict, XHTML 1.0 Transitional, XHTML 1.0 Frameset, XHTML 1.1.)

- `xml:space`—Set to `preserve` to preserve spacing. (XHTML 1.0 Strict, XHTML 1.0 Transitional, XHTML 1.0 Frameset, XHTML 1.1.)

This element does not support any XHTML events.

The `<style>` element usually goes in a Web page's head, and you can use it to set styles, just as you can with an external stylesheet. Here's an example that creates the same display as the example in the previous topic. Note that the type attribute is required in XHTML:

Listing ch17_10.html

```
<?xml version="1.0"?>
<!DOCTYPE html PUBLIC "-//W3C//DTD XHTML 1.0 Transitional//EN"
"http://www.w3.org/tr/xhtml1/DTD/xhtml1-transitional.dtd">
<html xmlns="http://www.w3.org/1999/xhtml" xml:lang="en" lang="en">
    <head>
        <title>
            Working With External Style Sheets
        </title>
        <style type="text/css">
            body {background-color: #FFFFCC; font-family: Arial}
            a:link {color: #0000FF}
            a:visited {color: #FFFF00}
            a:hover {color: #00FF00}
            a:active {color: #FF0000}
            p {font-style: italic}
        </style>
    </head>

    <body>
        <center>
            <h1>
                Working With External Style Sheets
            </h1>

            <p>
            This document is displayed using an external style sheet.
            </p>
        </center>
    </body>
</html>
```

Here's an important note: XHTML browsers are allowed to read and interpret every part of your document. If your stylesheet includes the characters < or & or]]> or --, you should make your stylesheet *external* so that those characters are not parsed and mistaken for markup. Also, XML parsers, like the ones inside XHTML browsers, are permitted to remove comments; the practice of "hiding" stylesheets inside comments as Web authors sometimes did to make documents backward compatible might not work as expected in XHTML.

Using Inline Styles in XHTML

In XHTML, you can also *create* inline styles, in which you apply styles to one XHTML element only. You create inline styles with the style attribute that most XHTML elements have. Here's an example. This example creates the same result as the previous two examples, but this time I'm using the style attribute, not the `<link>` element to link to an external stylesheet or the `<style>` element to create an embedded stylesheet:

Listing ch17_11.html

```
<?xml version="1.0"?>
<!DOCTYPE html PUBLIC "-//W3C//DTD XHTML 1.0 Transitional//EN"
"http://www.w3.org/tr/xhtml1/DTD/xhtml1-transitional.dtd">
<html xmlns="http://www.w3.org/1999/xhtml" xml:lang="en" lang="en">
    <head>
        <title>
            Working With External Style Sheets
        </title>
    </head>

    <body style="background-color: #FFFFCC; font-family: Arial">
        <center>
            <h1>
                Working With External Style Sheets
            </h1>

            <p style="font-style: italic">
            This document is displayed using an external style sheet.
            </p>
        </center>
    </body>
</html>
```

You usually use inline styles for short amounts of text; in fact, style purists insist that you should stay away from inline styles because this decentralizes the definition of styles, mixing markup with content more than they like. Note that, as with embedded stylesheets, if your stylesheet includes the characters <, or &, or]]>, or - -, you should make your stylesheet external.

<*script*>–Using Script Programming

You use the `<script>` element to embed a script, such as those written in JavaScript in an XHTML document. You usually place this element in a document's `<head>` section, except when the code writes directly to the document's body—in that case, you should place it in the document's body. This element is supported in XHTML 1.0 Strict, XHTML 1.0 Transitional, XHTML 1.0 Frameset, and XHTML 1.1. Here are the attributes of this element:

- `charset`—Gives the character encoding of the script contents. (XHTML 1.0 Strict, XHTML 1.0 Transitional, XHTML 1.0 Frameset, XHTML 1.1.)

- `defer`—Tells the browser that the script is not going to generate any document content. (XHTML 1.0 Strict, XHTML 1.0 Transitional, XHTML 1.0 Frameset, XHTML 1.1.)

- `language`—Specifies the scripting language. This attribute is required if the `src` attribute is not set; it is optional otherwise. (XHTML 1.0 Strict, XHTML 1.0 Transitional, XHTML 1.0 Frameset.)

- `src`—Holds a URI for the script code. (XHTML 1.0 Strict, XHTML 1.0 Transitional, XHTML 1.0 Frameset.)

- `type`—Required. Holds the Multipurpose Internet Mail Extension (MIME) type of the scripting code. (XHTML 1.0 Strict, XHTML 1.0 Transitional, XHTML 1.0 Frameset.)

- `xml:space`—Set to `preserve` to preserve spacing. (XHTML 1.0 Strict, XHTML 1.0 Transitional, XHTML 1.0 Frameset, XHTML 1.1.)

This element does not support any XHTML events.

You use the `<script>` element to embed a script in a document. In XHTML, the `type` attribute, which you set to `"text/javascript"` in JavaScript, is required. In the following listing, note that, normally, `<script>` goes in a document's `<head>` element; however, because this script writes a messge, `Welcome to XHTML scripting!`, to the document's body, it's supposed to be in the `<body>` element. (Note also that the `document.open()` and `document.close()` calls are not needed in Internet Explorer.)

Listing ch17_12.html

```
<?xml version="1.0"?>
<!DOCTYPE html PUBLIC "-//W3C//DTD XHTML 1.0 Transitional//EN"
"http://www.w3.org/tr/xhtml1/DTD/xhtml1-transitional.dtd">
<html xmlns="http://www.w3.org/1999/xhtml" xml:lang="en" lang="en">
    <head>
        <title>
            Welcome to XHTML scripting
        </title>
    </head>

    <body>
        <script type = "text/javascript" language="javascript">
            document.open()
            document.writeln("Welcome to XHTML scripting!")
            document.close()
        </script>
    </body>
</html>
```

You can see the results of this XHTML in Figure 17-6.

Figure 17-6
Running
JavaScript in
XHTML.

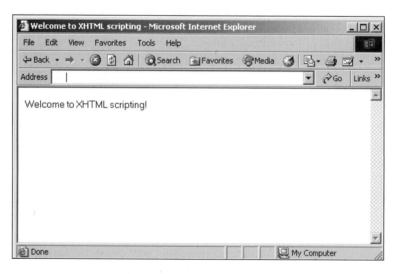

In HTML programming, you used to enclose the actual JavaScript in an HTML comment like this (note that I end the comment with a JavaScript comment marker, //; if I didn't, some HTML browsers would try to read --> as script):

```
<?xml version="1.0"?>
<!DOCTYPE html PUBLIC "-//W3C//DTD XHTML 1.0 Transitional//EN"
"http://www.w3.org/tr/xhtml1/DTD/xhtml1-transitional.dtd">
<html xmlns="http://www.w3.org/1999/xhtml" xml:lang="en" lang="en">
    <head>
        <title>
            Welcome To JavaScript
        </title>
    </head>

    <body>
        <script type = "text/javascript" language="javascript">
            <!--
            document.open()
            document.writeln("Welcome to XHTML scripting!")
            document.close()
            //-->
        </script>
    </body>
</html>
```

You used to do that because if a browser doesn't understand the `<script>` tag, it'll display what's inside the `<script>` element—the JavaScript code—as text. If you enclose that text in what looks like an HTML comment to the browser, it won't display the code. However, that's no good in XML because XML parsers are allowed to remove what they consider to be comments from the document entirely and not pass them on to the browser.

While we're on the topic, it's worth noting that if your script contains sensitive characters such as < and &, they may be treated as markup by an XHTML browser. To avoid that, the W3C helpfully suggests that you enclose the script in a CDATA section:

```
<?xml version="1.0"?>
<!DOCTYPE html PUBLIC "-//W3C//DTD XHTML 1.0 Transitional//EN"
"http://www.w3.org/tr/xhtml1/DTD/xhtml1-transitional.dtd">
<html xmlns="http://www.w3.org/1999/xhtml" xml:lang="en" lang="en">
    <head>
        <title>
            Welcome to XHTML scripting
        </title>
    </head>

    <body>
        <script type = "text/javascript" language="javascript">
            <![CDATA[
            document.open()
            document.writeln("Welcome to XHTML scripting!")
            document.close()
            ]]>
```

```
        </script>
    </body>
</html>
```

Unfortunately, no major HTML browser today has any idea what to do with CDATA sections in documents that the browsers consider to be HTML. Your only real alternative here is to store the script in an external file so that it won't be parsed and assign the src attribute the URI of that file. Here's how that looks—in this case, I'm storing the JavaScript code in a file named ch17_14.js:

Listing ch17_13.html

```
<?xml version="1.0"?>
<!DOCTYPE html PUBLIC "-//W3C//DTD XHTML 1.0 Transitional//EN"
"http://www.w3.org/tr/xhtml1/DTD/xhtml1-transitional.dtd">
<html xmlns="http://www.w3.org/1999/xhtml" xml:lang="en" lang="en">
    <head>
        <title>
            Welcome to XHTML scripting
        </title>
    </head>

    <body>
        <script type = "text/javascript" language="javascript"
        src="ch17_14.js">
        </script>
    </body>
</html>
```

Here, ch17_14.js, stored in the same directory as the Web page itself, contains this code:

Listing ch17_14.js

```
document.open()
document.writeln("Welcome to XHTML scripting!")
document.close()
```

This XHTML gives the same results as the earlier examples. What's important to remember here is that you should use external scripts if your script uses the characters <, or &, or]]>, or -- because an XHTML browser may interpret those characters as markup.

<form>—Creating XHTML Forms

You use the `<form>` element to create an XHTML form, which you use to contain XHTML controls such as buttons and text fields. This element is supported in XHTML 1.0 Strict, XHTML 1.0 Transitional, XHTML 1.0 Frameset, and XHTML 1.1. Here are its attributes:

- `accept`—Holds a comma-separated list of content types that a server processing this form must handle correctly. (XHTML 1.0 Strict, XHTML 1.0 Transitional, XHTML 1.0 Frameset, XHTML 1.1, 4.)

- `accept-charset`—Holds a list of possible language character sets for the form data. (XHTML 1.0 Strict, XHTML 1.0 Transitional, XHTML 1.0 Frameset, XHTML 1.1, 4.)

- `action`—Required. Gives the URI that will handle the form data. (XHTML 1.0 Strict, XHTML 1.0 Transitional, XHTML 1.0 Frameset, XHTML 1.1.)

- `class`—Gives the style class of the element. (XHTML 1.0 Strict, XHTML 1.0 Transitional, XHTML 1.0 Frameset, XHTML 1.1.)

- `dir`—Sets the direction of text that doesn't have an inherent direction in which you should read it, called directionally neutral text. You can set this attribute to `ltr`, for left-to-right text, or `rtl`, for right-to-left text. (XHTML 1.0 Strict, XHTML 1.0 Transitional, XHTML 1.0 Frameset, XHTML 1.1.)

- `enctype`—Sets the MIME type used to encode the name/value pairs when sent to the action URI. The default is `"application/x-www-form-urlencoded"`. (XHTML 1.0 Strict, XHTML 1.0 Transitional, XHTML 1.0 Frameset, XHTML 1.1.)

- `id`—Refers to the element; set this attribute to a unique identifier. (XHTML 1.0 Strict, XHTML 1.0 Transitional, XHTML 1.0 Frameset, XHTML 1.1.)

- `lang`—Specifies the base language used in the element. Applies only when the document is interpreted as HTML. (XHTML 1.0 Strict, XHTML 1.0 Transitional, XHTML 1.0 Frameset, XHTML 1.1.)

- `method`—Indicates a method or protocol for sending data to the target action URI. The `GET` method is the default; the other alternative is `POST`. (XHTML 1.0 Strict, XHTML 1.0 Transitional, XHTML 1.0 Frameset, XHTML 1.1.)

- name—Deprecated. Gives a name to the form so you can reference it in code. Use the `id` attribute instead in browsers that understand it. (XHTML 1.0 Transitional, XHTML 1.0 Frameset.)

- style—Inline style indicating how to render the element. (XHTML 1.0 Strict, XHTML 1.0 Transitional, XHTML 1.0 Frameset, XHTML 1.1.)

- target—Indicates a named frame for the browser to display the form results in. (XHTML 1.0 Transitional, XHTML 1.0 Frameset.)

- title—Contains the title of the element. (XHTML 1.0 Strict, XHTML 1.0 Transitional, XHTML 1.0 Frameset, XHTML 1.1.)

- xml:lang—Specifies the base language for the element when the document is interpreted as an XML document. (XHTML 1.0 Strict, XHTML 1.0 Transitional, XHTML 1.0 Frameset, XHTML 1.1.)

Here are the XHTML events this element supports: `onclick`, `ondblclick`, `onmousedown`, `onmouseup`, `onmouseover`, `onmousemove`, `onmouseout`, `onkeypress`, `onkeydown`, `onkeyup`, `onsubmit`, and `onreset`.

When you want to use controls, such as buttons and text fields, in a Web page, you should enclose the control elements in a `<form>` element. (Controls won't even appear in Netscape Navigator unless you enclose them in a `<form>` element.)

Forms were originally intended to be used to send data (such as the contents of text fields) back to the server. The target URI to send that data to is placed in the `action` attribute, and the W3C has made that attribute required for forms. We'll see how to send data to a server in Chapter 20, "WML, ASP, JSP, Servlets, and Perl," and we'll use the `action` attribute there; until then, I'll just set the `action` attribute to `"action"`. In addition, note that in XHTML, you're supposed to give XHTML forms an ID with the `ID` attribute. However, some browsers, such as Netscape Navigator, don't understand that attribute and use `name` instead. The only alternative in this case is to use both the `ID` and the `name` attributes here.

Let's see an example. Here, the document will display a message that, when clicked, displays `Hello from JavaScript.` in a text field. Here's the code (note that the `<br>` element will be deprecated in XHTML 2.0):

Listing ch17_15.html

```
<?xml version="1.0"?>
<!DOCTYPE html PUBLIC "-//W3C//DTD XHTML 1.0 Transitional//EN"
"http://www.w3.org/tr/xhtml1/DTD/xhtml1-transitional.dtd">
<html xmlns="http://www.w3.org/1999/xhtml" xml:lang="en" lang="en">
    <head>
```

```
<title>
    Using Forms in XHTML
</title>

<script language = "javascript">
    function displayMessage()
    {
        document.form1.textfield.value = "Hello from JavaScript."
    }
</script>
</head>

<body>
    <center>
        <h1>
            Using Forms in XHTML
        </h1>
        <form name = "form1" id = "form1" action = "action">
            <input type = "text" name = "textfield" size = "25" />
            <br />
            <br />
            <input type = "button" value = "Click Me"
                onclick = "displayMessage()" />
        </form>
    </center>
</body>
</html>
```

You can see the results of this XHTML in Figure 17-7.

Figure 17-7
Using an
XHTML form in
the Netscape
Navigator.

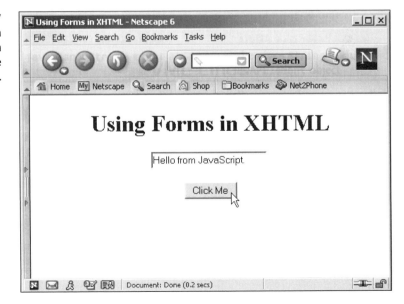

This document used both a button and a text field. I'll take a look at how to create those two controls in XHTML next.

<input type = "button">–Creating Controls

You use the `<input>` element to create controls such as buttons and text fields. Setting the `type` attribute indicates what kind of control you want to create, and this element supports different attributes based on control type. This element is empty and is supported in XHTML 1.0 Strict, XHTML 1.0 Transitional, XHTML 1.0 Frameset, and XHTML 1.1. Here are the attributes for `<input type="button">`:

- `accesskey`—Assigns a keyboard access key to the button. (XHTML 1.0 Strict, XHTML 1.0 Transitional.)

- `class`—Gives the style class of the element. (XHTML 1.0 Strict, XHTML 1.0 Transitional, XHTML 1.0 Frameset, XHTML 1.1.)

- `dir`—Sets the direction of text that doesn't have an inherent direction in which you should read it, called directionally neutral text. You can set this attribute to `ltr`, for left-to-right text, or `rtl`, for right-to-left text. (XHTML 1.0 Strict, XHTML 1.0 Transitional, XHTML 1.0 Frameset, XHTML 1.1.)

- `disabled`—Indicates that the element should be disabled when first displayed. (XHTML 1.0 Strict, XHTML 1.0 Transitional, XHTML 1.0 Frameset, XHTML 1.1.)

- `id`—Refers to the element; set this attribute to a unique identifier. (XHTML 1.0 Strict, XHTML 1.0 Transitional, XHTML 1.0 Frameset, XHTML 1.1.)

- `lang`—Specifies the base language used in the element. Applies only when the document is interpreted as HTML. (XHTML 1.0 Strict, XHTML 1.0 Transitional, XHTML 1.0 Frameset, XHTML 1.1.)

- `name`—Gives the element a name. (XHTML 1.0 Strict, XHTML 1.0 Transitional, XHTML 1.0 Frameset, XHTML 1.1.)

- `size`—Sets the size of the control. (XHTML 1.0 Strict, XHTML 1.0 Transitional, XHTML 1.0 Frameset, XHTML 1.1.)

- `style`—Inline style indicating how to render the element. (XHTML 1.0 Strict, XHTML 1.0 Transitional, XHTML 1.0 Frameset, XHTML 1.1.)

- tabindex—Specifies the tab sequence of hyperlinks in the page for keyboard navigation. (XHTML 1.0 Strict, XHTML 1.0 Transitional, XHTML 1.0 Frameset, XHTML 1.1.)

- title—Contains the title of the element. (XHTML 1.0 Strict, XHTML 1.0 Transitional, XHTML 1.0 Frameset, XHTML 1.1.)

- type—Specifies the type of the element. (XHTML 1.0 Strict, XHTML 1.0 Transitional, XHTML 1.0 Frameset, XHTML 1.1.)

- value—Specifies the caption of the element. (XHTML 1.0 Strict, XHTML 1.0 Transitional, XHTML 1.0 Frameset, XHTML 1.1.)

- xml:lang—Specifies the base language for the element when the document is interpreted as an XML document. (XHTML 1.0 Strict, XHTML 1.0 Transitional, XHTML 1.0 Frameset, XHTML 1.1.)

This element supports these XHTML events: onclick, ondblclick, onmousedown, onmouseup, onmouseover, onmousemove, onmouseout, onkeypress, onkeydown, onkeyup, onfocus, onblur, onselect, and onchange.

You can create buttons in XHTML with the <input type="button"> element (and also with the <button> element). We saw an example in the previous topic:

```
<?xml version="1.0"?>
<!DOCTYPE html PUBLIC "-//W3C//DTD XHTML 1.0 Transitional//EN"
"http://www.w3.org/tr/xhtml1/DTD/xhtml1-transitional.dtd">
<html xmlns="http://www.w3.org/1999/xhtml" xml:lang="en" lang="en">
    <head>
        <title>
            Using Forms in XHTML
        </title>

        <script language = "javascript">
            function displayMessage()
            {
                document.form1.textfield.value = "Hello from JavaScript."
            }
        </script>
    </head>

    <body>
        <center>
            <h1>
                Using Forms in XHTML
            </h1>
            <form name = "form1" id = "form1" action = "action">
```

```
                   <input type = "text" name = "textfield" size = "25" />
                   <br />
                   <br />
                   <input type = "button" value = "Click Me"
                       onclick = "displayMessage()" />
            </form>
        </center>
    </body>
</html>
```

You can create plenty of other controls, of course. I'll take a brief look at creating text fields next.

<input type="text">—Creating Text Fields

You use the `<input type = "text">` element to create text fields. This element is an empty element and is supported in XHTML 1.0 Strict, XHTML 1.0 Transitional, XHTML 1.0 Frameset, and XHTML 1.1. Here are its attributes:

- accesskey—Assigns a keyboard access key to the button. (XHTML 1.0 Strict, XHTML 1.0 Transitional.)

- class—Gives the style class of the element. (XHTML 1.0 Strict, XHTML 1.0 Transitional, XHTML 1.0 Frameset, XHTML 1.1.)

- dir—Sets the direction of text that doesn't have an inherent direction in which you should read it, called directionally neutral text. You can set this attribute to ltr, for left-to-right text, or rtl, for right-to-left text. (XHTML 1.0 Strict, XHTML 1.0 Transitional, XHTML 1.0 Frameset, XHTML 1.1.)

- disabled—Indicates that the element should be disabled when first displayed. (XHTML 1.0 Strict, XHTML 1.0 Transitional, XHTML 1.0 Frameset, XHTML 1.1.)

- id—Refers to the element; set this attribute to a unique identifier. (XHTML 1.0 Strict, XHTML 1.0 Transitional, XHTML 1.0 Frameset, XHTML 1.1.)

- lang—Specifies the base language used in the element. Applies only when the document is interpreted as HTML. (XHTML 1.0 Strict, XHTML 1.0 Transitional, XHTML 1.0 Frameset, XHTML 1.1, 3, 4, IE4, IE5.)

- `maxlength`—Sets the maximum number of characters that can be entered into the text field. The text field will scroll as needed if `maxlength` is greater than value of the `size` attribute. (XHTML 1.0 Strict, XHTML 1.0 Transitional, XHTML 1.0 Frameset, XHTML 1.1.)

- `name`—Gives the element a name. (XHTML 1.0 Strict, XHTML 1.0 Transitional, XHTML 1.0 Frameset, XHTML 1.1.)

- `readonly`—Specifies that the content of the text field is read-only, which means that it cannot be modified. (XHTML 1.0 Strict, XHTML 1.0 Transitional, XHTML 1.0 Frameset, XHTML 1.1.)

- `size`—Sets the size of the text field, as measured in characters. (XHTML 1.0 Strict, XHTML 1.0 Transitional, XHTML 1.0 Frameset, XHTML 1.1.)

- `style`—Inline style indicating how to render the element. (XHTML 1.0 Strict, XHTML 1.0 Transitional, XHTML 1.0 Frameset, XHTML 1.1.)

- `tabindex`—Specifies the tab sequence of hyperlinks in the page for keyboard navigation. (XHTML 1.0 Strict, XHTML 1.0 Transitional, XHTML 1.0 Frameset, XHTML 1.1.)

- `title`—Contains the title of the element. (XHTML 1.0 Strict, XHTML 1.0 Transitional, XHTML 1.0 Frameset, XHTML 1.1.)

- `type`—Specifies the type of the element. (XHTML 1.0 Strict, XHTML 1.0 Transitional, XHTML 1.0 Frameset, XHTML 1.1.)

- `value`—Holds the initial text in the text field. Set this to alphanumeric characters. (XHTML 1.0 Strict, XHTML 1.0 Transitional, XHTML 1.0 Frameset, XHTML 1.1.)

- `xml:lang`—Specifies the base language for the element when the document is interpreted as an XML document. (XHTML 1.0 Strict, XHTML 1.0 Transitional, XHTML 1.0 Frameset, XHTML 1.1.)

Here are the XHTML events this element supports: `onclick`, `ondblclick`, `onmousedown`, `onmouseup`, `onmouseover`, `onmousemove`, `onmouseout`, `onkeypress`, `onkeydown`, `onkeyup`, `onfocus`, `onblur`, `onselect`, and `onchange`.

You can create a text field with the `<input type="text">` element. You can set the size of the text field in characters with the `size` attribute and the maximum length of text (text fields will scroll if the maximum length is greater than its size) with the `maxlength` attribute.

Here's an example. In this case, I'm connecting JavaScript code to display the message Hello from JavaScript. in the text field to the onkeyup event; every time you type something in this text field, the text will be immediately replaced with that message:

Listing ch17_16.html

```
<?xml version="1.0"?>
<!DOCTYPE html PUBLIC "-//W3C//DTD XHTML 1.0 Transitional//EN"
"http://www.w3.org/tr/xhtml1/DTD/xhtml1-transitional.dtd">
<html xmlns="http://www.w3.org/1999/xhtml" xml:lang="en" lang="en">
    <head>
        <title>
            Using Forms in XHTML
        </title>

        <script language = "javascript">
            function displayMessage()
            {
                document.form1.textfield.value = "Hello from JavaScript."
            }
        </script>
    </head>

    <body>
        <center>
            <h1>
                Using Forms in XHTML
            </h1>
            <form name = "form1" id = "form1" action = "action">
                <input type = "text" name = "textfield" size = "25"
                onkeyup = "displayMessage()" />
            </form>
        </center>
    </body>
</html>
```

You can see the results in Figure 17-8.

Figure 17-8
Using a text
field in XHTML.

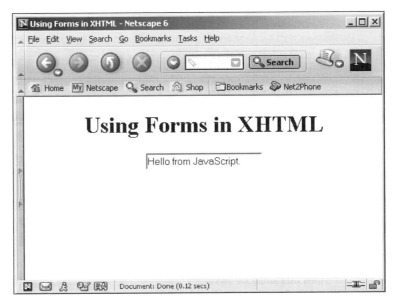

Extending XHTML—Creating New Elements and Attributes

Because XHTML is just an XML application, you can extend it simply by creating new elements and attributes. I'll take a look at an example here, creating a new element, `<underlinedredtext>`, that will style its contents as underlined red text. Here's how that element might be defined in a DTD:

```
<!ELEMENT underlinedredtext (#PCDATA)>
```

You can also add attributes to an element like this—I will do that here, calling the attribute `underlinedredtextattribute`:

```
<!ELEMENT underlinedredtext (#PCDATA)>
<!ATTLIST underlinedredtext underlinedredtextattribute CDATA #IMPLIED >
```

This is a new element that I'm adding to XHTML. To include the rest of the XHTML 1.0 Transitional DTD, I'll create a new parameter entity, `XHTML1.0TransitionalDTD`:

```
<!ELEMENT underlinedredtext (#PCDATA)>
<!ATTLIST underlinedredtext underlinedredtextattribute CDATA #IMPLIED >
<!ENTITY % XHTML1.0TransitionalDTD PUBLIC "-//W3C//DTD XHTML 1.0
Transitional//EN" "http://www.w3.org/TR/xhtml1/DTD/xhtml1-transitional.dtd">
```

All that remains is to include a reference to this parameter entity to make sure the entire XHTML 1.0 Transitional DTD is included:

Listing ch17_17.dtd

```
<!ELEMENT underlinedredtext (#PCDATA)>
<!ATTLIST underlinedredtext underlinedredtextattribute CDATA #IMPLIED >
<!ENTITY % XHTML1.0TransitionalDTD PUBLIC "-//W3C//DTD XHTML 1.0
Transitional//EN" "http://www.w3.org/TR/xhtml1/DTD/xhtml1-transitional.dtd">
%XHTML1.0TransitionalDTD;
```

The result is a fully functional DTD that supports the new element we've created. It's that easy to extend XHTML. As soon as you know how to work with XML, you can extend XHTML without problem. Here's an XHTML document, ch17_18.html, that uses this new element:

Listing ch17_18.html

```
<?xml version="1.0"?>
<!DOCTYPE html SYSTEM "ch17_18.dtd">
<html xmlns="ch17_17.dtd"
xml:lang="en" lang="en">
    <head>
        <title>
            Extending XHTML
        </title>
        <link rel="stylesheet" href="ch17_19.css" />
    </head>

    <body>
        <p>
            This text uses a new XHTML element for
            <underlinedredtext>emphasis</underlinedredtext>.
        </p>
    </body>
</html>
```

You can tell an XHTML browser how to handle your new element with a CSS stylesheet—here's an example, ch17_19.css:

Listing ch17_19.css

```
underlinedredtext {text-decoration: underline; color: #FF0000}
p (diplay:block}
```

Unfortunately, no major browser will handle ch17_18.html correctly yet because those browsers do not yet validate XHTML documents by checking the DTD (because ch17_18.html has the extension .html). You could try treating this page as XML, ch17_20.xml, if you use the `<?xml-stylesheet?>` XML processing instruction to include ch17_19.css instead of `<link>`:

Listing ch17_20.xml

```
<?xml version="1.0"?>
<?xml-stylesheet type="text/css" href="ch17_19.css"?>
<!DOCTYPE html SYSTEM "ch17_17.dtd">
<html xmlns="ch17_17.dtd"
xml:lang="en" lang="en">
    <head>
        <title>
        </title>
    </head>

    <body>
        <p>
            This text uses a new XHTML element for
            <underlinedredtext>emphasis</underlinedredtext>.
        </p>
    </body>
</html>
```

This used to work in Internet Explorer, but the current version (version 6) has problems with the XHTML DTDs; we'll have to wait a while until a browser appears that allows you to extend XHTML. It's easy enough to extend XHTML, but seeing the results with today's browsers is another story.

This example used only XHTML 1.0; in XHTML 1.1, the story is a little more involved. XHTML 1.1 is module-based, and any DTD that extends XHTML 1.1 must to declare its namespace using the XML parameter entity `%XHTML.ns;` (this is the same namespace you'll use in the `<html>` element in documents that use the DTD). You must do this because the XHTML 1.1 Structure module, which is central to XHTML 1.1, uses this parameter internally and needs to know the namespace you're using.

Doing this is easy enough; I'll use a URI as the new DTD's namespace (the namespace need not be a URI, of course—it can be any unique name):

```
<!ENTITY % XHTML1.ns "http://www.starpowder.com/DTDs/ch17_17.dtd" >
<!ELEMENT underlinedredtext (#PCDATA)>
<!ATTLIST underlinedredtext underlinedredtextattribute CDATA #IMPLIED >
<!ENTITY % XHTML1.1DTD PUBLIC "-//W3C//DTD XHTML 1.1//EN"
     "http://www.w3.org/TR/xhtml11/DTD/xhtml11.dtd">
%XHTML1.1DTD;
```

In addition, you should make sure that you use the same namespace in the xmlns attribute of the document element of documents that use this DTD, like this:

```
<?xml version="1.0"?>
<!DOCTYPE html SYSTEM "http://www.starpowder.com/DTDs/ch17_17.dtd">
<html xmlns="http://www.starpowder.com/DTDs/ch17_17.dtd"
xml:lang="en" lang="en">
    <head>
        <title>
        </title>
    </head>

    <body>
        <p>
            This text uses a new XHTML element for
            <underlinedredtext>emphasis</underlinedredtext>.
        </p>
    </body>
</html>
```

Extending Public XHTML DTDs

In the previous section, I created a new DTD to extend XHTML, and I put it to work in an XHTML document like this:

```
<?xml version="1.0"?>
<?xml-stylesheet type="text/css" href="ch17_19.css"?>
<!DOCTYPE html SYSTEM "ch17_17.dtd">
<html xmlns="ch17_17.dtd"
xml:lang="en" lang="en">
    <head>
        <title>
        </title>
    </head>

    <body>
```

```
    <p>
        This text uses a new XHTML element for
        <underlinedredtext>emphasis</underlinedredtext>.
    </p>
  </body>
</html>
```

In this case, I declared a local DTD for private use with the SYSTEM keyword. You can also make your DTD public with the PUBLIC keyword, but to do that, you've got to create a formal public identifier (FPI). Here are the rules for FPIs:

- The first field in an FPI specifies the connection of the DTD to a formal standard. For DTDs that you're defining yourself, this field should be [ms]. If a nonstandards body has approved the DTD, use +. For formal standards, this field is a reference to the standard itself (such as ISO/IEC 13449:2000).

- The second field must hold the name of the group or person that is going to maintain or be responsible for the DTD. In this case, you should use a name that is unique and that identifies your group easily (for example, the W3C simply uses W3C).

- The third field must indicate the type of document that is described, preferably followed by a unique identifier of some kind (such as Version 1.0). This part should include a version number that you'll update.

- The fourth field specifies the language your DTD uses (for example, for English you use EN). Note that two-letter language specifiers allow only a maximum of $24 \times 24 = 576$ possible languages. Expect to see three-letter language specifiers in the near future.

- Fields in an FPI must be separated by a double slash (//).

You can put these rules to work, changing the previous example to indicate that the DTD we're using is publicly available, like this:

Listing ch17_21.xml

```
<?xml version="1.0"?>
<?xml-stylesheet type="text/css" href="ch17_19.css"?>
<!DOCTYPE html PUBLIC "-//starpowder//ELEMENTS XHTML-Custom 1.0//EN"
"http://www.starpowder.com/DTDs/ch17_17.dtd">
<html xmlns="http://www.starpowder.com/DTDs/ch17_17.dtd"
xml:lang="en" lang="en">
    <head>
        <title>
```

continues

```
            </title>
        </head>

        <body>
            <p>
                This text uses a new XHTML element for
                <underlinedredtext>emphasis</underlinedredtext>.
            </p>
        </body>
</html>
```

Extending XHTML with a Driver DTD

So far, I've extended XHTML by adding elements and attributes to a DTD. You can also create a driver DTD to do the same thing (in fact, the W3C is working on creating schemas for XHTML as well as DTDs). A driver DTD does not contain any DTD declarations except for parameter entities. The parameter entities are what you use to include other DTD sections, creating one combined DTD.

For example, I can create a new DTD, ch17_22.dtd, with this new XHTML element:

Listing ch17_22.dtd

```
<!ELEMENT underlinedredtext (#PCDATA)>
<!ATTLIST underlinedredtext underlinedredtextattribute CDATA #IMPLIED >
```

Now I can put together a new driver DTD that includes both ch17_22.dtd and the XHTML 1.0 transitional DTD, like this:

Listing ch17_23.dtd

```
<!ENTITY % XHTMLExtensionDTD
      SYSTEM "http://www.starpowder.com/DTDs/ch17_22.dtd">
%XHTMLExtensionDTD;

<!ENTITY % XHTML1.0TransitionalDTD PUBLIC "-//W3C//DTD XHTML 1.0
Transitional//EN" "http://www.w3.org/TR/xhtml1/DTD/xhtml1-transitional.dtd">
%XHTML1.0TransitionalDTD;
```

That's all it takes. Now when you want to exclude a section of the combined DTD, you have to just comment out its parameter entity reference. One thing to note: When you're creating a DTD from multiple parts like this, make sure there are no declaration conflicts. If there are—for example, if there's a conflict between some elements in MathML and XHTML—make sure you use namespaces.

All About XHTML 1.1 Modules

The XHTML 1.1 DTD is a driver DTD that includes DTD *modules*. A DTD module is a section of a DTD that has two parts: an abstract part, which specifies what the DTD does in human-readable language, and the module itself, which is a DTD fragment that contains element types, a set of attribute list declarations, and a set of content model declarations.

You can find the XHTML 1.1 driver DTD at `www.w3.org/TR/xhtml11/xhtml11_dtd.html#a_xhtml11_driver` and the actual implementation of the XHTML 1.1 modules (there's one for forms, one for text, one for images, and so on) at `www.w3.org/TR/xhtml-modularization/dtd_module_defs.html#a_xhtml11_modules`. You'll find the XHTML 1.1 modules listed in Table 17-1.

Table 17-1
The XHTML 1.1 Modules

Module	Contents
xhtml-applet.module	Java Applet Element Module
xhtml-base.module	Base Element Module
xhtml-bdo.module	BIDI (bidirectional) Override Module
xhtml-csismap.module	Client-Side Image Map Module
xhtml-edit.module	Edit Module (`<del>` and `<ins>`)
xhtml-events.module	Events Module
xhtml-form.module	Forms Module
xhtml-framework.module	Modular Framework Module
xhtml-hypertext.module	Hypertext Module
xhtml-image.module	Image Module
xhtml-link.module	Link Element Module
xhtml-list.module	Lists Module

continues

Module	Contents
xhtml-meta.module	Document Metainformation Module
xhtml-param.module	Param Element Module
xhtml-postfw-redecl.module	Post-Framework Redeclaration Module
xhtml-prefw-redecl.module	Pre-Framework Redeclaration Module
xhtml-pres.module	Presentation Module
xhtml-ruby.module	Ruby (annotation text) Module
xhtml-script.module	Scripting Module
xhtml-ssismap.module	Server-side Image Map Module
xhtml-struct.module	Document Structure Module
xhtml-style.module	Stylesheets Module
xhtml-table.module	Tables Module
xhtml-text.module	Basic Text Module

Each module has two parts, and I'll take a look at them here in overview.

XHTML 1.1 Abstract Modules

Each XHTML 1.1 module has a description called an *abstract module* that specifies what elements and attributes are in the module. It also gives a minimal content model for each element. You can find these abstract versions of the XHTML 1.1 modules at www.w3.org/TR/xhtml-modularization/ xhtml_modules.html#s_xhtmlmodules. An abstract module is really just a table listing the elements, attributes, and minimal content models in the module. For example, the Basic Text abstract module appears in Table 17-2.

Table 17-2
The Basic Text Abstract Module

Element	Attributes	Minimal Content Model
abbr	Common	(PCDATA | Inline)*
acronym	Common	(PCDATA | Inline)*
address	Common	(PCDATA | Inline)*
blockquote	Common, cite	(PCDATA | Heading | Block)*
br	Core	EMPTY

Element	Attributes	Minimal Content Model
cite	Common	(PCDATA I Inline)*
code	Common	(PCDATA I Inline)*
dfn	Common	(PCDATA I Inline)*
div	Common	(Heading I Block I List)*
em	Common	(PCDATA I Inline)*
h1	Common	(PCDATA I Inline)*
h2	Common	(PCDATA I Inline)*
h3	Common	(PCDATA I Inline)*
h4	Common	(PCDATA I Inline)*
h5	Common	(PCDATA I Inline)*
h6	Common	(PCDATA I Inline)*
kbd	Common	(PCDATA I Inline)*
p	Common	(PCDATA I Inline)*
pre	Common	(PCDATA I Inline)*
q	Common, cite	(PCDATA I Inline)*
samp	Common	(PCDATA I Inline)*
span	Common	(PCDATA I Inline)*
strong	Common	(PCDATA I Inline)*
var	Common	(PCDATA I Inline)*

The Basic Text abstract module in Table 17-2 lists two attribute groups: Common and Core. Here's what they contain:

- The Common attribute groups contains the class, id, title, dir, xml:lang, style, onclick, ondblclick, onmousedown, onmouseup, onmouseover, onmousemove, onmouseout, onkeypress, onkeydown, and onkeyup attributes.

- The Core attribute group contains the class, id, and title attributes.

The content models in Table 17-2 also use the Heading, Block, and Inline content models, and here's what elements they contain:

- The Heading content model contains <h1>, <h2>, <h3>, <h4>, <h5>, and <h6>.

- The Block content model contains <address>, <blockquote>, <div>, <p>, and <pre>.

- The Inline content model contains <abbr>, <acronym>, <br>, <cite>, <code>, <dfn>, <em>, <kbd>, <q>, <samp>, <span>, <strong>, and <var>.

An abstract module such as the Basic Text module is useful only so you can find out what's in a module; it isn't actually used by any software, nor does it appear in any actual module implementation. What actually makes these modules work is their *implementations*.

XHTML 1.1 Module Implementations

As far as an XML processor is concerned, a module is really just a DTD fragment that is included in a driver DTD. This DTD fragment can contain element declarations, attribute declarations, and content model declarations. You can find the XHTML 1.1 module implementations at www.w3.org/TR/xhtml-modularization/dtd_module_defs.html. For example, here's the XHTML 1.1 images module, xhtml11-image-1.mod:

```
<!--
.............................................................
-->
<!-- XHTML 1.1 Images Module
......................................... -->
<!-- file: xhtml11-image-1.mod

     This is XHTML XHTML 1.1, a modular variant of XHTML 1.0.
     Copyright 1998-2000 W3C (MIT, INRIA, Keio), All Rights Reserved.
     Revision: $Id: dtd_module_defs.html,v 1.2 2000/01/05 20:58:33
shane Exp $ SMI

     This DTD module is identified by the PUBLIC and SYSTEM
identifiers:

     PUBLIC "-//W3C//ELEMENTS XHTML 1.1 Images 1.0//EN"
     SYSTEM "xhtml11-image-1.mod"

     Revisions:
```

```
    (none)
    ..............................................................
-->


<!-- Images

        img

    This module provides markup to support basic image embedding.
-->


<!-- To avoid problems with text-only UAs as well as to make
     image content understandable and navigable to users of
     non-visual UAs, you need to provide a description with
     the 'alt' attribute, and avoid server-side image maps.
-->


<!ENTITY % Img.element   "INCLUDE" >
<![%Img.element;[
<!ENTITY % Img.content   "EMPTY" >
<!ELEMENT img   %Img.content; >
<!-- end of Img.element -->]]>


<!ENTITY % Img.attlist   "INCLUDE" >
<![%Img.attlist;[
<!ATTLIST img
     %Common.attrib;
     src             %URI.datatype;              #REQUIRED
     alt             %Text.datatype;             #REQUIRED
     longdesc        %URI.datatype;              #IMPLIED
     height          %Length.datatype;           #IMPLIED
     width           %Length.datatype;           #IMPLIED
>
<!-- end of Img.attlist -->]]>


<!-- end of xhtml11-image-1.mod -->
```

Here's how that module is included in the XHTML 1.1 driver DTD:

```
<!-- Image Module .............................................  -->
<!ENTITY % xhtml-image.module "INCLUDE" >
<![%xhtml-image.module;[
<!ENTITY % xhtml-image.mod
PUBLIC "-//W3C//ELEMENTS XHTML 1.1 Images 1.0//EN" "xhtml11-image-1.mod" >
%xhtml-image.mod;]]>
```

Note the parameter entity `xhtml-image.module` here. This entity is set to `"INCLUDE"` by default, as you see here, but you can set it to `"IGNORE"` if you want to exclude the image module in a customized version of XHTML 1.1. The W3C calls the XHTML 1.1 DTD *fully parameterized,* and that's that it means: You can include or exclude modules just by changing parameter entities.

You'll find various suffixes used in the XHTML 1.1 driver DTD. For example, the name of the actual image module file is `xhtml-image.mod`. Here are the suffixes, including .mod, that you'll find in the XHTML 1.1 driver DTD, along with what they mean. Using these suffixes, you can decipher what the various parameter entities in the DTD do:

- `.attrib`—Specifies a group of tokens that indicate attribute specifications. Used in `ATTLIST` declarations.

- `.class`—Groups elements of the same class together.

- `.content`—Specifies the content model of a particular element. You specify what elements go inside what other elements with the content model. For example, here's how that looks for the `<head>` element: `<!ENTITY % Head.content "( %Head-opts.mix;, title, %Head-opts.mix; )" >`.

- `.mix`—Specifies a collection of elements from different classes.

- `.mod`—Used for DTD modules, as in the term `xhtml-image.mod`, which we've already seen.

- `.module`—Used for parameter entities that are used to control inclusion or exclusion of DTD modules. You can set them to `INCLUDE` (the default) to include a module, or `IGNORE` to exclude the module.

Modifying XHTML Content Models

In the examples so far, I've just added entirely new elements and attributes to XHTML, without making any effort to incorporate them into existing XHTML content models. But what if you wanted to change XHTML so that, for example, you add a new element named `<description>` to the `<object>` element? To do that, you can start by creating this new element, but you'll also need to modify the content model of the `<object>` element to include the `<description>` element.

The way you change an existing element's content model differs in XHTML 1.0 and XHTML 1.1, and I'll take a look at both ways in overview here.

Modifying XHTML 1.0 Content Models

Here's the content model for the `<object>` element in the XHTML 1.0 Transitional DTD:

```
<!ELEMENT object (#PCDATA | param | %block; | form | %inline; | %misc;)*>
```

After you've created the `<description>` element, you can easily add it to the `<object>` element's content model, which would look something like this:

```
<!ELEMENT object (#PCDATA | param | description | %block; | form | %inline; |
%misc;)*>
```

Now you're free to use the `<description>` element in the `<object>` element in valid documents, as in this example:

```
<object data="meeting.avi" type="video/msvideo"
    width="400"
    height="600">
    <description>
        Business meeting July 20, 2001
    </description>
</object>
```

You also can add attributes to existing elements just by changing the `<!ATTLIST>` list for the element. For example, that list looks like this for the `<object>` element (note the heavy use of parameter entity references here, such as `%attrs;`, which contains the common attributes used in most XHTML elements):

```
<!ATTLIST object
  %attrs;
  declare       (declare)        #IMPLIED
  classid       %URI;            #IMPLIED
  codebase      %URI;            #IMPLIED
  data          %URI;            #IMPLIED
  type          %ContentType;    #IMPLIED
  codetype      %ContentType;    #IMPLIED
  archive       %UriList;        #IMPLIED
  standby       %Text;           #IMPLIED
  height        %Length;         #IMPLIED
  width         %Length;         #IMPLIED
```

```
    usemap      %URI;         #IMPLIED
    name        NMTOKEN       #IMPLIED
    tabindex    %Number;      #IMPLIED
    align       %ImgAlign;    #IMPLIED
    border      %Pixels;      #IMPLIED
    hspace      %Pixels;      #IMPLIED
    vspace      %Pixels;      #IMPLIED
>
```

If you want to add an attribute to <object>, such as a description attribute, all you have to do is to add it to this list. That might look something like this:

```
<!ATTLIST object
    %attrs;
    declare     (declare)       #IMPLIED
    classid     %URI;           #IMPLIED
    codebase    %URI;           #IMPLIED
    data        %URI;           #IMPLIED
    description CDATA           #IMPLIED
    type        %ContentType;   #IMPLIED
    codetype    %ContentType;   #IMPLIED
    archive     %UriList;       #IMPLIED
    standby     %Text;          #IMPLIED
    height      %Length;        #IMPLIED
    width       %Length;        #IMPLIED
    usemap      %URI;           #IMPLIED
    name        NMTOKEN         #IMPLIED
    tabindex    %Number;        #IMPLIED
    align       %ImgAlign;      #IMPLIED
    border      %Pixels;        #IMPLIED
    hspace      %Pixels;        #IMPLIED
    vspace      %Pixels;        #IMPLIED
>
```

Modifying XHTML 1.1 Content Models

Modifying content models in XHTML 1.1 is the same as doing so in XHTML 1.0—in theory, anyway. In practice, you have to find the actual content model that you want to modify. You do that not by looking for an <!ELEMENT> declaration as in XHTML 1.0, but for the <!ENTITY> declaration for the element's content model, which ends with .content. For example, the content model for the <object> element corresponds to the entity Object.content, which is declared like this:

```
<!ENTITY % Object.content "( % Flow.mix | param )*">
```

You can add the `<description>` element to this content model easily enough, like this:

```
<!ENTITY % Object.content "( % Flow.mix | param | description )*">
```

Modifying an element's content in the XHTML 1.1 DTDs is easy enough, as long as you remember that those DTDs are highly parameterized—which just means that you have to track down the declaration of the content model parameter entity.

Adding attributes is easier because the XHTML 1.1 DTDs still use standard `<!ATTLIST>` declarations for attributes. For example, here is the `<!ATTLIST>` declaration for `<object>`:

```
<!ATTLIST object
      %Common.attrib;
      declare      ( declare )              #IMPLIED
      classid      %URI.datatype;           #IMPLIED
      codebase     %URI.datatype;           #IMPLIED
      data         %URI.datatype;           #IMPLIED
      type         %ContentType.datatype;   #IMPLIED
      codetype     %ContentType.datatype;   #IMPLIED
      archive      %URIs.datatype;          #IMPLIED
      standby      %Text.datatype;          #IMPLIED
      height       %Length.datatype;        #IMPLIED
      width        %Length.datatype;        #IMPLIED
      usemap       IDREF                    #IMPLIED
      name         CDATA                    #IMPLIED
      tabindex     %Number.datatype;        #IMPLIED
>
```

I can add a new attribute, `description`, just as I did in the XHTML 1.0 Transitional DTD:

```
<!ATTLIST object
      %Common.attrib;
      declare      ( declare )              #IMPLIED
      classid      %URI.datatype;           #IMPLIED
      codebase     %URI.datatype;           #IMPLIED
      data         %URI.datatype;           #IMPLIED
      description  CDATA                    #IMPLIED
      type         %ContentType.datatype;   #IMPLIED
      codetype     %ContentType.datatype;   #IMPLIED
      archive      %URIs.datatype;          #IMPLIED
      standby      %Text.datatype;          #IMPLIED
      height       %Length.datatype;        #IMPLIED
      width        %Length.datatype;        #IMPLIED
      usemap       IDREF                    #IMPLIED
      name         CDATA                    #IMPLIED
      tabindex     %Number.datatype;        #IMPLIED
>
```

That's all it takes.

And that's it for our look at XHTML. These two chapters have provided an introduction to the subject, and we've hit the major differences between HTML and XHTML. You're now ready to create XHTML documents of substantial complexity. However, there are more details in XHTML than we can cover in two chapters—for example, what attributes are required in each of the 100+ XHTML elements. For more information, see the W3C XHTML sites using the various URIs I've listed—everything you need is there. You can also check out New Riders' *XHTML* by Chelsea Valentine and Chris Minnick.

In the next chapter, I'm going to take a look at two more popular XML applications: the Simple Object Access Protocol (SOAP) and the Resource Description Framework (RDF).

CHAPTER 18
SOAP and RDF

This chapter is about two popular XML applications: the Simple Object Access Protocol (SOAP) and the Resource Description Framework (RDF).

SOAP is an XML-based communications protocol that lets applications communicate over the Web. As applications move to the Web, SOAP is becoming more popular. Web services let applications become distributed, with one part in the client's computer and other parts on the Internet; you can even call procedures across the Internet. Web services and SOAP are a big part of Microsoft's .NET initiative. In fact, it's easy to create Web services in .NET's Visual Studio if you're connected to the Microsoft Internet Information Server (IIS); you just select the Web Service icon for the type of project you want to create and then add the code you want for the procedures that you want client applications to call. Visual Studio uploads the project to the server automatically. Then you create a client application as a new project, add a reference to the Web service you created, and run the client application. It's practically the same as developing your entire application on the same machine—but your application is actually distributed over the Internet and uses SOAP to communicate among the various parts.

SOAP lets applications send data in messages in a platform-independent, language-independent way. It's an easy protocol to understand, as we'll see. SOAP was originally designed so that distributed applications could communicate through corporate firewalls. SOAP sends its XML-based messages using HTTP, which is already well established on the Internet, and that's a large reason for its success: It provides a backbone for distributed applications using existing technologies. You can also send attachments using SOAP messages, and we'll do that here too.

As you can gather from its name, the RDF is a language that lets you describe resources. Although it's typically used to describe Web documents and sites, you can also use it to describe CD collections, books in a library, a collection of antique pen knives, and more. It's a general-purpose XML application that is helping to standardize the way people handle data on the Internet. Some consistent way of working with vast amounts of data on the Internet is sorely needed, and RDF is one possible solution. You may recall our discussion of canonical XML, which puts XML documents into a format that may easily be compared. RDF is actually stored in documents separate from the resources that it describes, and it provides a standard description language.

We'll see both of these XML applications in this chapter. I'll start with SOAP.

SOAP

Because distributed applications are becoming so popular, SOAP, which lets such applications communicate, is becoming popular, too. Plenty of SOAP resources can be found on the Internet; here's a starter list, including W3C's documentation on it:

- `http://www.w3.org/TR/SOAP/`—The W3C SOAP 1.1 documentation. This is a W3C Note.

- `http://www.w3.org/TR/SOAP-attachments`—The W3C SOAP Messages with Attachments documentation. This is also a W3C Note.

- `http://www.zvon.org/xxl/soapReference/Output/index.html`—A SOAP 1.1 reference.

- `http://www.xml.com/pub/a/2001/04/04/soap.html`—A history of SOAP.

- `http://www.develop.com/soap/soapfaq.htm`—The SOAP Frequently Asked Questions (FAQ).

- `http://xml.apache.org/soap/faq/index.html`—The Apache project's SOAP FAQ.

- `http://www.xml.com/pub/a/2000/02/09/feature/index.html`—An article on SOAP.

- `http://www.soapware.org/bdg`—A "Busy Developer's Guide" to SOAP 1.1.

- `http://www.w3schools.com/SOAP/default.asp`—A SOAP tutorial.

- `http://www.javaworld.com/javaworld/jw-03-2001/`
  `jw-0330-soap.html`—Part 1 of a SOAP tutorial.

- `http://www.javaworld.com/javaworld/jw-04-2001/`
  `jw-0427-soap.html`—Part 2 of a SOAP tutorial.

- `http://www.javaworld.com/javaworld/jw-06-2001/`
  `jw-0601-soap.html`—Part 3 of a SOAP tutorial.

- `http://www.javaworld.com/javaworld/jw-07-2001/`
  `jw-0706-soap.html`—Part 4 of a SOAP tutorial.

- `http://www.javaworld.com/javaworld/jw-03-2001/`
  `jw-0302-xmlmessaging.html`—"XML Messaging with SOAP, Part 1."

- `http://www.javaworld.com/jw-06-2001/`
  `jw-0622-xmlmessaging2.html`—"XML Messaging with SOAP, Part 2."

Here are some SOAP resources for Microsoft's SOAP support:

- `http://msdn.microsoft.com/library/default.asp?url=/nhp/`
  `Default.asp?contentid=28000523`—Microsoft SOAP overview and toolkit. Also `http://msdn.microsoft.com/soap/`.

- `http://msdn.microsoft.com/msdnmag/issues/0900/`
  `WebPlatform/WebPlatform.asp`—"The Programmable Web: Web Services Provide Building Blocks for the Microsoft .NET Framework."

- `http://msdn.microsoft.com/msdnmag/issues/0800/`
  `webservice/webservice.asp`—"Develop a Web Service: Up and Running with the SOAP Toolkit for Visual Studio."

- `http://msdn.microsoft.com/xml/general/`
  `toolkit_intro.asp`—"Web Services and the SOAP Toolkit for Visual Studio 6.0."

- `http://msdn.microsoft.com/xml/general/`
  `soapspec.asp`—SOAP Specification, Version 1.1.

- `http://msdn.microsoft.com/library/default.asp?url=/`
  `library/en-us/dnsoap/html/soapsecurity.asp`—"Building Secure Web Services with Microsoft SOAP Toolkit 2.0."

Let's start digging into this topic now, beginning with the syntax that makes SOAP work.

SOAP Syntax

A SOAP message is simply an XML document that adheres to the SOAP syntax rules. There are three parts to a SOAP message:

- A SOAP envelope. The envelope indicates the content of the SOAP message.

- An optional SOAP header. The header holds information about the message.

- A SOAP body. The body contains the actual information in the message.

Here's a simple SOAP message, with an envelope and a body. This SOAP message is requesting the number of pens in stock at the warehouse (soap-env is the name the W3C uses for the envelope namespace in its documentation):

```
<soap-env:Envelope
    xmlns:soap-env="http://www.w3.org/2001/12/soap-envelope"
    soap:soap-enc="http://www.w3.org/2001/12/soap-encoding">
    <soap-env:Header>
        <m:Name xmlns:m="http://www.starpowder.com">
            ReallyReallyBigCo
        </m:Name>
    </soap-env:Header>
    <soap-env:Body>
        <m:NumberInStock xmlns:m="http://www.starpowder.com">
            <m:Item>Pens</m:Item>
        </m:NumberInStock>
    </soap-env:Body>
</soap-env:Envelope>
```

Note that although SOAP messages are XML documents, they must not contain references to DTDs, and they must not contain XML processing instructions.

Default namespaces already have been defined for the SOAP envelope and for SOAP encoding and data types. The default namespace for the envelope is http://schemas.xmlsoap.org/soap/envelope/. The default namespace for the document encoding and data types is http://schemas.xmlsoap.org/soap/encoding/.

So what elements are already defined for SOAP? That's coming up next.

SOAP Elements

SOAP messages are XML documents, and the root element is the <Envelope> element. There are three possible child elements: <Header>, <Body>, and <Fault>. All of these elements must use these names, although they can have child elements with different names. Here's what a SOAP envelope might look like:

```
<soap-env:Envelope
    xmlns:soap-env="http://schemas.xmlsoap.org/soap/envelope/"
    soap-env:encodingStyle="http://schemas.xmlsoap.org/soap/encoding/">
    .
    .
    .
</soap-env:Envelope>
```

The <Header> element is optional and contains application-specific information about the SOAP message. In this example, the locale-specific language is being set to U.S. English—here, <m:locale> and <m:language> are user-defined elements:

```
<soap-env:Envelope
    xmlns:soap-env="http://schemas.xmlsoap.org/soap/envelope/"
    soap-env:encodingStyle="http://schemas.xmlsoap.org/soap/encoding/">
    <soap-env:Header>
        <m:locale xmlns:m="http://www.starpowder.com">
            <m:language>EN-US</m:language>
        </m:locale>
    </soap-env:Header>
    .
    .
    .
</soap-env:Envelope>
```

The <Body> element contains the SOAP message itself:

```
<soap-env:Envelope
    xmlns:soap-env="http://schemas.xmlsoap.org/soap/envelope/"
    soap-env:encodingStyle="http://schemas.xmlsoap.org/soap/encoding/">
    <soap-env:Header>
        <m:locale xmlns:m="http://www.starpowder.com">
            <m:language>EN-US</m:language>
        </m:locale>
    </soap-env:Header>

    <soap-env:Body>
        <m:NumberInStock xmlns:m="http://www.starpowder.com">
            <m:Item>Pens</m:Item>
        </m:NumberInStock>
    </soap-env:Body>
</soap-env:Envelope>
```

The <Body> element may also contain a <Fault> element, which you use to hold errors that occurred while working with a message. This element can appear only in response messages, which you get in response to a SOAP message:

```
<soap-env:Envelope
    xmlns:soap-env="http://schemas.xmlsoap.org/soap/envelope/"
    soap-env:encodingStyle="http://schemas.xmlsoap.org/soap/encoding/">
    <soap-env:Header>
        <m:locale xmlns:m="http://www.starpowder.com">
            <m:language>EN-US</m:language>
        </m:locale>
    </soap-env:Header>

    <soap-env:Body>
        <m:NumberInStock xmlns:m="http://www.starpowder.com">
            <m:Item>Pens</m:Item>
        </m:NumberInStock>

        <soap-env:Fault>
            <faultcode>soap:Server</faultcode>
            <faultstring>Server Error</faultstring>
        </soap-env:Fault>
    </soap-env:Body>
</soap-env:Envelope>
```

There can only be one <Fault> element in a SOAP message, and it can have these subelements:

- <faultcode>—Holds the error code
- <faultstring>—Holds an error string
- <faultactor>—Indicates where the error came from
- <detail>—Holds error details

Here are the possible fault codes:

- VersionMismatch—The namespace for the SOAP Envelope element was not right.
- MustUnderstand—An element with the mustUnderstand attribute set to "1" could not be interpreted.
- Client—A general problem occurred with the message as sent from the client.
- Server—A general problem with the server occurred.

These SOAP elements can also support various attributes, which are coming up next.

SOAP Attributes

You can use these attributes in SOAP elements: `actor`, `encodingStyle`, and `mustUnderstand`. The `actor` attribute gives the URI for which the header elements are targeted. Here's an example showing how to use the `actor` attribute:

```
<soap-env:Header>
    <m:data xmlns:m="http://www.starpowder.com"
        soap-env:actor="http://www.starpowder.com/accounting" />
        <m:language>EN-US</m:language>
    </m:data>
</soap-env:Header>
```

You can use the `encodingStyle` attribute to specify the data types used in the document. `http://schemas.xmlsoap.org/soap/encoding/` is the URI of a schema that the W3C provides for SOAP data types:

```
<soap-env:Envelope
    xmlns:soap-env="http://schemas.xmlsoap.org/soap/envelope/"
    soap-env:encodingStyle="http://schemas.xmlsoap.org/soap/encoding/">
    .
    .
    .
</soap-env:Envelope>
```

The `encodingStyle` attribute is optional—you don't have to use a schema at all to specify the data types that you use in your SOAP message. SOAP schemas can use any of the data types defined for use in XML schemas (see `http://www.w3.org/TR/xmlschema-2/`) or combinations of them. For all the details on constructing SOAP schemas, see Section 5 of the W3C SOAP Note (`http://www.w3.org/TR/SOAP/`).

You use the `mustUnderstand` attribute in the <Header> element. It's used to specify whether the target of a message must interpret and process a header element. You set it to a Boolean value, `"0"` for false and `"1"` for true:

```
<soap-env:Header>
    <m:data xmlns:m="http://www.starpowder.com"
        soap-env:mustUnderstand="1" />
        <m:language>EN-US</m:language>
    </m:data>
</soap-env:Header>
```

That gives us an overview of how SOAP works. What about putting SOAP to work? How about using SOAP in code—creating a message, sending it, receiving it, and interpreting it to see how this all works in practice? That's coming up next.

A SOAP Example Using Java

Because SOAP relies on Web services, this Java example is going to be significantly more advanced than the Java examples we've already seen. You can use Java on the Internet in the form of Java servlets or JavaServer Pages, and it'll be easier to use servlets here.

SOAP in Java Versus .NET

Another major SOAP user is Microsoft's .NET initiative, of course. In fact, I wrote three complete SOAP examples using Visual Basic .NET for this chapter, but then I realized that the Java way of doing things provides us far greater insight into actually working with SOAP. In .NET, the details are handled behind the scenes (and there's a great deal of .NET-specific code); in Java, you do it yourself (including constructing and unpacking the SOAP messages themselves). For that reason, I'm sticking to Java here. If you want to see SOAP in .NET, however, just take a look at the excellent SOAP examples that come with VB .NET—they're ready to run.

A servlet is a Java application that runs on a Web server—sort of the analog of an applet that runs in the client browser. Our example will have two servlets, one that sends the SOAP message and one that receives that message. The receiving servlet will decode the data in the SOAP message and return a new SOAP message indicating that it has understood. Usually you don't see the actual SOAP message directly, but in this case, both the sent and returned SOAP messages will be stored to files so we can take a look at them directly.

You'll need a Web server that can run Java servlets for this example. You might not have access to such a Web server on the Internet, but that's not a problem—you can run one right on your own computer: the Tomcat server. Tomcat is the premier Web server for JavaServer Pages and servlets, and you can download it from `http://jakarta.apache.org/tomcat/`. The current version is version 4. Downloading and installing Tomcat is really not as hard as it sounds, even though you're installing a full Web server on your computer. Take a look at the installation directions that come with Tomcat. After you've gotten Tomcat installed and running (all the information you need comes with the Tomcat documentation), navigate to `http://localhost:8080/index.html`. (Tomcat uses port 8080, so it won't conflict with other local servers.) You should see Tomcat running, something like in Figure 18-1.

Figure 18-1
Running the
Tomcat server.

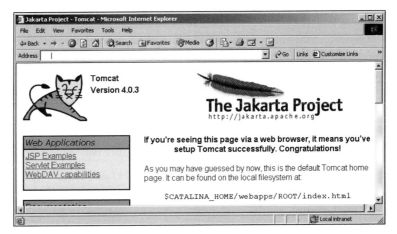

In addition, you'll need some added support from Java. As we've seen, Java
1.4 comes with considerable XML support. However, the standard edition
doesn't come with support to create XML Web services. A considerable
amount of Java support exists for Web services, however—take a look at
`http://java.sun.com/webservices/` for the details.

You have two options to start using SOAP with Java: You can download
the Java XML Pack, which is currently at `http://java.sun.com/xml/`
`downloads/javaxmlpack.html`, or you can download the Java Web Services
Developer's Pack, which is currently at `http://java.sun.com/`
`webservices/webservicespack.html`. The Java XML Pack is the smaller
of these two and is a simple zipped file that holds the JAR files you'll need:
jaxm-api.jar, saaj-api.jar, and activation.jar. You'll also need servlet.jar to
create servlets, and it comes with Tomcat (in the Tomcat `lib` directory).

You'll need to set up Tomcat to work with Java XML Messaging, or JAXM.
Stop Tomcat if it's running and copy jaxm-docs.war, which comes with the
Java XML Pack or the Java Web Services Developer's Pack, to the Tomcat
`webapps` directory. Then restart Tomcat and navigate to `http://`
`localhost:8080/jaxm-docs/tomcat.html` for directions (which just
involves copying Java Archive [JAR] and Web Archive [WAR] files).

And that's it. You've set up the needed environment; it's time to start writing some code. There will be two servlets here: the ch18_01 servlet will create a
SOAP message and send it to a servlet named ch18_02, which will read it and
send another SOAP message back to ch18_01.

I'll start with the ch18_01 servlet. This is the servlet that creates and sends the SOAP message in the first place. It begins by declaring itself part of a Java package that I'll call soapExample. It includes the other packages we'll need:

```
package soapExample;

import java.io.*;
import java.net.*;
import javax.servlet.*;
import javax.xml.soap.*;
import javax.activation.*;
import javax.servlet.http.*;
              .
              .
              .
```

Next, we'll create the actual SOAP connection that we'll use to send the SOAP message. The base class for servlets is HttpServlet, so this new class, ch18_01, is based on that class. When a new servlet starts, its init method is called first. We can use a SOAPConnectionFactory object to create a SOAPConnection object like this (the call to super.init(servletConfig) makes sure that the HttpServlet class's constructor is called):

```
public class ch18_01 extends HttpServlet
{
    private SOAPConnection connection;

    public void init(ServletConfig servletConfig) throws ServletException
    {
        super.init(servletConfig);

        try {
            SOAPConnectionFactory factory = SOAPConnectionFactory.newInstance();
            connection = factory.createConnection();
        } catch(Exception e) {}
    }
              .
              .
              .
```

This new SOAPConnection object, connection, is the object we'll use to send a SOAP message to the other servlet, ch18_02. You can see the methods of the SOAPConnectionFactory class in Table 18-1 and the methods of the SOAPConnection class in Table 18-2.

Table 18-1	Method	Does This
Methods of the *javax.xml. soap.SOAP Connection Factory* Class	`SOAPConnectionFactory()`	The default constructor
	`abstract SOAPConnection createConnection()`	Creates a new `SOAPConnection` object
	`static SOAPConnectionFactory newInstance()`	Creates an object of the default `SOAPConnectionFactory` class

Table 18-2	Method	Does This
Methods of the *javax.xml. soap.SOAP Connection* Class	`SOAPConnection()`	The default constructor
	`abstract SOAPMessage call (SOAPMessage request, java. lang.Object to)`	Sends the specified message to the indicated object and waits until there is a response
	`abstract void close()`	Closes the `SOAPConnection` object

When you call this servlet using the GET Http method, the servlet's doGet method is called. In that method, we want to create the new SOAP message, which you can do with a `MessageFactory` object. You use this object's createMessage method to create a new `SOAPMessage` object. Note that we're also creating the text string that will display the progress of this servlet to the user:

```
public void doGet(HttpServletRequest request, HttpServletResponse response)
throws ServletException
{
    String outString ="<HTML><H1>Sent and Received SOAP Message</H1><P>";

    try {
        MessageFactory messageFactory = MessageFactory.newInstance();
        SOAPMessage message = messageFactory.createMessage();
    .
    .
    .
```

You can see the methods of the `MessageFactory` class in Table 18-3 and the methods of the `SOAPMessage` class in Table 18-4.

Table 18-3	**Method**	**Does This**
Methods of the *javax.xml. soap.MessageFactory* Class	`MessageFactory()`	The default constructor
	`abstract SOAPMessage createMessage()`	Creates a new `SOAPMessage` object using default `SOAPPart`, `SOAPEnvelope`, `SOAPBody`, and `SOAPHeader` objects
	`abstract SOAPMessage createMessage(MimeHeaders headers, java.io.InputStream in)`	Creates a SOAP message and returns that object
	`static MessageFactory newInstance()`	Creates a new `MessageFactory` object

Table 18-4	**Method**	**Does This**
Methods of the *javax.xml. soap.SOAP Message* Class	`SOAPMessage()`	The default constructor
	`abstract  void addAttachmentPart (AttachmentPart AttachmentPart)`	Adds the specified `AttachmentPart` object to this `SOAPMessage` object
	`abstract  int countAttachments()`	Returns the number of attachments in this message
	`abstract  AttachmentPart createAttachmentPart()`	Creates an empty `AttachmentPart` object
	`AttachmentPart createAttachmentPart (javax.activation.DataHandler dataHandler)`	Creates an `AttachmentPart` object using the specified `DataHandler` object
	`AttachmentPart createAttachmentPart (java.lang.Object content, java.lang.String contentType)`	Creates an `AttachmentPart` object using data of the specified type
	`abstract java.util.Iterator getAttachments()`	Returns an iterator for all the `AttachmentPart` objects that are attached to this `SOAPMessage` object
	`abstract java.util.Iterator getAttachments(MimeHeaders headers)`	Returns an iterator over the `AttachmentPart` objects that have header entries that match the given headers

Method	Does This
abstract java.lang.String getContentDescription()	Returns a description of this SOAPMessage object's content
abstract MimeHeaders getMimeHeaders()	Returns the MIME headers for this SOAPMessage object
abstract SOAPPart getSOAPPart()	Returns the SOAP part of this SOAPMessage object
abstract void removeAllAttachments()	Removes all AttachmentPart objects attached to this SOAPMessage object
abstract void saveChanges()	Saves this SOAPMessage object, including all changes that have been made to it
abstract boolean saveRequired()	Returns true if this SOAPMessage object has had the saveChanges method called
abstract void setContentDescription (java.lang.String description)	Sets the description of this SOAPMessage object's content
abstract void writeTo (java.io.OutputStream out)	Writes this SOAPMessage object to the specified output stream

Now that we have a SOAPMessage object, we need to customize the message we want to send. You do that by getting access to the SOAP message's body. In this case, we might send a SOAP message informing the other servlet that there are 125 writing pens in stock at the current time, for example. To get access to the SOAP message's body, you first use the SOAPMessage object's getSOAPPart method to get the SOAP part of the message (as opposed to attachments). Then you can use the getEnvelope method to get the SOAP envelope. Finally, you can use the envelope's getHeader and getBody methods to get the message's header and body (we won't use the header here—this code just shows how to get access to it):

```
public void doGet(HttpServletRequest request, HttpServletResponse response)
throws ServletException
{
    String outString ="<HTML><H1>Sent and Received SOAP Message</H1><P>";

    try {
        MessageFactory messageFactory = MessageFactory.newInstance();
        SOAPMessage message = messageFactory.createMessage();
```

```
SOAPPart soappart = message.getSOAPPart();
SOAPEnvelope envelope = soappart.getEnvelope();
SOAPHeader header = envelope.getHeader();
SOAPBody body = envelope.getBody();
```

.
.
.

You can see the methods of the SOAPPart class in Table 18-5, the methods of the SOAPEnvelope interface in Table 18-6, the methods of the SOAPHeader interface in Table 18-7, and the methods of the SOAPBody interface in Table 18-8.

Table 18-5 Methods of the *javax.xml. soap.SOAP Part* Class	Method	Does This
	SOAPPart()	The default constructor
	abstract void addMimeHeader (java.lang.String name, java.lang.String value)	Adds a MimeHeader object with the given name and value to this SOAPPart object
	abstract java.util.Iterator getAllMimeHeaders()	Returns an iterator over all the headers for this SOAPPart object
	abstract Source getContent()	Returns the content of the SOAPEnvelope as a Source object
	java.lang.String getContentId()	Returns the value of the MIME header with the name "Content-Id"
	java.lang.String getContentLocation()	Returns the value of the MIME header with the name "Content-Location"
	abstract SOAPEnvelope getEnvelope()	Returns the SOAPEnvelope object associated with this SOAPPart object
	abstract java.util.Iterator getMatchingMimeHeaders (java.lang.String[] names)	Returns an iterator over all MimeHeader objects with names matching those in the specified array
	abstract java.lang.String[] getMimeHeader(java.lang.String name)	Returns the values of the MimeHeader object in this SOAPPart object identified by the specified String

Method	Does This
abstract java.util.Iterator getNonMatchingMimeHeaders (java.lang.String[] names)	Returns all MimeHeader objects whose name is not in the specified array
abstract void removeAllMimeHeaders()	Removes all the MimeHeader objects in this SOAPEnvelope object
abstract void removeMimeHeader (java.lang.String header)	Removes all MIME headers that match the specified name
abstract void setContent (Source source)	Sets the content of the SOAPEnvelope object using the given Source object
void setContentId(java.lang. String contentId)	Sets the MIME header named "Content-Id" to the given String
void setContentLocation(java. lang.String contentLocation)	Sets the MIME header "Content-Location" to the given String
abstract void setMimeHeader (java.lang.String name, java. lang.String value)	Sets the header entry that matches the specified header name

Table 18-6

Methods of the *javax.xml. soap.SOAP Envelope* Interface

Method	Does This
SOAPBody addBody()	Adds a SOAPBody object to this SOAPEnvelope object
SOAPHeader addHeader()	Adds a SOAPHeader object to this SOAPEnvelope object
Name createName(java.lang. String localName)	Creates a new Name object using the indicated local name
Name createName(java.lang.String localName, java.lang.String) prefix, java.lang.String uri	Creates a new Name object using the indicated local name, namespace prefix, and name-space URI
SOAPBody getBody()	Returns the SOAPBody object of this SOAPEnvelope object
SOAPHeader getHeader()	Returns the SOAPHeader object of this SOAPEnvelope object

Table 18-7	Method	Does This
Methods of the *javax.xml. soap.SOAP Header* Interface	`SOAPHeaderElement addHeaderElement(Name name)`	Creates a new SOAPHeaderElement object
	`java.util.Iterator examineHeaderElements(java.lang. String actor)`	Returns an iterator over all the SOAPHeaderElement objects in this SOAPHeader object with the given actor
	`java.util.Iterator extractHeaderElements(java.lang. String actor)`	Returns an iterator over all the SOAPHeaderElement objects in this SOAPHeader object with the given actor

Table 18-8	Method	Does This
Methods of the *javax.xml. soap.SOAP Body* Interface	`SOAPBody addBody()`	Adds a SOAPBody object to this SOAPEnvelope object
	`SOAPBodyElement addBodyElement (Name name)`	Adds a new SOAPBodyElement object with the given name to this SOAPBody object
	`SOAPFault addFault()`	Adds a new SOAPFault object to this SOAPBody object
	`SOAPFault getFault()`	Returns the SOAPFault object if there is one
	`boolean hasFault()`	Returns true if a SOAPFault object exists in this SOAPBody object

We can insert a new element into the body of our SOAP message, creating an element named `<pens:NumberInStock>` with the value 125 like this:

```
<soap-env:Envelope xmlns:soap-env="http://schemas.xmlsoap.org/soap/
envelope/">
    <soap-env:Header/>
    <soap-env:Body>
        <pens:NumberInStock
        ➡xmlns:pens="http://www.starpowder.com">125</pens:NumberInStock>
    </soap-env:Body>
</soap-env:Envelope>
```

Here's how you create that element and add it to the SOAP message's body—with the `SOAPBody` object's `addBodyElement` method and the `addText` method to add the text 125:

```
public void doGet(HttpServletRequest request, HttpServletResponse response)
throws ServletException
{
    String outString ="<HTML><H1>Sent and Received SOAP Message</H1><P>";

    try {
        MessageFactory messageFactory = MessageFactory.newInstance();
        SOAPMessage message = messageFactory.createMessage();
        SOAPPart soappart = message.getSOAPPart();
        SOAPEnvelope envelope = soappart.getEnvelope();
        SOAPHeader header = envelope.getHeader();
        SOAPBody body = envelope.getBody();

        body.addBodyElement(envelope.createName("NumberInStock", "pens",
        "http://www.starpowder.com")).addTextNode("125");
           .
           .
           .
```

We can also add an attachment to our SOAP message. Attachments hold the text of a file that you want to pass along with the SOAP message (and a receiving servlet can read a SOAP message's attachments with the `getAttachments` method). In this example, we'll use an HTML page, ch18_03.html (which will be developed in a few pages), to call the ch18_01 servlet and make that servlet run. Let's attach the text of that HTML page to our SOAP message as an example attachment. We start by going through a little work to find the actual URL of that document:

```
public void doGet(HttpServletRequest request, HttpServletResponse response)
throws ServletException
{
    String outString ="<HTML><H1>Sent and Received SOAP Message</H1><P>";

    try {
        MessageFactory messageFactory = MessageFactory.newInstance();
        SOAPMessage message = messageFactory.createMessage();
        SOAPPart soappart = message.getSOAPPart();
        SOAPEnvelope envelope = soappart.getEnvelope();
        SOAPHeader header = envelope.getHeader();
        SOAPBody body = envelope.getBody();

        body.addBodyElement(envelope.createName("NumberInStock", "pens",
        "http://www.starpowder.com")).addTextNode("125");
```

```
                    StringBuffer urlServer = new StringBuffer();
        urlServer.append(request.getScheme()).append("://")
        ➥.append(request.getServerName());
        urlServer.append(":").append(request.getServerPort()).append\
        ➥(request.getContextPath());
                    String requestBase = urlServer.toString();
                    URL url = new URL(requestBase + "/ch18_03.html");
```

.
.
.

Then we can add that document as an attachment to our SOAP message with an `AttachmentPart` object, like this:

```
public void doGet(HttpServletRequest request, HttpServletResponse response)
throws ServletException
{
    String outString ="<HTML><H1>Sent and Received SOAP Message</H1><P>";

    try {
        MessageFactory messageFactory = MessageFactory.newInstance();
        SOAPMessage message = messageFactory.createMessage();
        SOAPPart soappart = message.getSOAPPart();
        SOAPEnvelope envelope = soappart.getEnvelope();
        SOAPHeader header = envelope.getHeader();
        SOAPBody body = envelope.getBody();

        body.addBodyElement(envelope.createName("NumberInStock", "pens",
        "http://www.starpowder.com")).addTextNode("125");

        StringBuffer urlServer = new StringBuffer();
urlServer.append(request.getScheme()).append("://").append
➥(request.getServerName());

urlServer.append(":").append(request.getServerPort()).append
➥(request.getContextPath());
        String requestBase = urlServer.toString();
        URL url = new URL(requestBase + "/ch18_03.html");

        AttachmentPart attachmentpart = message.createAttachmentPart
        ➥(new DataHandler(url));
        attachmentpart.setContentType("text/html");
        message.addAttachmentPart(attachmentpart);
```

.
.
.

Now ch18_03.html will be sent to the target servlet as an attachment to our SOAP message. You can see the methods of the `AttachmentPart` class in Table 18-9.

Table 18-9	Method	Does This
Methods of the *javax.xml. soap. Attachment Part* Class	`AttachmentPart()`	The default constructor
	`abstract void addMimeHeader (java.lang.String name, java.lang.String value)`	Adds a MIME header with the given name and value to this `AttachmentPart` object
	`abstract void clearContent()`	Clears this `AttachmentPart` object's content
	`abstract java.util.Iterator getAllMimeHeaders()`	Returns an iterator over the headers for this `AttachmentPart`
	`abstract java.lang.Object getContent()`	Returns the content of this `AttachmentPart` object
	`java.lang.String getContentId()`	Returns the value of the MIME header named `"Content-Id"`
	`java.lang.String getContentLocation()`	Returns the value of the MIME header named `"Content-Location"`
	`java.lang.String getContentType()`	Returns the value of the MIME header `"Content-Type"`
	`abstract javax.activation. DataHandler getDataHandler()`	Returns the `DataHandler` object for this `AttachmentPart` object
	`abstract java.util.Iterator getMatchingMimeHeaders(java. lang.String[] names)`	Returns all `MimeHeader` objects that match a name in the indicated array
	`abstract java.lang.String[] getMimeHeader(java.lang.String name)`	Returns all values of the header specified by the passed `String`
	`abstract java.util.Iterator ) getNonMatchingMimeHeaders (java.lang.String[] names`	Returns all `MimeHeader` objects whose name is not in the given array
	`abstract int getSize()`	Returns the number of bytes in this `AttachmentPart` object
	`abstract void removeAllMimeHeaders()`	Removes all the MIME headers
	`abstract void removeMimeHeader) (java.lang.String header`	Removes all MIME headers that match the specified name

continues

Method	Does This
abstract void setContent (java.lang.Object object, java. lang.String contentType)	Sets the content of this attachment part to that of the given Object and sets the value of the Content-Type header to the given type
void setContentId(java.lang. String contentId)	Sets the MIME header "Content-Id" with the given value
void setContentLocation(java. lang.String contentLocation)	Sets the MIME header "Content-Location" with the given value
void setContentType(java.lang. String contentType)	Sets the MIME header "Content-Type" with the given value
abstract void setDataHandler (javax.activation.DataHandler dataHandler)	Makes the passed DataHandler object the data handler for this AttachmentPart object
abstract void setMimeHeader (java.lang.String name, java. lang.String value)	Sets the header entry matching the given name to the given value

Now that we have the base location of the application, we can get the URL of the target servlet, which I'll call getter:

```
StringBuffer urlServer = new StringBuffer();
urlServer.append(request.getScheme()).append("://").append(request.
➥getServerName());
urlServer.append(":").append(request.getServerPort()).append
➥(request.getContextPath());
String requestBase = urlServer.toString();
URL url = new URL(requestBase + "/ch18_03.html");

AttachmentPart attachmentpart = message.createAttachmentPart(new
➥DataHandler(url));
attachmentpart.setContentType("text/html");
message.addAttachmentPart(attachmentpart);

URL getter = new URL(requestBase + "/ch18_02");
    .
    .
    .
```

This URL is the URL we'll send the SOAP message to. Before sending that message, let's store it in a file so we can take a look at it afterward; in this case, I'll store our SOAP message in a file named put.msg. You can do that with the Java `FileOutputStream` class and the SOAP message's `writeTo` method this way:

```
        StringBuffer urlServer = new StringBuffer();
urlServer.append(request.getScheme()).append("://").append
➥(request.getServerName());
urlServer.append(":").append(request.getServerPort()).append
➥(request.getContextPath());
        String requestBase = urlServer.toString();
        URL url = new URL(requestBase + "/ch18_03.html");

        AttachmentPart attachmentpart = message.createAttachmentPart
➥(new DataHandler(url));
        attachmentpart.setContentType("text/html");
        message.addAttachmentPart(attachmentpart);

        URL getter = new URL(requestBase + "/ch18_02");

        FileOutputStream sentFile = new FileOutputStream("put.msg");
        message.writeTo(sentFile);
        sentFile.close();
            .
            .
            .
```

Now we'll be able to examine the SOAP message even after it has been sent. You can send the message using the `connection` object's `call` method, passing that method the message and the target URL like this (note that I also add the message "`Sent SOAP message stored in put.msg. <p>`" to the text this servlet will display in the user's browser):

```
        StringBuffer urlServer = new StringBuffer();
urlServer.append(request.getScheme()).append("://").append
➥(request.getServerName());
urlServer.append(":").append(request.getServerPort()).append
➥(request.getContextPath());
        String requestBase = urlServer.toString();
        URL url = new URL(requestBase + "/ch18_03.html");
            .
            .
            .
        URL getter = new URL(requestBase + "/ch18_02");
            .
            .
            .
```

```
outString += "Sent SOAP message stored in put.msg. <p>";

SOAPMessage receivedMessage = connection.call(message, getter);
```

.
.
.

The `call` method returns the SOAP message that the other servlet sent back
to us. We can save that SOAP message in a new file, get.msg:

```
SOAPMessage receivedMessage = connection.call(message, getter);
```

```
if (receivedMessage != null) {
    FileOutputStream receivedFile = new FileOutputStream("get.msg");
    receivedMessage.writeTo(receivedFile);
    receivedFile.close();
    outString += "Received SOAP message stored in get.msg.</HTML>";
}
```

And that's it. We've sent a SOAP message, gotten one back, and stored them
both in files for later examination. All that remains is to send the notification
text stored in the `outString` variable (which tells the user `Sent SOAP message
stored in put.msg.` and `Received SOAP message stored in get.msg.`)
back to the user's browser. You can do that in a servlet using an `OutputStream`
object. You can create this using the `response` object's `getOutputStream`
method (the `response` object is passed to the servlet's `doGet` method):

```
SOAPMessage receivedMessage = connection.call(message, getter);

if (receivedMessage != null) {
    FileOutputStream receivedFile = new FileOutputStream("get.msg");
    receivedMessage.writeTo(receivedFile);
    receivedFile.close();
    outString += "Received SOAP message stored in get.msg.</HTML>";
}

} catch(Throwable e) {}
```

```
try {
    OutputStream outputStream = response.getOutputStream();
    outputStream.write(outString.getBytes());
    outputStream.flush();
    outputStream.close();
} catch (IOException e) {}
```

And that's it. We've passed the text back to the user's browser, and that completes the ch18_01 servlet. Here's the full code:

Listing ch18_01.java

```
package soapExample;

import java.io.*;
import java.net.*;
import javax.servlet.*;
import javax.xml.soap.*;
import javax.activation.*;
import javax.servlet.http.*;

public class ch18_01 extends HttpServlet
{
    private SOAPConnection connection;

    public void init(ServletConfig servletConfig) throws ServletException
    {
        super.init(servletConfig);

        try {
          SOAPConnectionFactory factory =
          ➥SOAPConnectionFactory.newInstance();
            connection = factory.createConnection();
        } catch(Exception e) {}
    }

    public void doGet(HttpServletRequest request, HttpServletResponse
    ➥response)
    throws ServletException
    {
        String outString ="<HTML><H1>Sent and Received SOAP
        ➥Message</H1><P>";

        try {
            MessageFactory messageFactory = MessageFactory.newInstance();
            SOAPMessage message = messageFactory.createMessage();
            SOAPPart soappart = message.getSOAPPart();
            SOAPEnvelope envelope = soappart.getEnvelope();
            SOAPHeader header = envelope.getHeader();
            SOAPBody body = envelope.getBody();

            body.addBodyElement(envelope.createName("NumberInStock", "pens",
            "http://www.starpowder.com")).addTextNode("125");

            StringBuffer urlServer = new StringBuffer();
urlServer.append(request.getScheme()).append("://").append
➥(request.getServerName());
```

continues

```java
urlServer.append(":").append(request.getServerPort()).append
➥(request.getContextPath());
            String requestBase = urlServer.toString();
            URL url = new URL(requestBase + "/ch18_03.html");

            AttachmentPart attachmentpart = message.createAttachmentPart
            ➥(new DataHandler(url));
            attachmentpart.setContentType("text/html");
            message.addAttachmentPart(attachmentpart);

            URL getter = new URL(requestBase + "/ch18_02");

            FileOutputStream sentFile = new FileOutputStream("put.msg");
            message.writeTo(sentFile);
            sentFile.close();

            outString += "Sent SOAP message stored in put.msg. <p>";

            SOAPMessage receivedMessage = connection.call(message, getter);

            if (receivedMessage != null) {
                FileOutputStream receivedFile = new
                ➥FileOutputStream("get.msg");
                receivedMessage.writeTo(receivedFile);
                receivedFile.close();
                outString += "Received SOAP message stored in
                ➥get.msg.</HTML>";
            }

        } catch(Throwable e) {}

        try {
            OutputStream outputStream = response.getOutputStream();
            outputStream.write(outString.getBytes());
            outputStream.flush();
            outputStream.close();
        } catch (IOException e) {}
    }
}
```

The next step is to develop the ch18_02 servlet, which is the target of our
SOAP message. This servlet will read the incoming SOAP message, interpret
it, and send a message back indicating that it has understood that incoming
message. This servlet, which "listens" for incoming SOAP messages, is based
on the JAXMServlet class and implements the ReqRespListener interface:

```java
public class ch18_02 extends JAXMServlet implements ReqRespListener
{
        .
        .
        .
```

The JAXMServlet class lets you handle XML messages like SOAP messages. The ReqRespListener interface has only one method, the onMessage method that is called when a message is read. When that message is read, we will create and send back a new SOAP message, which means we'll need a new message factory object. I'll create that object when the servlet is first initialized:

```
public class ch18_02 extends JAXMServlet implements ReqRespListener
{
    static MessageFactory factory = null;

    public void init(ServletConfig servletConfig) throws ServletException
    {
        super.init(servletConfig);
        try {
            factory = MessageFactory.newInstance();
        } catch (Exception ex) {}
    }
        .
        .
        .
```

Now, in the onMessage method, we can handle the incoming SOAP message, which is passed to this method. We handle that message by getting the data in it (that there are 125 pens in stock). The code begins by getting the SOAP message's body:

```
public SOAPMessage onMessage(SOAPMessage msg)
{
    try {
        SOAPPart soappart = msg.getSOAPPart();
        SOAPEnvelope incomingEnvelope = soappart.getEnvelope();
        SOAPBody body = incomingEnvelope.getBody();
        .
        .
        .
```

To access the elements in the SOAP message's body, you can use the body object's getChildElements method. You pass this method a Name object for the element you want, which includes the name of the element as well as the element's namespace and namespace URI. You can create that Name object with the SOAP envelope object's createName method like this:

```
public SOAPMessage onMessage(SOAPMessage msg)
{
    try {
        SOAPPart soappart = msg.getSOAPPart();
```

```
        SOAPEnvelope incomingEnvelope = soappart.getEnvelope();
        SOAPBody body = incomingEnvelope.getBody();

        Iterator it = body.getChildElements(
        incomingEnvelope.createName("NumberInStock", "pens",
        ➥"http://www.starpowder.com"));
```

.
.
.

The getChildElements method returns a Java Iterator object, which lets you access all the returned elements with Iterator's next method. To get the body element's first (and only, in this case), element—the <pens:NumberInStock> element—you can use the Iterator's next method like this:

```
public SOAPMessage onMessage(SOAPMessage msg)
{
    try {
        SOAPPart soappart = msg.getSOAPPart();
        SOAPEnvelope incomingEnvelope = soappart.getEnvelope();
        SOAPBody body = incomingEnvelope.getBody();

        Iterator it = body.getChildElements(
        incomingEnvelope.createName("NumberInStock", "pens",
        ➥"http://www.starpowder.com"));

        SOAPElement element;
        element = (SOAPElement) it.next();
```

.
.
.

Now we have the <pens:NumberInStock> element in a SOAPElement object. You can see the methods of the SOAPElement interface in Table 18-10. This interface is based on the SOAP Node interface, and you can see the methods of the Node interface in Table 18-11. Note in particular the getValue method of the Node interface in Table 18-11—that's the method we'll use to extract the value of the <pens:NumberInStock> element.

Table 18-10	Method	Does This
Methods of the *javax.xml. soap.SOAP Element* Interface	`SOAPElement addAttribute (Name name, java.lang.String value)`	Adds an attribute with the given name and value to this SOAPElement object
	`SOAPElement addChildElement (Name name)`	Adds a new SOAPElement object with the given name to this SOAPElement object
	`SOAPElement addChildElement (SOAPElement element)`	Adds a SOAPElement object as a child of the current SOAPElement object
	`SOAPElement addChildElement (java.lang.String localName)`	Adds a new SOAPElement object with the given local name to this SOAPElement object
	`SOAPElement addChildElement (java.lang.String localName, java.lang.String prefix)`	Adds a new SOAPElement object with the given local name and prefix to this SOAPElement object
	`SOAPElement addChildElement (java.lang.String localName, java.lang.String prefix, java. lang.String uri)`	Adds a new SOAPElement object with the given local name, prefix, and URI to this SOAPElement object
	`SOAPElement addNamespaceDeclaration (java.lang.String prefix, java.lang.String uri)`	Adds a namespace declaration with the given prefix and URI to this SOAPElement object
	`SOAPElement addTextNode (java.lang.String text)`	Adds a new Text object holding the given String to this SOAPElement object
	`java.util.Iterator getAllAttributes()`	Returns an iterator over all the attribute names in this SOAPElement object
	`java.lang.String getAttributeValue(Name name)`	Returns the value of the attribute with the specified name
	`java.util.Iterator getChildElements()`	Returns an iterator over child elements of this element
	`java.util.Iterator getChildElements(Name name)`	Returns an iterator over all the child elements with the indicated name

continues

Method	Does This
`Name getElementName()`	Returns the name of this SOAPElement object
`java.lang.String getEncodingStyle()`	Returns the encoding style for this SOAPElement object
`java.util.Iterator getNamespacePrefixes()`	Returns an iterator over namespace prefixes
`java.lang.String getNamespaceURI (java.lang.String prefix)`	Returns the URI of the namespace that matches the specified prefix
`boolean removeAttribute (Name name)`	Removes the attribute with the given name
`boolean removeNamespaceDeclaration (java.lang.String prefix)`	Removes the namespace declaration corresponding to the specified prefix
`void setEncodingStyle (java.lang.String encodingStyle)`	Sets the encoding style for this SOAPElement object

Table 18-11
Methods of the
*javax.xml.
soap.Node*
Interface

Method	Does This
`void detachNode()`	Removes this Node object
`SOAPElement getParentElement()`	Returns the parent element of this Node object
`java.lang.String getValue()`	Returns the text value of the immediate child of this Node object
`void recycleNode()`	Indicates that you're done with the node and lets Java reuse it
`void setParentElement (SOAPElement parent)`	Makes the parent of this Node object the specified SOAPElement object

To send a SOAP message back to the ch18_01 servlet, we can use the message factory's `createMessage` method. Then we can use the new message's `getEnvelope` method to get the message's envelope, which is the first step in customizing that message:

```
public SOAPMessage onMessage(SOAPMessage msg)
{
    try {
        SOAPPart soappart = msg.getSOAPPart();
        SOAPEnvelope incomingEnvelope = soappart.getEnvelope();
        SOAPBody body = incomingEnvelope.getBody();

        Iterator it = body.getChildElements(
        incomingEnvelope.createName("NumberInStock", "pens",
        ➥"http://www.starpowder.com"));

        SOAPElement element;
        element = (SOAPElement) it.next();

        SOAPMessage message = factory.createMessage();
        SOAPEnvelope envelope = message.getSOAPPart().getEnvelope();
            .
            .
            .
```

All that's left is to add a new element to hold the data we want to send to the return message. I'll call this new element `<Response>`, and I'll add a text node to that element with text indicating that we've read how many pens are left in stock (the `element.getValue` method here returns the number of pens from the incoming SOAP message):

```
public SOAPMessage onMessage(SOAPMessage msg)
{
    try {
        SOAPPart soappart = msg.getSOAPPart();
        SOAPEnvelope incomingEnvelope = soappart.getEnvelope();
        SOAPBody body = incomingEnvelope.getBody();

        Iterator it = body.getChildElements(
        incomingEnvelope.createName("NumberInStock", "pens",
        ➥"http://www.starpowder.com"));

        SOAPElement element;
        element = (SOAPElement) it.next();

        SOAPMessage message = factory.createMessage();
        SOAPEnvelope envelope = message.getSOAPPart().getEnvelope();
```

```
      envelope.getBody().addChildElement(envelope.createName
   ➥("Response")).addTextNode(
         "Thanks for the SOAP message telling me there are " +
         ➥element.getValue() +
         " pens in stock"
   );
```

```
      return message;
   } catch(Exception e) {
      return null;
   }
```

At the end of this code, we return the completed message, which automatically sends it back to the original servlet, ch18_01. Here's the full code for the ch18_02 servlet:

Listing ch18_02.java

```
package soapExample;

import java.util.*;
import javax.servlet.*;
import javax.xml.soap.*;
import javax.servlet.http.*;
import javax.xml.messaging.*;

public class ch18_02 extends JAXMServlet implements ReqRespListener
{
    static MessageFactory factory = null;

    public void init(ServletConfig servletConfig) throws ServletException
    {
        super.init(servletConfig);
        try {
            factory = MessageFactory.newInstance();
        } catch (Exception ex) {}
    }

    public SOAPMessage onMessage(SOAPMessage msg)
    {
        try {
            SOAPPart soappart = msg.getSOAPPart();
            SOAPEnvelope incomingEnvelope = soappart.getEnvelope();
            SOAPBody body = incomingEnvelope.getBody();

            Iterator it = body.getChildElements(
            incomingEnvelope.createName("NumberInStock", "pens",
            ➥"http://www.starpowder.com"));
```

```
        SOAPElement element;
        element = (SOAPElement) it.next();

        SOAPMessage message = factory.createMessage();
        SOAPEnvelope envelope = message.getSOAPPart().getEnvelope();

        envelope.getBody().addChildElement(envelope.createName
        ➥("Response")).addTextNode(
            "Thanks for the SOAP message telling me there are " +
            ➥element.getValue() +
            " pens in stock"
        );

        return message;
    } catch(Exception e) {
        return null;
    }
    }
  }
}
```

And that's it. To compile these servlets, ch18_01.java and ch18_02.java, you'll need servlet.jar, jaxm-api.jar, saaj-api.jar, and activation.jar in your classpath environment variable. Here's what that looks like (this assumes that the .jar files are in the same directory as the .java files; if that's not so, make sure you preface every .jar filename with its correct path):

```
%set classpath=servlet.jar;jaxm-api.jar;saaj-api.jar;activation.jar
%javac ch18_01.java
%javac ch18_02.java
```

How do we get the first servlet, ch18_01, to run? In this example, I'll use an HTML page, ch18_03.html, to call that servlet. The user can open this HTML page and click a hyperlink to run ch18_01, which will send a SOAP message to ch18_02:

Listing ch18_03.html

```
<HTML>
    <HEAD>
        <TITLE>Using SOAP</TITLE>
    </HEAD>

    <BODY>
        <CENTER>
            <H1>Using SOAP</H1>
```

continues

Listing ch18_03.html   Continued

```
        </CENTER>
            <A HREF="ch18_01">Click me</a> to send and receive a SOAP message.
        </BODY>
</HTML>
```

And we're almost set. We also need to create a file named web.xml that will let Tomcat connect the class files ch18_01.class and ch18_02.class to URLs that you can enter into a browser. Here's what web.xml looks like (this file is included in the downloadable code for this book):

```xml
<?xml version="1.0" encoding="ISO-8859-1"?>

<!DOCTYPE web-app
    PUBLIC "-//Sun Microsystems, Inc.//DTD Web Application 2.2//EN"
    "http://java.sun.com/j2ee/dtds/web-app_2_2.dtd">

<web-app>
    <servlet>
        <servlet-name>
            ch18_01
        </servlet-name>
        <servlet-class>
            soapExample.ch18_01
        </servlet-class>
    </servlet>

    <servlet>
        <servlet-name>
            ch18_02
        </servlet-name>
        <servlet-class>
            soapExample.ch18_02
        </servlet-class>
    </servlet>

    <servlet-mapping>
        <servlet-name>
            ch18_01
        </servlet-name>
        <url-pattern>
            /ch18_01
        </url-pattern>
    </servlet-mapping>

    <servlet-mapping>
        <servlet-name>
            ch18_02
        </servlet-name>
```

```
        <url-pattern>
            /ch18_02
        </url-pattern>
    </servlet-mapping>
</web-app>
```

And that's it. Now we have the files we'll need, ch18_01.class, ch18_02.class, ch18_03.html, and web.xml. To install them in Tomcat, stop Tomcat and add a directory named soap to the Tomcat webapps directory with these files and subdirectories:

```
webapps (directory)
|__soap (directory)
    |__ch18_03.html
    |__WEB-INF (directory)
        |__web.xml
        |__classes (directory)
            |__soapExample (directory)
                |__ch18_01.class
                |__ch18_02.class
```

Then (re)start Tomcat. The whole application is ready to go. Navigate to http://localhost:8080/soap/ch18_03.html in your browser, as you see in Figure 18-2.

Figure 18-2 Starting our SOAP example.

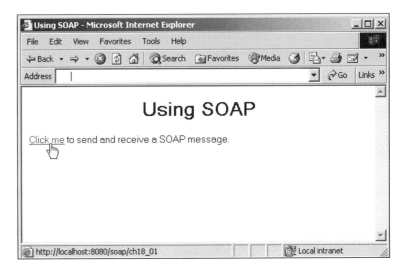

Click the link you see in Figure 18-2 to call the ch18_01 servlet, which will send a SOAP message to the ch18_02 servlet. This servlet, in turn, sends another SOAP message back to ch18_01. You can see the results that ch18_01 reports back to the user in Figure 18-3.

Figure 18-3
The status report by the SOAP example.

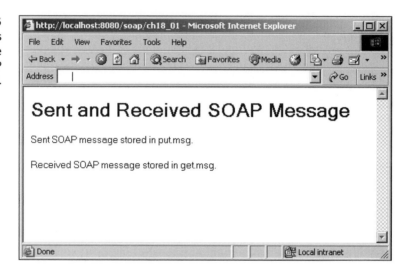

As you can see in Figure 18-3, a SOAP message was sent and another SOAP message was returned. What did those messages look like? We wrote this application to store the actual SOAP messages in the files put.msg and get.msg, which will be stored in the Tomcat bin directory. Here's the first SOAP message, as sent by ch18_01 and stored in put.msg. You can see the SOAP message here, including the <pens:NumberInStock> element that holds the number of pens in stock, as well as the attachment that holds ch18_03.html:

```
------=_Part_0_13526686.1026338101718
Content-Type: text/xml

<?xml version="1.0" encoding="UTF-8"?>
<soap-env:Envelope xmlns:soap-env="http://schemas.xmlsoap.org/soap/
➥envelope/">
    <soap-env:Header/>
    <soap-env:Body>
        <pens:NumberInStock xmlns:pens="http://www.starpowder.com">125<
        ➥/pens:NumberInStock>
    </soap-env:Body>
</soap-env:Envelope>
------=_Part_0_13526686.1026338101718
Content-Type: text/html
```

```
<HTML>
    <HEAD>
        <TITLE>Using SOAP</TITLE>
    </HEAD>

    <BODY>
        <CENTER>
            <H1>Using SOAP</H1>
        </CENTER>
        <A HREF="ch18_01">Click me</a> to send and receive a SOAP message.
    </BODY>
</HTML>

------=_Part_0_13526686.1026338101718--
```

Here's the returned SOAP message, as stored in get.msg, indicating that the second servlet, ch18_02, understood that 125 pens were in stock:

```
<?xml version="1.0" encoding="UTF-8"?>
<soap-env:Envelope xmlns:soap-env="http://schemas.xmlsoap.org/soap/
➥envelope/">
    <soap-env:Header/>
    <soap-env:Body>
        <Response>Thanks for the SOAP message telling me there are 125 pens
        ➥in stock</Response>
    </soap-env:Body>
</soap-env:Envelope>
```

Congratulations, you've sent and received SOAP messages in code now. As you can see, SOAP can form the communications backbone for a distributed application. And you don't need to program SOAP applications in Java, either. There are many other options these days, including Microsoft's Visual Studio .NET, which creates Web services that use SOAP. In fact, because SOAP is language- and platform-independent, you can use SOAP to communicate among various parts of a Web application that are written in different languages.

RDF

RDF is a language for describing resources. Although you can use it to describe any kind of resource, it's usually used to describe Web documents and sites. RDF is a W3C recommendation, and its main page is at www.w3.org/RDF. You can find the RDF model and syntax specification at www.w3.org/TR/REC-rdf-syntax, and you can find the RDF schema specification at www.w3.org/TR/rdf-schema. Here's what the W3C says about RDF:

The Resource Description Framework (RDF) is a foundation for XML documents to be read as metadata; it provides interoperability between applications that exchange machine-understandable information on the Web. RDF uses XML to exchange descriptions of Web resources, but the resources being described can be of any type, including XML and non-XML resources.

What does RDF look like? Here's an example:

```
<?xml version="1.0" ?>
<rdf:RDF
    xmlns:rdf="http://www.w3.org/1999/02/22-rdf-syntax-ns#">
    <rdf:Description about="http://www.starpowder.com/planets.html">
        <Creator>Nicolas Copernicus</Creator>
    </rdf:Description>
</rdf:RDF>
```

This RDF document describes the document at `www.starpowder.com/planets.html` and lists that document's creator, Nicolas Copernicus. RDF is general enough to support all kinds of resource descriptions, but complete generality may not be what you need. To be useful, descriptions should use agreed-upon terms. Several sublanguages or grammars use RDF and define specific XML elements for describing resources; I'll take a look at the most popular such sublanguage in this chapter, the Dublin Core. For example, RDF itself does not define an element named `<Creator>` to indicate the resource's creator; however, `<Creator>` is an element in the Dublin Core, which means that Web search engines that support the Dublin Core will know enough to search for `<Creator>` elements when they want to find a particular Web resource's author.

Support for RDF is growing. Here's a partial list of what's available in RDF today:

- `http://www710.univ-lyon1.fr/~champin/rdf-tutorial` is an RDF tutorial online. (It's in English, even though the Web page is in France.)

- `http://www.w3.org/1999/02/26-modules` is the PerlXmlParser, which is a set of Comprehensive Perl Archive Network (CPAN) modules by Eric Prud'Hommeaux (a W3C member). It supports an RDF SAX parser and a simple database interface for Perl.

- `http://www.ics.forth.gr/proj/isst/RDF` is a validating RDF parser by ICS-FORTH. It's a Java parser with some support for RDF schemas.

- `http://nestroy.wi-inf.uni-essen.de/xwmf` is the XWMF (eXtensible Web Modeling Framework). It offers a number of tools, including an RDF parser.

- `http://www.w3.org/Library/src/HTRDF` is John Punin's RDF parser in C.

- `http://www.mozilla.org/rdf/doc` explains about Mozilla's RDF implementation. I'll say more about this later.

- `http://www.w3.org/RDF/Validator/` is a Simple RDF validator.

- `http://lists.w3.org/Archives/Public/www-rdf-interest/2000May/0009.html` is an RDF parser in XSLT by Dan Connolly.

Although no major browser has yet supported RDF in a big way, Mozilla, Netscape Navigator's open source version, has a lot of RDF support built into it. Here are some of the documents covering RDF in Mozilla:

- `http://www.mozilla.org/rdf/50-words.html`—One of Mozilla's "In Fifty Words or Less" articles. This is an overview of RDF and how it fits with Mozilla. It also includes examples.

- `http://www.mozilla.org/rdf/back-end-architecture.html`— A very detailed document that describes how the RDF "back end" works in Mozilla. Although it doesn't have sample code now, it will some day: It will show how to use the back end directly as a client and how to write your own RDF data source.

- `http://www.mozilla.org/rdf/doc/faq.html`—The RDF-in-Mozilla FAQ. You'll also find some sample code.

- `http://www.mozilla.org/rdf/doc/datasource-howto.html`— A cookbook approach to creating an RDF datasource.

- `http://www.mozilla.org/rdf/rdf-nglayout.html`—How RDF is handled in Mozilla to create a content model consistent with W3C Level 1 DOM.

- `http://www.mozilla.org/rdf/doc/api.html`—The RDF Technical Overview. It provides an overview of the Mozilla RDF implementation.

- `http://www.mozilla.org/rdf/doc/vocabs.html`—The Mozilla RDF metadata vocabularies.

You can also get more information about software support for RDF in Mozilla at these locations:

- `http://www.mozilla.org/rdf/doc/SmartBrowsing.html`— Mozilla's SmartBrowsing system. It allows third-party metadata servers to provide XML/RDF "related link" annotations.

- `http://www.mozilla.org/rdf/doc/aurora.html`—Mozilla's Aurora project, which is the code name for the user interface in Mozilla that handle RDF data sources.

- `http://www.mozilla.org/rdf/doc/flash-spec.html`—The Mozilla Flash Specification. The Flash system offers an XML/RDF system for offering up-to-the-minute information about events that are of interest to the user.

- `http://www.mozilla.org/rdf/doc/z3950.html`—The Mozilla RDF/Z39.50 Integration Project, which lets you connect to digital library systems. This project is all about using the ANSI/NISO Z39.50 search protocol from inside Mozilla.

What about RDF support in Internet Explorer? There really isn't any—at least, not yet. However, Microsoft does offer an RDF viewer, which is currently at `http://msdn.microsoft.com/downloads/samples/Internet/xml/xml_rdf_viewer/sample.asp`. Here's Microsoft's description of the RDF viewer:

> *The sample is written in Visual Basic 6.0 and consists of a single form. Users can enter the URL of a known RDF file, or they can choose buttons that represent RDF files from three different sources. The form then retrieves the RDF file, which is then parsed using the MSXML parser. The contents of the RDF file are presented in a list box, and any URL links attached to each item are stored in an array. When an item in the list box is selected, the page represented by the associated URL is displayed in the Browser control.*

To run the viewer, however, you need Internet Explorer 5.0, Visual Basic 6.0, and Windows 98, Windows NT 4.0, or Windows 2000.

As you can see, there's a lot of material out there on RDF. It's time to get to the RDF details now, starting with RDF syntax.

RDF Syntax

RDF documents are made of RDF statements that describe resources. Each statement has three parts, so it's called a *triple*. Here are the three parts of an RDF statement:

- **A resource**. Resources are typically Web documents that you point to with a URI.

- **A named property**. Such a property is a specific characteristic or attribute of the resource, such as the resource's creator.

- **A property value**. The value of the property is the property's content. For example, the value of the `<Creator>` property is usually the name of the resource's creator.

An RDF statement, then, is made up of a resource, a named property, and a property value. In RDF, you name these three parts like this:

- The resource is called the *subject* of the statement.

- The named property is called the *predicate* of the statement.

- The property value is called the *object* of the statement.

Here's a simple example RDF document:

Listing ch18_04.rdf

```
<?xml version="1.0" ?>
<rdf:RDF
    xmlns:rdf="http://www.w3.org/1999/02/22-rdf-syntax-ns#">
    <rdf:Description about="http://www.starpowder.com/planets.html">
        <Creator>Nicolas Copernicus</Creator>
    </rdf:Description>
</rdf:RDF>
```

In this case, the subject is the document `http://www.starpowder.com/planets.html`, the predicate is the named property `Creator`, and the object is the name of the document's creator, Nicolas Copernicus. To understand RDF, I'm going to take this document apart piece-by-piece now.

RDF Root Element

RDF documents are also XML documents, so they start with the <?xml?> declaration. These documents also must have a specific root element, <RDF>, which encloses the rest of the document. Because the namespace that you use with RDF is usually given the prefix rdf, you often specify the <RDF> element as <rdf:RDF> like this:

```
<?xml version="1.0" ?>
<rdf:RDF

        .
        .
        .
</rdf:RDF>
```

Also note that RDF documents must use the RDF namespace.

RDF Namespace

The official W3C-defined RDF namespace is "http://www.w3.org/1999/02/22-rdf-syntax-ns#". (The # on the end, which may look pretty funny, is not an error; it's there to help applications create valid XPointers.) All RDF documents must use this namespace. The conventional prefix for this namespace is rdf, so I'll declare that prefix like this:

```
<?xml version="1.0" ?>
<rdf:RDF
    xmlns:rdf="http://www.w3.org/1999/02/22-rdf-syntax-ns#">
        .
        .
        .
</rdf:RDF>
```

RDF Description Element

Each resource that you want to describe in RDF gets its own <rdf:Description> element. This element has several attributes:

- about lets you specify what resource the element describes.
- aboutEach lets you make statements about each of the element's children.

- `aboutEachPrefix` lets you select RDF container items by prefix.

- `bagID` specifies the ID of an associated bag container.

- `ID` lets you give the element an ID value.

- `type` specifies the description's type.

In fact, you can also convert the properties that you list in the `<rdf:Description>` element into attributes, as we'll see when we take a look at the RDF abbreviated syntax.

In our example, the resource being described is the document `http://www.starpowder.com/planets.html`, so I assign that URI to the about attribute of the `<rdf:Description>` element:

```
<?xml version="1.0" ?>
<rdf:RDF
    xmlns:rdf="http://www.w3.org/1999/02/22-rdf-syntax-ns#">
    <rdf:Description about="http://www.starpowder.com/planets.html">
        .
        .
        .
    </rdf:Description>
</rdf:RDF>
```

In other words, you use the about attribute to specify the statement's subject. To actually say something about the resource, you use property elements.

RDF Property Elements

Inside the `<rdf:Description>` element, you store the actual elements that describe the subject. In the current example, the predicate is the Creator property, which specifies the document's author, and the object is the name of the author, Nicolas Copernicus:

```
<?xml version="1.0" ?>
<rdf:RDF
    xmlns:rdf="http://www.w3.org/1999/02/22-rdf-syntax-ns#">
    <rdf:Description about="http://www.starpowder.com/planets.html">
        <Creator>Nicolas Copernicus</Creator>
    </rdf:Description>
</rdf:RDF>
```

The `Creator` property is not built into the RDF specification—in fact, no properties are. It's up to you to create the named properties you want to use to describe a resource. In fact, a number of property sets, called RDF content description models, already are available. That's useful because they provide some agreement on property names. This means that applications such as Web search engines can make some sense out of the properties you use. The most popular and well supported of these RDF content-description models is the *Dublin Core*.

Dublin Core

The Dublin Core calls itself a "metadata initiative," and it provides an RDF content model that is in wide use to describe Web resources. The Dublin Core has attracted the attention of museums, libraries, government agencies, and commercial groups as a way of standardizing RDF for Web resources. You can find out all about the Dublin Core at its home page, `www.purl.org/dc`.

In the previous example, I used a `<Creator>` property without specifying a namespace for that property. However, when you create your own properties, you should use a namespace to avoid conflicts. The Dublin Core's namespace is `"http://purl.org/DC/"`. In fact, the `<Creator>` property I've been using is modeled after the Dublin Core's `<Creator>` property. I can declare the Dublin Core's namespace—which is usually given the prefix `dc`—in the example document, and I can indicate that `<Creator>` is part of that namespace like this:

```
<?xml version="1.0" ?>
<rdf:RDF
    xmlns:rdf="http://www.w3.org/1999/02/22-rdf-syntax-ns#"
    xmlns:dc="http://purl.org/DC/">
    <rdf:Description about="http://www.starpowder.com/planets.html">
        <dc:Creator>Nicolas Copernicus</dc:Creator>
    </rdf:Description>
</rdf:RDF>
```

The `<Creator>` property is just one Dublin Core property; you can find all the defined Dublin Core properties in Table 18-12.

Table 18-12	Element	Means this
Dublin Core Elements	Contributor	Person or organization that has contributed in some way to this resource.
	Coverage	The extent or scope of the content of the resource. For example, this might include location, time, or jurisdiction.
	Creator	Person, organization, or service responsible for creating the resource. This typically refers to the resource's author.
	Date	A date connected to the resource, such as its last update or its creation date. Recommended practice for encoding the date value is defined in ISO 8601, which follows the YYYY-MM-DD format.
	Description	The description of the resource. For example, this might be an abstract, table of contents, or text description of the resource.
	Format	The format used for the resource. Usually the format includes the media type or dimensions of the resource. Readers may use Format to determine the software, hardware, or other equipment needed. You usually use a MIME type here.
	Identifier	An ID value for the resource in its context. Recommended practice is to identify the resource by means of a string or number as part of a formal identification system. For example, you might use a URI or an International Standard Book Number (ISBN).
	Language	The language of the resource. Recommended practice is to use values defined by RFC 1766, which includes a two-letter language code (from the ISO 639 standard) with an optional two-letter country code (from the ISO 3166 standard).
	Publisher	The agent responsible for making the resource available. Usually this is a person, an organization, or a service.
	Relation	A reference to a related resource or relationship type.
	Rights	Rights information about the resource. For example, a Rights element can contain intellectual property rights, copyright, or various other property rights.

continues

Element	Means this
Source	A resource from which the current resource is derived.
Subject	The topic of the content of the resource. Recommended practice is to select a value from a formal classification scheme. For example, subjects might be keywords, key phrases, or classification codes.
Title	A name given to the resource.
Type	The type of the content of the resource, usually a term describing general categories or functions. Recommended practice is to select a value from a formally defined and publicly available vocabulary.

Each Dublin Core element also has 10 attributes, which are taken from the ISO/IEC 11179 standard:

- Comment—A comment about the use of the data in the element
- Datatype—The type of data in the element
- Definition—The concept behind the data in the element
- Identifier—A unique identifier assigned to the element that identifies it
- Language—The language of the data in the element
- Maximum Occurrence—A limit on how many times the element may occur
- Name—The name you've assigned to the data element
- Obligation—Whether the element is required
- Registration Authority—The agency or group authorized to register the element
- Version—The version of the element

In fact, 6 of these 10 attributes are common to all the Dublin Core elements, and they have fixed values. Here they are, along with their values:

- Version: 1.1
- Registration Authority: Dublin Core Metadata Initiative
- Language: en (that is, English)
- Obligation: Optional

- Datatype: Character String

- Maximum Occurrence: Unlimited

The Dublin Core also lists a set of default resource *types* that you can use with the `<Type>` element:

- collection
- dataset
- event
- image
- interactive resource
- model

- party
- physical object
- place
- service
- software
- sound
- text

Describing Multiple Properties

The example RDF document we've seen so far has defined only one property for the `http://www.starpowder.com/planets.html` resource—the `<Creator>` property. In fact, you can assign multiple properties to resources. Now that we've seen all the available Dublin Core elements, I'll put more of them to work. For example, here's how I describe that resource's creator, title, and type:

Listing ch18_05.rdf

```
<?xml version="1.0" ?>
<rdf:RDF
    xmlns:rdf="http://www.w3.org/1999/02/22-rdf-syntax-ns#"
    xmlns:dc="http://purl.org/DC/">

    <rdf:Description about="http://www.starpowder.com/planets.html">
        <dc:Creator>Nicolas Copernicus</dc:Creator>
        <dc:Title>Mercury</dc:Title>
        <dc:Type>text</dc:Type>
    </rdf:Description>

</rdf:RDF>
```

Describing Multiple Resources

An RDF document can also describe multiple resources. All you have to do is to use multiple `<rdf:Description>` elements. For example, here's an RDF document that describes three resources: mercury.html, venus.html, and earth.html:

Listing ch18_06.rdf

```
<?xml version="1.0" ?>
<rdf:RDF
    xmlns:rdf="http://www.w3.org/1999/02/22-rdf-syntax-ns#"
    xmlns:dc="http://purl.org/DC/">

    <rdf:Description about="http://www.starpowder.com/mercury.html">
        <dc:Creator>Nicolas Copernicus</dc:Creator>
        <dc:Title>Mercury</dc:Title>
        <dc:Type>text</dc:Type>
    </rdf:Description>

    <rdf:Description about="http://www.starpowder.com/venus.html">
        <dc:Creator>Nicolas Copernicus</dc:Creator>
        <dc:Title>Venus</dc:Title>
        <dc:Type>text</dc:Type>
    </rdf:Description>

    <rdf:Description about="http://www.starpowder.com/earth.html">
        <dc:Creator>Nicolas Copernicus</dc:Creator>
        <dc:Title>Earth</dc:Title>
        <dc:Type>text</dc:Type>
    </rdf:Description>

</rdf:RDF>
```

Nesting Resources

What if a property itself needs more description? For example, what if the creator of the resource is described by a Web page and you want to refer the reader to that page? In that case, you can nest `<rdf:Resource>` elements. For example, if you want to describe Nicolas Copernicus, the creator of planets.html, with another Web page, NickC.html, that might look like this:

Listing ch18_07.rdf

```
<?xml version="1.0" ?>
<rdf:RDF xmlns="http://www.w3.org/1999/02/22-rdf-syntax-ns#"
    xmlns:dc="http://www.purl.org/DC/">

    <rdf:Description about="http://www.starpowder.com/planets.html">
        <dc:Title>Mercury</dc:Title>
        <dc:Creator>
            <rdf:Description about="http://www.starpowder.com/NickC.html">
                <dc:Title>Nicolas Copernicus</dc:Title>
                <dc:Language>en</dc:Language>
            </rdf:Description>
        </dc:Creator>
    </rdf:Description>
</rdf:RDF>
```

Referring to Resources by Reference

There's another way to refer to a resource that describes a property: You can give the resource's URI using the rdf:resource attribute. You use this attribute in the property element. Here's an example; in this case, I'm referring to the resource NickC.html to describe the creator of various documents:

Listing ch18_08.rdf

```
<?xml version="1.0" ?>
<rdf:RDF
    xmlns:rdf="http://www.w3.org/1999/02/22-rdf-syntax-ns#"
    xmlns:dc="http://www.purl.org/DC/">

    <rdf:Description about="http://www.starpowder.com/mercury.html">
        <dc:Title>Mercury</dc:Title>
        <dc:Creator rdf:resource="http://www.starpowder.com/NickC.html"/>
    </rdf:Description>

    <rdf:Description about="http://www.starpowder.com/venus.html">
        <dc:Title>Venus</dc:Title>
        <dc:Creator rdf:resource="http://www.starpowder.com/NickC.html"/>
    </rdf:Description>

    <rdf:Description about="http://www.starpowder.com/earth.html">
        <dc:Title>Earth</dc:Title>
        <dc:Creator rdf:resource="http://www.starpowder.com/NickC.html"/>
    </rdf:Description>

</rdf:RDF>
```

As you can see, using the `rdf:resource` attribute makes it easy to connect the same property to a number of resources; in this case, I'm giving mercury.html, venus.html, and earth.html the same `Creator` properties.

Using XML in Property Elements

Although property values are mostly text or resources that you reference, they can also be straight XML. In that case, you just set the `parseType` attribute of the property to `"Literal"`.

For example, I'm using my own XML elements, such as `<BirthCity>` and `<BirthCountry>` in the `<Creator>` property here, and giving them their own namespace: `ns`:

Listing ch18_09.rdf

```
<?xml version="1.0" ?>
<rdf:RDF
    xmlns:rdf="http://www.w3.org/1999/02/22-rdf-syntax-ns#"
    xmlns:dc="http://www.purl.org/DC/"
    xmlns:ns="http://www.starpowder.com/namespace/">

    <rdf:Description about="http://www.starpowder.com/planets.html">
        <dc:Creator parseType="Literal">
            <ns:FirstName>Nicolas</nm:FirstName>
            <ns:LastName>Copernicus</nm:LastName>
            <ns:Birth>1473</nm:Birth>
            <ns:Death>1543</nm:Death>
            <ns:BirthCity>Torun</nm:BirthCity>
            <ns:BirthCountry>Poland</nm:BirthCountry>
        </dc:Creator>
    </rdf:Description>

</rdf:RDF>
```

Using Abbreviated RDF Syntax

The W3C also defines an abbreviated RDF syntax to make things a little easier. To use the abbreviated syntax, you just convert property elements to attributes of the `<rdf:Description>` element. For example, here's what an unabbreviated document might look like:

```
<?xml version="1.0" ?>
<rdf:RDF
    xmlns:rdf="http://www.w3.org/1999/02/22-rdf-syntax-ns#"
    xmlns:dc="http://purl.org/DC/">

    <rdf:Description about="http://www.starpowder.com/mercury.html">
        <dc:Creator>Nicolas Copernicus</dc:Creator>
        <dc:Title>Mercury</dc:Title>
        <dc:Type>text</dc:Type>
    </rdf:Description>

    <rdf:Description about="http://www.starpowder.com/venus.html">
        <dc:Creator>Nicolas Copernicus</dc:Creator>
        <dc:Title>Venus</dc:Title>
        <dc:Type>text</dc:Type>
    </rdf:Description>
        .
        .
        .
```

Here's the abbreviated form:

```
<?xml version="1.0" ?>
<rdf:RDF
    xmlns:rdf="http://www.w3.org/1999/02/22-rdf-syntax-ns#"
    xmlns:dc="http://purl.org/DC/">

    <rdf:Description about="http://www.starpowder.com/mercury.html"
        dc:Creator = "Nicolas Copernicus"
        dc:Title = "Mercury"
        dc:Type = "text">
    </rdf:Description>

    <rdf:Description about="http://www.starpowder.com/venus.html"
        dc:Creator = "Nicolas Copernicus">
        dc:Title = "Venus"
        dc:Type = "text">
    </rdf:Description>
        .
        .
        .
```

Why is this useful? One big reason is that it makes RDF easier to handle in HTML browsers in case that RDF is embedded in an HTML document. Recall that HTML browsers will ignore any tags that they don't understand and simply treat the element's content as plain text. If you convert the property elements to attributes, there are no property elements to be mishandled in that way.

The situation is a little more complex if your properties themselves contain resources. In that case, it's best to refer to those resources by reference using the `rdf:resource` attribute:

```
<?xml version="1.0" ?>
<rdf:RDF
    xmlns:rdf="http://www.w3.org/1999/02/22-rdf-syntax-ns#"
    xmlns:dc="http://www.purl.org/DC/">

    <rdf:Description about="http://www.starpowder.com/mercury.html"
        dc:Title = "Mercury">
        <dc:Creator rdf:resource="http://www.starpowder.com/NickC.html"/>
    </rdf:Description>

    <rdf:Description about="http://www.starpowder.com/venus.html"
        dc:Title = "Venus">
        <dc:Creator rdf:resource="http://www.starpowder.com/NickC.html"/>
    </rdf:Description>
    .
    .
    .
```

Even though this uses `<dc:Creator>` property elements, there is still no element content to be treated as plain text by an HTML browser.

RDF Containers

RDF also allows you to group properties together by defining property *containers*. There are three containers:

- `Bag`—A group of properties without any particular order.

- `Seq`—A sequence of properties in a specific order.

- `Alt`—A list of properties giving alternate choices. Only one of all these choices is actually chosen.

These containers are supported with the `<rdf:Bag>`, `<rdf:Seq>`, and `<rdf:Alt>` elements, which have `ID` and `aboutEach` attributes. (The W3C RDF syntax specification mistakenly defines these elements with only an `ID` attribute but then uses both attributes in the text.) I'll use both those attributes in this chapter.

Using the Bag Container

You use a Bag container to indicate that a property has multiple, although un-ordered, values. How do you specify the multiple items in a container? You use the `<rdf:li>` element (modeled after the HTML `<LI>`, list item, element).

Here's an example: In this case, I'm indicating that the planets.html resource has multiple subjects—Mercury, Venus, Mars, and Earth:

Listing ch18_10.rdf

```
<?xml version="1.0" ?>
<rdf:RDF
    xmlns:rdf="http://www.w3.org/1999/02/22-rdf-syntax-ns#"
    xmlns:dc="http://www.purl.org/DC#">

    <rdf:Description about="http://www.starpowder.com/planets.html">
        <dc:Title>Planets</dc:Title>
        <dc:Creator>Nicolas Copernicus</dc:Creator>
        <dc:Type>text</dc:Type>
        <dc:Subject>
            <rdf:Bag>
                <rdf:li>Mercury</rdf:li>
                <rdf:li>Venus</rdf:li>
                <rdf:li>Earth</rdf:li>
                <rdf:li>Mars</rdf:li>
            </rdf:Bag>
        </dc:Subject>
    </rdf:Description>

</rdf:RDF>
```

The items in a Bag container can also be resource references, of course, like this:

Listing ch18_11.rdf

```
<?xml version="1.0" ?>
<rdf:RDF
    xmlns:rdf="http://www.w3.org/1999/02/22-rdf-syntax-ns#"
    xmlns:dc="http://www.purl.org/DC#">

    <rdf:Description about="http://www.starpowder.com/planets.html">
        <dc:Title>Planets</dc:Title>
        <dc:Creator>Nicolas Copernicus</dc:Creator>
        <dc:Subject>
```

continues

Listing ch18_11.rdf   Continued

```
                <rdf:Bag>
                    <rdf:li
                        rdf:resource="http://www.starpowder.com/mercury.html"/>
                    <rdf:li
                        rdf:resource="http://www.starpowder.com/venus.html"/>
                    <rdf:li
                        rdf:resource="http://www.starpowder.com/earth.html"/>
                    <rdf:li
                        rdf:resource="http://www.starpowder.com/mars.html"/>
                </rdf:Bag>
            </dc:Subject>
        </rdf:Description>
</rdf:RDF>
```

Using the Seq Container

You use a Seq container to indicate that a property has multiple ordered values. In this case, you are indicating that the multiple property values have some order. For example, this document indicates that planet.html covers the topics Mercury, Venus, Earth and Mars, in that order:

Listing ch18_12.rdf

```
<?xml version="1.0" ?>
<rdf:RDF
    xmlns:rdf="http://www.w3.org/1999/02/22-rdf-syntax-ns#"
    xmlns:dc="http://www.purl.org/DC#">

    <rdf:Description about="http://www.starpowder.com/planets.html">
        <dc:Title>Planets</dc:Title>
        <dc:Creator>Nicolas Copernicus</dc:Creator>
        <dc:Subject>
            <rdf:Seq>
                <rdf:li>Mercury</rdf:li>
                <rdf:li>Venus</rdf:li>
                <rdf:li>Earth</rdf:li>
                <rdf:li>Mars</rdf:li>
            </rdf:Seq>
        </dc:Subject>
    </rdf:Description>

</rdf:RDF>
```

Using the Alt Container

The Alt container provides alternatives, such as different language versions of a resource or mirror sites. Here's an example: In this case, I'm listing various versions of a document in different formats, plain text, HTML, Rich Text Format (RTF), and XML:

Listing ch18_13.rdf

```
<?xml version="1.0" ?>
<rdf:RDF
    xmlns:rdf="http://www.w3.org/1999/02/22-rdf-syntax-ns#"
    xmlns:dc="http://www.purl.org/DC#">

    <rdf:Description about="http://www.starpowder.com/planets">
        <dc:Title>Planets</dc:Title>
        <dc:Creator>Nicolas Copernicus</dc:Creator>
        <dc:Format>
            <rdf:Alt>
                <rdf:li resource =
                  "http://www.starpowder.com/planets.html">
                    text/html
                </rdf:li>
                <rdf:li resource =
                  "http://www.starpowder.com/planets.txt">
                    text/plain
                </rdf:li>
                <rdf:li resource =
                  "http://www.starpowder.com/planets.rtf">
                    text/rtf
                </rdf:li>
                <rdf:li resource =
                  "http://www.starpowder.com/planets.xml">
                    text/xml
                </rdf:li>
            </rdf:Alt>
        </dc:Format>
    </rdf:Description>

</rdf:RDF>
```

Making Statements About Containers

You can use a container's ID attribute to make a statement about the container as a whole, separate from the items in the container. Here's an example: In this case, I'm giving a creation date for a Bag container. To do that, I give the Bag container the ID "planets" and then create a new <rdf:Description> element about "#planets" to describe the Bag container and give its date:

Listing ch18_14.rdf

```
<?xml version="1.0" ?>
<rdf:RDF
    xmlns:rdf="http://www.w3.org/1999/02/22-rdf-syntax-ns#"
    xmlns:dc="http://www.purl.org/DC#">

    <rdf:Description
        about="http://www.starpowder.com/planets.html">
        <dc:Title>XML Links</dc:Title>
        <dc:Creator>Nicolas Copernicus</dc:Creator>
        <dc:Subject>
            <rdf:Bag ID="planets">
                <rdf:li
                    rdf:resource="http://www.starpowder.com/mercury.html"/>
                <rdf:li
                    rdf:resource="http://www.starpowder.com/venus.html"/>
                <rdf:li
                    rdf:resource="http://www.starpowder.com/earth.html"/>
                <rdf:li
                    rdf:resource="http://www.starpowder.com/mars.html"/>
            </rdf:Bag>
        </dc:Subject>
    </rdf:Description>

    <rdf:Description about="#planets">
        <dc:Date>
            1501-10-15
        </dc:Date>
    </rdf:Description>

</rdf:RDF>
```

Making Statements About the Items in a Container

You can also make statements about each item in a container by using the container's aboutEach attribute. For example, suppose that I want to indicate that each item in a bag has the same creation date. In that case, I could assign the value "creationDate" to the Bag's aboutEach attribute and add a new <rdf:Description> element about "#creationDate", like this:

Listing ch18_15.rdf

```
<?xml version="1.0" ?>
<rdf:RDF
    xmlns:rdf="http://www.w3.org/1999/02/22-rdf-syntax-ns#"
    xmlns:dc="http://www.purl.org/DC#">

    <rdf:Description about="http://www.starpowder.com/planets.html">
        <dc:Title>Mercury</dc:Title>
        <dc:Creator>Nicolas Copernicus</dc:Creator>
        <dc:Subject>
            <rdf:Bag aboutEach="creationDate">
                <rdf:li
                    resource="http://www.starpowder.com/mercury.html"/>
                <rdf:li
            resource="http://www.starpowder.com/venus.html"/>
                <rdf:li
                    resource="http://www.starpowder.com/earth.html"/>
                <rdf:li
                    resource="http://www.starpowder.com/mars.html"/>
            </rdf:Bag>
        </dc:Subject>
    </rdf:Description>

    <rdf:Description aboutEach="#creationDate">
        <dc:Date>
            1501-10-15
        </dc:Date>
    </rdf:Description>
</rdf:RDF>
```

Selecting Container Items by Prefix

In fact, you can make statements about groups of resources that have the same prefixes (which may or may not be members of one container). For example, say I want to connect a date with all resources that start with `"http://www.starpowder.com/"`. I can do that with the `aboutEachPrefix` attribute of `<rdf:Description>` like this:

Listing ch18_16.rdf

```
<?xml version="1.0" ?>
<rdf:RDF
    xmlns:rdf="http://www.w3.org/1999/02/22-rdf-syntax-ns#"
    xmlns:dc="http://www.purl.org/DC#">

    <rdf:Description about="http://www.starpowder.com/planets.html">
        <dc:Title>Mercury</dc:Title>
        <dc:Creator>Nicolas Copernicus</dc:Creator>
        <dc:Subject>
            <rdf:Bag>
                <rdf:li
                    resource="http://www.starpowder.com/mercury.html"/>
                <rdf:li
        resource="http://www.starpowder.com/venus.html"/>
                <rdf:li
                    resource="http://www.starpowder.com/earth.html"/>
                <rdf:li
                    resource="http://www.starpowder.com/mars.html"/>
            </rdf:Bag>
        </dc:Subject>
    </rdf:Description>

    <rdf:Description aboutEachPrefix="#http://www.starpowder.com/">
        <dc:Date>
            1501-10-15
        </dc:Date>
    </rdf:Description>
</rdf:RDF>
```

Creating RDF Schemas

So far, the property elements that you use in RDF are up to you to define, unless you use someone else's RDF content model, such as the Dublin Core. Until recently, there was no real way to make sure that RDF software would be able to check the syntax of your RDF extensions.

However, the W3C has been working hard on creating an RDF schema language, and you can find the details at www.w3.org/TR/rdf-schema. It's not finalized yet (the specification is a working draft at this writing), and it is not supported by software. When it's available, though, it will let RDF parsers check the full syntax of the extensions you make to RDF.

And that's it for our coverage of SOAP and RDF in this chapter. In the next chapter, we'll take a look at Vector Markup Language (VML).

CHAPTER 19

Vector Markup Language

The way you present XML in browsers should not be limited to simple text. In fact, there are various initiatives to create graphics-based XML applications. We created graphical browsers in Chapter 11, "Java and the XML DOM," and Chapter 12, "Java and SAX," to use XML to display circles. I also discussed the W3C language, Scalable Vector Graphics (SVG), in Chapter 1, "Essential XML." SVG has been around for a long time but has not been very widely implemented. Today, the most widespread graphics-based XML application is the Vector Markup Language (VML) from Microsoft. Besides being supported in Microsoft applications, VML is supported by many leading software vendors such as Autodesk and Macromedia.

Here's how Microsoft describes VML:

> VML is an application of Extensible Markup Language (XML) 1.0 which defines a format for the encoding of vector information together with additional markup to describe how that information may be displayed and edited.

VML supports the markup of vector graphic information in the same way that HTML supports the markup of textual information. Besides its own XML elements, VML supports CSS, so you can style and position shapes as you like. VML is supported in Microsoft Office 2000 and XP—Microsoft Word, PowerPoint, and Excel. When you create graphics in those programs, the graphics are stored in VML. Internet Explorer also supports VML. You can use the tools that come with Microsoft Office to draw VML figures, or you can create VML yourself. We'll do it ourselves in this chapter.

Here's the primary online resource for VML, the note that Microsoft wrote and sent to W3C, which W3C has posted: www.w3.org/TR/NOTE-VML

VML was added to Internet Explorer before that browser added its built-in XML support, so the way you implement VML does not involve Internet Explorer XML islands or any such mechanism. Instead, you use a namespace for VML and then use the VML engine in Internet Explorer. This is actually implemented as an Internet Explorer *behavior* (an external code module). We saw this example in Chapter 1, and I'll take a closer look at it in this chapter:

Listing ch19_01.html

```
<HTML xmlns:v="urn:schemas-microsoft-com:vml">

    <HEAD>
        <TITLE>
            Using Vector Markup Language
        </TITLE>

        <STYLE>
        v\:* {behavior: url(#default#VML);}
        </STYLE>
    </HEAD>

    <BODY>
        <CENTER>
            <H1>
                Using Vector Markup Language
            </H1>
        </CENTER>
        <P>
        <v:oval STYLE='width:100pt; height:75pt'
            fillcolor="yellow" />
        <P>
        <v:rect STYLE='width:100pt; height:75pt' fillcolor="blue"
            strokecolor="red" STROKEWEIGHT="2pt"/>
        <P>
        <v:polyline
            POINTS="20pt,55pt,100pt,-10pt,180pt,65pt,260pt,25pt"
            strokecolor="red" STROKEWEIGHT="2pt"/>
    </BODY>
</HTML>
```

Internet Explorer Behaviors

You can find out more about Internet Explorer behaviors, which represent one of Microsoft's techniques for separating markup from document content, at http://msdn.microsoft.com/workshop/c-frame.htm#/workshop/author/default.asp.

This example just drew a few VML shapes; you can see the result of this page in Figure 19-1.

Figure 19-1
A VML sample
page.

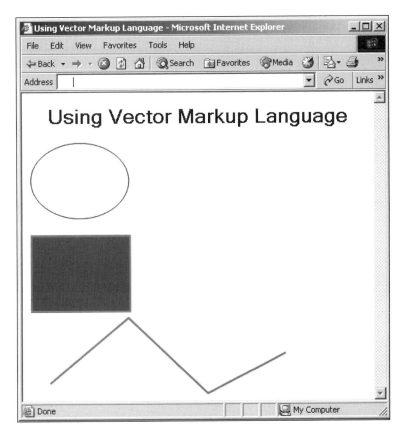

Now that we're discussing VML in depth, the syntax of this document bears a little examination.

Creating VML Documents

In Internet Explorer, VML is embedded in HTML documents. You start by declaring this namespace, v:

```
<HTML xmlns:v="urn:schemas-microsoft-com:vml">
    .
    .
    .
```

You must also instantiate the VML engine, which is implemented as an Internet Explorer behavior. To implement this behavior, you use a <STYLE> element, connecting the v namespace to the VML default behavior:

```
<HTML xmlns:v="urn:schemas-microsoft-com:vml">

    <HEAD>
        <TITLE>
            Using Vector Markup Language
        </TITLE>

        <STYLE>
            v\:* {behavior: url(#default#VML);}
        </STYLE>
    </HEAD>
        .
        .
        .
```

This indicates to Internet Explorer that the VML in the page should be handled by the VML engine. Now you can add VML elements such as <oval> if you use the proper namespace, v:

```
<HTML xmlns:v="urn:schemas-microsoft-com:vml">

    <HEAD>
        <TITLE>
            Using Vector Markup Language
        </TITLE>

        <STYLE>
            v\:* {behavior: url(#default#VML);}
        </STYLE>
    </HEAD>

    <BODY>
        <CENTER>
            <H1>
                Using Vector Markup Language
            </H1>
        </CENTER>
        <P>
        <v:oval STYLE='width:100pt; height:75pt'
            fillcolor="yellow" />
        <P>
        <v:rect STYLE='width:100pt; height:75pt' fillcolor="blue"
            strokecolor="red" STROKEWEIGHT="2pt"/>
        <P>
```

```
<v:polyline
     POINTS="20pt,55pt,100pt,-10pt,180pt,65pt,260pt,25pt"
     strokecolor="red" STROKEWEIGHT="2pt"/>
</BODY>
</HTML>
```

I'll take a look at what VML elements are available now.

The VML Elements

Twenty elements are defined in VML:

- `<arc>`—Draws an arc
- `<background>`—Adds a background
- `<curve>`—Draws a curve
- `<fill>`—Fills a shape
- `<formulas>`—Specifies a formula that lets you scale shapes
- `<group>`—Groups shapes
- `<handles>`—Draws handles on shapes
- `<image>`—Supports images
- `<imagedata>`—Specifies an image to be rendered on top of a shape
- `<line>`—Draws a line
- `<oval>`—Draws an oval
- `<path>`—Specifies a path for rendering
- `<polyline>`—Draws a shape from line segments
- `<roundrect>`—Draws a rounded rectangle
- `<shadow>`—Adds a shadow to a shape
- `<shape>`—Creates a basic shape
- `<shapetype>`—Defines a reusable shape
- `<stroke>`—Specifies how to draw a path
- `<textbox>`—Creates a text box
- `<textpath>`—Specifies a path for text to be drawn along

The overall structure of VML is based on two primary elements: `<shape>` and `<group>`. The `<shape>` element is the most basic VML element, and you use it to define general graphic shapes in VML. You can use the `<group>` element to group shapes together so they can be handled as a single unit.

Besides the `<shape>` and `<group>` elements, VML defines additional top-level elements to help make the editing and representation of complex graphical information more compact and convenient. For example, you can use the `<shapetype>` element to define a definition of a shape. A `<shape>` element may then reference a `<shapetype>` element to instantiate several copies of the same shape.

You also can use a number of predefined shapes based on the `<shape>` element. Using the predefined shapes means you don't have to explicitly declare the shape you want to use. These predefined shapes are `<line>`, `<polyline>`, `<curve>`, `<rect>`, `<roundrect>`, `<oval>`, `<arc>`, and `<image>`.

VML Elements' Common Attributes

You can find parts (but only parts) of the VML DTD in the VML note at www.w3.org/TR/NOTE-VML. Two important parts are the entity parameters `coreattrs` and `shapeattrs`, which define attribute lists, because many of the elements we'll see in this chapter use those attributes. Here's how `coreattrs` is defined:

```
<!entity %coreattrs
id id #implied -- document-wide unique id --
class cdata #implied -- space separated list of classes --
style cdata #implied -- associated style info --
title cdata #implied -- advisory title/amplification --
href cdata #implied -- URL link if the element is clicked on --
target cdata #implied -- target frame for href --
alt cdata #implied -- alternate text if element cannot be displayed --
coordsize cdata #implied -- size of coordinate space inside the element --
coordorigin cdata #implied -- coordinate at top-left corner of element --
wrapcoords cdata #implied -- outline to use for tight text wrapping --
>
```

Here is the `shapeattrs` parameter entity:

```
<!entity %shapeattrs
opacity cdata #implied -- opacity of the shape --
chromakey cdata #implied -- color to be made transparent --
stroke cdata #implied -- Boolean whether to stroke the outline or not --
strokecolor cdata #implied -- RGB color to use for the stroke --
strokeweight cdata #implied -- weight of the line to use for stroking --
fill cdata #implied -- Boolean whether to fill the shape or not --
fillcolor cdata #implied -- RGB color to use for the fill --
print cdata #implied -- Boolean whether the element is to be printed --
>
```

VML Uses CSS

VML uses CSS to position and orient shapes. In addition to standard CSS layout, the VML elements may be rotated or flipped. Each element also establishes a coordinate space for its content, which allows scaling of the content with respect to the containing elements.

VML uses a number of VML styles to augment CSS2, and I'll take look at them here.

The rotation *Property*

You can use the `rotation` property to specify a rotation for a shape or group. The rotation is measured in clockwise degrees about its center.

The flip *Property*

You use the `flip` property to specify that a shape or group should be flipped about its center about either the x or the y axis. Here are the two values you can assign to the `flip` property:

- x—Flips the rotated shape about the y axis
- y—Flips the rotated shape about the x axis

The center-x *and* center-y *Properties*

You use the `center-x` and `center-y` properties to specify the center of the block that contains the shape. These properties can be used as an alternative to the customary CSS positioning properties, `left` and `top`.

Local Coordinate Space

The `<shape>` and `<group>` elements are CSS block-level elements. Inside their blocks, a local coordinate system is defined for any subelements that use the `coordsize` and `coordorigin` attributes, and all CSS2 positioning information is expressed in terms of this local coordinate space. We'll run into these attributes in this chapter when we group shapes together.

The VML `coordsize` attribute defines how many units there are along the width of the containing block. The `coordorigin` attribute defines the coordinate at the top-left corner of the containing block. For example, if a group were defined as follows:

```
<v:shape style='width: 500px; height: 200px' coordsize="100,100"
coordorigin="-50,-50" />
```

the containing block would be 500 pixels wide by 200 pixels high. The coordinate system inside the block ranges from −50.0 to 50.0 along the x axis and −50.0 to 50.0 along the y axis. The point (0, 0) is right in the center of the block. Shapes inside the group are positioned and sized according to this local coordinate system. That's useful because, no matter how the width and height of the group is changed, the local coordinate system inside will remain the same.

The <*shape*> Element

The <shape> element is the primary one in VML, although I rarely find myself using it in practice (I mostly use the predefined shapes based on <shape>). This element may appear by itself or within a <group> element. The <shape> element includes all the attributes in coreattrs and shapeattrs, and it adds three more:

```
<!attlist shape %coreattrs; %shapeattrs;
type cdata #implied -- reference to shapetype --
adj cdata #implied -- list of adjust values for parameterized paths --
path cdata #implied -- string with command set describing a path --
>
```

For the sake of reference, all the attributes of this element and their descriptions appear in Table 19-1. Note that VML attributes can be part of either the VML or CSS namespaces.

Table 19-1 Attributes of the <*shape*> Element	Namespace	Attribute	Type	Default Value	Description
	CSS	flip	string	null	Specifies that the shape image inside the reference rectangle should be flipped along the given axes in the order specified. Takes the values x or y or both.
	CSS	height	number	100	Specifies the height of the containing block of the shape.
	CSS	left, margin-left, center-x, etc.	number	0	Sets the position of the left of the containing block of the shape.

Name-space	Attribute	Type	Default Value	Description
CSS	`position`	`string`	`"static"`	Sets the CSS type of positioning. When inside a group, this value must always be `"absolute"`.
CSS	`rotation`	`number`	`0`	Specifies the angle to rotate by.
CSS	`top, margin -top, center -y,` etc.	`number`	`0`	Sets the position of the top of the containing block of the shape.
CSS	`visibility`	`string`	`visible`	Sets the visibility of shapes.
CSS	`width`	`number`	`100`	Specifies the width of the container rectangle of the shape.
CSS	`z-index`	`number`	`0`	Specifies the `z-index` of the shape. Positive numbers come out of the screen, and negative ones come into it.
VML	`adj`	`string`	`null`	Gives a comma-separated list of numbers that are "adjusting" parameters for the formulas that define the path of the shape.
VML	`alt`	`string`	`null`	Gives text associated with the shape that may appear instead of the shape.
VML	`chromakey`	`color`	`null`	Sets a color value that will be transparent so that anything behind the shape will show through.

continues

Name-space	Attribute	Type	Default Value	Description
VML	class	string	null	Gives the CSS class of this shape.
VML	coordorigin	Vector2D	"0 0"	Gives the coordinates at the top-left corner of the containing block.
VML	coordsize	Vector2D	"1000 1000"	Gives the width and height of the coordinate space inside the containing block of this shape.
VML	fill	boolean	true	If "true", the path defining the shape will be filled.
VML	fillcolor	color	"white"	Gives the color of the brush to use to fill the path of this shape.
VML	href	string	null	Gives the URI to jump to when this shape is clicked.
VML	id	string	null	Is a unique identifier for the shape.
VML	opacity	number	1.0	Sets the opacity of the entire shape. Set to values between 0 (transparent) and 1 (opaque.)
VML	path	string	null	Gives the path that defines the shape. This is a string containing the commands that define the path.
VML	print	boolean	true	If true, this shape should be printed.
VML	stroke	boolean	true	If true, the path defining the shape will be stroked (rendered) using a solid line unless there is a stroke subelement.

Name-space	Attribute	Type	Default Value	Description
VML	strokecolor	color	"black"	Sets the color of the brush to use to draw the path of this shape.
VML	strokeweight	number	"0.75pt"	Sets the width of the brush to use to stroke the path.
VML	target	string	null	Gives the target frame URI.
VML	title	string	null	Gives the title of the shape.
VML	type	string	null	Holds a shapetype ID that describes the shape.
VML	v	string	null	Gives a string containing the commands that define the path.
VML	wrapcoords	string	null	Used for the wrapping text around an object.

Microsoft gives all VML elements an "XML template" that specifies default values for each of its attributes. Here's the XML template for the <shape> element:

```
<shape
type=null
adj=null
path=null
opacity="100%"
chromakey="none"
stroke="true"
strokecolor="black"
strokeweight="0.75pt"
fill="true"
fillcolor="white"
print="true"
id=null
class=null
style='visibility: visible'
```

```
title=null
href=null
target=null
alt=null
coordsize="1000, 1000"
coordorigin="0, 0"
wrapcoords=null
/>
```

Using the <shape> element to draw shapes can be a little complex because you need to define the whole shape yourself; you do this by specifying a VML *path*. That means giving the actual locations to use to draw the shape. To show how that works, I'll use a shape that Microsoft supports in its reference material and that draws a heart:

Listing ch19_02.html

```
<HTML xmlns:v="urn:schemas-microsoft-com:vml">

    <HEAD>
        <TITLE>
            Using Vector Markup Language
        </TITLE>

        <STYLE>
        v\:* {behavior: url(#default#VML);}
        </STYLE>
    </HEAD>

    <BODY>
        <CENTER>
            <H1>
                VML Shapes
            </H1>
            <v:shape fillcolor="red"
                strokecolor="red" coordsize="21600,21600"
                path="m10860,2187c10451,1746,9529,1018,9015,730,
                7865,152,6685,,5415,,4175, 152,2995,575,1967,
                1305,1150,2187,575,3222,242,4220,,5410,242,6560,
                575,7597l10860, 21600,20995,7597c21480,6560,
                21600,5410,21480,4220,21115,3222,20420,2187,19632,
                1305,18575,575,17425,152,16275,,15005,,13735,152,
                12705,730,12176,1018,11254,1746, 10860,2187xe"
                style='width:200;height:160;'/>
        </CENTER>
    </BODY>
</HTML>
```

You can see the result in Figure 19-2.

Figure 19-2
Using the
<shape>
element.

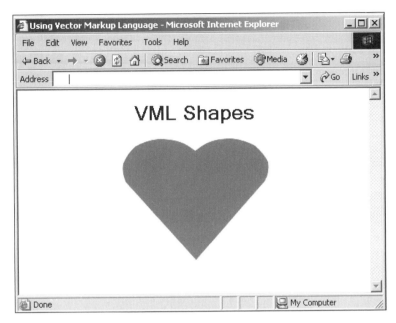

Another way of drawing this shape is to specify the shape's path in a
<shapetype> element and reference the <shapetype> element's ID with the
<shape> element's type attribute:

```
<HTML xmlns:v="urn:schemas-microsoft-com:vml">

    <HEAD>
        <TITLE>
            Using Vector Markup Language
        </TITLE>

        <STYLE>
        v\:* {behavior: url(#default#VML);}
        </STYLE>
    </HEAD>

    <BODY>
        <CENTER>
            <H1>
                VML Shapes
            </H1>
            <v:shapetype id="Valentine" fillcolor="red"
                strokecolor="red" coordsize="21600,21600"
                path="m10860,2187c10451,1746,9529,1018,9015,730,
                7865,152,6685,,5415,,4175, 152,2995,575,1967,
                1305,1150,2187,575,3222,242,4220,,5410,242,6560,
                575,7597l10860, 21600,20995,7597c21480,6560,
```

```
                21600,5410,21480,4220,21115,3222,20420,2187,19632,
                1305,18575,575,17425,152,16275,,15005,,13735,152,
                12705,730,12176,1018,11254,1746, 10860,2187xe">
            </v:shapetype>
            <v:shape type="#Valentine" style='width:200;height:160;'/>
        </CENTER>
    </BODY>
</HTML>
```

However, unless you have a drawing tool of some kind, it's pretty tedious to calculate all the points in a path; it's usually far easier to use the predefined shapes.

Using Predefined Shapes

Quite a few predefined shapes exist in VML, and using them can save you a lot of effort. In this section, I'll take a look at how to draw graphics using these elements.

The <rect> Element

The <rect> element just draws rectangles. This element supports both the coreattrs and shapeattrs attributes; here is its XML template showing the default values for those attributes:

```
<rect
id=null
href=null
target=null
class=null
title=null
alt=null
style='visibility: visible'
opacity="1.0"
chromakey="null"
stroke="true"
strokecolor="black"
strokeweight="1"
fill="true"
fillcolor="white"
print="true"
coordsize="1000,1000"
coordorigin="0 0"
/>
```

Here's an example; in this case, I'll draw a rectangle that will be red with a green border of 4 points width:

Listing ch19_03.html

```
<HTML xmlns:v="urn:schemas-microsoft-com:vml">

    <HEAD>
        <TITLE>
            Using Vector Markup Language
        </TITLE>

        <STYLE>
            v\:* {behavior: url(#default#VML);}
        </STYLE>
    </HEAD>

    <BODY>
        <CENTER>
            <H1>
                VML Rectangles
            </H1>
            <v:rect style='width:200pt;height:100pt'
                fillcolor="red" strokecolor="green"
                strokeweight="4pt"/>
        </CENTER>
    </BODY>
</HTML>
```

You can see the result in Figure 19-3.

Figure 19-3
Using the
<rect>
element.

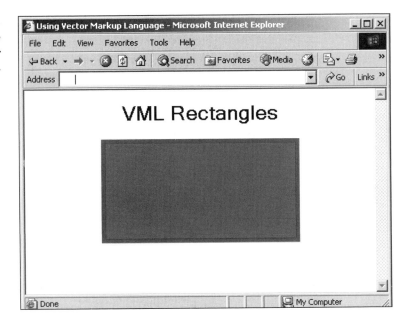

The <*line*> Element

You use the `<line>` element to create a straight line. Here are the attributes of this element:

```
<!attlist line %coreattrs; %shapeattrs;
from cdata #implied
to cdata #implied
>
```

Here are the two attributes specific to the `<line>` element:

- `from`—The starting point of the line. Specified using Vector2D format, like this: `"100 100"`.

- `to`—The ending point of the line. Specified using Vector2D format, like this: `"100 100"`.

And here's the XML template for this element:

```
<line
from="0 0"
to="10 10"
id=null
href=null
target=null
class=null
title=null
alt=null
style='visibility: visible'
opacity="1.0"
chromakey="null"
stroke="true"
strokecolor="black"
strokeweight="1"
fill="true"
fillcolor="white"
print="true"
coordsize="1000,1000"
coordorigin="0 0"
/>
```

Here's an example; in this case, I'm drawing a thick blue line from the pixel coordinates (20, 20) to (400, 100):

Listing ch19_04.html

```html
<HTML xmlns:v="urn:schemas-microsoft-com:vml">

    <HEAD>
        <TITLE>
            Using Vector Markup Language
        </TITLE>

        <STYLE>
            v\:* {behavior: url(#default#VML);}
        </STYLE>
    </HEAD>

    <BODY>
        <CENTER>
            <H1>
                VML Lines
            </H1>
            <v:line from="20px,20px" to="400px,100px"
                    strokecolor="blue" strokeweight="4pt">
        </CENTER>
    </BODY>
</HTML>
```

You can see the result of this VML in Figure 19-4.

Figure 19-4
Using the
<line>
element.

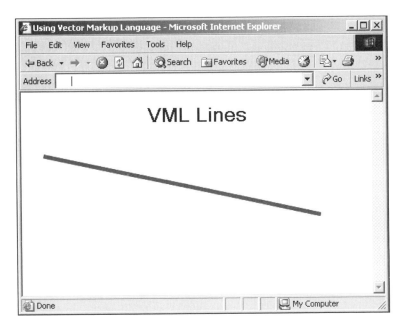

The <*oval*> Element

You use the <oval> element to draw ovals and circles. This element supports the coreattrs and shapeattrs attributes. Here is the <oval> element's XML template:

```
<oval
position="0 0"
size="100 100"
id=null
href=null
target=null
class=null
title=null
alt=null
style='visibility: visible'
opacity="1.0"
chromakey="null"
stroke="true"
strokecolor="black"
strokeweight="0.75pt"
fill="true"
fillcolor="white"
print="true"
coordsize="1000,1000"
coordorigin="0 0"
/>
```

Here's an example in which I'm drawing a blue oval. As with other elements, you can specify the size of the oval using the CSS style attribute:

Listing ch19_05.html

```
<HTML xmlns:v="urn:schemas-microsoft-com:vml">

    <HEAD>
        <TITLE>
            Using Vector Markup Language
        </TITLE>

        <STYLE>
            v\:* {behavior: url(#default#VML);}
        </STYLE>
    </HEAD>

    <BODY>
        <CENTER>
            <H1>
```

```
                    VML Ovals
              </H1>
              <v:oval style='width:200pt;height:100pt'
                    fillcolor="blue" />
          </CENTER>
      </BODY>
</HTML>
```

You can see the result of this VML in Figure 19-5.

Figure 19-5
Using the
<oval>
element.

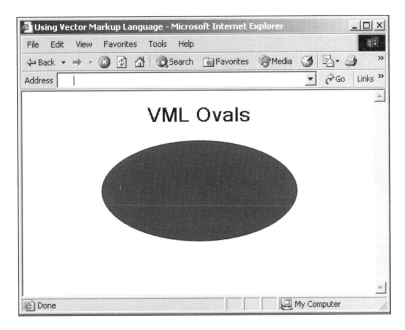

The *<polyline>* Element

You can use the <polyline> element to define shapes that are created from connected line segments. Here's the attribute list for this element:

```
<!attlist polyline %coreattrs; %shapeattrs;
points cdata #implied
>
```

The `points` attribute is a string that defines the polyline shape to draw using pairs of values that specify points, such as "0 0 10 10 40 40". Here is the XML template for this element:

```
<polyline
points="0 0 10 10 20 0"
id=null
href=null
target=null
class=null
title=null
alt=null
style='visibility: visible'
opacity="1.0"
chromakey="null"
stroke="true"
strokecolor="black"
strokeweight="1"
fill="true"
fillcolor="white"
print="true"
coordsize="1000,1000"
coordorigin="0 0"
/>
```

For example, to draw a polyline shape, here's some VML:

Listing ch19_06.html

```
<HTML xmlns:v="urn:schemas-microsoft-com:vml">

    <HEAD>
        <TITLE>
            Using Vector Markup Language
        </TITLE>

        <STYLE>
            v\:* {behavior: url(#default#VML);}
        </STYLE>
    </HEAD>

    <BODY>
        <CENTER>
            <H1>
                VML Polylines
            </H1>
            <v:polyline points="0pt,0pt,90pt,-9pt,180pt,60pt,0pt,20pt
                -180pt,60pt,-90pt,-9pt,0pt,0pt"
                strokecolor="red" strokeweight="2pt"/>
        </CENTER>
    </BODY>
</HTML>
```

You can see the result of this VML in Figure 19-6.

Figure 19-6
Using the
<polyline>
element.

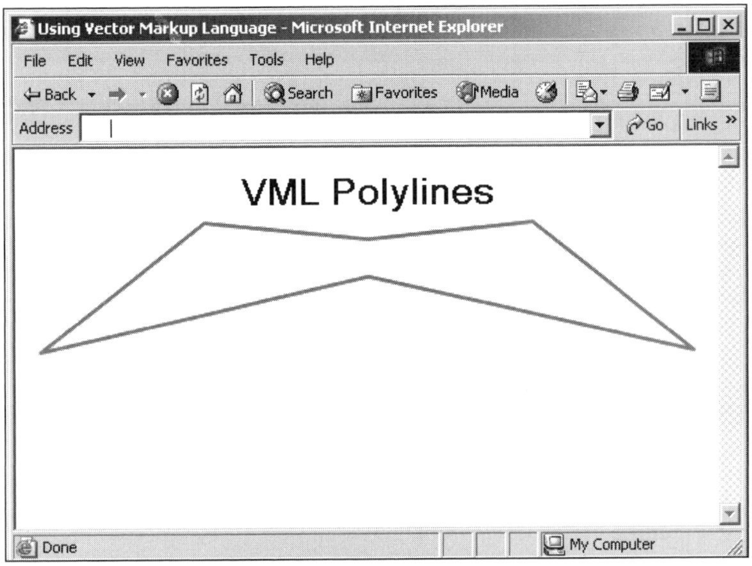

The *<curve>* Element

You can use the <curve> element to draw a cubic Bézier curve. Here is the attribute list of this element:

```
<!attlist curve %coreattrs; %shapeattrs;
from cdata #implied
control1 cdata #implied
control2 cdata #implied
to cdata #implied
>
```

Here are the custom attributes for this element:

- from—The starting point of the line in the coordinate space of the parent element. Specified using Vector2D format, like this: "100 100".

- control1—The first control point for the curve. Specified using Vector2D format, like this: "100 100".

- control2—The second control point for the curve. Specified using Vector2D format, like this: "100 100".

- to—The ending point of the line in the coordinate space of the parent element. Specified using Vector2D format, like this: "100 100".

The control points let you specify the bounding rectangle for the curve and thus specify its shape. Here is this element's XML template:

```
<curve
from="0 0"
control1="10 10"
control2="20 0"
to="10 10"
id=null
href=null
target=null
class=null
title=null
alt=null
style='visibility: visible'
opacity="1.0"
chromakey="null"
stroke="true"
strokecolor="black"
strokeweight="1"
fill="true"
fillcolor="white"
print="true"
coordsize="1000,1000"
coordorigin="0 0"
/>
```

For example, I'll draw a curve using this VML:

Listing ch19_07.html

```
<HTML xmlns:v="urn:schemas-microsoft-com:vml">

    <HEAD>
        <TITLE>
            Using Vector Markup Language
        </TITLE>

        <STYLE>
            v\:* {behavior: url(#default#VML);}
        </STYLE>
    </HEAD>

    <BODY>
        <CENTER>
            <H1>
                VML Curves
            </H1>
```

```
            <v:curve style='position:absolute'
            from="-100pt,0" control1="100pt,100pt"
            control2="200pt,100pt" to="100pt,0"
            strokecolor="blue" strokeweight="4pt"/>
        </CENTER>
    </BODY>
</HTML>
```

You can see the result of this VML in Figure 19-7.

Figure 19-7
Using the
<curve>
element.

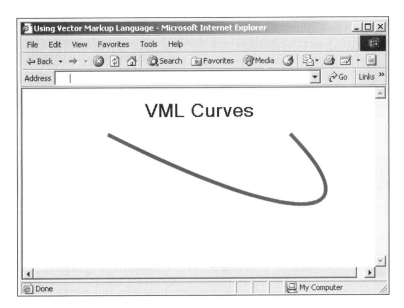

The *<arc>* Element

You can use the <arc> element to draw an arc. The arc is defined by the inter-section of the oval with the start and end radius vectors given by angles. Here is the attribute list of this element:

```
<!attlist arc %coreattrs; %shapeattrs;
startangle cdata #implied
endangle cdata #implied
>
```

Here are the custom attributes for this element:

- startangle—Specifies the angle where the arc starts
- endangle— Specifies the angle where the arc ends

Here is the XML template for this element:

```
<arc
startangle="0"
endangle="90"
id=null
href=null
target=null
class=null
title=null
alt=null
style='visibility: visible'
opacity="1.0"
chromakey="null"
stroke="true"
strokecolor="black"
strokeweight="0.75pt"
fill="true"
fillcolor="white"
print="true"
coordsize="1000,1000"
coordorigin="0 0"
/>
```

For example, here's how to take an arc from an oval, extending from 0° to 160°:

Listing ch19_08.html

```
<HTML xmlns:v="urn:schemas-microsoft-com:vml">

    <HEAD>
        <TITLE>
            Using Vector Markup Language
        </TITLE>

        <STYLE>
            v\:* {behavior: url(#default#VML);}
        </STYLE>
    </HEAD>

    <BODY>
        <CENTER>
            <H1>
                VML Arcs
            </H1>
            <v:arc style='width:200pt;height:100pt'
                startangle="0" endangle="160"
                strokecolor="blue" strokeweight="4pt"/>
        </CENTER>
    </BODY>
</HTML>
```

You can see the result of this VML in Figure 19-8.

Figure 19-8
Using the
<arc>
element.

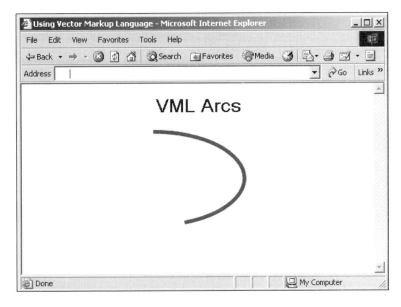

Coloring Shapes

You may have noticed that I've specified colors so far using words like `"red"`, `"blue"`, `"green"`, and so on. In fact, there are three ways to specify colors in VML:

- Using a predefined color name: `fillcolor="red"`
- Using the `rgb` function: `fillcolor="rgb(255,0,0)"`
- Specifying a direct value: `fillcolor="#FF0000"`

You can use the HTML 4.0 predefined color names in VML:

- `aqua`
- `black`
- `blue`
- `fuchsia`
- `gray`
- `green`
- `lime`
- `maroon`
- `navy`

- olive

- purple

- red

- silver

- teal

- white

- yellow

You can also specify colors by giving the red, green, and blue color values in the rgb function like this: rgb(*rrr*, *ggg*, *bbb*), where *rrr* is the red color value, *ggg* is the green color value, and *bbb* is the blue color value, all of which range from 0 to 255. Or, you can give those color values directly using hexadecimal digits, as you would in HTML, like this: "#*rrrgggbbb*". For example, "000000" is black, "#0000FF" is bright blue, "#FFFFFF" is white, and so on.

Scaling Shapes

You may also have noticed that you can set the size for shapes with the style attribute, as in this case, where I'm setting the size of the bounding rectangle of an oval:

```
<HTML xmlns:v="urn:schemas-microsoft-com:vml">

    <HEAD>
        <TITLE>
            Using Vector Markup Language
        </TITLE>

        <STYLE>
            v\:* {behavior: url(#default#VML);}
        </STYLE>
    </HEAD>

    <BODY>
        <CENTER>
            <H1>
                VML Ovals
            </H1>
            <v:oval style='width:200pt;height:100pt'
                fillcolor="blue" />
        </CENTER>
    </BODY>
</HTML>
```

To scale a shape, all you have to do is change the width and height as specified with the `style` attribute. For example, to double the oval's size in both dimensions, I could assign `style` a value of `"width:400pt;height:200pt"`.

Positioning Shapes

VML uses the same syntax defined in CSS2 to position shapes on a Web page. You can use static, relative, or absolute positioning to determine where the base point is located on a Web page. You can also use the `top` and `left` or `center-x` and `center-y` style attributes to specify the offset from the base point at which the containing box for the shape will be positioned.

You can also use `z-index` to specify the z-order of shapes on a Web page. In addition, VML provides `rotation` and `flip` to rotate or flip shapes. I'll take a look at a few of the position styles here.

The *static* Position Style

The default position style is `static`, which makes the browser insert a shape at the current point in the browser's text flow. Here's an example putting static positioning to work, in which I'm drawing a rectangle following some text:

Listing ch19_09.html

```
<HTML xmlns:v="urn:schemas-microsoft-com:vml">

    <HEAD>
        <TITLE>
            Using Vector Markup Language
        </TITLE>

        <STYLE>
            v\:* {behavior: url(#default#VML);}
        </STYLE>
    </HEAD>

    <BODY>
        <CENTER>
            <H1>
                VML Positioning
            </H1>
            Here is the rectangle:
            <v:rect style='width:200pt;height:100pt'
                fillcolor="red" strokecolor="green"
                strokeweight="4pt"/>
        </CENTER>
    </BODY>
</HTML>
```

The result appears in Figure 19-9. As you see there, the shape's baseline is aligned with the baseline of the text.

Figure 19-9
Using static
positioning.

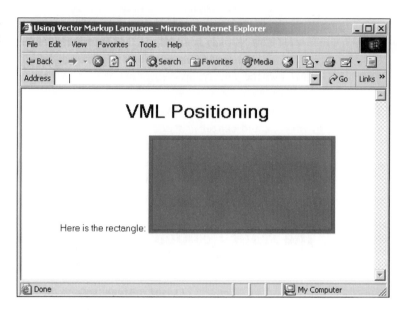

The *relative* Position Style

When you use static positioning, a shape is positioned with respect to the current location in the text flow. You can also position shapes *relative* to the current location in the text flow. To do so, you use the `position: relative` style and use the `top` and `left` style properties.

Here's an example in which I position a shape 30 points to the right of the current text location and 15 points higher:

Listing ch19_10.html

```
<HTML xmlns:v="urn:schemas-microsoft-com:vml">

    <HEAD>
        <TITLE>
            Using Vector Markup Language
        </TITLE>

        <STYLE>
            v\:* {behavior: url(#default#VML);}
        </STYLE>
    </HEAD>
```

```
<BODY>
    <CENTER>
        <H1>
            VML Relative Positioning
        </H1>
        Here is the rectangle:
        <v:rect style='position:relative;left:30pt;
            top:-15pt;width:200pt;height:100pt'
            fillcolor="red" strokecolor="green"
            strokeweight="4pt"/>
    </CENTER>
</BODY>
</HTML>
```

You can see the result in Figure 19-10. As you see in the figure, the shape is positioned relative to the current text flow location.

Figure 19-10
Using relative positioning.

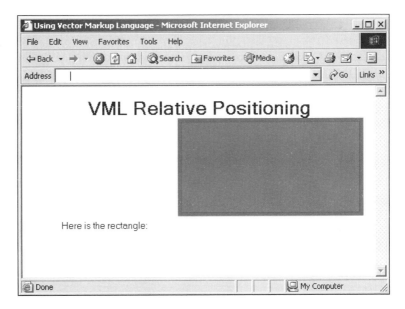

The *absolute* Position Style

You can also position shapes in *absolute* terms. When you set the position style property to absolute, the shape is positioned with respect to the upper-left corner of its container. You can use the top and left style properties to position the top left of the shape with regard to the container's origin.

Here's an example. In this case, I'll position a VML shape 100 points from the top and left of the shape's container, which is the browser's display area:

Listing ch19_11.html

```
<HTML xmlns:v="urn:schemas-microsoft-com:vml">

    <HEAD>
        <TITLE>
            Using Vector Markup Language
        </TITLE>

        <STYLE>
            v\:* {behavior: url(#default#VML);}
        </STYLE>
    </HEAD>

    <BODY>
        <CENTER>
            <H1>
                VML Absolute Positioning
            </H1>
            Here is the rectangle:
            <v:rect style='position:absolute;left:100pt;
                top:100pt;width:200pt;height:100pt'
                fillcolor="red" strokecolor="green"
                strokeweight="4pt"/>
        </CENTER>
    </BODY>
</HTML>
```

You can see the result in Figure 19-11. The rectangle is positioned in absolute terms in the browser's display area. Note that when you position shapes absolutely, they are not considered part of the text flow.

Figure 19-11
Using absolute
positioning.

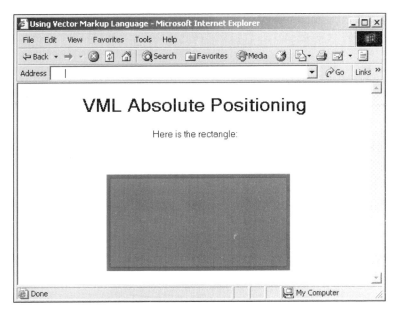

The *z-index* Position Style

It is possible to position a shape that overlaps another shape. In VML, you can control the z-order by using the z-index style attribute. You can set this attribute to zero, a positive integer, or a negative integer. The shape that has a larger z-index value appears on top of the shape that has a smaller z-index value. When both shapes have the same z-index value, the shape that was displayed last appears on top.

For example, in the following VML, the blue oval is displayed on top of the red rectangle. This is because the z-index value of the blue oval is greater than the z-index value of the red rectangle:

Listing ch19_12.html

```
<HTML xmlns:v="urn:schemas-microsoft-com:vml">

    <HEAD>
        <TITLE>
            Using Vector Markup Language
        </TITLE>

        <STYLE>
            v\:* {behavior: url(#default#VML);}
        </STYLE>
```

continues

Listing ch19_12.html   Continued

```
    </HEAD>

    <BODY>
        <CENTER>
            <H1>
                VML Z-Index Positioning
            </H1>
            <v:rect style='position:absolute;left:100pt;top:100pt;
             width:200pt;height:100pt;z-index:0'
                fillcolor="red" strokecolor="green"
                strokeweight="4pt"/>
            <v:oval style='position:absolute;left:150pt;top:60pt;
                width:100pt;height:100pt;z-index:1'
                fillcolor="blue" />
        </CENTER>
    </BODY>
</HTML>
```

You can see the result in Figure 19-12.

Figure 19-12
Reversing
z-index
positioning.

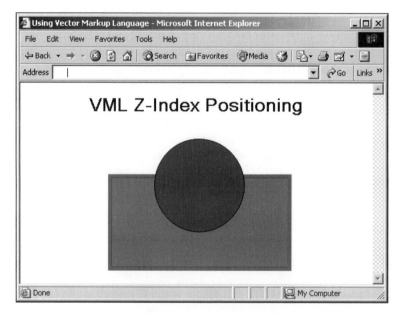

If you reverse the z-index of the shapes, the blue oval would move behind the red rectangle:

```
<v:rect style='position:absolute;left:100pt;top:100pt;
 width:200pt;height:100pt;z-index:1'
    fillcolor="red" strokecolor="green"
    strokeweight="4pt"/>
<v:oval style='position:absolute;left:150pt;top:60pt;
    width:100pt;height:100pt;z-index:0'
    fillcolor="blue" />
```

Positive z-index values are considered out of the screen, and negative values are considered into the screen. Note that if you provide a negative integer, you can use z-index to position graphics behind the normal flow of text.

The *rotation* Position Style

You can use the rotation style property to specify how many degrees you want a shape to be rotated. A positive value specifies a clockwise rotation, and a negative value specifies a counterclockwise rotation.

For example, if you specify style='rotation:45', you can rotate this rectangle 45° clockwise:

Listing ch19_13.html

```
<HTML xmlns:v="urn:schemas-microsoft-com:vml">

    <HEAD>
        <TITLE>
            Using Vector Markup Language
        </TITLE>

        <STYLE>
            v\:* {behavior: url(#default#VML);}
        </STYLE>
    </HEAD>

    <BODY>
        <CENTER>
            <H1>
                VML Rotation Positioning
            </H1>
            <v:rect style='position:absolute;left:100pt;top:100pt;
                width:200pt;height:100pt;rotation:45'
                fillcolor="red" strokecolor="green"
                strokeweight="4pt"/>
        </CENTER>
    </BODY>
</HTML>
```

You can see the result of this VML in Figure 19-13.

Figure 19-13
Rotation
positioning.

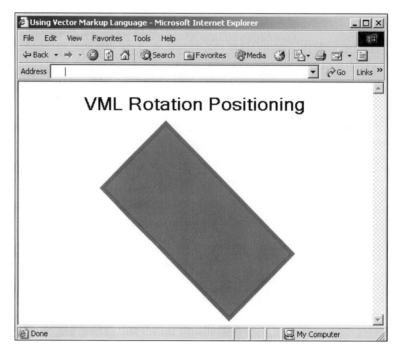

The *flip* Position Style

You can use the flip style attribute to flip a shape on its x or y axis. Here are the possible values of this property:

- x—Flips the rotated shape about the y axis
- y—Flips the rotated shape about the x axis

You can use either x or y or both. If you use style='flip:x y', the shape flips on both its x and y axis. As an example, here's how to flip the shape in Figure 19-7 with respect to the y axis:

Listing ch19_14.html

```
<HTML xmlns:v="urn:schemas-microsoft-com:vml">

    <HEAD>
        <TITLE>
            Using Vector Markup Language
        </TITLE>

        <STYLE>
            v\:* {behavior: url(#default#VML);}
        </STYLE>
    </HEAD>

    <BODY>
        <CENTER>
            <H1>
                VML Flip Positioning
            </H1>
            <v:polyline points="0pt,0pt,90pt,-9pt,180pt,60pt,0pt,
                20pt -180pt,60pt,-90pt,-9pt,0pt,0pt"
                style="flip: y"
                strokecolor="red" strokeweight="2pt"/>
        </CENTER>
    </BODY>
</HTML>
```

The flipped shape appears in Figure 19-14.

Figure 19-14
Flip
positioning.

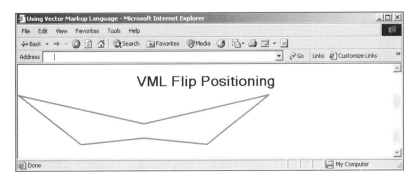

The *<group>* Element

You can group shapes with the <group> element, which allows you to treat a number of shapes as one unit. To create a group, you use the <group> element, which supports the `coreattrs` attributes. Here is this element's XML template:

```
<group
id=null
class=null
style='visibility: visible'
title=null
href=null
target=null
alt=null
coordsize="1000, 1000"
coordorigin="0, 0"
wrapcoords=null
/>
```

Here's an example. In this case, I'll group a rectangle and an oval together. I do that by creating a <group> element this way:

```
<HTML xmlns:v="urn:schemas-microsoft-com:vml">

    <HEAD>
        <TITLE>
            Using Vector Markup Language
        </TITLE>

        <STYLE>
            v\:* {behavior: url(#default#VML);}
        </STYLE>
    </HEAD>

    <BODY>
        <CENTER>
            <H1>
                VML Grouping Elements
            </H1>
            <v:group id="Group1" style='position:absolute;
                left:150pt;top:60pt;width:200pt;height:100pt'
                coordsize="100,100">
                .
                .
                .
            </v:group>
        </CENTER>
    </BODY>
</HTML>
```

You position grouped shapes together, so I'm specifying the absolute position and dimensions of the group with the <group> element's style property.

Here's an important point: The shapes in a group use the group's coordinate system because the group is their container. To specify the group's coordinates, you can use the coordsize and coordorigin attributes. By default, the coordinate size is set to 1000 × 1000, and the origin is set to (0, 0) in a group (there are no units for these values—they're relative measurements expressed simply as numbers).

In this example, I've set the coordinate size to 100 × 100, so I draw the contained shapes using that coordinate system:

Listing ch19_15.html

```
<HTML xmlns:v="urn:schemas-microsoft-com:vml">

    <HEAD>
        <TITLE>
            Using Vector Markup Language
        </TITLE>

        <STYLE>
            v\:* {behavior: url(#default#VML);}
        </STYLE>
    </HEAD>

    <BODY>
        <CENTER>
            <H1>
                VML Grouping Elements
            </H1>
            <v:group id="Group1" style='position:absolute;
                left:150pt;top:60pt;width:200pt;height:100pt'
                coordsize="100,100">
                <v:rect
                    fillcolor="red" strokecolor="green"
                    style='width:50;height:50'
                    strokeweight="4pt" />
                <v:oval
                    fillcolor="blue"
                    style='width:50;height:50' />
            </v:group>
        </CENTER>
    </BODY>
</HTML>
```

You can see the result of this VML in Figure 19-15. The group of shapes is treated as one unit, which is useful because it allows you to position and scale all the shapes in the group at once.

Figure 19-15
Grouping
elements.

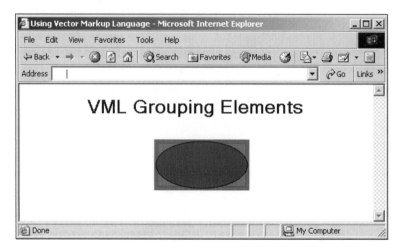

The *<shadow>* Element

You can use the <shadow> element to add shadows to VML shapes, as well as create embossing effects and even double shadows. Here's the attribute list for this element:

```
<!attlist shadow

id id #implied -- document-wide unique id --
on cdata #implied
type cdata #implied
obscured cdata #implied
color cdata #implied
opacity cdata #implied
offset cdata #implied
color2 cdata #implied
offset2 cdata #implied
origin cdata #implied
matrix cdata #implied
>
```

You can find the attributes of this element in Table 19-2.

Table 19-2	Name-space	Attribute	Type	Default Value	Description
Attributes of the *<shadow>* Element	VML	color	boolean	gray RGB (128,128, 128)	Sets the color of the primary shadow.
	VML	color2	boolean	gray RGB (203,203, 203)	Sets the color of the second shadow, or the highlight in an embossed shadow.
	VML	id	string	null	Gives a unique identifier for the shadow.
	VML	matrix	string	null	Gives a perspective transform matrix using the form "scalexx, scalexy,scaleyx, scaleyy,perspec-tivex,perspectivey". The perspective units are measured in inverse fractions of the shape size.
	VML	obscured	boolean	false	Determines whether you can see the shadow if the shape is not filled.
	VML	offset	vector2D	2pt,2pt	Gives the amount of x,y offset for the shadow from the shape's location.
	VML	offset2	vector2D	0pt,0pt	Gives the amount of x,y offset for the second shadow from the shape's location.
	VML	on	boolean	true	Turns the display of the shadow on and off.
	VML	opacity	number	1.0	Sets the opacity of the shadow.
	VML	origin	vector2D	0,0	Sets the origin. Set this to fractional values.
	VML	type	string	single	Sets the shadow type. Can be single, double, emboss, or perspective.

Here is the XML template for this element:

```
<shadow
id=null
on="false"
type="single"
obscured="false"
color="rgb(128,128,128)"
opacity="1.0"
offset="2pt,2pt"
color2="rgb(203,203,203)"
opacity2="1.0"
offset2="0pt,0pt"
origin="0,0"
matrix=null
</shadow>
```

You place the <shadow> element inside the <shape> or <shapetype> element or any predefined shape element to draw a shape with a shadow. When creating a shadow, the tricky part is getting the perspective transform matrix to indicate how to create the shadow as you want it. In this example, I've created a matrix that will add a shadow to any VML shape—that shape is a rectangle here, but you can use an oval or whatever you like—pointing to the right and up at 45°:

Listing ch19_16.html

```
<HTML xmlns:v="urn:schemas-microsoft-com:vml">

    <HEAD>
        <TITLE>
            Using Vector Markup Language
        </TITLE>

        <STYLE>
        v\:* {behavior: url(#default#VML);}
        </STYLE>
    </HEAD>

    <BODY>
        <CENTER>
            <H1>
                VML Shadows
            </H1>
            <v:rect style='width:120pt;height:100pt;'
                fillcolor="blue">
                <v:shadow on="true" type="perspective"
```

```
                origin=".5,.5"
                matrix="1,-1,0,1,0,-5e-7"/>
          </v:rect>
     </CENTER>
   </BODY>
</HTML>
```

The result appears in Figure 19-16, where you can see the shadow apparently coming from a light source at the lower left.

Figure 19-16
Creating VML
shadows.

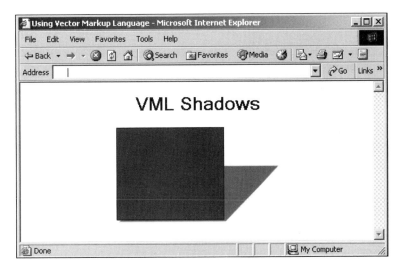

The <*fill*> Element

As we've seen, you can use the fill attribute to set fill colors. The <fill> element works like the fill attribute, except that it's an element you enclose in VML shape elements. I'll take a look at this element here, including some of its more advanced capabilities. Here is the attribute list for the <fill> element:

```
<!attlist fill
id id #implied -- document-wide unique id --
type cdata #implied
on cdata #implied
color cdata #implied
color2 cdata #implied
opacity cdata #implied
src cdata #implied
size cdata #implied
origin cdata #implied
position cdata #implied
alignshape cdata #implied
colors cdata #implied
angle cdata #implied
```

```
focus cdata #implied
focussize cdata #implied
focusposition cdata #implied
method cdata #implied
>
```

You can find these attributes explained in Table 19-3.

Table 19-3 Attributes of the *<fill>* Element	Name-space	Attribute	Type	Default Value	Description
	VML	alignshape	boolean	true	Aligns the image with the shape if true. Otherwise, aligns the image with the window.
	VML	angle	number	"0"	Specifies the angle along which the gradient is directed.
	VML	aspect	string	"ignore"	Set to "ignore" to ignore aspect issues, "atleast" to specify that the image is at least as big as imageSize, or "atmost" to specify that the image is no bigger than imageSize.
	VML	color	color	"white"	Sets the fill color.
	VML	color2	color	"white"	Sets the secondary fill color for patterns.
	VML	colors	string	null	Sets intermediate colors in the gradient and their relative positions along the gradient, as in "20% red, 60% blue, 80% green".
	VML	focus	number	"0"	Sets the focus point for linear gradient fill; possible values range from -100 to 100.

Name-space	Attribute	Type	Default Value	Description
VML	focus position	Vector2D	0,0	For radial gradients, sets the position of the inner-most rectangle.
VML	focussize	Vector2D	0,0	For radial gradients, sets the size of the innermost rectangle.
VML	id	string	null	Is a unique identifier for the shape.
VML	method	string	"sigma"	Sets the fill method. Set this to "none", "linear", "sigma", or "any".
VML	on	boolean	true	Turns the fill display on or off.
VML	opacity	number	1.0	Sets the opacity of the fill.
VML	origin	Vector2D	"auto"	Sets the origin, relative to the upper left of the image. By default, is set to the center of the image.
VML	position	Vector2D	"auto"	A point in the reference rectangle of the shape used to position the origin of the image. Specified as a fraction of the image size.
VML	size	Vector2D	"auto"	Gives the size of the image.
VML	src	string	null	Gives the URI of an image to load for image and pattern fills.
VML	type	string	"solid"	Sets the fill type. May be "solid", "gradient", "gradientradial", "tile", "pattern", or "frame".

Here is the XML template for this element, showing the default values for its attributes:

```
<fill
id=null
type="solid"
on="true"
color="white"
opacity="1.0"
color2="white"
opacity2="1.0"
src=null
size="auto"
origin="center"
position="center"
aspect="ignore"
alignshape="true"
colors=null
angle="0"
focus="0"
focussize="0,0"
focusposition="0,0"
method="sigma"
/>
```

You can create all kinds of fills, such as gradient fills, pattern fills, and picture fills.

Creating Gradient Fills

To draw a gradient-filled shape, you can set the `type` property attribute of the `<fill>` subelement to `"gradient"` or `"gradientRadial"`. Then you specify other property attributes of the `<fill>` subelement, such as `method`, `color2`, `focus`, and `angle`. Here's an example; in this case, I'm creating a shaded egg shape with a standard gradient fill:

Listing ch19_17.html

```
<HTML xmlns:v="urn:schemas-microsoft-com:vml">

    <HEAD>
        <TITLE>
            Using Vector Markup Language
        </TITLE>
```

```
        <STYLE>
        v\:* {behavior: url(#default#VML);}
        </STYLE>
    </HEAD>

    <BODY>
        <CENTER>
            <H1>
                VML Gradient Fills
            </H1>
            <v:oval style='width:200pt;height:100pt'
                fillcolor="blue" strokecolor="white">
                <v:fill method="linear sigma" angle="45"
                 type="gradient" />
            </v:oval>
        </CENTER>
    </BODY>
</HTML>
```

You can see the result of this VML in Figure 19-17.

Figure 19-17
A gradient fill.

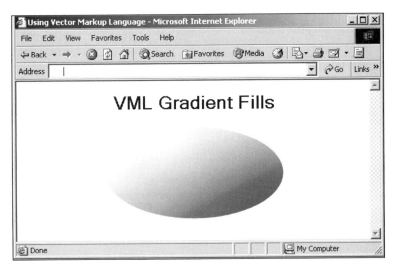

Another option is the `gradientRadial` fill type, in which the fill gradient is directed radially. Here's an example, this time with a rectangle:

Listing ch19_18.html

```
<HTML xmlns:v="urn:schemas-microsoft-com:vml">

    <HEAD>
        <TITLE>
            Using Vector Markup Language
        </TITLE>

        <STYLE>
        v\:* {behavior: url(#default#VML);}
        </STYLE>
    </HEAD>

    <BODY>
        <CENTER>
            <H1>
                VML Gradient Radial Fills
            </H1>
            <v:rect style='width:200pt;height:100pt'
                fillcolor="blue" strokecolor="white">
                <v:fill method="linear sigma" angle="45"
                    type="gradientradial" />
            </v:rect>
        </CENTER>
    </BODY>
</HTML>
```

You can see the result of this VML in Figure 19-18.

Figure 19-18
A gradient radial fill.

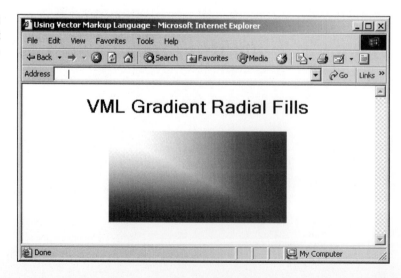

You can also set the origin of gradient radial fills, as in this case. I'm setting the gradient origin to the center of the rectangle for an intriguing effect:

Listing ch19_19.html

```
<HTML xmlns:v="urn:schemas-microsoft-com:vml">

    <HEAD>
        <TITLE>
            Using Vector Markup Language
        </TITLE>

        <STYLE>
        v\:* {behavior: url(#default#VML);}
        </STYLE>
    </HEAD>

    <BODY>
        <CENTER>
            <H1>
                VML Gradient Radial Fills
            </H1>
            <v:rect style='width:200pt;height:100pt' fillcolor="blue"
            ➥strokecolor="white">
                <v:fill method="linear sigma" angle="45"
                    focus="100%" focusposition=".5,.5" focussize="0,0"
                    type="gradientradial" />
            </v:rect>
        </CENTER>
    </BODY>
</HTML>
```

You can see the result of this VML in Figure 19-19.

Figure 19-19
A gradient radial fill with origin at the center.

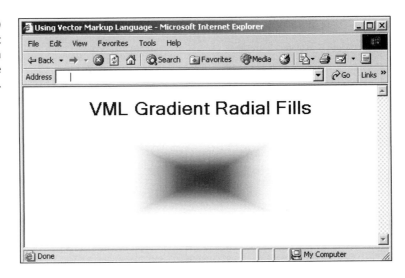

Creating Pattern Fills

To draw a pattern-filled shape, you can set the `type` property attribute of the `<fill>` element to `"pattern"` and then set the `src` property to the URI of an image file. For example, here's how I use the image ch19_21.jpg as a fill pattern:

Listing ch19_20.html

```
<HTML xmlns:v="urn:schemas-microsoft-com:vml">

    <HEAD>
        <TITLE>
            Using Vector Markup Language
        </TITLE>

        <STYLE>
        v\:* {behavior: url(#default#VML);}
        </STYLE>
    </HEAD>

    <BODY>
        <CENTER>
            <H1>
                VML Fill Patterns
            </H1>
            <v:rect style='width:200pt;height:100pt'
                fillcolor="red">
                <v:fill type="pattern" src="ch19_21.jpg"/>
            </v:rect>
        </CENTER>
    </BODY>
</HTML>
```

Note that you can also specify the color of the fill you want, as in this case, where I'm making it red. You can see the result of this VML in Figure 19-20, where the image is repeatedly tiled inside a rectangle.

Figure 19-20
A pattern fill.

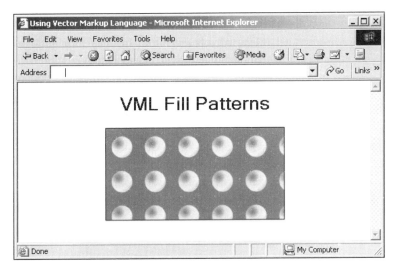

Creating Picture Fills

To draw a picture-filled shape, you can set the `type` property attribute of the `<fill>` element to `"frame"` and then set the `src` property to the URI of the image you want to use. Here's an example; in this case, I'll display the image ch19_23.jpg:

Listing ch19_21.html

```
<HTML xmlns:v="urn:schemas-microsoft-com:vml">

    <HEAD>
        <TITLE>
            Using Vector Markup Language
        </TITLE>

        <STYLE>
        v\:* {behavior: url(#default#VML);}
        </STYLE>
    </HEAD>

    <BODY>
        <CENTER>
            <H1>
                VML Picture Fills
            </H1>
```

continues

Listing ch19_21.html   Continued

```
                <v:rect style='width:673px;height:89px'>
                    <v:fill type="frame" src="ch19_23.jpg"/>
                </v:rect>
        </CENTER>
    </BODY>
</HTML>
```

You can see the result of this VML in Figure 19-21.

Figure 19-21
A picture fill.

Using the *<shapetype>* Element

You can parameterize the creation of shapes with the `<shapetype>` element. The `<shapetype>` element defines a shape type, and you can instantiate shapes of that type. You create a shape type and give it a name with the ID attribute of `<shapetype>`; you use that shape type with the `<shape>` element's type attribute.

Here's the attribute list of the `<shapetype>` element:

```
<!attlist shapetype %coreattrs; %shapeattrs;
adj cdata #implied -- list of adjust values for parameterized paths --
path cdata #implied -- string with command set describing a path --
>
```

Here are the custom attributes of this element:

- `adj`—A comma-separated list of numbers that are "adjusting" parameters for the formulas that define the path of the shape

- `path`—The path that defines the shape; a string containing the commands that define the path

Here is the `<shapetype>` element's XML template:

```
<shapetype
adj=null
path=null
opacity="100%"
chromakey="none"
stroke="true"
strokecolor="black"
strokeweight="0.75pt"
fill="true"
fillcolor="white"
print="true"
id=null
class=null
style='visibility: visible'
title=null
href=null
target=null
alt=null
coordsize="1000, 1000"
coordorigin="0, 0"
wrapcoords=null
/>
```

We've already seen an example using the `<shapetype>` element earlier in this chapter. In that example, the shape was defined with the path attribute like this:

```
<v:shapetype id="Valentine" fillcolor="red"
    strokecolor="red" coordsize="21600,21600"
    path="m10860,2187c10451,1746,9529,1018,9015,730,
    7865,152,6685,,5415,,4175, 152,2995,575,1967,
    1305,1150,2187,575,3222,242,4220,,5410,242,6560,
    575,7597l10860, 21600,20995,7597c21480,6560,
    21600,5410,21480,4220,21115,3222,20420,2187,19632,
    1305,18575,575,17425,152,16275,,15005,,13735,152,
    12705,730,12176,1018,11254,1746, 10860,2187xe">
</v:shapetype>
```

The path defined here defines the shape. Specifying a path in the `<shapetype>` element is a little involved. You specify pairs of points along the path and use commands such as m (start a path), x (close the path), e (end the path), and so on. You can find the available commands in Table 19-3. This table also indicates how many parameters each command takes, using DTD notation. For example, 2* indicates that the command takes pairs of parameters. You can also skip any values that are zero when specifying points, so the point specification 16275,,15005,,13735,152 is the same as 16275,0,15005,0,13735,152.

Table 19-2 Commands for the *path* Attribute	Command	Name	Parameters	Description
	ae	angleellipseto	6*	center (x,y) size(w,h) start-angle, end-angle. Draws a segment of an ellipse.
	al	angleellipse	6*	Same as angleellipseto, except that there is an implied move to the starting point of the segment.
	ar	arc	8*	left, top, right, bottom start(x,y) end(x,y). Same as arcto, except that a new subpath is started by an implied move to the start point.
	at	arcto	8*	left, top, right, bottom start(x,y) end(x,y). The first four values define the bounding box of an ellipse, and the second four define two radial vectors. This command draws a segment of the ellipse starting at the angle defined by the start radius vector and ending at the angle defined by the end vector.
	c	curveto	6*	Draws a cubic Bézier curve from the current point to

Command	Name	Parameters	Description
			the coordinate given by the final two parameters. The control points are given by the first four parameters.
e	end	0	Ends the current set of subpaths.
l	lineto	2*	Draws a line from the current point to the given point.
m	moveto	2	Begins a new sub-path at the given coordinate.
nf	nofill	0	Ensures that the current set of sub-paths will not be filled.
ns	nostroke	0	Ensures that the current set of sub-paths will not be drawn (stroked).
qb	quadraticbezier	2+2*	`(controlpoint(x,y))*, end(x,y).` Defines one or more quadratic Bézier curves with a set of control points and an end point.
qx	ellipticalquadrantx	2*	`end(x,y).` Draws a quarter ellipse from the current point to the end point.
qy	ellipticalquadranty	2*	`end(x,y).` Same as `ellipticalquad-rantx.` except that the segment starts out vertical.

continues

Command	Name	Parameters	Description
r	rlineto	2*	Draws a line from the current point to the given point.
t	rmoveto	2*	Starts a new subpath at the indicated coordinate.
v	rcurveto	6*	Creates a cubic Bézier curve using the given coordinate relative to the current point.
wa	clockwisearcto	8*	left, top, right, bottom start(x,y) end(x,y). Same as arcto, except that here the arc is drawn in a clockwise direction.
wr	clockwisearc	8*	left, top, right, bottom start(x,y) end(x,y). Same as arc, except that here the arc is drawn in a clockwise direction.
x	close	0	Closes the current subpath. Draws a straight line from the current point to the original moveto point.

Here's how you can use this <shapetype> element to create a shape as we've done earlier in the chapter:

```
<HTML xmlns:v="urn:schemas-microsoft-com:vml">

    <HEAD>
        <TITLE>
            Using Vector Markup Language
        </TITLE>

        <STYLE>
        v\:* {behavior: url(#default#VML);}
        </STYLE>
```

```
    </HEAD>

    <BODY>
        <CENTER>
            <H1>
                VML Shapes
            </H1>
            <v:shapetype id="Valentine" fillcolor="red"
                strokecolor="red" coordsize="21600,21600"
                path="m10860,2187c10451,1746,9529,1018,9015,730,
                7865,152,6685,,5415,,4175, 152,2995,575,1967,
                1305,1150,2187,575,3222,242,4220,,5410,242,6560,
                575,7597l10860, 21600,20995,7597c21480,6560,
                21600,5410,21480,4220,21115,3222,20420,2187,19632,
                1305,18575,575,17425,152,16275,,15005,,13735,152,
                12705,730,12176,1018,11254,1746, 10860,2187xe">
            </v:shapetype>
            <v:shape type="#Valentine" style='width:200;height:160;'/>
        </CENTER>
    </BODY>
</HTML>
```

The result of this VML appears in Figure 19-22.

You can list properties for the shape in the <shapetype> element, as in this example, which assigns a value to the fillcolor property. However, if you want to override those properties, you can; just specify new values in the <shape> element when you instantiate the shape. For example, here's how I turn the heart this VML draws to blue:

Listing ch19_22.html

```
<HTML xmlns:v="urn:schemas-microsoft-com:vml">

    <HEAD>
        <TITLE>
            Using Vector Markup Language
        </TITLE>

        <STYLE>
        v\:* {behavior: url(#default#VML);}
        </STYLE>
    </HEAD>

    <BODY>
        <CENTER>
            <H1>
                VML Shapes
```

continues

Listing ch19_22.html   Continued

```
            </H1>
            <v:shapetype id="Valentine" fillcolor="red"
                strokecolor="red" coordsize="21600,21600"
                path="m10860,2187c10451,1746,9529,1018,9015,730,
                7865,152,6685,,5415,,4175, 152,2995,575,1967,
                1305,1150,2187,575,3222,242,4220,,5410,242,6560,
                575,7597l10860, 21600,20995,7597c21480,6560,
                21600,5410,21480,4220,21115,3222,20420,2187,19632,
                1305,18575,575,17425,152,16275,,15005,,13735,152,
                12705,730,12176,1018,11254,1746, 10860,2187xe">
            </v:shapetype>
            <v:shape type="#Valentine" fillcolor="blue"
                style='width:200;height:160;'/>
        </CENTER>
    </BODY>
</HTML>
```

More Advanced VML

Besides the material we've seen in this chapter, there's plenty more in VML. Like many graphics languages, VML has a lot of depth. Here's a last example, adapted from the examples in the Microsoft VML reference, which displays text along a VML *text path*, specified using VML *formulas*:

Listing ch19_23.html

```
<HTML xmlns:v="urn:schemas-microsoft-com:vml">

    <HEAD>
        <TITLE>
            Using Vector Markup Language
        </TITLE>

        <STYLE>
        v\:* {behavior: url(#default#VML);}
        </STYLE>
    </HEAD>

    <BODY>
        <CENTER>
            <H1>
                VML Text Paths
            </H1>
            <v:shapetype id="MyShape"
                coordsize="21600,21600" adj="9931"
```

```
            path="m0@0c7200@2,14400@1,21600,
            0m0@5c7200@6,14400@6,21600@5e">
            <v:formulas>
                <v:f eqn="val #0"/>
                <v:f eqn="prod #0 3 4"/>
                <v:f eqn="prod #0 5 4"/>
                <v:f eqn="prod #0 3 8"/>
                <v:f eqn="prod #0 1 8"/>
                <v:f eqn="sum 21600 0 @3"/>
                <v:f eqn="sum @4 21600 0"/>
                <v:f eqn="prod #0 1 2"/>
                <v:f eqn="prod @5 1 2"/>
                <v:f eqn="sum @7 @8 0"/>
                <v:f eqn="prod #0 7 8"/>
                <v:f eqn="prod @5 1 3"/>
                <v:f eqn="sum @1 @2 0"/>
                <v:f eqn="sum @12 @0 0"/>
                <v:f eqn="prod @13 1 4"/>
                <v:f eqn="sum @11 14400 @14"/>
            </v:formulas>
            <v:path textpathok="t" />
            <v:textpath on="t" fitshape="t" xscale="t"/>
        </v:shapetype>

        <v:shape type="#MyShape"
            style='position:absolute; top:60pt; left:60pt;
            width:207pt;height:63pt;' adj="8717"
            fillcolor="blue" strokeweight="1pt">
            <v:fill method="linear sigma" focus="100%"
            type="gradient"/>
            <v:shadow on="t" offset="3pt"/>
            <v:textpath style='font-family:"Times New Roman";
                v-text-kern:t'trim="t" fitpath="t" xscale="f"
                string="VML"/>
        </v:shape>
    </CENTER>
  </BODY>
</HTML>
```

You can see the result of this VML in Figure 19-22. You may have seen text graphics like this in Microsoft Office products such as Word and PowerPoint, and now you know how it's done.

Figure 19-22
Using a VML
text path.

For more information on VML, take a look at the Microsoft VML site. VML is a powerful language, but it's limited to Internet Explorer. One day, browsers will implement a W3C language such as SVG, and I'll be able to rewrite this chapter.

It's time to take a look at using Perl and XML on the server side, as well as Wireless Markup Language (WML). I'm going to do that in the next chapter.

WML, ASP, JSP, Servlets, and Perl

This chapter is about a number of topics, such as using XML on the server side of things with Active Server Pages (ASP), JavaServer Pages (JSP), Java servlets, and Perl. It's also about Wireless Markup Language (WML), a popular XML application that is targeted at cordless phones, PDAs, and other relatively simple devices that support the Wireless Application Protocol (WAP) and WML browsers that are coming to be called "microbrowsers." WML is easy to use; you find it in more places these days, and WAP servers are popping up all over the place. In this chapter, I'll take a look at creating WML documents and viewing them in a WML browser.

In this chapter, I'm going to take a look at how to create XML documents from the server side. There are many ways to do that, and we don't have space to cover them all in depth. But we'll get a good idea of how things work in overview (for more details, check out the many books on the subjects we'll see in this chapter). Here, I'll extract data from a small database file, ch20_01.mdb, written in Microsoft Access format, on various different servers. Then I'll format that data using XML and send the resulting XML back to the client. This database file was written to be a simple example and just holds the names of eight students and a letter grade for each student, as you see in Table 20-1.

Table 20-1	Student	Grade
Students in ch20_01.mdb	Ann	C
	Mark	B
	Ed	A
	Frank	A
	Ted	A
	Mabel	B
	Ralph	B
	Tom	B

I'll start by using ActiveX Data Objects (ADO) on a server to search ch20_01.mdb and create an XML document displaying the results with ASP.

Server-Side Programming

In the first half of this chapter, which is on server-side programming, I'll be moving through many technologies fairly quickly. Unfortunately, there's no way to provide all the background you need to program in ASP, JSP, Java Servlets, and Perl here, so I'll assume that you can find that background elsewhere if you need it. When discussing WML, which is an XML application, in the second half of the chapter, I won't make any such assumptions. There, we'll start from the ground up.

XML and ASP

ASP is one of Microsoft's Internet server-side technologies that lets you create Web documents on the fly. It runs on servers such as the Microsoft Internet Information Server (IIS). In this case, I'll search ch20_01.mdb for the names of the students and return them in an XML document like this, using <document> as the document element and <student> for each student:

```
<?xml version="1.0"?>
<document>
    <student>
        Ann
    </student>
    <student>
        Mark
    </student>
    <student>
        Ed
```

```
        </student>
        <student>
            Frank
        </student>
        <student>
            Ted
        </student>
        <student>
            Mabel
        </student>
        <student>
            Ralph
        </student>
        <student>
            Tom
        </student>
</document>
```

The main trick in the .asp file is to make sure your code creates an XML document because the default document type is HTML. If you don't make sure that the content type item in the HTTP header indicates that a document is XML, the browser isn't going to treat it as an XML document (and will probably treat it as HTML). The way you do this in the ASP script is with `<% Response.ContentType %>`, setting the content type header item to `"application/xml"` this way:

```
<% Response.ContentType = "application/xml" %>
   .
   .
   .
```

I also add the XML declaration for the resulting document, and the document element, `<document>`:

```
<% Response.ContentType = "application/xml" %>
<?xml version="1.0"?>
<document>
   .
   .
   .
```

Now I've got to fetch the names of the students from ch20_01.mdb. I'll do this using Microsoft ADO since ASP is targeted to run on Microsoft platforms like IIS. I create an ADO connection to ch20_01.mdb and use a SQL statement to return a record set of all records:

```
<% Response.ContentType = "application/xml" %>
<?xml version="1.0"?>
<document>
```

```
<%

DIM adoConnect
DIM adoRecordset

Set adoConnect = Server.CreateObject("ADODB.Connection")

adoConnect.open "Provider=Microsoft.Jet.OLEDB.4.0;" _
    & "Data Source=C:\xml\ch20_01.mdb"

Set adoRecordset = adoConnect.Execute("SELECT * FROM Students")
    .
    .
    .
```

All that's left is to loop over each record and create the corresponding XML <student> element:

Listing ch20_02.asp

```
<% Response.ContentType = "application/xml" %>
<?xml version="1.0"?>
<document>

<%

DIM adoConnect
DIM adoRecordset

Set adoConnect = Server.CreateObject("ADODB.Connection")

adoConnect.open "Provider=Microsoft.Jet.OLEDB.4.0;" _
    & "Data Source=C:\xml\ch20_01.mdb"

Set adoRecordset = adoConnect.Execute("SELECT * FROM Students")

Do While Not adoRecordset.EOF
    Response.Write "<student>" + adoRecordset("Name") + "</student>"
    adoRecordset.MoveNext
Loop

adoRecordset.Close

set adoRecordset = Nothing

%>
</document>
```

And that creates the XML we want. You can see that result, as created by this ASP file, in Figure 20-1.

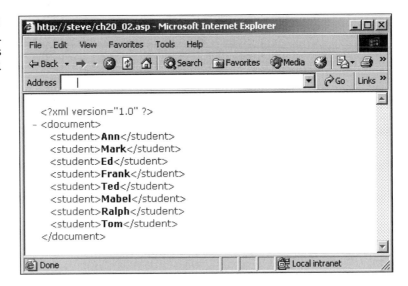

XML and Java Servlets

As you saw in Chapter 18, "SOAP and RDF," Java servlets are to Web servers what Java applets are to Web clients. You can use servlets to create Web documents on suitably enabled servers. To create servlets, you'll need servlet.jar, which comes with the Tomcat Web server used in Chapter 18, or you can download the Java Servlet Development Kit (JSDK) from java.sun.com (as of this writing, the main page for servlets is `http://java.sun.com/ products/servlet/index.html`).

To read the names of the students from ch20_01.mdb, I'll use the Java Database Connectivity package (JBDC), interfacing to ch20_01.mdb after registering that database as an Open Database Connectivity (ODBC) data source. After searching for all the students, I'll return their names in an XML document and send that document back to the client.

Again, the key here is to make sure we create an XML document, not the default HTML document. You do that in servlets with the `ServletResponse` class's `setContentType` method, setting the content type to `"application/xml"`. Here's what that looks like:

```
import java.net.*;
import java.sql.*;
import java.awt.*;
```

```
import java.awt.event.*;
import java.io.*;
import javax.servlet.*;

public class xml extends GenericServlet
{
    public void service(ServletRequest request, ServletResponse
        response) throws ServletException, IOException
    {
        response.setContentType("application/xml");
        .
        .
        .
```

Next, I send the XML declaration and document element back to the client:

```
import java.net.*;
import java.sql.*;
import java.awt.*;
import java.awt.event.*;
import java.io.*;
import javax.servlet.*;

public class xml extends GenericServlet
{
    Connection connection;
    Statement statement;

    public void service(ServletRequest request, ServletResponse
        response) throws ServletException, IOException
    {
        response.setContentType("application/xml");
        PrintWriter printwriter = response.getWriter();

        printwriter.println("<?xml version=\"1.0\"?>");
        printwriter.println("<document>");
        .
        .
        .
```

At this point, I can use JDBC to create a result set with all records from
ch20_01.mdb. I do that like this with a SQL statement:

```
import java.net.*;
import java.sql.*;
import java.awt.*;
import java.awt.event.*;
import java.io.*;
import javax.servlet.*;
```

```
public class xml extends GenericServlet
{
    Connection connection;
    Statement statement;

    public void service(ServletRequest request, ServletResponse
        response) throws ServletException, IOException
    {
        response.setContentType("application/xml");
        PrintWriter printwriter = response.getWriter();

        printwriter.println("<?xml version=\"1.0\"?>");
        printwriter.println("<document>");

        try
        {
            Class.forName("sun.jdbc.odbc.JdbcOdbcDriver");

            connection = DriverManager.getConnection(
                "jdbc:odbc:students", "Steve", "password");

            statement = connection.createStatement();

            String SQL = "SELECT Name FROM Students";
            ResultSet resultset = statement.executeQuery(SQL);
            .
            .
            .
```

All that's left is to loop over the result set with the next method, getting the student names and sending them back to the client in <student> elements like this:

Listing ch20_03.java

```
import java.net.*;
import java.sql.*;
import java.awt.*;
import java.awt.event.*;
import java.io.*;
import javax.servlet.*;

public class xml extends GenericServlet
{
    Connection connection;
    Statement statement;

    public void service(ServletRequest request, ServletResponse
        response) throws ServletException, IOException
    {
```

continues

Listing ch20_03.java   Continued

```java
        response.setContentType("application/xml");
        PrintWriter printwriter = response.getWriter();

        printwriter.println("<?xml version=\"1.0\"?>");
        printwriter.println("<document>");

        try
        {
            Class.forName("sun.jdbc.odbc.JdbcOdbcDriver");

            connection = DriverManager.getConnection(
                "jdbc:odbc:students", "Steve", "password");

            statement = connection.createStatement();

            String SQL = "SELECT Name FROM Students";
            ResultSet resultset = statement.executeQuery(SQL);

            while (resultset.next()) {
                printwriter.println("<student>" +
                ➥resultset.getString(1) + "</student>");
            }
        }
        catch(Exception e) {}

        printwriter.println("</document>");
        printwriter.close();
    }
}
```

And that's all it takes. You can see this servlet running in Figure 20-2, where you see the same XML document delivered to the client as we saw in the previous topic.

Figure 20-2
Creating XML
documents
with Java
servlets.

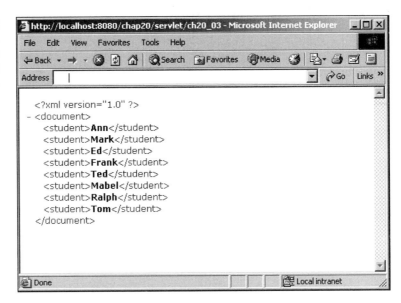

Another Java technology is becoming popular for serving XML documents: JavaServer Pages.

JSP

JSP are Java's answer to Active Server Pages. They let you create dynamic Web content in much the same way, by running scripts on the server. You can read all about them at the main JavaServer Pages page, which, as of this writing, is at `http://java.sun.com/products/jsp/index.html`. Using JSP is fairly close to using ASP.

In this example, I'm going to use the Tomcat server, which we saw in Chapter 18 and which is the official reference implementation for JSP (and Java servlets, for that matter). You can download Tomcat at the Tomcat main page, currently at `http://jakarta.apache.org/tomcat/` (see Chapter 18 for more on installing this Web server locally).

I'll create the same XML document as in the previous two examples here, by searching ch20_01.mdb for all students and returning them in an XML document. Because we're working in Java again here, I'll use JDBC to connect to ch20_01.mdb.

Once again, a major point here is to make sure that the content type of the document we send to the client is `"application/xml"`, not the default HTML type. In JSP, you do that with the `contentType` attribute of the `page` directive like this:

```
<%@ page language="java" contentType="application/xml"
    import="java.sql.*" %>
    .
    .
    .
```

I also initialize the JDBC driver like this:

```
<%@ page language="java" contentType="application/xml"
    import="java.sql.*" %>

<% Class.forName("sun.jdbc.odbc.JdbcOdbcDriver") ; %>
    .
    .
    .
```

And I send the XML declaration and the document element back to the client like this:

```
<%@ page language="java" contentType="application/xml"
    import="java.sql.*" %>

<% Class.forName("sun.jdbc.odbc.JdbcOdbcDriver") ; %>

<?xml version="1.0"?>
<document>
    .
    .
    .
```

Now I get a JDBC result set with all the students' records using a SQL statement:

```
<%@ page language="java" contentType="application/xml"
    import="java.sql.*" %>

<% Class.forName("sun.jdbc.odbc.JdbcOdbcDriver") ; %>

<?xml version="1.0"?>
<document>

<%
```

```
Connection connection = DriverManager.getConnection(
    "jdbc:odbc:students", "Steve", "password");

Statement statement = connection.createStatement() ;
ResultSet resultset =
    statement.executeQuery("select * from Students") ; %>
    .
    .
    .
```

All that's left is to loop over the students' records and send the matching <student> elements back to the client:

Listing ch20_04.jsp

```
<%@ page language="java" contentType="application/xml"
    import="java.sql.*" %>

<% Class.forName("sun.jdbc.odbc.JdbcOdbcDriver") ; %>

<?xml version="1.0"?>
<document>

<%
Connection connection = DriverManager.getConnection(
    "jdbc:odbc:students", "Steve", "password");

Statement statement = connection.createStatement() ;
ResultSet resultset =
    statement.executeQuery("select * from Students") ; %>

<% while(resultset.next()){ %>
  <student> <%= resultset.getString(1)  %>  </student>
<% } %>

</document>
```

And that's it. You can see the results of this JSP script in Figure 20-3. As you can see, JSP works as well as ASP when it comes to serving XML documents. In fact, I know plenty of XML developers that prefer JSP over ASP for this purpose because working with XML using Java is a natural, as we've seen in Chapter 11, "Java and the XML DOM," and Chapter 12, "Java and SAX."

Figure 20-3
A JSP and
XML page.

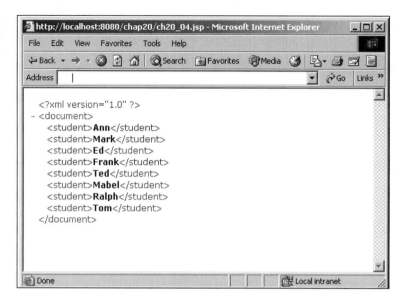

XML and Perl

The Practical Extraction and Reporting Language (PERL), has long been a mainstay of server-side programming and a foundation of Common Gateway Interface (CGI) programming. Perl has been getting into XML in a big way, and one could easily write a book on the subject.

Perl modules are distributed at the Comprehensive Perl Archive Network (CPAN) site, www.cpan.org, and plenty of them deal with XML (I counted 156). You can find a selection of Perl XML modules, along with their descriptions as given on the CPAN site, in Table 20-2.

Table 20-2
XML Modules
in Perl with
CPAN
descriptions

Module	Description
Apache::AxKit::XMLFinder	Detects XML files
Apache::MimeXML	mod_perl mime encoding sniffer for XML files
Apache::MimeXML	mod_perl mime encoding sniffer for XML files
Boulder::XML	XML format input/output for Boulder streams
Bundle::XML	A bundle to install all XML-related modules

Module	Description
CGI::XMLForm	Extension of CGI.pm, which reads/generates formatted XML
Data::DumpXML	Dump arbitrary data structures as XML
DBIx::XML_RDB	Perl extension for creating XML from existing DBI datasources
GoXML::XQI	Perl extension for the XML Query Interface at `xqi.goxml.com`
Mail::XML	Adds a `toXML()` method to Mail::Internet
MARC::XML	A subclass of MARC.pm to provide XML support
PApp::XML	`pxml` sections and more
XML::Catalog	Resolves public identifiers and remaps system identifiers
XML::CGI	Perl extension for converting CGI.pm variables to and from XML
XML::Checker	A Perl module for validating XML
XML::Checker::Parser	An XML::Parser that validates at parse time
XML::DOM	A Perl module for building DOM Level 1–compliant document structures
XML::DOM::NamedNodeMap	A hashtable interface for XML::DOM
XML::DOM::NodeList	A node list as used by XML::DOM
XML::DOM::PerlSAX	Old name of XML::Handler::BuildDOM
XML::DOM::ValParser	An XML::DOM::Parser that validates at parse time
XML::Driver::HTML	SAX driver for HTML that is not well formed
XML::DT	A package for down translation of XML to strings

continues

Module	Description
XML::Edifact	Perl module to handle XML::Edifact messages
XML::Encoding	A Perl module for parsing XML encoding maps
XML::ESISParser	Perl SAX parser using nsgmls
XML::Filter::DetectWS	A PerlSAX filter that detects ignorable whitespace
XML::Filter::Hekeln	A SAX stream editor
XML::Filter::Reindent	Reformats whitespace for attractively printing XML
XML::Filter::SAXT	Replicates SAX events to several SAX event handlers
XML::Generator	Perl extension for generating XML
XML::Grove	Perl-style XML objects
XML::Grove::AsCanonXML	Outputs XML objects in canonical XML
XML::Grove::AsString	Outputs content of XML objects as a string
XML::Grove::Builder	PerlSAX handler for building an XML::Grove
XML::Grove::Factory	Simplifies creation of XML::Grove objects
XML::Grove::Path	Returns the object at a path
XML::Grove::PerlSAX	A PerlSAX event interface for XML objects
XML::Grove::Sub	Runs a filter sub over a grove
XML::Grove::Subst	Substitutes values into a template
XML::Handler::BuildDOM	PerlSAX handler that creates XML::DOM document structures
XML::Handler::CanonXMLWriter	Output XML in canonical XML format

Module	Description
XML::Handler::Composer	Another XML printer/writer/ generator
XML::Handler::PrintEvents	Prints PerlSAX events (for debugging)
XML::Handler::PyxWriter	Converts Perl SAX events to ESIS of nsgmls
XML::Handler::Sample	A trivial Perl SAX handler
XML::Handler::Subs	A PerlSAX handler base class for calling user-defined subs
XML::Handler::XMLWriter	A PerlSAX handler for writing readable XML
XML::Handler::YAWriter	Another Perl SAX XML writer
XML::Node	Node-based XML parsing: a simplified interface to XML
XML::Parser	A Perl module for parsing XML documents
XML::Parser::Expat	Low-level access to James Clark's expat XML parser
XML::Parser::PerlSAX	Perl SAX parser using XML::Parser
XML::Parser::PyxParser	Converts ESIS of nsgmls or Pyxie to Perl SAX
XML::PatAct::Amsterdam	An action module for simplistic stylesheets
XML::PatAct::MatchName	A pattern module for matching element names
XML::PatAct::ToObjects	An action module for creating Perl objects
XML::PYX	XML-to-PYX generator
XML::QL	An XML query language
XML::RegExp	Regular expressions for XML tokens

Module	Description
XML::Registry	Perl module for loading and saving an XML registry
XML::RSS	Creates and updates RSS files
XML::SAX2Perl	Translates Perl SAX methods to Java/CORBA–style methods
XML::SAX2Perl	Translates Perl SAX methods to Java/CORBA–style methods
XML::Simple	Trivial API for reading and writing XML (especially config files)
XML::Stream	Creates and XML Stream connection and parses return data
XML::Stream::Namespace	Object to make defining namespaces easier
XML::Template	Perl XML template instantiation
XML::Twig	A Perl module for processing huge XML documents in tree mode
XML::UM	Converts UTF-8 strings to any encoding supported by XML::Encoding
XML::Writer	Perl extension for writing XML documents
XML::XPath	A set of modules for parsing and evaluating XPath
XML::XPath::Boolean	Boolean `true`/`false` values
XML::XPath::Builder	SAX handler for building an XPath tree
XML::XPath::Literal	Simple string values
XML::XPath::Node	Internal representation of a node
XML::XPath::NodeSet	A list of XML document nodes
XML::XPath::Number	Simple numeric values
XML::XPath::PerlSAX	A PerlSAX event generator
XML::XPath::XMLParser	The default XML parsing class that produces a node tree

Module	Description
XML::XQL	A Perl module for querying XML tree structures with XQL
XML::XQL::Date	Adds an XQL::Node type for representing and comparing dates and times
XML::XQL::DOM	Adds XQL support to XML::DOM nodes
XML::XSLT	A Perl module for processing XSLT
XMLNews::HTMLTemplate	A module for converting NITF to HTML
XMLNews::Meta	A module for reading and writing XMLNews metadata files

Most of the Perl XML modules that appear in Table 20-2 must be downloaded and installed before you can use them. (The process is a little lengthy, if straightforward; Download Manager tools exist for Windows and UNIX that will manage the download and installation process for you and make things easier.) The Perl distribution does come with some XML support built in, such as the XML::Parser module.

Here's an example that puts XML::Parser to work. In this case, I'll parse an XML document and print it using Perl. The XML::Parser module can handle callbacks, calling subroutines when the beginning of an element is encountered, as well as the text content in an element and the end of an element. Here's how I set up such calls to the handler subroutines start_handler, char_handler, and end_handler, respectively, creating a new parser object named $parser in Perl:

```
use XML::Parser;

$parser = new XML::Parser(Handlers => {Start => \&start_handler,
        End   => \&end_handler,
        Char  => \&char_handler});
    .
    .
    .
```

Now I need an XML document to parse. I'll use a document we've seen before, ch07_01.xml:

```xml
<?xml version="1.0"?>
<MEETINGS>
    <MEETING TYPE="informal">
        <MEETING_TITLE>XML In The Real World</MEETING_TITLE>
        <MEETING_NUMBER>2079</MEETING_NUMBER>
        <SUBJECT>XML</SUBJECT>
        <DATE>6/1/2003</DATE>
        <PEOPLE>
            <PERSON ATTENDANCE="present">
                <FIRST_NAME>Edward</FIRST_NAME>
                <LAST_NAME>Samson</LAST_NAME>
            </PERSON>
            <PERSON ATTENDANCE="absent">
                <FIRST_NAME>Ernestine</FIRST_NAME>
                <LAST_NAME>Johnson</LAST_NAME>
            </PERSON>
            <PERSON ATTENDANCE="present">
                <FIRST_NAME>Betty</FIRST_NAME>
                <LAST_NAME>Richardson</LAST_NAME>
            </PERSON>
        </PEOPLE>
    </MEETING>
</MEETINGS>
```

I can parse that document using the $parser object's parsefile method:

```perl
use XML::Parser;

$parser = new XML::Parser(Handlers => {Start => \&start_handler,
        End   => \&end_handler,
        Char  => \&char_handler});

$parser->parsefile('ch07_01.xml');
    .
    .
    .
```

All that remains is to create the subroutines start_handler, char_handler, and end_handler. I'll begin with start_handler, which is called when the start of an XML element is encountered. The name of the element is stored in item 1 of the standard Perl array @_, which holds the arguments passed to subroutines. I can display that element's opening tag like this:

```
use XML::Parser;

$parser = new XML::Parser(Handlers => {Start => \&start_handler,
        End   => \&end_handler,
        Char  => \&char_handler});

$parser->parsefile('ch07_01.xml');

sub start_handler
{
    print "<$_[1]>\n";
}
```

    .
    .
    .

I'll also print the closing tag in the end_handler subroutine:

```
use XML::Parser;

$parser = new XML::Parser(Handlers => {Start => \&start_handler,
        End   => \&end_handler,
        Char  => \&char_handler});

$parser->parsefile('ch07_01.xml');

sub start_handler
{
    print "<$_[1]>\n";
}

sub end_handler
{
    print "</$_[1]>\n";
}
```

    .
    .
    .

And I can print the text content of the element in the char_handler subroutine after removing discardable whitespace:

Listing ch20_05.pl

```
use XML::Parser;

$parser = new XML::Parser(Handlers => {Start => \&start_handler,
        End   => \&end_handler,
        Char  => \&char_handler});
```

continues

Listing ch20_05.pl   Continued

```
$parser->parsefile('ch07_01.xml');

sub start_handler
{
    print "<$_[1]>\n";
}

sub end_handler
{
    print "</$_[1]>\n";
}

sub char_handler
{
    if(index($_[1], " ") < 0 && index($_[1], "\n") < 0){
        print "$_[1]\n";
    }
}
```

That completes the code. Running this Perl script gives you this result, where you can see that ch07_01.xml was indeed parsed successfully:

```
<MEETINGS>
<MEETING>
<MEETING_TITLE>
XML
</MEETING_TITLE>
<MEETING_NUMBER>
2079
</MEETING_NUMBER>
<SUBJECT>
XML
</SUBJECT>
<DATE>
6/1/2002
</DATE>
<PEOPLE>
<PERSON>
<FIRST_NAME>
Edward
</FIRST_NAME>
<LAST_NAME>
Samson
</LAST_NAME>
</PERSON>
<PERSON>
<FIRST_NAME>
Ernestine
</FIRST_NAME>
<LAST_NAME>
Johnson
```

```
</LAST_NAME>
</PERSON>
<PERSON>
<FIRST_NAME>
Betty
</FIRST_NAME>
<LAST_NAME>
Richardson
</LAST_NAME>
</PERSON>
</PEOPLE>
</MEETING>
</MEETINGS>
```

Writing this script, parsing the document, and implementing callbacks like this in Perl may remind you quite closely of the Java SAX work we did in Chapter 12.

I'll take a look at serving XML documents from Perl scripts next. Unfortunately, Perl does not come with a built-in database protocol as powerful as JDBC and its ODBC handler, or ASP and its ADO support. The database support that comes built into Perl is based on DBM files, which are hash-based databases (although now, of course, you can install many Perl modules to interface to other database protocols, from ODBC to Oracle).

In this case, I'll write a Perl script that will let you enter a key (such as vegetable) and a value (such as broccoli) to store in a database built in the NDBM database format, which is a default format that Perl does support. This database will be stored on the server. When you enter a key into the page created by this script, the code checks the database for a match to that key and, if found, returns the key and its value. For example, when I enter the key vegetable in the database and the value broccoli, that key/value pair is stored in the database. When you subsequently search for a match to the key vegetable, the script returns both that key and the matching value, broccoli in an XML document using the tags <key> and <value>:

```
<?xml version="1.0" ?>
<document>
    <key>vegetable</key>
    <value>broccoli</value>
</document>
```

You can see the results of the CGI script we'll create in Figure 20-4. To add an entry to the database, you enter a key into the text field marked Key to Add to the Database, and you enter a corresponding value in the text field marked Value to Add to the Database. Then you click the Add to Database button. In Figure 20-4, I'm storing the value broccoli under the key vegetable.

Figure 20-4
A Perl CGI
script database
manager.

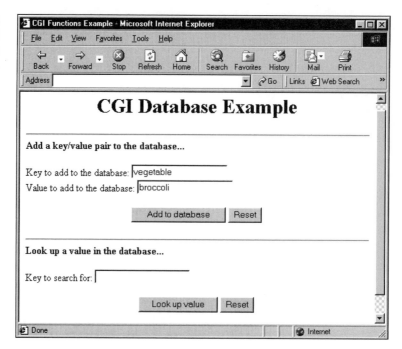

To retrieve a value from the database, you enter the value's key in the box marked Key to Search For, which you see in Figure 20-4. Then you click the Look Up Value button. When you do, the database is searched and an XML document with the results is sent to the client, as you see in Figure 20-5. In this case, I've searched for the key `vegetable`, and the result is as it should be, as you see in Figure 20-5. Although this XML document is displayed in a browser, it's relatively easy to use Internet sockets in Perl code to let you read and handle such XML without a browser.

Figure 20-5
An XML
document
generated by a
Perl script.

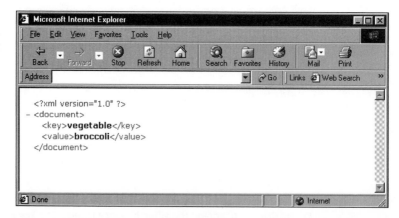

In this Perl script, I'll use CGI.pm, the official Perl CGI module, which comes with the standard Perl distribution. I begin by creating the Web page you see in Figure 20-4, including all the HTML controls we'll need:

```perl
#!/usr/local/bin/perl
use Fcntl;
use NDBM_File;
use CGI;
$co = new CGI;

if(!$co->param()) {
print $co->header,
$co->start_html('CGI Functions Example'),
$co->center($co->h1('CGI Database Example')),
$co->hr,
$co->b("Add a key/value pair to the database..."),
$co->start_form,
"Key to add to the database: ",$co->textfield(-name=>'key',-default=>'', -
override=>1),
$co->br,
"Value to add to the database: ",$co->textfield(-name=>'value',-default=>'',
-override=>1),
$co->br,
$co->hidden(-name=>'type',-value=>'write', -override=>1),
$co->br,
$co->center(
    $co->submit('Add to database'),
    $co->reset
),
$co->end_form,
$co->hr,
$co->b("Look up a value in the database..."),
$co->start_form,
"Key to search for: ",$co->textfield(-name=>'key',-default=>'', -over-
ride=>1),
$co->br,
$co->hidden(-name=>'type',-value=>'read', -override=>1),
$co->br,
$co->center(
    $co->submit('Look up value'),
    $co->reset
),
$co->end_form,
$co->hr;
print $co->end_html;
}
    .
    .
    .
```

This CGI creates two HTML forms, one for use when you want to store key/value pairs and one when you want to enter a key to search for. I didn't specify a target for these two HTML forms in this page to send their data to, so the data will simply be sent back to the same script. I can check whether the script has been called with data to be processed by checking the return value of the CGI.pm param method; if it's true, there is data waiting for us to work on.

The document that this script returns is an XML document, not the default HTML. So how do you set the content type in the HTTP header to indicate that? You do so with the header method, setting the type named parameter to "application/xml". This code follows the previous code in the script:

```
if($co->param()) {
    print $co->header(-type=>"application/xml");
    print "<?xml version = \"1.0\"?>";
    print "<document>";
    .
    .
    .
```

I keep the two HTML forms separate with a hidden data variable named type. If that variable is set to write, I enter the data the user supplied into the database:

```
if($co->param()) {
    print $co->header(-type=>"application/xml");
    print "<?xml version = \"1.0\"?>";
    print "<document>";
    if($co->param('type') eq 'write') {
        tie %dbhash, "NDBM_File", "dbdata", O_RDWR|O_CREAT, 0644;
        $key = $co->param('key');
        $value = $co->param('value');
        $dbhash{$key} = $value;
        untie %dbhash;
        if ($!) {
            print "There was an error: $!";
        } else {
            print "$key=>$value stored in the database";
        }
    }
    .
    .
    .
}
```

Otherwise, I search the database for the key the user has specified and return both the key and the corresponding value in an XML document:

```perl
if($co->param()) {
    print $co->header(-type=>"application/xml");
    print "<?xml version = \"1.0\"?>";
    print "<document>";
    if($co->param('type') eq 'write') {
        tie %dbhash, "NDBM_File", "dbdata", O_RDWR|O_CREAT, 0644;
        $key = $co->param('key');
        $value = $co->param('value');
        $dbhash{$key} = $value;
        untie %dbhash;
        if ($!) {
            print "There was an error: $!";
        } else {
            print "$key=>$value stored in the database";
        }
    } else {
        tie %dbhash, "NDBM_File", "dbdata", O_RDWR|O_CREAT, 0644;
        $key = $co->param('key');
        $value = $dbhash{$key};
        print "<key>";
        print $key;
        print "</key>";
        print "<value>";
        print $value;
        print "</value>";
        if ($value) {
            if ($!) {
                print "There was an error: $!";
            }
        } else {
            print "No match found for that key";
        }
        untie %dbhash;
    }
    print "</document>";
}
```

In this way, we've been able to store data in a database using Perl, and retrieve that data, formatted as XML. Here's the complete listing:

Listing ch20_06.cgi

```perl
#!/usr/local/bin/perl
use Fcntl;
use NDBM_File;
use CGI;
$co = new CGI;
```

continues

Listing ch20_06.cgi   Continued

```
if(!$co->param()) {
print $co->header,
$co->start_html('CGI Functions Example'),
$co->center($co->h1('CGI Database Example')),
$co->hr,
$co->b("Add a key/value pair to the database..."),
$co->start_form,
"Key to add to the database: ",$co->textfield(-name=>'key',-default=>'', -
override=>1),
$co->br,
"Value to add to the database: ",$co->textfield(-name=>'value',-default=>'',
-override=>1),
$co->br,
$co->hidden(-name=>'type',-value=>'write', -override=>1),
$co->br,
$co->center(
    $co->submit('Add to database'),
    $co->reset
),
$co->end_form,
$co->hr,
$co->b("Look up a value in the database..."),
$co->start_form,
"Key to search for: ",$co->textfield(-name=>'key',-default=>'', -over-
ride=>1),
$co->br,
$co->hidden(-name=>'type',-value=>'read', -override=>1),
$co->br,
$co->center(
    $co->submit('Look up value'),
    $co->reset
),
$co->end_form,
$co->hr;
print $co->end_html;
}

if($co->param()) {
    print $co->header(-type=>"application/xml");
    print "<?xml version = \"1.0\"?>";
    print "<document>";
    if($co->param('type') eq 'write') {
        tie %dbhash, "NDBM_File", "dbdata", O_RDWR|O_CREAT, 0644;
        $key = $co->param('key');
        $value = $co->param('value');
        $dbhash{$key} = $value;
        untie %dbhash;
        if ($!) {
            print "There was an error: $!";
```

```
    } else {
        print "$key=>$value stored in the database";
    }
} else {
    tie %dbhash, "NDBM_File", "dbdata", O_RDWR|O_CREAT, 0644;
    $key = $co->param('key');
    $value = $dbhash{$key};
    print "<key>";
    print $key;
    print "</key>";
    print "<value>";
    print $value;
    print "</value>";
    if ($value) {
        if ($!) {
            print "There was an error: $!";
        }
    } else {
        print "No match found for that key";
    }
    untie %dbhash;
}
print "</document>";
}
```

WML

One of the XML applications that has been getting a lot of attention there days is WML. WML and its associated protocol, the WAP, are targeted at handheld devices such as cellular phones, PDAs, and other devices with restricted hardware capabilities. WML represents a limited-syntax language that's relatively easy to implement for such devices. The programs that use WML in those devices are often called microbrowsers.

Here are some WML resources:

- www.wapforum.org—A great resource for all things WML. Acts as a clearinghouse for information. The WAP Forum was consolidated with the Open Mobile Architecture Initiative to form the Open Mobile Alliance Ltd, whose home page is at www.openmobilealliance.org. As of this writing, however, the WAP Forum site is still available.

- www.apachesoftware.com—All about Klondike, a popular WML browser.

- `www.apachesoftware.com/wml/wmldemo.wml`—Klondike WML examples.

- `http://www.zvon.org/xxl/WMLTutorial/Output/introduction.html`—A WML tutorial.

- `http://www.wirelessdevnet.com/channels/wap/training/wml.html`—Another WML tutorial.

- `http://www.wapforum.org/DTD/wml20-flat.dtd`—The WML 2.0 (the current version) DTD. A great place to check to resolve syntax questions.

- `http://updev.phone.com`—Openwave's WML SDK, which includes a browser.

You can find the WML 2.0 elements in Table 20-3. You'll find links to the various sections of the WML DTD at `http://www.wapforum.org/what/technical.htm`, and you can view the whole DTD as one file in `http://www.wapforum.org/DTD/wml20-flat.dtd`. If you want to check on WML elements or see what attributes an element has, `http://www.wapforum.org/DTD/wml20-flat.dtd` is a good resource.

Table 20-3	Element	Function
WML 2.0 Elements	a	Hyperlink
	abbr	Abbreviation
	access	Access element
	acronym	Acronym
	address	Addresses
	anchor	Creates an anchor
	b	Bold
	base	Base
	big	Big text
	blockquote	Block quotes
	br	Line break
	caption	Table caption
	card	Creates a card
	cite	Citations
	code	Code text
	dd	Definition description

Element	Function
dfn	Definitions
div	DIV sections
dl	Definition list
do	Do element
dt	Definition term
em	Emphasized
fieldset	Field set
form	Creates a form
getvar	Get variable
go	Navigates
h1–h6	Headings
head	Head section
hr	Horizontal rule
i	Italic
img	Handles images
input	Text field
kbd	Keyboard text
label	Label
li	List item
link	Link
meta	Holds metadata
noop	No operation
object	Object
ol	Ordered list
onevent	Handles an event
optgroup	Creates an option group
option	Creates an option
p	Paragraph
param	Parameter
postfield	Post field data
pre	Preformatted text
prev	Move to previous card
q	Quote

continues

Element	Function
refresh	Handles refreshes
samp	Sample text
select	Select control
setvar	Sets a variable
small	Small text
span	Spans text
strong	Strong
style	Style
sub	Subscript
sup	Superscript
table	Creates a table
td	Table cell data
template	Template
textarea	Text area
timer	Creates a timer
title	Title
tr	Table row
tt	Teletype text
u	Underlined
ul	Unordered list
var	Variables

In addition, WML supports these character entities:

- & is an ampersand (&).
- ' is an apostrophe (').
- > is the greater-than symbol (>).
- < is the less-than symbol (<).
-   is a nonbreaking space ( ).
- " is a quotation mark (").
- ­ is a soft hyphen (_).

In this chapter, I'll use the popular Apache Klondike WML browser, which you can download for free from links at www.apachesoftware.com. It's a well-designed browser; if you want to follow along, I encourage you to install it.

Getting Starting with WML

Microbrowsers do not have a lot of display area to spare, so WML documents are divided into *cards* that are displayed one at a time. A WML document is called a *deck* of such cards. A deck begins and ends with the <wml> tag, and each card in a deck begins and ends with the <card> tag. When a microbrowser reads a WML document, it reads the whole deck, although you see only one card at a time.

As you'd expect, you start WML documents with this XML declaration:

```
<?xml version="1.0"?>
    .
    .
    .
```

As with XHTML, WML uses a <!DOCTYPE> element with a formal public identifier, except that this time, the authorization body is the WAP Forum, not the W3C:

```
<?xml version="1.0"?>
<!DOCTYPE wml PUBLIC "-//WAPFORUM//DTD WML 2.0//EN"
    "http://www.wapforum.org/dtd/wml20.dtd" >
    .
    .
    .
```

The document, or deck, element is <wml>:

```
<?xml version="1.0"?>
<!DOCTYPE wml PUBLIC "-//WAPFORUM//DTD WML 2.0//EN"
    "http://www.wapforum.org/dtd/wml20.dtd" >
<wml>
    .
    .
    .
</wml>
```

You create a card in this deck with the <card> element. In this case, I'll give this card the ID "Card1" and the title "First WML Example" (which will appear in Klondike's title bar):

```
<?xml version="1.0"?>
<!DOCTYPE wml PUBLIC "-//WAPFORUM//DTD WML 2.0//EN"
    "http://www.wapforum.org/dtd/wml20.dtd" >
<wml>
    <card id="Card1" title="First WML Example">
        .
        .
        .
    </card>
</wml>
```

You can use comments in WML just as you can in XML:

```
<?xml version="1.0"?>
<!DOCTYPE wml PUBLIC "-//WAPFORUM//DTD WML 2.0//EN"
    "http://www.wapforum.org/dtd/wml20.dtd" >
<wml>
    <card id="Card1" title="First WML Example">
        <!-- This is a comment -->
        .
        .
        .
    </card>
</wml>
```

Every card must have a <p> (paragraph) element, and I'll place some greeting text in that element:

Listing ch20_07.wml

```
<?xml version="1.0"?>
<!DOCTYPE wml PUBLIC "-//WAPFORUM//DTD WML 2.0//EN"
    "http://www.wapforum.org/dtd/wml20.dtd" >
<wml>
    <card id="Card1" title="First WML Example">
        <!-- This is a comment -->
        <p>
            Greetings from WML.
        </p>
    </card>
</wml>
```

That's all it takes. You can see this WML document displayed in Klondike in Figure 20-6.

Figure 20-6
A first WML
document.

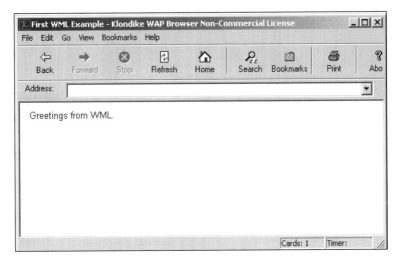

Setting Text Alignment

The <p> element has an `align` attribute, which is supported by Klondike and is useful for aligning text. You can assign this attribute the values `"left"`, `"center"`, or `"right"`. There's also a `mode` attribute that you can use to specify whether you want text wrapped; you can assign values of `"wrap"` or `"nowrap"` to this attribute.

Here's an example that demonstrates text alignment, using these attributes of the <p> element:

Listing ch20_08.wml

```
<?xml version="1.0"?>
<!DOCTYPE wml PUBLIC "-//WAPFORUM//DTD WML 2.0//EN"
    "http://www.wapforum.org/dtd/wml20.dtd" >
<wml>
    <card id="Card1" title="Text Alignment">
        <p align="center"><b>Text Alignment</b></p>
        <p align="left">Left-aligned text</p>
        <p align="center">Center-aligned text</p>
        <p align="right">Right-aligned text</p>
        <p mode="nowrap">Non-wrapped text in a long line of text....</p>
    </card>
</wml>
```

You can see what this WML document looks like in Klondike in Figure 20-7.

Figure 20-7
Aligning text in
a WML
document.

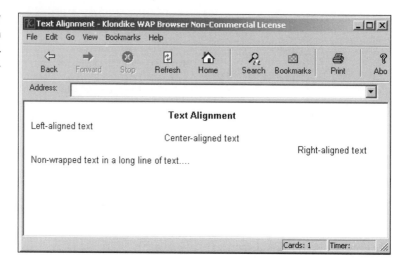

Basic Text Styling

WML also supports several basic text styling elements modeled after HTML, such as <b> for bold text, <i> for italic text, <u> for underlined text, and so on. Here's an example that puts these basic text styling elements to work (note that not all microbrowsers will support all these styling elements):

Listing ch20_09.wml

```
<?xml version="1.0"?>
<!DOCTYPE wml PUBLIC "-//WAPFORUM//DTD WML 2.0//EN"
    "http://www.wapforum.org/dtd/wml20.dtd" >
<wml>
    <card id="Card1" title="Text Formatting">
        <p align="center"><b>Text Formatting</b></p>
        <p>
            WML supports these text styles:
            <b>bold</b>,
            <big>big</big>,
            <em>emphasis</em>,
            <i>italic</i>,
            <small>small</small>,
            <strong>strong</strong>,
            and <u>underline</u>.
        </p>
    </card>
</wml>
```

You can see this WML displayed in the Klondike browser in Figure 20-8.

Figure 20-8
Text formatting
in WML.

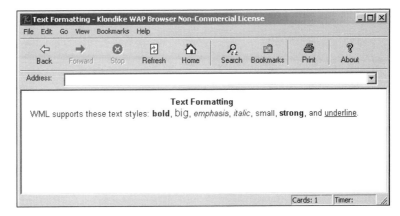

The *<do>* Element

WML <do> elements appear as bracketed text in Klondike, as bold text that you can click in devices such as cell phones. Clicking these elements performs some action. For example, say that I wanted to let the user navigate to the (nonexistent) WML document page at www.starpowder.com/planets.wml. In that case, I'd start with the <do> element, setting the type attribute to "accept" and adding a label with the label attribute, like this:

```
<?xml version="1.0"?>
<!DOCTYPE wml PUBLIC "-//WAPFORUM//DTD WML 2.0//EN"
    "http://www.wapforum.org/dtd/wml20.dtd" >
<wml>
    <card id="Card1" title="The do Element">
        <p align="center"><b>The do Element</b></p>
        <do type="accept" label="Go to a new page...">
            .
            .
            .
        </do>
    </card>
</wml>
```

You can navigate to the new document with the <go> element, specifying the URI to navigate to with the href element:

Listing ch20_10.wml

```
<?xml version="1.0"?>
<!DOCTYPE wml PUBLIC "-//WAPFORUM//DTD WML 2.0//EN"
    "http://www.wapforum.org/dtd/wml20.dtd" >
<wml>
    <card id="Card1" title="The do Element">
        <p align="center"><b>The do Element</b></p>
        <do type="accept" label="Go to a new page...">
            <go href="http://www.starpowder.com/planets.wml"/>
        </do>
    </card>
</wml>
```

The results of this WML document appear in Figure 20-9. As you can see there, the <do> element appears in the browser. Clicking that element makes the browser navigate to the (nonexistent) document at www.starpowder.com/planets.wml.

As you know, you can have multiple cards in a deck but see only one at a time. So how do you get to the others? Just as we have done: with <do> elements. In this case, you assign the ID of the target card to the href attribute in the <go> element.

Figure 20-9
Displaying a
<do> element
in a WML
document.

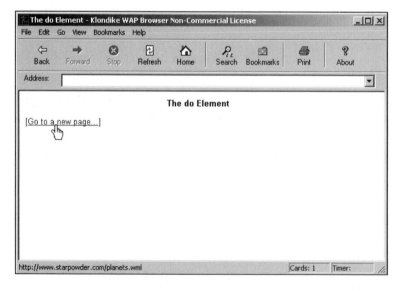

Here's an example with two cards and a <do> element that lets the user navigate from the first card to the second one. Note that the href attribute of the <go> element points to the ID value of the target card:

Listing ch20_11.wml

```
<?xml version="1.0"?>
<!DOCTYPE wml PUBLIC "-//WAPFORUM//DTD WML 2.0//EN"
    "http://www.wapforum.org/dtd/wml20.dtd" >
 <wml>
    <card id="Card1" title="Multiple Cards">
        <p align="center"><b>Multiple Cards</b></p>
        <do type="accept" label="Go to Card 2">
            <go href="#Card2"/>
        </do>
    </card>
    <card id="Card2" title="Card 2">
        <p>
            This is card 2.
        </p>
    </card>
</wml>
```

The results of this WML appear in Figure 20-10. When the user clicks the <do> element, the browser navigates to card 2 in the deck. That's how you get from card to card in WML: with browser navigation techniques.

So having navigated to card 2, how does the user get back to card 1? Take a look at the next topic.

Figure 20-10
Displaying a navigation element in a WML document.

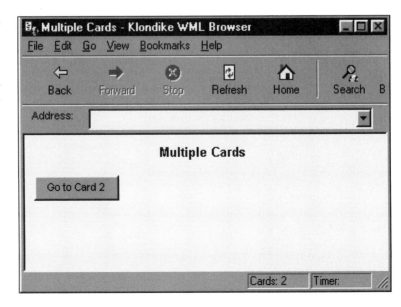

The *<prev>* Element

To add a <do> element that lets you move backward to card 2, I use the WML <prev> element like this:

Listing ch20_12.wml

```
<?xml version="1.0"?>
<!DOCTYPE wml PUBLIC "-//WAPFORUM//DTD WML 2.0//EN"
    "http://www.wapforum.org/dtd/wml20.dtd" >
 <wml>
    <card id="Card1" title="Multiple Cards">
        <p align="center"><b>Multiple Cards</b></p>
        <do type="accept" label="Go to Card 2">
            <go href="#Card2"/>
        </do>
    </card>
    <card id="Card2" title="Card 2">
        <p>
            This is card 2.
        </p>
        <do type="prev" label="Back">
            <prev/>
        </do>
    </card>
</wml>
```

That's all it takes. Now a <do> element appears in card 2 that lets you move backward, as you can see in Figure 20-11. When the user clicks this <do> element, the browser navigates back to the previous card. It's a good idea to include such an element on every card (microbrowsers typically won't have a built-in Back button, although Klondike does).

Figure 20-11
Displaying a Back element.

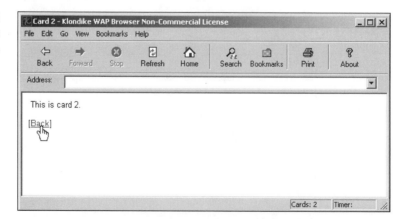

Hyperlinks

WML also supports an <a> element for hyperlinks. Like the HTML version of
this element, you use the href attribute to specify the URI you want to navigate to. Here's an example that takes the user to the Apache WML example:

Listing ch20_13.wml

```
<?xml version="1.0"?>
<!DOCTYPE wml PUBLIC "-//WAPFORUM//DTD WML 2.0//EN"
    "http://www.wapforum.org/dtd/wml20.dtd" >
 <wml>
    <card id="Card1" title="Hyperlinks">
        <p align="center"><b>Hyperlinks</b></p>
        <p>
            Want to see some WML examples?
            Take a look at the
            <a href="http://www.apachesoftware.com/wml/wmldemo.wml">
                Apache examples
            </a>.
        </p>
    </card>
    </card>
</wml>
```

You can see the results of this WML in Figure 20-12. When the user clicks the
hyperlink, Klondike will navigate to the target URI.

Figure 20-12
A WML
hyperlink.

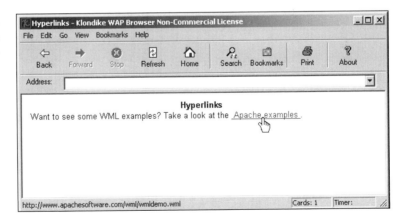

Tables

You can also create tables in WML, using markup that matches the HTML `<table>`, `<tr>`, and `<td>` elements (there are no `<th>`, `<tbody>`, `<thead>`, or `<tfoot>` elements). Here's an example—note how closely this resembles an HTML table:

Listing ch20_14.wml

```
<?xml version="1.0"?>
<!DOCTYPE wml PUBLIC "-//WAPFORUM//DTD WML 2.0//EN"
    "http://www.wapforum.org/dtd/wml20.dtd" >
<wml>
    <card id="Card1" title="Tables">
        <p align="center"><b>Tables</b></p>
        <p align="center">
            <table columns="3">
                <tr>
                    <td>TIC</td>
                    <td>TAC</td>
                    <td>TOE</td>
                </tr>
                <tr>
                    <td>x</td>
                    <td>o</td>
                    <td>x</td>
                </tr>
                <tr>
                    <td>o</td>
                    <td>x</td>
                    <td>o</td>
                </tr>
                <tr>
                    <td>x</td>
                    <td>o</td>
                    <td>x</td>
                </tr>
            </table>
        </p>
    </card>
</wml>
```

You can see the results of this WML in Figure 20-13.

Figure 20-13
WML tables.

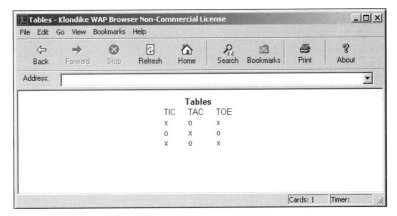

Text Input

WML also supports an `<input>` element. If you set this element's `type` attribute to `text`, you can display a text field, much like HTML text fields (note
that not all microbrowsers will support this element).

Here's an example. In this case, I'll let the user enter the URI of a local file
to navigate to in a text field. When the user clicks a `<do>` element labeled Go,
the browser will navigate to that URI. I begin by creating the text field:

```
<?xml version="1.0"?>
<!DOCTYPE wml PUBLIC "-//WAPFORUM//DTD WML 2.0//EN"
    "http://www.wapforum.org/dtd/wml20.dtd" >
<wml>
    <card id="Card1" title="Text Input">
        <p align="center"><b>Text Input</b></p>
        <p>
            Navigate to:
            <input type="text" name="uri"/>
        .
        .
        .
```

When the user clicks the `<do>` element, we'll need some way to read what he
has entered in the text field. Here, I've given the text field the name `uri`. That
means I can refer to the text in the text field as `$(uri)` this way in the `<go>`
element:

Listing ch20_15.wml

```
<?xml version="1.0"?>
<!DOCTYPE wml PUBLIC "-//WAPFORUM//DTD WML 2.0//EN"
    "http://www.wapforum.org/dtd/wml20.dtd" >
<wml>
    <card id="Card1" title="Text Input">
        <p align="center"><b>Text Input</b></p>
        <p>
            Navigate to:
            <input type="text" name="uri"/>
            <do type="accept" label="Go">
                <go href="$(uri)"/>
            </do>
        </p>
    </card>
</wml>
```

That's all it takes. The results of this WML appear in Figure 20-14. When the user enters a URI of a local document—I'm using ch20_07.wml in this figure—in the text field and clicks the <do> element labeled Go, the browser reads the name of the document from the text field and opens that document.

This topic has also introduced us to the concept of WML variables, such as $(uri). Being able to handle variables directly like this gives WML an interesting mix of markup and scripting capabilities. There's also a <setvar> element that lets you set the value of variables like this:

```
<setvar name="uri" value="ch20_07.wml" />
```

I'll put variables to work in the next topic as well.

Figure 20-14
Handling text
input.

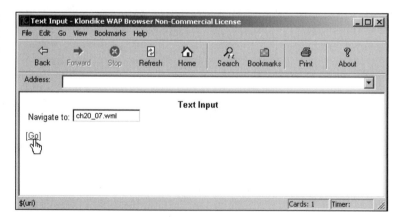

Select Elements

Like HTML, WML supports a `<select>` element to display a select control (which is like a drop-down list box). As an example, I'll create a select control here. After the user has made a selection, he can click a Read Selection `<do>` element, which will navigate to a new card that displays the selection they've made.

I start by creating the select control and giving it the name `"selection"`:

```
<?xml version="1.0"?>
<!DOCTYPE wml PUBLIC "-//WAPFORUM//DTD WML 2.0//EN"
    "http://www.wapforum.org/dtd/wml20.dtd" >
<wml>
    <card id="Card1" title="Select">
        <p align="center"><b>Select</b></p>
        <select name="selection">
            .
            .
            .
        </select>
```

As in HTML, you specify the items in the `select` control with `<option>` elements:

```
<?xml version="1.0"?>
<!DOCTYPE wml PUBLIC "-//WAPFORUM//DTD WML 2.0//EN"
    "http://www.wapforum.org/dtd/wml20.dtd" >
<wml>
    <card id="Card1" title="Select">
        <p align="center"><b>Select</b></p>
        <select name="selection">
            <option value="broccoli">Broccoli</option>
            <option value="green beans">Green Beans</option>
            <option value="spinach">Spinach</option>
        </select>
        .
        .
        .
```

Now I add the Read Selection `<do>` element that will navigate to a new card, card 2:

```
<?xml version="1.0"?>
<!DOCTYPE wml PUBLIC "-//WAPFORUM//DTD WML 2.0//EN"
    "http://www.wapforum.org/dtd/wml20.dtd" >
<wml>
    <card id="Card1" title="Select">
        <p align="center"><b>Select</b></p>
```

```
                <select name="selection">
                    <option value="broccoli">Broccoli</option>
                    <option value="green beans">Green Beans</option>
                    <option value="spinach">Spinach</option>
                </select>
                <do type="accept" label="Read selection">
                    <go href="#card2"/>
                </do>
        .
        .
        .
```

In card 2, I'll display the value in the select control, which I can refer to as $(selection). The value of a select control is the string in the value attribute of the currently selected item's <option> element. Here's what the WML to display the current selection looks like in card 2:

Listing ch20_16.wml

```
<?xml version="1.0"?>
<!DOCTYPE wml PUBLIC "-//WAPFORUM//DTD WML 2.0//EN"
    "http://www.wapforum.org/dtd/wml20.dtd" >
<wml>
    <card id="Card1" title="Select">
        <p align="center"><b>Select</b></p>
        <select name="selection">
            <option value="broccoli">Broccoli</option>
            <option value="green beans">Green Beans</option>
            <option value="spinach">Spinach</option>
        </select>
        <do type="accept" label="Read selection">
            <go href="#card2"/>
        </do>
    </card>
    <card id="card2" title="Card 2">
        <p>
            You selected $(selection).
        </p>
    </card>
</wml>
```

You can see how this works in Figure 20-15, where I've selected the item Broccoli.

Clicking the Read Selection <do> element takes us to card 2, which reports the selection, as you see in Figure 20-16.

Figure 20-15
Making
selections.

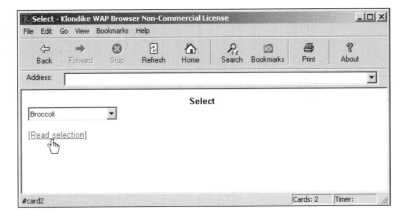

Figure 20-16
Reporting
selections.

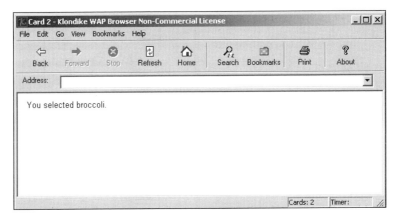

Another useful aspect of `select` controls is the `onpick` attribute of `<option>` elements, which allows you to navigate to new URIs as soon as the user chooses an item in a `select` control. Here's an example. All I have to do is to set the `onpick` attribute of a number of `<option>` elements to URIs; when the user chooses one, the browser will navigate to the corresponding URI:

Listing ch20_17.wml

```
<?xml version="1.0"?>
<!DOCTYPE wml PUBLIC "-//WAPFORUM//DTD WML 2.0//EN"
    "http://www.wapforum.org/dtd/wml20.dtd" >
<wml>
    <card id="Card1" title="Select">
        <p align="center"><b>Select</b></p>
        <select name="selection">
```

continues

Listing ch20_17.wml   Continued

```
            <option onpick="http://www.starpowder.com/mercury.wml">
                Mercury
            </option>
            <option onpick="http://www.starpowder.com/venus.wml">
                Venus
            </option>
            <option onpick="http://www.starpowder.com/earth.wml">
                Earth
            </option>
        </select>
    </card>
</wml>
```

Timers

In WML, you can use *timers* to perform timed actions. A timer measures a time period, and the browser undertakes some action when that period has expired. For example, if I assign a card's `ontimer` attribute to the ID of another card, the browser will navigate to that card when the timer finishes:

```
<?xml version="1.0"?>
<!DOCTYPE wml PUBLIC "-//WAPFORUM//DTD WML 2.0//EN"
    "http://www.wapforum.org/dtd/wml20.dtd" >
<wml>
    <card id="Card1" ontimer="#card2" title="Timers">
        .
        .
        .
    </card>
    .
    .
    .
```

You create a timer with the `<timer>` element and give it a time period (measured in tenths of seconds) with the `value` attribute, like this, where I'm giving this card's timer a period of 10 seconds:

```
<?xml version="1.0"?>
<!DOCTYPE wml PUBLIC "-//WAPFORUM//DTD WML 2.0//EN"
    "http://www.wapforum.org/dtd/wml20.dtd" >
<wml>
    <card id="Card1" ontimer="#card2" title="Timers">
        <p align="center"><b>Timers</b></p>
        <timer value="100"/>
        <p>
            In ten seconds, you'll be redirected
            to the second card.
        </p>
```

```
</card>
    .
    .
    .
```

All that remains is to add the targeted card, card2:

Listing ch20_18.wml

```
<?xml version="1.0"?>
<!DOCTYPE wml PUBLIC "-//WAPFORUM//DTD WML 2.0//EN"
    "http://www.wapforum.org/dtd/wml20.dtd" >
<wml>
    <card id="Card1" ontimer="#card2" title="Timers">
        <p align="center"><b>Timers</b></p>
        <timer value="100"/>
        <p>
            In ten seconds, you'll be redirected
            to the second card.
        </p>
    </card>
    <card id="card2" title="Welcome">
        <p>
            Welcome to card 2.
        </p>
    </card>
</wml>
```

Now when you open this deck, you'll see card 1, as shown in Figure 20-17. After 10 seconds, the browser will navigate to card 2. (Note that, as shown in the figure, Klondike features a timer counter at lower right; here, it's indicating that there are 7 seconds left in the timer.)

Figure 20-17
Using a timer.

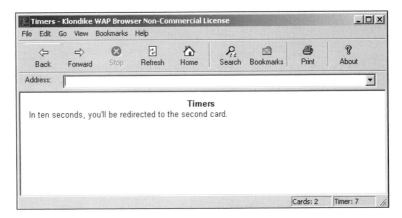

Connecting to the Server

In WML, you can also create forms, which are much like HTML forms. The data in a WML form is encoded just as in HTML, so it can be uploaded to CGI scripts (note that not all microbrowsers will support forms).

Here's an example. In this case, I'll ask for user comments and send them back to a CGI script named comments.cgi. To start, I create a <do> element with the label Upload Data, setting its method attribute to "post", and its href attribute to the URI to post to, "http://www.starpowder.com/comments.cgi", just as you might in an HTML form:

```
<?xml version="1.0"?>
<!DOCTYPE wml PUBLIC "-//WAPFORUM//DTD WML 2.0//EN"
    "http://www.wapforum.org/dtd/wml20.dtd" >
<wml>
    <card id="Card1" title="Uploading">
        <p align="center"><b>Uploading</b></p>
        <do type="accept" label="Upload data">
            <go method="post"
                href="http://www.starpowder.com/comments.cgi">
                .
                .
                .
            </go>
            .
            .
            .
```

All that's left is to indicate the value of the data to upload and how to name that data. You do that with the <postfield> element's name and value attributes. In this case, I'll upload the text from a text field named comments, like this:

```
<?xml version="1.0"?>
<!DOCTYPE wml PUBLIC "-//WAPFORUM//DTD WML 2.0//EN"
    "http://www.wapforum.org/dtd/wml20.dtd" >
<wml>
    <card id="Card1" title="Uploading">
        <p align="center"><b>Uploading</b></p>
        <do type="accept" label="Upload data">
            <go method="post"
                href="www.starpowder.com/comments.cgi">
                <postfield name="comments" value="$(comments)"/>
            </go>
        </do>
        <p>
        Please give us your comments:
```

```
            <input type="text" name="comments"/>
        </p>
    </card>
</wml>
```

And that's all it takes. The CGI script can now read the uploaded data as it would from any HTML document. Note that when you send back a response, you should format that response in WML, which means setting the content type HTTP header item to the WML MIME type "text/vnd.wap.wml".

Images

You can also display images in WMF, but there's a catch. Images must be in special WBMP format, and that format doesn't exactly permit the rich depth of colors you may be used to. In fact, WBMP format is black and white with no grayscale—just 1 bit per pixel. Here are some WBMP resources available online:

- `www.phnet.fi/public/jiikoo/`—WAPDraw, a useful WBMP drawing program.
- `www.teraflops.com/wbmp Teraflops`—An online converter that converts image files to WBMP files with a few simple clicks. Any HTML browser can download the resulting images, unless the browser understands WBMP format, in which case the image will be displayed.
- `http://www.hicon.nl/cgi-bin/library/clipart/clipart.pl`—A WBMP clip art library.

To display images, you probably won't be surprised to learn that WML has an `<img>` element. You set the `alt`, `src`, `width`, and `height` attributes of this element to display images; here's an example:

Listing ch20_19.wml

```
<?xml version="1.0"?>
<!DOCTYPE wml PUBLIC "-//WAPFORUM//DTD WML 2.0//EN"
    "http://www.wapforum.org/dtd/wml20.dtd" >
<wml>
    <card id="Card1" title="Images">
        <p align="center"><b>Images</b></p>
```

continues

Listing ch20_19.wml   Continued

```
            <p align="center">
                <img alt="WML Image"
                    src="ch20_20.wbmp" width="217" height="164"/>
            </p>
        </card>
    </wml>
```

You can see this WML document, along with a WBMP image I created for it to display, ch20_20.wbmp, in Figure 20-18.

That's it for our exploration of WML—and XML. We've come far in this book, from the very beginning up through valid and well-formed documents, DTDs, schemas, how to parse XML with JavaScript, data binding, CSS, XML and Java, DOM and SAX parsers, XSL transformations, XSL formatting objects, XLinks, XPointers, XHTML, RDF, SOAP, VML, and now WML and XML with JSP, ASP, Java servlets, and Perl. All that remains now is for you is to put all this incredible amount of technology to work for yourself.

Figure 20-18
Displaying an
image.

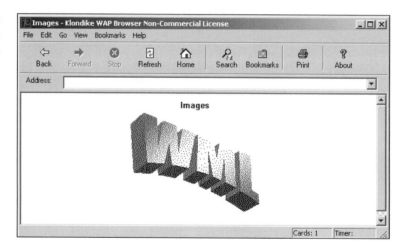

APPENDIX A

The XML 1.0 Recommendation (Second Edition)

This appendix lists the W3C XML 1.0 recommendation (second edition) from www.w3.org/TR/REC-xml, and was written by the authors listed at the end of the appendix. It is a W3C recommendation. Note that formal syntax of XML is given using a simple *Extended Backus-Naur Form notation* (EBNF). This notation is explained in Section 6 of the appendix.

Extensible Markup Language (XML) 1.0 (Second Edition)

W3C Recommendation 6 October 2000

This version:

http://www.w3.org/TR/2000/REC-xml-20001006 (XHTML, XML, PDF, XHTML review version with color-coded revision indicators)

Latest version:

http://www.w3.org/TR/REC-xml

Previous versions:

http://www.w3.org/TR/2000/WD-xml-2e-20000814
http://www.w3.org/TR/1998/REC-xml-19980210

Editors:

Tim Bray, Textuality and Netscape <tbray@textuality.com>

Jean Paoli, Microsoft <jeanpa@microsoft.com>

C. M. Sperberg-McQueen, University of Illinois at Chicago and Text Encoding Initiative <cmsmcq@uic.edu>

Eve Maler, Sun Microsystems, Inc. <eve.maler@east.sun.com> - Second Edition

Abstract

The Extensible Markup Language (XML) is a subset of SGML that is completely described in this document. Its goal is to enable generic SGML to be served, received, and processed on the Web in the way that is now possible with HTML. XML has been designed for ease of implementation and for interoperability with both SGML and HTML.

Status of this Document

This document has been reviewed by W3C Members and other interested parties and has been endorsed by the Director as a W3C Recommendation. It is a stable document and may be used as reference material or cited as a normative reference from another document. W3C's role in making the Recommendation is to draw attention to the specification and to promote its widespread deployment. This enhances the functionality and interoperability of the Web.

This document specifies a syntax created by subsetting an existing, widely used international text processing standard (Standard Generalized Markup Language, ISO 8879:1986(E) as amended and corrected) for use on the World Wide Web. It is a product of the W3C XML Activity, details of which can be found at `http://www.w3.org/XML`. The English version of this specification is the only normative version. However, for translations of this document, see `http://www.w3.org/XML/#trans`. A list of current W3C Recommendations and other technical documents can be found at `http://www.w3.org/TR`.

This second edition is not a new version of XML (first published 10 February 1998); it merely incorporates the changes dictated by the first-edition errata (available at `http://www.w3.org/XML/xml-19980210-errata`) as a convenience to readers. The errata list for this second edition is available at `http://www.w3.org/XML/xml-V10-2e-errata`.

Please report errors in this document to xml-editor@w3.org; archives are available.

> **Note:**
> C. M. Sperberg-McQueen's affiliation has changed since the publication of the first edition. He is now at the World Wide Web Consortium, and can be contacted at `cmsmcq@w3.org`.

Table of Contents

Appendices

1 Introduction

Extensible Markup Language, abbreviated XML, describes a class of data objects called XML documents and partially describes the behavior of computer programs which process them. XML is an application profile or restricted form of SGML, the Standard Generalized Markup Language [ISO 8879]. By construction, XML documents are conforming SGML documents.

XML documents are made up of storage units called entities, which contain either parsed or unparsed data. Parsed data is made up of characters, some of which form character data, and some of which form markup. Markup encodes a description of the document's storage layout and logical structure. XML provides a mechanism to impose constraints on the storage layout and logical structure.

[Definition: A software module called an **XML processor** is used to read XML documents and provide access to their content and structure.] [Definition: It is assumed that an XML processor is doing its work on behalf of another module, called the **application**.] This specification describes the required behavior of an XML processor in terms of how it must read XML data and the information it must provide to the application.

1.1 Origin and Goals

XML was developed by an XML Working Group (originally known as the SGML Editorial Review Board) formed under the auspices of the World Wide Web Consortium (W3C) in 1996. It was chaired by Jon Bosak of Sun Microsystems with the active participation of an XML Special Interest Group (previously known as the SGML Working Group) also organized by the W3C. The membership of the XML Working Group is given in an appendix. Dan Connolly served as the WG's contact with the W3C.

The design goals for XML are:

1. XML shall be straightforwardly usable over the Internet.
2. XML shall support a wide variety of applications.
3. XML shall be compatible with SGML.
4. It shall be easy to write programs which process XML documents.
5. The number of optional features in XML is to be kept to the absolute minimum, ideally zero.
6. XML documents should be human-legible and reasonably clear.
7. The XML design should be prepared quickly.
8. The design of XML shall be formal and concise.
9. XML documents shall be easy to create.
10. Terseness in XML markup is of minimal importance.

This specification, together with associated standards (Unicode and ISO/IEC 10646 for characters, Internet RFC 1766 for language identification tags, ISO 639 for language name codes, and ISO 3166 for country name codes), provides all the information necessary to understand XML Version 1.0 and construct computer programs to process it.

This version of the XML specification may be distributed freely, as long as all text and legal notices remain intact.

1.2 Terminology

The terminology used to describe XML documents is defined in the body of this specification. The terms defined in the following list are used in building those definitions and in describing the actions of an XML processor:

may

[Definition: Conforming documents and XML processors are permitted to but need not behave as described.]

must

[Definition: Conforming documents and XML processors are required to behave as described; otherwise they are in error.]

error

[Definition: A violation of the rules of this specification; results are undefined. Conforming software may detect and report an error and may recover from it.]

fatal error

[Definition: An error which a conforming XML processor must detect and report to the application. After encountering a fatal error, the processor may continue processing the data to search for further errors and may report such errors to the application. In order to support correction of errors, the processor may make unprocessed data from the document (with intermingled character data and markup) available to the application. Once a fatal error is detected, however, the processor must not continue normal processing (i.e., it must not continue to pass character data and information about the document's logical structure to the application in the normal way).]

at user option

[Definition: Conforming software may or must (depending on the modal verb in the sentence) behave as described; if it does, it must provide users a means to enable or disable the behavior described.]

validity constraint

[Definition: A rule which applies to all valid XML documents. Violations of validity constraints are errors; they must, at user option, be reported by validating XML processors.]

well-formedness constraint

[Definition: A rule which applies to all well-formed XML documents. Violations of well-formedness constraints are fatal errors.]

match

[Definition: (Of strings or names:) Two strings or names being compared must be identical. Characters with multiple possible representations in ISO/IEC 10646 (e.g. characters with both precomposed and base+diacritic forms) match only if they have the same representation in both strings. No case folding is performed. (Of strings and rules in the grammar:) A string matches a grammatical production if it belongs to the language generated by that production. (Of content and content models:) An element matches its declaration when it conforms in the fashion described in the constraint [VC: Element Valid].]

for compatibility

[Definition: Marks a sentence describing a feature of XML included solely to ensure that XML remains compatible with SGML.]

for interoperability

[Definition: Marks a sentence describing a non-binding recommendation included to increase the chances that XML documents can be processed by the existing installed base of SGML processors which predate the WebSGML Adaptations Annex to ISO 8879.]

2 Documents

[Definition: A data object is an **XML document** if it is well-formed, as defined in this specification. A well-formed XML document may in addition be valid if it meets certain further constraints.]

Each XML document has both a logical and a physical structure. Physically, the document is composed of units called entities. An entity may refer to other entities to cause their inclusion in the document. A document begins in a "root" or document entity. Logically, the document is composed of declarations, elements, comments, character references, and processing instructions, all of which are indicated in the document by explicit markup. The logical and physical structures must nest properly, as described in 4.3.2 Well-Formed Parsed Entities.

2.1 Well-Formed XML Documents

[Definition: A textual object is a **well-formed** XML document if:]

1. Taken as a whole, it matches the production labeled document.

2. It meets all the well-formedness constraints given in this specification.

3. Each of the parsed entities which is referenced directly or indirectly within the document is well-formed.

Document

```
[1] document ::= prolog element Misc*
```

Matching the document production implies that:

1. It contains one or more elements.

2. [Definition: There is exactly one element, called the **root**, or document element, no part of which appears in the content of any other element.] For all other elements, if the start-tag is in the content of another element, the end-tag is in the content of the same element. More simply stated, the elements, delimited by start- and end-tags, nest properly within each other.

[Definition: As a consequence of this, for each non-root element C in the document, there is one other element P in the document such that C is in the content of P, but is not in the content of any other element that is in the content of P. P is referred to as the **parent** of C, and C as a **child** of P.]

2.2 Characters

[Definition: A parsed entity contains **text**, a sequence of characters, which may represent markup or character data.] [Definition: A **character** is an atomic unit of text as specified by ISO/IEC 10646 [ISO/IEC 10646] (see also [ISO/IEC 10646-2000]). Legal characters are tab, carriage return, line feed, and the legal characters of Unicode and ISO/IEC 10646. The versions of these standards cited in A.1 Normative References were current at the time this document was prepared. New characters may be added to these standards by amendments or new editions. Consequently, XML processors must accept any character in the range specified for Char. The use of "compatibility characters", as defined in section 6.8 of [Unicode] (see also D21 in section 3.6 of [Unicode3]), is discouraged.]

Character Range

```
[2]  Char ::= #x9 | #xA | #xD | [#x20-#xD7FF]  /*   any Unicode character,
                  | [#xE000-#xFFFD]                   excluding the surrogate
                  | [#x10000-#x10FFFF]                blocks, FFFE, and FFFF. */
```

The mechanism for encoding character code points into bit patterns may vary from entity to entity. All XML processors must accept the UTF-8 and UTF-16 encodings of 10646; the mechanisms for signaling which of the two is in use, or for bringing other encodings into play, are discussed later, in 4.3.3 Character Encoding in Entities.

2.3 Common Syntactic Constructs

This section defines some symbols used widely in the grammar.

S (white space) consists of one or more space (#x20) characters, carriage returns, line feeds, or tabs.

White Space

```
[3]  S ::= (#x20 | #x9 | #xD | #xA)+
```

Characters are classified for convenience as letters, digits, or other characters. A letter consists of an alphabetic or syllabic base character or an ideographic character. Full definitions of the specific characters in each class are given in B Character Classes.

[Definition: A **Name** is a token beginning with a letter or one of a few punctuation characters, and continuing with letters, digits, hyphens, underscores, colons, or full stops, together known as name characters.] Names beginning with the string "xml", or any string which would match (('X' | 'x') ('M' | 'm') ('L' | 'l')), are reserved for standardization in this or future versions of this specification.

> **Note:**
> The Namespaces in XML Recommendation [XML Names] assigns a meaning to names containing colon characters. Therefore, authors should not use the colon in XML names except for namespace purposes, but XML processors must accept the colon as a name character.

An Nmtoken (name token) is any mixture of name characters.

Names and Tokens

```
[4] NameChar    ::=   Letter | Digit | '.' | '-' | '_' | ':' |
                      CombiningChar | Extender
[5] Name        ::=   (Letter | '_' | ':') (NameChar)*
[6] Names       ::=   Name (S Name)*
[7] Nmtoken     ::=   (NameChar)+
[8] Nmtokens    ::=   Nmtoken (S Nmtoken)*
```

Literal data is any quoted string not containing the quotation mark used as a delimiter for that string. Literals are used for specifying the content of internal entities (EntityValue), the values of attributes (AttValue), and external identifiers (SystemLiteral). Note that a SystemLiteral can be parsed without scanning for markup.

Literals

```
[9]  EntityValue    ::= '"' ([^%&"] | PEReference | Reference)* '"'
                      | "'" ([^%&'] | PEReference | Reference)* "'"
[10] AttValue       ::= '"' ([^<&"] | Reference)* '"'
                      | "'" ([^<&'] | Reference)* "'"
[11] SystemLiteral  ::= ('"' [^"]* '"') | ("'" [^']* "'")
[12] PubidLiteral   ::= '"' PubidChar* '"' | "'" (PubidChar - "'")* "'"
[13] PubidChar      ::= #x20 | #xD | #xA | [a-zA-Z0-9] |
                      [-'()+,./:=?;!*#@$_%]
```

Note:
Although the EntityValue production allows the definition of an entity consisting of a single explicit < in the literal (e.g., `<!ENTITY mylt "<">`), it is strongly advised to avoid this practice since any reference to that entity will cause a well-formedness error.

2.4 Character Data and Markup

Text consists of intermingled character data and markup. [Definition: **Markup** takes the form of start-tags, end-tags, empty-element tags, entity references, character references, comments, CDATA section delimiters, document type declarations, processing instructions, XML declarations, text declarations, and any white space that is at the top level of the document entity (that is, outside the document element and not inside any other markup).]

[Definition: All text that is not markup constitutes the **character data** of the document.]

The ampersand character (&) and the left angle bracket (<) may appear in their literal form only when used as markup delimiters, or within a comment, a processing instruction, or a CDATA section. If they are needed elsewhere, they must be escaped using either numeric character references or the strings "`&amp;`" and "`&lt;`" respectively. The right angle bracket (>) may be represented using the string "`&gt;`", and must, for compatibility, be escaped using "`&gt;`" or a character reference when it appears in the string "`]]>`" in content, when that string is not marking the end of a CDATA section.

In the content of elements, character data is any string of characters which does not contain the start-delimiter of any markup. In a CDATA section, character data is any string of characters not including the CDATA-section-close delimiter, "`]]>`".

To allow attribute values to contain both single and double quotes, the apostrophe or single-quote character (') may be represented as "`&apos;`", and the double-quote character (") as "`&quot;`".

Character Data

```
[14] CharData ::= [^<&]* - ([^<&]* ']]>' [^<&]*)
```

2.5 Comments

[Definition: **Comments** may appear anywhere in a document outside other markup; in addition, they may appear within the document type declaration at places allowed by the grammar. They are not part of the document's character data; an XML processor may, but need not, make it possible for an application to retrieve the text of comments. For compatibility, the string "`--`" (double-hyphen) must not occur within comments.] Parameter entity references are not recognized within comments.

Comments

[15] Comment   ::= '<!--' ((Char - '-') | ('-' (Char - '-')))* '-->'

An example of a comment:

```
<!-- declarations for <head> & <body> -->
```

Note that the grammar does not allow a comment ending in ```--->```. The following example is *not* well-formed.

```
<!-- B+, B, or B---->
```

2.6 Processing Instructions

[Definition: **Processing instructions** (PIs) allow documents to contain instructions for applications.]

Processing Instructions

```
[16] PI      ::=  '<?' PITarget (S (Char* - (Char* '?>' Char*)))? '?>'
[17] PITarget ::=  Name - (('X' | 'x') ('M' | 'm') ('L' | 'l'))
```

PIs are not part of the document's character data, but must be passed through to the application. The PI begins with a target (PITarget) used to identify the application to which the instruction is directed. The target names "XML", "xml", and so on are reserved for standardization in this or future versions of this specification. The XML Notation mechanism may be used for formal declaration of PI targets. Parameter entity references are not recognized within processing instructions.

2.7 CDATA Sections

[Definition: **CDATA sections** may occur anywhere character data may occur; they are used to escape blocks of text containing characters which would otherwise be recognized as markup. CDATA sections begin with the string "```<![CDATA[```" and end with the string "```]]>```":]

CDATA Sections

```
[18] CDSect  ::= CDStart CData CDEnd
[19] CDStart ::= '<![CDATA['
[20] CData   ::= (Char* - (Char* ']]>' Char*))
[21] CDEnd   ::= ']]>'
```

Within a CDATA section, only the CDEnd string is recognized as markup, so that left angle brackets and ampersands may occur in their literal form; they need not (and cannot) be escaped using "<" and "&". CDATA sections cannot nest.

An example of a CDATA section, in which "`<greeting>`" and "`</greeting>`" are recognized as character data, not markup:

```
<![CDATA[<greeting>Hello, world!</greeting>]]>
```

2.8 Prolog and Document Type Declaration

[Definition: XML documents should begin with an **XML declaration** which specifies the version of XML being used.] For example, the following is a complete XML document, well-formed but not valid:

```
<?xml version="1.0"?> <greeting>Hello, world!</greeting>
```

and so is this:

```
<greeting>Hello, world!</greeting>
```

The version number "`1.0`" should be used to indicate conformance to this version of this specification; it is an error for a document to use the value "`1.0`" if it does not conform to this version of this specification. It is the intent of the XML working group to give later versions of this specification numbers other than "`1.0`", but this intent does not indicate a commitment to produce any future versions of XML, nor if any are produced, to use any particular numbering scheme. Since future versions are not ruled out, this construct is provided as a means to allow the possibility of automatic version recognition, should it become necessary. Processors may signal an error if they receive documents labeled with versions they do not support.

The function of the markup in an XML document is to describe its storage and logical structure and to associate attribute-value pairs with its logical structures. XML provides a mechanism, the document type declaration, to define constraints on the logical structure and to support the use of predefined storage units. [Definition: An XML document is valid if it has an associated document type declaration and if the document complies with the constraints expressed in it.]

The document type declaration must appear before the first element in the document.

Prolog

```
[22] prolog       ::= XMLDecl? Misc* (doctypedecl Misc*)?
[23] XMLDecl      ::= '<?xml' VersionInfo EncodingDecl? SDDecl? S? '?>'
[24] VersionInfo  ::= S 'version' Eq ("'" VersionNum "'" | '"'
                      VersionNum '"')/* */
[25] Eq           ::= S? '=' S?
[26] VersionNum   ::= ([a-zA-Z0-9_.:] | '-')+
[27] Misc         ::= Comment | PI | S
```

[Definition: The XML **document type declaration** contains or points to markup declarations that provide a grammar for a class of documents. This grammar is known as a document type definition, or **DTD**. The document type declaration can point to an external subset (a special kind of external entity) containing markup declarations, or can contain the markup declarations directly in an internal subset, or can do both. The DTD for a document consists of both subsets taken together.]

[Definition: A **markup declaration** is an element type declaration, an attribute-list declaration, an entity declaration, or a notation declaration.] These declarations may be contained in whole or in part within parameter entities, as described in the well-formedness and validity constraints below. For further information, see **4 Physical Structures**.

Document Type Definition

[28] doctypedecl	::=	`'<!DOCTYPE' S Name`
		`(S ExternalID)? S?`
		`('[' (markupdecl | DeclSep)*`
		`']' S?)? '>'`
			[VC: Root Element Type]
			
			[WFC: External Subset]
			/ */*

[28a] DeclSep	::=	`PEReference	S`	[WFC: PE Between Declarations] */* */*
[29] markupdecl	::=	`elementdecl	AttlistDecl |` `EntityDecl	NotationDecl |` `PI	Comment`	[VC: Proper Declaration/PE Nesting] [WFC: PEs in Internal Subset]

Note that it is possible to construct a well-formed document containing a doctypedecl that neither points to an external subset nor contains an internal subset.

The markup declarations may be made up in whole or in part of the replacement text of parameter entities. The productions later in this specification for individual nonterminals (elementdecl, AttlistDecl, and so on) describe the declarations after all the parameter entities have been included.

Parameter entity references are recognized anywhere in the DTD (internal and external subsets and external parameter entities), except in literals, processing instructions, comments, and the contents of ignored conditional sections (see **3.4 Conditional Sections**). They are also recognized in entity value literals. The use of parameter entities in the internal subset is restricted as described below.

Validity constraint: Root Element Type

The Name in the document type declaration must match the element type of the root element.

Validity constraint: Proper Declaration/PE Nesting

Parameter-entity replacement text must be properly nested with markup declarations. That is to say, if either the first character or the last character of a markup declaration (markupdecl above) is contained in the replacement text for a parameter-entity reference, both must be contained in the same replacement text.

Well-formedness constraint: PEs in Internal Subset

In the internal DTD subset, parameter-entity references can occur only where markup declarations can occur, not within markup declarations. (This does not apply to references that occur in external parameter entities or to the external subset.)

Well-formedness constraint: External Subset

The external subset, if any, must match the production for extSubset.

Well-formedness constraint: PE Between Declarations

The replacement text of a parameter entity reference in a DeclSep must match the production extSubsetDecl.

Like the internal subset, the external subset and any external parameter entities referenced in a DeclSep must consist of a series of complete markup declarations of the types allowed by the non-terminal symbol markupdecl, interspersed with white space or parameter-entity references. However, portions of the contents of the external subset or of these external parameter entities may conditionally be ignored by using the conditional section construct; this is not allowed in the internal subset.

External Subset

```
[30]  extSubset       ::=   TextDecl? extSubsetDecl
[31]  extSubsetDecl   ::=   ( markupdecl | conditionalSect | DeclSep)*  /* */
```

The external subset and external parameter entities also differ from the internal subset in that in them, parameter-entity references are permitted *within* markup declarations, not only *between* markup declarations.

An example of an XML document with a document type declaration:

```
<?xml version="1.0"?> <!DOCTYPE greeting SYSTEM "hello.dtd"> <greeting>Hello,
➥ world!</greeting>
```

The system identifier "`hello.dtd`" gives the address (a URI reference) of a DTD for the document.

The declarations can also be given locally, as in this example:

```
<?xml version="1.0" encoding="UTF-8" ?>
<!DOCTYPE greeting [
  <!ELEMENT greeting (#PCDATA)>
]>
<greeting>Hello, world!</greeting>
```

If both the external and internal subsets are used, the internal subset is considered to occur before the external subset. This has the effect that entity and attribute-list declarations in the internal subset take precedence over those in the external subset.

2.9 Standalone Document Declaration

Markup declarations can affect the content of the document, as passed from an XML processor to an application; examples are attribute defaults and entity declarations. The standalone document declaration, which may appear as a component of the XML declaration, signals whether or not there are such declarations which appear external to the document entity or in parameter entities. [Definition: An **external markup declaration** is defined as a markup declaration occurring in the external subset or in a parameter entity (external or internal, the latter being included because non-validating processors are not required to read them).]

Standalone Document Declaration

```
[32] SDDecl    ::= S 'standalone' Eq (("'" ('yes' |    [VC: Standalone
                   'no') "'") | ('"'                    Document
                   ('yes' | 'no') '"'))                 Declaration]
```

In a standalone document declaration, the value "yes" indicates that there are no external markup declarations which affect the information passed from the XML processor to the application. The value "no" indicates that there are or may be such external markup declarations. Note that the standalone document declaration only denotes the presence of external *declarations*; the presence, in a document, of references to external *entities*, when those entities are internally declared, does not change its standalone status.

If there are no external markup declarations, the standalone document declaration has no meaning. If there are external markup declarations but there is no standalone document declaration, the value "no" is assumed.

Any XML document for which `standalone="no"` holds can be converted algorithmically to a standalone document, which may be desirable for some network delivery applications.

Validity constraint: Standalone Document Declaration

The standalone document declaration must have the value "no" if any external markup declarations contain declarations of:

- attributes with default values, if elements to which these attributes apply appear in the document without specifications of values for these attributes, or
- entities (other than `amp`, `lt`, `gt`, `apos`, `quot`), if references to those entities appear in the document, or
- attributes with values subject to *normalization*, where the attribute appears in the document with a value which will change as a result of normalization, or
- element types with element content, if white space occurs directly within any instance of those types.

An example XML declaration with a standalone document declaration:

```
<?xml version="1.0" standalone='yes'?>
```

2.10 White Space Handling

In editing XML documents, it is often convenient to use "white space" (spaces, tabs, and blank lines) to set apart the markup for greater readability. Such white space is typically not intended for inclusion in the delivered version of the document. On the other hand, "significant" white space that should be preserved in the delivered version is common, for example in poetry and source code.

An XML processor must always pass all characters in a document that are not markup through to the application. A validating XML processor must also inform the application which of these characters constitute white space appearing in element content.

A special attribute named `xml:space` may be attached to an element to signal an intention that in that element, white space should be preserved by applications. In valid documents, this attribute, like any other, must be declared if it is used. When declared, it must be given as an enumerated type whose values are one or both of "default" and "preserve". For example:

```
<!ATTLIST poem  xml:space (default|preserve) 'preserve'>

<!-- -->
<!ATTLIST pre xml:space (preserve) #FIXED 'preserve'>
```

The value "default" signals that applications' default white-space processing modes are acceptable for this element; the value "preserve" indicates the intent that applications preserve all the white space. This declared intent is considered to apply to all elements within the content of the element where it is specified, unless overriden with another instance of the xml:space attribute.

The root element of any document is considered to have signaled no intentions as regards application space handling, unless it provides a value for this attribute or the attribute is declared with a default value.

2.11 End-of-Line Handling

XML parsed entities are often stored in computer files which, for editing convenience, are organized into lines. These lines are typically separated by some combination of the characters carriage-return (#xD) and line-feed (#xA).

To simplify the tasks of applications, the characters passed to an application by the XML processor must be as if the XML processor normalized all line breaks in external parsed entities (including the document entity) on input, before parsing, by translating both the two-character sequence #xD #xA and any #xD that is not followed by #xA to a single #xA character.

2.12 Language Identification

In document processing, it is often useful to identify the natural or formal language in which the content is written. A special attribute named xml:lang may be inserted in documents to specify the language used in the contents and attribute values of any element in an XML document. In valid documents, this attribute, like any other, must be declared if it is used. The values of the attribute are language identifiers as defined by [IETF RFC 1766], *Tags for the Identification of Languages*, or its successor on the IETF Standards Track.

> **Note:**
> [IETF RFC 1766] tags are constructed from two-letter language codes as defined by [ISO 639], from two-letter country codes as defined by [ISO 3166], or from language identifiers registered with the Internet Assigned Numbers Authority [IANA-LANGCODES]. It is expected that the successor to [IETF RFC 1766] will introduce three-letter language codes for languages not presently covered by [ISO 639].

(Productions 33 through 38 have been removed.)

For example:

```
<p xml:lang="en">The quick brown fox jumps over the lazy dog.</p>
<p xml:lang="en-GB">What colour is it?</p>
<p xml:lang="en-US">What color is it?</p>
<sp who="Faust" desc='leise' xml:lang="de">
  <l>Habe nun, ach! Philosophie,</l>
  <l>Juristerei, und Medizin</l>
  <l>und leider auch Theologie</l>
  <l>durchaus studiert mit heißem Bemüh'n.</l>
</sp>
```

The intent declared with xml:lang is considered to apply to all attributes and content of the element where it is specified, unless overridden with an instance of xml:lang on another element within that content.

A simple declaration for xml:lang might take the form

```
xml:lang NMTOKEN #IMPLIED
```

but specific default values may also be given, if appropriate. In a collection of French poems for English students, with glosses and notes in English, the xml:lang attribute might be declared this way:

```
<!ATTLIST poem   xml:lang NMTOKEN 'fr'>
<!ATTLIST gloss  xml:lang NMTOKEN 'en'>
<!ATTLIST note   xml:lang NMTOKEN 'en'>
```

3 Logical Structures

[Definition: Each XML document contains one or more **elements**, the boundaries of which are either delimited by start-tags and end-tags, or, for empty elements, by an empty-element tag. Each element has a type, identified by name, sometimes called its "generic identifier" (GI), and may have a set of attribute specifications.] Each attribute specification has a name and a value.

Element

```
[39] element  ::= EmptyElemTag
                | STag content ETag      [WFC: Element Type Match]
                                         [VC: Element Valid]
```

This specification does not constrain the semantics, use, or (beyond syntax) names of the element types and attributes, except that names beginning with a match to `(('X'|'x')('M'|'m')('L'|'l'))` are reserved for standardization in this or future versions of this specification.

> **Well-formedness constraint: Element Type Match**
>
> The Name in an element's end-tag must match the element type in the start-tag.

> **Validity constraint: Element Valid**
>
> An element is valid if there is a declaration matching elementdecl where the Name matches the element type, and one of the following holds:

1. The declaration matches **EMPTY** and the element has no content.

2. The declaration matches children and the sequence of child elements belongs to the language generated by the regular expression in the content model, with optional white space (characters matching the nonterminal S) between the start-tag and the first child element, between child elements, or between the last child element and the end-tag. Note that a CDATA section containing only white space does not match the nonterminal S, and hence cannot appear in these positions.

3. The declaration matches Mixed and the content consists of character data and child elements whose types match names in the content model.

4. The declaration matches **ANY**, and the types of any child elements have been declared.

3.1 Start-Tags, End-Tags, and Empty-Element Tags

[Definition: The beginning of every non-empty XML element is marked by a **start-tag**.]

Start-tag

```
[40] STag       ::= '<' Name (S Attribute)      [WFC: Unique Att Spec]
                    * S? '>'
[41] Attribute  ::= Name Eq AttValue            [VC: Attribute Value Type]
                                                [WFC: No External Entity
                                                References]
                                                [WFC: No < in Attribute
                                                Values]
```

The Name in the start- and end-tags gives the element's **type**. [Definition: The Name-AttValue pairs are referred to as the **attribute specifications** of the element], [Definition: with the Name in each pair referred to as the **attribute name**] and [Definition: the content of the AttValue (the text between the ' or " delimiters) as the **attribute value**.] Note that the order of attribute specifications in a start-tag or empty-element tag is not significant.

Well-formedness constraint: Unique Att Spec

No attribute name may appear more than once in the same start-tag or empty-element tag.

Validity constraint: Attribute Value Type

The attribute must have been declared; the value must be of the type declared for it. (For attribute types, see 3.3 Attribute-List Declarations.)

Well-formedness constraint: No External Entity References

Attribute values cannot contain direct or indirect entity references to external entities.

Well-formedness constraint: No < in Attribute Values

The replacement text of any entity referred to directly or indirectly in an attribute value must not contain a <.

An example of a start-tag:

```
<termdef id="dt-dog" term="dog">
```

[Definition: The end of every element that begins with a start-tag must be marked by an **end-tag** containing a name that echoes the element's type as given in the start-tag:]

End-tag

```
[42]    ETag    ::=    '</' Name S? '>'
```

An example of an end-tag:

```
</termdef>
```

[Definition: The text between the start-tag and end-tag is called the element's **content**:]

Content of Elements

```
[43] content  ::= CharData? ((element | Reference | CDSect | PI | Comment) /* */
                   CharData?)
```

[Definition: An element with no content is said to be **empty**.] The representation of an empty element is either a start-tag immediately followed by an end-tag, or an empty-element tag. [Definition: An **empty-element tag** takes a special form:]

Tags for Empty Elements

[44] `EmptyElemTag  ::= '<' Name (S Attribute)* S? '/>'   [WFC: Unique Att Spec]`

Empty-element tags may be used for any element which has no content, whether or not it is declared using the keyword **EMPTY**. For interoperability, the empty-element tag should be used, and should only be used, for elements which are declared EMPTY.

Examples of empty elements:

```
<IMG align="left"
 src="http://www.w3.org/Icons/WWW/w3c_home" />
<br></br>
<br/>
```

3.2 Element Type Declarations

The element structure of an XML document may, for validation purposes, be constrained using element type and attribute-list declarations. An element type declaration constrains the element's content.

Element type declarations often constrain which element types can appear as children of the element. At user option, an XML processor may issue a warning when a declaration mentions an element type for which no declaration is provided, but this is not an error.

[Definition: An **element type declaration** takes the form:]

Element Type Declaration

```
[45] elementdecl ::= '<!ELEMENT' S Name S        [VC: Unique Element
                     contentspec S? '>'           Type Declaration]
[46] contentspec ::= 'EMPTY' | 'ANY' | Mixed |
                     children
```

where the Name gives the element type being declared.

Validity constraint: Unique Element Type Declaration

No element type may be declared more than once.

Examples of element type declarations:

```
<!ELEMENT br EMPTY>
<!ELEMENT p (#PCDATA|emph)* >
<!ELEMENT %name.para; %content.para; >
<!ELEMENT container ANY>
```

3.2.1 Element Content

[Definition: An element type has **element content** when elements of that type must contain only child elements (no character data), optionally separated by white space (characters matching the nonterminal S).][Definition: In this case, the constraint includes a **content model**, a simple grammar governing the allowed types of the child elements and the order in which they are allowed to appear.] The grammar is built on content particles (cps), which consist of names, choice lists of content particles, or sequence lists of content particles:

Element-content Models

```
[47] children  ::= (choice | seq) ('?' | '*' | '+')?
[48] cp         ::= (Name | choice | seq) ('?' | '*' | '+')?
[49] choice     ::= '(' S? cp ( S? '|' S? cp )+ S? ')'    /* */
                                                          /* */
                                                          [VC: Proper
                                                          Group/PE Nesting]
[50] seq        ::= '(' S? cp ( S? ',' S? cp )* S? ')'    /* */
                                                          [VC: Proper
                                                          Group/PE Nesting]
```

where each Name is the type of an element which may appear as a child. Any content particle in a choice list may appear in the element content at the location where the choice list appears in the grammar; content particles occurring in a sequence list must each appear in the element content in the order given in the list. The optional character following a name or list governs whether the element or the content particles in the list may occur one or more (+), zero or more (*), or zero or one times (?). The absence of such an operator means that the element or content particle must appear exactly once. This syntax and meaning are identical to those used in the productions in this specification.

The content of an element matches a content model if and only if it is possible to trace out a path through the content model, obeying the sequence, choice, and repetition operators and matching each element in the content against an element type in the content model. For compatibility, it is an error if an element in the document can match more than one occurrence of an element type in the content model. For more information, see **E Deterministic Content Models**.

Validity constraint: Proper Group/PE Nesting

Parameter-entity replacement text must be properly nested with parenthesized groups. That is to say, if either of the opening or closing parentheses in a choice, seq, or Mixed construct is contained in the replacement text for a parameter entity, both must be contained in the same replacement text.

For interoperability, if a parameter-entity reference appears in a choice, seq, or Mixed construct, its replacement text should contain at least one non-blank character, and neither the first nor last non-blank character of the replacement text should be a connector (| or ,).

Examples of element-content models:

```
<!ELEMENT spec (front, body, back?)>
<!ELEMENT div1 (head, (p | list | note)*, div2*)>
<!ELEMENT dictionary-body (%div.mix; | %dict.mix;)*>
```

3.2.2 Mixed Content

[Definition: An element type has **mixed content** when elements of that type may contain character data, optionally interspersed with child elements.] In this case, the types of the child elements may be constrained, but not their order or their number of occurrences:

Mixed-content Declaration

```
[51] Mixed    ::= '(' S? '#PCDATA' (S? '|' S? Name)
                * S? ')*'
                | '(' S? '#PCDATA' S? ')'       [VC: Proper Group/PE
                                                 Nesting]
                                                 [VC: No Duplicate
                                                 Types]
```

where the Names give the types of elements that may appear as children. The keyword **#PCDATA** derives historically from the term "parsed character data."

Validity constraint: No Duplicate Types

The same name must not appear more than once in a single mixed-content declaration.

Examples of mixed content declarations:

```
<!ELEMENT p (#PCDATA|a|ul|b|i|em)*>
<!ELEMENT p (#PCDATA | %font; | %phrase; | %special; | %form;)* >
<!ELEMENT b (#PCDATA)>
```

3.3 Attribute-List Declarations

Attributes are used to associate name-value pairs with elements. Attribute specifications may appear only within start-tags and empty-element tags; thus, the productions used to recognize them appear in 3**.1 Start-Tags, End-Tags, and Empty-Element Tags**. Attribute-list declarations may be used:

- To define the set of attributes pertaining to a given element type.
- To establish type constraints for these attributes.
- To provide default values for attributes.

[Definition: **Attribute-list declarations** specify the name, data type, and default value (if any) of each attribute associated with a given element type:]

Attribute-list Declaration

```
[52] AttlistDecl      ::= '<!ATTLIST' S Name AttDef* S? '>'
[53] AttDef           ::= S Name S AttType S DefaultDecl
```

The Name in the AttlistDecl rule is the type of an element. At user option, an XML processor may issue a warning if attributes are declared for an element type not itself declared, but this is not an error. The Name in the AttDef rule is the name of the attribute.

When more than one AttlistDecl is provided for a given element type, the contents of all those provided are merged. When more than one definition is provided for the same attribute of a given element type, the first declaration is binding and later declarations are ignored. For inter-operability, writers of DTDs may choose to provide at most one attribute-list declaration for a given element type, at most one attribute definition for a given attribute name in an attribute-list declaration, and at least one attribute definition in each attribute-list declaration. For inter-operability, an XML processor may at user option issue a warning when more than one attribute-list declaration is provided for a given element type, or more than one attribute definition is provided for a given attribute, but this is not an error.

3.3.1 Attribute Types

XML attribute types are of three kinds: a string type, a set of tokenized types, and enumerated types. The string type may take any literal string as a value; the tokenized types have varying lexical and semantic constraints. The validity constraints noted in the grammar are applied after the attribute value has been normalized as described in **3.3 Attribute-List Declarations**.

Attribute Types

```
[54] AttType          ::= StringType | TokenizedType |
                          EnumeratedType
[55] StringType       ::= 'CDATA'
[56] TokenizedType    ::= 'ID'                          [VC: ID]
                                                        [VC: One ID per
                                                        Element Type]
                                                        [VC: ID Attribute
                                                        Default]
                        | 'IDREF'                       [VC: IDREF]
                        | 'IDREFS'                      [VC: IDREF]
                        | 'ENTITY'                      [VC: Entity Name]
                        | 'ENTITIES'                    [VC: Entity Name]
                        | 'NMTOKEN'                     [VC: Name Token]
                        | 'NMTOKENS'                    [VC: Name Token]
```

Validity constraint: ID

Values of type **ID** must match the Name production. A name must not appear more than once in an XML document as a value of this type; i.e., ID values must uniquely identify the elements which bear them.

Validity constraint: One ID per Element Type

No element type may have more than one ID attribute specified.

Validity constraint: ID Attribute Default

An ID attribute must have a declared default of **#IMPLIED** or **#REQUIRED**.

Validity constraint: IDREF

Values of type **IDREF** must match the Name production, and values of type **IDREFS** must match Names; each Name must match the value of an ID attribute on some element in the XML document; i.e. **IDREF** values must match the value of some ID attribute.

Validity constraint: Entity Name

Values of type **ENTITY** must match the Name production, values of type **ENTITIES** must match Names; each Name must match the name of an unparsed entity declared in the DTD.

Validity constraint: Name Token

Values of type **NMTOKEN** must match the Nmtoken production; values of type **NMTOKENS** must match Nmtokens.

[Definition: **Enumerated attributes** can take one of a list of values provided in the declaration]. There are two kinds of enumerated types:

Enumerated Attribute Types

```
[57] EnumeratedType   ::= NotationType | Enumeration
[58] NotationType     ::= 'NOTATION' S '(' S? Name     [VC: Notation
                          (S? '|' S? Name)* S? ')'        Attributes]
                                                       [VC: One Notation
                                                        Per Element Type]
                                                       [VC: No Notation
                                                        on Empty Element]
[59] Enumeration      ::= '(' S? Nmtoken (S? '|'       [VC: Enumeration]
                          S? Nmtoken)* S? ')'
```

A **NOTATION** attribute identifies a notation, declared in the DTD with associated system and/or public identifiers, to be used in interpreting the element to which the attribute is attached.

Validity constraint: Notation Attributes

Values of this type must match one of the *notation* names included in the declaration; all notation names in the declaration must be declared.

Validity constraint: One Notation Per Element Type

No element type may have more than one **NOTATION** attribute specified.

Validity constraint: No Notation on Empty Element

For compatibility, an attribute of type **NOTATION** must not be declared on an element declared **EMPTY**.

Validity constraint: Enumeration

Values of this type must match one of the Nmtoken tokens in the declaration.

For interoperability, the same Nmtoken should not occur more than once in the enumerated attribute types of a single element type.

3.3.2 Attribute Defaults

An attribute declaration provides information on whether the attribute's presence is required, and if not, how an XML processor should react if a declared attribute is absent in a document.

Attribute Defaults

```
[60] DefaultDecl  ::= '#REQUIRED' | '#IMPLIED'
                      | (('#FIXED' S)? AttValue)        [VC: Required Attribute]
                                                        [VC: Attribute Default Legal]
                                                        [WFC: No < in Attribute
                                                         Values]
                                                        [VC: Fixed Attribute
                                                         Default]
```

In an attribute declaration, **#REQUIRED** means that the attribute must always be provided, **#IMPLIED** that no default value is provided. [Definition: If the declaration is neither **#REQUIRED** nor **#IMPLIED**, then the AttValue value contains the declared **default** value; the **#FIXED** keyword states that the attribute must always have the default value. If a default value is declared, when an XML processor encounters an omitted attribute, it is to behave as though the attribute were present with the declared default value.]

Validity constraint: Required Attribute

If the default declaration is the keyword **#REQUIRED**, then the attribute must be specified for all elements of the type in the attribute-list declaration.

Validity constraint: Attribute Default Legal

The declared default value must meet the lexical constraints of the declared attribute type.

Validity constraint: Fixed Attribute Default

If an attribute has a default value declared with the **#FIXED** keyword, instances of that attribute must match the default value.

Examples of attribute-list declarations:

```
<!ATTLIST termdef
          id       ID       #REQUIRED
          name     CDATA    #IMPLIED>
<!ATTLIST list
          type     (bullets|ordered|glossary)   "ordered">
<!ATTLIST form
          method   CDATA    #FIXED "POST">
```

3.3.3 Attribute-Value Normalization

Before the value of an attribute is passed to the application or checked for validity, the XML processor must normalize the attribute value by applying the algorithm below, or by using some other method such that the value passed to the application is the same as that produced by the algorithm.

1. All line breaks must have been normalized on input to #xA as described in **2.11 End-of-Line Handling**, so the rest of this algorithm operates on text normalized in this way.

2. Begin with a normalized value consisting of the empty string.

3. For each character, entity reference, or character reference in the unnormalized attribute value, beginning with the first and continuing to the last, do the following:

- For a character reference, append the referenced character to the normalized value.

- For an entity reference, recursively apply step 3 of this algorithm to the replacement text of the entity.

- For a white space character (#x20, #xD, #xA, #x9), append a space character (#x20) to the normalized value.

- For another character, append the character to the normalized value.

If the attribute type is not CDATA, then the XML processor must further process the normalized attribute value by discarding any leading and trailing space (#x20) characters, and by replacing sequences of space (#x20) characters by a single space (#x20) character.

Note that if the unnormalized attribute value contains a character reference to a white space character other than space (#x20), the normalized value contains the referenced character itself (#xD, #xA or #x9). This contrasts with the case where the unnormalized value contains a white space character (not a reference), which is replaced with a space character (#x20) in the normalized value and also contrasts with the case where the unnormalized value contains an entity reference whose replacement text contains a white space character; being recursively processed, the white space character is replaced with a space character (#x20) in the normalized value.

All attributes for which no declaration has been read should be treated by a non-validating processor as if declared **CDATA**.

Following are examples of attribute normalization. Given the following declarations:

```
<!ENTITY d  "&#xD;">
<!ENTITY a  "&#xA;">
<!ENTITY da "&#xD;&#xA;">
```

the attribute specifications in the left column below would be normalized to the character sequences of the middle column if the attribute a is declared **NMTOKENS** and to those of the right columns if a is declared **CDATA**.

Attribute specification	a is NMTOKENS	a is CDATA
a="		
xyz"	x y z	#x20 #x20 x y z
a="&d;&d;A&a;&a;B&da;"	A #x20 B	#x20 #x20 A #x20 #x20 B #x20 #x20
a=		
"A

B
"	#xD #xD A #xA #xA B #xD #xA	#xD #xD A #xA #xA B #xD #xD

Note that the last example is invalid (but well-formed) if a is declared to be of type **NMTOKENS**.

3.4 Conditional Sections

[Definition: **Conditional sections** are portions of the document type declaration external subset which are included in, or excluded from, the logical structure of the DTD based on the keyword which governs them.]

Conditional Section

```
[61] conditionalSect   ::= includeSect | ignoreSect
[62] includeSect       ::= '<![' S? 'INCLUDE' S? '['         /* */
                           extSubsetDecl ']]>'               [VC: Proper
                                                             Conditional
                                                             Section/PE
                                                             Nesting]

[63] ignoreSect        ::= '<![' S? 'IGNORE' S? '['          /* */
                           ignoreSectContents* ']]>'         [VC: Proper
                                                             Conditional
                                                             Section/PE
                                                             Nesting]

[64] ignoreSectContents ::= Ignore ('<!['
                            ignoreSectContents ']]>' Ignore)*
[65] Ignore            ::= Char* - (Char* ('<![' | ']]>') Char*)
```

Validity constraint: Proper Conditional Section/PE Nesting

If any of the "<![", "[," or "]]>" of a conditional section is contained in the replacement text for a parameter-entity reference, all of them must be contained in the same replacement text.

Like the internal and external DTD subsets, a conditional section may contain one or more complete declarations, comments, processing instructions, or nested conditional sections, intermingled with white space.

If the keyword of the conditional section is **INCLUDE**, then the contents of the conditional section are part of the DTD. If the keyword of the conditional section is **IGNORE**, then the contents of the conditional section are not logically part of the DTD. If a conditional section with a keyword of **INCLUDE** occurs within a larger conditional section with a keyword of **IGNORE**, both the outer and the inner conditional sections are ignored. The contents of an ignored conditional section are parsed by ignoring all characters after the "[" following the keyword, except conditional section starts "<![" and ends "]]>", until the matching conditional section end is found. Parameter entity references are not recognized in this process.

If the keyword of the conditional section is a parameter-entity reference, the parameter entity must be replaced by its content before the processor decides whether to include or ignore the conditional section.

An example:

```
<!ENTITY % draft 'INCLUDE' >
<!ENTITY % final 'IGNORE' >
<![%draft;[
<!ELEMENT book (comments*, title, body, supplements?)>
]]>
<![%final;[
<!ELEMENT book (title, body, supplements?)>
]]>
```

4 Physical Structures

[Definition: An XML document may consist of one or many storage units. These are called **entities**; they all have **content** and are all (except for the document entity and the external DTD subset) identified by entity **name**.] Each XML document has one entity called the document entity, which serves as the starting point for the XML processor and may contain the whole document.

Entities may be either parsed or unparsed. [Definition: A **parsed entity's** contents are referred to as its replacement text; this text is considered an integral part of the document.]

[Definition: An **unparsed entity** is a resource whose contents may or may not be text, and if text, may be other than XML. Each unparsed entity has an associated notation, identified by name. Beyond a requirement that an XML processor make the identifiers for the entity and notation available to the application, XML places no constraints on the contents of unparsed entities.]

Parsed entities are invoked by name using entity references; unparsed entities by name, given in the value of **ENTITY** or **ENTITIES** attributes.

[Definition: **General entities** are entities for use within the document content. In this specification, general entities are sometimes referred to with the unqualified term entity when this leads to no ambiguity.] [Definition: **Parameter entities** are parsed entities for use within the DTD.] These two types of entities use different forms of reference and are recognized in different contexts. Furthermore, they occupy different namespaces; a parameter entity and a general entity with the same name are two distinct entities.

4.1 Character and Entity References

[Definition: A character reference refers to a specific character in the ISO/IEC 10646 character set, for example one not directly accessible from available input devices.]

Character Reference

```
[66] CharRef    ::=    '&#' [0-9]+ ';'
                    |  '&#x' [0-9a-fA-F]+ ';'        [WFC: Legal Character]
```

Well-formedness constraint: Legal Character

Characters referred to using character references must match the production for Char.

If the character reference begins with "&#x", the digits and letters up to the terminating ; provide a hexadecimal representation of the character's code point in ISO/IEC 10646. If it begins just with "&#", the digits up to the terminating ; provide a decimal representation of the character's code point.

[Definition: An **entity reference** refers to the content of a named entity.] [Definition: References to parsed general entities use ampersand (&) and semicolon (;) as delimiters.] [Definition: **Parameter-entity references** use percent-sign (%) and semicolon (;) as delimiters.]

Entity Reference

```
[67] Reference      ::= EntityRef | CharRef
[68] EntityRef      ::= '&' Name ';'        [WFC: Entity Declared]
                                            [VC: Entity Declared]
                                            [WFC: Parsed Entity]
                                            [WFC: No Recursion]
[69] PEReference    ::= '%' Name ';'        [VC: Entity Declared]
                                            [WFC: No Recursion]
                                            [WFC: In DTD]
```

Well-formedness constraint: Entity Declared

In a document without any DTD, a document with only an internal DTD subset which contains no parameter entity references, or a document with "standalone='yes'", for an entity reference that does not occur within the external subset or a parameter entity, the Name given in the entity reference must match that in an entity declaration that does not occur within the external subset or a parameter entity, except that well-formed documents need not declare any of the following entities: amp, lt, gt, apos, quot. The declaration of a general entity must precede any reference to it which appears in a default value in an attribute-list declaration.

Note that if entities are declared in the external subset or in external parameter entities, a non-validating processor is not obligated to read and process their declarations; for such documents, the rule that an entity must be declared is a well-formedness constraint only if standalone='yes'.

Validity constraint: Entity Declared

In a document with an external subset or external parameter entities with "standalone='no'", the Name given in the entity reference must match that in an entity declaration. For interoperability, valid documents should declare the entities amp, lt, gt, apos, quot, in the form specified in 4.6 Predefined Entities. The declaration of a parameter entity must precede any reference to it. Similarly, the declaration of a general entity must precede any attribute-list declaration containing a default value with a direct or indirect reference to that general entity.

Well-formedness constraint: Parsed Entity

An entity reference must not contain the name of an unparsed entity. Unparsed entities may be referred to only in attribute values declared to be of type **ENTITY** or **ENTITIES**.

Well-formedness constraint: No Recursion

A parsed entity must not contain a recursive reference to itself, either directly or indirectly.

Well-formedness constraint: In DTD

Parameter-entity references may only appear in the DTD.

Examples of character and entity references:

```
Type <key>less-than</key> (&#x3C;) to save options.
This document was prepared on &docdate; and
is classified &security-level;.
```

Example of a parameter-entity reference:

```
<!-- declare the parameter entity "ISOLat2"... -->
<!ENTITY % ISOLat2
```

```
            SYSTEM "http://www.xml. com/iso/isolat2-xml.entities" >
<!-- ... now reference it. -->
%ISOLat2;
```

4.2 Entity Declarations

[Definition: Entities are declared thus:]

Entity Declaration

```
[70] EntityDecl   ::= GEDecl | PEDecl
[71] GEDecl       ::= '<!ENTITY' S Name S EntityDef S? '>'
[72] PEDecl       ::= '<!ENTITY' S '%' S Name S PEDef S? '>'
[73] EntityDef    ::= EntityValue | (ExternalID NDataDecl?)
[74] PEDef        ::= EntityValue | ExternalID
```

The Name identifies the entity in an entity reference or, in the case of an unparsed entity, in the value of an ENTITY or ENTITIES attribute. If the same entity is declared more than once, the first declaration encountered is binding; at user option, an XML processor may issue a warning if entities are declared multiple times.

4.2.1 Internal Entities

[Definition: If the entity definition is an EntityValue, the defined entity is called an **internal entity**. There is no separate physical storage object, and the content of the entity is given in the declaration.] Note that some processing of entity and character references in the literal entity value may be required to produce the correct replacement text: see **4.5 Construction of Internal Entity Replacement Text**.

An internal entity is a parsed entity.

Example of an internal entity declaration:

```
<!ENTITY Pub-Status "This is a pre-release of the
specification.">
```

4.2.2 External Entities

[Definition: If the entity is not internal, it is an **external entity**, declared as follows:]

External Entity Declaration

```
[75] ExternalID   ::= 'SYSTEM' S SystemLiteral
                    | 'PUBLIC' S PubidLiteral S SystemLiteral
[76] NDataDecl    ::= S 'NDATA' S Name                [VC: Notation Declared]
```

If the NDataDecl is present, this is a general unparsed entity; otherwise it is a parsed entity.

Validity constraint: Notation Declared

The Name must match the declared name of a notation.

[Definition: The SystemLiteral is called the entity's **system identifier**. It is a URI reference (as defined in [IETF RFC 2396], updated by [IETF RFC 2732]), meant to be dereferenced to obtain input for the XML processor to construct the entity's replacement text.] It is an error for a fragment identifier (beginning with a # character) to be part of a system identifier. Unless otherwise provided by information outside the scope of this specification (e.g. a special XML element type defined by a particular DTD, or a processing instruction defined by a particular application specification), relative URIs are relative to the location of the resource within which the entity declaration occurs. A URI might thus be relative to the document entity, to the entity containing the external DTD subset, or to some other external parameter entity.

URI references require encoding and escaping of certain characters. The disallowed characters include all non-ASCII characters, plus the excluded characters listed in Section 2.4 of [IETF RFC 2396], except for the number sign (#) and percent sign (%) characters and the square bracket characters re-allowed in [IETF RFC 2732]. Disallowed characters must be escaped as follows:

1. Each disallowed character is converted to UTF-8 [IETF RFC 2279] as one or more bytes.

2. Any octets corresponding to a disallowed character are escaped with the URI escaping mechanism (that is, converted to %*HH*, where HH is the hexadecimal notation of the byte value).

3. The original character is replaced by the resulting character sequence.

[Definition: In addition to a system identifier, an external identifier may include a **public identifier**.] An XML processor attempting to retrieve the entity's content may use the public identifier to try to generate an alternative URI reference. If the processor is unable to do so, it must use the URI reference specified in the system literal. Before a match is attempted, all strings of white space in the public identifier must be normalized to single space characters (#x20), and leading and trailing white space must be removed.

Examples of external entity declarations:

```
<!ENTITY  open-hatch
          SYSTEM "http://www.textuality.com/boilerplate/OpenHatch.xml">
<!ENTITY  open-hatch
          PUBLIC "-//Textuality//TEXT Standard open-hatch boilerplate//EN"
          "http://www.textuality.com/boilerplate/OpenHatch.xml">
<!ENTITY  hatch-pic
          SYSTEM "../grafix/OpenHatch.gif"
          NDATA gif >
```

4.3 Parsed Entities

4.3.1 The Text Declaration

External parsed entities should each begin with a **text declaration**.

Text Declaration

[77] TextDecl   ::= '<?xml' VersionInfo? EncodingDecl S? '?>'

The text declaration must be provided literally, not by reference to a parsed entity. No text declaration may appear at any position other than the beginning of an external parsed entity. The text declaration in an external parsed entity is not considered part of its replacement text.

4.3.2 Well-Formed Parsed Entities

The document entity is well-formed if it matches the production labeled document. An external general parsed entity is well-formed if it matches the production labeled extParsedEnt. All external parameter entities are well-formed by definition.

Well-Formed External Parsed Entity

[78] extParsedEnt ::= TextDecl? content

An internal general parsed entity is well-formed if its replacement text matches the production labeled content. All internal parameter entities are well-formed by definition.

A consequence of well-formedness in entities is that the logical and physical structures in an XML document are properly nested; no start-tag, end-tag, empty-element tag, element, comment, processing instruction, character reference, or entity reference can begin in one entity and end in another.

4.3.3 Character Encoding in Entities

Each external parsed entity in an XML document may use a different encoding for its characters. All XML processors must be able to read entities in both the UTF-8 and UTF-16 encodings. The terms "UTF-8" and "UTF-16" in this specification do not apply to character encodings with any other labels, even if the encodings or labels are very similar to UTF-8 or UTF-16.

Entities encoded in UTF-16 must begin with the Byte Order Mark described by Annex F of [ISO/IEC 10646], Annex H of [ISO/IEC 10646-2000], section 2.4 of [Unicode], and section 2.7 of [Unicode3] (the ZERO WIDTH NO-BREAK SPACE character, #xFEFF). This is an encoding signature, not part of either the markup or the character data of the XML document. XML processors must be able to use this character to differentiate between UTF-8 and UTF-16 encoded documents.

Although an XML processor is required to read only entities in the UTF-8 and UTF-16 encodings, it is recognized that other encodings are used around the world, and it may be desired for XML processors to read entities that use them. In the absence of external character encoding information (such as MIME headers), parsed entities which are stored in an encoding other than UTF-8 or UTF-16 must begin with a text declaration (see **4.3.1 The Text Declaration**) containing an encoding declaration:

Encoding Declaration

```
[80]  EncodingDecl  ::=  S 'encoding' Eq ('"'
                         EncName '"' | "'" EncName "'" )
[81]  EncName       ::=  [A-Za-z] ([A-Za-z0-9._] |  '-')  * /* Encoding name
                                                            contains only Latin
                                                            characters */
```

In the document entity, the encoding declaration is part of the XML declaration. The EncName is the name of the encoding used.

In an encoding declaration, the values "UTF-8", "UTF-16", "ISO-10646-UCS-2", and "ISO-10646-UCS-4" should be used for the various encodings and transformations of Unicode / ISO/IEC 10646, the values "ISO-8859-1", "ISO-8859-2", ... "ISO-8859-*n*" (where n is the part number) should be used for the parts of ISO 8859, and the values "ISO-2022-JP", "Shift_JIS", and "EUC-JP" should be used for the various encoded forms of JIS X-0208-1997. It is recommended that character encodings registered (as *charsets*) with the Internet Assigned Numbers Authority [IANA-CHARSETS], other than those just listed, be referred to using their registered names; other encodings should use names starting with an "x-" prefix. XML processors should match character encoding names in a case-insensitive way and should either interpret an IANA-registered name as the encoding registered at IANA for that name or treat it as unknown (processors are, of course, not required to support all IANA-registered encodings).

In the absence of information provided by an external transport protocol (e.g. HTTP or MIME), it is an error for an entity including an encoding declaration to be presented to the XML processor in an encoding other than that named in the declaration, or for an entity which begins with neither a Byte Order Mark nor an encoding declaration to use an encoding other than UTF-8. Note that since ASCII is a subset of UTF-8, ordinary ASCII entities do not strictly need an encoding declaration.

It is a fatal error for a TextDecl to occur other than at the beginning of an external entity.

It is a fatal error when an XML processor encounters an entity with an encoding that it is unable to process. It is a fatal error if an XML entity is determined (via default, encoding declaration, or higher-level protocol) to be in a certain encoding but contains octet sequences that are not legal in that encoding. It is also a fatal error if an XML entity contains no encoding declaration and its content is not legal UTF-8 or UTF-16.

Examples of text declarations containing encoding declarations:

```
<?xml encoding='UTF-8'?>
<?xml encoding='EUC-JP'?>
```

4.4 XML Processor Treatment of Entities and References

The table below summarizes the contexts in which character references, entity references, and invocations of unparsed entities might appear and the required behavior of an XML processor in each case. The labels in the leftmost column describe the recognition context:

Reference in Content

as a reference anywhere after the start-tag and before the end-tag of an element; corresponds to the nonterminal content.

Reference in Attribute Value

as a reference within either the value of an attribute in a start-tag, or a default value in an attribute declaration; corresponds to the nonterminal AttValue.

Occurs as Attribute Value

as a Name, not a reference, appearing either as the value of an attribute which has been declared as type **ENTITY**, or as one of the space-separated tokens in the value of an attribute which has been declared as type **ENTITIES.**

Reference in Entity Value

as a reference within a parameter or internal entity's literal entity value in the entity's declaration; corresponds to the nonterminal EntityValue.

Reference in DTD

as a reference within either the internal or external subsets of the DTD, but outside of an EntityValue, AttValue, PI, Comment, SystemLiteral, PubidLiteral, or the contents of an ignored conditional section (see **3.4 Conditional Sections**).

	Entity Type				
	Parameter	**Internal General**	**External Parsed General**	**Unparsed**	**Character**
Reference in Content	*Not recognized*	*Included*	*Included if validating*	*Forbidden*	*Included*
Reference in Attribute Value	*Not recognized*	*Included in literal*	*Forbidden*	*Forbidden*	*Included*
Occurs as Attribute Value	*Not recognized*	*Forbidden*	*Forbidden*	*Notify*	*Not recognized*
Reference in EntityValue	*Included in literal*	*Bypassed*	*Bypassed*	*Forbidden*	*Included*
Reference in DTD	*Included as PE*	*Forbidden*	*Forbidden*	*Forbidden*	*Forbidden*

4.4.1 Not Recognized

Outside the DTD, the % character has no special significance; thus, what would be parameter entity references in the DTD are not recognized as markup in content. Similarly, the names of unparsed entities are not recognized except when they appear in the value of an appropriately declared attribute.

4.4.2 Included

[Definition: An entity is **included** when its replacement text is retrieved and processed, in place of the reference itself, as though it were part of the document at the location the reference was recognized.] The replacement text may contain both character data and (except for parameter entities) markup, which must be recognized in the usual way. (The string "AT&T;" expands to "AT&T;" and the remaining ampersand is not recognized as an entity-reference delimiter.) A character reference is **included** when the indicated character is processed in place of the reference itself.

4.4.3 Included If Validating

When an XML processor recognizes a reference to a parsed entity, in order to validate the document, the processor must include its replacement text. If the entity is external, and the processor is not attempting to validate the XML document, the processor may, but need not, include the entity's replacement text. If a non-validating processor does not include the replacement text, it must inform the application that it recognized, but did not read, the entity.

This rule is based on the recognition that the automatic inclusion provided by the SGML and XML entity mechanism, primarily designed to support modularity in authoring, is not necessarily appropriate for other applications, in particular document browsing. Browsers, for example, when encountering an external parsed entity reference, might choose to provide a visual indication of the entity's presence and retrieve it for display only on demand.

4.4.4 Forbidden

The following are forbidden, and constitute fatal errors:

- the appearance of a reference to an unparsed entity.
- the appearance of any character or general-entity reference in the DTD except within an EntityValue or AttValue.
- a reference to an external entity in an attribute value.

4.4.5 Included in Literal

When an entity reference appears in an attribute value, or a parameter entity reference appears in a literal entity value, its replacement text is processed in place of the reference itself as though it were part of the document at the location the reference was recognized, except that a single or double quote character in the replacement text is always treated as a normal data character and will not terminate the literal. For example, this is well-formed:

```
<!-- -->
<!ENTITY % YN '"Yes"' >
<!ENTITY WhatHeSaid "He said %YN;" >
```

while this is not:

```
<!ENTITY EndAttr "27'" >
<element attribute='a-&EndAttr;'>
```

4.4.6 Notify

When the name of an unparsed entity appears as a token in the value of an attribute of declared type **ENTITY** or **ENTITIES**, a validating processor must inform the application of the system and public (if any) identifiers for both the entity and its associated notation.

4.4.7 Bypassed

When a general entity reference appears in the EntityValue in an entity declaration, it is bypassed and left as is.

4.4.8 Included as PE

Just as with external parsed entities, parameter entities need only be *included if validating*. When a parameter-entity reference is recognized in the DTD and included, its replacement text is enlarged by the attachment of one leading and one following space (#x20) character; the intent is to constrain the replacement text of parameter entities to contain an integral number of grammatical tokens in the DTD. This behavior does not apply to parameter entity references within entity values; these are described in **4.4.5 Included in Literal**.

4.5 Construction of Internal Entity Replacement Text

In discussing the treatment of internal entities, it is useful to distinguish two forms of the entity's value. [Definition: The **literal entity value** is the quoted string actually present in the entity declaration, corresponding to the non-terminal EntityValue.] [Definition: The **replacement text** is the content of the entity, after replacement of character references and parameter-entity references.]

The literal entity value as given in an internal entity declaration (EntityValue) may contain character, parameter-entity, and general-entity references. Such references must be contained entirely within the literal entity value. The actual replacement text that is included as described above must contain the *replacement text* of any parameter entities referred to, and must contain the character referred to, in place of any character references in the literal entity value; however, general-entity references must be left as-is, unexpanded. For example, given the following declarations:

```
<!ENTITY % pub    "&#xc9;ditions Gallimard" >
<!ENTITY    rights "All rights reserved" >
<!ENTITY    book   "La Peste: Albert Camus,
&#xA9; 1947 %pub;. &rights;" >
```

then the replacement text for the entity "book" is:

```
La Peste: Albert Camus,
© 1947 Éditions Gallimard. &rights;
```

The general-entity reference "&rights;" would be expanded should the reference "&book;" appear in the document's content or an attribute value.

These simple rules may have complex interactions; for a detailed discussion of a difficult example, see **D Expansion of Entity and Character References**.

4.6 Predefined Entities

[Definition: Entity and character references can both be used to **escape** the left angle bracket, ampersand, and other delimiters. A set of general entities (amp, lt, gt, apos, quot) is specified for this purpose. Numeric character references may also be used; they are expanded immediately when recognized and must be treated as character data, so the numeric character references "<" and "&" may be used to escape < and & when they occur in character data.]

All XML processors must recognize these entities whether they are declared or not. For interoperability, valid XML documents should declare these entities, like any others, before using them. If the entities lt or amp are declared, they must be declared as internal entities whose replacement text is a character reference to the respective character (less-than sign or ampersand) being escaped; the double escaping is required for these entities so that references to them produce a well-formed result. If the entities gt, apos, or quot are declared, they must be declared as internal entities whose replacement text is the single character being escaped (or a character reference to that character; the double escaping here is unnecessary but harmless). For example:

```
<!ENTITY lt      "&#38;#60;">
<!ENTITY gt      "&#62;">
<!ENTITY amp     "&#38;#38;">
<!ENTITY apos    "&#39;">
<!ENTITY quot    "&#34;">
```

4.7 Notation Declarations

[Definition: **Notations** identify by name the format of unparsed entities, the format of elements which bear a notation attribute, or the application to which a processing instruction is addressed.]

[Definition: **Notation declarations** provide a name for the notation, for use in entity and attribute-list declarations and in attribute specifications, and an external identifier for the notation which may allow an XML processor or its client application to locate a helper application capable of processing data in the given notation.]

Notation Declarations

```
[82] NotationDecl  ::= '<!NOTATION' S Name S          [VC: Unique
                       (ExternalID | PublicID) S? '>'  Notation Name]
[83] PublicID      ::= 'PUBLIC' S PubidLiteral
```

> **Validity constraint: Unique Notation Name**
>
> Only one notation declaration can declare a given Name.

XML processors must provide applications with the name and external identifier(s) of any notation declared and referred to in an attribute value, attribute definition, or entity declaration. They may additionally resolve the external identifier into the system identifier, file name, or other information needed to allow the application to call a processor for data in the notation described. (It is not an error, however, for XML documents to declare and refer to notations for which notation-specific applications are not available on the system where the XML processor or application is running.)

4.8 Document Entity

[Definition: The **document entity** serves as the root of the entity tree and a starting-point for an XML processor.] This specification does not specify how the document entity is to be located by an XML processor; unlike other entities, the document entity has no name and might well appear on a processor input stream without any identification at all.

5 Conformance

5.1 Validating and Non-Validating Processors

Conforming XML processors fall into two classes: validating and non-validating.

Validating and non-validating processors alike must report violations of this specification's well-formedness constraints in the content of the document entity and any other parsed entities that they read.

[Definition: **Validating processors** must, at user option, report violations of the constraints expressed by the declarations in the DTD, and failures to fulfill the validity constraints given in this specification.] To accomplish this, validating XML processors must read and process the entire DTD and all external parsed entities referenced in the document.

Non-validating processors are required to check only the document entity, including the entire internal DTD subset, for well-formedness. [Definition: While they are not required to check the document for validity, they are required to **process** all the declarations they read in the internal DTD subset and in any parameter entity that they read, up to the first reference to a parameter entity that they do not read; that is to say, they must use the information in those declarations to *normalize* attribute values, *include* the replacement text of internal entities, and supply *default attribute values*.] Except when standalone="yes", they must not process entity declarations or attribute-list declarations encountered after a reference to a parameter entity that is not read, since the entity may have contained overriding declarations.

5.2 Using XML Processors

The behavior of a validating XML processor is highly predictable; it must read every piece of a document and report all well-formedness and validity violations. Less is required of a non-validating processor; it need not read any part of the document other than the document entity. This has two effects that may be important to users of XML processors:

- Certain well-formedness errors, specifically those that require reading external entities, may not be detected by a non-validating processor. Examples include the constraints entitled *Entity Declared*, *Parsed Entity*, and *No Recursion*, as well as some of the cases described as *forbidden* in **4.4 XML Processor Treatment of Entities and References**.

- The information passed from the processor to the application may vary, depending on whether the processor reads parameter and external entities. For example, a non-validating processor may not *normalize* attribute values, *include* the replacement text of internal entities, or supply *default attribute values*, where doing so depends on having read declarations in external or parameter entities.

For maximum reliability in interoperating between different XML processors, applications which use non-validating processors should not rely on any behaviors not required of such processors. Applications which require facilities such as the use of default attributes or internal entities which are declared in external entities should use validating XML processors.

6 Notation

The formal grammar of XML is given in this specification using a simple Extended Backus-Naur Form (EBNF) notation. Each rule in the grammar defines one symbol, in the form

```
symbol ::= expression
```

Symbols are written with an initial capital letter if they are the start symbol of a regular language, otherwise with an initial lower case letter. Literal strings are quoted.

Within the expression on the right-hand side of a rule, the following expressions are used to match strings of one or more characters:

#xN

where N is a hexadecimal integer, the expression matches the character in ISO/IEC 10646 whose canonical (UCS-4) code value, when interpreted as an unsigned binary number, has the value indicated. The number of leading zeros in the #xN form is insignificant; the number of leading zeros in the corresponding code value is governed by the character encoding in use and is not significant for XML.

[a-zA-Z], [#xN-#xN]

matches any Char with a value in the range(s) indicated (inclusive).

[abc], [#xN#xN#xN]

matches any Char with a value among the characters enumerated. Enumerations and ranges can be mixed in one set of brackets.

[^a-z], [^#xN-#xN]

matches any Char with a value *outside* the range indicated.

[^abc], [^#xN#xN#xN]

matches any Char with a value not among the characters given. Enumerations and ranges of forbidden values can be mixed in one set of brackets.

"string"

matches a literal string matching that given inside the double quotes.

'string'

matches a literal string matching that given inside the single quotes.

These symbols may be combined to match more complex patterns as follows, where A and B represent simple expressions:

(expression)

`expression` is treated as a unit and may be combined as described in this list.

A?

matches A or nothing; optional A.

A B

matches A followed by B. This operator has higher precedence than alternation; thus A B | C D is identical to (A B) | (C D).

A | B

matches A or B but not both.

A - B

matches any string that matches A but does not match B.

A+

matches one or more occurrences of A. Concatenation has higher precedence than alternation; thus A+ | B+ is identical to (A+) | (B+).

A*

matches zero or more occurrences of A. Concatenation has higher precedence than alternation; thus A* | B* is identical to (A*) | (B*).

Other notations used in the productions are:

`/* ... */`

comment.

[wfc: ...]

well-formedness constraint; this identifies by name a constraint on well-formed documents associated with a production.

[vc: ...]

validity constraint; this identifies by name a constraint on valid documents associated with a production.

A References

A.1 Normative References

IANA-CHARSETS

(Internet Assigned Numbers Authority) *Official Names for Character Sets*, ed. Keld Simonsen et al. See ftp://ftp.isi.edu/in-notes/iana/assignments/character-sets.

IETF RFC 1766

IETF (Internet Engineering Task Force). *RFC 1766: Tags for the Identification of Languages*, ed. H. Alvestrand. 1995. (See http://www.ietf.org/rfc/rfc1766.txt.)

ISO/IEC 10646

ISO (International Organization for Standardization). ISO/IEC 10646-1993 (E). Information technology — Universal Multiple-Octet Coded Character Set (UCS) — Part 1: Architecture and Basic Multilingual Plane. [Geneva]: International Organization for Standardization, 1993 (plus amendments AM 1 through AM 7).

ISO/IEC 10646-2000

ISO (International Organization for Standardization). ISO/IEC 10646-1:2000. *Information technology — Universal Multiple-Octet Coded Character Set (UCS) — Part 1: Architecture and Basic Multilingual Plane.* [Geneva]: International Organization for Standardization, 2000.

Unicode

The Unicode Consortium. *The Unicode Standard, Version 2.0.* Reading, Mass.: Addison-Wesley Developers Press, 1996.

Unicode3

The Unicode Consortium. *The Unicode Standard, Version 3.0.* Reading, Mass.: Addison-Wesley Developers Press, 2000. ISBN 0-201-61633-5.

A.2 Other References

Aho/Ullman

Aho, Alfred V., Ravi Sethi, and Jeffrey D. Ullman. *Compilers: Principles, Techniques, and Tools.* Reading: Addison-Wesley, 1986, rpt. corr. 1988.

Berners-Lee et al.

Berners-Lee, T., R. Fielding, and L. Masinter. *Uniform Resource Identifiers (URI): Generic Syntax and Semantics.* 1997. (Work in progress; see updates to RFC1738.)

Brüggemann-Klein

Brüggemann-Klein, Anne. Formal Models in Document Processing. Habilitationsschrift. Faculty of Mathematics at the University of Freiburg, 1993. (See ftp://ftp.informatik.uni-freiburg.de/documents/papers/brueggem/habil.ps.)

Brüggemann-Klein and Wood

Brüggemann-Klein, Anne, and Derick Wood. Deterministic Regular Languages. Universität Freiburg, Institut für Informatik, Bericht 38, Oktober 1991. Extended abstract in A. Finkel, M. Jantzen, Hrsg., STACS 1992, S. 173-184. Springer-Verlag, Berlin 1992. Lecture Notes in Computer Science 577. Full version titled *One-Unambiguous Regular Languages* in Information and Computation 140 (2): 229-253, February 1998.

Clark

James Clark. Comparison of SGML and XML. See http://www.w3.org/TR/NOTE-sgml-xml-971215.

IANA-LANGCODES

(Internet Assigned Numbers Authority) Registry of Language Tags, ed. Keld Simonsen et al. (See http://www.isi.edu/in-notes/iana/assignments/languages/.)

IETF RFC2141

IETF (Internet Engineering Task Force). *RFC 2141: URN Syntax*, ed. R. Moats. 1997. (See http://www.ietf.org/rfc/rfc2141.txt.)

IETF RFC 2279

IETF (Internet Engineering Task Force). *RFC 2279: UTF-8, a transformation format of ISO 10646*, ed. F. Yergeau, 1998. (See http://www.ietf.org/rfc/rfc2279.txt.)

IETF RFC 2376

IETF (Internet Engineering Task Force). *RFC 2376: XML Media Types*. ed. E. Whitehead, M. Murata. 1998. (See http://www.ietf.org/rfc/rfc2376.txt.)

IETF RFC 2396

IETF (Internet Engineering Task Force). *RFC 2396: Uniform Resource Identifiers (URI):Generic Syntax*. T. Berners-Lee, R. Fielding, L. Masinter. 1998. (See http://www.ietf.org/rfc/rfc2396.txt.)

IETF RFC 2732

IETF (Internet Engineering Task Force). *RFC 2732: Format for Literal IPv6 Addresses in URL's*. R. Hinden, B. Carpenter, L. Masinter. 1999. (See http://www.ietf.org/rfc/rfc2732.txt.)

IETF RFC 2781

IETF (Internet Engineering Task Force). *RFC 2781: UTF-16, an encoding of ISO 10646*, ed. P. Hoffman, F. Yergeau. 2000. (See http://www.ietf.org/rfc/rfc2781.txt.)

ISO 639

(International Organization for Standardization). *ISO 639:1988 (E). Code for the representation of names of languages*. [Geneva]: International Organization for Standardization, 1988.

ISO 3166

(International Organization for Standardization). *ISO 3166-1:1997 (E). Codes for the representation of names of countries and their subdivisions — Part 1*: Country codes [Geneva]: International Organization for Standardization, 1997.

ISO 8879

ISO (International Organization for Standardization). *ISO 8879:1986(E). Information processing — Text and Office Systems — Standard Generalized Markup Language (SGML)*. First edition — 1986-10-15. [Geneva]: International Organization for Standardization, 1986.

ISO/IEC 10744

ISO (International Organization for Standardization). *ISO/IEC 10744-1992 (E). Information technology — Hypermedia/Time-based Structuring Language (HyTime)*. [Geneva]: International Organization for Standardization, 1992. Extended Facilities Annexe. [Geneva]: International Organization for Standardization, 1996.

WEBSGML

ISO (International Organization for Standardization). *ISO 8879:1986 TC2. Information technology — Document Description and Processing Languages*. [Geneva]: International Organization for Standardization, 1998. (See http://www.sgmlsource.com/8879rev/n0029.htm.)

XML Names

Tim Bray, Dave Hollander, and Andrew Layman, editors. *Namespaces in XML*. Textuality, Hewlett-Packard, and Microsoft. World Wide Web Consortium, 1999. (See http://www.w3.org/TR/REC-xml-names/.)

B Character Classes

Following the characteristics defined in the Unicode standard, characters are classed as base characters (among others, these contain the alphabetic characters of the Latin alphabet), ideographic characters, and combining characters (among others, this class contains most diacritics) Digits and extenders are also distinguished.

Characters

```
[84] Letter    ::= BaseChar | Ideographic
[85] BaseChar  ::= [#x0041-#x005A] | [#x0061-#x007A] | [#x00C0-#x00D6]
                 | [#x00D8-#x00F6] | [#x00F8-#x00FF] | [#x0100-#x0131]
                 | [#x0134-#x013E] | [#x0141-#x0148] | [#x014A-#x017E]
                 | [#x0180-#x01C3] | [#x01CD-#x01F0] | [#x01F4-#x01F5]
                 | [#x01FA-#x0217] | [#x0250-#x02A8] | [#x02BB-#x02C1]
                 | #x0386 | [#x0388-#x038A] | #x038C | [#x038E-#x03A1]
                 | [#x03A3-#x03CE] | [#x03D0-#x03D6] | #x03DA | #x03DC
                 | #x03DE | #x03E0 | [#x03E2-#x03F3] | [#x0401-#x040C]
                 | [#x040E-#x044F] | [#x0451-#x045C] | [#x045E-#x0481]
```

```
| [#x0490-#x04C4] | [#x04C7-#x04C8] | [#x04CB-#x04CC]
| [#x04D0-#x04EB] | [#x04EE-#x04F5] | [#x04F8-#x04F9]
| [#x0531-#x0556] | #x0559 | [#x0561-#x0586]
| [#x05D0-#x05EA] | [#x05F0-#x05F2] | [#x0621-#x063A]
| [#x0641-#x064A] | [#x0671-#x06B7] | [#x06BA-#x06BE]
| [#x06C0-#x06CE] | [#x06D0-#x06D3] | #x06D5
| [#x06E5-#x06E6] | [#x0905-#x0939] | #x093D
| [#x0958-#x0961] | [#x0985-#x098C] | [#x098F-#x0990]
| [#x0993-#x09A8] | [#x09AA-#x09B0] | #x09B2
| [#x09B6-#x09B9] | [#x09DC-#x09DD] | [#x09DF-#x09E1]
| [#x09F0-#x09F1] | [#x0A05-#x0A0A] | [#x0A0F-#x0A10]
| [#x0A13-#x0A28] | [#x0A2A-#x0A30] | [#x0A32-#x0A33]
| [#x0A35-#x0A36] | [#x0A38-#x0A39] | [#x0A59-#x0A5C]
| #x0A5E | [#x0A72-#x0A74] | [#x0A85-#x0A8B] | #x0A8D
| [#x0A8F-#x0A91] | [#x0A93-#x0AA8] | [#x0AAA-#x0AB0]
| [#x0AB2-#x0AB3] | [#x0AB5-#x0AB9] | #x0ABD | #x0AE0
| [#x0B05-#x0B0C] | [#x0B0F-#x0B10] | [#x0B13-#x0B28]
| [#x0B2A-#x0B30] | [#x0B32-#x0B33] | [#x0B36-#x0B39]
| #x0B3D | [#x0B5C-#x0B5D] | [#x0B5F-#x0B61]
| [#x0B85-#x0B8A] | [#x0B8E-#x0B90] | [#x0B92-#x0B95]
| [#x0B99-#x0B9A] | #x0B9C | [#x0B9E-#x0B9F]
| [#x0BA3-#x0BA4] | [#x0BA8-#x0BAA] | [#x0BAE-#x0BB5]
| [#x0BB7-#x0BB9] | [#x0C05-#x0C0C] | [#x0C0E-#x0C10]
| [#x0C12-#x0C28] | [#x0C2A-#x0C33] | [#x0C35-#x0C39]
| [#x0C60-#x0C61] | [#x0C85-#x0C8C] | [#x0C8E-#x0C90]
| [#x0C92-#x0CA8] | [#x0CAA-#x0CB3] | [#x0CB5-#x0CB9]
| #x0CDE | [#x0CE0-#x0CE1] | [#x0D05-#x0D0C]
| [#x0D0E-#x0D10] | [#x0D12-#x0D28] | [#x0D2A-#x0D39]
| [#x0D60-#x0D61] | [#x0E01-#x0E2E] | #x0E30
| [#x0E32-#x0E33] | [#x0E40-#x0E45] | [#x0E81-#x0E82]
| #x0E84 | [#x0E87-#x0E88] | #x0E8A | #x0E8D
| [#x0E94-#x0E97] | [#x0E99-#x0E9F] | [#x0EA1-#x0EA3]
| #x0EA5 | #x0EA7 | [#x0EAA-#x0EAB] | [#x0EAD-#x0EAE]
| #x0EB0 | [#x0EB2-#x0EB3] | #x0EBD | [#x0EC0-#x0EC4]
| [#x0F40-#x0F47] | [#x0F49-#x0F69] | [#x10A0-#x10C5]
| [#x10D0-#x10F6] | #x1100 | [#x1102-#x1103]
| [#x1105-#x1107] | #x1109 | [#x110B-#x110C]
| [#x110E-#x1112] | #x113C | #x113E | #x1140 | #x114C
| #x114E | #x1150 | [#x1154-#x1155] | #x1159
| [#x115F-#x1161] | #x1163 | #x1165 | #x1167
| #x1169 | [#x116D-#x116E] | [#x1172-#x1173] | #x1175
| #x119E | #x11A8 | #x11AB | [#x11AE-#x11AF]
| [#x11B7-#x11B8] | #x11BA | [#x11BC-#x11C2] | #x11EB
| #x11F0 | #x11F9 | [#x1E00-#x1E9B] | [#x1EA0-#x1EF9]
| [#x1F00-#x1F15] | [#x1F18-#x1F1D] | [#x1F20-#x1F45]
| [#x1F48-#x1F4D] | [#x1F50-#x1F57] | #x1F59 | #x1F5B
| #x1F5D | [#x1F5F-#x1F7D] | [#x1F80-#x1FB4]
| [#x1FB6-#x1FBC] | #x1FBE | [#x1FC2-#x1FC4]
| [#x1FC6-#x1FCC] | [#x1FD0-#x1FD3] | [#x1FD6-#x1FDB]
| [#x1FE0-#x1FEC] | [#x1FF2-#x1FF4] | [#x1FF6-#x1FFC]
| #x2126 | [#x212A-#x212B] | #x212E | [#x2180-#x2182]
| [#x3041-#x3094] | [#x30A1-#x30FA] | [#x3105-#x312C]
| [#xAC00-#xD7A3]
```

```
[86] Ideographic    ::= [#x4E00-#x9FA5] | #x3007 | [#x3021-#x3029]
[87] CombiningChar   ::= [#x0300-#x0345] | [#x0360-#x0361] | [#x0483-#x0486]
                       | [#x0591-#x05A1] | [#x05A3-#x05B9] | [#x05BB-#x05BD]
                       | #x05BF | [#x05C1-#x05C2] | #x05C4 | [#x064B-#x0652]
                       | #x0670 | [#x06D6-#x06DC] | [#x06DD-#x06DF]
                       | [#x06E0-#x06E4] | [#x06E7-#x06E8] | [#x06EA-#x06ED]
                       | [#x0901-#x0903] | #x093C | [#x093E-#x094C]
                       | #x094D | [#x0951-#x0954] | [#x0962-#x0963]
                       | [#x0981-#x0983] | #x09BC | #x09BE | #x09BF
                       | [#x09C0-#x09C4] | [#x09C7-#x09C8] | [#x09CB-#x09CD]
                       | #x09D7 | [#x09E2-#x09E3] | #x0A02 | #x0A3C
                       | #x0A3E | #x0A3F | [#x0A40-#x0A42] | [#x0A47-#x0A48]
                       | [#x0A4B-#x0A4D] | [#x0A70-#x0A71] | [#x0A81-#x0A83]
                       | #x0ABC | [#x0ABE-#x0AC5] | [#x0AC7-#x0AC9]
                       | [#x0ACB-#x0ACD] | [#x0B01-#x0B03] | #x0B3C
                       | [#x0B3E-#x0B43] | [#x0B47-#x0B48] | [#x0B4B-#x0B4D]
                       | [#x0B56-#x0B57] | [#x0B82-#x0B83] | [#x0BBE-#x0BC2]
                       | [#x0BC6-#x0BC8] | [#x0BCA-#x0BCD] | #x0BD7
                       | [#x0C01-#x0C03] | [#x0C3E-#x0C44] | [#x0C46-#x0C48]
                       | [#x0C4A-#x0C4D] | [#x0C55-#x0C56] | [#x0C82-#x0C83]
                       | [#x0CBE-#x0CC4] | [#x0CC6-#x0CC8] | [#x0CCA-#x0CCD]
                       | [#x0CD5-#x0CD6] | [#x0D02-#x0D03] | [#x0D3E-#x0D43]
                       | [#x0D46-#x0D48] | [#x0D4A-#x0D4D] | #x0D57
                       | #x0E31 | [#x0E34-#x0E3A] | [#x0E47-#x0E4E]
                       | #x0EB1 | [#x0EB4-#x0EB9] | [#x0EBB-#x0EBC]
                       | [#x0EC8-#x0ECD] | [#x0F18-#x0F19] | #x0F35
                       | #x0F37 | #x0F39 | #x0F3E | #x0F3F | [#x0F71-#x0F84]
                       | [#x0F86-#x0F8B] | [#x0F90-#x0F95] | #x0F97
                       | [#x0F99-#x0FAD] | [#x0FB1-#x0FB7] | #x0FB9
                       | [#x20D0-#x20DC] | #x20E1 | [#x302A-#x302F]
                       | #x3099 | #x309A
[88] Digit           ::= [#x0030-#x0039] | [#x0660-#x0669] | [#x06F0-#x06F9]
                       | [#x0966-#x096F] | [#x09E6-#x09EF] | [#x0A66-#x0A6F]
                       | [#x0AE6-#x0AEF] | [#x0B66-#x0B6F] | [#x0BE7-#x0BEF]
                       | [#x0C66-#x0C6F] | [#x0CE6-#x0CEF] | [#x0D66-#x0D6F]
                       | [#x0E50-#x0E59] | [#x0ED0-#x0ED9] | [#x0F20-#x0F29]
[89] Extender        ::= #x00B7 | #x02D0 | #x02D1 | #x0387 | #x0640 | #x0E46
                       | #x0EC6 | #x3005 | [#x3031-#x3035] | [#x309D-#x309E]
                       | [#x30FC-#x30FE]
```

The character classes defined here can be derived from the Unicode 2.0 character database as follows:

- Name start characters must have one of the categories Ll, Lu, Lo, Lt, Nl.

- Name characters other than Name-start characters must have one of the categories Mc, Me, Mn, Lm, or Nd.

- Characters in the compatibility area (i.e. with character code greater than #xF900 and less than #xFFFE) are not allowed in XML names.

- Characters which have a font or compatibility decomposition (i.e. those with a "compatibility formatting tag" in field 5 of the database -- marked by field 5 beginning with a "<") are not allowed.

- The following characters are treated as name-start characters rather than name characters, because the property file classifies them as Alphabetic: [#x02BB-#x02C1], #x0559, #x06E5, #x06E6.

- Characters #x20DD-#x20E0 are excluded (in accordance with Unicode 2.0, section 5.14).

- Character #x00B7 is classified as an extender, because the property list so identifies it.

- Character #x0387 is added as a name character, because #x00B7 is its canonical equivalent.

- Characters ':' and '_' are allowed as name-start characters.

- Characters '-' and '.' are allowed as name characters.

C XML and SGML (Non-Normative)

XML is designed to be a subset of SGML, in that every XML document should also be a conforming SGML document. For a detailed comparison of the additional restrictions that XML places on documents beyond those of SGML, see [Clark].

D Expansion of Entity and Character References (Non-Normative)

This appendix contains some examples illustrating the sequence of entity- and character-reference recognition and expansion, as specified in **4.4 XML Processor Treatment of Entities and References**.

If the DTD contains the declaration

```
<!ENTITY example "<p>An ampersand (&#38;#38;) may be escaped
numerically (&#38;#38;#38;) or with a general entity
(&amp;amp;).</p>" >
```

then the XML processor will recognize the character references when it parses the entity declaration, and resolve them before storing the following string as the value of the entity "`example`":

```
<p>An ampersand (&#38;) may be escaped
numerically (&#38;#38;) or with a general entity
(&amp;amp;).</p>
```

A reference in the document to "`&example;`" will cause the text to be reparsed, at which time the start- and end-tags of the p element will be recognized and the three references will be recognized and expanded, resulting in a p element with the following content (all data, no delimiters or markup):

```
An ampersand (&) may be escaped
numerically (&#38;) or with a general entity
(&amp;).
```

A more complex example will illustrate the rules and their effects fully. In the following example, the line numbers are solely for reference.

```
1 <?xml version='1.0'?>
2 <!DOCTYPE test [
3 <!ELEMENT test (#PCDATA) >
4 <!ENTITY % xx '&#37;zz;'>
5 <!ENTITY % zz '&#60;!ENTITY tricky "error-prone" >' >
6 %xx;
7 ]>
8 <test>This sample shows a &tricky; method.</test>
```

This produces the following:

- in line 4, the reference to character 37 is expanded immediately, and the parameter entity "xx" is stored in the symbol table with the value "%zz;". Since the replacement text is not rescanned, the reference to parameter entity "zz" is not recognized. (And it would be an error if it were, since "zz" is not yet declared.)

- in line 5, the character reference "<" is expanded immediately and the parameter entity "zz" is stored with the replacement text "<!ENTITY tricky "error-prone" >", which is a well-formed entity declaration.

- in line 6, the reference to "xx" is recognized, and the replacement text of "xx" (namely "%zz;") is parsed. The reference to "zz" is recognized in its turn, and its replacement text ("<!ENTITY tricky "error-prone" >") is parsed. The general entity "tricky" has now been declared, with the replacement text "error-prone".

- in line 8, the reference to the general entity "tricky" is recognized, and it is expanded, so the full content of the test element is the self-describing (and ungrammatical) string *This sample shows a error-prone method.*

E Deterministic Content Models (Non-Normative)

As noted in **3.2.1 Element Content**, it is required that content models in element type declarations be deterministic. This requirement is for compatibility with SGML (which calls deterministic content models "unambiguous"); XML processors built using SGML systems may flag non-deterministic content models as errors.

For example, the content model ((b, c) | (b, d)) is non-deterministic, because given an initial b the XML processor cannot know which b in the model is being matched without looking ahead to see which element follows the b. In this case, the two references to b can be collapsed into a single reference, making the model read (b, (c | d)). An initial b now clearly matches only a single name in the content model. The processor doesn't need to look ahead to see what follows; either c or d would be accepted.

More formally: a finite state automaton may be constructed from the content model using the standard algorithms, e.g. algorithm 3.5 in section 3.9 of Aho, Sethi, and Ullman [Aho/Ullman]. In many such algorithms, a follow set is constructed for each position in the regular expression (i.e., each leaf node in the syntax tree for the regular expression); if any position has a follow set in which more than one following position is labeled with the same element type name, then the content model is in error and may be reported as an error.

Algorithms exist which allow many but not all non-deterministic content models to be reduced automatically to equivalent deterministic models; see Brüggemann-Klein 1991 [Brüggemann-Klein].

F Autodetection of Character Encodings (Non-Normative)

The XML encoding declaration functions as an internal label on each entity, indicating which character encoding is in use. Before an XML processor can read the internal label, however, it apparently has to know what character encoding is in use—which is what the internal label is trying to indicate. In the general case, this is a hopeless situation. It is not entirely hopeless in XML, however, because XML limits the general case in two ways: each implementation is assumed to support only a finite set of character encodings, and the XML encoding declaration is restricted in position and content in order to make it feasible to autodetect the character encoding in use in each entity in normal cases. Also, in many cases other sources of information are available in addition to the XML data stream itself. Two cases may be distinguished, depending on whether the XML entity is presented to the processor without, or with, any accompanying (external) information. We consider the first case first.

F.1 Detection Without External Encoding Information

Because each XML entity not accompanied by external encoding information and not in UTF-8 or UTF-16 encoding *must* begin with an XML encoding declaration, in which the first characters must be '<?xml', any conforming processor can detect, after two to four octets of input, which of the following cases apply. In reading this list, it may help to know that in UCS-4, '<' is "#x0000003C" and '?' is "#x0000003F", and the Byte Order Mark required of UTF-16 data streams is "#xFEFF". The notation ## is used to denote any byte value except that two consecutive ##s cannot be both 00.

With a Byte Order Mark:

00 00 FE FF	UCS-4, big-endian machine (1234 order)
FF FE 00 00	UCS-4, little-endian machine (4321 order)
00 00 FF FE	UCS-4, unusual octet order (2143)
FE FF 00 00	UCS-4, unusual octet order (3412)
FE FF ## ##	UTF-16, big-endian
FF FE ## ##	UTF-16, little-endian
EF BB BF	UTF-8

Without a Byte Order Mark:

`00 00 00 3C`
`3C 00 00 00`
`00 00 3C 00`
`00 3C 00 00`
	UCS-4 or other encoding with a 32-bit code unit and ASCII characters encoded as ASCII values, in respectively big-endian (1234), little-endian (4321) and two unusual byte orders (2143 and 3412). The encoding declaration must be read to determine which of UCS-4 or other supported 32-bit encodings applies.

`00 3C 00 3F`	UTF-16BE or big-endian ISO-10646-UCS-2 or other encoding with a 16-bit code unit in big-endian order and ASCII characters encoded as ASCII values (the encoding declaration must be read to determine which)
`3C 00 3F 00`	UTF-16LE or little-endian ISO-10646-UCS-2 or other encoding with a 16-bit code unit in little-endian order and ASCII characters encoded as ASCII values (the encoding declaration must be read to determine which)
`3C 3F 78 6D`	UTF-8, ISO 646, ASCII, some part of ISO 8859, Shift-JIS, EUC, or any other 7-bit, 8-bit, or mixed-width encoding which ensures that the characters of ASCII have their normal positions, width, and values; the actual encoding declaration must be read to detect which of these applies, but since all of these encodings use the same bit patterns for the relevant ASCII characters, the encoding declaration itself may be read reliably
`4C 6F A7 94`	EBCDIC (in some flavor; the full encoding declaration must be read to tell which code page is in use)
Other	UTF-8 without an encoding declaration, or else the data stream is mislabeled (lacking a required encoding declaration), corrupt, fragmentary, or enclosed in a wrapper of some kind

Note:

In cases above which do not require reading the encoding declaration to determine the encoding, section 4.3.3 still requires that the encoding declaration, if present, be read and that the encoding name be checked to match the actual encoding of the entity. Also, it is possible that new character encodings will be invented that will make it necessary to use the encoding declaration to determine the encoding, in cases where this is not required at present.

This level of autodetection is enough to read the XML encoding declaration and parse the character-encoding identifier, which is still necessary to distinguish the individual members of each family of encodings (e.g. to tell UTF-8 from 8859, and the parts of 8859 from each other, or to distinguish the specific EBCDIC code page in use, and so on).

Because the contents of the encoding declaration are restricted to characters from the ASCII repertoire (however encoded), a processor can reliably read the entire encoding declaration as soon as it has detected which family of encodings is in use. Since in practice, all widely used character encodings fall into one of the categories above, the XML encoding declaration allows reasonably reliable in-band labeling of character encodings, even when external sources of information at the operating-system or transport-protocol level are unreliable. Character encodings such as UTF-7 that make overloaded usage of ASCII-valued bytes may fail to be reliably detected.

Once the processor has detected the character encoding in use, it can act appropriately, whether by invoking a separate input routine for each case, or by calling the proper conversion function on each character of input.

Like any self-labeling system, the XML encoding declaration will not work if any software changes the entity's character set or encoding without updating the encoding declaration. Implementors of character-encoding routines should be careful to ensure the accuracy of the internal and external information used to label the entity.

F.2 Priorities in the Presence of External Encoding Information

The second possible case occurs when the XML entity is accompanied by encoding information, as in some file systems and some network protocols. When multiple sources of information are available, their relative priority and the preferred method of handling conflict should be specified as part of the higher-level protocol used to deliver XML. In particular, please refer to [IETF RFC 2376] or its successor, which defines the `text/xml` and `application/xml` MIME types and provides some useful guidance. In the interests of interoperability, however, the following rule is recommended.

- If an XML entity is in a file, the Byte-Order Mark and encoding declaration are used (if present) to determine the character encoding.

G W3C XML Working Group (Non-Normative)

This specification was prepared and approved for publication by the W3C XML Working Group (WG). WG approval of this specification does not necessarily imply that all WG members voted for its approval. The current and former members of the XML WG are:

- Jon Bosak, Sun (*Chair*)
- James Clark (*Technical Lead*)
- Tim Bray, Textuality and Netscape (*XML Co-editor*)
- Jean Paoli, Microsoft (*XML Co-editor*)
- C. M. Sperberg-McQueen, U. of Ill. (*XML Co-editor*)
- Dan Connolly, W3C (*W3C Liaison*)
- Paula Angerstein, Texcel
- Steve DeRose, INSO
- Dave Hollander, HP
- Eliot Kimber, ISOGEN
- Eve Maler, ArborText
- Tom Magliery, NCSA
- Murray Maloney, SoftQuad, Grif SA, Muzmo and Veo Systems
- MURATA Makoto (FAMILY Given), Fuji Xerox Information Systems
- Joel Nava, Adobe
- Conleth O'Connell, Vignette
- Peter Sharpe, SoftQuad
- John Tigue, DataChannel

H W3C XML Core Group (Non-Normative)

The second edition of this specification was prepared by the W3C XML Core Working Group (WG). The members of the WG at the time of publication of this edition were:

- Paula Angerstein, Vignette
- Daniel Austin, Ask Jeeves
- Tim Boland
- Allen Brown, Microsoft
- Dan Connolly, W3C (*Staff Contact*)
- John Cowan, Reuters Limited
- John Evdemon, XMLSolutions Corporation
- Paul Grosso, Arbortext (*Co-Chair*)
- Arnaud Le Hors, IBM (*Co-Chair*)
- Eve Maler, Sun Microsystems (*Second Edition Editor*)
- Jonathan Marsh, Microsoft
- MURATA Makoto (FAMILY Given), IBM
- Mark Needleman, Data Research Associates
- David Orchard, Jamcracker
- Lew Shannon, NCR
- Richard Tobin, University of Edinburgh
- Daniel Veillard, W3C
- Dan Vint, Lexica
- Norman Walsh, Sun Microsystems
- François Yergeau, Alis Technologies (*Errata List Editor*)
- Kongyi Zhou, Oracle

I Production Notes (Non-Normative)

This Second Edition was encoded in the XMLspec DTD (which has documentation available). The HTML versions were produced with a combination of the xmlspec.xsl, diffspec.xsl, and REC-xml-2e.xsl XSLT stylesheets. The PDF version was produced with the html2ps facility and a distiller program.

Index

Symbols

[ ] operator, matching with, 652

{ } (curly braces) characters, 403

| (bar) character, 650

|| (or operator), 269

; (semicolon), in Java, 472

" (quotation marks) characters
in attribute values, 79–80

% (percent sign) character, 108

& (ampersand) character in entity references, 80–83

&& (and operator), 269

< (left angle bracket) character, in tags, 80–83

; (semicolon) character, 108
in entity references, 79
in JavaScript statements, 244

* (star) operator, 113
in choices, 122
in sequences, 117

+ (plus) operator, 112
in choices, 122
in sequences, 117

/ (forward slash) character, 421

/ (slash) character, closing empty tags with, 76

// (double forward slash) character in JavaScript, 263

= operator, matching with, 653–654

? (question mark) operator, 114
in choices, 122
in sequences, 117

?: operator (Java), in if...else statements, 492

@ (at sign) character, 644

A

<A> element, 741, 1057
attributes, 742–743
XHTML, 848–851
attributes, 848–850
events, 850

abbreviated syntax
RDF, 950–952
XPath, 665–667

abbreviations, XPointers, 780–782

absolute location paths, 655

absolute position style, 989–991

absolute positioning, 432–433

abstract keyword (Java), 506

abstract XHTML 1.1 modules, 894–896

access specifiers (Java), 469, 499

Active Server Pages. *See* ASP

actor attribute, 909

ADO (ActiveX Data Object), 357

Adobe Framemaker, 21

after regions, 706

all element, 205

all groups, 230

Alt container (RDF), 955

Amaya, 35

ampersand (&) character in entity references, 80–83

anchors, creating with <a> element (XHTML), 848–851

and operator (&&), 269

annotation element, 205, 225

annotations, adding with schemas, 225–226

anonymous type definitions, 220–222
including attribute declarations, 222

ANY content models, 108–109

any element, 205

anyAttribute element, 205

Apache Klondike WML browser, 1049

appinfo element, 205, 225

applets (Java), 463

applications (Java), 463–464
creating, 464–465, 468–472
running, 473–474
XML. *See* XML applications

<arc> element, 983–985

arcs, 761–765
VML, 983–985

arguments, 279–281
arguments arrays, 281

Array class, 286–287, 289
methods, JScript, 286

arrays, 286
Java, 481–485

ASCII (American Standard Code for Information Interchange), 32
converting to Unicode, 33

ASP (Active Server Pages), 1020
documents, creating, 1020–1023
setting content type, 1021

W